The Study of Law:
A Critical Thinking Approach

The Study of Law
A Critical Thinking Approach

KATHERINE A. CURRIER
Chair, Division of Business and Law
Elms College

THOMAS E. EIMERMANN
Paralegal Program Director
Illinois State University

ASPEN

PUBLISHERS

1185 Avenue of the Americas, New York, NY 10036
www.aspenpublishers.com

Permissions
Aspen Publishers
1185 Avenue of the Americas
New York, NY 10036

Printed in the United States of America

1   2   3   4   5   6   7   8   9   0

ISBN 0-7355-5253-3

Library of Congress Cataloging-in-Publication Data

Currier, Katherine A.
    The study of law : a critical thinking approach / Katherine A. Currier,
Thomas E. Eimermann.
            p.   cm.
    Includes index.
    ISBN 0-7355-5253-3 (alk. paper)
    1. Law—Study and teaching—United States.   2. Legal assistants—United
States—Handbooks, manuals, etc.   I. Eimermann, Thomas E.   II. Title.

KF386.C88 2005
340′.071′173—dc22

                                                            2004055416

About Aspen Publishers

Aspen Publishers, headquartered in New York City, is a leading information provider for attorneys, business professionals, and law students. Written by pre-eminent authorities, our products consist of analytical and practical information covering both U.S. and international topics. We publish in the full range of formats, including updated manuals, books, periodicals, CDs, and online products.

Our proprietary content is complemented by 2,500 legal databases, containing over 11 million documents, available through our Loislaw division. Aspen Publishers also offers a wide range of topical legal and business databases linked to Loislaw's primary material. Our mission is to provide accurate, timely, and authoritative content in easily accessible formats, supported by unmatched customer care.

To order any Aspen Publishers title, go to *www.aspenpublishers.com* or call 1-800-638-8437.

To reinstate your manual update service, call 1-800-638-8437.

For more information on Loislaw products, go to *www.loislaw.com* or call 1-800-364-2512.

For Customer Care issues, e-mail *CustomerCare@aspenpublishers.com*; or call 1-800-234-1660; or fax 1-800-901-9075.

Aspen Publishers
A Wolters Kluwer Company

About the Authors

Katherine A. Currier, J.D., is chair of the Division of Business and Law at Elms College. She has developed and taught many law-related courses, including Legal Reasoning, Research, and Writing; Introduction to Legal Studies I and II; Law Office Computer Literacy; Law Office Applications; Interviewing, Counseling, and Negotiating; and Law and Literature. She has publications in the areas of legal ethics as applied to paralegals and law office computing.

Professor Currier is actively involved in the development of undergraduate legal education at both the regional and the national levels, particularly through her work with the American Association for Paralegal Education (AAfPE) and the American Bar Association Approval Commission on Paralegals. Professor Currier has served on the national board of AAfPE, first as its parliamentarian and then later as the elected representative of four-year paralegal programs. She has also served many years as the AAfPE publications chair, charged with the final responsibility for overseeing the Journal of Paralegal Education and Practice and The Educator. Professor Currier frequently speaks at both the AAfPE Northeast regional meetings and the annual AAfPE conferences on topics as diverse as the use of computer shareware, paralegals and the unauthorized practice of law, creative teaching techniques, and conducting legal research on the Internet. Professor Currier also serves as chair of the American Bar Association Approval Commission on Paralegals, the body charged with conducting site visits of paralegal programs that are seeking their initial ABA approval or reapproval.

Prior to teaching at Elms College, Professor Currier taught at Suffolk Law School and Western New England College School of Law. She graduated magna cum laude with her B.A. in Political Science from Carelton College in 1971, with her M.A. in Political Philosophy from University of California, Berkeley, in 1973, and with her J.D. from Northeastern University Law School in 1979.

Thomas E. Eimermann is Professor of Political Science and Director of the Legal Studies Program at Illinois State University. Dr. Eimermann helped establish the paralegal program in 1976 and has been its director since its inception. He has taught the Introduction to Paralegal Studies and the Legal Research and Writing courses.

Professor Eimermann was a member of the American Association for Paralegal Education's Board of Directors from 1986-1993 and served as president of that organization in 1991-1992. He has also served on the Certification Board and Specialty Task Force of the National Association of Legal Assistants, as a member of the Illinois State Bar Association Committee on the Delivery of Legal Services, as a member of the Hearing Board of the Illinois Attorney Registration and Disciplinary Commission, and as a consultant for the Illinois Department of Corrections, where he designed the Uniform Law Clerk Training Program.

Professor Eimermann's publications include three editions of *Fundamentals of Paralegalism* and journal articles on paralegals, jury behavior, and free speech issues. He earned his B.A. in Political Science at North Central College. He went on to receive an M.A. and a Ph.D. in Political Science from the University of Illinois-Urbana/Champaign campus.

Katherine Currier and Thomas Eimermann also co-authored *Introduction to Law for Paralegals: A Critical Thinking Approach* and *Introduction to Paralegal Studies: A Critical Thinking Approach*.

To our spouses and children
for their understanding and support

Summary of Contents

Contents

List of Illustrations

Preface

As the title indicates, in this book we use a critical thinking approach to introduce the readers to the study of law. This book is designed for use in introductory law courses for general prelaw students, criminal justice majors, government majors, business students, paralegal students, and generally anyone wishing to know more about the law.

Rather than taking an approach that emphasizes the memorization of definitions and rules, *The Study of Law: A Critical Thinking Approach* focuses on the basic foundations of the law and on the legal reasoning process. In addition to presenting an overview of the legal system, this book teaches the basic skills necessary to read and understand statutes and court cases.

We use this critical thinking approach because we believe it is the best way for students to learn the fundamental principles of law. By learning how to read and interpret statutes, cases, regulations, and court documents, students will be better able to learn how the American legal system functions. Therefore this book emphasizes careful reading for detail, analytical thinking, and the written presentation of arguments. The hypothetical cases, Discussion Questions, Legal Reasoning Exercises, Practical Tips, and Ethics Alerts incorporated throughout the text all serve to help develop students' critical thinking skills.

Those familiar with *Introduction to Law for Paralegals: A Critical Thinking Approach* will recognize a great deal of similarity between that book and this one. Topics covered in both include information about the sources of law, the judicial system, legal analysis, civil and criminal procedure, and substantive law in the fields of torts, contracts, property, criminal, business, and family law. The primary difference is that for this text we have removed many of the paralegal specific references and practical applications contained in the *Introduction to Law for Paralegals* text. Most significantly, the chapter on legal ethics has been completely rewritten to focus on the ethical dilemmas attorneys face in the context of our adversary system.

ORGANIZATION OF THE BOOK

Part 1, The American Legal System, introduces students to the study of law and the organization of the legal system. It covers such topics as sources of the law, the different ways in which law is classified, and various stages involved in litigation.

Part 2, Finding and Analyzing the Law, presents the basic tools used to find and analyze the law. These chapters are the basis on which we build the critical thinking skills students need for reading and analyzing the law. Chapters 6 and 7 cover finding and interpreting statutory law and court opinions. Chapter 8 shows students how to apply what they have found to specific legal problems. Included in the last chapter of this section of the book is a discussion of how to use the IRAC approach to legal analysis and how to report research findings in a legal memorandum.

Part 3, Ethical Issues and Substantive Law, leads off with a chapter on ethical dilemmas attorneys face in the context of our adversary system. Other chapters in Part 3 introduce students to the basic terms and concepts in the areas of torts, contracts, property and estate, business, family, and criminal law and procedure. In each chapter we blend traditional case law with a discussion of cutting-edge developments to give students a solid foundation in traditional concepts and an appreciation of the dynamic nature of law.

Some instructors may wish to alter the sequence in which they cover the chapters. For example, some may wish to either include the ethics chapter in Part I or save it for the end of the course. However, students need to develop the skills taught in Part 2 to be able to fully benefit from the discussion questions and legal reasoning exercises included in Part 3.

KEY FEATURES

Among the many features that set this book apart are

- the nature of the included cases
- Ethics Alerts
- Practical Tips
- NetNotes
- Legal Reasoning Exercises
- Discussion Questions integrated into each chapter
- marginal definitions of key terms
- checklists
- Review Questions
- appendixes on legal research, good writing, and legal citation

Because this book stresses the critical thinking approach, we illustrate our points with hypothetical situations and with real case decisions that students will understand and to which they can relate. The cases cover such topics as AIDS-infected blood transfusions, battered woman's syndrome, same-sex marriage, flag burning, the insanity defense, search and seizure of automobiles, sexual harassment, surrogate motherhood, and spousal immunity. We have also included such "classics" as *McBoyle v. United States, Palsgraf v. Long Island Railroad*, and *Mapp v. Ohio*. Our philosophy in editing these and other cases was to retain enough of the court's wording to give students a realistic feel for how judges actually write and to allow students to develop their critical thinking skills. We deleted nonessential information in order to keep each case a reasonable length.

Furthermore, the cases are fully integrated into the text. Many times, these cases are cross-referenced in other cases and used to show how the courts build on precedent and modify it in response to changing societal conditions. Discussion Questions and Legal Reasoning Exercises call on students to carefully analyze these cases and apply them to hypothetical situations. Ethics Alert boxes are placed throughout the text to draw attention to the ethical issues involved in various aspects of the law. These boxes warn students of actions that would be considered unethical.

Practical Tip boxes provide checklists and other "words of wisdom" regarding practical problems that are involved in certain areas of the law. They are placed appropriately throughout the text.

Also of special note are the appendixes. Appendix B provides students with a convenient and easy-to-understand primer on the basics of grammar, including verb tense, pronoun agreement, modifier placement, punctuation, and style. Appendix C is a quick reference for proper legal citation form, and Appendix D provides an overview of legal research sources and strategies. Appendix E lists websites for legal resources.

An instructor's manual that includes suggested answers for all the Discussion Questions, Review Questions, and Legal Reasoning Exercises, as well as teaching tips, is available to help teachers make the most effective use of this book. Also available are PowerPoint slides to assist with classroom lectures and a computerized test bank.

ACKNOWLEDGMENTS

Naturally, we owe a great deal of thanks to the many students, educators, paralegals, and attorneys who contributed ideas for this book and the *Introduction to Law for Paralegals* book upon which much of this book is based. We would especially like to recognize Victoria Joseph for her contribution to the criminal law chapter.

We would also like to thank the staff at Aspen Publishers for the excellent support we have received on this project. We especially want to recognize the key roles that Carol McGeehan and Betsy Kenny have played in making this book a reality.

Finally, a special thanks goes to our spouses and children for their continued support and understanding of our professional activities

Katherine A. Currier
Thomas E. Eimermann

November 2004

Acknowledgments

We are grateful to copyright holders for permission to reprint excerpts from the following items:

Mike Barnicle, "Spouse Suits, a New Wave of Americana," Boston Globe, Aug. 1, 1980. Reprinted courtesy of The Boston Globe.

Lexis Law Publishing, United States Code Service, 42 U.S.C.S. 2000e-2, pages 449 and 452, Copyright 1989. The statute is reprinted from the United States Code Service, Lexis Law Publishing, a division of Reed Elsevier Inc., and is reprinted with the permission of Lexis Law Publishing. All rights reserved.

Shepard's, Massachusetts Citations, Case Edition, Part 4, 1993, page 318; and Northeastern Reporter Citations, Vol. 5, 1995, page 1408. Reproduced by permission of Shepard's. Further reproduction of any kind is strictly prohibited.

Supreme Court Historical Society, photograph of the Supreme Court Justices. Collection, The Supreme Court of the United States, courtesy The Supreme Court Historical Society, photographed by Richard Strauss, Smithsonian Institution.

West Group, *Callow v. Thomas*, 78 N.E.2d 637, 637–641. Reprinted with permission.

——, *Lewis v. Lewis*, 351 N.E.2d 526, 526–533. Reprinted with permission.

——, American Jurisprudence Second, Volume 41, pages 192–193. Reprinted with permission.

——, American Jurisprudence Second, Index, pages 448, 497. Reprinted with permission.

——, American Law Reports Annotated, 92 A.L.R.3d 901, page 926. Reprinted with permission.

——, Corpus Juris Secundum, Volume 41, page 407. Reprinted with permission.

——, Massachusetts Digest, 12 Mass. Digest 2d 523; Table of Cases, page 61; Index, page 461. Reprinted with permission.

——, Massachusetts General Laws Annotated, Ch. 209 § 6, pages 351–352, 354, Pocket Part. Reprinted with permission.

——, Massachusetts General Laws Annotated, Index, page 329. Reprinted with permission.

——, Massachusetts Practice, Vol. 37, pages 259–260. Reprinted with permission.

——, West's Law Finder, page 2, National Reporter System Map. Reprinted with permission.

The Study of Law:
A Critical Thinking Approach

PART 1

The American Legal System

Chapter 1

Introduction to the Study of Law and the Legal Profession

*The study of the law qualifies a [wo]man to be useful
to self, to neighbors, and to the public.*
Unknown

INTRODUCTION

Law plays an essential role in everyone's life. It provides guidelines on how people should interact with each other. The criminal codes prohibit theft, assault, battery, rape, murder, and many other offenses. The tax codes require that individuals and businesses give part of their income to the government. The environmental laws prohibit the dumping of raw sewage into lakes and rivers. The civil rights laws protect against discrimination and harassment.

In addition to defining what constitutes appropriate behavior, the law provides a mechanism for resolving the conflicts and disagreements that arise among us without resorting to personal violence. When individuals violate a section of the criminal law, the government takes responsibility for bringing them to trial and for administering an appropriate punishment. If one person's negligence injures others, that person can be required to compensate the injured parties for the damages caused by this negligent act. When persons fail to carry out the terms of a contract, the state can either force them to do so or force them to pay damages that resulted from their failure to live up to their agreement.

Legislators, government administrators, and lobbyists focus on developing the statutes and regulations that govern everything from the way we drive our cars to the procedures we have to follow to get a divorce. Most lawyers spend their time advising people as to what they should do to live within the requirements of the law. For example, a group of entrepreneurs may seek legal advice regarding the best way to organize their new business, or a young married couple may come to an attorney for help with the purchase of their first home. Alternatively, individuals may enlist the aid of an attorney when they have been injured in an automobile accident or have been charged with a crime.

Frequently, paralegals help attorneys solve people's legal problems by assisting in the gathering of factual information about the client's situation; by doing legal research to find appropriate statutes, regulations, and case law; by helping to draft various types of legal documents; and by helping to prepare and organize the information attorneys present in trials.

The purpose of this text is to help you understand the American legal system and how attorneys and paralegals work within it. In the chapters that follow, you will learn about the organization and structure of the legal system, the various forms that law takes, the procedures used in litigating civil and criminal cases, and the basic legal principles that form the basis of our law in areas such as torts, contracts, and property.

A. LEGAL ANALYSIS

In addition to helping you acquire this type of basic legal knowledge, this text is designed to develop the critical thinking skills you need to understand statutes, court opinions, and various types of legal documents. These critical thinking skills include analyzing the facts, identifying the appropriate legal rules, applying the legal rules to the facts, and reporting the results in a clear and understandable manner.

Throughout the text we will be presenting you with short factual scenarios to illustrate how people and businesses turn to the law for help. Two such scenarios follow. Take a moment to read the facts of the case of "The Distressed Grandfather" and the case of "The Harassed Student." In addition to studying these cases now, we will refer to them again in later chapters.

Case 1: The Distressed Grandfather

Approximately one year ago, Donald Drake and his six-year-old grandson, Philip, were walking down a residential road on their way home from visiting one of Philip's friends. Philip was walking on the sidewalk approximately thirty feet in front of Mr. Drake. Suddenly, a car sped past Mr. Drake, seemingly went out of control, jumped the curb, and hit Philip. Mr. Drake ran to Philip's side, but it was too late. Philip had been killed instantly. The driver of the car, Mrs. Wilma Small, was unhurt. Based on skid marks and testimony from both Mrs. Small and Mr. Drake, the police investigation following the accident determined that excessive speed was the cause of the accident.

Mr. Drake said that at the time of the accident his only concern was for the welfare of his grandson because he himself was clear of the danger. Naturally, Mr. Drake suffered a great deal of mental pain and shock because of seeing his grandson killed. While being driven home from the accident, he suffered a heart attack that necessitated a lengthy hospital stay.

One year later, he still does not feel completely recovered and often suffers from nightmares reliving the accident and his grandson's death. Following the advice of trusted friends, he decides to make an appointment at the law office of Darrow and Bryan to see if he can sue Mrs. Small to recover for his hospital bills and for his pain and suffering.

Case 2: The Harassed Student

Wanda Smith, a twenty-two-year-old college student, was walking past a construction site on campus when several of the construction workers began to whistle and make cat calls. Wanda did not appreciate being treated as a sex object and greatly resented the way in which these construction workers were behaving.

After talking it over with a few of her friends, Wanda decides to talk to one of the attorneys at Darrow and Bryan to see if she can take legal action. She does not want other women to have to undergo similar treatment and wonders if she can collect damages for mental suffering.

Keep these clients' situations in mind as we give you a quick overview of the four basic steps in analyzing a legal situation:

- analyze the facts;
- identify the appropriate legal rules (and, if necessary, conduct legal research);
- apply the legal rules to the facts; and
- report the results (usually in writing).

Once an attorney completes these steps, the attorney can advise the client as to the appropriate actions to take.

1. Analyzing the Facts

The first step in legal analysis is to review the facts. The answer to any legal question depends on the specific facts of the individual case. Even a minor change in the facts may alter the outcome of the case.

Just as a medical doctor cannot give a competent medical diagnosis without a thorough examination of the patient, a lawyer cannot render legal advice without a complete understanding of all of the relevant facts. Some areas of the law, such as those dealing with negligence or landlords and tenants, are particularly **fact bound.** For example, assume a stranger approaches an attorney at a party with a question such as: "My landlord is trying to evict me. Can he do that?" or "My husband is trying to get custody of my kids. Will he succeed?" It would be impossible for the attorney to answer without gathering a lot more information and personally reviewing key documents.

Fact bound
When even a minor change in the facts can change the outcome.

Cause of action
A claim that based on the
law and the facts is
sufficient to support a
lawsuit.

Legal research
The process of finding
the law.

Legal reasoning
The application of legal
rules to a client's specific
factual situation; also
known as *legal analysis*.

Paralegals often assist in the fact-gathering process by conducting interviews, summarizing those interviews, and reading and summarizing relevant documents. For example, when Donald Drake and Wanda Smith came to the law office of Darrow and Bryan to seek advice, they were each interviewed by Pat Harper, a senior attorney with the firm. Chris Kendall, one of the firm's paralegals sat in on the interviews to help take notes and to become familiar with the facts of their cases.

2. Identifying the Appropriate Legal Rules

After meeting with the clients, the first thing that attorney Harper needed to determine was whether either client had a valid cause of action. A **cause of action** can be defined as a claim that based upon the law and the facts is sufficient to support a lawsuit. For example, in Wanda Smith's case, she was clearly upset and disturbed by what had happened to her. However, that does not mean she has a legal remedy. Her lawyers will have to prove not only that the construction workers harassed and upset her but also that these actions violated some law. It is important to understand that not every problem is a problem for which the courts will supply a remedy.

Thus, the second stage of legal analysis involves the identification of the specific provisions of the law that are applicable to the client's situation. Because there are so many laws at the federal, state, and local levels, and because the law covers such a wide variety of topics, it is impossible for any lawyer to know everything there is to know about the law. The law is far too complex for any individual to be able to commit it all to memory. Furthermore, because the law is constantly changing, one's legal knowledge must be continually updated. Therefore, even lawyers who specialize and strive to keep current by reading legal newspapers, journals, and bar publications on a daily basis may still need to do legal research. Law books and on-line computer databases are the tools of the trade for the legal professional.

Because **legal research** is a very time-consuming process, attorneys often rely on paralegals to assist them in locating and summarizing the relevant statutes and cases they need to properly interpret the current status of the law. Because attorney Harper has not recently handled a similar case, Chris Kendall was assigned to research the law on sexual harassment. You can find a detailed discussion of legal research in Appendix D.

3. Applying the Legal Rules to the Facts

Even after an attorney has found the applicable legal rule through legal research, the job is far from completed. Because each client's problem is unique, simply knowing a general rule will not solve the client's problem. These general rules must be applied to the client's specific facts. We call this **legal reasoning**.

There are two basic types of legal reasoning. The first involves the analysis of court opinions and the second the analysis of constitutions, statutes, and administrative regulations. We will discuss these processes in great depth in Chapters 6, 7, and 8. For now, it is important that you understand that the result in a client's case will depend on how the courts have handled similar situations in the past. This is because our legal system is based on a doctrine

NETNOTE

One way to stay current with the changes in the law is through the Internet. You can find the latest legal news by going to the home page of Findlaw at *www.findlaw.com*. Then click on *Legal News*.

known as **stare decisis,** literally, the decision stands. Following stare decisis means that if a court has decided one way on a particular issue in the past, in all likelihood it and other courts in the same jurisdiction will decide the same way on that issue in future cases given a similar set of facts.

In order to find out how similar situations have been handled in the past, an attorney or a paralegal will examine prior court decisions, known as **precedent,** and then apply them to the client's situation. If the facts of the client's situation and a prior court decision are similar, the two situations are **analogous.** If they are analogous, it is likely that the result in the client's case will be similar to the result reached in the prior case. If the facts are significantly different, the two situations are **distinguishable.** Because they are distinguishable, it is likely that the result in the client's case will not be the same as the result reached in the prior case. As you progress through this text, you will learn a lot more about the importance of stare decisis to our legal system. But for now, it is enough to understand that the doctrine of stare decisis is what gives our system its stability and predictability. As we will see, however, stare decisis also gives the courts enough flexibility to allow for change as the needs of our society change.

Unfortunately for Ms. Smith, the research indicated that she did not appear to have a cause of action against the construction workers. If Ms. Smith had been employed as one of the construction workers and her boss had been harassing her in this way, she would have had the basis for a suit against the company. However, as a mere passerby she lacked such protection. Her facts combined with the law do not give her a cause of action.

Fifteen years ago, Ms. Smith would not even have had a cause of action if she had been harassed by her employer. But as societal values change, the law usually changes as well. In recent years our society has become more sensitive to issues of gender equality, and new laws have been developed to provide new protections. Fifteen years from now, someone in Ms. Smith's position may have a cause of action that does not exist today. Societal values will change, and the law will continue to evolve in order to respond to those changes.

Stare decisis
The doctrine stating that normally once a court has decided one way on a particular issue in the past, it and other courts in the same jurisdiction will decide the same way on that issue in future cases given a similar set of facts unless they can be convinced of the need for change.

Precedent
One or more prior court decisions.

Analogous
Similar.

Distinguishable
Different.

DISCUSSION QUESTIONS

1. Why do you suppose there are certain types of harm, such as the humiliation Ms. Smith felt when the construction workers whistled at her, that courts will not help individuals resolve?

2. Do you think it is right that employees can go to court and sue their bosses for sexual harassment? Why? If the harasser were a co-worker instead of a boss, how would you view the situation?

With regard to Mr. Drake's case, the research proved more promising. In one case a mother who saw her young child killed by a negligent driver was allowed to recover for the emotional distress the accident caused her. However, five years later, in another decision involving a similar situation, a female bystander who happened to witness the death of a young boy was not allowed to recover for her emotional distress.

In assessing the strength of Drake's case, attorney Harper must decide whether the courts would treat a grandfather as they did the mother or as they did the bystander. Take a few minutes to list as many arguments as you can muster for each side of the debate. The most important part of legal reasoning is seeking factual similarities and differences between prior decisions and your client's case and then explaining why you think those similarities or differences matter. In that process you will find that you and your classmates often differ as to the "right" answer.

In actuality there is no "right" answer, only better or worse arguments for your client. A judge may be the final arbiter as to what the answer is in a particular case, but even then it is not the "right" answer in any cosmic sense. Any decision about what the law should be is a choice between competing values. This is why some cases go to trial instead of settling—that is, because the two litigants have differing viewpoints as to which of two competing values is the more important. The important point to remember is that your goal is to learn how to develop arguments that will help persuade the other side that your answer is more correct than theirs.

4. Reporting the Results

At various points throughout the legal process attorneys and paralegals are required to commit their thoughts to writing. At some points, they will take informal working notes for their own use. At other times they will make more formal reports that are designed to be read by colleagues, clients, opposing attorneys, or judges. Examples of some of the more specialized forms of **legal writing** include case briefs, legal memoranda, and appellate briefs.

Legal writing
Examples of legal writing include case briefs, law office memoranda, and documents filed with the court.

Case briefs summarize specific court decisions. Attorneys and paralegals use case briefs to help them analyze court decisions and prepare legal memoranda and appellate briefs. A **law office memorandum** is an unbiased analysis of a client's case for use within the law firm. It serves as a means of fairly evaluating the likelihood of the client's winning should the case go to court. This type of memorandum is often followed by a letter written to the client advising the client as to what action should be taken. An **appellate brief** is written to persuade an appeals court of the merits of the client's case. These documents will be discussed more thoroughly at various points throughout this text.

B. TAKING ACTIONS ON BEHALF OF THE CLIENT

After an attorney has thoroughly analyzed the application of the law to the client's situation and has advised the client as to the options available under the law, the attorney and client may agree to take some action on the client's behalf. These actions might include drafting a demand letter, initiating a lawsuit, defending a client, or helping a client avoid future litigation through careful planning.

Sometimes a lawsuit can be avoided by sending a **demand letter**. A demand letter is a letter from the attorney demanding that some action be taken, with either an implicit or an explicit threat that the matter will be taken to court if the requested action is not forthcoming.

In some cases there may be ways to settle the dispute through means other than litigation, such as mediation or arbitration. If litigation cannot be avoided, the attorney may represent the client in a civil lawsuit. In these situations the attorney is responsible for submitting court documents called **pleadings** in order to initiate the lawsuit. Prior to trial, the attorney may also conduct **discovery** in order to find out as much about the case as possible from witnesses and the parties on the opposite side. If the case does proceed to trial, the attorney will also be responsible for conducting direct and cross-examinations of witnesses and making appropriate arguments to the judge and the jury. Paralegals often assist in all of these stages, from drafting the pleadings to preparing the witnesses and evidence for trial.

Finally, in many situations the best recourse is to help the client avoid future litigation through careful planning. That planning frequently takes the form of a written agreement. A **contract** is a legally binding agreement that creates an obligation to do or refrain from doing something. Common examples include purchase agreements, leases, and prenuptial agreements. Paralegals often assist in drafting these documents as well.

In Donald Drake's case, attorney Harper concluded that, although victory was not assured, there were good grounds for a lawsuit. Because Mr. Drake was anxious to proceed, the firm filed the documents needed to officially begin the lawsuit.

Pleadings
The papers that begin a lawsuit—generally, the complaint and the answer.

Discovery
The modern pretrial procedure by which one party gains information from the adverse party.

Legal Reasoning Exercises

John and Mary Kulig have been married for ten years. They are both thirty-five years old. For the past eight years they have unsuccessfully been trying to have children. After being told that there would be a ten-year wait before they could adopt an infant, they decided to seek the services of a surrogate mother.

1. What kinds of problems do you think this decision might raise? Personal, medical, moral, religious, legal? If you think this is a problem the legal system should address, should such practices be made illegal? Should they be legal but regulated by the government?

Responding to an advertisement in the classified section of their Sunday newspaper, the Kuligs visited the office of James Matchum, an attorney who acts as a broker in setting up surrogacy arrangements. This attorney introduced John and Mary to Barbara Tufflife, a twenty-five-year-old, divorced woman who has a child from her former marriage. Because she had been having a difficult time finding work and had an easy pregnancy with her own child, Barbara agreed to serve as a surrogate mother for the childless couple. The Kuligs got along well with Barbara and noted that her two-year-old daughter appeared to be energetic and in good health.

Attorney Matchum then drew up a contract in which Barbara agreed to (1) be artificially impregnated with John's sperm, (2) refrain from smoking or consuming alcoholic beverages during the pregnancy, (3) carry the child to term if medical evidence indicated it was healthy, (4) abort the fetus if medical evidence indicated it had major birth defects, and (5) turn over any and all parental rights to the Kuligs when the baby was born. John and Mary, in turn, agreed to pay (1) Barbara's medical costs and (2) a maintenance allowance of $8,000 per month during the time of the pregnancy and a three-month recovery period after the pregnancy.

2. What do you think of these contractual arrangements? Are they fair to both parties? Which, if any, of these provisions do you find objectionable? Why?

Both parties signed this agreement, and arrangements were made for Barbara to be artificially inseminated with John's sperm. The process was successful, and Barbara became pregnant with John's baby. The pregnancy went smoothly. Barbara did not smoke or drink alcoholic beverages, and the Kuligs met the financial obligations laid out in the contract. However, when the baby arrived, Barbara refused to release the baby to the couple or sign over her parental rights. When John and Mary turned to attorney Matchum for help, he told them he would have to update his research on the enforceability of surrogacy contracts. Attorney Matchum assigned one of his paralegals to conduct the initial research.

This research revealed that the state legislature still had not passed anything on the subject and that there were no court cases in the state dealing with surrogacy contracts. However, the paralegal found a case in which a man and a woman wrote a contract whereby the woman agreed to live with the man if he would pay her $500 per month for life. One year later the man stopped the payments, and the woman sued for breach of contract.

3. What do you think the court did in that situation? Do you think the court ordered the man to continue the payments?

One basis for refusing to enforce a contract is because it is against public policy. In the case of the live-in couple, the man argued that the contract was against public policy, as it was based on his giving the woman money in exchange for sex. The court agreed and said that because contracts for prostitution are illegal, the agreement could not be enforced.

4. What are the implications of this case for the Kuligs? Do you see any similarities between their case and that of the live-in couple? Is the surrogacy contract a contract for prostitution? How do you define that term? Even if it is not a contract for prostitution, is a surrogacy contract against public policy?

These are questions that can be answered only through the process of legal reasoning, which we discussed earlier—that is, taking the law and applying it to the facts. Based on how you answered the questions in 4 above, write one paragraph supporting the conclusion that the surrogacy contract should not be enforced. Then write one paragraph arguing just the opposite. Come to class prepared to defend either position. Remember there is no "right" answer, just better or worse arguments.

C. THE LEGAL PROFESSION

In hearing about the cases of Donald Drake and Wanda Smith, you met two of the main legal professionals from the law firm of Darrow and Bryan: Pat Harper, a senior attorney, and Chris Kendall, one of the firm's paralegals. Although attorneys and paralegals are certainly two of the main actors within the law firm setting, the legal profession also encompasses other lay personnel such as law clerks, investigators, and secretaries, as well as court personnel, such as judges, magistrates, and court reporters. In the following section we briefly describe the roles of the law firm personnel. We discuss court personnel in Chapter 4.

1. Attorneys

The terms "attorney" and "lawyer" are generally used interchangeably. In its most general sense, "attorney" denotes an agent, one who is authorized to act on behalf of another person or corporation. An "attorney at law" is a person who has been officially licensed to practice law in a state or federal jurisdiction. A "lawyer" is an equivalent term for an "attorney at law."

In some contexts, people use "lawyer" to refer to a person who is authorized to practice law and use "attorney" to refer to a job title. Thus an organizational chart may carry titles such as attorney, associate attorney, enforcement attorney, District Attorney, United States Attorney, or Attorney General.

Lawyers can be employees of federal, state, or local governments (e.g., an attorney-general's office, a public defender's office, the Securities and Exchange Commission, etc.); be "in-house" counsel for business corporations or private associations; or be employees of or partners in private "law firms." Lawyers can also be self-employed.

Becoming a licensed attorney involves attaining a bachelor's degree (not required in all states, but most attorneys have one), a graduate legal education (normally three years if attending full-time or four years part-time), passing a state bar exam, and passing a morals/character check. In some states, to be authorized to practice law, attorneys must also join their state bar association and fulfill annual continuing education requirements.

Although paralegals can draft legal documents, these documents cannot be filed with the court until an attorney has reviewed, approved, and signed them.

2. Paralegals

Paralegal
A person who assists an attorney and, working under the attorney's supervision, performs tasks that, absent the paralegal, the attorney would do. A paralegal cannot give legal advice or appear in court.

American Bar Association (ABA)
www.abanet.org
A national voluntary organization of lawyers.

Generally speaking, the terms "paralegal" and "legal assistant" are viewed as synonyms. Because the term **paralegal** is the most common and the most generic, it will be the term most often employed in this book.

The paralegal profession emerged in the late 1960s. It established its legitimacy in the early 1970s and underwent tremendous growth in the 1980s and 1990s. The role paralegals play in the delivery of legal services is likely to continue to expand. The U.S. Department of Labor predicts that the paralegal profession will grow faster than the average for other occupations, with an expected 33 percent increase in the number of paralegal jobs from the year 2000 to the year 2010.[1] This will make the paralegal profession one of the fastest-growing occupational groups in the twenty-first century.

The **American Bar Association (ABA)** is the largest and most prominent national organization of lawyers. Over the past thirty years it has taken a leadership role in recognizing the need for and helping establish the paralegal profession. As the profession has developed, the ABA has periodically modified and refined its definition of paralegal/legal assistant. Most recently in 1997 the ABA amended its officially adopted definition of a legal assistant/paralegal to read:

> A legal assistant or paralegal is a person, qualified by education, training or work experience who is employed or retained by a lawyer, law office, corporation, governmental agency or other entity and who performs specifically delegated substantive legal work for which a lawyer is responsible.[2]

Depending upon their particular job assignment, paralegals assist lawyers by performing a variety of functions that require knowledge of substantive and procedural law, such as doing legal and factual research, preparing drafts of various legal documents, organizing trial exhibits, coordinating witnesses, and taking notes at trials.

Unlike the qualifications for becoming an attorney, most states have no requirements for becoming a paralegal.

Figure 1-1 presents the differences in qualifications for becoming a paralegal and becoming an attorney. In most states nothing prevents a person with no college credits and no paralegal training from being hired to work as a paralegal. This is true because currently there are no minimum legal requirements, such as licensing statutes would create, that must be satisfied to be able to work as a paralegal. Nor are there any informal standards universally accepted by all attorneys who hire paralegals. To become a paralegal a person simply needs to find an attorney who is willing to hire him or her and assign the title paralegal.

Although it is possible for anyone to be hired as a paralegal, most employers do not wish to start from scratch in training their paralegals. Therefore, they limit their employment searches to individuals who already have experience in the field or who have completed some form of formal paralegal education they trust. For example, perhaps because attorneys in most states are required to graduate from an ABA-accredited law school, many employers limit their

---

[1] U.S. Bureau of Labor Statistics, Occupational Outlook Handbook (2002–2003 ed.).
[2] Adopted by the ABA House of Delegates, August 1997.

Qualifications	Paralegal	Attorney
Undergraduate education	None required (An associate's degree is rapidly becoming the minimum acceptable degree for employment; many employers require a bachelor's degree.)	Bachelor's degree
Specialized education	None required (Some employers give preference to graduates of ABA-approved paralegal programs.)	Usually a degree from an ABA-accredited law school
Testing	None required (Some employers give preference to those who pass a voluntary exam administered by one of the national paralegal associations.)	Passage of a state bar exam (Most exams have multi-state and state-specific questions.)
License and morals check	None required	Must be licensed

Figure 1-1   Paralegal versus Attorney Qualifications

employment search to paralegals who have graduated from an ABA-approved paralegal program.

3. Other Support Staff

Attorneys work with a variety of lay support staff in addition to paralegals, such as law students (usually called law clerks), secretaries, librarians, and special investigators. Police detectives serve as investigators for prosecuting attorneys. Many mid-sized and most large private law offices also employ special law office administrators to supervise lay personnel and manage the business aspects of the practice.

DISCUSSION QUESTIONS

3. If paralegals *are* working under the supervision of an attorney, do you think they should be allowed to give legal advice? What if they are *not* working under the supervision of an attorney?

4. Some argue that paralegals should be licensed, following a process similar to that used for attorneys. Do you agree?

SUMMARY

This chapter provided a brief introduction to the role of law in our society, the manner in which lawyers evaluate and respond to their clients' legal problems, and an overview of the legal profession. We have also introduced the nature of the legal reasoning process. Throughout the text we will be stressing the development of the critical thinking skills you will need to understand the legal system. Among these skills are the ability to analyze the facts, identify the appropriate legal rules, apply the legal rules to the facts, report the results, and take actions on behalf of the client.

Although we have presented each stage in a linear fashion, the reality is that these various stages are intertwined. Legal reasoning often reveals the need to do more research. In the process of reporting your findings, you may discover flaws in your analysis. Thinking, researching, and writing are inseparable.

In the chapters that follow, you will learn more about the organization and structure of the legal system, the various forms that law takes, the procedures used in litigating civil and criminal cases, and basic legal principles that form the basis of our law in areas such as torts, contracts, and property.

Do not be dismayed if you are sometimes overwhelmed by the complexity and the sheer volume of legal concepts and materials. Learning law is a lot like learning a foreign language. Although many of these terms may be new to you now, they will become increasingly familiar to you as you progress through the text. In the end you will be amazed at how these diverse pieces end up fitting into a logical and effective system.

REVIEW QUESTIONS

Pages 3 through 7

1. Why does the study of law involve more than simply memorizing rules?
2. What is legal reasoning?
3. What is the doctrine of stare decisis, and why is it important?
4. Why is it important to know whether a client's facts are analogous to or distinguishable from those in prior court decisions?
5. What is a cause of action? What does it mean to say that a person does not have a valid cause of action?
6. Why does law change? Should it?

Pages 8 through 13

7. Why is there no one "right" answer to a legal problem?
8. Should it be the attorney or the paralegal who signs a client letter that analyzes the law? Why?
9. What are the requirements for becoming an attorney? A paralegal?

Chapter 2

Functions and Sources of Law

We hold these truths to be self-evident. . . .
Declaration of Independence

INTRODUCTION

Clients are people who have problems or who are trying to avoid problems. They turn to attorneys hoping that the legal system will help them. In this chapter and the next we will be discussing another case that came to the law firm of Darrow and Bryan. When Diane Dobbs, a new client, met with attorney Pat Harper, she related the following story.

Case 3: The Pregnant Waitress

Ms. Diane Dobbs had been employed by the Western Rib Eye Restaurant for the past three years. Throughout that time her work record had been exemplary. Customers often spoke to the manager to tell him how Diane's service and personality contributed to their especially enjoyable dining experience at the restaurant.

Six months ago Diane, who is not married, found out that she was pregnant. When she approached her manager, Ben, to discuss arrangements for a maternity leave, instead of the favorable reception she had expected, Ben reached over, patted her stomach, and said, "Well, I guess we can't have you working for us any longer." Ben then grabbed her by the arm and escorted her out of the restaurant. Diane protested and asked to be allowed to collect her personal belongings from her locker, but the manager just laughed and said she was "history." When Diane began to cry, he softened his demeanor a little and said,

"Look, we simply can't have a pregnant lady working here. It just wouldn't be good for business."

Although she has been actively looking, Diane has not yet been able to find suitable employment.

When a client presents a problem to an attorney, the attorney may feel confident that the legal system can provide a remedy, but that will not always be so. As we indicated in Chapter 1, not every problem can be resolved by the legal system. In order to better appreciate why this is so, we need to study the function of law, the history of our American legal system, and the sources of our laws. You also need to understand the sources of law in order to do legal research and analysis.

A. FUNCTIONS AND THEORIES OF LAW

The development and enforcement of the law are essential governmental functions in all developed societies. Although the laws themselves sometimes differ, they serve the same essential functions in all fifty states and at the federal level.

1. Definition of Law

Laws
Rules of conduct promulgated and enforced by the government.

It is our **laws**—rules of conduct promulgated and enforced by the government—that define the types of conduct that are either prohibited or required. For example, a criminal code usually prohibits the unauthorized taking of property that belongs to someone else. Tax laws require that certain types of individuals or corporations give part of their income to the government. The laws can apply to the behavior of individuals, businesses, and even governments themselves. Thus municipalities may be prohibited from dumping raw sewage into lakes and rivers and the police prohibited from conducting unreasonable searches and seizures.

To be considered laws, these rules of conduct must be promulgated and enforced by the appropriate governmental bodies. For example, only the U.S. Congress can make federal statutory law, and only a state's highest court can authoritatively interpret the meaning of that state's laws.

These rules of conduct also carry with them certain sanctions that can be imposed on those who fail to follow the rules. When individuals violate a section of the criminal law, they may be fined, sent to prison, or in some cases even suffer loss of life. Persons who are found liable under the civil law may be forced to pay various penalties or damage awards or to perform some action, such as carrying out the terms of a contract. Police who conduct illegal searches and seizures may be denied the right to use in court any evidence they find and may even be forced to pay damages to the injured parties. Even presidents can be cited for contempt of court if they fail to turn over subpoenaed materials.

2. Functions of Law

While there may be a great deal of debate over the wisdom and appropriateness of a particular law (as there is, for example, over a mandatory seat belt law), there is general agreement that laws themselves are necessary. As the Task Force on Law and Law Enforcement reported to the National Commission on the Causes and Prevention of Violence:

> Human welfare demands, at a minimum, sufficient order to insure that such basic needs as food production, shelter and child rearing be satisfied, not in a state of constant chaos and conflict, but on a peaceful, orderly basis with a reasonable level of day-to-day security. . . . When a society becomes highly complex, mobile, and pluralistic; the beneficiary, yet also the victim, of extremely rapid technological change; and when at the same time, and partly as a result of these factors, the influence of traditional stabilizing institutions such as family, church, and community wanes, then that society of necessity becomes increasingly dependent on highly structured, formalistic systems of law and government to maintain social order. . . . For better or worse, we are by necessity increasingly committed to our formal legal institutions as the paramount agency of social control.[1]

It has thus been increasingly left to the legal system to define and enforce the rules of society. Some of these rules, such as restrictions on abortions, pornography, and gambling, are heavily influenced by the religious and moral beliefs of various groups in the society, while others, such as traffic regulations, have no moral content at all. In either case they help to provide the type of order and predictability that are essential elements of our modern society.

3. Theories of Jurisprudence

To help explain what the purpose of law is and how laws work (or should work in a just society), various theories of legal philosophy have been developed. This area of study, known as **jurisprudence,** has had an important impact on the development of our legal system and on the thinking of many judges.

One part of jurisprudence deals with theorizing about the source of laws. For example, since the time of the ancient Greeks, **natural law** theorists have believed that man-made law should be based on timeless and immutable principles that can be discovered through careful thought and humanity's innate sense of right and wrong. The purpose of having governments and laws is to protect the natural rights that are inherent in these principles. Therefore, the laws that governments enact are to be respected when they reflect these natural laws but should be resisted when they do not conform to these natural laws.

This natural law philosophy has had a great influence on the development of the American legal system and is reflected in our Declaration of Independence, which includes the following:

> We hold these truths to be self-evident, that all men are created equal, that they are endowed by their Creator with certain unalienable Rights, that among these are Life, Liberty, and the Pursuit of Happiness.

The Reverend Martin Luther King, Jr. used natural law as a justification for civil disobedience in his fight against racial segregation.

---

[1]J. Campbell, J. Sahid, & D. Strang, Law and Order Reconsidered: Report of the Task Force on Law and Law Enforcement to the National Commission on the Causes and Preventions of Violence 3, 5 (1970).

The alternative to the natural law theory is known as **legal positivism.** Supporters of this approach believe that the validity of a law is determined by the process through which it was made rather than by the degree to which it reflects natural law principles. To a legal positivist a law is valid as long as it was passed by the appropriate lawmaking agency.

A second area of jurisprudence is concerned with the extent to which judges simply apply the law versus create the law. **Formalists** believe that the proper role of the judge is to do the former, that is, simply to apply the law. They view the law as a complete and autonomous system of logically consistent principles. Judges can find the "correct result" by simply making logical deductions. Judges serve as impartial technicians who simply identify the proper, preexisting rule and then apply it to the facts of the case. Social policy and the judge's private views are considered irrelevant.

Legal realists, on the other hand, reject the formalist's assertion that judges' decisions are reached by a strict application of the principles of logic. First, judges must frequently decide between contradictory rules. Second, legal realists point to instances in which the law is vague and ambiguous. Because of the elastic nature of the English language, it is always possible for judges to expand or contract the meaning of any given rule. In these situations, the realists assert that judges can interpret the wording of the statutes and prior cases to justify different outcomes. The number of five-to-four split votes in controversial Supreme Court cases is often cited as proof of this assertion that there are always counterarguments.

But if, as the realists assert, logic alone is insufficient to explain judicial decisions, what then does determine how judges decide cases? Some realists suggest that judges simply seek interpretations that will advance the public values and social goals to which they subscribe. Others argue that realism involves going beyond the confines of the law to determine the social consequences of the alternative outcomes. To assist in this process, judges should look to the expertise that can be provided by the social sciences, specifically psychology, sociology, and economics.

An illustration of the realist approach can be found in the 1954 Supreme Court case of *Brown v. Board of Education.*[2] That case raised the question of whether segregated public schools could provide "separate but equal" education. In 1896 in *Plessy v. Ferguson*[3] the Court had found that segregated railway cars did not violate the Fourteenth Amendment so long as they provided "equal" accommodations. However, rather than relying on the legal precedent established by *Plessy,* the Court in *Brown* looked beyond the law and recognized studies done by social scientists that concluded that segregation in the public schools had a detrimental effect upon black children because it generated feelings of inferiority "that may affect their hearts and minds in a way unlikely ever to be undone."[4] Based upon this data, the Court concluded that "[s]eparate educational facilities are inherently unequal."[5] Today, lawyers routinely present policy

---

[2]347 U.S. 483 (1954).

[3]163 U.S. 537 (1896).

[4]347 U.S. at 494.

[5]Id. at 495.

arguments in support of their client's position in an effort to convince the court that finding for their side is not only "legally" but also "socially" desirable.

While few still argue that judicial decisions are determined solely by the rules of logic, there remains considerable disagreement as to how far judges should be given discretion, especially in the area of constitutional interpretation. Prominent political conservatives such as Supreme Court Justice Antonin Scalia argue for a strict construction that narrowly interprets the text of the Constitution in a manner that is consistent with what most people understood those words meant at the time that they were written.[6] This view is often referred to as **originalism.** Scalia argues that such an approach will keep judges from substituting their own political views for those of the original drafters.

In contrast to this strict construction approach, others argue that judges should seek to determine the underlying goal or value that the drafters had in mind at the time they wrote the law. Then they should select the modern-day option that best advances that goal or value. This view is sometimes labeled the **evolutionary** or "living law" approach.

In recent years scholars associated with the **Critical Legal Studies** (CLS) movement have been focusing their attention on identifying what they believe to be preferences and biases that are built into our law. The movement is called *Critical* Legal Studies because its members are openly critical of the manner in which our legal system currently operates. Adherents of CLS argue there can be no value-neutral process for enacting society's authoritative rules and any process will inherently favor some values over others. Rather than protecting against the illegitimate use of power, the rule of law protects certain groups and ideas at the expense of others. Some adherents of CLS utilize a Marxist analysis that focuses on economic supression of the poor by the wealthy. **Critical Race Studies** and **Feminist Jurisprudence** focus on alleged racial and gender biases within the legal system.

Of course, many legal thinkers embrace more than one theory of how law should be viewed. Consider the following remarks of Justice Benjamin Cardozo:

> My analysis of the judicial process comes then to this, and little more: logic, and history, and custom, and utility and the accepted standards of right conduct, are the forces which singly or in combination shape the progress of the law.[7]

As you read the cases that are contained in this book and are part of other courses you take, stop and analyze them in terms of these different perspectives of the role of law and how law is made. Did they include references to the natural law? How much discretion did the precedents leave to the judge? What values were aligned with each of the possible outcomes?

DISCUSSION QUESTIONS

1. Do you agree with the statement "Laws are necessary"? Many believe we have too many laws today. Do you agree? If you do, which laws should be eliminated? Do we need additional laws in some areas?

---

[6]Antonin Scalia, A Matter of Interpretation: Federal Courts and the Law (1997).
[7]Benjamin Cardozo, The Nature of the Judicial Process 112 (1949).

2. Can you think of ways, other than those mentioned in the text, that natural law theory has influenced the development of American law?

3. One of the basic principles of the natural law theory is that people should not have to obey an unjust law. Should it be left to the individual or to a judge to determine when a man-made law is unjust? If it is left to the judge, what criteria should the judge use?

4. Which of the theories of jurisprudence discussed in the text do you think best explains how law should work?

5. Would you expect to hear a follower of natural law, legal positivism, legal realism, or Critical Legal Studies making the following statements?

   a. The killing of another human is wrong.
   b. The penalty for first degree murder is life imprisonment or death.
   c. Studies have shown that a disproportionate number of minority men are sentenced to the death penalty.

6. There is an old joke about a lawyer who was asked, "What is two plus two?" The lawyer responded, "What do you *want* it to be?" Which legal theory does this best exemplify? Is it necessarily a bad thing that we live in a world where two plus two does not always have to be four?

B. SOURCES OF LAW

Most people can recall something from their high school civics class about the legislature making the law, the executive branch enforcing the law, and the courts interpreting the law. The truth is that the legislative, executive, and judicial branches are all involved in making the law.

1. Constitutional Law

Separation of powers
The division of governmental power among the legislative, executive, and judicial branches.

The United States was the first nation to adopt a written constitution, and it is that Constitution that provides the framework within which all our laws are made. The first major function of the federal Constitution is to establish an organizational structure that allocates governmental powers. On the national level, the Constitution divides governmental powers among the legislative, executive, and judicial branches. This is commonly referred to as the **separation of powers**.

The separate branches of government share power and have the ability to limit the actions of the other branches. In the Federalist Papers, James Madison explained that this system of **checks and balances** is designed to guard against "a gradual concentration of the several powers in the same department." Under the Constitution, Congress has the power to make laws, but the President has the power to veto them. The executive branch is responsible for administering the law, but it cannot spend money to do so unless Congress provides for the appropriate funding in the budget.

Federalism
A system of government in which the authority to govern is split between a single, nationwide central government and several regional governments that control specific geographical areas.

The Constitution also divides governmental power between the national government and the states. This division of power between the national government and the states is referred to as **federalism.** Certain powers are explicitly granted to the federal government, while all others are reserved to the states and the people.

The second major function of the Constitution is to protect individual rights from governmental overreaching. Because our founding fathers perceived a lack of such protection in the Constitution, as soon as it was ratified, the first Congress began work on the first ten amendments, commonly known as the **Bill of Rights.** These ten amendments include protections for freedom of speech and press, freedom of religion, a privilege against self-incrimination, the right to an attorney and a trial by jury, and protections against unreasonable searches and seizures. Along with the Thirteenth, Fourteenth, and Fifteenth Amendments (added during the Civil War), these amendments serve to prevent state or federal government officials from interfering with our civil rights and liberties.

Bill of Rights
The first ten amendments to the U.S. Constitution

The Constitution and its amendments constitute the "supreme law of the land." To be enforceable, all other laws must not conflict with the principles laid down in the Constitution. When there is a challenge to the constitutionality of a law, it is the courts that determine whether or not the law is valid. The process by which the courts make these types of judgments is referred to as **judicial review.**

Power of judicial review
A court's power to review statutes to decide if they conform to the federal or state constitution.

It could be argued that since the Constitution established three coequal branches, each branch should be free to interpret the Constitution as it sees fit. However, there are times in which there is disagreement among the three branches about the interpretation of the Constitution, and in those situations, someone has to have the final say.

In *Marbury v. Madison*[8] the U.S. Supreme Court claimed this power for itself. The Court held it was inherent in the nature of a court's work to have to resolve conflicting interpretations of the law before it can carry out its assigned task of applying the law. If a Court determines that a statute does not conform to the Constitution, then the statute is invalid and the court cannot enforce it.

Over the years, the U.S. Supreme Court has used this power of judicial review to invalidate a number of federal and state laws that it found to be in conflict with the U.S. Constitution. Some of the most controversial of the more recent applications of judicial review include decisions invalidating state laws involving racial segregation, abortions, and school prayer.

In addition to determining the constitutionality of statutes, the courts are often called upon to determine the meaning of the Constitution itself. The Constitution was written more than two hundred years ago and uses broad sweeping terminology such as "freedom of speech," "establishment of religion," "unreasonable searches and seizures," and "cruel and unusual punishment." It is often difficult to determine the meaning of such ambiguous phrases, especially when applied to a specific situation. Under the power of judicial review, the U.S. Supreme Court has the final say regarding the interpretation of those ambiguous constitutional provisions.

Each of the fifty states also has a written constitution that defines the organization and powers of its government. Most also include an equivalent of the federal Bill of Rights. In the past many attorneys tended to ignore their own state's constitutional provisions. Recently, however, there has been an increase in litigation based on state constitutional law. This is partly because many state constitutions provide for more protection of individual rights than does the federal Constitution. The highest state court is the final arbiter of what its state constitution means.

---

[8]5 U.S. (1 Cranch) 137 (1803).

NETNOTE

You can read the full text of the Declaration of Independence, the Constitution, and the Bill of Rights at the National Archives web site: *www.archives.gov*.

The Declaration of Independence:

www.archives.gov/national_archives_experience/declaration.htm

The Constitution:

www.archives.gov/national_archives_experience/constitution.html

The Bill of Rights:

www.archives.gov/national_archives_experience/bill_of_rights.html

You can also view the Constitution and the Bill of Rights at Findlaw:

http://caselaw.lp.findlaw.com/data/constitution/articles.html
(Note: The address does not start with www.)

http://caselaw.lp.findlaw.com/data/constitution/amendments.html

2. Statutory Law

Statute
A law enacted by a state legislature or by Congress.

As explained above, federal and state constitutions delineate the general framework within which the government must operate. Although these documents do list some major substantive and procedural rights, they were not designed to contain the types of detailed laws and regulations we need to operate in today's complex society. Rather, the federal and state constitutions specifically delegate the power to make these laws to the legislative branches of government.

At the federal level, the legislative power rests with the U.S. Congress. At the state level, it is exercised by state legislatures and a variety of local bodies such as city councils and village boards. Congress and state legislatures enact **statutes**, while city councils and village boards enact **ordinances**.

These statutes and ordinances lay down general rules that govern future conduct. They are general in the sense that they apply to broad categories of people rather than to specific individuals. Furthermore, the requirements they impose generally cannot be applied to actions taken *before* the law went into effect.

The formulation of such future oriented rules is a difficult task, because legislatures cannot foresee all the possible circumstances that might arise. Statutes therefore often contain general prohibitions that are somewhat ambiguous and open to differing interpretations. Ambiguity in statutes can also result from sloppy draftsmanship or be intentionally inserted to avoid creating conflicts among the legislation's supporters.

> **PRACTICAL TIP**
>
> In areas having to do with individual rights, sometimes a state constitution will give more protection than the U.S. Constitution.

An example of the ambiguity contained in statutes can be found in the following excerpt from Title VII of the 1964 Civil Rights Act. It states:

> It shall be an unlawful employment practice for an employer (1) to . . . discriminate against any individual . . . because of such individual's race, color, religion, sex, or national origin.[9]

Recall the situation of Diane Dobbs mentioned at the beginning of the chapter. Was the restaurant manager discriminating against Diane Dobbs because of her sex when he fired her for being pregnant? While the statute clearly states that employers cannot discriminate on the basis of sex, it is not clear what types of actions should be considered sex discrimination. After the enactment of Title VII some people argued that pregnancy discrimination should be considered a form of sex discrimination because only women can become pregnant. Others argued that it should not be considered sex discrimination because the differential treatment is based on the condition of being pregnant rather then on the employee's sex. Although only women can become pregnant, the employer was legitimately differentiating between two different types of women—those who were pregnant and those who were not—rather than discriminating between women and men.

As with ambiguities in constitutional provisions, when disagreements such as this arise over the meaning of a statute, a court must resolve the ambiguity. Thus in *Gilbert v. General Electric*,[10] the U.S. Supreme Court was called upon to determine if discrimination based on pregnancy was a form of sex discrimination under Title VII. The Supreme Court ruled in *Gilbert* that Title VII allowed employers to discriminate based on pregnancy.

The Supreme Court's interpretation would have left Diane without a remedy under the statute. However, luckily for her, if the legislative branch disagrees with the interpretation a court gives to one of its statutes, Congress can always introduce new legislation that amends the original statute to make clear that a different result or interpretation was intended. If this new legislation passes, the court's interpretation is superseded by the new statute. In this instance, Congress reacted by amending the statute to include pregnancy discrimination with the definition of sex discrimination.[11] Thus, under the amended statute it was unlawful for Diane's employer to fire her based upon her pregnancy.

Note, however, the difference between interpreting a statute and making a determination that it is unconstitutional. Whereas the legislative branch can amend one of its statutes to override a judicial interpretation, the courts retain the final authority with respect to deciding whether it is constitutional.

3. Administrative Law

Administrative agencies create administrative law. **Administrative law** is similar to statutory law in that it lays down rules designed to regulate future conduct. However, these rules are usually drawn more narrowly and directed to a more specialized group. Often the legislative branch intentionally leaves it

Administrative law
Rules and regulations created by administrative agencies.

---

[9]42 U.S.C. § 2000e-2(a) (2000).
[10]429 U.S. 125 (1976).
[11]Bennett Amendment, 42 U.S.C. § 2000e(k) (2000).

to the executive branch and to independent regulatory agencies to "fill in the details" of the law within a general structure set down by the legislature. Through the process of filling in these details the executive branch is actually making the law.

Assume a taxpayer wins $50 in the lottery. Must he pay taxes on it? The Internal Revenue Code, a federal statute, provides that he must pay tax on income but only includes general categories of income. The Internal Revenue Service (IRS), a federal agency, has developed **regulations** that define in much more detail what the word *income* means. Without the IRS, Congress would be forced to make constant revisions in the federal tax laws and would be hard-pressed to see that they were enforced.

Regulation
A law promulgated by an administrative agency.

Other examples of federal agencies include the Occupational Safety and Health Administration (OSHA), which oversees the federal statute requiring safe working conditions, and the Environmental Protection Agency (EPA), which oversees the federal statute governing the environment.

Just as the courts are drawn into the lawmaking process when they must interpret constitutions and statutes, so, too, are they called on to be the final arbiters of the meaning of administrative regulations. If someone disagrees with the administrative interpretation of a statute, the dissatisfied party can go to court to challenge the agency's interpretation. The court must support the agency's interpretation unless the court determines that the regulation is outside the authorization Congress gave to the administrative agency or that the regulation is unconstitutional. To determine whether the agency has stepped out of the bounds created for it by Congress, the court will examine the **enabling act,** the statute that created the agency. The court will also seek to determine the underlying legislative intent of the statute that the agency is attempting to interpret through its regulations.

Enabling act
A statute establishing and setting out the powers of an administrative agency.

Returning once again to the case of our pregnant waitress, attorney Pat Harper may also wish to consider suing Diane Dobbs's employer for sexual harassment. A sexual harassment case would be based on the same federal statute, Title VII, that we discussed above. The statute makes no specific reference to sexual harassment. However, the Equal Employment Opportunity Commission (EEOC), acting under authority given to it in the statute, has declared that acts of sexual harassment are a form of sex discrimination. One of its administrative regulations states:

> Unwelcome sexual advances, requests for sexual favors, and other verbal or physical conduct of a sexual nature constitute sexual harassment when (1) submission to such conduct is made either explicitly or implicitly a term or condition of an individual's

---

PRACTICAL TIP

Your understanding of a statute may be incomplete without also checking for related regulations. For example, policies such as the right of the police to conduct breathalizer tests may be set by state statute. However, how those policies are to be implemented (e.g., how a breathalizer test is to be conducted) may be set by administrative regulation.

employment, (2) submission to or rejection of such conduct by an individual is used as the basis for employment decisions affecting such individual, or (3) such conduct has the purpose or effect of unreasonably interfering with an individual's work performance or creating an intimidating, hostile, or offensive working environment.[12]

Note how much more specific the wording of the regulation is in comparison to the wording of the statute.

Recall that Diane Dobbs alleged that the manager patted her on the stomach as he was firing her for being pregnant. Do you think that is sufficient to support a claim of sexual harassment? Is there any language in the regulation that could support such a claim?

In addition to their power to promulgate regulations, and as part of their enforcement powers, most agencies have investigatory and adjudicative powers. For example, if Diane Dobbs wants to pursue her claim of sexual harassment, Title VII mandates that she first take her complaint to the EEOC or a comparable state agency. The agency will investigate her case and, if it deems it appropriate, will hold a hearing to determine the truth of her claims. If she or her employer is not satisfied with the results they obtain at the agency, they can then take the case to court. Ultimately, the court would be the final arbiter of whether Diane Dobbs's situation fits within the agency definition of sexual harassment.

Because administrative agencies combine legislative, executive, and judicial functions, they are sometimes referred to as the **fourth branch of government.**

4. Judicial Interpretation and the Common Law

As we have noted above, courts play a vital role in interpreting constitutions and the laws created by the legislatures and agencies. The courts also apply and interpret the **common law** when there is no statute, administrative regulation, or constitutional provision governing the case they are adjudicating.

> **Common law**
> Law created by the courts.

The common law consists of various legal principles that have evolved through the years from the analysis of specific court decisions. Ultimately, these principles can be traced back to early medieval England, though they have been modified through the years by various state courts. When a legal dispute involves a subject that is not adequately covered by the other types of law, the judge applies the principles of the common law. In other words, in the absence of pronouncements from the constitution or a legislative or administrative body, the judge looks to the earlier decisions of other judges in similar circumstances.

Indeed, courts existed in England long before there was a democratically elected legislature to enact legislation. The roots of the court's power to create law go back to the eleventh century and the Norman Conquest. Although reading about medieval history may seem irrelevant to your study of the modern American legal system, the principles followed by our American legal system originated in England in 1066. Until 1066 Anglo-Saxon kings ruled England. There was no central legislature or centralized court system. Disputes were decided locally based on local custom. In 1066 the king, Edward the Confessor, died without children. This left the succession to the throne to either his brother-in-law, Harold, a powerful English baron, or his French cousin,

---

[12]29 C.F.R. § 1604.11 (2000).

William, Duke of Normandy. Harold was elected king. Immediately William assembled an army of soldiers, knights, and horses.[13]

In the fall of 1066 William landed on the south coast of England with his soldiers and knights, mounted on horseback. The mounted Norman knights overwhelmed the English foot soldiers, defeating the English army. On Christmas Day, 1066, William, the Duke of Normandy, had himself crowned king of England.

England became a country where everyone who spoke English owned no land and was impoverished. The king and the upper classes spoke French and used French in the courts. As a result, one enduring reminder of the Norman Conquest was the infusion of French words, such as **acquit** and **voir dire**, into our legal vocabulary. In addition, Norman kings used Latin in their written documents, so many Latin words, such as **certiorari** and **actus reus,** were incorporated into our legal language.

The Norman Conquest left a much greater legacy, however, than the French and Latin words in our legal vocabulary. It created an entirely new method for resolving disputes. Before the Conquest most disputes were decided locally, and the "law" would vary from town to town. As part of unifying England, the English kings wanted to create a common law throughout the land.

How was this uniformity created? Remember that there was no central legislature. The solution was for the king to appoint judges and establish a court system so that disputes could be settled in a uniform manner. Initially, the "courts" were simply individual judges appointed by the king to "ride a circuit" around the countryside, settling disputes in the name of the king. Over time the judges realized that rather than deciding each case as though it were the first of its kind, it would be more efficient to share the results of their prior decisions with each other so that similar cases could be decided similarly. The resulting court-made law became known as the common law.

Unless a good reason dictated otherwise, it became the policy to follow the rules laid down in prior decisions. This was how the doctrine of **stare decisis** developed. Once courts had determined the law in an area, other courts followed that rule unless a court thought there was a good reason to change it.

By about 1200 the main structure of the common law system was in place. A body of centrally appointed judges applied a common law throughout the country, and a tradition of following precedent had been established. The commencement of a series of Year Books, each collecting cases from the most important courts for that year, further solidified this development. In 1535 this system was replaced by reporters, collections of court opinions as "reported" by various authors. Finally, in 1865 this process culminated in the United States with the practice of publishing official law reports.

Meanwhile, the common law had come to America and had formed the basis for our legal system. There are areas of the law that are still totally governed by the common law, such as most matters dealing with torts. However, over the years more and more areas of the common law have been enacted into statutes; that process is known as the **codification of the common law**. When the common law has been changed through legislation, the statute is said to be in **derogation of the common law.**

Stare decisis
The doctrine stating that normally once a court has decided one way on a particular issue, it and other courts in the same jurisdiction will decide the same way on that issue in future cases given similar facts unless they can be convinced of the need for change.

Codification of the common law
The process of legislative enactment of areas of the law previously governed solely by the common law.

Derogation of the common law
Used to describe legislation that changes the common law.

---

[13]This is a good illustration of what occurs when there is no established governmental structure for settling disagreements. The disputants resort to violence.

Before abandoning our history lesson, there was one more development in the English court system that has had a great impact on our system, and that was the development of equity courts. The courts we have discussed up to now had the power to settle disputes by requiring one party to compensate the other with money damages. But there are times when money is not what the litigants want. Rather they would like the court to order the other party to do something, such as living up to contractual obligations, or to cease doing something, such as having loud parties in the wee hours of the morning. In response to this need, the English created the **equity** courts.

Judges in the equity courts used their powers to "do justice." For example, equity powers allow judges to take preventive action when the law would otherwise limit their decisions to monetary awards after the damage has been done. Equity powers include a judge's ability to issue an **injunction** or to order **specific performance**. An injunction is a court order requiring someone to act or to refrain from acting. Specific performance requires that a party fulfill his or her contractual obligations. In the 1800s most states merged their law and equity courts. Therefore, today judges have the power to give either monetary awards or equitable relief or both, as they deem appropriate.

Equity
Fairness; a court's power to do justice. Equity powers allow judges to take action when otherwise the law would limit their decisions to monetary awards. Equity powers include a judge's ability to issue an injunction and to order specific performance.

Injunction
A court order requiring a party to perform a specific act or to cease doing a specific act.

Specific performance
A requirement that a party fulfill his or her contractual obligations.

DISCUSSION QUESTIONS

7. Assume Congress enacted a statute making it a federal crime for "anyone" to kidnap children and take them across state lines. Assume further that the U.S. Supreme Court decided that the word *anyone* did not include a parent. If it wanted to do so, could Congress amend the statute to say that the word *anyone* does include parents? Why? *Yes*

8. Assume Congress enacted a statute making it a federal crime to have an abortion. Assume further that the U.S. Supreme Court declared the statute to be unconstitutional because it interfered with a woman's constitutional right to privacy. If it wanted to do so, could the executive branch prosecute women for violating the statute? In other words, does Congress or the Supreme Court have the final word on what is constitutional? Why?

9. For each of the following, which source of law—a constitution, a statute, an administrative regulation, or a court opinion—would be best able to handle the problem and why?
    a. A requirement that all motorcycle riders wear helmets. *statute*
    b. A rule making a bar owner liable for any injuries caused by a patron to whom the bar sold drinks. *court opinion, statute*
    c. A rule that all semi-trailers traveling on interstate highways use concave mud flaps. *Ad detailed*
    d. A requirement that employers not discriminate on the basis of religion or sexual orientation. *constitution, statutory*
    e. A requirement that no more than a certain percentage of a known pollutant be released by factory smokestacks.
    f. A question as to whether a person not wearing a seat belt should be able to recover for injuries that person sustained in an automobile accident that was not his fault.
    g. A law prohibiting government from interfering with an individual's right to freedom of speech. *Constitution*

SUMMARY

Our country was the first to adopt a written constitution, and it is our federal constitution that provides the framework within which all our laws are made. Similarly, states' constitutions provide the legal basis for their governments to act.

Even though traditionally we say that the legislature makes the law, the executive branch enforces the law, and the courts interpret the law, the truth is that the legislative, executive, and judicial branches, as well as administrative agencies, are all involved in making the law. Legislatures create law by enacting statutes, agencies create law by promulgating regulations, and appellate courts create law through their written opinions known as court decisions. In addition, the executive branch occasionally creates law through executive orders.

The example with which we began this chapter provides a good illustration of how statutory, regulatory, and court-made law work together. Congress enacted a statute that prohibited "sex discrimination." Because this phrase is so broad, the EEOC, an administrative agency, has issued regulations that more clearly define some types of sex discrimination, such as sexual harassment. Finally, even the most detailed regulation cannot cover every individual case. Therefore, the courts are constantly called on to interpret the meanings of both statutes and regulations.

Figure 2-1   Sources of Law

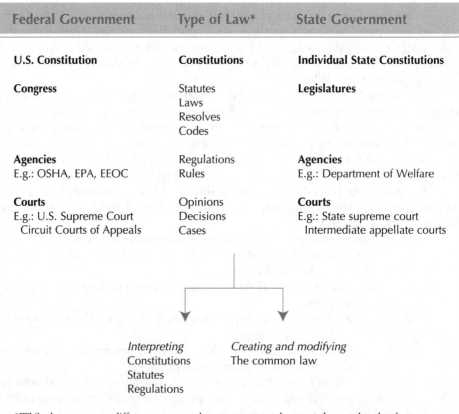

Federal Government	Type of Law*	State Government
U.S. Constitution	Constitutions	**Individual State Constitutions**
Congress	Statutes Laws Resolves Codes	**Legislatures**
Agencies E.g.: OSHA, EPA, EEOC	Regulations Rules	**Agencies** E.g.: Department of Welfare

Courts
E.g.: U.S. Supreme Court
  Circuit Courts of Appeals
	Opinions
	Decisions
	Cases
		Courts
		E.g.: State supreme court
		  Intermediate appellate courts

Interpreting
Constitutions
Statutes
Regulations

Creating and modifying
The common law

*While there are some differences among the terms *statutes, laws, resolves,* and *codes,* for our current purposes you can view them as synonyms. The same is true for the terms *regulations* and *rules,* as well as *opinions, decisions,* and *cases.*

Where no constitution, statute, or administrative regulation applies, the courts rely on the common law to resolve the problem. But it is in their role as interpreters of constitutional, statutory, and administrative provisions that courts have the greatest power: By interpreting the law, the courts end up creating the law. Figure 2-1, page 28, summarizes the major sources of law.

REVIEW QUESTIONS

Pages 15 through 21

1. What are the two primary functions of the U.S. Constitution?
2. What is the power of judicial review, and why is it so important to our legal system?
3. Read the excerpts from the U.S. Constitution and the Bill of Rights located in Appendix A. Then answer the following questions:
   a. Which article deals specifically with the legislature? With the executive? With the judiciary? (This may seem like trivia necessary only for Jeopardy contestants, but lawyers often refer to Article I, Article II, or Article III powers.)
   b. Which amendment states that the powers not specifically delegated to the federal government are reserved to the states?
   c. Make a list of the rights protected by the first ten amendments.

Pages 22 through 23

4. Why do constitutions and statutes frequently include ambiguous language?
5. How do courts become involved in the legislative process?
6. Who has the final say as to what a statute means, the legislature or the courts?
7. Who has the final say as to the constitutionality of a statute, the legislature or the courts?

Pages 23 through 25

8. How are statutes and administrative regulations similar? How do they differ?
9. Why are administrative agencies referred to as the fourth branch of government?

Pages 25 through 27

10. What impact did the Norman Conquest have on the American legal system?
11. What is the common law?
12. Why were equity courts created, and what special powers were they given?

Chapter 3

Classification of the Law

Logically, everything ought to come first.
Jean Jacques Rousseau

INTRODUCTION

In the previous chapter, we explained how law is made not only by legislatures, but also by administrative agencies and courts. Based on its source, we classified law in terms of constitutional, statutory, administrative, or common law. In this chapter we discuss other ways of classifying the law based on whether it involves

1. state, federal, or local law (every state as well as the federal government has its own laws);
2. civil and/or criminal law (**civil law** deals with harm against an individual—for example, a broken contract—whereas **criminal law** deals with harm against society as a whole—as when violence leads to someone's death); and
3. substantive and/or procedural law (**substantive law** defines our legal rights and duties—for example, the duty to obey speed limits and the right of freedom of speech—whereas **procedural law** is comprised of the rules that govern how the legal system operates).

Knowledge of these classification schemes is a necessary part of organizing your legal research plan. For example, depending upon how an attorney categorizes a problem, that attorney may decide to start research in state instead of federal law or to look at statutes instead of court opinions. Often these classifications will be obvious to an experienced attorney or paralegal. There will be times, however, when the categorizations are not so obvious.

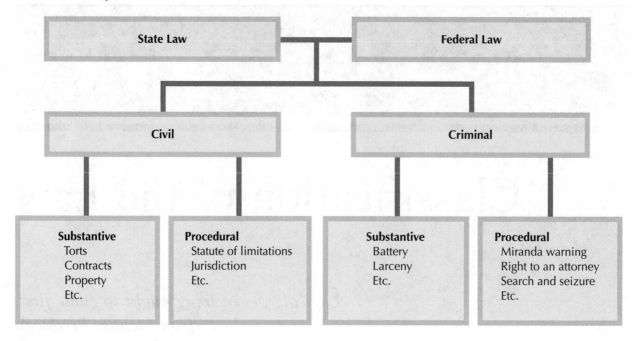

Figure 3-1   How Lawyers Classify the Law

Recall the case of Diane Dobbs, the pregnant waitress introduced at the beginning of the last chapter. In analyzing Diane's story, an attorney would think in terms of the three categories we just listed. While it is not necessary to proceed in any particular order in applying the three categories listed above to Diane's situation, all three must be evaluated. First, do Diane's problems relate to state or federal law? Are both state and federal laws involved? Second, does her situation involve any criminal laws, or does only civil law apply? Third, in addition to examining the substantive law issues, what procedural issues might be involved? As we proceed through the chapter, we will discuss each of these classifications.

Note that these are not mutually exclusive categories. A client's situation may involve both federal and state laws, both civil and criminal issues, and procedural as well as substantive questions. Figure 3-1 illustrates how these different categories relate to each other. At this point do not be concerned about understanding all of the terms listed in the figure. As the chapter proceeds, we will discuss each term in more detail.

Federalism
A system of government in which the authority to govern is split between a single, nationwide central government and several regional governments that control specific geographical areas.

A. FEDERAL VERSUS STATE LAW

Each of the fifty states, along with the federal government, has its own legal system. Each determines how its court system will be organized and what laws it will enforce. Although the laws of one state are often similar to the laws of another, each state ultimately decides for itself what those laws will be. This is because, as we mentioned in the last chapter, the United States operates under a system of government known as **federalism**. In our federal system the power to make various types of laws is divided between the federal government in

Washington, D.C., and the fifty state governments. A client's problem may involve state law or federal law or both state and federal law.

1. Federal Law

You will be in an area covered by federal law if the client's problem deals with any of the following:

1. a U.S. constitutional issue (such as freedom of speech or the rights of a criminal defendant);
2. a federal statute (such as the Internal Revenue Code); or
3. regulations of a federal agency (such as the IRS).

When a client's problem is covered by one of these three areas, you will hear attorneys referring to this as raising a federal issue or a federal question. As we will see later in the chapter on civil litigation, categorizing a legal problem in this way is very important as generally federal courts can only hear cases that either involve parties from different states or that raise a federal question.

When you hear people complaining about what they believe to be the excessive reach of the federal government, they are frequently referring to the second area of federal law, federal statutes. However, despite its growth in recent years, it is not true that eventually all areas of the law will be governed by federal law. The Constitution imposes important limits on the scope of Congress's law making power. Congress can enact legislation only if the Constitution has given Congress the power to legislate in that particular area. These delegated powers can be found in Article I, Section 8. In addition, several constitutional amendments, such as Section 5 of the Fourteenth Amendment, have provisions enabling Congress to pass legislation necessary to enforce that amendment.

For example, Congress could and does enact legislation regarding taxation because Article I, Section 8, provides that "[t]he Congress shall have Power To lay and collect Taxes, Duties, Imposts and Excises." On the other hand, Congress could not enact a national divorce law, as there is nothing in the Constitution to give Congress that power. Further, under the Tenth Amendment any power not specifically given to Congress by the Constitution is reserved to the people or to the states.

It is important to note, however, that after enumerating powers such as those to lay and collect taxes, establish post offices and post roads, raise armies, and declare war, Section 8 states that Congress has the power "to make all Laws which shall be necessary and proper for carrying into Execution" the specifically enumerated powers. The U.S. Supreme Court broadly interpreted this last clause in the 1819 case of *McCulloch v. Maryland*.[1] Even though the Constitution did not explicitly delegate to Congress the power to create banks, the Court ruled that Congress could create and operate a national bank as part of the exercise of its expressly delegated powers to collect taxes and to borrow money. This is known as the **"doctrine of implied powers."**

In addition, Congress has sweeping powers under Article I, Section 8. That section provides: "Congress shall have power to regulate commerce . . . among the

Doctrine of implied powers
Powers not stated in Constitution but that are necessary for Congress to carry out other, expressly granted powers.

---

[1] 4 Wheat. 316.

several states." This has come to be known as the "interstate commerce clause." Originally, the courts interpreted "interstate commerce" to mean exactly that: the movement of goods across state lines. However, in *Gibbons v. Ogden*[2] the Supreme Court interpreted this clause as giving the federal government the authority not only to regulate products that actually travel in interstate commerce, but also to regulate anything that has an "effect upon" interstate commerce.

In the 1930s Congress used this expansive reading of the interstate commerce clause as the basis for much of its "New Deal" economic legislation, including the Unfair Labor Standards Act (controlling the hours and wages of employees who manufactured goods destined for interstate commerce) and the National Labor Relations Act (creating the National Labor Relations Board and authorizing it to enjoin unfair labor practices).

A major challenge to Congress's use of the commerce clause powers came in the 1960s, following Congress's passage of the 1964 Civil Rights Act. In Title II of the Civil Rights Act Congress made it unlawful to discriminate in a place of public accommodation on the basis of race, color, religion, sex, or national origin. When this provision was challenged in *Heart of Atlanta Motel, Inc. v. United States*,[3] the Court held that the law was within the scope of the commerce clause because the existence of racially discriminatory practices made it more difficult for racial minorities to travel from one state to another and this had a negative impact on the free flow of interstate commerce. In a related case, *Katzenback v. McClung*,[4] the Court found that even a small, local, family-owned restaurant catering to local customers had enough of an impact on interstate commerce to justify Congress's actions in prohibiting discrimination.

In its decision in the *Heart of Atlanta* case the Court wrote that when reviewing a statute enacted by Congress pursuant to its commerce clause powers, the only questions the Court needs to ask are these: (1) Did Congress have a rational basis for finding that the proscribed activity affected interstate commerce, and if so, (2) were the means selected reasonable and appropriate?[5] If the answers are yes, the act is constitutional. In other words, the Court's role is to decide not whether Congress was right in finding the connection to interstate commerce, but only whether Congress had a rational basis for acting as it did. Thus, it did not matter that the Senate had made it quite clear that "the fundamental object of Title II was to vindicate the 'deprivation of personal dignity that surely accompanies denials of equal access to public establishments,'"[6] rather than something more directly related to interstate commerce. That "Congress was legislating against moral wrongs . . . rendered its enactments no less valid"[7] so long as Congress could reasonably have believed the legislation was necessary in order to regulate interstate commerce.

Throughout the sixties, seventies, eighties, and nineties this expansive reading of Congress's power under the commerce clause allowed Congress to address problems through federal statutes that Congress believed the states had failed to

---

[2] 9 Wheat. 1 (1824).
[3] 379 U.S. 241 (1964).
[4] 379 U.S 294 (1964).
[5] 379 U.S. at 258.
[6] Id. at 250.
[7] Id. at 257.

handle properly themselves. It was not until the 1995 case of *United States v. Lopez*[8] that the U.S. Supreme Court gave the first indication that there were limits to Congress's power under the interstate commerce clause. In *Lopez* the Court reversed a conviction under the federal Gun-Free School Zones Act of 1990. A twelfth-grade student had brought a concealed .38-caliber handgun to school with him. That statute made it a federal crime to possess a firearm in a school zone. The Court found that the interstate commerce clause did not give the federal government authority to regulate the possession of guns on public school grounds because Congress had failed to show the required connection between the unlawful possession of guns near schools and interstate commerce. In dissent, Justice Stevens argued that Congress had a reasonable basis for finding that education is inextricably intertwined with the nation's economy and that the decline in the quality of education brought about by violent crime in school zones had adversely affected interstate commerce.[9] The majority insisted, however, that Congress could act under the commerce clause only when an *economic* activity was involved.[10] To rule otherwise, the majority said, would permit Congress to "regulate not only all violent crime, but all activities that might lead to violent crime, regardless of how tenuously they relate to interstate commerce."[11] Therefore, the Court concluded that in order to maintain the proper distinction between what is truly national and what is truly local, the control of guns in school zones was a matter that had to be left solely for the individual states to regulate.

Five years later, in *United States v. Morrison,*[12] the Supreme Court struck down another federal statute, the federal Violence against Women Act of 1994. That statute authorized victims of violent acts directed at women to sue for damages in federal court. Before enacting the Violence Against Women Act, Congress had held four years of hearings and found that violence against women affected interstate commerce by deterring potential victims from traveling, seeking employment, and transacting business across state lines.

Relying upon this federal statute, a female college student filed a civil suit in federal court seeking damages from the university and the two male students she alleged had raped her in her dormitory room. When the case came before the Court, 36 states supported the plaintiff's right to sue her attackers in federal court based on the belief that the current system for dealing with violence against women was inadequate as "the problem of violence against women is a national one, requiring federal attention, federal leadership, and federal funds."[13] In spite of the congressional findings mentioned above and the support from the states, the Court, in a sharply divided five-four decision, held that Congress had overstepped its powers in enacting the statute because gender-motivated crimes are not the kind of *economic* activity that Congress has the power to regulate. Citing the *Lopez* case, the Court reasoned that the "regulation and punishment of intrastate violence that is not directed at the instrumentalities, channels, or

---

[8]514 U.S. 549 (1995).

[9]Id. at 620-623.

[10]Id. at 560.

[11]Id. at 564.

[12]529 U.S. 598 (2000).

[13]Id. at 615 (citing H.R. Conf. Rep. No. 103-711, at 385).

goods involved in interstate commerce has always been the province of the States,"[14] rather than the federal government.

The *Lopez* decision had left many legal analysts in doubt as to the future of Congress's commerce clause powers. The Court could simply have been sending a warning to Congress to justify its actions through congressional hearings and to take care not to overstep its bounds. Alternatively, the case could be interpreted as a signal that the Supreme Court was ready to return to an earlier, more limited view of the powers of the federal government. With the *Morrison* decision it appears that the latter is more likely to be the correct interpretation and that the constitutionality of additional federal statutes will be challenged.

Just as there are some areas where the federal government cannot legislate, there are a few areas where only the federal government may legislate. This occurs when a decision has been made that uniformity is necessary across state lines. In those cases the federal law preempts the state law. This **doctrine of preemption** allows the federal government to prevent the states from passing conflicting laws and sometimes even to prohibit states from passing any laws on a particular subject. Recent examples of preemption include *Geier v. American Honda Motor Co.,*[15] where the Supreme Court held that federal rules on air bags preempted lawsuits based on state tort law, and *Lorillard Tobacco Co. v. Reilly,*[16] in which the Court held that the Federal Cigarette Labeling and Advertising Act preempted Massachusetts state regulations restricting outdoor and point-of-sale cigarette advertising. On the other hand, in *Rush Prudential HMO, Inc. v. Moran,*[17] the Court held the federal Employee Retirement Income Security Act of 1974 (commonly referred to as ERISA) did not preempt an Illinois statute that allowed HMO patients to seek a second opinion if their HMO denied coverage. The Court, noting that the field of health care is traditionally subject to state regulation, stated that there could be no federal preemption in this area without a clear manifestation of congressional intent to do so.[18] For example, in *Aetna Health Inc. v. Davila,*[19] the Court determined that Congress did intend for ERISA to preempt state law when injuries allegedly result from an insurance provider's decision to disregard a treating physician's recommendations for treatment or services. The plaintiffs had argued that the insurance providers' decisions had been made negligently, causing them harm, and had sued under state law in state court. The Court concluded that such cases must be brought in federal court and resolved according to the terms of ERISA, not state law.

Preemption
The power of the federal government to prevent the states from passing conflicting laws, and sometimes even to prohibit states from passing any laws on a particular subject.

2. State Law

Whereas the federal government must trace all of its powers back to a specific constitutional authorization, the states are allowed to make any laws they deem appropriate for the health, welfare, safety, and morals of their citizens

---

[14]Id. at 618.
[15]529 U.S. 861 (2000).
[16]533 U.S. 525 (2001).
[17]536 U.S. 355 (2002).
[18]Id. at 403.
[19]124 S. Ct. 2488 (2004).

as long as those laws are not prohibited by the U.S. Constitution.[20] Typical examples of areas covered by state law are criminal behavior, contracts, torts, property, marriage, and family matters. While much of the law from one state to the next is quite similar, the states are free to create their own unique laws. Where one state may choose to legalize gambling, another may not; where one state may choose to allow no-fault divorces, another may not.

Some see this diversity as one of the great strengths of our political system. They argue that it encourages experimentation and innovation by allowing the residents of Georgia, for example, to establish rules of conduct that differ from those established by the residents of Nevada. Critics, on the other hand, point to the problems it creates for interstate business and travel—for example, forcing large corporations and other out-of-state parties to hire local attorneys and making it difficult for an attorney to move a practice from one state to another. They also point out that states are sometimes reluctant to impose needed regulations (in areas such as environmental protection and worker safety) for fear that the affected businesses will move to another state with fewer restrictions.

As we become an ever more interdependent nation, however, state laws are tending to become more and more uniform, especially in the area of commercial law. Businesses with dealings in more than one state do not like having to worry about a multiplicity of state laws. Therefore, most states have voluntarily moved to adopt uniform laws in areas such as commercial sales.

Finally, both federal and state laws cover some areas, such as employment discrimination. From our discussion above regarding preemption, you will recall that a state cannot pass laws that conflict with federal laws. However, if there is no conflict between state and federal law, a state is free to legislate in that area. For example, a Massachusetts statute states that an employer of six or more employees may not discriminate on the basis of race, color, religion, sex, or national origin. This is perfectly valid as it does not conflict with the federal statute, Title VII, that states an employer of fifteen or more employees may not discriminate on the basis of race, color, religion, sex, or national origin.

DISCUSSION QUESTIONS

1. For each question determine whether you think the law involved is federal, state, or both.
   a. A person is liable for slander if that person intentionally says that someone is a thief when she knows it is not true.
   b. To be valid, a contract for the sale of real estate must be in writing.
   c. Trucks traveling on interstate highways must be equipped with concave mud flaps.
   d. No employer with ten or more employees may discriminate on the basis of race, color, religion, sex, or national origin.
   e. A manufacturer of inherently dangerous products will be liable for any defective product that causes injury.

---

[20]The Tenth Amendment to the U.S. Constitution declares that "powers not delegated to the United States by the Constitution, nor prohibited by it to the States, are reserved to the States respectively, or to the people."

2. Can you think of any areas of the law that are not now regulated on a federal level but should be? What are those areas, and why do you think the federal government should take on a more active role?

3. Can you think of any areas of the law that should be left solely to state and local governments? If so, what are they, and why do you think the federal government should not be involved?

4. In what areas of the law do you think there should be uniformity across all of the states? In what areas should there be diversity? Why?

B. CRIMINAL LAW VERSUS CIVIL LAW

Another major classification within the law is the division between criminal law and civil law. Both provide mechanisms for addressing violations of the law, but they differ regarding the procedures you must use and the types of sanctions or remedies that are available. In this section we will first compare criminal and civil law. Next we will take a quick look at the major substantive areas of criminal and civil law. We cover substantive civil law in more depth in Chapters 10-14 and criminal law in Chapter 15.

1. A Comparison of Criminal and Civil Law

Some of the major differences between criminal and civil law are listed in Figure 3-2.

a. Type of Harm

Civil law
Law that deals with harm to an individual.

Criminal law
Law that deals with harm to society as a whole.

Civil law is invoked when one individual harms another. When an individual violates a part of the **criminal law,** society considers itself the offended party and takes an active role in the sanctioning process. Thus if Peter Jones burglarizes Sam Smith's home, the criminal law views that act as an offense against society itself rather than simply as a matter between Smith and Jones.

But what determines when an act such as burglarizing someone's home is a wrong against society as a whole? It is up to the legislative branch of government to decide when the consequences of certain acts are viewed as grave enough to classify the act as a crime against the state. Thus when the legislature perceives that a particular act, such as drunk driving, has that broader impact, it can criminalize such behavior.

b. Names of the Parties and the "Prosecutor" of the Claim

Plaintiff
A person who initiates a lawsuit.

Defendant
In a lawsuit the person who is sued; in a criminal case the person who is being charged with a crime.

The person who brings the civil suit (also known as a civil action or a civil lawsuit) is known as the **plaintiff,** and the person sued is called the **defendant.** For example, recall the situation involving the pregnant waitress presented at the beginning of Chapter 2. If Diane Dobbs were to sue the restaurant, she would be the plaintiff. Both the corporation that owns the Western Rib Eye Restaurant and the restaurant manager would probably be named as defendants. Although civil suits are usually between individuals, a governmental unit (federal, state, or local) can become a plaintiff in a civil suit. In a criminal case, the case is listed as *People v. Jones* or *State v. Jones.* Governmental attorneys prosecute the accused party (the defendant), and the victim is merely a witness.

	Civil	Criminal
Type of harm	Private injury	Harm to society
Names of the parties	Plaintiff/defendant	State*/defendant
"Prosecutor" of the claim	Usually an individual; sometimes the government	Government
Standard of proof	Proponderance of the evidence	Beyond a reasonable doubt
Judgment	Liable/not liable	Guilty/not guilty
Sanctions/remedies	Damages/injunction	Imprisonment/fines/death
Source of law	Common law/statutes	Statutes

*The State may also be referred to as the Commonwealth or the People. Although the state is the named party, it is actually a government employee, the **prosecutor** (also known as the **district attorney**, **state's attorney**, or **attorney general**), who brings the lawsuit as the state's representative.

Figure 3-2   A Comparison of Civil and Criminal Law

c. Standard of Proof

Because of the serious consequences of violating criminal laws, the standard of proof is different from that used in civil cases. On the criminal side, the prosecution is required to prove its case **beyond a reasonable doubt**. In civil actions the plaintiff need only meet the **preponderance of the evidence** standard. Judges usually explain the beyond a reasonable doubt standard to jurors as the degree of doubt that causes a reasonable person to refrain from acting. The proof must be so conclusive and complete that all reasonable doubts regarding the facts are removed from the jurors' minds. A preponderance of the evidence, on the other hand, is usually understood to mean that the facts asserted are more likely to be true than not true. One study showed that judges equate "beyond a reasonable doubt" with a median probability of approximately 8.8 out of 10. Jurors averaged approximately 8.6 out of 10. The judges interpreted preponderance of the evidence as a median probability of 5.4 out of 10. For jurors the median was 7.1 out of 10.[21] These results indicate that although judges and jurors may disagree as to the precise meaning of the standards, they agree that the criminal law requires a greater degree of proof before its sanctions can be applied.

Beyond a reasonable doubt
The standard of proof used in criminal trials. The proof must be so conclusive and complete that all reasonable doubts regarding the facts are removed from the jurors' minds.

Preponderance of the evidence
The standard of proof used in civil trials. The proof must indicate that it is more likely than than not the defendant committed the wrong.

---

[21]Simon & Mahan, Quantifying Burdens of Proofs, 5 Law & Socy. Rev. 319 (1971).

d. Judgment

The result of the court's actions in a civil suit is a finding of liability or no liability. Do not use the term *guilty* when referring to a civil defendant. In a criminal case we say that the defendant was found guilty or not guilty.

e. Sanctions/Remedies

Damages
Monetary compensation, including compensatory, punitive, and nominal damages.

The typical remedy in a civil case is either **damages,** where the defendant pays the plaintiff for the harm he or she has done, or an **injunction,** where the court orders the defendant to take some specific action or to cease acting in a specific way. For example, in Diane's situation she might ask to be paid for the time she has been out of work (damages) and request a court order requiring the restaurant to rehire her (an injunction).

While the focus of civil law is on redressing the losses of the plaintiff, in the criminal law the sanctions are designed to punish the offender and deter future offenders. If a court of law determines that a provision of the criminal law has been violated, it may impose two broad types of sanctions—loss of liberty and financial penalty. The loss of liberty can range from receiving unsupervised probation to spending a few days in the county jail to serving several years in a state penitentiary to receiving the death penalty. The fines assessed as part of the criminal process become the property of the state rather than the victim. Only occasionally will a negotiated settlement with a criminal defendant contain some provisions for restitution for the victim. Usually, if the victim wishes to receive money from the criminal defendant to compensate her for the harm done to her, she must hire a lawyer and initiate a civil suit.

PRACTICAL TIP

Even though we sometimes talk about civil versus criminal law, keep in mind that the same facts may give rise to both civil and criminal lawsuits. If a potential defendant in a civil case has been convicted at a criminal trial, that will make it easier for the plaintiff to win a civil case. However, even if the defendant was acquitted at the criminal trial, because of the different standards of proof and evidentiary requirements the plaintiff may still win in a civil case.

---

f. Sources of Law

A final difference relates to the sources of criminal and civil law. Criminal law is almost entirely statutory, while civil law is rooted in the common law (court-made law). Gradually, however, this distinction is being eroded as more and more areas of the civil law are becoming controlled by statutory law.

A single event can become the basis for actions in both the criminal and the civil courts. For example, the victim of a battery could sue the attacker for civil damages at the same time the state is prosecuting the attacker on a criminal charge. The driver of an automobile involved in a traffic accident may receive a traffic ticket from the police and at the same time be sued by someone else involved in the accident. In certain types of antitrust cases the government can choose between seeking criminal charges and seeking civil damages. As noted earlier regarding Diane's case, she might bring a civil action to recover money and obtain a court order. In addition, she might want to press criminal charges for the restaurant's refusal to let her collect her personal belongings. Charging a person with a criminal violation and suing that person civilly do not constitute **double jeopardy**. Double jeopardy is defined as being prosecuted twice for the same criminal offense.

> **Double jeopardy**
> A constitutional protection against being tried twice for the same crime.

In summary, common ways of differentiating criminal from civil law include the following: In a civil case the harm is to an individual, while in a criminal case the action is said to harm society itself; in a civil case the parties are labeled the plaintiff and the defendant, whereas in a criminal case they are the state and the defendant; the government prosecutes criminal cases, while individual plaintiffs initiate civil cases; in a criminal case the government must prove its case beyond a reasonable doubt, whereas in a civil case the plaintiff must prove his or her case by a preponderance of the evidence; a finding of guilt in a criminal case results in a fine or imprisonment, while a finding of liability in a civil case results in a monetary award or an injunction; and the source of law for civil cases is both court-made law and statutes, whereas almost all criminal law is based in statutes.

2. Criminal Law

Murder, robbery, and arson are examples of criminal behavior. However, it is much easier to list types of criminal behavior than it is to define the difference between criminal and civil law. As mentioned earlier, usually it is said that a criminal act harms not just the victim but also society as a whole. That definition does not get us very far. What is a wrong against society as a whole? One way of viewing that is to say that the act hurts not only the individual victim, but also society as a whole because the act's consequences are so grave as to cause concern to the rest of the population. When the legislature perceives that a particular act such as arson has that broader impact, it enacts a statute outlining the elements of the crime and its punishment.

In this section we will discuss the major types of criminal behavior, what is necessary to prove to a court that a crime has been committed, and what defenses might be raised to try to show the court that the defendant was justified in acting as he or she did.

a. Types of Crimes

Serious crimes, such as murder, rape, armed robbery, and aggravated assault, are classified as felonies, and they generally involve a punishment that can include a year or more in a state prison. **Misdemeanors** include such lesser charges as disorderly conduct and criminal damage to property. When incarceration is called for in these cases, it usually is for less than one year and is served in a county jail. Today the criminal law in most jurisdictions is entirely statutory in nature, and the legislature determines whether a given act is to be considered a felony or a misdemeanor.

The criminal codes of most states typically divide crimes into the following categories:

1. crimes against persons (homicide, kidnapping, sex offenses, assault, and battery),
2. crimes against property (theft, robbery, burglary, arson, and trespass),
3. crimes against the public health or decency (drug offenses, abortion, bribery, gambling, prostitution, and disorderly conduct), and
4. crimes against the government itself (treason and official misconduct).

The focus of federal criminal law is on interstate activities and unlawful interference with a federal agency or its workers.

b. Establishing a Prima Facie Case

In order for a person to be convicted in a criminal trial, the prosecution must establish that the defendant committed an act defined as being illegal in the criminal code. This involves proving that the accused both had the requisite bad intent (called **mens rea**) and committed the requisite bad behavior (called **actus reus**). Different acts—killing someone, burning down a building, robbing a store—can give rise to different crimes. It is also true that the same act accompanied by different types of intent can give rise to different crimes. For example, the act of killing could be categorized as murder or manslaughter depending on the defendant's state of mind when he or she committed the act.

At the trial the prosecution must first present a **prima facie case**, one that establishes the elements of the crime, the requisite bad intent and bad behavior. A prima facie case contains enough evidence to support a finding of guilty if the defense presents no contrary evidence. If the prosecution fails to present a prima facie case, the judge must issue a not guilty verdict without the defense even presenting its case.

Mens rea
Bad intent.

Actus reus
Bad act.

Prima facie case
What the prosecution or plaintiff must be able to prove in order for the case to go to the jury—that is, the elements of the prosecution's case or the plaintiff's cause of action.

DISCUSSION QUESTIONS

5. What do you think of the differences between judges' and jurors' definitions of "beyond a reasonable doubt" and a "preponderance of the evidence"? Do you think this causes any problems for our legal system?

6. Take a moment to read the following Massachusetts statute regarding larceny.

> Whoever steals . . . and with intent to steal . . . the property of another . . . shall be guilty of larceny. . . . [22]

a. Assume Alan got into a car, knowing that it was not his, "hot wired" it, and then drove off in it. Is he guilty of violating the statute? Why?
b. Assume Bill approached a car that he intended to steal but was scared away by a passerby. Is he guilty of violating the statute? Why?
c. Assume Charles got into a car, thinking he was getting into his friend's car, and "hot wired" it but only meant to borrow it. Is he guilty of violating the statute? Why?

---

[22]Mass. Gen. L. ch. 266, § 30 (2000).

c. Defenses

If the prosecution does present a prima facie case, the defense then has the opportunity to present evidence that either contradicts that presented by the prosecutor or establishes a legally recognized justification. This evidence could involve witnesses who contradict the testimony of prosecution witnesses or evidence that establishes an alibi, self-defense, or insanity.

There are essentially two types of criminal **defenses**. The first type justifies the act. The second type negates the requisite mens rea. An example of the first type of defense, which justifies the act, is self-defense. The defendant admits killing the victim but argues that he or she had no choice. Examples of the second type of defense, which negates the requisite intent, are insanity, infancy, and intoxication. Each of these defenses has as its premise the fact that the defendant was incapable of forming the requisite intent to commit the crime.

After the defense has presented its evidence, the prosecution has a chance to respond with rebuttal witnesses to attack these defenses and reestablish the credibility of its own witnesses.

3. Civil Law

Civil law involves private actions brought by individuals to address perceived wrongs. In this section we will discuss what is necessary to prove a civil prima facie case, the defenses to a civil suit, the damages that a plaintiff can recover, and the main areas of civil law.

a. Establishing a Prima Facie Case

Just as the prosecution has the burden of establishing a prima facie case in a criminal case, so, too, the plaintiff shares a similar burden in a civil case. The plaintiff has the burden of proving the various elements listed in his or her complaint that show the plaintiff has a valid **cause of action**. A cause of action is a claim that based on the law and the facts is sufficient to demand judicial action. The plaintiff must prove these elements by a preponderance of the evidence, which means it is more likely than not that the defendant committed the wrong.

Cause of action
A claim that based on the law and the facts is sufficient to support a lawsuit. If the plaintiff does not state a valid cause of action in the complaint, the court will dismiss it.

For example, assume a car and a truck collided at an intersection. The driver of the car is injured and wants to sue the truck driver, alleging the truck driver ran a red light. The car driver will be the plaintiff, and his cause of action will be based on the law of **negligence** (acting unreasonably under the circumstances) and the facts of what happened at the intersection. To succeed in a lawsuit, the plaintiff will have to present evidence that it is more likely than not that the truck driver was negligent. If the plaintiff/driver is able to do so, then he has satisfied his prima facie case. Every area of civil law has its own required elements that constitute the plaintiff's prima facie case. Later in this chapter as you read about torts, contracts, and property law, note the requirements of each for the plaintiff to prove a prima facie case.

b. Defenses

The defendant/truck driver can respond first by trying to negate the plaintiff's case. Perhaps he has a witness who will testify that the light was green for

Affirmative defense
A defense whereby the defendant offers new evidence to avoid judgment.

the truck driver and red for the plaintiff. In addition to attempting to negate the plaintiff's case, the defendant can raise defenses of his own, known as **affirmative defenses**. In effect, the defendant is saying this: Even if you are right and I did something wrong, I have a good excuse or a reason why my liability should be reduced.

For example, in the accident mentioned above, the truck driver might ask the car driver's passenger to testify that the car driver was not being as attentive to his driving as he should have been. This behavior could have contributed to the accident, thereby decreasing the defendant's share of the liability.

It is very important to keep these two approaches separate: First, the defendant tries to negate the plaintiff's case. Second, the defendant raises defenses that could limit his liability even if the plaintiff's version of the law and facts is true.

Depending on the area of law different defenses will be available. For example, it might be a valid defense to a contract claim that the defendant was only fifteen years old when he signed the contract. However, being fifteen years old may not be a defense to an intentional tort, such as battery.

In some cases, statutes or constitutions protect certain classes of people or institutions from being sued by granting them either full or partial immunity. One of the oldest and most important forms of immunity is **sovereign immunity**. Historically, the doctrine of sovereign immunity prohibited injured parties from suing the government, unless the government gave its consent. This protection can be traced back to the concept of the divine right of kings and the idea that "the king can do no wrong." In Chapter 10 we discuss how the doctrine of sovereign immunity has been modified over the years. Later in this book we also discuss the concepts of spousal and parental immunity.

Compensatory damages
Money awarded to a plaintiff in payment for his or her actual losses.

Punitive damages
Money awarded to a plaintiff in cases of intentional torts in order to punish the defendent and serve as a warning to others.

Nominal damages
A token sum awarded when liability has been found but monetary damages cannot be shown.

c. Damages

If a court determines that the plaintiff should recover, the issue of damages (monetary compensation) arises. There are three types of damages: compensatory, punitive, and nominal. **Compensatory damages** are intended to compensate the plaintiff for the harm done to her or him. In a tort action involving harm to a person, that might mean the cost of medical bills, lost time from work, and pain and suffering. **Punitive damages** are designed to punish the defendant and typically are awarded only for intentional torts when the court deems that the **tortfeasor** (the person who committed the tort) deserves an additional punishment beyond just compensating the plaintiff for the harm done to him or her. Finally, **nominal damages** are awarded when the law has been violated but the plaintiff cannot prove any monetary harm. As mentioned earlier, in addition to or instead of damages, the court might issue an injunction, an order to the defendant telling the defendant to do a specific act or to cease doing a specific act.

d. Areas of Civil Law

Civil law covers a very broad range of subjects, including adoption, admiralty, collections, corporate, divorce, employment, environmental, intellectual property, personal injury, probate, and real estate law. However, we believe it is helpful to think of civil law as falling into three main categories: making deals, owning property, and protecting people and property from harm. The most basic principles of each are covered in the standard law school courses of contracts, property, and torts, respectively. The various specialty fields listed above all involve applications of the principles taught in these three courses.

(1) Contracts

The formal definition of a **contract** is an agreement supported by consideration. Therefore, contract law deals with two-sided agreements or bargains. I agree to sell you my diamond ring, and you agree to give me $500 in return. We have struck a bargain, entered into a contract. If something should go wrong—if I refuse to hand over the ring or you refuse to give me the money—we would find our actions governed by contract law. For a contract to be valid there must be an offer, an acceptance of the offer, and **consideration**; that is, something of value must be exchanged. It is the consideration that differentiates a contract from a gift. Common defenses to a contract action include breach by the other side and incapacity to contract, as when one party is underage.

Contract
An agreement supported by consideration.

Consideration
Something of value exchanged to form the basis of a contract.

(2) Property

Property law deals with ownership. If two neighbors have a dispute over the correct placement of the boundary separating their land, property law will resolve it. Property law is divided into two main categories: (1) **real property,** land and objects permanently attached to land, and (2) **personal property,** all other property.

The first issue raised in a property law case may be how to classify the property. For example, is a room air conditioner real or personal property? If it is simply sitting in a window opening and can be easily removed without damage to the window, it is personal property. But what if the window has been taken out and the air conditioner screwed into the window frame? Is it now "permanently attached"? How you classify property is important because different rules may apply to real versus personal property.

Another common dispute that arises under property law relates to gift law. Above we noted that the difference between a contract and a gift is that a contract is two-sided (each party gives something to the other), while a gift is one-sided. The necessary elements for a valid gift include an offer, an acceptance of the offer, and delivery. Usually, the first two elements are not at issue, but the last element, delivery, can become a problem, especially when the gift is delivered symbolically, as by handing over the keys to a car. The question is, Has the car been delivered? The deciding factor is usually whether the owner has relinquished all control over the object. In the case of a car, that probably involves more than simply handing over a set of keys. This type of delivery is known as **constructive delivery.** (*Note:* A constructive delivery is one example of a **legal fiction.** Courts create a legal fiction when they need to make an assumption that is not based in fact in order to resolve a dispute. For example, courts frequently speak of corporations as though they were persons.) No actual delivery of the car is made, but the owner takes the necessary actions to allow the new owner to gain control over the gift.

Property law
Law dealing with ownership.

Real property
Land and objects permanently attached to land.

Personal property
All property that is not real property.

Constructive
Not factually true, but accepted by the courts as being legally true.

Legal fiction
An assumption that something that is not real is real—for example, saying that a corporation is a person for purposes of its being able to sue and be sued.

(3) Torts

Issues of **tort law** arise when one person harms another person or that person's property. A tort is defined as a private wrong (other than a breach of

Tort law
Law that deals with harm to a person or a person's property.

You are walking along the beach and see a young child drowning. No one else is in sight. Should the law require you to try to save the child? Should it matter if you are an off-duty lifeguard?

contract) in which a person is harmed because of another's failure to carry out a legal duty. Through the common law the courts have defined legal duties as occasionally including gthe affirmative obligation to take action to protect others. More commonly, courts require that everyone refrain from taking actions that inflict harm on others. Torts are traditionally categorized as intentional, negligent, or the result of strict liability.

Intentional tort
A tort committed by one who intends to do the act that creates the harm.

As the name indicates, an **intentional tort** occurs when someone intentionally harms a person or that person's property. If one of your classmates deliberately hits you, your classmate has committed the intentional tort known as battery. **Battery** is the intentional, harmful or offensive physical contact by one person with another person. Libel, slander, invasion of privacy, and false imprisonment are other examples of intentional torts.

Negligence
The failure to act reasonably under the circumstances.

The most common category of tort law is that of **negligence.** Negligence is the failure to act as a reasonably prudent and careful person is expected to act under the circumstances. This used to be known as the reasonable man standard but has more recently become known as the reasonable person standard.

Case 4: Mr. Whipple

Your client Mr. Whipple owns a grocery store. A customer breaks a bottle of apple juice and promptly reports it to Mr. Whipple. Nonetheless, Mr. Whipple fails to have the broken jar and spilled juice cleaned up. Twenty minutes later another customer slips on the wet floor, breaking her leg.

Mr. Whipple would probably be found liable for negligence. Clearly he did not intend for the customer to slip and break her leg. Therefore, there was no intentional tort. But a jury might find that a reasonable store owner would have ordered the spill cleaned up within the twenty minutes after learning of it.

In order for a plaintiff to prove negligence, he or she must show that

1. the defendant owed the plaintiff a duty of care;
2. the defendant breached that duty;
3. the breach caused
4. the plaintiff harm.

These four basic prerequisites (elements) in a negligence case are known as duty, breach, causation, and harm. In the case just mentioned Mr. Whipple had a duty to act as a reasonable store owner would under the circumstances. The circumstances were a broken jar of apple juice about which Mr. Whipple was informed and a twenty-minute time period in which he did nothing. If the jurors believe Mr. Whipple breached his duty to act as a reasonable store owner, then they will find liability if they also think that breach caused the customer harm.

As the store owner, Mr. Whipple would, of course, try to defend himself through rebutting the plaintiff's evidence. Perhaps it had only been two and not twenty minutes since he learned of the spill. In addition, he might try to raise an affirmative defense. As mentioned previously, an affirmative defense is a defense whereby the defendant offers new evidence to avoid or limit the judgment. The two main affirmative defenses to negligence are **contributory negligence** and **assumption of the risk.** Contributory negligence means that the plaintiff was also negligent and through that negligence contributed to his or her own injury. In Mr. Whipple's case, perhaps the customer was in a hurry and was not looking where she was going. Assumption of the risk means that the plaintiff voluntarily and knowingly subjected himself or herself to a known danger. Perhaps the customer saw the spilled juice but chose to walk through it anyway. In many states assumption of the risk is no longer a separate defense to negligence, as it has been subsumed under the more general category of contributory negligence.

Historically, any showing of contributory negligence or assumption of the risk meant that the plaintiff could recover nothing from the defendant even if the defendant's actions were much more culpable than those of the plaintiff. Legislatures and courts in many states have tried to rectify that situation by replacing contributory negligence with a new defense known as **comparative negligence.** Under comparative negligence, instead of the plaintiff's own negligence relieving the defendant of liability, the jury compares the negligence of the plaintiff to that of the defendant and apportions the responsibility. The plaintiff's recovery is reduced by his or her degree of negligence.

The third category of tort law is called **strict liability.** In some cases persons or corporations can be held liable for injuries that resulted from their actions, even when their actions were reasonable under the circumstances and they did not intend to harm anyone. The doctrine of strict liability holds that persons who engage in activities that are inherently dangerous are responsible for injury that results, even though they carried out the activities in the safest and most prudent way possible. For example, someone who uses explosives or who keeps wild animals is liable for all resulting injuries, even if that person used the utmost care. In recent years many courts have held manufacturers and sellers to be strictly liable when a defective product the defendant manufactured or sold caused harm to the user or consumer, even when the user or consumer could not show that the manufacturer's negligence caused the defect.

Contributory negligence Negligence by the plaintiff that contributed to his or her injury. Normally, any finding of contributory negligence acts as a complete bar to a plaintiff's recovery.

Assumption of the risk Voluntarily and knowingly subjecting oneself to danger.

Comparative negligence A method for measuring the relative negligence of the plaintiff and the defendant, with a commensurate sharing of the compensation for the injuries.

Strict liability Liability without a showing of fault.

Discussion Questions

7. For each question decide whether the facts raise an issue of tort, contract, or property law or more than one area of law.

    a. You buy a new car. Two days later as you are driving, the brakes fail, and you go off the road, hitting a telephone pole. Luckily you are unhurt, but the car is badly damaged.

    b. You rent an apartment. One night as you are leaving the building through the central stairway, the railing gives way, and you fall down, breaking your leg.
8. For each of the following situations decide if you think liability should be found based on an intentional tort, negligence, or strict liability or whether no liability should be found.
    a. Sally was angry with Martha. One night after leaving class, she deliberately drove her car into the side of Martha's car.
    b. One night after leaving class, Sally was in a hurry. When she arrived at the stop sign at the student parking lot entrance to Main Street, she did a "rolling stop." Martha was driving by on Main Street. Sally's auto hit the side of Martha's car.
    c. One night after leaving class, Sally got into her brand new Dodge van. When she arrived at the stop sign at the student parking lot entrance to Main Street, she pressed on the brakes, but nothing happened. Martha was driving by on Main Street. Sally's auto hit the side of Martha's car.
    d. One night after leaving class, Sally got into her car. When she arrived at the stop sign at the student parking entrance to Main Street, she suddenly got a tremendous cramp in her side and momentarily lost control of her car. Martha was driving by on Main Street. Sally's auto hit the side of Martha's car.

C. SUBSTANTIVE VERSUS PROCEDURAL LAW

Substantive law
Law that creates rights and duties.

In addition to being categorized on the basis of its source, we also classify law as being either substantive or procedural. **Substantive law** refers to the part of the law that defines our rights and duties. It defines what actions will violate the criminal law and what our obligations are to each other. For example, substantive law includes the statutes that govern the legal speed limits, the circumstances under which someone can be convicted of robbery, and when a contract is enforceable. **Procedural law,** on the other hand, deals with how the legal system operates. It defines the steps that someone must go through to file a lawsuit and the procedures the police must follow in conducting a search or interrogating a suspect.

Procedural law
Law that regulates how the legal system operates.

Statute of limitations
The law that sets the length of time from when something happens to when a lawsuit must be filed before the right to bring it is lost.

Every case is founded in substantive law, and attorneys must determine what their client's obligations and liabilities are. However, they must be equally aware of the procedural aspects of the case. Even if the substantive law is on the client's side, the case may be lost if a claim is not filed within the time prescribed in the **statute of limitations.** The legal system imposes a limitation on how long a plaintiff has before he or she can no longer bring suit. Those limitations vary given the type of case involved. A plaintiff could also lose if the complaint, the initial document that starts a lawsuit, fails to include all the required information.

We have all heard of the criminal who was set free due to a "technicality." The rules of criminal procedure have their roots in the Constitution and are intended to protect the innocent from the overreaching of possibly overzealous law enforcement officials. These rules govern everything from the way in which the arresting police officer must inform a suspect of his or her rights to how evidence is introduced at trial.

Civil law is also controlled by very specific rules of procedure. Those rules of civil procedure will be the focus of Chapter 5. Criminal procedure will be discussed in Chapter 15. You will be studying the various areas of substantive law throughout this book.

DISCUSSION QUESTION

9. Review the hypothetical case that began Chapter 2. How would you categorize Diane's legal problems?

SUMMARY

We have seen how lawyers categorize law as either state or federal, civil or criminal, and substantive or procedural. The first category, state or federal, arises because the United States operates under a system of federalism. Under our federal system governmental authority is split between the national government and the fifty state governments. Some areas of the law, such as divorce, are reserved exclusively to the states; some are reserved to the federal government; and some are shared by the states and the federal government. If you are in doubt as to which law applies, check state law first. Federal law will be involved only if the federal Constitution, a federal statute, or a federal regulation is involved.

Civil law involves harm to an individual, while criminal law deals with harms to society as a whole. In both criminal and civil cases the party with the burden of proof must first establish a prima facie case. Once that is established, the other side is given the opportunity to negate the prima facie case or to raise affirmative defenses. While the law has become increasingly specialized, the main areas of civil law are contracts, property, and torts. Tort law can be further subdivided into those involving intentional acts, those based on negligent behavior, and those that result from an imposition of strict liability.

Finally, substantive law defines our rights and duties. Procedural law deals with how the legal system operates.

REVIEW QUESTIONS

Pages 31 through 32

1. What are the three major ways in which attorneys categorize the law?
2. What is the difference between substantive and procedural law?
3. In terms of the type of harm caused, what is the difference between civil and criminal law?

Pages 32 through 37

4. What is federalism?
5. True or false: Every state must have the same laws regarding gambling. Why?
6. What does it mean to say that the federal government is a government of limited powers?
7. Do you think Congress could (not should) enact a national divorce statute? Why?
8. Why are some areas of the law preempted by the federal government?

Pages 38 through 41

9. Name at least four ways in which civil law differs from criminal law.
10. When is the burden of proof "beyond a reasonable doubt" and when is it a "preponderance of the evidence"? What is the difference between them?

11. In a civil case if a jury is evenly split, leaning equally toward the plaintiff's and the defendant's views of the facts, who will win, the plaintiff or the defendant? Why?

Pages 41 through 43

12. What two basic elements must be established for the government to prove the prima facie case in a criminal case?
13. Why can the same act constitute several different crimes?
14. What are the two basic defenses to a criminal action?
15. In a criminal case does the government or the defendant present its case first? Why?
16. What is the general definition of a civil cause of action?
17. In a civil case does the plaintiff or the defendant present its case first? Why?
18. What are the three types of damages available in a civil case?
19. In addition to damages, what might a plaintiff seek in a civil case?

Pages 43 through 49

20. What must be present for a contract to be valid?
21. What is the basic difference between a contract and a gift?
22. What are the three main areas of tort law?
23. Give the general definition of negligence, and list the elements necessary to prove a prima facie case.
24. What are the main defenses to negligence?

Chapter 4

Structure of the Court System

*Trial courts search for truth and appellate courts
search for error.*
Unknown

INTRODUCTION

The law provides rules about how people should behave in different types of
situations and provides remedies for when those rules are broken. However,
these rules are not self-enforcing. In order to enforce these rules, people often
have to go to court to have a judge or jury settle it for them. A court is a unit of the
judicial branch of government that has authority to decide legal disputes.
Jurisdiction refers to the ability of a specific court to hear a particular type of case.

One major way of classifying courts is in terms of whether they are trial or
appellate courts. They can also be classified in terms of whether they are federal
or state courts. In this chapter we will examine the structure of the various court
systems, the concept of jurisdiction, and the rules played by those who work in
the court system.

A. TRIAL VERSUS APPELLATE COURTS

Most court cases begin in a **trial court**.[1] Trial courts are said to be courts of
original jurisdiction because trial courts are where actions are initiated and heard

Jurisdiction
The power of a court to
hear a case.

Trial courts
Courts that determine
the facts and apply the
law to the facts.

Original jurisdiction
The authority of a court
to hear a case when it is
initiated, as opposed to
appellate jurisdiction.

---

[1]The primary exception to this pattern occurs when a dispute is adjudicated in an administrative agency
and then appealed to the courts. In very rare circumstances a case can be filed directly with the U.S.
Supreme Court under its original jurisdiction.

Questions of fact
Questions relating to what happened: who, what, when, where, and how.

Questions of law
Questions relating to the interpretation or application of the law.

Bench trial
A trial conducted without a jury.

for the first time. In addition to conducting trials, much of a trial court's time is spent in far less dramatic proceedings, such as receiving plea agreements and ratifying out-of-court settlements. When a trial is held, attorneys present witness testimony and other evidence. After considering the evidence and the attorneys' arguments, trial courts have two functions. First, they must determine whose version of the facts is most credible. Second, they must apply the law to those facts to reach a decision. Therefore, trial courts must determine both questions of fact and questions of law.

Questions of fact relate to the determination of what took place: Who, what, when, where, and how? **Questions of law** relate to how the judge interprets and applies the law and include such issues as how a statute is to be interpreted and whether a specific piece of evidence is admissible. In a jury trial questions of fact are determined by the jury, while questions of law are determined by the judge. If it is a **bench trial** rather than a **jury trial,** the judge will decide the factual questions as well as the legal ones.

In most cases that go to trial, the meaning of the law is clear, but the facts themselves are very much in dispute. For example, under the criminal codes of most states it is a violation of the law for a person to forcibly take someone else's property without the owner's permission. When someone is tried for robbery, the trial usually focuses on such factual questions as the identification of the alleged robber and the ownership of the property taken.

Although the primary focus of most trials is on factual issues, at times legal issues are involved as well. For example, a trial judge may have to decide if certain testimony or evidence is admissible. That is a question of law. If the judge decides that the testimony or evidence is not admissible, then the trial proceeds without it. Also, if the judge rules that a search was illegal or that disputed pictures are too prejudicial, then the objects discovered in that search or the pictures are not admitted as evidence. Based on the evidence that has been allowed, the jury then resolves the questions of fact.

Consider the following example. In most states it is a crime for someone other than a physician, pharmacist, or other authorized medical person to sell or distribute narcotic drugs. When someone is on trial for selling narcotics, the prosecution must present evidence that shows the accused did in fact sell a substance that fits the legal definition of a prohibited narcotic drug. These are issues of fact. The evidence usually consists of an undercover police agent testifying that the accused did sell the agent a substance that laboratory reports identify as a narcotic.

It is possible, however, that the defendant might admit to selling the drug but then claim **entrapment.** The entrapment doctrine prohibits law enforcement officers from instigating criminal acts to lure otherwise innocent persons into committing a crime. One question of fact relating to the entrapment defense is whether the defendant ever committed such a criminal act or thought of committing such an act before. However, in addition to the factual questions and depending on the circumstances of a given case, a legal issue of what constitutes entrapment could arise. For example, assume government agents supplied the defendant with a drug and then later arrested him for selling the very same drug to another government agent. Here no one would be disputing what happened, the facts. But an appellate court could be asked to decide whether such actions legally qualify as entrapment. In *Hampton v. United States*[2] the U.S. Supreme

---

[2]425 U.S. 484 (1976).

Court held that as long as the defendant is predisposed to commit the crime, it is not entrapment when government agents supply the defendant with a drug and then later arrest him for selling the very same drug to another government agent.

In sum, legal issues can arise in three ways. First, legal issues can arise regarding the meaning of the underlying cause of action, as in the example given above regarding whether entrapment had occurred. Second, during a trial numerous legal issues may be raised involving the conduct of the trial itself. Such issues might include whether a particular piece of evidence should be excluded because it is the product of an illegal search and seizure, whether the plaintiff's attorney should be allowed to pursue a certain line of questioning, whether the judge should present a particular set of instructions to the jury, and whether prejudicial publicity has tainted the defendant's trial—to give but a few examples. Finally, legal issues can involve challenges to the constitutionality of the law that is being applied. For example, a doctor charged with performing an illegal abortion could argue that the law he is charged with violating is itself unconstitutional.

Appellate courts review the actions taken by trial courts (and in some cases the actions of administrative agencies). The person who loses in a trial court may be able to appeal the decision to an appellate court. The party filing the appeal is called the **appellant** or the **petitioner**. The party who won in the trial court is called the **appellee** or the **respondent**. Most states and the federal government provide for one appeal as a matter of right. Additional appeals are usually at the discretion of the higher court.

Unlike trial courts, appellate courts do not hear testimony. They rely on the written record of what occurred in the trial court to determine whether the trial court made an error regarding the law. They do so because when conducting a review, appellate courts limit themselves to "legal" as opposed to "factual" issues that are specifically raised by the party who is bringing the appeal. Therefore, you can appeal a lower court decision only when you raise a valid legal issue. Appellate courts will not reconsider the facts; they will consider only whether the trial court made an error of law. Case 5: Alibi to a Murder illustrates this point.

Do you think there is any basis for launching an appeal in Mr. Jones's case? It is a question of fact whether on the night of the murder Mr. Jones was

Appellate courts
Courts that determine whether lower courts have made errors of law.

Appellant or petitioner
The party in a case who has initiated an appeal.

Appellee or respondent
The party in a case against whom an appeal has been filed.

Case 5: Alibi to a Murder

Frederick Jones could not believe it when he was arrested for murder because he thought he had an ironclad alibi.

At his trial an elderly gentleman testified that he saw Mr. Jones near the scene of the murder shortly after it took place. At one point in the trial, over the objection of the defendant's attorney, the prosecutor showed the jury bloody and gruesome pictures of the deceased victim.

Mr. Jones testified that not only did he not commit the murder, but also he was attending an out-of-town wedding at the time the murder was supposed to have taken place. Ten witnesses then took the stand in succession and testified that they had been at the wedding and seen the defendant there.

At the end of the trial the jury convicted Mr. Jones.

present at the scene of the murder (as testified to by one elderly witness) or out of town attending a wedding (as testified to by ten other witnesses). Therefore, his whereabouts on the night of the murder cannot form the basis for an appeal.

On the other hand, it is a question of law as to whether the judge should allow the jury to see pictures of the victim's bloody corpse. It can be argued that the viewing of those pictures was so inflammatory as to prejudice the jury. Therefore, the showing of the pictures could form the basis of an appeal. Keep in mind that this does not mean that Mr. Jones would win at the appellate level. It simply means that he will be given the opportunity to argue his case to the appellate court.

There is one exception to the rule that appellate courts review only questions of law. Occasionally they will review a case because they believe that what the jury did was something that no reasonable jury could do. Because appellate courts review only legal issues, normally they do not engage in this type of second-guessing regarding the trial court's findings. For example, in Mr. Jones's situation mentioned above, even though ten eyewitnesses testified that Mr. Jones was out of town on the night of the murder, Mr. Jones's attorney cannot appeal on the grounds that the jury was mistaken about his whereabouts on the night of the murder. Appellate courts will accept a jury's determination as to which witnesses were most credible. Only in rare instances will appellate courts reexamine the evidence.

If the appellate court determines that a legal error occurred but that it was minor and did not affect the result, the court labels it a **harmless error** and allows the decision to stand. If the court finds that a significant legal error was made in the way the trial was conducted, it will usually cancel the original outcome by **reversing** the trial court's decision. It may also direct that the case be retried by **remanding** the case to the trial court for further consideration.

In criminal cases a reversal of a conviction does not necessarily mean that the defendant will go free, as the government then has the option of retrying the case. However, if the appellate court rules that a key piece of evidence is inadmissible, the government may choose not to retry the defendant because it may feel that its case is too weak without the excluded evidence.

If the government chooses to proceed with a new trial, this does not violate the constitutional provision regarding **double jeopardy**. Double jeopardy occurs when a person is tried more than once for the same criminal offense. The Fifth and Fourteenth Amendments to the Constitution prohibit various forms of double jeopardy. However, when a defendant voluntarily appeals a conviction, he or she waives the right not to be retried for the same crime.

Appellate court judges reach their decisions by majority vote. Someone from the majority writes the **majority opinion** explaining the court's decision and how that decision was reached. In cases where the decision is not unanimous, judges may also write concurring or dissenting opinions to explain the nature of their disagreements. In a **concurring opinion** the judge agrees with the result reached by the majority but not with its reasoning. In a **dissenting opinion** the judge disagrees with the result and with the reasoning.

In summary, there are several major differences between trial and appellate courts. At the trial-court level the parties are called the plaintiff and the defendant in a civil case and the state and the defendant in a criminal case. At the appellate-court level the party who lost in the trial court is called either the

---

Harmless error
A trial court error that is not sufficient to warrant reversing the decision.

Reverse
A decision is reversed when an appellate court overturns or negates the decision of a lower court.

Remand
When an appellate court sends a case back to the trial court for a new trial or other action.

Majority opinion
An opinion in which a majority of the court joins.

Concurring opinion
An opinion that agrees with the majority's result but disagrees with its reasoning.

Dissenting opinion
An opinion that disagrees with the majority's decision and its reasoning.

	Trial Court	Appellate Court
Parties' names	Plaintiff/defendant State/defendant	Appellant/appellee or petitioner/respondent
Decision maker	Judge and sometimes a jury	Majority vote of three or more judges
Attorney arguments	Yes	Yes
Witness testimony	Yes	No
Evidence introduced	Yes	No
Questions of fact decided	Yes	No
Questions of law decided	Yes	Yes

Figure 4-1   Comparison of Trial and Appellate Courts

appellant or the **petitioner**, while the party who won is called either the **appellee** or the **respondent.** In the trial court either a single judge or a jury decides the facts, and the judge determines the law. In the appellate court, a panel of three or more judges decides questions of law based on the attorneys' briefs (written arguments) and oral arguments. There are no witnesses who give testimony in the appellate courts and no juries. The judges merely review the trial transcript and the written briefs from the lawyers. Sometimes oral arguments from the opposing attorneys are heard, during which the judges have an opportunity to pose questions. Lower-level appellate judges usually work in rotating panels of three, while in the upper-level appellate courts all the judges jointly decide each case.

Most of these differences are directly related to the most important distinction between trial and appellate courts: Trial courts determine the facts and apply the law to those facts; appellate courts deal only with questions of law. Three basic types of legal questions can arise at the appellate level. First are those that relate to the meaning of the underlying legal cause of action or defense, such as what qualifies as entrapment. Second, one of the parties can argue that the law being applied is unconstitutional, as when the doctor challenged an abortion law. Finally, legal issues can arise that have nothing to do with the underlying legal claim but rather relate to how the trial was conducted. Figure 4-1 summarizes the differences between trial and appellate courts.

Discussion Questions

1. Do you think it is a good or a bad idea that only questions of law can be appealed?

2. Can you think of a situation when an appellate judge might reverse and remand a case? When a judge might reverse but not remand a case?

3. It is not always easy to know whether something is a question of fact or a question of law. In fact, there have been cases when the issue on appeal was whether something was a question of fact or a question of law. That question is itself a question of law. To see how that can happen, assume there was a negligence trial in which a grocer was sued when a customer slipped and fell. The customer testified that she slipped on a banana peel in the produce section. The grocery store owner testified that when he came to the assistance of the customer, there was no peel on the floor. One of the store employees also testified that he had mopped the floor in that area just five minutes before the accident and that there were no banana peels on the floor. Nonetheless, the jury found the store liable. Can the store appeal on the grounds that it was telling the truth and the customer was lying? Why? Can the store appeal on the grounds that the jury should not have found that it acted negligently because even if there was a banana peel, such hazards are to be expected in the produce section and the store had done all it could to make the area safe? Is that issue—that is, whether the store acted as a reasonable store should—a question of fact or a question of law?

B. FEDERAL AND STATE COURT SYSTEMS

Trial and appellate courts exist in both the federal and the state court systems. At first glance the federal and state judicial systems of this country present a confusing mixture of titles and functions. In large part this is because there are actually fifty-one different court systems (the federal system plus one for each state). To complicate matters, the same types of courts often have different names. For example, the basic trial court is called the court of common pleas in Pennsylvania, the district court in Minnesota, the circuit court in Illinois, the superior court in California, and the supreme court in New York. Although New York uses the "supreme court" designation for its trial courts, most states reserve that title for their highest appellate court. Out of this confusion we will try to create some order by discussing the basic structure of both the federal court system and a typical state court system. Although both systems can seem quite complex, the federal system, as well as most state systems, has three levels: the trial courts, the intermediate appellate courts, and one appellate court of last resort.

1. The Federal System

A simplified organizational chart of the federal court system is shown in Figure 4-2. As you can see, it follows the basic pattern described above: trial courts, intermediate appellate courts, and one highest appellate court. The federal court system also includes a variety of other less-well-known judicial bodies, such as the U.S. Court of International Trade, which are not listed here. The arrows indicate the avenues for appeals.

U.S. Supreme Court
The highest federal appellate court, consisting of nine appointed members.

The **U.S. Supreme Court** sits at the top of the federal judicial branch, where it hears appeals from both federal and state courts. However, as we will discuss more fully later in this chapter, not all state cases can be appealed to the U.S. Supreme Court. Cases are appealed from state supreme courts only when federal issues are involved.

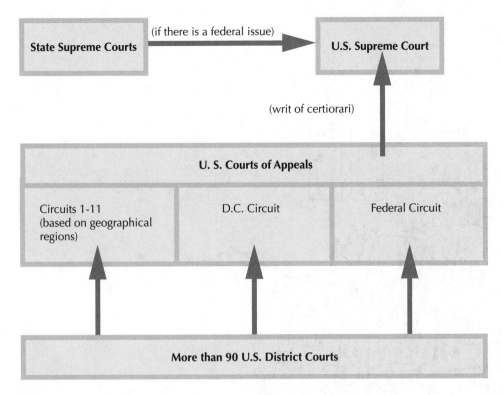

Figure 4-2 The Federal Court System

Immediately below the Supreme Court are the **U.S. courts of appeals.** Both the Supreme Court and the courts of appeals are appellate courts. The Supreme Court is the highest appellate court, while the courts of appeals are intermediate-level appellate courts. The country is divided geographically into twelve circuits, which include eleven numbered circuits and the District of Columbia as a separate circuit. The thirteenth circuit is called the Federal Circuit, where appeals in specialized cases from the entire country are heard. There is a court of appeals for each of the thirteen circuits. Most of the work, however, is done in the federal trial courts, the ninety-three **U.S. district courts** spread among the fifty states. There is at least one district court for each state. Most district court cases are appealed to the U.S. court of appeals in the circuit in which the district court is located. To gain an appreciation for how the circuits are organized, look at the map in Figure 4-3, page 58.

The basic outline for this three-tiered judicial structure is set forth in the federal Constitution. Article III, Section 1, provides that "[t]he judicial Power of the United States, shall be vested in one supreme Court, and in such inferior Courts as the Congress may from time to time ordain and establish." Those **"inferior Courts"** are the district courts and courts of appeals. Congress established the first inferior courts through the Judiciary Act of 1789. That act provided for thirteen districts and three circuits. Over the years, through further legislative action, the number of both district and federal circuits has grown to its present-day level.

U.S. courts of appeals
The intermediate appellate courts in the federal system.

U.S. district courts
The general jurisdiction trial courts in the federal system.

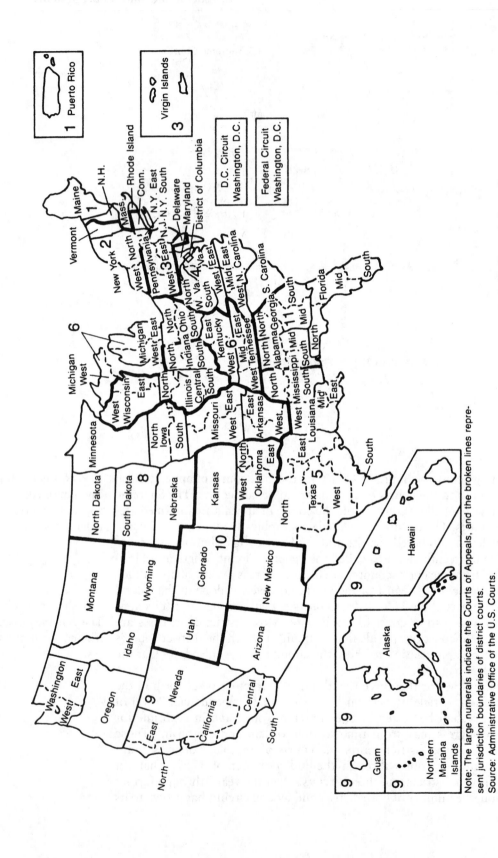

Figure 4-3 District and Circuit Court Boundaries

Note: The large numerals indicate the Courts of Appeals, and the broken lines represent jurisdiction boundaries of district courts.

Source: Administrative Office of the U.S. Courts.

a. The Primary Federal Courts

In the federal system, cases normally begin in one of the district courts, which serve as the federal trial courts. These district courts are courts of **general jurisdiction.** That means they are authorized to adjudicate all types of civil and criminal cases. Courts of **limited jurisdiction** hear only a narrow range of cases on a specific subject (such as probate, domestic relations, or traffic).

The number of judges assigned to each district varies from one to twenty-seven depending on the caseload of the district. Usually, cases are heard by a single judge or a judge and a jury. The district court judges are assisted by **magistrate judges** and **bankruptcy judges.**

The magistrate judges supervise court calendars, hear procedural motions, issue **subpoenas,** hear minor criminal offense cases, and conduct civil pretrial hearings. In some district courts the magistrate judges, with the consent of the parties involved, conduct trials and enter judgments in civil cases. Bankruptcy judges handle most bankruptcy cases entirely on their own. In a limited number of cases they conduct the trial but then must submit their proposed findings of fact to the district judge, who enters the final order or judgment.

The losing party takes an appeal from a district court decision to the appropriate court of appeals. For example, cases from California district courts are appealed to the Court of Appeals for the Ninth Circuit. Each of the twelve regular circuits has from four to twenty-three judges. In courts of appeals, a panel, normally comprised of three judges, hears appeals and reaches its decision through a majority vote. Occasionally all the judges sit together and decide a case **en banc.** This happens most frequently when the losing party in a case already decided by a panel of the court requests a rehearing before the full membership of the court.

Sitting at the top of the federal judicial system is the U.S. Supreme Court. The Court is composed of nine justices, who hear all appeals as a group. It is interesting to note that the Judiciary Act of 1789, mentioned above, provided for a Supreme Court with one chief justice and five associate justices. As with the number of courts, the number of Supreme Court justices has also grown over the years as the volume of the Court's work has increased. The Supreme Court justices also reach their decisions by majority vote. Figure 4-4 shows a picture of the U.S. Supreme Court taken in the fall of 1997.

A case seldom goes any further than a court of appeals, as the U.S. Supreme Court rarely is required to hear a case on appeal. Most cases that do reach the U.S. Supreme Court do so because the litigants have requested a **writ of certiorari.** In this writ the losing party asks the Supreme Court to review the case. The decision whether to grant a writ of certiorari is discretionary. The Supreme Court usually hears no more than 200 of the approximately 4,000 requests it receives each year. For the request to be granted, four of the nine justices must agree to hear the case. If the request is denied, this does not mean that the Court agrees with the lower court's decision. It simply means that the Court does not want to hear the case. When discussing the Court's response to a writ of certiorari, you will often hear lawyers refer to the granting or denial of cert.

All the courts discussed so far are known as **constitutional courts,** which means they were established under the provisions of Article III of the Constitution. Article II of the Constitution gives the president the power to appoint judges for life terms. For an appointment to become final, the Senate must confirm it. Article III, Section 1, provides that "[t]he Judges, both of the

General jurisdiction
A court's power to hear any type of case arising within its geographical area.

Limited jurisdiction
A court's power to hear only specialized cases.

Subpoena
A court order requiring a person to appear to testify at a trial or deposition.

Writ of certiorari
A means of gaining appellate review; in the U.S. Supreme Court the writ is discretionary and will be issued to another court to review a federal question if four of the nine justices vote to hear the case.

NETNOTE

The official web site of the Federal judiciary is *www.uscourts.gov/*. It contains links to the U.S. Supreme Court, the U.S. courts of appeals, the U.S. district courts, and the U.S. Bankruptcy courts. Emory University's web site at *www.law. emory.edu/caselaw/* has a map of the federal circuits that allows you link to a wide variety of information on each of the circuits. The U.S. Supreme Court's site at *www.supremecourtus.gov/* contains helpful information on the Court's procedures, its caseload, and biographies and pictures of the Justices.

supreme and inferior Courts, shall hold their Offices during good Behaviour, and shall, at stated Times, receive for their Services, a Compensation, which shall not be diminished during their Continuance in Office." This means that "constitutional" judges are guaranteed lifetime tenure unless they resign or are impeached and are protected from any salary reductions.

DISCUSSION QUESTIONS

4. Why do you think the framers of the Constitution chose to give federal judges lifetime tenure and to protect them from salary reduction? Do you think that was a wise decision?

5. Do you think it is appropriate that the Supreme Court hears no more than 200 of the approximately 4,000 requests it receives each year? What criteria should the Court use in deciding which cases it will hear?

b. Other Federal Courts

Figure 4-5, page 62, shows where the "core" courts, shown in Figure 4-2, fit into a more complete organizational chart of the federal court system. In addition to the primary courts discussed above, Congress has created

---

Figure 4-4 The U.S. Supreme Court (**Standing, from left to right:** *Ruth Bader Ginsberg*—the second woman to be appointed to the Supreme Court, in 1993; prior to her appointment was a law professor and served as a U.S. court of appeals judge; a moderate. *David H. Souter*—appointed in 1990; conservative to moderate. *Clarence Thomas*—appointed in 1991; his confirmation hearings will always be remembered because of the controversy created by Professor Anita Hill's accusations of sexual harassment; very conservative, usually voting with Justice Scalia. *Stephen Breyer*—the newest Supreme Court justice, appointed by President Clinton in July 1994; a moderate. **Sitting, from left to right:** *Antonin Scalia*—appointed in 1986; the most conservative member of the Court. *John Paul Stevens*—appointed in 1975; the oldest member of the Court; a moderate. *William H. Rehnquist*—chief justice since 1986; appointed by President Nixon in 1971; a conservative. *Sandra Day O'Connor*—appointed in 1981; the first woman to serve on the Court; conservative to moderate. *Anthony M. Kennedy*—appointed in 1988; also served as a law professor and U.S. court of appeals judge before his appointment to the Supreme Court; a conservative.)

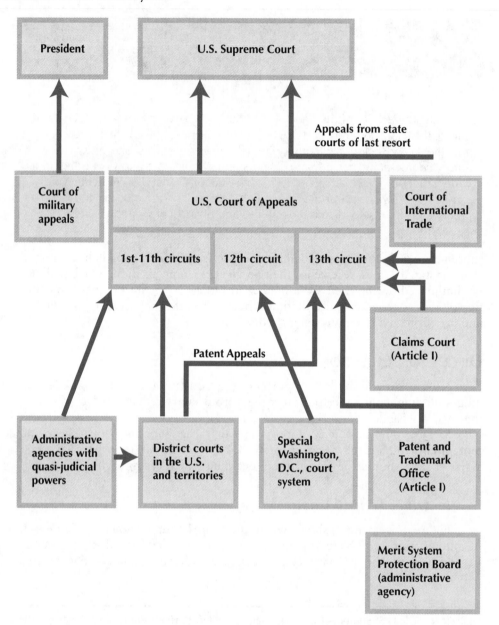

Figure 4-5 Organization of the Federal Courts and Quasi-Judicial Administrative Agencies

more-specialized courts, known as **legislative courts,** under Article I of the federal Constitution. These legislative courts include the U.S. Court of Military Appeals, the U.S. Tax Court, the U.S. Claims Court, and the U.S. Court of International Trade.

The U.S. Court of Military Appeals is the final appellate tribunal for court-martial convictions. The U.S. Tax Court (formerly the Board of Tax Appeals) considers challenges to Internal Revenue Service rulings. The U.S. Claims Court (formerly the Court of Claims) decides the validity of specific types of claims against the U.S. government, and the U.S. Court of International Trade (formerly the U.S. Customs Court) reviews decisions and appraisals of imported merchandise made in collecting customs duties.

Judges who serve on these courts, as well as district court magistrate and bankruptcy judges, are appointed for set terms and theoretically lack some of the independence of the constitutional judges. Magistrate judges, for example, are selected by a majority of the active judges of each district court for full-time terms of eight years or part-time terms of four years, and they can be removed for cause. Bankruptcy judges are appointed for fourteen-year terms by the court of appeals for the circuit in which the district is located.

2. State Court Systems

Due to the controversial nature of many of its decisions the U.S. Supreme Court gets the lion's share of the media coverage given to the courts on the evening news. While many important cases and significant constitutional issues are decided in the federal courts, it is in state courts where over 98 percent of all legal business occurs.[3] While paralegals may have some opportunities to work with federal courts, most will spend their time operating within state court systems.

Many states have court systems that are very similar to the federal system. Cases begin in a trial court and then proceed through one or two levels of appellate courts. Figure 4-6 shows the organization of a typical state court system. Note how closely it parallels Figure 4-2, showing the core of the federal court system. The path for appeals in most state court systems is from the trial court to an intermediate appellate court (if one exists) and then to the state's highest appellate court (usually called the supreme court).

Rather than attempting to describe each of these fifty-one court systems, we will review some general patterns and leave it to you to search out the details for your specific state. Relatively simple explanations of most state court systems can be found in books and pamphlets published by the individual states and are usually available in the reference section of local libraries. Other sources for such information are The American Bench and the Martindale-Hubbell Law Directory, Court Calendar section.

Starting at the bottom of Figure 4-6, you will find the trial courts. In some states, below the trial courts shown in Figure 4-6 is a system of inferior courts with names such as justice of the peace, city, and magistrate courts. Those courts are not **courts of record**. No permanent record is kept of the testimony, lawyers' remarks, or judges' rulings. The absence of a record eliminates the possibility of an appeal and requires the losing party to initiate a completely new trial in a higher-level trial court if that party wishes to have the matter reconsidered.

Many states have one basic trial court, similar to federal district courts, that can hear any type of case (i.e., it has **general jurisdiction**). This court typically carries a name like circuit court, district court, county court, or superior court. On the other hand, other states have a confusing variety of specialized courts with **limited jurisdiction**. These courts hear a narrow range of cases on a specific subject (such as probate, domestic relations, or traffic) and sometimes even overlap regarding the types of cases they can hear. For example, in

<aside>
**P R A C T I C A L
T I P**

Find the time to take a walking tour of your local courts. Note the location of the clerk's offices, the courtrooms, and the nearest law library.
</aside>

---

[3]Cooke & Goodman, The State of the Nation's State Courts, Natl. L.J., Mar. 19, 1984, at 23.

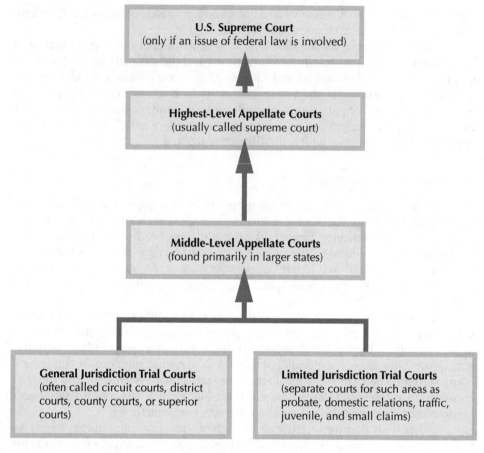

Figure 4-6 Organization of a Typical State Court System

Massachusetts both the probate court and the superior court can hear divorce cases.

States maintain either one or two levels of appellate courts. The larger states have generally gone to a two-tiered system like that in operation at the federal level. The intermediate-level appellate courts usually sit in panels, while the court of last resort sits **en banc.** On some matters appeals to the highest court are discretionary, while on others they are a matter of right. A few states have established separate courts to handle criminal versus civil appeals at the intermediate or highest level. Finally, as noted earlier in this chapter, even the name of the highest-level appellate court varies from state to state. While most states identify their highest court as the state supreme court, in New York and Maryland it is called the court of appeals.

In most cases a state's top appellate court is the end of the road because cases can be appealed to the U.S. Supreme Court only if they raise a federal issue. For example, in criminal cases state courts must accord the due process rights guaranteed by the U.S. Constitution. This can involve resolving issues regarding the right to counsel, the admissibility of evidence resulting from an allegedly illegal search, jury selection procedures, and so on. If the defendant thinks these constitutional rights have been violated, she or he may be able to appeal the case to the federal courts on the basis that a federal issue is involved. Whenever a federal

En banc
When an appellate court that normally sits in panels sits as a whole.

law or a provision of the U.S. Constitution is involved, the federal courts have the right to make the final determination as to what that law or constitutional provision means. But remember that a criminal defendant has no right to appeal his or her conviction in a state court to a federal court unless such federal issues are raised. Under the principles of federalism the state courts are the final arbiters as to the meaning of state statutes and state constitutional provisions.

State court judges are selected in a variety of ways. In some states they are appointed by the state's chief executive or the state legislature or both. In others they are selected in either partisan or nonpartisan elections. Still other states use a modification of what has become known as the Missouri plan. These systems generally convene a special panel of lawyers and lay persons who nominate a few candidates for a vacancy. The governor then appoints from among this select group. A year or two later the person who was appointed goes before the general electorate in a special retention election. In such an election the voters are asked simply whether that judge should be retained.

3. Exclusive and Concurrent Jurisdiction

If a specific court is the only one authorized to hear a particular type of case, it has **exclusive jurisdiction.** If more than one court is authorized to hear the same type of case, they each have **concurrent jurisdiction.** Where concurrent jurisdiction exists, a case can be heard by more than one court, and the parties can select the one they wish to use.

As we mentioned in Chapter 3, the federal government is a government of limited powers. Just as Congress can legislate only if the Constitution has given it the power to do so, federal courts can hear cases only if the Constitution has given them the power to do so. Article III, Section 2, of the Constitution spells out the jurisdiction of the federal courts in terms of (1) the nature of the subject matter of the case and (2) the parties involved. Figure 4-7 lists the requirements for federal court jurisdiction. Two of the grounds for federal court jurisdiction require particular emphasis, as they account for the bulk of federal cases. The federal courts have jurisdiction when the case involves

1. federal law. This is known as **federal question jurisdiction** and includes cases involving a federal statute, a federal regulation, or the U.S. Constitution.
2. opposing litigants from different states where the amount in controversy exceeds $75,000. This is known as **diversity jurisdiction.**

If a lawsuit does not fall within one of the categories listed in Figure 4-7, the parties have no choice but to bring the matter in a state court. Unlike the federal courts, state courts generally have the power to hear any type of case. The only time state courts are prohibited from hearing cases involving federal law is when Congress has expressly included that limitation in a federal statute.

In situations where both the state and the federal courts have concurrent jurisdiction, the plaintiff makes the initial decision as to which court to use. However, when the plaintiff selects a state court and the federal courts also have jurisdiction, the defendant may be able to **remove** the case to federal court.

Deciding whether to go to state or federal court is not the same as deciding whether the court will apply state or federal law to the case. For example, in a

Exclusive jurisdiction
When only one court has the power to hear a case.

Concurrent jurisdiction
When more than one court has jurisdiction to hear a case.

Federal question jurisdiction
The power of the federal courts to hear matters of federal law.

Diversity jurisdiction
The power of the federal courts to hear matters of state law if the opposing parties are from different states and the amount in controversy exceeds $75,000.

Removal
The transfer of a case from one state court to another or from a state court to a federal court.

Based on the subject matter (federal question):
Any case involving the interpretation or application of
1. the U.S. Constitution,
2. a federal law or regulation,
3. a treaty, or
4. admiralty and maritime laws.

Based on the parties involved:
Any case or controversy in law and equity in which
1. the case affects ambassadors or other public ministers and counsels,
2. the United States is a party to the suit,
3. the controversy is between two or more states,
4. the controversy is between a state and citizens of another state,*
5. the parties are citizens of different states (known as diversity jurisdiction),
6. the controversy is between citizens of the same state claiming lands under grants of different states, or
7. the controversy is between (a) a state or the citizens thereof and (b) foreign states, citizens, or subjects.*

Based on the amount of money involved:
In addition to the constitutional requirements stated above, Congress has the power to add a minimum dollar value to suits between citizens of different states. The current federal statute states that the amount in controversy in diversity actions must exceed $75,000 to qualify for original federal jurisdiction.

*The Eleventh Amendment modified this to exclude situations where the suit was commenced or prosecuted against a state by an individual.

Figure 4-7   Jurisdiction of Federal Courts

negligence case a federal court might have jurisdiction based on the diversity of citizenship of the parties. However, the federal court must follow state negligence law in deciding the case. If the case involves an area of unsettled state law, the federal court must base its decision on its best guess as to what the state's highest court would do if faced with the same situation. Because the federal court is only guessing at what the state court would do, the federal court's decision is binding on the current litigants but is not binding on the state courts. Therefore, no matter how the federal court decides the case, it will still be open to the state courts to change the law in that area the next time a litigant brings a case on the same issue to the state courts. Likewise, when a state court hears a case involving a federal matter, it must follow the guidance of the federal courts.

DISCUSSION QUESTION

6. For each of these situations determine whether you think the matter should be heard in state or federal *court*. Also decide whether you think a court would apply state or federal *law*.

    a. A wife wants to divorce her husband.

    b. Martha, a Massachusetts resident, wants to sue Susan, a Massachusetts resident, for $80,000 based on breach of contract.

c. Sam, a Massachusetts resident, wants to sue Jill, a Vermont resident, for $80,000 based on breach of contract.

d. A teacher in a public school wants to challenge a state law requiring all teachers to start each day of class with a minute of silent prayer.

C. COURT PERSONNEL

It takes many different participants to make the judicial system work effectively. Court personnel include not only the judges and attorneys appearing before them but also court clerks, court reporters, and bailiffs.

The trial court judge is, of course, one of the most powerful members of the judicial system. Within the limits of the law the judge decides whether to dismiss a case before it reaches trial, the extent of pretrial discovery, and the amount of time the lawyers will have to prepare their cases. Once the trial is under way, the judge acts as the presiding officer, rules on objections, and determines when recesses will occur. If a jury is involved, the judge supervises its selection, removes jury members from the courtroom at key times to protect them from improper influences, and instructs them on the meaning of the law they are to apply. When a jury is not involved, the judge also acts as the fact finder and decides whether the defendant is guilty (in criminal cases) or liable (in civil cases). In criminal cases the judge is also responsible for sentencing the convicted defendant. If the litigants want to contest a trial judge's findings, they must present their arguments to appellate judges.

Some states also use **justices of the peace, court commissioners,** and **magistrates** in their court systems. Individuals holding these titles are lower-level court personnel who perform limited judicial duties but are not considered full-fledged judges. In some states they do not have to be lawyers to perform these duties.

In addition to being advocates for their clients, attorneys are considered officers of the court. As such, they are responsible for maintaining proper decorum in the courtroom and acting within the ethical restraints imposed on them by the courts and their profession.

Court clerks are responsible for keeping the court files in proper condition and ensuring that the various motions filed by lawyers and the actions taken by judges are properly recorded. A head clerk of the courts is usually responsible for running the central records section of the courthouse; his or her assistants are assigned to sit in on the actual courtroom proceedings.

The **court reporter** prepares verbatim transcripts of courtroom proceedings. Most reporters use a stenotype machine rather than shorthand. Because it is expensive, they prepare a written transcript only if the case is being appealed.

Bailiffs are responsible for maintaining order in the courtrooms. They are also responsible for watching over the juries when they are in recess or when they have been sequestered. When a jury is sequestered, the members sleep at a hotel and are kept isolated from the public and their families to prevent them from being exposed to prejudicial publicity, threats, bribes, or any other improper influences.

Finally, sheriffs and marshals also serve as officers of the court. They serve summonses and other court documents, collect money as required by court judgments, and otherwise help in carrying out the court's orders.

SUMMARY

In this chapter we have seen that although the American legal system may seem to involve a confusing mix of names and functions, all courts can be classified in two ways:

1. They are either trial or appellate courts. Some trial courts have only limited jurisdiction; for example, they only hear cases worth less than a certain amount of money.
2. They are part of either the federal or a state system.

The federal court system and most state court systems are based on a three-tier model. At the bottom are the trial courts, which decide both factual and legal issues. Above the trial courts you will generally find an intermediate appellate court. At the top of every system is the highest appellate court. Appellate courts decide questions of law only. In the federal system the trial courts are called district courts, the intermediate appellate courts are called courts of appeals, and the highest court is the U.S. Supreme Court.

The power of a particular court to hear certain types of cases is known as its jurisdiction. The federal Constitution limits all federal courts' jurisdiction by allowing them to hear only the types of cases listed under Article III, Section 2. The two most common grounds for federal court jurisdiction are federal question and diversity of citizenship.

REVIEW QUESTIONS

Pages 51 through 56

1. What are the two basic functions of trial courts?
2. What is the difference between questions of law and questions of fact? Why is it important to know the difference?
3. Give an example of a question of fact that might arise during a murder trial. Give an example of a question of law that might arise in that same trial.
4. What is the difference between a bench and a jury trial?
5. What will an appellate court usually do if it finds that the trial court made a harmless error?
6. What is the difference between reversing and remanding a case?
7. What is the difference between a dissenting and a concurring opinion?
8. List the major differences between trial and appellate courts.

Pages 56 through 63

9. In the federal court system what are the names given to
   a. the highest appellate court,
   b. the intermediate appellate courts, and
   c. the trial courts?
10. Look at the map in Figure 4-3. How many district courts are there in your state? In which circuit is your state located?
11. If you hear that "cert." has been denied in a case, what does that mean?
12. In the federal system, what are the "inferior Courts"?

Pages 63 through 67

13. Describe a typical state court system. How is your state court system similar to or different from the "typical" state system?
14. True or false: In every state the highest appellate court is called the supreme court.

15. Jurisdiction refers to the power a court has to hear a case. Define each of the following types of jurisdiction:
    a. general jurisdiction,
    b. limited jurisdiction,
    c. original jurisdiction,
    d. appellate jurisdiction,
    e. exclusive jurisdiction, and
    f. concurrent jurisdiction.
16. What are the two major grounds for gaining federal court jurisdiction?

Chapter 5

Civil Litigation and Its Alternatives

There can be no equal justice where the kind of trial a man gets depends on the amount of money he has.
Justice Hugo L. Black

INTRODUCTION

When people have a dispute they cannot settle among themselves, they typically turn to the courts to have a judge or jury settle it for them. This process of using the courts is referred to as **litigation.** In this chapter we will present an overview of the procedural steps involved in civil litigation, as well as alternative forms of dispute resolution, such as arbitration and mediation.

Although the specific stages in the process and the specific court documents that must be completed differ in federal and state court systems, they also have much in common. The three basic stages to civil litigation are pretrial, trial, and appeal. These stages of litigation are governed by very specific sets of rules. In the federal system these rules are known as the **Federal Rules of Civil Procedure.** All states have adopted very similar rules. The state rules are usually identified as [state name] Rules of Civil Procedure (e.g., Massachusetts Rules of Civil Procedure and Illinois Criminal Law and Criminal Procedure).

Because most state rules are based on the federal rules, in this book we will focus on the federal rules. However, even though most states base their rules on those developed for the federal system, the procedures followed in state and federal courts vary somewhat, as do the procedures from one state to another.

Therefore, you must always consult the statutes and court rules for the particular court with which you are dealing.[1]

Many commentators see the litigation process as consuming too much of the courts' and litigants' time, as costing too much money, and as being needlessly draining on the emotions of all concerned. This has led to increasing interest in other ways in which people can resolve their conflicts, including administrative adjudication and alternative dispute resolution.

A. CIVIL PROCEDURE

To put the procedural rules into context, we will base our discussion of civil procedure on the case of Donald Drake from his first contact with a law firm through his appeal. From Chapter 1, you will recall that Mr. Drake witnessed the death of his grandson, Philip, when Philip was struck by the car Wilma Small was driving. As you proceed through this chapter, you will find that it is also important to know that Mr. Drake is a resident of Massachusetts, while Mrs. Small is a resident of Connecticut. The accident occurred in Massachusetts. Also take a few moments to study Figure 5-1, which provides an overview of the basic stages in the litigation process. Refer to it as you proceed through the chapter to help you keep track of the various stages.

1. The Pretrial Stage

Pleadings
The papers that begin a lawsuit—generally, the complaint and the answer.

A lawsuit officially begins when the plaintiff files the appropriate legal documents with the clerk of the court. However, before this can occur, the attorney must handle some preliminary matters: The attorney must decide whether there is a legal basis for a suit, who should be sued, and in which court the case should be brought. Once those issues have been resolved and a determination to sue has been made, the lawsuit enters the pleadings stage. The **pleadings** are the documents each side files with the court and serves on the other side to commence the lawsuit. In order to narrow the issues, either party may file **pretrial motions.** Finally, the parties will engage in **discovery,** an attempt by both sides to gather as much information as possible. The end result of this process may be a negotiated settlement, a court determination to dismiss the suit, or a decision to proceed to the trial stage.

Pretrial motion
A motion brought before the beginning of a trial either to eliminate the necessity for a trial or to limit the information that can be heard at the trial.

Discovery
The modern pretrial procedure by which one party gains information from the adverse party.

a. Preliminary Matters

The decisions as to what the grounds for the suit should be, who should be sued, and in which court the suit should be brought are not always easy to make and may involve extensive factual and legal research in order to determine the best course of action. Paralegals are often assigned the task of locating and

---

[1]Local federal district court rules are available in pamphlets from the district court office. You can also find federal court rules in the annotated codes and Supreme Court digests, as well as some specialized loose-leaf services. Complete texts of the court decisions that construe the federal rules of civil and criminal procedure are published in the Federal Rules Service (a loose-leaf service of Callaghan and Co.) and the Federal Rules Decisions (a West product, containing district court decisions involving the rules of procedure not published in the Federal Supplement). At the state level you can find the jurisdictional requirements of the courts in your state's constitution and statutes.

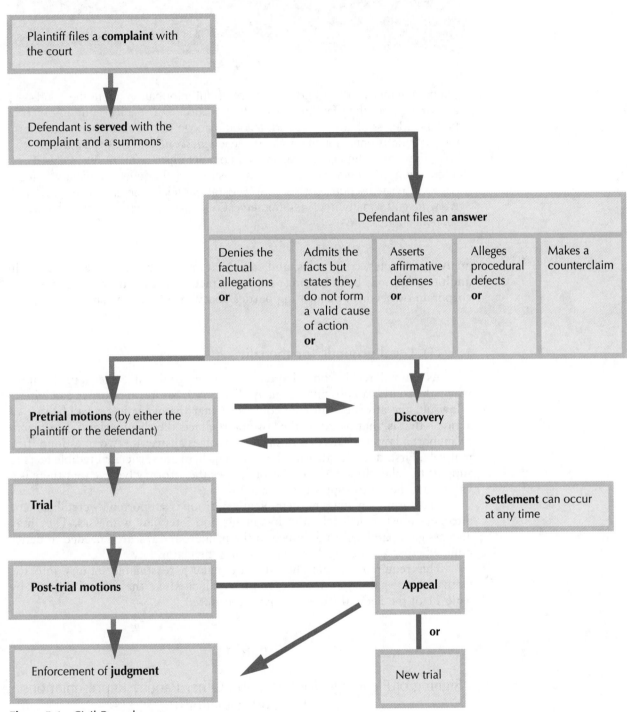

Figure 5-1 Civil Procedure

NETNOTE

On the Internet you can find all sorts of useful information about the courts—everything from their fax numbers to the location of a specific courthouse. To find the address of any state court, a good place to start is at the home page for the National Center for State Courts, *www.ncsconline.org/D_KIS/info_court_web_sites.html*. The center maintains a complete listing for all fifty states. For information on federal courts, you can visit either the federal judiciary home page at *www.uscourts.gov* or the Federal Judicial Center home page at *www.fjc.gov*. Finally, the U.S. Supreme Court has its own web site at *www.supremecourtus.gov*.

analyzing statutes, court rules, and cases that are relevant to these decisions. In addition, they may be called on to engage in factual investigation, such as tracing corporate ownerships or locating parties and witnesses to the suit.

(1) Legal grounds for the suit

As you will recall from Chapter 1, not every problem is a legal problem for which the courts can provide a remedy. Therefore, before an attorney can initiate a lawsuit, the attorney must be convinced that the client has a valid cause of action—that is, that based on the law and the facts the client's claim is sufficient to support a lawsuit. This determination involves answering two questions affirmatively. First, does the attorney believe that there are sufficient credible facts to support the plaintiff's position? Second, does the attorney believe that there is a valid legal theory to support the claim?

In determining whether their client's position is supported by credible facts, attorneys must review relevant documents and interview witnesses. They may also assign a paralegal to do much of the background research needed to determine whether a valid legal theory supports the claim.

This requirement that the attorney make a reasonable inquiry into the factual and legal bases for the claim is dictated in the federal system by Rule 11 of the Federal Rules of Civil Procedure:

Rule 11

Signing of Pleadings, Motions, and Other Papers; Representations to Court; Sanctions

(a) **Signature.** Every pleading, written motion, and other papers shall be signed by at least one attorney of record . . . or, if the party is not represented by an attorney, shall be signed by the party.

(b) **Representations to Court.** By presenting to the court . . . a pleading, written motion, or other paper, an attorney . . . is certifying that to the best of the person's

If attorneys file lawsuits without first conducting a reasonable investigation regarding the facts of the case, they may be subject to Rule 11 sanctions.

knowledge, information, and belief, formed after an inquiry reasonable under the circumstances,—

> (1) it is not being presented for any improper purpose, such as to harass or to cause unnecessary delay or needless increase in the cost of litigation;
> (2) the claims, defenses, and other legal contentions therein are warranted by existing law or by a nonfrivolous argument for the extension, modification, or reversal of existing law or the establishment of new law; . . . .
>
> **(c) Sanctions.** If, after notice and a reasonable opportunity to respond, the court determines that subdivision (b) has been violated, the court may . . . impose an appropriate sanction upon the attorneys, law firms, or parties. . . .

First, notice under subsection (a) that all pleadings, written motions, and other papers must be signed by the attorney, not a paralegal. Second, under subsection (b) the attorney can sign the pleading, written motion, or other paper only after conducting a reasonable inquiry into the facts and the law. This requirement of a reasonable inquiry was added in 1983. Prior to that time an attorney's signature on a document indicated that "to the best of his knowledge, information, and belief, there is a good ground to support it." The drafters of the 1983 amendment believed that this subjective standard did not sufficiently protect the legal system from frivolous lawsuits—hence the addition of the requirement of a reasonable inquiry, a standard that can be objectively measured based on what a reasonable attorney would have done rather than simply on what the attorney actually did.

DISCUSSION QUESTIONS

In Mr. Drake's case, assume Massachusetts courts have allowed mothers and fathers to recover in situations similar to that experienced by Mr. Drake but have never spoken about whether they would extend the rule to allow recovery by grandparents. Several other states, however, that have directly confronted this issue have ruled against grandparents. The most common reason for not allowing recovery is the fear that to do so would encourage people to bring too many potentially frivolous lawsuits.

1. With that as the legal precedent do you think Mr. Drake's attorney should feel any concern in signing her name to the complaint? Why?

2. Which language do you prefer: "that to the best of his knowledge, information, and belief there is good ground to support" the claim or "that to the best of the person's knowledge, information, and belief, formed after an inquiry reasonable under the circumstances," the claim is warranted? Why?

(2) Parties to the suit

Standing
The principle that courts cannot decide abstract issues or render advisory opinions; rather they are limited to deciding cases that involve litigants who are personally affected by the court's decision.

Under the legal principle called **standing,** only parties with a real stake in the outcome are allowed to participate in a lawsuit. Generally, courts are not supposed to decide abstract issues or render advisory opinions. (The one exception occurs in some states where courts are authorized to respond to requests for advice from other governmental bodies.) By requiring courts to decide concrete rather than abstract cases, they will have the benefit of parties who have a vested interest in the outcome and who will therefore vigorously argue their positions.

Why limit lawsuits to people who have been hurt? One reason is that they're likely to marshal the strongest arguments. It brings to mind the old line about the role of the chicken and the pig in furnishing your breakfast: The chicken is involved, but the pig is *committed*. Let chickens file lawsuits against bacon-and-egg combos, and they may lack the motivation to do a good job.[2]

Because of this requirement of standing, persons and organizations cannot file lawsuits simply because they do not approve of a certain governmental policy or some corporation's building project. For example, only persons who have been sentenced to death can challenge the death penalty. If the court determines that the parties do not have standing, it simply dismisses the case without making a determination on the merits.

A classic example of how the requirement of standing affects who can sue occurred in conjunction with the litigation that led up to the famous case of *Brown v. Board of Education.*[3] While the National Association for the Advancement of Colored People (NAACP) was opposed to the Kansas policy of segregating its public school system, it had no standing on its own to challenge the constitutionality of that policy. Before it could proceed, the organization had to recruit an African-American child who was actually turned away when she attempted to enter an all-white school located in her neighborhood.[4] Eventually, the NAACP was able to find thirteen parents and their children who were willing to serve as plaintiffs in the case.

After having determined that the plaintiff has the required standing to sue, the attorney must decide who should be named as defendants. Naturally the attorney will choose to sue the person who caused his or her client harm. However, the most logical person to sue may not be worth suing because he or she may not have money to pay the damages that a court might award. This is referred to as being **judgment proof.** If there is more than one possible defendant, the plaintiff will want to make sure to include the one with the "deepest pocket" (most assets).

Judgment proof
When the defendant does not have sufficient money or other assets to pay the judgment.

For example, under a theory known as **respondeat superior** an employer can sometimes be held responsible for the acts of its employees. Because employers usually have more money than employees, persons injured by an employee will frequently also sue the employer. Similarly, in an automobile accident case the plaintiff may sue the manufacturer of the auto or the governmental unit responsible for maintaining the roadway.

---

[2]Steve Chapman, No Decision Sometimes Best Decision, The Republican, June 22, 2004, at A9.
[3]347 U.S. 483 (1954).
[4]Paul E. Wilson, A Retrospective of Brown v. Board of Education: The Genesis of Brown v. Board of Education, 6 Kan. J.L. & Pub. Pol'y 7 (1996).

The attorney must also be certain that the parties to a lawsuit are legally capable of suing and being sued. For example, in many states a minor must sue or be sued through a named **guardian** or **"next friend."** A guardian is someone who has the legal right and duty to take care of another person's property when that person is a child or is otherwise incompetent. A next friend is not the legal guardian but is a responsible party that the court recognizes as being a legitimate representative. Allowing suit by such representatives is an exception to the requirement of standing mentioned above. The guardian or next friend is not suing in his or her own right but rather as a representative for the child or incompetent person. An interesting case intertwining the principles of standing and guardianship occurred when the U.S. Supreme Court was asked to decide the constitutionality of the words "under God" in the Pledge of Allegiance. Michael Newdow had brought a suit on behalf of his daughter. His daughter attended an elementary school where each day the classes were led in a group recitation of the Pledge of Allegiance. Newdow shared physical custody of his daughter with his daughter's mother, but the mother had exclusive legal custody. Therefore, the Court determined that he lacked standing to litigate as his daughter's next friend. Because Mr. Newdow lacked standing to bring the lawsuit, the Court could make no decision as to the constitutionality of the words "under God" and dismissed the case.[5]

Finally, there are times when a plaintiff cannot sue one potential defendant without including the others as well. This is known as **compulsory joinder.** Where such rules do not apply, the plaintiff may be selective in deciding who should be included in the suit. The defendant, however, may later file a motion to add a defendant that the plaintiff left out. Finally, in special circumstances when a number of people have been injured, such as in an airplane crash, the plaintiff may also wish to consider the possibility of a **class action suit.** The named plaintiff brings the suit on behalf of a large class of additional plaintiffs who are in a similar situation with respect to having been wronged by the defendant.

Guardian
A person appointed by the court to manage the affairs or property of a person who is incompetent due to age or some other reason.

Compulsory joinder
When a person must be brought into a lawsuit as either a plaintiff or a defendant.

Class action suit
A lawsuit brought by a person as a representative for a group of people who have been similarly injured.

(3) Selection of the court

The last preliminary issue requires the attorney to decide which court should hear the case. From your readings in Chapter 4 you know that lawsuits begin in a trial court and not an appellate court, but which trial court? That will depend on which trial courts have **jurisdiction** over the type of case that the attorney will be filing. Recall that jurisdiction relates to the power of a particular court to hear a case brought before it. In some cases the attorney may have the option of selecting among several different courts and must evaluate the advantages and disadvantages of using one versus the other.

In determining whether jurisdiction exists, you must consider both **subject matter jurisdiction** and **personal jurisdiction.** If a court does not have both subject matter jurisdiction and personal jurisdiction, it cannot hear the case.

(a) Subject matter jurisdiction As the term implies, subject matter jurisdiction is determined by the subject matter of the case—that is, the type of law that is involved. Take a moment to review the material in Chapter 4 on the jurisdiction of the federal and state courts. Do you think Mr. Drake's case could be filed in federal court? Federal courts and state courts are empowered to hear different

Jurisdiction
The power of a court to hear a case.

Subject matter jurisdiction
The power of a court to hear a particular type of case.

Personal jurisdiction
The power of a court to force a person to appear before it.

---

[5]Elk Grove Unified School District v. Newdow, 72 U.S.L.W. 4457 (2004).

types of cases. Generally, federal courts can hear only cases relating to federal law (such as federal constitutional or statutory issues) or cases in which the plaintiff and defendant are from different states and the amount in dispute exceeds $75,000. Rule 8 of the Federal Rules of Civil Procedure requires that the attorney filing a complaint include "a statement indicating why the federal court has jurisdiction to hear the case."

Mr. Drake's case does not involve federal law, as negligence is strictly state law. However, he and Mrs. Small, the defendant, are residents of different states. Therefore, Mr. Drake will be able to bring his case in federal court if the amount in dispute exceeds $75,000. Recall from Chapter 4, however, that even if he brings the case in federal court, because the accident happened in Massachusetts the federal court will apply Massachusetts state law.

Mr. Drake could also bring his action in state court. For his case the federal and state courts have concurrent jurisdiction. Mr. Drake's attorney is free to search for the best available forum. In deciding which court to choose, an attorney will usually consider such matters as filing requirements, deadline dates, the current backlog of cases, discovery procedures, the rules of evidence, and the personalities of the judges. The convenience of the physical location of the court may also be a factor.

Minimum contacts
A constitutional fairness requirement that a defendant have at least a certain minimum level of contact with a state before the state courts can have jurisdiction over the defendant.

(b) Personal jurisdiction   Personal jurisdiction relates to the court's power to force a person to appear before it—hence the name personal jurisdiction. Generally, for a state court to have personal jurisdiction over a defendant, the defendant must either be a resident of that state or have some **minimum contacts** with it. Because Mr. Drake's accident happened in Massachusetts, the accident supplies the minimum contacts that Massachusetts courts need to hear the lawsuit. Mr. Drake may sue Mrs. Small in Massachusetts.

To better understand this concept of personal jurisdiction, just for a moment assume the situation had been different, as illustrated in Figure 5-2.

Figure 5-2   Personal Jurisdiction

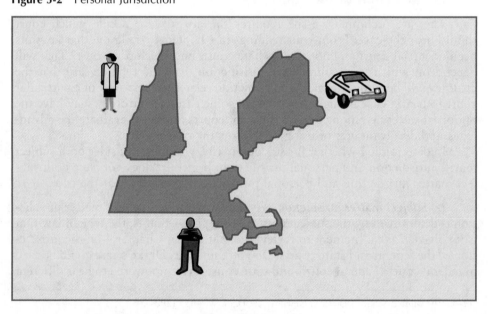

Assume that Mr. Drake, a Massachusetts resident, had been vacationing in Maine when the accident happened and that Mrs. Small, also vacationing in Maine, was a New Hampshire resident. Then the issue of personal jurisdiction would be much more complicated. As he lives in Massachusetts, Mr. Drake would like to commence his lawsuit there. Under these revised facts, however, Mrs. Small has had no contact with Massachusetts, and as at least minimum contacts are required, Mr. Drake would not be allowed to sue her in Massachusetts. He could sue her in New Hampshire because, as a resident of that state, the New Hampshire courts would have jurisdiction over Mrs. Small. He could also sue her in Maine, as the accident in that state provides the minimum contacts necessary to satisfy personal jurisdiction.

(4) Statutes of limitations

Statutes of limitations set the amount of time that a person has before he or she is forever barred from bringing a lawsuit. Such statutes vary depending on the type of situation involved. Some statutes of limitations set very short deadlines. A person complaining of discrimination at work has only 180 days in which to bring a complaint. Other statutes of limitations, such as that for murder, are really without limit. Typically, persons have two years from the date of a negligent act to file a lawsuit. Mr. Drake is fortunate in that he sought legal advice well within the time frame allowed by the statute of limitations.

Statutes of limitations
The law that sets the length of time from when something happens to when a lawsuit must be filed before the right to bring it is lost.

(5) Exhaustion of administrative remedies

If Mr. Drake's claim had involved a matter coming under the jurisdiction of an administrative agency, he might have had to consult that agency before being allowed to sue in a court of law. Such a requirement is known as the **exhaustion of administrative remedies.** The purpose behind this rule is to give the administrative agency a chance to resolve the problem without the parties having to resort to a lawsuit. The case of the pregnant waitress, discussed in Chapter 2, provides an example of when it is necessary to first go to an administrative agency. In employment discrimination cases there is a requirement that an employee who has experienced discrimination at work first complain to the state or federal agency that handles such claims before being allowed to proceed with a court suit. In Mr. Drake's situation, however, there is no administrative agency that has jurisdiction over his type of problem. Therefore, he can proceed directly to a court of law.

Exhaustion of administrative remedies
The requirement that relief be sought from an administrative agency before proceeding to court.

Mrs. Small may find herself before an administrative agency, however, if the police determine the accident was her fault. For example, she might have to argue before a state licensing agency that her driver's license should not be revoked. At the end of this chapter we have included a discussion on dispute resolution in administrative agencies.

Discussion Questions

3. Assume Mary was injured in an automobile accident while vacationing in California. Joe was driving the car that hit her. Mary is a resident of

Michigan. Joe is a resident of Florida. In which state(s) may Mary bring suit? Why?

4. For years the federal courts have been trying to persuade Congress to eliminate diversity jurisdiction. Do you think that would be a wise decision? What purpose do you suppose diversity jurisdiction was originally meant to serve? If diversity jurisdiction is maintained, should it be tied to any jurisdictional amount, and if so, how much? Why?

b. Pleadings

Complaint
The pleading that begins a lawsuit.

Answer
The defendant's reply to the complaint. It may contain statements of denial, admission, or lack of knowledge and affirmative defenses.

Counterclaim
A claim by the defendant against the plaintiff.

Cross-claim
A claim by one defendant against another defendant or by one plaintiff against another plaintiff.

Third-party claim
A claim by a defendant against someone in addition to the persons the plaintiff has already sued.

The pleadings are the documents that each side files with the court and serves on the other side in order to commence the lawsuit. Their purpose is to narrow and focus the issues involved. The initial document the plaintiff files is logically called a **complaint** because the plaintiff is the person starting the lawsuit and hence complaining of some behavior. A complaint states the allegations that form the basis of the plaintiff's case. The document the defendant files in response to the complaint is called an **answer** because it contains the defendant's answers to the charges laid out in the complaint. There are various other pleadings, including a **counterclaim** (a countersuit by the defendant against the plaintiff), a **cross-claim** (a suit by one defendant against another defendant), and a **third-party claim** (a suit by a defendant against someone not originally part of the lawsuit), but in most litigation the pleadings are simply the complaint and the answer. Figure 5-3 diagrams one example of how these various pleadings might be used in litigation. Here plaintiff Smith sued two defendants, Jones and Brown, by filing a complaint against them. Defendant Jones responded with an answer to the complaint and an additional counterclaim against the plaintiff. Defendant Brown filed an answer to the complaint, a cross-claim against defendant Jones, and a third-party claim against Jim Jackson, someone whom the plaintiff had not named as a defendant in the original complaint.

(1) The complaint

Assume that, after reviewing the facts and the jurisdictional questions involved, Pat Harper, Mr. Drake's attorney, has determined that the best

Figure 5-3 The Pleadings

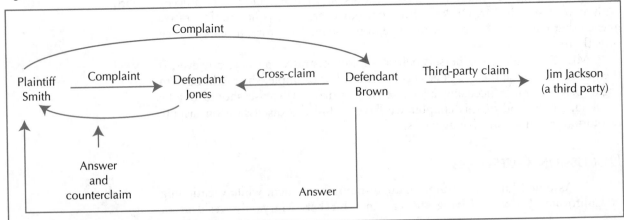

court in which to proceed is federal district court. Attorney Harper directs paralegal Chris Kendall to draft a complaint to initiate the lawsuit. The requirements for the format and the contents of the complaint are spelled out in the Federal Rules of Civil Procedure.

Rule 10 outlines the form required for all pleadings and motions in federal court. Each document must begin with a **caption,** and all claims and defenses must be in numbered paragraphs. The caption must include the names of the parties, the name of the court, the title of the action, the docket file number, and the name of the pleading. Exhibit 5-1 shows what the caption would look like in Mr. Drake's case. First, the caption would identify Donald Drake as the plaintiff and Wilma Small as the defendant. It would also indicate that the case is being filed in the U.S. District Court for the District of Massachusetts and would leave space for the eventual docket number to be entered by the court clerk. The court assigns the number at the time the attorney files the complaint.

Caption
The heading section of a pleading that contains the names of the parties, the name of the court, the title of the action, the docket or file number, and the name of the pleading.

Rule 8 determines what must appear in a claim, such as a complaint, that asks for relief. It requires that a complaint contain allegations as to why the case falls within the court's jurisdiction, the grounds that form the basis of the plaintiff's case, and the relief desired.

Rule 8

General Rules of Pleading

(a) **Claims for Relief.** A pleading which sets forth a claim for relief . . . shall contain (1) a short and plain statement of the grounds upon which the court's jurisdiction depends . . . (2) a short and plain statement of the claim showing that the pleader is entitled to relief, and (3) a demand for judgment for the relief the pleader seeks. Relief in the alternative or of several different types may be demanded.

Exhibit 5-1   Caption

UNITED STATES DISTRICT COURT FOR THE DISTRICT OF MASSACHUSETTS

Civil Action, File Number_____

Donald Drake, Plaintiff   }

                 v.   }   COMPLAINT

Wilma Small, Defendant   }

Therefore, in Mr. Drake's case, at a minimum, the complaint must include a statement indicating why he believes the federal district court has jurisdiction, a statement showing why Mr. Drake has a valid claim against Mrs. Small, and finally what relief he would like the court to grant him. After considering all of these issues, paralegal Kendall drafted the complaint that appears in Exhibit 5-2. Notice how he worked each of these items into the complaint.

The body of the complaint consists of the allegations of facts that constitute the cause of action. The federal rules allow for **notice pleading**; that is, the complaint must simply identify the transaction from which the plaintiff's claim arises. In many states, however, the facts being pleaded must be "ultimate" facts as opposed to conclusions of law.

Notice pleading
A method adopted by the federal rules in which the plaintiff simply informs the defendant of the claim and the general basis for it.

This sample complaint has only one **count** or basis for the lawsuit, the negligence of Mrs. Small. If the facts were different, however, the plaintiff could have alleged more than one basis for his lawsuit. For example, in Mr. Drake's case assume there were two people in Mrs. Small's car, Mrs. Small and Ms. Black. If Mr. Drake did not know which of them had been driving, he could allege in one count that Mrs. Small was the driver and alternatively allege in count two that Ms. Black was the driver. In addition, if he did not know whether the driver was simply being careless or had actually intended to hit Philip expressly to cause Mr. Drake's suffering, the complaint could include a count for the intentional infliction of emotional distress as well as one for negligence. This is known as **pleading in the alternative.**

Count
In a complaint, one cause of action.

Pleading in the alternative
Including more than one count in a complaint; the counts do not need to be consistent.

DISCUSSION QUESTION

5. Does it seem fair to you that plaintiffs should be allowed to plead in the alternative? Why?

If a paralegal has drafted the complaint, the supervising attorney must carefully review and sign it. In some states there is a final requirement that the client verify the complaint. A **verification** consists of an affidavit signed by the client indicating that he or she has read the complaint and that its contents are correct.

Verification
An affidavit signed by the client indicating that he or she has read the complaint and that its contents are correct.

Finally, the attorney or paralegal will file the complaint with the court. As provided in Rule 3, this action of filing the complaint with the court officially starts the lawsuit.

Ethics Alert

While paralegals may draft pleadings, they may *not* sign them. To do so would constitute the unauthorized practice of law.

UNITED STATES DISTRICT COURT FOR THE DISTRICT OF MASSACHUSETTS

Civil Action, File Number_____

Donald Drake, Plaintiff   }

v.   }   COMPLAINT

Wilma Small, Defendant   }

1. Jurisdiction of this court is founded on diversity of citizenship. Plaintiff is a citizen of Massachusetts, and defendant is a citizen of Connecticut. The matter in controversy exceeds, exclusive of interest and costs, the sum of seventy-five thousand dollars.

2. The plaintiff, Donald Drake, is a natural person residing at 56 Bancroft Way, Springfield, Massachusetts.

3. The defendant, Wilma Small, is a natural person residing at 106 Hemingway Lane, Hartford, Connecticut.

4. On September 1, 2004, while the plaintiff was walking on the sidewalk along a public way called Bishop Street in Springfield, Massachusetts, the defendant negligently drove a motor vehicle onto the sidewalk where the plaintiff's grandson, Philip Drake, was walking approximately thirty feet ahead of the plaintiff.

5. As a result of the defendant's negligence, the plaintiff's grandson was struck by the defendant's motor vehicle and instantly killed. The plaintiff viewed the entire accident.

6. As a direct result of viewing the death of his grandson, the plaintiff suffered a heart attack, great physical pain, mental suffering, and expenses for medical attention and hospitalization in the sum of one million dollars.

WHEREFORE the plaintiff demands judgment against the defendant in the sum of one million dollars, interest, and costs.

Plaintiff demands trial by jury.

Dated: _____   _____

Pat Harper
333 Main St.
Springfield, MA 01009
413-787-9999

Exhibit 5-2 Complaint

(2) The summons

Summons
A notice informing the defendant of the lawsuit and requiring the defendant to respond or risk losing the suit.

Service
The delivery of a pleading or other paper in a lawsuit to the opposing party.

Notice
Being informed of some act done or about to be done.

The plaintiff must arrange to have the defendant notified that the suit has been filed. The plaintiff's attorney does this by preparing a **summons** and then having that summons and a copy of the complaint served on (given to) the defendant. Proper service usually requires that the local sheriff (or a U.S. marshal in federal cases) personally deliver the notice in the form of a summons to the defendant. There are occasions where proper notice can be satisfied by mailing the summons to the defendant's last known address, publishing copies of it in newspapers of general circulation, or delivering it to an authorized agent. An attorney or a paralegal must consult the federal or state civil practice act on the type of service required in each case.

Courts require such **service** for reasons of basic fairness. Before a court will hear a lawsuit, it must be convinced that the defendant has received proper **notice** that the suit has been filed against her or them. The federal requirements for notice are listed in Rule 4.

Rule 4

Summons

(a) **Form.** The summons shall . . . be directed to the defendant and state the name and address of the plaintiff's attorney, ... It shall also state the time within which the defendant must appear and defend and notify the defendant that failure to do so will result in a judgment by default against the defendant for the relief demanded in the complaint.

Exhibit 5-3 shows the summons in the *Drake* case. This would be served along with a copy of the complaint in order to notify the defendant of the nature of the claim.

(3) The answer

Upon receiving the summons the defendant has a designated time within which to file a formal answer to the complaint. For example, the summons in the *Drake* case indicates that after Mrs. Small receives the complaint and summons, she has twenty days in which to answer the complaint. In an answer a defendant can choose a combination of responses from among the following alternatives:

1. deny the facts that the plaintiff says took place,
2. admit the facts but assert that those facts do not provide the plaintiff with a legal remedy,
3. claim that additional facts give rise to an affirmative defense,
4. assert that there are procedural defects in the complaint, and
5. bring a claim of one's own against either the plaintiff or another defendant.

Default judgment
A judgment entered against a party who fails to complete a required step, such as answering the complaint.

These options are not considered mutually exclusive.

A sixth alternative is simply not to respond at all—that is, not to file any documents with the court. However, the failure to take any action is viewed as an admission of the allegations contained in the complaint and creates a situation in which the plaintiff can seek a **default judgment.** In a default judgment the

```
┌─────────────────────────────────────────────────────────────────────────┐
```

UNITED STATES DISTRICT COURT FOR THE DISTRICT OF MASSACHUSETTS

Civil Action, File Number_____

Donald Drake, Plaintiff   }
                          }
              v.   }   } SUMMONS
                          }
Wilma Small, Defendant   }

To the above-named Defendant:

   You are hereby summoned and required to serve upon Pat Harper , plaintiff's attorney, whose address is 333 Main St., Springfield, MA 01009 , an answer to the complaint which is herewith served upon you, within 20 days after service of this summons upon you, exclusive of the day of service. If you fail to do so, judgment by default will be taken against you for the relief demanded in the complaint.

                     Witness _____ , Esq.
at _____ , the _____ day of _____ 20____ .

                     _____
                     Clerk of Court

(Seal of Court)

   This summons is issued pursuant to Rule 4 of the Federal Rules of Civil Procedure.

```
└─────────────────────────────────────────────────────────────────────────┘
```

Exhibit 5-3   Summons

judge awards the judgment against the party who fails to appear in court to contest the matter. While the plaintiff must still convince the judge that the claim is legitimate, the defendant has no right either to challenge the evidence presented or to present contrary evidence. Although it is possible to have a default judgment set aside, it is a very difficult task.

   The specific techniques you use to assert these options differ from state to state. At the federal level the general rules for what constitutes a proper answer are laid out in Rule 8(b) and (c). Counterclaims and cross-claims (alternative 5 above) are discussed in Rule 13.

Rule 8

General Rules of Pleading

   (a) **Claims for Relief.** . . .
   (b) **Defenses: Forms of Denials.** A party shall state in short and plain terms the party's defenses to such claims asserted and shall admit or deny the averments upon which the adverse party relies. If the party is without knowledge or information sufficient to form a belief as to the truth of an averment, the party shall so state and this has the effect of a denial. Denials shall fairly meet the substance of the averments denied. . . .

(c) **Affirmative Defenses.** In pleading to a preceding pleading, a party shall set forth affirmatively accord and satisfaction, . . . contributory negligence . . . statute of limitations . . . and any other matter constituting an avoidance or affirmative defense.

Rule 13

Counterclaim and Cross-claim

(a) **Compulsory Counterclaims.** A pleading shall state as a counterclaim any claim which at the time of serving the pleading the pleader has against any opposing party, if it arises out of the transaction or occurrence that is the subject matter of the opposing party's claim. . . .

(b) **Permissive Counterclaims.** A pleading may state as a counterclaim any claim against an opposing party not arising out of the transaction or occurrence that is the subject matter of the opposing party's claim. . . .

(g) **Cross-claim Against Co-party.** A pleading may state as a cross-claim any claim by one party against a co-party arising out of the transaction or occurrence that is the subject matter either of the original action or of a counterclaim. . . .

After reviewing these rules, think about the type of answer you might draft if you were working for the law firm that is representing Mrs. Small. Think through each of the alternatives mentioned above.

(a) Deny the facts that the plaintiff says took place.   Mrs. Small will naturally deny as many of the complaint's allegations as she can. She must be careful, however, to deny only those allegations that she truly intends to dispute. As to the other matters, she must either admit their validity or state that she is without the knowledge to form a belief as to the truth or falsity of these statements.

(b) Admit the facts but assert that those facts do not provide the plaintiff with a legal remedy.   As suggested earlier, under Massachusetts law it is unclear whether grandfathers can sue for the emotional distress they experience when seeing a grandchild harmed. Therefore, Mrs. Small may want to take advantage of the second option, arguing that even if the facts as alleged are true, they do not form a basis for a lawsuit.

Affirmative defense
A defense whereby the defendant offers new evidence to avoid judgment.

(c) Claim that additional facts give rise to an affirmative defense.   As to the third option, in her answer Mrs. Small will also include any **affirmative defense** that she thinks may decrease or even eliminate her liability. In this case there does not appear to be any such defense, but let us assume the facts were different. Assume that instead of walking down the sidewalk Mr. Drake was driving his car. Assume further that just as he was approaching an intersection, the light turned from green to yellow. He might have had time to stop, but he chose to proceed through the intersection. Mrs. Small, speeding toward him from his right, ran her red light and struck his car, killing Philip. Clearly Mrs. Small was negligent, and Mr. Drake would want to sue her. However, Mrs. Small might feel that Mr. Drake was also negligent given these changed facts. Therefore, in her answer Mrs. Small would allege the affirmative defense of contributory negligence.

Motion
A request made to the court.

(d) Assert that there are procedural defects in the complaint.   This option is usually raised through a separate **motion**. A motion is simply a request made to the court, asking for a court ruling on a particular matter. The assertion that the

complaint is defective will be discussed below under the heading Pretrial Motions.

(e) Bring a claim of one's own against either the plaintiff or another defendant. Finally, if Mrs. Small has a claim that she would like to bring against Mr. Drake based on the same factual situation on which he is relying, then she must bring that claim as part of her answer. In this case it does not appear that Mrs. Small has any basis for a counterclaim. However, let us suppose the same altered facts laid out above, where both Mr. Drake and Mrs. Small were driving their own vehicles. If Mrs. Small had been injured, in addition to alleging that she does not owe Mr. Drake any money because of his contributory negligence, she might countersue Mr. Drake to try to recover some money from him to compensate her for her own injuries. As noted above, Rule 13 governs counterclaims.

Given our original facts, Mrs. Small's answer might look like Exhibit 5-4.

c. Pretrial Motions

Sometimes the parties feel they have grounds for having the lawsuit dismissed without a trial. Therefore, in addition to or instead of filing an answer, the defendant may file a motion asking that the court immediately dismiss the case. A motion is a written request directed to the court. Rule 12 outlines the basic types of pretrial motions, as well as how they are presented to the court. For example, if Mrs. Small's attorney thinks the complaint is defective, the attorney can bring a motion under Rule 12.

Rule 12

Defenses and Objections—When and How Presented—by Pleading or Motion—Motion for Judgment on Pleadings

(a) **When Presented.** . . .

(b) **How Presented.** Every defense, in law or fact, to a claim for relief in any pleading . . . shall be asserted in the responsive pleading thereto if one is required, except that the following defenses may at the option of the pleader be made by motion:

    (1) lack of jurisdiction over the subject matter,
    (2) lack of jurisdiction over the person,
    (3) improper venue,
    (4) insufficiency of process,
    (5) insufficiency of service of process,
    (6) failure to state a claim upon which relief can be granted,
    (7) failure to join a party under Rule 19. . . .

If, on a motion asserting the defense numbered (6) to dismiss for failure of the pleading to state a claim upon which relief can be granted, matters outside the pleading are presented to and not excluded by the court, the motion shall be treated as one for summary judgment and disposed of as provided in Rule 56. . . .

Take a moment to study the various options under Rule 12. Probably the most important of the Rule 12 motions is (6), commonly referred to as a **12(b)(6) motion.** If the defendant can convince the court that she has a solid foundation for such a motion—that is, that the plaintiff has stated a claim for which the

12(b)(6) motion
A request that the court find the plaintiff has failed to state a valid claim and dismiss the complaint.

UNITED STATES DISTRICT COURT FOR THE DISTRICT OF MASSACHUSETTS

Civil Action, File Number 04-483

Donald Drake, Plaintiff }
                           }

v.   }   ANSWER
                           }

Wilma Small, Defendant }

First Defense

The complaint fails to state a claim against the defendant upon which relief can be granted as there is no right to recover for the injuries suffered by a grandparent upon seeing the negligently caused death of a grandchild.

Second Defense

1. The defendant has no knowledge as to the allegations in paragraph 1.

2. The defendant has no knowledge as to the allegations in paragraph 2.

3. The defendant admits the allegations in paragraph 3.

4. The defendant admits that the plaintiff was walking on a sidewalk along a public way called Bishop Street in Springfield, Massachusetts, on September 1, 2004. The defendant denies the allegation of negligence contained in paragraph 4. The defendant is without knowledge or information sufficient to form a belief as to the truth of the remaining allegations contained in paragraph 4.

5. The defendant denies the allegation of negligence contained in paragraph 5. The defendant is without knowledge or information sufficient to form a belief as to the truth of the remaining allegations contained in paragraph 5.

6. The defendant is without knowledge or information sufficient to form a belief as to the truth of the allegations contained in paragraph 6.

Dated: _____

_____
William Smith
886 State St.
Springfield, MA 01009
413-787-1111

Exhibit 5-4   Answer

court cannot give relief—then the court will be forced to dismiss the complaint. This means that there will be no trial. No judge or jury will ever hear about the accident or about Mr. Drake's injuries. In Mr. Drake's case the defendant might very well file such a motion, arguing that, in Massachusetts, trial courts have no right to grant relief to a grandfather who suffers injury upon seeing a grandchild negligently killed.

Another method that attorneys may use to try to end a case before trial is through filing a Rule 56 motion, known as a motion for **summary judgment.** An attorney's objective in filing a summary judgment motion is generally the same as that in filing a 12(b)(6) motion—to end the case without the need for a trial. The main difference between the two motions is that when faced with a 12(b)(6) motion, the court must make a determination based only on the facts as alleged in the complaint, and it must assume those facts are true for purposes of deciding the motion. (If the court denies the motion, all parties treat the facts as once again being in dispute.) In a summary judgment motion, however, the court will consider additional evidence as presented in documents other than the pleadings, such as depositions, answers to interrogatories, admissions on file, and affidavits. Rule 56 provides that if those documents show that "there is no genuine issue as to any material fact and that the moving party is entitled to a judgment as a matter of law," the court will grant the motion and enter judgment for the moving party. Sometimes the parties start off with a motion to dismiss but then find that they want to present additional facts not found in the pleadings. This is permissible, and indeed Rule 12 anticipates this development by stating that when "matters outside the pleading are presented to and not excluded by the court, the motion will be treated as one for summary judgment."

For example, assume in our case that the complaint did not state that Mr. Drake was Philip's grandfather but rather had simply stated that he was a relative. The defendant could request that the plaintiff admit he was the grandfather. With that admission in hand the defendant could then proceed to file a summary judgment motion on the same grounds as she would have filed a motion to dismiss. Again if the court granted the motion, there would be no trial. This is a very important fact to keep in mind. Assume that Mrs. Small did win either a motion to dismiss or a summary judgment motion. Assume further that on appeal the appellate court reversed that decision. At that point what has the plaintiff won? Only the right to continue with the lawsuit from where they left off.

Before leaving summary judgment motions, consider these two quick points. First, plaintiffs as well as defendants can bring summary judgment motions. The purpose of the motion is to avoid the necessity of a trial if there are no material facts in dispute. The purpose of a trial is to ferret out the facts. If the facts are already known, there is no need for a trial. Therefore, once the facts are known, either side can ask the court to determine that there is no need for a trial and to declare him or her the winner. Second, motions to dismiss and summary judgment motions can relate to just part of the case. For example, in Mr. Drake's situation assume that during her deposition Mrs. Small broke down and admitted that her speeding caused the accident. Her medical experts informed her, however, that they did not think Mr. Drake's heart attack was caused by seeing his grandson's death. The plaintiff might be able to convince the court to grant summary judgment on the issue of the defendant's negligence because even Mrs. Small agrees her speeding caused the accident. There would

Rule 56 motion (summary judgment motion) A request that the court grant judgment in favor of the moving party because there is no genuine issue as to any material fact and the moving party is entitled to judgment as a matter of law. It is similar to a 12(b)(6) motion except that the court also considers matters outside the pleadings.

still have to be a trial, however, to determine whether Mr. Drake's heart attack was caused by witnessing the accident.

While the motions just discussed challenge the validity of the claim, other pretrial motions are designed to expedite the discovery process or to affect how the trial will be conducted. For example, in a case involving sensitive material an attorney may make a **motion in limine**. A motion in limine is made to prevent reference to specific information in the presence of the jury. An attorney might also file a motion requesting that the judge inquire and permit the attorneys to inquire into certain areas during **voir dire**. Voir dire is the portion of the trial during which potential jurors are questioned to determine whether they are fit to serve on a jury.

Motion in limine
A request that the court order that certain information not be mentioned in the presence of the jury.

Voir dire
An examination of a prospective juror to see if he or she is fit to serve as a juror.

d. Discovery

Once the defendant files an answer, each side frequently begins using various **discovery** devices to find out more about the strength of the other side's case. The purpose of discovery is to help each side find out as much information as possible so that each can fairly evaluate the case and prepare for trial or settlement. The parties seek to discover information about the identification of witnesses, the nature of the testimony that such witnesses can be expected to provide, and the contents of relevant contracts, medical reports, and so forth. Such information is acquired through various discovery tools, including interrogatories, depositions, requests for admissions, motions to produce documents, and motions for physical and mental exams. What follows is a discussion of the most important methods.

(1) Interrogatories

Interrogatories are written questions sent by one party in a lawsuit to another party to obtain written answers in return. **Interrogatories** are used to help locate potential witnesses, establish dates, determine a person's medical or financial condition, and inquire about the existence of documentary evidence.

When a law office receives interrogatories directed at its client, the client usually is instructed to write out the answers as fully as possible. An attorney may then edit these answers and prepare the formal responses that will be returned to the other party's attorney. When answers to a firm's interrogatories are received from the other party, a paralegal may help in analyzing and organizing them.

Rule 33 provides that "[a]ny party may serve upon any other party written interrogatories." Note therefore that interrogatories cannot be served on nonparties. Also, in the federal system the number of interrogatories is limited to twenty-five. States usually impose a similar limitation.

A major advantage of interrogatories is that they are relatively inexpensive to prepare. A major disadvantage is that the answers can be closely reviewed by that person's attorney or paralegal before they are returned to the party submitting the questions.

Attorneys frequently ask their paralegals to draft interrogatories. A sample of the types of questions paralegal Kendall might draft in Mr. Drake's case can be found in Exhibit 5-5. In addition to these questions, what other types of information do you think paralegal Kendall attempted to gather through the interrogatories?

Interrogatories
Written questions sent by one side to the opposing side, answered under oath.

Boilerplate
Standard language found in a particular type of legal document.

UNITED STATES DISTRICT COURT FOR THE DISTRICT OF MASSACHUSETTS

Civil Action, File Number 04-483

Donald Drake, Plaintiff   }

v.   }   PLAINTIFF'S INTERROGATORIES

Wilma Small, Defendant   }   TO WILMA SMALL

[The interrogatories start with fairly standard boilerplate language. Attorneys use the word **boilerplate** to refer to standard language found in a particular type of legal document. In the case of interrogatories the boilerplate language at the beginning sets out basic information such as to whom the interrogatory answers are to be returned, the deadline for their return, and instructions for answering the interrogatories. This language is then followed by the specific questions.]

1. State your full name, age, full address, and telephone number.

2. At the time of the events referred to in paragraphs 4 and 5 of the complaint, did you have a valid driver's license?

3. Has your driver's license ever been suspended or revoked, and if so, state
   a. When and where it was suspended or revoked;
   b. The grounds upon which the license was suspended or revoked. . . .

15. During the 24 hours preceding the events referred to in paragraphs 4 and 5 of the complaint, had you consumed any medicines, drugs, or alcoholic beverages of any type, and if so, state
   a. The type and amount consumed;
   b. The length of time over which the substance was consumed;
   c. The names, addresses, and telephone numbers of every person who has knowledge as to your consumption of the substance. . . .

Dated: _____

Pat Harper
333 Main St.
Springfield, MA 01009
413-787-9999

Exhibit 5-5   Interrogatories

(2) Depositions

If an attorney would like to ask questions of a nonparty, such as the doctor who treated Mr. Drake, or would like to ask questions of either a party or a nonparty in person, that attorney will consider taking a deposition. A **deposition** is sworn testimony that is taken outside the courtroom without a judge being present. Although a judge is not present, there is a court reporter who administers the oath and records the testimony. The format of a deposition is similar to that of a trial in that one attorney questions the witness and the opposing

Deposition
The pretrial oral questioning of a witness under oath.

attorney has an opportunity to make objections and to cross-examine the witness.

Depositions are used primarily to preserve the testimony of a witness when that witness may not be available for the trial (as in the case of a physician) or when the attorney wants to ensure that the story of the individual being deposed cannot be changed. Because a person can be subpoenaed to be deposed, a statement may be obtained from a witness otherwise unwilling to talk to the attorney or to an investigator.

Deponent
The person who is being asked questions at a deposition.

An attorney is responsible for asking the questions during a deposition. The advantages of a deposition over interrogatories are that the deposing attorney is not limited in the number of questions he or she can ask, the **deponent's** answers are usually more spontaneous, the deposing attorney can view the demeanor of the person answering the questions, and under certain circumstances the answers may be used later in a court trial. The major disadvantages are the time and cost involved. At a minimum a deposition requires the time and presence of both attorneys, a court reporter, and the deponent. Without a special court order the federal rules limit the number of depositions to ten.

(3) Requests for admissions

Request for admissions
A document that lists statements regarding specific items for the other party to admit or deny.

A **request for admissions** is a written document that lists statements regarding specific facts for the other party to admit or deny. Once admitted, a matter cannot be contested. The purpose of the request for admissions is to clarify what is not in dispute and what therefore will not need to be resolved through a trial. Paralegals frequently draft requests for admissions.

(4) Requests for documents and physical examinations

Subpoena duces tecum
A court order that a person who is not a party to litigation appear at a trial or deposition and bring requested documents.

The motion to produce documents is used to obtain documents in the possession of one of the parties. Documents in the possession of third parties can be obtained through a **subpoena duces tecum.** The motion for a physical examination is usually used in personal injury cases or other situations where the health of one of the parties is at issue.

(5) Enforcing discovery rights

The parties to a lawsuit have an obligation to respond to discovery requests. If a party refuses to respond, the opposing attorney can go to court to seek a court order requiring the other side to comply with a valid discovery request. A plaintiff's failure to follow such a court order can result in one of the following sanctions: a prohibition against using certain evidence, a dismissal of some counts, and on rare occasions a **dismissal with prejudice** of the entire case. A dismissal with prejudice means that the case cannot be refiled.

Dismissal with prejudice
A court order that ends a lawsuit; the suit cannot be refiled by the same parties.

On the other hand, there are limits to the materials that each side must supply. If the judge is convinced that discovery attempts have gone beyond the bounds of reasonableness and amount to an undue burden or harassment, the judge can issue a protective order to allow the party to refuse to comply with certain types of discovery actions.

DISCUSSION QUESTIONS

6. If expense and time were not obstacles, would you prefer to use inter-rogatories or depositions? Why?

7. Some have likened the current discovery process to a guessing game whereby one side tries to guess what information the other side has and attempts to ferret it out through the clever use of interrogatories and depositions. Do you think the system would work better if all parties were automatically required to hand over all relevant information at the beginning of the lawsuit? Do you think that would be a workable system? A fair system? Recently the federal rules were amended to require automatic disclosure in certain circumstances. The change is contained in Rule 26(a)(1). It is too early to tell if the attempt to increase voluntary cooperation among attorneys will be successful.

8. If you were doing the discovery plan for Mr. Drake, what methods of discovery would you prefer? Why? Would your answer change if you were representing Mrs. Small? Why?

e. Settlement or Pretrial Conference

Most cases settle rather than going to trial. Settlement is a possibility at any time, even before the commencement of a lawsuit, but human nature being what it is, it often seems to happen on the very eve of trial. One method for trying to encourage settlement is the pretrial conference.

Pretrial conferences are informal sessions in which the opposing attorneys meet (usually in the presence of the judge) to discuss the case before it goes to trial. Such conferences focus on the issues to be presented at the trial and encourage the parties to agree to matters that they are not contesting. Such conferences make the trial more efficient and encourage out-of-court settlements. The hope is that as both sides learn more about the strengths and weaknesses of the case, they will be more likely to agree on the probable outcome of a trial and therefore reach a mutually agreeable accommodation. Such accommodations are encouraged because they serve the public interest by easing the pressure on an overburdened court system.

> **Pretrial conference**
> A meeting of the attorneys and the judge prior to the beginning of the trial.

2. The Trial

If the case is not settled, then it proceeds to trial. Although the majority of lawsuits filed never reach the trial stage, the results of those that are tried influence the results of future settlements. For example, there are companies that compile and publish reports of recently decided personal injury cases in different areas of the country. When parties learn of the amount of damages being awarded in similar cases, they may see the necessity for settling their case out of court.

a. The Right to a Jury Trial

The use of juries in our legal system is a product of our English common-law heritage. The system originated as a means of limiting the powers of the English monarchy and safeguarding citizens against corrupt or biased judges and prosecutors. Today the use of the jury system is most strongly entrenched in criminal cases, but it continues to play an important role in civil cases as well.

Ethics Alert

The right to a jury trial is the client's right, not the lawyer's decision.

The Seventh Amendment to the U.S. Constitution states that the right to a trial by jury shall be preserved in suits at common law where the value in the controversy exceeds $20. Although the word *preserved* might suggest that the constitutional right to a jury trial is limited to those actions tried by a jury in 1791, the right to a jury trial now extends to most types of federal civil cases. Because there is no federal right to a jury in civil cases tried in state courts, each state has defined for itself the extent to which juries are to be available in state courts. In most states you will not find juries in divorce and probate cases. But you will find juries provided for, either by statute or by constitution, in contractual and tort matters exceeding some dollar limit.

The basic function of the jury is to resolve the factual, as opposed to the legal, questions raised in the case. Generally, this comes down to deciding how much credibility to give to the often conflicting testimony of various witnesses. When damage awards are called for, the jury must decide how to measure pain and suffering in terms of dollars and cents. In cases where a jury is not used, the judge takes over the jury's function besides her or his normal duties of presiding over the trial and resolving the legal questions raised.

Finally, a word about the number of people on a jury. Under the common law a jury consisted of twelve people. However, the courts have ruled that there is nothing that is constitutionally significant about that number, and six-person juries have been used in civil cases at both the federal and the state levels. Furthermore, it is not unusual to select one or two extra jurors as alternates, especially where the trial is expected to last for more than a few days. These alternates sit in the jury box with their fellow jurors throughout the trial and are used as substitutes if regular jurors are unable to continue. An alternate does not participate in the deliberations, however, unless he or she has replaced one of the original jurors.

b. Jury Selection

If a jury is being used, the first formal step in the trial process is the selection of the individual jurors. This **voir dire** process marks the start of the trial itself. Jury selection, however, actually begins many months before that date when a computer randomly selects names off a list of registered voters. The manner in which jury pools are selected varies, but the description given here is representative of the most commonly used procedures.

Once potential jury names are selected, a jury commission screens them to determine their eligibility. Although the modern trend is to require almost everyone to serve as a juror, many states still have statutory exemptions for various occupational groups, such as government officials, attorneys, physicians, clergy, police officers, fire fighters, and others. In addition, people may be excused from jury service if they are in bad health, if service creates hardships for their employers, or if they have small children. Those who pass this screening process then have their names placed on a list of people eligible for jury service.

Judges schedule their jury trials during an agreed-on time period (usually referred to as a jury calendar) so that the jury commission officials can plan to have a pool of qualified jurors available. An appropriate number of eligible jurors are subpoenaed to report to the courthouse on a particular day or every day during a particular week.

When they arrive at the courthouse, the jurors usually assemble in a special lounge area from which they are then directed to specific courtrooms as they are needed. A random drawing usually is used to determine which jurors are to be assigned to which cases.

The voir dire itself consists of questioning potential jurors to determine whether they are fit to serve on the jury for that specific case. Although the jury commission has cleared these jurors to serve on a jury, there may be something about a particular person that disqualifies him or her from serving on a specific case. For example, a potential juror would be disqualified if he or she had some personal relationship with a party in the case or with one of the attorneys involved. Potential jurors may also be disqualified if they have been exposed to a great deal of prejudicial pretrial publicity or have been involved in similar lawsuits themselves.

The specific process used in voir dire varies from state to state and even from judge to judge. The judge usually begins by asking general questions about each person's occupation, family, and possible relationship to anyone involved in the case. When pretrial publicity has been extensive, the judge may question the jurors about what they remember from the media accounts and whether they think they can lay aside any opinions they may have formed and decide the case solely on the merits of what is presented in the courtroom. In some jurisdictions the lawyers are given a chance to ask their own questions after the judge is finished, while in others they are limited to submitting questions for the judge to ask. Most attorneys prefer to be able to question the jurors personally because they see it as an opportunity to begin to establish a rapport with them and to indoctrinate them to their view of the case.

Attorneys use two types of challenges when seeking to prevent specific individuals from serving on the jury in their case. The first line of attack is usually a **challenge for cause.** To exercise this challenge, the attorney must convince the judge that something about the juror's background or answers demonstrates that the person has some type of bias. If the judge agrees, the person will not be seated. There is no limit on the number of such challenges that can be raised or granted. In some well-publicized and highly controversial cases, attorneys have gone through hundreds of jurors before arriving at the final twelve.

Attorneys can also exercise **peremptory challenges.** These allow an attorney to have a potential juror removed without giving a reason for the dismissal. However, peremptory challenges are limited in number. In deciding whether to use one of these valuable peremptory challenges on a questionable juror, attorneys must weigh the risk of having to accept a worse juror later because they will have exhausted their limited supply of challenges.

If the court excuses a potential juror as the result of either a challenge for cause or a peremptory challenge, that individual usually returns to the jury

Challenge for cause
A method for excusing a prospective juror based on the juror's inability to serve in an unbiased manner.

Peremptory challenge
A method for excusing a prospective juror; no reason need be given.

lounge for reassignment on another case. The acceptable jurors are then seated in the jury box and are officially sworn in.

DISCUSSION QUESTIONS

9. Many people argue that life and lawsuits have become too complex for the average juror. For example, how can anyone but an economist understand the intricacies of an antitrust lawsuit or anyone but a computer expert comprehend the concept of reverse engineering? Do you think there are certain types of lawsuits where the jury should be composed only of experts in that field? Should jury trials be eliminated entirely in some areas of the law?

10. When litigants have sufficient money, they often hire jury experts, people who specialize in studying the characteristics of various groups. The theory is that certain types of people will be more likely, for example, in a medical malpractice case to lean toward the doctor, while others will favor the patient. Can you think of any groups that you could characterize in this way? Do you think this is a valid approach to choosing a jury? Even if valid, should it be used?

c. Opening Statements

Once the jury is selected, the attorneys make their opening arguments, in which they outline the evidence they hope to present. In these presentations the plaintiff's and defendant's attorneys state their theories of the case and describe, from their respective points of view, what allegedly took place and to what they expect the witnesses to testify. The jury is thus presented with a framework for viewing the upcoming testimony.

Because the plaintiff has the burden of proving his or her case, the plaintiff's attorney presents the first opening argument. In most cases the defendant's attorney makes an opening statement immediately following that of the plaintiff's attorney. At other times the defense waits until the plaintiff's attorney has finished presenting the plaintiff's witnesses and exhibits and the defense is about to present its case.

d. Presentation of Evidence

Direct examination
The questioning of your own witness.

Leading question
A question that suggests the answer; generally, leading questions may not be asked during direct examination of a witness.

After the opening statements the plaintiff's attorney presents evidence in the form of witness testimony and exhibits. The exhibits consist of such things as medical records, accident reports, and photographs of the accident scene. There are rules of evidence that dictate what types of evidence can be admitted and the manner in which witnesses can be questioned.

In considering evidence it is essential to be aware of the differences between facts and opinions. When a witness testifies that he saw the defendant's automobile strike the plaintiff's car broadside, he is testifying about a fact he observed. But when that same witness says the defendant was driving too fast for the icy condition of the road, he is stating an opinion. Generally, only expert witnesses, such as doctors and police officers, can testify as to their opinions, based on their expert knowledge.

In conducting the **direct examination** of a witness, an attorney usually cannot ask leading questions. A **leading question** is one that suggests the answer.

For example, "Wouldn't you say the defendant appeared to be very angry at that point in time?" is a leading question.

Once the plaintiff's attorney has completed questioning a witness, the defendant's attorney may **cross-examine** that same witness. The cross-examination clarifies any potentially misleading statements or half-truths and attacks the credibility of the witness. Therefore, the defense attorney attempts to bring out possible biases or the inability of the witness to have seen clearly what she or he claims to have seen. On cross-examination a lawyer may ask leading questions.

Cross-examination
The questioning of an opposing witness.

The defendant's cross-examination is then followed by redirect examination, where the plaintiff's attorney has the opportunity to ask additional questions of the witness. The plaintiff's attorney uses redirect questions to rehabilitate the witness after the defense's attack on the witness's credibility. These questions cannot be used to raise new subjects or to explore topics that were not covered as part of the cross-examination. The redirect is then followed by an opportunity for recross-examination by the defendant's attorney, but that must, in turn, be limited to topics raised during the redirect. At that point the witness is finally excused, and the plaintiff's attorney then proceeds to call the next witness.

Throughout the process of questioning witnesses and presenting evidence the attorneys must keep in mind that appellate courts usually require them to raise appropriate objections at the proper times during the trial. An attorney cannot complain later to an appellate court about something that he or she did not complain about at the proper time to the trial judge.

This requirement for "laying a proper foundation" places additional pressures on the trial attorney. A careless or incompetent attorney can simultaneously destroy the client's chances to win at the trial level and to successfully appeal an adverse decision. Attorneys will make objections for the record even when they do not expect the trial judge to accept them. This is sometimes called protecting the record or making a record for appeal.

After the plaintiff's attorney has finished calling witnesses and presenting evidence, the defense has its opportunity. Before this occurs, it is not unusual for the defense attorney to move for a **directed verdict**. This motion requests that the judge end the trial at that point and find in favor of the defendant on the basis that the plaintiff's side failed to meet its obligation of presenting a prima facie case supporting its position. The judge will enter a directed verdict if the judge concludes that the plaintiff's evidence is so weak that even considered in its most favorable light (without considering any rebuttal evidence from the defendant) it is not sufficient as a matter of law to merit a verdict in the plaintiff's favor. For example, in Mr. Drake's case, to present a prima facie case of negligence, his attorney must enter evidence of each element of negligence: duty, breach, cause, and harm. If she inadvertently omits one of the elements, then there is no way for the court to find a basis for the negligence claim, and a directed verdict in the defendant's favor is appropriate.

Directed verdict
A verdict ordered by a trial judge if the plaintiff fails to present a prima facie case or if the defendant fails to present a necessary defense.

If the court grants the motion, the trial is over. However, it is very unusual for a judge to accept a motion for a directed verdict at this point in the trial. Typically, the judge denies the motion, and the defense attorney goes on to present his or her witnesses. The same process of direct, cross, redirect, and recross is used. The defense strategy involves presenting evidence that contradicts evidence presented by the plaintiff and possibly attempting to raise a legally accepted defense for that particular type of case.

NETNOTE

You can read about and see video clips of current trials at:

www.courttv.com

Once the defendant's case is complete, the plaintiff can ask for a directed verdict on the basis that even if the defendant's evidence is taken in its most favorable light, it would be insufficient to rebut the plaintiff's case. If the judge also denies this motion, as is usually the case, the plaintiff can present witnesses who will attempt to rebut testimony and evidence presented by the defense. After that, either side can again renew its motion for a directed verdict. If these motions are again denied, both sides then give their closing arguments.

DISCUSSION QUESTIONS

11. Do you agree with the rule that only experts should be allowed to state their opinions? Why should it matter if a witness who saw Mrs. Small stumble just before she entered her car testifies that "Mrs. Small was drunker than a skunk"?

12. One of the all-time famous leading questions is "So, when did you stop beating your wife?" What is the problem with asking your witness this type of question during direct examination?

e. Closing Arguments

Perhaps the most dramatic part of any trial is the closing arguments. Here the attorneys review and interpret the evidence in its most favorable light and develop emotional appeals. Closing arguments are their final chance to persuade the jury. Although both the plaintiff and the defendant receive equal time, in some states the plaintiff has the advantage of splitting the time and speaking both first and last. The plaintiff is given this advantage because the plaintiff also has the burden of proof to overcome.

f. Jury Instructions

Before sending the jury members out to deliberate, it is the judge's responsibility to properly instruct them about the nature of their duties and the requirements of the law. The jury's duty is to determine the facts and then apply the requirements of the law to those facts. However, the jury is composed of a group of lay persons who do not know what the law requires. Therefore, it is the duty of the judge to explain the law in terms the jury can understand.

Rather than starting from scratch and risking reversal for failing to include some key element or for explaining some concept in a misleading way, judges frequently rely on **pattern jury instructions**. These are collections of instructions that have already been tested on appeal in other cases. Furthermore, the attorneys in the case have the opportunity to submit instructions they would like to see included. The judge then reviews their submissions and often discusses the issues with the attorneys in chambers before deciding which instructions to give at the trial.

g. Jury Deliberations, Verdict, and Judgment

Once they have been properly instructed, the jurors retire to a special room where they are kept isolated while they deliberate over their **verdict.** Their first task is always to select one of their number to act as a foreman. The person selected becomes the official spokesperson for the jury and the one who sends messages to the judge and delivers the verdict.

The actual deliberations take place in secrecy. No one other than the jurors themselves is allowed in the room. Not even the bailiffs, who are responsible for looking after the jury, are allowed to be present during the actual deliberations. By a series of discussions and votes the deliberations go on until either the jury reaches a verdict or the judge declares a **mistrial.** In most cases the jurors must come to a unanimous agreement regarding the verdict, although some states have provisions for less-than-unanimous verdicts in certain types of cases.

Usually, evidence is presented at the trial regarding the question of liability and the amount of damages. The jurors consider the amount of damages as soon as they decide that damages are in fact owed. In some cases, however, a bifurcated trial is held. During the first phase of the trial the jury hears testimony regarding liability and then deliberates on that issue alone. If the jury finds the defendant liable, the trial enters a second stage. Now the jury hears evidence about the nature of the damages and then deliberates regarding the amount of damages to award.

After the deliberations are complete, the jury files back into the courtroom, and the foreman either reads the verdict aloud or hands a piece of paper to the clerk for the judge or the clerk to read aloud. The judge then checks with the other jurors to ensure that the verdict read was indeed what they had agreed to.

When cases are tried to a judge without a jury, at the conclusion of the trial the judge usually calls a recess. The judge then announces the verdict later. This gives the judge time to consider the evidence and the law before reaching a decision.

The **judgment** is the court's official statement regarding the rights and obligations of the parties involved in the case. In order for the plaintiff to use the power of the state to enforce those rights, the clerk must enter a formal judgment into the record. Then, for example, if the defendant fails to pay damages that were part of the judgment, the plaintiff can request a **writ of execution.** The writ instructs the sheriff to seize the defendant's property, sell it at public auction, and then use the proceeds to pay the plaintiff. Usually, if the losing party does not appeal within a specified time period, the judgment automatically becomes effective. If the losing party does appeal, the court stays the judgment until the appellate court reaches its decision.

h. Post-Trial Motions

After the verdict has been announced, the losing party has a certain time period within which to file post-trial motions. The most common motions are

Verdict
The opinion of a jury on a question of fact.

Mistrial
A trial ended by the judge because of a major problem, such as a prejudicial statement by one of the attorneys.

Judgment
The decision of the court regarding the claims of each side. It may be based on a jury's verdict.

Writ of execution
A court order authorizing a sheriff to take property in order to enforce a judgment.

Judgment notwith-standing the verdict (judgment N.O.V.) A judgment that reverses the verdict of the jury when the verdict had no reasonable factual support or was contrary to law.

Motion for a new trial A request that the court order a rehearing of a lawsuit because irregularities, such as errors of the court or jury misconduct, make it probable that an impartial trial did not occur.

a motion for judgment notwithstanding the verdict and a motion for a new trial.

The motion for a **judgment notwithstanding the verdict,** also known as a **judgment N.O.V.** (judgment non obstante veredicto), is a request to the judge to reverse the jury's decision on the basis that the evidence was legally insufficient to support its verdict. If the judge grants the motion, the case is over, and the moving party has won.

An attorney usually bases the **motion for a new trial** on the assertion that some procedural error has tainted the outcome. The losing party might argue, for example, that some piece of evidence was admitted that should not have been admitted or that someone made improper contacts with a juror on the case. If the court grants the motion, the case has to be retried.

Both motions are frequently made but seldom granted. Nevertheless, they are important because they may be necessary to preserve the client's right to appeal to a higher court. The doctrine of **exhaustion** requires that the trial court be given every possible opportunity to correct its own errors before the appellate courts intervene.

3. The Appeal

"I'll take my case all the way to the Supreme Court" is a battle cry that has been echoed by many concerned litigants. No one likes to lose, and there are few attorneys who have not dreamed of arguing a case before the U.S. Supreme Court.

On the other hand, appeals consume time and money. The client's initial desire for appeal often pales because of costs. In addition, the option to appeal may be either very limited or even nonexistent. If the attorney did not make the correct objections during the trial or if the client's case did not involve any questions of law, there will be no basis for an appeal.

a. The Timing of the Appeal

A case cannot be appealed until a final judgment has been entered. This can occur at any time during the trial if the court grants a final judgment. For example, the court can grant a motion to dismiss, a summary judgment motion, a motion for a directed verdict, or one of the post-trial motions. Most commonly a final judgment comes after a jury verdict. The party wishing to have the case reviewed must file a notice of appeal within a specified time period after the final judgment is entered. If the notice is not filed within the proper time limits, the federal appellate courts will refuse to hear it. Most states are equally strict about the enforcement of their time limits.

b. The Scope of the Review

When an appellate court considers a case, it does not conduct a new trial. It simply reviews the official record of the proceedings at the trial court. Moreover, it limits its review to specific **appealable issues,** for which the party appealing the case must have laid a proper foundation at the trial level.

As you know, in general appellate courts consider only legal issues. Recall that legal issues involve the interpretation and application of the law; factual issues involve the determination of whether a given event took place as alleged.

Sometimes, however, appellate courts are asked to review a trial court's findings of fact. When they do so, it is on a very limited basis. Generally, appellate courts will resolve conflicts in the testimony and questions of the credibility of the witnesses in favor of the trial judge's position. They cannot disregard a trial court's findings of fact unless they determine that the findings were **clearly erroneous.** This means not simply that the appellate court would have found otherwise but that the appellate court is convinced that the trial court made a mistake, as, for example, when the trial court did not base its findings on sufficient evidence.

Clearly erroneous
Standard used by
appellate courts when
reviewing a trial court's
findings of fact.

However, when an appellate court reviews legal issues, it gives no deference to the trial court's findings but rather makes its own independent review. A legal issue might involve reviewing a trial judge's interpretation of a statute or legal document, such as a will or a lease. Similarly, questions about the nature of the jury instructions and the trial court's decision on the admissibility of evidence present legal issues.

Sometimes the resolution of a legal issue requires the court to review the facts. This creates a situation that is hard to categorize as either factual or legal. For example, when a party appeals based on the trial judge's decision to deny a motion for a directed verdict, the appellant is arguing that the evidence was so one-sided, it could support only one conclusion. Because it is a ruling on a motion, it is a legal question; but to reach a decision, the appellate court must make a judgment about the strength of the evidence itself. In these mixed fact/law situations, an appellate court often does an independent review—especially if the court believes the legal aspects predominate. An appellate court uses the **clearly erroneous** standard when factual aspects predominate, such as in questions involving negligence.

If the appellate court decides that the trial judge made a legal error, it must determine whether that error was prejudicial or merely harmless. Errors are defined as prejudicial when they probably affected the results. **Harmless errors** are errors so minor and peripheral that they had no significant effect on the outcome. Only **prejudicial errors** are considered to be **reversible errors.**

An example of a harmless error is a mistake in the pleadings. Such mistakes are usually considered to be harmless because the facts can be determined at trial. Also, errors in jury instructions will not be considered reversible unless there is reason to believe that they actually misled the jury. Generally it is assumed that a judge presiding at a bench trial is less likely to be affected by incompetent evidence than a jury exposed to the same incompetent evidence.

Another condition for a reversible error is that the attorney who appeals cannot be responsible for the error that attorney is appealing. In other words, the appellant cannot complain about the admission of inflammatory evidence if the appellant's attorney was the one who introduced it. An exception to this principle can occur in a criminal case when a different attorney is handling the appeal and is charging that the trial attorney's performance was incompetent.

Finally, sometimes an appeal is based upon a challenge to a trial judge's decision as to court procedure or how the case should be managed. Examples include permission to amend a complaint, denial of a request for a continuance, imposition of sanctions for filing an improper pleading, and the awarding of prejudgment interest. Because these types of decisions are generally left to the discretion of the trial judge, appellate courts review them using an **abuse of discretion** standard. They will reverse a trial court only if the appellant can prove the judge committed a clear error of judgment, lacked the authority to act, or acted with prejudice or malice.

c. Filing the Appeal

After the attorney files the notice of appeal with the trial court, the attorney or a paralegal contacts the court reporter and the court clerk to order appropriate portions of the official record. He or she instructs the court reporter to prepare a written transcript of either the entire trial or selected portions of the trial and asks the court clerk to prepare copies of various official court records relating to the case. The specific records ordered will depend on the nature of the case and the specific rules of the appellate court.

On behalf of the client, either the paralegal or another representative of the firm must pay a filing fee with the appellate court. In addition, the client may be required to file one or more bonds. In the federal courts, for example, the appellant must post a bond to secure payment of the costs on appeal. If a party wants to **stay the judgment** pending the outcome of the appeal, that party must file a bond in the trial court. When the court stays a judgment, it permits the party who owed the judgment to withhold paying until the appellate court has had an opportunity to review it. The bond guarantees the person to whom the judgment is owed that the money (plus interest) will be paid if either the appeal is dismissed or the judgment is affirmed.

Within a specified time period after filing the notice of appeal, the side bringing the appeal, the appellant, must file an **appellate brief.** The brief explains the facts of the case, lists the relevant statutes and court cases, and then presents legal arguments for overturning the lower court's decisions.

Then the other side, the appellee, must file an appellate brief that presents its version of the facts, relevant statutes and cases, and legal arguments that favor upholding the lower court decision. It is interesting to note that the lower court judge who made the decision plays no part in this appeal process and cannot present his or her own brief in defense of the contested decision.

After the appellee files a brief, the appellant can file a reply brief, which attempts to respond to the appellee's argument and to any new authorities cited in the appellee's brief. The appellee can file a reply brief only in situations where a cross-appeal is involved. A cross-appeal occurs when both sides are appealing different issues of the case.

d. Oral Arguments

Depending on the rules of the particular appellate court, the court may hear oral arguments on appeal. During oral argument the attorneys present their clients' positions. The court gives the attorneys a limited time to speak (often no more than twenty minutes), and the judges frequently interrupt the attorneys with questions. The purpose of the questioning is to probe weak points in the argument and to explore the implications of the attorney's line of reasoning.

e. The Decision and Its Publication

With or without the benefit of oral argument the judges study the matter until they reach a decision by majority vote. Usually, the case is assigned to one of the judges in the majority to prepare the official opinion of the court. As part

Stay the judgment
A suspension of the judgment. It is often requested when the trial court judgment is being appealed.

Appellate brief
An attorney's written argument presented to an appeals court, setting forth a statement of the law as it should be applied to the client's facts.

of this process the judge's law clerks verify the authorities cited in the briefs, sometimes finding additional cases that apply. The clerks typically prepare a rough draft of the opinion for the majority judges to edit and polish. The other judges on the court have the right to prepare either concurring or dissenting opinions if they want the record to reflect their differences. You will recall that in a concurring opinion the judge agrees with the outcome but disagrees with the reasoning in the court's opinion. In a dissenting opinion the writer disagrees with both the outcome and the reasoning. The court's decision is then published in the appropriate **reporters,** lawbooks that contain all of an appellate court's opinions.

Usually, the appellate decision is either to **affirm** the lower court's action or to **reverse** and **remand** (return) the case to the lower court for reconsideration. Sometimes, based on the nature of the case, a new trial is not needed to supplement the factual record. Then the judges may simply enter a final judgment based on the existing record.

Affirm
When a higher court agrees with what a lower court has done.

Reverse
When an appellate court overturns or negates the decision of a lower court.

Remand
When an appellate court sends a case back to the trial court for a new trial or other action.

f. Further Appeals

Depending on the court structure and the nature of the case, the party that loses at the appellate level (regardless of which party lost at the trial-court level) may have the option of appealing to yet a higher-level appellate court. The general rule, however, is that there is only one right of appeal. A second appeal to a higher court is usually discretionary rather than a matter of right: The judges on the higher appellate court choose to hear only the cases that they believe have the greatest judicial significance. For example, to have a case heard by the U.S. Supreme Court, the losing party must first petition the Court and request that it grant a writ of certiorari. In support of this request the applicant will file a written brief. The purpose of the brief is not to argue the merits of the case but to convince the Court to agree to hear the case. Common reasons are the importance of the case for others beyond the immediate litigants and the need to resolve conflicts among the circuits. For example, for many years the federal courts of appeals were reaching different results in sexual harassment cases. Some courts of appeals thought such situations were covered by Title VII, while others disagreed. In a federal system, leaving such a conflict unresolved is obviously undesirable, as the outcome of a case will vary based on where it is brought. Eventually the Supreme Court agreed to hear a case involving sexual harassment and resolved the issue by deciding that such situations are covered by Title VII.[6]

If the Court grants the petition for a writ of certiorari, the litigants will then file briefs arguing the merits of the case. However, the Court denies most petitions for certiorari.

Most state courts follow a similar procedure. For example, in Massachusetts there is one right of appeal to the intermediate appellate court. If a party wishes to be heard by the state's highest court, the Massachusetts Supreme Judicial Court, that person must file an application for **leave to obtain further appellate review.** Massachusetts Appellate Rule 27.1 provides that "[s]uch application shall be founded upon substantial reasons affecting the public interest or the interests of justice." Massachusetts Appellate Rule 11

---

[6]Meritor Savings Bank v. Vinson, 477 U.S. 57 (1986).

also makes it possible to bypass the intermediate appellate court and go directly to the Supreme Judicial Court if that court is convinced that the questions presented are

(1) questions of first impression or novel questions of law which should be submitted for final determination to the Supreme Judicial Court; (2) questions of law concerning the Constitution of the Commonwealth or questions concerning the Constitution of the United States which have been raised in a court of the Commonwealth; or (3) questions of such public interest that justice requires a final determination by the full Supreme Judicial Court.

If the higher appellate court accepts the appeal, the parties file new briefs, and the process described above begins all over again.

B. ADMINISTRATIVE PROCEDURE

As we learned in Chapter 2, administrative agencies have far-reaching powers, encompassing roles traditionally reserved for the legislative, executive, and judicial branches. Under their legislative powers most agencies have the authority to enact rules and regulations in order to further the purposes of their enabling statute. To aid them in drafting appropriate rules, they often hold rulemaking hearings to hear testimony regarding the proposed new regulations. In their executive role they can conduct investigations either at their own initiative or in response to a complaint filed with their agency. This is in stark contrast to the approach followed in the court system, where judges are not allowed to conduct independent investigations but must rely upon the parties to bring the evidence to them. Finally, in their judicial role agencies convene formal adjudicative hearings to decide issues that cannot be resolved by more informal means.

Most of the day-to-day work of administrative agencies, however, is done on a very informal basis with no need to resort to a formal hearing. For example, a pharmacist may have to go to an administrative agency to apply for a license to dispense drugs, or someone who has lost his or her job will seek the aid of an agency in applying for unemployment benefits.

If an individual or business is seeking a specific benefit from an administrative agency, such as a license or some type of compensation, the process ordinarily begins with the party filing an application or claim form that they get from the agency. The receipt of this form constitutes formal notification that the individual or business is applying for a specified benefit. Most licensing decisions, and many claim determinations, are made solely on the basis of the written documentation provided by the applicants. Formal hearings are most likely to occur only when the individual or business wishes to appeal the agency's initial decision. Even where an agency seeks to impose a fine or take some other type of punitive action, the affected individual or business may negotiate a "plea bargain," whereby there is an agreement to accept a penalty without having to take the matter to a formal hearing stage.

Sometimes, however, a formal hearing is required to resolve the dispute. The remainder of this section will focus on what happens when a formal hearing is needed and the procedures that typically lead up to such hearings. To assist us in understanding how a typical state agency operates, we will view the agency process through the eyes of Diane Dobbs, the waitress you met at the beginning of Chapter 2. You may recall that she was fired when she announced to her boss that she was pregnant. While the discussion that follows is typical of the process to be found in a state agency handling discrimination claims, administrative procedures, like court procedures, vary among the states and between the federal and state agencies. The federal government and each of the states have adopted administrative procedure acts that establish basic ground rules for the organization and operation of their administrative agencies. For example, at the federal level the Administrative Procedure Act[7] provides the basic legal structure within which federal administrative agencies function.

Procedures also vary among agencies within the same state and within the federal government because individual agencies use their rulemaking powers to specify additional procedures that apply only to their own agency's hearings. Thus, if you were preparing for a hearing on a Social Security disability claim, you would consult Part 422 of Title 20 of the Code of Federal Regulations for a more detailed description of the specific procedures used by the Social Security Administration. If you were preparing for a workers' compensation claim before the Illinois Industrial Commission, you would consult Part 7020 of the Illinois Administrative Code.

In the case of Diane Dobbs, to understand the agency law governing the substance of Diane's allegations of discrimination as well as the procedures that the agency follows, an attorney would look for information in at least three sources:

1. the state statute that made it unlawful for employers to discriminate and that created the agency authorized to enforce the law in that area;
2. the state administrative procedure act that would set forth the basic rules governing that state's agencies; and
3. regulations enacted by the agency itself that have interpreted what it means to discriminate and that have established the procedures that must be followed by someone who wants to complain of alleged unlawful discrimination.

1. Prehearing Procedures

Dispute resolution through administrative agencies is designed to relieve the courts of the burden of resolving certain types of disagreements. As noted earlier in this chapter, when a claim involves a matter coming under the jurisdiction of an administrative agency, the aggrieved party may have to consult that agency before being allowed to sue in a court of law. Such a requirement is known as the **exhaustion of administrative remedies.** The purpose behind this rule is to give the administrative agency a chance to resolve the problem without the parties having to resort to a lawsuit. Diane's case provides an example of when it is necessary to first go to an administrative agency. In employment discrimination cases there is a requirement that an employee who has experienced discrimination at work first complain to the state or federal agency that handles such claims before being allowed to proceed with a court suit. Therefore, after talking with her, the attorneys at Darrow and Bryan suggested she first file a complaint with

---

[7]5 U.S.C. § 500 (2000).

the appropriate local state agency before pursuing a lawsuit through the court system.

Just as with court-based litigation, dispute resolution through administrative agencies follows certain prescribed steps. The first involves the prehearing procedures, including the proper method for commencing an action, providing notice to all parties, conducting an investigation, and reaching an initial determination.

a. Commencing the Action

Individuals or businesses usually become involved in administrative adjudication when they seek review of an agency decision with which they disagree or when the agency charges them with some violation of its regulations. For example, when a person applies for but is denied Social Security disability benefits, he or she can seek an agency review of that decision. However, agencies can themselves take the initial steps, such as when a state agency might seek to revoke a real estate broker's license or to charge an employer with unfair labor practices. Other examples include the Environmental Protection Agency seeking to fine a business for the improper disposal of dangerous chemicals or a state agency taking steps to shut down a restaurant for repeated violations of the local health code.

In Diane's case, her first step was to file a written complaint with her local antidiscrimination agency. The complaint identified both herself (the complainant) and her employer (the respondent), indicated the date of the alleged unlawful acts, and provided a concise statement of the grounds for her complaint.

b. Notice of Alleged Violations

Once an action has been initiated, either through an individual's complaint or the agency's own actions, the agency must formally serve the defendant (in some agencies referred to as the respondent) with notice as to which of its rules may have been violated and the circumstances under which those violations are alleged to have occurred. It must also provide information about what steps the defendant must take to dispute these charges and avoid being penalized.

Once the state agency received Diane's complaint, it sent her a notice acknowledging the agency had received the complaint and informing her of her rights. It also sent a copy of the complaint to the employer along with a statement as to the employer's rights. The receipt of Diane's complaint also served as the prerequisite for the agency beginning a formal investigation into her allegations.

c. Investigation

A unique feature of administrative agencies is that they are able to conduct their own investigations. In Diane's case the agency was authorized to engage in informal investigations by conducting field visits, making written or oral inquiries, interviewing witnesses, and even issuing subpoenas that would require people to present themselves or their books, papers, and other tangible possessions to the agency. In addition, if the parties are represented by an attorney, the attorneys can engage in some limited forms of discovery.

In some cases very helpful information can be obtained under the Freedom of Information Act. The act declares in part that an agency shall

> upon request by an individual to gain access to his record or to any information pertaining to him which is contained in the system, permit him and upon his request, a person of his own choosing to accompany him, to review the record and have a copy made of all or any portion thereof in a form comprehensible to him.[8]

Finally, the agency may be able to convene an investigative conference for the purposes of obtaining evidence, identifying the issues in dispute, ascertaining the positions of the parties, and exploring the possibility of a negotiated settlement. Before such a conference can be held, the parties must receive adequate notice.

d. Initial Determination

After concluding its investigation, the agency reaches an initial decision. If the parties are in agreement with the proposed outcome, a negotiated settlement can often be reached at this stage. However, if the parties disagree with the agency's proposed resolution, they can request that the matter be reviewed through a formal administrative hearing.

In Diane's case the agency's task was to determine whether the evidence it found through its investigation was sufficient to indicate probable cause to believe that discrimination had occurred. If the agency had determined that there was insufficient evidence, then Diane could have asked for a review of that decision. However, in Diane's case, the agency found probable cause to believe her employer had acted unlawfully in firing her. It then sent notice of its decision to Diane and the employer along with a statement alerting them to their rights to choose to appeal the decision either by requesting an administrative hearing or by taking the matter to court. Both Diane and the employer opted to remain within the agency system. Usually at this stage, the agency also makes another attempt to get the parties to reach a mutually agreeable resolution. If that is not possible, then the next stage is the formal hearing.

e. Notice of Hearing

Before a formal hearing can be convened, however, the agency must send notice to all parties of the date, time, and place of the hearing along with a summary of the issues to be determined. For example, Section 554 of the federal Administrative Procedure Act (APA) states that notice should consist of

1. the time, place, and nature of the hearing;
2. the legal authority and jurisdiction under which the hearing is being held; and
3. the matters of fact and law asserted.[9]

---

[8]5 U.S.C. § 552a(d)(1) (2000).
[9]5 U.S.C. § 554(b) (2000).

2. Hearings

Rulemaking hearing
An administrative
agency hearing that
resembles a legislative
hearing in which
interested parties present
evidence and arguments
to an administrative
agency about what the
general law should be.

Adjudicatory hearing
A mechanism through
which parties to a
dispute can present
arguments and evidence
about their case to an
administrative law judge.

As mentioned at the beginning of this section, administrative agencies conduct two types of hearings: adjudicatory and rulemaking. **Rulemaking hearings** resemble legislative hearings in which interested parties present evidence and arguments about proposed agency rules or regulations. An **adjudicatory hearing,** on the other hand, is similar to a trial. It is a mechanism through which parties to a dispute can present arguments and evidence about their case to an administrative decision maker. In this section we will focus on procedure followed in adjudicatory hearings.

In preparing for the hearing, the attorney should carefully examine the policy statements and interpretative rules of the agency. For the federal agencies some of these are published in the **Code of Federal Regulations**. Similarly, most states publish a state code of regulations. However, there may be additional unpublished procedures that the agency follows. Finally, administrative staff manuals and other instructions to field staff may prove to be helpful, as they often provide explicit and detailed information on how factors are measured and evaluated. The presentation at the hearing can then be geared to meeting these criteria.

a. The Participants

A **hearing officer,** known as an **administrative law judge** in federal agencies, controls the proceedings during the hearing in much the same way that a judge does during a trial. However, because administrative hearings are usually less structured than trials, the hearing officer has more flexibility in organizing the hearing and influencing the atmosphere surrounding it. Federal administrative law judges are appointed for a life term (contingent on good behavior) in order to ensure their independence and impartiality.

In addition to conducting the hearing, in federal agencies the administrative law judge has the power to administer oaths, issue subpoenas, take depositions or have depositions taken, and hold settlement conferences.[10] Most states give their hearing officers similar powers.

A court reporter or a hearing assistant may be present to record the proceedings. Tape recorders are used more frequently than the special shorthand machines used by most court reporters.

As is true in most agencies, in Diane's case she had the option of representing herself, being represented by an attorney, or being represented by a nonlawyer advocate. In fact, many agencies have provisions that allow paralegals to provide formal representation in administrative hearings. For example, the section of the federal regulations governing representation of parties at Social Security Administration hearings explicitly allows for persons other than attorneys to provide representation if they are "capable of giving valuable help" in connection with the claim.[11] A representative is authorized to obtain information about the claim, submit evidence, and make statements about facts and law.[12]

---

[10]See 5 U.S.C. § 556(c) (2000).
[11]20 C.F.R. § 404.1705 (2000).
[12]20 C.F.R. § 404.1710(a) (2000).

The parties may also ask witnesses to give testimony at the hearing. These witnesses may be classified as either expert or lay witnesses. Given the technical nature of many regulatory agencies, expert witnesses often play a vital role in administrative hearings. Because most hearing officers hear cases involving only a single agency, they rapidly develop their own expertise in their assigned area.

b. Hearing Procedures

The hearing itself resembles a trial except that it tends to be more informal and, as noted above, the hearing officer takes a more active role than does a judge. The hearing usually begins with the hearing officer reading the case name and number into the record, identifying for the record who is present at the hearing, and briefly explaining the purpose of the hearing to the people involved. Opening statements by attorneys are rare.

Before taking testimony from witnesses, the hearing officer usually decides what documentary evidence is to be admitted. After all the participants have had an opportunity to examine the documents, the hearing officer gives those involved a chance to raise objections. The hearing officer then decides what will be admitted into the official record.

Witness testimony is presented in much the same way as during a trial except that the hearing officer takes a much more active role in the questioning than would a trial judge. The hearing officer may even question the witness before giving the attorneys an opportunity to do so.

The hearing officer is usually not bound to follow the strict rules of evidence that are applicable in court trials. In fact, because of the cost of requiring all witnesses to appear in person, hearing officers frequently admit **hearsay evidence**. That is, they allow the introduction of testimony about what was said outside of the courtroom. For example, one of the parties may offer to introduce medical records rather than requiring the doctor who wrote the records to testify. However, the hearing officer is required to evaluate the worth of the testimony and may discount it because of its tendency to be unreliable. In some agencies there is also no absolute right to cross-examine witnesses. Rather, parties must establish that cross-examination is necessary for a full disclosure of the facts.

Hearsay
Testimony or evidence introduced in court regarding what someone said out of court for the purpose of establishing the truth of what was said.

The standard of proof in administrative hearings is usually the same as in most civil cases, a preponderance of the evidence. However, in some situations where the possible outcome is very serious, such as the loss of citizenship or parental rights, the agency may use a higher standard of proof, often referred to as "clear and convincing." **Clear and convincing** evidence is something more than a preponderance of the evidence but less than the criminal standard of beyond a reasonable doubt.

Clear and convincing
An evidentiary standard that requires more than a preponderance of the evidence but less than beyond a reasonable doubt.

Closing arguments, if used at all, are usually submitted to the hearing officer as written memoranda rather than being given as oral statements at the hearing itself.

For Diane's hearing, one of the attorneys from the law firm of Darrow and Bryan accompanied her. The attorney called Diane as a witness as well as the bartender who had been on duty the day Diane was fired. Finally, he cross-examined the restaurant manager.

c. The Form of the Decision

After all of the evidence has been presented, the hearing officer takes the matter under consideration, reviews the testimony and the documentary evidence, and prepares a written decision. The decision usually begins by listing the date and location of the hearing and who attended. It then identifies the issues, cites the relevant statutes and regulations, and offers summaries of witnesses' testimony.

The three most important sections are (1) the evaluation of the evidence, in which the hearing officer explains the relative weight or credibility given to different testimony and documents; (2) the findings, in which the hearing officer states his or her opinion of the facts; and (3) the decision, in which the hearing officer clearly states the legal effect of the decision (whether, for example, the party will or will not receive disability benefits).

In Diane's case, the hearing officer determined that the employer had engaged in unlawful discrimination. The hearing officer wrote a decision that included findings of fact and conclusions of law. In addition, the hearing officer issued an order to the employer to cease and desist from future discriminatory actions and to take the following affirmative actions: to reinstate Diane Dobbs into her former position and to grant her back pay for the time she has been unable to work.

3. Appeals

Before a single hearing officer's decision becomes the final decision of the agency, most agencies provide the parties a right to appeal within the agency itself. The appeal does not provide the participants with a new hearing. Rather, it is limited to a review of the record of the hearing, and no new evidence can be introduced. Generally, the agency will set aside the decision only if the hearing officer committed an error of law, the decision was not supported by substantial evidence, or the decision was arbitrary, capricious, or an abuse of discretion.

NETNOTE

You can find the federal Administrative Procedure Act at many places on the Internet. We recommend starting with Findlaw's home page *www.findlaw.com.* Click on "US Law: Cases & Codes." Next click on "U.S. Code." In the dialog box under U.S. Code for Title enter 5 and for Section enter 500. Click on the search button.

To review the content of the Code of Federal Regulations, again start with Findlaw's home page *www.findlaw.com.* Click on "US Law: Cases & Codes." Next click on "Code of Federal Regulations." Enter your search information.

To use the Internet to review state administrative materials, again start with Findlaw's home page *www.findlaw.com.* Below the link for "US Law: Cases & Codes," click on "states." Click on the desired state. Select either the state's statutes (codes) or its administrative regulations.

If one of the participants is still dissatisfied with the result, that party may be able to have the matter reviewed in the courts as well. State and federal statutes specify the circumstances under which administrative actions are subject to such judicial review. Generally, as with the appeal to the full agency, judicial review involves only a review of the record developed at the hearing. In exercising this judicial review, courts tend to defer to administrative expertise, especially as to questions of fact or policy, and only invalidate such decisions when they determine that the agency made an error of law, such as misinterpreting a statutory provision.

In Diane's case the employer appealed the hearing officer's decision to the full agency. After the agency affirmed that decision, the employer decided to comply with the hearing officer's order and to waive his right to judicial review within the state court system.

C. ALTERNATIVE DISPUTE RESOLUTION

As mentioned at the beginning of this chapter, increasing numbers of people are expressing dissatisfaction with the time and expense involved in resolving conflicts through the courts. In response to these concerns many commentators have urged greater use of what is commonly referred to as **alternative dispute resolution (ADR)**. While mediation and arbitration are the most commonly used forms of ADR, the term sometimes includes activities such as mini-trials and summary jury trials, which are designed to encourage out-of-court settlements.

In 1998 Congress enacted legislation requiring that each U.S. district court establish and implement a plan to decrease costs and delays in the federal court system. Specifically, the legislation mandated that all district courts establish programs to offer alternative dispute resolution to all litigants. In addition, nearly all of the U.S. courts of appeals have established mediation programs to assist parties in resolving their appeals. Many state and local court systems have also incorporated ADR, especially in the area of family law, where the

Alternative dispute resolution (ADR) Techniques for resolving conflicts that are alternatives to full-scale litigation. The two most common are arbitration and mediation.

NETNOTE

If you are interested in learning more about various forms of ADR, there are several web sites you can visit, including the American Arbitration Association at *www.adr.org,* the Mediation Information and Resource Center at *www.mediate .com,* and the ABA Section on Dispute Resolution at *www.abanet.org/dispute.* A particularly interesting site is that of the Victim Offender Mediation Association (VOMA) at *www.voma.org.* VOMA supports mediation between victims and offenders, so that victims are given an opportunity to have their questions answered and their emotional and other needs met and offenders are held accountable and given an opportunity to make restitution to their victims and the community.

parties are often required to participate in formal mediation regarding issues of child custody and visitation.

The business community has long been a strong supporter of ADR because it is viewed as being a faster and less expensive way of settling disputes that arise in the course of doing business. It is a common practice for businesses to include arbitration clauses in their contracts. Under these clauses the parties are legally bound to refer disputes over the interpretation of a contract to arbitration rather than taking them to court. In addition to saving time and money, ADR often allows a company to settle a dispute without attracting the public attention that may accompany a lawsuit.

1. Arbitration

Arbitration
An ADR mechanism whereby the parties submit their disagreement to a third party whose decision is binding.

When a dispute is sent to **arbitration,** the matter is delegated to a neutral third-party arbitrator. Both parties agree in advance to accept the arbitrator's decision. In many cases the arbitrator's decision is binding, and the dissatisfied party cannot challenge it in court unless the award was obtained by fraud.

An arbitrator functions much as a judge in a court of law, but the arbitrator follows a much simpler set of procedures that do not require as much time or expense. The arbitrator is usually selected from a panel of individuals who have special training in the area. These individuals are often affiliated with the American Arbitration Association or one of the other organizations that are set up specifically to provide arbitration services. In addition to being speedier and less expensive than traditional litigation, the results of arbitration can frequently be kept confidential.

In the field of labor law, arbitration is often used as a way of avoiding strikes. Sports fans are familiar with the role arbitration has played in determining the salaries of baseball players. Also, public employees are often required to use arbitration when state law prohibits them from striking.

> **PRACTICAL TIP**
>
> Sometimes the best way to win is to refuse to play. Often it is more cost effective and easier to get what you want if you stay out of court.

2. Mediation

Mediation
An ADR mechanism whereby a neutral third party assists the parties in reaching a mutually agreeable, voluntary compromise.

Although both arbitration and **mediation** involve the disputants meeting with a neutral third party, they differ greatly with respect to the role this third party plays. Whereas an arbitrator imposes a solution, a mediator attempts to guide the disputants toward a compromise that is voluntarily accepted by both sides.

The basic premise of mediation is that the best solution is the solution that the parties themselves devise. After all, they (not the mediator) best understand their positions, and they (not the mediator) will have to live with the solution they reach.

The mediator's role is therefore like that of a Sherpa guide. The guide's role is not tell the explorers which mountain to climb or even whether to climb a mountain at all. The guide simply helps the climbers find the best way to reach whatever summit they have chosen to climb. In mediation the mediator helps the disputants identify the issues that divide them and explore possible solutions for bridging the divide.[13]

---

[13]See Mori Irvine, Serving Two Masters: The Obligation under the Rules of Professional Conduct to Report Attorney Misconduct in a Confidential Mediation, 26 Rutgers L.J. 155, 158 n.13 (1994).

While the parties often enter mediation in a combative posture, the goal of mediation is to change the position of the parties to one of collaboration whereby they can jointly construct a win-win solution. If the parties reach a resolution, they (not their attorneys and not the mediator) draft a written agreement. The agreement may be a court-enforceable contract. If they do not reach agreement, they can simply walk away from the mediation and seek other approaches to resolving their differences.

a. Cases Most Suitable for Mediation

Generally, some types of cases are better suited for mediation than others. Mediation is particularly appropriate in those situations where the parties will be required to deal with each other in the future, such as after a divorce when children are involved, or when the parties simply wish to have amiable future relations, such as in the case of a dispute between neighbors. It is hoped that the mediation process will not only resolve the current situation but will also improve the participants' interpersonal and conflict management skills as they continue to deal with each other in the future.

In tort cases, mediation works best in situations where liability is clear-cut and the dispute is primarily over the amount of the damages. In this type of situation, both sides can usually see the advantage to settling for an "average" damage award rather than spending a significant amount of money on trial preparation and then gambling on the outcome.

There are, of course, some situations that do not lend themselves to mediation. For example, Rosa Parks, a black woman, was arrested in 1955 for refusing to give up her seat on a city bus to a white person. Civil rights leaders used her situation to bring public attention to racial discrimination in the South and organized the famous Montgomery bus boycott. This type of political mobilization could not have occurred through mediation.[14]

Mediation may also not be appropriate in situations involving domestic violence. Not only may the contact between the abuser and the victim during mediation result in further violence following the mediation session, but the victim may perceive the mediation session itself as another form of abuse. Further, as mediation works best when the parties are of fairly equal bargaining power, it is not as effective in situations of abuse, where the victim perceives herself as powerless against the abuser.

b. Mediation Formats and Styles

In mediation the role of the mediator is to encourage the parties to work together. The mediator helps the parties search for common ground. Once they have found some areas of agreement, then they can work toward creating solutions to resolve their dispute.

At the initial session the mediator meets with the parties and, if the parties are represented, their attorneys as well. The mediator starts by making some

---

[14]Drew Peterson, Getting Together: Conflict Triage—Appropriate and Inappropriate Cases for Mediation, 23 Alaska Bar Rag 9 (1999).

preliminary comments to inform the participants of the mediator's role as a neutral and of how the process will proceed. Next the mediator usually asks each of the parties (or if they are represented by attorneys, the attorneys) to describe the dispute from his or her point of view. The mediator identifies the different issues and sets an agenda for their further discussion.

Following this opening session, most mediators begin a series of caucuses in which the mediator meets separately with each party. As it is imperative that the parties be open with the mediator, the mediator stresses his or her commitment to confidentiality. The mediator assures the parties that he or she will not reveal any information to the other party without the express permission of the party that revealed it. The purpose of these first private meetings is not to convince the parties to accept a solution but rather to gather information.

After the private meetings with each side, the mediator usually begins the process of floating various compromise solutions. "Would you be willing to give up ___ if you were able to get ___." The mediator tries to get the parties to stop reacting emotionally to the situation and instead to focus on compromise.

There are two basic styles of mediation: facilitative and evaluate. The facilitative model is based on a very nondirective approach. The mediator does not give legal advice, provide an opinion as to the relative value of the parties' positions, or make predications as to the possible outcome should the parties fail to settle and the case proceed to litigation. The mediator does not propose any particular solution and does not draft the agreement for the parties. On the other hand, in the evaluative model, the mediator is more likely to voice both legal and personal opinions and to give the parties his or her view of the likely outcome should the case proceed to court. The evaluative mediator may also try to encourage the parties to reach an agreement that the mediator thinks is in the best interests of both parties. Many attorneys are most comfortable with the evaluative approach, as it provides a natural fit with their legal education, which taught them to be "problem solvers."

Those critical of the evaluative approach argue that it strips the parties of self-determination by substituting the mediator's point of view for that of the disputants. There is also the danger that the mediator will no longer be seen as an impartial neutral. Proponents of the evaluative approach argue, however, that the parties need to understand their legal rights and the likely outcome should their case proceed to trial in order to make informed decisions and to avoid the feeling after the session is over that they had unknowingly "given away the farm."[15]

In practice it is likely that no mediator completely follows either approach. Even the decision to encourage a certain line of discussion could be seen as directive and hence evaluative, and even the most evaluative mediator strives to create an environment that will be perceived as neutral and safe to the parties. Therefore, the two styles, instead of being seen as mutually exclusive, perhaps can best be viewed as the two ends of a continuum. Also some situations

---

[15]See Ellen A. Waldman, The Evaluative-Facilitative Debate in Mediation: Applying the Lens of Therapeutic Jurisprudence, 82 Marq. L. Rev. 155 (1998); Jacqueline M. Nolan-Haley, Court Mediation and the Search for Justice through Law, 75 Wash. U. L.Q. 47 (1996).

may be more appropriate for one approach than the other. For example, the evaluative approach may best serve the needs of the parties when the main goal is to reach a monetary settlement and the parties do not expect to have any future interactions with each other, such as in a dispute between an insurance company and someone injured in an automobile accident. On the other hand, the facilitative approach might be more appropriate when solutions other than a money settlement are sought and the disputants will of necessity have future dealings with each other, such as in an employer-employee dispute or in a case involving child custody and support.[16]

A third style of mediation, known as transformative mediation, is an extreme version of the facilitative approach in which mediators are entirely nondirective. Rather than seeing the conflict as something negative, as something that must be "fixed," a transformative mediator sees conflict as positive, as a way to empower the disputants. Conflicts are not problems to be solved but rather opportunities for personal growth. The twin goals of the mediation process are to help the participants gain a greater understanding of themselves and an ability to understand the concerns of the other disputants. Therefore, the mediator's role is to help the participants learn new attitudes and skills that will help them resolve not only the current dispute but also conflicts they face in the future. This places the main emphasis on the process of the mediation rather than on the resolution of the dispute. In fact, whether the case settles is almost irrelevant so long as the parties are positively transformed by the mediation process. The ultimate goal is to heal the negative feelings between the parties and to improve their ability to deal with conflict in the future.

While settlement is not the primary goal of transformative mediation, it is believed that this approach encourages the parties to use creative problem-solving skills to find new solutions that better satisfy each party than the solutions each party had originally hoped to attain. For example, nonmonetary solutions, such as a public apology, may give the parties a better sense of resolution than money alone can accomplish.

c. Mandatory Mediation Programs

While it may at first appear to be a contradiction in terms, many states are now imposing "mandatory mediation" in selected types of disputes. It is mandatory in the sense that both parties are required to engage in a formal mediation process before a court can hear the case. In effect the dispute is diverted into mediation where either it is settled or it returns to the court for a final resolution. However, it is still mediation, rather than arbitration, because after a given time limit the parties can still end the mediation process and continue with the court proceedings.

---

[16]See Scott H. Hughes, Alternative Dispute Resolution: Facilitative Mediation or Evaluative Mediation: May Your Choice Be a Wise One, 59 Ala. Law. 246 (1998).

Ethics Alert

If a paralegal works as a mediator, has that paralegal committed the unauthorized practice of law? If mediation is seen as the practice of law, mediation would be closed to nonlawyers, thereby leading to the loss of effective mediators. Because evaluative mediators are sometimes called upon to give legal advice and to predict the outcome should the case proceed to trial, nonlawyers engaged in evaluative mediation may be committing the unauthorized practice of law. However, at least one writer has argued that mediators engaged in facilitative mediation are not practicing law. The role of the facilitative mediator is to remain neutral and to refrain from giving the mediator's point of view or suggesting any particular outcome to the participants.[17]

d. Mediation Training

People are being trained to be mediators by community groups, educational institutions, and court-annexed programs. In those cases where mediation is formally incorporated into the litigation process, some governmental agency, either the courts or an administrative agency, is responsible for licensing or certifying the individuals who are designated to act as mediators. Although attorneys and retired judges frequently serve as mediators, many state and local courts also allow nonlawyers to serve as mediators. For example, clergy, psychologists, and social workers often serve as mediators in family law cases. All mediators, regardless of their formal education, are usually required to undergo a set number of hours of formal training in mediation skills. This training emphasizes the need to lay aside one's personal views and to assist both sides in finding a "win-win" solution to their problems.

3. Summary Jury Trials

Summary jury trial
A nonbinding process in which attorneys for both sides present synopses of their cases to a jury, which renders an advisory opinion on the basis of these presentations.

Summary jury trials are nonbinding mock trials in which attorneys for both sides present synopses of their cases to a jury, which then renders an advisory opinion on the basis of these presentations. Time is saved because the attorneys give summaries of what key witnesses are expected to say rather than going through complete direct and cross-examinations. It is hoped that the parties will agree to a settlement that approximates the results reached by the mock jury.

4. Evaluation of ADR Techniques

As mentioned above, proponents of ADR have argued that its use will save time and avoid at least some of the expenses associated with going to court. It is also generally thought that the parties will feel better about a solution they worked out through mediation than they will about an unpopular decision imposed on

---

[17]For a fuller discussion of this topic, see Note: Laymen Cannot Lawyer, But Is Mediation the Practice of Law?, 20 Cardozo L. Rev. 1715 (May/July 1999).

them by the courts. This is especially true in child custody cases, where the parents will often continue to have regular contact with each other and consult with each other about the welfare of their children.

Not everyone agrees with this assessment. For example, a study conducted by the Rand Institute for Civil Justice found that ADR was not extensively used when it was voluntary and that when it was used, it did not result in great savings of time or expenses. Furthermore, its use was not found to affect the participants' views of fairness or attorney satisfaction.[18]

Nevertheless, other studies indicate that ADR participants are extremely satisfied with both the process and the result, at least when the ADR method used is mediation and not arbitration. For example, a recent survey conducted by the National Law Journal and the American Arbitration Association found that of those who responded to the survey, a majority of litigators and in-house counsel preferred nonbinding mediation over binding arbitration. Not only did mediation save money and time, but also the respondents felt it provided a more satisfactory process, as it was most likely to preserve the relationship between the disputing parties. The attorneys' complaints about arbitration included distrust of the arbiters themselves, the costs (which can approach those of litigation), and the inability to appeal an arbiter's decision. The president of the American Arbitration Association was quoted as saying: "Mediation is to the millennium what arbitration was to the 1990s . . . But while mediation is growing by leaps and bounds, there's no abatement in arbitrations. The process is about party choice."[19]

DISCUSSION QUESTIONS

13. If two disputants want to settle their differences other than by going to court, what options do they have?

14. If you were involved in a dispute, which alternative dispute resolution method would you prefer?

15. Do you think either mediation or arbitration would be appropriate in Mr. Drake's case? Why?

SUMMARY

Litigation is a complex, time-consuming, and expensive way of settling disputes. The three main stages of litigation are pretrial, trial, and post-trial. In the pretrial stage the parties use pleadings, discovery, and pretrial conferences to identify the facts and the legal issues involved in the dispute. The majority of cases are settled "out of court" during this stage. At the trial stage the parties present their evidence to either a judge or a jury. The rules of evidence dictate the form in which the evidence must be presented and what types of questions witnesses can be required to answer. Following the trial verdict, the losing party may challenge the trial court's decision in an appellate court.

[18]Van Duch, Case Management Reform Ineffective, Natl. L.J., Feb. 3, 1997, at A3.
[19]Lisa Brennan, What Lawyers Like: Mediation, Natl. L.J., Nov. 15, 1999, at A1.

In some circumstances it may be necessary to exhaust administrative remedies prior to filing a lawsuit. Adjudicatory hearings in administrative agencies follow the general outline of a civil trial, but they are less formal and do not involve as many due process protections. A hearing officer presides over the hearing, acting much as a judge would. Although it is relatively easy to get evidence admitted into the record, the hearing officer has a great deal of discretion over the weight given to that evidence. Once all avenues of appeal within an agency have been exhausted, a party can often seek review within the judicial system.

Increasingly the courts are turning to forms of alternative dispute resolution (ADR) in the hope of increasing "customer" satisfaction, decreasing court costs, and increasing the speed with which disputes can be resolved. The most common types of ADR are arbitration, mediation, and summary jury trials.

REVIEW QUESTIONS

Pages 71 through 79

1. What are the three basic stages of civil litigation?
2. What rules govern civil litigation in federal courts?
3. What issues have to be considered in deciding who should be sued?
4. How does a class action lawsuit differ from one brought by and on behalf of one individual?
5. If someone says that a particular court does not have jurisdiction over a lawsuit, what is meant by that?
6. What is the difference between subject matter jurisdiction and personal jurisdiction?
7. What is the purpose of requiring litigants to first exhaust their administrative remedies?

Pages 80 through 87

8. What is the purpose of each of the following pleadings:
   a. the complaint,
   b. the answer,
   c. a counterclaim,
   d. a cross-claim, and
   e. a third-party claim?
9. Under the federal rules what three items must be included in a complaint?
10. What is a caption?
11. Who must sign all pleadings? Why?
12. What is the purpose of a summons?
13. What is the danger to the defendant in failing to answer a complaint?
14. What are the five basic ways that a defendant can respond to a complaint, and what is the purpose of each?

Pages 87 through 90

15. What are the grounds for a 12(b)(6) motion, and what is its purpose?
16. What is the difference between a 12(b)(6) motion and a summary judgment motion?

Pages 90 through 93

17. What is the main goal of discovery?
18. What are interrogatories and depositions, and how do they differ?
19. Besides interrogatories and depositions, what are the main discovery tools available to the parties?
20. What is the purpose of a pretrial conference?

Pages 93 through 100

21. What is the function of the jury?
22. What is a voir dire, and what is its purpose?
23. What are the differences between challenges for cause and peremptory challenges, and what is the function of each?
24. What do attorneys hope to accomplish in their opening statements?
25. Who presents evidence first, the plaintiff or the defendant, and why?
26. When can either side move for a directed verdict? What is the purpose of that motion?
27. What is the difference between a verdict and a judgment?
28. What is the difference between the motion for a judgment notwithstanding the verdict (a judgment N.O.V.) and a motion for a new trial? Give an example of when each could be used.

Pages 100 through 104

29. Describe the limitations on a litigant's right to appeal.
30. What is the difference between a harmless error and a reversible error?

Pages 104 through 111

31. Why must some disputes be taken to an administrative agency before going to court?
32. What is the difference between an adjudicatory hearing and a rulemaking hearing?
33. How does an administrative hearing differ from a civil trial?
34. What is contained in a typical administrative agency decision?

Pages 111 through 117

35. What are the most common forms of ADR, and how do they differ from each other?
36. What do the proponents of ADR see as the advantages of ADR over traditional litigation?
37. Describe the different styles of mediation and the types of situations for which each style might be most appropriate.

PART 2

Finding and Analyzing the Law

Chapter 6

Finding and Interpreting Statutory Law

A word is not a crystal, transparent and unchanged, it is the skin of a living thought and may vary greatly in color and content according to the circumstances and the time in which it is used.
Justice Oliver Wendell Holmes

INTRODUCTION

In Chapter 1 we gave a brief overview of the process involved in legal reasoning. You begin with an analysis of the client's facts and the identification of the legal rules applicable to that set of facts. You then apply those rules to the facts in order to predict the likely outcome, analyzing both the weaknesses and the strengths of the client's case. In this and the next chapter we look at how to find the law and the methods you can use to interpret the law.

Recall that the two main sources of law are

1. court-made law (common law) and
2. enacted law.

Enacted law can be further subdivided into constitutional, statutory, and administrative law. In this chapter we will explore the methods you use to analyze enacted law. While the emphasis will be on analyzing statutes, you can apply the same principles to constitutional provisions and agency regulations.

Although all four areas of the law—common, constitutional, statutory, and administrative law—must be considered in any legal situation, most attorneys begin their legal analysis of a specific legal problem with a review of statutes. They initially focus on statutes because statutes supersede the common law. In addition, reading an annotated statute will alert the attorney to administrative agencies and regulations that may also be relevant. (In annotated statutes, in addition to finding the text of the statute, you will find summaries of court decisions that have interpreted the statute, citations to administrative regulations, and cross-references to secondary sources that will help explain or summarize the law.) Thus if a client has been arrested for murder, an attorney will start by locating and then analyzing the state statutes on homicide. If a client is seeking a divorce, alimony, and child support, the attorney will locate and then analyze the state's domestic relations statutes.

A. LOCATING THE APPROPRIATE STATUTE

Before you can interpret a statute, you have to have a copy of what it is you are being asked to interpret. In this section we will discuss the ways in which you can locate a statute if you have its "popular name" or its official **citation.** A statutory citation is a formalized method for referring to a statute's chapter (or title) and section numbers. In Appendix C you can read more about citation form, and in Appendix D we will discuss other methods for locating relevant statutes.

State and federal statutes are usually published in three primary forms:

1. individual slip laws,
2. periodic compilations of new laws passed within a certain time period, and
3. unified codes.

When laws are first officially enacted, they are usually published individually as **slip laws.** At the end of a legislative term the federal and most state governments publish the laws passed during that term as one or more volumes in a continuing set. They are usually arranged in chronological order by date of passage and are referred to as either **statutes at large** or **session laws.**

The above publications are arranged chronologically by date of passage and contain only those laws passed during a particular time period. **Codes,** on the other hand, arrange the laws by subject matter and contain all public laws currently in force in a particular area. The United States Code is the official codification of federal statutes and is printed and distributed by the U.S. Government Printing Office. The United States Code Annotated and the United States Code Service are published by West and Lexis Law Publishing, respectively. In addition to the text of the laws themselves, these two **annotated** versions of the code have information about the legislative history and references to court decisions that have interpreted the statutes. Some state

Citation
A statutory citation is a formalized method for referring to a statute's chapter (or title) and section numbers.

Slip laws
A form in which statutes are published; they are printed individually at the time they are first enacted.

Statutes at large or session laws
The chronological publication of statutes at the end of a legislative session.

Code
A compilation of federal or state statutes in which the statutes are organized by subject matter rather than by year of enactment.

Annotated statutes
A privately published statutory code that includes editorial features, such as summaries of court opinions that have interpreted the statutes.

statutes are also published by West and other private publishers in annotated form. Figure 6-1 lists the most common publications and abbreviations for federal statutes and gives a few examples for state statutes. These abbreviations, as well as those for any statutory compilation, can be found in citation manuals such as The Bluebook: A Uniform System of Citation and the ALWD Citation Manual. Citation manuals are discussed in Appendix C.

A reference to a specific statute should include enough information so that others can easily locate and check the source. This is known as giving the statute's **citation**. If you would like to read more about citation form, take a look at Appendix C. For now, you need to know that a complete statutory citation includes the name of the book in which the statute is found, the statute's chapter number (sometimes referred to as its title number), and its section number. Sometimes the citation will also include the name of the statute. For example, you might see

> Administrative Procedure Act, 5 U.S.C. § 552(b)(3) (2000)
> Cannabis Control Act, Ill. Rev. Stat. ch. 56[42], § 701 (2000)

PRACTICAL TIP

In the annotated version of statutes you can locate not only the relevant statute but also the cases that have interpreted the statute.

Figure 6-1   Common Publications Containing the Texts of Federal and State Statues

Publication	Abbreviation	Coverage
United States Code	U.S.C.	Official codification of federal statutes arranged by subject matter.
United States Code Annotated	U.S.C.A.	West's unofficial codification of federal statutes arranged by subject matter with annotations.
United States Code Service	U.S.C.S.	Lexis Law Publishing's unofficial codification of federal statutes arranged by subject matter with annotations.
Alabama Code	Ala. Code	Official codification of Alabama statutes arranged by subject matter.
West's Annotated California Code, Business and Professions	Cal. Bus. & Prof. Code	West's unofficial codification of California statutes relating to business and the professions with annotations.
General Laws of the Commonwealth of Massachusetts	Mass. Gen. L.	Official codification of Massachusetts statutes arranged by subject matter.
Massachusetts General Laws Annotated	Mass. Gen. Laws Ann.	West's unofficial codification of Massachusetts statutes arranged by subject matter with annotations.

NETNOTE

At the Cornell Law School site you can find an "Introduction to Basic Legal Citation," an on-line tutorial designed to teach the Bluebook rules. Go to *www.law.cornell.edu/citation.*

The first citation is to a federal statute. You can tell it is a federal statute because of the abbreviation U.S.C., which stands for United States Code. The number 5 preceding the U.S.C. designation indicates that the statute is part of Title 5; 552(*b*)(*3*) is the section number (the symbol § stands for section). The second citation is to an Illinois state statute (*ch.* stands for chapter). In each the date in parentheses refers to the date the book in which the statute is published was last updated. It does not refer to the date when the statute was enacted.

As you can see, the citation gives you the information you need to locate a specific statute. If you have only the name of a statute (e.g., the Freedom of Information Act), you can use the table of names index found in most state and federal codes to find the citation.

B. THE FORMAT OF STATUTES

Statutes can be quite lengthy, containing many subsections and cross-references to other statutes. For example, the Illinois Criminal Code is more than 200 pages long. There are separate sections defining key terms, spelling out the jurisdiction of the state criminal courts, listing requirements for different mental states, determining who can be considered parties to a crime, and listing affirmative defenses. All these are separated from the section that actually lists specific crimes, and to find the punishments that go with the crimes, you have to turn to a separate one-hundred-page Code of Corrections. To find sections of the law relevant to juvenile offenses and domestic violence, you must consult other Illinois statutes.

Statutes are usually subdivided into subsections, sometimes called **articles**. Note in Exhibit 6-1 how the Illinois Domestic Violence Act of 1986 is organized into four articles: General Provisions, Orders of Protection, Law Enforcement Responsibilities, and Health Care Services. Notice also how the General Provisions article is subdivided into Short title, Purposes—Rules of construction, and Definitions. This last subsection contains definitions of key words used in the statute.

Therefore, the first step in reading and understanding a statute is to pay attention to its overall organizational layout. Here

Chapter 750 deals with families
Act 60 is the Illinois Domestic Violence Act
Article I contains General Provisions of that act
§ 103 gives definitions
(1) defines the word *abuse*

CHAPTER 750

FAMILIES

Act
60. Illinois Domestic Violence Act of 1986.
70. Parental Notice of Abortion Act of 1995.

ACT 60. ILLINOIS DOMESTIC VIOLENCE ACT OF 1986

Article
I   General Provisions.
II   Orders of Protection.
III   Law Enforcement Responsibilities.
IV.   [Health Care Services].

ARTICLE I—GENERAL PROVISIONS

Section
60/101.   Short title.
60/102.   Purposes—Rules of construction.
60/103.   Definitions.

60/101.   Short title

§ 101. Short Title. This Act shall be known and may be cited as the "Illinois Domestic Violence Act of 1986".
P.A. 84-1305, Art. I, § 101, eff. Aug. 21, 1986.
Formerly Ill.Rev.Stat.1991, ch. 40, ¶ 2311-1.

Title of Act:

An Act concerning domestic violence, amending and repealing certain Acts and parts of Acts herein named. P.A. 84-1305, approved and eff. Aug. 21, 1986.

60/102.   Purposes—Rules of construction

§ 102. Purposes; rules of construction. This Act shall be liberally construed and applied to promote its underlying purposes, which are to:

(1) Recognize domestic violence as a serious crime against the individual and society which produces family disharmony in thousands of Illinois families, promotes a pattern of escalating violence which frequently culminates in intra-family homicide, and creates an emotional atmosphere that is not conducive to healthy childhood development;

(2) Recognize domestic violence against high risk adults with disabilities, who are particularly vulnerable due to impairments in ability to seek or obtain protection, as a serious problem which takes on many forms, including physical abuse, sexual abuse, neglect, and exploitation, and facilitate accessibility of remedies under the Act in order to provide immediate and effective assistance and protection.

(3) Recognize that the legal system has ineffectively dealt with family violence in the past, allowing abusers to escape effective prosecution or financial liability, and has not adequately acknowledged the criminal nature of domestic violence; that, although many laws have changed, in practice there is still widespread failure to appropriately protect and assist victims;

(4) Support the efforts of victims of domestic violence to avoid further abuse by promptly entering and diligently enforcing court orders which prohibit abuse and, when necessary, reduce the abuser's access to the victim and address any related issues of child custody and economic support, so that victims are not trapped in abusive situations by fear of retaliation, loss of a child, financial dependence, or loss of accessible housing or services;

(5) Clarify the responsibilities and support the efforts of law enforcement officers to provide immediate, effective assistance and protection for victims of domestic violence, recognizing that law enforcement officers often become the secondary victims of domestic violence, as evidenced by the high rates of police injuries and deaths that occur in response to domestic violence calls; and

(6) Expand the civil and criminal remedies for victims of domestic violence; including, when necessary, the remedies which effect physical separation of the parties to prevent further abuse.
P.A. 84-1305, Art. I, § 102, eff. Aug. 21, 1986. Amended by P.A. 86-542, § 1, eff. Jan. 1, 1990; P.A. 87-1186, § 3, eff. Jan. 1, 1993.
Formerly Ill.Rev.Stat.1991, ch. 40, ¶ 2311-2.

60/103.   Definitions

§ 103. Definitions. For the purposes of this Act, the following terms shall have the following meanings:

(1) "Abuse" means physical abuse, harassment, intimidation of a dependent, interference with personal liberty or willful deprivation but does not include reasonable direction of a minor child by a parent or person in loco parentis.

(2) "Adult with disabilities" means an elder adult with disabilities or a high-risk adult with disabilities. A person may be an adult with disabilities for purposes of this Act even though he or she has never been adjudicated an incompetent adult. However, no court proceeding may be initiated or continued on behalf of an adult with disabilities over that adult's objection, unless such proceeding is approved by his or her legal guardian, if any.

(3) "Domestic violence" means abuse as defined in paragraph (1).

(4) "Elder adult with disabilities" means an adult prevented by advanced age from taking appropriate action to protect himself or herself from abuse by a family or household member.

(5) "Exploitation" means the illegal, including tortious, use of a high-risk adult with disabilities or of the assets or resources of a high-risk adult with disabilities. Exploitation includes, but is not limited to, the misappropriation of assets or resources of a high-risk adult with disabilities by undue influence, by breach of a fiduciary relationship, by fraud, deception, or extortion, or the use of such assets or resources in a manner contrary to law.

(6) "Family or household members" include spouses, former spouses, parents, children, stepchildren and other persons related by blood or by present or prior marriage, persons who share or formerly shared a common dwelling, persons who have or allegedly have a child in common,

718

Exhibit 6-1   Illinois Domestic Violence Act

When reading specific sections, pay close attention to the use of punctuation and indentation. Both give you further clues as to the statute's organizational scheme. Finally, be sure to notice the use of "or" and "and." For example, in the definition of *abuse* notice the use of the word "or." This means that any of those items listed could by itself constitute abuse.

In an annotated set the statutes will be followed by editorial information, including summaries of the court opinions that have interpreted the statute. To see an example of an annotated statute, look at Exhibit D-7 in Appendix D.

C. AMBIGUITY IN STATUTES

Before we begin our discussion of how to analyze a statutory problem, we need to remember that when a legislative body formulates a statute, it is setting down general rules that will be applied to a variety of future situations. Trying to lay down rules today for situations that will arise in the future is a difficult task, as illustrated by the following classic example.

Assume a town council passed the following ordinance:

> It shall be unlawful to operate any vehicle on town park paths. Violators will be subject to a $100 fine for the first offense and up to a $500 fine for each additional offense.

The council passed the ordinance in response to citizen complaints about a group of teenagers who had been riding their motorcycles on the paths of the town's parks. Not only are motorcycles noisy, but also the citizens were afraid that one day an accident would occur and a child walking down one of the paths would be injured.

Following the passage of this ordinance the following four events took place in a town park:

1. For a "lark," two teenagers drove a Jeep Cherokee down one of the park paths.
2. Once a week the garbage collector backs his truck approximately six feet down one of the park paths to pick up garbage from one of the trash receptacles.
3. A child pushed her doll's baby carriage along a park path.
4. An ambulance drove down one of the park paths to pick up a man who had collapsed in the middle of the park.

Based on a literal reading of the town's new ordinance, all four of these situations are violations of the law. All four involve a "vehicle" being on a park path. However, while the town council undoubtedly wished to ban joyriding Jeep Cherokee drivers as much as it wanted to ban joyriding motorcycle riders, it is highly unlikely that it actually wished to prohibit situations 2, 3, and 4. The problem is that the town council members chose language that was more inclusive than they really intended, and now all four parties are technically guilty of violating the ordinance.

This example illustrates how slippery language can be and how difficult it is to draft a law that encompasses only what you are trying to prohibit. It also illustrates how ambiguities in a statute may not appear until you apply it to individual factual situations. Therefore, even though on its face statutory interpretation may seem straightforward, always remember that even the most seemingly clear language can appear ambiguous when applied to a new factual situation.

STEPS TO STATUTORY INTERPRETATION

1. Get the facts.
2. Locate a relevant statute.
3. Analyze the statute.
   ■ Determine if it applies to the client's facts.
   ■ Divide the statute into its elements.
   ■ Determine the issues raised by the statute's language or the client's facts, and develop arguments for each side.
4. Conclude.

Sometimes statutory ambiguities result from sloppy draftsmanship. More often, however, ambiguities arise when the statute is applied to unanticipated circumstances. There are also times when the drafters purposely write the ambiguity into the statute in order to provide a basis for compromise by glossing over conflicts among the legislators.

D. THE FOUR BASIC STEPS TO STATUTORY INTERPRETATION

There are four steps involved in finding and applying a statute to a client's situation. First, attorneys must obtain the facts from the client or other sources. Second, they must determine whether any statute governs the situation and locate that statute. Third, they must analyze the statute by first reading it carefully to make sure that it does apply to the client's case. Then they must determine its requirements. This is known as dividing the statute into its elements. If there is any ambiguity as to whether the client's facts satisfy any of the

Case 6: The Clearance Sale

Last week Mary, a cellist with the local symphony orchestra, was doing some shopping at Ajax's Country Hardware Store. Mary had gone to Ajax's specifically in response to an ad announcing a clearance sale. When she got to the store, most of the clearance items were gone, but she did spot one last 50-foot tape measure. Just as she was about to pick it up, another customer grabbed it. Outraged, Mary picked up a hammer that had been lying on the counter and told the other customer to hand over the tape measure. The other customer quickly did so, and Mary put the hammer back on the counter. At home the next day Mary answered the door to find herself confronted by a police officer who had a warrant for her arrest. Based on the incident in the store, Mary had been charged with the crime of carrying a dangerous weapon. That statute reads:

It is unlawful for anyone, other than a police officer, ~~to carry~~ a <u>dangerous weapon</u>.

elements, those ambiguities must be resolved. This will involve legal analysis—that is, applying the statutory elements to the client's facts to develop arguments on each side of each issue. Finally, attorneys decide which arguments are most persuasive, thereby determining the most likely outcome for the client. In this section we will look at each of these four steps in more detail.

1. Get the Facts

The first step is to get as many of the relevant facts as possible. Often this is accomplished through a combination of interviewing the client, talking to witnesses, and obtaining information through other sources, such as police or doctor reports. Assume Mary Smith met with attorney Pat Harper and related the events described in Case 6: The Clearance Sale, located on page 129.

2. Locate a Relevant Statute

The next step is to locate statutes that appear to be applicable to the client's facts. Sometimes the initial research will already be done for you. For example, as in Mary's case, when representing a criminal defendant, you will frequently know the statute that the client has been charged with violating. However, there will be other times when you have to go out and find relevant statutes on your own. We will discuss some of the methods you can use to locate such statutes in Appendix D.

After finding an arguably relevant statute, you must take a close look at its language and purpose to make sure it does apply to your client's facts. For example, assume your client has a problem with his apartment lease, a type of contract. There is a statute, the Uniform Commercial Code, that sets out uniform rules governing business relationships. Article Two deals specifically with contracts. You might wonder if Article Two applies to your client's problem with his lease. While Article Two does deal with contracts, it applies only to those contracts that involve "transactions in goods." Therefore, the statute would apply to your client's lease only if an apartment lease qualifies as a "transaction in goods." To find the answer to that question, you would consult the section in Article Two that defines the most important terms used within the statute. That section defines "goods" as "all things . . . which are moveable." Because an apartment is not moveable, you would conclude that Article Two does not apply to your client's case.

In addition to analyzing whether the statute's language was intended to cover your client's situation, be sure to check the statute's effective date. Usually, the events of your client's case must have occurred after the statute's effective date for the statute to govern the outcome of your client's case. Occasionally, the legislature will give a statute a retroactive effect, but that is very rare. You must also check to be sure the statute has not been superseded by a more recent statute.

3. Analyze the Statute

Once you have located a statute that appears to be relevant, you must decide how it will affect your client's case. This involves a two-step process. First, you must

NETNOTE

To find an on-line copy of the United States Code, the Code of Federal Regulations, and state statutes, start at *www.findlaw.com*. Then click on the link to "US Law: Cases & Codes."

break the statute down into separable parts, known as elements, each of which must be satisfied for the statute to apply. Then you must apply those elements to your client's facts.

a. Divide the Statute into Its Elements

The first step in statutory interpretation is to break the relevant statute down into its elements. A **statutory element** can be defined as a separable part of the statute that must be satisfied for the statute to apply. Another way of stating this is to say that an element is a precondition to the application of the statute. In Mary's case the statute contains three elements. For Mary to be found guilty,

1. she must not be a police officer and
2. she must have "carried"
3. a "dangerous weapon."

Statutory element
A separable part of a statute that must be satisfied for the statute to apply.

b. Determine the Issues and Develop Arguments for Each Side

Next you must apply the statutory elements to your client's facts. Sometimes this will be a straightforward process. For example, because the facts state that Mary is not a police officer, the first element of the crime is satisfied. However, sometimes ambiguities will be created either by the statutory language or by the client's facts. For example, it is not clear that Mary "carried" a "dangerous weapon." While she did pick up the hammer, most people think of carrying something as more than just picking it up and then setting it back down in the same place. Similarly, while a hammer could be used to harm someone, most people think of a hammer as a common household tool rather than as a weapon. Therefore, the facts in Mary's case, when combined with the statutory language of two of the elements, create issues. An **issue** arises whenever an element applied to the specific facts fails to give you a clear-cut answer.

When trying to determine whether an element will create an issue, first ask yourself whether you detect any ambiguity in the statute's words. Sometimes the words will seem to have only one possible meaning. However, as we just demonstrated in Mary's case, when you try to apply statutory language to a specific factual situation, often you will find that the language is ambiguous and that it can be interpreted in more than one way.

Issue
When the law is applied to the client's facts and the result is not obvious, an issue is created.

Ask yourself which of the possible interpretations makes the most sense. That is, which interpretation do you think would best further the purposes for which the statute was enacted? As we will see in a moment, courts have devised several methods to assist them when they are asked to interpret statutory language. These methods can assist you as well. However, before resorting to any of those methods, focus on the statutory language, and use your common sense to try to ferret out a sensible legislative purpose.

(1) Think creatively

One of the most powerful legal reasoning skills that you can acquire is the ability to think creatively about a problem. The best way to develop that skill is to try to work with a statute on its own terms before turning to other sources, such as court opinions and legislative history, for guidance. Take the time to develop arguments that you think would best convince a court that the language should or should not be applied to your client's case. Ask yourself, What was the legislature trying to accomplish with the statute, and will that purpose be better fulfilled by saying that an element is or is not satisfied given the client's particular set of facts?

To help you brainstorm the statute, develop a chart. List the elements, and then under each element list the facts that you would use to make arguments both for and against satisfying the element. Figure 6-2 is a sample chart that you might develop for Mary's case.

At this stage do not worry about finding the "right" answer. Let yourself feel free to explore all the possible arguments on both sides of each issue. This process of looking at the language of the statute and at the facts of your client's case is an ongoing one. Each time you look at the statute, you may see new ambiguities, and each time you look at your client's facts, you may see new arguments about whether or not the statute's language applies to your client's facts.

Figure 6-2   Sample Chart of Statutory Elements

Element 1—"to carry"
  Element satisfied—moved hammer from counter.

  Element not satisfied—did not move it from the building; legislature used specific term of "carry" rather than a broader term, such as "possess."

Element 2—"dangerous weapon"
  Element satisfied—a hammer is a heavy, hard object capable of causing physical harm; purpose of legislation is to protect people from physical harm.

  Element not satisfied—hammers are normally viewed as tools, not weapons.

Legal Reasoning Exercise

1. Before the enactment of the following statute, under the common law a married woman was not allowed to sue in her own name. Instead the lawsuit was brought in her husband's name. Assume you have a client who wishes to sue her spouse for negligence. Read the statute. Do you think she will be able to sue her husband? Why?

Mass. Gen. L. ch. 209, § 6
> A married woman may sue and be sued in the same manner as if she were sole; but this section shall not authorize suits between husband and wife.

(2) Understand the methods used for interpreting statutes

Up to this point, our efforts to analyze statutes have involved variations of what is commonly referred to as the "literal" or "plain meaning" approach. It involves giving the words of the statute their ordinary dictionary definition. Although this is generally considered to be the preferred approach to statutory interpretation, there are many situations in which the "plain meaning" is not very plain. When that occurs, judges and lawyers must rely on alternative methods of statutory construction, such as canons of construction, reference to other parts of the statute, and consideration of evidence external to the statute. These methods may be used separately or in combination. The judges' own views as to the role of the courts relative to the legislature will also have an impact on how they interpret a statute. No matter which method or combination of methods is used, the court's goal is to ascertain the **legislature's intent** when it enacted the statute. As Charles Evans Hughes, former Chief Justice of the U.S. Supreme Court, once put it:

Legislative intent
The purpose of the legislature at the time it enacted the statute.

> In the interpretation of statutes, the function of the courts is easily stated. It is to construe the language so as to give effect to the intent of Congress.[1]

The court's objective is to interpret the statute in such a way as to frustrate whatever evil the legislature wanted to prevent or to further whatever positive goals the legislature wanted to achieve.

(a) Plain meaning Courts usually begin the process of statutory interpretation by using the **plain meaning** approach because it is generally thought to be the most objective approach. In fact, courts will frequently say that if the language's meaning is clear, then there is no need for the court to search further for the legislature's intent. Based on a literal reading of the statute's language, this plain meaning approach assumes that

Plain meaning
A method for interpreting statutes in which the ordinary meaning of the statute's language is examined.

1. the words used reflect the true intentions of the legislature (i.e., they meant what they said); and
2. the legislature intended that the words used would be interpreted in light of their common, ordinary meanings.

---

[1]United States v. American Trucking Assn., 310 U.S. 534, 542 (1940).

One place to search for the plain meaning of statutory language is in definitions contained within the statute itself. Many statutes begin with a list of key terms to clarify the meaning of the most important terms used in the statute. However, many times either the legislative body did not choose to define the word in question or the definition is itself ambiguous.

Another problem arises when there is more than one commonly accepted, ordinary meaning for a term. Return for a moment to the problem we discussed earlier with regard to the interpretation of "carrying" when Mary lifted the hammer from the counter. The American Heritage Dictionary lists thirty-two different meanings for the word *carry*. One definition involves conveying something from one place to another, while another definition speaks in terms of simply holding something. Mary's criminal liability will thus depend on which of these two competing definitions the court decides is the common, ordinary meaning. Or consider a federal statute that provided for a stiffer penalty if, "during and in relation to . . . [a] drug trafficking crime," the defendant "uses . . . a firearm."[2] What constitutes "use of a firearm"? Should it be interpreted as actually discharging the firearm, or should it include merely showing the gun and threatening to shoot it? What if someone traded an unloaded firearm in exchange for drugs?

The plain meaning approach fails to resolve statutory ambiguity when its use causes portions of the statute to stand in apparent contradiction to each other. For example, assume the phrase "every wife and mother" is used in a statute. Should you interpret this phrase as applying to everyone who is either a wife or a mother or just to those who are both a wife and a mother?

Occasionally a court will openly reject the plain meaning approach and ignore the literal meaning of the words in a statute. This occurs when the court is convinced that such a reading does not properly reflect the "true intent" of the legislature. For example, a court might decide to reject a literal interpretation of the town ordinance prohibiting vehicles on park paths if it were being applied to the little girl pushing her doll carriage or to the ambulance picking up the injured man.

Canons of construction
General principles that guide the courts in their interpretation of statutes.

Ejusdem generis
A canon of construction meaning "of the same class."

(b) Canons of construction In situations in which the plain meaning approach fails to resolve statutory ambiguities, judges often turn to what are known as the **canons of construction**. For example, when a series of specific items is followed by a catchall phrase, such as "and others," the courts may assume that the legislature intended to limit the statute to matters that are like the ones specifically listed. This is known as the principle of **ejusdem generis** (of the same class). Assume a statute prohibited the outdoor sale of perishables, such as food, drink, beverages, and the like. Does it apply to flowers? You could argue that the legislature did not intend for the statute to cover the sale of flowers, as all items on the list are edible and flowers are not.

A major problem in relying on a canon of construction is that most canons can be negated by yet other canons. For example, when looking at a list, another rule of statutory construction states that the members of that list are only examples and are not meant to be exclusive. Because all the items on the list are examples of perishable items and because flowers are perishable, you could argue that they were not meant to be excluded.

---

[2]See, for example, 18 U.S.C.S. § 924(c)(1) (2004).

In the 1917 case of *Caminetti v. United States*,[3] two U.S. Supreme Court justices illustrated how the use of the same canon, in this instance ejusdem generis, could lead them to reach entirely different conclusions. In that case Caminetti was convicted of violating the Mann Act after he transported a woman from Sacramento, California, to Reno, Nevada, where she was to become his mistress. At the time of the *Caminetti* decision, the Mann Act stated that

> any person who shall knowingly transport . . . in interstate or foreign commerce . . . any woman or girl for the purpose of prostitution or debauchery, or for any other immoral purpose . . . shall be punished by a fine not exceeding five thousand dollars, or by imprisonment of not more than five years, or by both. . . .

Relying on the doctrine of ejusdem generis, Justice Day quoted an earlier Supreme Court opinion in which the Court had stated:

> "Now the addition in the last statute of the words, 'or for any other immoral purpose,' after the word 'prostitution,' must have been made for some practical object. . . . [I]n accordance with the familiar rule of ejusdem generis, the immoral purpose referred to by the words 'any other immoral purpose' must be one of the same general class or kind as the particular purpose of 'prostitution' specified in the same clause of the statute. . . . [T]he immoral purpose charged in the indictment is of the same general class or kind as the one that controls in the importation of an alien woman for the purpose strictly of prostitution. The prostitute may, in the popular sense, be more degraded in character than the concubine, but the latter nonetheless must be held to lead an immoral life, if any regard whatever be had to the views that are almost universally held in this country as to the relations which may rightfully, from the standpoint of morality, exist between man and woman in the matter of sexual intercourse. . . ."[4]

Therefore, Justice Day, along with the majority of the Court, concluded that Caminetti had violated the statute. The dissenters disagreed.

> Our present concern is with the words "any other immoral practice," . . . . "Immoral" is a very comprehensive word. It means a dereliction of morals. In such sense it covers every form of vice, every form of conduct that is contrary to good order. It will hardly be contended that in this sweeping sense it is used in the statute. . . .
>
> [I]t is vice as a business at which the law is directed, using interstate commerce as a facility to procure or distribute its victims. . . .[5]

Therefore, the dissenters concluded that because Caminetti's case did not involve commercial prostitution, the statute did not apply, and he should not be convicted under it.

Two general rules of statutory construction are particularly important. First, normally courts **strictly construe** criminal statutes and **statutes in derogation of the common law**—that is, those that change the common law. When courts strictly construe a statute, they narrow the scope of its coverage. For example, a court interpreting the phrase "dangerous weapon" in the statute dealing with "carrying a dangerous weapon" would say that it does not include

Strict construction
An approach whereby the courts give a statute a narrow interpretation.

Statute in derogation of the common law
A statute that changes the common law.

---

[3]242 U.S. 470 (1917).

[4]Id. at 487 (quoting United States v. Bitty, 208 U.S. 393, 401-402 (1908)).

[5]Id. at 496-497, 498.

Remedial statute
A statute enacted to correct a defect in prior law or to provide a remedy where none existed.

Liberal construction
An approach whereby the courts give a statute a broad interpretation.

hammers. Courts strictly construe criminal statutes because of the severe penalties that defendants face. It is thought to be unfair to make someone suffer criminal sanctions if the legislature did not clearly intend to include that particular behavior within the statute. Similarly, courts strictly construe statutes in derogation of the common law because they assume the legislature meant to change the common law no more than was necessary to achieve its purpose.

On the other hand, courts normally give **remedial statutes** a **liberal construction.** When the courts give a statute a liberal construction, they broaden the scope of its coverage. The courts presume that when the legislature is trying to remedy a situation, it does not want its intent thwarted by too narrow an interpretation. An example of a remedial statute is Title VII, the federal statute outlawing discrimination in employment. As we saw earlier, the court liberally construed the term *sex discrimination* to include sexual harassment.

However, even these two basic rules of construction can conflict. For example, what should a court do when interpreting a statute such as one creating a workers' compensation system? Under the common law if a worker was hurt on the job, the worker's only recourse was to sue the employer under tort law. State legislatures created workers' compensation laws so that employers would automatically be required to compensate injured employees. Therefore, it is a statute that both serves a remedial purpose and is in derogation of the common law.

Legal Reasoning Exercises

2. Assume John shipped obscene phonograph records from Massachusetts to California. He has been charged with violating a federal criminal statute that prohibits interstate shipment of any obscene "book, pamphlet, picture, motion-picture film, paper, letter, writing, print or other matter of indecent character." Has he violated the statute?

3. Assume Gary knowingly transported a stolen airplane from Illinois to Oklahoma. He is charged with violating the following federal statute:

National Motor Vehicle Theft Act, 18 U.S.C. § 408
    Sec. 2. That when used in this Act: (a) The term "motor vehicle" shall include an automobile, automobile truck, automobile wagon, motor cycle, or any other self-propelled vehicle not designed for running on rails;
    Sec. 3. That whoever shall transport or cause to be transported in interstate or foreign commerce a motor vehicle, knowing the same to have been stolen, shall be punished by a fine of not more than $5,000, or by imprisonment of no more than five years, or both.

Do you think Gary should be found guilty? Why?

4. On the basis of the U.S. Supreme Court's decision in the *Caminetti* case, which, if any, of the following situations would be a violation of the Mann Act?

> **a.** A man drives a woman whom he knows to be a prostitute from Los Angeles to Las Vegas. The man receives no compensation for providing this transportation, nor does he receive any share of any money she makes as a prostitute. He took her as a favor to a friend and to have someone to talk to on the trip.
>
> **b.** A man drives his girlfriend from Newark, New Jersey, to New York City so that she can perform a striptease at a stag party.
>
> **c.** A man picks up his girlfriend in Sacramento, California, and drives her to Seattle, Washington, where they cohabit without getting married.

(c) Reference to other parts of the statute Judges often look for clues to the meaning of a particular statutory section by focusing on the context in which the disputed clause occurs. This **contextual analysis** involves looking at the overall structure of the larger legislative package. For example, under the discussion of the plain meaning approach we mentioned that one place courts sometimes look for guidance is a definitions section. A contextual analysis requires you to think about the following questions:

- What title did the legislature give the act? (It is usually assumed that the name chosen for the act is significant.)
- Are relevant subheadings provided?
- Does the statute contain a definitions section?
- Even if there is no definitions section, is the same term used elsewhere in the statute or in a related statute? (One can assume that any given clause is intended to be read as part of a larger, more comprehensive regulatory scheme and that the legislature intended to be consistent in its approaches to the problem.)

As with the canons of construction, reference to other parts of the statute (even the statute's title) can lead to contradictory results. In *Caminetti*, the dissenting justices used the official title of the statute to support their interpretation of the statute.

> [O]f the purpose of the statute Congress itself has given us illumination. It devotes a section to the declaration that the "act shall be known and referred to as the 'White Slave Traffic Act.'" And its prominence gives it prevalence in the construction of the statute. It cannot be pushed aside or subordinated by indefinite words in other sentences, limited even there by the context. It is a peremptory rule of construction that all parts of a statute must be taken into account in ascertaining its meaning, and it cannot be said that § 8 has no object. Even if it gives only a title to the act, it has especial weight. . . . But it gives more than a title; it makes distinctive the purpose of the statute. The designation "white slave traffic" has the sufficiency of an axiom. If apprehended, there is no uncertainty as to the conduct it describes. It is commercialized vice, immoralities having a mercenary purpose, and this is confirmed by other circumstances.[6]

Justice Day, for the majority, disagreed with the dissent's reliance on the statute's title.

---

[6]Id. at 497.

It is true that § 8 of the act provides that it shall be known and referred to as the "White Slave Traffic Act," . . . . Still, the name given to an act by way of designation or description . . . cannot change the plain import of its words. If the words are plain, they give meaning to the act, and it is neither the duty nor the privilege of the courts to enter speculative fields in search of a different meaning.[7]

(d) Evidence external to the statute In addition to the previously discussed methods of statutory interpretation, courts frequently look for evidence of legislative intent beyond the wording of the statute itself. This type of evidence includes decisions by other courts, the act's legislative history, current events at the time the statute was enacted, a comparison of this statute with similar statutes from the same or other jurisdictions, administrative agency interpretations, and scholarly works.

(1) Other court opinions Following the doctrine of stare decisis courts will normally consider the manner in which other courts have interpreted the same words. In addition to looking to decisions from their own state, courts will frequently look to judicial interpretations of similar statutes in other states.

(2) Legislative history The term **legislative history** refers to the background documents created during the process of a bill becoming a statute. These documents can include alternative versions of the legislation, proceedings of committee hearings and reports, and transcripts of floor debates. The exact nature of the materials that exist for a particular statute will vary depending on the importance of the statute and the type of legislative body involved. For example, generally there is more recorded legislative history for federal statutes than there is for state statutes.

To understand why certain documents form a statute's legislative history, you need to recall the steps that the legislature follows to create a statute. Statutes begin as **bills**. A legislator introduces a draft of what the proposed law should look like. Before passage there may be amendments that change various sections of the bill. The pattern that emerges from examining multiple bills and amendments can sometimes provide insight into the legislative intent of the final act. The court, for example, would probably not read the act as applying to a particular situation if the legislative history shows that an amendment that would have applied to that situation was defeated.

Before bills are presented on the floor of the legislative body, they are usually sent to a committee. Committees often hold public hearings where interested parties can testify about the proposed law. The proceedings of these **committee hearings** are published, and the transcript becomes a part of the statute's legislative history. A committee sometimes will issue an official report discussing the nature of the proposed legislation and what it is expected to accomplish. The **committee report** also becomes part of the legislative history.

When the bill is debated on the floor of the legislative body, proponents and opponents often make statements about what they expect the bill to do or not do. The transcripts of these **floor debates** are another source of information about legislative intent. In determining legislative intent courts may quote from any of these sources.

When you see a court relying on legislative history or when you are thinking of relying on it yourself, keep in mind that legislative history should be viewed with an open mind. First, it is frequently incomplete, especially at the state level.

Legislative history
The background documents created during the process of a bill becoming a statute. These documents can include alternative versions of the legislation, proceedings of committee hearings and reports, and transcripts of floor debates.

---

[7]Id. at 489.

PRACTICAL TIP

A legislature often enacts legislation as a reaction to a specific event. Therefore, to gain insight into the legislative thinking at the time, you can search through archived newspaper reports for major events around the time the legislation was enacted.

Second, it is usually based on what just one or a few of the legislators said. There is no way of knowing if the other legislators agreed or even knew of the statements. Ultimately it was not what the other legislators said, but what the statute says that got enacted. Third, legislative history is similar to the canons of construction in that you can usually find history to support opposing points of view.

For example, in the 1975 case of *United States v. Powell*,[8] both the majority and the dissenting justices attempted to use the legislative history of a federal gun control statute to justify their differing interpretations. Powell was convicted of violating a federal statute, 18 U.S.C. § 1715, when he mailed a sawed-off shotgun. The statute prohibits the mailing of "pistols, revolvers, and other firearms capable of being concealed on the person." The issue was whether sawed-off shotguns qualify as "other firearms capable of being concealed on the person." In the Court's opinion, Justice Rehnquist stated:

> The legislative history of this particular provision is sparse, but the House report indicates that the purpose of the bill upon which § 1715 is based was to avoid having the Post Office serve as an instrumentality for the violation of local laws which prohibited the purchase and possession of weapons. H.R. Rep. No. 610, 69th Cong., 1st Sess. (1926). It would seem that sawed-off shotguns would be even more likely to be prohibited by local laws than would pistols and revolvers. A statement by the author of the bill, Representative Miller of Washington, on the floor of the House indicates that the purpose of the bill was to make it more difficult for criminals to obtain concealable weapons. 66 Cong. Rec. 726 (1924). To narrow the meaning of the language Congress used so as to limit it to only those weapons which could be concealed as readily as pistols or revolvers would not comport with that purpose.[9]

In dissent, Justice Stewart stated:

> The legislative history of the bill on which § 1715 was based contains persuasive indications that it was not intended to apply to firearms larger than the largest pistols or revolvers. Representative Miller, the bill's author, made it clear that the legislative concern was not with the "shotgun, the rifle, or any firearm used in hunting or by the sportsman." 66 Cong. Rec. 727. As a supporter of the legislation stated: "The purpose . . . is to prevent the shipment of pistols and revolvers through the mails." 67 Cong. Rec. 12,041. The only reference to sawed-off shotguns came in a question posed by Representative McKeown: "Is there anything in this bill that will prevent the citizens of Oklahoma from buying sawed-off shotguns to defend themselves against these bank-robbing bandits?" Representative Blanton, an opponent of the bill, responded: "That may come next. Sometimes a revolver is more necessary than a

---

[8] 423 U.S. 87 (1975).
[9] Id. at 91.

sawed-off shotgun." 66 Cong. Rec. 729. In the absence of more concrete indicia of legislative intent, the pregnant silence that followed Representative Blanton's response can surely be taken as an indication that Congress intended the law to reach only weapons of the same general size as pistols and revolvers.[10]

Sometimes the legislative history can include the failure of the legislative body to react to administrative or judicial interpretations. This aspect of the judicial reasoning process is well illustrated in the continuing controversy over the antitrust status of professional sports. In *Federal Baseball Club v. National League*[11] and *Toolson v. New York Yankees, Inc.*,[12] the Supreme Court held that professional baseball was not covered by federal antitrust laws. In subsequent cases the Court ruled that other professional sports, such as football, hockey, and boxing, were covered. In 1972 in a decision involving baseball the Court was faced with having to justify this inconsistency.[13] The majority asserted that because Congress, knowing of the Court's position on baseball, had not passed a specific law to include it under the antitrust laws, Congress must have approved the Court's earlier position excluding it.

Of course, it is always dangerous to make assumptions about why some group or individual did not act. In the case of Congress and baseball, Congress may have remained silent not because it agreed with the Supreme Court ruling, but because it was simply too hazardous politically to attack America's favorite pastime.

(3) Other external sources of evidence   In addition to legislative history, courts will sometimes take into account events that occurred at the time the statute was enacted. They may also compare the statute in question to similar statutes from the same or other jurisdictions. If the legislature has empowered an administrative agency to write regulations interpreting the statute, the court will defer to the administrative agency's interpretation unless the court thinks it does not support the intent of the legislation. Finally, the courts will occasionally rely on scholarly works for gaining insight into the legislative intent.

(e) Summary of interpretation methods   When courts are asked to interpret the meaning of statutes, they can use several techniques. For example, they can use a dictionary and a grammar book to give a literal interpretation, or they can study committee hearings and floor debates from the legislature to try to ascertain the legislative intent. The following list summarizes the major principles of statutory interpretation:

1. Statutes should be interpreted to be consistent with the intent of the legislators who enacted them.
2. Statutes should be read literally and their words given meanings that were commonly used at the time the statutes were written.
3. Individual parts of a statute should be interpreted so that they will be consistent with the other parts of the statute.
4. Unless the legislative intent is clearly to the contrary, statutes should be interpreted to be consistent with other statutes and with the common law.

---

[10]Id. at 95.

[11]259 U.S. 200 (1922).

[12]346 U.S. 356 (1953).

[13]Flood v. Kuhn, 407 U.S. 258 (1972).

5. Statutes should be interpreted to be consistent with committee reports, floor debates, and other aspects of the legislative history.

The legislative intent is often unclear, and sometimes the application of these principles can lead to contradictory results. When the legal advocate is attempting to persuade a court to interpret a statute in a way favorable to a client, that advocate urges the court to adopt the method of interpretation that favors the client. Therefore, legal professionals need to develop the ability to work comfortably with each approach to finding legislative intent.

(3) Recognize the role of judicial philosophy

Ultimately how a particular court interprets a statute will also be influenced by the judicial philosophy of the judges deciding the case. Some judges are strong believers in **judicial restraint** and will tend to rely on the plain meaning of the statute, giving it the narrowest construction possible. They do not view their role as one of second-guessing the legislature. Even if they think something beyond the strict language of the statute would produce a better result, they will not so interpret the statute. It is not their role to correct legislative omissions. Finally, they tend to think that legislative intent is static. That is, the courts should give the statute the meaning that the original drafters of the legislation intended. The meaning of the statute should not change as the needs of society change.

Judges who believe in **judicial activism** see the issue of statutory construction a little differently. While they, too, will search for legislative intent, they are more willing to see the need for the meaning of a statute to change over time as society changes. They are also more likely to search for a more general purpose behind the statute as opposed to a specific intent in the minds of the legislators. For example, in the situation regarding the prohibition against vehicles in public parks, while the immediate concern and intent of the city council were to ban motorcycles, the broader purpose of the ordinance was to protect life. With that in mind a judicial activist would have no problem saying that the prohibition against vehicles would not apply to an ambulance driving through the park for the very purpose of saving a human life.

Judicial restraint
A judicial philosophy that supports a limited role for the judiciary in changing the law, including deference to the legislative branch.

Judicial activism
A judicial philosophy that supports an active role for the judiciary in changing the law.

4. Conclude

You should consider each of the methods that we discussed when you analyze a statute. There will be times when you find that these alternative methods suggest contradictory interpretations. At some point, however, you will have to reach a conclusion on each issue. Based on those individual conclusions, you will decide about the question as a whole.

Returning to the case of Mary and the hammer, assume you conclude that Mary did possess a "dangerous weapon" but that she did not "carry" it. Therefore, one of the statute's elements is not satisfied. Because we have defined an element as a precondition to the applicability of the rule and because one element has not been met, the statute would not apply to Mary's case. She would not be convicted of carrying a dangerous weapon. Of course, a court might not agree with your analysis and might instead find that both elements had been satisfied. If that were to happen, Mary would be convicted.

Keep in mind that often there is no one right answer. At this stage of learning legal reasoning, developing sound arguments in support of your conclusions is more important than the conclusions you reach.

In summary, the process of analyzing a statute and applying it to your client's facts is as follows:

1. Find the main facts of the client's case.
2. Research the law.
3. Analyze the statutory language.
   a. Determine if there is a statute applicable to your client's situation.
   a. Break the statute down into its elements, specifically noting any ambiguous language.
   b. State the issues raised by the specific language of the statute and the specific facts of the client's case. Analyze the problem.
      ■ Determine how each element applies to the facts of your client's case, striving to see the arguments that hurt as well as those that help your client. (*Hint:* Based on our definition of an issue, if you cannot find two sides to the argument, you are probably not dealing with an issue.)
      ■ Think about why the legislature enacted the statute. Thinking about the purpose behind the statute will help you determine how best to interpret ambiguous statutory language.
4. Given the statute's language and the likely purpose behind the statute, conclude as to the statute's effect on your client's facts.

E. THE CASE OF THE UNHAPPY CUSTOMER

To reinforce the four steps of legal analysis, we will examine how that process applies to a situation involving a civil statute. The steps are the same. All that varies is that now you will be dealing with a civil rather than a criminal statute.

Case 7: The Unhappy Customer

Last week Sarah and a friend were enjoying a delightful dinner at the Westly Inn. Everything had gone well until it was time for dessert. The waiter offered Sarah's companion the dessert menu. When Sarah asked for one for herself, the waiter replied, "Absolutely not. The last thing you need is more calories, you fat cow." Naturally Sarah was outraged. She jumped up, threw $50 on the table, and proceeded toward the doorway.

Unfortunately her napkin hid the money, and the waiter thought she was trying to leave the restaurant without paying. He grabbed her by the arm and in front of all the customers accused her of trying to leave without paying.

When the waiter grabbed her arm, the strap to her purse broke. The purse fell to the floor, spilling its contents.

Sarah began to search under the tables and chairs, looking for her valuables. Five minutes later the waiter discovered the $50 Sarah had left on the table and told her she was free to go. However, it took Sarah nearly twenty more minutes to collect all of her purse's contents. She then left the restaurant.

Sarah is understandably upset over what occurred at the restaurant and wants to know whether or not she has grounds for a lawsuit, based on the waiter's actions.

Assume an attorney met with Sarah Howard. During the initial interview she related the following facts as described in Case 7: The Unhappy Customer, located on page 142.

The first step is to determine if there is any immediate need to gather additional facts beyond those you obtained through the client interview. For now, we will assume the supervising attorney decided that you have sufficient facts to proceed with the next step.

Based on the facts from the interview the supervising attorney could decide that Sarah might have a good claim for **false imprisonment**. False imprisonment is an intentional tort. It occurs whenever one person unlawfully detains another person against his or her will. In your search to determine if there are any statutes that might govern the situation, you find the following state statute:

> In an action for false imprisonment by reason of having been detained for questioning on or in the immediate premises of a merchant, if such person was detained in a reasonable manner and for not more than a reasonable length of time by the merchant or his servant and if there were reasonable grounds to believe that the person so detained was committing or attempting to commit larceny of goods for sale on such premises, it shall be a defense to such action.[14]

Because this statute provides a defense to a charge of false imprisonment in some situations, it may help the restaurant avoid liability in Sarah's case.

Step three involves deciding whether the statute even applies to Sarah's situation. Is a restaurant a "merchant"? If it is not, the statute will not apply. Assume the statute does not define the term *merchant*. How would you argue that a restaurant should be considered a merchant? That it should not? Besides using your common sense about the plain meaning of the term, remember to think about why the legislature enacted such a statute. Who were the legislators trying to protect and why? Should that protection be extended to restaurant owners?

If you are unsure about whether the statute would apply to the restaurant, the safest course is to assume that it would and to continue with your analysis. Never analyze only part of a problem and then stop. Why? Because you might be wrong. For example, assume you decided a restaurant is not a "merchant" and stopped your analysis there. If a court were later to decide otherwise and asked your boss his thoughts on the remaining issues and if he relied solely on your work, he would be unprepared to answer.[15] Therefore, you should continue with your analysis of the statute. To do that, you must break the statute down into the following elements:

It will be a defense to false imprisonment if the person was

1. detained for questioning on or in the immediate premises of a merchant,
2. if such person was detained in a reasonable manner and
3. for not more than a reasonable length of time
4. by the merchant or his servant and
5. if there were reasonable grounds to believe

---

[14]Based on Mass. Gen. L. ch. 231, § 94B (2000).

[15]This advice is also applicable to exam taking. Assume your instructor hands out a test question worth one hundred points. If your instructor thinks the question involves four issues, she may develop a grading sheet whereby she will award up to twenty-five points for the discussion on each of the four issues. If you decide that your analysis of one issue answers the problem and therefore do not write about the other three issues, you will have just made it impossible to earn more than twenty-five points for your answer.

6. that the person so detained was committing or attempting to commit larceny of goods for sale on such premises.

When reading statutes, you must pay careful attention to every word. Some words are especially important. For example, always take note of whether the legislature used a mandatory word, such as *shall*, or a discretionary word, such as *may*. Double-check to see whether the elements of the statute are connected with "and" or "or." If the statute uses "and," each part connected by "and" must be satisfied. If the statute uses "or," the parts are alternatives to each other. Note how many times "and" and "or" are used in this statute.

Now, based on your client's facts, you need to determine which, if any, of these elements create an issue—that is, an argument for or against the applicability of that particular element to the client's case. Under different facts the first element, "detained for questioning on or in the immediate premises of a merchant," could give rise to an issue. Assume the questioning had taken place in the restaurant's parking lot. Would that qualify as being "in the immediate premises"? However, given the facts of our case, it does not appear that the first element raises any issues.

The second element, however, "if such person was detained in a reasonable manner," raises a host of issues. Was it reasonable for the waiter to grab Sarah with such force as to break the strap on her purse? Should he have done so in front of other customers? The answers to these and similar questions suggest that there could be at least some argument that the manner was not reasonable.

There is also an issue as to whether the detention was for a reasonable length of time. While the questioning itself took only a few minutes, it took Sarah another twenty minutes to collect the contents of her purse.

The fourth element, "by the merchant or his servant," may seem to raise an issue but does not. While a waiter would probably not appreciate being called a **servant**, the law sometimes uses such antiquated terms. For example, children are often called **infants**. Similarly, employers are sometimes called **masters**.

The fifth and sixth elements also present issues: Did the waiter have "reasonable grounds" to believe Sarah was attempting to leave without paying her bill? Do food and drink served in a restaurant qualify as "goods for sale"?

In developing your arguments on each side of every issue, you should, of course, use any of the methods of statutory interpretation available to you. However, focus first on the language of the statute, the facts of your client's case, and your commonsense reasoning as to which interpretations would best satisfy the legislation's intent. Then you can look to other sources, such as prior court opinions interpreting the statute and legislative history, for assistance.

Legal Reasoning Exercises

5. For Sarah's case develop a chart listing each element and the arguments you could make under each for Sarah and for the restaurant. For each issue reach a conclusion. Finally, decide whether you think the restaurant has a valid defense to detaining Sarah.

6. Assume Carl Clay has been charged with burglary. Briefly the facts are as follows:

> Last Friday Carl was watching As the Word Turns, his favorite soap opera, when suddenly the TV screen went blank. Nothing he could do would cause it to work. Unfortunately Carl did not have enough money to buy a new set. He decided to help himself to someone else's.
>
> He drove to the nearby Sleep Well Motel because he knew that the owners had recently purchased new nineteen-inch TVs. When he got to the motel around 5:00 p.m., he waited in his car until he saw a lady leave her room, ice bucket in hand. She had left the door to her room slightly ajar. Carl quickly ran to the door, opened it, and saw the TV. He went over to the TV, unplugged it, and picked it up. He was about to leave when the woman unexpectedly returned. Knowing karate, she felled him on the spot and then called the office manager, who, in turn, called the police. The TV, which was purchased for $600 and had a resale price of approximately $400, was returned to its rightful place in the room.

Carl has been charged with violating the following statutes:

General Laws ch. 228, § 1
Burglary is defined as the breaking and entering of a dwelling at nighttime with the intent to commit a felony therein.

General Laws ch. 228, § 2
Theft of personal property over the value of $500 is a felony.
Theft of personal property of a value less than $500 is a misdemeanor.

    a. Develop a chart listing the elements of each statute.
    b. For each element determine whether the facts raise an issue.
    c. For each issue list arguments that both Carl's attorney and the prosecution would raise. Reach a conclusion on each issue.
    d. Do you think Carl can be convicted of burglary?

In the final step you conclude whether or not the restaurant could use the statute to defend itself against Sarah's charge of false imprisonment.

F. WRITTEN ANALYSIS—THE USE OF IRAC

The results of your legal analysis should be put in writing so that they are preserved for future reference by you or by others with an interest in the legal problem. In addition, writing your analysis will force you to rethink the assumptions you have made. Your written analysis will mirror your thought process thus far. That is, you will discuss each issue raised by the statute's elements and the client's facts.

Legal readers do not appreciate reading something that simply reproduces your stream of consciousness thinking. An attorney or judge wants to know four things:

    1. what your client's problem (the issue) is,
    2. what the law (the rule) is,

3. how that law will affect your client's case (the analysis), and
4. what your answer as to the likely result (the conclusion) is.

One widely accepted method for conveying your thoughts in a logical order is known as **IRAC**. IRAC is an acronym for Issue-Rule-Analysis-Conclusion. The IRAC approach is not the only or necessarily always the best approach for every legal issue, but it is an excellent starting point. If you consciously try to write using IRAC, you will find that you will be forced to think about what you are writing and you will be less likely to leave out important information. The result will be better-organized and clearer paragraphs. Figure 6-3 describes each of the IRAC elements.

To see a practical application of the use of the IRAC technique, consider the following problem.

Case 8: The Book Battery

Mark Brown was at home one night. He had been studying in bed when he fell asleep. He was awakened when he heard and then saw a stranger in his darkened bedroom. He shouted, and the stranger moved toward the door. Frightened of what the stranger might do next, Mark took one of his heavy law books and threw it at the man's departing back. Unfortunately the man's spine was broken. Analyze whether Mark is guilty of committing a criminal battery.

Mark has been charged with violating a criminal statute:

> Any person committing an intentional, harmful, unprivileged touching of another shall be guilty of battery.

From our earlier discussions we know that one of the first steps in analyzing this statute is to break it down into its elements.

> Battery is
>
> 1. the intentional,
> 2. harmful,
> 3. unprivileged
> 4. touching
> 5. of another.

The following is a brief description of each of the IRAC elements with an example of how each would be used to analyze Mark's problem.

1. Issue

Have a topic sentence that states the issue you will be discussing in that paragraph. This sentence should be brief and clear. It should also contain only one

Issue:	Have a topic sentence that states the issue you will be discussing in that paragraph.
Rule:	State the rule of law that arguably governs the particular issue in question.
Analysis:	Explain how the statutory language and policy behind the statute determine the outcome given your client's specific facts.
Conclusion:	Conclude. State what you think the result will be. Do not leave your reader to decide what the bottom line is. That is why your supervisor asked you to analyze the problem.
Transition:	Use a short transition sentence to lead to the next issue that you want to discuss.

Figure 6-3   Elements of an IRAC Analysis

idea: the one to be discussed in that particular paragraph. If there is more than one issue, devote a separate IRAC paragraph to each one.

> The issue is whether Mark Brown can be found guilty of battery.

2. Rule

State the rule of law that arguably governs the particular issue in question. Quote the exact statutory language. If the statute is quite long, quote only the relevant language. Use ellipses[16] to show any omissions. Make sure your omissions do not change the statute's meaning.

> Battery requires "an intentional . . . unprivileged touching of another."

3. Analysis

Explain how the statutory language and policy behind the statute determine the outcome given your client's specific facts. Note the strengths as well as the weaknesses in your client's case. You will be doing your client a great disservice if you only point out the helpful arguments and leave out the harmful ones.

> Because Mark threw a book at a stranger he found in his bedroom, there was a touching. The touching, however, was privileged. The stranger was a trespasser

---

[16]Note the use of three dots. Each is separated by a space. If you omit the end of a sentence, use four dots: three to show the omission and one for the period.

> in Mark's house. He awoke Mark from his sleep, thereby frightening him. Mark had a right to defend himself. Although the man had his back turned to Mark and was possibly leaving the room when Mark threw the book at him, it was quite dark in the room. In his half-awake state Mark could not be held responsible for making a necessary and quick decision to defend himself.

4. Conclusion

Conclude. Do not leave your reader to decide what the bottom line is. That is why you were asked to analyze the problem.

> Therefore, while Mark did touch the stranger, the touching was privileged. Mark should not be found guilty of battery.

If you are discussing more than one issue, use a short transition sentence to lead to the next element you want to discuss. When you put all of the IRAC elements together, the final discussion would look like this.

> The issue is whether Mark Brown can be found guilty of battery. Battery requires "an intentional . . . unprivileged touching of another." Because Mark threw a book at a stranger he found in his bedroom, there was a touching. The touching, however, was privileged. The stranger was a trespasser in Mark's house. He awoke Mark from his sleep, thereby frightening him. Mark had a right to defend himself. Although the man had his back turned to Mark and was possibly leaving the room when Mark threw the book at him, it was quite dark in the room. In his half-awake state Mark could not be held responsible for making a necessary and quick decision to defend himself. Therefore, while Mark did touch the stranger, the touching was privileged. Mark should not be found guilty of battery.

Some attorneys prefer the CRAC as opposed to the IRAC method. With CRAC you start with the conclusion. For now, it is better to use IRAC. IRAC forces you to support your conclusion with a well-developed analysis. When you start your writing with a conclusion, the answer may seem so self-evident that you will not see any need to justify it with an analysis. However, when you start your paragraph with a statement of the issue and end it with a conclusion, there is all that space in between just crying out to be filled with an explanation that will convince your reader of how you logically moved from your issue to your conclusion. This will help prevent the most common error in legal writing: stating the rule and simply jumping to the conclusion with no supporting reasoning. Look at the following paragraph. What is missing?

The issue is whether Mark Brown can be found guilty of battery. Battery requires both that there be an intentional touching of another and that the touching be "unprivileged." While Mark did touch the stranger, the touching was privileged. Mark should not be found guilty of battery.

After reading this you would be left wondering: But why? Why was the touching privileged? The writer gave an answer but not the reasons for that answer. Always double-check your writing to make sure you are not leaving your reader with any questions about how you reached your conclusion.

If the statute you are analyzing contains more than one issue, start with an introductory paragraph, also known as a **road map paragraph,** that tells your reader where you will be going. In that paragraph very briefly outline the facts, the rule, and the issues you will be discussing. This is not the place to completely retell the client's story. Give just enough of the facts to set the stage. Follow that paragraph with an IRAC analysis of each major issue, using the rest of the facts to make arguments based on the statute's elements.

Sometimes an issue will be simple enough that you can put all the IRAC elements into a single paragraph. At other times you may want to divide the IRAC elements into more than one paragraph. For example, you might wish to set out the issue and the rule of law in one paragraph. Then in the next paragraph you could include the arguments for one side of the issue. You could follow this with a third paragraph outlining the arguments for the other side and your conclusion on that issue, along with a transitional phrase or sentence to lead into the next issue.

You need to use **transitions** between your issues to help lead your reader from one issue to the next. A transition can be as simple as "The next issue is. . . ." More sophisticated transitions are discussed in Appendix B. Finally, wrap up your discussion with a **concluding paragraph** that summarizes your analysis.

When using IRAC remember that each paragraph should contain one and only one idea. A paragraph, indeed any written work, is a structure. It should build, grow, and develop toward a denouement. If you cannot discern such a progression in your own work, go back and rework it until you do.

Finally, do not view IRAC as a straightjacket. It is meant not to limit your creative abilities but simply to provide a structure for your writing.

Exhibit 6-2 is a sample analysis using the IRAC format for the problem of Mary and the hammer, introduced earlier in the chapter. We have added the marginal notes to help you locate each of the IRAC elements. When writing a legal analysis yourself, do not include these marginal notations.

Road map paragraph
An introductory paragraph listing issues to be discussed in the order they are to be discussed.

Transition
In writing, a technique used to help your reader move from one thought to the next and to see the connections between them.

Concluding paragraph
The final paragraph in a written legal analysis that summarizes the writer's conclusions.

Road map paragraph	Mary is concerned about whether she can be convicted of carrying a dangerous weapon. During an argument with another customer in a local store Mary briefly picked up a hammer from the counter. The statute under which she has been charged makes it unlawful for "anyone, other than a police officer, to carry a dangerous weapon." Because Mary is not a police officer, the first element of the statute is satisfied. However, as Mary only picked up the hammer, there is an issue as to whether she "carried" it. Second, there is an issue as to whether a hammer can be considered a "dangerous weapon."	
Issue 1 **Rule** **Analysis** **Conclusion on issue 1**	As to the first issue of whether her lifting of the hammer constituted "carrying," the statute simply reads that it is unlawful "to carry" a dangerous weapon. While in the hardware store Mary did move the hammer from the counter into the air. However, she did not take it from one location to another, such as from the store out into the street. Therefore, while she may have "possessed" the hammer, she cannot be said to have "carried" the hammer. The second issue, however, is not as clear-cut.	**Transition**
Issue 2 **Rule** **Analysis** **Conclusion on issue 2**	The second issue is whether the hammer should be viewed as a "dangerous weapon." The statute does not define "dangerous weapon." A hammer is normally viewed as a tool and not as a weapon. However, being a large, hard object, a hammer certainly has the capacity to become a dangerous weapon. Also, it was only when Mary lifted the hammer and told the other customer to hand over the item that Mary wanted that the other customer did as Mary wished. Because the legislature was probably more concerned about the potential harm that a dangerous weapon could cause than about the specific identity of any particular weapon, the hammer should be seen as a dangerous weapon.	

Exhibit 6-2 Sample IRAC Analysis

(continued)

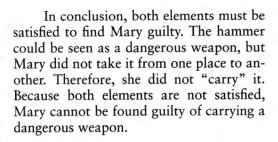

In conclusion, both elements must be satisfied to find Mary guilty. The hammer could be seen as a dangerous weapon, but Mary did not take it from one place to another. Therefore, she did not "carry" it. Because both elements are not satisfied, Mary cannot be found guilty of carrying a dangerous weapon.

Concluding paragraph

Exhibit 6-2   Sample IRAC Analysis (*concluded*)

Legal Reasoning Exercises

7. Use the IRAC approach to write an analysis of one of the issues you outlined for Exercise 5 regarding Sarah and the defenses to her possible false imprisonment claim.

8. Apply the principles we have been discussing to Carl's situation, described in Exercise 6, and write an IRAC analysis of his problem.

G. LOCATING AND INTERPRETING ADMINISTRATIVE REGULATIONS

Legislatures often delegate considerable lawmaking authority to administrative agencies. Therefore, frequently you must look beyond the statutes to administrative regulations that interpret the statute. For example, you may recall from Chapter 2 that Congress enacted a statute prohibiting discrimination in employment on the basis of sex. In that same statute Congress also created an administrative agency, the Equal Employment Opportunity Commission (EEOC), and gave that agency the power to write regulations interpreting the statute. One such regulation defines sex discrimination to include sexual harassment.

> Unwelcome sexual advances, requests for sexual favors, and other verbal or physical conduct of a sexual nature constitute sexual harassment when (1) submission to such conduct is made either explicitly or implicitly a term or condition of an individual's employment, (2) submission to or rejection of such conduct by an individual is used as the basis for employment decisions affecting such individual, or (3) such conduct has the purpose or effect of unreasonably interfering with an individual's work performance or creating an intimidating, hostile, or offensive working environment.[17]

---

[17]29 C.F.R. § 1604.11 (2000).

Code of Federal Regulations (C.F.R.)
A compilation of federal administrative regulations arranged by agency.

As you can see, administrative regulations are published in formats that resemble those used for statutes. Federal regulations are published in the **Code of Federal Regulations (C.F.R.).** The C.F.R. is analogous to the United States Code in that it contains only those regulations that are of a general, permanent nature and are currently in force. The regulations are arranged by agency.

Some states publish codes of regulations that correspond to the Code of Federal Regulations in that they contain all the current state regulations and are organized by subject matter. In other states you must obtain the regulations from each individual agency. At both the state and the federal levels some private publishers issue loose-leaf reporters that contain administrative regulations in specialized areas such as taxes and labor law.

Citations for administrative regulations follow a form that is analogous to that for statutes. For example:

> 49 C.F.R. § 6.1 (2003)
> Ill. Admin. Code tit. 5, § 4430 (1995)

In the first citation *C.F.R.* tells you that it is a reference to the Code of Federal Regulations. The number *49* stands for title 49, while *§ 6.1* refers to section 6.1 of title 49. As with statutes, the date in parentheses refers to the last publication date for the book in which the regulation appears, not the date the regulation was promulgated. The second citation is to an Illinois regulation.

Administrative regulations have the same basic features as statutes, and they are similarly future oriented. However, they tend to be more detailed than statutes, as their function is to spell out the specifics of the statute. Nonetheless, the basic approaches you use when interpreting statutes can also be used to interpret regulations. In addition, keep in mind that the courts will seek an interpretation that is consistent with the intent of the statute that established and controls the agency in question.

H. LOCATING AND INTERPRETING CONSTITUTIONS

Constitutions set out the structure of the government itself, as well as the limitations on the government's power. Therefore, you would turn to a constitutional provision to challenge an objectionable statute or the manner in which government agents conducted themselves (as in a Fourth Amendment challenge to an allegedly unreasonable search).

State and federal constitutions are usually included in the corresponding statutory compilation. For example, the U.S. Constitution can be found in the United States Code, the United States Code Annotated, and the United States Code Service. Similarly, a state statute compilation usually includes a copy of its state constitution, and a few even feature a copy of the U.S. Constitution with annotations to decisions from their own state courts.

Sections of constitutions are cited as follows:

> U.S. Const. art. I, § 8, cl. 3
> U.S. Const. amend. XX, § 3
> Ill. Const. art. IV, § 2(b)

Just as you will see ambiguity in statutes and administrative regulations, you will see it in constitutions. Indeed, the broader and more general the document, the greater the likelihood that ambiguity will occur. Consider, for example, the following clauses contained in the U.S. Constitution:

The Congress shall have Power . . .
To regulate *Commerce* with foreign Nations, and among the several States, and with the Indian Tribes. . . .

To make all Laws which shall be *necessary and proper* for carrying into Execution the foregoing Powers, and all other Powers vested by this Constitution in the Government of the United States, or in any Department or Officer thereof. (art. I, § 8) (emphasis added)

Congress shall make *no law* respecting an *establishment of religion*, or prohibiting the *free exercise thereof*; or abridging the *freedom of speech*, or *of the press*, or the right of the people peaceably to assemble, and to petition the Government for a redress of grievances. (amend. I) (emphasis added)

The right of the people to be secure in their persons, houses, papers, and effects, against *unreasonable searches and seizures*, shall not be violated. . . . (amend. IV) (emphasis added)

We added the italics to emphasize the ambiguity of various words and phrases. Note that these provisions are broadly written and hence contain a great deal of ambiguity.

Over the years the courts have interpreted these and other parts of the Constitution. To do so, the courts generally use the same approaches discussed in the section on statutory construction. They attempt a literal reading of the words themselves (plain meaning), consider the relationship of the clause in question to similar clauses located elsewhere in the document (contextual analysis), and go back to the minutes of the Constitutional Convention and to the legislative history of amendments (external analysis).

Once a court has formally interpreted the meaning of a particular clause of the Constitution, that court decision takes on precedential value and becomes case law on the meaning of the Constitution. Therefore, rather than going back to begin the interpretive process over again, succeeding courts follow the lead of previous decisions, and gradually a series of cases develops that explains, for example, that the words *no law* as they are used in the First Amendment really mean that the government can pass laws restricting obscene materials or punishing libelous statements. As the case law expands, it becomes clearer as to when something might be considered obscene and when it might not or as to when a search is a reasonable search and when it is not.

It is important to realize that it is in the area of constitutional law that the courts (particularly the U.S. Supreme Court) have the greatest freedom to exercise discretion. By virtue of being a constitution rather than a statute, a constitution contains far more generalized and thus ambiguous language. This increased ambiguity creates more opportunities for judges' decisions to be influenced by their judicial philosophies.

As we noted in Chapter 2, U.S. Supreme Court Justice Antonin Scalia and other conservatives support a judicial philosophy they call **originalism** that holds that the Constitution should be interpreted to reflect what the average person

Originalism
An approach to constitutional interpretation that narrowly interprets the text of the Constitution in a manner that is consistent with what most people understood those words to mean at the time that they were written.

thought it meant at the time the provision in question was adopted. For example, originalists argue that the Eighth Amendment provision against "cruel and unusual punishment" should not be interpreted as prohibiting capital punishment, because capital punishment was an accepted form of sentencing at the time the Bill of Rights was ratified.

Living Constitution
Judicial philosophy that seeks to interpret the Constitution in light of existing societal values.

Liberal judges and legal scholars support an approach that views the Constitution as a **living constitution.** This approach is sometimes labeled the **evolutionary** or "living law" approach. With this approach judges first seek to identify the underlying principles reflected in the Constitution. Judges then interpret any particular provision by applying those basic principles to contemporary conditions. For example, when the Fourth Amendment was adopted, no one anticipated technological developments, such as telephones or thermo-imaging cameras. However, an underlying Constitutional principle is concern for the protection of individual privacy rights. Therefore, those who see the Constitution as a living and evolving document would argue that the Fourth Amendment provisions against unreasonable searches and seizures prohibit wiretapping phone lines and using thermo-imaging devices to determine if illegal activities are being carried on inside somebody's private residence.

SUMMARY

Once you have located a relevant statute, you must analyze it by breaking it down into its elements and then applying those elements to your client's facts. In analyzing the statute you should look at the plain meaning of the statutory language and try to ascertain the legislative intent in enacting the statute. You can use several strategies to assist you in this process, including relying on the canons of construction, reading legislative history, and seeing how the courts have interpreted the statute. Once you have analyzed the statute, you may be asked to summarize your thinking in writing. One form of written analysis is known as IRAC (Issue-Rule-Analysis-Conclusion).

As we suggested in the first chapter, many view studying law as a skill that simply requires the memorization of rules: If you know the right rule, you will know the right answer. By now we hope you more fully understand why that is not true. While a lot of memorization is involved in learning about the law, applying the law is a process. You do need to know the rules, but that is only the beginning and not the end of the process. Furthermore, the rules change as we apply them to new situations. It is only when the rules are applied to facts that we are forced to give a clearer definition to otherwise ambiguous language.

REVIEW QUESTIONS

Pages 123 through 145

1. Why do statutes often contain ambiguous language?
2. What is meant by looking for the plain meaning of a statute?
3. What are the canons of construction? How do courts use them in interpreting statutes?
4. What types of statutes are courts most likely to strictly construe? To liberally construe?

5. What types of documents could make up a statute's legislative history?
6. What are the dangers in relying on legislative history?
7. What type of judge would be more likely to interpret Title VII's prohibition against employment discrimination based on sex to include discrimination based on sexual preference: one who believes in judicial restraint or judicial activism? Why?
8. What are the main steps in analyzing a statutory problem?
9. What is a statutory element?
10. How does an issue differ from an element?
11. When reading a statute, why is it important to pay attention to the use of "and" and "or"?

Pages 145 through 154

12. What does IRAC stand for, and why does it provide a useful structure for your legal writing?
13. What is the function of a road map paragraph? Of a concluding paragraph?
14. Why is it important to use transitions?
15. We asked you this question at the end of Chapter 1, but we want to ask it again. Why does the study of law involve more than the mere memorization of rules?

Chapter 7

Finding and Interpreting Court Opinions

The picture of the bewildered litigant lured into a course of action by the false light of a decision, only to meet ruin when the light is extinguished and the decision is overruled, is for the most part a figment of excited brains.
Justice Benjamin Cardozo

INTRODUCTION

In Chapter 6 we discussed how to locate and interpret statutes, administrative regulations, and constitutions. In this chapter we will discuss how to locate and interpret court opinions. The terms *court opinion, case,* and *decision* are synonymous.

As you will recall from Chapter 4, there are two basic types of courts: trial and appellate courts. While trial courts determine the facts and apply the law to those facts, appellate courts act as the final interpreters of the law. As the final interpretation of the law, appellate court opinions serve as precedent for future court decisions. For that reason it is principally appellate decisions that you will be studying and briefing. **Case briefing** is a stylized method that you will use to summarize those court opinions.

A. TYPES OF COURT OPINIONS

Court opinions generally fall in one of four categories:

1. those interpreting and applying enacted law, such as statutes;
2. those deciding the constitutionality of a law;
3. those applying established common-law principles; and
4. those creating new common-law principles.

The first type of opinion, which interprets and applies enacted law, consumes a great deal of the courts' time. As we said in Chapter 6, statutes, administrative regulations, and constitutional provisions often contain ambiguous words and phrases. When interpreting enacted law and attempting to determine legislative intent, the courts rely on the same methods we have discussed: looking at the plain meaning, relying on the canons of construction, examining other parts of the statute, and searching for external evidence, such as legislative history and prior court decisions. Under the doctrine of stare decisis, if previous courts have already interpreted the same or similar language, a court will generally try to reach a decision that is consistent with those earlier interpretations.

Judicial review
The court's power to review statutes to decide whether they conform to the Constitution.

A second type of case involves challenges to the constitutionality of a law. Under the power of **judicial review** the courts are responsible for ensuring that all laws comport with the Constitution's requirements. In this type of decision the court's focus is on the intent of the Constitution's framers and the purpose the constitutional provision was meant to fulfill. Then the court determines whether the law in question is consistent with the Constitution's intended purpose.

Mandatory authority
Court decisions from a higher court in the same jurisdiction.

The third and fourth types of cases involve the common law rather than enacted law. Despite the tremendous growth in statutory law, there are times when no statute covers a litigant's situation. Then the courts rely on the common law, or court-made law. Usually, the court will be faced with a group of prior cases and will use them to form an opinion on the current case. Those cases will be seen as either mandatory or persuasive authority.

A decision is **mandatory authority** when it comes from

1. a higher court
2. in the same jurisdiction.

Persuasive authority
Court decisions from an equal or a lower court from the same jurisdiction or from a higher court in a different jurisdiction; also includes secondary authority.

For state cases, that means higher courts within that state's own court system. Federal courts deciding a case involving state law must follow the interpretations given by that state's courts. Within the federal court system it means cases from within that circuit and the U.S. Supreme Court.

Persuasive authority consists of the decisions of courts that do not constitute mandatory authority and the writings of legal scholars. It may therefore include primary authority, such as decisions of other state courts, and secondary authority, such as legal treatises or law review articles.

Figure 7-1 shows the hierarchical nature of mandatory authority. A decision handed down by a court is mandatory authority for those courts below it connected by an arrow. For example, a federal district court in the First Circuit is required to follow the decisions of the federal court of appeals for the First Circuit. But the decisions of the Second Circuit court of appeals are only persuasive authority for the First Circuit district courts. Likewise, the decisions of state A's highest appellate court are mandatory authority for state A's intermediate appellate and trial courts but are only persuasive authority for state B's courts.

When looking to mandatory authority, unless there is a good reason not to do so, a court will decide a new case based on how courts have held in prior **analogous cases**—that is, cases that involved similar facts and rules of law. If the court decides that the prior cases and the present one are dissimilar, on either the facts or the law, the court will **distinguish** the prior cases and reach a contrary decision in the case before it. As you will recall, this process of looking to **precedent**, prior cases, for guidance is known as following the doctrine of **stare decisis**.

However, there will be times when a court will create new common law. This can occur either because there is no law governing the situation or because the court decides to overrule its own prior decisions. When there is no law covering a situation, the court is faced with an **issue of first impression**. If

Analogous cases
Cases that involve similar facts and rules of law.

Distinguishable cases
Cases that involve different facts and/or rules of law.

Issue of first impression
An issue that the court has never faced before.

Figure 7-1 Mandatory Authority

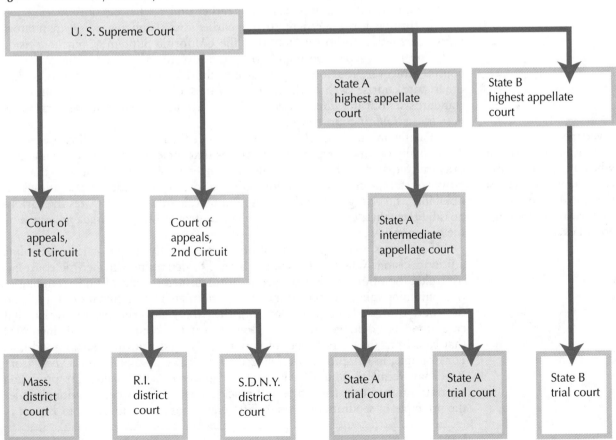

there are decisions from other jurisdictions, the court may look to those decisions for guidance. In addition, the court may look to secondary authority, such as law reviews and treatises. In cases of first impression the court has the option of creating new common-law rules to cover the situation or refusing to do so and deferring to the legislature. If the court defers to the legislature, it does so because it thinks the case involves an area of law that an elected body can handle better than the courts.

Landmark decision

A court opinion that establishes new law in an important area.

A leading example of a court deciding to change the current law, thereby creating a new common-law rule, occurred in the 1968 **landmark decision** of *Dillon v. Legg.*[1] Prior to that decision bystanders could not recover for the emotional distress they suffered when witnessing an accident. Then in *Dillon v. Legg* the California Supreme Court created new law. The court stated that a mother could recover for the emotional injury she suffered when she saw her child injured. When deciding this type of case, the courts are literally making new law, and at times this can create quite dramatic and swift changes in the law. This can be contrasted with cases that revolve around the application of established legal principles to a set of facts. Then the law slowly evolves as the courts evaluate new fact patterns. For example, once the California Supreme Court had established that a mother could recover for seeing a child injured, questions were raised as to whether the mother actually had to see the accident or whether hearing it was enough, whether other family members could recover, and so on. The courts were then flooded with cases in which the issue was no longer whether a bystander could recover but rather under what circumstances.

Returning for a moment to our earlier discussion regarding mandatory versus persuasive authority, note that the California Supreme Court's decision in *Dillon v. Legg* became mandatory authority for all lower California state courts. However, it is only persuasive authority in the federal courts and in other state courts. Each of those courts is free to decide whether to follow the standards set out in *Dillon* based solely on each court's view of the persuasiveness of the *Dillon* court's arguments.

Overrule

A decision is overruled when a court in a later case changes the law so that the decision in the earlier case is no longer good law.

Finally, in rare cases the court will change the law by **overruling** precedent. This usually occurs when the court decides that society's needs have changed so drastically that the old rules should no longer apply. This illustrates the true power of stare decisis. While it normally is a force for stability, it also allows for flexibility and change when the times require it. Figure 7-2 illustrates the various possibilities that a court can pursue when confronted with an issue governed by the common law.

Sometimes a court implies but does not explicitly state that it is overruling a prior decision. When that occurs, it is hard to determine whether the court has overruled the prior decision or merely distinguished it. For an understanding of the continuing validity of the prior court decision, such a determination is crucial. If the court overruled the prior decision, then the legal principle for which that case stood is no longer the law. However, if the court merely distinguished that case from the current one, the prior case's legal principle is still good law. For example, in Chapter 2, we referred to the 1896 case of *Plessy v. Ferguson.* You may recall that in *Plessy* the U.S. Supreme Court held that providing separate railway cars for white and black passengers was constitutional under the principle of separate but equal. Fifty-eight years later, in 1954, in *Brown v.*

---

[1] 441 P.2d 912 (Cal. 1968).

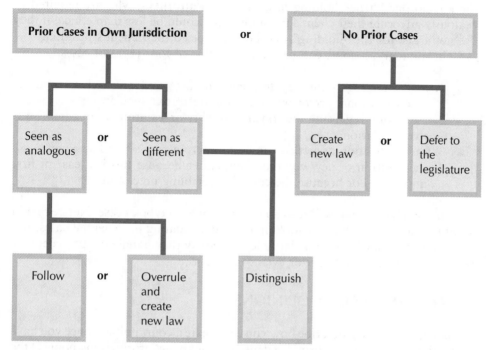

Figure 7-2   Four Routes Open to a Court Faced with a Common-Law Problem

Board of Education, a case involving segregation of public schools, the Supreme Court stated: "We conclude that in the field of public education the doctrine of 'separate but equal' has no place."[2] Did the Court in *Brown* overrule *Plessy*? If so, then the doctrine of separate but equal could no longer be applied in any situation. Or did the Court merely distinguish *Plessy*? If it merely distinguished *Plessy*, then while the principle of separate but equal could not be applied to educational facilities, it could still be applied in other situations, such as transportation.

While it could be argued that the Court had merely distinguished *Plessy*, in reality the Court did not have to utter the precise words "We hereby overrule *Plessy v. Ferguson*" for that to be the effect of the decision. All subsequent courts faced with cases involving separate facilities assumed the *Brown* decision had overruled *Plessy*. In fact, two years after the *Brown* decision a federal court in a case involving transportation (city buses) stated: "[W]e think that *Plessy v. Ferguson* has been impliedly, though not explicitly, overruled, and that . . . there is now no rational basis upon which the separate but equal doctrine can be validly applied to public carrier transportation."[3]

As you can see, on a theoretical level it can be difficult to decide if a court has overruled or merely distinguished a prior case. However, because of the nature of our legal system this problem basically disappears in practice. Attorneys are hired to present their client's point of view and therefore will argue that a prior case has been overruled or distinguished based upon the needs of their client's position. To some this may seem disingenuous, reinforcing the popular notion that attorneys are nothing more than hired guns. However, if

---

[2]347 U.S. 483, 495 (1954).

[3]Browder v. Gayle, 142 F. Supp. 707, 717 (M.D. Ala. 1956).

there is no one, "true" holding of a case, then attorneys, who are required to zealously advocate their client's point of view, would be less than ethical if they did not argue for the "holding" that best supported their client's position.

In summary, a court can be faced with one of four types of cases:

1. a question regarding the interpretation of enacted law, such as a statute, a constitutional provision, or an administrative regulation;
2. a question regarding the constitutionality of a statute or an administrative regulation;
3. the application of settled common law to a new set of facts; and
4. the creation of new common law, either because this is a case of first impression or because the court is overruling precedent.

In this chapter you will read an example of each type of case. Notice that in all of the cases the judges are looking for and evaluating precedential cases. But also note how they have some latitude in the way they handle the precedent; at times they are able to ignore or even overrule it.

B. LOCATING COURT OPINIONS

Case reporters
Books that contain appellate court decisions. There are both official and unofficial reporters.

Official reporter
Governmental publication of court opinions.

Unofficial reporter
Private publication of court opinions—for example, the regional reporters, such as N.E.2d, published by West.

Case citation
Information that tells the reader the name of the case, where it can be located, the court that decided it, and the year it was decided. The Bluebook gives precise rules as to how case citations are to be written.

In this chapter we will describe how you can locate a court opinion once you have its citation. A **citation** is a formalized method for giving information about (1) the name of the case, (2) where it can be located, (3) the court that decided the case, and (4) the year in which it was decided. In Appendix D we will discuss various ways in which you can locate relevant court cases without this information.

Case reporters are sets of books, consisting of hundreds of volumes, that contain copies of appellate court opinions. They are usually arranged in chronological order and divided into volumes named for the court that rendered the opinions. Thus opinions of the Massachusetts Supreme Judicial Court, the highest appellate court in Massachusetts, are found in the Massachusetts Reports. Likewise, those of the highest appellate court in Illinois are reported in the Illinois Reports. The federal government publishes U.S. Supreme Court cases in the United States Reports.

West is the major publisher of case reporters, and the West National Reporter System covers all appellate court decisions in the fifty states. The complete West system is outlined in Appendix C, Figures C-2 and C-3.

Reporters are generally divided into two categories—**official** and **unofficial**. They are official when published at the direction of state or federal statutes. All others are unofficial. The texts of the opinions published in the unofficial reporters are the same as those in the official ones. What differs are the editorial features, such as case summaries, that the publishers add at the beginning of the unofficial reports.

At a minimum a **case citation** to a court opinion will include the names of the parties, the volume and page number of the reporter(s) in which the opinion is published, and the date of the case. Here is a typical citation for a state court case:

Callow v. Thomas, 322 Mass. 550, 78 N.E.2d 637 (1948)

Each part of the citation is explained in Figure 7-3. Starting at the left the parties' last names are listed. Notice that their names are underlined, as is the

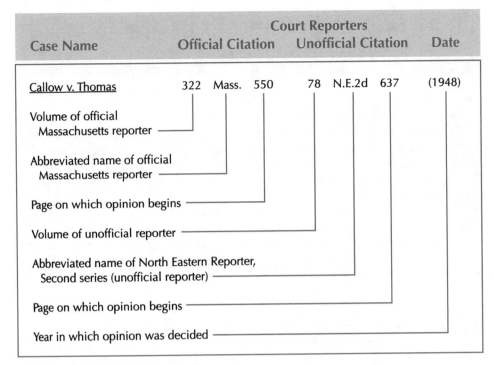

Figure 7-3 Case Citation

small *v.* The *v.* stands for "versus." The party bringing the appeal (the **appellant** or **petitioner**) is usually listed first, and the opposing side (the **appellee** or **respondent**) is listed second. However, some states follow the practice of listing the name of the original plaintiff first, no matter which party brought the appeal.

When there is more than one party on any side of a dispute or when several cases have been consolidated, the citation uses only the names of the first parties listed on each side or the first case listed. When the state is a party to a case in its own courts, it is usually listed as *People v.* or *State v.* On the other hand, if a state is a party to a suit in federal court, the case name would include the state name—for example, *Illinois v. Smith*.

After the parties' names, the reporters where the case can be found are listed. Some state court opinions are published in two reporters, the official state reporter and a West unofficial regional reporter. Some state opinions are only published in the West unofficial reporter.

State reporters use abbreviated versions of the state name—for example, Mass. for Massachusetts and Cal. for California. West regional reporters are abbreviated as follows:

P., P.2d, or P.3d for the Pacific region
N.W. or N.W.2d for the North Western region
S.W., S.W.2d, or S.W.3d for the South Western region
So., So. 2d, or So. 3d for the Southern region
S.E. or S.E.2d for the South Eastern region
N.E. or N.E.2d for the North Eastern region
A. or A.2d for the Atlantic region

Appellant or petitioner
A person who initiates an appeal.

Appellee or respondent
The party in a lawsuit against whom an appeal has been filed.

NETNOTE

The courts are beginning to post their appellate opinions on-line. In fact, you can find U.S. Supreme Court opinions dating back to the 1800s at Findlaw: *www.findlaw.com*. On Findlaw's home page click on "US Law: Cases & Codes" and then click on "US Supreme Court-Opinions & Web Site." However, do not expect to find most other federal and state opinions older than the early 1990s.

To locate appellate court opinions on-line for your circuit, start by going to *www.findlaw.com*. Click on "US Law: Cases & Codes." Next scroll down and select your circuit. To locate court opinions for your state, again begin at Findlaw's home page. Below "US Law: Cases & Codes" click on "States." Select your state.

A map showing these regions is located in Appendix C, Figure C-2.

The number immediately in front of the reporter abbreviation indicates the volume in which the case is found. The number immediately after the reporter abbreviation is the page number on which the case begins. Thus you could find *Callow v. Thomas* either on page 550 of volume 322 of the Massachusetts Reports or on page 637 of volume 78 of the North Eastern Reporter, Second Series.

Following the volume and page numbers of the reporters, the year of the decision appears in parentheses. *Callow v. Thomas* was decided in 1948.

In those cases where the identification of the court is not obvious from the name of the reporter, there will be additional information about the court in parentheses. In the *Callow v. Thomas* citation, you can tell that the Massachusetts Supreme Judicial Court wrote the decision because only Massachusetts Supreme Judicial Court decisions are published in the Massachusetts Reports. However, if the citation had been only to N.E.2d, then the abbreviation for the state would have to be included in the parentheses:

Callow v. Thomas, 78 N.E.2d 637 (Mass. 1948)

For more discussion of when it is correct to include only the regional citation, refer to Appendix C.

Whenever you see a citation to a federal district court or court of appeals case, you will see the name of the district or the circuit in the parentheses:

Chambers v. Maroney, 409 F.2d 1186 (3d Cir. 1969)
Brown v. Merkel, 355 F. Supp. 90 (D. Mass. 1990)

Pinpoint cite
The reference to a particular page within an opinion.

Sometimes a writer will refer to a specific part of the court decision where a particular quote appears or where an issue is discussed. This reference to a particular page within an opinion is sometimes referred to as a **pinpoint cite**. In those instances a second page number will appear after the page number on which the case begins. For example, a quotation taken from page 1189 of the *Chambers v. Maroney* decision would be cited as follows:

Chambers v. Maroney, 409 F.2d 1186, 1189 (3d Cir. 1969)

Finally, citations will sometimes include information about the **subsequent history** of the case. For example:

Telex Corp. v. International Business Machines Corp., 367 F. Supp. 258 (N.D. Okla. 1973), rev'd, 510 F.2d 894 (10th Cir.), cert. denied, 423 U.S. 802 (1975)

This citation indicates that the case was first decided by the U.S. District Court for the Northern District of Oklahoma and can be found on page 258 of volume 367 of the Federal Supplement. The case was then appealed to the Tenth Circuit, where the decision was reversed and reported on page 894 of volume 510 of the Federal Reporter, Second Series. The U.S. Supreme Court's decision not to grant certiorari is reported on page 802 of volume 423 of the United States Reports.

C. THE ELEMENTS OF A COURT OPINION

All court opinions contain some preliminary information, such as the names of the parties, followed by the decision itself. The decision usually contains a statement of the facts on which the case is based; a discussion of the law and how that law, combined with the facts, created legal issues; the court's decision; and an explanation why the decision was reached. If the opinion is one printed by West, there will also be the additional editorial features added by West.

1. Preliminary Material and West Editorial Features

The court opinion in *Callow v. Thomas* is reprinted for you beginning on page 194. It is reprinted exactly as it appears in West's North Eastern Reporter. We have added explanatory material in the right and left margins in order to help you identify the various editorial features that West adds to the opinion.

First, notice that West uses its trademarked key number symbol to separate the cases. Following that are the names of the parties, the name of the court that rendered the decision, and the dates the case was argued and decided. This, in turn, is followed by the **headnotes** and the **syllabus**. The headnotes are short summaries of each of the legal issues decided by the court in this decision as West has identified them. The headnote title and key number (e.g., Husband and Wife, key 205(2)) are cross-references to the West Digest System, which will be explained in Appendix D. The syllabus is a summary of the facts and the court's decision.

Below that is a listing of the judges who decided the case and the attorneys involved in the case. The actual opinion itself begins with the name of the judge who drafted the majority opinion.

2. Facts of the Case

Because court decisions are based on the facts of the case, you must have a thorough knowledge of these facts in order to understand the true meaning

---

Prior case history
Information about what happened procedurally to the cited case before it was heard by the cited court. Do not include this information in a citation.

Subsequent case history
Information about what happened procedurally to the litigation after the case cited. Include this information in a citation.

Headnote
Summary of one legal point in a court opinion; written by the editors at West.

Syllabus
A summary of a court opinion that appears at the beginning of the case.

and impact of a case. Facts can be divided into two groups: substantive and procedural.

Substantive facts
In a case brief, facts that deal with what happened to the parties before the litigation began.

The **substantive facts** deal with what happened to the parties before the litigation began—that is, why one party is suing the other. Under the principle of **standing**, courts cannot decide abstract issues or render advisory opinions. Rather they are limited to deciding cases that involve litigants who are personally affected by their decisions. The facts must therefore establish that a true adversarial relationship exists and that the legal requirement of a "case or controversy" is met.

In approaching a civil case ask yourself the following questions:

Who was the original plaintiff (the person who first brought the matter to court)?
Who was the original defendant?
What was the nature of the injury?
What was the plaintiff asking the trial court to do about it?

In criminal cases your questions should include

Who is the defendant?
What is the nature of the alleged criminal activity?
Did the police use any questionable methods in obtaining the evidence used against the defendant?
Was the trial conducted in accordance with the requirements of the due process clause?

Procedural facts
In a case brief, facts that relate to what happened procedurally in the lower courts or administrative agencies before the case reached the court issuing the opinion.

Procedural facts refer to what happened in the lower courts or administrative agencies as well as the action taken by the appellate court issuing the opinion. For example, in the trial court did the plaintiff win after a jury verdict, or did the plaintiff lose on a motion to dismiss? These procedural facts are sometimes referred to as the **judicial history** of the case.

Look again at the *Callow v. Thomas* case, beginning on page 194, and you will see that Justice Spalding began his opinion with a brief discussion of the substantive facts. The parties were married at the time they were involved in an automobile accident. Several months later the wife sought and received an annulment. The wife then sued her former husband for negligence in causing the accident. At that time the law in Massachusetts was that spouses could not sue each other for negligence. Therefore, this case raised the interesting question of whether or not she could sue her former husband for something that happened before the annulment. The trial court, obviously at a loss as to how it should decide the case, agreed to the parties' request to send the case to the Massachusetts Supreme Judicial Court for a determination. The parties stipulated (agreed on) the amount of damages should the Supreme Judicial Court decide as a matter of law that the defendant could be held liable for his negligence.

In *Callow v. Thomas*, Justice Spalding followed his discussion of the substantive facts with a review of that procedural history. Justice Spalding stated: "The judge at the request of the parties reported the case to this court without decision . . . 'upon the stipulation that if the plaintiff is entitled to recover, judgment shall be entered for the plaintiff in the sum of $3,000, otherwise judgment for the defendant.' "

3. Law Analyzed

A trial court must base its decision on the law as it exists when the litigants arrive in court. The court's statement of the current law may involve a quotation from the relevant statute or a discussion of a series of prior cases. In *Callow v. Thomas* the court stated that the rule that prohibited spouses from suing each other was "too well settled to require citation of authority."

4. Issues Raised

A trial court applies the law to what it determines are the facts of the case. When that case is appealed, the appellate court can either approve or disapprove of the manner in which the trial was conducted and either accept or reject the way in which the lower court interpreted and applied the law. A single appellate case may involve several issues. In *Callow v. Thomas*, immediately following the facts, Justice Spalding gave his view of the issue as follows: "The question for decision is whether a wife after the marriage has been annulled can maintain an action against her former husband for a tort committed during coverture."

5. Decisions Reached

In its decision the court will reach a result not only for these particular litigants but also for future litigants faced with a similar situation. The result reached in this particular case is known as the **disposition**. The result reached not only for these particular litigants but also for future litigants is known as the **holding**.

The disposition usually consists of **affirming** (approving) or **reversing** (disapproving) the judgment of the lower court. If the case is affirmed, the matter is considered settled unless a higher-level appellate court decides to review it. If the lower court's decision is reversed, the appellate court either sends the case back to the lower court for review or substitutes its own judgment for that of the lower court. If the appellate court sends the case back to the lower court, it is with the understanding that the lower court must act consistently with the principles of law the higher court laid down in its decision.

As mentioned above, the new rule of law created by this case that will apply to future litigants is known as the **holding**. The holding is the court's answer to the issue and will be looked to by future courts and litigants for assistance in deciding similar cases. Therefore, the court decision should be analyzed at two different levels: How was the issue settled in this particular case? What general principle of law has been enunciated by the way in which the court resolved this issue?

In *Callow v. Thomas* the court combined its holding with the disposition for these particular litigants:

> The better rule, we think, is that in the case of voidable marriage transactions which have been concluded and things which have been done during the period of the supposed marriage ought not to be undone or reopened after the decree of annulment. Applying that principle here, the plaintiff is not entitled to recover.

Finally, do not confuse reversing a decision with **overruling** a case. An appellate court reverses a decision when it concludes that a lower court failed to properly apply the law. An appellate court overrules a prior appellate court decision when it determines that the law needs to be changed.

Disposition
The result reached in a particular case.

Affirm
A decision is affirmed when the litigants appeal the trial court decision and the higher court agrees with what the lower court has done.

Reverse
A decision is reversed when the litigants appeal the trial court decision and the higher court disagrees with the decision of a lower court.

Holding
The new legal principle established by a court opinion.

6. The Reasoning

Most written court opinions devote considerable space to justifying the court's decision. In the reasoning section of an opinion the court reviews the relevant provisions of the constitutions, statutes, and case law and then specifies the logical reasoning process used to arrive at the court's judgment.

Dictum
A statement in a judicial opinion not necessary for the decision of the case.

In reviewing the reasoning section it is important to distinguish between the **ratio decidendi** and the **obiter dictum**. The ratio decidendi is a decision on the legal issues raised in that specific case, whereas obiter dictum refers to a comment the judge makes that is not necessary to the resolution of the issues of the case and that is in effect a discussion of a hypothetical situation. For example, it is dictum when a judge talks about what might have been if the facts had been different from the ones presented. Even though courts have power to decide only the precise case with which they are faced, human nature being what it is, judges often cannot resist discussing issues that were not really presented to them. While that part of the opinion will have no effect on the litigants, it could give you a very good clue as to how the court might decide a different case in the future.

7. Concurring and Dissenting Opinions

Concurring opinion
An opinion that agrees with the majority's result but disagrees with the reasoning.

Following the court's opinion, there may also be one or more **concurring** or **dissenting opinions**. Judges write concurring opinions when they agree with the disposition of the case but disagree with respect to the reasoning. Judges write dissenting opinions when they disagree with the holding.

Dissenting opinion
An opinion that disagrees with the majority's decision and reasoning.

D. CASE BRIEFING

The word *brief* has several meanings. In this chapter we use the term *briefing a case* to mean using your own words to make a brief written summary of a court opinion. This is to be contrasted with an **appellate brief**, which is a formal written argument to an appellate court, in which a lawyer argues why that court should affirm or reverse a lower court's decision.

1. An Overview of Case Briefing

Briefing court opinions serves two purposes. First, and most important, it makes you read the case thoroughly. You have to go back and dig out the essentials, organize them, and state them in your own words. This is necessary for an adequate understanding of the court opinion. Second, it gives you a permanent condensed record of each case. You can use your case briefs later to refresh your memory about the cases without having to go back and reread whole opinions.

Be warned: There are almost as many different briefing styles as there are attorneys writing briefs. Everyone develops his or her own favorite method for summarizing a court opinion. Therefore, if you are not writing a brief just for yourself, you should always ask the person for whom you are writing the brief about his or her preferred method. Also keep in mind the purpose for which you are writing the brief. For this course the principal reason is so that you can learn to analyze and criticize court opinions. Therefore, we will ask you to follow a very structured method, designed to teach you that process. Later when you are working, your boss may have a very different purpose for asking you to brief cases. For example, your boss may want a factual comparison among a series of cases and so ask you to summarize (brief) only the facts of each case. The bottom line: Follow a briefing style that accomplishes your purpose.

2. Format for a Case Brief

The case briefing method we will be using in this chapter breaks the case down into the following elements: (1) case citation, (2) facts—both procedural and substantive, (3) rule, (4) issue, (5) holding, (6) reasoning, and (7) criticism. After you read the opinion once, put the case citation at the top of your paper, and list the next six items on the left side of the paper, leaving enough room opposite each for the appropriate information. Reread the opinion and fill in the various items.

Although you list the items in a specific order, you may find yourself filling them in out of order. That is fine. Case briefing is a circuitous process. You will often rewrite one part of your brief as your understanding of that part changes based on your work on other parts. As with any type of writing, thinking and writing are intertwined.

To illustrate how a case brief is done, we will start by using a simplified fictional case of Jim Jones and Sam Smith.

Jim Jones v. Sam Smith
440 Mass. App. Ct. 99, 548 N.E.2d 50
Decided June 4, 1990

The defendant appeals from a judgment for the plaintiff in the amount of $30,000. The plaintiff, Jim Jones, who is blind, was walking on the sidewalk in front of his house, located on Lily Street. He had just returned from classes he was taking at the local community college. A group of youths approached him. One of the youths, 16-year-old Sam Smith, said, "Hey, man, what a cool cane." He then knocked Jim's cane from his hand. In knocking the cane from his hand, the defendant never touched the plaintiff's body. Jim began to search for his cane. While searching, Jim fell over the curb and broke his ankle. We hereby affirm the trial court's decision.

We have long held that an intentional, offensive contact to a person's body constitutes battery. Here the 16-year-old defendant intended to knock the cane from the plaintiff's hand. While the defendant did not actually touch the plaintiff's body, the plaintiff was holding the cane at the time it was knocked away from him. Because the plaintiff was able to go about on his own only with the use of the cane, it was as though the cane were a part of his body. The cane was so closely connected to his person that touching it was tantamount to touching the plaintiff himself. We also note the increased awareness that the legislature has exhibited in recent years for the needs of the disabled.

Affirmed.

---

a. Case Citation

At the top of a sheet of paper write the **case citation**. If this is a case that you are reading for class, you may also want to indicate its page number in your textbook. As we discussed earlier, the citation contains enough information to let the reader know (1) the name of the case, (2) the court that decided it, (3) where the reader can locate it, and (4) the year of decision. For example, this case was between Jim Jones and Sam Smith. The Massachusetts Appeals Court decided the case in 1990. If this were a real case (and not a fictional case we created to illustrate case briefing), you would be able to find it on page 99 of volume 440 of the Massachusetts Appeals Court Reports. You could also find it on page 50 of volume 548 of the North Eastern Reporter, Second Series. Therefore, you cite this case in the following manner.

Jones v. Smith, 440 Mass. App. Ct. 99, 548 N.E.2d 50 (1990).

Notice that there is more information supplied with the case, such as the parties' first names, than you actually need to provide for a complete citation. Also notice that in the citation, but not in the case, there is a comma after the case name.

b. Facts

Include a summary of both kinds of facts: substantive and procedural. Recall that the **substantive facts** deal with what happened to the parties before the litigation began; that is, why are they suing each other? These are the facts that caused the lawsuit. Be sure to state the relevant facts in your own words rather than copying them directly from the opinion. Omit any facts that you think did not form the basis of the court's decision, but be sure to include all facts that the court relied on in reaching its decision.

When giving the facts, it is always best to be as precise as possible. For example, if the case involves an eight-year-old girl, say so. Do not say that it involves simply a girl or a child. If you give specific details, you can always generalize later. If you start with a generalization, such as that the plaintiff was a child, later you may have difficulties remembering the specifics.

For the **procedural facts** be sure to include what happened in the lower court or courts. For example, in the trial court did the plaintiff or the defendant win? Did the lower court proceedings conclude after a motion or a jury verdict? You should conclude the procedural facts with a statement as to how this court responded by way of disposition; that is, did it reverse, reverse and remand, or affirm the lower court's decision? You will usually find the court's disposition near the end of the opinion, stated in a few words, such as reversed or vacated and remanded. Some legal writers prefer to put the court's disposition in a separate section rather than including it with the other procedural facts. If you include the disposition with the procedural facts, however, then the reader can see the "whole story" right at the beginning of the brief. Study the following example of a facts section.

Facts: The plaintiff, Jim Jones, is blind. A group of youths approached him. One of the youths, sixteen-year-old Sam Smith, knocked Jim's cane from his hand. In knocking the cane from the plaintiff's hand the defendant never touched the plaintiff's body. In searching for his cane, Jim fell, breaking his ankle. Judgment for plaintiff; affirmed.

First are the substantive facts: who did what to whom. Notice how specific facts that could have changed the outcome of the case are included: Jim is blind. Sam is sixteen years old. However, facts that would not influence the outcome, such as the name of the street down which Jim was walking, are not included. The last sentence gives the procedural facts. "Judgment for plaintiff" means the plaintiff won at the trial court level. "Affirmed" means this court, the court that issued the opinion you are reading, agreed with that result. The amount of the trial court award is not included because it was not an issue in this case. If the parties were disagreeing about the amount of the award, as opposed to whether there should have been an award at all, then it would be appropriate to include it.

c. Rule

The **rule** is a general legal principle in existence *before* the case began. The court might base it either on prior court decisions or on a statute.

First, explicitly state the area of law, such as burglary. Then give a precise definition of the law in that area: For example, burglary occurs when there is a breaking and entering of the dwelling of another at nighttime with the intention of committing a felony therein. You do not always need to give the complete definition of a rule. For example, if the only issue in the case is whether breaking into a house at 5 P.M. qualifies as nighttime, you would state only the relevant part of the rule: Burglary occurs when there is a breaking and entering at nighttime.

Our sample brief would contain the following statement of the rule.

Rule
In a case brief, the general legal principle in existence before the case began.

> Rule: A battery occurs when there is an intentional, offensive contact to a person's body.

Notice how the general area of law, battery, is given first. We will call that the *label*. The label is followed by a definition of what constitutes battery.

d. Issue

Phrase this as a "whether" question. The **issue** has two components: first, the rule of law that the court used to resolve the current dispute (section c above) and, second, the specific facts of the case to which the rule of law is being applied (section b above). This is the hardest part of briefing a case. In one sentence you want to let your reader know exactly why the parties are in court. Include facts that make it clear why the issue is an issue; that is, let the reader see what the fight is all about. Modeling your issue after the following formula will assist you in making sure that you have included both the rule and the specific facts in your issue statement.

Issue
In a case brief, the rule of law applied to the case's specific facts.

Whether the defendant is [guilty of or liable for]
   (name the general area of law involved—e.g., battery or murder),
which requires that
   (give the specific part of the rule at issue—e.g., intended contact or willful intent)
when
   (give the specific facts—e.g., the defendant accidentally bumped into the plaintiff).

Keep in mind that this is just a model. There are times when you will need to vary the pattern. Learning to state the issue precisely is a skill you will be working on throughout your legal career; therefore, do not feel discouraged if it seems difficult now.

If a court opinion deals with more than one issue, brief each issue separately.

> Issue: Whether the defendant is liable for battery, which requires that there be an intentional, offensive contact to a person's body, when the sixteen-year-old defendant did not touch the blind plaintiff but did knock his cane from his hand.

Notice how the issue contains both the rule and the specific facts involved in the case. Given the rule of law in existence prior to these parties going to court and given the specific facts of the case, what problem must the court resolve? That is the issue.

Never state your issue as follows: whether or not the trial court erred. Although technically that would be correct, it is not very helpful, as it would be true of all cases; that is, no one would have appealed unless there was an allegation that the court made an error. Remember to include the specific rule of law and the facts involved so that your reader, hearing only your statement of the issue, will know exactly why the litigants were in court.

Finally, be sure to state the issue in an unbiased manner. Do not slant the issue by giving conclusions. Stick to the facts. For example, the following issue is too biased.

> **Example of a biased statement of the issue:**
> Whether the defendant was negligent, which requires failing to act as a reasonable person, when he got drunk, sped down the highway, and crashed into the plaintiff's car.

To keep it unbiased, you must state the facts underlying your conclusions. And you must include facts that show both sides of the issue.

> **Example of an unbiased statement of the issue:**
> Whether the defendant was negligent, which requires failing to act as a reasonable person, when he drank one beer, drove 55 mph in a 50-mph zone, and hit the plaintiff's car as he ran a red light.

Holding
In a case brief, the court's answer to the issue presented to it; the new legal principle established by a court opinion.

e. Holding

The **holding** is the court's answer to the issue. The holding is the new version of the rule, a rule that future courts will look to for assistance in deciding similar cases.

If you have given a complete issue statement, technically the holding could be a simple yes or no answer. However, it is always best to give the holding as a complete sentence. Therefore, include the same elements as you did for the issue statement except state them as a positive sentence. That is, make sure the holding contains both the rule of law the court was relying on to resolve the dispute and the specific facts of the case.

One of the most difficult aspects of developing the holding is determining how narrow or broad it should be. A **narrow holding** contains many of the case's specific facts, thereby limiting its future applicability to a narrow range of cases. A **broad holding** states the facts in very general terms so that the holding will apply to a wider range of cases. See Figure 7-4.

To be useful, a holding should be broad enough to help courts resolve similar cases. But a holding should not be so broad that it stands for no more than a general legal principle. Learning how to state a holding either very narrowly, by including very specific facts, or very broadly, by stating the facts as generalizations only, is a skill you will acquire over time. For now, state your holdings narrowly. As with the facts portion of the brief you will find it easier to amend a narrow holding to make it broader than you will to amend a broad holding to make it narrower. However, even with a narrow holding, include only those facts that you think truly affected the court's decision.

Narrow holding
A statement of the court's decision that contains many of the case's specific facts, thereby limiting its future applicability to a narrow range of cases.

Broad holding
A statement of the court's decision in which the facts are either omitted or given in very general terms so that it will apply to a wider range of cases.

Holding: Yes, the defendant should be liable for battery, which requires that there be an intentional, offensive contact to a person's body, when the sixteen-year-old defendant did not touch the blind plaintiff but did knock his cane from his hand. (Narrow)

Yes, the defendant should be liable for battery, which requires that there be an intentional, offensive contact to a person's body, when something closely connected to the plaintiff's body was touched. (Broad)

A battery occurs whenever a person's sense of bodily integrity is threatened. (Probably too broad; really a policy statement)

Also be sure to include any possible limitations to the holding. If the court specifically states that its decision covers only a certain set of circumstances, let

Figure 7-4   Possible Holdings for a Case

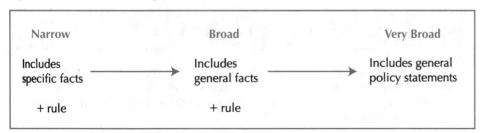

your reader know that. For example, in a case dealing with a social host's liability for serving alcohol to a minor, a court might relieve the social host of any responsibility but limit its holding to situations where alcohol is not being served for a profit.

Finally, note that the court's procedural answer—reversed, remanded, affirmed, and so on—can never be the holding. The holding is always a statement of the new rule that results from the court's decision.

f. Reasoning

This is an explanation of *why* the court ruled as it did, stated in your own words. The court's reasoning gives you your best clue as to how the court may act in the future in a different but similar situation.

Pinpoint as far as is possible the explicit and implicit reasons that the court gave to justify its holding. But do not quote the court's exact language unless the precise phrasing is critical. It will be easier for the reader to understand your summary if it is primarily in your own words.

In this section you may want to note reasoning that is really dictum. As we mentioned earlier, **dictum** (the plural is *dicta*) is language unnecessary to the decision of the case. For example, if the court talks about how it might decide a future case based on different facts, that is dictum. Courts have power to decide only the precise case with which they are faced. By definition the court's dicta are not relevant to the case's litigants, but they do give you an idea of how the court might be predisposed to rule in a future case. Therefore, dicta are often worth noting in your brief.

> Reasoning: While the defendant did not touch the plaintiff's body, the cane was so closely connected to his person that touching it was tantamount to touching the plaintiff himself. (In dicta the court noted the increased awareness in recent years of the needs of persons with disabilities.)

g. Criticism

Take a few minutes to think critically about the case. Do you agree with the result? Even if you agree with the result, do you think the court gave the best or only reasons for reaching that result? If the court included a limitation in the holding, what problems do you think that will cause for future litigants?

PRACTICAL TIP

When briefing cases, once you have entered the important facts and the rule, you have essentially written the issue and the holding. Just copy the important facts and the rule from the prior sections, and insert the appropriate connective phrases.

If there were **concurring** or **dissenting opinions**, include a discussion of their reasoning. Remember that a concurring decision is one in which the judge agrees with the majority's result but not with the reasoning. A dissenting opinion is one in which the judge disagrees with both the majority's result and its reasoning. While only the majority opinion represents the court's view, what individual concurring and dissenting judges have to say can influence later courts.

The reason for including a criticism section is to accustom you to thinking critically about court decisions. There will be times when an opinion will harm your client's case and you will need to argue either that the decision was incorrectly decided or that the reasoning does not apply to your client's case. Practice in thinking critically about court decisions now will prepare you to assist your clients later.

Criticism:	The court left open the question of what constitutes an object so closely connected to a person's body as to be considered a part of it. Because the case involved a blind person, it is unclear whether the court meant to limit future cases to objects used by persons with disabilities, such as canes, hearing aids, and the like, or whether the court meant to include anything closely connected to a person's body, such as clothing.

Do not be discouraged if you find the criticism section one of the most difficult parts of the brief to write. It is the court's job to convince you that it has reached the right result for the right reasons. Therefore, your first reaction may be to simply agree with everything it says. Resist that inclination. Remember that the case would not have been appealed unless someone thought there were two sides to the issue.

Once put together, the entire brief should look similar to the sample brief in Exhibit 7-1. You can find a summary of case briefing in Exhibit 7-2.

3. Six Hints for Better Brief Writing

Here are six hints to help you with your brief writing.

a. Read the Case First, Then Brief

Do not try to brief the case as you read it for the first time. Read it through, underlining if you wish and making notes in the margin, before you start your brief. When you are reading more than one case on a particular topic, it may save time to first read all of the cases and then begin briefing.

b. Develop a Workable Style

Develop a briefing style that works best for you. As mentioned above, there is no right or wrong method. However, if your brief is to serve its intended purpose, you must write it in such a way that you can return to it later and easily find the information for which you are looking.

> **PRACTICAL TIP**
>
> Do not overlook the power of a dissent. It may help you predict the path the court may take in the next case.

Jones v. Smith, 440 Mass. App. Ct. 99, 548 N.E.2d 50 (1990).

Facts: The plaintiff, Jim Jones, is blind. A group of youths approached him. One of the youths, sixteen-year-old Sam Smith, knocked Jim's cane from his hand. In knocking the cane from the plaintiff's hand the defendant never touched the plaintiff's body. In searching for his cane, Jim fell, breaking his ankle. Judgment for plaintiff; affirmed.

Rule: A battery occurs when there is an intentional, offensive contact to a person's body.

Issue: Whether the defendant is liable for battery, which requires that there be an intentional, offensive contact to a person's body, when the sixteen-year-old defendant did not touch the blind plaintiff but did knock his cane from his hand.

Holding: Yes, the defendant should be liable for battery, which requires that there be an intentional, offensive contact to a person's body, when the sixteen-year-old defendant did not touch the blind plaintiff but did knock his cane from his hand.

Reasoning: While the defendant did not touch the plaintiff's body, the cane was so closely connected to his person that touching it was tantamount to touching the plaintiff himself. (In dicta the court noted the increased awareness in recent years of the needs of persons with disabilities.)

Criticism: The court left open the question of what constitutes an object so closely connected to a person's body as to be considered a part of it. Because the case involved a blind person, it is unclear whether the court meant to limit future cases to objects used by persons with disabilities, such as canes, hearing aids, and the like, or whether the court meant to include anything closely connected to a person's body, such as clothing.

Exhibit 7-1 Sample Brief

Exhibit 7-2 Summary of Case Briefing

Citation goes here

Facts: Provide both the substantive and the procedural facts, including what this court decided.

Rule: This is the rule *before* this case was decided. Include both the label and the definition.

Issue: This is the rule applied to the facts. You may want to use the following format:

Whether the defendant is [guilty of or liable for]
   (name the general area of law involved—for example, battery or murder),
which requires that
   (give the specific part of the rule that is creating the problem)
when
   (give the specific facts; this is not the place for generalizations).

Holding: In a complete sentence give the court's answer to the issue. If the court puts any limits on its holding, include those limitations.

Reasoning: Include all the major reasons the court gives in support of its decision.

Criticism: Explain what you think is wrong with either the court's holding or its reasoning. If there is a concurrence or dissent, include that reasoning here as well.

c. Write Based on the Needs of Your Reader

If you will be using the brief just as a reference for yourself, abbreviate commonly used terms. For example, use π or P. for plaintiff and Δ or D. for defendant. You may also want to write in phrases rather than complete sentences. However, if you are writing the brief for another person, whether it is your instructor now or your boss later on, make sure to ask whether that person wants you to use abbreviations and phrases or prefers that you use complete words and sentences.

d. Cross-reference

Develop a cross-reference system that will allow you to find the court's full discussion of the points you summarized in your brief. For example, you could place numbers in the margin of the case to correspond to the points you discuss in your brief.

e. Paraphrase

Write the brief in your own words. A brief should not be a long series of quotations, so do not copy large parts of the opinion. A brief is your summary of the case, not merely a listing of quotations from it.

f. Use a Dictionary

Make sure you understand every unfamiliar legal term. Initially, you will find the courts using many unfamiliar terms. Do not hesitate to turn to a legal dictionary for help.

4. A Sample Case Brief

Before we tackle a real court opinion, we would like to give you some practice in case briefing. Below you will find a hypothetical court opinion based on the case of *People v. Blair*.[4]

Read *People v. Blair*, and then try your hand at briefing it. We have included a sample brief in Exhibit 7-3. It will be tempting to turn to the sample brief before trying it yourself, but resist the temptation. Now is the time to experiment with briefing. Write the case citation at the top of a sheet of paper. Then write each of the six parts of a standard brief in the left-hand margin. Fill in each part of the case brief as best you can. Finally, when you can no longer stand it, turn to the sample brief. Remember that the sample brief is only a sample. Your approach may be different and yet be just as valid.

Remember that everyone has his or her own style for briefing, and the court may not follow the definitions we have given you for the different elements of the brief. A court may not even include every element of a case brief in its decision. Also, courts do not always explicitly label the parts of their opinion that contain the issue, holding, reasoning, and so on. Nor do they tell you which of the facts or reasons they give are the most important. Therefore, while the language of the court often provides helpful clues, do not be surprised if you do not always find every part of the brief in every case. Also do

---

[4]288 N.E.2d 443 (Ill. 1972).

People v. Blair
52 Ill. 2d 371, 288 N.E.2d 443 (1972)

UNDERWOOD, Chief Justice.

In February 1969, defendant Gary Blair was convicted in superior court of burglary for actions that took place in a carwash. He was sentenced to imprisonment for two to four years. The defendant appealed his conviction, and the intermediate appellate court vacated the judgment of conviction, finding that the carwash structure here involved was not a building as that word is used in the burglary statute. We granted leave to appeal. The statute in part provides:

> A person commits burglary when without authority he knowingly breaks into and enters a building or house trailer with intent to commit a felony or theft therein.

The carwash in question consists of wash bays or stalls completely open at each end (there are no doors), a roof, concrete side walls and floor; attached to the side walls are the washing apparatus and a coin box. The defendant allegedly drove into one of the stalls, washed his car, and then forced open the coin box, took the coins, and fled.

The burglary statute contains no definition of the word "building," and, in the absence of a statutory definition indicating a different legislative intention, the courts will assume that statutory words have their ordinary and popularly understood meanings. In the past, this court has defined a building to be any structure designed for the habitation of men or animals or for the shelter of property. The carwash comes within this definition. It is a structure designed for the shelter and protection of the carwash equipment and the fact that it is not completely enclosed does not necessitate a contrary conclusion.

The judgment of the appellate court is reversed, and the trial court's judgment of conviction for burglary is affirmed.

not be surprised if the court appears to be "mislabeling" various parts of the case. For example, in *People v. Blair* assume the court had stated:

> The legislature did not see fit to include a definition of "building" within the statute. Over the years, this court has had to decide whether other structures such as barns and garages were meant to fit the statutory meaning of a "building." Likewise, in this case there is no need for us to wait until the legislature decides to act and amend the statute so as to include a definition that might or might not encompass carwashes. We hold that we have the power to include a partially enclosed carwash within the definition of "building."

It would not be correct to give the last sentence in the holding section of your brief. We have defined a holding as the current rule applied to the case's specific facts. This statement by the court therefore is not a holding but rather is reasoning. That is, the reason the court thinks it can hold that a carwash comes within the definition of a "building" is that the court has the power to do so. Words can have more than one meaning, and this is just one example of how the courts may use words differently from the way we have been using them.

5. Briefing Cases Involving Statutes

Now that you have experience with the purpose of case briefing, it is time to try your hand with real court opinions. In this section we will look at two court opinions that illustrate the first two types of cases that courts face: interpreting statutes and ruling on their constitutionality.

<u>People v. Blair</u>
52 Ill. 2d 371, 288 N.E.2d 443 (1972)

Facts: Inside a carwash the defendant forced open a coin box and took the coins. The carwash had concrete walls and floor but was completely open at each end and covered the washing apparatus and a coin box. Convicted; vacated; reversed, affirming trial court's judgment.

Rule: "A person commits burglary when without authority he knowingly breaks into and enters a building or house trailer with intent to commit a felony or theft therein."

Issue: Whether the defendant committed burglary, which requires entering a building or house trailer, when he entered a partially enclosed carwash.

Holding: Yes, burglary, which requires the entering of a building or house trailer, is committed when someone enters a partially enclosed carwash.

Reasoning: The statute did not contain a definition for "building." Therefore, the court followed the ordinary meaning of the word and looked to past decisions, where a building was defined as a structure meant to protect people or property. Here the carwash protected property and so should be considered a building.

Criticism: In the statute the word "building" is coupled with the words "house trailer." This suggests that the legislature intended to limit the statute to dwellings. Also, the carwash was not entirely enclosed. Therefore, although the defendant definitely "entered" the carwash, it is difficult to see how he could have been charged with "breaking" into the carwash.

Exhibit 7-3 Sample Brief

a. Interpreting a Statute

Recall the situation from a legal reasoning question in Chapter 6 in which you were asked to apply a federal statute to a situation where a client had been charged with illegally transporting an airplane across state lines. This was the very situation that the Supreme Court had to face in the following case, *McBoyle v. United States*. We have reprinted the *McBoyle* opinion exactly as it appears in the official United States Reports in Exhibit 7-4. The U.S. government pays for the printing and publishing of all U.S. Supreme Court decisions in a series of books called the United States Reports. The opinions are printed and published in chronological order as they are decided. In the margins we have added labels to describe the different parts of a typical court opinion.

Read and then brief *McBoyle v. United States*, paying special attention to the methods of statutory analysis that the Court relied on in reaching its decision. There is a sample brief following the opinion (see Exhibit 7-5). However, as you did with *People v. Blair*, wait to look at the sample until after you have briefed the opinion yourself. That way you will have a better idea as to whether you are on the right track with your case briefing. Also, as with the *People v. Blair* sample brief, the sample brief for *McBoyle* is just that, a sample. Do not worry if yours does not match the sample exactly. However, if yours is significantly different, reread the prior section on the functions of each part of the brief.

Now that you have read *McBoyle v. United States*, take a close look at how the procedural facts are given in the sample brief shown in Exhibit 7-5. Ask your instructor about his or her preferred method for including the procedural facts.

The case name; McBoyle was the petitioner and the U.S. government was the respondent.

McBOYLE *v.* UNITED STATES.   25

Page in volume 283 of the United States Report where the case begins.

15   Opinion of the Court.

U. S. 192; *Jacob Ruppert* v. *Caffey,* 251 U. S. 264; *Lambert* v. *Yellowley,* 272 U. S. 581.   *Affirmed.*

End of a different decision.

McBOYLE *v.* UNITED STATES.

This lets you know the court is hearing a case from the Tenth Circuit.

CERTIORARI TO THE CIRCUIT COURT OF APPEALS FOR THE TENTH CIRCUIT.

Docket number and dates the case was argued and decided.

No. 552.   Argued February 26, 27, 1931.—Decided March 9, 1931.

The National Motor Vehicle Theft Act, U. S. C., Title 18, § 408, which punishes whoever transports, or causes to be transported, in interstate or foreign commerce a motor vehicle knowing it to have been stolen, and which defines "motor vehicle" as including "an automobile, automobile truck, automobile wagon, motor cycle, or any other self-propelled vehicle not designed for running on rails," does not apply to aircraft.   P. 26.

43 F. (2d) 273, reversed.

Known as the syllabus, this is a summary of the court's opinion.

Where it is reported that cert, was granted.*

CERTIORARI, 282 U. S. 835, to review a judgment affirming a conviction under the Motor Vehicle Theft Act.

Mr. Harry F. Brown for petitioner.

Petitioner's attorney.

Mr. Claude R. Branch, Special Assistant to the Attorney General, with whom *Solicitor General Thacher, Assistant Attorney General Dodds* and *Messrs. Harry S. Ridgely* and *W. Marvin Smith* were on the brief, for the United States.

Responder's attorneys.

MR. JUSTICE HOLMES delivered the opinion of the Court.

This is where the opinion begins.

This is where the Tenth Circuit court's decision is reported.

The petitioner was convicted of transporting from Ottawa, Illinois, to Guymon, Oklahoma, an airplane that he knew to have been stolen, and was sentenced to serve three years' imprisonment and to pay a fine of $2,000.   The judgment was affirmed by the Circuit Court of Appeals for the Tenth Circuit.   43 F. (2d) 273.   A writ of certiorari was granted by this Court on the question whether the National Motor Vehicle Theft Act applies to aircraft.

*This one sentence contains a lot of information. Combined with what you already know about the structure of the federal court system, it gives you the complete procedural history of the case. Start at the end of the sentence and work your way forward. First, we read that McBoyle was convicted. As he was tried in the federal system, his trial and conviction would have occurred in a federal district court. Next the conviction was affirmed. This would have occurred in a court of appeals. In fact, right under the case name we see that the Tenth Circuit court of appeals decided this case. Finally, the U.S. Supreme Court agreed to hear the case by granting certiorari.

Exhibit 7-4   *McBoyle v. United States*   *(continues)*

26   OCTOBER TERM, 1930.

Opinion of the Court.   283 U.S.

Act of October 29, 1919, c. 89; 41 Stat. 324; U. S. Code, Title 18, § 408. That Act provides: "Sec. 2. That when used in this Act: (a) The term 'motor vehicle' shall include an automobile, automobile truck, automobile wagon, motor cycle, or any other self-propelled vehicle not designed for running on rails; . . . Sec. 3. That whoever shall transport or cause to be transported in interstate or foreign commerce a motor vehicle, knowing the same to have been stolen, shall be punished by a fine of not more than $5,000, or by imprisonment of not more than five years, or both."

Section 2 defines the motor vehicles of which the transportation in interstate commerce is punished in § 3. The question is the meaning of the word 'vehicle' in the phrase "any other self-propelled vehicle not designed for running on rails." No doubt etymologically it is possible to use the word to signify a conveyance working on land, water or air, and sometimes legislation extends the use in that direction, e. g., land and air, water being separately provided for, in the Tariff Act, September 22, 1922, c. 356, § 401 (b), 42 Stat. 858, 948. But in everyday speech 'vehicle' calls up the picture of a thing moving on land. Thus in Rev. Stats. § 4, intended, the Government suggests, rather to enlarge than to restrict the definition, vehicle includes every contrivance capable of being used "as a means of transportation on land." And this is repeated, expressly excluding aircraft, in the Tariff Act, June 17, 1930, c. 997, § 401 (b); 46 Stat. 590, 708. So here, the phrase under discussion calls up the popular picture. For after including automobile truck, automobile wagon and motor cycle, the words "any other self-propelled vehicle not designed for running on rails" still indicate that a vehicle in the popular sense, that is a vehicle running on land, is the theme. It is a vehicle that runs, not something, not commonly called a vehicle, that flies. Airplanes were well known in 1919, when this statute was passed; but it is admitted that they were not mentioned in the reports or in the debates in Congress.

Exhibit 7-4 *McBoyle v. United States (continued)*   *(continues)*

CARBICE CORP. *v.* AM. PATENTS CORP.   27

It is impossible to read words that so carefully enumerate the different forms of motor vehicles and have no reference of any kind to aircraft, as including airplanes under a term that usage more and more precisely confines to a different class. The counsel for the petitioner have shown that the phraseology of the statute as to motor vehicles follows that of earlier statutes of Connecticut, Delaware, Ohio, Michigan and Missouri, not to mention the late Regulations of Traffic for the District of Columbia, Title 6, c. 9, § 242, none of which can be supposed to leave the earth.

Although it is not likely that a criminal will carefully consider the text of the law before he murders or steals, it is reasonable that a fair warning should be given to the world in language that the common world will understand, of what the law intends to do if a certain line is passed. To make the warning fair, so far as possible the line should be clear. When a rule of conduct is laid down in words that evoke in the common mind only the picture of vehicles moving on land, the statute should not be extended to aircraft, simply because it may seem to us that a similar policy applies, or upon the speculation that, if the legislature had thought of it, very likely broader words would have been used. *United States* v. *Thind*, 261 U. S. 204, 209.

Judgment reversed.

The court's decision

CARBICE CORPORATION OF AMERICA *v.* AMERICAN PATENTS DEVELOPMENT CORPORATION ET AL.

The beginning of the next case

CERTIORARI TO THE CIRCUIT COURT OF APPEALS FOR THE SECOND CIRCUIT.

No. 54. Argued January 16, 19, 1931.—Decided March 9, 1931.

1. A patentee can not lawfully exact, as the condition of a license, that unpatented materials used in connection with the invention shall be purchased only from himself. P. 31.

Exhibit 7-4   *McBoyle v. United States (concluded)*

What is given here is a shorthand way of saying that the defendant was convicted. His conviction was affirmed by the U.S. Court of Appeals for the Tenth Circuit. The Supreme Court granted certiorari and then reversed the decision of the court of appeals. For someone versed in the structure of the court system, the method used in the sample brief is quick and to the point. However, when you first start briefing, you may feel more comfortable avoiding abbreviations and writing out each of the procedural steps.

Also notice that the entire procedural story is given, including the final resolution by the U.S. Supreme Court—that is, that it reversed the lower appellate court.

Exhibit 7-5   Sample Brief

<u>McBoyle v. United States</u>, 283 U.S. 25 (1931)

Facts: The defendant transported across state lines an airplane that he knew was stolen. He was convicted; aff'd; cert. granted; rev'd.

Rule: National Motor Vehicle Theft Act, Section 3
              Whoever transports in interstate commerce a motor vehicle, knowing it to be stolen, shall be punished.

              Section 2
              A motor vehicle shall include "any other self-propelled vehicle not designed for running on rails."

Issue: Whether the defendant violated the National Motor Vehicle Theft Act, which requires that the defendant transport across state lines a stolen motor vehicle, defined as "any other self-propelled vehicle not designed for running on rails," when he transported a stolen plane across state lines.

Holding: No, the defendant did not violate the National Motor Vehicle Theft Act, which requires that the defendant transport across state lines a stolen motor vehicle, defined as "any other self-propelled vehicle not designed for running on rails," when he flew a stolen plane across state lines.

Reasoning: The Court based its decision on what it saw as the plain meaning of the statute. In support of this view the Court also looked to other statutes and to other portions of this statute. The legislative history also favored this interpretation, as airplanes were in existence when the statute was enacted and yet no mention was made of them. Also, because this is a criminal statute, the Court said that it should be construed narrowly so as to give any potential defendant fair warning of what was not allowed. Finally, the Court showed great deference to the legislature. The Court stated that it would not extend the statute simply because it might seem to the justices that "a similar policy applies, or upon the speculation that, if the legislature had thought of it, very likely broader words would have been used" (p. 27).

Criticism: The plain meaning approach could also be used to argue that the statute uses the word "including" but does not say "excluding." Therefore, presumably it would cover other "self-propelled vehicles," such as airplanes. Also, it does not stand to reason that the defendant would not have suspected that it was a crime to transport a stolen airplane across state lines.

In the reasoning section, notice the use of the verbs *saw, said,* and *stated.* Never use language that suggests that the court was emotional about the case. For example, do not say the court "felt" something was so. Say the court *thought, explained, discussed,* and the like.

DISCUSSION QUESTIONS

1. Do you agree with the Court's reasoning and holding in *McBoyle?* Why?
2. Did you notice the similarities between the Court's approach to analyzing a statute and those discussed in Chapter 6? List the methods of statutory interpretation that the *McBoyle* Court used.
3. Why would each of the following not be a correct issue for *McBoyle?*
   a. whether the defendant knew the airplane was stolen
   b. whether the defendant stole the airplane
   c. whether the defendant was guilty
   d. whether the trial court erred

The role of the courts in interpreting ambiguous language is to strive to find the meaning that the legislature intended. In this they are engaged in something of a guessing game, and if they guess wrong, the legislature has the power to amend the statute. For example, sometime after the Supreme Court decided *McBoyle* the legislature amended the statute to include airplanes within the definition of motor vehicles.

b. Ruling on a Statute's Constitutionality

As you will recall from Chapter 4, most cases decided by state courts cannot be appealed to the U.S. Supreme Court. The major exception is if a federal law is involved. In the following case, because the constitutionality of the state statute was in doubt, the U.S. Supreme Court had jurisdiction to hear it.

As you read the U.S. Supreme Court's decision in *Texas v. Johnson,* decide whether you agree with the majority, the concurrence, or the dissent. Recall that the majority opinion represents the final decision of a court and is binding. In a concurrence the judge agrees with the result but not with the reasoning or simply wants to add his or her own thoughts. The judge who writes the dissent disagrees with the majority opinion, but the dissent is not binding and does not represent the law in that jurisdiction.

Because a dissent has no effect in the present case, you might wonder why judges bother writing dissents. There are at least three reasons to do so.[5] First, it keeps the majority honest. Because a dissent is being written, the majority knows that what they write can be contradicted. Second, a dissent limits the precedential effect of the opinion. An opinion with a strong dissent does not carry the same weight with future courts as does a unanimous opinion. Finally, there is always the hope that someday a later court will see the wisdom of the dissent and decide to follow that path. Although that hope is not always realized, it can be the motivating force behind continued dissents on such issues as capital punishment. One Supreme Court justice dissented in every capital punishment case,

---

[5]For a fascinating discussion of this topic view the PBS series This Honorable Court.

arguing that it always represented cruel and unusual punishment. To date, the Court has not accepted that argument.

We have omitted the footnotes and most of the citations to the cases the Court cites. Also we have greatly condensed the opinion for you. The original was over thirty pages long. The numbers in brackets, such as [*399], refer to the page numbers in the United States Reports.

— petitioner

Texas v. Johnson
491 U.S. 397 (1989)

[*399] Justice BRENNAN delivered the opinion of the Court.

After publicly burning an American flag as a means of political protest, Gregory Lee Johnson was convicted of desecrating a flag in violation of Texas law. This case presents the question whether his conviction is consistent with the First Amendment. We hold that it is not.

I

While the Republican National Convention was taking place in Dallas in 1984, respondent Johnson participated in a political demonstration dubbed the "Republican War Chest Tour." . . . [T]he purpose of this event was to protest the policies of the Reagan administration and of certain Dallas-based corporations. . . .

The demonstration ended in front of Dallas City Hall, where Johnson unfurled the American flag, doused it with kerosene, and set it on fire. While the flag burned, the protestors chanted: "America, the red, white, and blue, we spit on you." . . . [*400] Of the approximately 100 demonstrators, Johnson alone was charged with a crime. The only criminal offense with which he was charged was the desecration of a venerated object in violation of Tex. Penal Code Ann. § 42.09(a)(3) (1989). After a trial, he was convicted, sentenced to one year in prison, and fined $2,000. The Court of Appeals for the Fifth District of Texas at Dallas affirmed Johnson's conviction, 706 S.W.2d 120 (1986), but the Texas Court of Criminal Appeals reversed, 755 S.W.2d 92 (1988), holding that the State could not, consistent with the First Amendment, punish Johnson for burning the flag in these circumstances. . . .

We granted certiorari, 488 U.S. 907 (1988), and now affirm.

II . . .

[*404] The First Amendment literally forbids the abridgment only of "speech," but we have long recognized that its protection does not end at the spoken or written word. While we have rejected "the view that an apparently limitless variety of conduct can be labeled 'speech' whenever the person engaging in the conduct intends thereby to express an idea," *United States v. O'Brien*, supra, at 376, we have acknowledged that conduct may be "sufficiently imbued with elements of communication to fall within the scope of the First and Fourteenth Amendments," [*Spence v. Washington*, 418 U.S. 405, 409 (1974) (reversing the conviction of a college student who displayed the flag with a peace symbol affixed to it by removable black tape)]. . . .

The State of Texas conceded for purposes of its oral argument in this case that Johnson's conduct was expressive conduct, . . . and this concession seems to us as [*406] prudent. . . . Johnson burned an American flag as part—indeed, as the culmination—of a political demonstration that coincided with the convening of the Republican Party and its renomination of Ronald Reagan for President. The expressive, overtly political nature of this conduct was both intentional and overwhelmingly apparent. At his trial, Johnson explained his reasons for burning the flag as follows: "The American Flag was burned as Ronald Reagan was being renominated as President. And a more powerful statement of symbolic speech, whether you agree with it or not, couldn't have been made at that time. It's quite a just position [juxtaposition]. We had new patriotism and no patriotism." 5 Record 656. In these circumstances, Johnson's burning of the flag was conduct "sufficiently imbued with elements of communication," *Spence*, 418 U.S., at 409, to implicate the First Amendment.

III . . .

The State offers two separate interests to justify this conviction: preventing breaches of the peace and preserving the flag as a symbol of nationhood and national unity. We hold that the first interest is not implicated on this record and that the second is related to the suppression of expression.

A

Texas claims that its interest in preventing breaches of the peace justifies Johnson's conviction for flag desecration. [*408] However, no disturbance of the peace actually occurred or threatened to occur because of Johnson's burning of the flag. . . .

The State's position, therefore, amounts to a claim that an audience that takes serious offense at particular expression is necessarily likely to disturb the peace and that the expression may be prohibited on this basis. Our precedents do not countenance such a presumption. On the contrary, they recognize that a principal "function of free speech under our system of government is to invite dispute. It may indeed best serve its high purpose when it induces a condition of unrest, creates dissatisfaction with conditions as they are, or [*409] even stirs people to anger." . . .

Nor does Johnson's expressive conduct fall within that small class of "fighting words" that are "likely to provoke the average person to retaliation, and thereby cause a breach of the peace." *Chaplinsky v. New Hampshire*, 315 U.S. 568, 574 (1942). No reasonable onlooker would have regarded Johnson's generalized expression of dissatisfaction with the policies of the Federal Government as a direct personal insult or an invitation to exchange fisticuffs. . . .

[*410] We thus conclude that the State's interest in maintaining order is not implicated on these facts. The State need not worry that our holding will disable it from preserving the peace. We do not suggest that the First Amendment forbids a State to prevent "imminent lawless action." *Brandenburg*, supra, at 447. And,

in fact, Texas already has a statute specifically prohibiting breaches of the peace, Tex. Penal Code Ann. § 42.01 (1989), which tends to confirm that Texas need not punish this flag desecration in order to keep the peace. See *Boos v. Barry*, 485 U.S., at 327–329.

B

[T]he State's claim is that it has an interest in preserving the flag as a symbol of nationhood and national unity, a symbol with a determinate range of meanings. Brief for Petitioner 20-24. According to Texas, if one physically treats the flag in a way that would tend to cast doubt on either the idea that nationhood and national unity are the flag's referents or that national unity actually exists, the message conveyed thereby is a harmful one and therefore may be prohibited. . . .

If there is a bedrock principle underlying the First Amendment, it is that the government may not prohibit the expression of an idea simply because society finds the idea itself offensive or disagreeable. . . .

To conclude that the government may permit designated symbols to be used to communicate only a limited set of messages would be to enter territory having no discernible or defensible boundaries. Could the government, on this theory, prohibit the burning of state flags? Of copies of the Presidential seal? Of the Constitution? In evaluating these choices under the First Amendment, how would we decide which symbols were sufficiently special to warrant this unique status? To do so, we would be forced to consult our own political preferences, and impose them on the citizenry, in the very way that the First Amendment forbids us to do. See *Carey v. Brown*, 447 U.S., at 466-467. . . .

We are fortified in today's conclusion by our conviction that forbidding criminal punishment for conduct such as Johnson's will not endanger the special role played by our flag or the feelings it inspires. To paraphrase Justice Holmes, we submit that nobody can suppose that this one gesture of an unknown [*419] man will change our Nation's attitude towards its flag. See *Abrams v. United States*, 250 U.S. 616, 628 (1919) (Holmes, J., dissenting). . . .

We are tempted to say, in fact, that the flag's deservedly cherished place in our community will be strengthened, not weakened, by our holding today. Our decision is a reaffirmation of the principles of freedom and inclusiveness that the flag best reflects, and of the conviction that our toleration of criticism such as Johnson's is a sign and source of our strength. Indeed, one of the proudest images of our flag, the one immortalized in our own national anthem, is of the bombardment it survived at Fort McHenry. It is the Nation's resilience, not its rigidity, that Texas sees reflected in the flag—and it is that resilience that we reassert today.

The way to preserve the flag's special role is not to punish those who feel differently about these matters. It is to persuade them that they are wrong. . . . And, precisely because it is our flag that is involved, one's response to the flag [*420] burner may exploit the uniquely persuasive power of the flag itself. We can imagine no more appropriate response to burning a flag than waving one's own, no better way to counter a flag burner's message than by saluting the flag that burns, no surer means of preserving the dignity even of the flag that burned than by—as one witness here did—according its remains a respectful burial. We do not consecrate the flag by punishing its desecration, for in doing so we dilute the freedom that this cherished emblem represents.

V

Johnson was convicted for engaging in "expressive conduct." The State's interest in preventing breaches of the peace does not support his conviction because Johnson's conduct did not threaten to disturb the peace. Nor does the State's interest in preserving the flag as a symbol of nationhood and national unity justify his criminal conviction for engaging in political expression. The judgment of the Texas Court of Criminal Appeals is therefore

Affirmed.

Justice KENNEDY, concurring.

I write not to qualify the words Justice Brennan chooses so well, for he says with power all that is necessary to explain our ruling. I join his opinion without reservation, but with a keen sense that this case, like others before us from time to time, exacts its personal toll. This prompts me to add to our pages these few remarks.

The case before us illustrates better than most that the judicial power is often difficult in its exercise. We cannot here ask another Branch to share responsibility, as when the argument is made that a statute is flawed or incomplete. For we are presented with a clear and simple statute to be judged against a pure command of the Constitution. The outcome can be laid at no door but ours.

The hard fact is that sometimes we must make decisions we do not like. We make them because they are right, right [*421] in the sense that the law and the Constitution, as we see them, compel the result. And so great is our commitment to the process that, except in the rare case, we do not pause to express distaste for the result, perhaps for fear of undermining a valued principle that dictates the decision. This is one of those rare cases. . . .

Though symbols often are what we ourselves make of them, the flag is constant in expressing beliefs Americans share, beliefs in law and peace and that freedom which sustains the human spirit. The case here today forces recognition of the costs to which those beliefs commit us. It is poignant but fundamental that the flag protects those who hold it in contempt.

For all the record shows, this respondent was not a philosopher and perhaps did not even possess the ability to comprehend how repellent his statements must be to the Republic itself. But whether or not he could appreciate the enormity of the offense he gave, the fact remains that his acts were speech, in both the technical and the fundamental meaning of the Constitution. So I agree with the Court that he must go free.

Chief Justice REHNQUIST, with whom Justice WHITE and Justice O'CONNOR join, dissenting.

In holding this Texas statute unconstitutional, the Court ignores Justice Holmes' familiar aphorism that "a page of history is worth a volume of logic." *New York Trust Co. v.* [*422] *Eisner,* 256 U.S. 345, 349 (1921). For more than 200 years, the American flag has occupied a unique position as the symbol of our Nation, a uniqueness that justifies a governmental prohibition against flag burning in the way respondent Johnson did here. . . .

[T]he Court insists that the Texas statute prohibiting the public burning of the American flag infringes on respondent Johnson's freedom of expression. Such freedom, of course, is not absolute. . . . In *Chaplinsky v. New Hampshire*, 315 U.S. 568 (1942), a unanimous Court said: "Allowing the broadest scope to the language and purpose of the Fourteenth Amendment, it is well understood that the right of free speech is not absolute at all times and under all circumstances. There are certain well-defined and narrowly limited classes of speech, the prevention and punishment of which have never been thought to raise any Constitutional problem. These include the lewd and obscene, the profane, the libelous, and the insulting or 'fighting' words— those which by their very utterance inflict injury or tend to incite an immediate breach of the peace. It has been well observed that such utterances are no essential part of any exposition of ideas, and are of such slight social value as a step to truth that any benefit that may be derived from them is clearly outweighed by the social interest in order and morality." Id., at 571-572 (footnotes omitted). The Court upheld Chaplinsy's conviction under a state statute that made it unlawful to "address any offensive, derisive or annoying word to any person who is lawfully in any street or other public place." Id., at 569. Chaplinsky had told a local marshal, " ' "You are a God damned racketeer" and a "damned Fascist and the whole government of Rochester are Fascists or agents of Fascists." ' " Ibid.

Here it may equally well be said that the public burning of the American flag by Johnson was no essential part of any exposition of ideas, and at the same time it had a tendency to incite a breach of the peace. Johnson was free to make any verbal denunciation of the flag that he wished; indeed, he was [*431] free to burn the flag in private. He could publicly burn other symbols of the Government or effigies of political leaders. He did lead a march through the streets of Dallas, and conducted a rally in front of the Dallas City Hall. He engaged in a "die-in" to protest nuclear weapons. He shouted out various slogans during the march, including: "Reagan, Mondale which will it be? Either one means World War III"; "Ronald Reagan, killer of the hour, Perfect

example of U.S. power"; and "red, white and blue, we spit on you, you stand for plunder, you will go under." Brief for Respondent 3. For none of these acts was he arrested or prosecuted; it was only when he proceeded to burn publicly an American flag stolen from its rightful owner that he violated the Texas statute. . . .

[*432] The result of the Texas statute is obviously to deny one in Johnson's frame of mind one of many means of "symbolic speech." Far from being a case of "one picture being worth a thousand words," flag burning is the equivalent of an inarticulate grunt or roar that, it seems fair to say, is most likely to be indulged in not to express any particular idea, but to antagonize others. . . . It was Johnson's use of this particular symbol, and not the idea that he sought to convey by it or by his many other expressions, for which he was punished. . . .

The Court concludes its opinion with a regrettably patronizing civics lecture, presumably addressed to the Members of both Houses of Congress, the members of the 48 state legislatures that enacted prohibitions against flag burning, and the troops fighting under that flag in Vietnam who objected to its [*435] being burned: "The way to preserve the flag's special role is not to punish those who feel differently about these matters. It is to persuade them that they are wrong." Ante, at 419. The Court's role as the final expositor of the Constitution is well established, but its role as a Platonic guardian admonishing those responsible to public opinion as if they were truant schoolchildren has no similar place in our system of government. The cry of "no taxation without representation" animated those who revolted against the English Crown to found our Nation—the idea that those who submitted to government should have some say as to what kind of laws would be passed. Surely one of the high purposes of a democratic society is to legislate against conduct that is regarded as evil and profoundly offensive to the majority of people—whether it be murder, embezzlement, pollution, or flag burning. . . .

I would uphold the Texas statute as applied in this case.

DISCUSSION QUESTIONS

4. Did you notice that more and slightly different facts were brought out by the dissenting justices? This frequently happens. Why do you think the majority did not include all the facts?

5. Were you surprised by the tone of the opinion, especially the way in which the dissent was written? Do you think it is appropriate for U.S. Supreme Court justices to criticize each other? Each other's opinions?

6. In the past few years many U.S. Supreme Court decisions have been decided by a divided court. It is not uncommon to find five/four splits. What do you think this does to the public's perception of the power and role of the Court?

6. Briefing Cases Involving the Common Law

So far in this chapter, in addition to learning the basics of case briefing, we have explored the responsibility of courts to interpret statutes and to strike down unconstitutional statutes. In areas where there are no statutory or constitutional issues involved, the courts are free to develop the common law. In dealing with common-law issues much of what the courts do involves areas where the law is well settled. What is not so settled is whether a particular litigant's facts fit within the law. Occasionally, however, the court is faced not with applying the established law to new facts, but with deciding what the common-law rule should be.

To make the process of reading cases more interesting and practical, we will introduce you to a new client and ask you to assist in the evaluation of her case by briefing three court opinions. In the first opinion, *Keller*, the court relies on a long and well-established line of cases to decide liability in a negligence action. In the other two opinions, *Callow* and *Lewis*, the court has the much more difficult task of deciding whether to create a new rule of law to meet society's changing values.

For these final three cases assume paralegal Chris Kendall has just received the following memorandum from senior partner Pat Harper. The firm is located in Springfield, Massachusetts.

a. Applying Estalished Law

Memorandum

TO: Chris Kendall
FROM: Pat Harper
RE: Miller Intake Interview; Possible Negligence Claim
DATE: March 25

Last week Ms. Janice Miller came to our office seeking advice about whether she could sue Mr. George Booth for the injuries that she received due to his alleged negligence. She initially presented the facts to me as follows: She and Mr. Booth were cutting firewood. Mr. Booth was using a chain saw, and Ms. Miller was stacking the pieces of wood as Mr. Booth cut them. Neither was wearing safety glasses although each owned a pair. Ms. Miller explained the omission by saying that they had both thought that they would only be cutting wood for a short time and neither wanted to be bothered by putting on the glasses.

As it turned out, the wood-cutting session took longer than anticipated. After about an hour, both Mr. Booth and Ms. Miller were getting tired. In particular, Mr. Booth complained that he was feeling fatigued and that it was getting harder and harder to hold the saw sufficiently perpendicular to the wood to cut a straight line. Ms. Miller suggested that they quit for the day, but Mr. Booth wanted to cut just a few more pieces. On his next attempt, probably due to his tired condition, he allowed the chain saw to slip slightly so that it hit the log at a slant, slicing off a piece of bark that flew into Ms. Miller's right eye. Unfortunately the accident has left Ms. Miller totally blind in that eye. Neither she nor Mr. Booth has medical or homeowners' insurance to cover her medical bills, which currently amount to almost $50,000. In addition, Ms. Miller would like to be compensated for her loss of sight, as well as her pain and suffering. I have tentatively attached a value of $400,000 for the former and $150,000 for the latter, for a total possible claim of $600,000.

Attorney Harper first wants to address the issue of whether Mr. Booth can be held liable for negligence. Because the injury occurred in Massachusetts, the ideal situation would be to find cases from Massachusetts that have dealt with a similar situation. The only authorities that are binding on a state court are statutes and court opinions from higher courts within that same state. Similarly, in the federal system the courts are bound only by federal statutes and court opinions from higher federal courts. This constitutes **mandatory authority**—authority from a higher court within the same jurisdiction. All else is **persuasive authority**, and the courts need not follow it. But if the court finds an argument in nonbinding authority persuasive, it may choose to follow it. Researchers usually rely on such persuasive authority when they cannot find any useful mandatory authority because the cases are too old, they go against the client's position, or the facts are not sufficiently similar to the client's facts or when there simply are no prior court opinions dealing with that area of the law.

As it happens, neither attorney Harper nor paralegal Kendall could find any Massachusetts cases dealing with a similar issue of negligence. They did, however, find the following New Hampshire court opinion. The bracketed numbers refer to the pages within the Atlantic Reporter, Second Series. As is true in most states, New Hampshire Supreme Court decisions are published in both an official reporter, New Hampshire Reports, and an unofficial reporter, Atlantic Reporter.

Read and brief *Keller v. DeLong*. Because negligence is a well-established area of the law, most negligence cases, such as this one, involve applying settled principles to new factual situations. Therefore, make sure throughout your brief that you are very specific about which facts seemed to matter to the litigants and the court.

Keller v. DeLong
108 N.H. 212, 231 A.2d 633 (1967)

Case, for wrongful death. Trial was by the Court (Grimes, J.), without a jury. The Court made findings and rulings in writing and returned a verdict for the defendant. Reserved and transferred by the Presiding Justice upon the plaintiff's exceptions. Exceptions sustained; new trial.

Westcott, Millham & Dyer (Mr. Harold E. Westcott orally), for the plaintiff.
[*634] Wiggin, Nourie, Sundeen, Nassikas & Pingree and Dort S. Bigg (Mr. Bigg orally), for the defendant.

DUNCAN, Justice. *— deceased person*

The plaintiff's intestate, a registered nurse who was twenty-eight years of age, died in consequence of injuries suffered at Tyngsboro, Massachusetts at approximately 11:40 P.M. on April 14, 1963, when her automobile, operated by the defendant, collided with a utility pole at the side of the highway. She and the defendant had left Laconia late in the afternoon of the same day. Until shortly before the accident, the decedent had done the driving. A stop had been made at Bow, at which time both parties had some beer to drink. Thereafter they had sandwiches at a restaurant in Concord, and then proceeded toward Lowell, Massachusetts with the decedent at the wheel. At some place near the Massachusetts line, the defendant took the wheel at the decedent's request, and the decedent went to sleep. The accident occurred a few miles from where the defendant commenced to drive.

The Trial Court found "that the sole cause of the accident was the fact that the defendant dozed off to sleep and did not awaken in time to avoid collision with the pole." It further found: "While the defendant had been drinking, the evidence does not convince me that he was unable properly to control the vehicle while awake or that he had difficulty in doing so before dozing off. Neither is it found that after he took the wheel he had any warning that he was going

to fall asleep." The Court granted the defendant's request as follows: "After taking over the wheel, Carl DeLong had no advance warning that he was about to doze, but suddenly and unexpectedly dozed at the time of the occurrence of the accident." After reasoning that dozing as a passenger "does not mean that a person cannot keep awake when charged with the responsibility of driving," the Trial Court was "not convinced ... that in taking over the wheel ... under all the circumstances was anything different than the ordinary man of average prudence would have done and I therefore do not find the defendant was negligent in doing so."

Under principles which receive general recognition an operator of a motor vehicle who permits himself to fall asleep while driving is guilty of ordinary negligence if he has continued to drive without taking reasonable precautions against sleeping after premonitory symptoms of drowsiness or fatigue. Annot. 28 A.L.R.2d 12, 44 et seq.; *Bushnell v. Bushnell*, 103 Conn. 583; *Bernosky v. Greff*, 350 Pa. 59; *Carvalho v. Oliveria*, 305 Mass. 304. Cf. *Theisen v. Milwaukee Automobile Mut. Ins. Co.*, 18 Wis. 2d 91. ...

[*635] We are of the opinion that in the case before us, the Trial Court erred in the application of the law to the evidence. The error is best illustrated by the finding made at the defendant's request: "After taking over the wheel, Carl DeLong had no advance warning that he was about to doze, but suddenly and unexpectedly dozed at the time of occurrence of the accident." The effect of this finding, and of the like finding made by the Court of its own motion, was to isolate selected portions of the evidence, in disregard of the evidence upon which the Court found that the defendant had dozed on a "couple of occasions" before he undertook to drive, and was "drowsy just before taking the wheel."

This evidence disclosed ample warning to the defendant that he might fall asleep. It was not disputed that when he took the wheel, the windows of the automobile were closed, and the heater turned on. There was no evidence that he took any precaution to arouse himself before proceeding, whether by walking around the vehicle, opening windows, or reducing the heat. See *Sater v. Owens*, 67 Wash. 2d 699. On the contrary, it appeared that it was the decedent who left the vehicle and walked to the opposite side, to permit the defendant to slide under the wheel without leaving the seat.

Under these circumstances, a finding that "after taking over the wheel" the defendant had "suddenly and unexpectedly dozed at the time of . . . the accident" cannot be sustained. Such an occurrence could not be unexpected in the absence of precaution to prevent it. Thus it was error to judge the defendant's care solely with reference to what occurred after he took the wheel, in disregard of the evidence of "advance warning" which he had just prior thereto. See *Shine v. Wujick*, 89 R.I. 22, 27-28. The plaintiff was entitled to have the defendant's care determined upon a basis of all of the evidence, rather than just what occurred after he took the wheel. See *Murray v. Boston & Maine R.R.*, 107 N.H. 367, 373-374; *Lynch v. Sprague*, 95 N.H. 485, 490. The verdict for the defendant must therefore be set aside.

Exceptions sustained; new trial.

GRIMES, J., did not sit; the others concurred.

Once you have finished briefing a case, the next step is to use that opinion to help you predict how a court will rule in your client's case. If you think the opinion and your client's situation share many similarities, you can assume that a court will decide your client's case as courts have done in the past. If, however, you find many dissimilarities, that could lead you to believe that the court might rule differently than it has in the past. In Chapter 8 we will spend more time on this process of applying court opinions to our client's facts. For now, however, it is important to realize that once you are in the workforce, you will rarely have the luxury of reading cases just for the enjoyment of reading them. You will be reading them to gain insight into how courts have handled similar situations and hence how they might rule in your client's case.

One method for finding similarities and differences between a court decision and your client's case is to make a chart. First, list all the key facts from the court decision. Then list all the key facts from your client's case. For each fact, note whether it is similar to or different from one of the facts in the prior court decision. Most important, decide if any similarities and differences matter. Then based on your chart make an educated guess as to what a court would do.

Legal Reasoning Exercise

1. Analyze whether, based on the same reasoning used by the *Keller* court, a court would find George negligent. (*Note:* The question is not, Was Janice contributorily negligent? Think only about George's potential liability.) Recall from Chapter 3 our discussion regarding the importance of distinguishing between a prima facie case and the defenses. Here you are being asked to focus exclusively on the prima facie case of negligence.

Make a chart in which you list all the ways in which you think *Keller* and George's situation are analogous and all the ways in which you think they are distinguishable. (*Hint*: To argue that two situations are analogous, think in general terms. For example, both situations involved a dangerous activity. To argue that two situations are distinguishable, think specifically. For example, *Keller* involved a motor vehicle, while George's case involved a chain saw.) Then ask yourself whether the similarities or the differences are more important. If you think the similarities are more important, then you will assume the court will find George negligent. If you think the differences are more important, then you will assume the court will not find George negligent.

b. Creating New Law

Memorandum

TO: Chris Kendall
FROM: Pat Harper
RE: Miller Intake Interview; Possible Spousal Immunity Defense
DATE: April 15

There is a development in the Miller situation. It seems that Ms. Miller and Mr. Booth are married. Since the accident they have been living apart, but they are not legally separated or divorced. This may create a problem for us because to the best of my recollection I do not believe spouses can sue each other. However, it has been quite a while since I researched that area of the law. Would you please do so for me and report on your findings?[6]

We have reproduced the two cases in Exhibits 7-6 and 7-7 exactly as you would find them in the North Eastern Reporter. We have added the marginal notes to help explain some of the editorial features that West adds.

After reading *Callow* (Exhibit 7-6) try writing a brief. In the procedural history, note that there was no trial in this case. The case was sent from the trial court directly to the Supreme Judicial Court. (This usually happens when the parties agree as to what happened but disagree as to what the law should be.) In your holding be particularly careful to note any limitations the court places on its holding. View a limitation as a red flag. A limitation is an indication that the court has left some area open that can be resolved only through future litigation.

---

[6]All research materials are contained in your readings. *Do not* do any additional research.

CALLOW v. THOMAS
Cite as 78 N.E.2d 637

Mass. 637

N.E.2d 729, 731. Consequently, no error of fact or of law being made to appear, we cannot modify this provision of the decree.

The matter of allowance of attorney's fees, briefs and expenses in this court will be settled by a separate order of a single justice upon presentation of an itemized list of the expenses.

Decree affirmed.

CALLOW v. THOMAS.

Supreme Judicial Court of Massachusetts. Middlesex.

April 1, 1948.

1. Husband and wife ⬅205(2)

No cause of action arises in favor of either spouse for a tort committed by the other during coverture.

2. Husband and wife ⬅205(2)

Where either spouse commits a tort upon the other during coverture recovery is denied, not merely because of the disability of one spouse to sue the other during coverture, but because of the marital relationship, no cause of action ever came into existence.

3. Divorce ⬅313

After divorce, no action can be maintained by either spouse for a tort committed by the other during coverture.

4. Marriage ⬅57, 67

Generally an "annulment" is distinguished from a "divorce" in that annulment is not a dissolution of the marriage but is a judicial declaration that no marriage has ever existed, and decree of annulment makes the marriage void ab initio even though the marriage be voidable only at the instance of the injured party. G.L.(Ter.Ed.) c. 207, § 14.

See Words and Phrases, Permanent Edition, for all other definitions of "Annulment" and "Divorce".

5. Marriage ⬅67

Where marriage was voidable and not void and so was valid until set aside by decree of nullity, wife could not after annulment, recover for a tort committed upon her by husband during coverture because of his gross negligence in operation of automobile in which wife was a guest passenger. G.L.(Ter.Ed.) c. 207, § 14.

6. Marriage ⬅67

Where a voidable marriage has been annulled things which have been done during the period of the supposed marriage ought not be undone or reopened after the decree of annulment. G.L.(Ter.Ed.) c. 207, § 14.

Report from Superior Court, Middlesex County.

Action by Muriel Callow against Frederick Thomas for injuries sustained when plaintiff was riding as a gratuitous passenger in an automobile owned and operated by defendant. The case was reported to Supreme Judicial Court without decision.

Judgment for defendant.

Before QUA, C. J., and LUMMUS, DOLAN, WILKINS, and SPALDING, JJ.

M. Harry Goldburgh and J. Finks, both of Boston, for plaintiff.

K. C. Parker, of Boston, for defendant.

SPALDING, Justice.

The plaintiff and the defendant were married in this Commonwealth on August 6, 1944, and thereafter lived together here as husband and wife. On November 9, 1944, while riding as a "gratuitous passenger" in an automobile owned and operated by the defendant, the plaintiff was injured when the automobile, due to the gross negligence of the defendant, ran into a tree. The plaintiff was in the exercise of due care. The accident occurred on a public way in this Commonwealth and the defendant's automobile was registered in accordance with the laws thereof. On June 28, 1945, upon the petition of the plaintiff to annul the marriage because of the defendant's fraud, the Probate Court decreed that the marriage was "null and

---

Margin annotations:

The bold word or phrase is called a West topic. There are 414 West topics. The number preceded by a key symbol is called a key number.

West key symbol

These are headnotes, so called because they appear at the head of the case. They are written by the editors at West, not by the court. Do not quote them, and do not rely on them.

Syllabus

Judges hearing the case.

Attorneys of the parties.

This is where the opinion begins.

Each headnote summarizes one legal point. You can find those points in the opinion by locating the bracketed numbers corresponding to the headnote numbers. For example, you can find the points summarized in headnotes 1-3 in one long paragraph beginning at the bottom of the left-hand column on the next page. Headnote 4 is covered in five paragraphs beginning on page 639 of the opinion.

Exhibit 7-6 *Callow v. Thomas*

(continues)

void."[1] Two months later the plaintiff commenced this action of tort to recover compensation for her injuries.

The foregoing facts were submitted to a judge of the Superior Court upon a case stated in which it was agreed that no inferences should be drawn. See G.L.(Ter.Ed.) c. 231, § 126. The judge at the request of the parties reported the case to this court without decision. G.L.(Ter.Ed.) c. 231, § 111; Scaccia v. Boston Elevated Railway Co., 317 Mass. 245, 248, 249, 57 N.E.2d 761, "upon the stipulation that if the plaintiff is entitled to recover, judgment shall be entered for the plaintiff in the sum of $3,-000, otherwise judgment for the defendant."

The question for decision is whether a wife after the marriage has been annulled can maintain an action against her former husband for a tort committed during coverture. The question is one of first impression in this Commonwealth. Indeed no case in any other jurisdiction has been brought to our attention, and we have found none, in which this question has been presented.

[1-3] That no cause of action arises in favor of either husband or wife for a tort committed by the other during coverture is too well settled to require citation of authority. Recovery is denied in such a case not merely because of the disability of one spouse to sue the other during coverture, but for the more fundamental reason that because of the marital relationship no cause of action ever came into existence.[2] That this is so is revealed by the fact that it has uniformly been held that even after divorce no action can be maintained by either spouse for a tort committed by the other during coverture. Phillips v. Barnet, 1 Q.B.D. 436; Abbott v. Abbott, 67 Me. 304, 24 Am.Rep. 27; Bandfield v. Bandfield, 117 Mich. 80, 75 N.W. 287, 40 L.R.A. 757, 72 Am.St.Rep. 550; Strom v. Strom, 98 Minn. 427, 107 N.W. 1047, 6 L.R.A.,N.S., 191, 116 Am.St.Rep. 387; Lillienkamp v. Rippetoe, 133 Tenn. 57, 179 S.W. 628, L.R.A.1916B, 881, Ann.Cas. 1917C, 901; Schultz v. Christopher, 65 Wash. 496, 118 P. 629, 38 L.R.A.,N.S., 780. There is nothing in our statutes enlarging the rights of married women that can be construed as altering this rule.[3] See Lubowitz v. Taines, 293 Mass. 39, 198 N.E. 320; Luster v. Luster, 299 Mass. 480, 482, 483,

[1] The material portions of the decree are as follows: "On the libel of Muriel Gladys Thomas, of Sudbury, in said county of Middlesex, representing that she and Frederick A. Thomas, now of Lexington, in said county, were joined in marriage lawfully solemnized at Boston, in the county of Suffolk, on August 6, 1944; and that they last lived together in this Commonwealth at said Sudbury; that she now doubts the validity of said marriage for the reason that at the time of said marriage said libellee fraudulently concealed from her the fact that he was afflicted with a contagious disease, thereby practicing a fraud upon her; and praying that said marriage between the said libellant and libellee be annulled and declared void: Said Frederick A. Thomas having had due notice of said libel, objection being made, and after hearing, it appearing to the court that said libellant entered into said marriage in good faith but that said libellee practiced a fraud upon her: It is decreed that said marriage between the said libellant and libellee be and the same hereby is declared to be null and void."

[2] There are, to be sure, instances where one spouse may have a cause of action against the other but cannot enforce it because of the rule prohibiting, with certain exceptions, legal proceedings between husband and wife. See G.L. (Ter.Ed.) c. 209, § 6. Thus in Giles v. Giles, 279 Mass. 284, 181 N.E. 176, it was held that a wife could not maintain a suit in equity against her husband to recover money lent to him before the marriage. But after the parties had been divorced it was held that the suit could be maintained. Giles v. Giles, 293 Mass. 495, 200 N.E. 378. The right to sue was merely suspended during coverture. In Charney v. Charney, 316 Mass. 580, 55 N.E.2d 917, it was held that a wife who, without the intervention of a trustee, had entered into a separation agreement with her husband in New York could not, although the contract was valid by the law of that State, enforce the agreement in the courts of this Commonwealth. Compare Whitney v. Whitney, 316 Mass. 367, 55 N.E.2d 601. See Lubowitz v. Taines, 293 Mass. 39, 198 N.E. 320; Mertz v. Mertz, 271 N.Y. 466, 3 N.E.2d 597, 108 A.L.R. 1120.

[3] In other jurisdictions it has usually been held that statutes removing the common law disabilities of the wife do not

Footnotes can be very important. They are part of the opinion. Always read them.

Exhibit 7-6   *Callow v. Thomas (continued)*   *(continues)*

CALLOW v. THOMAS
Cite as 78 N.E.2d 637
Mass.   639

13 N.E.2d 438. Recognizing the common law rule and the fact that it has not been changed by statute, the plaintiff argues that the decree of nullity "effaced the marriage between the plaintiff and defendant ab initio, and, therefore, at the time of the accident the relationship of husband and wife did not exist."

[4] General Laws (Ter.Ed.) c. 207, § 14, which governs proceedings for annulment, so far as material, reads as follows: "If the validity of a marriage is doubted, either party may file a libel for annulling such marriage. * * * Upon proof of validity or nullity of the marriage, it shall be affirmed or declared void by a decree of the court." In general it may be said that an annulment is to be distinguished from a divorce in that it is not a dissolution of the marriage but is a judicial declaration that no marriage has ever existed. In other words, the decree of annulment makes the marriage void ab initio. Restatement: Conflict of Laws, § 115(1), comment b; Clarke v. Menzies, [1922] 2 Ch. 298; Dodworth v. Dale, [1936] 2 K.B. 503, 511; Mason v. Mason, [1944] N.I. 134; Millar v. Millar, 175 Cal. 797, 804, 805, 167 P. 394, L.R.A.1918B, 415, Ann.Cas.1918E, 184; McDonald v. McDonald, 6 Cal.2d 457, 461, 58 P.2d 163, 104 A.L.R. 1290; Griffin v. Griffin, 130 Ga. 527, 61 S.E. 16, 16 L.R.A.,N.S., 937, 14 Ann.Cas. 866; Henneger v. Lomas, 145 Ind. 287, 298, 44 N.E. 462, 32 L.R.A. 848; Ridgely v. Ridgely, 79 Md. 298, 305,

29 A. 597, 25 L.R.A. 800; Steerman v. Snow, 94 N.J.Eq. 9, 13, 14, 118 A. 696; Jones v. Brinsmade, 183 N.Y. 258, 76 N.E. 22, 3 L.R.A.,N.S., 192, 111 Am.St.Rep. 746, 5 Ann.Cas. 378; Leventhal v. Liberman, 262 N.Y. 209, 211, 186 N.E. 675, 88 A.L.R. 782. See Loker v. Gerald, 157 Mass. 42, 45, 31 N.E. 709, 16 L.R.A. 497, 34 Am.St. Rep. 252; Hanson v. Hanson, 287 Mass. 154, 157, 191 N.E. 673, 93 A.L.R. 701. And this is true even though, as here, the marriage be only voidable at the instance of the injured party. Dodworth v. Dale, [1936] 2 K.B. 503, 511–512; Mason v. Mason, [1944] N.I. 134; McDonald v. McDonald, 6 Cal.2d 457, 461, 58 P.2d 163, 104 A.L.R. 1290; Matter of Moncrief's Will, 235 N.Y. 390, 139 N.E. 550, 27 A.L.R. 1117; Sleicher v. Sleicher, 251 N.Y. 366, 369, 167 N.E. 501, 502.

But the doctrine that such a decree makes the marriage void ab initio has not always been applied unqualifiedly. See Sleicher v. Sleicher, 251 N.Y. 366, 369, 167 N.E. 501, 502.[4] In England, where the question of the effect of a decree of annulment seems to have been considered to a greater extent than in this country, the rule is that such a decree is void for most purposes but not for all. In discussing the effect of such a decree in Mason v. Mason, [1944] N.I. 134, it was said by Lord Chief Justice Andrews, "It is further to be observed that the marriage, after such decree absolute, is void for almost every purpose;

permit her to maintain an action against her husband for a tort committed during coverture. Libby v. Berry, 74 Me. 286, 43 Am.Rep. 589; Bandfield v. Bandfield, 117 Mich. 80, 75 N.W. 287, 40 L. R.A. 757, 72 Am.St.Rep. 550; Strom v. Strom, 98 Minn. 427, 107 N.W. 1047, 6 L.R.A.,N.S., 191, 116 Am.St.Rep. 387; Longendyke v. Longendyke, 44 Barb., N. Y., 366; Lillienkamp v. Rippetoe, 133 Tenn. 57, 179 S.W. 628, L.R.A.1916B, 881, Ann.Cas.1917C, 901; Thompson v. Thompson, 218 U.S. 611, 31 S.Ct. 111, 54 L.Ed. 1180, 30 L.R.A.,N.S., 1153, 21 Ann. Cas. 921. But some statutes have been construed to permit actions in such cases. Johnson v. Johnson, 201 Ala. 41, 77 So. 335, 6 A.L.R. 1031; Brown v. Brown, 88 Conn. 42, 89 A. 889, 52 L.R.A.,N.S., 185, Ann.Cas.1915D, 70; Gilman v. Gilman, 78 N.H. 4, 95 A. 657, L.R.A.1916B, 907. See note in 38 Harv.L.Rev. 383.

4 In that case the defendant was directed by a decree of divorce to pay alimony to the plaintiff "so long as she remains unmarried." Thereafter the plaintiff remarried but the marriage was subsequently annulled on the ground of fraud. Alimony payments ceased at the time of the second marriage. In an action to recover unpaid instalments of alimony it was held that the plaintiff could recover instalments of alimony falling due from the time of the annulment but not for the period during which the second marriage was in force. The court refused to give retroactive effect to the decree of annulment, saying, "The retroactive effect of rescission from the beginning is not, however, without limits, prescribed by policy and justice."

Exhibit 7-6   *Callow v. Thomas (continued)*

(continues)

and, speaking in general terms, the only exception to the rule—an exception founded on general equitable principles—may be said to be such transactions as have been concluded and such things as have been done during the period of the supposed marriage. These cannot be undone or reopened after the marriage has been declared null and void" (page 163).

This exception has been recognized in several decisions. Thus in Anstey v. Manners, Gow. 10, the plaintiff, after a sentence of nullity had been pronounced by the Ecclesiastical Court, brought suit against the former husband to recover for necessaries which he (the plaintiff) had supplied to the wife. Some of the necessaries were supplied during the supposed marriage and some were supplied afterwards. In a very brief opinion which is somewhat obscure it was held that the defendant was not liable for debts contracted after the date of the decree. The case has been considered as impliedly holding that the defendant was liable for necessaries furnished prior to that date. See Dodworth v. Dale, [1936] 2 K.B. 503, 512.

In Dunbar v. Dunbar, [1909] 2 Ch. 639, it was held that a completed and executed transaction, namely, an advancement, effected while the plaintiff and the defendant were living together as man and wife, was unaffected by a subsequent decree annulling a marriage which was voidable but not void.

In Dodworth v. Dale, [1936] 2 K.B. 503, it was held that a husband who had obtained an annulment of his marriage on the ground of his wife's impotency and who during the period of his purported marriage had filed tax returns as a married man, could not be compelled to pay additional taxes for that period on the ground that the deductions which he had taken for the support of his wife were improper. The court stated "that what has been done during the continuance of the de facto marriage cannot be undone—cannot be overturned by the operation of law" (page 519).

In Fowke v. Fowke, [1938] Ch. 774, it was held that a decree of nullity granted on the ground of the wife's impotency did not affect a previous deed of separation whereby the husband convenanted to pay the wife an annuity so long as she continued to lead a chaste life. See also P. v. P. [1916] 2 Ir.R. 400; De Reneville v. De Reneville, [1947] A.C.[5]

[5, 6] We are of opinion that the exception recognized in these cases is sound and that the present case falls within it. At the time of the accident the parties were husband and wife for all intents and purposes. Had no proceedings been brought to annul the marriage, this status would have endured until the marriage was terminated by death or divorce. In other words, the marriage here was voidable and not void and was valid until it was set aside by the decree of nullity. 1 Bish.Mar. Div. & Sep. §§ 258, 259, 271, 281; Anders v. Anders, 224 Mass. 438, 441, 113 N.E. 203, L.R.A.1916E, 1273; Sleicher v. Sleicher, 251 N.Y. 366, 369, 167 N.E. 501, 502. It is to be observed that this is not a case of a marriage prohibited by law such as a bigamous marriage or one prohibited by reason of consanguinity or affinity between the parties. G.L.(Ter.Ed.) c. 207, §§ 1, 2, 4. Such a marriage is no marriage at all and is "void without a decree of divorce or other legal process." G.L.(Ter. Ed.) c. 207, § 8. While it doubtless is true that a decree of nullity ordinarily has the effect of making a marriage, even one which is voidable, void ab initio, this is a legal fiction which ought not to be pressed too far. To say that for all purposes the marriage never existed is unrealistic. Logic must yield to realities. Public policy requires that there must be some limits to the retroactive effects of a decree of annulment. It was said by Cardozo, C. J., in American Surety Co. v. Conner, 251 N.Y. 1, 9, 166 N.E. 783, 786, 65 A.L.R. 244, "The decree of annulment destroyed the marriage from the beginning as a source of rights and duties * * * but it could not obliterate the past and make events unreal." The better rule, we think, is that in the case of a voidable marriage transactions which have been concluded and things which have been done during

[5] 64 T. L. R. 82.

Exhibit 7-6   *Callow v. Thomas* (continued)   *(continues)*

the period of the supposed marriage ought not to be undone or reopened after the decree of annulment. Applying that principle here, the plaintiff is not entitled to recover. On the day after the accident if the plaintiff had brought suit against the defendant it could not have been maintained, for the marriage at that time had not been declared invalid. The situation was unaffected by the subsequent decree of annulment.

It follows that in accordance with the stipulation judgment is to be entered for the defendant.

So ordered.

JOYCE et al. v. DEVANEY et al.

Supreme Judicial Court of Massachusetts. Middlesex.

April 1, 1948.

1. Easements ⟨⟩16

The owner of realty may make use of one part of his realty for the benefit of another part in such a way that, on severance of the title, an easement, which is not expressed in the deed, may arise, which corresponds to the use which was previously made of the realty while it was under common ownership.

2. Easements ⟨⟩15

Implied easements, whether by grant or by reservation, do not arise out of necessity alone, and their origin must be found in presumed intention of parties, to be gathered from language of instruments when read in the light of circumstances attending their execution, physical condition of premises, and knowledge which parties had or with which they are chargeable.

3. Easements ⟨⟩15

The creation in deeds of express easements that were unambiguous and definite negatived any intention to create easements by implication, since the expression of one thing is the exclusion of another.

78 N.E.2d—41
Mass.Dec.76–79 N.E.2d—23

4. Easements ⟨⟩17(1)

Where deeds of adjoining lots at time of severance created specific easements shown by plan providing for an 8-foot wide driveway 4 feet of which was to be on each lot, but 10-foot wide driveway was constructed, 8½ feet of which was on defendant's lot, and 1½ feet of which was on plaintiff's lot, there was no implied easement entitling plaintiff to use driveway as constructed, and plaintiff was entitled only to easement expressly set forth in deeds.

————◆————

Appeal from Superior Court, Middlesex County; Goldberg, Judge.

Bill in equity by John J. Joyce and another against John T. Devaney and another to restrain defendants from interfering with plaintiff's use of a common driveway, and for a determination of plaintiff's rights in the driveway, wherein the defendants filed a counterclaim to restrain plaintiffs from trespassing on defendant's land. From an adverse decree, plaintiffs appeal.

Interlocutory decree affirmed and final decree affirmed.

Before QUA, C. J., and LUMMUS, DOLAN, WILKINS, and SPALDING, JJ.

R. B. Brooks, of Boston, for plaintiffs.

M. E. Gallagher, Jr., of Boston, and A. J. Kirwan, of Medford, for defendants.

SPALDING, Justice.

The plaintiffs by this bill in equity seek to restrain the defendants from interfering with their use of a common driveway; they also ask that their rights in the driveway be determined. The answer of the defendants included a counterclaim in which they ask that the plaintiffs be restrained from trespassing on their land. The case was referred to a master whose report, to which there were no objections, was confirmed by an interlocutory decree. The case comes here on the plaintiffs' appeal from a final decree.

We summarize the findings of the master as follows: On April 30, 1931, MacNeil Bros. Corporation, hereinafter called the corporation, acquired for development purposes a parcel of vacant land in West Med-

Exhibit 7-6   *Callow v. Thomas (concluded)*

The beginning of the text case.

Discussion Questions

7. In Chapter 6 (Legal Reasoning Exercise 1) we looked at the following statute, which would seem to govern Janice's case. What does the *Callow* court say about it?

> A married woman may sue and be sued in the same manner as if she were sole; but this section shall not authorize suits between husband and wife.

8. What is the difference between a void and a voidable marriage? Do you think the court would have ruled the same way if the marriage had been void? Should such technicalities matter?

9. The result here was the finding that Muriel Callow could not sue her ex-husband. This does not mean that the court thought he was not negligent. Because the court said she could not sue, the court never heard any evidence regarding his behavior that caused his car to run into a tree. Do you think that there should be such absolute bars to even having a case heard? If so, can you think of other situations where the courts should not allow potential litigants to sue each other?

Legal Reasoning Exercise

2. Based on *Callow* analyze whether you think the doctrine of spousal immunity will bar Janice's claim.

In 1975 the Massachusetts Supreme Judicial Court was asked to change the law regarding parental immunity. A child was hurt when his father allegedly caused an automobile accident. After considering the two major arguments against allowing such suits, the possibility of disrupting the family's peace and harmony and the tendency to promote fraud, the court allowed the child to sue his father. One year later, and twenty-eight years after the Supreme Judicial Court decided *Callow*, the court revisited the issue of spousal immunity in *Lewis*, reprinted here in Exhibit 7-7.

As you read and brief this opinion, ask yourself why the court went to such lengths to explain itself and whether you agree with its reasoning. Pay particular attention to why the court said this was not a matter in which they should defer to the legislature. In the holding section, again be particularly careful to note any limitations the court puts on its holding.

As in *Callow*, there was no trial in *Lewis*. The court granted Mr. Lewis's summary judgment motion. The case then went to the Supreme Judicial Court by way of *direct appellate review*. This occurs when the courts think a case is so significant that the highest appellate court will eventually hear it, no matter how the intermediate court decides. Therefore, to save time, the middle step of going through the intermediate appellate court on the way to the highest court is simply omitted.

Court is not barred by the principle of double jeopardy. Accordingly the defendant's motion is to be denied, and the indictments are to stand for trial in the Superior Court.

So ordered.

Blanche LEWIS

v.

Larry C. LEWIS.

Supreme Judicial Court of Massachusetts, Hampden.

Argued Jan. 6, 1976.

Decided July 9, 1976.

Syllabus

Action was brought by wife against husband for personal injuries sustained in automobile accident. The Superior Court, Moriarty, J., granted defendant's motion for summary judgment, and plaintiff's motion for direct appellate review was allowed. The Supreme Judicial Court, Reardon, J., held that it was open to the Supreme Judicial Court to reconsider common-law rule of interspousal immunity, and that such rule no longer barred wife's action against husband for injuries sustained in automobile accident.

Judgment vacated.

Headnotes

1. Husband and Wife 🔑205(2)

Arguments that tort actions between husband and wife would tend to disrupt peace and harmony of family and that such actions would tend to promote fraud and collusion on part of husband and wife for purpose of reaping undeserved financial reward at expense of family's liability insurer are insufficient to justify common-law rule of interspousal immunity.

2. Constitutional Law 🔑70.1(11)

Statute which provides that a married woman may sue and be sued in same manner as if she were sole but provides that such statute does not authorize suit between husband and wife except in connection with certain contracts left interspousal immunity rule in its common-law status susceptible to reexamination and alteration by Supreme Judicial Court. M.G.L.A. c. 209 § 6.

3. Courts 🔑90(6)

It is within power and authority of court to abrogate judicially created rule and mere longevity of rule does not by itself provide cause for Supreme Judicial Court to stay its hand if to perpetuate rule would be to perpetuate inequity.

4. Courts 🔑90(6)

When rationales which gave meaning and coherence to judicially created rule are no longer vital, and rule itself is not consonant with needs of contemporary society, court not only has authority but also duty to reexamine its predecents rather than to apply by rote an antiquated formula.

5. Constitutional Law 🔑70.1(11)

Where legislature recognized rule of interspousal immunity but left rule in its common-law form, expressing preference, at least implicitly, that Supreme Judicial Court continue to evaluate usefulness and propriety of rule, it was open to Supreme Judicial Court to reconsider common-law rule of interspousal immunity. M.G.L.A. c. 209 § 6.

6. Husband and Wife 🔑205(2)

Wife's action against her husband for personal injuries sustained in automobile accident was not barred by common-law rule of interspousal immunity.

7. Torts 🔑5

If there is tortious injury there should be recovery, and only strong arguments of public policy can justify judicially created

Exhibit 7-7 *Lewis v. Lewis*

(continues)

immunity for tort-feasors and bar recovery for injured victims.

Morton J. Sweeney, Springfield (Patricia A. Bobba, Springfield, with him), for the plaintiff.

George J. Shagory, Boston (Edward J. Shagory, Boston, with him), for defendant.

Robert M. Fuster, Pittsfield, for Juliette G. Pevoski, amicus curiae, submitted a brief.

J. Norman O'Connor and John D. Lanoue, Adams, for Joseph J. Pevoski, amicus curiae, submitted a brief.

Before HENNESSEY, C. J., and REARDON, BRAUCHER, KAPLAN and WILKINS, JJ.

REARDON, Justice.

This matter raises the question of the continuance in Massachusetts of the doctrine of interspousal immunity. The case originated as a civil action of tort for personal injuries brought by the plaintiff Blanche Lewis against her husband, the defendant Larry Lewis. The defendant's motion for summary judgment was granted, and we allowed the plaintiff's motion for direct appellate review. Blanche Lewis was a passenger in a car owned and driven by her husband on July 27, 1973, when about 9 P.M., on a public highway in the town of Agawam, the car slid on a wet pavement, struck a light pole and rolled over on its side, causing injury to the plaintiff. The motion for summary judgment which was allowed was based on the common law doctrine of interspousal immunity and on the provisions of G.L. c. 209, § 6, as amended by St.1963, c. 765, § 2. In addition to briefs filed by the parties we also reviewed briefs filed by counsel in a case raising a similar question commenced in the Superior Court for Berkshire County. We are thus led to a discussion of the current status of the doctrine of inter-

spousal immunity and our opinion relative to the argument here presented by the plaintiff.

The fundamental basis for the common law rule of interspousal immunity was the special unity of husband and wife within the marital relationship. For most purposes the common law treated husband and wife as "a single person, represented by the husband." *Nolin v. Pearson*, 191 Mass. 283, 284, 77 N.E. 890, (1906). See *Butler v. Ives*, 139 Mass. 202, 203, 29 N.E. 654 (1885). This merger of legal identities has been described in the following terms: "By marriage, the husband and wife are one person in law: . . . that is, the very being or legal existence of the woman is suspended during the marriage, or at least is incorporated and consolidated into that of the husband; under whose wing, protection, and *cover*, she performs everything . . . . Upon this principle, of a union of a person in husband and wife, depend almost all the legal rights, duties, and disabilities, that either of them acquire by the marriage." 1 W. Blackstone, Commentaries *442.

Among the many disabilities visited upon a woman once she took her marriage vows was an inability to sue or be sued in her own name. To enforce any right of action for tortious injury to her person her husband had to be joined as a plaintiff; and, furthermore, he was entitled to the proceeds of any judgment obtained. Conversely, to enforce an action against a married woman it was necessary to join the husband as a defendant, and a judgment, if obtained during coverture, became the obligation of the husband. McCurdy, Personal Injury Torts Between Spouses, 4 Vill.L.Rev. 303, 304 (1959). 1 F. Harper & F. James, Torts § 8.10 at 643 (1956).

Within this framework a rule prohibiting suits between husband and wife made some sense. Not only was there the conceptual problem of the single marital entity suing itself but, as a practical matter, the rules of liability would have rendered such suits

Exhibit 7-7   *Lewis v. Lewis (continued)*   *(continues)*

528   Mass.   351 NORTH EASTERN REPORTER, 2d SERIES

idle exercises. As Dean Prosser pointed out: "If the man were the tort-feasor, the woman's right would be a chose in action which the husband would have the right to reduce to possession, and he must be joined as a plaintiff against himself and the proceeds recovered must be paid to him . . . . . If the wife committed the tort, the husband would be liable to himself for it, and must be joined as a defendant in his own action." W. Prosser, Torts § 122 at 860 (4th ed. 1971).

These antediluvian assumptions concerning the role and status of women in marriage and in society which animated and gave support to the common law rule of interspousal immunity were soon perceived as inconsistent with the principles and realities of a progressing American society. Beginning in the middle of the nineteenth century, women's emancipation acts were passed in all American jurisdictions in order to secure to married women their own independent legal identities. See W. Prosser, Torts § 122 at 861 (4th ed. 1971); McCurdy, Torts Between Persons in Domestic Relation, 43 Harv.L.Rev. 1030, 1036–1037 (1930). In Massachusetts, beginning with St.1845, c. 208, the Legislature through a series of enactments now found in G.L. c. 209, §§ 1–13, has moved to recognize and invigorate the legal identity of the married woman. Most of the disabilities which rendered women second class citizens under the common law were removed by these statutes in Massachusetts. They provide inter alia that a married woman may hold and dispose of both real and personal property (G.L. c. 209, § 1), may enter into contracts in her own name (G.L. c. 209, § 2), and may sue and be sued in her own name without joinder of her husband, and without her husband's

being liable for judgments against her (G. L. c. 209, §§ 6, 8). As we recognized as early as 1906 in *Nolin v. Pearson, supra,* 191 Mass. at 285, 77 N.E. at 890, "This remedial legislation has resulted in very largely impairing the unity of husband and wife as it existed at common law." The old order has been changing and the doctrine of the legal unity of husband and wife is no longer a satisfactory foundation on which to base a rule of interspousal tort immunity.[1]

Despite the demise of the unity theory of husband and wife and the enactment of married women's acts, the rule of interspousal tort immunity has survived in Massachusetts and in many other jurisdictions. This court could say in 1948 in very broad and dogmatic terms, "That no cause of action arises in favor of either husband or wife for a tort committed by the other during coverture is too well settled to require citation of authority. Recovery is denied in such a case not merely because of the disability of one spouse to sue the other during coverture, but for the more fundamental reason that because of the marital relationship no cause of action ever came into existence." *Callow v. Thomas,* 322 Mass. 550, 551–552, 78 N.E.2d 637, 638 (1948). Indeed at that time interspousal immunity was the rule in a substantial majority of jurisdictions. However, in the interim there has been a significant trend in other jurisdictions toward abrogating the doctrine. Currently, State jurisdictions are about evenly divided between those which have abandoned and those which have maintained the interspousal immunity rule. Furthermore, among commentators who have considered the topic, criticism of the rule is pratically universal. See, e. g., 1 F. Harper & F. James, *supra* at 643–647;

1. What we have said is not to be interpreted as a derogation of the spiritual and emotional unity that many hold as an ideal in marriage. As the Supreme Court of Washington pointed out, "The 'supposed unity' of husband and wife, which serves as the traditional basis of interspousal disability, is not a reference to the common nature or loving oneness

achieved in a marriage of two free individuals. Rather, this traditional premise had reference to a situation, coming on from antiquity, in which a woman's marriage for most purposes rendered her a chattel of her husband." *Freehe v. Freehe,* 81 Wash.2d 183, 186, 500 P.2d 771, 773 (1972).

Exhibit 7-7   *Lewis v. Lewis (continued)*

(continues)

LEWIS v. LEWIS   **Mass. 529**
Cite as, Mass., 351 N.E.2d 526

W. Prosser, *supra* at 859–864; McCurdy, Torts Between Persons in Domestic Relation, 43 Harv.L.Rev. 1030 (1930); McCurdy, Personal Injury Torts Between Spouses, 4 Vill.L.Rev. 303 (1959); Comment Tort Liability Between Husband and Wife: The Interspousal Immunity Doctrine, 21 U.Miami L.Rev. 423 (1966); Note, Interspousal Immunity—Time for a Reappraisal, 27 Ohio St.L.J. 550 (1966).

[1] While most jurisdictions recognize that the theory of the legal identity of husband and wife can no longer support the interspousal immunity rule, those courts which have upheld the rule have generally done so on grounds of public policy. The two arguments most frequently advanced in favor of the rule are, first, that tort actions between husband and wife would tend to disrupt the peace and harmony of the family, and, second, that such actions would tend to promote fraud and collusion on the part of husband and wife for the purpose of reaping an undeserved financial reward at the expense of the family's liability insurer. Both of these arguments were considered and rejected in the analogous context of parental immunity in the recent case of *Sorensen v. Sorensen*, —— Mass. —— [a], 339 N.E.2d 907 (1975), decided this term. We refer to our discussion and resolution of these issues in that case. *Id.* at —— – —— [b], 339 N.E.2d 907. Suffice it to say that just as we did not find the arguments concerning the preservation of family harmony and the avoidance of family fraud sufficient to justify a rule barring tort suits for personal injuries by a

child against a parent, we are similarly unconvinced by these arguments in the present context of interspousal immunity. We further note that most of the jurisdictions which have rejected the rule of interspousal immunity have considered these very same arguments and found them wanting. See *Self v. Self*, 58 Cal.2d 683, 689–691, 26 Cal.Rptr. 97, 376 P.2d 65 (1962) (intentional torts); *Klein v. Klein*, 58 Cal.2d 692, 694–696, 26 Cal.Rptr. 102, 376 P.2d 70 (1962) (negligent torts); *Brooks v. Robinson*, 259 Ind. 16, 20–22, 284 N.E.2d 794 (1972); *Rupert v. Stienne*, 90 Nev. 397, 401–402, 528 P.2d 1013 (1974); *Immer v. Risko*, 56 N.J. 482, 488–495, 267 A.2d 481 (1970); *Flores v. Flores*, 84 N. M. 601, 603, 506 P.2d 345 (Ct.App.1973) (intentional torts); *Maestas v. Overton*, 87 N.M. 213, 531 P.2d 947 (1975) (negligent torts); *Surratt v. Thompson*, 212 Va. 191, 192, 183 S.E.2d 200 (1971); *Freehe v. Freehe*, 81 Wash.2d 193, 187–189, 500 P.2d 771 (1972).

However, the defendant argues that, unlike the situation prevailing in most other jurisdictions, the rule of interspousal immunity has taken on statutory dimensions in Massachusetts. The argument is based on G.L. c. 209, § 6, as appearing in St. 1963, c. 765, § 2, which provides: "A married woman may sue and be sued in the manner as if she were sole; *but this section shall not authorize suits between husband and wife* except in connection with contracts entered into pursuant to the authority contained in section two" (emphasis supplied).[2] By including the italicized lan-

---

a. Mass.Adv.Sh. (1975) 3662.

b. Mass.Adv.Sh. (1975) at 3674–3683.

2. As to the historical development of G.L. c. 209, § 6, briefly, married women were first given a limited right to sue and be sued in their own names in St.1845, c. 208, which provided for the separate ownership of property by married women and authorized suits by and against married women "in respect to such property." The first mention of tort actions appears in St.1871, c. 312, which

351 N.E.2d—34

provided that a married woman could sue and be sued in tort in the same manner as if she were unmarried but contained no reference to suits by or against her husband. In 1874 the interspousal language we are concerned with in this case was added in substantially the same form as it appears today in G.L. c. 209, § 6. Statute 1874, c. 184, § 3, read: "A married woman may sue and be sued in the same manner and to the same extent as if she were sole, but nothing herein contained shall authorize suits between hus-

---

Exhibit 7-7   *Lewis v. Lewis (continued)*

(continues)

530 Mass.   **351 NORTH EASTERN REPORTER, 2d SERIES**

guage in the statute, the Legislature, according to the defendant's argument, has chosen to incorporate the rule of interspousal immunity into the statutory law of the Commonwealth and, therefore, this court is without power to abrogate the rule. With this contention we do not agree. The Supreme Court of New Jersey was faced with similar statutory language when called on to reëxamine the doctrine of interspousal immunity in *Immer v. Risko*, 56 N.J. 482, 267 A.2d 481 (1970). New Jersey's Married Persons' Act included the following provision: "Nothing in this chapter contained shall enable a husband or wife to contract with or to sue each other, except as heretofore, and except as authorized by this chapter." N.J.Stat.Ann. tit. 37:2–5 (1968). The court held that this provision did not incorporate the doctrine of interspousal immunity but merely left the common law undisturbed and " 'intact with its inherent capacity for later judicial alteration.' " *Id.* 56 N.J. at 486, 267 A.2d at 483. The court went on to scrutinze the reasons behind the rule of interspousal immunity and abrogated the rule at least with respect to automobile negligence torts.

The Supreme Court of Indiana in abrogating interspousal immunity in the case of *Brooks v. Robinson*, 259 Ind. 16, 284 N.E.

2d 794 (1972), construed a similar statutory limitation to the same effect, holding that the Legislature was not barring tort actions between husband and wife but was preserving the rule of interspousal immunity in its common law form "subject to amendment, modification, or abrogation by this Court." *Id.* at 24, 284 N.E.2d at 798.[3]

[2] With respect to G.L. c. 209, § 6, it was open to the Legislature to take the position that while it did not wish to abolish the common law rule of interspousal immunity neither did it wish to convert the common law rule into a mandate of statutory law. In G.L. c. 209, § 6, it chose apt language to express such an intention. The Legislature apparently recognized the broad scope of the language, "A married woman may sue and be sued in the same manner as if she were sole," and realized that unless some limiting provision were included the statute itself could be construed as authorizing suits between spouses. By making clear that the statute itself does not alter the rule of interspousal immunity, the Legislature closed the path taken by many courts in other jurisdictions in interpreting the broad, general provisions of their married women's acts as in and of themselves removing the barrier of interspousal immunity. See, e. g., *Katzenberg v. Katzenberg*,

band and wife." This statutory language was adopted with minor changes in subsequent consolidations and revisions of the laws of the Commonwealth. See Pub.Sts. (1882), c. 147, § 7; R.L. (1902), c. 153, § 6. Finally, in St.1963, c. 765, § 2, the Legislature added the language authorizing interspousal suits on contracts entered into pursuant to G.L. c. 209, § 2, which section was simultaneously amended to authorize such contracts (St. 1963, c. 765, § 1) and now reads, "A married woman may make contracts, oral and written, sealed and unsealed, in the same manner as if she were sole, and may make such contracts with her husband."

3. The court in the *Brooks* case was concerned with the following statutory language of TR. 17(D) of the Indiana Rules of Procedure: "*Sex, marital and parental status.* For the purposes of suing or being sued there shall

be *no distinction* between men and women or between men and women because of marital or parental status; *provided, however, that this subsection (D) shall not apply to actions in tort.*" The court held that this language should not be construed as "anything more than *legislative awareness* of the judicially created doctrine of the common law. The proviso in TR. 17(D) does not purport to abolish tort actions between husband and wife. Rather it merely provides that if any distinction between husband and wife exists in tort actions, such distinction is not removed by the rule as adopted. The 'distinction' which has existed up to the present is, of course, the common law doctrine of interspousal immunity which is, and always has been, subject to amendment, modification, or abrogation by this Court." *Brooks v. Robinson, supra* at 23–24, 284 N.E.2d at 798 (emphasis in the quoted opinion).

Exhibit 7-7 *Lewis v. Lewis (continued)*   *(continues)*

LEWIS v. LEWIS   Mass. **531**
Cite as, Mass., 351 N.E.2d 526

183 Ark. 626, 37 S.W.2d 696 (1931); *Lorang v. Hays,* 69 Idaho 440, 209 P.2d 733 (1949); *Brown v. Gosser,* 262 S.W.2d 480 (Ky.1953); *Gilman v. Gilman,* 78 N.H. 4, 95 A. 657 (1915); *Wait v. Pierce,* 191 Wis. 202, 209 N.W. 475 (1926). On the other hand, G.L. c. 209, § 6, does not directly forbid tort suits between husband and wife. The Legislature could have used language more prohibitory in nature had it been its intention to bar such suits; and its choice of the words, "shall not authorize" cannot be considered inadvertent or accidental. Compare with G.L. c. 209, § 6, the Married Women's Property Act of the English Parliament, 45 & 46 Vict., c. 75, § 12 (1882), which provides that "no husband or wife shall be entitled to sue the other for a tort," and Ill.Rev.Stat. c. 68, § 1 (1973), which provides: "A married woman may, in all cases, sue and be sued without joining her husband with her, to the same extent as if she were unmarried; *provided, that neither husband nor wife may sue the other for a tort to the person committed during coverture*" (emphasis supplied).

In *Frankel v. Frankel,* 173 Mass. 214, 53 N.E. 398 (1899), holding that the enactment of the statutory language now contained in G.L. c. 209, § 6, did not abolish the equitable remedies previously available between husband and wife, this court noted that "[t]he section referred to above does not forbid suits between husband and wife, but simply provides that it shall not be construed to authorize them." *Id.* at 215, 53 N.E. at 398. See *Zwick v. Goldberg,* 304 Mass. 66, 70, 22 N.E.2d 661 (1939). In addition, in *Gahm v. Gahm,* 243 Mass. 374, 375, 137 N.E. 876 (1923), a case decided prior to the amendments to G.L. c. 209, §§ 2, 6, contained in St.1963, c. 765, §§ 1, 2, which authorize contracts between husband and wife and suits on those contracts, the court observed that "[t]he common-law disabilities of married women as to the making of contracts have been removed by statute so that they now can contract and

sue and be sued in the same manner as if single, subject, however, to the limitation that contracts and suits between husband and wife are not permissible but *stand on the same footing as heretofore*" (emphasis supplied). The "footing" which was the basis of the prohibition of suits between husband and wife "heretofore" was the *common law rule* of interspousal immunity. See *Fowle v. Torrey,* 135 Mass. 87, 89-90 (1883). The "shall not authorize" language of G.L. c. 209, § 6, would appear then to be a reference to, not an incorporation of, the common law rule of interspousal immunity. We conclude that the statute has left the rule in its common law status susceptible to reëxamination and alteration by this court.

[3, 4] The defendant further argues that even if interspousal immunity is not mandated by statute, a common law rule of such long standing should be abolished, if at all, by legislative and not judicial action. The defendant concedes, as he must, that it is within the power and authority of the court to abrogate this judicially created rule; and the mere longevity of the rule does not by itself provide cause for us to stay our hand if to perpetuate the rule would be to perpetuate inequity. When the rationales which gave meaning and coherence to a judicially created rule are no longer vital, and the rule itself is not consonant with the needs of contemporary society, a court not only has the authority but also the duty to reëxamine its precedents rather than to apply by rote an antiquated formula. Chief Justice Vanderbilt described this interaction between the judiciary and the evolving common law in an oft cited passage from *State v. Culver,* 23 N.J. 495, 505, 129 A.2d 715, 721, cert. denied, 354 U.S. 925, 77 S.Ct. 1387, 1 L.Ed.2d 1441 (1957): "One of the great virtues of the common law is its dynamic nature that makes it adaptable to the requirements of society at the time of its application in court. There is not a rule of the common

---

Exhibit 7-7 *Lewis v. Lewis (continued)*   *(continues)*

532   Mass.   351 NORTH EASTERN REPORTER, 2d SERIES

law in force today that has not evolved from some earlier rule of common law, gradually in some instances, more suddenly in others, leaving the common law of today when compared with the common law of centuries ago as different as day is from night. The nature of the common law requires that each time a rule of law is applied it be carefully scrutinized to make sure that the conditions and needs of the times have not so changed as to make further application of it the instrument of injustice. Dean Pound posed the problem admirably in his *Interpretations of Legal History* (1922) when he stated, 'Law must be stable, and yet it cannot stand still.' "

This court has frequently had occasion to effect through its decisions not insignificant changes in the field of tort law. See, e. g., *Sorensen v. Sorensen*, — Mass. —**c**, 339 N.E.2d 907 (1975); *Mone v. Greyhound Lines, Inc.*, — Mass. —**d**, 331 N. E.2d 916 (1975); *Diaz v. Eli Lilly & Co.*, 364 Mass. 153, 302 N.E.2d 555 (1973), and cases cited at 166 n. 43, 302 N.E.2d 555. In the *Diaz* case, in rejecting the argument that the court should defer to the Legislature on the question of recovery for loss of consortium, we noted that "the Legislature may rationally prefer to act, if it acts at all, after rather than before the common law has fulfilled itself in its own way." *Id.* at 166, 302 N.E.2d at 563. We are of opinion that this is an especially appropriate comment in the context of this case where the Legislature in G.L. c. 209, § 6, has recognized the rule of interspousal immunity but has left the rule in its common law form, expressing the preference, at least implicitly, that this court continue to evaluate the usefulness and propriety of the rule. We further note that the argument that any change in the doctrine of interspousal immunity should come from the Legislature, not the judiciary, has been considered and rejected in many decisions

abrogating the common law rule. See, e. g., *Brooks v. Robinson*, 259 Ind. 16, 22–23, 284 N.E.2d 794 (1972); *Beaudette v. Frana*, 285 Minn. 366, 370–371, 173 N.W.2d 416 (1969); *Rupert v. Stienne*, 90 Nev. 397, 399–401, 528 P.2d 1013 (1974); *Immer v. Risko*, 56 N.J. 482, 487, 267 A.2d 481 (1970); *Flores v. Flores*, 84 N.M. 601, 603–604, 506 P.2d 345 (Ct.App.1973); *Freehe v. Freehe*, 81 Wash.2d 183, 189, 500 P.2d 771 (1972).

[5–7] We conclude therefore that it is open to this court to reconsider the common law rule of interspousal immunity and, having done so, we are of opinion that it should no longer bar an action by one spouse against another in a case such as the present one. We believe this result is consistent with the general principle that if there is tortious injury there should be recovery, and only strong arguments of public policy should justify a judicially created immunity for tortfeasors and bar to recovery for injured victims. See *Morash & Sons, Inc. v. Commonwealth*, 363 Mass. 612, 621, 296 N.E.2d 461 (1973); *Freehe v. Freehe, supra*, 81 Wash.2d at 192, 500 P.2d 771. We have examined the reasons offered in support of the common law immunity doctrine and, whatever their vitality in the social context of generations past, we find them inadequate today to support a general rule of interspousal tort immunity. In arriving at this conclusion we are mindful that the rights and privileges of husbands and wives with respect to one another are not unaffected by the marriage they have voluntarily undertaken together. Conduct, tortious between two strangers, may not be tortious between spouses because of the mutual concessions implied in the marital relationship. For this reason we limit our holding today to claims arising out of motor vehicle accidents. Further definition of the scope of

c. Mass.Adv.Sh. (1975) 3662.

d. Mass.Adv.Sh. (1975) 2326.

Exhibit 7-7   *Lewis v. Lewis (continued)*

(continues)

COMMONWEALTH v. LODER   Mass. **533**
Cite as, Mass.App., 351 N.E.2d 533

the new rule of interspousal tort liability will await development in future cases.[4]

It follows that the motion for summary judgment should not have been allowed and that the judgment is to be vacated.

So ordered.

COMMONWEALTH

v.

Robert D. LODER.

Appeals Court of Massachusetts, Middlesex.

Argued May 10, 1976.

Decided July 27, 1976.

Defendant was convicted in Superior Court, Middlesex County, of rape, armed robbery, burglary and the commission of an unnatural and lascivious act, and he appealed. The Appeals Court held that the trial court acted correctly in denying in part defendant's motion to suppress in-court and out-of-court identifications by the victims.

Affirmed.

Criminal Law ☞339.7(1), 339.8(1)

In prosecution for rape and related offenses, trial court acted properly in refusing to suppress photographic and other pretrial identifications of defendant by victims.

4. In *Sorensen v. Sorensen*, —— Mass. ——, ——, 339 N.E.2d 907 (1975) (Mass.Adv.Sh. [1975] 3662, 3665), in abrogating parental immunity in automobile tort cases we limited the liability to the extent of the parent's automobile liability insurance coverage. In the present case there is nothing in the record concerning the availability or the amount of

Daniel F. Toomey, Boston, for defendant.

Bonnie H. MacLeod-Griffin, Asst. Dist. Atty., for the Commonwealth.

Before HALE, C. J., and KEVILLE and GOODMAN, JJ.

RESCRIPT.

The defendant appeals under G.L. c. 278, §§ 33A–33G from convictions, after a jury trial, of rape, armed robbery and burglary, and the commission of an unnatural and lascivious act. He claims error in the denial in part, after a voir dire, of his motion to suppress in-court and out-of-court identifications by the victims, a young man and woman. At the time of the crimes the victims were occupying the bedroom of an apartment of the young woman. Two men entered and assaulted them during a period of one and one-half to two hours. The only light in the room came from a street light opposite the window and lights from the park across the street. These dimly illuminated the room. In the course of the episode the young man, despite being nearsighted, was able to view both assailants for a total period of ten minutes. For one minute, the face of the individual, later identified by the victims as the defendant, was only several inches distant from his eyes. The young woman was assaulted by the defendant for approximately thirty minutes. During that time her face was within inches of his face. Later that day the young man selected the defendant's photograph from an array of more than one hundred photographs shown him by the police and the young woman separately selected the defendant's photograph from six to ten

the defendant's liability insurance, and we do not refer to insurance as a limiting factor in our holding. We do not interpret the logic (as opposed to the precise holding) of *Sorensen* as turning on the availability of insurance in each case, and we decline to limit liability in interspousal tort actions in such a fashion.

Do not overlook this footnote. It is part of the *Lewis* decision.

Exhibit 7-7 *Lewis v. Lewis (concluded)*

DISCUSSION QUESTIONS

10. Compare the court's view in *Lewis* regarding the need to defer to the legislative branch with that of the court in *McBoyle*. Those cases, as well as the dissent in *Johnson*, illustrate a constant tension in our system between the elected legislature and the appointed judiciary. While the court will often defer to the legislative branch, there are times when it will not, especially in areas of law not yet touched by legislation. It is then that you will probably see a phrase similar to the one used by the *Lewis* court: "[T]he court not only has the authority but also the duty to reexamine its precedents." Do you think it is appropriate in a democratic society for a court to wield such power?

11. What exactly did Mrs. Lewis win?

12. On page 529 of the opinion, the court cites *Sorensen v. Sorensen*, a case in which a child wanted to sue his father for negligent driving. By citing this case the court seems to suggest that the same principles that apply to children suing their parents should apply to spouses suing each other. Do you agree?

Legal Reasoning Exercise

3. Based on *Lewis* analyze whether you think the doctrine of spousal immunity will bar Janice's claim.

E. THE POWER OF THE COURTS TO MAKE NEW LAW

In this chapter we have examined how to interpret the four major types of court opinions. In *McBoyle* the Court thought it was bound to narrowly interpret the statute. In another, *Johnson*, the Court struck down a state statute as unconstitutional. In *Callow* the court clung to stare decisis, whereas in *Lewis* the same court chose to remake the law.

How can you know whether a court will take a more liberal or a more conservative view of its role in changing the law? You can never know for sure, but here are some general guidelines. First, remember that all courts, even the U.S. Supreme Court, are bound to follow the Constitution. Therefore, the first question to ask is whether the issue involves a constitutional provision. If it does, then the court has the power to invalidate any statute or common law principle that is not in conformity with the Constitution.

If there is no constitutional provision involved, then the court's only role in statutory cases is to interpret the statute. The court is not free to rewrite the statute to reach a result that it thinks is more just. This is the type of case where the court has the least amount of freedom. (Of course, a determined court can often find ambiguity in the seemingly clearest of language and thereby "rewrite" the statute.) If there is no constitutional provision and no statute involved, then the court has the most freedom to shape the common law as it deems best to meet the needs of justice. See Figure 7-5.

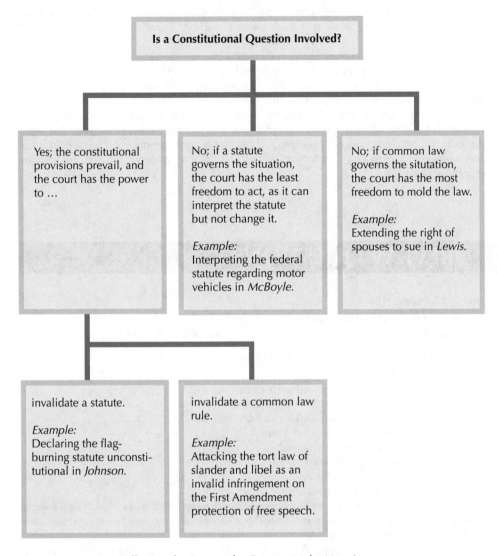

Figure 7-5 Factors Affecting the Power of a Court to Make New Law

---

SUMMARY

When interpreting a court opinion you must first determine if it is mandatory or persuasive authority. Mandatory authority comes from a higher court in the same jurisdiction. Second, you should be aware of the standard elements of any court opinion: the headnotes (in West editions) and the syllabus (prepared by the court or by West), the facts of the case, the statement of existing law, the issues raised, the decision reached, the reasoning, and, if they exist, concurring and/or dissenting opinions.

The traditional method for summarizing court opinions is known as case briefing. In this chapter we have examined one approach to case briefing that emphasizes the analytical skills that are the focus of this book. Depending on your purpose, however, you or your supervising attorney may wish to follow another method. There is no one right way to brief. Use the method that best serves your purpose.

As you can see from reading the cases in this chapter, the theory of stare decisis plays a vital role in our legal system: While it provides for stability, it also allows for change. In Chapter 8 we will continue to explore this topic as we discuss the next step in legal analysis: drafting a written discussion that compares your client's case to statutory rules and prior cases. Before that, however, we need to take a more detailed look at how to find the law. Although you may have appreciated how we have thus far supplied you with the statutes and court opinions, you probably have been wondering what you would do if someone asked you to go to a law library and find them for yourself. That is the topic of Appendix D.

REVIEW QUESTIONS

Pages 157 through 168

1. What are the four basic categories of court opinions?
2. What is the difference between mandatory and persuasive authority? Why does it matter?

Listed below are the possible answers for Questions 3 through 8.

a. U.S. Supreme Court
b. U.S. Court of Appeals for the First Circuit
c. U.S. Court of Appeals for the Second Circuit
d. U.S. District Court for the District of Massachusetts
e. Massachusetts Supreme Judicial Court
f. New Hampshire Supreme Court
g. Massachusetts Appeals Court
h. Massachusetts Superior Court
i. New Hampshire trial court

3. If the U.S. District Court for the District of Massachusetts heard a case regarding a federal statutory issue, which of the courts listed above could issue decisions that the district court would have to follow? Why?
4. If the U.S. Court of Appeals for the First Circuit heard a case regarding a federal statutory issue, which of the courts listed above could issue decisions that the court of appeals would have to follow? Why?
5. If the U.S. Supreme Court heard a case regarding a federal statutory issue, which of the courts listed above could issue decisions that the U.S. Supreme Court would have to follow? Why?
6. If a Massachusetts superior court (a trial court) heard a case regarding a Massachusetts state law issue, which of the courts listed above could issue decisions that the superior court would have to follow? Why?
7. If the Massachusetts Appeals Court (an intermediate-level appellate court) heard a case regarding a Massachusetts state law issue, which of the courts listed above could issue decisions that the appeals court would have to follow? Why?
8. If the Massachusetts Supreme Judicial Court (the highest appellate court in Massachusetts) heard a case regarding a Massachusetts state law issue, which of the courts listed above could issue decisions that the Supreme Judicial Court would have to follow? Why?

9. For each of the situations listed in Questions 3-8, indicate which of the following would be seen as mandatory authority by the court hearing the case. Give a short explanation for each of your answers. (Assume all constitutional provisions and statutes deal with the same issue that the court is facing.)
   a. U.S. constitutional provision
   b. U.S. statute
   c. Massachusetts statute
   d. Massachusetts constitutional provision
   e. New Hampshire constitutional provision
   f. New Hampshire statute
10. What is the difference between analogizing a case and distinguishing a case?
11. Give an example of when a court decided to overrule precedent and thereby dramatically changed the current law.
12. Why does court-made law generally evolve slowly?

Pages 168 through 209

13. Explain the difference between overruling a decision and reversing a decision.
14. List each part of a brief, and describe the function of each.
15. Look at each of the following potential case holdings for the *Blair* case. Which one do you think best represents a holding as it should appear in a case brief? Why? What is wrong with the others? Which is the broadest holding? The narrowest?
    a. Yes.
    b. Yes, burglary is committed when someone enters a partially enclosed carwash.
    c. Yes, it is unlawful to enter a partially enclosed carwash.
    d. Yes, the defendant should be found guilty.
    e. Yes, burglary, which requires the entering of a building or house trailer, is committed when someone enters any partially enclosed building designed to protect people or property.
    f. Yes, burglary, which requires the entering of a building or house trailer, is committed when someone enters a partially enclosed carwash.
    g. Reversed.
    h. The trial court's decision was correct.
16. Why is it sometimes important to include the reasoning of concurring and/or dissenting opinions in a case brief?

Chapter 8

Applying the Law

If you do not know where you are going, it is damnably hard to get there. It is even harder for the instructor to see how you got there.
Karl Llewellyn

INTRODUCTION

Written analysis based on court opinions is similar to what we discussed in Chapter 6 on statutory interpretation. Now, however, instead of gleaning the rule from the statutory language and presumed legislative intent, the rule comes from the holding of a court decision or a series of court decisions. Also, your analysis section will now be very fact based as you compare and contrast your client's facts with those of the cases you cite.

A. PREDICTING THE OUTCOME IN YOUR CLIENT'S CASE

As a practical matter few people (lawyers and paralegals included) read cases in a vacuum just for the fun it. Usually, they read cases because they are striving to keep current in their area of expertise or because they have a client and need to see whether prior cases will help or hurt the client's situation.

1. Looking for Analogies and Distinctions

In determining the extent to which a court opinion applies to a client's facts, you engage in a process of comparing the facts involved in the prior cases with those of the client's situation. As we have discussed, this process of looking at two decisions and deciding that they are similar is called analogizing. If you find that the two cases are similar, then the doctrine of **stare decisis** will suggest that they should be decided the same way. If they are different in important respects, the prior case is distinguishable and is not applicable to the client's problem.

Therefore, after case briefing, the next step is to use the opinions that you have briefed as a basis for predicting the likely outcome in your client's situation. To do that, you must find both the factual similarities (analogies) and the factual differences (distinctions) between your client's situation and that of the prior decision.

The steps that are necessary to evaluate whether a prior decision and a client's case will be seen as essentially similar or dissimilar follow.

a. Determine Whether the Governing Rules of Law and Issues Are the Same in Both Cases

Obviously, you should not rely on a case dealing with wills to decide a situation involving an intentional tort. However, if yours is one of those situations when there is no established law in the area, you will need to rely on cases in closely related, though not identical, areas of the law, where a logical extension can be made. For example, if there are no cases in your jurisdiction on parental immunity, you might look to cases on spousal immunity for guidance. Because the rules and issues are not identical, however, you will have to work at convincing the court why the same policies that applied in the prior cases should apply to your case.

b. Decide Which Facts Are the Key Facts in the Prior Case

Key facts are those facts that, if changed, might have caused the court to reach a different result.

c. Decide How Those Facts Are Similar to or Different from the Facts of Your Client's Case

To find similarities between the prior decision and the client's situation, think in general terms. For example, both the prior case and your client's situation might involve children who were injured in the daytime. To find distinctions between the prior case and your client's situation, be as specific as possible, within reason. For example, you might find the following differences between your case and the prior case: In your case the child was a six-year-old, but in the prior case the child was thirteen years old. In both cases the accident happened in the daytime; however, in the prior case it was at noon on a bright sunny day, and in your case it was at 4:30 in the afternoon on a cold wintery overcast day. All these differences might matter. On the other hand, it probably is irrelevant that the child's name in the prior case was Mark and your client's name is Bill.

Generally, whenever you have a precedent that you like and that you would like the court to apply to your client's situation, you should search for as many similarities as possible between your facts and the key facts in the prior case. For any facts that do differ you must find ways to convince the court that those differences are so insignificant that they do not matter. On the other hand, if you have a precedent that you do not like, try to find as many differences as possible between the facts in your client's situation and those in the precedent. It is only by thus distinguishing the two situations that you can convince the court it should not apply the precedent to your client's situation. If there are any similar facts, you must argue that they are insignificant and should not affect the court's view that the two situations are fundamentally different. (*Note*: There are times, however, when a difference between two cases actually supports an argument that they should be decided the same way. For example, assume a court found that a store owner who had detained a suspected shoplifter for one hour had acted unreasonably. If in the next case the shopkeeper detained a suspected shoplifter for two hours, the facts in the two cases would differ. However, rather than helping the shopkeeper in the second case, the difference actually reinforces the argument that he, too, acted unreasonably.)

As a tool to help you find similarities and differences, it is often a good idea to draw a chart. In the chart explicitly label specific facts as facts that tend to show how the two situations are analogous or distinguishable. This is the most important step in legal analysis. If you take the time to note as many analogies and distinctions as possible, most of your work will be done.

d. Explain Why Those Similarities or Differences Matter

A mere listing of the factual similarities and differences is not enough. You must explain to your reader why particular similarities or differences should affect the outcome of your client's case. In the example given above assume our six-year-old client accidentally shot a neighbor child with his father's hunting rifle. The issue is whether or not he should be tried for manslaughter. If in the prior case under similar facts a thirteen-year-old child was tried for manslaughter, we would, of course, point to the differences in the children's ages. But do not assume that pointing to differences, even obvious differences, is enough. Explain why a six-year-old should be treated differently from a thirteen-year-old.

2. Selecting among Precedents

Once you have completed your initial thinking about the similarities and differences between your case and those cases that you found through your research, you must decide which of the cases to emphasize and which to mention only briefly or not at all.

Naturally you will rely on primary authority over secondary authority and mandatory authority over persuasive authority. Among mandatory authority you will usually rely more on cases from the highest appellate court in your jurisdiction than on those from an intermediate-level appellate court. Other factors that will influence your choice include the age of the case and how close the facts are to your client's facts. Two similar cases are said to be **on point** with each other. If the facts of the two cases are almost identical, they are said to be **on all fours.** You would also rather rely on a unanimous decision or one written by a well-known jurist. Therefore, all things being equal, you would prefer to use

1. a case from the highest appellate court in your jurisdiction
2. that was decided recently

On point
A term used to describe a case that is similar to another case.

On all fours
A term used to describe two cases that are almost identical, with similar facts and legal issues.

3. with facts similar to your own and
4. decided by a unanimous court and
5. written by a well-known and respected judge.

In addition to following these rules for deciding on which precedents to rely, you must develop an ability to analyze the cases in the light most favorable to your client.

It will be your job, as well as that of someone working on the opposing side, to develop a list of what you believe are the most relevant cases and statements of what you believe the holdings of those cases to be. You will frequently find that you disagree with your colleagues, as well as with those representing the opposing side, as to which cases belong on that list and what those cases stand for. In fact, not even courts are immune from this ability to, in effect, see "both sides of a case." A good example of this was illustrated in a U.S. Supreme Court decision, *Texas v. White*.[1] In that case Mr. White was arrested at 1:30 in the afternoon. The police had his car towed to the police station, where they conducted a warrantless search. Based on the evidence found in the case Mr. White was convicted. Both Mr. White's attorneys and the attorneys for the state argued that the holding in the prior U.S. Supreme Court decision of *Chambers v. Maroney* supported their point of view. Take a few minutes to read the following excerpts from *Chambers v. Maroney*, and decide whether you think the holding in *Chambers* should have helped or hurt Mr. White.

Chambers v. Maroney
399 U.S. 42 (1970)

Mr. Justice WHITE delivered the opinion of the Court.

The principal question in this case concerns the admissibility of evidence seized from an automobile, in which petitioner was riding at the time of his arrest, after the automobile was taken to a police station and was there thoroughly searched without a warrant. The Court of Appeals for the Third Circuit found no violation of petitioner's Fourth Amendment rights. We affirm.

I

During the night of May 20, 1963, a Gulf service station in North Braddock, Pennsylvania, was robbed by two men, each of whom carried and displayed a gun. . . . Two teenagers, who had earlier noticed a blue compact station wagon circling the block in the vicinity of the Gulf station, then saw the station wagon speed away from a parking lot close to the Gulf station. About the same time, they learned that the Gulf station had been robbed. They reported to police, who arrived immediately, that four men were in the station wagon and one was wearing a green sweater. Kovacich told the police that one of the men who robbed him was wearing a green sweater and the other was wearing a trench coat. A description of the car and the two robbers was broadcast over the police radio. Within an hour, a light blue compact station wagon answering the description and carrying four men was stopped by the police about two miles from the Gulf station. Petitioner was one of the men in the station wagon. He was wearing a green sweater and there was a trench coat in the car. The occupants were arrested and the car was driven to the police station. In the course of a

[1] 423 U.S. 67 (1975).

thorough search of the car at the station, the police found concealed in a compartment under the dashboard two .38-caliber revolvers (one loaded with dumdum bullets), a right-hand glove containing small change, and certain cards bearing the name of Raymond Havicon, the attendant at a Boron service station in McKeesport, Pennsylvania, who had been robbed at gun-point on May 13, 1963. . . .

II

We pass quickly to the claim that the search of the automobile was the fruit of an unlawful arrest. Both the courts below thought the arresting officers had probable cause to make the arrest. We agree. . . .

In terms of the circumstances justifying a warrantless search, the Court has long distinguished between an automobile and a home or office. In *Carroll v. United States*, 267 U.S. 132 (1925), the issue was the admissibility in evidence of contraband liquor seized in a warrantless search of a car on the highway. After surveying the law from the time of the adoption of the Fourth Amendment onward, the Court held that automobiles and other conveyances may be searched without a warrant in circumstances that would not justify the search without a warrant of a house or an office, provided that there is probable cause to believe that the car contains articles that the officers are entitled to seize. . . .

On the facts before us, the blue station wagon could have been searched on the spot when it was stopped since there was probable cause to search and it was a fleeting target for a search. The probable-cause factor still obtained at the station house and so did the mobility of the car unless the Fourth Amendment permits a warrantless seizure of the car and the denial of its use to anyone until a warrant is secured. In that event there is little to choose in terms of practical consequences between an immediate search without a warrant and the car's immobilization until a warrant is obtained. [It was not unreasonable in this case to take the car to the station house. All occupants in the car were arrested in a dark parking lot in the middle of the night. A careful search at that point was impractical and perhaps not safe for the officers, and it would serve the owner's convenience and the safety of his car to have the vehicle and the keys together at the station house.] The same consequences may not follow where there is unforeseeable cause to search a house. Compare *Vale v. Louisiana*, ante, 399 U.S. 30. But as *Carroll*, supra, held, for the purpose of the Fourth Amendment there is a constitutional difference between houses and cars. . . .

Affirmed.

What do you think the Court's holding in *Chambers* was? Certainly the Court ruled that the police did have probable cause to stop the automobile and arrest the occupants. The Court also ruled that the police had a legal right to search the car at the station without first obtaining a search warrant. But what is the significance of this decision for future defendants? What general principles of law emerged that were likely to be applied to future cases?

More specifically, do you think the Court held that the police have the right to search any vehicle at the police station if they had probable cause to search it at the scene of the arrest? Or do you think the police can conduct warrantless searches of vehicles at the police station only when they stopped the automobile in a dark parking lot at night, the facts that existed in *Chambers*? Justice White's opinion specifically mentioned that the arrests took place "in a dark parking lot in the middle of the night" and that a "careful search at the point was impractical and perhaps not safe for the officers."

In *Texas v. White*[2] lawyers for the state of Texas argued that *Chambers* stood for the principle that whenever the police had the right to conduct a

---

[2]423 U.S. 67 (1975).

warrantless search of an automobile at the scene of the arrest, they also had the right to conduct such a warrantless search at the police station.

White's lawyers disagreed. They argued that *Chambers* stood for the principle that police could conduct a warrantless search of an automobile at the station only when conditions at the scene of the arrest made it unsafe to conduct a search there. White's lawyers argued that because the police could have safely searched White's car in daylight, the *Chambers* decision did not apply to White's situation.

In a per curiam decision the U.S. Supreme Court agreed with the state, declaring that

> [i]n *Chambers v. Maroney* we held that police officers with probable cause to search an automobile on the scene where it was stopped could constitutionally do so later at the station house without first obtaining a warrant.[3]

Justices Marshall and Brennan, writing for the dissent, argued that Mr. White's conviction should be reversed and that the majority had misstated the true holding of the *Chambers* case:

> Only by misstating the holding of *Chambers v. Maroney*, can the Court make that case appear dispositive of this one. The court in its brief *per curiam* opinion today extends *Chambers* to a clearly distinguishable factual setting. . . .
>
> *Chambers* did not hold as the court suggests, "that police officers with probable cause to search an automobile on the scene where it was stopped could constitutionally do so later at the station house without first obtaining a warrant." . . . *Chambers* simply held that to be the rule when it is reasonable to take the car to the station house in the first place.[4]

This discussion regarding more than one possible "right" holding for a case should remind you of the one we had in Chapter 7. In that discussion we observed that in briefing a case you can state a holding either broadly so that it is not limited by the specific facts of the case or quite narrowly so that it is limited to those facts. When you are faced with a case that is harmful to your client, develop a narrow statement of the holding so that it is limited to the facts of the prior case. That is what the attorneys for White attempted to do by pointing out that the arrest in the prior case had occurred "in a dark parking lot in the middle of the night," whereas their client had been arrested in the middle of the day. If you have a case that is beneficial to your client, state the holding in broad enough terms so that it will cover both the facts of the prior case and those of your client's case. That is what the attorneys for the government did in *Texas v. White*.

B. A NOTE ON LOGIC

As we have seen, legal reasoning requires that we identify and evaluate arguments. This is a form of deductive logic. While learning about logic will not teach

---

[3]Id. at 68.

[4]Id. at 69.

you all there is to know about legal reasoning, an understanding of deductive reasoning will help you understand the basic structure of legal thinking.

All arguments involve evidence, assumptions, and the conclusion the speaker wants you to reach. Politicians make arguments so that you will conclude you should vote for them, car salespersons make arguments so that you will conclude you should buy your next car from them, and lawyers make arguments so that courts or opponents will conclude that the law should be interpreted in favor of their clients.

The strength of an argument's conclusion ultimately rests on the strength of the **evidence** in support of it. Strong evidence strengthens an argument, while weak evidence dilutes the strength of the conclusions. A car salesperson will be more persuasive if the evidence includes a Consumer Reports article highly rating the particular model that dealership sells. In a criminal trial the prosecutor has to present compelling evidence that a crime was committed and that the defendant was the person who did it.

Assumptions serve as a bridge between the evidence and the conclusion. An assumption is often an unstated belief that justifies the author in arguing his conclusion on the basis of the evidence presented. To take an example from daily life, a mother may note that her three-year-old child is crying and generally cranky. The conclusion she reaches is that he needs a nap. Her unstated assumption is that the crying and crankiness are due to a lack of sleep.

In legal reasoning it is important to know what your assumptions are. An argument is only **valid** if the assumptions that underlie it are valid. To take the prior example one step further, if the child is crying not because he needs sleep but because a dog just bit him, then the mother's conclusion, or solution, to the problem—putting the child to bed—is invalid.

Most legal arguments are presented in the form of **deductive reasoning**. Deductive reasoning involves a major premise, a minor premise, and a conclusion. The major and minor premises are assumptions. The most famous example of deductive reasoning is the following:

MAJOR PREMISE	All men are mortal.
MINOR PREMISE	Socrates is a man.
CONCLUSION	Therefore, Socrates is mortal.

In legal reasoning, the **major premise** is a statement of a legal rule that you can find in a statute or a court opinion. The **minor premise** consists of the client's facts. The conclusion is the answer you reach when you apply the law to the facts.

MAJOR PREMISE	Anyone intentionally taking the life of another human being is guilty of murder.
MINOR PREMISE	John intentionally shot Bill, taking his life.
CONCLUSION	Therefore, John is guilty of murder.

It is important to understand that "logic is concerned with form and not with truth. Perfectly ridiculous arguments can be logically correct."[5]

---

[5]Landau, Logic for Lawyers, 13 Pac. L.J. 59, 62 (1981).

Evidence
The way in which a question of fact is established. Evidence can consist of witness testimony or documents and exhibits. It is the proof presented at a trial.

Assumption
In logic, a belief that justifies one in arguing a conclusion.

Valid
In logic, an argument is considered to be valid or sound if the assumptions underlying the argument are true.

Deductive reasoning
A form of logical reasoning based on a major premise, a minor premise, and a conclusion.

Major premise
In deductive reasoning, the statement of a broad proposition that forms the starting point; in law, the statement of a legal rule that you can find in a statute or court opinion.

Minor premise
In deductive reasoning, the second proposition, which along with the major premise leads to the conclusion; in law, the minor premise consists of the client's facts.

Take the following example:

MAJOR PREMISE   All men are twenty feet tall.
MINOR PREMISE   George is a man.
CONCLUSION   Therefore, George is twenty feet tall.

Because the major premise is false, the conclusion is false. Nonetheless, because the form follows the deductive model, the conclusion is logically correct. It is just not true. Take a more serious example:

MAJOR PREMISE   Anyone intentionally taking the life of another human being is guilty of murder.
MINOR PREMISE   As required by his job, Sam, the state executioner, intentionally takes the life of prisoners sentenced to die in the electric chair.
CONCLUSION   Therefore, Sam is guilty of murder.

Again the conclusion is false because the major premise is not true. It is not true that *anyone* taking the life of another is guilty of murder. Clearly there are exceptions.

Therefore, while the deductive model provides the structure for legal argument, logic can never tell us whether our conclusions are right. The conclusions we reach depend on us using the correct law for the major premise and accurately reflecting the facts in the minor premise. In the first example given above assume John shot Bill as they were struggling with a gun that Bill had aimed at John's head. These additional facts suggest that the minor premise as stated is false because it does not contain all the relevant information. With that additional information, we might conclude that John did not "intentionally" shoot Bill.

When you are presented with a deductive argument, there are two ways to attack it. First, you can argue that there is something wrong with the major premise. Perhaps it has been stated too broadly, as in the second example. Second, you can try to find flaws with the minor premise. Examine whether the writer has omitted or distorted the facts.

When creating deductive arguments yourself, you must ensure not only that the facts that make up the minor premise are accurate but also that you portray them in the light most favorable to your client. For example, it is not only permissible but also necessary to interpret ambiguous facts in the best way to help your client. However, be aware that there is a definite line between interpreting facts and changing facts. You must interpret the facts. You must not distort them.

This leads us to our last reason for including this short lesson on logic. The deductive model requires three things: a major premise, a minor premise, and a conclusion. As we have mentioned before, one of the most common and fatal flaws in legal analysis is the omission of the reasoning. Keeping the three components of the deductive model in mind will remind you that legal analysis is more than the statement of a major premise (the law) and a conclusion. It also requires that you discuss the minor premise (the facts) that provides the logical link between the major premise and the conclusion and that you supply your reasoning, justifying your conclusion.

In a famous quotation Justice Oliver Wendell Holmes said that "the life of the law has not been logic: it has been experience."[6] Justice Holmes was right: The process of legal analysis is a very human, creative process. However, logic still plays an important role in legal analysis. Logic provides the structure of legal reasoning even when judges and lawyers appeal to other factors to justify their conclusions.

C. THE FORMAT FOR A WRITTEN ANALYSIS

In Chapter 6 we discussed how the IRAC (Issue-Rule-Analysis-Conclusion) format can help you organize your arguments when you write a statutory analysis. Likewise, when writing an analysis based on court opinions, following the IRAC format will help ensure that your writing follows a logical pattern. In addition, you should develop a style that allows you to synthesize the points raised by a group of cases rather than a style whereby you simply report the cases one by one.

1. Using IRAC

The breakdown of each of the IRAC elements, when writing an analysis based on court opinions, is as follows:

ISSUE — Have a topic sentence that states the issue you will be discussing in that paragraph. This sentence should be brief and clear. It should also contain only one idea: the one to be discussed in that particular paragraph.

RULE — State the rule of law that arguably governs the particular issue in question.

ANALYSIS — Explain how prior court opinions determine the outcome for your client's case. When citing a court opinion, briefly give the facts, holding, and reasoning to demonstrate how and why that case relates to the facts and issues of your own situation. Note the strong parallels (analogies) and the critical differences (distinctions) between the cited opinion and your own situation. Be very specific both when referring to facts from the cited court opinions and when referring to facts from your client's situation. Be sure to explain *why* you think those similarities or differences matter. Remember that the reasoning in the court's opinion will determine whether a court will see your case and the precedent as fundamentally similar or different.

CONCLUSION — Conclude! Do not leave your reader to decide what the bottom line is. That is why your supervisor asked you to analyze the problem.

---

[6]Oliver Wendell Holmes, Jr., The Common Law 1 (1881).

Ethics Alert

If you use information from a dissent in your analysis, *always* tell your reader that it came from a dissent. Failure to do so would seriously mislead your reader as to the correct status of the law.

TRANSITION   Use a short transition sentence to lead to the next issue that you want to discuss.

When faced with a fairly simple legal problem, all the IRAC elements may fit into a single paragraph. At other times you may want to divide the IRAC elements. For example, you might wish to set out the issue and the rule of law in one paragraph, the analysis for the plaintiff in a second paragraph, the analysis for the defendant and your conclusion in a third paragraph, and the transitional phrase or sentence in the first sentence of yet a fourth paragraph.

The amount of emphasis that you place on the factual comparisons between your case and the cited cases will vary, however, depending on whether you are working for a change in the law or are dealing with well-established legal principles that require you to analogize and distinguish your client's case relative to existing case law. If you are engaging in the first type of analysis, arguing for a change in the law, then your analysis section will be more policy based. For example, recall the case of Janice Miller, the woman who was injured when she was working with her husband cutting and stacking wood. If you were representing Janice in 1977, shortly after the Massachusetts Supreme Judicial Court decided that spouses could sue each other but limited their holding to motor vehicle accidents, you would be arguing for a change in the law that would allow suits in any negligence claim. Your analysis would be primarily based not on the factual issues, but on the policy reasons for extending the holding in *Lewis*. Such an analysis might look similar to the following:

Our client Janice Miller would like to sue her husband for injuries that she received when they were working together in their backyard cutting wood. The current law in Massachusetts is that spouses can sue each other only for injuries sustained in motor vehicle accidents. *Lewis v. Lewis*, 351 N.E.2d 526 (Mass. 1976). In the *Lewis* decision the court changed the long-standing rule that spouses could never sue each other for injuries sustained during their marriage. While recognizing the spiritual unity of marriage, *id.* at 528, n.1, the court stated that the doctrine of the legal unity of marriage was no longer a sufficient reason to bar such suits. *Id.* at 528. The principal motivating force behind this decision was the "general principle that if there is tortious injury there should be recovery." *Id.* at 532. Similarly, in our case the wife was injured by the negligence of her husband, and spousal immunity should not shield her husband from suit.

The court did, however, limit its holding to motor vehicle accidents. *Id.* While recognizing that injured parties should be able to pursue their claims, the court was mindful that "[c]onduct, tortious between two strangers, may not be tortious because of the mutual concessions implied in the marital relationship." *Id.* This is such a case. The spouses were working together on a joint project. This was not the situation where one spouse was solely responsible for the enterprise as is true when driving a car. If the court were to allow suit in this case, it would open the court system to every injury that occurs when spouses are working together on household chores. For example, if one winter morning a husband were to forget to salt the front steps and his wife were to slip on them, expanding the holding in *Lewis* would allow such suits into the courthouse. Therefore, in acknowledgment of the special unity of marriage, suits between spouses should be limited to situations such as motor vehicle accidents, where one party is solely responsible for the safety of the undertaking. In conclusion, Janice Miller should not be allowed to sue her husband for a nonmotor vehicle accident.

The purpose of an analysis is to present the arguments that each side will make and to predict how a court will resolve the issue. In the analysis you should candidly evaluate both the strengths and the weaknesses of the client's case. An analysis that tells only about the strengths of a client's case will do little good, as a supervising attorney needs to know not only what arguments to make but also how to combat the arguments that the opposing side will make. As one well-known authority on legal writing has said, the purpose of an analysis

> is to explore and evaluate candidly the strength and weakness of the client's case. It should therefore be as much concerned with the weaknesses of the case as with the favorable aspects, and should devote at least as much attention to precedents and other authorities against the client's position as to those that are for him. The cases and authorities contra should, of course, be carefully analyzed too so if they can be distinguished or otherwise minimized, but this too should be done with complete willingness to face the situation realistically.
>
> . . . Try to put yourself in the position of your opposite number. Ask yourself: If I were he, how would I answer the analysis or argument just made? How would I rebut or distinguish the cases cited? What countervailing arguments could I offer? Minimizing or covering up what may prove to be fatal weaknesses is the worst thing you can do. It is your responsibility to point out where the dangers lie, where the decisive battles are going to be fought.[7]

While it is always nice to turn out to be right in your prediction of how the court will ultimately resolve the issue, it is more important that you fairly present both sides of the issue than that you select the correct result. Remember, until a

---

[7]Henry Weihofen, Legal Writing Style 230 (2d ed. 1980).

court resolves the issue, there is no correct result, just better or worse arguments. As it turns out, the Massachusetts Supreme Judicial Court did not think it was so ridiculous to let a wife sue her husband for failing to salt the front steps. In 1980, in *Brown v. Brown*,[8] a case involving that very fact scenario, the court expanded the *Lewis* decision to allow spouses to sue each other in all types of negligence cases. As in *Lewis*, the trial court had dismissed the case at the pretrial stage. Therefore, the appellate court was not in a position to determine whether the husband should be found negligent. All the appellate court decided was that the wife had the right to take her case to court and to let a jury hear the facts in order to determine whether her husband should be found liable for negligence.

Legal Reasoning Exercise

1. Read the following article that appeared in the Boston Globe shortly after the Massachusetts Supreme Judicial Court decided *Brown v. Brown*. What do you think of the author's comments? Why is the statement "the Superior Court agreed, more or less, with defendant Bill that the wife would have hauled ashes" misleading?

By MIKE BARNICLE

Spouse suits, a new wave of Americana

Here, in the middle of summer, comes the perfect story to put your mind on vacation. It is the story of Brown vs. Brown.

It begins in Wakefield at 8 o'clock in the morning on the 21st day of December, 1978. It is a miserable day with snow and sleet drawing a gray shade over the dawn.

A husband gets out of bed to go to work. He leaves the house about 7 o'clock.

A wife gets out of bed. She leaves the house about 8 o'clock.

The wife walks from the front door to the driveway. She slips and falls on the ice.

She lands on her pelvis. Shortly, you will think she landed on her head.

She goes to the hospital. Two pelvic bones are broken.

Guess where she goes later? Figure it out: This is America. What is the absolutely most American thing to do when anything bothers you?

Right: The wife goes to court. She sues the husband. For $35,000: says the husband should have shoveled the walk before he went to work.

The couple used to be known as William and Shirley Brown. Since December of 1978, they have been affectionately called the plaintiff and the defendant.

"Do they still live together?" the wife's lawyer Charles Blumstack was asked.

"They live together and they love each other," the lawyer said.

"Can they settle out of court?" the husband's lawyer, Anil Madan was asked.

---

[8]409 N.E.2d 717 (Mass. 1980).

"The question you want to ask is will they?" Madan answered. "And I can't answer that."

You are nothing in this country today unless you go to court. It is a badge of honor: proof that you are alive.

Plaintiff Shirley took her damage suit to the courts in 1979. Then, the Superior Court agreed, more or less, with defendant Bill that the wife could have hauled ashes to sprinkle on the ice that infamous morning. Case dismissed.

However, worse than not going to court is going and giving up at the first level. Naturally, Shirley Brown went forward to the Supreme Judicial Court.

Wednesday, Justice Robert Braucher knocked the Superior Court ruling over and said that Mrs. Brown should have the right to sue her husband. The Browns now go back to the lower court to fight the thing out.

There will be a discovery motion. This is the process where both parties are asked written questions and come up with written lies for answers. Lies are the things that keep courts in business, especially in anything involving a husband and wife.

Then there will be a trial. This will be the most fun of all.

The defense, the lawyers for Plaintiff Bill, could call Bella Abzug as a witness. They could ask her if a woman should not be given the right to handle a snow blower or a shovel.

As a matter of fact, this whole bizarre case raises the question: Where is the women's movement? Why isn't Bill Brown being praised by the feminists?

A snowstorm is an equal opportunity employer. Ice can be chipped by both women and men. Salt can be spread by a construction worker or a housewife. You don't need special muscles to put ashes on a sidewalk.

Instead of settling the thing in the kitchen though, we might now have the spectacle of a jury being asked to decide whether the husband was guilty for not scraping the walk clean before he went to work. You do not have to be a genius to figure out the ramifications of such a trial.

Imagine what the courts would be flooded with next.

Broken garbage disposal, bookshelves that fall down, clogged toilets, stuck windows, ripped screens, carpets with holes and walls with cracks . . . all of it could become the potential property of the judicial system. Unless a husband uses common sense and makes sure the wife knows he is totally irresponsible and thus, judgment proof, Brown vs. Brown is just the beginning.

"I even make my wife go out and start the car on cold mornings," Joe Buccieri of the East Boston Buccieris was saying. "It's only fair."

"She's grown to like it, too. It gives her a chance to get out of the house once in awhile. She goes out, takes the paper and a cup of coffee with her and sits there and reads until the car and the seat are both warm."

"Sounds to me like they should give the husband a saliva test," my friend Albert Baranello was saying. "His old lady sues him for something like that and he's still in the house with her. That's crazy."

"What would you do?" he was asked.

"Do what I've done four times already," Baranello answered. "Get divorced. You don't even need a trial for that."

Mike Barnicle is a Globe columnist.[9]

---

[9] Barnicle, Spouse Suits, A New Wave of Americana, Boston Globe, Aug. 1, 1980.

If your client's case requires you to work not at changing the law but rather at analyzing or distinguishing the case from existing law, then your analysis will be much more fact based. However, not all factual distinctions and similarities are equally important. Therefore, you will still need to turn to policy arguments to explain why some facts are more important than others. For example, if Janice were to overcome the hurdle of spousal immunity, then the next issue should be whether her husband would be found negligent. Look at the following two possible approaches to analyzing this problem. In the margins of each approach label each of the IRAC elements. Then decide which approach is better and why.

Approach 1

The issue is whether Mr. Booth can be found negligent because of the injuries his wife suffered when Mr. Booth allowed the chain saw he was using to slip, slicing off a piece of bark that flew into Ms. Miller's eye. The general rule is that to avoid negligence a person should take precautions once warned of drowsiness or fatigue. *Keller v. DeLong*, 231 A.2d 633, 634 (N.H. 1967). In *Keller* the defendant, while a passenger, felt sleepy. Before taking over at the wheel he did not take any precautions against falling asleep, such as rolling down the windows or turning on the radio. Soon after that he fell asleep and hit a utility pole, killing his passenger. The court held that the defendant was negligent because he had felt sleepy as a passenger but had taken no precautions before taking over at the wheel. *Id.* at 635. The court reasoned that because the defendant did not take any precautions to avoid the accident, the accident was foreseeable. *Id.*

Unlike the *Keller* case, Mr. Booth would argue that the harm to Ms. Miller was not foreseeable. There are significant differences between driving a car and operating a chain saw. If someone drives a car negligently, the passengers are just as likely as the driver to be injured. But when using a chainsaw, the person most likely to be hurt is the one using it, in this case Mr. Booth and not Ms. Miller.

However, while the person most likely to be hurt may be the operator of the chain saw, any dangerous instrument, if used carelessly, can easily inflict injury on others. Indeed, that is what happened in this case. As in *Keller*, the defendant was warned of the impending danger. In *Keller* the driver felt drowsy as a passenger and yet took no precautions before taking over at the wheel. In Mr. Booth's case, he told his wife that he was feeling fatigued just before the accident occurred. If anything, the negligence in Mr. Booth's case is greater because the defendant felt tired while operating the chain saw and yet continued to operate it. It would have been a simple matter to have taken a break, but Mr. Booth chose to continue with a dangerous activity even while knowing he was fatigued. As in *Keller*, once the defendant is warned of his fatigue, an injury is foreseeable. Therefore, Mr. Booth should be found negligent.

Approach 2

Mr. Booth's wife suffered injuries when they were working together in their backyard sawing wood. Mr. Booth had told his wife that he was feeling fatigued just before the accident happened. In *Keller* the defendant, while a passenger, felt sleepy. Before taking over at the wheel he did not take any precautions against falling asleep, such as rolling down the windows or turning on the radio. Soon thereafter he fell asleep and hit a utility pole, killing his passenger. On its face that case is easily distinguishable from our own. There are significant differences between driving a car and operating a chain saw. However, both a chain saw and an automobile can cause injuries.

In Approach 1 the writer uses the IRAC format. The paragraph starts with a statement of the issue, followed by the rule that will be applied. The analysis section gives both the holding and the reasoning of a prior court decision, *Keller*. This is followed by two paragraphs comparing and contrasting the facts of the client's case with those of *Keller*. Finally, the writer concludes that Mr. Booth should be found negligent. In Approach 2 the writer begins with a statement of the facts without first putting those facts into context by starting with an issue statement. Next the writer begins a discussion of a prior case without first explaining what the general rule of law is or why the writer is discussing that particular case. For an analysis the writer simply states that the facts are similar or different without explaining why the similarities or differences matter. Finally, the writer forgets to conclude. Therefore, Approach 2 fails in its mission to start off with a clear issue statement, explain the current state of the law, apply that law to the client's facts, and conclude.

In sum, when writing an analysis you may be trying to argue for a change in the law, or you may be working to show how your client's case fits into a pattern of well-established case law. In this latter type of case, however, you should be aware that you are still asking the court to "change the law," even if only in an evolutionary sense, in that after your case we will know more about exactly what the law means than we knew before the case was decided. Finally, besides

PRACTICAL TIP

Here are some hints for a successful analysis:

- Tell enough about each case so that the reader will not have to read the cases.
- Give both sides of the argument.
- Work with the facts.
- Explain *why* the court should care that the facts are the same or that the facts are different.

analyzing cases there will be times when, as we discussed in Chapter 6, a statute will govern your problem. In that situation you will begin with an analysis of the statute itself, but then you will probably add an analysis of any cases that have interpreted the statute. The three legal reasoning exercises at the end of this section will give you practice with each of these three types of analysis.

2. Synthesizing Cases

When you are doing research, you read cases one at a time and summarize them one at a time. If that is then how you report them to your reader, you have done little more than hand over your case briefs. What you need to do is to synthesize them so that the reader understands what principles of law arise out of reading the series of cases as a unit. The following is an example taken from Writing and Analysis in the Law by Helene S. Shapo, Marilyn R. Walter, and Elizabeth Fajans.[10] Read each approach and then decide which you like better and why.

Approach 1

Two factors determine parental immunity for a tort suit in Kent: the type of tort involved and the age of the child. First, immunity extends to suits for negligence only. Parents are not immune from suits for intentional torts. The Kent Supreme Court has held that parents are not immune from their child's suit for assault, *Brown v. Brown*, and for battery, *White v. White*. But the court has held that parents are immune from a negligence suit brought by their child. *Abbott v. Abbott*. Second, parental immunity extends only to a suit brought by a minor child. *Id.* (immunity against twelve-year-old child's suit for negligence); *Black v. Black* (no immunity against twenty-four-year-old's suit for negligence).

Approach 2

The Kent Supreme Court has decided four cases on parental immunity from tort suits by their children. In the first case in 1965, the court decided that a parent was immune from suit for negligence brought by his twelve-year-old son. *Abbott v. Abbott* (1965). However, in the next suit, in 1968, the court held that a parent was not immune from suit for battery brought by a ten-year-old son. *White v. White* (1968). Only a year later in *Brown v. Brown* (1969), the court affirmed that a parent is not immune from suit for assault brought by a twenty-four-year-old daughter. The most recent case on this topic is *Black v. Black*, decided in 1982. In *Black*, the court decided another suit by a twenty-four-year-old against his parent, this time for negligence. The court still decided that the parent is not immune.

---

[10]Helen S. Shapo, Marilyn R. Walter, and Elizabeth Fajans, Writing and Analysis in the Law 51 (3d ed. 1995).

Hopefully, you found the first example much easier to understand. The author starts by giving you a frame of reference: There will be two factors determining parental immunity. The author then goes on to discuss each of these factors. In the second example the author simply lists the cases in chronological order. The first approach does a much better job of explaining to the reader the principles for which these cases stand.

Legal Reasoning Exercises

2. In this problem you need to argue for a change in the law.

Your firm represents Amanda and Sam Baker, grandparents of two-year-old Brian Baker. Brian was recently injured in a home accident. The two-year-old stuck a hairpin into an electrical outlet and was severely burned. The parents had not installed safety plugs in the outlets because they felt the plugs gave a false sense of security. The plugs are easily removed and were not present in many of their friends' homes. The grandparents want to bring a negligence suit on the child's behalf against the parents.

Assume the Massachusetts Supreme Judicial Court has decided the following cases:

- *Sorensen v. Sorensen* (1975)—A child was injured when his father negligently caused an automobile accident. The court held that children could sue their parents but limited the holding to motor vehicle cases and limited the recovery to the amount of available insurance. For its reasoning the court stated that neither the argument that such suits would disrupt the peace and harmony of the family nor the argument that such actions would tend to promote fraud and collusion was valid.
- *Lewis v. Lewis* (1976)—A wife was injured when her husband negligently caused an automobile accident. The court held that the wife could sue her husband but limited the holding to motor vehicle cases. The court did not limit the recovery to the amount of insurance, stating: "In the present case there is nothing in the record concerning the availability or the amount of the defendant's liability insurance, and we do not refer to insurance as a limited factor in our holding. We do not interpret the logic (as opposed to the precise holding) of *Sorenson* as turning on the availability of insurance in each case, and we decline to limit liability in interspousal tort actions in such a fashion." The court cited *Sorenson* with approval as standing for the proposition that such suits would not disrupt the peace and harmony of the family or tend to promote fraud and collusion. Finally, while acknowledging that some actions that would constitute torts between strangers might not constitute torts if committed between spouses, the court based its decision on the general principle that normally there should be recovery for tortious injury.
- *Brown v. Brown* (1980)—A wife was injured when she slipped on the front steps that her husband had forgotten to salt. The court held that

the wife could sue her husband. The court reasoned that while certain behavior between spouses might not be tortious, that was for a trial court to determine at trial, and the case should not be dismissed as a matter of immunity.

Based on the prior case law develop arguments both for and against the child's being able to sue his parents for negligence.

3. In this problem you need to show how your case fits with established law.

Your firm represents the Gilberts. Last week the Gilberts went out to dinner at a fashionable lakeshore restaurant. After dinner they decided to take a stroll down a boardwalk that leads from the restaurant out onto a pier. The walkway was not lighted. About halfway down the pier Ms. Gilbert stepped on a board that gave way due to dry rot. She fell and was seriously injured. About five years ago the restaurant, which owns the pier, decided it was too expensive to keep up with the necessary repairs and had done nothing to maintain the pier since. The restaurant owners posted a sign near the entry to the pier that said "Danger."

Assume the Nebraska Supreme Court decided the following case:

■ *Weiss v. Autumn Hills* (1986)—One night the plaintiff, a tenant in the defendant landlord's apartment building, was walking across the unlighted grassy area adjoining the patio of her street-level apartment. Although there was a sidewalk leading to the parking lot, taking the sidewalk took longer than cutting across the grass, and many people chose this shorter route. The area was eroded due to water falling from a defective rain gutter. The plaintiff stepped in a rut covered by weeds and fell. The landlord was found negligent.

Based on the *Weiss* decision, will your client be able to show that the restaurant was negligent? List all the factual similarities that make you think the restaurant might be negligent. Then list all the factual differences that make you think the restaurant might not be negligent. Decide which of the factual differences or similarities are most important and why.

4. In this last problem you need to base your analysis on a statute and a case interpreting that statute.

Assume you have a client, Jack Brilliant, who has been charged with violating the National Motor Vehicle Theft Act. Last weekend a friend of his, Sam Slick, told your client that he had just acquired a new motorboat but that he did not know how to run it. He asked your client if he would go out for a ride with him on the Connecticut River and show him how to drive the boat. Your client agreed. They left from a marina in Massachusetts and headed south with your client at the wheel. Soon after they crossed the Connecticut border, they were flagged down by the marine patrol and arrested. Apparently Sam had stolen the motorboat.

Based on the language of the statute and the *McBoyle* decision (p. 180), what are the arguments that your client should be convicted of violating the National Motor Vehicle Theft Act? What are the arguments that he should not be convicted?

D. INTERNAL OFFICE MEMORANDA

We have been focusing on how to analyze prior court opinions in order to predict how a court will decide your client's case. In a law office setting your supervisor may ask you to include this analysis within a law office memorandum. A law office memorandum is made up of various sections. The most important section is the Discussion section. It is in that section that you include your analysis.

You write a law office memorandum to inform the person to whom it is addressed of what you have discovered. But you will also be creating a concise, permanent record that can be used by you, your supervisor, or someone else working on the same or a similar problem in the future. Such memoranda are usually placed in a permanent file. Later, when the firm has a similar case, attorneys and paralegals can take advantage of the work that has already been done and avoid needless duplication of effort. As we have discussed, to fully understand the issues, the analysis section should fairly evaluate both sides. Another reason for this two-sided approach is that someone in your firm representing a client on the other side of a similar issue may later use your memorandum.

As the quotation at the beginning of this chapter suggests, before you start to write, you must have thoroughly thought through the problem. It may be tempting to just sit down and hope the good thoughts will come to you as you write your memo. Do not fool yourself. It usually does not work that way. Legal analysis is complicated enough in its own right without being further complicated by stream of consciousness writing.

First, think about the problem. Then write an outline. The purpose of the outline is to force you to think through everything you want to say and the order in which you want to say it. To do that, you have to organize your ideas into issues and subissues, with some logical progression between issues. Be clear in your own mind why you are citing a particular case or including a specific argument. Ask yourself, How does this idea fit into the general structure of my argument? As you write your outline, many new thoughts probably will come to you. That is the time to organize them into a logical order—not as you write.

1. Format and Content

The degree of detail and the precise elements of a legal memorandum vary from one law office to another (or even from one lawyer within an office to another), but a law office memorandum usually consists of a heading, a listing of the issues raised (called the questions presented), brief answers to those issues, a statement of the facts, a discussion of the law and how it applies to the client's case, and a conclusion. The following outlines how a law office memorandum is ordinarily organized.

a. Heading

Use a traditional To:, From:, Re:, Date: format. Identify the person to whom you are directing the memo; yourself; the client's name, the office file number, and the memo's subject matter; and the date on which you prepared the memo.

b. Question Presented (Issue)

State the legal issues raised by the facts of the problem in as concrete a fashion as possible; that is, the legal issues should be related to the specific facts of the case. A general legal proposition or abstract question of law will do little to inform your reader of the specific facts and issues involved in your client's specific problem. The issue identification process is similar to that used in case briefs. It contains a general statement of the law and the specific facts to which that law will be applied.

You should carefully identify your issues before you begin your research because in writing the memorandum you should organize the analysis section around these issues.

Here are some general guidelines you should follow in formulating the Question Presented section:

1. State the question in terms of the *facts* of the case.
2. Identify the specific narrow legal question raised by the problem's facts.
3. Make sure the reader can understand the question on the first reading.
4. Eliminate all unnecessary verbiage.
5. Only include issues—that is, questions for which there are more than one possible answer.

Following these guidelines serves two purposes: (1) It will ensure that the question informs the reader of the content of this specific memorandum, and (2) it will aid you in your analysis by requiring you to focus on the specific issues of your client's problem. To arrive at such a precise statement, you may have to rewrite the question several times. Do not let that discourage you. If you can write a clear, simple statement of the issue, you will have gone a long way toward understanding how to analyze your client's problem.

c. Brief Answer

The brief answer should be brief. Write a short, specific answer to the question presented. First, give a definite answer. Follow that with a brief statement of the reasons that led you to that conclusion. A good check is to see if you have included a "because" in your answer. Generally, this section should not include restatements of the facts, citations, or argumentation. If you have researched more than one issue, you should write separate Question Presented and Brief Answer sections.

d. Facts

State the relevant facts of the legal problem you researched. Begin with a short summary of the general nature of the case and continue with a review of the key events in chronological order. As with case briefing be very specific about the facts. For example, rather than saying that a car was new, give the car's model year; instead of merely stating that a day was cold, provide the day's actual temperature. Do not omit facts that might influence the analysis of the problem. One good practice is to be sure that every fact you refer to in the Discussion section is set out in the statement of facts. Conversely, a fact you do not need for analysis is an irrelevant fact and should be omitted. Of course, you may also need to include some facts that are not strictly relevant to the issue to give the reader necessary background information. If you are unsure about how much to include, err on the side of including too many rather than too few facts.

e. Applicable Statutes

If the problem is controlled by a statute, a constitution, or an administrative regulation, quote the relevant language in this section. However, if it is only tangentially related to your main analysis, you may omit this section and quote the necessary language in the Discussion section.

f. Discussion

Start your discussion with an introductory paragraph that sets out the issues you will be discussing. Often this can be simply an expanded version of your question presented. The function of this paragraph is to tell the reader what issues you will be discussing and in what order you will be discussing them. This paragraph can also contain background information if your problem involves an area of the law that would not be familiar to most attorneys.

Following your introductory paragraph, use IRAC to help you frame your analysis for each issue. For each case that you cite, decide how much you want to say about it. At one extreme you can list a bare ruling of law followed by one or more case citations. This is known as a naked cite and should be avoided unless you are citing a case only for a nondisputed rule of law. At a minimum always tell the reader why you are citing the case, what its facts were, what it stands for, and how it relates to your case. At the other extreme you do not have to convince your reader that you read the case by setting forth all the facts. The trick, of course, is to be selective in your statement of the facts of a particular case so that you include only those that show the case's relevance. The discussion of the holding should be similarly limited. Therefore, for each major case you cite you should tell the reader why you are citing the case (it is the most recent case, the leading case, etc.) and then briefly state the facts, the nature of the case, the holding, and how it applies to your case.

Whatever you do, do not simply give a series of case descriptions. As discussed earlier under the section Synthesizing Cases, if your supervisor had merely wanted to know what the cases said, she could have read them for herself. Your job is much more difficult. You must analyze those cases and apply them to your client's problem. Your discussion should constantly be shifting back and forth between a discussion of your client's facts and a discussion of how the cases you read relate to those facts.

Similarly, do not give long quotations. Again, if your supervisor had wanted to read the cases, she would not have asked you to do it. Generally, it is better to restate the court's holding in your own words and then to apply that holding to the facts of your case. In that way you are not simply parroting the court but fulfilling your job of translating the court's language for your reader. The only exception to this rule is if it is important for the reader to see the exact language of the court to understand your analysis.

Finally, remember that your basic job in writing a memorandum of law is to relate the law to the facts of your case. Keep in mind the famous observation of Justice Oliver Wendell Holmes that "general propositions do not decide concrete cases." Do not engage in extended abstract discussions of the law;

PRACTICAL TIP

Busy people are most likely to read the first and last sentences of a paragraph. Therefore, to make sure you are conveying your main points, go through your analysis reading only the first and last sentences of each paragraph.

devote your energy to applying the law to your facts. One quick method to ascertain the effectiveness of your Discussion section is to review it with an eye toward learning the facts of the case. A successful discussion will continually refer to the facts and thus paint a picture, as well as analyze.

In sum, in this section you should analyze relevant constitutional provisions, statutes, administrative regulations, and court cases. Quote from the key provisions of statutory materials. With cases, state the holdings of relevant cases. Also discuss the similarities and differences between the facts of the case being cited and the facts involved in the problem being researched. All references to legal authorities should include proper citations. Be sure to report the extent to which intervening court cases have modified any statutes or earlier court opinions. In assessing the strengths and the weaknesses of the client's case be as objective as possible. Specify which courses of action appear most promising, and when relevant also identify facts that need to be clarified or additional legal materials that need to be examined.

g. Conclusion

Give a brief review of the most significant conclusions. Do not introduce new ideas or authorities in this paragraph. This final section of the memo should provide a brief and concise summary that points out the strengths and weaknesses of the client's position. It also may include the writer's recommendations for further action, including additional factual investigation and further legal research on specific points.

2. Sample Law Office Memorandum

TO: Janice Brown, Senior Partner

FROM: Chris Parker

RE: Janice Miller; File No. 04-483

        Possibility of Proving Mr. Booth's Negligence

DATE: April 5, 2004

Questions Presented

Issue 1: Whether Mr. Booth can be found negligent for failing to take precautions once warned of his fatigue; when Mr. Booth stated to Ms. Miller that he was tired, he continued to use a chain saw to cut wood, and the chain saw slipped, slicing off a piece of bark that flew into Ms. Miller's eye, blinding her.

Issue 2: Whether Ms. Miller will be barred from recovering for Mr. Booth's negligence if the jury determines that she was negligent in failing to wear a pair of safety goggles.

Brief Answers

Issue 1: Yes, Mr. Booth will be found negligent. If someone is fatigued while using a chain saw, it is foreseeable that an injury will occur. Mr. Booth was warned of his fatigue but continued to use the chain saw. Therefore, Ms. Miller's injury was foreseeable, and Mr. Booth was negligent in failing to heed the warning.

Issue 2: Ms. Miller will not be barred from recovering for Mr. Booth's negligence so long as she was not more than 50 percent responsible for her injuries. However, based on Massachusetts statutory law the amount that she can recover will be decreased by the percentage of her negligence.

Facts

Last March our client, Janice Miller, was injured in an accident that occurred in her backyard. She and her husband, George Booth, were cutting firewood. Mr. Booth was using a chain saw, and Ms. Miller was stacking the pieces of wood as Mr. Booth cut them. Neither was wearing safety glasses although each owned a pair. Ms. Miller explained the omission by saying that they had both thought they would be cutting wood only for a short time and neither wanted to be bothered by putting on the glasses.

As it turned out, the wood-cutting session took longer than anticipated. After about an hour both Mr. Booth and Ms. Miller were getting tired. In particular, Mr. Booth complained that he was feeling fatigued and that it was getting harder and harder to hold the saw sufficiently perpendicular to the wood to cut a straight line. Ms. Miller suggested that they quit for the day, but Mr. Booth wanted to cut just a few more pieces. On his next attempt, probably due to his tired condition, he allowed the chain saw to slip slightly so that it hit the log at a slant, slicing off a piece of bark that flew into Ms. Miller's right eye. Unfortunately the accident has left Ms. Miller totally blind in that eye.

Applicable Statutes

Issue 1: There are no statutes that apply.

Issue 2:

> Contributory negligence shall not bar recovery in any action by any person . . . to recover damages for negligence . . . if such negligence was not greater than the total amount of negligence attributable to the person . . . against whom recovery is sought, but any damages allowed shall be diminished in proportion to the amount of negligence attributable to the person for whose injury . . . recovery is made.

Mass. Gen. L. ch. 231, § 85 (2004).

Discussion

The resolution of two issues will determine whether Mr. Booth will be found liable for the injuries Ms. Miller sustained. The first relates to whether Mr. Booth was negligent for continuing to use his chain saw after he acknowledged that he was feeling fatigued. The second is whether Ms. Miller will be barred from recovery because of her failure to wear safety goggles.

Issue 1—Mr. Booth's Actions Constitute Negligence

Mr. Booth will be found liable for negligently causing his wife's injuries if the injury was foreseeable and Mr. Booth did nothing to prevent it. To avoid negligence, a person should take precautions once warned of drowsiness or fatigue. *Keller v. DeLong*, 231 A.2d 633, 634 (N.H. 1967). In *Keller* the defendant, while a passenger, felt sleepy. Before taking over at the wheel he did not take any precautions against falling asleep, such as rolling down the windows or turning on the radio. Soon after that he fell asleep and hit a utility pole, killing his passenger. The court held that the defendant was negligent because he had felt sleepy as a passenger but had taken no precautions before taking over at the wheel. *Id.* at 635. The court reasoned that because the defendant did not take any precautions to avoid the accident, the accident was foreseeable. *Id.*

Unlike the *Keller* case, Mr. Booth would argue that the harm to Ms. Miller was not foreseeable. There are significant differences between driving a car and operating a chain saw. If someone drives a car negligently, the passengers are just as likely as the driver to be injured. But when using a chain saw, the person most likely to be hurt is the one using it, in this case Mr. Booth and not Ms. Miller.

However, while the person most likely to be hurt may be the operator of the chain saw, any dangerous instrument, if used carelessly, can easily inflict injury on others. Indeed, that is what happened in this case. As in *Keller*, the defendant was warned of the impending danger. In *Keller* the driver felt drowsy as a passenger and yet took no precautions before taking over at the wheel. In Mr. Booth's case, he told his wife that he was feeling fatigued just before the accident occurred. If anything, the negligence in Mr. Booth's case is greater because the defendant felt tired while operating the chain saw and yet continued to operate it. It would have been a simple matter to have taken a break, but Mr. Booth chose to continue with a dangerous activity even while knowing he was fatigued. As in *Keller*, once the defendant is warned of his fatigue, an injury is foreseeable. Therefore, Mr. Booth should be found negligent.

Issue 2—Ms. Miller's Contributory Negligence Will Reduce Her Damages

The second issue is whether a jury, finding that Ms. Miller failed to use reasonable care by not protecting her eyes with safety glasses, would bar her from recovering. A jury finding of contributory negligence will not bar a plaintiff from recovery so long as her negligence "was not greater than" the defendant's negligence. Mass. Gen. L. ch. 231, §85 (2004). Therefore, so long as the jury finds that Mr. Booth's negligence was at least 50 percent of the reason for Ms. Miller's injury, she will not be barred from recovery.

However, the statute also provides that "any damages allowed shall be diminished in proportion to the amount of negligence attributable" to Ms. Miller's actions. For example, if the jury were to decide that Ms. Miller's own actions contributed 25 percent to her injuries and that her damages are $400,000, she would be able to recover $300,000. Therefore, so long as the jury finds that Ms. Miller's actions contributed 50 percent or less to her injuries, she will be allowed to recover for her injuries, with the total damages reduced by the amount of her contributory negligence.

Conclusion

On the first issue, regarding Mr. Booth's failure to stop using the chain saw after experiencing warning symptoms of fatigue, he will be found negligent. Once he felt tired, an accident was foreseeable, and Mr. Booth was negligent in continuing to use a dangerous tool, such as a chain saw. On the second issue, regarding Ms. Miller's failure to use safety goggles, if the jury determines that her contributory negligence did not cause more than 50 percent of the harm, then she will still be allowed to recover, but her damages will be reduced by the amount of her negligence.

SUMMARY

The purpose of analyzing court opinions is to try to predict the outcome of your client's case. The process involves searching for analogies and distinctions between prior court opinions and the facts of your client's situation. Generally, to find analogies, you will think in general terms, while to find distinctions, you will think as specifically as possible about the facts. Legal analysis also involves selecting among available precedents based on such factors as the court that decided the case, the age of the case, and the number of factual similarities or differences between that case and your own.

In writing an analysis, the deductive model—major premise (rule of law), minor premise (facts), and conclusion—can provide a structure for your argument. Another method is to rely on IRAC (Issue-Rule-Analysis-Conclusion). Finally, whenever you are analyzing more than one case, you are engaging in synthesis, the process of integrating the concepts you find in the cases so that the reader can appreciate the principles of law that arise from seeing the series of cases as a unit.

REVIEW QUESTIONS

1. Why is it important to find both analogies and distinctions between your client's facts and the facts of prior cases?
2. Why is it not enough simply to list the similarities and differences between your client's facts and the facts of prior cases?
3. What factors help determine whether you should use a particular case in support of your client's position?

4. Assume you have been asked to write an analysis of whether a client is guilty of murder. The case occurred and will be tried in California. List the following in order from most to least authoritative. Explain your choices.
   a. A 1995 Illinois Supreme Court decision, with facts similar to your client's facts, in which the defendant was found not guilty of murder.
   b. A 1989 law review article that surveys all of the murder statutes in the fifty states.
   c. A 1980 California Supreme Court decision, with facts similar to your client's facts, in which the defendant was found guilty of murder.
   d. A 1990 California intermediate court decision, with facts similar to your client's facts, in which the defendant was found guilty of manslaughter.
   e. A California state statute defining murder and manslaughter.
   f. A section from Am. Jur. 2d explaining the differences between murder and manslaughter.
   g. A 1995 California Supreme Court decision on breach of warranty in automobile sales.
5. What does it mean to say a case is on all fours?
6. What is the relationship between deductive reasoning and legal reasoning?

PART 3

Ethical Issues and Substantive Law

Chapter 9

Ethical Dilemmas Facing Attorneys

Virtually all difficult ethical problems arise from conflict between a lawyer's responsibilities to clients, to the legal system and to the lawyer's own interest in remaining an ethical person.
Model Rules of Professional Conduct, Preamble, Comment 9 (2003)

INTRODUCTION

Legal decisions often involve ethical and moral choices. You have already encountered several examples in the early chapters of this text: Should the law support a system whereby couples who cannot have children of their own pay a surrogate mother; should spouses be able to sue each other for tortious injuries that occur while they are married; should the court recognize the rights of an unborn child? These and other legal decisions involve a balance between conflicting goals and values in the search to reach the just or ethical result. In this chapter we will focus on the particular ethical dilemmas that are presented to attorneys in their role as advocates for their clients.

As advocates, attorneys sometimes find themselves confronted with situations in which they are torn between their loyalty to their client, their role as a member of the legal system, and their own sense of morality. For example, consider the following true story.

Attorney Belge, along with his colleague Frank Armani, was appointed to represent a criminal defendant charged with murder. In the course of their conversations, the client revealed that not only had he committed the murder but three others as well. The attorneys went to the location where his client had said one of the bodies was buried and found the corpse of a young girl, Alicia Hauck. For six months, neither attorney reported their gruesome discovery despite repeated frantic pleas by Alicia's parents for any information they might have that would let them know if their daughter was still alive. Finally, the truth was revealed in court when the attorneys used the information to try and mount an insanity defense for their client. The townspeople were outraged. How could these attorneys, members of this small community, have kept silent so long, while the parents agonized over whether their little girl was dead or alive?[1]

Stories like this raise complex issues that do not have simple solutions. Did Belge and Armani act appropriately? Should they have notified the police or at least the parents either directly or through an anonymous telephone call? What harm would have been done if they had notified either the police or the parents? Before you answer these questions, you need to learn more about the principles and assumptions that underlie our adversary system and the ethical rules that govern attorney behavior. We will then return to the *Belge* case and the tension created by the need to keep client confidences when doing so can cause harm to others. We will also examine two other areas that raise ethical dilemmas: conflict of interest and access to justice. Conflict-of-interest issues arise when attorneys find themselves with divided loyalties. This can occur when attorneys try to represent two clients with differing interests or when an attorney's personal loyalties jeopardize his or her ability to give impartial representation. We end the chapter with a discussion of access-to-justice issues, including the need to represent unpopular clients and to ensure that those with limited resources receive representation.

A. THE ADVERSARIAL SYSTEM

In Chapter 4, we saw how our courts are organized to discover the facts underlying a case and then to interpret and apply the law to those facts. In Chapter 5, we learned about the variety of things lawyers do in preparing cases for trial. The legal system described in those chapters is known as an "adversarial system" because it places lawyers in an adversarial relationship and then relies on them to present all of the relevant facts and arguments needed for a neutral judge or jury to reach a proper decision.

To better understand our adversarial system, we need to contrast it with the "inquisitorial system" used in many European nations where judges are active participants in the search for truth rather than neutral arbitrators. It is judges, rather than lawyers, who determine who will be called as witnesses, and it is the judges who ask most of the questions of the witnesses. Lawyers are present in the courtroom to assist the judge, and the lawyers' duty to the litigants is clearly secondary to their duty to the court.

---

[1]For a fascinating discussion of the events that led up to this case, read Richard Zitrin & Carol M. Langford, The Moral Compass of the American Lawyer (Ballantine Publishing Group 1999).

The primary criticism of the inquisitorial system is that it puts too much power in the hands of judges, thereby creating an imbalance of power between the individual and the government. Our adversary system is thought to better serve the needs of the individual litigants because it places greater emphasis on the lawyer's responsibility to serve the client's interests and limits the judge's role to that of a neutral arbitrator of the rules.

A Constitutional basis for our adversary system can be found in the Bill of Rights. The adoption of the Sixth Amendment guarantee of the right to counsel recognizes the importance placed on the role of lawyers in our adversarial legal system. The Fourth Amendment prohibition against unreasonable searches and seizures and the Fifth Amendment privilege against self-incrimination demonstrate that due process rights take precedence over the government's search for the truth. Although the use of these rights may result in allowing some guilty persons to go free, they help ensure the innocent are not unjustly convicted.

Critics of the adversary system argue that it places too much reliance on the quality of the lawyers handling the case. It assumes that the lawyers will use skillful examinations of witnesses and well-researched arguments about the interpretation of the law to present the strongest possible case for their clients. However, if a lawyer is poorly prepared or lacks certain key skills, justice is not necessarily done and the client will suffer for the lawyers' inadequacies.

DISCUSSION QUESTIONS

1. Approximately 90 percent of all criminal cases scheduled for trial are instead resolved through plea bargaining. In a plea bargain, the two sides work together to reach a compromise. Does this undermine the very notion that ours is an adversarial system?

2. It is often said that the function of the adversarial system is to find the truth. How is it then that courts frequently block access to information that would assist in that search for truth? For example, courts routinely exclude evidence if the police officers used unconstitutional means to acquire it, and they do not require spouses to testify against each other.

B. REGULATION OF ATTORNEYS

Because lawyers play such a vital role in the adversary system, we need to examine how they are regulated. Historically, state supreme courts have claimed the power to determine who can or cannot "practice law." Typically they establish specialized boards or agencies to administer bar exams, investigate the character and fitness of applicants, review complaints against attorneys, and discipline those who violate their rules of professional conduct.

While each state is responsible for establishing its own rules of professional conduct, the content of these rules generally follows model rules promulgated by the American Bar Association. In 1908 the American Bar Association adopted the first set of rules dealing directly with attorney behavior. Entitled the Canons of Ethics, this document contained suggestions for what attorneys should do. It was almost sixty years (1969) before the ABA produced a more detailed document, the **Model Code of Professional Responsibility,** that for the first time told lawyers what they must do or be in danger of being disciplined through

Model Code of Professional Responsibility
An older set of standards governing attorney ethics developed by the American Bar Association.

NETNOTE

You can locate the ABA Model Rules of Professional Conduct at *www.abanet .org/cpr/mrpc/mrpc_toc.html.*

Model Rules of Professional Conduct
A set of ethical rules developed by the American Bar Association in the 1980s. The Model Rules have been adopted by more than half the states.

reprimand, suspension, or loss of their license to practice law. Then came a serious of incidents, including the Watergate scandal of the Nixon presidency, that increased the public's sensitivity to the issue of attorneys and ethics. Working quickly, it took the ABA only a little more than eleven years to produce an entirely new set of rules, the **Model Rules of Professional Conduct**. Adopted in 1983, these rules have been amended many times, most recently in 2003 as a result of an ABA initiative known as Ethics 2000.

While most states have adopted some version of the Model Rules of Professional Conduct, a few states still follow the Model Code of Professional Responsibility. Therefore, as you read this text, keep in mind that in any given state attorneys in that state may be subject to any one of the following:

1. The Model Code of Professional Responsibility;
2. The Model Rules of Professional Conduct (pre-2003 version);
3. The Model Rules of Professional Conduct (as revised in 2003); or
4. A state's individual variation on any of the above three.

With so many different approaches in existence, you may well ask how can any of these sets of rules claim to guide attorneys as to ethical behavior? One answer is that neither the Code nor the Rules are actually ethical codes based on moral values but rather are simply rules to govern attorney behavior. This possibility is even reflected in the change in their name from the Canon of *Ethics* to the Code of *Professional Responsibility* and the Rules of *Professional Conduct*. That is, these rules are not meant to offer attorneys moral guidance but rather to set forth a strict set of rules that attorneys must follow at peril of losing their license to practice law. Arguably, when they study these rules in law school, law students are not really studying a code of ethics but rather a series of rules governing behavior, violation of which could result in disbarment. Therefore, when confronted with what might be seen as an ethical dilemma, attorneys may not immediately ask "what is right?" but rather "what does the rule say I have to do?"[2] Perhaps it should not be surprising therefore that, at least in the public's view, at times lawyers do engage in immoral behavior.

The drafters of the Model Rules had as one of their goals the creation of more definitive answers than could be found in the older Model Code. Theoretically, lawyers would be able to find specific guidance in order to avoid disciplinary sanctions. However, as we will see later, the Model Rules

---

[2]American Bar Association, Section on Tort Trial & Insurance Practice, Leonard Bucklin, Ethics in a Time of Historical Change, available at *www.edicta.org/NeoethicsBucklin/Neoethics04 history.htm* (last visited July 10, 2004).

are often ambiguous and offer less than complete instructions on how to behave in difficult situations. Even on their own terms, the Model Rules cannot be seen simply as a set of proscriptions. Rule 2.1 provides that in "rendering advice, a lawyer may refer not only to law but to other considerations such as moral, economic, social and political factors, that may be relevant to the client's situation." Even more telling is this statement from Comment 7 of the Preamble: "Many of a lawyer's professional responsibilities are prescribed in the Rules. . . . However, a lawyer is also guided by personal conscience and the approbation of professional peers."

For an attorney mired in an ethical dilemma, this acknowledgment—that at times attorneys may have to look to their own consciences rather than at the exact rules—does not provide much assistance. Also, it appears that the very purpose of a set of rules—to make it easy for attorneys to know the right thing to do—is completely undercut if there is a general acknowledgment that the rules will not provide for an efficacious result in many situations. We will see this tension between following the rules versus doing "the right thing" throughout our discussions in this chapter.

In sum, probably it should not surprise us that following any set of rules will not always provide attorneys with the best answer in any individual situation. After all, rules are simply society's best guess as to what is the most appropriate behavior most of the time. But because by their nature a set of rules is designed to apply to the usual situation, the rules cannot provide answers for the unusual. For the unusual, attorneys are thrown back onto their individual senses of morality, having to make individual choices in situations where the rule no longer "works." In the next section, we will explore some of these difficult situations in the context of the rules regarding attorney-client confidentiality and conflict of interest. Later in the chapter, we will discuss the impact these regulations have on the availability of legal services.

DISCUSSION QUESTIONS

3. On a basic level, do you think attorneys have to face ethical dilemmas that are fundamentally different from those faced by other professionals, such as physicians or accountants?

4. In the popular media, attorneys are often referred to as "hired guns." We have also all heard the lawyer jokes: "How do you know when a lawyer is lying? His lips are moving." Why do you think there is this negative perception of lawyers and what they do? Do you think it is a fair characterization?

5. What do you think of the statement "At times following the rules may not lead to the best moral response and indeed may produce an amoral or even immoral response"?

C. THE ATTORNEY-CLIENT RELATIONSHIP

As we learned earlier in this chapter, the attorney-client relationship is critical to the successful operation of the adversary system of justice. To fulfill this critical role, the lawyer must be able to obtain confidential information about the client's situation and must not have any interests that might conflict with those of the client.

1. Confidentiality

Confidentiality
The ethical rule prohibiting attorneys and paralegals from disclosing information regarding a client or a client's case.

While there is little empirical data to support the claim, it is generally assumed that without the assurance of **confidentiality**, many clients would be reluctant to reveal potentially embarrassing or incriminating information to their attorneys. There is also the assumption that only if an attorney knows of a client's planned bad acts can the attorney have the opportunity to try to talk the client out of proceeding with those acts. Because of these concerns, there is a general rule prohibiting attorneys from revealing client confidences. Except in very rare situations, an attorney can never mention any aspect of a client's case to those outside the law firm. In fact, the very presence of the client in the firm must be kept confidential. This confidentiality covers any information that clients tell their attorneys as well as any information that attorneys learn from a third party, such as witnesses or an investigator. The prohibition against revealing client confidences applies to potential clients, clients, and prior clients. It even remains in effect after the client's death.[3]

Attorney-client privilege
A rule of evidence that prevents an attorney or a paralegal from being compelled to testify about confidential client information.

Confidentiality is also protected by the doctrine of "attorney-client privilege." The **attorney-client privilege** is a rule of evidence that prevents an attorney from being compelled by a court to reveal confidential information unless certain conditions are satisfied. Therefore, the rule on attorney-client privilege governs when a court can order an attorney to testify, despite the fact that otherwise the attorney would be required to keep the information confidential. It is similar to the concept of spousal privilege, which prohibits the use of a spouse's statement against the other spouse. The attorney-client privilege also protects the attorney's work product from being subpoenaed. This protected work product includes private memoranda, written statements of witnesses, and mental impressions, conclusions, or legal strategies related to litigation.

For the attorney-client privilege to apply, the client, while seeking legal advice, must speak directly to an attorney or his or her employee, with no unnecessary third parties present. This is more restrictive than the ethical rule protecting client confidences. The ethical rule applies no matter how the attorney acquired the confidential information, so long as it was during the course of the representation. The rules regarding client confidentiality have always been very broad, requiring that the attorney keep secret almost all information learned from any source during the course of representation. The evidentiary rule of attorney-client privilege is much narrower because it keeps out testimony during trials—the purpose of which is to reveal as much information as possible to the court in its search for the truth.

Figure 9-1 summarizes the differences between the attorney-client privilege and the ethical rules regarding confidentiality. As you can see from Figure 9-1, the attorney-client privilege does not cover as many situations as do the ethical rules regarding confidentiality. The ethical rules generally cover any confidence regarding the client, no matter the source. Therefore, an attorney cannot voluntarily repeat that information without the client's consent. However, a court

---

[3]Swidler v. U.S., 524 U.S. 399 (1998), discussing whether communications made by White House counsel Vincent Foster Jr. and his lawyer, James Hamilton, made nine days before Foster's suicide remained confidential. The Court determined the communications were still protected by the attorney-client privilege.

Ethical Rule Regarding Confidentiality	Attorney-Client Privilege
Under the Model Code applies to ■ confidences and secrets ■ learned from any source ■ regarding anything and ■ made anywhere	*Applies to* ■ a client statement ■ to an attorney ■ made while seeking legal advice and ■ made in confidence (no unnecessary persons present)
Under the Model Rules applies to ■ information ■ relating to representation of the client	
Result: If all of the conditions are present, the attorney may not voluntarily reveal the information (but may be compelled to testify unless statements also satisfy criteria for the attorney-client privilege).	*Result:* If any of these four conditions is missing, the attorney can be compelled to testify.

Figure 9-1   A Comparison of the Ethical Rule Regarding Confidentiality and the Attorney-Client Privilege

could require the attorney to testify regarding that information unless it also meets the four-part test for satisfying the attorney-client privilege:

1. The *client* made a statement
2. to the attorney
3. while seeking legal advice and
4. no unnecessary persons were present.

Therefore, you can think of information covered by the attorney-client privilege as a subset of all confidential information. See Figure 9-2.

With this background information on client confidentiality and the attorney-client privilege, think back to the situation mentioned at the beginning of this chapter. Attorneys Belge and Armani chose not to report their knowledge of the death of Alicia Hauck or the location of her body because they believed that they would be violating the confidentiality of attorney-client communications. Did they do the right thing, or should the obligation to maintain client confidentiality take a back seat to other, more important societal needs?

More than a hundred years ago, Lord Broughham, while representing Queen Caroline in a divorce trial that threatened to end the reign of King George IV, declared:

> [A]n advocate . . . knows but one person in all the world, and that person is the client. To save that client by all means and expedients, and at all hazards and costs to

Figure 9-2   Attorney-Client Privilege: A Subset of Confidentiality

Confidences

Attorney-client privilege

other persons, and among them, to himself, is his first and only duty; *and in performing this duty he must not regard the alarm, the torments, the destruction which he may bring upon others.*[4]

On the other hand, Rule 1.6 of the Model Rules of Professional Conduct, which has been adopted in most states, specifically authorizes attorneys to reveal confidential information about their clients in specified situations.

Model Rule 1.6

(a) A lawyer shall not reveal information relating to representation of a client unless the client consents after consultation, except for disclosures that are impliedly authorized in order to carry out the representation, and except as stated in paragraph (b).

(b) A lawyer may reveal such information to the extent the lawyer reasonably believes necessary:

(1) to prevent the client from committing a criminal act that the lawyer believes is likely to result in imminent death or substantial bodily harm; or

(2) to establish a claim or defense on behalf of the lawyer in a controversy between the lawyer and the client, to establish a defense to a criminal charge or civil claim against the lawyer based upon conduct in which the client was involved, or to respond to allegations in any proceeding concerning the lawyer's representation of the client.

Before returning to our discussion of the situation involving attorneys Belge and Armani, we will explore the most controversial exception to the rule requiring attorneys to keep their client confidences: the one regarding situations in which the attorney has knowledge that the client is planning a "criminal act that the lawyer believes is likely to result in imminent death or substantial bodily harm."

a. Harm to Others Involving Death or Substantial Bodily Harm

The Model Code provides that

DR 4-101 (C) A lawyer may reveal:

(3) The intention of his client to commit a crime and the information necessary to prevent the crime. . . .

while the Model Rules state that

DR 4-101 (b) A lawyer may reveal such information to the extent the lawyer reasonably believes necessary:

(1) to prevent the client from committing a criminal act that the lawyer believes is likely to result in imminent death or substantial bodily harm.

Under both the Model Code and the Model Rules, the exemption applies only to *future* crimes that may be committed *by the client*. Therefore, if the client reveals past criminal conduct, the attorney may not reveal it. If the client reveals

---

[4]2 Trial of Queen Caroline 83 (1879) (emphasis added).

he or she is planning a criminal act, the attorney may, but is not required to, reveal the planned crime. In only a few states an attorney may reveal a confidence in those situations where the criminal activity is over, but there is the potential for ongoing harm. The main area of disagreement relates primarily to the nature of the crime that would warrant revealing a client confidence. While the Model Code simply speaks of "a crime," the Model Rules specify a criminal act "that the lawyer believes is likely to result in *imminent death or substantial bodily harm.*"

As noted above, both the Model Code and the Model Rules allow for confidences to be revealed only when it is the client who is planning the criminal activity. For example, if Mrs. Smith was to tell her attorney that her husband was so upset with the course of her litigation that he was planning to kill the opposing attorney, under the Model Rules in effect in most states, Mrs. Smith's attorney could not breach that confidence. Only a few states would allow the attorney to breach the client's confidence in situations such as that involving Mrs. Smith's husband, i.e., when persons other than the client plan the criminal acts, and those plans are discovered by the attorney through a conversation with the client.

As a result of the Ethics 2000 initiative, the ABA amended Rule 1.6. An attorney may now reveal information to "prevent reasonably certain death or substantial bodily harm."[5] Note there is no longer a requirement that the actor be the client, that the harm be imminent, or that there be planned future criminal behavior. According to the comments this means that the rules recognize

> the overriding value of life and physical integrity. . . . Thus, a lawyer who knows that a client has accidentally discharged toxic waste into a town's water supply may reveal this information to the authorities if there is a present and substantial risk that a person who drinks the water will contract a life-threatening or debilitating disease and the lawyer's disclosure is necessary to eliminate the threat or reduce the number of victims.[6]

In a very few states the rules differ significantly from either the original Model Rules or the 2003 proposed revisions. For example, in some the verb "may reveal" has been changed to "shall reveal." In those states, attorneys are given no option but instead must report their client's planned criminal activities. In

---

[5]The full text of proposed Rule 1.6(b) reads:

> A lawyer may reveal information relating to the representation of a client to the extent the lawyer reasonably believes necessary:
>   (1) to prevent reasonably certain death or substantial bodily harm;
>   (2) to prevent the client from committing a crime or fraud that is reasonably certain to result in substantial injury to the financial interests or property of another and in furtherance of which the client has used or is using the lawyer's services;
>   (3) to prevent, mitigate or rectify substantial injury to the financial interests or property of another that is reasonably certain to result or has resulted from the client's commission of a crime or fraud in furtherance of which the client has used the lawyer's services;
>   (4) to secure legal advice about the lawyer's compliance with these Rules;
>   (5) to establish a claim or defense on behalf of the lawyer in a controversy between the lawyer and the client, to establish a defense to a criminal charge or civil claim against the lawyer based upon conduct in which the client was involved, or to respond to allegations in any proceeding concerning the lawyer's representation of the client; or
>   (6) to comply with other law or a court order.

[6]Model Rules of Professional Conduct, Rule 1.6, Comment 6 (2003).

Source of Rule	Who must commit the act	Type of act that can be revealed	Discretionary or mandatory
Model Code	Client	A crime	May
Model Rules	Client	Criminal act likely to result in imminent death or substantial bodily harm	May
Revised Model Rules (2003)	Anyone	Reasonably certain death or substantial bodily harm	May
	Client	Crime or fraud that is reasonably certain to result in substantial injury to financial or property interests (but only if in furtherance the client has used or plans to use the lawyer's services)[7]	
	Client	To rectify substantial injury to financial or property interests (but only if in furtherance the client has used the lawyer's services)	
Massachusetts[8]	Anyone	Criminal or fraudulent act likely to result in death or substantial bodily harm or substantial injury to the financial interests or property of another or to prevent the wrongful execution or incarceration of another	May
Connecticut[9]	Client	Criminal act likely to result in death or substantial bodily harm	Shall
		A criminal act likely to result in substantial injury to the financial interest or property of another	May
		To rectify the consequences of a client's criminal or fraudulent act (but only if the lawyer's services were used).	May
Virginia[10]	Client	A crime	Shall

Figure 9-3   Exceptions to Client Confidentiality

others, attorneys are also allowed to reveal a confidence to prevent the incarceration or execution of an innocent person. To help you visualize these many variations, a few of the main differences in the provisions regarding disclosure are included in Figure 9-3.

---

[7] It has been suggested that the ABA added this and the next provision in reaction to the "public's post-Enron outrage, i.e., to the idea that lawyers could be required to sit back and say nothing if they thought their clients were about to engage in massive fraud that was going to result in billions of dollars' worth of loss." Robert Black, Dilemmas in Attorney-Client Confidentiality, *www.dcbar.org/for_lawyers/washington_lawyer/january_2004/privilege.cfm* (quoting David B. Wilkins, Harvard Law School professor).

[8] Massachusetts 1.6(b):

A lawyer may reveal . . . such [confidential] information:
>   (1) to prevent the commission of a criminal or fraudulent act that the lawyer reasonably believes is likely to result in death or substantial bodily harm, or in substantial injury to the financial interests or property of another, or to prevent the wrongful execution or incarceration of another.

[9] Connecticut 1.6(b):

(b) A lawyer shall reveal such information to the extent the lawyer reasonably believes necessary to prevent the client from committing a criminal act that the lawyer believes is likely to result in death or substantial bodily harm.

(c) A lawyer may reveal such information to the extent the lawyer reasonably believes necessary to:
>   (1) prevent the client from committing a criminal act that the lawyer believes is likely to result in substantial injury to the financial interest or property of another;
>   (2) rectify the consequence of a client's criminal or fraudulent act in the commission of which the lawyer's services had been used.

[10] Virginia 1.6(c):

A lawyer shall promptly reveal:
>   (1) the intention of a client, as stated by the client, to commit a crime and the information necessary to prevent the crime, but before revealing such information, the attorney shall, where feasible, advise the client of the possible legal consequences of the action, urge the client not to commit the crime, and advise the client that the attorney must reveal the client's criminal intention unless thereupon abandoned, and, if the crime involves perjury by the client, that the attorney shall seek to withdraw as counsel.

DISCUSSION QUESTIONS

6. As you can see, there is substantial disagreement as to when an attorney should be required or even allowed to report a client's future crime. Do you think there are any instances when such reporting should be required instead of merely permitted?[11] Classify each of the following according to whether you think an attorney should be required to report the future crime, allowed to do so at his or her discretion, or prohibited from disclosing it at all. You should also consider whether the test should be a subjective one, based on what the attorney actually thought was likely to happen, or an objective test, based on what a reasonable person would think would happen.

    a. A deliberately wrongful act
    b. Harm to a financial or property interest
    c. Substantial harm to a financial or property interest
    d. Any crime
    e. A serious violent crime
    f. Bodily harm
    g. Substantial bodily harm
    h. Death
    i. Imminent death

7. Take a look at Figure 9-3. Given your answers to number 6, which rule or combination of rules do you prefer?

8. Do you think that clients will seriously be dissuaded from revealing confidences if they know that their attorney may be allowed to reveal that information after the client's death?

b. Harm to Others Not Involving Death or Substantial Bodily Harm

With these rules in mind, let us return to the situation facing attorneys Belge and Armani. After the townspeople found out that the attorneys had kept quiet for months about the location of the girl's body, their outrage put pressure on the local district attorney to prosecute the men for their inaction. The problem was in finding a law that the attorneys had violated. Remarkably, the district attorney did not charge Belge and Armani with obstruction of justice or being accessories after the fact. Instead, the indictment was based on two little-known statutes: one that requires a decent burial be accorded the dead and the other that anyone knowing that a person died without medical attendance must report that death to the proper authorities. The grand jury indicted one of the attorneys, Francis Belge. Prior to trial, his attorney brought a motion seeking dismissal of the indictment. The following is the trial court's decision regarding whether or not the charges against attorney Belge should be dropped.

---

[11]See, e.g., the argument presented in Harry L. Subin, The Lawyer as Superego: Disclosure of Client Confidences to Prevent Harm, 70 Iowa L. Rev. 1091 (July 1985), to the effect that in the case of threatened criminal activity the rules should provide for mandatory disclosure because the present rules give attorneys no guidance as to how and when to exercise their discretion. Contrast this with the position of others who view the duty of confidentiality as a sacred trust between attorney and client. Therefore, almost always the balance should be tipped toward silence. This may cause individualized harm, but it will prevent harm to the system as a whole. Allegiance to that system is viewed as necessary. Without the maintenance of client confidences, the attorney-client relationship, the very foundation of the adversary system, would be destroyed.

New York v. Belge
County Court of New York, Onondaga County
83 Misc. 2d 186, 372 N.Y.S.2d 798 (1975)

GALE, J.

In the summer of 1973 Robert F. Garrow, Jr., stood charged in Hamilton County with the crime of murder. The defendant was assigned two attorneys, Frank H. Armani and Francis R. Belge. A defense of insanity had been interposed by counsel for Mr. Garrow. During the course of the discussions between Garrow and his two counsel, three other murders were admitted by Garrow, one being in Onondaga County. On or about September of 1973 Mr. Belge conducted his own investigation based upon what his client had told him and with the assistance of a friend the location of the body of Alicia Hauck was found in Oakwood Cemetery in Syracuse. Mr. Belge personally inspected the body and was satisfied, presumably, that this was the Alicia Hauck that his client had told him that he murdered.

This discovery was not disclosed to the authorities, but became public during the trial of Mr. Garrow in June of 1974, when to affirmatively establish the defense of insanity, these three other murders were brought before the jury by the defense in the Hamilton County trial. Public indignation reached the fever pitch. . . . [T]he District Attorney of Onondaga County . . . caused the Grand Jury of Onondaga County, then sitting, to conduct a thorough investigation. As a result of this investigation . . . Indictment No. 75-55 was returned as against Francis R. Belge, Esq., accusing him of having violated subdivision 1 of *section 4200 of the Public Health Law*, which, in essence, requires that a decent burial be accorded the dead, and *section 4143 of the Public Health Law*, which, in essence, requires anyone knowing of the death of a person without medical attendance, to report the same to the proper authorities. Defense counsel moves for a dismissal of the indictment on the grounds that a confidential, privileged communication existed between him and Mr. Garrow, which should excuse the attorney from making full disclosure to the authorities.

The National Association of Criminal Defense Lawyers, as *amicus curiae (Times Pub. Co. v Williams, 222 So 2d 470, 475* [Fla]), succinctly state the issue in the following language: If this indictment stands, "The attorney-client privilege will be effectively destroyed. No defendant will be able to freely discuss the facts of his case with his attorney. No attorney will be able to listen to those facts without being faced with the Hobson's choice of violating the law or violating his professional code of Ethics."

Initially in England the practice of law was not recognized as a profession, and certainly some people are skeptics today. However, the practice of learned and capable men appearing before the court on behalf of a friend or an acquaintance became more and more demanding. Consequently, the King granted a privilege to certain of these men to engage in such practice. There had to be rules governing their duties. These came to be known as "Canons". The King has, in this country, been substituted by a democracy, but the "Canons" are with us today, having been honed and refined over the years to meet the changes of time. Most are constantly being studied and revamped by the American Bar Association and by the bar associations of the various States. While they are, for the most part, general by definition, they can be brought to bear in a particular situation. Among those is the following . . . : "Confidential communications between an attorney and his client are privileged from disclosure * * * as a rule of necessity in the administration of justice."

In the most recent issue of the New York State Bar Journal (June, 1975) there is an article by Jack B. Weinstein, entitled "Educating Ethical Lawyers". In a subcaption to this article is the following language which is pertinent: "The most difficult ethical dilemmas result from the frequent conflicts between the obligation to one's client and those to the legal system and to society. It is in this area that legal education has its greatest responsibility, and can have its greatest effects." In the course of his article Mr. Weinstein states that there are three major types of pressure facing a practicing lawyer. He uses the following language to describe these: "First, there are those that originate in the attorney's search for his own well-being. Second, pressures arise from the attorney's obligation to his client. Third, the lawyer has certain obligations to the courts, the legal system, and society in general."

Our system of criminal justice is an adversary system and the interests of the State are not absolute, or even paramount. "The dignity of the individual is respected to the point that even when the citizen is known by the state to have committed a heinous offense, the individual is nevertheless accorded such rights as counsel, trial by jury, due process, and the privilege against self incrimination."

A trial is in part a search for truth, but it is only partly a search for truth. The mantle of innocence is flung over the defendant to such an extent that he is safeguarded by rules of evidence which frequently keep out absolute truth, much to the chagrin of juries. Nevertheless, this has been a part of our system since our laws were taken from the laws of England and over these many years has been found to best protect a balance between the rights of the individual and the rights of society.

The concept of the right to counsel has again been with us for a long time, but . . . [t]he effectiveness of counsel is only as great as the confidentiality of its client-attorney relationship. If the lawyer cannot get all the facts about the case, he can only give his client half of a defense. This, of necessity, involves the client telling his attorney everything remotely connected with the crime.

Apparently, in the instant case, after analyzing all the evidence, and after hearing of the bizarre episodes in the life of their client, they decided that the only possibility of salvation was in a defense of insanity. For the client to disclose not only everything about this particular crime but also everything about other crimes which might have a bearing upon his defense, requires the strictest confidence in, and on the part of, the attorney. . . .

The following language [is] from the brief of the *amicus curiae* . . . : "The client's Fifth Amendment rights cannot be violated by his attorney. . . . Because the discovery of the body of Alicia Hauck would have presented 'a

significant link in a chain of evidence tending to establish his guilt', Garrow was constitutionally exempt from any statutory requirement to disclose the location of the body. And Attorney Belge, as Garrow's attorney, was not only equally exempt, but under a positive stricture precluding such disclosure. Garrow, although constitutionally privileged against a requirement of compulsory disclosure, was free to make such a revelation if he chose to do so. Attorney Belge was affirmatively required to withhold disclosure. The criminal defendant's self-incrimination rights become completely nugatory if compulsory disclosure can be exacted through his attorney."

. . . In the case at bar we must weigh the importance of the general privilege of confidentiality in the performance of the defendant's duties as an attorney, against the inroads of such a privilege on the fair administration of criminal justice as well as the heart tearing that went on in the victim's family by reason of their uncertainty as to the whereabouts of Alicia Hauck. In this type situation the court must balance the rights of the individual against the rights of society as a whole. There is no question but Attorney Belge's failure to bring to the attention of the authorities the whereabouts of Alicia Hauck when he first verified it, prevented bringing Garrow to the immediate bar of justice for this particular murder. This was in a sense, obstruction of justice. This duty, I am sure, loomed large in the mind of Attorney Belge. However, against this was the Fifth Amendment right of his client, Garrow, not to incriminate himself. If the Grand Jury had returned an indictment charging Mr. Belge with obstruction of justice under a proper statute, the work of this court would have been much more difficult than it is.

There must always be a conflict between the obstruction of the administration of criminal justice and the preservation of the right against self incrimination which permeates the mind of the attorney as the alter ego of his client. But that is not the situation before this court. We have the Fifth Amendment right, derived from the Constitution, on the one hand, as against the trivia of a pseudo-criminal statute on the other, which has seldom been brought into play.

Clearly the latter is completely out of focus when placed alongside the client-attorney privilege. . . .

It is the decision of this court that Francis R. Belge conducted himself as an officer of the court with all the zeal at his command to protect the constitutional rights of his client. Both on the grounds of a privileged communication and in the interests of justice the indictment is dismissed.

CASE DISCUSSION QUESTIONS

1. What do you think the court meant when it said that a "trial is in part a search for truth, but it is only partly a search for truth"?

2. Ultimately, why did the court find that the indictment against attorney Belge should be dismissed?

3. Do you think the result would have been the same if attorney Belge had been charged with obstruction of justice?

Because New York follows the Model Code, which provides that the only time an attorney can reveal a client confidence is to prevent a crime, attorney Belge would have been violating the attorney's code of ethics if he had revealed the girl's location. After the town learned what the lawyers knew and when they knew it, one of the lawyers made the following statement: "I caused pain, I prolonged their pain. What can you say . . . How do you . . . Nothing I could say would justify it in their minds. You couldn't justify it to me."[12] Even the lawyers in the case were troubled by having to follow what they considered to be binding ethical rules. If New York adopts the newly proposed Model Rule revisions, an attorney in a situation identical to the one in which attorney Belge found himself still would not be able to act.

But however much pain attorney Belge's actions caused him and others, no life was at stake. What if a client's past actions create the possibility for future harm of a more serious nature? That is what we will discuss in the next section.

DISCUSSION QUESTIONS

9. The common justification for having such strict limits on when an attorney can reveal client confidences is because without such restrictions, clients would be afraid to give their attorneys the complete story. Do you think this is really true? Given the complexities of the legal system and hence the need for an attorney to help others through it, do you think a client would risk not getting adequate representation by not being forthcoming to the attorney?

10. What do you make of the fact that in every jurisdiction the confidentiality rules do not apply where the litigation is between a lawyer and the client and the issue is the attorney's fees?

c. Substantial Bodily Harm or Death Due to Past Actions

Some have argued that the *Belge* case does not really present a clear conflict between the attorneys' duty of maintaining client confidences and preventing harm to others because in *Belge*, the crime had already been committed and could not be undone. Nothing attorney Belge could have done would have

---

[12]Zitrin & Langford, supra, at 19.

NETNOTE

You can find links to all of the states' ethical rules and opinions at *www.law .cornell.edu/ethics.*

prevented further harm except perhaps to shorten the time of the parents' not knowing of their daughter's death. But who is to say learning of her death several months later caused them any more harm than the time they spent with some hope she was still alive. A more striking conflict was presented by a case that arose in Minnesota.

> Late in the day of August 24, 1956, in Brandon, Minnesota, two cars approached each other on country roads. One car, driven by John Zimmerman, age nineteen, was traveling west; the second car, driven by Florian Ledermann, age fifteen, was heading south toward the intersection. There were no stop signs at the crossing, and sight of approaching traffic was obscured by the mature corn in the surrounding fields. The cars collided, resulting in the deaths of two young persons, one from each car, and serious injury to nine of the ten other persons involved in the accident.[13]

David Spaulding, who was twenty years old at the time and considered a minor under Minnesota law, was a passenger in a car driven by John Zimmerman. He was injured in the collision with the car driven by Florian Ledermann. Theodore Spaulding, David's father, sued on behalf of his son for the injuries David sustained. During the discovery phase of the lawsuit David was examined by his own physician as well as an orthopedic specialist, both of whom found David had suffered severe, but not life-threatening, injuries.

On the eve of settlement, the defendants' attorneys learned for the first time that David was also suffering from a life-threatening medical condition caused by the car accident. The information came from one of the defendant's doctors who had also examined David. In a report to the defendants' attorneys, the doctor wrote:

> The one feature of the case which bothers me more than any other part of the case is the fact that this boy of 20 years of age has an aneurysm, which means a dilatation of the aorta and the arch of the aorta. . . . Of course an aneurysm or dilatation of the aorta in a boy of this age is a serious matter as far as his life. This aneurysm may dilate further and it might rupture with further dilatation and this would cause his death.

The defendants were poised to settle the case. Obviously, the doctor's report contained critical information that David and his physicians needed to have him properly treated. But if the defendants' attorneys revealed this information to the plaintiffs, they could count on seeing the projected amount of the settlement multiplied many times over. The defendants' attorneys decided

---

[13]Roger C. Cramton & Lori P. Knowles, Professional Secrecy and Its Exceptions: Spaulding v. Zimmerman Revisited, 83 Minn. L. Rev. 63, 63 (Nov. 1998).

not to share this information with David, David's father, or David's attorneys. Without this piece of information, the parties reached a pretrial settlement of $6,500.

Because David was a minor, the parties had to submit the settlement to the court for its approval, which it gave. Two years later, before entering the army reserve, David was given a physical examination. During that examination, his family physician for the first time discovered the aorta aneurysm that had been caused by the automobile accident and that was threatening David's life. David underwent immediate surgery that repaired the aneurysm but left David with permanent severe speech loss. Shortly thereafter David petitioned the court to set aside the settlement so that he could recover additional compensation. The trial court set aside the settlement, and the defendants appealed. In the following case the supreme court of Minnesota discussed whether the settlement should have been set aside. After the court's decision in this case, David entered into a new settlement with the defendants for a larger but undisclosed amount.

Spaulding v. Zimmerman
263 Minn. 346, 116 N.W.2d 704 (1962)

GALLAGHER, J.

... On appeal defendants contend that the court was without jurisdiction to vacate the settlement ... because (1) no mutual mistake of fact was involved; [and] (2) no duty rested upon them to disclose information to plaintiff which they could assume had been disclosed to him by his own physicians. ...

The case was called for trial on March 4, 1957. ... On the following day an agreement for settlement was reached wherein, in consideration of the payment of $6,500, David and his father agreed to settle in full for all claims arising out of the accident. ... Richard S. Roberts, counsel for David, thereafter presented to the court a petition for approval of the settlement. ... Attached to the petition were affidavits of David's physicians, Drs. James H. Cain and Paul S. Blake. ... At no time was there information disclosed to the court that David was then suffering from an aorta aneurysm which may have been the result of the accident. Based upon the petition for settlement and such affidavits of

Drs. Cain and Blake, the court on May 8, 1957, made its order approving the settlement.

Early in 1959, David was required by the army reserve, of which he was a member, to have a physical checkup. For this, he again engaged the services of Dr. Cain. In this checkup, the latter discovered the aorta aneurysm. He then reexamined the X rays which had been taken shortly after the accident and at this time discovered that they disclosed the beginning of the process which produced the aneurysm. He promptly sent David to Dr. Jerome Grismer for an examination and opinion. The latter confirmed the finding of the aorta aneurysm and recommended immediate surgery therefor. This was performed by him at Mount Sinai Hospital in Minneapolis on March 10, 1959.

Shortly thereafter, David, having attained his majority, instituted the present action for additional damages due to the more serious injuries including the aorta aneurysm which he alleges proximately resulted from the accident. As indicated above, the prior order for settlement was vacated. In a memorandum made a part of the order vacating the settlement, the court stated: . . .

"The mistake concerning the existence of the aneurysm was not mutual. For reasons which do not appear, plaintiff's doctor failed to ascertain its existence. By reason of the failure of plaintiff's counsel to use available rules of discovery, plaintiff's doctor and all his representatives did not learn that defendants and their agents knew of its existence and possible serious consequences. Except for the character of the concealment in the light of plaintiff's minority, the Court would, I believe, be justified in denying plaintiff's motion to vacate, leaving him to whatever questionable remedy he may have against his doctor and against his lawyer.

"That defendants' counsel concealed the knowledge they had is not disputed. . . . There is no doubt of the good faith of both defendants' counsel. There is no doubt that during the course of the negotiations, when the parties were in an adversary relationship, no rule required or duty rested upon defendants or their representatives to disclose this knowledge. However, once the agreement to settle was reached, it is difficult to characterize the parties' relationship as adverse. At this point all parties were interested in securing Court approval. * * * . . .

"When the adversary nature of the negotiations concluded in a settlement, the procedure took on the posture of a joint application to the Court, at least so far as the facts upon which the Court could and must approve settlement is [sic] concerned. It is here that the true nature of the concealment appears, and defendants' failure to act affirmatively, after having been given a copy of the application for approval, can only be defendants' decision to take a calculated risk that the settlement would be final. * * *

"To hold that the concealment was not of such character as to result in an unconscionable advantage over plaintiff's ignorance or mistake, would be to penalize innocence and incompetence and reward less than full performance of an officer of the Court's duty to make full disclosure to the Court when applying for approval in minor settlement proceedings." . . .

2. From the foregoing it is clear that in the instant case the court did not abuse its discretion in setting aside the settlement which it had approved on plaintiff's behalf while he was still a minor. It is undisputed that neither he nor his counsel nor his medical attendants were aware that at the time settlement was made he was suffering from an aorta aneurysm which may have resulted from the accident. The seriousness of this disability is indicated by Dr. Hannah's report indicating the imminent danger of death therefrom. This was known by counsel for both defendants but was not disclosed to the court at the time it was petitioned to approve the settlement. While no canon of ethics or legal obligation may have required them to inform plaintiff or his counsel with respect thereto, or to advise the court therein, it did become obvious to them at the time that the settlement then made did not contemplate or take into consideration the disability described. This fact opened the way for the court to later exercise its discretion in vacating the settlement. . . .

Affirmed.

CASE DISCUSSION QUESTIONS

1. Why did the Minnesota Supreme Court agree that the trial court could set aside the settlement? Do you think the result would have been the same if the settlement had involved an adult plaintiff rather than a child? Should it matter?

2. Did the court view the attorney's decision not to reveal the extent of David's injury as a violation of an ethical obligation or rather as a strategic move that in this case simply did not work out?

3. Do you think the court should have tackled head on the ethical and moral issues involved in choosing to keep a client's confidence over saving a child's life?

4. David Spaulding was represented by a young, inexperienced attorney. Perhaps the attorney was not aware that he was entitled to ask for a copy of the defendant doctor's examination. Or perhaps he just thought it would duplicate the information his own doctors had found. Or perhaps in the rush to settle the case, he simply forgot to ask for a copy. No matter the answer, should the system develop better protections for clients against the inexperience or incompetence of their attorneys?

5. It appears in this case that the defendants' attorneys never even consulted with the defendants about what they wanted to do but rather just assumed they would not want the information revealed. Should the attorneys have made such an assumption?

6. Assuming the attorneys had discussed with their clients the decision regarding whether to reveal this information, and the clients had said they did not wish to have the information revealed, what options would the attorneys have had?

7. Consider whether you think your answer to number 6 would change under the newly revised Model Rules. Do you think the defense attorney would have an ethical obligation to reveal the injury? Would you change your answer if David had been suffering from an inoperable tumor rather than a correctable, but life-threatening condition?

Legal Reasoning Exercises

1. In *Belge*, the principal harm had already been done. The client had committed the crime of murder and the girl was dead. Nothing the attorney could do would change that. In *Spaulding*, the harm had also been done, but revealing it would serve to save a life and would not lead to the client's trial for murder. Suppose, however, that a case arose in which the attorney had a chance to still "save the girl" but that his actions would lead to the criminal conviction of his client. Consider the following.[14] On December 17, Gary Krist went to the motel room of Barbara Mackle. He told her he was a detective and that there had been an accident involving a young man driving a white Ford. The young man was in the hospital and asking for her. As her boyfriend owned a white Ford, she believed Krist and opened the door. Krist entered brandishing a knife and forced her into the backseat of his car where he then tied her up. After driving her out into the country, he ordered her into a coffin-like box, equipped with a method for getting air, and buried her alive. He then called her father, told him he had kidnapped his daughter, and demanded $500,000 in ransom. Arrangements were made for Krist to receive the money. On December 19 following Krist's instructions, the father left the money in a suitcase. Krist retrieved the money and left without revealing the whereabouts of Barbara. Two days later on December 21 Krist was arrested when he tried to spend part of the money in order to rent a boat and motor at a local marina.

---

[14]These facts are based on the case of Krist v. State, 179 S.E.2d 56 (Ga. 1970).

Assume that Krist meets with his court-appointed attorney and reveals where Barbara is located. He thinks she is still alive but does not know. He said that he left her with a limited amount of food and water but does not know how long it will last. The attorney encourages Krist to tell the police where Barbara is buried. Krist refuses to do so, feeling that so long as they do not find Barbara, the police have no direct proof that he was the kidnapper. What should the attorney do? What are his options under the Model Code, the Model Rules, and the recently proposed changes to the Model Rules?

2. Consider the case of Leo Frank. Although innocent, he had been convicted of the rape and murder of a fourteen-year-old girl. While he was waiting to be executed, an attorney, who was not involved in the *Frank* case, found out from a prospective client the name of the true murderer. The attorney never revealed the information, and Frank was killed when a mob kidnapped him from prison and lynched him. Later in his memoirs, the attorney wrote: "I am one of the few people who know that Leo Frank was innocent of the crime for which he was convicted and lynched. . . . [B]ut the information came to me in such a way that, though I wish I could do so, I can never reveal it so. . . . We lawyers . . . take an oath never to reveal the communications made to us by our clients; and this includes facts revealed in an attempt to employ the lawyer, though he refuses the employment."[15] Consider this attorney's behavior under the Model Code, the Model Rules, the recently proposed changes to the Model Rules, and the Massachusetts Rule that you can find in footnote 8.

3. William Macumber was on trial for first-degree murder. His attorney wanted to call attorney Brown to the stand. Attorney Brown had been the attorney for James Smith in a different murder trial. During his representation of Smith, Smith had confessed to attorney Brown that he was the murderer and had acted alone in the case for which Macumber was on trial. Sometime prior to the Macumber trial, Smith died. After his death, attorney Brown approached Macumber's attorney and volunteered to testify as to what Brown had told him. Should the court allow this testimony?[16]

d. Revelation of a Client's Plan to Cause Substantial Bodily Harm or Death

In both the *Belge* and *Spaulding* cases, neither the Model Code nor the Model Rules, prior to the 2003 revision, would permit disclosure of the confidential information. When, however, a client directly tells his attorney that he is planning on killing someone or causing substantial bodily harm, both the Model Code and the Model Rules would allow but not mandate that the attorney reveal this information. Assuming for the moment that the attorney does tell the police of a client's plans and thereby saves a life, can that information then be

---

[15]Arthur G. Powell, I Can Go Home Again 291 (1943).
[16]These facts are based on State v. Macumber, 544 P.2d 1084 (Ariz. 1976).

used in court against the client? If the answer is yes, would knowledge of such potential use of the information further discourage attorneys from revealing the information?

Specifically, in situations where attorneys may reveal a confidence without breaking the code of ethics, what impact does that have on the attorney-client privilege? If an attorney makes the decision to reveal a client's plan to harm another person, can that information be used against the client later in court? If so, it seems that very few attorneys would be willing to reveal a confidence, even to save a life.

In a relatively recent case from Massachusetts, the Supreme Judicial Court discussed the intersection between the ethical rules of client confidentiality and the evidentiary rule of attorney-client privilege. In that case,[17] Joseph Tyree met with attorney Purcell, a legal services attorney. Mr. Tyree was seeking advice about being evicted. He was about to lose his apartment because he had been fired as the maintenance man for his apartment complex. In the course of the conversation, the client told the attorney he planned to burn down the building. After thinking long and hard, the attorney reported this information to the police. When they investigated, they found gas cans and fuses in Tyree's apartment. Also all of the fire detectors had been disabled. At Tyree's trial for arson, the prosecution called attorney Purcell to testify. Purcell invoked the attorney-client privilege, and the judge agreed he did not have to testify. The jury was unable to reach a verdict, and the judge was forced to call a mistrial. At the second trial, a different judge ordered Purcell to testify, and when he refused, the judge determined Purcell was not protected by the attorney-client privilege and held him in contempt for refusing to testify. Purcell appealed to the Massachusetts Supreme Judicial Court, the highest appellate court in Massachusetts. That court determined that he should not have to testify, concluding "lawyers will be reluctant to come forward if they know that the information that they disclose may lead to adverse consequences to their clients."[18]

Three years later, the Ohio Supreme Court was confronted with a similar case. Attorney Helmick was representing a defendant in a capital murder trial. While he was preparing for trial, one of his investigators gave him a letter written by his client that the investigator had gotten from the client's mother. The letter contained death threats. After consulting with the state ethics committee, attorney Helmick revealed the contents of the letter to the police and then filed a motion to withdraw as defense counsel. The district attorney served attorney Helmick with a subpoena ordering him to produce the letter in his former client's murder trial. Helmick refused, and he was found in contempt of court. In the following case, the Supreme Court of Ohio discusses whether attorney Helmick can be required to turn over the letter to the prosecution.

---

[17]Purcell v. District Attorney for the Suffolk District, 676 N.E.2d 436 (Mass. 1997).
[18]Id. at 440.

In re Original Grand Jury Investigation
89 Ohio St. 3d 544, 2000 Ohio 170, 733 N.E.2d 1135 (2000)

SWEENEY, SR., J. The issue presented in this case is whether an attorney can be compelled to disclose to the grand jury a letter written by a client and discovered by an investigator that contains evidence of a possible crime or whether the Ohio Code of Professional Responsibility prohibits such disclosure. . . .

DR 4-101(B) states, "Except when permitted under DR 4-101(C), a lawyer shall not knowingly * * * reveal a confidence or secret of a client."

We must first determine whether the letter sought falls within the definition of a client "secret." Unlike "confidence," which is limited to information an attorney obtains directly from his or her client, the term "secret" is defined in broad terms. Therefore, a client secret includes information obtained from third-party sources, including "information obtained by a lawyer from witnesses, by personal investigation, or by an investigation of an agent of the lawyer, disclosure of which would be embarrassing or harmful to the client." . . .

[W]e find that the letter falls within the definition of a client "secret," since it was obtained in the professional attorney-client relationship, by appellant's agent (the investigator), and since it contains detrimental information detailing a possible crime committed by appellant's former client.

Although the letter is a client secret, this does not necessarily mean that disclosure of the letter is absolutely prohibited. An attorney may disclose a client secret if one of the four listed exceptions in DR 4-101(C) applies.

Appellant concedes that DR 4-101(C)(3) permits him to "reveal * * * the intention of his client to commit a crime and the information necessary to prevent the crime." . . .

We agree with appellant that he was authorized by DR 4-101(C)(3) when he chose to reveal the intent of his client to commit a

crime. . . . However, the fact that he revealed this information does not answer the question whether he is obligated to produce the letter itself. Thus, the question that remains is whether appellant is required to relinquish the letter itself and present it to the grand jury. We find that the exception found in DR 4-102(C)(2) governs disposition of this issue.

DR 4-101(C)(2) provides that an attorney may reveal "confidences or secrets when permitted under Disciplinary Rules or required by law or court order." . . .

The exception of DR 4-101(C)(2) for disclosures required by law has been applied in the context of mandating that attorneys relinquish evidence and instrumentalities of crime to law-enforcement agencies. Thus, the rule has emerged that, despite any confidentiality concerns, a criminal defense attorney must produce real evidence obtained from his or her client or from a third-party source. . . . *State v. Green (La.1986), 493 So. 2d 1178* (holding that the attorney had an obligation to relinquish client's gun, an instrumentality of a crime, to authorities). In essence, the confidentiality rules do not give an attorney the right to withhold evidence.

Appellant contends, however, that there are strong policy reasons against mandating disclosure. Appellant believes that mandatory disclosure will discourage attorneys from reporting possible threats made by their clients and will therefore run contrary to the intent of the code, which is to prevent crimes from occurring. Appellant cites the Massachusetts decision of *Purcell v. Dist. Atty. for Suffolk Dist. (1997), 424 Mass. 109, 676 N.E.2d 436*, which highlights these concerns.

In *Purcell*, an attorney informed police about his client's intention to commit arson. The trial court ordered the attorney to testify about the conversation he had with his client concerning his client's intention to commit this crime, and the state defended the order on the basis of the crime-fraud exception to the attorney-client privilege. The Massachusetts Supreme Court vacated the trial court's order and held that the attorney did not have to testify against his client. In so holding, the court noted:

"We must be cautious in permitting the use of client communications that a lawyer has revealed only because of a threat to others. Lawyers will be reluctant to come forward if they know that the information that they disclose may lead to adverse consequences to their clients. A practice of the use of such disclosures might prompt a lawyer to warn a client in advance that the disclosure of certain information may not be held in confidence, thereby chilling free discourse between lawyer and client and reducing the prospect that the lawyer will learn of a serious threat to the well-being of others."

Although these may be valid concerns, we find that the *Purcell* decision is distinguishable from the instant case, and that the policy reasons cited in *Purcell* have less validity here. *Purcell* involved direct communications between an attorney and client. The issue in that case was whether the attorney was required to testify against his client. In this case, the attorney-client privilege is not at issue. Nor is appellant being asked to testify against his former client. Instead, the instant case revolves around whether a physical piece of evidence must be relinquished to the grand jury. While we recognize the importance of maintaining a client's confidences and secrets and understand that an attorney may have concerns in turning over incriminating evidence against his or her client, we do not believe that these concerns should override the public interest in maintaining public safety and promoting the administration of justice by prosecuting individuals for their alleged criminal activity.

Since the letter sought in this case contains evidence of a possible crime, we find that the letter must be turned over to the grand jury. Accordingly, we hold that where an attorney receives physical evidence from a third party relating to a possible crime committed by his or her client, the attorney is obligated to relinquish that evidence to law-enforcement authorities and must comply with a subpoena issued to that effect. . . .

Judgment affirmed.

CASE DISCUSSION QUESTIONS

1. On what basis did the court decide that the attorney should turn over the client's letter?

2. The dissent argued that the reasoning in *Purcell* should have been followed and that the court's failure to do so will mean "attorneys and their clients will be less likely to discuss potential crimes, which will decrease the likelihood that the crimes can be prevented."[19] Do you agree? Why or why not?

Arguably under the current rules governing attorney-client privilege, the information the Ohio attorney received was not privileged, and he could be forced to testify. After all, he did not receive the letter directly from his client. But should that be the rule? Should the outcome turn on from whom the attorney got the information—the investigator or directly from the client—or simply on whether the information was discovered as part of the attorney's representation? So long as the ethical rule regarding revealing confidences is discretionary, would it not better serve the interests of society (and certainly the victim) if the rule was that any confidences revealed would not lead to admissible evidence against the accused?

---

[19]733 N.E.2d at 1141.

e. Responding to Client Perjury

One of the most difficult ethical challenges attorneys face involves balancing a client's confidentiality interests against the attorney's responsibility to be truthful to the court. While attorneys must act as the zealous advocates of their clients, they also owe a duty of candor toward the court. Rule 3.3(a)(4) of the Model Rules states: "A lawyer shall not knowingly offer evidence that the lawyer *knows* to be false. If a lawyer has offered material evidence and comes to know of its falsity, the lawyer shall take reasonable remedial measures." However, Rule 3.3(c) states: "A lawyer may refuse to offer evidence that the lawyer *reasonably believes* is false."

Note that the rule makes a distinction between testimony the attorney "knows" will be false and testimony the attorney "reasonably believes" will be false. If the attorney knows the testimony will be false, he cannot present it, and if it has already been given, he must take reasonable remedial measures. If, however, the attorney simply believes it is or will be false, it is at the discretion of the attorney whether or not to present the evidence.[20]

There is often ambiguity over what is or is not truthful testimony. Was President Clinton testifying falsely when he said he and Monica Lewinsky were never alone? There were always other persons present somewhere in the White House even if no one else was present in the same room as they were. The problem is that people may give different definitions to the same word. By giving uncommon definitions to common words, the statements may be technically true but misleading.

Consider the following exchange that occurred during a bankruptcy hearing. The questioner was trying to determine if Mr. Bronston in the past or currently had any personal accounts in Swiss banks.

Q. Do you have any bank accounts in Swiss banks, Mr. Bronston?
A. No, sir.
Q. Have you ever?
A. The company had an account there for about six months, in Zurich.

Mr. Bronston's last answer, while truthful, was incomplete. For five years he had a Swiss bank account. He was charged with perjury based on the "theory that in order to mislead his questioner, [he] answered the second question with literal truthfulness but unresponsively addressed his answer to the company's assets and not to his own—thereby implying that he had no personal Swiss bank account at the relevant time."[21] The court reversed his conviction, finding that he could not be found guilty of perjury for giving a nonresponsive answer. The court distinguished this from the situation where a witness has visited a store fifty times in a given day and when asked how many times she entered the store, replied "five." While technically true (she did enter five times, and ten times, and etc.), such a responsive answer would do nothing to alert the questioner to probe further.

---

[20]Under the revised Rules this has been modified to read: "A lawyer may refuse to offer evidence, *other than the testimony of a defendant in a criminal matter,* that the lawyer reasonably believes is false." (Emphasis added.)

[21]*Bronston v. United States,* 409 U.S. 352, 355 (1973).

In our adversarial system, cross-examination is supposed to be used to ferret out the truth if a witness is evasive or misleading. That is not possible, however, when the answer is given in such a way, as in the example of the answer of having entered five times, that the questioner will not be alerted that only a partial answer has been given.

Assuming, however, that the attorney "knows" that the statements a witness plans to make will be "false," the rules clearly state that the attorney must refuse to offer the testimony. When that witness is a criminal defendant, the defense attorney is faced with what Monroe Freedman termed "the defense lawyer's trilema."[22] A lawyer in this situation must balance three separate and sometimes conflicting responsibilities:

- To best represent the client's interests, the lawyer must discover all relevant facts about the case.
- The lawyer must keep in strictest confidence all disclosures made by the client in the course of their professional relationship.
- As an "officer of the court," the lawyer must not knowingly present false evidence.

The ideal ethical solution is for the lawyer to talk the client out of presenting perjured testimony. The attorney can point out the dangers of lying: the potential of being charged with the additional crime of perjury and the consequences if the defendant's statement is proved to be false in court. But what if the client insists on going ahead with the perjured testimony? Can the attorney threaten to withdraw from the case without violating the client's Sixth Amendment right to assistance of counsel? The U.S. Supreme Court addressed this issue in *Nix v. Whiteside*.

Nix v. Whiteside
475 U.S. 157 (1986)

BURGER, J.

We granted certiorari to decide whether the Sixth Amendment right of a criminal defendant to assistance of counsel is violated when an attorney refuses to cooperate with the defendant in presenting perjured testimony at his trial.

Whiteside and two others went to one Calvin Love's apartment late [at] night, seeking marihuana. Love was in bed when Whiteside and his companions arrived; an argument between Whiteside and Love over the marihuana ensued. At one point, Love directed his girlfriend to get his "piece," and at another point got up, then returned to his bed. According to Whiteside's testi-

mony, Love then started to reach under his pillow and moved toward Whiteside. Whiteside stabbed Love in the chest, inflicting a fatal wound.

Whiteside was charged with murder, and when counsel was appointed he objected to the lawyer initially appointed, claiming that he felt uncomfortable with a lawyer who had formerly been a prosecutor. Gary L. Robinson was then appointed and immediately began an investigation. Whiteside gave him a statement that he had stabbed Love as the latter "was pulling a pistol from underneath the pillow on the bed." Upon questioning by Robinson, however, Whiteside indicated that he had not actually seen a gun, but

---

[22]See Monroe Freedman, Lawyers' Ethics in an Adversary System (Bobbs-Merrill Company 1975).

that he was convinced that Love had a gun. No pistol was found on the premises; shortly after the police search following the stabbing, which had revealed no weapon, the victim's family had removed all of the victim's possessions from the apartment. Robinson interviewed Whiteside's companions who were present during the stabbing, and none had seen a gun during the incident. Robinson advised Whiteside that the existence of a gun was not necessary to establish the claim of self-defense, and that only a reasonable belief that the victim had a gun nearby was necessary even though no gun was actually present.

Until shortly before trial, Whiteside consistently stated to Robinson that he had not actually seen a gun, but that he was convinced that Love had a gun in his hand. About a week before trial, during preparation for direct examination, Whiteside for the first time told Robinson and his associate Donna Paulsen that he had seen something "metallic" in Love's hand. When asked about this, Whiteside responded:

> [In] Howard Cook's case there was a gun. If I don't say I saw a gun, I'm dead.

Robinson told Whiteside that such testimony would be perjury and repeated that it was not necessary to prove that a gun was available but only that Whiteside reasonably believed that he was in danger. On Whiteside's insisting that he would testify that he saw "something metallic" Robinson told him, according to Robinson's testimony:

> [We] could not allow him to [testify falsely] because that would be perjury, and as officers of the court we would be suborning perjury if we allowed him to do it; . . . I advised him that if he did do that it would be my duty to advise the Court of what he was doing and that I felt he was committing perjury. . . .

Robinson also indicated he would seek to withdraw from the representation if Whiteside insisted on committing perjury.

Whiteside testified in his own defense at trial and stated that he "knew" that Love had a gun and that he believed Love was reaching for a gun and he had acted swiftly in self-defense. On cross-examination, he admitted that he had not actually seen a gun in Love's hand. Robinson presented evidence that Love had been seen with a sawed-off shotgun on other occasions, that the police search of the apartment may have been careless, and that the victim's family had removed everything from the apartment shortly after the crime. Robinson presented this evidence to show a basis for Whiteside's asserted fear that Love had a gun.

The jury returned a verdict of second-degree murder. . . .

[W]e [have] recognized counsel's duty of loyalty and his "overarching duty to advocate the defendant's cause." Plainly, that duty is limited to legitimate, lawful conduct compatible with the very nature of a trial as a search for truth. Although counsel must take all reasonable lawful means to attain the objectives of the client, counsel is precluded from taking steps or in any way assisting the client in presenting false evidence or otherwise violating the law. . . .

It is universally agreed that at a minimum the attorney's first duty when confronted with a proposal for perjurious testimony is to attempt to dissuade the client from the unlawful course of conduct. A statement directly in point is found in the commentary to the Model Rules of Professional Conduct under the heading "False Evidence":

"When false evidence is offered by the client, however, a conflict may arise between the lawyer's duty to keep the client's revelations confidential and the duty of candor to the court. Upon ascertaining that material evidence is false, the lawyer *should seek to persuade the client that the evidence should not be offered* or, if it has been offered, that its false character should immediately be disclosed." Model Rules of Professional Conduct, Rule 3.3, Comment (1983) (emphasis added).

The commentary thus also suggests that an attorney's revelation of his client's perjury to the court is a professionally responsible and acceptable response to the conduct of a client who has actually given perjured testimony. Similarly, the Model Rules . . . expressly permit withdrawal from representation as an appropriate response of an attorney when the client threatens to commit perjury. . . . The essence of the brief *amicus* of the American Bar Association reviewing practices long accepted by ethical lawyers is that under no circumstance may a lawyer either advocate or passively tolerate a client's giving false testimony. This, of course, is consistent with the governance of trial conduct in what we have long called "a search for truth." The suggestion sometimes made that "a lawyer must believe his client, not judge him" in no sense means a lawyer can honorably be a party to or in any way give aid to presenting known perjury.

Considering Robinson's representation of respondent in light of these accepted norms of professional conduct, we discern no failure to adhere to reasonable professional standards that would in any sense make out a deprivation of the Sixth Amendment right to counsel. Whether Robinson's conduct is seen as a successful attempt to dissuade his client from committing the crime of perjury, or whether seen as a "threat" to withdraw from representation and disclose the illegal scheme, Robinson's representation of Whiteside falls well within accepted standards of professional conduct. . . .

Nothing counsel did in any way undermined Whiteside's claim that he believed the victim was reaching for a gun. . . . We see this as a case in which the attorney successfully dissuaded the client from committing the crime of perjury. . . .

Robinson's admonitions to his client can in no sense be said to have forced respondent into an *impermissible* choice between his right to counsel and his right to testify as he proposed for there was no *permissible* choice to testify falsely. For defense counsel to take steps to persuade a criminal defendant to testify truthfully, or to withdraw, deprives the defendant of neither his right to counsel nor the right to testify truthfully. In *United States v. Havens,* we made clear that "when defendants testify, they must testify truthfully or suffer the consequences." When an accused proposes to resort to perjury or to produce false evidence, one consequence is the risk of withdrawal of counsel.

. . . An attorney's duty of confidentiality, which totally covers the client's admission of guilt, does not extend to a client's announced plans to engage in future criminal conduct. In short, the responsibility of an ethical lawyer, as an officer of the court and a key component of a system of justice, dedicated to a search for truth, is essentially the same whether the client announces an intention to bribe or threaten witnesses or jurors or to commit or procure perjury. No system of justice worthy of the name can tolerate a lesser standard. . . .

[Authors' Note: The Court affirmed the District Court's denial of a habeas corpus petition, meaning that the defendant had no valid grounds for contesting his conviction.]

STEVENS, J., concurring in the judgment.

Justice Holmes taught us that a word is but the skin of a living thought. A "fact" may also have a life of its own. From the perspective of an appellate judge, after a case has been tried and the evidence has been sifted by another judge, a particular fact may be as clear and certain as a piece of crystal or a small diamond. A trial lawyer, however, must often deal with mixtures of sand and clay. Even a pebble that seems clear enough at first glance may take on a different hue in a handful of gravel.

As we view this case, it appears perfectly clear that respondent intended to commit perjury, that his lawyer knew it, and that the lawyer had a duty—both to the court and to his client, for perjured testimony can ruin an otherwise meritorious case—to take extreme measures to prevent the perjury from occurring. The lawyer was successful and, from our unanimous and remote perspective, it is now pellucidly clear that the client suffered no "legally cognizable prejudice."

Nevertheless, beneath the surface of this case there are areas of uncertainty that cannot be resolved today. A lawyer's certainty that a change in his client's recollection is a harbinger of intended perjury . . . should be tempered by the realization that, after reflection, the most honest witness may recall (or sincerely believe he recalls) details that he previously overlooked. . . . Thus, one can be convinced—as I am—that this lawyer's actions were a proper way to provide his client with effective representation without confronting the much more difficult questions of what a lawyer must, should, or may do after his client has given testimony that the lawyer does not believe. . . .

CASE DISCUSSION QUESTIONS

1. The court assumes, without really discussing, that Robinson "knew" Whiteside was going to commit perjury. Given the nature of memory and how a person's recollections can change over time, is it fair to say that Robinson "knew" that Whiteside was lying when he said he had seen something metallic?

2. What guidance does this case provide for other attorneys confronted with a client who recalls events one way shortly after first meeting with the attorney and then differently right before trial?

3. Why did Justice Stevens concur?

Because the absolute prohibition against offering testimony only applies when the attorney *knows* the client is lying, several commentators have suggested that attorneys often work very hard to "not know." The classic literary presentation of this approach occurred in Robert Traver's *Anatomy of a Murder* in the famous scene where the defense attorney meets with a client who has been arrested for murder. The attorney first describes the elements of an insanity defense and then asks for the client's version of the events.

While some lawyers may indeed coach their clients or tell them that they do not want to know "if they did it," these lawyers are not fulfilling their duty to know all the facts and as a result they may fail to provide the most effective defense. For example, while a client charged with murder may indeed have "done it" by stabbing the victim to death, telling all of the facts may reveal information that could lead to a valid self-defense argument.

In situations in which a lawyer is concerned about a client's committing perjury, some state courts allow the attorney to call the client to testify in a narrative fashion. Rather than having the client respond to specific questions posed by the attorney, the attorney simply asks the client to give an account of what happened. While the attorney cannot ask any follow-up questions, the prosecuting attorney conducts a regular cross-examination. Additionally, the defense attorney may not refer to the client's false testimony during closing argument. The obvious problem with this procedure is that it signals the judge and the opposing attorney, and possibly the jury, that the client is lying.

Another option is for the lawyer to withdraw from the case when the client insists on going ahead with perjured testimony. While the Court in *Nix v. Whiteside* decided that there is no Sixth Amendment claim of ineffective assistance of counsel when an attorney threatens to withdraw from the case and expose the perjury if the client lies on the stand, the Court did not decide whether such a withdrawal violates the lawyer's ethical duty not to reveal confidential information or whether a refusal to call the defendant to the stand violates the client's due process right to testify in his or her own behalf. Furthermore, lawyers are usually not allowed to withdraw from a case without giving the judge a good reason for doing so. But the lawyer cannot tell the judge the reasons for withdrawing without revealing confidential information about the client.

In summary, the issue of client perjury presents many difficult issues for the advocate. As one court has stated:

> The problem of representing a defendant who insists on testifying falsely has been called, correctly, one of the hardest questions a criminal defense lawyer faces. The attorney is faced simultaneously with a duty to represent [the] client effectively, a duty to protect

[the] client's right to testify, a duty not to disclose the confidential communications of [the] client, a duty to reveal fraud on the court, and a duty not to knowingly use perjured testimony. . . . Experienced and conscientious people can come to different conclusions about the best way to deal with the conflict.[23]

DISCUSSION QUESTIONS

11. Under the Model Rules an attorney has an obligation not to present false evidence, but there is no affirmative obligation to reveal truthful material *facts* unless asked to do so by the other side. However, attorneys are under an obligation to disclose to the court *legal authority* in the controlling jurisdiction that is directly adverse to their clients' position if it has not already been disclosed by the opposing counsel. While there can be arguments as to why the obligation only runs to law from the "controlling jurisdiction" (the state or federal district in which the case is being tried) and what it means for the law to be "directly" adverse, this raises an even more fundamental question: If the goal of a trial is the search for truth, why is there an affirmative obligation to reveal law but not facts?

12. Former Supreme Court Justice Byron White said that if a defense attorney "can confuse a witness, even a truthful one, or make him appear at a disadvantage, unsure or indecisive, that will be his normal course." But is it ethical for an attorney to impeach the credibility of a witness when the attorney knows that the testimony given was in fact truthful? In essence, how is that different from putting on the stand a client the attorney knows is going to lie?

f. Inadvertent Disclosure of Confidential Information

Under our adversarial system, attorneys are expected to serve as zealous advocates for their clients. However, there may be times when zealous advocacy should give way to other interests, such as professionalism, respect for the courts, and respect for innocent bystanders. We have already discussed the requirement that lawyers not use false evidence to help win their cases. An additional limitation on zealous representation involves the decision regarding what to do with confidential information that the other side has inadvertently disclosed.

Consider the following fact scenario. You are an attorney working on a major case. Things are not going so well. Imagine your surprise and delight when in opening the day's mail you find the proverbial smoking gun: the one piece of evidence that seals your opponent's fate and guarantees victory for your side. Unfortunately, the piece of paper that contains this information is a letter from the opposing attorney to her client. Apparently, this letter was accidentally mixed in with a group of other documents that you had legitimately received through a document request. Should you try to forget what the letter said, notify the opposing attorney you have the letter, and then return or destroy it at the opposing attorney's direction? Or should you remind yourself that you are a zealous advocate, that your first duty is to your client, keep the fact that you have it secret, and then use the information to win your case?

The receipt of such misdirected confidential information raises this fundamental question: In an adversarial system, just how adversarial do the adversaries have to be? Is there a place for cooperation and even assistance when one adversary makes a mistake?

---

[23]Maddox v. State, 613 S.W.2d 275, 280 (Tex. Crim. App. 1980).

When an adversary fails to make a crucial motion or ask the right questions on cross-examination, it is not incumbent on the other attorney to point out or even correct the mistake. However, in the area of inadvertent disclosure of confidential information, ethics committees and courts seem to be moving in the direction of saying an attorney should "help out the opponent" when that opponent makes a mistake, even though that assistance interferes with the attorney's loyalty to the client. As first the fax and now e-mail have become major modes of communication, the danger of misdialing a fax number or hitting "reply all" rather than "reply" to an e-mail are obvious. But are these errors fundamentally different from other mistakes that attorneys make? The leading ethics opinion on this issue was issued by the ABA in 1992.

American Bar Association Standing Committee on Ethics and Professional Responsibility Formal Opinion 92-368

The Committee has been asked to opine on the obligations under the Model Rules of Professional Conduct of a lawyer who comes into possession of materials that appear on their face to be subject to the attorney-client privilege or otherwise confidential, under circumstances where it is clear that the materials were not intended for the receiving lawyer. . . . This opinion is intended to answer a question which has become increasingly important as the burgeoning of multi-party cases, the availability of xerography and the proliferation of facsimile machines and electronic mail make it technologically ever more likely that through inadvertence, privileged or confidential materials will be produced to opposing counsel by no more than the pushing of the wrong speed dial number on a facsimile machine.

A satisfactory answer to the question posed cannot be drawn from a narrow, literalistic reading of the black letter of the Model Rules. But it is useful, and necessary, to bear in mind the thoughts in the Preamble to the Model Rules that "many difficult issues of professional discretion . . . must be resolved through the exercise of sensitive professional and moral judgment guided by the basic principles underlying the Rules," and that "the Rules do not exhaust the moral and ethical considerations that should inform a lawyer, for no

worthwhile human activity can be completely defined by legal rules." . . .

[I]t is the view of the Committee that the receiving lawyer, as a matter of ethical conduct contemplated by the precepts underlying the Model Rules, (a) should not examine the materials once the inadvertence is discovered, (b) should notify the sending lawyer of their receipt and (c) should abide by the sending lawyer's instructions as to their disposition. . . .

The concept of confidentiality is a fundamental aspect of the right to the effective assistance of counsel. As reflected in each iteration of the rules of professional responsibility, the obligation of the lawyer to maintain and to refuse to divulge client confidences is virtually absolute.

The confidentiality principle rests on the vital importance society places upon the "full, free and frank" exchange between lawyer and client, shielded from the intrusive eyes and ears of adverse parties, the government, the media and the public. The principle's primary basis is that, absent the guarantee of confidentiality, critical discussions will be either proscribed, circumscribed or intruded upon in a way that will impact directly on the ability of the lawyer to serve his or her client. If the lawyer cannot gather all the necessary information and is not free to explore with the client the client's options, free from the threat that these confidential communications will be shared with those whose interests may be adverse to the client, the chilling effect on the lawyer-client relationship becomes plain. . . .

A. Competing Principles

. . . First, it might be argued that keeping the confidential materials and not letting the sending lawyer know they were received will punish carelessness on the part of the sending lawyer and those with whom that lawyer works. However, loss of confidentiality is a very high penalty to pay for a mere slip, particularly when the person or entity paying the "price" is not the individual lawyer responsible for the inadvertent conduct, but rather the client who presumably had nothing to do with the mis-sending of the materials.

Second, it could be asserted that letting the receiving lawyer keep the confidential materials in this situation will encourage more careful conduct on the part of other counsel in the future. Once the catastrophic consequences of a misstep are recognized, lawyers and their clients will conform their future conduct to avoid such an unfortunate result. . . . The argument . . . ignores the persistence of human frailty. The possibility of "punishment," no matter how severe, will never prevent, in this modern age of electronic transmission, unlimited photocopies and cases with hundreds of parties, accidents from occurring. The wrong number on the facsimile machine will still be "mis-speed-dialed;" the contents of two envelopes will get switched; "send copies to all defense counsel" will be misunderstood as "send copies to all counsel." . . .

IV. Good Sense and Reciprocity

. . . The immediate reaction of receiving counsel might be that the use of the missent materials can only serve to advantage his client. Nonetheless, it is clear there are advantages to doing just the opposite. First, instances of inadvertent production of documents tend not to occur only on one side. While a lawyer today may be the beneficiary of the opposing lawyer's misstep, tomorrow the shoe could be on the other foot. Second, when it is discovered that the confidential materials were retained and used the result could be similar to that which occurred recently in Baltimore when the court learned after jury selection that defendants' jury selection strategy was misdirected to plaintiffs' counsel by fax. "I find that the plaintiffs' attorneys have an advantage over the defense attorneys. Specifically, the plaintiffs know pretty well which prospective jurors the defense is going to strike. . . . They knew the inner-most thinking of the defense counsel." The judge struck the jury and ordered the entire process to begin again, at no small cost to plaintiffs, a cost that would have been expanded exponentially if the judge had not learned of this fact until the trial was over or when it was on appeal. . . . "Taking a bet" on what reaction a court may have when an inadvertent disclosure becomes known can be a risky proposition indeed. Third, the credibility and professionalism inherent in doing the right thing can, in some significant ways, enhance the strength of one's case, one's standing with the other party and opposing counsel, and one's stature before the Court.

Conclusion

The preamble to the Model Rules correctly notes that "virtually all difficult ethical problems arise from the conflict between a lawyer's responsibility to clients, to the legal system and to the lawyer's interest in remaining an upright person while earning a satisfactory living." Similarly, the same introduction observes that "a lawyer is also guided by personal conscience and the approbation of professional peers." . . . [R]eceiving counsel's obligations under those circumstances are to avoid reviewing the materials, notify sending counsel if sending counsel remains ignorant of the problem and abide sending counsel's direction as to how to treat the disposition of the confidential materials. This result not only fosters the important principle of confidentiality [and] avoids punishing the innocent client, . . . but also achieves a level of professionalism which can only redound to the lawyer's benefit.

CASE DISCUSSION QUESTIONS

1. The American Bar Association concluded that an attorney should not read inadvertently received confidential documents. Instead, the attorney should notify the other lawyer and comply with any request, such as to return the unread documents. Do you agree?

2. The Committee discussed the need for protecting client confidentiality, but generally that right is seen as running from the client to the client's attorney, not from the client to the opposing attorney. How does that factor into your thinking about the Committee's conclusion?

3. If attorneys are not to follow the "narrow, literalistic reading" of the Model Rules but rather, as the Committee suggests, are to be governed by "basic principles," is there any value in having a set of specific rules?

4. Many attorneys see a move toward "professionalism" as a misguided attempt to subvert the adversarial system. What do you suppose is the basis of their argument?

DISCUSSION QUESTIONS

13. In the ABA Opinion, the Committee raised the following hypotheticals to bolster its position that it would be unethical for an attorney to use missent information. Example 1: During a lunch break in a deposition, lawyer B left notes in a conference room either in an unlocked briefcase or on the conference room table. Lawyer A, arriving back from lunch early, could not ethically review the materials to which he now has easy access. Example 2: After a closing at lawyer A's office, lawyer B accidentally leaves a file or a briefcase behind. Lawyer A could not ethically take advantage of this inadvertence and rifle the file or inspect the briefcase before returning it. Example 3: In positioning an overhead projector on a shared counsel table in a courtroom during a recess, court personnel inadvertently moves the prosecutor's notes into a position in front of the defense counsel's place at the table. Again, ethically the defendant's attorney could not take a quick peek at those notes. If an attorney were to take advantage of any of the above situations and read the confidential information, do you think that presents a different situation than the one presented in the Ethics Opinion? Why?

14. In this day of fax machines and e-mails, it is all too easy to pick the wrong fax number off a list or the wrong address from a computerized address book. Is it fair to penalize attorneys when they mistakenly dial the wrong number?

Not all state bars have agreed with the ABA approach. For example, the Massachusetts Bar Association's Committee on Professional Ethics advised that a lawyer's primary ethical duty is to zealously advocate for the client's interests, and therefore, the documents do not have to be returned. In Opinion No. 99-4, the Committee stated that the attorney's main ethical obligation is to "represent [the] client zealously within the bounds of the law." A lawyer had received a letter written by the opposing attorney to that attorney's client. An associate thought their firm had simply been copied on the letter and filed it in the firm's file. When preparing for a hearing, the lawyer reviewed the file and read the letter for the first time. The Committee determined that not only did the attorney not have to return the letter but that it would be unethical to do so as that would conflict with the lawyer's ethical obligation to represent his client "zealously within the bounds of the law."[24]

The Maine Board of Bar Overseers was presented with a similar issue when it was asked to decide whether an attorney (Counsel Z) who received from Counsel A a number of documents, one of which was clearly privileged, could use that information and whether Counsel Z had to notify Counsel A of the error. Their response is strikingly different from that of the ABA.

Professional Ethics Commission of the Maine Board of Overseers of the Bar Opinion No. 146 (1994)

... For the reasons stated herein, the Commission concludes that Counsel Z may use the document and the information contained in it ... but that she should notify Counsel A, the sending lawyer, of the fact that the document has been received and provide a copy of the document to Counsel A on request.

In so holding, we are mindful that the ABA Standing Committee on Ethics and Professional Responsibility reached a contrary result in Formal Opinion 92-368. We do not find that Opinion to be persuasive. The ABA Committee was unable to cite any specific provision of the Model Rules of Professional Conduct in support of its conclusion. Indeed, Committee Opinion 92-368 expressly acknowledged that it was not based on any "black letter of the Model Rules." ...

The fundamental purpose behind the creation of the Bar Rules was to establish a clear codified set of standards for attorneys, the violation of which could result in professional sanctions. With that purpose ... in mind, we strongly believe that this Commission is not free to add ethical limitations not expressed by the Bar Rules. ...

Rule 3.2(f)(4) states that "A lawyer shall not: ... (4) engage in conduct that is prejudicial to the administration of justice." While that rule is very broad, nothing in its history suggests that the language of the Rule on its face would apply to the question before us. ... We do not believe that Rule 3.2(f)(4), standing alone, requires

Counsel Z to return the document to the sending lawyer, nor does that rule prohibit a lawyer from taking advantage of any other mistake of opposing counsel such as the failure to (1) plead an affirmative defense, (2) assert a counterclaim, (3) argue a theory of law, (4) assert an evidentiary objection at trial, (5) introduce an essential piece of evidence or (6) demand an important provision during contract negotiations. ...

The ABA Committee opinion ... [is] based in part on the view that lawyers owe to each other a level of courtesy that obligates them to return an inadvertently disclosed privileged document. ... However appealing such rationale is in theory, we find no support for that conclusion in the Maine Bar Rules. ...

We join the ... concern for maintaining and improving the level of civility, honor and common courtesy in the profession, however we do not believe that we can enforce those values through the Bar Rules in the absence of specific provisions to that effect. ...

Dissent

... In the debate about how the ethical question discussed in the majority opinion should be resolved, several Commission members indicated that, acting as individuals, they would return the papers as requested. However, absent any specific disciplinary rule which required otherwise, these members felt constrained to follow the client's wishes that they retain the

---

[24]Mass. R. Prof. C. 1.3 (Opinion No. 99-4).

documents even though they would have preferred to do otherwise.

In an article entitled "uncivil Law," ... former B.C. Law School Dean Dan Coquillette states that the "legal culture" must change before the public's perception of lawyers will improve. He suggests that attorneys cannot separate their private views of justice and morality from the standards which they practice as professionals:

> One lawyer I talked to who was very embarrassed about the profession said to me, "You know, one thing I keep telling myself is that being a lawyer is what I do. It's not what I am." I said, "You've got it wrong. Aristotle said you are what you do every day. You are the product of what you do day in, day out, hour in, hour out. You can't say that being a lawyer

is what you do and not what you are. . . . There's no way you can split these roles. If you act like a jerk in court, you're not an aggressive advocate pursuing an assertive strategy—you're just a jerk."

... Indeed, Dean Coquillette attributes much of the profession's present image problem to its failure to maintain a proper balance between the duty to uphold the system of justice embodied in the lawyers' oath, and the obligation to promote the interests of individual clients.

The foregoing considerations suggest that conduct which attorneys would find repugnant in their private lives, e.g., refusing to return something which clearly belongs to another, should not be tolerated on a professional level.

CASE DISCUSSION QUESTIONS

1. The majority opinion seems to be that an attorney should not be responsible for correcting the mistakes of the opposing attorney. Even the dissent stated, "After all, Attorney Z should not be expected to rectify every mistake made by opposing counsel in the course of litigation." Do you agree? Are there some mistakes that so fundamentally alter the adversarial process that an attorney should be required to rectify opposing counsel's errors?

2. Why should the lawyer be required to notify the sending lawyer of the document's receipt? See *Aerojet General Corp. v. Transport Indemnity Insurance*, 22 Cal. Rptr. 2d 862 (Cal. App. 1993), in which the court stated that the attorney had not violated any ethical rules by not notifying the opposing attorneys immediately after he inadvertently received documents originating from them, including a memorandum that revealed the existence of a witness about whom he had not known and whom he subsequently deposed.

3. Do you think a different result should occur if an attorney left a file folder behind during a break in a deposition and while out of the room, the opposing attorney took the folder and surreptitiously copied it? What if a disgruntled staff member working in the opposing attorney's firm had sent the document to the attorney?

When the ABA's Ethics 2000 Commission reviewed the Rules, they added this provision to Rule 4.4:

(b) A lawyer who receives a document relating to the representation of the lawyer's client and knows or reasonably should know that the document was inadvertently sent shall promptly notify the sender.

Notice that the new rule only addresses part of the issue, i.e., the need to notify the opposing side of the receipt of the document. It gives no guidance as to whether the attorney may use the information contained in the document nor whether the attorney must return it if requested to do so.

This revised rule was adopted by the ABA in February of 2002. It will not be in effect in any state, however, until that state accepts the recommendation as binding on the attorneys in that state. In states that choose to do so, because the rule uses the mandatory verb "shall," attorneys who fail to follow Rule 4.4(b) will be subject to discipline including suspension and possible disbarment.

DISCUSSION QUESTIONS

15. When an attorney receives information that the opposing side has sent accidentally, that attorney has four options:

- To refrain from reading the information, and then to contact the opposing attorney and return the document unread.
- To read the information, contact the opposing attorney, and return the document.
- To read the information, contact the opposing attorney, and refuse to return the document.
- To read the information and use it.

Given our adversarial system and your own sense of justice, which approach do you think is best?

16. Attorney White represents the plaintiff, who was injured in an automobile accident. She and her client have decided to settle the case if they can obtain at least $200,000. The settlement talks are set to begin tomorrow, and her strategy is to start by asking for $300,000, hoping to end up at $200,000. As attorney White is reviewing the files in preparation for the settlement talks, she discovers a one-page fax that she had not noticed before. It is from the defendant's insurer and was obviously intended to reach the defendant's attorney. It contains just one line: "Offer $100,000, but you have authority to settle for up to $500,000."

  a. What should attorney White do?
  b. Do you think that it should matter if the fax was intermixed with other documents?
  c. What if attorney White was wandering by the fax machine as it came in? As she pulled it out, she saw the cover sheet that contained the following language:

Privileged and Confidential—All information transmitted hereby is intended only for the use of the addressee(s) named above. If the reader of this message is not the intended recipient or the employee or agent responsible for delivering the message to the intended recipient(s), please note that any distribution or copying of this communication is strictly prohibited. Anyone who receives this communication in error should notify us immediately by telephone and return the original to us at the above address via the U.S. mail.

The cover sheet showed that the fax was to be sent to the opposing attorney, but the fax number was for Ms. White's office. What should she do?

2. Avoiding Conflict of Interest

In an adversarial system, an attorney may not represent both sides. By representing both the plaintiff and the defendant in a negligence action, or acting as both prosecutor and defense attorney in a criminal case, an attorney would have a clear **conflict of interest**. Any action that would help the plaintiff or the government would at the same time hurt the defendant.

Conflict of interest
The ethical rule prohibiting attorneys and paralegals from working for opposite sides in a case.

However, many conflicts are not this obvious. Take, for example, a situation in which the chief executive officer (CEO) of a corporation comes to the corporation's attorney for advice. Is the corporation's attorney supposed to be representing the interests of the CEO, the interests of the board of directors, the interests of the employees, or the interests of the shareholders?

Conflicts of interest can generally be divided into two categories. The first involves situations in which lawyers have a personal or business interest that suggests they cannot give their undivided loyalty to a client. The second involves either present or past client representation that presents a conflict with the representation of a new client.

Conflicts of the first type can occur when a lawyer is related to another lawyer who represents the opposite side of a case. Other examples include entering into certain types of business relationships with clients, preparing instruments for a client that give some benefit to the lawyer or a family member of the lawyer (such as a bequest in a will), providing financial assistance to a client in connection with pending litigation, and accepting compensation from third parties. Each of these situations poses either a real or a potential conflict of interest.

As an example of the first type of conflict, assume Mrs. Abbot is an attorney working for a defendants' firm. Her husband is an attorney who works for a plaintiffs' firm. One of Mr. Abbot's clients is suing the local grocery store for allegedly selling tainted meat. Mrs. Abbot represents the grocery store. See Figure 9-4. Mr. and Mrs. Abbot had been hoping for some time to get away from the pressures of work for a week or so, but their lack of finances was standing in their way. If Mr. Abbot wins his case against the grocery store (through either a settlement or a court judgment), he will earn 33 percent of the amount awarded to his client. Defendants' attorneys, however, usually receive a fee that does not vary based on whether their clients win. Can you see any potential conflict of interest? Would anyone knowing all the facts think that perhaps Mrs. Abbot might not be quite as diligent in her representation of the grocery store as she would be if another attorney were representing the plaintiff? In addition, do you think anyone might be concerned that in

Figure 9-4 Personal Conflict

> *Example:* Husband and wife represent opposing sides at litigation.
>
> π Store customer ——————————————▶ Δ Grocery store
> (Attorney, Mr. Abbot)   (Attorney, Mrs. Abbot)
> Receives 33 percent   Receives fee no matter the outcome.
> if he wins   Might the store question Mrs. Abbot's
>   zealous representation?

a careless moment either Mr. or Mrs. Abbot might let some confidential information slip?

Because of the ever-increasing number of women entering the profession and because of the variety of lifestyle choices other than traditional marriage that are becoming commonplace, one type of personal conflict that we may expect to see more frequently is the one created when the opposing attorneys share a close personal relationship. One such case was *Commonwealth v. Croken*.

Commonwealth v. Croken
432 Mass. 266, 733 N.E.2d 1005 (2000)

SPINA, J.

The defendant, Richard H. Croken, was convicted on two indictments charging forcible rape of a child under sixteen years, *G. L. c. 265, § 22A*, and one indictment charging indecent assault and battery on a child under fourteen years, *G. L. c. 265, § 13B*. Represented by new counsel on appeal the defendant filed a motion for a new trial raising claims . . . that trial counsel was impaired by a conflict of interest due to an undisclosed intimate relationship he had at the time of representation with an assistant district attorney (to whom he is now married) employed by the office which prosecuted the defendant. The motion was denied by the trial judge without an evidentiary hearing. . . . The Appeals Court held that the defendant was entitled to an evidentiary hearing on his motion and ordered that the case be remanded to the Superior Court. We granted the Commonwealth's application for further appellate review. We . . . remand the case to the Superior Court for an evidentiary hearing on that motion.

We summarize the evidence. . . . The defendant frequently babysat for the victims, whom we shall call Steve and Chris. Steve and Chris are cousins, and they are related to the defendant by marriage. One night when Chris was eight years old he slept at the defendant's home during a February vacation. The defendant fondled the boy's penis during the night and performed fellatio on him. Chris struck the defendant, then ran into the bathroom. The next morning the defendant told Chris not to tell anyone what happened or he would get hurt and disappear, and his mother would never find him. On several other occasions the defendant put his fingers or his penis into Chris's anus. When Chris was ten or eleven years old the defendant again fondled his penis and performed fellatio on him during the night. He also put his penis into the boy's anus. Chris first disclosed these events after Steve made a similar disclosure in 1993. . . .

2. *Motion for a new trial.* The defendant argues that the motion judge, who was also the trial judge, erred by denying his motion for a new trial without an evidentiary hearing after concluding that it did not raise a substantial issue. The thrust of the motion was that trial counsel was impaired by an actual conflict of interest created by his intimate relationship with an assistant district attorney, now his wife, who was employed by the same office that prosecuted the defendant, and that he never disclosed the conflict to the defendant. . . .

Affidavits of the defendant and his appellate counsel were filed with his motion. An affidavit by the prosecutor was filed with the Commonwealth's opposition to the motion. The following facts are undisputed or appear from those affidavits. Attorney Robert LaLiberte was appointed to represent the defendant from his arraignment in the District Court on June 3, 1993, through sentencing in the Superior Court on July 18, 1996, and until August 13, 1996, when appellate counsel was appointed. For much if not all of that time, LaLiberte was involved in a close relationship with an assistant district attorney whom we, like the Appeals Court, shall call Jane Doe.

Doe was employed as an assistant district attorney for the Plymouth district from 1989 through December, 1994. Thereafter she practiced law in the private sector until April, 1997;

then served as an attorney for the Department of Social Services until February, 1998. In March, 1998, she returned to a position of supervising assistant district attorney in the District Court for the Plymouth district. At the start of LaLiberte's representation, one of Doe's colleagues was James M. Sullivan, the assistant district attorney in Plymouth County who was responsible for prosecuting the defendant throughout the proceedings in the trial court. Area telephone directories for July, 1996, through June, 1998, listed LaLiberte and Doe at the same residential address, a home purchased by LaLiberte in July, 1995. Doe and LaLiberte lived together during a portion of the time that LaLiberte represented the defendant.

Much more than this we do not know. Nor, apparently, does the defendant, whose affidavit states that he knew during the representation that LaLiberte had a girl friend with whom he was living, but that he did not know her name or her occupation. The defendant avers that he would never have consented to LaLiberte's representing him had he known that she worked for the district attorney's office for the Plymouth district. He became aware of this fact only by chance. His appellate counsel was speaking casually one day at a courthouse with an assistant district attorney, who informed her that Doe and LaLiberte were now married. The date of that marriage is not known. Appellate counsel investigated and brought to light some of the few details that are known. . . .

At the time LaLiberte represented the defendant, the Canons of Ethics and Disciplinary Rules were still in effect. . . . Disciplinary Rule 5-101(A), as appearing in *382 Mass. 779 (1981),* provided: "Except with the consent of his client after full disclosure, a lawyer shall not accept employment if the exercise of his professional judgment on behalf of his client will be or reasonably may be affected by his own financial, business, property, or personal interests." A lawyer's personal interests surely include his interest in maintaining amicable relations with his relatives, his spouse, and anyone with whom he is comparably intimate.

This interest is, of course, often significantly pecuniary in character, but it also has irreducible emotional and moral dimensions, and it heavily bears on how any ordinary human being goes about making important decisions. It follows that in a case where a lawyer's representation of a client may be significantly limited by his ties to his relatives and intimate companions, professional ethics are implicated just as they would in a case where the lawyer represents a second client with litigation interests potentially adverse to those of the first client. . . .

Before agreeing to represent the defendant, LaLiberte should have determined whether he reasonably believed his representation would be adversely affected by his relationship with Doe. If he concluded that it would, then he should have withdrawn from the case. If, on the other hand, he determined that he could represent the defendant vigorously, LaLiberte should then have asked the defendant whether he consented to being represented by him in light of his relationship with Doe. Informed consent would of course include disclosure of the fact that Doe was an assistant district attorney who worked in the same office as the prosecutor who was trying to convict the defendant.[4]

We think that the motion and affidavits raise a substantial question as to whether there was an actual conflict. The issue is certainly serious. Although factually underdeveloped, the papers demonstrate sufficient basis for a reasonable belief that the core of the attorney-client relationship might have been impaired, and that some probing of the matter by way of an evidentiary hearing was required. . . .

Marital and similar intimate relationships between lawyers have potential for creating unique problems. "The marriage relationship may be conducive to inadvertent breaches of confidentiality. A spouse may have knowledge of out-of-town investigative trips at or around the time of preparation for a particular case; clients and witnesses may contact the lawyer at home or leave messages on the home answering machine that may reveal a tactic or a confidence. Working

---

[4] "A possible conflict does not itself preclude the representation. The critical questions are the likelihood that a conflict will eventuate and, if it does, whether it will materially interfere with the lawyer's independent professional judgment in considering alternatives or foreclose courses of action that reasonably should be pursued on behalf of the client. Consideration should be given to whether the client wishes to accommodate the other interest involved." Mass. R. Prof. C. 1.7 comment [4], *426 Mass. 1330 (1998).*

papers left at home or work performed at home may reveal confidences of a client. The needs of a lawyer to work early or late or on weekends may give rise to the need for explanation in a marriage relationship that could inadvertently reveal client confidences or secrets." ABA Criminal Justice Section, Ethical Problems Facing the Criminal Defense Lawyer at 248 (1995). In addition, a "potential conflict of interest that may arise can be financial or personal. A district attorney or public defender may have a special interest in the outcome of a case based on a concern for a promotion or political benefit for one's spouse. A lawyer's loyalty to a client may be impaired by a personal interest in the success of a spouse. . . ." Id. at 249. We see no appreciable difference between marriage and other intimate relationships in this regard.

Sullivan's affidavit leaves some key questions unanswered, and it raises serious questions because of what it does not say. Sullivan simply did not have the information to tell what Doe knew and did. . . .

The Commonwealth would have done better in this case to submit an affidavit by Doe, who at present is in its employ. Doe could aver—assuming, of course, that the averments were true—that she never worked on the case, that she never discussed the case with LaLiberte or anyone from the district attorney's office, that no information concerning the case was ever made known to her or conveyed by her to the office or to LaLiberte, and that she had never understood that whether she regained employment with the district attorney's office would depend in any way on how LaLiberte handled his representation of the defendant. The existence of a strictly observed office policy designed to eliminate even inadvertent breaches of confidence in circumstances involving interoffice relationships, whose numbers appear to be increasing significantly, is also something that could have been included in an affidavit. Similarly, LaLiberte could have submitted an affidavit stating—again, assuming it were true—that he never discussed the case with Doe, and that he never expected that his performance in this case would affect Doe's chances of becoming reemployed by the district attorney's office . . . .We do not imply that affidavits addressing these particular issues would have obviated the need for a hearing. That is a question that can only be answered on a case-by-case basis. There are obvious and serious questions in this case that should have been addressed, but were not. The woeful inadequacy of the Commonwealth's response to the defendant's motion and affidavits compel the need for an evidentiary hearing. . . .

The hearing must not intrude unnecessarily on the privacy of LaLiberte and Doe. The details of their relationship need not be explored, as it is not disputed that LaLiberte and Doe were involved in an intimate relationship during most of LaLiberte's representation of the defendant. We think the hearing should focus upon (1) whether an actual conflict of interest existed between LaLiberte and the defendant; and (2) whether the potential conflict, i.e., the relationship between LaLiberte and Doe caused any material prejudice to the defendant, including (a) whether LaLiberte and Doe discussed the defendant's case, and if so, what was said; (b) whether Doe discussed the case with anyone in the district attorney's office, or in the office of the Department of Social Services if that office had any involvement in this matter, and if so, what information was disclosed which may have harmed the defense; (c) whether, during LaLiberte's representation of the defendant, Doe had any expectation of returning to the district attorney's office, and if so, whether LaLiberte's representation was directly or indirectly affected thereby (e.g., did LaLiberte show any special deference to the prosecutor that harmed the defense). . . .

The . . . matter is remanded to the Superior Court for an evidentiary hearing consistent with this opinion. . . .

So ordered.

After the case was remanded for an evidentiary hearing, the trial court determined that there was no actual conflict, finding Jane Doe and Attorney LaLiberte's testimony credible when they stated that they had no conversations regarding the case and that the prosecuting attorney never discussed the case with Doe. Finally, the court concluded that any potential conflict that may have arisen did not result in any showing of ineffective assistance of counsel. When the case was once again appealed, the court found that there was nothing in the record to show that LaLiberte's "independent professional judgment" was impaired by his own personal interest arising from his relationship with Doe.[25]

CASE DISCUSSION QUESTIONS

1. What is the danger to a client when his or her attorney is having a personal relationship with another attorney who works for the same organization that is prosecuting the client?

2. Do you think this case would have been decided differently if Jane Doe had been the prosecuting attorney instead of simply being an attorney working in the office?

3. The defendant stated that he would never have retained attorney LaLiberte as his attorney had he known of LaLiberte's and Ms. Doe's relationship. Why is this statement and the attorney's total failure to reveal the potential conflict not enough to form the basis for a new trial?

4. How is a client ever truly to know whether confidences and secrets were shared if the majority of the evidentiary hearing is based on the testimony of the two individuals who have the alleged conflict?

The second type of conflict of interest occurs when the attorney has information about the client on the opposite side of the case and therefore may know something that will be detrimental to that person. For example, assume attorney Smith worked for Mr. Brown when he was getting a divorce. During the divorce proceedings, attorney Smith naturally became quite informed on Mr. Brown's financial state, including his partnership interest in a local gymnasium. It is now two years later, and one of Mr. Brown's partners has approached the firm seeking representation in a case he wants to bring against Mr. Brown. If attorney Smith is allowed to take the case, his knowledge of Mr. Brown's finances that he gained while he represented him in his divorce might put Mr. Brown at an unfair disadvantage.

As you can see, client confidentiality and conflicts of interest are very closely related. In the situation involving Mr. and Mrs. Abbot and the *Croken* case, there is the fear that confidentiality might be breached because of the close relationship between the attorneys representing the two sides. In the situation involving information gained from a client, the fear is more real, as attorney Smith actually knows confidential information and the only issue is whether he might use it against his former client. Because of this possibility, the ethics codes require that attorney Smith either obtain Mr. Brown's consent to proceed as the attorney representing the partner or resign from the case. In addition, all other attorneys at attorney Smith's firm would be barred from representing Mr. Brown's partner.

---

[25] Commonwealth v. Croken, 797 N.E.2d 403 (Mass. App. C. 2003).

To summarize, in cases of actual conflict, an attorney can never represent both sides. In those situations involving potential conflict, a court might allow the representation so long as the client consented after being fully informed of the potential problems. However, the court could still disallow the representation if the court thought that there was in fact an actual conflict or that the client had not been fully informed.

Discussion Questions

17. Why should Mr. Brown's partner be penalized in his choice of attorney just because attorney Smith happened to represent Mr. Brown years ago in an unrelated matter?

18. Model Rule 1.7 states that "notwithstanding the existence of a concurrent conflict of interest . . . a lawyer may represent a client if the lawyer reasonably believes that the lawyer will be able to provide competent and diligent representation." Is that a bit like asking the fox to guard the hen house?

D. ACCESS TO JUSTICE

In this chapter we have discussed the key role lawyers play in the adversary system. But what if no lawyer wants to take the person's case? Can a lawyer be forced to represent a guilty client or to advocate for a cause that is contrary to the lawyer's personal beliefs? What if a person cannot afford to hire a lawyer? While the Constitution guarantees the right to an attorney in criminal matters, that is not true in civil cases. In this section we will explore these access-to-justice issues.

1. Providing Services to Unpopular Clients and Causes

Generally, lawyers are free to accept or reject clients. However, lawyers who work for others, whether it is in a law firm, public agency, corporation, or advocacy group, generally lose the ability to pick and choose the individuals they wish to represent. Perhaps the most obvious example of this is the lawyer who works for the public defenders' office representing individuals who have been charged with a crime. That lawyer is not free to represent only those whom the lawyer believes are innocent.

One of the most common questions asked of lawyers is, "How can you defend a guilty client?" There are several possible responses to this question.[26] The first response is to point out that guilt is a legal concept that is determined by a judge or a jury and not by the lawyer. A person is not considered guilty until after the trial has been completed. The second response is that in representing a guilty client, the attorney is just playing a role, similar to the actor who plays the part of the villain in a movie. The third response is based on the belief that the very legitimacy of our adversary system depends upon having lawyers willing to represent the "guilty" as well as the innocent. If criminal defendants cannot find

---

[26] For an interesting discussion of this topic found in the world of fiction, you might enjoy reading *A Cinderella Affidavit* by Michael Fredrickson. In that novel, when discussing the difficulties that confront attorneys, the main character concludes that attorneys must proceed on "the curious faith that the localized permissible evil we do on behalf of our clients will dissolve in the higher justice served by the adversary system." Id. at 446.

NETNOTE

An excellent site for up-to-date information on legal ethics is *www.legalethics.com*.

attorneys willing to represent them, "the foundation of the judicial system is eroded and the lawyers become the judges of guilt or innocence by their very decision to accept or reject those criminal clients."[27] The importance of attorneys being willing to accept court appointments is stated in Model Rule 6.2: "A lawyer shall not seek to avoid appointment by a tribunal to represent a person except for good cause." Examples of good cause include where the lawyer is not competent to handle the particular type of case or the representation would result in a conflict of interest.

One exception to Rule 6.2 provides that an attorney may decline representation if "the client or the cause is so repugnant to the lawyer as to be likely to impair the client-lawyer relations or the lawyer's ability to represent the client."[28] Because of this provision, no doubt there are limits as to the types of situations in which a court would order an attorney to represent a client. For example, it is not likely that a court would force an African-American attorney to represent a member of the Ku Klux Klan accused of placing a burning cross on the front lawn of an integrated church. Similarly, a court would not order a Jewish attorney to defend a Nazi organization that wished to march in a town parade. Nonetheless, some attorneys who have found themselves in such situations have voluntarily chosen to represent such unpopular clients in order to defend constitutional principles, such as freedom of speech and assembly.[29]

DISCUSSION QUESTION

19. Attorney Judith Nathanson is an attorney who earned her law degree with the purpose of helping to advance the status of women in the legal system. In her divorce practice, she only represents wives. As she only has a certain amount of time and energy to devote to her clients, she feels it essential to use her resources to redress social and legal wrongs done to women. Therefore, when Mr. Stropnicky asked her to represent him in his divorce, she refused. Should she be required to represent him? Should it matter that in his marriage he had assumed the role of homemaker and childcare giver? Is this analogous to an attorney with white supremacist views arguing that she should be able to decline to represent non-white clients?

---

[27] Stephen Jones, A Lawyer's Ethical Duty to Represent the Unpopular Client, 1 Chap. L. Rev. 105, 107 (1998).

[28] Model Rule 6.2(c).

[29] See, for example, the case of Anthony Griffin, an attorney for the NAACP who represented the Grand Dragon of the Texas Knights of the Ku Klux Klan, and David Goldberger, an ACLU lawyer who defended the Nazis' right to march in Skokie, Illinois.

2. Making Legal Services Available to Low-Income Clients

Over the past twenty years there has been an increasingly large unmet need for legal services, particularly amongst the poor and middle class. One American Bar Association study concluded that at least 70 to 80 percent of low-income persons who require legal assistance are unable to obtain it.[30]

Legal services agencies that were created in the 1970s by the federal government to serve the poor have not been able to keep up with this demand for legal assistance. They lack sufficient funding and typically can represent only the very poor. Attorney pro bono work is also not filling this need for legal services. Rule 6.1 of the Model Rules of Professional Conduct states that every lawyer should "aspire to render at least (50) hours of pro bono publico legal services per year," but this provision has not been adopted in all states, and even in the ones where it has, the rule is aspirational only. It does not require attorneys to provide pro bono representation.

In this section we will look at two different approaches to increasing access to justice: the contingency fee system and increased representation by nonattorney advocates.

a. The Contingency Fee System

Lawyers use various methods to charge for their services. The three most common methods are flat fee, hourly rate, and contingency fee. Typically attorneys charge a flat fee for simple matters where the total time that will need to be spent can be estimated fairly accurately before the services are rendered. Examples include drafting a simple will, preparing the documents for an uncontested divorce when children and substantial assets are not involved, and representing a criminal client on a misdemeanor charge. When it is more difficult to estimate the total amount of time that will be required to complete a project, attorneys frequently charge by the hour.

The third method is also the traditional method for providing representation to those who have been injured and who could not otherwise afford an attorney: the **contingency fee**. Clients can hire an attorney and only owe a fee "contingent upon" the attorney's winning the case. If the plaintiff loses, the plaintiff is responsible for the costs of litigation but owes the attorney nothing. If the plaintiff wins, however, then the attorney's fee is a percentage of what the plaintiff has won. Typically that amount is 33 percent of the plaintiff's recovery. Because typically lower-income clients do not have enough money to pay an attorney on an hourly basis, many argue that contingency fees make it possible for those clients to pursue claims that they would otherwise have to abandon.

However, some have questioned if it is ethical for an attorney to take one-third of the money that would otherwise be going to compensate the client for his or her injuries. If the goal in awarding a plaintiff money, either through a jury award or settlement, is to compensate the plaintiff 100 percent for the plaintiff's loss, that will not happen if the attorney takes one-third of the payment. Consider the following case.

Attorney Goodman represented Donald Gagnon, who was severely injured in a highway accident. At the time of the accident, Gagnon was trying to help another

Contingency fee
Attorney compensation as a percentage of the amount recovered rather than a flat amount of money or an hourly fee.

---

[30] Commission on Nonlawyer Practice, American Bar Association, Nonlawyer Activity in Law-Related Situations (1995).

motorist. The driver of a tractor-trailer had pulled completely off the travel lane of the highway and was parked in the breakdown lane. The driver had stopped because she had noticed that the mud flaps on her truck were rubbing against her rear trailer wheels. To help the woman, Gagnon pulled off the highway behind the truck in the breakdown lane. He then went underneath the rear of the trailer to attempt to correct the problem. While he was in that position, Donald Shoblom, driving a loaded garbage truck, veered off the highway into the breakdown lane and crashed into the tractor-trailer. The woman was killed as the result of the collision, and Gagnon sustained massive injuries, leaving him a paraplegic.

Gagnon v. Shoblom
409 Mass. 63, 565 N.E.2d 775 (1991)

On June 9, 1988, at 1 P.M., a truck operated by Donald Shoblom crashed into a parked trailer, killing Susan J. Thompson and severely injuring Donald Gagnon. Gagnon retained Attorney Alan R. Goodman in pursuit of his claim against Shoblom and Shoblom's employer, and for his workers' compensation claim. Gagnon and Mr. Goodman signed a contingent fee agreement in which Gagnon agreed that Mr. Goodman's compensation would amount to $33\frac{1}{3}$% of the recovery in his personal injury claim. The entire contingent fee agreement is set forth as an appendix to this opinion.

Mr. Goodman commenced an action and, after extensive discovery and investigation, a structured settlement of $ 2,925,000 (present cash value) was reached[3] . . . .

A Superior Court judge conducted a hearing and indicated his approval of the terms of the settlement agreement except the provision for recovery of $33\frac{1}{3}$% of the settlement which amounted to $ 975,000. The judge called this fee unconscionable. There was an evidentiary hearing on the reasonableness of the settlement agreement. Gagnon testified that he voluntarily signed the contingent fee agreement and that he was satisfied that Mr. Goodman had earned his agreed fee. Additionally, a leading member of the bar who specializes in prosecuting personal injury claims for plaintiffs testified as to the reasonableness of the fee. The attorney who defended the action

in the case testified as to the impressive work performed by Mr. Goodman. There was no evidence tending to prove that the fee was anything but reasonable.

However, the judge filed a carefully crafted memorandum and order in which he ordered payment of legal fees to Mr. Goodman as follows: "Mr. Goodman handled the case expeditiously and well. He obtained what I consider to be a very fine result. As stated above, he is entitled to handsome compensation.

"Taking those factors into account, as well as Mr. Goodman's ability and reputation (both of which are good) the demand for his services by others, the time reasonably spent, the expenses reasonably incurred by him and the charges usually made for similar services by others in Western Massachusetts, I am satisfied that the $33\frac{1}{3}$% maximum rate provided for in his contingent fee agreement should only be applied to the first $ 300,000.00 of the recovery. A rate of 25% of the next $ 1,200,000.00, plus a rate of 20% of all amounts in excess of $ 1,500,000 would be reasonable. At those rates Mr. Goodman is entitled to an attorney's fee of $ 695,000.00, which I consider to be 'handsome' compensation. Anything in excess of that amount would be unreasonable and excessive."

We allowed Mr. Goodman's request for direct appellate review of the correctness of the judge's order regarding the fee. We hold that it was error for the judge to disapprove the agreed fee. . . .

---

[3] The settlement called for immediate cash payment of $ 800,000 to Gagnon and . . . for substantial annual payments to Gagnon for life and deferred payments to Gagnon and his daughter.

The courts are not powerless to act in disapproving a fee which exceeds the percentage in the agreement, a fee to which the client never agreed, or a fee which is plainly unreasonable. . . . However, we need not discuss the court's inherent power in this case because no one is challenging the fee.

Accordingly, an order shall enter approving the entire settlement, including the amount of compensation due to Mr. Goodman under the contingent fee agreement.

So ordered.

GREANEY, J. (concurring). . . . I agree with the court that the attorney's fee in this case should not have been reduced. The evidence before the judge sufficiently indicated that the contingent fee agreement was reasonable "in light of the circumstances prevailing at the time of [the] making [of the agreement]." This conclusion is reinforced by the fact that the client, Gagnon, has made no objection to the contingent fee agreement and has affirmatively stated his satisfaction both with the work done and the percentage charged by Goodman. It is also a consideration that the one-third percentage has become institutionalized in the practice of the litigation bar as the minimum rate to be charged in the typical tort case. Change, if it is to come, should not come suddenly and to the disappointment of long-standing expectations.

The judge, however, has touched upon a larger issue. His memorandum frames that issue in this manner:

> "Contingent fee agreements . . . serve a very beneficial public purpose. They have been said to be the 'poor man's key to the courthouse' because they do provide a method whereby civil claims can be filed and litigated by persons who would otherwise be unable to afford the assistance of counsel. . . ."

> "I am satisfied (both on thxe basis of my own experience as a practicing attorney and as a trial judge as well as by the evidence presented at the hearings) that in the case of a civil tort action in which damages are sought for personal injuries a contingent fee of $33\frac{1}{3}$% of the amount recovered is reasonable to a point; depending (among other factors of course) upon the size of the recovery ultimately obtained. I am also satisfied, however, that as the size of the recovery (and hence the size of the fee) increases, the spread between the attorney's fee and the fair value of the time, effort and skill that he devoted to earning that fee widens—and at some point the fee becomes unreasonable and even (if the spread becomes wide enough) outrageous or unconscionable.

> "One should not lose sight of the fact that under our law a recovery for a personal injury is limited, at least in theory, to the fair and reasonable value of the pain and suffering, mental anguish, reasonable medical expenses, disfigurement, disability and lost earning capacity, both past and future, *sustained by the client*. However, attorney's fees incurred by the client are not recoverable in such a case, either as part of or in addition to his damages. Any fee that the attorney exacts from the client under a contingent fee agreement must therefore reduce the client's compensation for his injury below what is fair and reasonable. When, as in this case, the injury sustained by the client is catastrophic, the amount of the reduction can become enormous unless some rule of reason is applied to the application of the contingent fee. It is, after all, Mr. Gagnon and not Mr. Goodman who must spend the remainder of his life confined to a wheelchair with no bowel or bladder control and with constant dependence upon others to assist him in the normal tasks of day-to-day living . . ." (Emphasis in original; citation omitted). . . .

At a time when the gap between the service and the fee in tort cases appears to be becoming more and more pronounced, there may be a need to establish a better sense of proportion. This case is illustrative of the problem. The question raised by the judge deserves honest debate.

APPENDIX TO THE OPINION OF THE COURT

Law firm of

= ALAN R. GOODMAN =

CONTINGENT FEE AGREEMENT

Date .... 6-23-88 ....

The Client .... Donald A. Gagnon   38 Felicia St., Springfield, MA
............................(Name).............................(Street & Number).............................(City or Town)

retains the Law Firm of   ALAN R. GOODMAN   1350 Main Street   Springfield, MA 01103
to perform the legal services mentioned in paragraph (1) below. The attorney agrees to perform them faithfully and with due diligence.

(1) The claim, controversy, and other matters with reference to which the services are to be performed are:
an accident which occurred on or about   6 / 9 /88

(2) The contingency upon which compensation is to be paid is:
33.3% if settled before suit
35% if settled after suit before trial or after arbitration/mediation
40% if settled after trial but before verdict or judgement
45% if verdict or judgement
50% if appeal taken
An additional 15% (minimum $100.00) of PIP and Med. Pay collected in auto cases.

(3) The client is not to be liable to pay compensation otherwise than from amounts collected for him by the attorney, except that is responsible for following costs:
Out of pocket expenses, such as costs of medical reports and opinions, filing fees, sheriff's fees, service of subpoena, witness fees, photographs, excessive postage and photocopying, long distance telephone calls, research materials, expert witness opinions and fees, file initialization, travel costs, investigator's reports. Said costs are deducted from gross settlement after calculation of attorney's fees.   to be included in

(4) Reasonable compensation on the foregoing contingency is to be paid by the client to the attorney, but such compensation (including that of any associated counsel) is not to exceed the maximum percentages of the gross amount collected as specified in (2) above.

(5) The client is in any event to be liable to the attorney for his reasonable expenses and disbursements (3) above even if no settlement is made.

(6) If the attorney is discharged by the client prior to the conclusion of this representation, the attorney is entitled to be then compensated for his reasonable expenses and disbursements. Further, the attorney is to be compensated for the fair value of the services rendered to the client up to the time of discharge, but the amount of the fee shall not be due to the attorney until the subject matter litigation is concluded pursuant to Paragraphs 2 and 3 above.

This agreement and its performance are subject to Rule 3:05 of the Supreme Judicial Court of Massachusetts

WE EACH HAVE READ THE ABOVE AGREEMENT BEFORE SIGNING IT.
CLIENT ACKNOWLEDGES RECEIPT OF CARBON COPY.

Witnesses to Signatures
(To Client) .... Nancy A. Nall .... Donald A. Gagnon ....
                                                             (Signature of Client)
(To Attorney) ....
                                                             (Signature of Client)
                      6/25/88   .... Alan R. Goodman ....
                                                             (Signature of Attorney)

Practice Limited to Personal Injury Law

350 MAIN STREET, BANK OF BOSTON BUILDING, 12th FLOOR, SPRINGFIELD, MA 01103 413-736-1616
App-60

Form No. G-100 Rev # 87

Exhibit 9-1   Contingent Fee Agreement

CASE DISCUSSION QUESTIONS

1. Why did the Massachusetts Supreme Judicial Court think the trial court had erred in disapproving the agreed-upon fee?

2. Mr. Gagnon received a structured settlement in this case. How do you think that might have affected his ability to pay his attorney's fees?

3. Do you agree with the trial court judge that the percentage an attorney earns should decrease as the size of the client's award increases? Why or why not?

4. Specifically, how do you answer the trial judge's assertion that "[a]ny fee that the attorney exacts from the client under a contingent fee agreement must therefore reduce the client's compensation for his injury below what is fair and reasonable"?

5. What do you think of the contingency fee agreement in this particular case? Given the facts outlined before the case, it seems apparent that when Goodman had his client sign the contingent fee agreement, he knew that the liability aspect of Gagnon's case would not be difficult to prove, that his client's injuries were catastrophic, and as Shoblom was employed as a driver for a large corporate employer, that it was likely Gagnon would receive a very substantial judgment or settlement from that corporate employer.

6. In addition to representing Donald Gagnon, attorney Goodman had also been retained to represent the administrator of the dead woman's estate in her claim for wrongful death and the dead woman's mother for her claim of negligent infliction of emotional distress. Clearly, Goodman could make use of much of the work he had already done on the *Gagnon* case in preparing those additional cases, for which he was also charging a fee. Do you think those clients should receive some sort of a discount for work that had already been done and paid for?

b. Nonattorney Representation

Since the mid-seventies, there has been a continuing dialogue about expanding the role of nonattorneys, especially in those areas where there is a shortage of attorneys, either because potential clients cannot afford attorneys' fees or because attorneys have no desire to practice in those areas.

Unauthorized practice of law
When nonlawyers do things that only lawyers are allowed to do. In most states this is a crime.

However, state **unauthorized practice of law** (UPL) statutes have historically been used to protect lawyers from competition from accountants, real estate agents, paralegals, and "legal technicians." These UPL statutes are defended as being necessary to protect the "public interest." The following statement from *West Virginia State Bar v. Earley* is typical of the manner in which courts have justified these restrictions:

> The justification for excluding from the practice of law persons who are not admitted to the bar and for limiting and restricting such practice to licensed members of the legal profession is not the protection of the members of the bar from competition or the creation of a monopoly for the members of the legal profession, but is instead the protection of the public from being advised and represented in legal matters by unqualified and undisciplined persons over whom the judicial department of the government could exercise slight or no control.[31]

---

[31] 109 S.E.2d 420, 534 (W. Va. 1959).

However, as Deborah Rhode pointed out in a Stanford Law Review article:

> Courts have not required any factual showing that unqualified restraints on lay practice are necessary—or even closely related—to the states' interest in preventing incompetent assistance. Nor have courts inquired whether that interest could be realized through less restrictive means. Existing research in the most active areas of unauthorized practice enforcement suggests that states would have considerable difficulty making either demonstration.[32]

One major empirical study found that only 2 percent of the 1,188 cases concerning lay advocates originated from complaints by dissatisfied customers, and few of those involved claims of incompetence.[33]

This appears to make little difference to the courts. For example, in *State ex rel. Johnson v. Childe* the court conceded that Childe, a nonlawyer,[34] may have been more knowledgeable about one specialized area of the law than most lawyers; however,

> [t]his is not a defense. We do not doubt that respondent possesses high qualifications in the transportation rate field. But the fact that he can qualify as an expert in a particular field will not permit his engaging lawfully in the profession of the law without a license to do so.[35]

A key factor in the courts' justification of unauthorized practice statutes is that lawyers are governed by ethical restraints that do not apply to their lay competitors. In response to this argument, advocates of the legal technician movement and other legal reformers point out that limited licensing approaches could also impose these types of fiduciary duties and provide a mechanism for enforcing them. Thus, they argue, nonlawyers could be licensed to practice in limited designated areas of the law without endangering the public interest.

In recent years, state and federal administrative agencies have increasingly allowed nonlawyers to act in a representative capacity at administrative hearings. At the federal level the Administrative Procedure Act states:

> A person compelled to appear in person before an agency or representative thereof is entitled to be accompanied, represented, and advised by counsel or, if permitted by the agency, *by other qualified representatives.*[36]

The Patent Office, the Social Security Administration, and the Immigration and Naturalization Service have all made provisions for such lay representation.

At the state level some statutes and administrative regulations also permit lay representation in many agencies. Workers' compensation boards, unemployment compensation boards, and public utility commissions are most apt to have made such allowances. However, as can be seen in the next case, not all states

---

[32] Deborah Rhode, Policing the Professional Monopoly: A Constitutional and Empirical Analysis of Unauthorized Practice of Law Prohibitions, 34 Stan. L. Rev. 1, 85 (1991).

[33] Id.

[34] It is interesting to note that lawyers call all others "nonlawyers." Why is it that electricians do not refer to the rest of the human race as nonelectricians or doctors to all others as nondoctors?

[35] 295 N.W. 381, 382 (Neb. 1941).

[36] 5 U.S.C. § 555(b) (2004) (emphasis added).

agree that it is appropriate for nonlawyers to act as advocates in state administrative proceedings.

Here are the facts that led up to the state of Delaware challenging a nonlawyer who advocated for the rights of disabled children. Polly DeCrease had a ten-year-old son who could not read. His school was about to expel him for having brought a knife to class and setting a fire in a bathroom. Ms. DeCrease was sure that his behavior problems were due to a disability, and she wanted to force the school to give him help for that disability rather than expel him. However, none of the three lawyers she contacted would take her case and none could recommend anyone who would. Finally she turned to Marilyn Arons, a nonlawyer special education expert.

In 1977, Ms. Arons had established the Parent Information Center of New Jersey because she believed that her neurologically impaired daughter was not getting the special education she needed.[37] Since that time the center has helped more than 20,000 families, and in about 500 cases has represented parents at hearings before administrative law judges. In the late 1990s, Ms. Arons moved to Delaware where she continued her advocacy for children's rights, including agreeing to help Ms. DeCrease. Ms. Arons acted as the DeCreases' advocate at an administrative due process hearing.

These administrative hearings are similar to a trial. They can last for days and each side (with the school always represented by a lawyer) has an opportunity to make opening and closing statements, to call witnesses, and to cross-examine the witnesses called by the other side.

Ms. Arons prevailed at the hearing, forcing the school district to send Nick DeCrease to a private school at a cost of $70,000 a year. (The average cost for a student in public school in Delaware is $8,000.) Ms. Arons, and her colleague, Ruth Watson, successfully helped four other families receive special services before the Delaware Board on the Unauthorized Practice of Law investigated their activities. The Board acknowledged that Arons and Watson were "vigorous and knowledgeable advocates."[38] However, the Board also determined that they must stop advocating for families at such hearings because their representation amounted to the unauthorized practice of law.

Ms. Arons and Ms. Watson appealed the board's decision to the Delaware Supreme Court. In oral argument before the court, the attorney representing the Board stated that even though the administrative due process hearings were mandated by federal law, it was the state law of unauthorized practice that governs who should be allowed to appear as a representative at those hearings. Second, he also stated that there was an "important public-policy concern at stake in curtailing the unauthorized practice of law, where there is no guarantee of the advocates' professionalism and no disciplinary procedures to sanction them."[39] In the following case the supreme court of Delaware discussed whether Ms. Arons's activities constituted the unlawful practice of law.

---

[37] Richard B. Schmitt, Advocates Act as Lawyers, and States Cry "Objection!," Wall Street Journal, Jan. 14, 1999.

[38] For a further discussion of the facts leading up to the *Arons decision,* see Carl Wieser, Advocates Fight for the Right to Help, The News Journal, Mar. 3, 2001, accessed at *www.delawareonline.com/ newsjournal/local/1001/03/02advocates.html.*

[39] Celia Cohen, Preventing Overdue Process, Delaware Law Weekly (May 31, 2000).

In re Arons
756 A.2d 867 (Del. 2000)

WALSH, J.

This is an appeal from a decision of the Board on the Unauthorized Practice of Law (the "Board"), an arm of the Supreme Court of Delaware, concluding that the appellants had engaged in the unauthorized practice of law. The appellants, supported by the United States Department of Justice as *amicus curiae*, contend that the Board erred in not recognizing their entitlement under federal law to represent parents of children with disabilities before State administrative agencies. That entitlement, it is argued, preempts state law and is supported by due process considerations. We conclude, however, that the Board's decision is supported by the evidence and free of any error of law. Accordingly, we affirm.

I

The appellants, Marilyn Arons and Ruth Watson, are, respectively, the founder and Executive Director of Parent Information Center of New Jersey, Inc. (collectively "Appellants"). The Parent Information Center is a non-profit organization founded in 1977 that provides advice, counseling and advocacy services to families of children with disabilities. On five occasions, the Center has represented families of children with disabilities in "due process" hearings held by the Delaware Department of Public Instruction pursuant to the federal Individuals with Disabilities Education Act ("IDEA"), *20 U.S.C. § 1400 et seq.* Four of these five hearings were handled by Arons, while the other hearing was handled by Watson. Although neither Arons nor Watson is an attorney, both possess special knowledge and training with respect to the problems of children with disabilities.

The IDEA is intended to "ensure that children with disabilities and their parents are guaranteed procedural safeguards with respect to the provision of free appropriate public education." *20 U.S.C. § 1415*(a). Under the IDEA, the parents of a disabled child are entitled to challenge any proposal to change or initiate, or refusal to change or initiate, the identification, evaluation, educational placement or any other aspect of the provision of a free appropriate public education service to that child. *See id.* at § 1415(b)(3). When complaints are received, "the parents involved in such complaint shall have the opportunity for an impartial due process hearing." *Id.* at § 1415(f).

Due process hearings in Delaware are conducted in a manner typical of contested, adjudicatory hearings. The parties include the parent(s), the local school board and the Department of Public Instruction. The hearing is conducted by a three-member panel consisting of an attorney admitted to practice in Delaware; an educator who is either certified in the area of special education or who has been a post-secondary educator in the area of programs for students with disabilities; and a lay person with demonstrated interest in the education of students with disabilities from an approved list compiled by the Governor's Advisory Counsel for Exceptional Citizens. Hearings are chaired by the attorney member of the panel.

Due process hearings usually last from two to four days. The school board and the Department of Public Instruction are always represented by counsel. The hearing begins with opening statements from each party. Evidence is then presented through witnesses, who are subjected to direct and cross-examination. Although the rules of evidence do not apply strictly, the Chair rules on legal issues, the qualification of experts and objections to relevance, materiality and admissibility. Following the presentation of evidence, the parties make closing statements and may be asked to file written submissions on key questions.

On August 8, 1996, the Office of Disciplinary Counsel ("ODC") filed a petition with the Board requesting that Arons, Watson and the Parent Information Center be declared to have engaged in activities constituting the unauthorized practice of law by representing families of children with disabilities in due process hearings. While admitting the representation of at least five such families in Delaware due process hearings, Appellants denied that their activities, even if amounting to the practice of law, constitute the *unauthorized* practice of law. They argued that section 1415(h)(1) of the IDEA permits the representations in which they have engaged and preempts any state-law proscription against the unauthorized practice of law that might otherwise apply. That section provides that any party to a due process hearing "shall be accorded . . . the right to be accompanied and advised by counsel and by individuals with special knowledge or training with respect to the problems of children with disabilities." They also claimed that Delaware is alone among the fifty states in precluding non-lawyer representation in these circumstances. . . .

II

. . . .

Appellants and the ODC each argue that the pertinent language of the IDEA in dispute—"the right to be accompanied and advised by counsel and by individuals with special knowledge or training with respect to the problems of children with disabilities"—unambiguously supports their respective positions. We do not share the parties' vision of clarity. In our view, section 1415(h)(1) is ambiguous to the extent it appears to confer joint authority on lawyers and non-lawyers to accompany and advise parents and others affected by the operation of the due process hearings provided under the IDEA. . . .

[S]upportive of the ODC's proposed interpretation of the IDEA are a Senate Conference Report addressing the statute and remarks made by the original author of the Senate bill, Senator Harrison Williams of New Jersey. The Conference Report states that in administrative due process hearings a party is entitled to "the right to counsel and to be advised and accompanied by individuals with special knowledge, training or skills with respect to the problems of handicapped children." S. Conf. Rep. No. 94-455 (1975). . . . This language confirms the clear distinction that Congress envisioned between the representational role of counsel and the advisory role of non-lawyers. . . .

Congress has explicitly included language in other federal statutes to permit lay representation

where such a result was intended. *See, e.g., 7 U.S.C. § 2020*(e)(7) (Food Stamp Act provision allowing households in certification process to "be represented by a person other than a member of the household so long as that person has been clearly designated as the representative . . . and . . . is an adult."). Congress obviously knows how to provide such authority when it wishes to do so. The absence of similar language in the IDEA strongly suggests that Congress chose not to create a right to lay representation in due process hearings. . . .

III

In addition to their statutory interpretation argument, Appellants contend even if the IDEA does not expressly entitle them to represent parents in due process hearings, due process would be violated by forbidding parents from having non-lawyer representation in hearings under the IDEA. They note that due process hearings are formal adversarial proceedings in which the State of Delaware funds the attorneys who argue for the parents' adversaries. Denying parents and children access to "the only assistance available to them," the argument goes raises "unyielding due process problems." . . .

The ODC acknowledges that the individual liberty interest at stake in due process hearings under the IDEA is substantial. It also concedes that some parents will forego their statutory right to contest changes to their child's education plan because they cannot afford legal counsel and will opt not to proceed *pro se* due to the complexity of the hearings and the prospect of facing two sets of government lawyers. The ODC submits, however, that Appellants "grossly and unfairly" exaggerate the risk that Delaware will deprive children of that interest unless the children and their parents are allowed to be represented by lay advocates. In this regard, the ODC notes that Delaware's Community Legal Aid Society has, on occasion, provided representation at IDEA due process hearings to parents and children whose cases satisfy the organization's case acceptance criteria. The ODC further contends that the State of Delaware has a compelling interest in regulating the practice of law within its boundaries, and that this interest significantly outweighs any potential benefit that some individual parents and children may obtain through the services of lay advocates.

We agree. A balancing of . . . factors suggests that procedural due process would not be violated by forbidding parents from having non-lawyer representation in hearings under the IDEA. While there is no question of the importance of the individual interests involved, it seems clear that parties to an IDEA hearing are already provided with substantial procedural safeguards. The hearings are conducted in a manner typical of contested, adversarial adjudicatory hearings, including the direct and cross-examination of witnesses and the required exchange of witness lists and documents in advance of the hearing. While we recognize that Appellants possess some expertise in the area of the educational needs of disabled children, they admittedly lack the training and skills that lawyers are expected to exhibit in matters of evidence and procedure. . . . [L]ay advocates are unregulated and, unlike members of the Bar, are not answerable to the disciplinary process that operates as an arm of this Court. . . . Our role is to insure that the public will enjoy the representation of individuals who have been found to possess the necessary skills and training to represent others. . . .

IV

For the foregoing reasons, the language of section 1415(h)(1) cannot be interpreted as granting any clear right to lay representation. This conclusion renders moot Appellants' claim that the IDEA preempts any state-law proscription against the unauthorized practice of law that might otherwise apply to the activities of such individuals with special knowledge or training in this context. Accordingly, we affirm the decision of the Board.

CASE DISCUSSION QUESTIONS

1. The court seems to be stating that it is better for parents to have no representation at all than nonlawyer representation. Do you agree?

2. The court conceded that Ms. Arons was a specialist in education law. Why did they refuse to allow her to advocate on behalf of the parents at due process hearings?

3. Ms. Arons and her colleague prevailed in all five of the Delaware cases in which they appeared on behalf of the families. In an interview with the Wall Street Journal, Ms. Arons was quoted as saying that she never felt at a disadvantage in court, "I found it a piece of cake." Contrast that statement with the court's declaration that "they admittedly lack the training and skills that lawyers are expected to exhibit in matters of evidence and procedure."[40]

In 2001 the United States Supreme Court denied certiorari,[41] thereby leaving the decision as final. Perhaps based on the promise in the opinion that if "it could be demonstrated that an unmet need exists and that the local bar could not adequately respond, this Court would consider the adoption of a rule allowing lay representation in a certain limited class of cases,"[42] a parent petitioned the court for a one-time suspension of the Court's decision in *Arons* so that a nonlawyer could represent her and her child at an upcoming hearing. She alleged that she had not been able to find an attorney. The court denied her request, saying that

---

[40] 756 A.2d at 874.

[41] Arons v. Office of Disciplinary Counsel, 532 U.S. 1065 (2001).

[42] 756 A.2d at 874.

there had been no "changes, proposed or adopted, to the Court's rules since the *Arons* decision that would allow lay representation in this matter."[43]

SUMMARY

In this chapter we have focused on some of the most important ethical and moral issues related to the role of attorneys in our adversarial system of justice. We have seen how the need to protect the interests of their clients may come in direct conflict with the needs and even safety of others. Specifically, we examined these conflicts in the context of client confidentiality, conflict of interest, and access to justice.

In dealing with these issues, attorneys often have to choose between competing values and interests. While the ABA and state bar associations have addressed many of these issues in their ethical guidelines, we saw that the provisions of these codes do not always provide individual attorneys with the answers they need.

Clearly, knowing and following a code of ethics does not ensure moral behavior. In fact, at times it could even be argued that it leads to immoral or at least amoral behavior. However, if attorneys follow general rules, the belief is that over the long run more morally right than wrong choices will be made. The only other alternative is the anarchy that would result if each individual attorney is allowed to decide on a course of action based on his or her individual conscience. A compromise position acknowledges that the rules are meant to govern the "normal," while attorneys must exercise discretion in the case of the extraordinary.

We ended the chapter with a look at the issue of access to justice. In this context we considered an attorney's responsibility for taking on unpopular clients and causes as well as ways to increase access to justice for those who otherwise could not afford legal services.

REVIEW QUESTIONS

Pages 241 through 243

1. Describe the adversarial system. How does it vary from a system based on the inquisitorial model?
2. Explain the relationship between the rights contained in the Fourth, Fifth, and Sixth Amendments and our adversarial system.
3. Some have described litigation as a battleground. Why is that?

Pages 243 through 245

4. Attorneys are governed by either the Code of Professional Responsibility or the Rules of Professional Conduct. Who originally drafted these documents, and how is it that they govern the behavior of attorneys in a particular state?
5. Are attorneys in your state bound by the Code of Professional Responsibility or the Rules of Professional Conduct?
6. What can happen to attorneys who violate the ethical rules in effect in their state?

Pages 245 through 274

7. Why does our legal system place such a high value on attorneys' maintaining their clients' confidences?

---

[43] In re Machette, 2004 Del. LEXIS 250 (decided June 17, 2004).

8. How does the attorney-client privilege differ from the ethical rules regarding confidentiality?

9. Mrs. Smith, who is seeking a divorce, entered attorney Black's office for her first interview. Because she was very disturbed over the prospect of a divorce, Mrs. Smith brought her best friend along with her to the interview. Should attorney Black let Mrs. Smith's best friend sit in on the interview? Why?

10. At a cocktail party attorney Sims sees one of his firm's clients kissing someone not the client's wife. At the client's divorce hearing could attorney Sims be required to testify about what he saw at the party? Could attorney Sims ethically tell his wife about what he saw at the party? Why?

11. For each of the following discuss whether the attorney can reveal the information. Be sure to indicate if your answer would vary depending on whether the state in which this occurred had adopted the Model Code, the Model Rules, or the recently revised 2003 Model Rules.

   a. A client tells her attorney that she murdered her husband.

   b. A client tells her attorney that she is planning to murder her husband.

   c. A client tells her attorney that at the end of the week she is planning to steal all of her employer's cash receipts as she has access to his safe.

   d. A client tells her attorney that her husband is so upset with how the litigation is going that he is planning to kill the opposing attorney.

   e. A client tells her attorney that it was she, and not the woman who is on trial for murder, who killed the victim.

12. What are the major differences and similarities between the Model Rules and the Model Code's approach to allowing attorneys to reveal planned criminal behavior?

13. If a client tells an attorney she is going to commit perjury, what are the attorney's options?

14. If an attorney suspects but does not know that a client is going to commit perjury, what should the attorney do? Does it matter if the client is the defendant in a criminal case?

15. What should attorneys do when they inadvertently receive confidential information from the other side?

16. Give some examples of when an attorney might find her duty of loyalty to her client conflicting with other values she holds.

Pages 275 through 280

17. What are the two major causes of conflict of interest?

18. In each of the following situations determine whether you see any potential conflict-of-interest problems.

   a. Sam was injured in an automobile accident when the car he was riding in was struck in an intersection by a pickup truck. Both Sam and the driver of the car want attorney Black to represent them against the driver of the pickup truck.

   b. Sara and Emily were arrested for the attempted robbery of United Bank. They would like attorney Jones to represent both of them.

   c. Attorney Lacy is the prosecuting attorney for the murder trial of Tom Black. Jim White represents the defendant. Halfway through the murder trial, attorney Lacy and attorney White start dating.

Pages 280 through 292

19. What reasons do attorneys usually give for why they are willing to represent guilty or unpopular clients?

20. What are the three most common methods that attorneys use for charging clients?

21. What is a contingency fee and how does it arguably increase access to justice?

22. What is the major justification for enforcing unauthorized practice of law statutes?

Chapter 10

Torts

The risk reasonably to be perceived defines
the duty to be obeyed.
Justice Benjamin Cardozo

INTRODUCTION

A **tort** occurs when someone's person or property is hurt. More specifically, a tort is defined as a private wrong (other than a breach of contract) in which a person or property is harmed because of another's failure to carry out a legal duty. In most instances this legal duty is an obligation to refrain from taking actions that harm others. Occasionally, a duty will consist of an affirmative obligation to act in order to protect others.

A tort is considered to be a "private wrong," as opposed to criminal acts, which are seen as "public wrongs." Therefore, while the state prosecutes crimes, the individual harmed must pursue a tort action. The end results of a criminal action and a civil tort suit also differ: A finding of guilt in a criminal action can result in a fine paid to the state or imprisonment, while a finding of liability in a tort action usually leads to a damage award to the harmed party. However, as we discussed in Chapter 3, because both criminal acts and torts can result in harm to a person or property, sometimes the same set of facts will give rise to both a tort action and a criminal action.

Tort actions must also be distinguished from contract actions. In a tort action the legal duties are established by the courts through the common law and more recently also by statutory modifications of the common law. In contrast, contract actions are based on the legal duties the parties established in their contract. A further difference between a contract action and a tort action lies in the remedy sought. In a contract action the purpose of the lawsuit is to give the injured party the benefit of the bargain. In a tort action the purpose is to compensate the plaintiff for any losses suffered. For example, assume you purchase an automobile with defective brakes. Because of the defect you are unable to stop at a red light and are in a minor accident. The purpose of a breach of contract action would be to "get the benefit of your bargain"—that is, a car without defective brakes. The purpose of a tort action would be to fully compensate you for any harm to yourself or the car, including your medical bills, lost time from work, and pain and suffering. As this example suggests, at times one set of facts can give rise to both a breach of contract action and a tort action. For example, if a manufacturer intentionally lies about a product he is selling and the buyer relies on that lie to her detriment, the buyer might be able to sue for both breach of contract (thereby invalidating the sale) and fraud (thereby recovering for damages caused by the product).

Tort law has ancient roots, and tort rules have been created by the courts on a case-by-case basis. Therefore, looking to precedent for analogous situations plays a large role in any analysis of a tort problem. In addition, the courts frequently look to an authoritative secondary source, the **Restatement of the Law of Torts, Second.** This Restatement was drafted by a group of legal scholars in order to summarize the existing common law rules in a set of black letter principles. At times, instead of simply "restating" the law, the drafters also included their vision of what tort law should become. This is most notable in the area of products liability. Although the Restatement is a secondary source and is therefore only persuasive authority, you will frequently see courts citing to it and even formally adopting some of its provisions.

In spite of its ancient common law roots, tort law has never been static. Historically, judges have seen the need to adapt the common law principles to changing conditions. Most recently some of those conditions have included the development of modern modes of transportation and other scientific advances, such as the ability to artificially create and prolong life. In addition, when the need arises, instead of simply adapting the currently existing common law rules, the courts will even recognize new torts. One example is the new tort of battered woman's syndrome, which we will discuss later in this chapter.

While tort law is still predominately court-created law, legislatures are playing an increasingly active role. For example, both Congress and state legislatures have enacted "tort reform" statutes, with the purpose of modifying some of the perceived abuses of the tort system. One example is legislation to place limits on the amount of damages that can be awarded in certain types of tort cases. Such tort reform measures have even been included in the national platforms of the major political parties.

Torts have traditionally been classified into one of three major categories based on whether they involve intentional acts, negligence, or strict liability. See Figure 10-1. When people intentionally seek to violate a duty toward others, their purposeful conduct is classified as an **intentional tort,** and the **tortfeasor** (the person who committed the tort) is subject to a greater range of damages. When the harm occurs as a result of a careless act done with no conscious intent to injure anyone, the act is classified as **negligence.** Finally, there are times when for policy reasons the defendant is held responsible even though the defendant acted neither negligently nor intentionally to harm the plaintiff. These are classified as **strict liability** torts.

Restatement of the Law of Torts, Second
An authoritative secondary source, written by a group of legal scholars, summarizing the existing common law, as well as suggesting what the law should be.

Figure 10-1   Degrees of Fault

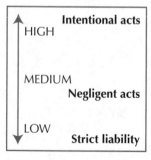

A. INTENTIONAL TORTS

An intentional tort occurs whenever someone intends an action that results in harm to a person's body, reputation, emotional well-being, or property. Almost any harm that you can imagine, if caused intentionally, can be classified as an intentional tort. In this section of the chapter we will discuss just a few of the most common intentional torts. First, there are the torts that cause harm to a person's body, reputation, or emotional well-being: assault and battery, false imprisonment, defamation, invasion of privacy, and intentional infliction of emotional distress. Second, there are the torts that cause harm to a person's property: trespass, trespass to personal property, and conversion. Third, we will briefly discuss a variety of other torts, including false arrest, malicious prosecution, abuse of process, fraud, and business torts.

In order to prove that an intentional tort occurred, the plaintiff must prove each of that tort's elements. The defendant then has the opportunity to raise any defenses. The primary defenses available in intentional tort cases are consent, self-defense, defense of third parties, and various types of privilege.

As we will see, one set of facts can give rise to more than one type of intentional tort. In addition, many intentional torts are also crimes. Consider the following fact scenario.

One day attorney John Bloom met with a new client, Mrs. Day. Mrs. Day told the following story.

Mrs. Day has been living with Mr. David Day for the past five years. While their marriage has never been a happy one, Mrs. Day never thought of divorce until last night. Mr. Day came home very late from an adult co-ed softball game. Mrs. Day said it was obvious that he had been drinking. They soon got into a verbal fight. Among other things, Mr. Day yelled at Mrs. Day that he had told her boss she had been skimming money from the company's petty cash drawer. Mrs. Day had never done any such thing. He also told her that he had received a call earlier in the day from the local hospital, telling him that Mrs. Day's mother had been admitted following a massive heart attack. (Later Mrs. Day found out that this was not true, but at the time she believed Mr. Day and became very upset.) The fight escalated, and Mr. Day began waving his baseball bat in front of Mrs. Day. Mrs. Day said that she was not frightened, as Mr. Day had never hit her, and she did not believe he would do so then. In fact, she turned her back on him and started to leave the room. He then yelled at her and, before she could turn around, hit her on the back of her arm with the bat, breaking her arm. Mrs. Day then fled to the bathroom, locking the door behind her. Mrs. Day remained in the bathroom for over two hours until she felt it was safe to leave. She found Mr. Day asleep on the living room couch. She fled to a neighbor's, who drove her to the hospital. The next morning Mrs. Day returned home to find Mr. Day as well as her purse gone. There was a message on the answering machine from her boss saying that she was fired.

While Mrs. Day is contemplating divorce proceedings, her more immediate concern is to learn what actions she can take to compensate her for her broken arm, emotional distress, missing purse, and lost job.

1. Harm to a Person's Body, Reputation, or Emotional Well-Being

The following torts will be discussed in this section: assault and battery (harm or threatened harm to a person's body), false imprisonment (a wrongful detention), defamation (harm to a person's reputation), and invasion of privacy and the intentional infliction of emotional distress (harm to a person's emotional well-being).

a. Assault and Battery

Assault
An intentional act that creates a reasonable apprehension of an immediate harmful or offensive physical contact.

Battery
An intentional act that creates a harmful or offensive physical contact.

An **assault** occurs when someone reasonably fears that he or she is about to suffer a harmful or offensive physical contact. A **battery** is the intentional harmful or offensive physical contact. While we usually think of assault and battery as one tort, in reality they are two torts. They can be present together, as, for example, when Tom first waves a fist in front of Sam's face and then proceeds to punch Sam in the nose. However, there can also be an assault with no battery whenever there is the threat of a battery but no ensuing physical contact. And there can also be a battery with no assault, as, for example, when the person being attacked does not see the threat of physical contact before it actually occurs.

(1) The elements of assault and battery

To prove an assault, the plaintiff must show that each of the following elements occurred:

1. an intentional act
2. that creates a reasonable apprehension of
3. an immediate harmful or offensive physical contact.

Notice the requirement in element 3 that the apprehension be of an *immediate* physical contact. A threat to go and get a gun is not an assault because there is no threat of an immediate contact.

To prove a battery, the plaintiff must show that each of the following elements occurred:

1. an intentional act
2. that creates a harmful or offensive physical contact.

Notice that for both assault and battery the contact does not have to actually be physically painful. It simply must be harmful or offensive. An unwanted kiss from a stranger could qualify as an offensive contact.

Contact also includes contact with anything attached to the person, such as clothing. In the classic case of *Fisher v. Carrousel Motor Hotel, Inc.,*[1] the court found that a battery had been committed when a hotel employee grabbed a plate from a customer. Also, the defendant need not actually do the touching if the defendant set the action in motion, such as by throwing a rock or ordering a dog to attack.

---

[1]424 S.W.2d 627 (Tex. 1967).

In discussing battery there are three important concepts to keep in mind. First, the intent involved must be the intent to perform the act, not necessarily to cause the plaintiff harm. Assume a boy, as a practical joke, pulls out a chair just as his friend is about to sit on it. The friend falls to the ground, breaking his arm. Even though the boy did not mean to hurt his friend, he is liable for battery. He intentionally did an act that caused physical injury. This example also illustrates the difference between intent, the desire to do an act, and motive, the reason for the act. The court is concerned with the intent (the boy's desire to pull out the chair) and not with his motive (his wish to play a practical joke).

Second, usually defendants will be liable for any consequences of their actions, even if the consequences were unforeseeable. Often this is phrased as follows: "The defendant must take the plaintiff as the defendant finds her." For example, if the plaintiff has an "eggshell skull" and the defendant merely taps the plaintiff's head lightly, the tap may seriously injure the plaintiff. The defendant is liable, even if such a tap would not have harmed most people.

Third, assume John swung his fist, meaning to hit Bill. However, Bill moved aside and John hit Sara instead. John is liable to Sara for battery under the theory of **transferred intent.**

The following case involves a friendly backyard touch football game that unfortunately ends in injury. While reading the case, decide for yourself whether you think the plaintiff should have been allowed to succeed on her claim of battery.

Transferred intent
A legal fiction that if a person directs a tortious action toward A but instead harms B, the intent to act against A is transferred to B.

Knight v. Jewett
3 Cal. App. 4th 1022, 275 Cal. Rptr. 292 (1990)

TODD, Acting P.J.

Kendra Knight appeals a summary judgment granted in favor of Michael Jewett in her lawsuit against Jewett for . . . assault and battery stemming from a touch football game in which she was injured. . . .

Facts

On January 25, 1987, Knight and several other individuals, including Jewett, gathered at the Vista home of Ed McDaniels to observe the Super Bowl football game. Knight and Jewett were among those who decided to play a game of coed touch football during half-time using a "peewee" football often used by children. Apparently, no explicit rules were written down or discussed before the game, other than the requirement that to stop advancement of the player with the ball it was necessary to touch that player above the waist with two hands. Knight and Jewett were on different teams.

Previously, Knight had played touch football and frequently watched football on television. Knight voluntarily participated in the Super Bowl half-time game. It was her understanding that this game would not involve forceful pushing, hard hitting or hard shoving during the game. She had never observed anyone being injured in a touch football game before this incident.

About five to ten minutes after the game started, Jewett ran into Knight during a play and afterward Knight asked Jewett not to play so rough. Otherwise, she told him, she would stop playing.

On the next play, Knight suffered her injuries, when she was knocked down by Jewett and he stepped on the little finger of her right hand. Kendra had three surgeries on the finger, but they proved unsuccessful. The finger was amputated during a fourth surgery.

According to Jewett, he had jumped up to intercept a pass and as he came down he knocked Knight over. When he landed, he stepped back and onto Knight's hand.

According to Knight's version, her teammate, Andrea Starr, had caught the ball and was proceeding up the field. Knight was headed in the same direction, when Jewett, in pursuit of Starr, came from behind Knight and knocked her down. Knight put her arms out to break the fall and Jewett ran over her, stepping on her hand. Jewett continued to pursue Starr for another 10 to 15 feet before catching up with her and tagging her. Starr said the tag was rough enough to cause her to lose her balance and fall and twist her ankle. . . .

Discussion . . .

Inasmuch as this case reaches us on appeal from a summary judgment in favor of Jewett, it is only necessary for us to determine whether there is any possibility Knight may be able to establish her case.

A requisite element of assault and battery is intent. Here, however, there is no evidence that Jewett intended to injure Knight or commit a battery on her. Moreover, the record affirmatively shows Knight does not believe Jewett had the intent to step on her hand or injure her.[7] Without the requisite intent, Knight cannot state a cause of action for assault and battery. . . .

Affirmed.

---

[7]The deposition of Kendra Knight was taken on October 19, 1988, and offered in support of the motion for summary judgment. Ms. Knight testified as follows:

"Q. Do you believe that Mr. Jewett was trying to step on your hand? Do you have any reason to believe he had any intention to hurt you?"

"A. No."

CASE DISCUSSION QUESTIONS

1. Did the court think that a battery had occurred? Why?
2. What role do you think Ms. Knight's deposition played in the court's reasoning?
3. Do you think the result would have been different if Ms. Knight had never watched football or played touch football prior to her accident?

(2) The defenses to assault and battery

The first step in winning a tort claim is for the plaintiff to prove each of the elements of that tort. Then only if the plaintiff is able to do so, the defendant raises any defenses. The defenses that can be raised to an assault or battery claim are consent, self-defense, defense of others, and sometimes defense of property.

Consent to a tortious act can sometimes be implied from the nature of the plaintiff's conduct. When one goes to a barber or hair stylist, there is an implied consent for that person to touch and cut the customer's hair. Some types of consent are implied by law, such as when a doctor administers medical treatment in an emergency. Because the court in *Knight v. Jewett* did not think that Ms. Knight had established a prima facie case for battery, it did not consider whether the defendant had any valid defenses. If the court in *Knight* had thought Mr. Jewett intentionally stepped on Ms. Knight, it next would have discussed the issue of whether she had consented to the battery. How do you think the court would have resolved that issue?

For self-defense and defense of others to be valid, the plaintiff must reasonably believe that a threat exists and then must use only as much force as is necessary to stop the battery. Self-defense, for example, could be used as a valid defense against a battery charge if the plaintiff had threatened the defendant with a knife and the defendant had defended himself with his fists. However, if the plaintiff was unarmed and struck the defendant with his fists, it might not be a valid self-defense for the defendant to stab the plaintiff with a knife.

Perhaps one of the most controversial defenses is that of defense of property. The following case from Iowa illustrates a rejection of its use.

Katko v. Briney
183 N.W.2d 657 (Iowa 1971)

MOORE, C.J.

The primary issue presented here is whether an owner may protect personal property in an unoccupied boarded-up farm house against trespassers and thieves by a spring gun capable of inflicting death or serious injury.

We are not here concerned with a man's right to protect his home and members of his family. Defendants' home was several miles from the scene of the incident to which we refer infra.

Plaintiff's action is for damages resulting from serious injury caused by a shot from a 20-gauge spring shotgun set by defendants in a bedroom of an old farm house which had been uninhabited for several years. Plaintiff and his companion, Marvin McDonough, had broken and entered the house to find and steal old bottles and dated fruit jars which they considered antiques.

At defendants' request plaintiff's action was tried to a jury consisting of residents of the community where defendants' property was located. The jury returned a verdict for plaintiff and against defendants for $20,000 actual and $10,000 punitive damages.

After careful consideration of defendants' motions for judgment notwithstanding the verdict and for new trial, the experienced and capable trial judge overruled them and entered judgment on the verdict. Thus we have this appeal by defendants. . . .

II. Most of the facts are not disputed. In 1957 defendant Bertha L. Briney inherited her parents' farm land in Mahaska and Monroe Counties. Included was an 80-acre tract in southwest Mahaska County where her grandparents and parents had lived. No one occupied the house thereafter. . . .

For about 10 years, 1957 to 1967, there occurred a series of trespassing and housebreaking events with loss of some household items, the breaking of windows and "messing up of the property in general." The latest occurred June 8, 1967, prior to the event on July 16, 1967 herein involved.

Defendants through the years boarded up the windows and doors in an attempt to stop the intrusions. They had posted "no trespass" signs on the land several years before 1967. The nearest one was 35 feet from the house. On June 11, 1967 defendants set "a shotgun trap" in the north bedroom. After Mr. Briney cleaned and oiled his 20-gauge shotgun, the power of which he was well aware, defendants took it to the old house where they secured it to an iron bed with the barrel pointed at the bedroom door. It was rigged with wire from the doorknob to the gun's trigger so it would fire when the door was opened. Briney first pointed the gun so an intruder would be hit in the stomach but at Mrs. Briney's suggestion it was lowered to hit the legs. He admitted he did so "because I was mad and tired of being tormented" but "he did not intend to injure anyone." He gave no explanation of why he used a loaded shell and set it to hit a person already in the house. Tin was nailed over the bedroom window. The spring gun could not be seen from the outside. No warning of its presence was posted.

Plaintiff lived with his wife and worked regularly as a gasoline station attendant in Eddyville, seven miles from the old house. He had observed it for several years while hunting in the area and considered it as being abandoned. He knew it had long been uninhabited. In 1967 the area around the house was covered with high weeds. Prior to July 16, 1967 plaintiff and McDonough had been to the premises and found several old bottles and fruit jars which they took and added to their collection of antiques. On the latter date about 9:30 P.M. they made a second trip to the Briney property. They entered the old house by removing a board from a porch window which was without glass. While McDonough was looking around the kitchen area plaintiff went to another part of the house. As he started to open the north bedroom door the shotgun went off striking him in the right leg above the ankle bone. Much of his leg, including part of the tibia, was blown away. Only by McDonough's assistance was plaintiff able to get out of the house and after crawling some distance was put in his vehicle and rushed to a doctor and then to a hospital. He remained in the hospital 40 days. . . .

III.   Plaintiff testified he knew he had no right to break and enter the house with intent to steal bottles and fruit jars therefrom. He further testified he had entered a plea of guilty to larceny in the nighttime of property of less than $20 value from a private building. . . .

Prosser on Torts, Third Edition, pages 116-118, states:

". . . the law has always placed a higher value upon human safety than upon mere rights in property, it is the accepted rule that there is no privilege to use any force calculated to cause death or serious bodily injury to repel the threat to land or chattels, unless there is also such a threat to the defendant's personal safety as to justify self-defense. . . . spring guns and other man-killing devices are not justifiable against a mere trespasser, or even a petty thief. They are privileged only against those upon whom the landowner, if he were present in person would be free to inflict injury of the same kind."

Restatement of Torts, section 85, page 180, states: . . . A possessor of land cannot do indirectly and by a mechanical device that which, were he present, he could not do immediately and in person. . . . Study and careful consideration of defendants' contentions on appeal reveal no reversible error.

Affirmed.

All Justices concur except LARSON, J., who dissents.

CASE DISCUSSION QUESTIONS

1. Why did the court uphold the jury's verdict in favor of the plaintiff trespasser?

2. The dissent stated: "When such a windfall comes to a criminal as a result of his indulgence in serious criminal conduct, the result is intolerable and indeed shocks the conscience. If we find the law upholds such a result, the criminal would be permitted by operation of law to profit from his own crime." What do you think?

3. Because the defendants did not raise the issue, this court did not deal directly with whether punitive damages were appropriate. What facts would support such a finding; what facts would argue against such a finding? Do you think punitive damages were appropriate in this case? Why?

4. Should a landowner who sets a trap such as in this case also be found criminally liable if an intruder is seriously injured? Why?

5. Do you think the result in this case would have been different if the house had been occupied? Why?

6. At trial Mr. Briney testified that "[p]rior to this time . . . he had locked the doors, posted seven no trespassing signs on the premises, and complained to the sheriffs of two counties on numerous occasions. . . . [A]ll these efforts were futile and the vandalism continued." What else could the defendants have done to protect their property?

b. False Imprisonment

False imprisonment occurs whenever one person, through force or the threat of force, unlawfully detains another person against his or her will. Issues of false imprisonment most frequently arise in situations in which store employees seek to detain suspected shoplifters or employers wish to detain and interview employees they suspect of unlawful activities.

> **False imprisonment**
> Occurs whenever one person, through force or the threat of force, unlawfully detains another person against his or her will.

(1) The elements of false imprisonment

In order to prove false imprisonment, the plaintiff must show the following:

1. an intentional act
2. that caused confinement or restraint
3. through force or the threat of force.

The plaintiff must actually be confined with no means of escape. For example, leaving someone alone in an unlocked office does not constitute false imprisonment.

(2) Defenses to false imprisonment

The most common defense to false imprisonment is that the defendant was justified in restraining the plaintiff. For example, many states have enacted statutes to protect merchants who want to question a suspected shoplifter. Usually, these statutes provide that a shopkeeper may detain a suspected shoplifter only if the shopkeeper can show probable cause to justify the delay and that even then the shopkeeper may detain the suspected shoplifter only for a reasonable time and in a reasonable manner. As you can imagine, because of the way these three statutory requirements are worded, each has given rise to a great deal of litigation.

In the following case notice how each individual fact becomes very important in determining, first, whether the shopkeeper had falsely imprisoned the plaintiff and, second, whether the shopkeeper could prove a valid defense.

Coblyn v. Kennedy's, Inc.
359 Mass. 319, 268 N.E.2d 860 (1971)

SPIEGEL, JJ.

This is an action of tort for false imprisonment. At the close of the evidence the defendants filed a motion for directed verdicts which was denied. The jury returned verdicts for the plaintiff in the sum of $12,500. The case is here on the defendants' exceptions to the denial of their motion and to the refusal of the trial judge to give certain requested instructions to the jury.

We state the pertinent evidence most favorable to the plaintiff. On March 5, 1965, the plaintiff went to Kennedy's, Inc. (Kennedy's), a store in Boston. He was seventy years of age and about five feet four inches in height. He was wearing a woolen shirt, which was "open at the neck," a topcoat and a hat. "[A]round his neck" he wore an ascot which he had "purchased . . . previously at Filenes." He proceeded to the second floor of Kennedy's to purchase a sport coat. He removed his hat, topcoat and ascot, putting the ascot in his pocket. After purchasing a sport coat and leaving it for alterations, he put on his hat and coat and walked downstairs. Just prior to exiting through the outside door of the store, he stopped, took the ascot out of his pocket, put it around his neck, and knotted it. The knot was visible "above the lapels of his shirt." The only stop that the plaintiff made on the first floor was immediately in front of the exit in order to put on his ascot.

Just as the plaintiff stepped out of the door, the defendant Goss, an employee, "loomed up" in front of him with his hand up and said: "Stop. Where did you get that scarf?" The plaintiff responded, "[W]hy?" Goss firmly grasped the plaintiff's arm and said: "[Y]ou better go back and see the manager." Another employee was standing next to him. Eight or ten other people were standing around and were staring at the plaintiff. The plaintiff then said, "Yes, I'll go back in the store" and proceeded to do so. As he and Goss went upstairs to the second floor, the plaintiff paused twice because of chest and back pains. After reaching the second floor, the salesman from whom he had purchased the coat recognized him and asked what the trouble was. The plaintiff then asked: "[W]hy 'these two gentlemen stop me?'" The salesman confirmed that the plaintiff had purchased a sport coat and that the ascot belonged to him.

The salesman became alarmed by the plaintiff's appearance and the store nurse was called. She brought the plaintiff into the nurse's room and gave him a soda mint tablet. As a direct result of the emotional upset caused by the incident, the plaintiff was hospitalized and treated for a "myocardial infarct."

Initially, the defendants contend that as a matter of law the plaintiff was not falsely imprisoned. They argue that no unlawful restraint was imposed by either force or threat upon the plaintiff's freedom of movement. However, "[t]he law is well settled that '[a]ny general restraint is sufficient to constitute an imprisonment . . .' and '[a]ny demonstration of physical power which, to all appearances, can be avoided only by submission, operates as effectually to constitute an imprisonment, if submitted to, as if any amount of force had been exercised.' 'If a man is restrained of his personal liberty by fear of a personal difficulty, that amounts to a false imprisonment' within the legal meaning of such term." *Jacques v. Childs Dining Hall Co.*, 244 Mass. 438, 438-439.

We think it is clear that there was sufficient evidence of unlawful restraint to submit this question to the jury. Just as the plaintiff had stepped out of the door of the store, the defendant Goss stopped him, firmly grasped his arm and told him that he had "better go back and see the manager." There was another employee at his side. The plaintiff was an elderly man and there were other people standing around staring at him. Considering the plaintiff's age and his heart condition, it is hardly to be expected that with one employee in front of him firmly grasping his arm and another at his side the plaintiff could do other than comply with Goss's "request" that he go back and see the manager. . . .

In addition, as this court observed in the *Jacques* case, supra, at p. 441, the "honesty and veracity [of the plaintiff] had been openly . . . challenged. If she had gone out before . . . [exonerating herself], her departure well might have been interpreted by the lookers on as an admission of guilt". . . .

The defendants next contend that the detention of the plaintiff was sanctioned by G.L. c. 231, § 94B, inserted by St. 1958, c. 337. This statute provides as follows: "In an action for false arrest or false imprisonment brought by any person by reason of having been detained for questioning on or in the immediate vicinity of the premises of a merchant, if such person was detained in a reasonable manner and for not more than a reasonable length of time by a person authorized to make arrests or by the merchant or his agent or servant authorized for such purpose and if there were reasonable grounds to believe that the person so detained was committing or attempting to commit larceny of goods for sale on such premises, it shall be a defense to such action. . . ."

The defendants argue in accordance with the conditions imposed in the statute that the plaintiff was detained in a reasonable manner for a reasonable length of time and that Goss had reasonable grounds for believing that the plaintiff was attempting to commit larceny of goods held for sale.

It is conceded that the detention was for a reasonable length of time. We need not decide whether the detention was effected in a reasonable manner for we are of opinion that there were no reasonable grounds for believing that the plaintiff was committing larceny and, therefore, he should not have been detained at all. However, we observe that Goss's failure to identify himself as an employee of Kennedy's and to disclose the reasons for his inquiry and actions, coupled with the physical restraint in a public place imposed upon the plaintiff, an elderly man, who had exhibited no aggressive intention to depart, could be said to constitute an unreasonable method by which to effect detention.

The pivotal question before us as in most cases of this character is whether the evidence shows that there were reasonable grounds for the detention. . . .

The defendants assert that the judge improperly instructed the jury in stating that "grounds are reasonable when there is a basis which would appear to the reasonably prudent, cautious, intelligent person." In their brief, they argue that the "prudent and cautious man rule" is an objective standard and requires a more rigorous and restrictive standard of conduct than is contemplated by G.L. c. 231, § 94B. The defendants' requests for instructions, in effect, state that the proper test is a subjective one, viz., whether the defendant Goss had an honest and strong suspicion that the plaintiff was committing or attempting to commit larceny.

We do not agree. . . . [T]he words "reasonable grounds" and "probable cause" have traditionally been accorded the same meaning. In the case of *Terry v. Ohio*, 392 U.S. 1, involving the question whether a police officer must have probable cause within the Fourth Amendment to "stop-and-frisk" a suspected individual, the Supreme Court of the United States held that the "probable cause" requirement of the Fourth Amendment applies to a "stop-and-frisk" and that a "stop-and-frisk" must "be judged against an objective standard: would the facts available to the officer at the moment . . . 'warrant a man of reasonable caution in the belief' that the action taken was appropriate? . . . Anything less would invite intrusions upon constitutionally guaranteed rights based on nothing more substantial than inarticulate hunches, a result this Court has consistently refused to sanction." Pp. 21–22.

If we adopt the subjective test as suggested by the defendants, the individual's right to liberty and freedom of movement would become subject to the "honest . . . suspicion" of a shopkeeper based on his own "inarticulate hunches" without regard to any discernible facts. In effect, the result would be to afford the merchant even greater authority than that given to a police officer. . . .

Applying the standard of reasonable grounds as measured by the reasonably prudent man test to the evidence in the instant case, we are of opinion that the evidence warranted the conclusion that Goss was not reasonably justified in believing that the plaintiff was engaged in shoplifting. There was no error in denying the motion for directed verdicts and in the refusal to give the requested instructions.

Exceptions overruled.

CASE DISCUSSION QUESTIONS

1. Why did the court think that there was sufficient evidence of unlawful restraint? Do you agree?

2. Did the court think that the detention had taken place in a reasonable manner? Why?

3. Did the court think that finding reasonable grounds to detain someone should be based on an objective or a subjective standard? Why? Do you agree?

Legal Reasoning Exercise

1. Martha Smith went to a K-Mart store at about 7:30 P.M. on September 8 to purchase some diapers and several cans of motor oil. She took her small child along to enable her to purchase the correct size diapers, carrying the child in an infant seat which she had purchased at K-Mart two or three weeks previously. A large K-Mart price tag was still attached to the infant seat.

Martha purchased the diapers and oil and some children's clothes. She was in a hurry to leave because it was then 8:00 P.M., her child's feeding time, and she rushed through the checkout lane. She paid for the diapers, oil, and clothing. Just after leaving the store she heard someone ask her to stop. She turned around and saw a K-Mart security guard, who asked, "Would you please come back into the store?" Martha replied, "What for?" The security guard pulled out a store badge, showed it to her, and said that if she would just come back into the store, he would like to talk to her about it.

When Martha hesitated, the security guard grabbed her by the arm and led her back into the store, stopping just inside the doors. The guard then told Martha that one of the K-Mart employees had informed him that she saw Martha steal the car seat. Martha denied that she had stolen the seat and explained that she had purchased the seat previously. She demanded to see the person who accused her of stealing the seat. The security guard said that it would take a while to find the employee. Martha asked if they could wait in a more private place, but the guard said that they could not.

After approximately twenty minutes, the employee was found. The employee stated that she saw Martha steal the infant seat by taking it off a table and putting her baby in it. Martha pointed out to the security guard that the seat had cat hairs, food crumbs, and milk stains on it. The guard then said, "I'm really sorry; there's been a terrible mistake. You can go." Martha looked at the clock as she left. The time was 8:30 P.M.

Assume Martha has sued K-Mart for false imprisonment. Your firm represents K-Mart, and your boss wants to know if the store has a valid defense. Research revealed the following statute:

ch. 203, § 99

A merchant or merchant's adult employee who has probable cause for believing that a person has stolen store merchandise may detain such person in a reasonable manner for a reasonable length of time.

Using the IRAC method, write an analysis of the issues in this case. Include arguments that will be raised by both Martha's attorney and the store's attorney. (Remember, if there are not two sides, you have not selected an issue.)

DISCUSSION QUESTION

1. Many argue that shoplifting is a major cause of increased costs. Do you think shopkeepers should be given more or less leeway in deciding when to detain suspected shoplifters?

c. Defamation

Defamation can consist of either oral or written remarks that harm a person's reputation. Oral defamation is known as **slander** (remember "s" for spoken), and written defamation is known as **libel** (remember "l" for literary). To be considered defamatory, the material must tend to injure a person's reputation, to hold a person up to ridicule, or to excite adverse, derogatory, or unpleasant feelings or opinions about that person. Furthermore, the statement must present the defamatory information as being factual rather than merely the opinion of the speaker. For example, a movie review or editorial is generally viewed as a statement of opinion rather than fact.

Defamation
The publication of false statements that harm a person's reputation.

Slander
Spoken defamation.

Libel
Written defamation.

(1) The elements of defamation

Whether it is oral or written, defamation consists of the following elements:

1. publication
2. of false statements
3. that cause harm to reputation.

The first element, publication, means that someone other than the plaintiff and the defendant must read or hear the defamatory comments. The offending material cannot harm someone's reputation if it is never seen or heard by a third party.

Second, and perhaps most important, the defamatory material must be false. No matter how damaging the information, a tort of defamation has not been committed if the statement was true. Note, however, that the plaintiff may still be able to recover damages by suing under the theory of invasion of privacy or intentional infliction of emotional distress.

As to the third element, the plaintiff must show that the publication of this false information damaged his or her reputation. This is usually established by showing that the plaintiff lost a job, a contract, or something else of value as a result of people having read or heard the defamatory material. However, historically some remarks are considered to be so bad that they are automatically viewed as damaging and thus constitute **defamation per se**. Examples of such remarks include the following:

Defamation per se
Remarks considered to be so harmful that they are automatically viewed as defamatory.

1. that someone has a loathsome communicable disease,
2. that someone committed business improprieties,
3. that someone has been imprisoned for a serious crime, and
4. that an unmarried woman is unchaste.

When dealing with comments that are defamatory per se, the plaintiff does not need to prove the statements caused him or her harm, as it is presumed they did so.

(2) Defamation of public figures

In order to protect the First Amendment rights of a free press to act as a watchdog and critic of government, the courts have made it more difficult for certain classes of people, public officials and "public figures," to win defamation suits. This rule was first enunciated by the U.S. Supreme Court in *New York Times Co. v. Sullivan,*[2] when the Court stated: "The constitutional guarantees require, we think, a federal rule that prohibits a public official from recovering damages for a defamatory falsehood relating to his official conduct unless he proves that the statement was made with 'actual malice'—that is, with knowledge that it was false or with reckless disregard of whether it was false or not."[3] This rule was extended to "public figures" in a 1974 Supreme Court case.[4]

What this means in practical terms is that when the plaintiff is a public official or public figure, the plaintiff must prove a fourth element, actual malice, in addition to the three elements that everyone else has to also prove—that is, (1) publication (2) of false statements (3) that cause harm to reputation. While it is clear that this fourth requirement comes into play only if the plaintiff is a public official or a public figure, it is less clear whether the defendant must also be a member of the media.

First, to qualify as a public figure, a person must either have achieved widespread fame or notoriety or be someone who became well known through involvement in a public controversy. Second, as noted above, to prove actual **malice,** the plaintiff must show that the defendant either knew the material was false but went ahead and published it anyway or acted with a "reckless disregard" for whether or not it was true. This can involve an examination of the editors as to what they knew and when they knew it in reaching their decision to publish the material. The courts take into consideration such factors as the nature of the news being reported, the historical trustworthiness of the source of the information, and the time constraints publishers are under to meet a deadline.

Malice
Making a defamatory remark either knowing the material was false or acting with a "reckless disregard" for whether or not it was true.

A prominent California case involving television personality Carol Burnett illustrates how these principles have been applied. In *Burnett v. National Enquirer, Inc.,*[5] Burnett sued the National Enquirer for publishing a four-sentence item that read:

> In a Washington restaurant, a boisterous Carol Burnett had a loud argument with another diner, Henry Kissinger. Then she traipsed around the place offering everyone a bite of her dessert. But Carol really raised eyebrows when she accidentally knocked a glass of wine over one diner and started giggling instead of apologizing. The guy wasn't amused and "accidentally" spilled a glass of water over Carol's dress.[6]

As a preliminary matter the court determined that the National Enquirer should be viewed as a magazine rather than a newspaper. In defamation cases, courts show more leniency toward newspapers because their short deadlines

---

[2]376 U.S. 254 (1964).
[3]Id. at 279-280.
[4]Gertz v. Robert Welch, Inc., 418 U.S. 323 (1974).
[5]144 Cal. App. 3d 991 (1983).
[6]Id. at 997.

prevent them from having enough time to fully investigate their stories. The Enquirer's normal lead time, however, was one to three weeks, during which time staff could verify the accuracy of its stories.

Next the court determined that the story was patently false and that the Enquirer knew that to be so: "There was no 'row' with Mr. Kissinger, nor any argument between the two, and what conversation they had was not loud or boisterous. Respondent never 'traipsed around the place offering everyone a bite of her dessert,' nor was she otherwise boisterous, nor did she spill wine on anyone."[7] Further, the court held that the statement was libelous on its face: "a message which reasonably carried the implication respondent's actions were the result of some objectionable state of inebriation."[8]

The jury awarded Ms. Burnett $300,000 in compensatory damages and $1.3 million in punitive damages. The trial court reduced this to $50,000 compensatory damages and $750,000 punitive damages. On appeal the court sustained the compensatory award but remanded the case for a retrial on the issue of punitive damages, stating that the amount of the punitive damages was disproportionate when compared to the compensatory award. The dissent disagreed, stating:

> The fact is that this is a publication read nationally by 16 million people. The potential for harm through a repetition of a libel by such an institution is tremendous. There are others to be protected from the harm. If the risk to an intentional wrongdoer that he will be adequately punished is slight, the defendant may well chance it again. It can in effect "write it off" as an expense or cost of doing business. Thus punitive damages need to be more than "an expense" item or "cost of doing business" which the defendant can calculate and absorb. . . .[9]

(3) Defenses to defamation

Because one of the elements of defamation is that the statement is false, truth is an absolute defense. There are also some circumstances when even the publication of a false statement can be privileged. For example, judges, attorneys, jurors, and other court personnel are protected against being held liable for comments that are made as part of their official duties, even if the statements turn out to be false. In 1979, in *Hutchinson v. Proxmire*,[10] the U.S. Supreme Court held that Wisconsin's Senator William Proxmire could not be sued for derogatory comments he made on the Senate floor when giving out one of his "Golden Fleece Awards." However, he could be sued for making those same remarks at a press conference and in a press release.

DISCUSSION QUESTION

2. In the case against the National Enquirer, Carol Burnett testified that the statements were particularly offensive to her because of her nationally known **work** against alcoholism.

   a. Do you think that should affect the amount of the damage award?

---

[7]Id. at 999.

[8]Id. at 1013.

[9]Id. at 1020 (dissenting opinion).

[10]443 U.S. 111 (1979).

b. During the trial Johnny Carson on his program The Tonight Show denounced the National Enquirer. How do you think the trial judge should have handled that situation?

c. Do you agree with the dissent that a large punitive award was justified in this case? Why?

d. Invasion of Privacy

Invasion of privacy
An intentional tort that covers a variety of situations, including disclosure, intrusion, appropriation, and false light.

The tort of **invasion of privacy** covers a variety of different situations. They include

1. disclosure,
2. intrusion,
3. appropriation, and
4. false light.

Disclosure
The intentional publication of embarrassing private affairs.

Intrusion
The intentional unjustified encroachment into another person's private activities.

Appropriation
An intentional unauthorized exploitive use of another person's personality, name, or picture for the defendant's benefit.

False light
The intentional false portrayal of someone in a way that would be offensive to a reasonable person.

Disclosure and intrusion best fit our common conception of what would be an invasion of privacy. **Disclosure** is the publicizing of embarrassing private affairs, and **intrusion** is the unjustified intrusion in another's private activities. Examples of intrusion include a neighbor eavesdropping and a photographer hounding a movie star by following that person everywhere he or she goes. **Appropriation** is defined as the unauthorized exploitive use of one's personality, name, or picture for the defendant's benefit. For example, Johnny Carson sued a Michigan corporation for renting and selling "Here's Johnny" portable toilets. The corporation acknowledged that "Here's Johnny" was the introductory slogan for The Tonight Show and in fact coupled the phrase with a second one, "The World's Foremost Commodian." The court determined that the defendant unfairly appropriated Carson's identity and used it for the sale of its products.[11] Finally, **false light** involves the use of a picture or some other means to infer a connection between the person and an idea or a statement for which the individual is not responsible.

In cases involving invasion of privacy, truth is not considered to be a valid defense. For example, it is not considered acceptable to publicize that someone is having an affair with his or her neighbor, even if it is true. However, "newsworthiness" is a valid defense. If the material is of legitimate public interest—for example, the mayor having an affair with a member of city council—then its publication is considered to be privileged unless it was done with malice. That is why it is so difficult for movie stars to prove this tort against tabloids and gossip columnists. Finally, as with other intentional torts, consent is a defense.

e. Intentional Infliction of Emotional Distress

Traditionally, plaintiffs could recover for their emotional distress that was caused by another tort, such as battery or false imprisonment. More recently the courts have created a new tort that allows plaintiffs to recover for emotional

---

[11]Carson v. Here's Johnny Portable Toilets, Inc., 698 F.2d 831 (6th Cir. 1983).

distress even absent another type of injury. This tort of intentional infliction of emotional distress is sometimes referred to as the tort of outrage. In order to ensure that such claims are valid, most courts have placed severe restrictions on what the plaintiff must prove, such as requiring that the intentional act that causes the emotional distress be extreme and outrageous and the emotional distress suffered be severe.

Therefore, to prove the intentional infliction of emotional distress, a plaintiff must show

1. an intentional act
2. that is extreme and outrageous
3. and causes
4. severe emotional distress.

As to the fourth requirement some courts add that the emotional distress must be so severe that it results in physical injury.

In the following case a restaurant manager was concerned about stealing occurring in the restaurant. He lined up the waitresses and told them that until he found out who the culprit was, he would fire them in alphabetical order. Plaintiff Debra Agis had the misfortune of having a name at the top of the alphabet. As you read this case, ask yourself whether you think the manager's actions were such that they would give rise to a claim of intentional infliction of emotional distress. This case also raises issues of **loss of consortium**. The loss of consortium is the loss by one spouse of the other spouse's companionship, services, or affection.

Loss of consortium
The loss by one spouse of the other spouse's companionship, services, or affection.

Agis v. Howard Johnson Co.
371 Mass. 140, 355 N.E.2d 315 (1976)

QUIRICO, JJ.

This case raises the issue, expressly reserved in *George v. Jordan Marsh Co.,* 359 Mass. 244, 255 (1971), whether a cause of action exists in this Commonwealth for the intentional or reckless infliction of severe emotional distress without resulting bodily injury. Counts 1 and 2 of this action were brought by the plaintiff Debra Agis against the Howard Johnson Company and Roger Dionne, manager of the restaurant in which she was employed, to recover damages for mental anguish and emotional distress allegedly caused by her summary dismissal from such employment. Counts 3 and 4 were brought by her husband, James Agis, against both defendants for loss of the services, love, affection and companionship of his wife. This case is before us on the plaintiffs' appeal from the dismissal of their complaint.

Briefly, the allegations in the plaintiffs' complaint, which we accept as true for purposes of ruling on this motion, are the following. Debra Agis was employed by the Howard Johnson Company as a waitress in a restaurant known as the Ground Round. On or about May 23, 1975, the defendant Dionne notified all waitresses that a meeting would be held at 3 P.M. that day. At the meeting, he informed the waitresses that "there was some stealing going on," but that the identity of the person or persons responsible was not known, and that, until the person or persons responsible were discovered, he would begin firing all the present waitresses in alphabetical order, starting with the letter "A." Dionne then fired Debra Agis.

The complaint alleges that, as a result of this incident, Mrs. Agis became greatly upset, began to cry, sustained emotional distress, mental anguish, and loss of wages and earnings. It further alleges that the actions of the defendants were reckless, extreme, outrageous and intended to cause emotional distress and anguish. In addition, the complaint states that the defendants knew or should have known that their actions would cause such distress.

The defendants moved to dismiss the complaint pursuant to Mass. R. Civ. P. 12(b)(6) on the ground that, even if true, the plaintiffs' allegations fail to state a claim on which relief can be granted because damages for emotional distress are not compensable absent resulting physical injury. The judge allowed the motion, and the plaintiffs appealed. . . .

The most often cited argument for refusing to extend the cause of action for intentional or reckless infliction of emotional distress to cases where there has been no physical injury is the difficulty of proof and the danger of fraudulent or frivolous claims. There has been a concern that "mental anguish, standing alone, is too subtle and speculative to be measured by any known legal standard," that "mental anguish and its consequences are so intangible and peculiar and vary so much with the individual that they cannot reasonably be anticipated," that a wide door might "be opened not only to fictitious claims but to litigation over trivialities and mere bad manners as well," and that there can be no objective measurement of the extent or the existence of emotional distress. There is a fear that "[i]t is easy to assert a claim of mental anguish and very hard to disprove it."

While we are not unconcerned with these problems, we believe that "the problems presented are not . . . insuperable" and that "administrative difficulties do not justify the denial of relief for serious invasions of mental and emotional tranquility. . . ." "That some claims may be spurious should not compel those who administer justice to shut their eyes to serious wrongs and let them go without being brought to account. It is the function of courts and juries to determine whether claims are valid or false. This responsibility should not be shunned merely because the task may be difficult to perform." . . .

In light of what we have said, we hold that one who, by extreme and outrageous conduct and without privilege, causes severe emotional distress to another is subject to liability for such emotional distress even though no bodily harm may result. However, in order for a plaintiff to prevail in a case for liability under this tort, four elements must be established. It must be shown (1) that the actor intended to inflict emotional distress or that he knew or should have known that emotional distress was the likely result of his conduct, (2) that the conduct was "extreme and outrageous," was "beyond all possible bounds of decency" and was "utterly intolerable in a civilized community," (3) that the actions of the defendant were the cause of the plaintiff's distress, and (4) that the emotional distress sustained by the plaintiff was "severe" and of a nature "that no reasonable man could be expected to endure it." These requirements are "aimed at limiting frivolous suits and avoiding litigation in situations where only bad manners and mere hurt feelings are involved," and we believe they are a "realistic safeguard against false claims. . . ."

Testing the plaintiff Debra Agis's complaint by the rules stated above, we hold that she makes out a cause of action and that her complaint is therefore legally sufficient. . . . While the judge was not in error in dismissing the complaint under the then state of the law, we believe that, in light of what we have said, the judgment must be reversed and the plaintiff Debra Agis must be given an opportunity to prove the allegations which she has made.

2. Counts 3 and 4 of the complaint are brought by James Agis seeking relief for loss of consortium as a result of the mental distress and anguish suffered by his wife Debra. There is no question that an action for loss of consortium by either spouse may be maintained in this Commonwealth where such loss is shown to arise from personal injury to one spouse caused by the negligence of a third person. The question before us is whether an action for loss of consortium may be maintained where the acts complained of are intentional, and where the injuries to the spouse are emotional rather than physical.

[T]he fact that there is no physical injury should not bar the plaintiff's claim. . . . [T]he underlying purpose of such action is to compensate for the loss of the companionship, affection and sexual enjoyment of one's spouse, and it is clear that these can be lost as a result of psychological or emotional injury as well as from actual physical harm.

Accordingly, we hold that, where a person has a cause of action for intentional or reckless infliction of severe emotional distress, his or her spouse also has a cause of action for loss of consortium arising out of that distress. . . .

CASE DISCUSSION QUESTIONS

1. The court stated that "for purposes of ruling on the motion dismissing plaintiff's complaint" it was accepting as true the allegations in the plaintiff's complaint. Why?

2. What is the most common reason given for refusing to allow a claim for intentional infliction of emotional distress when there is no physical injury? What was the court's response?

3. What four elements does the court require for a successful claim for intentional infliction of emotional distress?

4. Procedurally, what had to happen next in this case for the plaintiff to recover?

DISCUSSION QUESTIONS

3. What constitutes "extreme and outrageous" conduct is obviously a troubling issue, as is how debilitating the emotional distress must be to be seen as "severe." Consider the facts of *Harris v. Jones,* 380 A.2d 611 (Md. 1977). The plaintiff sued his employer (General Motors) and one of his supervisors, H. Robert Jones. Jones knew that the plaintiff suffered from a speech impediment that caused him to stutter. Jones also knew that the plaintiff was very sensitive about his disability. "Jones approached Harris over 30 times at work and verbally and physically mimicked his stuttering disability. . . . As a result of Jones' conduct Harris was 'shaken up' and felt 'like going into a hole and hide.'" However, the court concluded that Harris's humiliation was not so intense as to meet the requirement of being severe. Do you agree?

4. The March 1984 issue of Hustler magazine ran a parody of an advertisement for Campari Liqueur that featured various celebrities describing the first time they tasted Campari. Hustler's version presented a supposed interview with the Reverend Jerry Falwell, a nationally prominent Protestant minister, conservative political figure, and head of the now defunct "Moral Majority." The "advertisement" claimed that Falwell's first experience with Campari was part of an incestuous sexual encounter with his mother in an outhouse. Shortly after the issue hit the newsstands, Falwell sued the magazine for libel, invasion of privacy, and intentional infliction of emotional distress. If you were the judge, how would you rule on each of these issues?

2. Harm to a Person's Property

Property can be classified as either real property (land and anything permanently attached to land) or personal property. When someone invades your rights to real property, that is the tort of trespass. An invasion of your rights to personal property can be classified as either trespass to personal property or conversion.

a. Trespass to Land

A trespass occurs whenever

1. someone enters or causes something to enter or remain
2. on the land of another
3. without permission.

Examples of trespass include entering land that is posted with "No Trespassing" signs, standing alongside someone else's property and throwing rocks onto the property, and tying your boat to someone else's dock during a storm. The last situation raises the most common defense to trespass—that is, that the trespass was warranted to save the defendant's property or life.

b. Trespass to Personal Property and Conversion

Trespass to personal property occurs when someone harms or interferes with the owner's exclusive possession of the property but has no intention of keeping the property. For example, if your neighbor intentionally lets your dog loose, hoping it will never return, your neighbor has committed the tort of trespass to personal property. **Conversion** is considered the "big brother" of trespass in that it involves the more serious taking of someone else's property with the intent of permanently depriving the owner. It is the civil side of theft.

c. Defenses to Torts against Property

As mentioned above, private necessity, such as the need to tie up a boat to someone else's dock during a storm, may serve as a defense to trespass. Also, generally there is the right to invade another's land as a public necessity (such as to put out a fire or to catch a fleeing felon). Another defense to trespass to personal property and conversion is rightfully retaining someone's property. For example, a car mechanic may rightfully retain an auto on which he has worked until he is paid for his labor. This is known as an **artisan's lien**.

3. Other Intentional Torts

False arrest, malicious prosecution, and abuse of process are all intentional torts that are designed to provide some protection against misuse of the legal system. **False arrest** occurs when a person is arrested (by either a law officer or a citizen) without probable cause and when not covered by special privilege. **Malicious prosecution** and **abuse of process** both involve malicious and improper use of the courts or other forms of legal proceedings. Note that the plaintiff must prove that the behavior was malicious (that is, that the person proceeded even though the charges were known to be invalid) and not just a mistake.

Finally, there are intentional torts related to business dealings. **Fraud**, or intentional misrepresentation, involves (1) the intent to induce reliance on the misrepresentation, (2) knowledge that the misrepresentation is false or a reckless disregard for the truth, (3) justifiable reliance, and (4) harm. Fraud can form the basis for either a tort or a contract claim. We will discuss it more fully in the next chapter on contracts. The tort of **interference with a contractual relationship** prohibits one from inducing a party to breach a contract or interfering with the performance of a contract. Figure 10-2 summarizes the elements and defenses of the most common intentional torts.

Prima Facie Case	Defenses
Assault 1. an intentional act 2. that creates a reasonable apprehension of 3. an immediate harmful or offensive physical contact	1. consent 2. self-defense 3. defense of others 4. sometimes defense of property
Battery 1. an intentional act 2. that creates a harmful or offensive physical contact	

Prima Facie Case	Defenses
False imprisonment 1. an intentional act 2. that caused confinement or restraint 3. through force or the threat of force	1. consent 2. justification (e.g., shopkeeper's statute)
Defamation 1. publication 2. of false statements 3. that cause harm to reputation	1. truth 2. privilege
Invasion of privacy covers a variety of different situations, including 1. disclosure 2. intrusion 3. appropriation 4. false light	1. consent 2. newsworthiness
Intentional infliction of emotional distress 1. an intentional act 2. that is extreme and outrageous 3. and causes 4. severe emotional distress	1. consent
Trespass to land 1. someone enters or causes something to enter or remain 2. on the land of another 3. without permission	1. consent 2. private necessity 3. public necessity

Prima Facie Case	Defenses
Trespass to personal property 1. interference with the owner's exclusive possession 2. of personal property	1. rightful retention (e.g., under a mechanic's lien) 2. necessity
Conversion 1. taking 2. personal property 3. of another 4. with the intent of permanently depriving the owner	

Figure 10-2 Summary of Intentional Torts

Legal Reasoning Exercise

2. Review the situation of Mrs. Day, presented at the beginning of the chapter. Using the IRAC method, write an analysis of the issues in the case. Include arguments that will be raised by both Mrs. Day's attorney and Mr. Day's attorney. For example, if you represented Mrs. Day, what torts would you argue Mr. Day committed? If you were representing Mr. Day, how would you respond?

B. NEGLIGENCE

The most common tort actions involve **negligence.** Negligence is a failure to act as a reasonably prudent and careful person is expected to act in similar circumstances. It is a careless inflicting of an injury as opposed to an intentional one. Negligence actions can arise from such diverse circumstances as a slip on a wet spot on a supermarket floor to alleged medical malpractice. The four basic elements in a negligence case are duty, breach of duty, causation, and harm.

1. The Elements of Negligence

To be found negligent, a person must have acted unreasonably under the circumstances. More specifically, the courts look to the following four elements to establish negligence:

1. The defendant must owe a duty to the plaintiff to act reasonably, and
2. the defendant must have breached that duty
3. thereby causing
4. the plaintiff harm.

a. Duty

The law imposes a duty to act with "due care." This due care standard is defined in terms of how a "reasonably prudent person" would act in the same situation. If the person has some specialized type of training, such as a medical degree, then that individual is expected to act not just as a reasonable person would act but also as a reasonable person with medical training would act. Furthermore, the greater the inherent danger is in a particular situation, the more cautious the individual is expected to be. The duty is owed by all persons within the society to a degree that is consistent with their ages and physical and mental conditions. Jurisdictions differ, however, as to whom it is owed. Most states take the position that this duty to act with due care is owed to anyone who suffers injuries as a proximate or direct result of the person's actions. Other states say the duty applies only to those persons for whom there was a foreseeable risk.

What legal duty you owe to others also varies depending on your relationship to that other person. The closer and more direct the relationship, the greater the likelihood that a court will find a duty. For example, a doctor clearly has a duty to use due care in treating her patients. However, does the doctor also owe a duty to the patient's family? For instance, if the doctor failed to diagnose a contagious disease and the patient transmitted that disease to his wife, should the wife be able to sue the doctor?

Another example of how the relationship between the parties can determine the degree of duty owed is seen in the varying levels of duty a landowner owes to different types of people on his or her land. Many states, using a standard based solely on the status of the person injured, hold that a higher duty is owed to someone lawfully invited and present than to a trespasser. Further, they may view the duty owed to an adult trespasser as less than that owed to a child trespasser. Other states simply say that landowners owe a duty of care to everyone on their land. However, the level of duty varies with the circumstances, including whether the person harmed was a trespasser. While the result may be the same, the approaches are fundamentally different. A court in the latter type of jurisdiction would not base its analysis solely on the status of the person injured but would take into account everything that contributed to the injury.

One of the circumstances that might influence a finding of negligence is whether the defendant was acting under an emergency situation. For example, in a very colorful opinion, *Cordas v. Peerless Transportation Co.*,[12] New York's highest court was faced with the following situation: A thief was running down a Manhattan street being chased by his victim and a group of concerned citizens. The thief, armed with a pistol, jumped into a parked taxicab and ordered the driver to drive. The driver proceeded about fifteen feet and then

> quickly threw his car out of first speed in which he was proceeding, pulled on the emergency, jammed on his brakes, and, although he [thought] the motor was still running, swung open the door to his left and jumped out of his car. He confesses that the only act that smacked of intelligence was that by which he jammed the brakes in order to throw off balance the hold-up man who was half-standing and half-sitting with his pistol menacingly poised.[13]

Mrs. Cordas and her two children were standing on an adjacent sidewalk and were injured by the driverless taxi. They sued the taxicab company, claiming that the driver acted negligently in jumping to safety and leaving the moving vehicle uncontrolled.

The court stated that "the test of actionable negligence is what reasonably prudent men would have done under the same circumstances."[14] The court then held that when faced with an emergency a person is not required to exercise the same mature judgment that is expected under circumstances where there is an opportunity for deliberation. In this case the driver "—the ordinary man in this case—acted in a split second in a most harrowing experience. . . . The court is loathe to see the plaintiffs go without recovery even though their damages were

---

[12]27 N.Y.S.2d 198 (N.Y. 1941).

[13]Id. at 199-200.

[14]Id. at 200.

slight, but cannot hold the defendant liable upon the facts adduced at the trial."[15] Therefore, plaintiffs were not entitled to recover from the cab driver.[16]

Misfeasance
Acting in an improper or a wrongful way.

Nonfeasance
Failing to act.

Finally, the courts sometimes couch their discussion of duty in terms of **misfeasance** versus **nonfeasance**. Generally, you only owe a duty to refrain from harming someone. If you do actually harm someone, that is misfeasance. Further, there is no duty to prevent harm to those with whom you have no direct contact. Therefore, generally nonfeasance, the absence of action, cannot lead to liability. However, in order to find liability, a court might label an activity as misfeasance even though on the surface it appeared as though the defendant had not directly caused the injury. This was the case in *Weirum v. RKO General Inc.*[17] In order to increase its listening audience, a rock station held a contest wherein a traveling disk jockey gave out clues to his location. The first to arrive on the scene would receive a prize. Two teenagers, in an attempt to beat each other to the prize, drove in excess of eighty miles an hour and forced the plaintiff's car off of the road. The court stated:

> The primary question for our determination is whether defendant owed a duty to decedent arising out of its broadcast of the giveaway contest. The determination of duty is primarily a question of law. It is the court's "expression of the sum total of those considerations of policy which lead the law to say that the particular plaintiff is entitled to protection." (Prosser, Law of Torts (4th ed. 1971) pp. 325-326). Any number of considerations may justify the imposition of duty in particular circumstances, including the guidance of history, our continually refined concepts of morals and justice, the convenience of the rule, and social judgment as to where the loss should fall. While the question whether one owes a duty to another must be decided on a case-by-case basis, every case is governed by the rule of general application that all persons are required to use ordinary care to prevent others from being injured as the result of their conduct. However, foreseeability of the risk is a primary consideration in establishing the element of duty.[18]

The court found that the risk to the plaintiff was foreseeable. While acknowledging that normally, absent a special relationship, no one owes a duty to control the conduct of third parties, the court stated that the rule does not apply in a case such as this one where the radio station's conduct is what created the undue risk of harm.

> Misfeasance exists when the defendant is responsible for making the plaintiff's position worse, i.e., defendant has created a risk. Conversely, nonfeasance is found when the defendant has failed to aid plaintiff through beneficial intervention. As section 315 [of the Restatement of the Law of Torts, Second] illustrates, liability for nonfeasance is largely limited to those circumstances in which some special relationship can be established. If, on the other hand, the act complained of is one of misfeasance, the question of duty is governed by the standards of ordinary care discussed above. Here, there can be little doubt that we review an act of misfeasance to which section 315

---

[15]Id. at 202.
[16]Id.
[17]539 P.2d 36 (Cal. 1975).
[18]Id. at 39.

is inapplicable. Liability is not predicated upon defendant's failure to intervene for the benefit of decedent but rather upon its creation of an unreasonable risk of harm to him.[19]

DISCUSSION QUESTION

5. In the *Weirum* case the defendants argued that finding them liable would lead to situations in which "entrepreneurs will henceforth be burdened with an avalanche of obligations: an athletic department will owe a duty to an ardent sports fan injured while hastening to purchase one of a limited number of tickets; a department store will be liable for injuries incurred in response to a 'while-they-last' sale."[20] How do you think the court responded?

As the *Weirum* court noted, issues of duty usually revolve around whether the plaintiff was someone whom the defendant could foresee would be harmed by his actions. Courts frequently say that duty is a question of law to be determined by the judge, while foreseeability is a question of fact to be determined by the jury.

It is always to the defendant's benefit to end a lawsuit as early as possible to save litigation expenses and to put the matter to rest. On the other hand, it is often to the benefit of the plaintiff to go to trial, especially when the facts may arouse the jury's sympathy. Therefore, in a negligence action the defendant will try to argue whenever possible that the defendant owed no duty to the plaintiff. As duty is a question of law, the judge can resolve the matter on a motion to dismiss. If the judge determines that there was no duty, then the plaintiff loses, and the case is dismissed. However, the plaintiff will try to characterize the issue as a question of foreseeability, thereby necessitating a trial. Then the jury, after hearing all of the evidence and seeing the extent of the plaintiff's injuries, can resolve the issue of foreseeability as a question of fact.

At times, even though the person injured was a "foreseeable plaintiff," for policy reasons the courts will state that no duty is owed to the plaintiff. For example, in New York, until the courts were confronted with the following case, an infant harmed while a fetus had no right to sue for his or her negligently caused injuries. While reading the case, pay particular attention to the reasons the court gives for its decision to expand the range of those to whom a duty is owed to include a viable fetus.

Woods v. Lancet
303 N.Y. 349, 102 N.E.2d 691 (1951)

DESMOND, J.

The complaint served on behalf of this infant plaintiff alleges that, while the infant was in his mother's womb during the ninth month of her pregnancy, he sustained, through the negligence of defendant, such serious injuries that he came into this world permanently maimed and disabled. Defendant moved to dismiss the complaint as not

---

[19]Id. at 41.

[20]Id.

stating a cause of action, thus taking the position that its allegations, though true, gave the infant no right to recover damages in the courts of New York. The Special Term granted the motion and dismissed the suit, citing *Drobner v. Peters* (232 N.Y. 220). In the Appellate Division one Justice voted for reversal with an opinion in which he described the obvious injustice of the rule, noted a decisional trend (in other States and Canada) toward giving relief in such cases, and suggested that since *Drobner v. Peters* (supra) was decided thirty years ago by a divided vote, our court might well re-examine it.

The four Appellate Division Justices who voted to affirm the dismissal below, wrote no opinion except that one of them stated that, were the question an open one and were he not bound by *Drobner v. Peters* (supra), he would hold that "when a pregnant woman is injured through negligence and the child subsequently born suffers deformity or other injury as a result, recovery therefore may be allowed to the child, provided the causal relation between the negligence and the damage to the child be established by competent medical evidence." (278 App. Div. 913.) It will hardly be disputed that justice (not emotionalism or sentimentality) dictates the enforcement of such a cause of action. The trend in decisions of other courts, and the writings of learned commentators, in the period since *Drobner v. Peters* was handed down in 1921, is strongly toward making such a recovery possible. The precise question for us on this appeal is: shall we follow *Drobner v. Peters*, or shall we bring the common law of this State, on this question, into accord with justice? I think, as New York State's court of last resort, we should make the law conform to right.

Drobner v. Peters (supra), like the present case, dealt with the sufficiency of a complaint alleging prenatal injuries, tortiously inflicted on a nine-month foetus, viable at the time and actually born later. There is, therefore, no material distinction between that case and the one we are passing on now. However, *Drobner v. Peters* must be examined against a background of history and of the legal thought of its time and of the thirty years that have passed since it was handed down. . . . The movement toward a more just treatment of such claims seems to have commenced with the able dissent in the *Allaire* case, which urged that a child viable but in utero, if injured by tort, should, when born, be allowed to sue. . . .

In *Drobner v. Peters* (supra), this court, finding no precedent for maintaining the suit, adopted the general theory of *Dietrich v. Northampton* (supra), taking into account, besides the lack of authority to support the suit, the practical difficulties of proof in such cases, and the theoretical lack of separate human existence of an infant in utero. It is not unfair to say that the basic reason for *Drobner v. Peters* was absence of precedent. However, since 1921, numerous and impressive affirmative precedents have been developed. . . . Of law review articles on the precise question there is an ample supply. They justify the statement in Prosser on Torts, at page 190, that: "All writers who have discussed the problem have joined in condemning the existing rule, in maintaining that the unborn child in the path of an automobile is as much a person in the street as the mother, and urging that recovery should be allowed upon proper proof."

What, then, stands in the way of a reversal here? Surely, as an original proposition, we would, today, be hard put to it to find a sound reason for the old rule. Following *Drobner v. Peters* (supra) would call for an affirmance but the chief basis for that holding (lack of precedent) no longer exists. And it is not a very strong reason, anyhow, in a case like this. Of course, rules of law on which men rely in their business dealings should not be changed in the middle of the game, but what has that to do with bringing to justice a tort-feasor who surely has no moral or other right to rely on a decision of the New York Court of Appeals? Negligence law is common law, and the common law has been molded and changed and brought up-to-date in many another case. Our court said, long ago, that it had not only the right, but the duty to re-examine a question where justice demands it. That opinion notes that Chancellor Kent, more than a century ago, had stated that upwards of a thousand cases could then be pointed out in the English and American reports " 'which had been overruled, doubted or limited in their application,' " and that the great Chancellor had declared that decisions which seem contrary to reason " 'ought to be examined without fear, and revised without reluctance, rather than to have the character of our law impaired, and the beauty and harmony of the system destroyed by the perpetuity of error.'" And Justice Sutherland, writing for the Supreme Court in *Funk v. United States* (290 U.S. 371, 382), said that while legislative bodies have the power to change old rules of law, nevertheless, when they fail to act, it is the duty of the court to bring the law into accordance with present day standards of wisdom and justice rather than "with some outworn and antiquated rule of the past." No reason appears why there should not be the same approach when traditional common-law rules of negligence result in injustice.

The sum of the argument against plaintiff here is that there is no New York decision in which such a claim has been enforced. Winfield's answer to that (see U. of Toronto L.J. article, supra, p. 29) will serve: "if that were a valid objection, the common law would now be what it was in the Plantagenet period." And we can borrow from our British friends another mot: "When these ghosts of the past stand in the path of justice clanking their mediaeval chains the proper course for the judge is to pass through them undeterred" (Lord Atkin in *United Australia, Ltd., v. Barclay's Bank, Ltd.*, [1941] A.C. 1, 29). We act in the finest common-law tradition when we adapt and alter decisional law to produce common-sense justice.

The same answer goes to the argument that the change we here propose should come from the Legislature, not the courts. Legislative action there could, of course, be, but we abdicate our own function, in a field peculiarly nonstatutory, when we refuse to reconsider an old and unsatisfactory court-made rule. . . .

Two other reasons for dismissal (besides lack of precedent) are given in *Drobner v. Peters* (supra). The first of those, discussed in many of the other writings on the subject herein cited, has to do with the supposed difficulty of proving or disproving that certain injuries befell the unborn child, or that they produced the defects discovered at birth, or later. Such difficulties there are, of course, and, indeed, it seems to be commonly accepted that only a blow of tremendous force will ordinarily injure a foetus, so carefully does nature insulate it. But such difficulty of proof or finding is not special to this particular kind of lawsuit (and it is beside the point, anyhow, in determining sufficiency of a pleading). Every day in all our trial courts (and before administrative tribunals, particularly the Workmen's Compensation Board), such issues are disposed of, and it is an inadmissible concept that uncertainty of proof can ever destroy a legal right. The questions of causation, reasonable certainty, etc., which will arise in these cases are no different, in kind, from the ones which have arisen in thousands of other negligence cases decided in this State, in the past.

The other objection to recovery here is the purely theoretical one that a foetus in utero has no existence of its own separate from that of its mother, that is, that it is not "a being in esse." We need not deal here with so large a subject. It is to be remembered that we are passing on the sufficiency of a complaint which alleges that this injury occurred during the ninth month of the mother's pregnancy, in other words, to a viable foetus, later born. Therefore, we confine our holding in this case to prepartum injuries to such viable children. Of course such a child, still in the womb is, in one sense, a part of its mother, but no one seems to claim that the mother, in her own name and for herself, could get damages for the injuries to her infant. To hold, as matter of law, that no viable foetus has any separate existence which the law will recognize is for the law to deny a simple and easily demonstrable fact. This child, when injured, was in fact, alive and capable of being delivered and of remaining alive, separate from its mother. We agree with the dissenting Justice below that "To deny the infant relief in this case is not only a harsh result, but its effect is to do reverence to an outmoded, timeworn fiction not founded on fact and within common knowledge untrue and unjustified."

The judgments should be reversed, and the motion denied, with costs in all courts.

LEWIS, J. (dissenting). I agree with the view of a majority of the court that prenatal injury to a child should not go unrequited by the one at fault. If, however, an unborn child is to be endowed with the right to enforce such requital by an action at law, I think that right should not be created by a judicial decision on the facts in a single case. Better, I believe, that the right should be the product of legislative action taken after hearings at which the Legislature can be advised, by the aid of medical science and research, not only as to the stage of gestation at which a foetus is considered viable, but also as to appropriate means—by time limitation for suit and otherwise—for avoiding abuses which might result from the difficulty of tracing causation from prenatal injury to postnatal deformity. . . .

Accordingly, I dissent and vote for affirmance.

CASE DISCUSSION QUESTIONS

1. Reading this case we learned almost nothing about the facts that gave rise to this lawsuit. What procedural reason explains why we do not know very many of the facts?

2. Why did the court decide to overrule *Drobner v. Peters*?

3. What limitations did the court put on its holding? What difficulties can you foresee this creating for future litigants?

4. Do you agree with the court that this issue was a matter for judicial as opposed to legislative change? Why?

Legal Reasoning Exercises

3. Prosenjit Podar killed Tatiana Tarasoff. Two months earlier Prosenjit had told Dr. Lawrence Moore, a psychologist, that he intended to kill Tatiana. Dr. Moore did not warn Tatiana or her parents of Prosenjit's intention. What policy considerations would argue against finding the psychologist liable? If you represented Tatiana's parents, how would you reply to those arguments?

4. The defendant company entered a float in a parade. As the float traveled down the street, employees threw candy to the crowd. Children running to collect the candy injured a spectator. Develop an argument for why the spectator should be allowed to sue the company.

5. A grocery store customer was mugged on a sidewalk adjacent to the shopping center. The mugging occurred immediately after the customer left the store. The sidewalk was owned not by the grocery store but by the shopping center. The grocery store knew of numerous similar muggings on the sidewalk. The store employees used the sidewalk to carry bags to customers' cars, and its lease provided that the store could hold sidewalk sales there. Analyze whether the grocery store should be held liable for the customer's injuries.

b. Breach

In order to determine if someone has breached the duty of due care, the court considers all the circumstances. In evaluating those circumstances, the actions of the defendant are measured by an objective standard. That is, the jury is asked to consider what a reasonable person would have done.

In order to prove how a reasonable professional would have acted, the plaintiff will be required to call an expert witness to testify as to the professional standard of care and how in the expert's opinion the defendant breached that standard. For example, in a case involving alleged medical malpractice by a pediatric oncologist, the plaintiff would call as an expert witness a doctor specializing in that field.

Sometimes the defendant's actions violate a statute. If that statute's purpose is to protect the public, the plaintiff belongs to the group of persons the statute was meant to protect, and violation of the statute was a direct cause of the plaintiff's injury, then some states will hold that violation of the statute is negligence per se. In other states violation of such a statute is only evidence of negligence and can be rebutted. For example, assume there is a state statute prohibiting the sale of firearms to minors. A store owner sells a gun to a minor, and the minor, while playing a game of "chicken," discharges the gun, injuring another minor. If the injured minor sued the store owner, he would argue that the purpose of the statute was public protection, that he belonged to that group the statute was designed to protect, and finally that the seller's violation of the statute directly caused his injury. In those states that hold that violation of such a statute is negligence per se, the store owner would be found liable based on his violation of the statute. In those states where the presumption of negligence can be rebutted, the store owner would try to introduce evidence showing that his act of selling the gun and its accidental discharge were too removed from each other to make it fair to hold him responsible.

Another concept that can sometimes be used by the plaintiff to show negligence is the doctrine of **res ipsa loquitur**—the thing speaks for itself. Res ipsa loquitur applies in those situations where the event ordinarily would not have happened unless someone was negligent, the cause of the injury was under the defendant's exclusive control, and the injury was not due to the plaintiff's actions. For example, elevators usually do not drop, panes of glass usually do not fall out of windows, and planes do not crash absent someone's negligence. In those types of situations the court will assume that the defendant was negligent without the plaintiff having to prove the precise nature of that negligence.

Res ipsa loquitur "The thing speaks for itself"; the doctrine that suggests negligence can be presumed if an event happens that would not ordinarily happen unless someone was negligent.

Because in each case involving breach the court must evaluate the behavior given all the circumstances, the specific facts become very important. In reading the following case pay attention to the particular facts that you think influenced the court's determination that there was no breach of duty. Even though the plaintiff in this case was thirteen, notice how the court uses the archaic term "infant" when referring to him.

Sauer v. Hebrew Institute of Long Island, Inc.
17 A.D.2d 245, 233 N.Y.S.2d 1008 (1962)

BERGAN, J.

The infant plaintiff, a camper at defendant's Summer camp, was injured while playing a game supervised by defendant's personnel. The infant was 13 years old and the game was a "water fight" between groups of campers of similar age, played on a grass-covered area in which opposing groups of boys doused each other with water from cups or water pistols.

In running away from an opponent, the infant plaintiff slipped on the grass and struck his head on a concrete walk at the side of the grass area. After a trial before the court without a jury, an award of $15,000 has been made to infant plaintiff and nominal damages to his father.

In our view of the record, this result is not warranted. The defendant, as the operator of a camp for boys, could not reasonably be made responsible in damages for the consequences of every possible hazard of play activity. It was required, rather, to guard against dangers which ought to have been foreseen in the exercise of reasonable care.

It has not been demonstrated that the water fight game was more hazardous than any ordinary camp activity involving running. It was inevitable in the game that the grass would become wet; and, indeed, in any such game among 13-year-old boys, that there would be tumbles and falls whether it was wet or dry.

To impose liability in this situation is to interdict the game itself, which in turn would so sterilize camping activity for boys as to render it sedentary. It would take a keen sense of the prescient to envisage that in running in the game the infant plaintiff would slip at the very point in the area where there was a concrete walk. Nor is it, indeed, clearly demonstrated that, in view of the infant's plaintiff's bare feet, the wetness of the grass played any effective part in his falling.

The Trial Judge felt that the game itself "[had] every aspect of innocent play"; that the supervision was adequate and there was no "defect in the grounds on which the contest took place." (33 Misc. 2d 785, 786.) He felt, however, that the game should have been played on sand and not on grass. This retrospective view of how the camp should have managed the game, upon which there can be reasonable difference of opinion, is insufficient to impose a liability on defendant, either as an evaluation of the facts of the case, or as a matter of law.

The judgment for plaintiffs should be reversed on the law and the facts and judgment entered for defendant, without costs. . . .

CASE DISCUSSION QUESTIONS

1. Why did the court find that the camp was not liable for the boy's injury? Do you agree with that decision? Why?

2. What facts do you think were most important in helping the court reach its decision?

DISCUSSION QUESTIONS

6. Most states have statutes prohibiting the sale of alcohol to a minor. If a store sold alcohol to a minor and the minor while intoxicated drove an automobile that collided with and killed a cyclist, would the liquor store owner be held liable as to the deceased cyclist?

7. On an icy, snow-covered road the plaintiff lost control of her car, skidded across the center line, and collided with a road grader, driven by the defendant. The defendant did not have the statutorily required class B driver's license. The plaintiff, who was severely injured in the accident, sued the defendant under the theory of negligence per se. How do you think the court ruled and why?

Legal Reasoning Exercise

6. Every year Camp Good Times holds a hike to the top of Mount Snow or to the top of Barton Hill. Of the two hikes the one up Mount Snow is a bit more arduous, but either can be accomplished in under an hour. This past year the campers, who ranged in age from seven to twelve, voted to hike up Mount Snow. The fifty campers and two camp counselors made it to the top of the hill in about half an hour with no problems. On the way back down, however, eight-year-old Timmy tripped over a large moss-covered log lying across the path. As a result of his fall he suffered a broken leg. His parents now want to know whether they can successfully sue the camp for Timmy's injury. Please evaluate their claim based on *Sauer*.

c. Cause

In a tort action the defendant's actions must be the cause of the plaintiff's injuries. Under one commonly used test, referred to as the **"but for" standard,** it is necessary to establish that if the defendant had not acted in that manner, the plaintiff would not have been injured. This is also known as the **actual cause** or **cause in fact.** Sometimes there is more than one "cause" of an injury. When there are concurrent causes, the court asks if any one of them was a substantial factor in causing the injury. Under the "substantial factor" test, liability is imposed if the defendant's action is shown to be a substantial factor in causing the plaintiff's injuries.

Sometimes it is impossible for the plaintiff to know who of several defendants was responsible for the injury. Such was the situation in the classic case of *Summers v. Tice*.[21] The two defendants and the plaintiff had gone hunting. Both defendants shot at the same time, and the plaintiff was injured. The plaintiff was unable to show whose gun had caused the injury. The court held that the burden was on the defendants to show who was liable, and absent such a showing, both were liable. A more modern variant of this theory was adopted by the California Supreme Court in *Sindell v. Abbott Laboratories*.[22] In that case the plaintiff had developed cancer, allegedly because her mother took the product diethylstilbestrol (DES) while pregnant. The plaintiff's major roadblock in proving her case was that approximately 200 manufacturers had produced DES, and she had no way of knowing which specific company had produced the DES her mother had taken. Under a **market share theory,** the court held that each of the manufacturers would be held responsible based on its market share at the time the mother took DES.

The second prong of the requirement that the defendant's actions "cause" the injury is known as **proximate cause.** For a defendant's actions to be considered the proximate cause, a natural and continuous causal sequence must be

Actual cause
Also known as cause in fact, this is measured by the "but for" standard: But for the defendant's actions, the plaintiff would not have been injured.

Market share theory
A legal theory that allows plaintiffs to recover proportionately from a group of manufacturers when the identity of the specific manufacturer responsible for the harm is unknown.

Proximate cause
Once actual cause is found, as a policy matter, the court must also find that the act and the resulting harm were so foreseeably related as to justify a finding of liability.

[21]199 P.2d 1 (Cal. 1948).
[22]607 P.2d 924 (Cal. 1980).

shown between action and harm that is unbroken by any efficient intervening cause. In deciding cases in which determining the proximate cause is a key issue, the courts frequently wrestle with unforeseeable consequences and intervening forces. For example, the courts are sometimes faced with chain-reaction situations in which a person's actions lead to an event that in turn leads to several other events that eventually impact other people. Is everyone along the chain to be held responsible under the theory that but for their actions, no injury would have happened, or is it more just to say that only those actors most immediately involved in the injury should be held responsible?

As you will see, this notion of proximate cause is not really about cause at all but rather represents a policy decision that at some point a defendant will not be held responsible for every consequence of every action. Just as a pebble thrown into a pond sends out ripples of ever-decreasing strength, every action sends out repercussions of ever-decreasing importance. At some point we say that the consequences are too remote from the original action to hold the actor responsible.

Assume Ms. Farmer takes a lantern with her to her barn in order to milk her cow and thoughtlessly places the lantern next to the cow, who kicks it over. The barn catches on fire. The fire spreads to the neighbor's field, which also catches on fire. No major harm is done except that the ensuing group of gawkers, as well as the multiple fire-fighting and police vehicles, blocks traffic for over an hour. As a result, Mr. Smith, who is on his way to an important appointment, misses the appointment and consequently is fired. Should the neighbor be able to sue Ms. Farmer for the damage to his field? Most certainly. Should Mr. Smith be able to sue Ms. Farmer for his lost job? Most likely no. Why? In both cases Ms. Farmer was the "but for" cause of the injury. But most courts would probably say that the foreseeability of the harm to Mr. Smith was too remote to hold Ms. Farmer accountable. They might phrase this either as a lack of duty to Mr. Smith (an unforeseeable plaintiff) or as a lack of proximate cause (an unforeseeable injury). In either case the issue boils down to one of policy; that is, is this the type of injury for which we want to hold Ms. Farmer accountable?

As you read negligence cases, you will notice that the courts often confuse the issues of duty of care and proximate cause. This is because both are based on the concept of foreseeability. In order for a duty to be present, harm to that person must be foreseeable. However, even if the defendant's actions caused the harm, if that particular harm was not foreseeable, the concept of proximate cause says that, for policy reasons, we will no longer hold the defendant liable.

(1) Palsgraf v. Long Island Railroad Co.

The following classic case is probably the most famous tort decision ever written. However, as you will see from reading the case, even the most gifted legal jurists have difficulty differentiating between duty and proximate cause, as both are based on the concept of foreseeability. As you read the case, ask yourself, Was the railroad not liable because it owed no duty to Mrs. Palsgraf or because its employee's actions were not the proximate cause of her harm?

Palsgraf v. Long Island Railroad Co.
248 N.Y. 339, 162 N.E. 99 (1928)

CARDOZO, Ch.J.

Plaintiff was standing on a platform of defendant's railroad after buying a ticket to go to Rockaway Beach. A train stopped at the station, bound for another place. Two men ran forward to catch it. One of the men reached the platform of the car without mishap, though the train was already moving. The other man, carrying a package, jumped aboard the car, but seemed unsteady as if about to fall. A guard on the car, who had held the door open, reached forward to help him in, and another guard on the platform pushed him from behind. In this act, the package was dislodged, and fell upon the rails. It was a package of small size, about fifteen inches long, and was covered by a newspaper. In fact it contained fireworks, but there was nothing in its appearance to give notice of its contents. The fireworks when they fell exploded. The shock of the explosion threw down some scales at the other end of the platform, many feet away. The scales struck the plaintiff, causing injuries for which she sues.

The conduct of the defendant's guard, if a wrong in its relation to the holder of the package, was not a wrong in its relation to the plaintiff, standing far away. Relatively to her it was not negligence at all. Nothing in the situation gave notice that the falling package had in it the potency of peril to persons thus removed. Negligence is not actionable unless it involves the invasion of a legally protected interest, the violation of a right. "Proof of negligence in the air, so to speak, will not do" (Pollock, Torts [11th ed.], p. 455). . . . If no hazard was apparent to the eye of ordinary vigilance, an act innocent and harmless, at least to outward seeming, with reference to her, did not take to itself the quality of a tort because it happened to be a wrong, though apparently not one involving the risk of bodily insecurity, with reference to some one else. "In every instance, before negligence can be predicated of a given act, back of the act must be sought and found a duty to the individual complaining, the observance of which would have averted or avoided the injury" (McSherry, C.J., in *W. Va. Central R. Co. v. State*, 96 Md. 652, 666). The plaintiff sues in her own right for a wrong personal to her, and not as the vicarious beneficiary of a breach of duty to another.

A different conclusion will involve us, and swiftly too, in a maze of contradictions. . . . One who jostles one's neighbor in a crowd does not invade the rights of others standing at the outer fringe when the unintended contact casts a bomb upon the ground. The wrongdoer as to them is the man who carries the bomb, not the one who explodes it without suspicion of the danger. Life will have to be made over, and human nature transformed, before prevision so extravagant can be accepted as the norm of conduct, the customary standard to which behavior must conform.

The argument for the plaintiff is built upon the shifting meanings of such words as "wrong" and "wrongful," and shares their instability. What the plaintiff must show is "a wrong" to herself, i.e., a violation of her own right, and not merely a wrong to some one else, nor conduct "wrongful" because unsocial, but not "a wrong" to any one. . . . The risk reasonably to be perceived defines the duty to be obeyed. . . . Here, by concession, there was nothing in the situation to suggest to the most cautious mind that the parcel wrapped in newspaper would spread wreckage through the station. . . .

The judgment of the Appellate Division and that of the Trial Term should be reversed, and the complaint dismissed, with costs in all courts.

ANDREWS, J. (dissenting). . . .

What is a cause in a legal sense, still more what is a proximate cause, depend in each case upon many considerations, as does the existence of negligence itself. Any philosophical doctrine of causation does not help us. A boy throws a stone into a pond. The ripples spread. The water level rises. The history of that pond is altered to all eternity. It will be altered by other causes also. Yet it will be forever the resultant of all causes combined. Each one will have an influence. How great only omniscience can say. You may speak of a chain, or if you please, a net. An analogy is of little aid. Each cause brings about future events. Without each the future would not be the same. Each is proximate in the sense it is essential. But that is not what we mean by the word. Nor on the other hand do we mean sole cause. There is no such thing. . . .

As we have said, we cannot trace the effect of an act to the end, if end there is. Again, however, we may trace it part of the way. A murder at Serajevo may be the necessary antecedent to an assassination in London twenty years hence. An overturned lantern may burn all Chicago. We may follow the fire from the shed to the last building. We rightly say the fire started by the lantern caused its destruction. A cause, but not the proximate cause. What we do mean by the word "proximate" is, that because of convenience, of public policy, of a rough sense of justice, the law arbitrarily declines to trace a series of events beyond a certain point. This is not logic. It is practical politics. Take our rule as to fires. Sparks from my burning haystack set on fire my house and my neighbor's. I may recover from a negligent railroad. He may not. Yet the wrongful act as

directly harmed the one as the other. We may regret that the line was drawn just where it was, but drawn somewhere it had to be. We said the act of the railroad was not the proximate cause of our neighbor's fire. Cause it surely was. The words we used were simply indicative of our notions of public policy. . . .

The act upon which defendant's liability rests is knocking an apparently harmless package onto the platform. The act was negligent. For its proximate consequences the defendant is liable. If its contents were broken, to the owner; if it fell upon and crushed a passenger's foot, then to him. If it exploded and injured one in the immediate vicinity, to him also. . . . Mrs. Palsgraf was standing some distance away. How far cannot be told from the record—apparently twenty-five or thirty feet. Perhaps less. Except for the explosion, she would not have been injured. . . .

Under these circumstances I cannot say as a matter of law that the plaintiff's injuries were not the proximate result of the negligence. That is all we have before us. The court refused to so charge. No request was made to submit the matter to the jury as a question of fact, even would that have been proper upon the record before us.

The judgment appealed from should be affirmed, with costs.

CASE DISCUSSION QUESTIONS

1. Why did the majority hold that there was no negligence as to Mrs. Palsgraf? Do you agree?

2. The dissent stated: "What we do mean by the word 'proximate' is, that because of convenience, of public policy, of a rough sense of justice, the law arbitrarily declines to trace a series of events beyond a certain point. This is not logic. It is practical politics." Compare that to the quote at the beginning of this chapter.

3. Part of the dissent that we omitted included the following illustration: "A chauffeur negligently collides with another car which is filled with dynamite, although he could not know it. An explosion follows. A, walking on the sidewalk nearby, is killed. B, sitting in a window of a building opposite, is cut by flying glass. C, likewise sitting in a window a block away, is similarly injured. And a further illustration. A nursemaid, ten blocks away, startled by the noise, involuntarily drops a baby from her arms to the walk." Who out of A, B, C, and the baby should recover from the chauffeur? Why?

(2) Intervening cause

Sometimes after the defendant has acted negligently, another factor intervenes that contributes to the plaintiff's injury. If the intervening cause is great enough, the court may find that the defendant's negligence is no longer the proximate cause. In those situations the intervening cause is deemed to be a **superseding cause,** and the defendant's negligence no longer makes him or her liable. If, however, the intervening cause was foreseeable, the court may still find the defendant liable. Perhaps surprisingly, the classic case of a foreseeable intervening cause is malpractice. For example, assume a man is injured through a motorcyclist's negligent driving. If the injured man is taken to the hospital and his injuries are made worse through a doctor's malpractice, the motorcyclist will be responsible for all the injuries, not just those caused by the initial accident. Also, tavern owners are liable for injuries caused by their intoxicated patrons. An interesting variant of that will be discussed in the next section of this chapter when we look at two different approaches to the issue of social host liability. The following case graphically illustrates the problem of deciding where liability should end.

Anglin v. State Department of Transportation
472 So. 2d 784, 10 Fla. Law W. 1622 (Dist. Ct. App. 1985)

ZEHMER, JJ.

In these consolidated personal injury cases, plaintiffs below appeal a final summary judgment, contending the trial court erred in ruling as a matter of law that appellees were insulated from liability by unforeseeable independent intervening causes. We reverse.

On the night of September 3, 1979, Cleopatra Anglin, her husband, and her brother were traveling through drizzling rain in a 1965 Chevrolet pickup truck. Upon crossing a Seaboard Coastline Railroad track on Alternate U.S. 27 in rural Polk County, they unexpectedly hit an accumulation of water that covered both lanes of travel and was approximately six inches deep. The truck motor was doused with water, sputtered for some distance after hitting the pool of water, and then died. The Anglins attempted to start the motor by pushing the truck down the road and then "popping" the clutch once the truck reached a moderate speed. Approximately fifteen minutes after their truck hit the water, during which time they attempted in vain to push-start the truck several times, a car driven by Edward DuBose passed the Anglin truck heading in the opposite direction. A short distance after passing the truck, which was still on the road and, according to some witnesses, still being pushed, Mr. DuBose turned his car around and headed back toward the truck to render assistance. Unfortunately, Mr. DuBose failed to timely see the truck, hit his brakes, slid into the rear of the truck, and pinned Mrs. Anglin between the two vehicles, causing injury resulting in amputation of both legs. The distance between the pool of water and the accident scene was estimated by some witnesses as approximately 200 yards, by others up to three-tenths of a mile.

On February 16, 1981, Mrs. Anglin and her husband filed a complaint against the state Department of Transportation and Seaboard Coastline Railroad Company, alleging negligence in the design and maintenance of the road and railroad tracks by allowing the accumulation of water on the roadway immediately adjacent to the railroad tracks. Defendants filed a motion for summary judgment and, in addition to numerous depositions already taken, plaintiffs filed affidavits in opposition to the motion. A final summary judgment in favor of the defendants was entered on June 9, 1983, upon the trial judge's ruling as a matter of law that the actions of the plaintiffs in attempting to push-start their disabled pickup truck and the actions of Mr. DuBose in negligently losing control of his car and colliding with the plaintiffs' truck were independent, efficient intervening causes of the accident that were unforeseeable by the defendants, thereby breaking the chain of causation between the purported negligence of the defendants and the injury.

As a general rule, a tort feasor is liable for all damages proximately caused by his negligence. The term "proximate cause" (or "legal cause," in the language of the standard jury instructions) consists of two essential elements: (1) causation in fact, and (2) foreseeability. See generally, 38 Fla. Jur. 2d, Negligence, §§ 29–48. Causation in fact is often characterized in terms of a "but for" test, i.e., but for the defendant's negligence, the resulting damage would not have occurred. In the present case, there is no question as to causation in fact because "but for" the defendants' alleged negligence in causing the pooling of water on the highway, there would have been no accidental stopping of plaintiff's truck and resulting injury.

The second element of proximate cause, foreseeability, is, unlike causation in fact, a concept established through considerations of public policy and fairness whereby a defendant whose conduct factually "caused" damages may nevertheless be relieved of liability for those damages. Thus, proximate cause may be found lacking where the type of damage or injury that occurred is not within the scope of danger or risk created by the defendant's negligence and, thus, not a reasonably foreseeable result thereof. . . . It is not necessary, however, that the defendants "be able to foresee the exact nature and extent of the injuries or the precise manner in which the injuries occur"; all that is necessary to liability is that "the tort feasor be able to foresee that some injury will likely result in some manner as a consequence of his negligent acts." . . . In the instant case, it cannot be said as a matter of law that an injury to plaintiff was not within the scope of danger or risk arising out of the alleged negligence. In the field of human experience, one should expect that negligently permitting a pool of water on an open highway would likely pose a substantial hazard to motorists because a vehicle crashing unexpectedly into the water is likely to experience a stalled motor or other difficulty causing the vehicle to stop on the highway, thereby subjecting its occupants to the risk of injury from collision by other cars.

Proximate cause may be found lacking, however, where an unforeseeable force or action occurring independently of the original negligence causes the injury or damage. This force or action is commonly referred to as an "independent, efficient intervening cause." For the original negligent actor to be relieved of liability under this doctrine, however, the intervening cause must be "efficient," i.e., truly independent of and not "set in motion" by the original negligence. The trial court's ruling that the conduct of the plaintiffs in pushing their truck down the road was an independent, efficient intervening cause of the accident was error because the existence of the pool of water set into motion the plaintiffs' subsequent actions in attempting to restart the motor that was stalled by driving through the water. These actions, having been "set in motion" by defendants' negligence, did not constitute an independent, efficient intervening cause. Whether the plaintiffs' conduct was negligent and caused the injury should be submitted to the jury under appropriate instructions on comparative negligence.

The trial court correctly characterized Mr. DuBose's negligent operation of his car as an independent intervening cause. The negligent pooling of water did not cause Mr. DuBose to negligently operate his vehicle into collision with the plaintiffs.[2] The trial court erred, however, in ruling as a matter of law that such intervening cause warranted entry of summary judgment for defendants. If an intervening cause is reasonably foreseeable, the negligent defendants may be held liable. Whether an intervening cause is foreseeable is ordinarily for the trier of fact to decide. Only if reasonable persons could not differ as to the total absence of evidence to support any inference that the intervening cause was foreseeable may the court determine the issue as a matter of law. In the circumstances of this case (the night was dark, it was raining, and the collision occurred in a rural area where traffic customarily moves rapidly), had DuBose come on the scene and collided with plaintiffs' stalled truck immediately after plaintiffs hit the pooled water, the question of foreseeability of that occurrence would most assuredly present a jury issue. The fact that plaintiffs attempted to push-start their stalled truck for approximately fifteen minutes and that Mr. DuBose collided with it while attempting to stop and provide assistance does not change this jury issue to a question of law. The plaintiffs' exposure to danger was created by defendants' negligence, and the fact that a collision might occur while plaintiffs were extricating themselves from such danger up to fifteen minutes later presents a jury issue on foreseeability. That is so because the defendants need not have notice of the particular manner in which an injury would occur; it is enough that the possibility of some accidental injury was foreseeable to the ordinarily prudent person.

Reversed and Remanded.

BOOTH, J., Dissenting

We should affirm the summary judgment entered below based on lack of proximate cause. The chain of events here between alleged negligent act and injury is too attenuated and is broken, in fact, by the independent, intervening actions of others.

For the purpose of this appeal, we assume that defendants were negligent in maintaining a depression on a rural roadway, a depression which, in the aftermath of Hurricane David, was filled with six inches of water. It would be foreseeable that a driver who unexpectedly traversed such a depression in the road could lose control of his vehicle, causing an accidental injury to himself or others. Stalling and the immediate consequences thereof are also not unforeseeable. Other results of the puddle could be termed as "foreseeable" in a philosophical, but not a legal, sense. For example, the disabled vehicle could have been struck by lightning, or the occupants

could have been robbed or become ill but unable to seek medical care. In each instance, it could be said that, but for the stalling of their car caused by the defendant these subsequent events would not have occurred. Although there would be cause and effect relationship, such consequences would generally not be within the scope of the risk created by the negligent party who caused the vehicle to become immobile. The law does not impose liability because of the concept of "proximate cause," as stated in Prosser and Keeton:

> In a philosophical sense, the consequences of an act go forward to eternity, and the causes of an event go back to the dawn of human events, and beyond. But any attempt to impose responsibility upon such a basis would result in infinite liability for all wrongful acts, and would "set society on edge and fill the courts with endless litigation." As a practical matter, legal responsibility must be limited to those causes which are so closely connected with the result and of such significance that the law is justified in imposing liability. Some boundary must be set to liability for the consequences of any act, upon the basis of some social idea of justice or policy.

Therefore, I would agree with the majority that there could be a jury question as to causation in fact. But, as to proximate cause, in this case at least, the principle is one of law. . . .

The issue, then, is the scope of the legal duty to protect the plaintiff against intervening causes which are possible but not probable. . . . Plaintiff's injury occurred more than a quarter of an hour after, and three-tenths of a mile down the road from, the puddle. The accident occurred after, and as the result of, negligence of others, each acting independently of defendants.

The law does not impose unlimited liability for all consequences that may result from a puddle of water on the road. . . .

---

[2]The result would be otherwise if, for example, Mr. DuBose had driven through the pool of water and failed to stop because his brakes became wet and ineffective.

CASE DISCUSSION QUESTIONS

1. Do you agree with the majority or the dissent? Why?

2. Two years later, in 1987, this decision was reversed by the Supreme Court of Florida in *Department of Transportation v. Anglin,* 502 So. 2d 896, 900 (Fla. 1987) (as they so quaintly put it in Florida, "[W]e quash the decision below and remand for proceedings consistent with this opinion"). On what basis do you think the court reached its decision?

(3) Duty of care to third parties

As we have seen, sometimes the court will hold a person responsible for the actions of someone else. For example, traditionally a bar owner can be held responsible if an intoxicated patron negligently injures a third party. Liability is based on what are known as **dramshop laws.** In a sense the bar owner is held responsible for the patron's negligence.

A related and emerging area of the law is the degree of responsibility a social host has for the actions of an intoxicated guest. In some states the courts have refused to find liability, stating that such a change in the law is better left to the legislature. For example, in *Charles v. Seigfried,*[23] Alan Seigfried held a party at which he provided drinks for everyone, including sixteen-year-old Lynn Sue. Alan knew of Lynn Sue's "advanced state of drunkenness," knew that she had driven her own car to the party, and allowed her to leave the party while still extremely intoxicated. While driving, Lynn Sue died in a fatal collision. In refusing to find the host liable for Lynn Sue's death, the court noted that "the drinking of the intoxicant, not the furnishing it, is the proximate cause of the intoxication and the resulting injury. As a matter of public policy, the furnishing of alcoholic beverages is considered as too remote to serve as the proximate cause of the injury."[24] The court also based its decision on the belief that such a change in the law should come from the legislature.[25]

Other courts have disagreed. For example, the Massachusetts Supreme Judicial Court thought it was appropriate for the court, and not the legislature, to tackle the problem of social host liability. In *McGuiggan v. New England Telephone & Telegraph Co.*[26] the court concluded that "in certain circumstances liability properly could be imposed on such a social host."[27] Those circumstances arise when the social host knew or should have known the guest was drunk, knowingly gave the guest an alcoholic drink anyway, and knew or should have known that the guest would operate a motor vehicle.[28] The court noted that every case

> in which social host liability was acknowledged as a possibility or as a fact has been decided in the past decade. This trend toward imposing liability is no doubt a response to the greater concern of society in recent years regarding the problems of drunken driving. It is understandable that the law of torts, which in many aspects measures one's duty by what is reasonable conduct in the circumstances, should begin to respond to society's increasing concern.[29]

---

[23] 651 N.E.2d 154 (Ill. 1995).

[24] Id. at 157.

[25] Id. at 160.

[26] 496 N.E.2d 141 (Mass. 1986).

[27] Id. at 141.

[28] Id. at 146.

[29] Id.

Legal Reasoning Exercises

7. Two crime victims were killed, having been shot. The families wanted to sue the handgun manufacturer under the theory that manufacturers of handguns negligently marketed them in such a way as to create an underground market, making it easy to obtain the guns. However, the plaintiffs were not able to identify which specific manufacturer made the handguns used in the shootings. Should they be allowed to pursue their lawsuit and, if so, against whom?

8. An alarm company delayed calling the fire department. By the time the firefighters arrived, the fire had advanced to such a stage that one of the firefighters was killed. The firefighter's widow sued the alarm company, alleging its negligent delay in calling in the fire resulted in her husband's death. How do you think the court decided? Why?

9. Assume you are a legislator and want to draft a statute dealing with social host liability. How would you fashion such a rule? For example, would you limit liability to those cases

where minors are involved?
where the host knows the guest is intoxicated?
where the host actually serves the alcohol?

How would you avoid the concern that finding liability in some cases would potentially lead to unlimited liability for social hosts?

10. Do you think a social host should be liable for accidents caused by drivers who obtained alcohol from the social host? Why? For example, consider the following facts. Margaret Davis gave her daughter, a high school student, permission to hold a party. Davis did not keep alcoholic beverages in her home, and there were none on the night of the party. Before the party began, Davis left. During the unchaperoned party a seventeen-year-old guest obtained beer brought to the party by another guest. While driving home intoxicated, the guest lost control of his car and injured Ruth Langemann. Should Langemann be allowed to sue Davis for her injuries?

d. Harm

As we have seen, the purpose of negligence law is to compensate the plaintiff for any harm suffered. Until recently, however, that harm could include emotional distress only if the plaintiff also suffered physical harm and only if the plaintiff was in the "zone of danger" created by the defendant's actions. Therefore, a parent standing at her kitchen window, seeing her child negligently harmed by a speeding motorist, could not recover for her emotional distress. Then in a landmark decision, *Dillon v. Legg*,[30] the California Supreme

---

[30] 441 P.2d 912 (Cal. 1968).

Court held that a mother could recover for her emotional distress caused by seeing her daughter negligently injured. This was the result even though the mother was not "in the zone of danger," as she never feared for her own safety. Since *Dillon* many state courts have followed the lead of the California courts by adopting the tort of negligent infliction of emotional distress. Others have expanded on the *Dillon* holding, both as to how contemporaneous the injury and the plaintiff's emotional distress must be and as to who beyond parents and children is covered. For example, in *Leong v. Takasaki*[31] a ten-year-old boy was allowed to recover for nervous shock and psychic injuries after he witnessed his step-grandmother's death, when she was struck by the defendant's vehicle. In 1979 the New Hampshire Supreme Court held that the trial court erred in dismissing a case where the father did not hear the accident that harmed his daughter but was near enough to immediately become aware of the accident and go to her aid.[32]

DISCUSSION QUESTION

8. A woman sees her live-in boyfriend run over by a car and killed. Should she be allowed to sue for emotional distress? Why?

2. Defenses to Negligence

In representing the defendant in a negligence case the attorney usually attempts to rebut the plaintiff's evidence on as many of the above four elements as possible. In other words, the defense tries to show that no duty was owed to the plaintiff, that no breach occurred, and that the defendant's action was not the cause of the plaintiff's injuries. Another approach to defending such cases involves raising an affirmative defense, in which it is admitted that negligence was established, but it is argued that the defendant should not be held liable because of actions taken by the plaintiff. Traditionally, the two major affirmative defenses were contributory negligence and assumption of the risk. Today most states have adopted a form of comparative negligence.

a. Contributory Negligence

Contributory negligence
Negligence by the plaintiff that contributed to his or her injury. Normally, it is a complete bar to the plaintiff's recovery.

The doctrine of **contributory negligence** asserts that the plaintiff contributed to his or her own injuries or otherwise failed to protect himself or herself from risks that were foreseeable. In other words, it was the plaintiff's breach of a duty to protect himself or herself that was the proximate cause of the injuries. The defendant therefore is relieved of any liability connected with the defendant's negligence, no matter how great the defendant's negligence and how slight the plaintiff's contributory negligence.

Last clear chance
The doctrine that states that despite the plaintiff's contributory negligence, the defendant should still be liable if the defendant was the last one in a position to avoid the accident.

One way that a plaintiff can sometimes avoid the defense of contributory negligence is to argue that the defendant had the **last clear chance** to avoid the accident. Applied mainly in automobile accident cases this doctrine states that the negligence of the plaintiff does not preclude a recovery for the negligence of the defendant where it appears that the defendant, by exercising

---

[31]520 P.2d 758 (Haw. 1974).
[32]*Corso v. Merrill*, 406 A.2d 300 (N.H. 1979).

reasonable care and prudence, might still have been able to avoid the accident or at least reduce some of the plaintiff's injuries. For example, assume the plaintiff driver is hit by the defendant driver's car. The defendant was speeding at the time and therefore was negligent. However, the plaintiff was contributorily negligent in that she ran a stop sign. In a state that follows contributory negligence, the plaintiff will be barred from recovery. However, if she can show that the defendant had the last clear chance to avoid the accident, perhaps by veering off the road or shifting lanes, then she may be able to shift responsibility back to the defendant.

One area that has given the courts a great deal of difficulty is whether a plaintiff's failure to wear a seat belt should be considered a defense in a negligence action. Some courts have held that the failure to wear a seat belt, especially when there is a statutory duty to do so, shows a lack of ordinary care and hence is contributory negligence. Others have pointed out that as the failure to wear a seat belt did not cause the accident, such a failure cannot be seen as contributory negligence. However, if the failure to wear a seat belt caused an increase in the injuries, then that could be factored into the question of damages, analogously to the contract concept of mitigation of damages. Finally, a third approach is to ignore the presence or absence of a seat belt. These courts agree with the second approach—that failure to wear a seat belt is not contributory negligence, as it had no part in causing the accident—but disagree that it should be a factor in reducing the damage award. These courts argue that the failure to wear a seat belt is not analogous to the duty to mitigate damages. The duty to mitigate arises only after and not before an injury occurs.

b. Assumption of the Risk

Another affirmative defense involves the concept of **assumption of the risk**. According to this doctrine a plaintiff may not recover for an injury received as a result of voluntarily subjecting himself or herself to a known danger. Successful use of this defense requires proof that the plaintiff knew about the dangerous nature of the situation before voluntarily exposing himself or herself to that danger. It is argued, for example, that when people choose to attend a baseball game, they assume the risk of being hit by a foul ball. Take another example: If you know that a parking lot is covered with ice and yet you proceed to walk across it, the court will probably say that you assumed the risk of any injury from falling on the ice.

> **Assumption of the risk**
> Voluntarily and knowingly subjecting oneself to danger.

Notice that assumption of the risk involves a subjective standard. The plaintiff must voluntarily and knowingly assume the danger; that is, he or she must actually understand the risk. This can be contrasted with contributory negligence, which is measured not by what the plaintiff was thinking but by what a reasonable person would have done.

Under the traditional view, assumption of the risk, like contributory negligence, was a complete bar to recovery. Today many states have eliminated assumption of the risk as a separate defense, having subsumed it under the defense of comparative negligence. This eliminates many of the proof problems (i.e., having to prove what the plaintiff was actually thinking) and the problems of categorizing specific behavior as either negligence or assumption of the risk. For example, if you get into a car being driven by someone you know is intoxicated, is that an unreasonable act on your part (contributory negligence) or assumption of the risk (knowingly subjecting yourself to a dangerous situation)? In those states that have subsumed assumption of the risk under comparative negligence, the plaintiff's recovery can be reduced either if it can be shown that a reasonable person would have acted differently or if the plaintiff actually knew and voluntarily assumed the risk.

Exculpatory clause
A provision that purports to waive liability.

An example of an express assumption of the risk is the signing of a waiver of liability. Such waivers are frequently called **exculpatory clauses** because their purpose is to relieve tortfeasors of liability. In certain circumstances the courts have upheld such waivers, particularly when the parties are of fairly equal bargaining power and the event involves inherent danger, such as skydiving or mountain climbing. Increasingly, however, courts are refusing to enforce such waivers. Sometimes the refusal is based on the public policy argument that the parties were of very unequal bargaining power. Other times the courts have invalidated such waivers by requiring specific language or by finding an ambiguity and construing the language against the drafter. In addition, the courts usually disallow exculpatory clauses in cases of gross negligence.

An example of the recent trend disfavoring releases is the Virginia Supreme Court case of *Heitt v. Lake Barcroft Community Assn.*[33] The plaintiff was injured while participating in an athletic event sponsored by a homeowners' association. During the swimming portion of the event he dove into the water, struck his head, and sustained severe injuries, leaving him a quadriplegic. Prior to entering the event, he had signed an entry form that provided in part:

> "In consideration of this entry being accepted to participate in the Lake Barcroft Teflon Man Triathlon I hereby . . . waive, release and forever discharge any and all rights and claims for damages . . . for any and all injuries suffered by me in said event."[34]

The Virginia Supreme Court held that "an agreement entered into prior to injury, releasing a tortfeasor from liability for negligence resulting in personal injury, is void because it violates public policy."[35] The court distinguished prior decisions upholding waivers as having been limited to situations involving only property damage.

Legal Reasoning Exercises

11. Mr. Alack joined a local health club. He signed a two-page, single-spaced contract that included the following language:

> Member assumes full responsibility for any injuries, damages or losses and does hereby fully and forever release and discharge [the health club] from any and all claims, demands, damages, rights of action, or causes of action, present or future . . . resulting from or arising out of the Member's . . . use or intended use of said gymnasium or the facilities and equipment thereof.

---

[33]418 S.E.2d 894 (Va. 1992).

[34]Id. at 895.

[35]Id.

One day while he was exercising, the handle of a rowing machine disengaged from the weight cable and smashed into Mr. Alack's mouth. It was discovered that the machine's handle was not connected with the necessary clevis pin and that the health club did not require periodic inspections of its equipment. If you were representing Mr. Alack, how would you argue that the release would not bar him from suing the health club for its negligent failure to maintain the rowing machine?

12. Before taking part in a horseback riding tour at the Loon Mountain Equestrian Center, Ms. Wright signed the following release:

> I understand and am aware that horseback riding is a HAZARDOUS ACTIVITY. . . . I therefore release Loon Mountain Recreation Corporation . . . FROM ANY AND ALL LIABILITY FOR DAMAGES AND PERSONAL INJURY TO MYSELF . . . RESULTING FROM THE NEGLIGENCE OF LOON MOUNTAIN RECREATION CORPORATION TO INCLUDE NEGLIGENCE IN SELECTION, ADJUSTMENT OR ANY MAINTENANCE OF ANY HORSE.

While on the tour, the guide's horse kicked Ms. Wright in the leg. Ms. Wright sued for negligence, arguing that the tour guide had failed to control the horse after it had given signs it was about to "act out." If you were representing Ms. Wright, how would you argue that the release should not bar her from suing the tour company?

c. Comparative Negligence

Both contributory negligence and assumption of the risk prevent a plaintiff from being compensated for very serious injuries, even when the injuries resulted from rather minor breaches when compared to the extreme negligence of the defendant. In response to the perceived unfairness of this situation, all but a handful of states, through statutes and court decisions, have moved to adopt **comparative negligence.** Under comparative negligence, negligence is measured in terms of percentages, and damages are distributed proportionately. There are three alternative theories of comparative negligence:

Comparative negligence A method for measuring the relative negligence of the plaintiff and the defendant, with a commensurate sharing of the compensation for the injuries.

1. A plaintiff can recover when the plaintiff's negligence is slight but may not recover when the plaintiff's negligence is gross.
2. Under a "pure" comparative negligence statute a plaintiff can recover actual damages less a percentage, calculated as the amount of negligence attributable to the plaintiff.
3. Under modified comparative negligence a plaintiff's recovery is reduced by the percentage of the plaintiff's own negligence if the defendant's negligence is greater than that of the plaintiff. However, the plaintiff is barred from recovering anything if the plaintiff's negligence is greater than the defendant's.

d. Immunities

For policy reasons certain defendants, even though negligent, are immune from suit. Traditionally, immunity meant a complete bar to recovery. Recently, however, the courts have been reexamining many immunities and in some instances limiting their effect or even eliminating them entirely. For example, in Chapter 7 you read the case of *Lewis v. Lewis,* in which the Massachusetts Supreme Judicial Court removed the bar of spousal immunity. Similarly, many states have eliminated parental immunity, thereby allowing children to sue their parents in tort actions. The doctrine of charitable immunity has also been abolished or limited in most states.

The doctrine of **sovereign immunity** prohibits suits against the government without the government's consent. It can be traced back to the concept of the divine right of kings and the idea that the king could do no wrong. In modern times federal and state governments have passed legislation that modifies this concept. For example, at the federal level Congress has enacted the Federal Tort Claims Act (FTCA).[36] Under that statute someone can sue the government for harm caused by a government employee's negligence but not for an intentional tort or for something that resulted from a discretionary function. These limitations are a cause for much litigation, as it is often difficult to determine whether a particular action is the result of negligence or an intentional act and whether the action falls within a "discretionary function." Similarly, on the state and local level, governmental acts are often protected from suit if the public employee's action involved basic policy choices.

In circumstances where one is prohibited from suing the government for the employee's actions, he or she may sometimes be able to sue the government official directly. Limitations apply here as well. For example, judicial and legislative officials have an absolute privilege against being held liable for any actions performed as part of their official duties. The reasoning behind this absolute bar is that such officials must be able to perform their daily work without constant fear of being sued. Other administrative personnel receive only a qualified immunity. In order to recover damages under the terms of this qualified immunity, the plaintiff must prove that the defendant acted in bad faith.

In the following case the police stopped an intoxicated driver. An eyewitness stated that the driver "Fuller was swaying, unsteady on his feet, holding his hands up to his head, moving back and forth and holding onto the top of the door to steady himself." The police officer talked to Fuller for about one minute, did not conduct a field sobriety test, and did not detain him. Ten minutes later, driving at approximately seventy-five miles per hour, Fuller's car collided head-on with a car being driven by Mark Irwin. The collision killed Fuller, Mark Irwin, and a passenger in Irwin's car and seriously injured Debbie Irwin and her son. When Mrs. Irwin brought suit against the town, the court had to determine whether the town should be held liable for the police officer's actions. Massachusetts has a tort claims act that is similar to the federal statute in that it prohibits lawsuits based on a "discretionary function."

---

[36]28 U.S.C. § 1346(B) (1994).

Irwin v. Town of Ware
392 Mass. 745, 467 N.E.2d 1292 (1984)

Judges: HENNESSEY, C.J., WILKINS, LIACOS, ABRAMS, NOLAN, LYNCH, & O'CONNOR, JJ. NOLAN, J., dissenting, with whom LYNCH and O'CONNOR, JJ., join.

HENNESSEY, C.J.

The plaintiffs commenced this action against the defendant town of Ware (town). They charge that police officers of the town negligently failed to take into protective custody a motor vehicle operator who was under the influence of intoxicating liquor and who subsequently caused an accident resulting in harm to the plaintiffs. The jury returned special verdicts for the plaintiffs in the amount of $873,697. . . .

2. Applicability of G.L. c. 258, § 2.

Whether the town is liable to the plaintiffs for the negligence of its police officers depends initially upon the scope of G.L. c. 258, the so-called Massachusetts Tort Claims Act (Act). As to scope, the Act provides in relevant part that "[p]ublic employers shall be liable for injury or loss of property or personal injury or death caused by the negligent or wrongful act or omission of any public employee while acting within the scope of his office or employment, in the same manner and to the same extent as a private individual under like circumstances." G.L. c. 258, § 2, as appearing in St. 1978, c. 512, § 15. The Act exempts from such liability, however, "any claim based upon the exercise or performance or the failure to exercise or perform a discretionary function or duty on the part of a public employer or public employee, acting within the scope of his office or employment, whether or not the discretion involved is abused." G.L. c. 258, § 10(b). As a threshold matter, therefore, we must determine whether the challenged actions of the police officers were outside the Act as "discretionary functions" within the meaning of G.L. c. 258, § 10(b).

The town contends that the statutes setting forth an officer's authority with respect to intoxicated motor vehicle operators "indicate that the arrest of Fuller, assuming, arguendo, that he was

intoxicated, was discretionary and not mandatory." Whether an act is itself discretionary, of course, does not turn on whether that act was negligently or nonnegligently performed. Therefore, we need not consider how the act was performed in this case to determine whether it is discretionary. Rather, we must address only a more general question: Is the decision of a police officer to remove from the roadways a driver who he knows or has reason to know is intoxicated a discretionary act within the meaning of G.L. c. 258, § 10(b). We conclude it is not.

. . . In *Whitney v. Worcester,* 373 Mass. 208, 219 (1977), we noted that immunity for discretionary functions did not extend to all acts requiring judgment because "the performance of all functions involves the exercise of discretion and judgment to some degree." We described discretionary acts as those "characterized by the high degree of discretion and judgment involved in weighing alternatives and making choices with respect to public policy and planning." In contrast, we explained that not counted among such acts are those which involve "the carrying out of previously established policies or plans." Id. at 218.

No reasonable basis exists for arguing that a police officer is making a policy or planning judgment in deciding whether to remove from the roadways a driver who he knows is intoxicated. Rather, the policy and planning decision to remove such drivers has already been made by the Legislature. ["Any officer authorized to make arrests . . . may arrest without warrant any person . . . who the officer has probable cause to believe has operated or is operating a motor vehicle while under the influence of intoxicating liquor," G.L. c. 90, § 21.] This is not to say every harm resulting from the conscious failure of a police officer to remove an intoxicated driver from the roadway will give rise to liability for the public employer. There may be situations in which an officer's failure to remove an intoxicated driver from the roadway will not lead to such liability. Where liability does not result, however, it will be because some element of the tort alleged will not have been established. It will not be because the act of the officer is discretionary within the meaning of G.L. c. 258, § 10(b). . . .

7. Conclusion.

In sum, we conclude that, under G.L. c. 258, a town or city may be held liable in damages for the negligent failure of its police officers to remove from the highway a motor vehicle operator who is under the influence of intoxicating liquor and who subsequently causes injuries or death to other travellers. . . . [The case was remanded for a new trial because of erroneously admitted evidence regarding Fuller's blood alcohol content.]

CASE DISCUSSION QUESTIONS

1. Why didn't the court think the police officer's actions fell under the "discretionary functions" exception?

2. This case established that the defense of sovereign immunity was not available in these circumstances. However, to recover, the plaintiff still had to establish that the police officer was negligent. What elements of the negligence claim do you think might give the plaintiff problems?

3. Many charitable and sovereign immunity statutes cap the allowable recovery. In the *Irwin* case the statute provided that the public employer would not be liable "for any amount in excess of one hundred thousand dollars." There were four plaintiffs in this case. How do you think the parties argued this language should be interpreted?

See Figure 10-3 for a summary of the prima facie case and defenses in a negligence cause of action.

C. STRICT LIABILITY

Strict liability
Liability without having to prove fault.

Both negligence and intentional torts impose liability for improper behavior. In the former the injury is caused by carelessness, and in the latter it is intentional. In both cases the tortfeasor acts in an unreasonable manner and violates an established standard of care. When the concept of **strict liability** is applied, however, a person is held responsible for injuries that resulted from actions that were not necessarily unreasonable and that did not violate a standard of due care. In other words, it imposes liability even though the defendant is not at fault. Rather the courts impose liability for the policy reason that, as between the defendant and the injured plaintiff, the defendant is in a better position to absorb the costs of the injury. The courts have applied the doctrine of strict liability in two situations: those involving ultrahazardous activities and products liability.

When persons engage in activities that are inherently dangerous, they should be responsible for any injuries that result, even though the activities may be carried out in the safest and most prudent way possible. Examples of areas in which strict liability has been imposed through the common law include the use of explosives, the building of dams, and the keeping of wild animals. In recent years the doctrine of strict liability has also been widely applied in product liability cases, in which the manufacturer is held liable for

Plaintiff's Prima Facie Case	Defenses
1. The defendant must owe a duty to the plaintiff to act reasonably, and 2. the defendant must have breached that duty 3. causing (i.e., being both the cause in fact and the proximate cause) 4. the plaintiff harm.	1. **Contributory negligence** The plaintiff fails to use due care; traditionally, this has been a complete bar to the plaintiff's suit. Most states have abandoned contributory negligence and have adopted comparative negligence. 2. **Comparative negligence** The plaintiff fails to use due care; the plaintiff's negligence is compared to the defendant's negligence, and damages are reduced accordingly. 3. **Assumption of the risk** The plaintiff knowingly and voluntarily subjects himself or herself to danger; traditionally, this has been a complete bar to the plaintiff's suit. Today assumption of the risk has been eliminated in many states that have adopted comparative negligence. 4. **Immunity** This complete bar to a lawsuit is based on policy considerations, such as preventing suits between family members and protecting charitable organizations.

Figure 10-3   Negligence Summarized

defects that occur in the product. A product is considered to be defective if it is unreasonably dangerous for use in the ordinary manner.

1. Ultrahazardous Activities

The Restatement of the Law of Torts, Second lists the six factors that courts review in determining whether a defendant should be held strictly liable when engaging in dangerous activities. Not all six factors have to be present. However, enough of the factors must be present for a court to feel justified in imposing strict liability—that is, liability even though the defendant did not intentionally or negligently cause the harm. The six factors listed in Section 520 are

(a) existence of a **high degree of risk of some harm** to the person, land or chattels of others;
(b) likelihood that the **harm** that results from it **will be great;**

Ultrahazardous activities
Those activities that have an inherent risk of injury and therefore may result in strict liability.

    (c) **inability to eliminate the risk** by the exercise of reasonable care;

    (d) extent to which the **activity is not a matter of common usage;**

    (e) **inappropriateness** of the activity **to the place** where it is carried on; and

    (f) extent to which its **value to the community is outweighed by its dangerous attributes.** (Emphasis added.)

The classic case for finding strict liability is the use of dynamite in blasting. The rationale for finding strict liability in such cases is that blasting as a business carries with it extreme risks that cannot be guarded against. Therefore, as between a for-profit company that chooses to engage in blasting and an innocent person harmed by the results of the blasting, the company should be held accountable, with the damages to be absorbed as part of the costs of doing business. Of course, any company engaging in such dangerous activities would be wise to purchase liability insurance.

In addition to such dangerous business activities as using or storing explosives, courts have frequently found the owners of wild animals strictly liable for injuries the animals cause. Applying the factors listed in the Restatement you can see why keeping a lion, for example, in a backyard cage would lead to a finding of strict liability.

Products liability
The theory holding manufacturers and sellers liable for defective products when the defects make the products unreasonably dangerous.

2. Products Liability

When a product proves to be defective, an injured party can sue under any one of three theories: negligence, breach of warranty, or strict liability. Which theory to use depends on the facts of the case and how the plaintiff's state has chosen to categorize products liability cases. For example, a plaintiff might bring a case under a negligence theory if the plaintiff has proof of a manufacturing defect. The classic case is *MacPherson v. Buick Motor Co.*[37] The plaintiff's car had wooden wheel spokes, and one of the wheels was made of defective wood, causing the car to collapse, injuring the plaintiff. Another basis for a negligence claim would be proof of a design defect. For example, a hockey helmet with cutouts around the ears that allows penetration of a hockey puck is arguably defectively designed. Finally, a failure to warn of a danger known to the manufacturer but probably unknown to the user would form the basis for a negligence suit.

There are times, however, when a plaintiff cannot point to any one act of negligence. Nonetheless, the product was defective, and that defect caused an injury. In those cases the plaintiff might rely either on a warranty theory—the product failed to meet the buyer's expectations for a safe product—or on a tort strict liability theory. In the following case the court discusses the history of the development of products liability and why it thinks a tort as opposed to a contracts approach best meets the needs of consumers.

---

[37]111 N.E. 1050 (N.Y. 1916).

NETNOTE

The Consumer Product Safety Commission has a web site where you can find information on recalls and unsafe products. Start at *www.cpsc.gov.*

Doe v. Miles Laboratories, Inc.
675 F. Supp. 1466 (D. Md. 1987)

Norman P. RAMSEY, United States District Judge

A plague inflicts society and this Court is called upon to adjudicate the extent to which the effects will be visited upon its victims. The facts are tragic. In the autumn of 1983, plaintiff Jane Doe, who a week previous had given birth, sought emergency medical treatment for vaginal bleeding. During the course of treatment, the attending physician ordered the administration of 500 units of "Konyne," a blood-coagulation-factor concentrate produced by Cutter Laboratories, a division of Miles. Treatment appeared successful and plaintiff eventually was discharged.

Over the course of the months to follow, plaintiff suffered from a succession of ailments, ultimately being diagnosed as infected by the HTLV-III virus, and as having Acquired Immuno-Deficiency Syndrome-Related Complex (ARC), a predecessor of AIDS. . . . Defendant Miles . . . filed this motion for summary judgment on plaintiffs' counts for breach of warranties, for strict liability in tort, and for strict liability in tort—failure to warn; and further seeks summary judgment on the counts for loss of consortium and punitive damages to the extent they are derivative of the first three. . . .

Products Liability Law

Defective products cause accidents that result in both economic losses and injuries either to persons or property. Allowing victims to recover for such losses was long a controversial issue. Indeed, the common law has followed a confusing and torturous path in perceiving and remedying the situation.

Originally caveat emptor prevailed. Both English and early American courts found no liability on a seller's part—either in contract or in tort—toward anyone, either purchaser or bystander, for injuries caused by products. . . .

It is not surprising the rule faded away. As societies shifting from agriculture to industry, more manufactured products entered the stream of commerce. Purchasers understandably expected products both to be what they were said to be and to perform in the manner predicted. As commerce expanded, courts propounded rules to protect people's expectations.

Arising as it did in the context of commerce, early products liability law adopted the concepts and parameters of contract law. Present in seedling form in *Chandelor v. Lopus,* the notion of warranties took root until it became widely recognized there could be either 1) express warranties resulting from representations or affirmations of fact about the characteristics of goods sold, or 2) implied warranties resulting simply from the act of selling where the seller was a merchant. Being based on conduct of the parties, either express or implied, such obligations are inherently contractual in nature, as compared to tort law which imposes obligations as a matter of policy independent of any express assumption on the part of a person. . . .

Historically, contracts law never provided a credible basis for recovery for more than a few of the total numbers of persons injured in accidents. First, allowing warranties to be restricted limited the remedy. A manufacturer could contract out of liability by making disclaimers an express term of the contract. Second, the concept of privity severely restricted the class of persons who could recover. Consumers, for example, seldom buy directly from manufacturers. Instead people usually buy products from intervening distributers or retailers, and courts seized upon this intervention as a reason for cutting off manufacturers' liability. Similarly, persons injured in on-the-job accidents faced equally bleak prospects of obtaining recovery from manufacturers of defective machinery and other equipment. Employees seldom purchase the tools they work with. Whenever manufacturers sold defective items to the employer, they were held to have no liability to the injured employee since he or she was not a party to the contract of sale. . . .

Where contract law slammed the door, tort law served to pry it open a crack. . . .

This law evolved dramatically when Judge Cardoza articulated negligence in products liability as we know it today. In *MacPherson v. Buick Motor Co.*, 217 N.Y. 382, 111 N.E. 1050 (1916), he [stated:]

> If the nature of a thing is such that it is reasonably certain to place life and limb in peril when negligently made, it is then a thing of danger. Its nature gives warning of the consequences to be expected. If to the elements of danger there is added knowledge that the thing will be used by persons other than the purchaser, and used without new tests, then irrespective of contract, the manufacturer of this thing of danger is under a duty to make it carefully. . . . We have put aside the notion that the duty to safeguard life and limb, when the consequences of negligence may be foreseen, grew out of contract and nothing else. We have put the source of the obligation where it ought to be. We have put its source in the law.

Id. at 389-90, 111 N.E. at 1053. By 1966 the rule from *MacPherson v. Buick Motor Co.* had been universally recognized as the law in the United States. Thus manufacturers and vendors are held liable in tort for injury to consumers or ultimate users when found negligent.

Once liability in negligence became established, the concept of strict products liability gained favor as an alternative theory of recovery for injuries from defective products. It is commonly stated that there are three reasons for holding manufacturers and dealers strictly liable for personal or property injury caused by defective products. First, innocent victims should not be forced to bear the costs of accidents, which still occurs far too often, for even a negligence action may impose an evidentiary burden impossible to meet. Second, that strict liability promotes accident prevention, for the manufacturers are in a better position to ascertain and control the risks associated with their products. Third, that manufacturers are in a better position than victims to bear the costs, for they can distribute the losses across the many who purchase the product, whereas an individual victim, unless he or she is exceptionally well-to-do or heavily insured, will be driven into bankruptcy or into social welfare programs. . . .

[I]n *Greenman v. Yuba Power Products, Inc.*, 59 Cal. 2d 57, 27 Cal. Rptr. 697, 377 P.2d 897 (1963), [the court] inaugurated strict products liability in tort as an alternative theory of recovery. . . .

The *Greenman* court predicated liability on the idea a manufacturer "is strictly liable in tort when an article he places on the market, knowing that it is to be used without inspection for defects, proves to have a defect that causes injury to a human being." *Id.*, 377 P.2d at 900. The court expressly moved away from an implied warranty theory of recovery, reasoning:

> The abandonment of the requirement of a contract between [the plaintiff and the defendant], the recognition that the liability is not assumed by agreement but imposed by law [citations omitted], and the refusal to permit the manufacturer to define the scope of its own responsibility for defective products [citations omitted] make clear that the liability is not one governed by the law of contract warranties but by the law of strict liability in tort. Accordingly, rules defining and governing warranties that were developed to meet the needs of commercial transactions cannot properly be invoked to govern the manufacturers' liability to those injured by their defective products unless these rules also serve the purpose for which liability is imposed.
> *Id.* at 701, 377 P.2d at 901.

Shortly thereafter, the American Law Institute in 1965 in the Restatement (Second) of Torts included section 402A, which provides:

(1) One who sells any product in a defective condition unreasonably dangerous to the user or consumer or to his property is subject to liability for physical harm thereby caused to the ultimate user or consumer, or to his property, if (a) The seller is engaged in the business of selling such a product, and (b) It is expected to and does reach the user or consumer without substantial change in the condition in which it is sold. (2) The rule stated in subsection (1) applies although (a) The seller has exercised all possible care in the preparation and sale of his product, and (b) The user or consumer has not bought the product from or entered into any contractual relation with the seller.

. . . In 1976 the Maryland court explicitly adopted Section 402A's strict products liability in tort in *Phipps v. General Motors Corp.*, 278 Md. 337, 363 A.2d 955 (1976).

The court in *Phipps* iterated four essential elements for strict liability:

1) the product was in a defective condition at the time that it left the possession or control of the seller,
2) that it was unreasonably dangerous to the user or consumer,
3) that the defect was a cause of the injuries, and
4) that the product was expected to and did reach the consumer without substantial change in its condition.

Id. at 344, 363 A.2d at 958. The product had to be both "defective" and "unreasonably dangerous," with the latter described as "'dangerous to an extent beyond which would be contemplated by the ordinary consumer who purchases it, with the ordinary knowledge common to the community as to its characteristics.'" Id., 363 A.2d at 959 (quoting Comment i to section 402A). Proof of both a "defective" and "unreasonably dangerous"

product are required, for "the seller is not an insurer, as absolute liability is not imposed on the seller for any injury resulting from the use of his product." Id. at 352, 363 A.2d at 963. In essence the two characteristics create the legal cause requisite to liability. A plaintiff who cannot show that a product was both defective and unreasonably dangerous has failed to establish the basis for the defendant's liability.

Whatever the theory of recovery, whether negligence or strict liability, it is now clear that the test in products liability is the same. A plaintiff must show 1) the existence of a defect; 2) the attribution of the defect to the seller; and 3) a causal relation between the defect and the injury. *Jensen v. American Motors*, 50 Md. App. 226, 234, 437 A.2d 242, 247 (1981).

Analysis

Defendant's motion for summary judgment leads the Court into ambiguous territory. Many of the issues raised are new. The Court is in a position common to *Erie* cases, namely being a federal court required to determine state law when the state courts have not directly addressed the issues. In such a case the federal court is obliged to view the matter as a state court would find the law, not necessarily as it would find the law to be. . . . [The court then went on to discuss whether policy considerations warranted exempting blood and blood products from strict liability in tort and decided they did not.]

Entrepreneurs by their nature are risk taking individuals. To the extent they need an incentive to engage in socially beneficial activities, the law already provides it in the form of a corporate shield on personal liability. To do as defendant argues, and exempt blood from strict liability would be to subsidize the product by forcing either victims or government through its social welfare programs to bear accident costs. . . .

Accordingly, the Court will deny defendant's motion for summary judgment on plaintiffs' claim for strict products liability. . . .

CASE DISCUSSION QUESTIONS

1. The court discusses a doctrine known as privity of contract. What does privity of contract mean, and why did the court see it as limiting the ability of plaintiffs to sue for defective products?

2. Why did the court think a tort-based approach to products liability was preferable to one based on contract and warranty law?

3. The court stated: "The argument is often made that strict products liability has the potential to bankrupt manufacturers. Such an argument misses the salutory economic role strict products liability plays. Understood properly, it can be seen that strict liability promotes a rational market place." How so?

As the court in *Doe v. Miles Laboratories, Inc.*, pointed out, a very influential development in the history of products liability law was the 1965 passage of Section 402A of the Restatement of the Law of Torts, Second. Under Section 402A a manufacturer or seller is liable if it sells a defective product that harms a consumer and that defect made the product unreasonably dangerous. Unlike other provisions of the Restatement, Section 402A was not really a restatement of existing law. Rather it was the American Law Institute's vision of what the law should be. When it was passed, it had little support. Over the years that has changed, and today Section 402A has been adopted by many state courts and legislatures. See Figure 10-4 for the history of products liability law.

Nonetheless, it has not been uniformly supported, and in May 1997 the American Law Institute passed the Restatement of the Law of Torts, Third: Products Liability. The most notable way in which this new provision changes Section 402A is in requiring a plaintiff in a design defect case to prove that there was an alternative design that would have prevented the harm. It is too early to know whether the states will adopt this latest version of the Restatement.

3. Defenses to Strict Liability Torts

Product misuse
When the product was not being used for its intended purpose or was being used in a dangerous manner; it is a defense to a products liability claim so long as the misuse was not foreseeable.

A plaintiff's contributory negligence is usually not considered a defense to strict liability; however, assumption of the risk and **product misuse** may be. For a manufacturer to assert the affirmative defense of product misuse, the manufacturer must prove that the product was not being used for its intended purpose or was being used in a dangerous manner that could not reasonably have been foreseen by the manufacturer. However, even if a plaintiff misuses a product, if that use is foreseeable, the manufacturer may be liable for a design defect. For example, assume a young child opened a stove door in order to step on it in an attempt to reach a shelf located above the stove. Although clearly a stove is not meant to be used as a stepping stool, a court might hold that this misuse was foreseeable and could have been avoided by a different design.

Figure 10-4   History of Products Liability Law

Caveat Emptor	Contract/Breach of Warranty	Negligence	Strict Liability
No liability	Liability unless disclaimed or lack of privity of contract	Liability if can prove unreasonable behavior	Liability if sold defective product that was unreasonably dangerous

Figure 10-5 summarizes the prima facie case for and defenses to strict liability.

D. NEW TORTS

As you have seen, tort law is aspirational, striving to protect our interests in being free from unlawful intrusion into our privacy, reputation, and bodily integrity. As such, tort law is not a rigid doctrine but rather is ever changing to meet society's needs. In this section we will look at three developing areas of tort law. It is too soon to know whether any of these areas will become established, but they all illustrate the evolving nature of the law.

1. Wrongful Life or Wrongful Birth

Should a defendant be liable for negligently causing the birth of a healthy child? The courts have arrived at inconsistent answers to this question. These situations typically arise when a physician negligently failed to diagnose a pregnancy or negligently performed a sterilization procedure. One difficulty for the courts has been the problem of trying to weigh the costs of raising a healthy child against

Figure 10-5 Summary of Strict Liability

Prima Facie Case	Defenses
Ultrahazardous Activities 1. Existence of a high degree of risk of some harm to the person, land, or chattels of others; 2. likelihood that the harm that results from it will be great; 3. inability to eliminate the risk by the exercise of reasonable care; 4. extent to which the activity is not a matter of common usage; 5. inappropriateness of the activity to the place where it is carried on; and 6. extent to which its value to the community is outweighed by its dangerous attributes.	1. Assumption of the risk
Strict Liability 1. The product was in a defective condition at the time that it left the possession or control of the seller, 2. that it was unreasonably dangerous to the user or consumer, 3. that the defect was a cause of the injuries, and 4. that the product was expected to and did reach the consumer without substantial change in its condition.	1. Assumption of the risk 2. Unforseeable product misuse

the value of the life and the joy of parenthood. Another problem relates to the difficulty in assessing damages. Frequently courts have simply allowed recovery for the costs of the failed medical procedure. On the other hand, when the child is born deformed, then the courts are more willing to allow recovery for the costs associated with raising the child minus the costs associated with raising a healthy child.

2. Battered Woman's Syndrome

A new tort, recognized in only a few states, is the tort of battered woman's syndrome. One of the reasons a plaintiff might want to bring her claim under this new theory rather than under traditional battery or emotional distress is that those torts typically have a fairly short statute of limitations, often two years, whereas the tort of battered woman's syndrome is considered to be a "continuing tort," thereby eliminating the statute of limitations problem.

Giovine v. Giovine
284 N.J. Super. 3, 663 A.2d 109 (1995)

On July 1, 1994, plaintiff Christina Giovine filed an eleven count complaint against defendant Peter J. Giovine denominated: "Complaint for divorce, domestic torts, equitable claims and jury trial demand." . . .

On August 8, 1994, defendant filed a motion to strike certain causes of action contained within plaintiff's complaint. . . . On September 20, 1994, the motion judge granted defendant's motion, striking all tortious claims occurring prior to June 30, 1992 based upon the applicable statute of limitations, and limiting plaintiff's proofs on her claims for emotional distress or negligence to those acts alleged to have occurred after June 30, 1992. . . . We granted plaintiff's motion seeking leave to appeal those rulings. . . .

Interspousal tort immunity no longer exists to bar the suit of one spouse against another for injuries sustained by one spouse due to the tortious conduct of the other. *Merenoff v. Merenoff*, 76 N.J. 535, 557, 388 A.2d 951 (1978). . . . If the circumstances surrounding a domestic tort and a claim for monetary damages are relevant to a divorce proceeding, the domestic tort must be joined with the divorce proceeding under the "single controversy doctrine" in order to avoid protracted, repetitious and fractionalized litigation.

On appeal, plaintiff contends that the motion judge erred in refusing to follow the decision in *Cusseaux v. Pickett*, 279 N.J. Super. 335, 652 A.2d 789 (Law Div. 1994), which concluded that "battered-woman's syndrome is the result of a continuing pattern of abuse and violent behavior that causes continuing damage." Id. at 345. As such, "it must be treated in the same way as a continuing tort." Ibid. Battered woman's syndrome would therefore be an exception to N.J.S.A. 2A:14-2, that "every action at law for an injury to the person caused by the wrongful act, neglect or default of any person within this state shall be commenced within 2 years next after the cause of any such action shall have occurred." Ibid. The decision in *Cusseaux* substantially relied upon *State v. Kelly*, 97 N.J. 178, 478 A.2d 364 (1984).

In *Kelly*, the Supreme Court, relying in part on the research of Lenore E. Walker, The Battered Woman (1979), noted that battered woman's syndrome is a recognized medical condition. By definition, a battered woman is one who is repeatedly physically or emotionally abused by a man in an attempt to force her to do his bidding without regard for her rights. *State v. Kelly*, supra, 97 N.J. at 193. According to experts, in order to be a battered woman, the woman and her abuser must go through the "battering cycle" at least twice.

The battering cycle consists of three stages. Stage one, the "tension-building stage," involves some minor physical and verbal abuse while the woman tries to prevent an escalation of the abuse by assuaging the abuser with her passivity. Stage two, the "acute battering incident," is characterized by more severe battering due to either a triggering event in the abuser's life or the woman's inability to control the anger and fear she experienced during stage one. Ibid. During stage three, the abuser pleads for forgiveness and promises that he will not abuse again. This period of relative calm and normalcy eventually ends when the cycle begins anew. "The cyclical nature of battering behavior helps explain why more women simply do not leave their abuser." The caring and attentive behavior of the abuser during stage three fuels the victim's hope that her partner has reformed and keeps her tied to the relationship. In addition, some women who grew up in violent families do not leave abusive relationships because they perceive their situations as normal. Others cannot face the reality of their situations. Some victims "become so demoralized and degraded by the fact that they cannot predict or control the violence that they sink into a state of psychological paralysis and become unable to take any action at all to improve or alter the situation." Victims are often afraid to seek help out of shame, fear that no one will believe them, or fear of retaliation by their abusers. "They literally become trapped by their own fear."

In *Kelly,* the Supreme Court held that expert testimony on battered woman's syndrome was admissible to show that a woman on trial for murder who was repeatedly beaten during her marriage honestly believed that she was in imminent danger of death when she stabbed her husband, and therefore, she acted in self-defense. Id. at 187, 202-04. . . .

Cusseaux v. Pickett, supra, recognized for the first time in this state, that a woman who suffers from the medically diagnosable condition of battered woman's syndrome is entitled to seek compensation for the physical and emotional injuries attributable to the abusive conduct during the course of the relationship. The trial judge found that: Because the battered-woman's syndrome is the result of a continuing pattern of abuse and violent behavior that causes continuing damage, it must be treated in the same way as a continuing tort. It would be contrary to the public policy of this State, not to mention cruel, to limit recovery to only those individual incidents of assault and battery for which the applicable statute of limitations has not yet run. The mate who is responsible for creating the condition suffered by the battered victim must be made to account for his actions— all of his actions. Failure to allow affirmative recovery under these circumstances would be tantamount to the courts condoning the continued abusive treatment of women in the domestic sphere. This the courts cannot and will never do.

Cusseaux established a four-part test to state a cause of action for battered woman's syndrome: 1) involvement in a marital or marital-like intimate relationship; and 2) physical or psychological abuse perpetrated by the dominant partner to the relationship over an extended period of time; and 3) the aforestated abuse has caused recurring physical or psychological injury over the course of the relationship; and 4) a past or present inability to take any action to improve or alter the situation unilaterally. Id. at 344 (footnotes omitted).

We agree with the premise espoused in *Cusseaux* and conclude that a wife diagnosed with battered woman's syndrome should be permitted to sue her spouse in tort for the physical and emotional injuries sustained by continuous acts of battering during the course of the marriage, provided there is medical, psychiatric, or psychological expert testimony establishing that the wife was caused to have an "inability to take any action to improve or alter the situation unilaterally." In the absence of expert proof, the wife cannot be deemed to be suffering from battered woman's syndrome, and each act of abuse during the marriage would constitute a separate and distinct cause of action in tort, subject to the statute of limitations. . . .

The Supreme Court in *Kelly* and the Law Division in *Cusseaux* placed substantial weight on the legislative findings which led to the enactment of the Prevention of Domestic Violence Act, N.J.S.A. 2C:25-1 to -16. Those findings deserve repeating: The Legislature finds and declares that domestic violence is a serious crime against society;

that there are thousands of persons in this State who are regularly beaten, tortured and in some cases even killed by their spouses or cohabitants; that a significant number of women who are assaulted are pregnant; that victims of domestic violence come from all social and economic backgrounds and ethnic groups; that there is a positive correlation between spousal abuse and child abuse; and that children, even when they are not themselves physically assaulted, suffer deep and lasting emotional effects from exposure to domestic violence. . . . We recognize that the motion judge was not bound to follow *Cusseaux*, as that opinion was rendered by a court of concurrent jurisdiction. However, as we now subscribe to the concept articulated in *Cusseaux*, we reverse the motion judge's decision and direct that plaintiff shall be entitled to present proof that she has the medically diagnosed condition of battered woman's syndrome. Plaintiff shall be entitled to sue her husband for damages attributable to his continuous tortious conduct resulting in her present psychological condition, provided she has medical, psychiatric, or psychological expert proof to establish that she was caused to have an inability "to take any action at all to improve or alter the situation." *Cusseaux*, supra, 279 N.J. Super. at 341. . . .

CASE DISCUSSION QUESTIONS

1. Why couldn't the plaintiff, Christina Giovine, simply have sued for assault and battery?

2. The plaintiff testified that "[d]uring these Friday night incidences he would call me 'bitch,' 'C-nt,' 'whore,' 'f-ing son-of-a-bitch' and other vile names." The dissent suggested that the type of emotional distress the defendant caused the plaintiff could not be the basis for a claim of intentional infliction of emotional distress because such behavior in a marital context is not "so outrageous in character, and so extreme in degree, as to go beyond all possible bounds of decency, and to be regarded as atrocious, and utterly intolerable in a civilized community." What do you think?

3. The court did not allow the plaintiff to sue her husband for a battery that occurred in March 1972, which caused her to suffer a perforated eardrum, resulting in surgery and two weeks in the hospital. The reason the court disallowed this claim is that this was the first time her husband had hit her and the court noted that "the medical condition of battered woman's syndrome does not occur until a woman is battered at least twice." Do you agree with the court's analysis?

4. In *Kyle v. Green Acres at Verona, Inc.*, 207 A.2d 513 (N.J. 1965), the defendant's negligence caused the plaintiff to become insane. Insanity was defined as a condition that prevented the "sufferer from understanding his [or her] legal rights." The court held that the statute of limitations would be tolled until a reasonable time after the plaintiff's sanity was restored. In *Jones v. Jones*, 576 A.2d 316 (N.J. App. Div. 1990), the court held that the statute of limitations was tolled for a victim of incest. Should these cases be seen as analogous to *Giovine*? Why?

3. Drug Dealer Liability Act

Assume a baby is born already addicted to cocaine because of his mother's substance abuse while she was pregnant. Whom can the baby sue? Recalling the case of *Woods v. Lancet*, one possibility is that the baby could sue the person who supplied the drug or his mother for negligence.

In addition, in a few states there is now another possible defendant: anyone who sold or gave away cocaine to anyone (not necessarily the mother) in the same county and during the same time period that the mother used cocaine. Liability is based on a new statute, the Drug Dealer Liability Act, which has been adopted in at least five states. Under that statute anyone who distributes an illegal drug can be sued by anyone harmed by that type of drug. The only limitations are that the distribution must have been in the same geographic area and during the same time period as the user took the drugs. Obviously, such a statute has far-reaching consequences. At a backyard barbecue a business-man shares some marijuana with a friend. Two weeks later a teenager buys some marijuana on the street from an unknown dealer. The teenager is then injured in an automobile accident when he loses control due to his marijuana "high." That teenager could sue the businessman—someone he has never met—for his inju-ries. The difficulty, of course, would lie in locating potential defendants, such as the businessman, who have sufficient "deep pockets" to make such a lawsuit worthwhile.

Some have argued that the Drug Dealer Liability Act violates substantive due process in that it "shocks the conscience."[38] Others think that such a suit might violate double-jeopardy protections if the suit is brought by the government against someone who has already been convicted of drug dealing.

Discussion Questions

9. Should tort law be an ever-expanding concept, or should there be some limits put on liability? Why? If the latter, what should those limits be?

10. Some argue that there is a litigation explosion; that instead of taking responsibility for their own actions, people are resorting in increasing numbers to the legal system for relief. Do you agree? Why? If you do agree, what should be done about it?

E. REMEDIES

As you have seen from reading the cases in this chapter, the most common form of remedy that a plaintiff seeks in a tort action is the awarding of some form of damages. From Chapter 3 you will recall that there are basically three types of damage awards: compensatory, punitive, and nominal. In addition to or instead of damages, the court might issue an **injunction**. An injunction is an order to the defendant ordering the defendant to do a specific act or to cease doing a specific act.

Compensatory damages (sometimes referred to as **actual damages**) are awarded to compensate the plaintiff for the harm done to him or her. In a tort action involving harm to a person, that might mean the cost of medical bills, lost time from work, and pain and suffering.

Compensatory damages can be further divided into general damages and special damages. **General damages** are those damages that you would natu-rally expect to occur given the type of harm suffered. For example, if Tom

---

[38]Dam, Injured Parties Can Sue Any Drug Dealer, 95 L.W.U.S.A. 869 (Sept. 11, 1995).

intentionally hit Sam's arm, thereby breaking it, Tom should expect to have to pay for Sam's pain and suffering. **Special damages** (sometimes called **consequential damages**) are damages that also flow naturally from the injury, but they may vary depending on the special circumstances of the case. They include the cost of repairing or replacing the damaged property, paying any medical bills, and replacing plaintiff's income lost while unable to work. For example, if, unbeknownst to Tom, Sam was a major league pitcher and due to his injury he could no longer pitch, Sam could recover his future lost wages as special damages.

Unlike compensatory damages, which are designed to pay plaintiffs for harm done to them, **punitive damages** (also called **exemplary damages**) serve the dual functions of punishing and deterring tortfeasors. Because their purpose is to punish and deter, typically punitive damages are awarded only for intentional torts and only when the court determines that the defendant deserves an additional punishment beyond just compensating the plaintiff for the harm done to him or her.

Once the decision has been made to award punitive damages, courts often struggle with the appropriate ratio between those damages and the compensatory damages. For example, if a plaintiff were awarded $10,000 in compensatory damages, would adequate punishment be meted out with punitive damages that were twice, ten times, or even a hundred times the compensatory amount? The courts have never set an exact formula. However, the U.S. Supreme Court has held that under the Constitution's due process protections, a defendant must "receive fair notice not only of the conduct that will subject him to punishment, but also of the severity of the penalty that a state may impose."[39] Therefore, if a punitive award is so large that the defendant could not have been expected to be on notice that he could be subjected to such a severe punishment, a court must set it aside as excessive. To help courts with this process, the Supreme Court developed three "guideposts" to analyze the appropriateness of the size of the punitive award:

1. the degree of reprehensibility of the defendant's action,
2. the ratio of punitive to compensatory damages, and
3. a comparison of the punitive award and the civil or criminal sanctions that could be imposed for similar conduct.

Using these guideposts, in *BMW v. Gore*, the Supreme Court reversed a $2 million punitive award. A BMW owner claimed that BMW had intentionally defrauded him. When the car he had ordered was shipped to the United States, it was damaged by acid rain. Instead of informing him of the damage, BMW simply repainted the car. Nine months later, the owner found out that his car had been repainted and sued BMW. The trial court determined that his actual damages were only $4,000 (the decreased value of his car). After applying the three guideposts, the U.S. Supreme Court stated that $2 million in punitive damages was a "grossly excessive award," setting it aside because it "transcend[ed] the constitutional limit."[40]

Most recently, the Supreme Court applied the three guideposts in a case where an insurance company was ordered to pay $1 million in compensatory

[39]BMW v. Gore, 517 U.S. 559, 574 (1996).
[40]Id. at 585.

damages and $145 million in punitive damages. The case originated when Mr. Curtis Campbell caused an automobile accident. He was sued, and his insurance carrier, State Farm, refused settlement offers from the plaintiffs. The offers were within Campbell's policy limits of $50,000. Because they refused to settle, the case went to trial. The jury found against Campbell and awarded damages of $185,000. Campbell sued State Farm. The jury found that State Farm knew that if the case went to trial, it was likely to result in a verdict over the policy limits and so had acted in bad faith when it refused to settle. In reviewing this award of damages, the Supreme Court relied heavily on the first guidepost, noting that "while State Farm's handling of the claims against the Campbells merits no praise," State Farm's actions were not so reprehensible as to justify the large amount of punitive damages in this case.[41] As to the second guidepost, the Court noted:

> [I]n practice, few awards exceeding a single-digit ratio between punitive and compensatory damages, to a significant degree, will satisfy due process. In *Haslip*, in upholding a punitive damages award, we concluded that an award of more than four times the amount of compensatory damages might be close to the line of constitutional impropriety. We cited that 4-to-1 ratio again in *Gore*. While these ratios are not binding, they are instructive. They demonstrate what should be obvious: Single-digit multipliers are more likely to comport with due process, while still achieving the State's goals of deterrence and retribution, than awards with ratios in the range of 500 to 1, [as found in *Gore*] or, in this case, of 145 to 1.[42]

The Court spent little time on the third guidepost, simply stating that a relevant civil sanction of a $10,000 fine for fraud was "dwarfed" by the $145 million punitive damages award.[43]

At trial, the Campbells introduced evidence that State Farm's decision was not due to an isolated mistake in judgment but rather was part of a nationwide scheme to maximize profits by capping payouts on claims. This was a significant factor in the state court's awarding such a large punitive award. The Supreme Court rejected this argument, stating that "a defendant should be punished for the conduct that harmed the plaintiff, not for being an unsavory individual or business. Due process does not permit courts, in the calculation of punitive damages, to adjudicate the merits of other parties' hypothetical claims against a defendant."[44] Critics of the Supreme Court's approach argue that this raises the same issue we mentioned earlier in this chapter in our discussion of Carol Burnett and her suit against the National Enquirer. That is, if the ratio of punitive to compensatory damages is set at too low a level, there is the danger that punitive damages will cease to serve their deterrence function. Businesses may determine that a certain course of action will produce more profits than will be offset by any punitive damages award. Where, then, is the incentive for the business to choose a different and more socially responsible course of action?

---

[41]State Farm Automobile Insurance Co. v. Campbell, 538 U.S. 408 (2003).

[42]Id. at 426.

[43]Id. at 429.

[44]Id. at 422-423.

Both *BMW v. Gore* and *State Farm* involved economic harm. In fact, in *BMW v. Gore,* the plaintiff suffered minimal damages: the difference in value between a new BMW and a new BMW that had been repainted. In *State Farm,* the plaintiff suffered greater economic harm as well as emotional distress. However, neither of these cases involved conduct that endangered anyone's physical health or safety. Therefore, it is unclear whether the Court would be as willing to set aside punitive damages awards in cases involving personal injury. As one clue to a possible answer, it is interesting to note that the Court has stated that it is the first guidepost, the degree of the defendant's reprehensibility, that is the "most important indicium of a punitive damages award's reasonableness."[45] The Court also stated that in determining the degree of reprehensibility, a court must consider several factors, including whether the harm was physical rather than economic.[46]

Finally, **nominal damages** are awarded when a right has been violated but the plaintiff cannot prove any monetary harm. For example, a trespasser may have caused no harm to the land, but the landowner would still be entitled to a nominal award.

DISCUSSION QUESTIONS

11. Some argue that the quotation from *State Farm* cited above indicates that the Court will look most favorably on punitive damages awards that are four times that of the compensatory award. Do you agree?

12. Do you think it is fairer to defendants to apply "guideposts" such as the Supreme Court has been using or a simple ratio, such as mandating that punitive damages awards in non–personal injury cases cannot exceed nine times the compensatory award? Would such a rule satisfy society's need to deter future bad conduct?

13. Typically, punitive damages are awarded to the plaintiff because it was the plaintiff who brought the lawsuit. However, punitive damages are designed to punish the defendant rather than compensate the victim. Some have argued, therefore, that punitive damages should be paid to the state (society as a whole) rather than to the individual plaintiff. Indeed, a few states have passed laws that split punitive damages awards between the plaintiff and the state. Alaska, Missouri, and Utah split awards equally between plaintiff and state; Oregon takes 60 percent of the awards; Georgia, Indiana, and Iowa take 75 percent; and Illinois leaves the allocation up to the discretion of the judge.[47] In Ohio the state supreme court on its own initiative recently allocated almost two-thirds of a $30 million punitive damages award to a cancer research fund the court established.[48] What do you think of these various approaches?

---

[45]Id. at 420.

[46]Id.

[47]David Hechler, "California Eyes Share of Punitives," 26 Nat'l L.J. no. 38 (May 24, 2004).

[48]Dardinger v. Anthem Blue Cross & Blue Shield, 781 N.E.2d 121 (Ohio 2002).

SUMMARY

A tort is a private wrong that causes harm to a person or property. Torts are generally classified as involving intentional acts, negligence, or strict liability. Intentional torts occur whenever someone intends an action that results in harm. Examples include assault and battery, false imprisonment, defamation, invasion of privacy, intentional infliction of emotional distress, and trespass. Negligence involves a breach of duty that causes harm. Cause includes both actual cause and proximate cause. Strict liability includes both ultrahazardous activities and products liability, where an unreasonably dangerous defective product is sold.

Tort law is constantly evolving. The courts are still developing new torts to cover changing societal views as to what should be protected. Examples include the torts of wrongful life or birth and battered woman's syndrome.

Finally, in bringing a tort action a plaintiff is generally seeking either an injunction or damages. Damages can take the form of a compensatory, punitive, or nominal award.

REVIEW QUESTIONS

Pages 295 through 302

1. How can the same set of facts result in both a tort and a crime? Will every tort also create criminal liability?
2. How can a tort be distinguished from a contract action?
3. What are the elements of assault? Of battery?
4. How can there be an assault and no battery? A battery without an assault?
5. Review the situation of Mrs. Day presented at the beginning of the chapter. Do you think she has a valid claim for either assault or battery? Why?

Pages 303 through 306

6. What are the elements of false imprisonment?
7. When does a shopkeeper have a valid defense to a detained person's allegation of false imprisonment?

Pages 307 through 309

8. What are the elements of libel? The defenses?
9. In *New York Times v. Sullivan,* what limitations did the Supreme Court put on the ability of public figures to sue the press?
10. Assume Robin Barker dictates a letter to her secretary. The letter is addressed to Ms. Wanda Jones. In the letter Ms. Barker tells Ms. Jones that she thinks Ms. Jones is a thief. The secretary types and mails the letters to Ms. Jones. Can Ms. Jones sue for defamation? What element is arguably missing?
11. A grocery store employee followed a customer to the parking lot and accused her of having meat in her purse. The customer opened her purse and showed that she did not have any meat, and the employee left. Several passersby heard the remarks, but the plaintiff could not identify any of them. Should the customer be barred from proceeding with a defamation suit? Why?

Pages 310 through 315

12. How do the torts of defamation and invasion of privacy differ?
13. What must a plaintiff prove to win a case of intentional infliction of emotional distress?

Pages 316 through 322

14. What are the four basic elements of a negligence claim?
15. Do you think the result in the *Cordas* case would have been different if Mrs. Cordas and her two children had been in the taxicab rather than standing on the sidewalk? Why?

Pages 322 through 324

16. Explain the doctrine of res ipsa loquitur.
17. When might the court find that a defendant was negligent per se?

Pages 325 through 334

18. What is the difference between "but for" causation and proximate cause?

Pages 334 through 340

19. Describe the three basic affirmative defenses to negligence. How do they differ from each other?
20. A state court judge approved a mother's petition to have her "somewhat retarded" daughter sterilized. The daughter was told that she was to have her appendix removed. Later the daughter married and found out that she had been sterilized. She sued the judge. How do you think the court resolved the case?
21. A public high school required parents to sign a release-of-liability form before allowing their children to participate in interscholastic athletics. The parents objected to having to sign the form and went to court, requesting that the school district be enjoined from requiring the release. How do you think the court decided the issue?
22. State building codes set forth requirements for safe buildings. If a building inspector fails in his duty to carefully inspect a building, do you think a purchaser of such premises would have a cause of action for buying a building that was developed in violation of the governmental requirements? Why?

Pages 340 through 351

23. Describe the three theories that a plaintiff can use to sue a manufacturer when harmed by that manufacturer's product.
24. A woman keeps a pit bull dog as a pet. One day the neighbor children accidentally throw a Frisbee into her yard. In attempting to retrieve the Frisbee one of the children is severely bitten by the dog. Should the dog's owner be held strictly liable? Why?
25. Manuel Sanchez began smoking at the age of ten. Over his lifetime he smoked several different brands of cigarettes. At the age of fifty-three he was diagnosed with throat cancer and died within six months. His widow sued nine different cigarette manufacturers on the theory of strict liability. To win her case, what would Mrs. Sanchez have to prove? Do you think she was successful?
26. Five-year-old Daphne took a disposable lighter from her mother's purse that was stored on the top shelf of a closet in a bedroom in her grandparents' home. While playing with the lighter, she started a fire that severely burned her two-year-old brother, Ruben. While the lighter manufacturer produced lighters both with and without child safety mechanisms, this lighter did not have one. The children's mother sued the manufacturer of the lighter. If you represented the mother, how would you argue the manufacturer should be held liable for the boy's injury? How do you think the lawyers for the manufacturer would respond?

Pages 351 through 354

27. What are the three basic types of damages that a plaintiff can recover in a tort action, and what is the purpose of each?
28. What is the difference between general and special damages?

Chapter 11

Contract Law

*A contract has, strictly speaking, nothing to do with
the personal, or individual, intent of the parties....
If ... it were proved by twenty bishops that either
party, when he used the words, intended something
else than the usual meaning which the law imposes
upon them, he would still be held.*
Judge Learned Hand

INTRODUCTION

Contracts are involved in almost every aspect of our lives, from day-to-day
commercial transactions to corporate mergers—from purchasing and financing
a home to insuring that home, automobile, life, or health. A contract is nothing
more than an agreement, oral or written, that can be enforced in court. Contract
law sets out the basic elements that must be present for an agreement to be
considered legally enforceable. It also spells out when the court will excuse
one of the parties for not living up to that side of the agreement. In sum, contract
law reflects society's values regarding what promises we think should be kept
and what excuses we will allow.

You will discover that contract law is very rule bound. That is, to become
an expert in contract law, you must master a vast array of technical rules.
However, do not let yourself feel overwhelmed by the seemingly endless rules
and exceptions to those rules. What is most important is that you come to
understand the basic concepts that lie behind contract law and learn how to

recognize when there is a problem that you will then need to bring to the attention of your supervisor. In addition, the rules vary by jurisdiction. Therefore, memorizing the very specific rules that are valid in most states is not as important as is gaining an understanding of the basic requirements for a valid contract. Then, when you are faced with a contract problem, you will understand the issues that you will need to research.

Uniform Commercial Code (UCC)
Originally drafted by the National Conference of Commissioners on Uniform State Law, it governs commercial transactions and has been adopted by all states, entirely or in part.

A. THE UNIFORM COMMERCIAL CODE (UCC)

Contract law has strong common-law roots, and in areas that do not deal with the business world, the common-law rules still govern. However, if a contract involves a business setting, then you may also have to consult legislation, in the form of the **Uniform Commercial Code (UCC)**. The UCC is a series of model statutory provisions drafted by prominent legal scholars. It was developed with the intent that states would voluntarily incorporate these provisions into their own statutes, thus providing a uniform set of legal principles that would facilitate commercial transactions among persons in different states.

Although all states, as well as the District of Columbia, have adopted the UCC entirely or in part, it is not a federal law. That would require its enactment by Congress. While the UCC was created by a group of learned scholars in the hopes of establishing uniformity for businesses that deal across state lines, the terms of the UCC are valid only if they have been adopted by the state. In addition, while most states have adopted the UCC as it was originally written, each state has the option of changing the terms. Therefore, when dealing with the UCC in a specific state be sure to check that state's precise wording.

Figure 11-1 The Uniform Commercial Code

Article 1	General Provisions
Article 2	Sales
Article 2A	Leases [New]
Article 3	Commercial Paper
Article 4	Bank Deposits and Collections
Article 5	Letters of Credit
Article 6	Bulk Transfers
Article 7	Warehouse Receipts, Bills of Lading, & Other Documents of Title
Article 8	Investment Securities
Article 9	Secured Transactions
Article 10	Effective Date and Repealer

The UCC is divided into eleven articles (Figure 11-1). The four articles that are most relevant to contract law are Articles 1, 2, 2A, and 9. Article 1 sets forth general provisions, such as definitions that apply to the entire UCC. Article 2 deals with the sale of goods, and Article 9 deals with secured transactions, a method whereby a creditor can be assured that if the debtor fails to repay the debt, the creditor can obtain specific property as an alternative form of payment. Therefore, while the UCC applies to some contract situations, it does not apply to all. For example, the UCC does not apply to real estate or service contracts. The discussion in this chapter is based on the law of contracts as developed by the common law. However, wherever Article 2 of the UCC has made a significant change to the common law, we will also discuss that change. Article 2A on leases is a new provision. To see whether it has been adopted in your state, you need to check your state statutes. We will discuss Article 9 in Chapter 13, Laws Affecting Business.

Article 1 sets forth the basic principles that underlie the entire UCC. First, Article 1 states that the UCC is to be liberally construed in order to best fulfill its underlying purposes to "simplify, clarify and modernize the law governing commercial transactions," to "permit the continued expansion of commercial practices through custom, usage and agreement of the parties," and "to make uniform the law among the various jurisdictions." UCC § 1-102(2). Second, the parties are almost always free to set their own terms, even if they are at variance with the UCC's requirements. UCC § 1-102(3). Third, unless displaced by a particular part of the UCC, the common-law rules of contract still apply. UCC § 1-103. Therefore, unless there is a conflict between the common law and the UCC, both apply, for example, to contracts for the sale of goods. Finally, under the UCC everyone is under an obligation to act in good faith, defined as honesty in fact. UCC § 1-203.

Article 2 applies to sales of goods. A *sale* is defined as "the passing of title from the seller to the buyer for a price." UCC § 2-106(1). Goods are "all things (including specially manufactured goods) which are movable . . . other than the money in which the price is to be paid, investment securities (Article 8) and things in action. 'Goods' also includes the unborn young of animals and growing crops and other identified things attached to realty as described in the section on goods to be severed from realty (Section 2-107)." UCC § 2-105(1). When you run across terms such as "things in action," first consult the definitions section to see whether the UCC has defined the term. If not, refer to a standard legal dictionary. In this case a thing in action, also known as a chose in action, means a right to sue. If the situation does not involve a contract for the sale of goods, Article 2 of the UCC does not apply at all. Therefore, it does not apply, for example, to employment or service contracts. One area of confusion is the mixed services/ goods situation. For example, assume you go to a beauty parlor to have your hair dyed. Are you there to purchase the services of the beautician or to purchase the dye? In those situations the court will try to determine which element predominates—the service or the sale of the goods. Only if the court perceives the transaction as being principally for the sale of goods will it apply the UCC.

As the UCC was specially developed to make the commercial world more uniform and efficient, there are special rules that apply only to merchants. For example, a merchant's obligation of good faith includes "honesty in fact and the observance of reasonable commercial standards of fair dealing in the trade." UCC § 2-103(b). Therefore, merchants are expected not only to deal honestly but also to be aware of the normal business practices for their trade.

A merchant is someone who

1. deals in the goods that are the subject of the contract, or
2. "holds himself out as having knowledge or skill peculiar to the practices or goods involved" in the contract, or
3. who employs someone who has such knowledge and skill. Under this last standard the employee's knowledge and skill are then attributed to the employer. UCC § 2-104(1).

Notice how broad this definition is. Normally we would all think of the person referred to in the first definition as a merchant. However, under the second

NETNOTE

The Uniform Commercial Code as revised through 1992 can be found on the Internet at:

www.law.cornell.edu/ucc/ucc.table.html

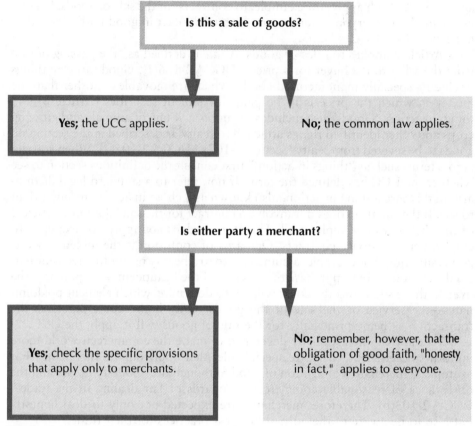

Figure 11-2   Does Article 2 of the UCC Apply?

definition even someone with a great deal of knowledge in an area, such as a law professor who as a hobby also happens to be a knowledgeable collector of antiques, could be declared a merchant when dealing in the sale or purchase of antiques. Finally, notice under the third definition that a person will also be considered a merchant if that person employs someone who meets the second definition.

Therefore, in summary, whenever you are faced with a contract situation, first ask yourself, Does this contract deal with the sale of goods? If the answer is yes, then ask whether either or both of the parties can be classified as a merchant. If yes, then be sure to check the special provisions that apply only to merchants. Finally, keep in mind the UCC's overall commitment to ensuring that all parties act in good faith and in such a way as to promote the expansion of commerce. See Figure 11-2.

B. TYPES OF CONTRACTS

As you may recall from Chapter 3, for a contract to be valid there must be an offer, an acceptance of the offer, and consideration; that is, something of value must be exchanged. However, before proceeding with our discussion of the elements of a binding contract, we need to mention the various ways in which courts classify contracts. Contracts can be either bilateral or unilateral, express or implied in fact, formal or informal, executed or executory, and valid, void, voidable, or unenforceable. These are mutually exclusive terms. A contract is always either bilateral or unilateral, and either express or implied in fact, and either formal or informal, and either executed or executory, and valid, void, voidable, or unenforceable.

A **bilateral contract** is one where a promise is exchanged for a promise. In a **unilateral contract** a promise is exchanged for an act. For example, I say to you, "I promise to pay you $5 if you will promise to mow my lawn." If you reply, "O.K., for $5 I promise to mow your lawn," we have formed a bilateral contract. However, if I say, "I promise to pay you $5 if you will mow my lawn," I have made an offer for a unilateral contract. I promise to pay in return for your act of mowing the lawn. This may seem like a lot of quibbling over a difference that should not matter, but it can matter if both parties do not fully perform. In the first case we have a completed contract: an offer, an acceptance, and something of value to be exchanged. Both parties are bound to perform. In the second situation, however, we only have an offer. Acceptance cannot come except by doing the act of mowing. The question is, Does simply starting the act of mowing create an acceptance, or must the entire job be completed before the acceptance is finalized? For example, if you begin mowing my lawn, am I free to take back my offer, or do we at that point have a binding contract? The traditional view is that we do not. I am free to withdraw my offer at any time up until the act is completed. Because of the obvious unfairness of that approach, the more modern view states that once substantial performance has begun, the contract is binding. The obvious question is, What constitutes substantial performance? That must be determined on a case-by-case basis.

Contracts can also be express or implied in fact. **Express contracts** are formed through words, either oral or written. **Implied-in-fact contracts** are formed through conduct. For example, if you say to Susan, "I would like to sell you my watch for $10," and Susan says, "I accept," through your words you have formed an express contract. On the other hand, assume you go to the college bookstore. There is a long line at the cash register, and you are late for class. You grab a candy bar, wave it at the cash register clerk, and put 50¢ on the counter. The clerk nods and picks up the 50¢. No words were spoken, but by your acts and those of the clerk you have formed an implied-in-fact contract.

Third, contracts can be either **formal** or **informal**. For most contracts today there are no special formalities that must be followed. Therefore, most contracts are classified as informal. There are a few exceptions, however. Certain contracts, such as those that transfer real estate, still require certain formalities. Other formal contracts include those under seal; a recognizance, which is an acknowledgment in court that a person will pay or act; negotiable instruments, such as a check; and letters of credit. All other contracts are classified as informal.

Once the parties have exchanged binding promises, a contract has been formed. Until it is fully performed, it is considered to be **executory**. Once both sides have fully performed, it is said that the contract has been **executed**. Be careful here. *Executed* also has another meaning in contract law: that a contract has been signed.

Bilateral	*or*	Unilateral	*and*			
Express	*or*	Implied in fact	*and*			
Formal	*or*	Informal	*and*			
Executory	*or*	Executed	*and*			
Valid	*or*	Void	*or*	Voidable	*or*	Unenforceable

Figure 11-3   Contract Classifications

Finally, most contracts are classified as **valid,** having all the essential elements needed for a binding agreement. If a court finds, however, that the contract is for an illegal purpose, it will be declared **void.** In certain circumstances, if one of the parties was under a disability, such as being a minor, when he or she signed it, the court will say that the contract is **voidable** at the option of that party. Finally, there are times when two parties have entered into a perfectly valid contract, but because of a procedural error, such as the passage of the statute of limitations or the failure to put the contract in writing, the court will say the contract is **unenforceable.** Each of these possible contract classifications is summarized in Figure 11-3.

DISCUSSION QUESTION

1. We all enter into contracts every day. Think back over the past week, and list all the contracts that you have entered into.

C. THE ELEMENTS OF A BINDING CONTRACT

A contract can be either oral or written, but in order to be considered valid, each of its three key elements must be present:

1. An offer must be made,
2. an acceptance must be given, and
3. something of value must be exchanged (consideration).

Some writers list only two elements: an agreement and consideration. In such formulations an agreement is defined as both an offer and an acceptance, and consideration is defined as the exchange of something of value.

It is important to clearly distinguish a contract from a gift. A gift may also involve an offer (someone offers to give you something), an acceptance (you respond that you would like the gift), and the passage of something of value (the gift itself). The difference is that in a gift situation the consideration is one-sided. Only one of the parties receives something of value. On the other hand, in a contract situation each party gives up something of value. Because of this difference, a contract is completed and binding on both parties once the parties have reached their agreement. However, a gift is not completed until the thing of value is actually delivered. This difference becomes important if one of the parties tries to take back a promise. In a contract situation the taking back of the promise creates a right in the other party to sue for breach of contract. In a gift situation, prior to delivery of the gift, the giver is free to take back the promise with no legal consequences. Consider the situation described in the following fact scenario.

Sally had often told her friend Jill how much she admired Jill's Mickey Mouse watch. Last Monday, as the two were walking to class, Sally noticed that Jill was wearing a different watch and asked Jill about it. Jill replied that at her birthday party yesterday her boyfriend gave her this new watch. "In that case," Sally inquired, "would you be interested in selling your Mickey Mouse watch to me?" Jill replied, "I paid $200 for it, but because we are friends, I will sell it to you for $100 and will bring the watch with me tomorrow." Sally said, "Great, it's a deal." Unnoticed by Sally and Jill, Mike had overheard the conversation. "Wait," Mike said. "I have always wanted a Mickey Mouse watch. I will give you $150 for the watch." Jill thought about it for a moment and then turned to Sally and said, "Gosh, I'm sorry, Sally, but I'm afraid that unless you can match Mike's offer, I will have to sell the watch to him." Sally replied that she could not raise her offer. Mike, feeling a bit guilty, told Sally that on Tuesday when he got the Mickey Mouse watch, he would no longer need his current watch and would give it to Sally. The next day Jill sold her watch to Mike. Mike, however, had a change of heart and refused to give his old watch to Sally. Sally is understandably upset by the turn of events. Does she have any legal rights against either Jill or Mike?

Sometimes in analyzing contract situations it is helpful to diagram them. The arrow indicates something of value passing from one party to the other.

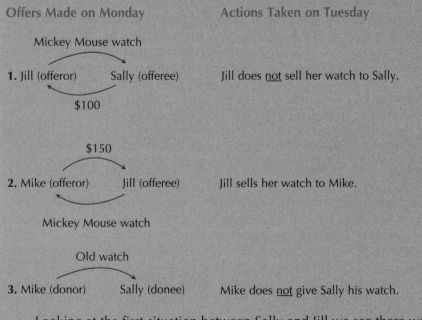

Offers Made on Monday	Actions Taken on Tuesday

Mickey Mouse watch

1. Jill (offeror)   Sally (offeree)   Jill does <u>not</u> sell her watch to Sally.

$100

$150

2. Mike (offeror)   Jill (offeree)   Jill sells her watch to Mike.

Mickey Mouse watch

Old watch

3. Mike (donor)   Sally (donee)   Mike does <u>not</u> give Sally his watch.

Looking at the first situation between Sally and Jill we see there was an agreement to exchange something of value. Recall that to form a binding contract, there must be an agreement to sell (Jill said she would sell the watch for $100 [an offer] and Sally said, "I agree" [an acceptance]); also, something of value must be exchanged (Sally was going to give $100 in return for the Mickey Mouse watch). Therefore, Sally and Jill had a binding contract. By selling the watch to someone else Jill is in breach of contract. Sally is entitled to the benefit of her bargain. However, it is unlikely that the court would order Jill to sell the watch to Sally. Such an order for specific performance occurs only when the item is unique. Instead Sally would be entitled to money damages. In this case she can purchase a similar watch, and if it costs more than the $100 she had agreed to spend, she can recover that difference.

The second situation illustrates a fully executed contract. Mike made an offer, Jill accepted, and they agreed to exchange something of value. A binding contract was formed. Then when they fulfilled their promises, the contract was fully executed.

In the third situation, involving Sally and Mike, there was no contract. Sally did not agree to exchange anything with Mike. Mike simply offered to give Sally his old watch. For a gift to be complete, however, delivery must occur. Because Mike never handed Sally the watch, there was no completed gift, and Sally has no rights to Mike's watch.

The courts treat these situations so differently because in a contract negotiation *both* parties give up something of value. In the second situation, however, the transaction is one-sided. Because gift givers receive nothing in return, they should be allowed time to reconsider up until actual delivery. The delivery then provides proof that there was intent for a gift to occur.

1. Offer and Acceptance

In order for a valid contract to be formed, there must be mutual agreement to create a legally binding relationship. Whether there is a valid offer and acceptance is determined by the objective theory of contract. An objective theory means that the parties' intent is determined by whether an outside observer could discern a serious intent to be bound. A subjective theory would ask what the parties actually intended. Therefore, the objective theory calls for a review of what was said, how the offeror acted, and the circumstances rather than of what the parties claim they were thinking at the time.

a. Offer

An offer is a promise to do something—for example, to sell a product or provide a service—that is conditioned on the other party's promising to do something in return—for example, to pay money or provide some other type of goods or services. The offer sets the parameters of the agreement and gives the other party the power to bind them to a contract.

Sometimes it may be difficult, however, to determine whether a statement really was an offer. For example, it could merely have been an expression of an intention to enter into further negotiations. In other circumstances a person making the statement might argue that the alleged offer was intended as a joke rather than as a serious offer. In all situations, for an offer to be valid, it must be obvious to an outside observer that the offeror meant to be bound.

In addition, the terms of the offer must be sufficiently definite so that a court can fashion a remedy. To be definite, the offer must contain at least the following four items:

1. the parties,
2. the subject matter of the contract,
3. the price, and
4. the time for performance.

When the time for performance is very important to the parties, as in the case of the sale of perishable fruit, then the time for performance may be stated along with the phrase "time is of the essence."

Finally, and perhaps obviously, the offer must be communicated to the offeree. Usually, this last requirement does not present any problems except in the case of rewards. Some courts have held that if a person fulfills the terms of a reward—for example, returning a lost dog to its owner—without knowing beforehand of the reward, that person cannot claim the reward, as it was never communicated to him or her.

(1) Statements of intent and preliminary negotiations

Problems can arise if the offeror uses words that indicate an intention to begin negotiations but no intention to be bound. For example, assume Sam says, "I am thinking of selling my car. What would you give me for it?" If John replies, "I will give you $750 for it," Sam has made only a statement of intent, not an offer. John's reply is the offer, and it is up to Sam whether he wants to accept or not. When an offeror asks, "Will you buy?" or says, "I plan to sell," this also gives rise to the inference that the offeror was only beginning the process of negotiation but was not yet ready to be bound by the statements. Review the facts set out in the following Legal Reasoning Exercise. Pay special attention to whether the letter sent should be seen as an offer or merely as an invitation to bid.

Legal Reasoning Exercise

1. Emma Johnson was the owner of two parcels of land. On March 27 Ms. Johnson's son-in-law, Edward Hicks, who was her agent to sell the property, wrote the following letter to James Mellen.

You will perhaps remember that we spent a pleasant visit on the breakwater at Nahant last summer. On that occasion either you or your brother-in-law expressed an interest in my Mother's property which is the Johnson cottage. . . . [Mother's] health is such that she will not be able to open the cottage this year. She has, therefore, decided that it will be best to place the property on the market; however, before turning it over to the real estate agents, I am writing to several people, including yourself, who have previously expressed an interest in the property. Our price is $7,500. This property consists of the lot and cottage on the south side of Willow Road, and also a very large plot on which a two-car garage is situated running from Willow Road clear through the block to the next street. Just how much property there is in this tract, I cannot tell you at the moment. . . . I will be interested in hearing from you further if you have any interest in this property, for as I said before, I am advising those who have asked for an opportunity to consider it. I might just add that the property would be available for immediate occupancy. By that I mean within such time as the present furnishings could be removed and title transferred.

On March 28 Mr. Hicks received a telegram from Mr. Mellon's brother-in-law that read:

We are interested in your offer. Will look at house tomorrow. Communicate with you first of week.

On the same day shortly after the telegram was received, Mr. Hicks telegraphed Mr. Mellon:

Have heard from three interested buyers tonight which means we must accept highest bid for Nahant property. Suggest you wire or phone us Elmsford N.Y. 7292 Saturday your best offer on cash basis.

Before this was received, Mr. Mellon telegraphed Mr. Hicks:

I accept your offer on Nahant cottage. Letter in mail.

When Mr. Hicks entered into a written contract to sell the property to someone else, Mr. Mellon sued to stop the sale from being completed.

   a. Do you think an offer was ever made? Why?
   b. Do you think Mr. Mellon's suit was successful? Why?

(2) Terms definite

The courts require that the basic contract terms be definite not only as a basis on which they can fashion a remedy but also as evidence that a bargain was truly struck. For example, assume Sam says, "I want to sell my car," and John replies, "Done!" There is no contract. How can either Sam or John be bound if neither knows the price? Similarly, ads are usually not viewed as offers because their terms are too indefinite to constitute an offer. The following case, however, presents an interesting exception to that rule. As you read the case, look for what differentiated this ad from the usual ad.

Lefkowitz v. Great Minneapolis Surplus Store, Inc.
251 Minn. 188, 86 N.W.2d 689 (1957)

This case grows out of the alleged refusal of the defendant to sell to the plaintiff a certain fur piece which it had offered for sale in a newspaper advertisement. It appears from the record that on April 6, 1956, the defendant published the following advertisement in a Minneapolis newspaper:

"Saturday 9 A.M. sharp
3 Brand New
Fur Coats
Worth to $100.00
First Come
First Served
$1
Each"

On April 13, the defendant again published an advertisement in the same newspaper as follows:

"Saturday 9 A.M.
2 Brand New Pastel
Mink 3-Skin Scarfs
Selling for $89.50
Out they go
Saturday. Each $1.00
1 Black Lapin Stole
Beautiful,
worth $139.50 $1.00
First Come
First Served"

The record supports the findings of the court that on each of the Saturdays following the publication of the above-described ads the plaintiff was the first to present himself at the appropriate counter in the defendant's store and on each occasion demanded the coat and the stole so advertised and indicated his readiness to pay the sale price of $1. On both occasions, the defendant refused to sell the merchandise to the plaintiff, stating on the first occasion that by a "house rule" the offer was intended for women only and sales would not be made to men, and on the second visit that plaintiff knew defendant's house rules.

The trial court properly disallowed plaintiff's claim for the value of the fur coats since the value of these articles was speculative and uncertain. The only evidence of value was the advertisement itself to the effect that the coats were "Worth to $100.00," how much less being speculative especially in view of the price for which they were offered for sale. With reference to the offer of the defendant on April 13, 1956, to sell the "1 Black Lapin Stole . . . worth $139.50 . . ." the trial court held that the value of this article was established and granted judgment in favor of the plaintiff for that amount less the $1 quoted purchase price.

1. The defendant contends that a newspaper advertisement offering items of merchandise for sale at a named price is a "unilateral offer" which may be withdrawn without notice. He relies upon authorities which hold that . . . such advertisements are not offers which become contracts as soon as any person to whose notice they may come signifies his acceptance. . . . Such advertisements have been construed as an invitation for an offer of sale on the terms stated, which offer, when received, may be accepted or rejected and which therefore does not become a contract of sale until accepted by the seller; and until a contract has been so made, the seller may modify or revoke such prices or terms. . . .

The test of whether a binding obligation may originate in advertisements addressed to the general public is "whether the facts show that some performance was promised in positive terms in return for something requested." 1 Williston, Contracts (Rev. ed.) § 27.

The authorities above cited emphasize that, where the offer is clear, definite, and explicit, and leaves nothing open for negotiation, it constitutes an offer, acceptance of which will complete the contract. . . .

Whether in any individual instance a newspaper advertisement is an offer rather than an invitation to make an offer depends on the legal intention of the parties and the surrounding circumstances. We are of the view on the facts before us that the offer by the defendant of the sale of the Lapin fur was clear, definite, and explicit, and left nothing open for negotiation. The plaintiff having successfully managed to be the first one to appear at the seller's place of business to be served, as requested by the advertisement, and having offered the stated purchase price of the article, he was entitled to performance on the part of the defendant. We think the trial court was correct in holding that there was in the conduct of the parties a sufficient mutuality of obligation to constitute a contract of sale.

2. The defendant contends that the offer was modified by a "house rule" to the effect that only women were qualified to receive the bargains advertised. The advertisement contained no such restriction. This objection may be disposed of briefly by stating that, while an advertiser has the right at any time before acceptance to modify his offer, he does not have the right, after acceptance, to impose new or arbitrary conditions not contained in the published offer.

Affirmed.

CASE DISCUSSION QUESTIONS

1. Why did the court hold that in this case there was a binding contract for the black lapin stole?

2. Why was there no binding contract for the fur coats?

3. On the plaintiff's first visit the store informed him of its "house rule" limiting the offer to women. Why didn't the court find that term to be part of the second offer?

The *Lefkowitz* case is an example of an ad that fulfilled all the requirements for a valid contract by including the four basic terms: (1) the parties; (2) the subject matter of the contract, especially quantity; (3) the price; and (4) the time for performance. Traditionally, when any of these terms is missing, the courts have refused to find a binding contract. For example, assume Sara states to Judy, "I would like to purchase some TV's from you," and Judy says, "Agreed." If Judy then sells Sara only two TV's, a court would have no basis for deciding if Judy has breached their agreement. "Some TV's" is simply too indefinite.

The UCC has made some major changes in this area of the law. Under the UCC a contract can be formed even if there are missing terms. The missing terms are supplied by the UCC itself. For example, a missing price term becomes a reasonable price. UCC § 2-305(1). If time and place of payment are left out, payment is due at the time and place where the buyer is to receive the goods. UCC § 2-310(a). If the delivery term is left open, it is to be the seller's place of business. UCC § 2-308(a). However, if too many terms are missing, this may show that the parties were still only in the preliminary negotiation stage. In that situation the court will not force a contract on the parties. In addition, quantity must always be included in the contract. Therefore, in the example given above even the UCC could not help Sara. With the quantity term missing there is no way of knowing whether Judy was in breach.

There is one exception when a missing quantity term is not fatal: requirements and output contracts. When a buyer agrees to buy all of a commodity that he requires from a specific seller or a seller agrees to sell all of her output to a particular buyer, a requirements or an output contract has been created. UCC § 2-306(1). Even though the quantity is not stated in the contract, it can be determined by the court. A **requirements contract** means the buyer's actual requirements, not just what it ordered, and an **output contract** means the seller's actual output. Therefore, the quantity is based on an objective standard, enforceable by the court.

Requirements contract
A contract in which one party agrees to buy all its requirements for a particular product from the other party.

Output contract
A contract in which one party agrees to deliver its entire output of a particular product to the other party.

Figure 11-4 Termination of an Offer

- By offeror's revocation Unless option contract or merchant's firm offer
- By offeree's rejection or counteroffer
- By operation of law

(3) Termination of an offer

An offer can be terminated in one of three ways: by the offeror's actions, by the offeree's actions, or by operation of law. See Figure 11-4. First, normally the offeror can revoke the offer by words or acts if done before acceptance. In some cases this notice of revocation can be indirect, such as by selling the item to a third party. A revocation terminates the offer as soon as the offeree learns of it.

An exception is the **option contract.** In an option contract the potential buyer gives the seller consideration, usually money, to keep the offer open for a stated time period. This creates a separate contract between the potential buyer and seller. The buyer gives the seller consideration for keeping the offer open. If during that time period the seller sells the product to someone else, the seller is in breach of contract.

In addition to the option contract, the UCC provides for a **merchant's firm offer.** A merchant can make an offer that is irrevocable for a reasonable time, even without the requirement of additional consideration. For such a firm offer to occur, the following requirements have to be met:

1. The offer has to be made by a merchant
2. in a signed writing
3. that assures the buyer that the offer will remain open for a specific period of time or, if no time is stated, for a reasonable time.

If these requirements are met, then the merchant must keep the offer open even though the buyer has not paid any consideration for the arrangement. UCC § 2-205.

Second, the offeree can terminate the offer by rejecting it or by changing the terms of the bargain by attempting to add new or different terms. Instead of an acceptance, such an attempt to vary the terms is seen as a rejection of the offer and a counteroffer. This allows the original offeror the chance to accept or reject it. This requirement that the acceptance completely agree with the terms of the offer is known as the **mirror image rule.** That rule and its exceptions under the UCC are discussed more fully in the next section on Acceptance.

Third, offers can be terminated by operation of law. By operation of law we simply mean that certain events will make it impossible for the offeree to accept the offer. These include lapse of time, destruction of the subject matter, death of one of the parties, and supervening illegality. As to lapse of time, frequently the offer includes a specific time frame within which the other party must reach a decision about accepting or rejecting the offer. If the other party has not accepted it by that date, it is automatically withdrawn. If no specific time limit is established, it is assumed to be valid for a reasonable period of time. As you would expect, that phrase is open to interpretation and will vary depending on the circumstances. For example, if Sam offers to sell John his car in a face-to-face meeting, a reasonable time might last only until the end of that meeting. However, if Sam and John live in different states and Sam makes his offer by mailing John a letter, a reasonable time might be at least as long as it would take John to receive the letter and mail his reply.

b. Acceptance

Once an offer is made, it is up to the other party to accept, reject, or propose a counteroffer. Earlier we saw that in a bilateral contract situation the offer invites acceptance by the offeree giving a return promise and that in a unilateral contract the offer invites acceptance only by the offeree doing the act itself. In commercial dealings, however, if the offeror indicates that either a promise to act or the action itself will suffice, then when either the promise is made or a substantial start is made on the act, the contract is formed. The UCC explicitly states that an offer can be accepted either by sending notification of such acceptance or by performing the act requested. If Alice offers to pay Bruce

---

Option contract
A contract in which the buyer gives the seller consideration to keep the offer open for a stated period of time.

Merchant's firm offer
An offer made by a merchant in a signed writing that assures the buyer the offer will remain open for a specific period of time. It does not require consideration to be binding.

Mirror image rule
The requirement that the acceptance exactly mirror the offer or the acceptance will be viewed as a counter-offer.

$10 for Bruce's bicycle, Bruce's acceptance can take the form of making a telephone call stating that he will sell her the bicycle or by delivering the bicycle to her. UCC § 2-206(b).

If the offeree decides to accept, then the mirror image rule requires that the acceptance exactly mirror the offer. The offeree cannot add new terms or vary the original terms. If he or she attempts to do so, the acceptance becomes a counteroffer. A counteroffer takes away the power of the offeree to then accept the original offer. For example, if Johns states, "I accept; please send a written contract," then there is an acceptance. However, if John says, "I accept if you send a written contract," then there is no acceptance because John has added an additional term to the contract. A mere inquiry as to the possibility of changing the terms usually will not be seen as a counteroffer. Here again the exact language used can be determinative of whether there was a counteroffer. If Sam offers to sell John his guitar for $200 and John replies, "I will give you $150 for the guitar," that is a counteroffer. If, however, John replies, "Would you consider $150?" that will probably not be seen as a counteroffer, and if Sam says no, John still has the power to accept the original offer.

The UCC has made some major changes to this mirror image rule. Basically the UCC states that if the parties intend to make a contract, then the use of additional or different terms in the acceptance will not prevent the contract from being formed. This provision recognizes that often the parties will assume they have made a contract and will act on that assumption even if the offer and acceptance do not match in every detail. It was also included in response to what is known as the "battle of the forms." In commercial dealings it is usual for both buyers and sellers to use their own preprinted forms, with blanks left to fill in the essential terms, such as quantity and price. These forms also often include a great deal of boilerplate language regarding other terms, such as whether in the case of a dispute the matter is to be sent to arbitration. However, because this provision essentially states that a contract will be found, even though the parties disagree as to some of the terms, it has given the courts some difficult problems of interpretation. Generally, the new terms are viewed as suggestions for addition to the contract. Between merchants they become a part of a contract unless the original offer limited acceptance to its terms, the new terms "materially alter" the contract, or the offeror objects to the terms. However, there will be no contract if the acceptance states that the offeror must agree to the new terms. UCC § 2-207.

Legal Reasoning Exercise

2. UCC § 2-207 provides as follows:

(1) A definite and seasonable expression of acceptance or a written confirmation which is sent within a reasonable time operates as an acceptance even though it states terms additional to or different from those offered or agreed upon, unless acceptance is expressly made conditional on assent to the additional or different terms.

(2) The additional terms are to be construed as proposals for addition to the contract. Between merchants such terms become part of the contract unless:

(a) the offer expressly limits acceptance to the terms of the offer;

(b) they materially alter it; or

(c) notification of objection to them has already been given or is given within a reasonable time after notice of them is received.

Please evaluate each of the following situations and determine whether a contract exists and, if so, what its terms are.

a. Value City, a Georgia retailer, sends an order form to RCV, a Mississippi manufacturer, ordering 100 televisions at $200 each. On the back of the form in fine print is the following:

> Seller expressly warrants that the goods are fit for the ordinary purposes for which they are sold. Seller shall assume all costs of shipping.

RCV sends back an acknowledgment form. On the back of the form in small print is the following:

> All disputes arising out of the agreement must be submitted to binding arbitration.

b. Value City, a Georgia retailer, sends an order form to RCV, a Mississippi manufacturer, ordering 100 televisions at $200 each. On the back of the form in fine print is the following:

> Seller shall assume all costs of shipping.

RCV sends back an acknowledgment form. On the back of the form in small print is the following:

> All goods are sold "as is" with no warranties of any kind.

c. Value City, a Georgia retailer, sends an order form to RCV, a Mississippi manufacturer, ordering 100 televisions at $200 each. On the back of the form in fine print is the following:

> Seller expressly warrants that the goods are fit for the ordinary purposes for which they are sold. Seller shall assume all costs of shipping.

RCV sends back an acknowledgment form. On the back of the form in small print is the following:

> All goods are sold "as is" with no warranties of any kind.
> Buyer shall assume all costs of shipping.

c. Quasi-Contract

Quasi means "as if." Therefore, a **quasi-contract** is not a real contract, but the situation is treated "as if" there was one. Usually, a quasi-contract situation arises when there is no agreement, but in order to avoid unjust enrichment, the

Quasi-contract
Although no contract was formed, the courts will fashion an equitable remedy to avoid unjust enrichment.

court orders the party that benefited to pay. For example, in an emergency an injured party might not be able to ask for assistance. Therefore, there could be no agreement between the injured person and the doctor. However, once the doctor gives medical aid, it would be unjust to let the patient benefit without compensating the doctor. This is an example of a court using its equitable powers to do what it views as fair in order to avoid allowing one side to be unjustly enriched.

DISCUSSION QUESTION

2. Much of contract law is based on the theory of freedom of contract; that is, the parties are free to create their own contract terms as they, and not the court, choose. How can you reconcile the courts' equitable power to find a quasi-contract when no contract exists with the notion of freedom of contract?

2. Consideration

Consideration

Anything of value; it must be present for a valid contract to exist, and each side must give consideration.

Consideration must be present for a valid contract to exist. Each party must give something of value as part of the bargain. It can be money, services, goods, or anything else that is a benefit to one party or a detriment to the other. The key is that something of real value has to be exchanged by both parties. In other words, a contract must be distinguished from a gift. When a person promises to give something without expecting to receive anything in return, that promise does not constitute an enforceable contract.

At times it may appear as though something of value has been exchanged when in actuality it has not. For example, if someone promises to hire you and pay you "what you are worth," the phrase is so vague as to make the promise illusory. In addition, if someone makes a promise because he or she feels morally obligated to do so but receives nothing else in return, there is no consideration. For example, assume Julie is friends with Martha. Martha feels ill but does not have a doctor. Julie takes Martha to her doctor. Once Martha is cured, she refuses to pay the doctor bill. Julie may feel morally obligated to pay the bill because she took Martha to the doctor, but she is under no contractual obligation to do so.

Also, past consideration will not support a contract. Assume I volunteer to take care of your cat while you are away on vacation. When you return, if you are very pleased with the job I have done and offer to pay me for my services, no contract has been formed. I have already done my job, and there is no new consideration for me to give in return for your promise. Finally, if someone is under a preexisting duty to act, performing that duty cannot serve as the consideration for a new contract. If your house is on fire and you offer a firefighter $2,000 to put out the fire, you will be under no obligation to pay the money. The fire fighter is already under a preexisting duty to put out the fire.

a. Detriment to Promisee or Benefit to Promisor

Both parties must exchange something of value to ensure that the promise is not illusory and that it was bargained for. Whatever is exchanged has to be detrimental to the party giving it up *or* beneficial to the party receiving it. It need not be both. In the following case ask yourself whether the uncle meant to give his nephew a gift or to be bound to a contractual arrangement.

Hamer v. Sidway
124 N.Y. 538, 27 N.E. 256 (1891)

SYLLABUS:

The plaintiff presented a claim to the executor of William E. Story, Sr., for $5,000 and interest from the 6th day of February, 1875. . . . The claim being rejected by the executor, this action was brought. It appears that William E. Story, Sr., was the uncle of William E. Story, 2d; that at the celebration of the golden wedding of Samuel Story and wife, father and mother of William E. Story, Sr., on the 20th day of March, 1869, in the presence of the family and invited guests he promised his nephew that if he would refrain from drinking, using tobacco, swearing and playing cards or billiards for money until he became twenty-one years of age he would pay him a sum of $5,000. The nephew assented thereto and fully performed the conditions inducing the promise. When the nephew arrived at the age of twenty-one years and on the 31st day of January, 1875, he wrote to his uncle informing him that he had performed his part of the agreement and had thereby become entitled to the sum of $5,000. The uncle received the letter and a few days later and on the sixth of February, he wrote and mailed to his nephew the following letter:

"Buffalo, Feb. 6, 1875." W.E. Story, Jr.:
"Dear Nephew—Your letter of the 31st ult. came to hand all right, saying that you had lived up to the promise made to me several years ago. I have no doubt but you have, for which you shall have five thousand dollars as I promised you. I had the money in the bank the day you was 21 years old that I intend for you, and you shall have the money certain. Now, Willie I do not intend to interfere with this money in any way till I think you are capable of taking care of it and the sooner that time comes the better it will please me. I would hate very much to have you start out in some adventure that you thought all right and lose this money in one year. The first five thousand dollars that I got together cost me a heap of hard work. . . . This money you have earned much easier than I did besides acquiring good habits at the same time and you are quite welcome to the money; hope

you will make good use of it. . . . To-day is the seventeenth day that I have not been out of my room, and have had the doctor as many days. Am a little better to-day; think I will get out next week. You need not mention to father, as he always worries about small matters.

Truly Yours,

"W.E. STORY.

"P.S.—You can consider this money on interest."

The nephew received the letter and thereafter consented that the money should remain with his uncle in accordance with the terms and conditions of the letters. The uncle died on the 29th day of January, 1887, without having paid over to his nephew any portion of the said $5,000 and interest.

OPINION: The question which provoked the most discussion by counsel on this appeal, and which lies at the foundation of plaintiff's asserted right of recovery, is whether by virtue of a contract defendant's testator William E. Story became indebted to his nephew William E. Story, 2d, on his twenty-first birthday in the sum of five thousand dollars. . . .

The defendant contends that the contract was without consideration to support it, and, therefore, invalid. He asserts that the promise by refraining from the use of liquor and tobacco was not harmed but benefited; that that which he did was best for him to do independently of his uncle's promise, and insists that it follows that unless the promisor was benefited, the contract was without consideration. A contention, which if well founded, would seem to leave open for controversy in many cases whether that which the promisee did or omitted to do was, in fact, of such benefit to him as to leave no consideration to support the enforcement of the promisor's agreement. Such a rule could not be tolerated, and is without foundation in the law. The

Exchequer Chamber, in 1875, defined consideration as follows: "A valuable consideration in the sense of the law may consist either in some right, interest, profit or benefit accruing to the one party, or some forbearance, detriment, loss or responsibility given, suffered or undertaken by the other." Courts "will not ask whether the thing which forms the consideration does in fact benefit the promisee or a third party, or is of any substantial value to anyone. It is enough that something is promised, done, forborne or suffered by the party to whom the promise is made as consideration for the promise made to him." (Anson's Prin. of Con. 63.) . . .

Pollock, in his work on contracts, page 166, after citing the definition given by the Exchequer Chamber already quoted, says: "The second branch of this judicial description is really the most important one. Consideration means not so much that one party is profiting as that the other abandons some legal right in the present or limits his legal freedom of action in the future as an inducement for the promise of the first."

Now, applying this rule to the facts before us, the promisee used tobacco, occasionally drank liquor, and he had a legal right to do so. That right he abandoned for a period of years upon the strength of the promise of the testator that for such forbearance he would give him $5,000. We need not speculate on the effort which may have been required to give up the use of those stimulants. It is sufficient that he restricted his lawful freedom of action within certain prescribed limits upon the faith of his uncle's agreement, and now having fully performed the conditions imposed, it is of no moment whether such performance actually proved a benefit to the promisor, and the court will not inquire into it, but were it a proper subject of inquiry, we see nothing in this record that would permit a determination that the uncle was not benefited in a legal sense. . . .

The order appealed from should be reversed and the judgment of the Special Term affirmed, with costs payable out of the estate.

CASE DISCUSSION QUESTIONS

1. Why didn't the court simply view the uncle's offer to pay his nephew $5,000 as a gift?

2. If the court had decided it was a gift instead of a contract situation, how would that have changed the result?

b. Problems with Consideration

Generally, the court will not look into the adequacy of the consideration. Simply put, the court does not care if you made a poor bargain. The philosophy behind freedom of contract is that you are free to make any bargain you like, even a bad one. In addition, if people could sue to get out of their contractual obligations every time it turned out they had made a poor bargain, the courts would be flooded with lawsuits. Finally, the security of being able to rely on contractual performance would be gone.

Unconscionable contract

A contract formed between parties of very unequal bargaining power where the terms are so unfair as to "shock the conscience."

Traditionally, courts would look at the adequacy of the consideration only if it was so inadequate as to raise a question, first, as to whether some factor such as undue influence or duress was affecting one of the parties or, second, as to whether the situation was actually one of a gift masquerading as a contract. In recent years the courts have also questioned the adequacy of the consideration in those situations where the parties are of very uneven bargaining power, and the bargain is so unfair as to "shock the conscience." For example, if a poor, illiterate person were to purchase a $300 freezer, agreeing to pay 24 monthly installments of $50 each, the seller would net a $900 profit (24 × $50 = $1,200 − $300 = $900). The court might declare this an **unconscionable contract** and refuse to enforce it.

The normal rule, however, is that a court will not invalidate a contract because one party turns out to have made a bad bargain. Nor will the court allow the parties to renegotiate the terms of the contract, unless there is new consideration given on both sides, because of the preexisting duty rule mentioned earlier. Parties typically want to renegotiate the terms of their contract when unforeseen difficulties arise before the contract is completed. The first hurdle is to convince the court that the unforeseen difficulties were truly unforeseen rather than the normal types of risks that should have been part of the original contract negotiations. Even if the other party agrees to a change in the terms of the contract, it is often unclear why that party agreed. It is possible that that party also thought the changes in circumstances were unforeseeable and justified the change. However, it is also possible that that party had no choice and was effectively being "held up" by the party wanting the change. For example, assume Harry hired William to build his house. Halfway through shingling the roof William refused to continue work unless Harry agreed to increase the price by $5,000. A major storm was approaching, and if the roof was not finished that day, the house would be severely damaged. Assume Harry agreed to the increase but then later refused to pay it. The court would have to determine whether the storm was an unforeseen circumstance necessitating extra work on William's part and thereby justifying the increase or whether it was just the sort of circumstance that William should have foreseen. If the latter is true, then he was already under a duty to finish the house at the agreed-on price, and the homeowner would not be required to pay the additional $5,000. In the following case, the court took the very firm position that there can be no change in a contract without new consideration.

Alaska Packers' Association v. Domenico
117 F. 99 (9th Cir. 1902)

Ross, Circuit Judge. . . . On March 26, 1900, at the city and county of San Francisco, the libelants entered into a written contract with the appellant, whereby they agreed to go from San Francisco to Pyramid Harbor, Alaska, and return, on board such vessel as might be designated by the appellant, and to work for the appellant during the fishing season of 1900, at Pyramid Harbor, as sailors and fishermen, agreeing to do "regular ship's duty, both up and down, discharging and loading; and to do any other work whatsoever when requested to do so by the captain or agent of the Alaska Packers' Association." By the terms of this agreement, the appellant was to pay each of the libelants $50 for the season, and two cents for each red salmon in the catching of which he took part.

On the 15th day of April, 1900, 21 of the libelants signed shipping articles by which they shipped as seaman on the Two Brothers, a vessel chartered by the appellant for the voyage between San Francisco and Pyramid Harbor, and also bound themselves to perform the same work for the appellant provided for by the previous contract of March 26th; the appellant agreeing to pay them therefor the sum of $60 for the season, and two cents each for each red salmon in the catching of which they should respectively take part. Under these contracts, the libelants sailed on board the Two Brothers for Pyramid Harbor, where the appellant had about $150,000 invested in a salmon cannery. The libelants arrived there early in April of the year mentioned, and began to unload the vessel and fit up the cannery. A few days thereafter, to wit, May 19th, they stopped work in a body, and demanded of the company's superintendent there in charge $100 for services in operating the vessel to and from Pyramid Harbor, instead of the sums stipulated for in and by the contracts; stating that unless they were paid this additional wage they would stop work entirely, and return to San Francisco. The evidence showed, and the court below found, that it was impossible for the appellant to get other men to take the places of the libelants, the place being remote, the season short and just opening; so that, after endeavoring for several days without success to induce the libelants to proceed with their work in accordance with their contracts, the company's superintendent, on the 22nd day of May, so far yielded to their demands as to instruct his clerk to copy the contracts executed in San Francisco, including the words "Alaska Packers' Association" at the end, substituting, for the $50 and $60 payments, respectively, of those contracts, the sum of $100, which document, so prepared, was signed by the libelants. . . .

The real questions in the case as brought here are questions of law, and, in the view that we take of the case, it will be necessary to consider but one of those. Assuming that the appellant's superintendent at Pyramid Harbor was authorized to make the alleged contract of May 22nd, and that he executed it on behalf of the appellant, was it supported by a sufficient consideration? From the foregoing statement of the case, it will have been seen that the libelants agreed in writing, for certain stated compensation, to render their services to the appellant in remote waters where the season for conducting fishing operations is extremely short, and in which enterprise the appellant had a large amount of money invested; and, after having entered upon the discharge of their contract, and at a time when it was impossible for the appellant to secure other men in their places, the libelants, without any valid cause, absolutely refused to continue the services they were under contract to perform unless the appellant would consent to pay them more money. Consent to such a demand, under such circumstances, if given, was, in our opinion, without consideration, for the reason that it was based solely upon the libelants' agreement to render the exact services, and none other, that they were already under contract to render. The case shows that they willfully and arbitrarily broke that obligation. . . . The circumstances of the present case bring it, we think, directly within the sound and just observations of the supreme court of Minnesota in the case of *King v. Railway Co.*, 61 Minn. 482, 63 N.W. 1105:

> No astute reasoning can change the plain fact that the party who refuses to perform, and thereby coerces a promise from the other party to the contract to pay him an increased compensation for doing that which he is legally bound to do, takes an unjustifiable advantage of the necessities of the other party. Surely it would be a travesty on justice to hold that the party so making the promise for extra pay was estopped from asserting that the promise was without consideration. A party cannot lay the foundation of an estoppel by his own wrong, where the promise is simply a repetition of a subsisting legal promise. There can be no consideration for the promise of the other party, and there is no warrant for inferring that the parties have voluntarily rescinded or modified their contract. The promise cannot be legally enforced, although the other party has completed his contract in reliance upon it.

. . . It results from the views above expressed that the judgment must be reversed, and the cause remanded, with directions to the court below to enter judgment for the respondent, with costs. It is so ordered.

CASE DISCUSSION QUESTIONS

1. What does this court say is the rule about allowing a modification of a contract with no new consideration? Why does the court think that is the only just result?

2. How do you reconcile this decision with the notion of freedom of contract? That is, shouldn't the parties be free to change the terms of their contract at any time?

3. Can you think of any circumstances when it would be fair to allow the parties to modify their contract without new consideration?

Note: Once again the UCC has changed one of the common law rules. Under the UCC, merchants can modify a contract with no new consideration being given. UCC § 2-209(1).

c. Promissory Estoppel

Sometimes people rely on promises to their detriment, but they cannot sue for breach of contract because while promises were made, they were not definite enough to amount to consideration. Nonetheless, some courts think it would be unfair not to compensate the person who relied on the promise. In that situation the promisor is estopped, or prevented, from revoking his promise. This is known as **promissory estoppel** or detrimental reliance. For the courts to find a case of promissory estoppel:

1. a promise must be made with the intent to induce action,
2. it must do so, and
3. the court must believe that it would be unjust not to enforce the promise.

Promissory estoppel Occurs when the courts allow detrimental reliance to substitute for consideration.

Assume an elderly relative induces you to give up your job in order to care for her with the promise of being remembered in her will. Her promise would not fulfill the requirements of valid consideration, as her promise of remembering you in her will is too indefinite to be enforceable. If, however, you give up your job and care for your relative for a number of years, the court might view your detrimental reliance on her promise as a substitute for consideration and enforce her promise to pay.

The Wisconsin Supreme Court was one of the first to adopt the theory of promissory estoppel as an alternative to a breach of contract action. In the case of *Hoffman v. Red Owl Stores, Inc.,*[1] Mr. Hoffman and his wife engaged in extensive negotiations with agents of the Red Owl grocery store chain in an attempt to obtain a Red Owl franchise, only to "have the rug pulled out from under them." The agents had originally promised the Hoffmans that for $18,000 they could establish a store. The figure was then changed to $24,100. Relying on further promises that the deal was about to go through and at the urging of the Red Owl representatives, Mr. Hoffman sold his own grocery store to raise the necessary money. While waiting to be placed in his new store, he began working the night shift at a local bakery. Finally, the Red Owl representatives said it would take $34,000 to close the deal. At that point Mr. Hoffman informed them that he could not afford to go through with the proposal. Mr. Hoffman

---

[1] 133 N.W.2d 267 (Wis. 1965).

then sued Red Owl for the damages he had incurred in relying on the promises of its representatives.

Because the negotiations had never gotten far enough for the parties to establish the precise terms of the contract, such as the size, layout, and design of the store, Mr. Hoffman was not able to sue on a breach of contract theory. He also could not sue for fraud. There was no evidence that the Red Owl representatives intended to misrepresent the facts. Relying instead on the doctrine of promissory estoppel, the court stated that each of the following questions must be answered in the affirmative:

> (1) Was the promise one which the promisor should reasonably expect to induce action or forbearance of a definite and substantial character on the part of the promisee? (2) Did the promise induce such action or forbearance? (3) Can injustice be avoided only by enforcement of the promise?[2]

The court noted that the first two questions are issues of fact for the jury to decide. The third question, however, involves a policy decision that must be made by the court. In the Hoffmans' case the court concluded that "injustice would result here if plaintiffs were not granted some relief because of the failure of defendants to keep their promises which induced plaintiffs to act to their detriment."[3]

D. DEFENSES TO A VALID CONTRACT

In addition to offer, acceptance, and consideration, you will sometimes hear that contractual capacity, legality, and genuineness of assent are necessary elements for a valid contract to be formed. While this is true, in this text we will treat these last three elements as defenses. Generally, it is assumed that those elements are present so the plaintiff has no obligation to allege their existence in the complaint. Rather it is incumbent on the defendant to raise their absence in the answer. First, the defendant can argue that one or both of the parties lacked contractual capacity. Second, the defendant can contend that the contract should not be enforced because it is illegal or because it violates public policy. Third, the defendant can assert that there was no true genuineness of assent because of fraud, mistake, or undue influence. Fourth, the defendant may argue that he or she owes nothing on a contract for sale because the product was defective in violation of the seller's warranties. Finally, at times the defendant may be able to show that the proper format was not followed, as, for example, with some contracts that must be in writing.

1. Lack of Contractual Capacity

The parties to a contract can be either people or corporations. However, an individual may be considered incapable of contracting if that person is a child, is mentally retarded or mentally ill, or is under the influence of drugs or alcohol.

---

[2]Id. at 275.
[3]Id.

a. Minors

If one of the parties is a minor, the contract may be **voidable.** Therefore, the terms of the contract are enforceable against the adult party to the contract but not against the minor party. Under the common law one had to be at least twenty-one years old in order to enter into binding contracts, but today many states have established a lower age limit.

Minors can **disaffirm** a contract and thereby avoid any contractual liability at any time during their minority or for a reasonable time thereafter. If the contract involves the sale of goods, in a majority of states the minor must return the goods, but the minor does not have to fulfill the terms of the contract, even if the goods are damaged. In a minority of states the minor must act so as to return the other party to his or her position prior to the contract. Even if a minor misrepresents his or her age, in a majority of states the minor can still disaffirm the contract. The one exception is that minors are liable for **necessaries.** Although they can disaffirm the contract, they must pay the reasonable value of the goods or services they received. Housing, food, and clothing are commonly classified as necessaries. However, what is "necessary" can vary with the circumstances. For example, in one case a court held that a lease for an apartment was not necessary because the minor tenants were able to return home to their parents at any time.[4]

Once minors reach the age of majority, they can ratify the contract, thereby binding themselves to the terms of the contract. This can occur by the minor expressly stating that he or she wishes to be bound, by the minor's conduct, or by operation of law after a reasonable time has passed once the minor is of age.

This next case graphically illustrates how dangerous it can be for an adult to deal with minors.

Voidable
A valid contract that can be set aside at the option of one of the parties.

Disaffirm
The ability to take back one's contractual obligations.

Necessaries
Normally food, clothing, shelter, and medical treatment.

Quality Motors, Inc. v. Hays
216 Ark. 264, 225 S.W.2d 326 (1949)

DUNAWAY, J.

Johnny M. Hays, by his next friend, Dr. D.J. Hays, brought this suit to disaffirm his purchase of a Pontiac automobile and recover the purchase price of $1,750 from defendant Quality Motors, Inc.

On January 21, 1949, Johnny Hays, a minor sixteen years old, went to the Quality Motors, Inc., to inspect and test a Pontiac car. When E.C. Buttry, salesman for Quality Motors, raised the question of Johnny's age, he was told that Johnny's father in New York had sent him the money to buy the car. The salesman then refused to sell unless the purchase was made by an adult. Johnny left the salesman and returned shortly with Harry R. Williams, a young man twenty-three years of age, whom he met that day for the first time. Johnny then gave to Quality Motors, Inc., a cashier's check on the Citizens Bank of Jonesboro, in the sum of $1,800 which was made payable to him, in payment for the car. A bill of sale was made to Harry Williams. The salesman then recommended a Notary Public who could prepare the necessary papers for transferring title

---

[4]Webster Street Partnership, Ltd. v. Sheridan, 368 N.W.2d 439 (Neb. 1985).

to the car to Johnny, and drove the two boys to town for this purpose. Williams did transfer title, and the Pontiac was delivered by the salesman to Johnny at Arkansas State College, where Dr. Hays, Johnny's father, was a teacher.

When Dr. Hays learned of his son's purchase he called E.C. Perkins, one of the owners of Quality Motors, Inc., on the night of January 25, 1949. Perkins knew nothing of the transaction and suggested that Dr. Hays call the motor company the next morning. On the morning of January 26, Dr. Hays talked to the salesman who had handled the transaction, and asked that defendant company take the car back. This the defendant refused to do. No physical tender of the car was made; Johnny had it out of town. The car was returned to Jonesboro on January 26, when Dr. Hays had his son arrested; it was then stored in a hangar at Arkansas State College. On January 27 Dr. Hays again called Quality Motors, Inc., and was informed the car would not be taken back. He then went to the office of his attorney where he once more called Quality Motors, Inc., and was told by W.E. Ebbert, one of the owners, that they would not accept the car and return the consideration for its purchase, but would try to sell it for him if they could. . . .

On February 12, 1949, while Dr. Hays was out of town, Johnny found the car keys and bill of sale and took the car to Kentucky where his grandmother lived.

On March 21, he returned to Jonesboro and asked Quality Motors for an estimate on repairs to the car which had been in a wreck. On this occasion he had an extended conversation with Buttry and Ebbert, who tried to persuade him to leave the car there and not go back to Kentucky as he told them he planned to do at once. At this time Quality Motors was still refusing to accept the car and return the purchase price. The suggestion was that the car be left with them for repairs "until this thing is settled." Johnny made a telephone call to his mother and immediately departed for Kentucky where the car was in a second and more serious wreck. At the time of trial the car was in Kentucky, subject to a repair bill for $557, and an attachment for $125, and not in running condition.

The special chancellor ordered the plaintiff to return the car within seven days and withheld final decree until this was done. When the wrecked car was returned, recovery of $1,750 from defendant was decreed. . . .

The law is well settled in Arkansas that an infant may disaffirm his contracts, except those made for necessaries, without being required to return the consideration received, except such part as may remain in specie in his hands.

We do not find any merit in appellant's contention that no proper tender of the car was made when appellee sought to disaffirm his purchase. The undisputed testimony shows that Dr. Hays and his attorney offered to return the car on several occasions, but were informed that appellant would not accept it. That it was not actually delivered to Quality Motors when the suit was filed is appellant's own fault. The law does not require that a tender be made under circumstances where it would be vain and useless.

Appellant's most serious contention is that the plaintiff is liable for damages to the car which occurred while he was driving over the country, after he had slipped the car from its storage place and while the suit to disaffirm was pending. In order to obtain any relief on this score, it must be shown that plaintiff was guilty of conversion in taking the automobile. Conversion is the exercise of dominion over property in violation of the rights of the owner or person entitled to possession. In advancing this argument appellant is in an inconsistent position.

. . . Until the court decreed return of the car and recovery of the consideration paid, plaintiff still had title to the car. One cannot be liable for conversion in taking his own property. . . .

Appellant knowingly and through a planned subterfuge sold an automobile to a minor. It then refused to take the car back. Even after the car was wrecked once, it was in appellant's place of business, and appellant was still resisting disaffirmance of the contract. The loss which appellant has suffered is the direct result of its own acts.

The decree is affirmed.

CASE DISCUSSION QUESTIONS

1. What does the court say is the general rule about the right of minors to disaffirm contracts?

2. What should this dealer have done differently in this case?

3. In general, how can merchants protect themselves in dealings with minors?

4. Some states simply require the return of the goods, no matter their condition. Others require that the adult be placed in the same position that he or she was in prior to the contract. Which approach do you think is better?

b. Intoxication

Intoxication is rarely used successfully to void a contract. The courts look with disfavor on this defense because the condition is self-inflicted. However, if the defendant can show the intoxication prevented him from understanding the import of his actions, a court might find that there was no meeting of the minds. In the next case notice how the defendant tried to raise two defenses: that he was intoxicated and that he was only playing a joke on his friend.

Lucy v. Zehmer
196 Va. 493, 84 S.E.2d 516 (1954)

BUCHANAN, J., delivered the opinion of the court.

This suit was instituted by W.O. Lucy and J.C. Lucy, complainants, against A.H. Zehmer and Ida S. Zehmer, his wife, defendants, to have specific performance of a contract by which it was alleged the Zehmers had sold to W.O. Lucy a tract of land owned by A.H. Zehmer in Dinwiddie county containing 471.6 acres, more or less, known as the Ferguson farm, for $50,000. J.C. Lucy, the other complainant, is a brother of W.O. Lucy, to whom W.O. Lucy transferred a half interest in his alleged purchase. . . .

W.O. Lucy, a lumberman and farmer, thus testified in substance: He had known Zehmer for fifteen or twenty years and had been familiar with the Ferguson farm for ten years. Seven or eight years ago he had offered Zehmer $20,000 for the farm which Zehmer had accepted, but the agreement was verbal and Zehmer backed out. On the night of December 20, 1952, around eight o'clock, he took an employee to McKenney, where Zehmer lived and operated a restaurant, filling station and motor court. While there he decided to see Zehmer and again try to buy the Ferguson farm. He entered the restaurant and talked to Mrs. Zehmer until Zehmer came in. He asked Zehmer if he had sold the Ferguson farm. Zehmer replied that he had not. Lucy said, "I bet you wouldn't take $50,000.00 for that place." Zehmer replied, "Yes, I would too; you wouldn't give fifty." Lucy said he would and told Zehmer to write up an agreement to that effect. Zehmer took a restaurant check and wrote on the back of it, "I do hereby agree to sell to W.O. Lucy the Ferguson Farm for $50,000 complete." Lucy told him he had better change it to "We" because Mrs. Zehmer would have to sign it too. Zehmer then tore up what he had written, wrote the agreement quoted above and asked Mrs. Zehmer, who was at the other end of the counter ten or twelve feet away, to sign it. Mrs. Zehmer said she would for $50,000 and signed it. Zehmer brought it back and gave it to Lucy, who offered him $5 which Zehmer refused, saying, "You don't need to give me any money, you got the agreement there signed by both of us."

The discussion leading to the signing of the agreement, said Lucy, lasted thirty or forty minutes, during which Zehmer seemed to doubt that Lucy could raise $50,000. Lucy suggested the provision for having the title examined and Zehmer made the suggestion that he would sell it "complete, everything there," and stated that all he had on the farm was three heifers.

Lucy took a partly filled bottle of whiskey into the restaurant with him for the purpose of giving Zehmer a drink if he wanted it. Zehmer did, and he and Lucy had one or two drinks together. Lucy said that while he felt the drinks he took he was not intoxicated, and from the way Zehmer handled the transaction he did not think he was either. . . .

Mr. and Mrs. Zehmer were called by the complainants as adverse witnesses. Zehmer testified in substance as follows: . . .

On this Saturday night before Christmas it looked like everybody and his brother came by there to a drink. He took a good many drinks during the afternoon and had a pint of his own. When he entered the restaurant around eight-thirty Lucy was there and he could see that he was "pretty high." He said to Lucy, "Boy, you got some good liquor, drinking, ain't you?" Lucy then offered him a drink. "I was already high as a Georgia pine, and didn't have any more better sense than to pour another great big slug out and gulp it down, and he took one too."

After they had talked a while Lucy asked whether he still had the Ferguson farm. He replied that he had not sold it and Lucy said, "I bet you wouldn't take $50,000.00 for it." Zehmer asked him if he would give $50,000 and Lucy said yes. Zehmer replied, "You haven't got $50,000 in cash." Lucy said he did and Zehmer replied that he did not believe it. They argued "pro and con for a long time," mainly about "whether he had $50,000 in cash that he could put up right then and buy that farm."

Finally, said Zehmer, Lucy told him if he didn't believe he had $50,000, "you sign that piece of paper here and say you will take $50,000.00 for the farm." He, Zehmer, "just grabbed the back off of a guest check there" and wrote on the back of it. At that point in his testimony Zehmer asked to see what he had writ-ten to "see if I recognize my own handwriting." He examined the paper and exclaimed, "Great balls of fire, I got 'Firgerson' for Ferguson. I have got satisfactory spelled wrong. I don't recognize that writing if I would see it, wouldn't know it was mine."

After Zehmer had, as he described it, "scribbled this thing off," Lucy said, "Get your wife to sign it." Zehmer walked over to where she was and she at first refused to sign but did so after he told her that he "was just needling him [Lucy], and didn't mean a thing in the world, that I was not selling the farm." Zehmer then "took it back over there . . . and I was still looking at the dern thing. I had the drink right there by my hand, and I reached over to get a drink, and he said, 'Let me see it.' He reached and picked it up, and when I looked back again he had it in his pocket and he dropped a five dollar bill over there, and he said, 'Here is five dollars payment on it.' . . . I said, 'Hell no, that is beer and liquor talking. I am not going to sell you the farm. I have told you that too many times before.'" . . .

The defendants insist that the evidence was ample to support their contention that the writing sought to be enforced was prepared as a bluff or dare to force Lucy to admit that he did not have $50,000; that the whole matter was a joke; that the writing was not delivered to Lucy and no binding contract was ever made between the parties.

It is an unusual, if not bizarre, defense. When made to the writing admittedly prepared by one of the defendants and signed by both, clear evidence is required to sustain it.

In his testimony Zehmer claimed that he "was high as a Georgia pine," and that the transaction "was just a bunch of two doggoned drunks bluffing to see who could talk the biggest and say the most." That claim is inconsistent with his attempt to testify in great detail as to what was said and what was done. It is contradicted by other evidence as to the condition of both parties, and rendered of no weight by the testimony of his wife that when Lucy left the restaurant she suggested that Zehmer drive him home. The record is convincing that Zehmer was not intoxicated to the extent of being unable to comprehend the nature and consequences of the instrument he executed, and hence that instrument is not to be invalidated on that ground. It was in fact conceded by defendants' counsel in oral argument that under the evidence Zehmer was not too drunk to make a valid contract.

... The appearance of the contract, the fact that it was under discussion for forty minutes or more before it was signed; Lucy's objection to the first draft because it was written in the singular, and he wanted Mrs. Zehmer to sign it also; the rewriting to meet that objection and the signing by Mrs. Zehmer; the discussion of what was to be included in the sale, the provision for the examination of the title, the completeness of the instrument that was executed, the taking possession of it by Lucy with no request or suggestion by either of the defendants that he give it back, are facts which furnish persuasive evidence that the execution of the contract was a serious business transaction rather than a casual, jesting matter as defendants now contend. ...

If it be assumed, contrary to what we think the evidence shows, that Zehmer was jesting about selling his farm to Lucy and that the transaction was intended by him to be a joke, nevertheless the evidence shows that Lucy did not so understand it but considered it to be a serious business transaction and the contract to be binding on the Zehmers as well as on himself. The very next day he arranged with his brother to put up half the money and take a half interest in the land. The day after that he employed an attorney to examine the title. The next night, Tuesday, he was back at Zehmer's place and there Zehmer told him for the first time, Lucy said, that he wasn't going to sell and he told Zehmer, "You know you sold that place fair and square." After receiving the report from his attorney that the title was good he wrote to Zehmer that he was ready to close the deal.

Not only did Lucy actually believe, but also the evidence shows he was warranted in believing, that the contract represented a serious business transaction and a good faith sale and purchase of the farm.

In the field of contracts, as generally elsewhere, "We must look to the outward expression of a person as manifesting his intention rather than to his secret and unexpressed intention. 'The law imputes to a person an intention corresponding to the reasonable meaning of his words and acts.'" ...

An agreement or mutual assent is of course essential to a valid contract but the law imputes to a person an intention corresponding to the reasonable meaning of his words and acts. If his words and acts, judged by a reasonable standard, manifest an intention to agree, it is immaterial what may be the real but unexpressed state of his mind.

So a person cannot set up that he was merely jesting when his conduct and words would warrant a reasonable person in believing that he intended a real agreement.

Whether the writing signed by the defendants and now sought to be enforced by the complainants was the result of a serious offer by Lucy and a serious acceptance by the defendants, or was a serious offer by Lucy and an acceptance in secret jest by the defendants, in either event it constituted a binding contract of sale between the parties. ...

Reversed and remanded.

CASE DISCUSSION QUESTIONS

1. What did the court think was the appropriate test for determining whether there was a serious intent to be bound?

2. Specific performance is not an absolute right but rather a question of equity. Do you think it was "fair" to enforce this contract?

3. The court stated: "Seven or eight years ago [Lucy] had offered Zehmer $20,000 for the farm which Zehmer had accepted, but the agreement was verbal and Zehmer backed out." Why was Zehmer able to back out of that agreement but not this one?

c. Mental Incompetence

Mental incompetence can cause a contract to be voidable, a situation analogous to that of minors. Also as is true with minors, the incompetent person nonetheless remains responsible for the reasonable value of necessaries. However, if someone has been adjudged mentally incompetent and the court has appointed a guardian to handle the incompetent's affairs, then that individual is without the capacity to make contracts. Instead of being merely voidable, any contract the incompetent individual tries to make is **void**. Only the guardian can enter into valid contracts.

Void
A contract that is invalid even if it is not repudiated by either party.

2. Illegal Contracts and Those That Violate Public Policy

Contracts can be declared unenforceable if they are found to be either illegal or against public policy. A contract involves illegality if it calls for behavior that violates the criminal law, such as robbery, gambling, or prostitution. In addition, a contract will be seen as involving illegality if it violates a licensing statute that explicitly states that it is for the protection of the public, antitrust laws, or state usury laws. Contracts for an illegal purpose are void and cannot be enforced by either party. For example, usury laws regulate interest rates. A loan that imposes an interest charge that exceeds the legal limit is said to be usurious and therefore illegal.

In addition, the courts hold that some contracts are unenforceable because they are contrary to public policy. For example, **covenants not to compete** by their very nature are against public policy in that they restrict the right of an individual to earn a living or they tend to decrease competition. However, they can also be a form of necessary business protection. For example, if a pharmaceutical company expends a great deal of time and money training a chemist, the company will want the chemist to sign a noncompetition clause, promising not to work for another pharmaceutical plant for a certain amount of time after leaving employment with the first company. The courts are generally willing to enforce that type of covenant so long as

Covenant not to compete
A promise not to compete within a given geographical area for a specific time period.

1. it is tied to employment or to the sale of a business and
2. its terms call for a reasonable time and
3. a reasonable geographic area.

A second type of contract that the courts may refuse to enforce as being against public policy is an **adhesion contract.** As you will recall from our discussion of inadequate consideration, normally courts will adhere to the theory of freedom of contract and will not inquire into the fairness of the bargain. However, when a contract is formed between two parties of very unequal bargaining power and the contract is drafted by the party with the greater power and then presented to the other party, who has no opportunity to negotiate the terms, the court may view this as a contract of adhesion. The court may then hold that such a contract is unconscionable and refuse to enforce it. Generally, a contract is considered unconscionable if, in the context of general commercial practices and under the specific circumstances in which the contract was made, it is so one-sided as to be oppressive and grossly unfair. An example would be a sale to a low-income family

Adhesion contract
A contract formed where the weaker party has no realistic bargaining power. Typically a form contract is offered on a "take it or leave it" basis.

who speaks little English where the contract is drawn up by the seller and includes a clause that disclaims all warranties that traditionally go with such a transaction.

While the UCC holds that the terms of a contract that are unconscionable cannot be enforced, it does not attempt to define unconscionability. UCC § 2-302. One must rely on court cases for specific application of the doctrine. The courts are more responsive to low-income consumers who raise this defense than they are to merchants who deal with other merchants.

Third, some contracts contain provisions that purport to release parties from all liability for their own negligence. These are known as **exculpatory clauses**. These clauses were discussed in Chapter 10, as they are frequently raised as a defense in negligence actions. As we discussed there, the courts generally disfavor such clauses and frequently refuse to enforce them.

Exculpatory clause
A provision that purports to waive liability.

Finally, society's changing mores, as well as advances in medical science, have presented some interesting dilemmas to the courts. For example, courts have recently been confronted with the issue of whether to enforce a surrogacy contract. They have also been asked to decide whether a contract regarding the "ownership" of frozen embryos should be enforced. The argument against enforcement is that such contracts are against public policy. We will discuss these and similar problems more fully in Chapter 14, which covers laws affecting the family.

3. Lack of Genuineness of Assent

As we have seen, normally the courts apply an objective reasonable person standard in interpreting whether an agreement was reached between the parties. However, a court will not enforce a contract if one of the parties can convince the court that there was no true "meeting of the minds" because of fraud, mistake, undue influence, or duress.

a. Fraud

In order to prove fraud, it must be demonstrated that the other party made intentional misrepresentations or intentional nondisclosures of material facts during the course of the negotiations. Therefore, the four requirements for a defense based on fraud are as follows:

1. an intent to deceive
2. regarding material facts and
3. justifiable reliance on the deception
4. that causes harm.

A successful defendant can recover damages or ask the contract be **rescinded**. In addition, fraud can be brought under a tort theory, thereby creating the possibility of also receiving a punitive damage award.

Rescission
The act of canceling the contract and returning the parties to the positions they were in prior to the contract having been formed.

For the reliance to be justified, it must be shown that the defendant did not know of the fraud and had no way to find out. Note that the misrepresentations must be material and that they must be made regarding a factual statement, not merely opinion or sales puffery. It is expected that the reasonable person engaged in contract negotiations will realize that she or he should not rely on opinions or on overblown sales statements that are obviously made simply as part of the sales pitch. However, in certain circumstances the opinion of an expert can be viewed as a fact when it is reasonable to rely on the opinion of an expert and the other party has no independent means of testing the statement's validity. The issue of whether a dance student was justified in relying on the statements of a dance instructor is presented in the following case.

Vokes v. Arthur Murray, Inc.
212 So. 2d 906 (Fla. Dist. Ct. App. 1968)

PIERCE, Judge. LILES, C.J., and MANN, J., concur.

. . . Defendant Arthur Murray, Inc., a corporation, authorizes the operation throughout the nation of dancing schools under the name of "Arthur Murray School of Dancing" through local franchised operators, one of whom was defendant J.P. Davenport whose dancing establishment was in Clearwater.

Plaintiff Mrs. Audrey E. Vokes, a widow of 51 years and without family, had a yen to be "an accomplished dancer" with the hopes of finding "new interest in life." So, on February 10, 1961, a dubious fate, with the assist of a motivated acquaintance, procured her to attend a "dance party" at Davenport's "School of Dancing" where she whiled away the pleasant hours, sometimes in a private room, absorbing his accomplished sales technique, during which her grace and poise were elaborated upon and her rosy future as "an excellent dancer" was painted for her in vivid and glowing colors. As an incident to this interlude, he sold her eight ½-hour dance lessons to be utilized within one calendar month therefrom, for the sum of $14.50 cash in hand paid, obviously a baited "come-on."

Thus she embarked upon an almost endless pursuit of the terpsichorean art during which, over a period of less than sixteen months, she was sold fourteen "dance courses" totalling in the aggregate 2302 hours of dancing lessons for a total cash outlay of $31,090.45, all at Davenport's dance emporium. . . .

These dance lesson contracts and the monetary consideration therefor of over $31,000 were procured from her by means and methods of Davenport and his associates which went beyond the unsavory, yet legally permissible, perimeter of "sales puffing" and intruded well into the forbidden area of undue influence, the suggestion of falsehood, the suppression of truth, and the free exercise of rational judgment, if what plaintiff alleged in her complaint was true. . . .

All the . . . sales promotions, illustrative of the entire fourteen separate contracts, were procured by defendant Davenport and Arthur Murray, Inc., by false representations to her that she was improving in her dancing ability, that she had excellent potential, that she was responding to instructions in dancing grace, and that they were developing her into a beautiful dancer, whereas in truth and in fact she did not develop in her dancing ability, she had no "dance aptitude," and in fact had difficulty in "hearing the musical beat." The complaint alleged that such representations to her "were in fact false and known by the defendant to be false and contrary to the plaintiff's true ability, the truth of plaintiff's ability being fully known to the defendants, but withheld from the plaintiff for the sole and specific intent to deceive and defraud the plaintiff and to induce her in the purchasing of additional hours of dance lessons." It was averred that the lessons were sold to her "in total disregard to the true physical, rhythm, and mental ability of the plaintiff." In other words, while she first exulted that she was entering the "spring of her life," she finally was awakened to the fact there was "spring" neither in her life nor in her feet.

The complaint prayed that the Court decree the dance contracts to be null and void and to be cancelled, that an accounting be had. . . . The Court held the complaint not to state a cause of action and dismissed it with prejudice. We disagree and reverse.

The material allegations of the complaint must, of course, be accepted as true for the purpose of testing its legal sufficiency. Defendants contend that contracts can only be rescinded for fraud or misrepresentation when the alleged misrepresentation is as to a material fact, rather than an opinion, prediction or expectation, and that the statements and representations set forth at length in the complaint were in the category of "trade puffing," within its legal orbit. It is true that "generally a misrepresentation, to be actionable, must be one of fact rather than of opinion." But this rule has significant qualifications, applicable here. It does not apply where there is a fiduciary relationship between the parties, or where there has been some artifice or trick employed by the representor, or where the parties do not in general deal at "arm's length" as we understand the phrase, or where the representee does not have equal opportunity to become apprised of the truth or falsity of the fact represented. ". . . A statement of a party having . . . superior knowledge may be regarded as a statement of fact although it would be considered as opinion if the parties were dealing on equal terms." . . .

Even in contractual situations where a party to a transaction owes no duty to disclose facts within his knowledge or to answer inquiries respecting such facts, the law is if he undertakes to do so he must disclose the whole truth. . . .

We repeat that where parties are dealing on a contractual basis at arm's length with no inequities or inherently unfair practices employed, the Courts will in general "leave the parties where they find themselves." But in the case sub judice, from the allegations of the unanswered complaint, we cannot say that enough of the accompanying ingredients, as mentioned in the foregoing authorities, were not present which otherwise would have barred the equitable arm of the Court to her. In our view, from the showing made in her complaint, plaintiff is entitled to her day in Court.

It accordingly follows that the order dismissing plaintiff's last amended complaint with prejudice should be and is reversed.

Reversed.

CASE DISCUSSION QUESTIONS

1. Why did the court categorize the dance studio's statements as "fact" rather than "opinion"?

2. Which facts do you think the court found particularly relevant in reaching that decision?

3. What do you think would have kept the statements of the dance studio in the realm of mere "sales puffing"?

b. Mistake

Mistakes about facts can sometimes form the basis for rescinding a contract. If the mistake is bilateral, then both parties had a different concept of what was to be included in the contract. Therefore, there never was a meeting of the minds, and the failed contract can be rescinded by either. The classic case that illustrates this principle took place in England in 1864. A buyer purchased a shipment of cotton from a seller, the cotton to be shipped on the Peerless. Unknown to either party there were two ships named the Peerless, one to depart in October and one in December. The buyer was thinking of the ship destined to leave in October and the seller the other in December. Consequently, the seller did not ship the cotton until December. By that time the buyer no longer needed the cotton. The court held that because there never was a "meeting of the minds" as to which ship was intended, no contract had been formed and the buyer was not obligated to pay for the cotton.[5]

Usually, however, if the mistake is unilateral and only one party is mistaken, both parties are bound. The only exceptions are if the other party knew or should have known of the mistake and if the mistake was the result of a mathematical error.

Keep in mind that we are talking only about factual mistakes. Mistakes as to the value of the subject matter can never be the basis for rescission. For example, assume Joan contracts to sell her diamond ring to Bertha. Both think the ring is worth about $500, and they set $500 as the contract price. Later Bertha has the ring appraised and is delighted to learn that it is actually worth $5,000. Joan cannot ask to have the contract rescinded on the ground that she was mistaken as to the value of the diamond. On the other hand, if Joan had contracted to sell what she thought was a zirconium ring to Bertha and upon appraisal it turned out to be a diamond ring, some courts could see that as a mutual mistake as to a fact and allow the contract to be rescinded.

c. Undue Influence

Sometimes a party will try to avoid contractual obligations by arguing that undue influence was exerted by the other party. Generally, for a court to find undue influence there must first be a showing that a special relationship existed between the parties. Then, because of the special relationship, one party is in a position of trust and misuses that trust to influence the actions of another. Situations alleging undue influence are frequently brought by family members against caretakers of the elderly or ill.

d. Duress

A contract is also not valid if it was agreed to under duress rather than as a result of a truly voluntary action. The actions of the second party must be sufficient for the court to find that the first party was forced into the agreement. Duress is difficult to prove because the defendant must show that the pressure exerted was so great as to overwhelm his or her ability to make a free choice.

4. Breach of Warranty

Warranty
A guarantee, made by the seller or implied by law, regarding the character, quality, or title of the goods being sold.

Among the most frequently contested issues is the nature of the warranties involved in commercial transactions. In this context a **warranty** is a statement or representation, made by the seller as part of the contract of sale or implied in law, regarding the character, quality, or title of the goods being sold. If such warranted facts later prove to be untrue, the seller has an obligation to compensate the buyer for any losses incurred as a result of the misrepresentation.

Implied warranty of merchantability
An implied promise that the goods being sold will be usable for the purpose for which they were sold.

Under the terms of the UCC any contract of sale automatically includes a warranty of title, an implied promise that the seller owns the goods being offered for sale and that they will be delivered free from any security interest, lien, or encumbrance. UCC § 2-312. There is also an **implied warranty of merchantability,** an implied promise that the goods being sold will be usable for the purpose for which they were sold.

---

[5]Raffles v. Wichelhaus, 159 Eng. Rep. 375 (1864).

(1) Unless excluded or modified by section 2-316, a warranty that the goods shall be merchantable is implied in a contract for their sale if the seller is a merchant with respect to goods of that kind. Under this section the serving for value of food or drink to be consumed either on the premises or elsewhere is a sale. (2) Goods to be merchantable must at least be such as . . . (c) are fit for the ordinary purposes for which such goods are used.

UCC § 2-314. This is a warranty regarding the fitness of the goods for the ordinary purpose for which these types of goods are used.

When a more specialized use of the goods is communicated to the seller during the course of negotiations, an **implied warranty of fitness** is also created. UCC § 2-315. This is a warranty regarding the fitness of the goods for that special purpose. For example, if you go to a hardware store and ask the clerk for electrical wiring and say nothing more, the wire will be warranted for its usual purpose of carrying household current. If instead you want the wire for outside use, you tell the clerk your special purpose, and you rely on the clerk's expertise in picking out the wire, then there will be an implied warranty of fitness for that particular purpose.

> **Implied warranty of fitness**
> An implied promise that the goods being sold will satisfy a special purpose.

In addition to these implied warranties, a contract can create **express warranties.** UCC § 2-313. The term *warranty* or *guarantee* does not have to be used in order for a warranty to be created. However, the seller's conduct or statements must have been communicated to the buyer so that the warranty becomes part of the "basis of the bargain." UCC § 2-313(1). Express warranties can be created by an affirmation of fact or a promise made by the seller; a description of the goods being sold, including technical specifications and blueprints; or a sample or a model provided. A mere expression of opinion as to the value of an item is considered "puffing" and does not constitute a warranty.

As you can imagine, two of the most common issues that arise in trying to resolve whether an express warranty exists are (1) whether the statement or actions were part of the "basis of the bargain" and (2) whether a statement is an affirmation of fact or merely the seller's opinion. There is no clear definition of either. The UCC does not define "basis of the bargain," and the courts have reached differing conclusions. Some have held that it means the warranty terms must have been bargained for; others hold that the buyer must have relied on the warranties in deciding to make the purchase; still others state that the buyer need not show any reliance but must have been aware of the warranty at the time the sale was made.

Warranties may be excluded or modified by disclaimers. UCC § 2-316. In many states, however, merchants are limited in their ability to exclude or modify the implied warranty of merchantability when the sale is to a consumer. For each type of warranty, Figure 11-5 summarizes how it is created and what actions a seller must take to exclude the warranty.

PRACTICAL TIP

Even if a seller states that all warranties have been disclaimed, do not assume that is true. Many states have enacted special protections for consumers that prohibit the exclusion of certain warranties.

Type of Warranty	Created by	Excluded by
Implied warranty of merchantability	the sale of goods by a merchant. The goods must be fit for their ordinary purpose.	language that includes the word *merchantability* or a disclaimer that includes the word *merchantability* or phrases such as "as is" or "with all faults." If in writing, it must be conspicuous.
Implied warranty of fitness	a seller ■ knowing the particular purpose the buyer has in mind *and* ■ being aware that the buyer is relying on the seller's expertise.	a writing that is conspicuous.
Express warranty	■ an affirmation of fact or a promise made by the seller, *or* ■ a description of the goods being sold, including technical specifications and blueprints, *or* a sample or model *and* that becomes a basis of the bargain.	words or conduct tending to limit or negate the warranty so long as such interpretation is reasonable.

Figure 11-5   Warranties Summarized

An interesting example of when implied warranties can be applied to food occurred in the following classic case.

(handwritten margin note: ✗ This case ✗ warranty of fitness)

Webster v. Blue Ship Tea Room, Inc.
347 Mass. 421, 198 N.E.2d 309 (1964)

REARDON, JJ. This is a case which by its nature evokes earnest study not only of the law but also of the culinary traditions of the Commonwealth which bear so heavily upon its outcome. It is an action to recover damages for personal injuries sustained by reason of a breach of implied warranty of food served by the defendant in its restaurant. . . .

On Saturday, April 15, 1959, about 1 P.M., the plaintiff, accompanied by her sister and her aunt, entered the Blue Ship Tea Room operated by the defendant. The group was seated at a table and supplied with menus.

This restaurant, which the plaintiff characterized as "quaint," was located in Boston "on the third floor of an old building on T Wharf which overlooks the ocean."

The plaintiff, who had been born and brought up in New England (a fact of some consequence), ordered clam chowder and crabmeat salad. Within a few minutes she received tidings to the effect that "there was no more clam chowder," whereupon she ordered a cup of fish chowder. Presently, there was set before her "a small bowl of fish chowder. . . . The chowder was milky in color and not clear. The haddock and potatoes were in chunks" (also a fact of consequence). . . . She ate about 3 or 4 spoonfuls then stopped. She looked at the spoonfuls as she was eating. She saw equal parts of liquid, potato and fish as she spooned it into her mouth. She did not see anything unusual about it. After 3 or 4 spoonfuls she was aware that something had lodged in her throat because she couldn't swallow and couldn't clear her throat by gulping and she could feel it. This misadventure led to two esophagoscopies at the Massachusetts General Hospital, in the second of which, on April 27, 1959, a fish bone was found and removed. The sequence of events produced injury to the plaintiff which was not insubstantial.

We must decide whether a fish bone lurking in a fish chowder, about the ingredients of which there is no other complaint, constitutes a breach of implied warranty under applicable provisions of the Uniform Commercial Code, the annotations to which are not helpful on this point. As the judge put it in his charge, "Was the fish chowder fit to be eaten and wholesome? . . . [N]obody is claiming that the fish itself wasn't wholesome. . . . But the bone of contention here—I don't mean that for a pun—but was this fish bone a foreign substance that made the fish chowder unwholesome or not fit to be eaten?" . . .

The defendant asserts . . . "[f]ish chowder, as it is served and enjoyed by New Englanders, is a hearty dish, originally designed to satisfy the appetites of our seamen and fishermen"; that "[t]his court knows well that we are not talking of some insipid broth as is customarily served to convalescents." We are asked to rule in such fashion that no chef is forced "to reduce the pieces of fish in the chowder to miniscule size in an effort to ascertain if they contained any pieces of bone." . . .

It is not too much to say that a person sitting down in New England to consume a good New England fish chowder embarks on a gustatory adventure which may entail the removal of some fish bones from his bowl as he proceeds. We are not inclined to tamper with age old recipes by any amendment reflecting the plaintiff's view of the effect of the Uniform Commercial Code upon them. We are aware of the heavy body of case law involving foreign substances in food, but we sense a strong distinction between them and those relative to unwholesomeness of the food itself. . . . In any event, we consider that the joys of life in New England include the ready availability of fresh fish chowder. We should be prepared to cope with the hazards of fish bones, the occasional presence of which in chowders is, it seems to us, to be anticipated, and which, in the light of a hallowed tradition, do not impair their fitness or merchantability. While we are buoyed up in this conclusion by *Shapiro v. Hotel Statler Corp.* 132 F. Supp. 891 (S.D. Cal.), in which the bone which afflicted the plaintiff appeared in "Hot Barquette of Seafood Mornay," we know that the United States District Court of Southern California, situated as are we upon a coast, might be expected to share our views. We are most impressed, however, by *Allen v. Grafton,* 170 Ohio St. 249, where in Ohio, the Midwest, in a case where the plaintiff was injured by a piece of oyster shell in an order of fried oysters, Mr. Justice Taft (now Chief Justice) in a majority opinion held that "the possible presence of a piece of oyster shell in or attached to an oyster is so well known to anyone who eats oysters that we can say as a matter of law that one who eats oysters can reasonably anticipate and guard against eating such a piece of shell. . . ." (P. 259.) Thus, while we sympathize with the plaintiff who has suffered a peculiarly New England injury, the order must be

Exceptions sustained. Judgment for the defendant.

CASE DISCUSSION QUESTIONS

1. Why did the court think Ms. Webster failed in her claim for breach of an implied warranty?

2. Why did it matter that the plaintiff was brought up in New England? Would the result have been different if she lived in the Midwest and this was her first trip to the East Coast?

3. Do you agree with the court that this is a different case from one in which the food is contaminated? Why?

Legal Reasoning Exercise

3. Janice Jones, along with her family, visited a Big Bill's Family Restaurant, a national chain. She was eating a piece of fried chicken when she bit into something that she thought was a worm. Naturally she became quite upset and has been unable to eat chicken since. Expert witnesses are likely to state that, instead of a worm, the object was actually either the chicken's aorta or its trachea, both of which would appear wormlike. Ms. Jones wants to know whether she can successfully sue the restaurant for breach of warranty. Please evaluate her claim based on *Webster v. Blue Ship Tea Room, Inc.*

---

5. Lack of Proper Format—Writing

A commonly held misunderstanding is that all contracts must be in writing to be enforceable. That is not so. In many situations an oral contract is perfectly valid. However, contractual disputes arise not just about whether a valid contract exists but also about what the terms of the contract actually require. Deciding these disputes is particularly difficult when the agreement was oral rather than set down in writing. When the dispute is reduced to one person's word against the other's, the courts find it difficult to determine who is telling the truth. Even though many oral contracts are legally enforceable, it is always wiser to put them in writing.

Statute of frauds
A statutory requirement that in order to be enforceable certain contracts must be in writing.

In addition to the fact that it simply makes sense to reduce any important contract to writing, all states have a statute known as the **statute of frauds,** which lists those contracts that must be in writing in order to be enforceable. The purpose of such statutes is to ensure that there will be reliable evidence of important or complex matters. The required writing does not have to be a formal contract, however. It can take the form of any writing—for example, a check or a memo—so long as it fully expresses the terms of the agreement. The writing can also be in multiple pieces, so long as it is clear the pieces were intended to constitute one agreement. A common example is a written offer and a separate written acceptance. Finally, the signature can be any authentication, even initials. Generally, the types of contracts that must be in writing fall into one of the following categories:

1. contracts involving land, including fixtures, and documents dealing with land, such as mortgages and leases;
2. contracts that cannot be performed in one year;
3. collateral contracts, those that involve a secondary as opposed to a primary obligation, unless the main purpose is to secure a personal benefit;
4. promises made in consideration of marriage, such as prenuptial agreements; and
5. contracts for the sale of goods valued at $500 or more.

Note the exact wording regarding the second type of contract—those that *cannot* be performed in one year. If it is possible, even though unlikely, that it can be performed in one year, then a writing is not necessary. For example, a contract for life could be performed in one year and so need not be in writing.

Article 2 of the UCC contains its own statute of frauds that applies to the sale of goods. UCC § 2-201. It requires something in writing if the price of the goods is $500 or more. The writing needs to be signed only by "the party to be charged." For example, Tom calls Jim, offering to buy his television for $600, and Jim mails back his signed reply agreeing to the arrangement. If Jim fails to perform his end of the bargain, Tom can sue Jim, the party to be charged, because Jim signed the letter agreeing to the arrangement. However, Jim would not be allowed to sue Tom, as there is no writing containing Tom's signature.

The statute of frauds does allow for some exceptions. The first is part performance. For example, if John made a partial payment for some land, took possession of the land, and made improvements, then the court might see this as enough evidence of an intended contract to enforce it. Also, under the UCC a contract will be enforced to the extent payment or delivery was accepted. Admissions in pleadings or testimony will also bind the party as to the quantity admitted. Finally, the court may invoke the doctrine of promissory estoppel when there is justifiable reliance.

A written agreement usually contains an integration clause that merges all previous oral agreements into the new written document. Under the **parol evidence rule** a written contract cannot be modified or changed by prior oral agreements.

Parol evidence rule
An evidentiary rule that a written contract cannot be modified or changed by prior verbal agreements.

Attorney Smith is always very careful to explain his contingency fee arrangement with his clients. The client is responsible for any court costs and other expenses, and attorney Smith receives 33 percent of any settlement or court award. Attorney Smith has never seen any need to put this arrangement in writing. Do you see any problems with attorney Smith's approach?

Substantial performance
Although a breach of contract, performance of all the essential terms of the contract will entitle the breaching party to the contractual price minus any damages caused by the breach.

Material breach
Such a grave failure to fulfill the contractual terms that the other party is relieved of all contractual obligations.

E. TERMINATION OF CONTRACTUAL DUTIES

A contract is typically discharged by performance. However, there are times when the parties may agree to end their agreement prior to complete performance. Also, at times a court may declare a party's obligations over when performance is impossible or commercially impracticable.

1. By Performance

Complete performance ends both parties' obligations. At times, however, a party will perform most but not all of the required duties. If the party **substantially performs,** that party is in breach of contract and is liable for damages caused by the breach. However, the other party is not relieved of his or her obligations. If, however, the failure to perform is seen as a **material breach,** it is a breach of contract that excuses the other party from any obligations. Whether the performance is so complete as to amount to only a minor breach or so insufficient as to constitute a material breach is often a difficult question. In the next case the court grapples with what to do when a construction contract is not fully performed.

Jacob & Youngs, Inc. v. Kent
230 N.Y. 239, 129 N.E. 889 (1921)

CARDOZO, J. The plaintiff built a country residence for the defendant at a cost of upwards of $77,000, and now sues to recover a balance of $3,483.46, remaining unpaid. The work of construction ceased in June, 1914, and the defendant then began to occupy the dwelling. There was no complaint of defective performance until March, 1915. One of the specifications for the plumbing work provides that "all wrought iron pipe must be well galvanized, lap welded pipe of the grade known as 'standard pipe' of Reading manufacture." The defendant learned in March, 1915, that some of the pipe, instead of being made in Reading, was the product of other factories. The plaintiff was accordingly directed by the architect to do the work anew. The plumbing was then encased within the walls except in a few places where it had to be exposed. Obedience to the order meant more than the substitution of other pipe. It meant the demolition at great expense of substantial parts of the completed structure. The plaintiff left the work untouched, and asked for a certificate that the final payment was due. Refusal of the certificate was followed by this suit.

The evidence sustains a finding that the omission of the prescribed brand of pipe was neither fraudulent nor willful. It was the result of the oversight and inattention of the plaintiff's subcontractor. Reading pipe is distinguished from Cohoes pipe and other brands only by the name of the manufacturer stamped upon it at intervals of between six and seven feet. Even the defendant's architect, though he inspected the pipe upon arrival, failed to notice the discrepancy. The plaintiff tried to show that the brands installed, though made by other manufacturers, were the same in quality, in appearance, in market value and in cost as the brand stated in the contract—that they were, indeed, the same thing, though manufactured in another place. The evidence was excluded, and a verdict directed for the defendant. The Appellate Division reversed, and granted a new trial.

We think the evidence, if admitted, would have supplied some basis for the inference that the defect was insignificant in its relation to the project. The courts never say that one who makes a contract fills the measure of his duty by less than full performance. They do say, however, that an omission, both trivial and innocent, will sometimes be atoned for by allowance of the resulting damage, and will not always be the breach of a condition to be followed by a forfeiture. . . .

Those who think more of symmetry and logic in the development of legal rules than of practical adaptation to the attainment of a just result will be troubled by a classification where the lines of division are so wavering and blurred. Something, doubtless, may be said on the score of consistency and certainty in favor of a stricter standard. The courts have balanced such considerations against those of equity and fairness, and found the latter to be the weightier. The decisions in this state commit us to the liberal view, which is making its way, nowadays, in jurisdictions slow to welcome it. Where the line is to be drawn between the important and the trivial cannot be settled by a formula. "In the nature of the case precise boundaries are impossible" (2 Williston on Contracts, sec. 841). The same omission may take on one aspect or another according to its setting. Substitution of equivalents may not have the same significance in fields of art on the one side and in those of mere utility on the other. Nowhere will change be tolerated, however, if it is so dominant or pervasive as in any real or substantial measure to frustrate the purpose of the contract. There is no general license to install whatever, in the builder's judgment, may be regarded as "just as good." The question is one of degree, to be answered, if there is doubt, by the triers of the facts, and, if the inferences are certain, by the judges of the law. We must weigh the purpose to be served, the desire to be gratified, the excuse for deviation from the letter, the cruelty of enforced adherence. Then only can we tell whether literal fulfillment is to be implied by law as a condition. This is not to say that the parties are not free by apt and certain words to effectuate a purpose that performance of every term shall be a condition of recovery. That question is not here. This is merely to say that the law will be slow to impute the purpose, in the silence of the parties, where the significance of the default is grievously out of proportion to the oppression of the forfeiture. The willful transgressor must accept the penalty of his transgression.

For him there is no occasion to mitigate the rigor of implied conditions. The transgressor whose default is unintentional and trivial may hope for mercy if he will offer atonement for his wrong.

In the circumstances of this case, we think the measure of the allowance is not the cost of replacement, which would be great, but the difference in value, which would be either nominal or nothing. . . . It is true that in most cases the cost of replacement is the measure. The owner is entitled to the money which will permit him to complete, unless the cost of completion is grossly and unfairly out of proportion to the good to be attained. When that is true, the measure is the difference in value. . . . The rule that gives a remedy in cases of substantial performance with compensation for defects of trivial or inappreciable importance, has been developed by the courts as an instrument of justice. The measure of the allowance must be shaped to the same end.

The order should be affirmed, and judgment absolute directed in favor of the plaintiff upon the stipulation, with costs in all courts.

McLAUGHLIN, J. (dissenting). I dissent. The plaintiff did not perform its contract. . . .

. . . The defendant had a right to contract for what he wanted. He had a right before making payment to get what the contract called for. It is no answer to this suggestion to say that the pipe put in was just as good as that made by the Reading Manufacturing Company, or that the difference in value between such pipe and the pipe made by the Reading Manufacturing Company would be either "nominal or nothing." Defendant contracted for pipe made by the Reading Manufacturing Company. What his reason was for requiring this kind of pipe is of no importance. He wanted that and was entitled to it. It may have been a mere whim on his part, but even so, he had a right to this kind of pipe, regardless of whether some other kind, according to the opinion of the contractor or experts, would have been "just as good, better, or done just as well." He agreed to pay only upon condition that the pipe installed were made by that company and he ought not to be compelled to pay unless that condition be performed. . . .

CASE DISCUSSION QUESTIONS

1. Why did the court find for the plaintiff contractor?

2. The dissent essentially states that people have a right to get what they contract for. The majority does not see things in such black-and-white terms, saying, "We must weigh the purpose to be served, the desire to be gratified, the excuse for deviation from the letter, the cruelty of enforced adherence." Which view do you think best serves the needs of the contracting parties?

3. What could the owner have done to ensure that there would be no deviations from his specifications?

4. Would this case have had a different outcome if the contractor had deliberately substituted the pipe in order to save money? Why?

Perfect tender rule
The requirement that the goods delivered exactly meet the contractual specifications.

The issue of not performing to the letter of the contract is one area where the UCC, instead of liberalizing the rules, has tightened them. Under Section 2-601, the UCC states that failure in any respect to supply conforming goods means that the buyer is free to accept the goods, reject them, or accept part and reject part. This is known as the **perfect tender rule.** The only relief from this rule involves the following exceptions: (1) if the parties agree to overlook the lack of conformity; (2) if "cure" is possible—that is, if the time for performance has not yet expired, the seller notifies the buyer of his intent to rectify the matter, and he then does so; and (3) in some cases of commercial impracticability.

If the goods cannot be returned without their perishing, they must be sold in order to minimize the seller's losses. UCC § 2-603. If substandard goods are accepted and retained, the buyer can seek damages that amount to the difference between the value of the goods promised and the value of the goods received. UCC § 2-714.

2. By Agreement

Rescission
The act of canceling the contract and returning the parties to the positions they were in prior to the contract having been formed.

Novation
When a third party is substituted for one of the original parties.

Accord and satisfaction
The agreement and then the performance of something different than originally promised.

Contractual obligations can be ended by agreement through rescission, novation, or accord and satisfaction. **Rescission** involves an agreement by both parties to cancel the contract. Rescission is generally viewed as appropriate if the contract is still completely executory. If one side has performed, a rescission will not be enforced unless the other side gives consideration for the rescission.

In a **novation** a third party is substituted for one of the original parties. This creates a new contract and as such differs from assignments or delegations. Because it is a new contract, it must be supported by new consideration.

Finally, the parties may enter into an **accord and satisfaction.** An accord is an agreement to do something different than originally promised. The satisfaction is the performance of the accord. For example, if John owes Sally $4,000 and they agree that Sally will accept John's Rolex watch in payment instead, their agreement is the accord. If John gives Sally his watch, there is a satisfaction. If he does not, then Sally can still sue John for the $4,000.

3. When Performance Is Impossible

A party can assert the defense of impossibility of contractual performance. This occurs when one party either dies or becomes too sick to carry through with the contractual responsibilities. It also could occur when the object to be sold is destroyed or stolen before the agreed-on transfer takes place or when there is a change in the law that makes the contract illegal. A party that hopes to win under the defense of impossibility must show that the contract cannot be performed, not simply that the party cannot perform it.

4. Due to Commercial Impracticability

As we saw from our discussion of consideration, freedom of contract allows parties to make and be held to a bad bargain. When circumstances change, leaving one party at a disadvantage, that party may ask to be excused from the contract under the doctrine of commercial impracticability. The argument is not that the contract is impossible to perform but rather that it has become too costly for one of the parties. If the change of circumstances should have been foreseen, then generally the courts will not supply any relief. For example, in one case a farm agreed to sell to a school district all the milk it required. During the course of the contract the price of raw milk increased by 23 percent. If the farm was required to abide by the terms of the contract, it would lose a substantial amount of money. The court held the farm to its contract, refusing to allow it to pass the increase on to the school district, because the rise in price was a foreseeable occurrence.[6]

F. THIRD-PARTY RIGHTS

There are three ways in which a person or corporation not a party to the contract can have a legal interest in enforcing part of the terms of that agreement. The most common of these is through the process of assignment. Third-party rights also arise through delegation and the creation of beneficiaries.

1. Assignment

An **assignment** occurs when one of the original parties to a contract transfers part or all of his or her interest to a third party. See Figure 11-6. For example, assume a consumer signs a sales contract with a furniture store. In the contract the consumer agrees to make certain monthly payments. The furniture store then assigns the right to receive those payments to a finance company, and in return the finance company gives the furniture store ready cash. The finance company now has a legal interest in receiving the monthly payments that the consumer agreed to pay to the store.

An assignment involves an assignor, an assignee, and an obligor. The assignee gets the same rights that the assignor had, but no more. The assignee is also subject to the same defenses as could have been raised against the assignor. Assignment is usually possible unless

Assignment
The transfer by one of the original parties to the contract of part or all of his or her interest to a third party.

1. the contract itself prohibits it,
2. the contract involves personal services, or
3. the assignment will materially alter the duties of the obligor.

---

[6]Maple Farms, Inc. v. City School District of Elmira, 352 N.Y.S.2d 784 (Sup. Ct. 1974).

Original Contract

Assignor ⇄ **Obligor**
(person under a contractual
obligation)

Assigns rights to

Assignee

Figure 11-6   Assignment of a Contract

Delegation
The transfer by one of
the original parties to the
contract of his or her
obligations to a third
party.

2. Delegation

Most duties can be delegated unless the contract prohibits it or the duty requires personal skill or special trust. The primary duty is not extinguished if the delegatee fails to perform. The original party remains obligated to fulfill the terms of the contract. See Figure 11-7.

3. Third-Party Beneficiaries

Assignment and delegation happen after the contract is formed. However, if at the time the contract is formed one or both of the parties want to benefit a third party, a third-party beneficiary relationship is created. There are two types of beneficiaries: intended (creditor or donee) and incidental. See Figure 11-8.

a. Intended Beneficiaries

Contracts often contain provisions in which one of the parties agrees to provide some direct benefit to a third party, or beneficiary. For example, in purchasing a house the buyer might agree to assume the seller's current mortgage.

Figure 11-7   Delegation of Duties under a Contract

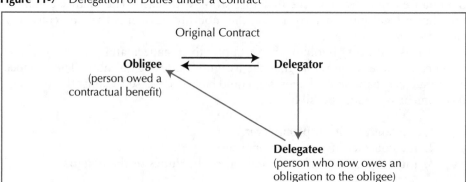

Original Contract

Obligee ⇄ **Delegator**
(person owed a
contractual benefit)

Delegatee
(person who now owes an
obligation to the obligee)

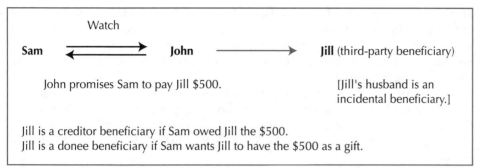

Figure 11-8   Third-Party Beneficiaries

In that case the mortgage lender is a third party that has been given a specific benefit under the terms of the contract; it is considered to be a creditor beneficiary. In a situation in which a father contracts with a bank to administer a trust fund for his children, those children would be considered donee beneficiaries.

If it is clear from the contract that the parties intended a third party to benefit, that party is an intended beneficiary. Consider two further examples: If in return for Sam's watch John promises Sam to pay the $500 debt Sam owes to Jill, Jill becomes a creditor beneficiary. If in return for Sam's car John promises Sam to give a $4,000 gift to Joan, then Joan is a donee beneficiary. In both cases the third party has a right to see that the contract terms are fulfilled, including the right to sue.

b. Incidental Beneficiaries

An incidental beneficiary is someone whom the original parties did not explicitly intend to benefit from the contract. An incidental beneficiary cannot enforce rights under the contract. For example, in the last example assume Bill is Joan's husband. If Joan plans on taking the two of them on a vacation with the $4,000, Bill will benefit, but if John fails to deliver the money, Bill has no right to enforce the contract.

G. DAMAGES

When one party fails to live up to the terms of a contract, a variety of remedies may be available to the other party. We have already discussed several actions that the parties can take on their own without court intervention: rescission, novation, and accord and satisfaction.

Alternatively, the nonbreaching party can go to court to seek monetary damages or specific performance. **Specific performance** is used in situations where there is no alternative comparable product available, such as a particular parcel of land or a rare piece of art. Under this remedy the injured party obtains a court order requiring the breaching party to fulfill the terms of the agreement. Specific performance is a wonderful remedy because the contracting party gets exactly what was contracted for. Also, there is no need to worry about collecting a judgment, the nonbreaching party need not expend time and effort to find another deal, and the actual performance may be more valuable than dollars.

Specific performance
When money damages are inadequate, a court may use this equitable remedy and order the breaching party to perform his or her contractual obligations.

However, keep in mind that specific performance is possible only if dollars are inadequate. In addition, specific performance cannot be used to enforce personal service contracts. Not only would that constitute involuntary servitude, but it would impose an impossible task for the court due to the difficulty of monitoring the party's performance.

The purpose of monetary damages is to give the injured party the benefit of the bargain. Monetary damages can be classified as compensatory, consequential, incidental, nominal, or punitive. In addition, the injured party may be required to take steps to lessen his or her loss. This is known as **mitigation of damages.**

Mitigation of damages
The requirement that the nonbreaching party take reasonable steps to limit his or her damages.

Compensatory damages are awarded to compensate for the loss of the bargain. Their purpose is to place the injured party in the same position that party would have been in had the contract been performed. The classic case describing this form of damages is a 1929 New Hampshire case, known by law students everywhere as the "hairy hand" case.[7] In that case a father took his son to a doctor. The boy had burned his hand, leaving it scarred. The doctor promised to give the boy a "hundred percent perfect hand" by grafting a piece of skin taken from the boy's chest. Everything went well until a few years passed, and the boy entered puberty. When he did so, his hand began sprouting hair, leaving him with a hand uglier than when he had started. The court calculated the damages as the difference between a "perfect hand" and what the boy received, a hairy hand. Not included in the damage award was any pain the boy suffered from the operation or the cost of the operation. The boy would have had to undergo the pain and cost of the operation even if the operation had been successful. Therefore, to compensate the plaintiff for the pain and the cost of the operation, in addition to the difference in the hand, would give the plaintiff more than what was necessary to put him in the position he would have been in had the operation been successful.

In calculating compensatory damages, courts frequently use the following formula:

Promised performance – actual performance – mitigation
    + expenses (incidental damages)

For example, if John agrees with Bill to sell Bill his watch for $500, but Bill only pays $300, John can sue Bill for $200. If Bill had paid nothing and simply reneged on the deal, John could have sold the watch to someone else and could have recovered the difference between that price and the contract price, along with any expenses incurred in finding the new buyer (incidental damages).

Cover
Finding substitute goods.

On the other hand, if John refuses to sell the watch, then Bill has two options. First, he can try to find another watch. The UCC calls this finding of substitute goods **cover.** Then his damages are the cost of the substitute watch minus the contract price. For example, if Bill finds a similar watch but has to pay $700, his damages are $200. Alternatively, he can decide to forgo a new watch. In that case his damages would be the difference between the market price and the contract price.

---

[7]Hawkins v. McGee, 146 A. 641 (N.H. 1929).

Consequential damages arise out of special circumstances that must be foreseeable to the other party. Typically this is handled by notifying the other party of any such circumstances. The classic case setting forth this rule is an English case from 1854.[8] The Hadley family ran a flour mill. Their crankshaft broke, and they gave it to Baxendale to deliver to a foundry for repair. Baxendale promised to deliver the shaft the next day. However, it was not delivered for several days. As a result, the mill was closed for those days. Despite the common practice, the Hadleys did not have an extra crankshaft. Because the Hadleys had not notified Baxendale of that special circumstance, he could not be held liable for their lost profits.

Punitive damages are not allowed in contract actions. However, if the plaintiff can also bring a tort action—for example, for fraud—then punitives are possible. Finally, nominal damages are possible when there has been a breach but no provable damages.

In order to avoid having to litigate damages issues, some contracting parties put **liquidated damages clauses** in their contracts. Such clauses specify what will happen in case of breach. Such clauses are valid so long as they bear a reasonable relationship to the true loss and are not seen as penalty clauses.

Finally, when the parties imperfectly express themselves, sometimes the court will **reform the contract**. For example, assume a covenant not to compete is included in a sale of a business. While it is limited geographically to one county, its duration is for ten years. The court might reform the contract so that the duration is for a shorter period of time.

Consequential damages
Indirect damages that must be foreseeable to be recovered.

Liquidated damages clause
A contract provision that specifies what will happen in case of breach.

Contract reformation
An equitable remedy that allows the courts to "rewrite" contract provisions.

SUMMARY

A contract is an agreement that can be enforced in court. The basic elements of a contract are offer, acceptance, and consideration. Contracts can be classified as bilateral or unilateral; express or implied in fact; formal or informal; executory or executed; and valid, void, voidable, or unenforceable. The most common defenses are lack of contractual capacity, illegality, violation of public policy, lack of genuineness of assent, breach of warranty, and the statute of frauds. Third parties can attain contractual rights either through assignment or delegation or through being an intended beneficiary. A plaintiff bringing a contract action may be under a duty to mitigate damages and is usually seeking specific performance or compensatory or consequential damages.

While many contracts are still controlled by the common law, contracts for the sale of goods are generally governed by Article 2 of the Uniform Commercial Code (UCC). The UCC was drafted by a group of legal scholars with the hope of making commercial law more unified among the states. Most of the UCC's provisions apply to everyone, but some sections contain specific rules that apply to merchants only. Under the UCC everyone is under the obligation to act in good faith.

---

[8]Hadley v. Baxendale, 9 Exch. 341, 156 Eng. Rep. 14 (1854).

‖‖‖ REVIEW QUESTIONS

Pages 357 through 362

1. How do the courts determine if the UCC governs a contract situation?
2. Why does it matter under the UCC whether one or both of the parties are merchants? Give at least two examples.
3. Describe each of the following contracts according to the categories listed in Figure 11-3.
   a. Carlos says to Mary, "Will you paint my house for $2,000?" Mary replies, "Yes, I would be happy to."
   b. Carlos says to Mary, "I will pay you $2,000 if you paint my house next week." The next week Mary begins to paint the house and gets about half-way done when severe weather forces her to wait until the next week to finish the job.
   c. Janet writes to Jim, "I will give you $600 for your car." Jim sends back a letter that says, "I accept."
   d. Joan says to Bill, "I will give you $5,000 if you kill Robert." Bill kills Robert, but Joan refuses to give him the $5,000.
   e. Every Saturday Jimmy came to the Booths' home and mowed their lawn for $15. One Saturday Jimmy arrived while Mr. Booth was on the phone. Mr. Booth simply waved at Jimmy, who then mowed the lawn.

Pages 362 through 369

4. What are the three basic elements of a valid contract claim?
5. What is the objective view of contract law?
6. What are the four basic elements that every offer should contain?
7. Juan says to Jim, "I would like to sell my watch to you." Jim replies, "Great. I will be happy to give you a fair price for it." Has a contract been formed? Why?
8. Sally offers Tom a job as a paralegal, saying she will pay him "what he is worth." Tom accepts. Has a contract been formed? Why?
9. Janet says to Joan, "I am eager to sell my antique vase to you." Joan says, "Would you consider $400 for it?" Has a contract been formed? Why?
10. We Growum, a garden center, places the following advertisement in the Sunday paper.

Spring Planting Sale
Lilac bushes $20

Tuesday John goes to the garden center. All the lilac bushes have been sold. He sues for breach of contract. Will he succeed? Why?
11. Acme Lawn Care receives a call asking them to mow a lawn at 423 Main Street. Unfortunately the mowers misread the address as 432 Main Street. They arrive at that address, unload their mowers, and begin their work. Mr. Adams, the owner, is home and sees what they are doing. He says nothing and lets them complete the job. When they finish and ask to be paid, he refuses. Would a court require Mr. Adams to pay and, if so, under what theory?
12. What are the three ways an offer can be terminated?
13. When may an offeror not revoke an offer?
14. What is the difference between an option contract and a merchant's firm offer?
15. What is the name of the rule that states that the acceptance must completely agree with the terms of the offer?
16. How has the UCC changed the mirror image rule?

Pages 369 through 378

17. An uncle offers his nephew $5,000 if the nephew promises not to smoke marijuana or use other illegal drugs during the next four years while he is away at college. Has a binding contract been formed? Why?

18. John volunteers to take care of Sam's pet rabbit while he is away on vacation. When Sam returns, he is very pleased with the good care John gave his rabbit and tells him that he is going to pay him $50. When John arrives the next day to receive his money, Sam said that he has changed his mind. Is Sam under a contractual obligation to pay John for the care of his rabbit? Why?

19. Anna Sacks was an employee of the Ajax Company for thirty-seven years. The president of the company told her that (in consideration for her outstanding service) when she retired, the company would pay her $200 per month for life. Two years later she retired and began receiving the payments. Shortly thereafter, the company was sold, and the new president refused to continue the payments, arguing that there had never been a valid contract between Ms. Sacks and the company. How do you think the court resolved the case?

20. Millie requested bids from three different contractors for a price to repair the roof on her house. The bids ranged from $5,000 to $20,000. Naturally, Millie accepted the $5,000 bid from We'gottcha Roofing. On a Monday We'gottcha began work by first removing all of the old shingles. The weather prediction was for rain by the end of the week. We'gottcha told Millie she had a choice. Either she could pay them a "bonus" of $15,000 and they would continue work on her roof, or they would have to take the rest of the week to finish other jobs they had started. Millie, afraid all of her household contents would be ruined if rain hit her "deshingled" roof, agreed to the extra money. Will Millie be required to pay the $15,000 bonus? Why?

21. Marvin began negotiations with the Big-W food chain to open a franchise store. The Big-W representative said that first Marvin would have to sell his bakery to raise the necessary money. Marvin was hesitant to do so, but based upon Big-W's representations that his selling the bakery was the only thing preventing them from finalizing the contract, Marvin did so. However, once he had sold the bakery, Big-W said they had found someone else and refused to sign a franchise contract with Marvin. If Marvin were to sue Big-W, would he win under a contract action? Why? Is there any alternative?

Pages 378 through 393

22. Name the six major defenses to a contract action.

23. Jim, who is sixteen years old, buys a stereo from Circuit Playground. Jim takes the stereo to the beach and ruins it when it becomes filled with sand. Jim takes it back to the store and demands the return of the money he paid for the stereo. Will the store have to refund his payment?

24. Mark and Bill are sitting at a bar drinking. They discuss the possibility of Mark selling Bill his watch for $50. Bill leaves, but Mark remains and continues to drink. Two hours later Bill calls Mark and offers him $5 for the watch. Now very intoxicated, Mark mutters, "Whatever." The next day Mark has no memory of the phone call. Will the court enforce this arrangement? Why?

25. Sara offers to sell her car to Janet for $800. Janet thinks Sara means her 1978 VW Beetle and agrees. Sara was thinking of her 1970 VW van. Has a contract been formed? Why?

26. A law firm requires all new attorneys to sign an agreement that states that if they leave the firm for any reason, they will not work for another law firm or open their own practice within a fifty-mile radius for two years. How do you think the court would treat such an agreement? Why?

27. What is the difference between a warranty of merchantability and an implied warranty of fitness? How do both of those differ from an express warranty?

28. Joan offers to buy Bill's sailboat for $2,000. Bill agrees and asks Joan to put it in writing. Joan leaves an e-mail message for her secretary, stating that she wants him to draft a

contract stating that she agrees to buy Bill's sailboat for $2,000. The next day Joan changes her mind. If Bill sues for breach of contract, will he succeed? Why?

Pages 394 through 399

29. What are the four ways in which the parties' contractual obligations can be discharged?
30. How does each of the following differ from the others—complete performance, substantial performance, and material failure to perform?
31. Jones contracted with Smith to log all the timber from his land between the months of September and December. Jones found he was not able to complete the work in the agreed time because his operations were slowed (a) by a local ordinance prohibiting logging during the hunting season, which occurred in September, and (2) by unusually heavy rains in the remaining months. Should Jones's lack of performance be excused? Why?
32. The city of Portage contracts with Get Going Builders to demolish a vacant building and replace it with a park. John Jakes is delighted, as his property is right across the street from the intended park. He envisions a significant increase in his property value. At the last minute the city decides to forgo the park in favor of increased pay for its firefighters. John is dismayed and wants to sue the city. Will he succeed in his suit? Why?
33. Martha contracts with Sam, a noted concert pianist, to take a series of ten music lessons. After the second lesson Sam is offered the opportunity to go on a world tour. He contacts William, a lesser known pianist, to take over his lessons. Martha is upset. Does she have any grounds to complain?
34. What is the difference between an assignment and a delegation?
35. What is the difference between assignments and delegations, on the one hand, and third-party-beneficiary contracts, on the other?

Pages 399 through 401

36. When is specific performance an appropriate remedy?
37. What is cover?
38. What are consequential damages?
39. Sara Smith is a struggling young artist. Recently, however, she was "discovered" when an art dealer saw one of her paintings hanging in a local art gallery. The art dealer contracted with Sara to hold a major showing of her work in six months, November 1. Under the contract Sara was to show no less than ten original paintings. In preparation for the show Sara contracted with Paint Masters, Inc., for four cases of her favorite oil paints to be shipped no later than July 1. Sara heard nothing more from Paint Masters, Inc., until September 1 when one case arrived. Sara attempted to find the same paint from other sources but was able to procure only one more case at $200 more than she had contracted to pay Paint Masters. Because of the delay in shipment, Sara was able to complete only six paintings and the show was canceled. Sara would like to sue Paint Masters, Inc., for the lost profits she would have received from her heightened recognition had the show gone as planned, for the money she had to spend on alternate paints, and for punitive damages to teach Paint Masters a lesson. Please evaluate Sara's situation.
40. Kate contracts with Bennett to buy 100 guitars at $300 each. Kate hopes to resell the guitars for $400 each. When the time for delivery arrives, Bennett refuses to deliver the guitars. Kate then spends $100 in phone calls trying to obtain an alternate supplier. Finally, she finds substitute guitars, but has to pay $350 each for them. She saved $50, however, because in her contract with Bennett she was going to have to pay the shipping. In her new contract, the seller paid the shipping. How much is Kate owed in compensatory damages?
41. The city of Kalamazoo hired Good Builders, Inc., to build a new courthouse for $560,000. Good Builders had barely broken ground when the city notified them that it would not be able to pay for the building after all and asked Good Builders to stop all work. Good

Builders refused, saying, "Hey, you guys signed a contract. We know our rights." At the time the city asked them to stop, Good Builders had expended $5,000 on materials, approximately $3,000 of which could have been returned at no loss to themselves. By completing the project, however, Good Builders expended an additional $400,000. In a breach of contract action by Good Builders against the city, how much money do you think the court should award Good Builders? Why?

Chapter 12

Property and Estate Law

In no country in the world is the love of property more active and more anxious than in the United States.
Alexis de Tocqueville

INTRODUCTION

Property law affects everyone, as it governs ownership rights in both real and personal property. When you buy a home, rent an apartment, or sell a car, you are dealing with property law. Estate law determines how that property is distributed after death: either according to the terms of a will or, in the absence of a will, by following a statutory scheme. This chapter first covers the ownership, leasing, and sale of real and personal property. Then we discuss estate planning, including the importance of writing a will. The chapter ends with an overview of the probate process.

A. PROPERTY LAW

In its broadest sense the legal concept of **property** refers to any valuable right or interest that belongs to a person. Property is usually thought of as being a tangible object, such as a house or an automobile, that is "owned" by an individual, a corporation, or a government. However, the term also applies to the set of rights that specify how a tangible object is to be used. Examples include

Property
A tangible object or a right or ownership interest.

leases, easements, contractual rights, promissory notes, and even admission tickets to concerts or sporting events. There are also circumstances under which a person can have a "property interest" in a job, an idea, or a reputation.

There are two basic types of property: real property and personal property. **Real property,** also referred to as **real estate,** consists of land and whatever is growing on or built on that land. It includes not only the houses, garages, sheds, and other types of buildings that are on the land but also everything that is permanently attached to those buildings—such as light fixtures, plumbing fixtures, and built-in shelves. At times it can be difficult to determine whether something is "permanently" attached. For example, normally a room air conditioner is seen as personal property. However, if the window frame has been removed and the air conditioner bolted to the wall, it might be seen as "permanently" attached, and hence a fixture. When determining whether something should be considered a fixture, the courts look to the amount of damage that would be caused either to the item or to the underlying property if the item was removed from the premises. The courts will also take into account the intention of the parties. In addition, real estate includes the trees and plants growing on the land, as well as the rights to gas and minerals under the land and to the air space above it. In recent years the common law right to air space has been modified so as to not interfere with modern aviation.

All property other than real property is classified as **personal property.** Personal property is sometimes referred to in the law as **chattel.** Personal property is often classified as being either tangible or intangible. **Tangible** property consists of goods that can be touched and moved, such as automobiles, jewelry, clothing, and television sets. **Intangible** property is personal property that cannot be touched, such as a stock certificate or a patent. While you can certainly touch the piece of paper that documents the stock ownership or the awarding of the patent, it is not the paper itself that has value. The term **intellectual property** is used to cover intangible assets such as trademarks, copyrights, and patents that are the product of someone's intellectual creation. **Trademarks** are terms, names, combinations of letters or numbers, and logos that identify particular products or services. Familiar examples include "Dodge," "IBM," and "V-8." **Service marks** are symbols that are used in connection with service-oriented businesses. The law gives the registered holders of these trademarks and service marks the right to control their use. **Copyrights** give authors, composers, and artists the right to control, with certain limitations related to "fair use," the use of their writings, musical performances, and artistic creations. A **patent** gives its owner the right to exclude others from making, using, or selling his or her invention.

Property can change its nature from real to personal or, as noted above, from personal to real. For example, while oil is still in the ground, it is considered to be real property, but once it has been extracted from the ground and loaded on a tanker or sent down a pipeline, it becomes personal property. When trees are still in the forest, they are real property. When they are cut, they become personal property. It is not always easy to determine when this change occurs. For example, a mobile home on the sales lot is personal property. If it is moved to a mobile home park, has its tires removed, and is affixed to a foundation, it becomes real property. However, what if its tires are not removed and it is simply placed on the lot? Is it still personal property?

Real property
Also known as *real estate;* land and items growing on or permanently attached to that land.

Personal property
All property that is not real property.

Freehold Estates	Leasehold Estates
Fee simple absolute estate	Tenancy for a term (estate for years)
Conditional fee estate	Periodic tenancy
Life estate	Tenancy at will
	Tenancy at sufferance

Figure 12-1   Freehold versus Leasehold Estates

Determining whether property is real or personal can have important consequences, as the courts apply different rules to the different types of property. For example, the selling and leasing of personal property are covered by the general principles of contract law and the Uniform Commercial Code, discussed in Chapter 11. The selling and leasing of real estate will be covered below.

1. Ownership of Real Property

The nature of the rights and responsibilities of ownership varies with the type of ownership interest a person holds in the property. As Figure 12-1 illustrates, ownership of land can be categorized as being either a freehold estate or a leasehold estate. When the term **estate** is used as a means of classifying different types of ownership, it refers to an interest or a title in a parcel of real property. Be careful to avoid confusing this use of the term with the way *estate* is used in the probate context. There it is used to refer to the total property, real and personal, that the decedent owned at the time of death.

A **freehold estate** is a right of title to real property that extends for life or some other indeterminate period of time. It involves what we ordinarily think of as "ownership" of a tract of land or a building. It is what you mean when you say that you own your house. A **leasehold estate,** on the other hand, gives a person certain "ownership rights" for a limited period of time, but the title to the property remains in the hands of the "owner." In everyday language these leasehold estates involve renting or leasing property.

The most common form of ownership is what is called a **fee simple absolute estate.** This is ownership that is free from any conditions or restrictions. A **conditional fee estate** is one in which the current owner retains ownership only as long as certain conditions are met. If those conditions are not met, the ownership reverts to the previous owner, the **grantor.** As an example, assume someone donates a piece of property to a charity but places conditions on how that property is to be used. If the charity fails to meet those conditions, the ownership of the property reverts to the person who made the gift or to her or his heirs.

A **life estate** gives the **life tenant** ownership that lasts only as long as that person, or some other named individual, lives. After the named person dies, the ownership reverts to the original owner or passes to a third party. An example might be where the wife of a second marriage is given a life estate to remain in a family home as long as she lives. Upon her death the ownership then reverts to the husband's estate or to his children from a previous marriage.

Estate
An interest in or a title to real property. (Note that this term has a different meaning when used in probate matters.)

Joint tenancy
Ownership by two or more persons who have equal rights in the use of that property. When a joint tenant dies, that person's share passes to the other joint tenant(s).

Tenancy in common
Ownership by two or more people. Ownership shares do not have to be equal, but each has an undivided interest in the property. When a tenant in common dies, that person's share passes either by will or by intestate statute.

Tenancy by the entirety
A special type of joint tenancy applicable only to married couples.

Restrictive covenant
A provision in a deed that prohibits specified uses of the property.

Ownership of property can be sole or shared, through either a joint tenancy or a tenancy in common. A **joint tenancy** occurs when a single estate of land is acquired by two or more persons who have equal rights in the use of that property during their respective lives. A **tenancy in common** is very similar in that it also involves two or more people who share use of the property. The ownership shares do not have to be equal, however, nor do they have to have been acquired at the same time. In addition, on death the ownership interest of a tenant in common passes to his or her heirs, while with a joint tenancy it passes to the co-owner(s). A **tenancy by the entirety** is a special type of joint tenancy applicable only to married couples. It is essentially a joint tenancy modified by the common law theory that the husband and wife are one person. During their lifetimes neither the wife nor the husband can transfer the property without the other's consent. As with any joint tenancy, on the death of one of the spouses the other takes whole title to the exclusion of any other heirs. In some condominium arrangements the individual living units are individually owned or owned in joint tenancy, and the common halls, walks, parking lots, and garden areas are a form of tenancy in common.

The distinction between joint tenancy and tenancy in common is very important. While both represent ways to jointly own property, the part owner of property held as a tenancy in common can bequeath that share to whomever the owner pleases. However, the owner of property held in joint tenancy cannot choose to whom the property will pass on the owner's death. Even if the owner provides in a will that the property will pass to a named individual, it will nonetheless pass to the other joint tenant. In fact, you will often hear the term *joint tenancy* referred to as **joint tenancy with a right of survivorship.**

An owner's rights to use a piece of real estate can be limited by the existence of either a **restrictive covenant** or an **easement.** The former is a provision in a deed that prohibits specified uses of the property and commonly is added at the time a developer subdivides and improves the property before it is marketed for housing. Common provisions include requirements relating to minimum square footage, set-back, and architectural styles. Others may prohibit the installation of satellite dishes in yards or the overnight parking of boats or recreational vehicles in driveways. These covenants are recorded in the county land records and become part of the title for all subsequent owners.

Given the close relationship between the value of an individual condominium unit and the condition and use of other units in the same building or complex, it is not surprising to find that condominium agreements often contain many restrictive covenants. Condominium developers trying to appeal to senior citizens have sometimes included covenants that prohibit young children from living in their units. Such restrictions have usually been upheld as a valid accommodation to the needs of older citizens for "peace and quiet." However, a court would probably not uphold the same restriction if applied to apartments or as part of a zoning plan, as it would violate fair housing laws, which prohibit age discrimination.

Historically, restrictive covenants were also used to exclude some racial and ethnic groups from living in certain areas. In *Shelly v. Kraemer,*[1] however,

---

[1]344 U.S. 1 (1948).

the U.S. Supreme Court ruled that such racially restrictive covenants could not be judicially enforced, and in *Jones v. Alfred H. Mayer Co.*[2] the Court interpreted the federal Civil Rights Act of 1866 as prohibiting racial discrimination in the purchasing and leasing of property. In addition, the federal Civil Rights Act of 1968 and many state and local open housing ordinances now prohibit such discrimination.

An **easement** is the right to use property owned by another for a limited purpose. Utility companies acquire easements that allow them to install and maintain electrical cables and gas pipes. Another common type of easement allows a neighbor to drive over a small section of someone else's lot in order to gain access to his or her own land.

Easement
A right to use property owned by another for a limited purpose.

DISCUSSION QUESTIONS

1. Should a condominium association that wishes to appeal to seniors be allowed to prohibit children from living in its units? What are the policy arguments for and against? How would you distinguish between children living in the unit versus those just visiting? Specifically, if you cannot discriminate on the basis of race, why should you be able to discriminate on the basis of age?

2. Sam and Mary are planning to marry and build a home. With her own money Mary plans on purchasing a piece of property. She wants Sam's name to appear on the deed as a joint tenant. Do you think this is advisable?

2. Rental of Real Property

A **lease** is an agreement in which the property owner, called either the **lessor** or the **landlord,** gives someone else, the **lessee** or the **tenant,** the right to use that property for a designated period of time. A **leasehold** is a parcel of real estate held under a lease. Look again at Figure 12-1. As you can see, leasehold estates can be classified as a tenancy for a term, a periodic tenancy, a tenancy at will, or a tenancy at sufferance.

With a **tenancy for a term,** also sometimes called an **estate for years,** the lease establishes a set period of time during which the lessee will have control and after which all rights revert to the lessor. With a **periodic tenancy** the rental periods are established at a set interval—for example, week to week, month to month, or year to year. At the end of each rental period the lease can be terminated with proper notice. However, if neither party gives such notice, the lease automatically continues. When no time period is specified, it is called a **tenancy at will,** and either the lessee can leave or the lessor can reclaim the land at any time. The law in many states requires that the owner give 30 days' notice before reclaiming possession. This has the effect of converting a tenancy at will into a month-to-month periodic tenancy.

A **tenancy at sufferance** denotes a situation in which the person in possession of the land has no legal right to be there. An example of this would be homeless people occupying an abandoned building.

Lease
An agreement in which the property owner gives someone else the right to use that property for a designated period of time.

Lessor or landlord
The owner of the property being leased.

Lessee or tenant
The person with right of possession during the term of the lease.

---

[2]392 U.S. 409 (1968).

When real estate is leased, a landlord-tenant relationship is created between the lessor and the lessee. The common law favored landlords. The tenant had to take the property in the condition it was in at the time that the lease was entered into, even if the tenant was not aware of defects at the time the lease was signed. The tenant also had to repair any damage resulting from natural disasters or the acts of other people, the tenant, or the tenant's family. The landlord's only obligation to the tenant was that of not interfering with the tenant's "quiet enjoyment" of the premises. **Quiet enjoyment** meant that the landlord could not interfere with the tenant's use of the property with respect to such things as what crops were planted or who was invited onto the property. The tenant's primary obligation was to pay the rent.

Over the years many state legislatures have enacted statutes that provide for a more equitable relationship between landlords and tenants. Such laws often require the owner to repair and maintain the premises at certain minimum levels. The plumbing and heating must work, the windows and the doors have to close, and so on. If an apartment is being rented as a residential unit, then it must come complete with running water, a working furnace, and other minimum living essentials. This requirement is present even if not written into the lease and is known as the **implied warranty of habitability.** It requires that the property be fit for the purpose for which it is being rented. These minimum standards are often equated with whatever is required in the local housing code.

A **constructive eviction** occurs when the landlord does something to deprive the tenant of quiet enjoyment of the land, such as shutting off the water or changing the locks. If the tenant is forced to abandon the property, then the tenant can rely on the constructive eviction as a defense to any further requirement to pay rent.

State laws also frequently regulate the handling of security deposits. A **security deposit** is an amount of money, usually equal to one month's rent, that is collected at the time the lease is signed and then held by the landlord to cover the cost of repairs that may be needed when the tenant moves out. Tenants are held responsible for any damage done to the property beyond what is considered to be "normal wear and tear." State laws often place limits on the amount of money that can be held as a security deposit, require the landlord to return the security deposit within a set amount of time after the tenant vacates, require the landlord to document the cost of repairs that are deducted from the deposit, and may even require the payment of interest on the amount of money held.

Some states and cities have rent control statutes and ordinances that regulate the amount of rent that can be charged for existing apartments. In addition, most states have "open housing" laws that prohibit landlords from discriminating in terms of the types of tenants to whom they rent. As mentioned above in the context of restrictive covenants, while some restrictions are possible in relation to the sale of condominiums, such restrictions are usually not allowed with the rental of real estate. One area that is currently causing a great deal of controversy is the interpretation of state statutes that make it unlawful to discriminate on the basis of marital status. The courts are split on whether a landlord can refuse to rent to an unmarried couple. Even in states that have a fair housing statute prohibiting discrimination on the basis of marital status, some courts have allowed the discrimination under the theory that the denial was based on the couple's engaging in criminal conduct, "cohabiting," and not on their marital status.

Quiet enjoyment
The tenant's right to be free from interference from the landlord with respect to how the property is used.

Implied warranty of habitability
A requirement that property be fit for the purpose for which it is being rented. Owners are required to repair and maintain the premises at certain minimum levels.

Constructive eviction
An act by a landlord that makes the premises unfit or unsuitable for occupancy.

PRACTICAL TIP

Before signing a lease, write a list describing any damaged areas and, if possible, photograph them. Have the landlord date and sign the list.

Baiz v. Hoffius
222 Mich. App. 210, 564 N.W.2d 493 (1997)

CORRIGAN, P.J.

In these consolidated appeals, plaintiffs appeal by right the orders granting summary disposition to defendants in this fair housing action. We affirm.

Defendants John and Terry Hoffius, a married couple, rent residential property in Jackson, Michigan. In June 1993, plaintiffs Kristal Mc-Cready and Keith Kerr contacted defendants in response to defendants' advertisement about housing for rent. Defendants refused to rent to plaintiffs when they learned that McCready and Kerr were not married but intended to live in the same rental unit. Similarly, plaintiff Rose Baiz telephoned defendants in July 1993 about the property. Defendants also declined to rent to Baiz when they learned that she was not married to plaintiff Peter Perusse yet planned to live with him. Defendant John Hoffius told plaintiffs that unmarried cohabitation violated his religious beliefs.

Plaintiffs filed two separate complaints with the Jackson Fair Housing Commission. Testers from the Commission posed as potential renters and contacted defendants. Defendants did not ask the marital status of all the testers. Defendants, however, refused to permit unmarried testers to inspect the apartments, claiming that the units only were available to married couples. Defendants stated that they usually did not rent to unmarried couples.

Defendants moved for summary disposition on plaintiffs' complaints, arguing in part that plaintiffs failed to state a claim upon which relief could be granted because the Elliott-Larsen Civil Rights Act, MCL 37.2502(1); MSA 3.548(502)(1), did not protect unmarried cohabitation. Defendants also argued that, if the Civil Rights Act protected unmarried cohabitation, it was unconstitutional because it would force defendants to violate their sincerely held religious beliefs against unmarried cohabitation.

The cases were heard separately, but decided similarly. Both circuit court judges opined that the cases involved statutory interpretation, and both declined to address the constitutional issues. The judges noted that the Civil Rights Act protected status, not conduct. They opined that unmarried cohabitation was unprotected conduct, not protected marital status. Accordingly, they determined that the Civil Rights Act did not protect unmarried cohabitation. We agree.

Plaintiffs first assert that defendants violated the Civil Rights Act by discriminating against them based on their marital status. Whether unmarried cohabitation enjoys protection from housing discrimination under the Civil Rights Act is an issue of first impression in this state. Cases from other jurisdictions reflect divergent opinions on this issue. For example, in *Smith v. Fair Employment & Housing Comm.*, 12 Cal. 4th 1143; 913 P.2d 909 (1996) *cert. pending,* the landlord presented arguments similar to those of defendants in this case. The California Supreme Court ruled that the California Fair Employment and Housing Act protected unmarried cohabitants against housing discrimination and rejected the landlord's argument that the unmarried tenants' sexual conduct, rather than their marital status, was at issue. Id. at 915-918. *See also Swanner v. Anchorage Equal Rights Comm.*, 874 P.2d 274, *cert. den.*, 115 S. Ct. 460 (1994); *Attorney General v. Desilets*, 418 Mass. 316; 636 N.E.2d 233 (1994), both of which held in accordance with *Smith.*

In contrast, the Supreme Court of Wisconsin decided that a landlord's refusal to rent to unmarried tenants was based on their conduct of living together and not on their marital status in *County of Dane v. Norman*, 174 Wis. 2d 683; 497 N.W.2d 714, 717-718 (1993). The Minnesota Supreme Court considered that state's criminal fornication statute when deciding this same issue in *State by Cooper v. French*, 460 N.W.2d 2 (Minn. 1990). The Court concluded that the Minnesota Human Rights Act did not extend to protect unmarried, cohabiting couples in housing cases. Id. at 7. The Court added:

Before abandoning fundamental values and institutions, we must pause and take stock of our present social order: millions of drug abusers; rampant child abuse; a rising underclass without marketable job skills; children roaming the streets; children with only one parent or no parents at all; and children growing up with no one to guide them in developing any set of values. How can we expect anything else when the state itself contributes, by arguments of this kind, to further erosion of fundamental institutions that have formed the foundation of our civilization for centuries? [Id. at 11.]

Whether the Civil Rights Act protects unmarried cohabitants from housing discrimination raises questions of statutory interpretation. Statutory interpretation is a question of law, which we review de novo. When courts construe statutory meaning, their primary goal is to ascertain and give effect to legislative intent. This Court first considers the specific statutory language to determine the intent of the Legislature. The Legislature is presumed to intend the meaning that the statute plainly expresses. Judicial construction of a statute is not permitted where the plain and ordinary meaning of the language is clear.

MCL 37.2502(1); MSA 3.548(502)(1) provides in relevant part:

> (1) A person engaging in a real estate transaction, or a real estate broker or salesman, shall not on the basis of religion, race, color, national origin, age, sex, familial status, or marital status of a person or a person residing with that person:

> (a) Refuse to engage in a real estate transaction with a person.

The Civil Rights Act does not define the term "marital status." In defining a term, courts should attempt to give effect to the legislative intent. *Miller v. CA Muer Corp.*, 420 Mich. 355, 362; 362 N.W.2d 650 (1984). The Civil Rights Act's purpose is to prevent discrimination based on membership in certain classes and to "eliminate the effects of offensive or demeaning stereotypes, prejudices and biases." Id. at 363. "By including marital status as a protected class, the Legislature manifested its intent to prohibit discrimination based on whether a person is married." Id.

The public policy of this state, as reflected in our laws, favors the institution of marriage. . . .

When promulgating new laws, the Legislature is charged with the knowledge of existing laws on the same subject and is presumed to have considered the effect of new laws on existing laws. . . . Because the Legislature would not have intended the Civil Rights Act to insulate criminal conduct, cohabitation is not protected conduct under the act. . . . Although courts are to construe liberally remedial statutes, we decline to recognize the Civil Rights Act as preventing housing discrimination against unmarried couples and at the same time legitimizing criminal conduct.

Further, if two statutes lend themselves to a construction that avoids conflict, that construction should control. . . . Our construction avoids conflict between the Civil Rights Act and the criminal cohabitation statute. The Civil Rights Act prohibits discrimination against couples who enjoy marital status, but the act is not violated when a landlord refuses to rent to unmarried persons who will be engaging in criminal unmarried cohabitation.

When two acts relate to the same subject, courts presume against repeal of the former statute by implication. If possible, courts give effect to both acts. . . .

Plaintiffs have not met their heavy burden of demonstrating that the Legislature intended to repeal the criminal cohabitation statute. Had the Legislature intended to repeal the criminal cohabitation statute, it would have done so. . . . Making social policy is a job for the Legislature, not for this Court. Indeed, the appropriate branch for resolution of the moral issue presented is the legislative branch, which is well equipped to weigh these issues.

Plaintiffs next contend that society's need to provide equal access in housing outweighs defendants' religious beliefs that they should not rent to an unmarried couple. Neither trial court addressed this issue in its opinion; therefore, the issue is not preserved for review. Additionally, our Supreme Court has refused to reach constitutional claims that are unnecessary to the resolution of a case. We decline to review this unpreserved issue, and we will not reach the constitutional issue because it is unnecessary in deciding this matter.

Affirmed.

CASE DISCUSSION QUESTIONS

1. The court in *Baiz* quoted from *State of Minnesota v. French,* 460 N.W.2d 2 (Minn. 1990), for the general proposition that the state's requesting protection for unmarried couples in acquiring rental housing was the cause for much of society's problems. In that case, the dissent had this to say:

> Religious and moral values include not discriminating against others solely because of their color, sex, or whom they live with, avoiding unnecessary emotional suffering, showing tolerance for nontraditional lifestyles, and treating others as one would wish to be treated. . . . It may be difficult for some individuals to recognize invidious discrimination, but one must not lose sight of the continuing fight of minorities to be protected from a "probable majority" point of view. It was not long ago that blacks and women were widely viewed as second-class citizens. Discrimination usually comes in less obvious forms—such as against single parents, those with AIDS, homosexuals, the elderly, and those living together—but no less invidious forms. The majority, in effect, would have us return to the day of "separate but equal" where individuals such as French would be permitted to keep their neighborhoods free of "undesirables" and "nonbelievers." . . .
>
> Discriminating against unmarried individuals living with members of the opposite sex is neither the cause or the solution to societal woes.

Id. at 17, 20. Who do you think presents the better argument, and why?

2. What did the court state was the first step in statutory analysis?

3. Why did the court think that the refusal to rent to an unmarried couple did not violate the state's fair housing laws?

4. Why did the court refuse to discuss the issue of whether the landlord's religious beliefs justified the discrimination?

State laws also determine the procedures landlords must use to retake possession of their property. Under the common law a landlord could forcibly **evict** a tenant who was in default of any term in the lease. The landlord or the landlord's agent could go in and literally throw the tenant and a tenant's personal possessions out on the street. As a result of the hardship and the frequent violence such procedures brought about, most states now require that a landlord first give an appropriate eviction notice and then go to court to get local law enforcement agents, such as police or sheriff's deputies, to supervise the physical removal of the tenant and any possessions. In some states these eviction procedures are known as **forcible entry and detainer** or **unlawful detainer** actions. Note, however, that the phrase *forcible entry and detainer* can be confusing, as in some states such an action can be brought by anyone, including the tenant, who has been unlawfully deprived of rightful possession of the property.

In an eviction proceeding most state courts have held that an implied warranty of habitability defense can be used. Therefore, the landlord cannot evict a tenant for failure to pay rent if the landlord has failed to maintain the premises at minimum standards.

3. Transfer of Real Property

Real property can be transferred (1) through a sales transaction, (2) at the death of the owner, (3) as a gift, (4) through a seizure by a creditor, (5) through an eminent domain proceeding, or (6) by adverse possession.

a. Sale

In the typical residential real estate transaction the seller either advertises the availability of the property or lists it for sale with a real estate agent. If a real estate agent is involved, the seller will sign a **listing agreement,** which spells out the nature of the services the agent will perform and how the agent will be compensated for those services.

The legal aspects of the sale start when the potential buyer makes an offer to purchase the property. Real estate agents usually carry standardized fill-in-the-blank offer forms, and the buyer's agent fills in the information regarding the description of the property, the amount of money being offered, a listing of the fixtures and appliances that are to be included, and the date of possession. The offer sheet also usually contains a number of clauses that make the offer contingent on the buyer's being able to obtain financing, often at a specified interest rate; the building's passing a termite inspection; and so forth. The buyer then turns over a specified sum of money to the real estate agent as **earnest money.** This money is applied to the purchase price at the time the sale is completed and may be forfeited if the buyer defaults prior to the completion of the sale. The seller, in turn, accepts the offer, rejects it, or proposes a counteroffer. To accept the offer, the seller simply signs the appropriate line on the offer sheet. A counteroffer usually consists of a lower asking price, somewhere between the buyer's offer and the original asking price.

While an offer and acceptance create a binding contract, one of the conditions of the offer sheet is frequently that a more formal contract be drawn up within a specified time. In a typical residential sale this is the stage at which lawyers first become directly involved in the transaction. Real estate brokers and bar associations disagree about how much legal assistance real estate professionals should provide and how much of the work should be done by attorneys. Local practices differ based on the nature of the accommodations that have been worked out between the two groups.

While the buyer arranges for financing, the seller arranges for a title search, and sometimes title insurance. A **title search** is an examination of documents recording title to the property to ensure the owner has a clear title to the property. A **clear title,** also known as **marketable title,** is an ownership right that is free from encumbrances or other defects. An **encumbrance** is a lien or other type of security interest that signifies that some other party has a legitimate claim to the property as a means of satisfying debts of the current owner. Examples of encumbrances include mortgages, liens for unpaid taxes, and mechanic's liens. A **mechanic's lien** is a claim by a contractor or repair person who had done work on the house for which he or she has not been fully paid.

The buyer guarantees the title by either obtaining an up-to-date abstract or purchasing title insurance. An **abstract** is a condensed history of the title, which includes the chain of ownership and a record of all liens, taxes, or other encumbrances that may impair the title. **Title insurance** is an insurance policy in which the insurer agrees to indemnify the purchaser or mortgage holder against any loss due to a defective title. If defects in the title are found and the seller is unwilling or unable to correct these defects, the buyer can refuse to complete the transaction.

A **real estate closing** is a meeting at which the buyer and the seller or their representatives sign and deliver a variety of legal documents associated with the sale and transfer of the property. The most important part of the closing is the

Listing agreement
A document that spells out the nature of the services a real estate agent will perform with respect to selling real property and how the agent will be compensated for those services.

Earnest money
The money the buyer turns over to the real estate agent to be applied to the purchase price of property.

Title search
An examination of documents recording title to a property to ensure the owner has a clear title.

Clear title
Also known as **marketable title;** an ownership right that is free from encumbrances or other defects.

Abstract
A condensed history of the title, which includes the chain of ownership and a record of all liens, taxes, or other encumbrances that may impair the title.

Title insurance
Insurance against any loss due to a defective title.

delivery of the deed. The **deed** is the legal document that formally conveys title to the property to the new owner. In most sales a **warranty deed** is used. With this type of deed the seller, also known as the *grantor,* promises "clear title" to the property, one that has no encumbrances or other defects.

As part of a divorce settlement one spouse will often use a quitclaim deed to sign over his or her share of the real estate they held in joint ownership. With a **quitclaim deed** the grantor gives up any claims to the property without making any assertions about there being a clear title.

At the closing the buyer signs the mortgage documents, and the seller receives the proceeds of the sale. A **closing statement** is prepared to itemize and allocate all costs and moneys exchanged among the various parties, including financial institutions and real estate brokers. In many states, property taxes assessed for one year are not collected until the next year, and the new owner is responsible for paying taxes that were incurred by the previous owner. If this is the case, the seller will give the buyer a credit that corresponds to the amount of taxes still owed for the period preceding the sale. If the actual possession of the property does not correspond to the closing date, credits are given to reflect the rent being paid by the seller to the buyer or by the buyer to the seller.

As an alternative to the standard sale process described above, real estate is sometimes sold through a **land contract.** In essence it is an installment sales contract. The buyer takes physical possession of the property and begins making monthly payments to the seller, which will be applied to the agreed-on sale price of the property. However, the seller retains legal title to the property until all the agreed-on installment payments have been made. If the buyer for some reason defaults in making the payments, the contract is broken, and the seller gets to keep title to the property, as well as any payments that were made during the course of the contract.

b. Death of the Owner

What happens to people's property when they die depends on the type of ownership they had and whether they had a will. If the property was held as a **joint tenancy,** the **decedent's** share passes automatically to the surviving joint owner(s). Such a transaction occurs independently of any provisions in the decedent's will, and the property is not considered to be part of her or his estate.

If property was owned individually or as a tenancy in common, it becomes part of the decedent's estate and is then transferred according to the provisions of the will. A gift of real estate by will is called a **devise.** If the person died without a will, the property is distributed according to the special procedures set out in state statutes for those who do not leave a will. These procedures are explained in more detail in the section on estate planning below.

c. Gift

Property can also be transferred as a gift. The elements for a valid gift include an offer, an acceptance, and delivery. Wealthy parents might give a child a house as a wedding gift or elderly parents might wish to transfer ownership of a vacation condo to their children before they die rather than having it become part of their estate. Such gifts are encouraged by the fact that federal tax laws allow gifts of less than a designated amount to be transferred tax free.

Deed
The legal document that formally conveys title to the property to the new owner.

Warranty deed
A deed in which the seller promises clear title to the property.

Quitclaim deed
A deed in which the grantor gives up any claims to the property without making any assertions about there being a clear title.

Closing statement
An itemized allocation of all the costs and moneys exchanged among the various parties, including financial institutions and real estate brokers, when a property is sold.

Land contract
An installment contract for the sale of land.

Decedent
A person who died.

Devise
A gift of real estate that is given to someone through a will.

d. Seizure by a Creditor

Foreclosure
The process by which a creditor who holds a mortgage or some other form of a lien on real property can force the sale of that property in order to satisfy the debt to the mortgagee or lien holder.

Power of sale clause
A clause authorizing a private foreclosure sale that does not require court action.

Eminent domain
The power of government to take private property for public purposes.

Just compensation
The amount of money the government must pay the owner of property it seizes through eminent domain.

Foreclosure is the process by which a creditor who holds a mortgage or some other form of a lien on real property can force the sale of that property in order to satisfy the debt to the mortgagee or lien holder. Many mortgages include **power of sale clauses,** authorizing private foreclosure sales that do not require court action.

e. Eminent Domain

Eminent domain is the power of government to take private property for public purposes. Although the government does not need the owner's consent, it is required to provide the owner with **just compensation** for the property. If the government and the owner cannot agree on a "fair" price, the government initiates an action for eminent domain, and the courts determine what constitutes fair market value for the property.

In recent years controversies over eminent domain have centered around the use of zoning laws. For example, some zoning laws regulate the way in which property can be used, such as prohibiting the construction of a factory on land that is zoned residential. Other regulations require the owner to turn over a portion of the land as a condition of being granted a variance or special use permit. The issue in these cases usually revolves not around whether the government had the power to make the regulation but rather around whether compliance with the regulation amounted to a taking so that the owner would have to be compensated.

An example of the first type of restriction—when a zoning law regulates the way the property may be used—occurred in *Lucas v. South Carolina Coastal Council.*[3] In 1986 Mr. Lucas purchased two beach-front lots with the intention of building single-family houses. He paid $975,000 for the lots. Then in 1988, before he could start construction on the lots, the legislature enacted the Beachfront Management Act. The act prohibited Mr. Lucas from building any permanent structure on his land. He sued, contending that the act constituted a "taking" under the Fifth and Fourteenth Amendments that required payment of just compensation. The U.S. Supreme Court agreed.

The second type of zoning case—one dealing with a requirement that the owner dedicate a portion of the land for public purposes—was the focus of *Dolan v. City of Tigard.*[4] Florence Dolan, the owner of a plumbing and electric store, applied to the city for a permit to redevelop the site. The city agreed to give her the permit so long as she dedicated fifteen feet as a public greenway and an additional fifteen-foot strip as a pedestrian/bicycle pathway. The case eventually reached the U.S. Supreme Court. The Court first noted that the takings clause of the Fifth Amendment, applicable to the states through the Fourteenth Amendment, provides that the government cannot take land for public use without providing just compensation. On the other hand, the Court cited an earlier case for the proposition that

> "[g]overnment hardly could go on if to some extent values incident to property could not be diminished without paying for every such change in the general law." A land use

---

[3] 505 U.S. 1003 (1992).
[4] 512 U.S. 374 (1994).

regulation does not effect a taking if it "substantially advances legitimate state interests" and does not "deny an owner economically viable use of his land."[5]

The court next stated that it must determine whether there was an "essential nexus" between a "legitimate state interest" and the conditions that the city applied to Ms. Dolan's permit. The court stated that

[un]doubtedly, the prevention of flooding along Fanno Creek and the reduction of traffic congestion in the Central Business District qualify as the type of legitimate public purposes we have upheld. It seems equally obvious that a nexus exists between preventing flooding along Fanno Creek and limiting development within the creek's 100-year floodplain. Petitioner proposes to double the size of her retail store and to pave her now-gravel parking lot, thereby expanding the impervious surface on the property and increasing the amount of stormwater run-off into Fanno Creek.

The same may be said for the city's attempt to reduce traffic congestion by providing for alternative means of transportation. In theory, a pedestrian/bicycle pathway provides a useful alternative means of transportation for workers and shoppers.[6]

However, that was not the end of the Court's decision. The second part of the analysis required a particularized look at the petitioner's case, specifically a determination of whether the "required dedication is related both in nature and extent to the impact of the proposed development."[7] The Court noted that "the city has never said why a public greenway, as opposed to a private one, was required in the interest of flood control."[8] The Court went on to explain the importance of the distinction. "The difference to petitioner, of course, is the loss of her ability to exclude others. As we have noted, this right to exclude others is 'one of the most essential sticks in the bundle of rights that we commonly characterized as property.'"[9] Similarly, the city had not demonstrated how the dedication of the pedestrian/bicycle pathway would offset the increased traffic demand caused by the increased size of Ms. Dolan's store. The Court concluded by stating that

[c]ities have long engaged in the commendable task of land use planning, made necessary by increasing urbanization particularly in metropolitan areas such as Portland. The city's goals of reducing flooding hazards and traffic congestion, and providing for public greenways, are laudable, but there are outer limits to how this may be done. "A strong public desire to improve the public condition [will not] warrant achieving the desire by a shorter cut than the constitutional way of paying for the change."[10]

The Court then remanded the case to the lower court for further proceedings consistent with its opinion.

To summarize, in this second type of zoning case, when the government places a zoning restriction on how a landowner may use a portion of his or her

---

[5]Id. at 384-385.

[6]Id. at 387.

[7]Id. at 391.

[8]Id. at 392.

[9]Id. at 384.

[10]Id. at 396.

land, the government will not have to pay the landowner if the restriction advances legitimate state interests and does not deny the owner the economically viable use of the land. However, if the restriction does deny the owner an economically viable use of the land and there is no clear relationship between a legitimate state interest to be served by the restriction and the restriction, the government will have to pay just compensation. The restriction then qualifies as a taking for which the government must pay.

DISCUSSION QUESTION

3. Why should the government be able to take somebody's property without his or her consent? Give some examples of what you would view as legitimate uses of eminent domain.

f. Adverse Possession

Each night as Greg drove up his driveway, he paused to appreciate the lovely flowers he had planted alongside his fence, bordering his land. One night, however, he drove home to find the flowers dug up and the fence gone. After a few frantic calls he discovered that when he erected the fence, he had inadvertently placed it two feet over the property line and onto his neighbor's land. Does Greg have any legal recourse? The answer will depend on who owns the land—Greg or his neighbor. Even if the neighbor holds the deed to the property, it is possible for Greg to obtain real property rights through a process known as **adverse possession.** For someone to qualify for ownership in this manner, that person's use of someone else's property must be

Adverse possession
A transfer of real property rights that occurs after someone other than the owner has had actual, open, adverse, and exclusive use of the property for a statutorily determined number of years.

1. actual,
2. open,
3. adverse, and
4. exclusive

for a statutorily determined number of years, usually between five and twenty. If all these conditions are met, many states grant a right to assume legal control of that property. In this case Greg's use of the property was actual—he built a fence on the land. It was also open—anyone could view the fence. Adverse simply means that the use of the land interfered with that of the rightful owner. That element is also satisfied. Finally, because Greg placed a fence and not just flowers in the area, his use of the land was also exclusive. The only question that remains is whether in Greg's state he has used the land for the requisite number of years. If that element is also satisfied, then Greg and not his neighbor owns that strip of land. However, to ensure his claim, Greg should go to court and request that the court quiet title so that Greg, the adverse possessor, will have a marketable title to the land.

4. Transfer of Personal Property

Personal property changes hands in much the same way real property does. It can be sold, it can be given away, it can be seized for nonpayment of a debt, and it can become part of a person's estate. In addition, with personal property there is a distinction among lost, abandoned, and mislaid property. Property is classified as lost if the owner has involuntarily parted with it and does not know where to find it. On the other hand, if the owner deliberately placed it somewhere and then forgot where it had been placed, it is classified as mislaid rather than lost. It is considered abandoned property when the owner left it with no intention of coming back to reclaim it. If you find lost property, you acquire title that is good against everyone except the true owner. However, you may have to turn the property over to the police for a certain amount of time to ensure that the rightful owner does not return to claim it. On the other hand, if you find mislaid property, property that was inadvertently left behind, such as a ring next to a sink, then you acquire no ownership rights in it. Finally, if you find abandoned property, you become the owner.

When personal property is only temporarily transferred to someone other than the owner for a specified purpose, a **bailment** occurs. For example, a bailment occurs when you take your clothes to be dry cleaned or your car to be repaired. A bailment also occurs when you contract with a moving company to move your furniture from one location to another. The owner is called the **bailor**, and the party taking temporary control of the property is called the **bailee**. The law imposes a duty on the bailee to exercise reasonable care toward the property while it is under the bailee's control.

B. ESTATE PLANNING

Estate planning is the analysis of a person's future financial needs and the development of strategies to meet those needs while the individual is alive, to expedite the probate process that follows death (see Section 4 below), and to avoid inheritance and estate taxes. In this context an **estate** is the total property of whatever kind, both real and personal, that a person owns at the time of his or her death. At the time of a person's death this property is distributed on the basis of the person's will and the terms of state laws with respect to such things as joint ownership rights, life insurance contracts, and probate laws.

1. Wills

A **will** is a legal expression of a person's wishes as to how his or her property should be distributed upon death. When someone dies without a valid will, that person is said to have died **intestate**. When this occurs, the person's property is distributed on the basis of guidelines laid down by the legislature of the state in which the deceased was domiciled (i.e., had his or her legal residence) at the time of death. Although these laws usually favor the spouse and the children, they may not correspond to how the deceased wanted to dispose of the estate. For this reason, as well as to take advantage of potential tax savings, it is generally desirable to have an up-to-date will.

In judging the validity of a will the courts focus on three factors: whether the testator was an adult, usually eighteen or older; his or her testamentary capacity; and whether the testator voluntarily executed the will. As to the second requirement of testamentary capacity, all that is required is that the testator know what he or she owns and what he or she wants to do with it, as well as

Bailment
A temporary transfer of personal property to someone other than the owner for a specified purpose.

Bailor
The owner of the personal property that is being temporarily transferred as part of a bailment.

Bailee
The party taking temporary control of the personal property during a bailment.

Estate
The total property of whatever kind, both real and personal, that a person owns at the time of his or her death.

Will
The document used to express a person's wishes as to how his or her property should be distributed upon death.

Intestate
When a person dies without a valid will.

Testator/Testatrix
The person making a will to direct how his or her assets will be distributed at death.

Bequest
Also known as a legacy; a gift of personal property in a will.

Beneficiary
The person named in a will, insurance policy, or trust who receives a benefit.

Executor/Executrix
A person appointed by the testator to carry out the directions and requests in his or her will.

Self-proving clause
A notarized affidavit, signed by the attesting witnesses, that may eliminate the need to call witnesses during the probate process to attest to the validity of the will.

Codicil
A supplement or addition to a will that modifies, explains, or adds to its provisions.

knowing the "natural objects of the testator's bounty"—that is, the testator's spouse and other close relatives. The third requirement is intended to invalidate a will that the testator signed due to fraud or undue influence.

Wills are classified as formal, informal, and nuncupative. A **formal will** is one that has been prepared on a word processor or typewriter and has been properly signed by the **testator** (the person making the will) and the required witnesses. (*Note:* In some states a female testator is known as a *testatrix*.) Will contests often revolve around arguments that the testator either was not competent or was unduly influenced. Should there be a will contest, the witnesses will be asked to testify as to whether the testator knew the extent of the testator's property and knew who the natural beneficiaries were. In addition, they will be asked to testify regarding whether the testator signed voluntarily, understood what was signed, knew it was a will, and asked the witnesses to sign.

A **holographic will,** or informal will, is one that was handwritten by the testator, without the witness signatures necessary for a formal will. Only about half the states recognize such wills as valid. A **nuncupative will** is an oral will. Few states recognize such wills, and those that recognize them do so only when the testator was in fear of imminent death and usually require at least two witnesses.

The standard will consists of a clause that identifies the testator, clauses making specific legacies or bequests, and signature clauses for the testator and witnesses. A gift of real estate in a will is called a **devise,** while a gift of personal property in a will is called a **bequest** or a **legacy.** The person named to receive the gift is called a **beneficiary.** The typical will also includes provisions for the payment of taxes and expenses, funeral arrangements, and appointment of executors and guardians and a simultaneous death clause. An **executor** (or **executrix**) is a person appointed by the testator to carry out the directions and requests in the will. A **guardian** is one who is given the responsibility of managing the affairs or property of a person who is incapable of administering his or her own affairs. For example, a guardian might be appointed to care for the decedent's minor children. A **simultaneous death clause** states that if a person named as a beneficiary in the will dies within a short period of time after the decedent dies, it will be assumed for purposes of the will that the person in question failed to survive the decedent. Such clauses are normally inserted for tax purposes. Without such a clause the estate of each decedent might be taxed as though each survived the other and hence inherited the property from the other. Therefore, estate taxes would have to be paid twice.

In some jurisdictions the courts will dispense with the need to call in witnesses to attest to the validity of a will if it contains a **self-proving clause.** Such a clause is actually a notarized affidavit, signed by the attesting witnesses. The clause simply states that the witnesses swear to the information that a probate court would need in order to admit the will to probate—that is, that the testator was at least eighteen years old, appeared to be of sound mind, and was not acting under any outside influence.

A testator can change a will with a codicil. The **codicil** has to be signed and witnessed like a will. Alternatively, the testator can destroy the old will and draft a new one.

2. Living Wills

A **living will** is not really a "will." It does not express a person's wishes as to how his or her property should be distributed upon death. Rather it is the expression of a person's wishes regarding the withholding or withdrawal of life-support equipment and other heroic measures to sustain life if the individual has an incurable or irreversible condition that will cause death. These documents are also sometimes referred to as **medical directives.** Closely related are **health care proxies** and **durable powers of attorney,** in which individuals delegate legal authority to make medical or financial decisions for them if they are too incapacitated to make them themselves.

Living will
Also known as a **medical directive;** a document expressing a person's wishes regarding the withholding or withdrawal of life-support equipment and other heroic measures to sustain life if the individual has an incurable or irreversible condition that will cause death.

3. Trusts

In order to avoid some aspects of probate and to minimize tax liabilities, modern estate planning often includes the creation of specialized trusts. A **trust** is a legal relationship in which one party holds property for the benefit of another. In this context the property is transferred to a trust fund, where it is to be used for the benefit of a designated person or persons rather than passing directly to them as part of the probate process. The person who creates the trust is called the **donor, grantor,** or **settlor.** The person appointed to administer the trust is the **trustee,** and the person who receives the benefits of the trust is the **beneficiary.**

The two types of trusts most commonly used in estate planning are inter vivos trusts and testamentary trusts. An **inter vivos trust** is one that is created before a person's death. *Inter vivos* is Latin for "among the living." A **living trust** is a commonly used type of inter vivos trust specifically designed to avoid probate. This type of trust allows a person, while still living, to benefit another. For example, parents might set up a trust that provides annual stipends to their children. Such inter vivos trusts can be either revocable or irrevocable. With a **revocable trust** the donor can change the beneficiaries and the terms, and even terminate the trust completely at any time and take back full ownership and control of the property. On the other hand, with an **irrevocable trust** the terms cannot be changed, and the donor cannot regain ownership or control of the property. A **testamentary trust** is created by a will and does not become effective until after the testator's death.

Trust
A legal relationship in which one party holds property for the benefit of another.

Donor
Also known as a **grantor** or **settlor;** a person who creates a trust.

Trustee
The person appointed to administer a trust.

4. Probate Process

Probate is the process of the court overseeing the distribution of property left by someone with a will or by someone who dies without a will. Jointly owned property does not have to go through probate, as it automatically passes to the joint owner. Also, unless the estate is named as the beneficiary, life insurance proceeds go directly to the named beneficiary.

The formal probate proceedings start with the filing of a petition in the probate court. This petition is usually accompanied by a certified copy of the death certificate and a will, if one exists. After payment of required fees, letters of testamentary are issued to give the **executor,** or a court-appointed **administrator** (or **administratrix**) if no executor is named in the will, the power to take control of the deceased's assets, pay the bills, and distribute the

Probate
The process of court supervision over the distribution of a deceased person's property.

Administrator/ Administratrix
A person appointed by the court to carry out the directions and requests of someone's will.

NETNOTE

The Uniform Probate Code has been adopted by eighteen states. You can access the text of the code as it has been adopted by each of those states by going to *www.law.cornell.edu/uniform/probate.html.*

proceeds of the estate. Various inventories and other reports have to be filed with the court at several stages of this process. The probate process provides an opportunity for unsecured creditors of the decedent to submit claims for payment from the estate.

a. Intestate Succession

The first step in the probate process is to determine whether the deceased had a will. As discussed earlier, if no will exists, the deceased is said to have died **intestate,** and the probate property will be distributed according to a series of rules established in state statutes. Most intestate laws give a set proportion of the estate to the surviving spouse, with the rest going to the children. If there are no children, the estate assets usually go first to the spouse, second to the decedent's parents, and then to brothers and sisters.

Heir is the generic term for someone entitled to inherit property left by the decedent. **Kindred** are those persons related to the decedent by blood. A relationship through blood is also known as **consanguinity.** Persons related by marriage are said to be related by **affinity.** A **lineal heir** is someone who is a grandparent, parent, child, grandchild, or great-grandchild of the decedent. **Descendants** or **issue** are those lineal heirs who descend from, or issue from, the decedent, such as children and grandchildren. A **collateral heir** is one who has the same ancestors but does not descend from the decedent. A brother or sister of the decedent would be a collateral heir. Figure 12-2 illustrates these relationships.

If an heir is not alive at the time the assets are distributed, the dead heir's share passes to that person's heirs **per stirpes.** This is also known as the **right of representation.** For example, if a parent is dead, the children inherit the dead parent's share. Referring to Figure 12-2, assume the decedent's wife has predeceased him. If all three sons are still living, under most intestate statutes each son will receive one-third of the estate. If Son 1 has also predeceased his father, then his child, Grandchild A, will receive Son 1's one-third share. However, if Son 2 has predeceased his father, his children, Grandchild B and Grandchild C, will only receive one-sixth each: their father's one-third, divided in half.

Adopted children have the same rights to inheritance as naturally born children. If there are no children, parents, siblings, aunts or uncles, nephews or nieces, or cousins, the property reverts, or **escheats,** to the state.

Kindred
Also known as **con-sanguinity;** persons related to the decedent by blood.

Affinity
Persons related to the decedent by marriage.

Per stirpes
Also known as **right of representation;** a method of dividing an intestate estate whereby a person takes in place of the dead ancestor.

Escheat
A reversion of property to the state when there are no heirs.

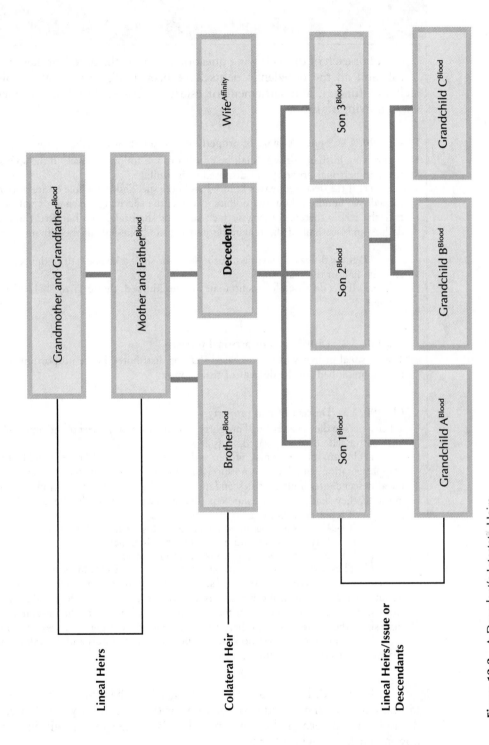

Figure 12-2 A Decedent's Intestate Heirs

Legal Reasoning Exercise

1. For each of the following questions, assume the decedent died without a will and all the decedent's debts have been paid, as have all of his last sickness, funeral, and settlement of estate expenses. Base your answers on the following statutes:

Ch. 190, § 1   Spouse's share of property not disposed of by will

A surviving husband or wife shall be entitled to the following share in the spouse's real and personal property not disposed of by will:

(1) If the deceased leaves kindred and no issue, and the whole estate does not exceed two hundred thousand dollars in value, the surviving husband or wife shall take the whole thereof; otherwise such survivor shall take two hundred thousand dollars and one-half of the remaining personal and one-half of the remaining real property.

(2) If the deceased leaves issue, the survivor shall take one-half of the personal and one-half of the real property.

(3) If the deceased leaves no issue and no kindred, the survivor shall take the whole.

Ch. 190, § 2   Distribution of personal property

The personal property of the deceased shall be distributed in the proportions hereinafter prescribed for the descent of real property.

Ch. 190, § 3   Descent of real property

When a person dies seized of real property, it shall descend, subject to the rights of the husband or wife of the deceased, as follows:

(1) In equal shares to his children and to the issue of any deceased child by right of representation; and if there is no surviving child of the intestate then to all his other lineal descendants. If all such descendants are in the same degree of kindred to the intestate, they shall share the estate equally; otherwise, they shall take according to the right of representation.

(2) If he leaves no issue, in equal shares to his father and mother.

(3) If he leaves no issue and no mother, to his father.

(4) If he leaves no issue and no father, to his mother.

(5) If he leaves no issue and no father or mother, to his brothers and sisters and to the issue of any deceased brother or sister by right of representation; and if there is no surviving brother or sister of the intestate, to all the issue of his deceased brothers and sisters. If all such issue are in the same degree of kindred to the intestate, they shall share the estate equally; otherwise, according to the right of representation.

(6) If an intestate leaves no kindred and no widow or husband, his estate shall escheat to the commonwealth.

a. Juan died, leaving a wife, Carmen, whom he adored, and a brother, James, whom he hated and had not seen for the past thirty years. For each of the following determine how much of Juan's estate Carmen will inherit and how much James will inherit.

(1) Juan leaves $180,000.

Wife Carmen:
Brother James:

(2) Juan leaves $500,000.

Wife Carmen:
Brother James:

(3) Juan leaves $500,000. Assume James had predeceased Juan but has a living child, James, Jr., whom Juan has never met.

Wife Carmen:
Nephew James, Jr.:

b. William died with an estate of $500,000. He left a wife, June, but no issue and no kindred. How much will June inherit?

c. Mary died with an estate of $500,000. She left a husband, John, and two living children, Rachel and Albert. How will the estate be divided among her husband and children?

Husband John:
Daughter Rachel:
Son Albert:

d. Roberto died with an estate of $500,000. He left a wife, Maria, and a living child, Bill, who has a child, Jill. His other child, Sam, predeceased him. Sam has two living children, Tracy and Tim. How will the estate be divided among his wife, Maria; his child, Bill; his grandchild Jill; and his grandchildren Tracy and Tim?

Wife Maria:
Son Bill:
Grandchild Jill:
Grandchild Tracy:
Grandchild Tim:

e. Samantha died with an estate of $500,000. She left no husband and no children. They had all predeceased her. However, she did leave five grandchildren. Two of the grandchildren, Amy and Albert, are the children of her deceased son, Robert. The other three grandchildren, Bonnie, Brad, and Bennett, are the children of her deceased daughter, Emily. How will the estate be divided among the five grandchildren?

Grandchild Amy:
Grandchild Albert:
Grandchild Bonnie:
Grandchild Brad:
Grandchild Bennett:

b. Probating a Will

Although a will may exist, it may not be a valid will. There is always the possibility that the will in question may have been superseded by another will completed at a later date. The will may also be challenged on the grounds of **testamentary capacity.** Such a challenge argues that the testator was not of **sound mind.** In other words, the person lacked the required mental capacity to understand the nature of his or her property or the identity of the people named in the will.

Testamentary capacity
The mental capacity, also known as **sound mind**, whereby the testator understands the nature of his or her property and the identity of those most closely related to him or her.

As indicated earlier, in order to protect against these types of claims, state laws usually require that the will be in writing, signed by the testator, and properly witnessed. In cases where the will is challenged the attorney who drafted the will and the persons who witnessed it are called on to testify as to the mental state of the testator at the time at which the will was signed.

In the following case there was a question as to whether the testator was suffering from undue influence. When Frank Till was eighty-three years old, he met Julie, the sixteen-year-old daughter of an old friend. Over the next four years the two became friends. Although Julie lived several hundred miles away from Frank, she frequently sent him letters and visited him while on vacation visiting her parents. In addition, when she learned that he was unhappy with his current nursing home, she helped him arrange to move to a new nursing home. She also drove him to an attorney when Frank wanted to cancel his power of attorney that he had given to one of his nephews and to change his will. On July 19 Frank prepared a new will that revoked his prior wills and gave the majority of his estate to Julie and her husband. When Frank died less than a month later, Frank's relatives, who were the sole beneficiaries under his prior will, contested the will, claiming it was a product of Julie's undue influence.

In the Matter of the Estate of Franklin J. Till
458 N.W.2d 521 (S.D. 1990)

This is an appeal from a will contest in which the circuit court held that the Last Will and Testament of the decedent, Frank Till (Frank), was a product of undue influence. As a result, the circuit court held this will to be invalid. We reverse. . . .

The first allegation of error raised by the executor regards the trial court's finding a confidential relationship existed between Julie and Frank. . . .

In the present case, the trial court not only found that Julie and Frank had a confidential relationship, but it also found that Julie actively participated in the preparation and execution of the will and that she unduly profited therefrom.

As a result, the trial court further found that a presumption of undue influence had arisen in this case. Based upon our review of the entire evidence, we are firmly and definitely convinced that the trial court made a mistake in finding that a confidential relationship existed between Julie and Frank. Hence, Julie should not have been given the burden of going forward with the evidence to show she did not take advantage of her supposed dominant position. Also, a presumption of undue influence should not have arisen due to the absence of a confidential relationship between Julie and Frank. . . .

In prior cases in which we have been presented with the question of whether a confidential relationship existed between a testator and a beneficiary, we have looked to such factors as the amount of time that the beneficiary spent with the testator, whether the beneficiary handled many of the testator's personal or business affairs, and also whether the testator had ever sought the advice of the beneficiary. Although these are not the only factors that may be considered in determining if a confidential relationship exists between a testator and a beneficiary, they are nevertheless significant factors which demand consideration in the resolution of this issue.

Our review of the record reveals that none of the above-mentioned factors are present in this case. Julie spent very little time with Frank. . . . Julie never handled any of Frank's personal or financial affairs. Rather, Frank handled much of his own personal affairs and Robert [Frank's nephew] handled Frank's financial affairs. Finally, we note there is nothing in the record which indicates Frank ever sought the advice of Julie regarding any of his affairs. While Frank did give consideration to some of Julie's suggestions, Frank did not rely on Julie in any respect for advice.

Considering all of the aforementioned facts, we conclude there is not sufficient evidence to show that a confidential relationship existed between Julie and Frank. Hence, we conclude the trial court erred in finding a confidential relationship existed in this case. Furthermore, having reached this conclusion, we must also conclude the trial court erred in finding a presumption of undue influence had arisen in this case since in order to establish this presumption, one must first establish that a confidential relationship existed between the beneficiary and the testator.

Although we have concluded a presumption of undue influence had not been established in this case, this does not end our review in this particular case. The record reflects that the trial court also found that the will contestants had established, by a preponderance of the evidence, the four elements necessary to prove the existence of undue influence. These elements include: (1) decedent's susceptibility to undue influence; (2) opportunity to exert such influence and effect the wrongful purpose; (3) a disposition to do so for an improper purpose; and (4) a result clearly showing the effects of undue influence. . . .

We first address the trial court's finding that Frank was susceptible to the undue influence of Julie. The preponderance of the evidence in this case clearly indicates that Frank was not a person who was susceptible to undue influence. During the trial of this matter, several people who were acquainted with Frank, including two long-time friends, testified Frank was a very strong willed person. . . .

In finding that Frank was susceptible to the undue influence of Julie, the trial court emphasized that Frank was an old person who was in poor health. While it is true that Frank had some physical problems, there is no evidence that Frank was incapacitated to any significant extent as a result of these physical problems. . . .

Finally, the fact Frank was lonely at the nursing home with few relatives and friends to visit him was also listed as a factor indicating Frank's susceptibility to undue influence. This fact gives little support to the contention that Frank was susceptible to the undue influence of Julie, however, since Julie lived hundreds of miles away from Frank and obviously could not visit him on a regular basis. In fact, the finding that Frank was lonely and had few family and friends to visit him weighs more in the favor of upholding the will since Frank may very well have decided not to provide for those people who did not see fit to visit him. This is particularly true when one considers the undisputed fact that Frank was a strong-willed person. It is for these reasons that we hold, based upon an entire review of the evidence, that the preponderance of the evidence clearly does not support the conclusion that Frank was susceptible to the undue influence of Julie. Hence, we conclude the trial court was clearly erroneous in finding to the contrary. . . .

In resolving the issue of whether Julie had an opportunity to influence Frank it is important to note Julie lived hundreds of miles away from Frank. While it may have been true Frank was lonely and had few visitors, it is unlikely Julie could influence Frank by promising to keep him company since she lived so far away from Frank and since Frank did not like to use the telephone. Hence, Julie could not influence Frank by promising to visit him on a regular basis. . . .

We next address the issue of whether Julie had the disposition to exert undue influence upon

Frank. The trial court held the preponderance of the evidence established that Julie did have such a disposition. Based upon our entire review of the record, we are firmly convinced the trial court erred in making this finding. The record clearly reveals Julie and Frank had a close relationship. Prior to Frank's death, Julie was accustomed to doing kind things for Frank including sending him letters and planning a birthday party for Frank. The record is devoid of any evidence which suggests that Julie ever tried to obtain any of Frank's property. In fact, the evidence points to the contrary. In assisting Frank to remove Robert as power of attorney, Julie sought to have the bank, not herself serve in that capacity. Nothing in the record reflects an attempt by Julie to obtain a power of attorney over Frank's property. If Julie did have a strong desire to gain control over Frank's property, it is likely she would have requested Frank to grant her a power of attorney. No such request was ever made. This strongly indicates that Julie did not have the disposition to exert undue influence upon Frank. . . .

Finally, we address the issue of whether, in the present case, there was a result clearly showing the effects of undue influence. . . . Prior to the 1988 will, the last will Frank had executed was in 1980. In the 1980 will, Frank left all of his estate to his relatives. What the trial court failed to note, however, was the fact that in 1980, Frank and Julie had not been acquainted with each other. Frank and Julie first became acquainted with each other in 1984 and thereafter developed what the trial court conceded was a close and loving relationship. Such a relationship is clearly revealed in the letters Frank and Julie sent to one another. Considering this strong relationship, it would be extremely unlikely for Frank not to provide for Julie after his death.

In the present case, there was an abundance of evidence showing Frank and Julie had a close and loving relationship. On the other hand, there was very little evidence, if any, which indicated Frank had a close and loving relationship with any of his collateral relatives. In fact, the greater weight of the evidence indicates Frank was upset with his relatives. It is undisputed that Frank's relatives placed him in a nursing home which he hated and considered as a "jail." Rather than making life more pleasant by frequent visits and contacts, Frank's relatives (at least in Frank's mind) ignored him. This is evidenced by the fact that Frank had to send Julie to Robert's house to recover several of his personal belongings and also some spending money. If Frank's relatives had paid more attention to Frank's needs and desires, Frank would not have had to make this request of Julie. . . .

Considering all of the above-mentioned facts, it is hardly surprising that Frank's "blood relatives" were excluded from the bulk of his estate. Also, considering the loving relationship that existed between Julie and Frank, it is not surprising that Frank decided to leave the bulk of his estate to Julie. . . .

As a final matter concerning the trial court's finding of undue influence, we note that in order for undue influence to exist, the influence "must be such as to destroy the free agency of the testator and substitute the will of the person exercising it for that of the testator." Considering the close relationship between Frank and Julie, it is extremely likely that Frank desired to provide for Julie to a significant extent after his death. This very likely was Frank's will or desire. Hence, if Julie did exercise influence over Frank, it is extremely unlikely that this amounted to undue influence since it is unlikely that Julie's will was substituted for that of Frank's insofar as Frank's last will and testament is concerned. This further supports the conclusion the trial court erred in finding Frank's last will was the product of undue influence.

From our examination of the entire record we are left with a firm and definite conviction the trial court erred in its findings of fact and conclusions of law. Accordingly, we reverse as to the denial of probate on the grounds of undue influence and we remand the matter to the court with instructions to admit the will to probate.

Judgment is reversed.

[Dissent omitted.]

CASE DISCUSSION QUESTIONS

1. The court noted that a presumption of undue influence arises if there was a confidential relationship between the testator and the beneficiary. What factors determine whether there was a confidential relationship? Did the court find such a relationship in this case? Why?

2. In the absence of proof of a confidential relationship, what are the four elements the court stated are necessary to prove the existence of undue influence?

3. The court concluded that there was no undue influence. Do you agree?

Because the probate process can require expensive fees and can delay the transfer and use of property in the estate, there has been a national movement to simplify the process, as well as allowing people with small estates to avoid it entirely. Some states exempt very small estates from this formal process and provide a simplified probate administration for intermediate-sized estates.

DISCUSSION QUESTION

4. Under what circumstances do you think people should be able to withdraw life-support equipment from someone who is in an irreversible coma? Should doctors be allowed to "help" a patient die by giving the patient a lethal dose of morphine or some other drug when the patient has an incurable disease, is in great pain, and wishes to end the misery? What should be done if that person is in a coma and did not have a formal living will but did tell a close relative that he or she did not wish to be kept alive in such a situation?

SUMMARY

Property law deals with ownership rights in real and personal property. Real property is land and anything permanently attached to land. Personal property is everything else. Property can be owned either individually or with others. Joint ownership that vests ownership rights upon death in the other co-owner(s) is known as joint tenancy with the right of survivorship. With a tenancy in common the joint owner can pass his or her share to heirs at death. Real property can be transferred through sale, at the death of the owner, as a gift, through seizure by a creditor, by eminent domain, or through adverse possession.

Residential landlords are obligated to provide habitable living areas, and tenants can sue for constructive eviction if landlords fail to do so. Currently the states are divided as to whether their state open housing laws permit landlords to deny housing to cohabiting couples.

Estate planning involves the analysis of a person's future financial needs and of ways to ensure that the person's desires regarding distribution of assets will be accomplished after death. Wills and trusts are two of the most common estate-planning tools. If a person dies without a will, that person is said to have died intestate, and the property passes to the decedent's heirs according to that state's statutory intestacy scheme.

REVIEW QUESTIONS

Pages 407 through 411

1. Define the two basic types of property.
2. Why is it important to know if property is classified as personal or real?
3. Describe the three basic types of freehold estates.
4. Why might it be important to know whether two friends shared ownership in a house as joint tenants or as tenants in common?
5. Describe two ways in which an owner's right to use his or her property may be limited by private arrangement.

Pages 411 through 421

6. Describe the four basic types of leasehold estates.
7. What is a constructive eviction, and how does it relate to the implied warranty of habitability?
8. What are land contracts? Can you envision any problems with their use? For example, do you think the terms of a standard land contract generally favor the buyer or the seller?
9. How does someone acquire property through adverse possession?
10. According to the dictates of the Fifth Amendment, if a state wants to take private property, what must it do?
11. What is the distinction between lost and mislaid property? Why does it matter?

Pages 421 through 431

12. What does it mean to say someone died intestate?
13. Why is it not a good idea to die without a will?
14. Define each of the following:
    a. formal will
    b. holographic will
    c. nuncupative will
15. What is the purpose of a simultaneous death clause? Give an example of when such a clause would be relevant and why it would be important.
16. What is the purpose of a trust?
17. What types of property do not have to go through the probate process?

Chapter 13

Laws Affecting Business

*[Title VII of the Civil Rights Act of 1964] proscribes not only overt discrimination but also practices that are fair in form, but discriminatory in operation....
[A]ny tests used must measure the person for the job and not the person in the abstract.*
Chief Justice Burger, U.S. Supreme Court

INTRODUCTION

In Chapters 10 and 11, we presented the basic legal concepts of tort and contract law. Those legal principles impact on a wide range of activities in both our business and our personal lives. In this chapter we introduce more specialized concepts, such as business formation, agency law, commercial paper, secured transactions, and employment law, as they relate to common business activities. Then in the next chapter we will focus on those specialized areas of the law that have the greatest impact on our personal lives.

In this chapter, to help illustrate business law concepts, we will use the experiences of an energetic group of entrepreneurs seeking the American dream of owning their own business. That group consists of four friends—Alice, Betty, Claire, and Dan—who meet once a week to play bridge. During the course of one such meeting they began discussing the possibility of going into business together. Alice, who is thirty years old, is currently working as a baker for

FreshStuff Bakeries, earning $22,000 a year. She loves her work but has long dreamed of opening her own bakery. She even has a name picked out—We BakeUm Fresh. Unfortunately she is a single parent raising two small children and does not feel she can afford to invest any of her approximately $5,000 in savings into such a business. Her friends, however, think that they may be able to help.

Betty, a sixty-two-year-old retired schoolteacher, just won $150,000 in the state lottery. In addition, she has $80,000 in retirement savings. Enjoying her retirement, she does not feel she would want anything to do with the day-to-day running of a business. However, assuming her money would not be at risk, she would be willing to invest up to $100,000 in the business.

Claire, a twenty-year-old college student, recently inherited a small two-story building, worth $50,000, in the downtown area that could easily house a bakery. She would be too busy with classes to help run the business, but she would be willing to let the others use her building to house the bakery.

Finally, Dan is twenty-five years old. He currently works odd jobs for a local landscaping company. However, he feels that he is a born salesperson and manager. Of the $10,000 he has in savings, he feels he could contribute up to $5,000 toward the business. He would love to quit his current job, at which he earns $19,000 a year, to serve as the bakery salesperson and manager.

If the four friends decide to go into business together, there will be many basic legal issues that they will have to confront. The first will be to decide what form they would like their business to take. While they have at least four basic forms from which to choose—**sole proprietorship, partnership, corporation, and limited liability company**—each has its own unique advantages and disadvantages. Second, they will probably need to secure financing for their new business. In return, the creditor may ask for their written promise that they will repay the debt. Such a promise to pay is one form of **commercial paper**. Most suppliers and other creditors will want some additional guarantee that they will be repaid beyond the friends' simple promise that they will do so. Such a guarantee often takes the form of a **security interest**; that is, the debtor agrees to put up something as collateral that the creditor can then claim if the debtor fails to pay his or her debt. If the friends decide to share responsibility for running the business, they must also have a basic understanding of agency law. An **agent** is someone who has the power to act in place of another, known as the **principal**. Finally, unless they are able to run the business on their own, they will want to hire employees. The hiring and firing of employees raises a whole series of legal

NETNOTE

You can find business ownership information, such as the names of the resident agent and the corporate officers, at various places on the Internet, including *www.westlaw.com* (Westlaw), *www.lexis.com* (Lexis), and many state government web sites.

issues. We will concentrate on just two: at-will employment and federal discrimination law.

A. THE FOUR BASIC BUSINESS FORMS

As indicated above, the first basic legal decision involved in the formation of a business is the legal form the business will take. Until recently the choices were limited to three basic business forms: sole proprietorship, partnership, or corporation. Starting in the mid-1990s, however, a new business form emerged: the limited liability company. This new form is quite appealing to many businesses, as it provides some of the best benefits of both the partnership and the corporate form. Figure 13-1 summarizes the major features of each business type.

1. Sole Proprietorship

The sole proprietorship is the most common form of business organization. Approximately two-thirds of all businesses are sole proprietorships. However, while they account for the greatest number of businesses, as most are small businesses, their revenues do not begin to approach those produced by corporations.

There are several advantages to forming a business as a sole proprietorship. First, it is the simplest form to start and maintain, requiring a minimum of paperwork and expense. No forms have to be filed with any state agency unless the owner chooses to use a fictitious business name, such as We BakeUm Fresh. In that case the owner may have to file a "doing business as" (DBA) certificate. Another primary advantage of the sole proprietorship is that the business's profits and losses are treated as personal profits and losses of the owner. Therefore, business profits are taxed as ordinary personal income, and the owner pays taxes on these business profits only once. In the corporate form of organization, on the other hand, the business's profits are taxed first at the corporate level and then again when they are distributed to the individual. Perhaps the major advantage, however, is that the owner retains complete control over the business operation.

The major disadvantage of the sole proprietorship is that all the owner's personal assets, regardless of whether they are related to the operation of the business, are available to satisfy business-incurred debts. For example, if the business is not able to pay its debts, in addition to seizing the assets of the business, creditors can take the business owner's home, automobiles, jewelry, or any other personal assets. Another disadvantage of this type of business operation is that the business dies with the owner. Finally, the owner of a sole proprietorship is often limited in funding to his or her own resources. One of the most common reasons for changing from a sole proprietorship to a partnership or corporate form is the need for additional capital to finance the business's expansion.

As the name implies, a sole proprietorship can have only one owner. In the hypothetical example we presented, only one of the four friends could be designated as the owner. They could not share ownership. (The remaining three

Type of Business	Sole Proprietorship	Partnership	Corporation	Limited Liability Company	Limited Liability Partnership
Number of Owners	One	Two or more	One or more	Usually one or more	Two or more
Taxation	Single	Single	Double	Single	Single
Liability	Unlimited	Unlimited	Limited to capital contribution	Limited to capital contribution	Usually limited to capital contribution; sometimes liable for business debts and for own negligent acts
Ease of Formation	Very easy; nothing to file except "DBA" certificate if using fictitious name	Very easy; formed by partners' oral or written agreement; no filing required except for "DBA" certificate if using fictitious name (can also be established by partners' words or conduct—partnership by estopppel)	File articles of organization; pay annual fee; elect board of directors and officers; hold annual meetings; keep corporate records; use designation such as Corp. or Inc.	File certificate of organization; pay annual fee; use designation such as LLC	Register with the state; pay annual fee; use designation such as LLP
Managed by	Sole owner	Partners	Board of directors and officers	Manager (either an ower or a nonowner) or the owners	Usually the partners

Figure 13-1 A Comparison of the Basic Types of Businesses

could be either investors or employees or both, but they could not be owners.) If they want their business to have more than one owner, they will have to form a partnership, a corporation, or a limited liability company.

2. Partnership

Under the Uniform Partnership Act a partnership is defined as "an association of two or more persons to carry on as co-owners a business for profit." Notice that this provision requires that there be (1) two or more persons (2) who serve as co-owners and (3) run the business for profit. As with a sole proprietorship, partnership assets are only taxed once as personal income to the partners. However, a partnership must file an informational tax return with the Internal Revenue Service that indicates how the profits and losses were divided among the partners.

One of the major disadvantages to doing business as a partnership is that every partner assumes liability for the actions of every other partner. And as with a sole partnership, personal assets can be taken to pay for business liabilities. Thus partners share in the liability for the actions of the partnership and for every other partner. This is known as **joint liability**. Usually, a plaintiff suing a partnership has the option of suing just the partnership, or the partnership and one or more selected partners, or just one of the partners. This is known as **joint and several liability**. For example, someone harmed by partner A's actions could sue the partnership, partner A and partner B, only partner B, or any combination of the above.

Some partnerships have both general and limited partners. This type of partnership is known as a **limited partnership**. The general partners (there must be at least one) have all the rights and liabilities of a normal partner within a **general partnership**. The limited partners, however, are only investors and do not actively participate in the management of the business. Therefore, their liability is limited to the extent of their investment in the partnership. In our example of the four friends both Betty and Claire might be interested in becoming limited partners, thereby limiting their liability to their investment. However, if either of them actually takes part in making business decisions for the partnership, she forfeits her limited partner status.

A partnership can be created in one of three ways: by a written agreement, by an oral agreement, or by operation of law. While there is no requirement that a partnership agreement be in writing, by far the safest course is to use a written partnership agreement listing the rights and duties of each of the partners. Recall also that most states have a statute of frauds requiring any contract that cannot be performed in a year to be in writing.

If there is no written partnership agreement, then the provisions of the **Uniform Partnership Act (UPA)** will govern. The UPA has been adopted in all states except Louisiana. The UPA is a "gap filler." That is, its provisions control only if the partners have not covered a particular area in their written agreement. For example, if two people form a partnership, the UPA will assume they intend to share profits on a 50/50 basis. If the partners want the profits to be divided differently, they can provide for that so long as they explicitly state their intentions. It is obviously prudent to do so.

If two or more individuals through their actions of sharing control, profits, and losses act as though they are a partnership but have no written partnership agreement, it may be difficult to determine whether the parties intended to do business as partners. In those situations the court will frequently be called on to determine whether a partnership has been formed. There is no single requirement that determines whether a partnership exists. Rather, most courts have adopted a three-part test. They will look at the facts of each individual case to see whether there is

1. common ownership,
2. a sharing of the profits and losses, and
3. a shared right to management.

Limited partnership
A partnership of at least one general partner and one or more limited partners. The limited partners' liability is limited to their investments so long as they do not participate in management decisions.

Uniform Partnership Act (UPA)
Known as a gap filler, the UPA comes into play only if terms are left out of a partnership agreement.

Consider, for example, a 1978 case from Michigan,[1] in which the court had to determine whether a surviving wife had worked with her now-deceased husband as a partner or as an employee. If Mrs. Miller could prove she and her husband were partners, she would be entitled to keep her half of the business, and only his half would have to be probated. However, if the business was found to be solely his, then the entire business would be subject to inheritance taxes.

In court she showed that in 1959 she met her future husband, Philip Miller. Mr. Miller asked her to marry him, to move to Jackson, and to help him run his nursery business. She agreed and gave up a well-paying job to move to Jackson. "Although Mr. Miller had been operating the business for some time, it was close to failing at the time of their marriage. However, by 1974, the time of Mr. Miller's death, the business was prosperous."[2] Although she had not invested any money in the business, Mrs. Miller had acted as manager, keeping the books and hiring and firing employees. She and her husband also shared the profits 50/50. In addition, their business registration certificate said they were a partnership, and their checking account, vehicles, and equipment were in the partnership name. However, on their annual tax forms they listed the husband's occupation as sole proprietor and the wife's as housewife. Also, the husband's retirement fund listed him as owning a sole proprietorship.

Applying the traditional three-part test used to determine the existence of a partnership, the court found that the second element, sharing of profits, was not conclusive. The money given to the wife could be seen as wages or simply as her wifely due rather than as her partnership share. As to the third element, sharing the right of control, there was no evidence that she did anything other than what any trusted employee could do. Also, there was no written agreement to prove that she had the right to control the business. Therefore, the court concluded that a partnership had not been formed.

A partnership can also be created without any explicit agreement but rather by operation of a law, even when the parties involved do not want to form a partnership. While Mrs. Miller wanted to prove a partnership existed, in the following case a group of doctors tried to argue that they had not been working together as partners in order to escape liability for the malpractice of another doctor with whom they had worked.

Van Dyke v. Bixby
388 Mass. 663, 448 N.E.2d 353 (1983)

The plaintiffs recovered judgments against the defendants solely on the theory that as partners of Richard E. Alt (Dr. Alt), a physician who died in 1975, they were liable for Dr. Alt's negligent treatment of the plaintiff Edwin S. Van Dyke (Van Dyke). In this appeal the defendants argue that the admissible evidence did not warrant a finding that a partnership existed. . . . We affirm the judgments and the order denying the defendants' motion for a new trial. . . .

1. We start with the question whether the jury were warranted in finding that the defendants

---

[1] Miller v. City Bank & Trust Co., 266 N.W.2d 687 (Mich. 1978).

[2] Id. at 689.

were partners of Dr. Alt because, if not, they could not be held liable for his negligent conduct. The defendants concede, by implication, that, if certain challenged evidence was admissible, the jury would have been warranted in finding that a partnership involving Dr. Alt and the defendants existed between 1962 and the end of 1969. . . .

We turn our attention then to the defendants' challenges to the admission of evidence offered to show that The Johnson Clinic was a partnership from 1962 through 1969.[6] The judge properly admitted a certificate filed with the city clerk in Beverly in 1962 . . . stating that ten doctors, all of whom signed the certificate, were conducting a business in Beverly under the name THE JOHNSON CLINIC. Five of the defendants signed the certificate, as well as Dr. Peer P. Johnson and Dr. Alt. The certificate was relevant, although certainly not conclusive, on the question whether a partnership had been formed. A person conducting business under any title other than his real name, "whether individually or as a partnership," must file such a certificate.

The judge properly admitted, solely on the issue of the existence of a partnership, the endorsement page only of a professional liability insurance policy stating that the defendants and Dr. Alt were insured "individually and as copartners dba [doing business as] Johnson Clinic." The fact that the defendants insured their liability as partners is some evidence that a partnership existed.

An October 31, 1969, billing statement of The Johnson Clinic was properly admitted. It showed that the defendants, Dr. Alt, and other physicians were associated with the clinic and stated that all checks should be made payable to The Johnson Clinic. It was relevant on the question whether the defendants were associated with Dr. Alt in the business at that time.

The statements of certain defendants in answers to interrogatories that they were partners and the testimony of two of those defendants that they were partners were admissible as tending to prove that they were partners. That evidence was admissible only against the defendant who made the statements. It was not binding on such a defendant, but it did show his state of mind concerning his relationship with Dr. Alt. Such questions do involve a legal conclusion. One might believe that he was a partner when, as a matter of law, he was not. The jury, therefore, must be made aware, as they were in this case through the judge's charge, that the partnership question must be determined on all the evidence.

2. There was evidence to warrant a finding that during the period when a partnership existed Dr. Alt was negligent in his treatment or failure to treat Van Dyke. . . . The jury could have found that Dr. Alt failed to remove the Penrose drain from Van Dyke after the 1969 operation. They could have found that, in his treatment of Van Dyke in 1969 after the drainage persisted, Dr. Alt failed to conform to accepted medical practice because he delayed taking substantial affirmative measures to investigate and to correct the cause of the condition. . . .

Order denying motion for a new trial affirmed.

Judgments affirmed.

---

[6]The partnership was succeeded by a corporation on January 1, 1970. The judge instructed the jury not to consider the acts of Dr. Alt after January 1, 1970, on the issue of partnership. From the judge's charge, it is reasonably clear that the jury were informed that the defendants could be liable only for negligent acts or omissions of Dr. Alt during the time a partnership existed.

CASE DISCUSSION QUESTIONS

1. Why was it crucial to the plaintiff's case to prove that Dr. Alt and the other doctors were working together as a partnership?
2. What evidence do you think was particularly relevant in answering that question?

As this case illustrates, if business owners give the appearance that they are partners, the courts may hold them liable for each other's actions, just as though

Partnership by estoppel
A partnership created by the words or actions of persons acting as though they were a partnership.

they had intentionally formed a partnership. Sometimes this is referred to as **partnership by estoppel**. In other words, if the persons doing business together, through their words or conduct, lead others reasonably to believe that they are working as partners and others rely on that belief, a court may prevent (estop) the business owners from denying they are a partnership. Once a court finds a partnership by estoppel, the partners by estoppel are held liable for the actions of all the other partners.

The death or withdrawal of any partner results in the dissolution of the partnership. However, the business entity often continues under a new restructured partnership agreement. The partnership can also end by the agreement of the partners.

3. Corporation

If our four friends are worried about assuming unlimited liability for their business actions, they may choose to form a corporation. A corporation can sue, be sued, own property, and make contracts in its own name. In a corporation, therefore, the investors have the advantage of being owners without having to assume any liability beyond the cost of their individual shares. While this limitation on liability may be important in the context of lawsuits, it may be somewhat illusionary when it comes to seeking credit because banks and other creditors often require shareholders in small corporations to provide personal guarantees to secure loans.

Another benefit of the corporate form is perpetual existence and transferability of shares. Unlike a partnership, it has a continuing life of its own that is not affected by the death of a stockholder or the exchange of shares of stock.

The major disadvantage of a corporation is the "double taxation" involved. The corporation's profits are taxed at the corporate level before dividends are distributed to shareholders. The shareholders then are taxed again on the dividends they receive. A **dividend** is a distribution of the corporate profit as ordered by the directors.

The primary document needed to form a corporation is the **articles of incorporation**. The articles of incorporation must include the legal name of the corporation, the purpose of the corporation, a list of the incorporators and directors, the name and address of a **registered agent** (the person designated to receive service of legal documents), and the share structure. Sometimes a business has its main place of business in one state but chooses to incorporate

NETNOTE

The Electronic Data Gathering, Analysis, and Retrieval (EDGAR) system contains information that companies are required to file with the U.S. Securities and Exchange Commission (SEC). Two places to locate EDGAR filings are *www.sec.gov/edgarhp.htm* and *www.freeedgar.com*.

in another state. The articles of incorporation must be filed with the secretary of state for the state in which the corporation wishes to incorporate. Once a certificate of incorporation has been issued, the corporation must maintain certain types of records, file periodic reports to the appropriate state and federal agencies, and pay an annual fee. Its name must also include a designation such as Corp. or Inc. to alert those doing business with the company that it enjoys the benefits of corporate limited liability.

Most corporate capital comes from the sale of shares of stock to **shareholders**. Shareholders have no responsibility for the daily management of the corporation. They do, however, elect the board of directors. Also, they must approve fundamental changes, such as amending the articles of incorporation or agreeing to the sale of all of the corporation's assets. They receive a share of the corporation's profits when the board chooses to distribute some of those profits through dividends on its stock. The corporation can also borrow money when it needs capital.

The **board of directors** is responsible for the management of the corporation. The board stands in a **fiduciary** relationship to the corporation and to the shareholders. A fiduciary relationship is one in which a person in a position of trust is responsible for acting in the best interests of another party. In this case the board is responsible for doing what is best for the stockholders of the corporation. The board typically makes major policy and investment decisions, as well as appointing, supervising, and removing corporate officers.

The officers of the corporation are elected by the board and are responsible for executing the board's policies. They are also expected to provide leadership for the corporation. In addition, officers have a fiduciary duty to act in the best interests of the corporation and its shareholders. They can be held liable for their actions if they fail to live up to this obligation.

Some corporations are relatively small operations in which one person or the members of one family own all the stock. Such corporations are referred to as close or **closely held corporations**. The rights of shareholders of a closely held corporation usually are restricted with respect to the transfer of shares to others. Most larger corporations are publicly held, meaning that their stock is openly traded on the New York and American Stock Exchanges.

When a corporation incorporated in one state does business in another state, it is called a **foreign corporation**. In its own state it is referred to as a **domestic corporation**. A corporation formed in another country is known as an **alien corporation**.

Persons wishing to sue a corporation may try to "pierce the corporate veil," that is, prove that the corporate form is really a sham and that the business should be treated as a sole proprietorship or partnership. This would mean that the personal assets of the owners could then be used to pay business debts. In order to pierce the corporate veil, the court would have to be convinced that it should set aside the normal protections offered by the corporate form. Factors that a court might look to in deciding whether to set aside the corporate form include situations in close corporations where the principal shareholder or shareholders did not follow the corporate formalities, such as by failing to issue stock, or commingled personal assets with corporate assets, such as by failing to set up a separate checking account for the corporation.

Piercing the corporate veil
When a court sets aside the unlimited liability protection normally given to corporate shareholders.

4. Limited Liability Company and Limited Liability Partnership

After reviewing the pros and cons of forming a sole proprietorship, a partnership, and a corporation, our four friends may wish to take advantage of one of the two new business forms, the **limited liability company (LLC)** and the **limited liability partnership (LLP)**, that are particularly attractive to small businesses. These forms are entirely creatures of statute and offer the best of two worlds—the limited liability that is afforded by the corporate form and the single taxation that occurs in a partnership. Because the statutes authorizing these new forms are of very recent origin (generally the early 1990s), there is very little case law as yet to guide us in understanding how the courts will view these new business forms.

The purpose of these new forms is to give a business the main advantage of the corporate form—limited liability—along with the main advantage of the partnership form—single taxation. The profits from the LLC or LLP are "passed through" to the members. Also, the limited liability protects the members from being sued for the negligent actions of their partners, but as is true with corporate limited liability, it cannot protect them from their own personal conduct.

Because limited liability companies and partnerships are creatures of statute, you must consult the statute in your individual state for the specific requirements for forming and running these business forms. Generally, most businesses appear to be following the route of becoming LLCs for two basic reasons. First, in most states the LLC form offers more liability protection. In an LLP the partners are protected from being personally liable for the wrongful acts of the other partners. However, in some states they remain liable for other business debts, such as rent or utilities. In an LLC personal liability is limited to the amount the person has invested in the company. Second, the LLC form avoids some of the disadvantages of having to use a partnership structure. For example, as you learned earlier, in a partnership each partner has authority to bind the business. With an LLC the business can provide that only some members have that authority and in fact may appoint a manager.

Usually, to become a limited liability company, a business must file articles of organization with the appropriate state office, such as the secretary of state, and pay an annual fee. The articles contain the name of the company, the period of its duration, the address, and the name and address of a statutory agent. The company name must include the words "Limited Liability Company," "Limited," or "Ltd." In addition, an operating agreement should set forth the basics of how the LLC will be run. Typical provisions would include information about how the LLC is to be managed; its purpose; the type and amount of contributions by each member, whether in cash, property, or service; how periodic allocations of income are to be made; transferability of a member's interest in the LLC; and when and how the LLC can dissolve.

Professional partnerships, such as law firms, appear to be gravitating more toward the LLP form. Because this form is essentially identical to a general partnership, except for obtaining the benefits of limited liability, law firms can easily make the change to a limited liability partnership with minimal disruption of the firm's internal workings. Typically, to attain LLP status, a business must register with the state and pay an annual fee. The partnership name must also add the LLP designation.

Limited liability company (LLC)
A new form of business ownership that gives small businesses the advantage of liability limited to the amount of the owner's investment along with single taxation.

Today, all fifty states have adopted LLC and LLP statutes. However, one of the biggest disadvantages to operating as an LLC or LLP remains the uncertainty of how the LLC and LLP statutes will be applied and interpreted by the courts.

Legal Reasoning Exercises

1. Write a memorandum analyzing the advantages and disadvantages of each of the four major business forms in light of the needs of Alice and her friends. Be sure to take into account the special life situation of each person and how that would impact that person's choice of business form.

2. Assume Alice and her friends have decided to form a partnership. Draft a partnership agreement that will best satisfy all the parties' needs.

B. BORROWING MONEY

At some point most businesses will need to buy supplies or equipment on credit or to borrow cash. If a business writes a check to pay for new equipment or signs a promissory note promising to repay a loan, the law of **commercial paper** is involved. Whenever a supplier or creditor asks for a guarantee of repayment in the form of collateral, a **secured transaction** is created. Then if the debtor fails to repay the debt, the creditor can seize the collateral (the asset) that was used to secure the loan.

1. Commercial Paper

Commercial paper refers to a variety of instruments (written documents) used for making payments. Commercial paper has two basic functions: as a substitute for money and as a credit device. For example, if you pay for a new stereo with a check, you have just used a form of commercial paper (the check) to substitute for cash and to give yourself some free credit until the store cashes the check.

There are a lot of terms involved in how commercial paper is categorized. The important point is not to memorize all the terminology but to become familiar with it so that later when you encounter your first client who has a legal problem involving commercial paper, you will be conversant with the basic terms. Commercial paper is categorized in the following ways:

1. as two- or three-party instruments,
2. as orders or promises to pay,
3. as bearer or order paper, and
4. as negotiable or nonnegotiable.

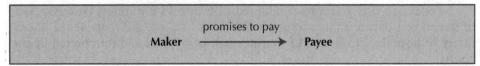

Figure 13-2 A Note

Therefore, the first way of categorizing commercial paper is by how many parties are involved. Notes only involve two parties. A **note** is a promise to pay money, whereby the **maker** signs the instrument promising to pay money to the **payee**. See Figure 13-2. These notes can be collectable either on a specific date in the future (time notes) or at any time the payee wishes to collect (demand notes). Installment notes establish a series of dates on which portions of the money are to be paid.

Three-party instruments include drafts and checks. A **draft** is a three-party instrument in which the **drawer** orders the **drawee**, usually a bank, to pay money to the **payee**. A **check** is a specialized form of a draft in which a bank depositor names a specific payee to whom funds are to be paid from the drawer's account. See Figure 13-3.

Second, drafts and checks are classified as orders to pay, as each contains an order by the drawer to the drawee to pay money to the payee. Notes are promises to pay.

Third, instruments are also classified as being either **bearer paper** or **order paper**. Bearer paper will have written on its front a statement that it is payable to cash or payable to the bearer, or it will have a signature on the back, causing it to be indorsed in blank. An **indorsement in blank** occurs when an indorser simply signs his or her name and does not specify to whom the instrument is payable. Order paper states on its face "pay to the order of" a specific payee and has not been indorsed in blank on its back.

Negotiable instrument
Commercial paper that can be transferred by indorsement or delivery. It must meet the requirements of UCC § 3-104 to be negotiable. If it does not, a transferee cannot become a holder but only gets the rights along with the liabilities of a contract assignee.

The fourth category, **negotiable** versus nonnegotiable, is the most essential category. Only if the paper is seen as negotiable can it be treated as a substitute for money. This is important because, as we mentioned above, one of the two main functions of commercial paper is as a substitute for cash. If the paper does not satisfy the requirements to be negotiable, that purpose has not been satisfied. Article 3 of the Uniform Commercial Code (UCC) spells out the requirements for an instrument to be negotiable. It must

1. be in writing,
2. be signed by the maker or drawer,
3. be an unconditional promise or order to pay,
4. state a specific sum of money,
5. be payable on demand or at a definite time, and
6. be payable to order or to bearer.

Figure 13-3 A Draft or Check. (For a check, the drawee is a bank.)

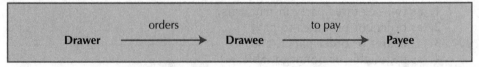

A person becomes a **holder** of a negotiable instrument that is bearer paper by proper delivery. If it is order paper, it must be properly delivered *and* have all necessary indorsements.

The reason all these steps are important is that if a note, check, or draft meets the requirements of negotiability, a holder can become a **holder in due course** and have the right not only to enforce the agreement but also to be exempt from some of the defenses that could have been asserted against the original payee. Under the UCC a person becomes a holder in due course only if that person receives the instrument under the following conditions. A holder in due course is someone

1. who gives value
2. in good faith (a subjective standard) and
3. without notice that the instrument is overdue or has been dishonored or has any claims against it or defenses to it (an objective standard).

Again, the main benefit of being a holder in due course, rather than a mere holder, is that a holder in due course takes the instrument free of most claims against payment. A holder, on the other hand, takes the instrument along with any defenses to its payment. Therefore, for commercial paper to truly work as a substitute for cash, it must be negotiable, and the person owning it must be a holder in due course. The steps by which commercial paper becomes negotiable and its owner becomes a holder in due course are outlined in Figure 13-4.

For example, assume a bakery owner signs a contract with a furniture store. The store gives the bakery owner a loan so that she can purchase new tables and chairs for her reception area. In return, the bakery owner promises to repay the loan on an installment basis. Later a finance company purchases that installment contract from the furniture store. The finance company becomes the holder in due course. Assume the furniture proves to be defective. If the store had not sold the installment contract, the bakery owner might have been able to stop paying on the loan to the furniture store by raising a defense of breach of warranty. However, the holder in due course doctrine prevents the bakery owner from being able to raise those defenses against the finance company. Therefore, even though the furniture is defective, the bakery owner will have to pay what it owes to the finance company. It can separately sue the furniture store for breach of warranty, but the results of the lawsuit do not affect the bakery owner's obligation to pay the finance company.

2. Secured Transactions

Often a creditor will demand more than the mere promise to repay a debt. The creditor will want assurance that if the debtor fails to repay the debt, the creditor can take something of value from the debtor. Therefore, promises to repay a debt are often secured by a pledge of something of value, such as a house, an automobile, or a stock certificate, that the creditor can seize and sell if the debtor does not repay the loan. Such an arrangement is known as a **secured transaction** and is governed by Article 9 of the UCC.

A creditor who has obtained a security interest has two main concerns if a debtor defaults. First, the creditor wants to be able to obtain the secured collateral from the debtor. This is done through an **attachment**. Second, the creditor

Front of the Paper	Do you have a negotiable instrument? ■ in writing and ■ signed by maker or drawer and ■ unconditional promise or order and ■ sum certain in money and ■ payable on demand or at a definite time and ■ to order or bearer If any are missing ≠ a negotiable instrument—STOP. If all present, continue on.
Back of the Paper	Is the transfer proper? ■ bearer paper—transfer alone enough ■ order paper—transfer plus proper indorsements If transfer was not proper—STOP. If transfer was proper, continue on; you have a HOLDER.
What Happened	Did the holder do all of the following? ■ give value ■ in good faith ■ with no notice that the instrument is overdue or has been dishonored or that there is a defense or a claim to it. If all were not met—STOP. If all were met, you have a HOLDER IN DUE COURSE.
Type of Defense Being Raised	Is the defense a **personal defense,** such as a defense to a breach of contract claim? Then the holder in due course takes the instrument clear of that defense. Is the defense a **real defense,** such as forgery of the instrument? Then the defense is good even against the holder in due course.

Figure 13-4   How to Determine Whether a Holder in Due Course Has Been Created

wants to have priority over other creditors who may also have rights to the same collateral. This is done through a process called **perfection**.

As to the first concern, for a creditor to have an enforceable security interest against the debtor, the following must be true:

1. The creditor must either possess the collateral or have a signed **security agreement,**
2. the creditor must have given something of value, and
3. the debtor must have rights in the collateral.

If all three requirements are satisfied, it is said that the security interest has attached. The creditor's first concern is satisfied. If the debtor fails to pay, the creditor can take the collateral from the debtor unless another creditor has a higher right to the collateral by having a perfected security interest.

For a creditor to establish priority over other creditors, the creditor must obtain a **perfected security interest** by taking additional steps. The requirements for perfection are

1. possessing the collateral, or
2. filing a **financing statement**, or
3. giving money to purchase consumer goods.

The purpose behind each of these three methods is to give third parties notice that the creditor has "first dibs" on the property. This gives the perfected creditor first rights to the collateral over other creditors.

Therefore, the difference between attachment and **perfection** is that with attachment the creditor has an enforceable security interest as against the debtor. With perfection the creditor also has priority to the collateral over other creditors. See Figure 13-5.

A special type of perfected security interest, a **purchase money security interest**, arises when a seller gives credit to a debtor so that the debtor can purchase an item. For example, if a car dealership lets you purchase a car on credit, the dealership will have a purchase money security interest in the car you buy. Also, if another creditor, such as a bank, gives value to a debtor so that the debtor can purchase the item, a purchase money security interest is formed. This could occur in the prior example if you obtained your loan from a credit union instead of the car dealership. The credit union would then have a purchase money security interest in your car. If you purchased the car for your own use, as opposed to that of your business, then the security interest would also be classified as a purchase money security interest in consumer goods.

While those with a perfected security interest will prevail over those whose interest has only attached, even a creditor with a perfected security interest will lose to a **buyer in the ordinary course of business**. If this were not so, once a store took out a secured loan, everyone would stop shopping at that store. For

Figure 13-5 A Comparison of Attachment and Perfection

Attachment (must occur first)	**Perfection** (can occur only after attachment)
Notice to the debtor that the creditor has an interest in the goods:	*Notice to third parties* that the creditor has an interest in the goods:
1a. actual possesion	**1a.** possession
or	*or*
1b. a security agreement, signed by the debtor, describing the collateral	**b.** a filed financing statement that was signed, describing the collateral, with addresses of the debtor and creditor
and	*or*
2. the creditor has received something of value	**c.** a purchase money security interest in consumer goods.
and	
3. the debtor has rights in the collateral.	

example, assume Sears took out a secured loan in order to increase its inventory of refrigerators. Without the rule protecting the ordinary buyer, if Sears failed to pay back the debt, the bank could go after customers, trying to reclaim the refrigerators they had purchased from Sears.

In sum, keeping in mind the two purposes of obtaining a security interest, to get repaid and to be first in line for the security, the general order of priorities among creditors and buyers is as follows:

1. buyers in the ordinary course of business,
2. perfected purchase money security interests,
3. perfected security interests,
4. lien creditors (such as a trustee in bankruptcy),
5. unperfected security interests, and
6. general creditors.

Finally, a security interest can be retained in collateral even when the collateral changes in character or location. For example, there can be a security interest in proceeds or after-acquired property. This is known as a **floating lien**. Assume our four entrepreneurs introduced at the beginning of the chapter obtain a loan to purchase an oven for their bakery. In addition to getting a security interest in the oven, the creditor who loans the money for the oven's purchase can also acquire a security interest in the proceeds from the bakery sales and in property, such as a new refrigerator, that the bakery later acquires.

C. AGENCY LAW AND AN EMPLOYER'S RESPONSIBILITY FOR AN EMPLOYEE'S ACT

Returning to the hypothetical we introduced at the beginning of the chapter, unless Alice chooses to run her business as a sole proprietorship with no employees, she will need to worry about how her potential partners' or employees' actions can affect her business. If she and her friends decide to form a partnership, corporation, or limited liability company, each will be seen as an agent of the others and of the business. Therefore, the actions of one of them would affect all of them. Their employees may also be given agency powers. Finally, a business is always responsible for the negligent acts of its employees when the employees are acting within the scope of their duties.

1. Agency Law

Agent
Someone who has the power to act in the place of another.

Principal
A person who permits or directs another person to act on the principal's behalf.

An **agent** is someone who has the power to act in the place of another. A **principal** is a person who permits or directs another person, the agent, to act on his or her behalf, subject to the principal's direction and control. When an agent is authorized to act in the principal's place, the acts of the agent become binding on the principal. For example, in a partnership each partner is an agent for the partnership. Therefore, each partner has the right to make decisions that will bind the partnership as a whole.

Many of the ethical requirements governing the attorney-client relationship are grounded in the fiduciary duties that any agent owes her or his principal. For example, the agent's duty of loyalty requires that the agent not represent two principals at the same time unless both know and consent to the representation. Similarly, an attorney cannot represent two clients if to do so would be against the best interests of either. An agent must keep all information confidential; an attorney must always respect the client's confidences. Finally, the agent's duty to give an accounting of all dollars received and paid is similar to the requirement that attorneys keep all client accounts separate and never commingle the client's and the firm's funds.

In a principal-agent relationship the agent owes a **fiduciary duty** to the principal. As explained earlier, a fiduciary duty is a legally imposed obligation to act in the best interests of the party to whom this duty is owed. Because of this fiduciary duty, agents owe their principals competent performance, notification of any important information (notice to the agent is considered to be notice to the principal, so the agent must keep the principal informed), loyalty, obedience, and an accounting of all moneys spent and earned. Therefore, agents must not place themselves in a conflict of interest situation and must exercise reasonable care, skill, and diligence in carrying out the principal's instructions. An agent who fails to fulfill these duties is liable for damages that result from this failure.

The principal, in turn, must cooperate with the agent and compensate the agent for losses incurred in the course of discharging the assigned duties. The principal must also pay the agreed-on fee for the agent's services.

Fiduciary duty
A legally imposed obligation to act in the best interests of the party to whom the duty is owed.

2. Employees versus Independent Contractors

When a business, whether a sole proprietorship, partnership, corporation, or limited liability partnership, pays people to work for it, these individuals can be hired either as employees or as independent contractors. An **employee** is someone who works for another person or an organization in what the law has defined as an employer-employee relationship. In such a relationship the worker is typically paid an hourly wage or a monthly salary to perform a variety of tasks assigned by the employer, and the employer is responsible for withholding money for taxes and Social Security. Finally, the employer maintains control over both the task and how the task is to be performed.

An **independent contractor**, on the other hand, is someone who contracts to perform a specific service for a set fee. The employer does not withhold taxes or make contributions to retirement funds or health insurance for an independent contractor. Another difference is that contractors are usually expected to supply their own tools. Ultimately the employer dictates the task to be done, but the independent contractor determines how the task is to be performed.

Employee	Independent Contractor
Can be agent of employer	Can be agent of employer
Employer responsible for negligent acts under doctrine of respondeat superior	Employer not responsible for negligent acts unless they involve ultrahazardous activities
Must be covered by worker's compensation, unemployment, etc.	Not covered by employer's worker's compensation, unemployment, etc.
Works for hire belong to employer	Works for hire belong to the independent contractor unless a writing gives rights to employer

Figure 13-6   The Employee versus the Independent Contractor

The distinction between employees and independent contractors is important because the duties, responsibilities, and liabilities of the employer differ between the two classes of workers. The courts have developed various tests to help determine if an employer-employee or an employer-independent contractor relationship exists. While no one factor will be determinative, the courts look to who controls the details of the job, who owns the tools, who sets the hours, how the worker is paid, whether the worker receives training from the employer, whether the worker is engaged in a business different from the employer's, and how long the worker has been employed.

Figure 13-6 shows some of the important differences between employees and independent contractors.

3. Employees and Independent Contractors as Agents

If an employee's duties include dealing with third parties, the employee may be seen as an agent of the employer. Therefore, an employee's acts can bind the employer. An employer-independent contractor relationship may involve an agency relationship if the independent contractor is hired to act on the employer's behalf in making arrangements with third parties. For example, if you wish to sell your house, you will most likely hire a real estate agent. The agent will then negotiate on your behalf and can through his or her actions bind you to contracts formed with third parties. However, because you will have little control over how the agent performs the job, the real estate agent will not be seen as your employee.

4. Employer's Liability for Acts of Employees

When someone is hurt by an employee's negligence, that person will often choose to sue the employer rather than or in addition to the employee because the employer has "deeper pockets"—that is, more resources to pay a large damage award. The extent to which an employer is held accountable for the acts of a worker depends on three factors. First, was the worker an employee or an independent contractor? Second, if the worker was an employee, did the employee act negligently? Third, at the time of the injury was the employee engaged in work of the type the employee was hired to perform? This last question requires an assessment of whether the employee was working within the "scope of employment" or, as the courts so quaintly put it, whether the employee was "on a frolic of the employee's own."

The employer-employee relationship follows common law principles that grew out of the master-servant relationship. Under the doctrine of **respondeat superior**, a Latin term translated as "Let the master answer," a business may be sued for the negligent acts of one of its employees. On the other hand, an employer is generally not responsible for the negligent actions of an independent contractor unless the contractor is engaged in an ultrahazardous activity, such as dynamiting. In such a case the employer is still held liable because not to do so would encourage employers to hire independent contractors simply to avoid liability in admittedly dangerous situations.

> **Respondeat superior**
> The tort theory that an employer can be sued for the negligent acts of its employees.

Therefore, to find an employer responsible under the doctrine of respondeat superior, a plaintiff must prove that

1. a true employer-employee relationship existed,
2. the employee was legally responsible for the injury, and
3. at the time of the negligent action the employee was "working within the scope of his or her employment."

In order to establish that the employee was working within the "scope of employment," the plaintiff will have to show that the employee responsible for the injury was at that time engaged in work of the type he or she was hired to perform. If the employee was on a "frolic of his or her own," the employer is not responsible. For example, if Joe, a driver for Pizzas Are Us, negligently causes an accident while delivering a pizza, the company will be liable. However, if while returning from a delivery Joe decides to take an unauthorized side trip to visit his girlfriend and negligently injures someone, the company should not be held responsible for Joe's unauthorized side trip. In the following case the court acknowledges that it is much easier to state the rule than it is to apply it to the facts of a specific case.

O'Connor v. McDonald's Restaurants of California, Inc.
220 Cal. App. 3d 25, 269 Cal. Rptr. 101 (1990)

Plaintiff Martin K. O'Connor appeals summary judgment favoring defendants McDonald's Restaurants of California, Inc., and McDonald's Corporation (together McDonald's) on his complaint for damages for personal injuries on a theory of McDonald's vicarious liability for the negligence of its employee Evans. . . .

I
Facts

In reviewing the propriety of the summary judgment, we state the facts in the light most favorable to O'Connor.

From about 8 P.M. on August 12, 1982, until between 1 and 2 A.M. the next day, Evans and several McDonald's coworkers scoured the children's playground area of McDonald's San Ysidro restaurant. The special cleaning prepared the restaurant for inspection as part of McDonald's "spring-blitz" competition. Evans—who aspired to a managerial position—worked without pay in the cleanup party at McDonald's request. Evans's voluntary contribution of work and time is the type of extra effort leading to advancement in McDonald's organization.

After completing the cleanup, Evans and four fellow workers went to the house of McDonald's employee Duffer. Duffer had also participated in the evening's work. At Duffer's house, Evans and the others talked shop and socialized into the early hours of the morning. About 6:30 A.M., as Evans drove from Duffer's house toward his own home, his automobile collided with O'Connor's motorcycle.

II

Superior Court Proceedings

O'Connor filed a lawsuit for negligence against Evans, McDonald's and others. O'Connor complained of serious injuries resulting in permanent disability and the loss of his left leg below the knee. The suit claimed McDonald's was liable for negligence on a theory of respondeat superior.[1] ...

III

Analysis

The central issue before us is of some antiquity. In 1834 Baron Parke addressed the issue: "The master is only liable where the servant is acting in the course of his employment. If he was going out of his way, against his master's implied commands, when driving on his master's business, he will make his master liable; but if he was going on a frolic of his own, without being at all on his master's business, the master will not be liable." *Joel v. Morison* (1834) 6 Car. & P. 501, 503, 172 Eng. Rep. 1338, 1339.

Unfortunately, as an academic commentator observed in 1923, "It is relatively simple to state that the master is responsible for his servant's torts only when the latter is engaged in the master's business, or doing the master's work, or acting within the scope of his employment; but to determine in a particular case whether the servant's act falls within or without the operation of the rule presents a more difficult task." ...

Whether there has been a deviation so material as to constitute a complete departure by an employee from the course of his employment so as to release employer from liability for employee's negligence, is usually a question of fact. ...

Here the evidence ... raises triable issues on the factors bearing on whether Evans completely abandoned the special errand in favor of pursuing a personal objective.

A. Evans's Intent

... The record contains evidence McDonald's encourages its employees and aspiring managers to show greater dedication than simply working a shift and going home. O'Connor presented McDonald's operations and training manual and employee handbook to demonstrate McDonald's fosters employee initiative and involvement in problem solving. Such evidence could reasonably support a finding of "a direct and specific connection" between McDonald's business and the gathering at Duffer's because the gathering was consistent with the "family" spirit and teamwork emphasized by McDonald's in its communications with employees. Such evidence could also reasonably support a finding McDonald's emphasis on teamwork made a group discussion of McDonald's business at Duffer's house a foreseeable continuation of Evans's special errand. ...

B. Nature, Time, and Place of Evans's Conduct

McDonald's contends the gathering at Duffer's house after normal business hours was an informal social function unconnected to Evans's special errand for his employer. However, O'Connor submitted evidence suggesting the gathering benefited McDonald's, occurred at Evans's fellow employee's house immediately

---

[1]"Under the doctrine of respondeat superior, an employer is liable for the torts of his employees committed within the scope of their employment."

after McDonald's place of business closed, consisted of continuation of employees' discussion about the spring blitz, and was inspired by the spirit of competition engendered by McDonald's. . . .

C. Work Evans Was Hired to Do

McDonald's contends the asserted managerial discussions at Duffer's house went beyond the scope of work Evans was hired to do. However, O'Connor introduced evidence suggesting Evans was in training to become a manager and was expected to show initiative in his work to be worthy of future promotion. Such evidence raises an inference Evans's participation in discussions at Duffer's house did not exceed the scope of his assigned work. . . .

F. Amount of Time Consumed in Personal Activity

McDonald's contends Evans stopped at Duffer's home for four hours on his own volition, for his own enjoyment and without McDonald's explicit direction or suggestion. However, O'Connor presented evidence showing much of the discussion at Duffer's home was related to

Evans's employment at McDonald's. Such evidence raises a triable factual issue about the combination of personal entertainment and company business at Duffer's house. "Where the employee may be deemed to be pursuing a business errand and a personal objective simultaneously, he will still be acting within the scope of his employment."

G. Conclusion

The superior court found—and the parties here do not challenge—Evans's voluntary participation in the spring blitz until after midnight constituted a special errand on McDonald's behalf. The question here is whether the gathering at Duffer's to discuss the spring blitz and socialize constituted a complete departure from the special errand.

Because disputed factual questions and reasonable inferences preclude determination as a matter of law of the issue whether Evans completely abandoned his special errand, the court should have denied McDonald's motion for summary judgment.

The summary judgment is reversed.

CASE DISCUSSION QUESTIONS

1. What factors will be particularly important in determining whether an employee is on a "frolic of his or her own"?

2. Why did the court reverse summary judgment in this case? Does this mean the plaintiff will be able to hold McDonald's liable for his injury?

D. EMPLOYMENT LAW

Prior to the Industrial Revolution most workers in the United States were either self-employed or worked as part of a family unit. After the Civil War the percentage of people working for businesses grew rapidly, and the courts applied the concept of employment "at will" to allow employers to hire and fire employees without government interference. When Congress first tried to curb the use of child labor and set limits on the number of hours employees could be required to work, the U.S. Supreme Court struck down such legislation on the grounds that it violated the business owners' substantive due process right to "freedom of contract."

Although the doctrine of at-will employment still remains, the Supreme Court rejected the right to "freedom of contract" in a series of cases beginning in 1934. Today, with a few limited exceptions (usually based on the number of

NETNOTE

The EEOC home page is located at *www.eeoc.gov*.

employees), most businesses in the United States are covered by federal and state statutes that limit the freedom of employers with regard to their employees' working conditions. For example, statutes set a minimum age at which someone is eligible to work, prohibit discrimination in hiring and promotion, establish minimum wages, establish overtime pay requirements, impose safety standards for the workplace, and establish procedures whereby workers can seek union representation and collective bargaining. Worker's compensation laws, unemployment insurance requirements, and regulations of employee benefit plans represent other areas of employment law. In this section we will focus on federal antidiscrimination law and contemporary interpretations of the concept of employment at will.

1. Title VII: Discrimination Based on Race, Color, Religion, Sex, or National Origin

Until 1964 it was perfectly legal for private employers to discriminate against current and potential employees based on their race, sex, or national origin. Congress dramatically changed this with the passage of Title VII of the Civil Rights Act of 1964. With the passage of the Civil Rights Act Congress hoped to stop all forms of discrimination, whether in voting, education, public accommodations, or employment.

a. Introduction to Title VII

Title VII of the Civil Rights Act of 1964 deals specifically with employment. It states that

> [i]t shall be an unlawful employment practice for an employer (1) to fail or refuse to hire or to discharge any individual, or otherwise to discriminate against any individual with respect to his compensation, terms, conditions, or privileges of employment, because of such individual's race, color, religion, sex, or national origin.[3]

In Title VII Congress also established the Equal Employment Opportunity Commission (EEOC) and delegated to it the task of developing regulations to more specifically delineate what is unlawful behavior. It also provided that persons who feel they have been discriminated against must first file claims with the EEOC, or a similar state agency, before taking their cases to court.

---

[3] 42 U.S.C. § 2000e-2(a) (2004).

As you will recall from Chapter 2, the federal government is a government of limited powers. Congress can legislate only in those areas listed in the U.S. Constitution. One of those areas involves regulating interstate commerce. To ensure that it was acting within its constitutional powers, before the passage of the Civil Rights Act Congress held hearings during which numerous witnesses testified how commerce was being impeded by various segregation practices, including those that prevented some traveling salespersons from staying in local motels and eating in local restaurants.

In addition, to meet the argument that only those employers who have an effect on interstate commerce should be covered, Congress limited the definition of employer to those with twenty or more employees. Since then Congress has amended the statute to reduce that number to fifteen employees. Does that mean that employers with less than fifteen employees can still freely discriminate? Perhaps. The answer depends on state law. Although Congress has prohibited discrimination by employers with fifteen or more employees, it has not preempted the field. States are free to legislate so long as their statutory scheme does not conflict with the federal prohibition. For example, in Massachusetts, employers of six or more employees may not discriminate on the basis of race, color, religious creed, national origin, sex, sexual orientation, or age.

In addition, in 1997 the U.S. Supreme Court ruled that "employee" includes any employee on the weekly payroll no matter how many days the employee actually worked in a given week. Therefore, under the federal statute an employer could have fifteen part-time employees and still be covered by Title VII.[4] Note, however, that Title VII covers only employees, not independent contractors. For example, in a Seventh Circuit decision the court held that a staff doctor could not sue his employing hospital, as he was an independent contractor and not an employee of the hospital.[5]

As originally proposed, Title VII would not have prohibited sex discrimination. However, a congressman from the South proposed an amendment from the floor to add sex to the list of protected categories. The legislative history recording the debate[6] on this amendment is an interesting study in politics. From the following brief excerpt see if you can divine why Congressman Smith proposed the amendment and why some congresswomen, whom you would think would favor it, instead were opposed to the amendment.

> *Mr. Smith of Virginia.* Mr. Chairman, this amendment is offered . . . with our desire to prevent discrimination against another minority group, the women, but a very essential minority group, in the absence of which the majority group would not be here today. . . .
>
> *Mr. Cellar.* Mr. Chairman, I heard with a great deal of interest the statement of the gentleman from Virginia that women are in the minority. Not in my house. I can say as a result of 49 years of experience . . . that I usually have the last two words, and those words are, "Yes, dear." . . . You know, the French have a phrase for it when they speak of women and men. When they speak the difference, they say "vive la difference."
>
> I think the French are right.

---

[4]Walters v. Metropolitan Educational Enterprises, Inc., 519 U.S. 202 (1997).
[5]Alexander v. Rush North Shore Medical Center, 101 F.3d 487 (7th Cir. 1996).
[6]110 Cong. Rec. 2,577-2,584 (1964).

Imagine the upheaval that would result from adoption of blanket language requiring total equality. Would male citizens be justified in insisting that women share with them the burdens of compulsory military service? What would become of traditional family relationships? What about alimony? Who would have the obligation of supporting whom? Would fathers rank equally with mothers in the right of custody to children? What would become of the crimes of rape and statutory rape? . . . Would the many State and local provisions regulating working conditions and hours of employment for women be struck down? . . .

Mrs. Griffiths. . . . Some people have suggested to me that labor opposes "no discrimination on account of sex" because they feel that through the years protective legislation has been built up to safeguard the health of women. Some protective legislation was to safeguard the health of women, but it should have safeguarded the health of men, also. Most of the so-called protective legislation has really been to protect men's rights in better paying jobs. . . .

Mrs. George. . . . Protective legislation prevents, as my colleague from the State of Michigan just pointed out—prevents women from going into the higher salary brackets. Yes, it certainly does.

Women are protected—they cannot run an elevator late at night and that is when the pay is higher.

They cannot serve in restaurants and cabarets late at night—when the tips are higher—and the load, if you please, is lighter. . . .

But what about the offices, gentlemen, that are cleaned every morning about 2 or 3 o'clock in the city of New York and the offices that are cleaned quite early here in Washington, D.C.? Does anybody worry about those women? I have never heard of anybody worrying about the women who do that work. . . .

The addition of that little, terrifying word "s-e-x" will not hurt this legislation in any way. In fact, it will improve it. It will make it comprehensive. It will make it logical. It will make it right.

Mrs. Green. . . . I wish to say first to the gentleman who offered this amendment and to others who by their applause I am sure are giving strong support to it that I, for one, welcome the conversion, because I remember when we were working on the equal pay bill that, if I correctly understand the mood of the House, those gentlemen of the House who are most strong in their support of women's rights this afternoon, probably gave us the most opposition when we considered the bill which would grant equal pay for equal work just a very few months ago. I say I welcome the conversion and hope it is of long duration. . . .

[A]s the author of the equal pay bill and as a member of the President's Commission on the Status of Women, I believe I have demonstrated my concern and my determination to advance women's opportunities in every reasonable way possible. But—I do not believe this is the time or place for this amendment.

Let me say first that I agree with many of the statements my women colleagues have made about the great amount of discrimination against women. . . . This is true when I am invited to a club in Washington as a guest to attend a conference, and when I arrive at the front door to attend that conference, solely because I am a woman, I have to go to the side door to gain admittance.

After I have said all of this Mr. Chairman, I honestly cannot support the amendment. For every discrimination that has been made against a woman in this country there has been 10 times as much discrimination against the Negro of this country. There has been 10 times maybe 100 times as much humiliation for the Negro woman, for the Negro man and for the Negro child. Yes: and for the Negro baby who is born into a world of discrimination. . . . [T]his bill is primarily for the purpose of ending discrimination against Negroes in voting and in public accommodations and in education and, yes, in employment. . . . As much as I hope the day will come when discrimination will be ended against women, I really and sincerely hope that this amendment will not be added to this bill. It will clutter up the bill and it may later—very well—be used to help destroy this section of the bill by some of the very people who today support it. And I hope that no other amendment will be added to this bill on sex or age or anything else, that would jeopardize our primary purpose in any way.

DISCUSSION QUESTIONS

1. What do you think Mr. Smith was trying to accomplish by amending the statute to include sex discrimination?

2. In Chapter 6 we said that one way to try to discover the intent of the legislature is to look at legislative history. Having just read an excerpt from legislative history for Title VII, what can you extrapolate about the value of relying on legislative history?

3. In addition to the categories that Congress included in Title VII, can you think of any other categories that should be included to completely protect individuals from employment discrimination?

The end result was the passage of Mr. Smith's amendment, as well as of Title VII. Therefore, the category of sex discrimination was added to race, color, religion, and national origin discrimination. The precise meaning of "sex discrimination," however, was hotly debated for many years. For example, it was not until 1998 that the United States Supreme Court decided that same-sex harassment qualified as prohibited sex discrimination under Title VII.[7]

Race, color, religion, sex, and national origin are known as **protected categories**. Title VII does not mean that an employer can never make an employment decision adverse to a member of a protected class. For example, an employer can refuse to hire an African American because that person lacks the skills required for the job, withhold a woman's promotion because of a bad attendance record, or fire a Muslim because that employee was caught embezzling company funds. The key is the reason behind the employer's actions. A negative action against a member of a protected class is unlawful only when the action was taken *because* that person is a member of a protected class.

The most difficult part of the typical employment discrimination case is the determination of the employer's true motivation behind the allegedly discriminatory action. While some employers may admit to discriminatory motives, most employers will claim that their decisions were based on legitimate considerations, such as educational credentials or work record. The sections that follow will identify the three major approaches the courts have taken to this problem.

b. The Three Theories of Discrimination

The three theories of discrimination are overt discrimination, disparate treatment, and disparate impact. First, there are those rare cases of **overt discrimination**, where the employer openly refuses to treat all applicants or employees equally. The only defense to such an action is proof that sex, religion, or national origin is a requirement of the job. This is known as establishing a **bona fide occupational qualification (BFOQ)**. Note that race can never be a bona fide job requirement.

> **Bona fide occupational qualification (BFOQ)** A defense to an overt discrimination claim, alleging that the qualification is necessary to the essence of the business operation.

---

[7]Oncale v. Sundowner Offshore Services, Inc., 523 U.S. 75 (1998).

Disparate treatment
The legal theory applied when a rejected applicant claims the reason for rejection was based on a discriminatory intent but the employer alleges a nondiscriminatory reason.

Disparate impact
The legal theory applied when the use of a neutral standard has a disproportionate impact on one protected group.

The second type of case involves **disparate treatment**, where a rejected applicant or employee thinks the reason for the rejection is based on discrimination, but the employer alleges a nondiscriminatory reason. Here the main issue is one of proof; that is, the plaintiff must find a way to prove that the real reason for the rejection was discrimination.

Third, there are times when an employer uses a neutral standard, such as a requirement that all employees have a high school education, that nonetheless excludes a large number of one classification of potential employees. This type of case does not require any proof of discriminatory intent, but the plaintiff must show that the neutral standard has a disproportionate negative impact on one protected group. This last type of case is known as a **disparate impact** case.

(1) Overt discrimination and the BFOQ defense

Sometimes an employer will state that it will hire only members of a particular sex, religion, or national origin. Because the discrimination is done openly, this is called overt discrimination. Title VII allows a limited exception for such overt discrimination when sex, national origin, or religion is "a bona fide occupational qualification reasonably necessary to the normal operation of that particular business or enterprise."[8] Notice how specific this provision is. First, it applies only to religion, sex, and national origin discrimination. Second, the occupational qualification must be "reasonably necessary" to the "normal operation" of that "particular" business. Figure 13-7 shows what the plaintiff in an overt discrimination case must prove and the requirements of the defendant's rebuttal.

A valid BFOQ defense would arise when an employer limits applicants for a locker room attendant's job to women if it is a women's locker room and to men if it is a men's locker room. The defense becomes more problematical when, for example, the owner of a Chinese restaurant argues that being Chinese is a valid BFOQ for working as a waiter in order to meet customer expectations. Similarly, an upscale restaurant might argue that its clientele expects to be assisted only by a male maître d'. Read the following landmark case to see how the U.S. Court of Appeals for the Fifth Circuit dealt with a similar argument.

Figure 13-7   Summary of the Order of Proof in Overt Discrimination Cases

1. Plaintiff's Prima Facie Case	Must prove overt discrimination against a member of a protected group
2. Defendant's Rebuttal	Must prove that discrimination is the result of a bona fide occupational qualification—that is, that the qualification is necessary to the essence of the business operation.

---

[8]42 U.S.C. § 2000e(a) (2004).

Diaz v. Pan American World Airways, Inc.
442 F.2d 385 (5th Cir. 1971)

TUTTLE, C.J.

This appeal presents the important question of whether Pan American Airlines' refusal to hire appellant and his class of males only on the basis of their sex violates § 703(a)(1) of Title VII of the 1964 Civil Rights Act. Because we feel that being a female is not a "bona fide occupational qualification" for the job of flight cabin attendant, appellee's refusal to hire appellant's class solely because of their sex, does constitute a violation of the Act.

The facts in this case are not in dispute. Celio Diaz applied for a job as flight cabin attendant with Pan American Airlines in 1967. He was rejected because Pan Am had a policy of restricting its hiring for that position to females. He then filed charges with the Equal Employment Opportunity Commission (EEOC) alleging that Pan Am had unlawfully discriminated against him on the grounds of sex. The Commission found probable cause to believe his charge, but was unable to resolve the matter through conciliation with Pan Am. Diaz next filed a class action in the United States District Court for the Southern District of Florida on behalf of himself and others similarly situated, alleging that Pan Am had violated Section 703 of the 1964 Civil Rights Act by refusing to employ him on the basis of his sex; he sought an injunction and damages.

Pan Am admitted that it had a policy of restricting its hiring for the cabin attendant position to females. Thus, both parties stipulated that the primary issue for the District Court was whether, for the job of flight cabin attendant, being a female is a "bona fide occupational qualification (hereafter BFOQ) reasonably necessary to the normal operation" of Pan American's business.

The trial court found that being a female was a BFOQ. Before discussing its findings in detail, however, it is necessary to set forth the framework within which we view this case.

Section 703(a) of the 1964 Civil Rights Act provides, in part:

(a) It shall be an unlawful employment practice for an employer—(1) to fail or refuse to hire or to discharge any individual, or otherwise to discriminate against any individual with respect to his compensation, terms, conditions, or privileges of employment, because of such individual's race, color, religion, sex or national origin. . . .

The scope of this section is qualified by § 703(e) which states:

(e) Notwithstanding any other provision of this sub-chapter,

(1) it shall not be an unlawful employment practice for an employer to hire and employ employees . . . on the basis of his religion, sex, or national origin in those certain instances where religion, sex, or national origin is a bona fide occupational qualification reasonably necessary to the normal operation of that particular business or enterprise. . . .

Since it has been admitted that appellee has discriminated on the basis of sex, the result in this case turns, in effect, on the construction given to this exception. . . .

In construing this provision, we feel . . . that it would be totally anomalous to do so in a manner that would, in effect, permit the exception to swallow the rule. Thus, we adopt the EEOC guidelines which state that "the Commission believes that the bona fide occupational qualification as to sex should be interpreted narrowly." 29 CFR 1604.1(a). Indeed, close scrutiny of the language of this exception compels this result. As one commentator has noted:

"The sentence contains several restrictive adjectives and phrases: it applies only 'in those certain instances' where there are 'bona fide' qualifications 'reasonably necessary' to the operation of that 'particular' enterprise. The care with which Congress has chosen the words to emphasize the function and to limit the scope of the exception indicates that it had no intention of opening the kind of enormous gap in the law which would exist if an employer could legitimately discriminate against a group solely because his employees, customers, or clients discriminated against that group. Absent much more explicit language, such a broad exception should not be assumed for it would largely emasculate the act." 65 Mich. L. Rev. (1967).

Thus, it is with this orientation that we now examine the trial court's decision. Its conclusion was based upon (1) its view of Pan Am's history of the use of flight attendants; (2) passenger preference; (3) basic psychological reasons for the preference; and (4) the actualities of the hiring process.

Having reviewed the evidence submitted by Pan American regarding its own experience with both female and male cabin attendants it had hired over the years, the trial court found that Pan Am's current hiring policy was the result of a pragmatic process. . . . The performance of female attendants was better in the sense that they were superior in such non-mechanical aspects of the job as "providing reassurance to anxious passengers, giving courteous personalized service and, in general, making flights as pleasurable as possible within the limitations imposed by aircraft operations."

The trial court also found that Pan Am's passengers overwhelmingly preferred to be served by female stewardesses. Moreover, on the basis of the expert testimony of a psychiatrist, the court found that an airplane cabin represents a unique environment in which an air carrier is required to take account of the special psychological needs of its passengers. These psychological needs are better attended to by females. This is not to say that there are no males who would not have the necessary qualities to perform these non-mechanical functions, but the trial court found that the actualities of the hiring process would make it more difficult to find these few males. . . .

Because of the narrow reading we give to section 703(e), we do not feel that these findings justify the discrimination practiced by Pan Am.

We begin with the proposition that the use of the word "necessary" in section 703(e) requires that we apply a business necessity test, not a business convenience test. That is to say, discrimination based on sex is valid only when the essence of the business operation would be undermined by not hiring members of one sex exclusively.

The primary function of an airline is to transport passengers safely from one point to another. While a pleasant environment, enhanced by the obvious cosmetic effect that female stewardesses provide as well as, according to the finding of the trial court, their apparent ability to perform the non-mechanical functions of the job in a more effective manner than most men, may all be important, they are tangential to the essence of the business involved. No one has suggested that having male stewards will so seriously affect the operation of an airline as to jeopardize or even minimize its ability to provide safe transportation from one place to another. Indeed the record discloses that many airlines including Pan Am have utilized both men and women flight cabin attendants in the past and Pan Am, even at the time of this suit, has 283 male stewards employed on some of its foreign flights.

We do not mean to imply, of course, that Pan Am cannot take into consideration the ability of individuals to perform the non-mechanical functions of the job. What we hold is that because the non-mechanical aspects of the job of flight cabin attendant are not "reasonably necessary to the normal operation" of Pan Am's business, Pan Am cannot exclude all males simply because most males may not perform adequately. . . .

Appellees also argue, and the trial court found, that because of the actualities of the hiring process, "the best available initial test for determining whether a particular applicant for employment is likely to have the personality characteristics conducive to high-level performance of the flight attendant's job as currently defined is consequently the applicant's biological sex." Indeed, the trial court found that it was simply not practicable to find the few males that would perform properly.

We do not feel that this alone justifies discriminating against all males. Since, as stated above, the basis of exclusion is the ability to perform non-mechanical functions which we find to be tangential to what is "reasonably necessary" for the business involved, the exclusion of all males because this is the best way to select the kind of personnel Pan Am desires simply cannot be justified. Before sex discrimination can be practiced, it must not only be shown that it is impracticable to find the men that possess the abilities that most women possess, but that the abilities are necessary to the business, not merely tangential.

Similarly, we do not feel that the fact that Pan Am's passengers prefer female stewardesses should alter our judgment. On this subject, EEOC guidelines state that a BFOQ ought not be based on "the refusal to hire an individual because of the preferences of co-workers, the employer, clients or customers. . . ." 29 CFR § 1604.1 (iii).

As the Supreme Court stated in *Griggs v. Duke Power Co.,* 401 U.S. 424, 91 S. Ct. 849, 28 L. Ed. 2d 158 (1971), "the administration interpretation of the Act by the enforcing agency is entitled to great deference. . . . While we recognize that the public's expectation of finding one sex in a particular role may cause some initial difficulty, it would be totally anomalous if we were to allow the preferences and prejudices of the customers to determine whether the sex discrimination was valid. Indeed, it was, to a large extent, these very prejudices the Act was meant to overcome. Thus, we feel that customer preference may be taken into account only when it is based on the company's inability to perform the primary function or service it offers. . . .

The judgment is Reversed and the case is Remanded for proceedings not inconsistent with this opinion.

CASE DISCUSSION QUESTIONS

1. Why did the male plaintiff win his claim of sex discrimination?

2. In the district court trial, Pan Am introduced evidence of a survey that indicated 79 percent of all passengers, both men and women, preferred female stewardesses. What did the court of appeals have to say about an employer using such customer preferences to make hiring decisions?

3. During the trial Dr. Eric Berne, author of *Games People Play,* testified, trying to explain in psychological terms why most passengers prefer female stewardesses.

"Dr. Berne explained that the cabin of a modern airliner is, for passengers, a special and unique psychological environment ('sealed enclave'), characterized by the confinement of a number of people together in an enclosed and limited space, by their being subjected to the unusual physical experience of being levitated off the ground and transported through the atmosphere at high speed, by their being substantially out of touch with their accustomed world, and by their own inability to control events. That environment . . . creates three typical passenger emotional states . . . a sense of apprehension, . . . a sense of boredom . . . and . . . a feeling of excitement. . . . [F]emale stewardesses . . . would be better able to deal with each of these psychological states. . . . [P]assengers of both sexes would . . . respond better to the presence of females than males. He explained that many male passengers would subconsciously resent a male flight attendant perceived as more masculine than they, but respond negatively to a male flight attendant perceived as less masculine, whereas male passengers would generally feel themselves more masculine and thus more at ease in the presence of a young female attendant. He further explained that female passengers might consider personal overtures by male attendants as intrusive and inappropriate, while at the same time welcoming the attentions and conversation of another woman."[9]

How do you think this testimony should have been factored into the court's decision?

---

[9]Diaz v. Pan American World Airways, Inc., 311 F. Supp. 559, 565-566 (S.D. Fla. 1970).

DISCUSSION QUESTION

4. Johnson Controls, Inc., manufactures batteries. In the process, lead is a primary ingredient. Because the company was afraid that exposure to lead could lead to harm to any fetus carried by a female employee, the company excluded women who were pregnant or "capable of bearing children" from jobs that exposed them to lead. When a group of women challenged this policy, the company argued that it was a BFOQ. How do you think the court resolved this issue?

(2) Intentional discrimination—disparate treatment

In most cases of alleged discrimination the employer does not broadcast its intent to discriminate. Rather the employer argues that its reasons are totally justified and nondiscriminatory. For example, the employer might argue that a decision to fire an employee was justified because the worker had a poor job performance rating. In this second type of employment discrimination case, known as **disparate treatment,** the plaintiff has the burden of proving that the decision was based on race, color, sex, religion, or national origin rather than on the alternative explanation offered by the employer.

For example, in the following case a laid-off worker applied for reinstatement. When his employer did not rehire him, he alleged it was due to his race. His employer argued, however, that its only reason for refusing to rehire him was his illegal labor union activities, which included, among other actions, being involved in a "stall in." The U.S. Supreme Court grappled with the issue of how such cases should be presented and proven and in the process laid down guidelines for future disparate treatment cases.

McDonnell Douglas Corp. v. Green
411 U.S. 792 (1973)

Certiorari to the United States Court of Appeals for the Eighth Circuit.

POWELL, J.

The case before us raises significant questions as to the proper order and nature of proof in actions under Title VII of the Civil Rights Act of 1964, 78 Stat. 253, 42 U. S. C. § 2000c et seq.

Petitioner, McDonnell Douglas Corp., is an aerospace and aircraft manufacturer headquartered in St. Louis, Missouri, where it employs over 30,000 people. Respondent, a black citizen of St. Louis, worked for petitioner as a mechanic and laboratory technician from 1956 until August 28, 1964 when he was laid off in the course of a general reduction in petitioner's work force.

Respondent, a long-time activist in the civil rights movement, protested vigorously that his discharge and the general hiring practices of petitioner were racially motivated. As part of this protest, respondent and other members of the Congress on Racial Equality illegally stalled their cars on the main roads leading to petitioner's plant for the purpose of blocking access to it at the time of the morning shift change. The District Judge described the plan for, and respondent's participation in, the "stall-in" as follows:

"Five teams, each consisting of four cars would 'tie up' five main access roads into McDonnell at the time of the morning rush hour. The drivers of the cars were instructed to line up next to each other completely blocking the intersections or roads. The drivers were also instructed to stop their cars, turn off the engines, pull the emergency brake, raise all windows, lock the doors, and remain in their cars until the police arrived. The plan was to have the cars remain in position for one hour.

Acting under the 'stall in' plan, plaintiff [respondent in the present action] drove his car onto Brown Road, a McDonnell access road, at approximately 7:00 A.M., at the start of the morning rush hour. Plaintiff was aware of the traffic problems that would result. He stopped his car with the intent to block traffic. The police arrived shortly and requested plaintiff to move his car. He refused to move his car voluntarily. Plaintiff's car was towed away by the police, and he was arrested for obstructing traffic. Plaintiff pleaded guilty to the charge of obstructing traffic and was fined." 318 F. Supp. 846, 849. . . .

[O]n July 25, 1965, petitioner publicly advertised for qualified mechanics, respondent's trade, and respondent promptly applied for re-employment. Petitioner turned down respondent, basing its rejection on respondent's participation in the "stall-in." . . . Shortly thereafter, respondent filed a formal complaint with the Equal Employment Opportunity Commission. . . .

In order to clarify the standards governing the disposition of an action challenging employment discrimination, we granted certiorari, 409 U.S. 1036 (1972). . . .

In this case respondent, the complainant below, charges that he was denied employment "because of his involvement in civil rights activities" and "because of his race and color." Petitioner denied discrimination of any kind, asserting that its failure to re-employ respondent was based upon and justified by his participation in the unlawful conduct against it. Thus, the issue at the trial on remand is framed by those opposing factual contentions. . . .

The complainant in a Title VII trial must carry the initial burden under the statute of establishing a prima facie case of racial discrimination. This may be done by showing (i) that he belongs to a racial minority; (ii) that he applied and was qualified for a job for which the employer was seeking applicants; (iii) that, despite his qualifications, he was rejected; and (iv) that, after his rejection, the position remained open and the employer continued to seek applicants from persons of complainant's qualifications.[13] In the instant case, we agree with the Court of Appeals that respondent proved a prima facie case. 463 F.2d 337, 353. Petitioner sought mechanics, respondent's trade, and continued to do so after respondent's rejection. Petitioner, moreover, does not dispute respondent's qualifications and acknowledges that his past work performance in petitioner's employ was "satisfactory."

The burden then must shift to the employer to articulate some legitimate, nondiscriminatory reason for the employee's rejection. We need not attempt in the instant case to detail every matter which fairly could be recognized as a reasonable basis for a refusal to hire. Here petitioner has assigned respondent's participation in unlawful conduct against it as the cause for his rejection. We think that this suffices to discharge petitioner's burden of proof at this stage and to meet respondent's prima facie case of discrimination. . . .

Nothing in Title VII compels an employer to absolve and rehire one who has engaged in such deliberate, unlawful activity against it.[17]

Petitioner's reason for rejection thus suffices to meet the prima facie case, but the inquiry must not end here. While Title VII does not, without more, compel rehiring of respondent, neither does it permit petitioner to use respondent's conduct as a pretext for the sort of discrimination prohibited by § 703(a)(1). On remand, respondent must . . . be afforded a fair opportunity to show that petitioner's stated reason for respondent's rejection was in fact pretext. Especially relevant to such a showing would be evidence that white employees involved in acts against petitioner of comparable seriousness to the "stall-in" were nevertheless retained or rehired. Petitioner may justifiably refuse to rehire one who was engaged in unlawful, disruptive acts against it, but only if this criterion is applied alike to members of all races.

[13]The facts necessarily will vary in Title VII cases, and the specification above of the prima facie proof required from respondent is not necessarily applicable in every respect to differing factual situations.

[17]The unlawful activity in this case was directed specifically against petitioner. We need not consider or decide here whether, or under what circumstances, unlawful activity not directed against the particular employer may be a legitimate justification for refusing to hire.

Other evidence that may be relevant to any showing of pretext includes facts as to the petitioner's treatment of respondent during his prior term of employment; petitioner's reaction, if any, to respondent's legitimate civil rights activities; and petitioner's general policy and practice with respect to minority employment. On the latter point, statistics as to petitioner's employment policy and practice may be helpful to a determination of whether petitioner's refusal to rehire respondent in this case conformed to a general pattern of discrimination against blacks. . . . In short, on the retrial respondent must be given a full and fair opportunity to demonstrate by competent evidence that the presumptively valid reasons for his rejection were in fact a coverup for a racially discriminatory decision. . . .

The judgment is vacated and the cause is hereby remanded to the District Court for further proceedings consistent with this opinion.

So ordered.

CASE DISCUSSION QUESTIONS

1. What do you think happened next in this case?
2. Why do you think the court established such an elaborate procedure for establishing the plaintiff's prima facie case?
3. How do you think the test proposed in this case could be modified to cover a case of a person denied a promotion?

As articulated in *McDonnell Douglas* and the cases that have followed it, the person bringing a disparate treatment case must first establish through the prima facie case that

1. he or she is a member of a protected class,
2. he or she applied and was qualified for the position,
3. his or her application was rejected, and
4. the employer continued to seek other applicants for the same position or filled the position with someone who was not within the protected class.

This four-part test can also be adjusted to fit firing and failure-to-promote cases.

Once the plaintiff has established this prima facie case, the employer has to articulate a valid reason for not hiring, for not promoting, or for firing the plaintiff. Note that this is a **burden of production** as opposed to a **burden of proof**. It means the employer will lose the case if it cannot come up with a reason that does not involve discrimination based on a protected class criterion, but it does not mean the defendant has the burden of proving that the reason offered is true. After this alternative reason is presented, the plaintiff has the burden of proving by a preponderance of the evidence that the employer's reason is really just a pretext and that the employer actually acted with a discriminatory intent. See Figure 13-8.

Because the focus in a discriminatory treatment case remains on the actual intent of the defendant, any evidence that the employer was motivated by a discriminatory animus is relevant. For example, in one case involving a nationwide professional accounting firm,[10] a female senior manager became a candidate for partnership. When she failed to get the promotion, the rejected

Burden of production
The necessity to produce some evidence, but it need not be so strong as to convince the trier of fact of its truth.

Burden of proof
The necessity of proving the truth of the matter asserted.

[10]Price Waterhouse v. Hopkins, 490 U.S. 228 (1989).

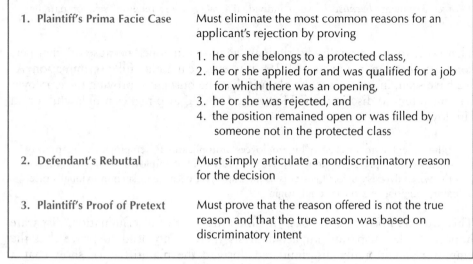

1. Plaintiff's Prima Facie Case	Must eliminate the most common reasons for an applicant's rejection by proving
	1. he or she belongs to a protected class,
	2. he or she applied for and was qualified for a job for which there was an opening,
	3. he or she was rejected, and
	4. the position remained open or was filled by someone not in the protected class
2. Defendant's Rebuttal	Must simply articulate a nondiscriminatory reason for the decision
3. Plaintiff's Proof of Pretext	Must prove that the reason offered is not the true reason and that the true reason was based on discriminatory intent

Figure 13-8   Three-Part *McDonnell Douglas* Analysis

employee sued. Supporters of her candidacy described her as "an outstanding professional" with a "strong character, independence and integrity." However, those that denied her the promotion appeared to react negatively to her personality because she was a woman. Evidence that the Court looked at in making this determination included the fact that one of the partners suggested she "take a course at charm school." In addition, "[s]everal partners criticized her use of profanity; in response, one partner suggested that those partners object to her swearing only 'because it[']s a lady using foul language.'"[11] Finally, one of the partners, in advising Hopkins how to advance her candidacy, suggested that she should "walk more femininely, talk more femininely, dress more femininely, wear make-up, have her hair styled, and wear jewelry."[12] Such "smoking gun" evidence can be used by the plaintiff to convince the court that any proffered nondiscriminatory reason for her rejection is really pretext.

With the passage of the Civil Rights Act of 1991 Congress made it easier for plaintiffs to win mixed motive cases by amending Title VII to add this provision: "[A]n unlawful employment practice is established when the complaining party demonstrates that race, color, religion, sex, or national origin was a motivating factor for any employment practice, even though other factors also motivated the practice."[13]

(3) Unintentional discrimination—disparate impact

As we have seen, Title VII makes it unlawful for any employer

(1) to fail or refuse to hire or to discharge any individual, or otherwise to discriminate against any individual with respect to his compensation, terms, conditions, or privileges

---

[11]Id. at 235.

[12]Id.

[13]Civil Rights Act of 1991, § 107(a), 42 U.S.C. § 2000e-2(m) (2004).

of employment, *because of* such individual's race, color, religion, sex, or national origin.[14]

Therefore, to intentionally discriminate against someone "because of" that person's membership in a protected class is to engage in unlawful discrimination. As we have seen, in such cases the plaintiff has the burden of proving the employer had the intent to discriminate. However, Title VII also makes it unlawful for an employer to

> (2) limit, segregate, or classify his employees or applicants for employment in any way which would deprive or tend to deprive any individual of employment opportunities or otherwise adversely affect his status as an employee, because of such individual's race, color, religion, sex, or national origin.[15]

This provision provides the basis for the third type of discrimination, **disparate impact.** Under disparate impact analysis there is no need to prove that the employer intentionally discriminated. Instead the plaintiff must show that a neutral employment practice deprived the plaintiff of "employment opportunities" because the practice had a disproportionate impact on the plaintiff's protected class. This theory of discrimination was originally developed by the U.S. Supreme Court in the following landmark decision.

Griggs v. Duke Power Co.
401 U.S. 424 (1971)

BURGER, C.J., delivered the opinion of the Court, in which all members joined except BRENNAN, J., who took no part in the consideration or decision of the case.

We granted the writ in this case to resolve the question whether an employer is prohibited by the Civil Rights Act of 1964, Title VII, from requiring a high school education or passing of a standardized general intelligence test as a condition of employment in or transfer to jobs when (a) neither standard is shown to be significantly related to successful job performance, (b) both requirements operate to disqualify Negroes at a substantially higher rate than white applicants, and (c) the jobs in question formerly had been filled only by white employees as part of a longstanding practice of giving preference to whites.

The District Court found that prior to July 2, 1965, the effective date of the Civil Rights Act of 1964, the Company openly discriminated on the basis of race in the hiring and assigning of employees at its Dan River plant. The plant was organized into five operating departments. . . . Negroes were employed only in the Labor Department where the highest paying jobs paid less than the lowest paying jobs in the other four "operating" departments in which only whites were employed. Promotions were normally made within each department on the basis of job seniority. Transferees into a department usually began in the lowest position.

In 1955 the Company instituted a policy of requiring a high school education for initial assignment to any department except Labor, and for transfer from the Coal Handling to any "inside" department (Operations, Maintenance, or Laboratory). When the Company abandoned its policy of restricting Negroes to the Labor

---

[14] 42 U.S.C. § 2000e-2(a)(1) (2004) (emphasis added).
[15] 42 U.S.C. § 2000e-2(a)(2) (2004).

Department in 1965, completion of high school also was made a prerequisite to transfer from Labor to any other department. From the time the high school requirement was instituted to the time of trial, however, white employees hired before the time of the high school education requirement continued to perform satisfactorily and achieve promotions in the "operating" departments. Findings on this score are not challenged.

The Company added a further requirement for new employees on July 2, 1965, the date on which Title VII became effective. To qualify for placement in any but the Labor Department it became necessary to register satisfactory scores on two professionally prepared aptitude tests, as well as to have a high school education. Completion of high school alone continued to render employees eligible for transfer to the four desirable departments from which Negroes had been excluded if the incumbent had been employed prior to the time of the new requirement. In September 1965 the Company began to permit incumbent employees who lacked a high school education to qualify for transfer from Labor or Coal Handling to an "inside" job by passing two tests—the Wonderlic Personnel Test, which purports to measure general intelligence, and the Bennett Mechanical Comprehension Test. Neither was directed or intended to measure the ability to learn to perform a particular job or category of jobs. The requisite scores used for both initial hiring and transfer approximated the national median for high school graduates.[3] . . .

The objective of Congress in the enactment of Title VII is plain from the language of the statute. It was to achieve equality of employment opportunities and remove barriers that have operated in the past to favor an identifiable group of white employees over other employees. Under the Act, practices, procedures, or tests neutral on their face, and even neutral in terms of intent, cannot be maintained if they operate to "freeze" the status quo of prior discriminatory employment practices. . . .

Congress did not intend by Title VII, however, to guarantee a job to every person regardless of qualifications. In short, the Act does not command that any person be hired simply because he was formerly the subject of discrimination, or because he is a member of a minority group. Discriminatory preference for any group, minority or majority, is precisely and only what Congress has proscribed. What is required by Congress is the removal of artificial, arbitrary, and unnecessary barriers to employment when the barriers operate invidiously to discriminate on the basis of racial or other impermissible classification.

Congress has now provided that tests or criteria for employment or promotion may not provide equality of opportunity merely in the sense of the fabled offer of milk to the stork and the fox. On the contrary, Congress has now required that the posture and condition of the job-seeker be taken into account. It has—to resort again to the fable—provided that the vessel in which the milk is proffered be one all seekers can use. The Act proscribes not only overt discrimination but also practices that are fair in form, but discriminatory in operation. The touchstone is business necessity. If an employment practice which operates to exclude Negroes cannot be shown to be related to job performance, the practice is prohibited.

On the record before us, neither the high school completion requirement nor the general intelligence test is shown to bear a demonstrable relationship to successful performance of the jobs for which it was used. Both were adopted, as the Court of Appeals noted, without meaningful study of their relationship to job-performance ability. Rather, a vice president of the Company testified, the requirements were instituted on the Company's judgment that they generally would improve the overall quality of the work force.

The evidence, however, shows that employees who have not completed high school or taken the tests have continued to perform satisfactorily and make progress in departments for which the high school and test criteria are now used. The promotion record of present employees who would not be able to meet the new criteria thus

---

[3]The test standards are thus more stringent than the high school requirement, since they would screen out approximately half of all high school graduates.

suggests the possibility that the requirements may not be needed even for the limited purpose of preserving the avowed policy of advancement within the Company. . . .

The Court of Appeals held that the Company had adopted the diploma and test requirements without any "intention to discriminate against Negro employees." 420 F.2d, at 1232. We do not suggest that either the District Court or the Court of Appeals erred in examining the employer's intent; but good intent or absence of discriminatory intent does not redeem employment procedures or testing mechanisms that operate as "built-in headwinds" for minority groups and are unrelated to measuring job capability. . . .

The Company contends that its general intelligence tests are specifically permitted by § 703(h) of the Act. That section authorizes the use of "any professionally developed ability test" that is not "designed, intended or used to discriminate because of race. . . ." (Emphasis added.) . . .

Nothing in the Act precludes the use of testing or measuring procedures; obviously they are useful. What Congress has forbidden is giving these devices and mechanisms controlling force unless they are demonstrably a reasonable measure of job performance. Congress has not commanded that the less qualified be preferred over the better qualified simply because of minority origins. Far from disparaging job qualifications as such, Congress has made such qualifications the controlling factor, so that race, religion, nationality, and sex become irrelevant. What Congress has commanded is that any tests used must measure the person for the job and not the person in the abstract.

CASE DISCUSSION QUESTIONS

1. What did the U.S. Supreme Court understand to be the objective of Title VII? That is, precisely what does it proscribe, and what does it require?

2. Do you think the *Griggs* decision is a fair reading of the statute? Should an employer be found in violation of an antidiscrimination statute when there is no proof of prejudice or biased motive?

3. What does business necessity mean, and what is its role in the order of proof discussed in this case?

4. Did the employer prove business necessity? Why?

5. In footnote 6 the *Griggs* Court noted that "[i]n North Carolina, 1960 census statistics show that, while 34% of white males had completed high school, only 12% of Negro males had done so. . . . Similarly, with respect to standardized tests, the EEOC in one case found that use of a battery of tests, including the Wonderlic and Bennett tests used by the Company in the instant case, resulted in 58% of whites passing the tests, as compared with only 6% of the blacks." What do you make of these statistics?

Following *Griggs* the courts have grappled with many situations involving disparate impact. To prove such a case, the plaintiff must first show that the employer's facially neutral practices have a disproportionately discriminatory impact on a protected class. To prove the disproportionate impact, the plaintiff frequently will resort to statistics to show the disparity between the numbers of available workers belonging to that classification versus those actually able to qualify for employment under the employer's neutral test. The burden is then shifted to the employer to prove that the practice was necessary for its business operation. If it does so, then the plaintiff has the opportunity to prove that an alternative practice would also accomplish the employer's purposes but without the negative discriminatory impact. See Figure 13-9. In the Civil Rights Act of

1. **Plaintiff's Prima Facie Case**	Must prove that the facially neutral practice disproportionately discriminates against a protected class (often demonstrated through statistics)
2. **Defendant's Rebuttal**	Must prove business necessity—that is, that the practice "bears a demonstrable relationship to successful performance of the jobs for which it was used"
3. **Plaintiff's Proof of a Nondiscriminatory Alternative**	Must prove that an equally useful but less discriminatory alternative exists that could be used by the employer.

Figure 13-9   Summary of the Order of Proof in Disparate Impact Cases

1991 Congress codified the concepts of "business necessity" and "job related" as they had been developed in *Griggs*.

c. Sexual Harassment

Until the mid-1980s it was unclear whether Title VII's prohibition against sex discrimination also prohibited sexual harassment. Then in *Meritor Savings Bank v. Vinson*[16] the U.S. Supreme Court held that, even in the absence of a tangible job loss (such as a failure to receive a raise), an employee can maintain an action for unlawful sex discrimination if the employer creates a hostile or abusive work environment. The Court cited an Eleventh Circuit opinion with approval:

> Sexual harassment which creates a hostile or offensive environment for members of one sex is every bit the arbitrary barrier to sexual equality at the workplace that racial harassment is to racial equality. Surely, a requirement that a man or woman run a gauntlet of sexual abuse in return for the privilege of being allowed to work and make a living can be as damaging and disconcerting as the harshest of racial epithets.[17]

Therefore, today it is clear that Title VII prohibits **quid pro quo sexual harassment,** as well as sexual harassment based on an **offensive work environment.** The EEOC has developed guidelines that detail each form of discrimination. Quid pro quo situations involve an exchange of sexual favors for employment benefits. For example, this type of situation would occur if an employee were passed by for a promotion because she refused to have sex with her supervisor. Sexual harassment can also consist of

> [u]nwelcome sexual advances, requests for sexual favors, and other verbal or physical conduct of a sexual nature . . . [that have] the purpose or effect of unreasonably interfering with an individual's work performance or creating an intimidating, hostile, or offensive working environment.[18]

---

[16]477 U.S. 57 (1986).

[17]Id. at 67 (citing Henson v. Dundee, 682 F.2d 897, 902 (11th Cir. 1982)).

[18]29 C.F.R. § 1604.11.

In 1993 the U.S. Supreme Court held that it is not necessary for the victim in a hostile work environment case to prove it seriously harmed his or her psychological well-being.[19] It is enough that "a reasonable person" would find it to be hostile or abusive and that the victim perceived the environment to be abusive. The Court noted that "Title VII comes into play before the harassing conduct leads to a nervous breakdown."[20]

Also, as noted earlier in this chapter, in 1998 the U.S. Supreme Court held that same-sex sexual harassment is actionable under Title VII so long as there is a proven connection between the sexual harassment and gender discrimination; that is, the plaintiff must still be able to prove the harassment was "because of" the person's gender.[21] The Court noted that while same-sex harassment was not the "primary evil" Congress hoped to eliminate through Title VII, it was a "reasonably comparable evil."[22]

However, there are still many unanswered questions in the area of sexual harassment, such as how to distinguish between voluntary sexual activity and "unwelcome" sexual advances. Also, from whose point of view should you judge whether a "hostile or offensive environment" was created? In the following case the U.S. Court of Appeals for the Ninth Circuit discussed whether that point of view should be that of a "reasonable woman" or that of a "reasonable person."

Ellison v. Brady
924 F.2d 872 (9th Cir. 1991)

BEEZER, Circuit Judge

I

Kerry Ellison worked as a revenue agent for the Internal Revenue Service in San Mateo, California. During her initial training in 1984 she met Sterling Gray, another trainee, who was also assigned to the San Mateo office. The two co-workers never became friends, and they did not work closely together.

Gray's desk was twenty feet from Ellison's desk, two rows behind and one row over. Revenue agents in the San Mateo office often went to lunch in groups. In June of 1986 when no one else was in the office, Gray asked Ellison to lunch. She accepted. Gray had to pick up his son's forgotten lunch, so they stopped by Gray's house. He gave Ellison a tour of his house.

Ellison alleges that after the June lunch Gray started to pester her with unnecessary questions and hang around her desk. On October 9, 1986, Gray asked Ellison out for a drink after work. She declined, but she suggested that they have lunch the following week. She did not want to have lunch alone with him, and she tried to stay away from the office during lunch time. One day during the following week, Gray uncharacteristically dressed in a three-piece suit and asked Ellison out for lunch. Again, she did not accept.

On October 22, 1986 Gray handed Ellison a note he wrote on a telephone message slip which read:

I cried over you last night and I'm totally drained today. I have never been in such constant term oil

---

[19]Harris v. Forklift Systems, 510 U.S. 17 (1993).

[20]Id. at 22.

[21]Oncale v. Sundowner Offshore Services, Inc., 523 U.S. 75 (1998).

[22]Id. at 79.

(sic). Thank you for talking with me. I could not stand to feel your hatred for another day.

When Ellison realized that Gray wrote the note, she became shocked and frightened and left the room. Gray followed her into the hallway and demanded that she talk to him, but she left the building.

Ellison later showed the note to Bonnie Miller, who supervised both Ellison and Gray. Miller said "this is sexual harassment." Ellison asked Miller not to do anything about it. She wanted to try to handle it herself. Ellison asked a male co-worker to talk to Gray, to tell him that she was not interested in him and to leave her alone. The next day, Thursday, Gray called in sick.

Ellison did not work on Friday, and on the following Monday, she started four weeks of training in St. Louis, Missouri. Gray mailed her a card and a typed, single-spaced, three-page letter. She describes this letter as "twenty times, a hundred times weirder" than the prior note. Gray wrote, in part:

> I know that you are worth knowing with or without sex. . . . Leaving aside the hassles and disasters of recent weeks. I have enjoyed you so much over these past few months. Watching you. Experiencing you from O so far away. Admiring your style and elan. . . . Don't you think it odd that two people who have never even talked together, alone, are striking off such intense sparks . . . I will [write] another letter in the near future.

Explaining her reaction, Ellison stated: "I just thought he was crazy. I thought he was nuts. I didn't know what he would do next. I was frightened."

She immediately telephoned Miller. Ellison told her supervisor that she was frightened and really upset. She requested that Miller transfer either her or Gray because she would not be comfortable working in the same office with him. . . . Gray subsequently transferred to the San Francisco office on November 24, 1986. . . .

After three weeks in San Francisco, Gray filed union grievances requesting a return to the San Mateo office. The IRS and the union settled the grievances in Gray's favor, agreeing to allow him to transfer back to the San Mateo office. . . . Ellison was "frantic." She filed a formal complaint alleging sexual harassment on January 30, 1987 with the IRS. She also obtained permission to transfer to San Francisco temporarily when Gray returned.

Gray sought joint counseling. He wrote Ellison another letter which still sought to maintain the idea that he and Ellison had some type of relationship. . . .

Ellison filed a complaint in September of 1987 in federal district court. The court granted the government's motion for summary judgment on the ground that Ellison had failed to state a prima facie case of sexual harassment due to a hostile working environment. Ellison appeals.

II

Congress added the word "sex" to Title VII of the Civil Rights Act of 1964 at the last minute on the floor of the House of Representatives. 110 Cong. Rec. 2,577-2,584 (1964). Virtually no legislative history provides guidance to courts interpreting the prohibition of sex discrimination. In *Meritor Savings Bank v. Vinson*, 477 U.S. 57, 91 L. Ed. 2d 49, 106 S. Ct. 2399 (1986), the Supreme Court held that sexual harassment constitutes sex discrimination in violation of Title VII.

Courts have recognized different forms of sexual harassment. In "quid pro quo" cases, employers condition employment benefits on sexual favors. In "hostile environment" cases, employees work in offensive or abusive environments. . . .

III

. . . The Supreme Court cautioned, however, that not all harassment affects a "term, condition, or privilege" of employment within the meaning of Title VII. For example, the "mere utterance of an ethnic or racial epithet which engenders offensive feelings in an employee" is not, by itself, actionable under Title VII. To state a claim under Title VII, sexual harassment "must be sufficiently severe or pervasive to alter the conditions of the victim's employment and create an abusive working environment." . . .

[W]e believe that Gray's conduct was sufficiently severe and pervasive to alter the conditions of Ellison's employment and create an abusive working environment. We first note that the required showing of severity or seriousness of the harassing conduct varies inversely with the pervasiveness or frequency of the conduct. . . .

Next, we believe that in evaluating the severity and pervasiveness of sexual harassment, we should focus on the perspective of the victim. . . . If we only examined whether a reasonable person would engage in allegedly harassing conduct, we would run the risk of reinforcing the prevailing level of discrimination. Harassers could continue to harass merely because a particular discriminatory practice was common, and victims of harassment would have no remedy.

We therefore prefer to analyze harassment from the victim's perspective. A complete understanding of the victim's view requires, among other things, an analysis of the different perspectives of men and women. Conduct that many men consider unobjectionable may offend many women. See, e.g., *Lipsett v. University of Puerto Rico*, 864 F.2d 881, 898 (1st Cir. 1988) ("A male supervisor might believe, for example, that it is legitimate for him to tell a female subordinate that she has a 'great figure' or 'nice legs.' The female subordinate, however, may find such comments offensive"). . . .

We realize that there is a broad range of viewpoints among women as a group, but we believe that many women share common concerns which men do not necessarily share. For example, because women are disproportionately victims of rape and sexual assault, women have a stronger incentive to be concerned with sexual behavior. Women who are victims of mild forms of sexual harassment may understandably worry whether a harasser's conduct is merely a prelude to violent sexual assault. Men, who are rarely victims of sexual assault, may view sexual conduct in a vacuum without a full appreciation of the social setting or the underlying threat of violence that a woman may perceive.

In order to shield employers from having to accommodate the idiosyncratic concerns of the rare hyper-sensitive employee, we hold that a female plaintiff states a prima facie case of hostile environment sexual harassment when she alleges conduct which a reasonable woman[11] would consider sufficiently severe or pervasive to alter the conditions of employment and create an abusive working environment.[12]

We adopt the perspective of a reasonable woman primarily because we believe that a sex-blind reasonable person standard tends to be male-biased and tends to systematically ignore the experiences of women. The reasonable woman standard does not establish a higher level of protection for women than men. Instead, a gender-conscious examination of sexual harassment enables women to participate in the workplace on an equal footing with men. By acknowledging and not trivializing the effects of sexual harassment on reasonable women, courts can work towards ensuring that neither men nor women will have to "run a gauntlet of sexual abuse in return for the privilege of being allowed to work and make a living."

We note that the reasonable victim standard we adopt today classifies conduct as unlawful sexual harassment even when harassers do not realize that their conduct creates a hostile working environment. Well-intentioned compliments by co-workers or supervisors can form the basis of a sexual harassment cause of action if a reasonable victim of the same sex as the plaintiff would consider the comments sufficiently severe or pervasive to alter a condition of employment and create an abusive working environment.[13] That is because Title VII is not a fault-based tort scheme.

---

[11]Of course, where male employees allege that co-workers engage in conduct which creates a hostile environment, the appropriate victim's perspective would be that of a reasonable man.

[12]We realize that the reasonable woman standard will not address conduct which some women find offensive. Conduct considered harmless by many today may be considered discriminatory in the future. *Rogers*, 454 F.2d at 238. Fortunately, the reasonableness inquiry which we adopt today is not static. As the views of reasonable women change, so too does the Title VII standard of acceptable behavior.

[13]If sexual comments or sexual advances are in fact welcomed by the recipient, they, of course, do not constitute sexual harassment. Title VII's prohibition of sex discrimination in employment does not require a totally desexualized workplace.

"Title VII is aimed at the consequences or effects of an employment practice and not at the . . . motivation" of co-workers or employers. To avoid liability under Title VII, employers may have to educate and sensitize their workforce to eliminate conduct which a reasonable victim would consider unlawful sexual harassment. See 29 C.F.R. § 1604.11(f). ("Prevention is the best tool for the elimination of sexual harassment.")

The facts of this case illustrate the importance of considering the victim's perspective. Analyzing the facts from the alleged harasser's viewpoint, Gray could be portrayed as a modern-day Cyrano de Bergerac wishing no more than to woo Ellison with his words. There is no evidence that Gray harbored ill will toward Ellison. He even offered in his "love letter" to leave her alone if she wished. Examined in this light, it is not difficult to see why the district court characterized Gray's conduct as isolated and trivial.

Ellison, however, did not consider the acts to be trivial. Gray's first note shocked and frightened her. After receiving the three-page letter, she became really upset and frightened again. She immediately requested that she or Gray be transferred. Her supervisor's prompt response suggests that she too did not consider the conduct trivial. When Ellison learned that Gray arranged to return to San Mateo, she immediately asked to transfer, and she immediately filed an official complaint.

We cannot say as a matter of law that Ellison's reaction was idiosyncratic or hypersensitive. We believe that a reasonable woman could have had a similar reaction. After receiving the first bizarre note from Gray, a person she barely knew, Ellison asked a co-worker to tell Gray to leave her alone. Despite her request, Gray sent her a long, passionate, disturbing letter. He told her he had been "watching" and "experiencing" her; he made repeated references to sex; he said he would write again. Ellison had no way of knowing what Gray would do next. A reasonable woman could consider Gray's conduct, as alleged by Ellison, sufficiently severe and pervasive to alter a condition of employment and create an abusive working environment.

Sexual harassment is a major problem in the workplace.[15] Adopting the victim's perspective ensures that courts will not "sustain ingrained notions of reasonable behavior fashioned by the offenders." Congress did not enact Title VII to codify prevailing sexist prejudices. To the contrary, "Congress designed Title VII to prevent the perpetuation of stereotypes and a sense of degradation which serve to close or discourage employment opportunities for women." We hope that over time both men and women will learn what conduct offends reasonable members of the other sex. When employers and employees internalize the standard of workplace conduct we establish today, the current gap in perception between the sexes will be bridged. . . .

Reversed and remanded.

STEPHENS, District Judge, dissenting:

. . . Nowhere in section 2000e of Title VII . . . is there any indication that Congress intended to provide for any other than equal treatment in the area of civil rights. . . . I believe that it is incumbent upon the court in this case to use terminology that will meet the needs of all who seek recourse under this section of Title VII. Possible alternatives that are more in line with a gender neutral approach include "victim," "target," or "person." . . .

The focus on the victim of the sexually discriminatory conduct has its parallel in rape trials in the focus put by the defense on the victim's conduct rather than on the unlawful conduct of the person accused. Modern feminists have pointed out that concentration by the defense upon evidence concerning the background, appearance and conduct of women claiming to have been raped must be carefully controlled by

---

[15]Over 40 percent of female federal employees reported incidents of sexual harassment in 1987, roughly the same number as in 1980. Victims of sexual harassment "pay all the intangible emotional costs inflicted by anger, humiliation, frustration, withdrawal, dysfunction in family life," as well as medical expenses, litigation expenses, job search expenses, and the loss of valuable sick leave and annual leave. Sexual harassment cost the federal government $267 million from May 1985 to May 1987 for losses in productivity, sick leave costs, and employee replacement costs.

the court to avoid effectively shifting the burden of proof to the victim. It is the accused, not the victim, that should be subjected to scrutiny. Many state legislatures have responded to this viewpoint, and rules governing the presentation of evidence in rape cases have evolved accordingly. . . .

The creation of the proposed "new standard" which applies only to women will not necessarily come to the aid of all potential victims of the type of misconduct that is at issue in this case. I believe that a gender neutral standard would greatly contribute to the clarity of this and future cases in the same area.

CASE DISCUSSION QUESTIONS

1. Why did Ellison wait so long before making a formal complaint against Gray?

2. Is every utterance of a sexual or racial epithet grounds for a Title VII lawsuit? Why?

3. Why did the majority adopt a reasonable woman standard? Why did the dissent disagree? Who do you think made the better argument and why?

4. Why did the court think it appropriate to classify conduct as unlawful sexual harassment even when the harasser does not realize his conduct creates a hostile working environment?

d. Damages Awards and Other Relief under Title VII

Until 1991 a plaintiff prevailing in a Title VII case was entitled to a court order enjoining the employer from engaging in unlawful employment practices and requiring affirmative action as appropriate, including reinstatement or hiring with or without back pay and other equitable relief. In 1991 Congress amended Title VII in the Civil Rights Act of 1991 so that in cases of intentional discrimination the complaining party may also recover compensatory and punitive damages. Punitive damages are possible if the plaintiff can show that the employer acted "with malice or reckless indifference" to his or her federally protected rights. Compensatory damages can include "future pecuniary losses, emotional pain, suffering, inconvenience, mental anguish, loss of enjoyment of life, and other nonpecuniary losses."[23] However, damages are limited based on the size of the employer, from $50,000 for the smallest employers to $300,000 for those with over 500 employees.

DISCUSSION QUESTION

5. A Fox one day invited a Stork to dinner and, being disposed to divert himself at the expense of this guest, provided nothing for the entertainment but some thin soup in a shallow dish. This the Fox lapped up very readily, while the Stork, unable to gain a mouthful with her long narrow bill, was as hungry at the end of dinner as at the beginning. The Fox meanwhile professed his regret at seeing his guest eat so sparingly and feared that the dish was not seasoned to her liking. The Stork said little but begged that the Fox would do her the honor of returning her visit. Accordingly, he agreed to dine with her on the following day. He arrived true to his appointment, and the dinner was ordered. But when it was

---

[23]42 U.S.C. § 1981a (2004).

served up, he found to his dismay that it was contained in a narrow-necked vessel, down which the Stork readily thrust her long neck and bill, while the Fox was obliged to content himself with licking the neck of the jar.

Is this fable about disparate treatment or disparate impact? Why?

2. ADEA: Age Discrimination

In 1967 Congress passed the Age Discrimination in Employment Act (ADEA).[24] This act prohibits employers from discriminating against persons aged 40 or older because of their age. While the protected classes found under Title VII are generally described by immutable characteristics, such as race or sex, everyone will move into the protected age category.

As with other forms of discrimination, enforcement of the ADEA involves proof problems. In cases of alleged disparate treatment employees can use a modified version of the *McDonnell Douglas* four-part analysis:

1. The plaintiff belongs to the protected class of persons forty years of age or older,
2. the plaintiff applied for a job for which the plaintiff was qualified,
3. the plaintiff was rejected, and
4. the position remained open or was filled by someone substantially younger than the plaintiff.

Note that the fourth part of this test has been modified from requiring "someone not in the protected class" to "someone substantially younger than the plaintiff." Without this change, if the person who replaces the plaintiff is younger than the plaintiff but is also from the protected age group, the plaintiff would be left without a cause of action. The U.S. Supreme Court was faced with that situation in *O'Connor v. Consolidated Coin Caterers Corp.*[25] The Court was called on to decide if the ADEA was violated when the Consolidated Coin Caterers Corporation fired a fifty-six-year-old middle manager and then gave his job to a forty-year-old. The company argued that by replacing one protected class individual with another it had not violated the law. The Court, however, rejected this argument and ruled that the law had been violated because the evidence showed that O'Connor had been fired because of his age.

> Or to put the point more concretely, there can be no greater inference of age discrimination (as opposed to "40 or over" discrimination) when a 40 year-old is replaced by a 39 year-old than when a 56 year-old is replaced by a 40 year-old. Because it lacks probative value, the fact that an ADEA plaintiff was replaced by someone outside the protected class is not a proper element of the *McDonnell Douglas* prima facie case.[26]

Therefore, the Court concluded that age discrimination can be more reliably indicated by a showing that the replacement is substantially younger than by a showing that the replacement is not a member of the protected class.

---

[24] 42 U.S.C. 623 (2004).

[25] 517 U.S. 308 (1996).

[26] Id. at 312.

Because the ADEA prohibits discrimination on the basis of age and not class membership, the fact that a replacement is substantially younger than the plaintiff is a far more reliable indicator of age discrimination than is the fact that the plaintiff was replaced by someone outside the protected class.[27]

This statement would seem to indicate that the replacement worker must be substantially younger than the plaintiff. However, the Tenth Circuit has ruled that all that is necessary is proof that age was the motivating factor. The court found that a fifty-seven-year-old replaced by a fifty-two-year-old could win an age discrimination case where he had direct proof that the reasons given for his firing were pretextual.[28]

While it is clear that an older worker can bring a claim of disparate treatment, the courts disagree as to whether it is possible to bring a case based on disparate impact. For example, when seeking to decrease operating expenses, employers often choose to reduce the number of highest paid workers. As increased pay and longevity at work tend to run together, such work reductions can lead to the difficult proof problem of having to show that the employees were laid off because of their age and not because of their cost to the company. Such a situation would obviously raise the issue of disparate impact.

At least one federal court of appeals has held that a disparate impact claim is not possible under the ADEA. In that case two women, aged thirty-eight and forty, applied for flight attendant positions. They were rejected because they were not able to meet the airline's maximum weight requirements. They argued that the requirements fell more harshly on older applicants. The court, in denying their claim, said, "You are not part of a discrete minority when you are over 40." The court stated that in enacting the ADEA Congress was interested in preventing age stereotypes but not in preventing unintentional discrimination.[29]

Another area in which there has been uncertainty regarding the reach of the ADEA relates to whether the ADEA's prohibition against age discrimination prohibits employers from favoring older employees over younger employees. In *General Dynamics Land Systems, Inc. v. Cline*,[30] the U.S. Supreme Court confronted that issue. General Dynamics and the union representing the employees reached a collective bargaining agreement that eliminated the company's obligation to provide health benefits to subsequently retired employees. However, an exception was made for current workers who were at least 50 years old. Cline and other employees who were at least 40 years old (and thus protected by the ADEA) but less than 50 years old (and therefore not entitled to the benefits) claimed that the agreement discriminated against them because of their age and hence violated the ADEA.

The U.S. Supreme Court disagreed. "We see the text, structure, purpose, and history of the ADEA, along with its relationship to other federal statutes, as showing that the statute does not mean to stop an employer from favoring an older employee over a younger one."[31] Therefore, the collective bargaining agreement favoring the older workers was not unlawful discrimination.

---

[27]Id.

[28]Greene v. Safeway Stores, Inc., 98 F.3d 554 (10th Cir. 1996).

[29]Ellis v. United Airlines, 73 F.3d 999 (10th Cir.), cert. denied, 517 U.S. 1245 (1996).

[30]124 S. Ct. 1236 (2004).

[31]Id. at 1248.

NETNOTE

The U.S. Department of Justice maintains information on the Americans with Disabilities Act at *www.usdoj.gov/crt/ada/adahom1.htm.* Another good source of information is the Americans with Disabilities Act Document Center, *http://www.jan.wvu.edu/links/adalinks.htm.*

3. ADA: Disability Discrimination

In 1990 Congress enacted the Americans with Disabilities Act (ADA).[32] As is true under Title VII this act applies to employers with fifteen or more employees. An employer cannot discriminate against a qualified individual with a disability if reasonable accommodations are possible.

A **disability** is defined as a physical or mental impairment that substantially limits a major life activity. An individual with a disability is someone who has such an impairment, or who has a record of such an impairment, or who is being regarded as impaired. A **qualified individual with a disability** is an individual with a disability who can perform the essential job functions. Examples of conditions that the courts have found to qualify as disabilities include alcoholism, cancer, heart disease, paraplegia, and obesity. Finally, the employer is only required to make **a reasonable accommodation.** An accommodation is not considered reasonable if it would create an undue hardship for the employer. In such situations the employer is excused from compliance. Examples of reasonable accommodations might include providing flexible working hours or installing a ramp to make an office wheelchair accessible.

Cases in this area tend to focus on two issues: (1) defining what a disability is and (2) determining what constitutes essential job functions. When looking at the first issue courts focus on the abilities of the individual rather than on the condition. Because every individual is affected differently, there must be a showing that the condition in that individual affected a "major life activity." As you can imagine, the phrase "major life activity" is itself open to interpretation. Also, in 1999 the U.S. Supreme Court determined that if the plaintiff has a condition that can be corrected with medication, glasses, or other corrective devices, he or she is not disabled.[33] As to the second issue, determining what constitutes essential job functions, employees must be able to show that although they are disabled, they can perform all essential functions. For example, regular job attendance is usually seen as an essential job function; however, the courts are divided on whether absenteeism disqualifies a claimant under the statute.

This is a new area of the law. The issues will become more clearly defined as more claims are brought and litigated on a case-by-case basis.

---

[32]42 U.S.C. § 12101 (2004).

[33]Sutton v. United Air Lines, Inc., 527 U.S. 471 (1999).

4. Limitations on Employee Lawsuits against State and Local Governmental Employers

The Eleventh Amendment makes the states immune from "any suit in law or equity, commenced or prosecuted . . . by Citizens of any Foreign State." While the amendment appears to prohibit only those suits brought by citizens of another state, the U.S. Supreme Court has determined that it also applies to any suit brought by a state's own citizens unless the state consents to the suit.

This prohibition creates problems when aggrieved state workers want to sue their state employer for alleged violations of Title VII, the ADEA, the ADA, or other federal statutes that prohibit unlawful employment discrimination. Such suits are authorized, however, if two conditions are met. First, the court must find that when Congress wrote the legislation, Congress's intent to authorize such suits was made clear. Second, as you will recall from our earlier discussion of federal legislative power, Congress can only legitimately enact statutes if it does so pursuant to a specific constitutional provision. The courts have determined that in the case of statutes prohibiting discrimination, in appropriate situations Congress does have this power under the Fourteenth Amendment's § 5 enforcement powers. Therefore, the second step is to ensure that Congress was validly exercising that power.

The Supreme Court's application of this two-part test has had varying results. In 2001 in *Board of Trustees of University of Alabama v. Garrett,*[34] the U.S. Supreme Court ruled that disabled state employees could not use the federal courts to sue their employers for money damages under Title I of the ADA. However, just two years later, the Court ruled in *Nevada Department of Human Resources v. Hibbs*[35] that state employees could sue state employers for money damages in federal court for violations of the Family and Medical Leave Act. The Court distinguished *Hibbs* from *Garrett* by saying that *Garrett* involved discrimination against the disabled, a classification that is not subjected to the heightened scrutiny required in cases of sex discrimination, such as that found in *Hibbs.*[36] And in 2004 they ruled in *Tennessee v. Lane*[37] that private individuals could sue states under Title II of the ADA when the suit concerned access to a county courthouse. The Court found that the interest being challenged here, like the one in *Hibbs,* was deserving of heightened judicial scrutiny as it involved the right of access to the courts.[38]

5. Common-Law Approaches: At-Will Employment

As mentioned at the beginning of this chapter, most employees work on an at-will basis. That is, they have not signed formal contracts with their employers governing their employment relationships, and they are not working in companies that have unions to protect the rights of employees. Therefore, they are free to leave work at any time, and likewise their employers are allowed to fire them

---

[34]531 U.S. 356 (2001).
[35]538 U.S. 721 (2003).
[36]Id. at 1981.
[37]124 S. Ct. 1978 (2004).
[38]Id. at 1988.

at any time so long as the reasons for the dismissal do not violate any federal or state statutes, such as the antidiscrimination statutes covered above.

Under traditional interpretations of the at-will doctrine, employers have been free to fire their employees for a good reason, a bad reason, or no reason at all so long as that reason does not conflict with specific statutes to the contrary. For example, if a paralegal reports late for work, the employer is free to fire that employee, even if this is the first instance of the paralegal's arriving late. Employees thus had no protection from arbitrary and even unreasonable employer actions.

However, in recent years some courts have begun to give at-will employees more protection. In some cases where employers have established employee handbooks that spell out various personnel procedures, the courts have generally required those employers to follow their own rules. In addition, a few courts have stated that employers owe employees an implied covenant to act in good faith. Finally, many courts have found a public policy exception that prevents an employer from firing an employee when the employer's actions are seen as harming not only the employee but also society as a whole. Examples include an employer firing an employee for asserting a legally guaranteed right, such as applying for worker's compensation; for doing what the law requires, such as reporting for jury duty; and for refusing to do an unlawful act, such as committing perjury.

At-will employment is another area of the law that is rapidly changing. You should expect to see the rights of employers to freely fire at-will employees come under increased judicial scrutiny in the coming years.

Legal Reasoning Exercises

3. Dianne Rawlinson sought employment with the Alabama Board of Corrections as a correctional officer. Alabama had established minimum height and weight requirements for all correctional officers of 120 pounds and 5 feet 2 inches. These combined requirements excluded 41.13 percent of the female population and less than 1 percent of the male population. Ms. Rawlinson was refused employment because she failed to meet the minimum 120-pound weight requirement. The prison argued that the requirements were necessary because they have a relationship to strength. Ms. Rawlinson filed a charge of discrimination with the EEOC. While her claim was pending, the Alabama Board of Corrections adopted another regulation prohibiting female correctional officers in any maximum-security institution housing men. In those prisons the inmate living area was divided into large dormitories with communal showers and toilets that are open to the dormitories and hallways. The main duty of correctional officers in such a setting is to maintain security. Because of inadequate staff and facilities, no attempt was made in the four maximum-security male prisons to segregate inmates according to their offenses or levels of dangerousness, leading to what some described as a "jungle atmosphere." Ms. Rawlinson then amended her charge to also challenge this regulation. Write an analysis discussing whether you think Ms. Rawlinson was successful on either claim.

4. Judith Smith was a unit director at a facility for the mentally retarded. Ms. Smith's six-month rating was "outstanding." She came in conflict, however, with the superintendent over an issue regarding the reorganization of the facility. The superintendent wanted to centralize all power within his office. Ms. Smith and the other unit directors thought it would be in the best interest of the patients and staff to also give them an opportunity to participate in policy decisions. The superintendent refused to consider that option. The unit directors then wrote a letter critical of the superintendent. Shortly thereafter Ms. Smith was fired. Ms. Smith sued, alleging that her dismissal was against public policy. Write an analysis explaining how you think the court resolved this issue.

5. A hospital administrator promoted a fifty-two-year-old "fishing buddy" because he wanted to help his friend. A better qualified, younger black woman sued, saying that her rights under Title VII had been violated. Write an analysis of the arguments each side would make.

SUMMARY

Businesses must be concerned with many areas of the law, including business formation, agency, commercial paper, secured transactions, and employment discrimination. One of the first decisions a business makes relates to its business form: whether it be a sole proprietorship, partnership, corporation, or limited liability company. When a company borrows money, commercial paper is involved. The business may also have to guarantee repayment by supplying collateral, thereby creating a secured transaction.

Any employer who hires employees must be aware of agency law. Generally, an agent is someone who has the power to act in the place of another. If an employee/agent acts within the scope of his or her responsibilities, the employer can be held liable for the agent's actions.

Finally, employment law is dominated by federal statutes, including Title VII of the Civil Rights Act of 1964, prohibiting discrimination based on race, color, religion, sex, or national origin; the Age Discrimination in Employment Act (ADEA), prohibiting discrimination based on age; and the Americans with Disabilities Act (ADA), prohibiting discrimination based on disability. If the case is not one of overt discrimination, the plaintiff can usually bring a discrimination claim under a theory of either disparate treatment or disparate impact.

REVIEW QUESTIONS

Pages 433 through 443

1. What are the four basic forms of business organizations, and what are the main advantages and disadvantages of each?
2. What is the most common reason for changing from a sole proprietorship to a partnership or a corporation?
3. Name the ways that a general partnership can be terminated.
4. What are the essential elements that the court looks for in trying to determine whether a partnership exists?

5. What types of information are contained in a business's articles of incorporation?
6. List the general responsibilities of a corporate board of directors.
7. Why might forming a limited liability company be preferable to forming either a partnership or a corporation?

Pages 443 through 448

8. Name the requirements for an instrument to be negotiable.
9. What must be satisfied for someone to be a holder in due course?
10. What are the two basic functions of commercial paper?
11. How does one become a holder of a negotiable instrument?
12. Buyer pays Seller $600 in cash for 1,000 calculators. Seller then takes the $600 and uses it to pay for a cruise.

                     Calculators   Cruise
Buyer ⟵⟶ Seller ⟵⟶ 3rd party
         $600 cash $600 cash

If the calculators prove to be defective and the seller is insolvent, who loses, the buyer or the third party who accepted $600 from the seller?

13. Buyer signs a contract with Seller promising to pay $600 for 1,000 calculators on or before 6/6/98. Seller then assigns the contract to the owner of a travel agency in payment for a cruise.

               Calculators   Cruise
Buyer ⟵⟶ Seller ⟵⟶ 3rd party

In contract Buyer   Assigns contract
promises to pay $600   to 3rd party
on or before 6/6/98

If the calculators prove to be defective and the seller is insolvent, who loses, the buyer or the third party who accepted the assigned contract rights from the buyer?

14. Buyer signs a note promising to pay Seller $600 for 1,000 calculators on or before 6/6/98. Seller then delivers the note to the owner of a travel agency in payment for a cruise.

               Calculators   Cruise
Buyer ⟵⟶ Seller ⟵⟶ 3rd party

Buyer signs a   Delivers note
note promising
to pay $600 on
or before 6/6/98

If the calculators prove to be defective and the seller is insolvent, who loses if the note is a negotiable instrument? Who loses if the note is not a negotiable instrument? Why?

15. In a secured transaction what is the difference between attachment and perfection?
16. Name the requirements that a creditor must meet in order to have an enforceable security interest against a debtor (to have the interest attach).
17. How may a creditor perfect a security interest?
18. What are the two main concerns of a creditor if a debtor defaults?
19. Define a *floating lien,* and give an example.

20. Define a *purchase money security interest*.
21. What is the main benefit of being a holder in due course rather than a mere holder?
22. List the following creditors in order of priority, starting with those that have the highest level of priority: general creditors, perfected security interest holders, unperfected security interest holders, buyers in the ordinary course of business, lien creditors, and perfected purchase money security interest holders.

Pages 448 through 453

23. What are the four basic duties that a principal owes an agent?
24. What are the basic duties that an agent owes a principal?
25. Name two of the factors a court will look to in trying to determine if an employer-employee or an employer-independent contractor relationship exists.
26. Give two examples of why it would matter whether a relationship is one of employer-employee or one of employer-independent contractor.
27. When will an employer be held responsible for an employee's act?

Pages 453 through 480

28. In a Title VII case alleging discriminatory treatment, how does the plaintiff prove the prima facie case? What must the defendant do in response? What must the plaintiff do to rebut the defendant's response?
29. After *Griggs* can employers use tests to evaluate people for hiring and promotion purposes? Why?
30. In a Title VII case alleging discriminatory impact, how does the plaintiff prove the prima facie case? What must the defendant do in response? What must the plaintiff do to rebut the defendant's response?
31. How does the presentation of an age discrimination case differ from that of one under Title VII?
32. Under the ADA who is a qualified individual?
33. What is employment at will?
34. Name two exceptions to the employment at-will doctrine.

Chapter 14

Family Law

Children are our most valuable national resource.
President Herbert Hoover

INTRODUCTION

This chapter presents an introduction to the basic legal principles of what is commonly called **family law.** The first section will cover the legal aspects of marriage and divorce. It will include a discussion of what marriage is, the requirements for a valid marriage, and how the marital bond can be dissolved. The second section will explore the legal aspects of the parent-child relationship, including problems related to adoption and paternity. It will also cover parental rights and responsibilities and problems related to the enforcement of those rights and responsibilities.

Family law
The area of the law that covers marriage, divorce, and parent-child relationships.

Family law is one of the most dynamic areas of the law. The very notion of what constitutes a family has become a politically and emotionally charged issue. No longer can we limit our definition of a family to a unit made up of a husband, a wife, and children. Today a family might mean an unmarried mother and her children; a single father and his children; a mother, her children, and a step-father; or a mother, her child, and her female companion. Legislatures and courts are struggling to update the law in this area as our societal views on these issues change.

Family law also illustrates the inability of the courts to solve basic social problems. The breakdown of the traditional family, advances in medical science, and changing societal mores are all pressing the courts with increasingly complex issues that can be only imperfectly resolved within the legal arena. Family law decisions go to the very heart of what we feel is important. For example, should the best interests of the child or the rights of a natural parent govern the outcome

483

of a custody dispute? Should the courts enforce a contract whereby a woman agrees to serve as a surrogate parent? Should couples who choose to live together without getting married receive the same legal benefits as do married couples? These are just a few of the issues that we will grapple with in this chapter on family law.

Because family law is dominated by state statutes and the court decisions interpreting those statutes, there is a great deal of variation from one state to the next. However, while state law is the principal source of family law, recently the federal government has enacted legislation in certain areas of family law, such as those laws assisting states with the collection of child support and trying to prevent divorced or separated parents from kidnapping their own children and taking them across state lines.

Most aspects of family law—governing who can be married, how marriages take place, the property rights of marital partners, how marriages are dissolved, how children are adopted—are part of the civil law. However, criminal statutes cover some aspects of family law, such as child and spousal abuse.

As is true of any law, the laws that state and federal legislatures develop governing family relationships must conform to the restrictions of state constitutions, as well as the U.S. Constitution. For example, laws regulating who may marry and those concerning parental rights have at times been challenged on the grounds that they violate either the due process or the equal protection guarantees of the Fourteenth Amendment.

A. MARRIAGE

Marriage has traditionally been defined as a legally recognized union in which a man and a woman form a family unit and take on special legal rights and obligations. In states such as Pennsylvania, where the marriage statute does not actually define marriage, the courts have relied on common-law cases and standard dictionary definitions in order to conclude that marriage is "the legal union of one man and one woman as husband and wife."[1] Later in this chapter we will examine recent court opinions, legislation, and proposed constitutional amendments related to same-sex marriages and civil unions.

Solemnized marriage
A marriage in which the couple has obtained the proper marriage license from a local government official and has then taken marriage vows before either a recognized member of the clergy or a judge and a designated number of witnesses.

In addition to being members of the opposite sex, state regulations have traditionally required persons applying for a marriage license to be over a minimum age (usually eighteen), not be too closely related by blood to their spouses, and be "of sound mind" (i.e., mentally capable of giving consent). Minors of a certain age are often allowed to marry if they have the consent of their parents or guardians. While a requirement for some sort of health certificate or blood test for sexually transmitted diseases was becoming less common, with the increased public concern over AIDS, the pendulum may be swinging back toward more premarital testing requirements.

The legal system recognizes two forms of marriage. In the first and most common type, known as a **solemnized marriage,** the parties first apply for and receive an official marriage license from a local governmental official. Usually after a brief waiting period, they then have their commitment solemnized by

---

[1] See DeSanto v. Barnsley, 476 A.2d 952, 954 (Pa. Super. Ct. 1984) (quoting Black's Law Dictionary).

saying their vows either through a religious ceremony presided over by a recognized member of the clergy or a civil ceremony presided over by a judge. The marriage becomes official once the license is signed and filed with the appropriate governmental office.

The second type of marriage is much less common and is referred to as **common-law marriage.** It is one in which the parties have mutually agreed to enter into a relationship in which they accept all the duties and responsibilities that correspond to those of a marital relationship and have openly cohabitated together but have never obtained a marriage license or had their marriage solemnized by someone who is legally authorized to do so. Most states no longer recognize the validity of such common-law marriages unless the couple established their common-law marital relationship in one of the few states that still formally recognize common-law marriages and then moved into the state.

Common-law marriage
A marriage that has not been solemnized but in which the couple has mutually agreed to enter into a relationship in which they accept all the duties and responsibilities that correspond to those of marriage.

DISCUSSION QUESTIONS

1. The following section from the Illinois Marriage and Dissolution of Marriage Act illustrates the types of prohibitions that appear in many state statutes:

750 Ill. Comp. Stat. 5/212
(a) The following marriages are prohibited:
  (1) a marriage entered into prior to the dissolution of an earlier marriage of one of the parties;
  (2) a marriage between an ancestor and a descendant or between a brother and a sister, whether the relationship is by the half or the whole blood or by adoption;
  (3) a marriage between an uncle and a niece or between an aunt and a nephew, whether the relationship is by the half or the whole blood;
  (4) a marriage between cousins of the first degree; however, a marriage between first cousins is not prohibited if:
    (i) both parties are 50 years of age or older; or
    (ii) either party, at the time of application for a marriage license, presents for filing with the county clerk of the county in which the marriage is to be solemnized, a certificate signed by a licensed physician stating the party to the proposed marriage is permanently and irreversibly sterile;
  (5) a marriage between 2 individuals of the same sex.

What do you think is the legislative purpose behind each of these provisions? With which ones do you agree or disagree?

2. List as many valid reasons as you can for why states require a marriage license.

3. As part of the legal requirements for getting married many states require a waiting period between the time the license is issued and the time the actual marriage can take place. Do you think states should impose these types of waiting periods? If yes, why and how long should they be? If no, why not?

4. As part of the legal requirements for getting a marriage license some states require a blood test for such things as sexually transmitted diseases or AIDS. Would you support such requirements? Why?

1. Consequences of Marriage

In the romantic haze that surrounds courtship and marriage a couple may not fully realize all the legal consequences that flow from their decisions to marry. Under our common-law traditions marriage was viewed as a contract in which a man and woman relinquished their former independence to merge themselves into a new joint enterprise. For example, married persons have a legal obligation to support each other not only during the marriage but often even after a divorce. Property purchased by one spouse may be seen as marital property, in which both have rights. Through a legal right known as a *forced share*, each of the married partners is given a statutory right to inherit from the other, even if the other spouse seeks to prevent it. One spouse may also be immune from being sued by the other spouse for torts committed against the first spouse. There are also many legal benefits to being married that are not given to nonmarital partners. For example, if a spouse is injured, the other spouse may recover loss of consortium damages. Marriage partners normally qualify for employer and governmental benefits not available to nonmarried couples. They also have the right to be taxed as a marital unit. Finally, both partners generally may not be forced to testify against each other.

As with other areas of family law the liabilities and benefits of marriage are constantly being altered. For example, many states now allow one spouse to sue the other for tortious injuries. Also, in what may start a trend, the Alaska Supreme Court recently held that a state statute prohibiting discrimination based on "marital status" means that employers must give cohabiting partners the same health insurance benefits offered to employee spouses.[2]

Of course, choosing to live together instead of getting married also has legal consequences. In the famous case of *Marvin v. Marvin*[3] a woman who had lived with the actor Lee Marvin for six years sought enforcement of an oral agreement regarding the division of their property when they separated. The court held that the agreement was a valid, enforceable contract so long as it was not based solely on immoral consideration.

2. Same-Sex Marriages and Civil Unions

Starting in the 1990s gay and lesbian groups began seeking legal recognition of and legal rights for "committed relationships" between partners of the same sex. Advocates for same-sex marriage usually focus on the need for equal treatment of all citizens, thereby allowing same-sex couples to enjoy all the traditional privileges accorded married persons. They emphasize practical concerns such as inheritance rights, child custody situations, and employee and government benefits for partners. At the symbolic level gays and lesbians stress the importance of receiving the legal recognition that their committed relationships are equal to those of opposite-sex partners.

Opponents of same-sex marriage rely on arguments that relate principally to religious values and to the traditional notion that the purpose of marriage is procreation. They argue that God has ordained that a marriage can only consist of one man and one woman and that official recognition of same-sex

---

[2]University of Alaska v. Tumeo, 933 P.2d 1147 (Alaska 1997).
[3]557 P.2d 106 (Cal. 1976).

partnerships threatens the stability of traditional families. Further they contend that homosexual couples could use contractual law to resolve problems involving issues such as inheritances, child custody, and visitation rights.

The first significant court challenge to the traditional view of marriage as being limited to opposite-sex partners occurred in Hawaii in 1990 when two women applied for a marriage license. When their application was denied, they went to the courts, seeking a judicial declaration that Hawaii's statute limiting marriage to men and women was unconstitutional sex discrimination. They based their argument on the Hawaii Constitution, which, unlike the U.S. Constitution, specifically prohibits discrimination based on sex. The Hawaii Supreme Court held that the statute was unconstitutional unless at trial the state could prove that the statute furthered compelling state interests.[4]

In 1996 the trial court ruled that the state had failed to present compelling reasons why the public interest in the well-being of children and families would be adversely affected by same-sex marriages. The court noted that expert witnesses for both sides testified that it was the nurturing ability of the parents, rather than their sexual orientation, that determined whether they would make good parents. The quality of parenting that a child received was more important than a biological connection or the gender of the parent. The trial court entered judgment in favor of the plaintiffs, ruling that the statute limiting marriage to opposite-sex couples was unconstitutional, as it violated the Hawaii state constitution's equal protection clause.

While the case was again on appeal to Hawaii's supreme court, the Hawaii legislature worked on a proposed amendment to the state constitution that would give the legislature the power to limit marriage to opposite-sex couples. After that amendment was ratified in November of 1999, the Hawaii Supreme Court ruled that in light of this change to the Hawaii constitution, the statute limiting marriage to opposite-sex couples was now constitutional and dismissed the plaintiff's case.[5]

Eleven days later, in an unrelated case, the Vermont Supreme Court held that the common benefits clause of the Vermont Constitution required the state to give same-sex couples the same benefits and protections that opposite-sex couples receive from marriage under Vermont law. The court noted that under the Vermont Constitution legislative classifications must "reasonably relate to a legitimate public purpose," and Vermont's marriage statute failed that test. It was not reasonably related to safeguarding the interests of children and was inconsistent with public policy against discrimination based on sexual orientation.

After deciding that same-sex couples were being denied their common rights and benefits, the court left it to the legislature to choose between allowing same-sex marriages or creating a parallel domestic partnership system that would provide legal benefits equivalent to those that married couples enjoyed.[6] The legislature reacted by passing a "civil union" statute. In April 2000 the Vermont governor signed the law, making Vermont the first state to grant same-sex couples the benefits of marriage, such as preferential tax status, the

---

[4]Baehr v. Lewin, 853 P.2d 44 (Haw. 1993).

[5]Baehr v. Miike, 92 Haw. 634, 994 P.2d 566 (table) (1999).

[6]Baker v. State, 744 A.2d 864, 867 (Vt. 1999).

ability to make medical decisions for each other should one of the parties become incapacitated, and the ability to inherit under state statutes.

While the Hawaii courts and legislature were debating the constitutionality of denying same-sex couples the right to marry, the U.S. Congress passed the Defense of Marriage Act. This federal law declared first, that states do not have to recognize same-sex marriages created in another state,[7] and second, that at the federal level "the word 'marriage' means only a legal union between one man and one woman as husband and wife, and the word 'spouse' refers only to a person of the opposite sex who is a husband or a wife."[8]

Three years after Vermont settled on the solution of civil unions, Massachusetts surprised the rest of the nation when its highest appellate court found that under the Massachusetts constitution, the state could not deny the benefits of marriage to two individuals of the same sex who wish to marry. When the state legislature then asked for the court's advisory opinion on a statute that would instead allow for same-sex civil unions, the court specifically rejected that approach, stating that "[t]he history of our nation has demonstrated that separate is seldom, if ever, equal."[9]

Opinions of the Justices to the Senate, Supreme Judicial Court of Massachusetts
440 Mass. 1201, 802 N.E.2d 565 (2004)

To the Honorable the Senate of the Commonwealth of Massachusetts:

The undersigned Justices of the Supreme Judicial Court respectfully submit their answers to the question set forth in an order adopted by the Senate. . . . The order indicates that there is pending before the General Court a bill, Senate No. 2175, entitled "An Act relative to civil unions." . . . [T]he bill . . . provides for the establishment of "civil unions" for same-sex "spouses," provided the individuals meet certain qualifications described in the bill.

The order indicates that grave doubt exists as to the constitutionality of the bill if enacted into law and requests the opinions of the Justices on the following "important question of law":

Does Senate No. 2175, which prohibits same-sex couples from entering into marriage but allows them to form civil unions with all 'benefits, protections, rights and responsibilities' of marriage, comply with the equal protection and due process requirements of the Constitution of the Commonwealth and *articles 1, 6, 7, 10, 12* and *16* of the Declaration of Rights?[2] . . .

1. Background of the proposed legislation. In *Goodridge v. Department of Pub. Health, 440 Mass. 309, 798 N.E.2d 941 (2003) (Goodridge)*, the court considered the constitutional question "whether the Commonwealth may use its formidable regulatory authority to bar same-sex couples from civil marriage. . . ." *Id. at 312-313*. The court concluded that it may not do so, determining

---

[2]*Article I of the Massachusetts Declaration of Rights* . . . provides: . . . "Equality under the law shall not be denied or abridged because of sex, race, color, creed or national origin."

---

[7]28 U.S.C.S. § 1738C (2004).

[8]1 U.S.C.S. § 7 (2004).

[9]Opinions of the Justices to the Senate, 802 N.E.2d 565 (Mass. 2004).

that the Commonwealth had failed to articulate a rational basis for denying civil marriage to same-sex couples. The court stated that the Massachusetts Constitution "affirms the dignity and equality of all individuals" and "forbids the creation of second-class citizens." *Id. at 312.* The court concluded that in "limiting the protections, benefits, and obligations of civil marriage to opposite-sex couples," the marriage licensing law "violates the basic premises of individual liberty and equality under law protected by the Massachusetts Constitution." *Id. at 342.*

In so concluding, the court enumerated some of the concrete tangible benefits that flow from civil marriage, including, but not limited to, rights in property, probate, tax, and evidence law that are conferred on married couples. *Id. at 322-325.* The court also noted that "intangible benefits flow from marriage," *id. at 322,* intangibles that are important components of marriage as a "civil right." *Id. at 325.* The court stated that "marriage also bestows enormous private and social advantages on those who choose to marry . . . [and] is at once a deeply personal commitment to another human being and a highly public celebration of the ideals of mutuality, companionship, intimacy, fidelity, and family." *Id. at 322.* "Because it fulfils yearnings for security, safe haven, and connection that express our common humanity, civil marriage is an esteemed institution, and the decision whether and whom to marry is among life's momentous acts of self-definition." *Id.* Therefore, without the right to choose to marry, same-sex couples are not only denied full protection of the laws, but are "excluded from the full range of human experience." *Id. at 326.*

The court stated that the denial of civil marital status "works a deep and scarring hardship on a very real segment of the community for no rational reason." *Id. at 341.* These omnipresent hardships include, but are by no means limited to, the absence of predictable rules of child support and property division, and even uncertainty concerning whether one will be allowed to visit one's sick child or one's partner in a hospital . . . All of these stem from the status of same-sex couples and their children as "outliers to the marriage laws." *Id. at 335 . . .*

In response to the plaintiffs' specific request for relief, the court preserved the marriage licensing statute, but refined the common-law definition of civil marriage to mean "the voluntary union of two persons as spouses, to the exclusion of all others." *Id. at 343. . . .*

2. Provisions of the bill . . . The proposed law states that "spouses" in a civil union shall be "joined in it with a legal status equivalent to marriage." Senate No. 2175, § 5. The bill expressly maintains that "marriage" is reserved exclusively for opposite-sex couples by providing that "persons eligible to form a civil union with each other under this chapter shall not be eligible to enter into a marriage with each other under *chapter 207.*" *Id.* Notwithstanding, the proposed law purports to make the institution of a "civil union" parallel to the institution of civil "marriage." For example, the bill provides that "spouses in a civil union shall have all the same benefits, protections, rights and responsibilities under law as are granted to spouses in a marriage." In addition, terms that denote spousal relationships, such as "husband," "wife," "family," and "next of kin," are to be interpreted to include spouses in a civil union "as those terms are used in any law." The bill goes on to enumerate a nonexclusive list of the legal benefits that will adhere to spouses in a civil union, including property rights, joint State income tax filing, evidentiary rights, rights to veteran benefits and group insurance, and the right to the issuance of a "civil union" license, identical to a marriage license under G. L. c. 207, "as if a civil union was a marriage."

3. Analysis. . . . We have now been asked to render an advisory opinion on Senate No. 2175, which creates a new legal status, "civil union," that is purportedly equal to "marriage," yet separate from it. The constitutional difficulty of the proposed civil union bill is evident in its stated purpose to "preserve the traditional, historic nature and meaning of the institution of civil marriage." . . . We recognize the efforts of the Senate to draft a bill in conformity with the *Goodridge* opinion. Yet the bill, as we read it, does nothing to "preserve" the civil marriage law, only its constitutional infirmity. This is not a matter of social policy but of constitutional interpretation. As the court concluded in

Goodridge, the traditional, historic nature and meaning of civil marriage in Massachusetts is as a wholly secular and dynamic legal institution, the governmental aim of which is to encourage stable adult relationships for the good of the individual and of the community, especially its children. The very nature and purpose of civil marriage, the court concluded, renders unconstitutional any attempt to ban all same-sex couples, as same-sex couples, from entering into civil marriage.

. . . Because the proposed law by its express terms forbids same-sex couples entry into civil marriage, it continues to relegate same-sex couples to a different status. The holding in *Goodridge*, by which we are bound, is that group classifications based on unsupportable distinctions, such as that embodied in the proposed bill, are invalid under the Massachusetts Constitution. The history of our nation has demonstrated that separate is seldom, if ever, equal.

In *Goodridge*, the court acknowledged, as we do here, that "many people hold deep-seated religious, moral, and ethical convictions that marriage should be limited to the union of one man and one woman, and that homosexual conduct is immoral. Many hold equally strong religious, moral, and ethical convictions that same-sex couples are entitled to be married, and that homosexual persons should be treated no differently than their heterosexual neighbors." *Id. at 312.* The court stated then, and we reaffirm, that the State may not interfere with these convictions, or with the decision of any religion to refuse to perform religious marriages of same-sex couples. These matters of belief and conviction are properly outside the reach of judicial review or government interference. But neither may the government, under the guise of protecting "traditional" values, even if they be the traditional values of the majority, enshrine in law an invidious discrimination that our Constitution, "as a charter of governance for every person properly within its reach," forbids.

The bill's absolute prohibition of the use of the word "marriage" by "spouses" who are the same sex is more than semantic. The dissimilitude between the terms "civil marriage" and "civil union" is not innocuous; it is a considered choice of language that reflects a demonstrable assigning of same-sex, largely homosexual, couples to second-class status. The denomination of this difference . . . as merely a "squabble over the name to be used" so clearly misses the point that further discussion appears to be useless. If . . . the proponents of the bill believe that no message is conveyed by eschewing the word "marriage" and replacing it with "civil union" for same-sex "spouses," we doubt that the attempt to circumvent the court's decision in *Goodridge* would be so purposeful. For no rational reason the marriage laws of the Commonwealth discriminate against a defined class; no amount of tinkering with language will eradicate that stain. The bill would have the effect of maintaining and fostering a stigma of exclusion that the Constitution prohibits. It would deny to same-sex "spouses" only a status that is specially recognized in society and has significant social and other advantages. The Massachusetts Constitution, as was explained in the *Goodridge* opinion, does not permit such invidious discrimination, no matter how well intentioned. . . .

We are well aware that current Federal law prohibits recognition by the Federal government of the validity of same-sex marriages legally entered into in any State, and that it permits other States to refuse to recognize the validity of such marriages. The argument . . . that . . . society will still accord a lesser status to those marriages is irrelevant. Courts define what is constitutionally permissible, and the Massachusetts Constitution does not permit this type of labeling. That there may remain personal residual prejudice against same-sex couples is a proposition all too familiar to other disadvantaged groups. That such prejudice exists is not a reason to insist on less than the Constitution requires. . . . Indeed, we would do a grave disservice to every Massachusetts resident, and to our constitutional duty to interpret the law, to conclude that the strong protection of individual rights guaranteed by the Massachusetts Constitution should not be available to their fullest extent in the Commonwealth because those rights may not be acknowledged elsewhere. We do not resolve, nor would we attempt to, the consequences of our holding in other jurisdictions. But, as the court held in *Goodridge*, under our

Federal system of dual sovereignty, and subject to the minimum requirements of the *Fourteenth Amendment to the United States Constitution*, "each State is free to address difficult issues of individual liberty in the manner its own Constitution demands." *Id. at 341.*

4. Conclusion. We are of the opinion that Senate No. 2175 violates the equal protection and due process requirements of the Constitution of the Commonwealth and the Massachusetts Declaration of Rights. . . .

The answer to the question is "No."

CASE DISCUSSION QUESTIONS

1. According to the court, what tangible and intangible benefits flow from marriage? What hardships are created by denying same-sex couples the right to marry?

2. How does the Massachusetts Constitution's equal protection provision differ from the U.S. Constitution's Fourteenth Amendment protections?

3. In what ways did the statutory proposal for civil unions differ from marriage?

4. Why do the justices who wrote this opinion think there is more involved than just "a squabble over the name to be used"?

5. Do you agree that the decision to allow same-sex marriages should be only a matter of constitutional interpretation and not a matter of social policy?

6. How does the court respond to the argument that Massachusetts's same-sex marriages may not be recognized in other states or by the federal government?

7. Unlike the Massachusetts Supreme Judicial Court, the U.S. Supreme Court does not give advisory opinions. What do you think are the advantages and disadvantages of this type of action?

Following the Massachusetts court's rejection of the civil union option, the governor and various legislators took the approach that had been used in Hawaii. They proposed that the state constitution be amended to reserve marriage for a union of a husband and a wife. Because of Massachusetts's constitutional amendment procedure, the earliest that such an amendment could be placed on the ballot is in November of 2006. Until then, same-sex couples will continue to marry in Massachusetts, but they will also find themselves in the uncomfortable position of not being "married" under the terms of the previously mentioned federal Defense of Marriage Act. This suggests that same-sex married couples from Massachusetts may not be able to file a joint federal income tax return, and same-sex "spouses" may not be able to collect some types of social security and other federal benefits.

These situations will most certainly lead to a challenge to the constitutionality of the Defense of Marriage Act. One of the problems with this legislation is that it appears to conflict with Article IV, Section 1, of the U.S. Constitution. This provision states: "Full Faith and Credit shall be given in each State to the public Acts, Records, and judicial Proceedings of every other State." In addition, such federal legislation treads heavily in the field of family law, an area that traditionally has been reserved for individual state regulation.

The Massachusetts situation also has led some to argue that the U.S. Constitution should be amended to define and protect marriage as a "union of man and woman as husband and wife." Others contend that this is an area of law that should be left for the states to resolve. Finally, federal legislation has been proposed that would strip federal courts of their jurisdiction to rule on challenges to state laws prohibiting same-sex marriages. Because such legislation would significantly erode the courts' power of judicial review, its constitutionality is questionable.

DISCUSSION QUESTIONS

5. Until 1967 Virginia had an antimiscegenation law, prohibiting interracial marriage. An interracial couple was convicted of violating the statute and given a one-year jail sentence. The sentence was suspended but only on the condition that the couple leave Virginia and not return for twenty-five years. The couple appealed their conviction. In *Loving v. Virginia*, 388 U.S. 1 (1967), the U.S. Supreme Court held that Virginia's statute violated the due process clause of the Fourteenth Amendment. Marriage is a fundamental right that states cannot regulate absent a compelling state interest. Should the Supreme Court be asked to decide whether statutes prohibiting same-sex marriages are unconstitutional, the *Loving* decision might form a basis for arguing by analogy that statutes banning same-sex marriages are unconstitutional. Do you think the two situations are analogous? If you were arguing for preserving the statutes prohibiting same-sex marriage, how would you distinguish the *Loving* decision?

6. Every state has laws against polygamy—that is, having more than one husband or wife at a time. What do you think are the arguments for and against allowing a man to have more than one wife at a time or a woman to have more than one husband at a time? Are such laws a form of religious discrimination against Mormons and Islamics, who have traditionally allowed men to have more than one wife?

7. M.T., a transsexual, was born a male but had the mental and emotional reactions of a female. She underwent surgery to become female. In a state that bans same-sex marriages do you think she would be able to obtain a marriage license to marry a man? Explain the basis for your answer.

3. Premarital Agreements

Prenuptial agreement
Also known as an **antenuptial agreement;** a document that prospective spouses sign prior to marriage regarding financial and other arrangements should the marriage end.

Premarital agreements, also known as **prenuptial** or **antenuptial agreements,** are becoming increasingly popular. Their basic purpose is to set forth the financial arrangements should one of the parties die or the marriage end in divorce. Premarital agreements are becoming especially common in situations involving second marriages in which the spouses have children from a previous marriage. Usually, the focus of such agreements is financial considerations. For example, a premarital agreement would be used when a couple in their sixties marries and wishes to ensure that the property they bring with them to the marriage will be passed on to their children rather than to the surviving spouse. Such an agreement in this type of situation can put to rest the children's concerns that the parent's new spouse will cut them out of their inheritance.

Traditionally, the courts saw such agreements as encouraging divorce, and therefore they found such contracts to be void as against public policy. Today,

> When preparing a prenuptial agreement, both parties must be represented individually by an attorney. Not to do so invites ethical charges of conflict of interest. In addition, if it is later discovered that through a lack of zealous representation one party had not been fully informed of all the marital assets and liabilities, the court will probably refuse to enforce the agreement.

however, most courts will enforce these agreements if the standard contract requirements were met. First, in most states to satisfy the statute of frauds, premarital agreements must be in writing. Second, there must be an offer, an acceptance, and consideration. Usually, the agreement to marry satisfies the consideration requirement.

The extent to which a court will enforce premarital agreements regarding matters other than financial arrangements depends on the nature of the specific provision. For example, although courts will generally enforce reasonable provisions relating to the distribution of property, they will not enforce provisions relating to third parties, such as those dealing with child custody.

Normal contract defenses are also available. For example, if the agreement was not based on full disclosure of all financial assets or was the result of undue influence, the courts might see it as against public policy and either modify its provisions or refuse to enforce it. Also, as noted above, the courts view some provisions, especially those trying to predetermine the rights of children, as against public policy and hence unenforceable. An example would be a provision that states that the custodial spouse will not seek child support if the couple divorces.

DISCUSSION QUESTIONS

8. The prenuptial agreement between a Catholic woman and a Jewish man stated that any children born of the marriage would be raised in the Jewish faith. After the couple divorced, the wife was given custody of the children. The father went to court, seeking to have the prenuptial agreement enforced. How do you think the court responded?

9. A prenuptial agreement stated that the wife could not share in her husband's property. During the early years of their marriage the couple kept their businesses and bank accounts separate. Eventually, however, the wife left her job to work full-time for no pay in the pro shop at her husband's golf course. When the golf course ran into financial troubles, she cashed in her retirement plan and took out a loan to keep the business going. Now the couple has divorced, and the wife wants "her share" of the husband's golf course. What do you think the court decided?

4. Consequences of Broken Engagements

Under common law the victim of a broken engagement could sue for an array of tort and contractual damages for mental and emotional suffering, damage to

Anti-heart-balm statute
A law that prohibits lawsuits for such things as breach of a promise of marriage, alienation of affection, and seduction of a person over the legal age of consent.

reputation, humiliation, embarrassment, and even "loss of worldly advantage." However, most states have adopted "**anti-heart-balm**" statutes, which prohibit lawsuits for such things as breach of a promise of marriage, alienation of affection, and seduction of a person over the legal age of consent.

Nevertheless, issues ranging from the return of the engagement ring to disposition of joint property may still find their way to the courts when wedding plans fall through. Such conflicts are illustrated in the following case. Note that this suit is not barred by the New Jersey anti-heart-balm statute because it is a suit to recover conditional gifts, not an action for damages for breach of a contract to marry.

Aronow v. Silver
223 N.J. Super. 344, 538 A.2d 851 (1987)

Option by Judge HAINES.

Philip Aronow, plaintiff, and Elizabeth Silver, defendant, were engaged to be married. The engagement was a stormy one. Problems arose involving the parties themselves and their relatives. On three occasions, Elizabeth cancelled the engagement and returned the engagement ring, only to recant. Finally, with the marriage ceremony a few days away, the engagement was broken irretrievably. Each party, in this resulting litigation, faults the other. Each claims the engagement ring, certain shares of stock and a jointly-owned condominium. . . .

A. The Law Concerning Engagement Rings

The majority rule in this country concerning the disposition of engagement rings is a fault rule: the party who unjustifiably breaks the engagement loses the ring. The minority rule rejects fault. . . . New Jersey courts have considered the question in only four published opinions, with split results. This court, not bound by any of those opinions, joins the minority.

Our earliest case is *Sloin v. Lavine*, 11 N.J. Misc. 899 (Sup. Ct. 1933), in which the court, citing the law of foreign jurisdictions, said:

So we have on the merits the simple case of an engagement ring and engagement broken and ring not returned. The decisions are not numerous, but we follow those holding what we deem the correct rule, viz., that such a gift is impliedly conditional, and must be returned, particularly when the

engagement is broken by the donee, as the court was entitled to find in this case.

Sloin's implication that the person who breaks the engagement loses the ring was rejected by Judge (later Justice) Sullivan in *Albanese v. Indelicato*, 25 N.J. Misc. 144 (D. Ct. 1947). The decision involved ownership of an engagement ring and a dinner ring. The court said:

As far as the engagement ring is concerned, the defendant had no right to keep it. An engagement ring is a symbol or pledge of the coming marriage and signifies that the one who wears it is engaged to marry the man who gave it to her. If the engagement is broken off the ring should be returned since it is a conditional gift. True, no express condition was imposed but the law implies a condition because of the symbolic significance of the ring. It does not matter who broke the engagement. A person may have the best reasons in the world for so doing. The important thing is that the gift was conditional and the condition was not fulfilled.

The giving of the dinner ring is an entirely different proposition. True, it was given after the parties became engaged. No doubt plaintiff would not have given the ring to defendant if they had not been engaged. The dinner ring though, has no symbolic meaning and is only a token of the love and affection which plaintiff bore for the defendant. Many gifts are made for reasons that sour with the passage of time. Under the law though, there is no consideration required for a gift and it is absolute once made unless a condition is imposed. There was no express condition here and the law will not imply one as in the case of the engagement ring since the dinner ring has no symbolic meaning attached to it. Defendant was under no obligation to return the dinner ring. . . .

The fault rule is sexist and archaic, a too-long enduring reminder of the times when even the law discriminated against women. The history is traced in 24 A.L.R.2d at 582–586. In ancient Rome the rule was fault. When the woman broke the engagement, however, she was required not only to return the ring, but also its value, as a penalty. No penalty attached when the breach was the man's. In England, women were oppressed by the rigidly stratified social order of the day. They worked as servants or, if not of the servant class, were dependent on their relatives. The fact that men were in short supply, marriage above one's station rare and travel difficult abbreviated betrothal prospects for women. Marriages were arranged. Women's lifetime choices were limited to a marriage or a nunnery. Spinsterhood was a centuries-long personal tragedy. Men, because it was a man's world, were much more likely than women to break engagements. When one did, he left behind a woman of tainted reputation and ruined prospects. The law, in a de minimis gesture, gave her the engagement ring, as a consolation prize. When the man was jilted, a seldom thing, justice required the ring's return to him. Thus, the rule of life was the rule of law—both saw women as inferiors.

To accept the ancient rule of law is to ignore our constitutional insistence upon the equality of women, to further the unfortunate reality that society still discriminates. That reality is one which courts must not promote. Our obligation is to enforce the law, which bars discrimination. By doing so we move reality in the right direction.

The majority rule, even without its constitutional infirmity, will not withstand elementary scrutiny. Its foundation is fault, and fault, in an engagement setting, cannot be ascertained.

What fact justifies the breaking of an engagement? The absence of a sense of humor? Differing musical tastes? Differing political views? The painfully learned fact is that marriages are made on earth, not in heaven. They must be approached with intelligent care and should not happen without a decent assurance of success. When either party lacks that assurance, for whatever reason, the engagement should be broken. No justification is needed. Either party may act. Fault, impossible to fix, does not count. . . .

Philip's gift of a ring to Elizabeth was conditioned upon marriage. When the promise of marriage was not kept, regardless of fault, the condition was not fulfilled and the ring must be returned to him. . . .

C. The Stock Purchases

During their engagement, the parties, in anticipation of their marriage, purchased stock with Philip's money upon the understanding that the stock certificate was to be placed in joint names. The broker, however, had the certificate issued in Elizabeth's name only. She sold it without Philip's knowledge after the engagement was broken and kept the proceeds. Other stock previously owned by Elizabeth was placed in joint names. That stock has not been sold. Quite clearly, these stock arrangements were conditioned upon marriage. When the engagement was broken, the stocks should have been returned to the parties who donated them. Philip's stock should not have been sold and Elizabeth must pay the proceeds of the sale to him. Philip is directed to transfer his interest in the jointly-held stock to Elizabeth.

CASE DISCUSSION QUESTIONS

1. The *Silver* court refused to apply a "fault standard." Do you think it should matter who was at fault for breaking off the engagement? Why?

2. In the cited case of *Albanese v. Indelicato* why did the court treat the diamond ring and the engagement ring differently? The *Silver* court did not apply

different standards to the engagement ring and stock. Can you reconcile these seemingly different approaches? Do you think one approach reaches a fairer result?

3. Elizabeth's parents also sued, seeking recovery of various wedding expenses paid by them. Do you think they should be able to recover? Why?

5. Termination of the Marital Relationship

Once the state has recognized a couple as being married, they will continue to be treated as married persons until one of the spouses dies or a court grants either an **annulment** or a **divorce**. The latter is sometimes referred to as **dissolution**. The major difference between an annulment and a divorce is that an annulment can be granted only for causes that existed at the time the marriage took place, whereas divorces are based on causes that occurred before or during the marriage.

a. Annulment

An annulment proceeding has the effect of rescinding the marriage and returning the parties to the status they had before the marriage took place. Therefore, if an annulment is granted, it is, from the legal perspective, as if the marriage had never taken place. Because the marriage never existed, normally there are no continuing matrimonial obligations, such as a duty to pay support or attorney's fees. On the other hand, a divorce or dissolution ends but does not erase the existence of the marital relationship. Although the parties are no longer married to each other, it does not necessarily cancel legal obligations that arose out of the marriage. One exception to this difference between annulment and marriage relates to children born during the marriage. Under the common law, children born during a marriage later annulled were considered illegitimate. Many state statutes have changed this, at least as to **voidable marriages.** However, if it was a **void marriage,** some states still consider the children to be illegitimate.

Recall the contract law distinction between void and voidable. A void contract is a legal nullity, even without court intervention. A voidable contract remains valid unless one of the parties takes steps to void it through legal proceedings. Similarly, marriages are considered void in certain situations, as when they involve incest or bigamy. A voidable marriage, on the other hand, is one where the marriage remains valid until a court has determined that it should be voided.

The grounds for voiding a marriage that are typically listed in state statutes include such things as the following:

1. One of the parties to the marriage lacked capacity to consent to the marriage because of being either mentally incapacitated or under the influence of alcohol, drugs, or other incapacitating substances.
2. One of the parties lacks the physical capacity to consummate the marriage, and the other party did not know of the incapacity.
3. One of the parties was under the prescribed age for marriage and did not have a parent's or guardian's consent.

Annulment
A legal (or religious) judgment that a valid marriage never existed.

Divorce
Also called **dissolution;** a legal judgment that dissolves a marriage.

Voidable marriage
A marriage that was valid when it was entered into and that remains valid until either party obtains a court order dissolving it.

Void marriage
A marriage that is invalid from its inception and that does not require court action for the parties to be free of any marital obligations.

4. The parties are too closely related to each other—for example, siblings or first cousins.
5. One of the parties was induced to enter into the marriage by force, duress, or fraud.

Most of the criteria listed in these statutes are fairly straightforward and relatively objective, but the language in the last provision relating to **fraud** often leads to difficult and controversial cases. For example, courts in some states have ruled that it is appropriate to annul a marriage on the grounds that the woman falsely represented herself as being pregnant or was pregnant but lied about who the father was. On the other hand, it has also been ruled that false representations as to being a virgin at the time of marriage do not constitute a basis for granting an annulment. Another interesting line of cases involves fraudulent representations regarding one's wealth and ability to support and maintain a certain lifestyle after the marriage. In such situations the courts have generally adopted a "buyer beware" attitude and have not recognized such representations as being the basis for granting an annulment. An example of a situation that would be the basis for an annulment based on fraud would be one where a spouse made promises of love, devotion, and living together in a normal marital relationship and then fled with the other spouse's bank account a few days after the wedding.

Keep in mind that there is a difference between legal annulments and religious ones. The two are completely separate processes, and clients must take additional steps to attain a religious annulment.

Fraud
A false representation of facts or intentional perversion of the truth to induce someone to take some action or give up something of value.

DISCUSSION QUESTIONS

10. Most statutes require the parties to be "mentally competent" in order to marry, but what does that mean? Should someone who has a mental or genetic disability, such as Down's syndrome, be allowed to marry? Should a court annul a marriage if the parties later allege they were so intoxicated at the time of the ceremony that they did not realize the significance of their actions?

11. Before the honeymoon was even over, Ashley Jones realized that her new husband had a major drinking problem. When he refused to seek help for his drinking problem or look for a job, she sought to have the marriage annulled. If you were the judge, would you grant her an annulment? Why?

b. Divorce/Dissolution

Traditionally, marriage meant that the norm was for spouses to be together for life, and divorce was seen as the exception. Therefore, the spouse wishing a divorce had to convince the court that there were extraordinary reasons justifying that request. Those reasons, called grounds, included such behavior as adultery and desertion. Today, every state also allows a divorce based on "**no fault.**" Rather than having to assess blame for the breakup, either party can end the marriage, with or without the consent of the partner. Either spouse can simply file a petition for dissolution. The parties merely must allege that the marriage has

No-fault divorce
A form of divorce that allows a couple to end their marital relationship without having to assess blame for the breakup.

NETNOTE

You can find various uniform laws governing the family, such as the Uniform Child Custody Jurisdiction Act, the Uniform Interstate Family Support Act, the Uniform Premarital Agreement Act, and the Uniform Marriage and Divorce Act at *www.law.cornell.edu/uniform/vol9.html.*

suffered an irretrievable breakdown, with no hope for reconciliation. In some states the parties must also allege that they are living separate and apart.

The "costs" of divorce are many. First, when couples seek a divorce, they relinquish to the state the power to make major life decisions for them. State courts can oversee a divorced family's financial arrangements in ways not permitted for intact families. For example, normally a court will not interfere with an intact family's decision as to whether to send a child to college. However, during divorce proceedings child support orders can include a requirement that the parents pay for their child's college education. In *LeClair v. LeClair*[10] the court stated that it could enforce such an order because the state had an interest in promoting higher education and in protecting children of divorce.

In addition, divorce can have severe economic consequences. This is especially true for women. The money that may have been insufficient to maintain one household is now being asked to maintain two homes. Studies have consistently shown that in the first year after divorce the standard of living for men increases anywhere from 17 to 43 percent, while that for women and children decreases by 29 to 73 percent.[11] Finally, for many divorcing parents the greatest cost is the loss of daily contact with their children.

(1) Divorce procedures

Whichever method is used, there are basic divorce procedures that must be followed. First, the grounds, even under no-fault, must exist to end the marriage. Then the party wishing a divorce must file a petition or complaint, requesting the divorce and including the reasons why one should be granted. Most states require the petition to include the following information:

1. the age, occupation, and residence of each party;
2. the length of time each party has resided in the state;
3. the date of the marriage and the place at which it was registered;
4. the names, ages, and addresses of all living children of the marriage and whether the wife is pregnant;

---

[10]624 A.2d 1350 (N.H. 1993).

[11]Lenore Weitzman, The Divorce Revolution: The Unexpected Social and Economic Consequences for Women and Children in America xii (1995); Joseph I. Lieberman, Child Support in America: Practical Advice for Negotiating and Collecting a Fair Settlement 11 (1988), cited in J. Shoshanna Ehrlic, Family Law for Paralegals 181 (1997).

Before an attorney can agree to represent a client, the attorney must take care to check for potential conflicts of interest. In a divorce case, for example, another attorney in the firm could not be simultaneously representing the client's spouse. In addition, conflicts could arise if either the attorney or other attorneys in the office previously represented the client's spouse in various business transactions. The general rule on so-called successive representation is that an attorney will be disqualified when the interests of the former and current clients are truly adverse and the attorney had access to confidential information that would be relevant to the current client's case.

5. any arrangements as to support, custody, and visitation of the children and maintenance of a spouse; and
6. the relief sought.

If the petitioner wants to proceed on a fault basis, then there will also be an identification of the grounds. Exhibit 14-1 on pp. 500-501 provides an example of a no-fault petition.

As you can see from the sample petition, usually other documents, such as affidavits, must be filed along with the petition. Paralegals are often involved in the preparation and filing of the petition and these other documents. They interview the client to gather relevant personal and financial information (locations and balances of bank accounts, investments, insurance policies, etc.) and then incorporate that information into the appropriate court documents that need to be filed.

Once the petition is filed with the court, the opposing party must be notified. This can be accomplished as in other civil suits through service of process. If the other spouse cannot be found, then an alternative method of notification must be used, such as publication in a newspaper. When both parties are agreeable to the divorce, the defendant may willingly appear in court without the need for formal service of process.

The other party can indicate he or she does not want to contest the divorce or can countersue. Then both sides may engage in discovery.

Many states incorporate alternative dispute resolution mechanisms into the decisions regarding distribution of property and child custody and support. Mediation is becoming increasingly common, on either a voluntary or a court-ordered basis, especially if minor children are involved. The philosophy behind mediation is that it can create a win-win atmosphere as opposed to the courtroom mentality of winner take all. In addition, it allows the participants to have a sense of ownership in the decision, as they craft it themselves rather than allowing a judge to impose it on them.

After the filing of the petition, the court will hold a hearing to deal with such matters as temporary child custody; child and spousal support; who remains in the house and who leaves; liability for home mortgages, car payments, and credit card bills; and orders protecting existing joint assets. In cases where there have been allegations of domestic abuse, there may also be a hearing on the issuance of a **temporary restraining order (TRO),** sometimes also called a **protection order,** to keep one spouse away from the other spouse, the children,

Temporary restraining order (TRO)
A court order of limited duration designed to maintain the status quo pending further court action at a later date.

Protection order
A court order issued in domestic violence and abuse cases to keep one spouse away from the other, the children, or the home.

[FACE SIDE OF FORM]

Commonwealth of Massachusetts
The Trial Court
Probate and Family Court Department

_____ Division   Docket No. _____

Joint Petition For Divorce Under M.G.L. Ch. 208, Sec. 1A

_____ and _____
         Petitioner   Petitioner
of _____   of _____
      (Street and No.)   (Street and No.)

_____   _____
(City or Town) (State) (Zip)   (City or Town) (State) (Zip)

1. Now come the Husband and Wife in a joint petition for divorce pursuant to Massachusetts General Laws, Chapter 208, Sec. 1A.

2. The parties were lawfully married at _____ on _____ and last lived together at _____ on _____ 19___.

3. The minor child _____ of this marriage and date(s) of birth is/are:

   _____   _____

   _____   _____

4. The parties certify that no previous action for divorce, annulment, affirmation of marriage, separate support, desertion, living apart for justifiable cause, or custody of child _____ has been brought by either party against the other except _____.

5. On or about _____, 19___, an irretrievable breakdown of the marriage under M.G.L. Ch. 208, Sec. 1A occurred and continues to exist.

6. Wherefore, the parties pray that the Court:
   [ ] grant a divorce on the ground of irretrievable breakdown
   [ ] approve the separation agreement executed by the parties
   [ ] incorporate and merge said agreement executed by the parties
   [ ] incorporate but not merge said agreement, which shall survive and remain as an independent contract
   [ ] allow Wife to resume her former name _____
   [ ] _____

Date _____

_____   _____
SIGNATURE OF WIFE OR ATTORNEY   SIGNATURE OF HUSBAND OR ATTORNEY

_____   _____
(Print address if not pro se)   (Print address if not pro se)

_____   _____
Tel. No. (   ) _____   Tel. No. (   ) _____
B.B.O. # _____   B.B.O. # _____

CJ-D 101A (6/90)

Exhibit 14-1 Joint Petition for Divorce   *(continues)*

[BACK SIDE OF FORM]

Joint Petition For Divorce Under M.G.L. Ch. 208, Sec. 1A

For Wife:

_____

Address _____

_____

Tel. No. (   ) _____

For Husband:

_____

Address _____

_____

Tel. No. (   ) _____

Docket No. _____

Filed _____ 19__

Agreement Approved _____ 19__

Judgment _____ 19__

Documents filed:

Marriage Certificate	[ ]
Wife's Financial Statement	[ ]
Husband's Financial Statement	[ ]
Separation Agreement	[ ]
Affidavit of Irretrievable Breakdown	[ ]
Affidavit Disclosing Care or Custody Proceedings	[ ]
Child Support Guidelines Worksheet	[ ]

Exhibit 14-1   Joint Petition for Divorce *(concluded)*

and the home. Although these are labeled temporary orders, do not be fooled. If the proceedings drag on for any length of time, when it is finally time to frame the permanent orders it may prove very difficult to change the "temporary" arrangements.

In an effort to help parents appreciate the needs of their children during the divorce process, some states are starting to mandate parent education programs for all divorcing parents. A certificate of attendance must be submitted to the court prior to a hearing on the merits of the case.

At any point in this process a **settlement agreement** can be reached and submitted to the court. The most important aspect of divorce is the separation agreement, as it sets out the rights and obligations of the parties, including the custody and support arrangements for the children, the distribution of **marital property**, and **alimony (maintenance)**. In most cases these negotiations eventually lead to agreements that are then formalized in the final court decree. In those instances in which the parties cannot reach agreement, a trial is held at which witnesses testify to such things as the spouses' fitness as parents, how and when various financial assets were obtained, the fair market value of various assets, and the nature of the children's or spouses' future financial needs. This is often a poor solution, as all major decisions as to custody, alimony, property division, and child support will be taken away from the parties and left for the judge to decide. The judge then renders a decision on the basis of this evidence and issues the final divorce decree and related orders. The court retains jurisdiction in matters of child and spousal support, and at a later date the parties may come back to seek a modification of the original order based on such things as a change in marital status, a significant change in income, or a child's unanticipated needs.

Settlement agreement
A document that contains the arrangements agreed on by the parties to a dispute.

Marital property
Property that is subject to court distribution upon termination of the marriage.

Alimony
Also known as **maintenance** or **support**; financial support and other forms of assistance required to supply the "necessities" of life.

(2) Property settlements

When a marriage ends, decisions need to be made regarding how jointly owned property will be divided. Such decisions relate not only to major assets, such as a home, but also to such specifics as who gets the living room sofa or the good china. In fact, some of the most hotly contested property fights relate to who gets "custody" of the family pet. Because only jointly owned property is subject to distribution, the first task is to determine which property is joint and which is separate.

Traditionally, there were three methods the courts used to determine what qualifies as marital property: by who holds title, by community property law, or through equitable distribution. Only the last two methods are still in use. Under a **community property** statute everything acquired during the marriage, with the exception of gifts or inheritances, is owned 50/50. Property acquired prior to the marriage is separate property, but it can lose its status if it is commingled. For example, if money acquired before the marriage is placed in a joint bank account, it loses its separate identity. At the time of divorce each spouse retains his or her share of separate property, but all property classified as community property is divided 50/50.

In non-community property states courts follow the **doctrine of equitable distribution** and award a "marital interest" in any property that was acquired during the marriage through the efforts of both spouses. This acknowledges the contributions of both spouses, whether that contribution be financial or through a spouse's work in the home, regardless of whose name is on the legal title. Typically a statute will provide that the judge must look at several factors, including the length of the marriage, the age and health of the spouses, and their ability to make a living. While this process may also result in a 50/50 division, under the theory of equitable distribution such an equal split is not mandated.

Where the specific piece of property, such as a house, cannot be literally split between the parties, the court can either require that it be sold with a distribution of the profits or that a portion of its assessed value be given to the other spouse, either in cash or through some other item of equal value.

Community property states
States that classify all property acquired by either the husband or the wife during the marriage, with the exception of gifts or inheritance, as marital property to be equally distributed between the spouses at the time of the divorce.

Doctrine of equitable distribution
A system for distributing property acquired during a marriage on the basis of such factors as the contributions of the spouses, the length of the marriage, the age and health of the spouses, and their ability to make a living.

Legal Reasoning Exercise

1. Brian LeClair lives in Tucson, Arizona. In early 1994 he bought a small home for $50,000, $45,000 of which he financed through a mortgage. Later that year, Brian met Monica, and they married within the week. Brian was later to regret his quick decision.

Shortly after they were married, Brian discovered that Monica liked to shop. In fact, she entered the marriage with approximately $5,000 in credit card bills. During their marriage this pattern persisted, with Monica on average charging $500 per month for clothes and jewelry for herself. Brian and Monica each deposited their earnings in a joint checking account, and each paid half of the monthly mortgage payments.

When Brian's father died in 1995, he left Brian 100 shares of stock, valued at $10 per share. Brian, knowing little about investments, asked Monica to handle his stock for him. She did so, and through careful buying and selling Brian now owns 150 shares of stock, valued at $15 a share. Brian's father also left Brian his mother's wedding ring, which as part of his father's estate was valued at $1,000. A jeweler recently appraised it at $1,500. Finally, his father left him $5,000, which he deposited into his and Monica's joint banking account.

In 1996 Monica stated that she was tired of living in Brian's tiny house and wanted to buy some land so that they could build a new, larger home. Brian was against the purchase both because of the cost and because of the rumors the land was about to be rezoned industrial. Monica went ahead anyway and took out a $20,000 loan from Commercial Savings to purchase the land. Brian did not sign the loan papers. The deed, however, lists them as joint owners. When the rumors proved to be true, the value of the land plummeted to $2,000.

Last week Monica informed Brian that she was tired of being married and that she needed some "space." When Brian got home from work the next day, he found that she was gone. Later that day when he opened the mail, he found a letter from Commercial Savings notifying him that the remaining amount of the loan ($18,000) was due immediately, as Monica had not made any payments in the last year. Also, there was a letter from the credit card company showing Monica's total balance of $12,000. As far as Brian could tell, at least $4,000 was money she had charged before they were married.

Brian has come to your firm because he is thinking of initiating divorce proceedings against Monica. He realizes, however, that Arizona is a community property state and is concerned, first, that he may be liable for what he considers to be Monica's debts and, second, that she may claim some of his property should be categorized as community property, thereby allowing her to take one-half. Your boss wants you to research (1) whether Brian is liable for either the Commercial Savings loan or Monica's credit card bills, (2) which assets would qualify as community assets and hence be available to satisfy a community debt if the court were to find him liable, and (3) which remaining assets Monica might be able to claim belong one-half to her as her share of community property.

The contested assets include the stock valued at $2,250, the house (with a mortgage of $40,000 and a resale value of $60,000), the diamond ring valued at $1,500, the land worth $2,000, and $10,000 in their joint checking account. As to the latter, Brian claims that $5,000 is from his inheritance, $4,000 came from money he earned, and the remaining $1,000 came from Monica's earnings.

In doing your research, you found the following Arizona statutes:

Chapter 25-211 All property acquired by either husband or wife during the marriage, except that which is aquired by gift, devise or descent, is the community property of the husband and wife.

Chapter 25-213 All property . . . of each spouse, owned by such spouse before marriage . . . is the separate property of such spouse.

> *Chapter 25-214* C. Either spouse separately may acquire, manage, control or dispose of community property, or bind the community. . . .
>
> *Chapter 25-215* A. The separate property of a spouse shall not be liable for the separate debts or obligations of the other spouse. . . .
>
> *Chapter 25-215* D. [E]ither spouse may contract debts and otherwise act for the benefit of the community. In an action on such a debt or obligation the spouse shall be sued jointly and the debt or obligation shall be satisfied: first, from the comunity property, and second, from the separate property of the spouse contracting the debt or obligation.

In addition to the types of property that you would normally view as being available for distribution, the courts have recently been faced with the necessity of deciding whether such items as frozen embryos, personal injury awards, pension plans, and professional degrees qualify as marital property. One of the first cases discussing frozen embryos was *Davis v. Davis.*[12] Mrs. Davis was unable to carry a pregnancy to term. She and her husband turned to a new medical technique, in vitro fertilization, for help. The doctors removed eggs from Mrs. Davis and fertilized them in vitro. Two were unsuccessfully implanted, and seven were frozen for future use. When the Davises decided to divorce, the embryos' fate was called in question. Mrs. Davis wanted to donate the frozen embryos to a childless couple. The husband did not want to become a parent. The court held that the father's right not to procreate won out over the wife's desire to donate the embryos.

Once the spouse has a vested interest in either a personal injury award or a pension plan, most states will view it as a divisible marital asset. However, the courts have come to varying conclusions as to how they should classify professional degrees. At one end of the spectrum, some courts do not factor it into a property or alimony agreement. Others view it as valuable marital property that must be valued and divided. Somewhere in between, other courts do not view it as property but do award the party without the degree reimbursement for the time and money expended in assisting the other spouse in attaining the degree. Finally, some courts simply take it into account when calculating possible future earning power and alimony awards. The following case illustrates the difficulty in determining whether a professional degree should qualify as a marital asset.

Woodworth v. Woodworth
126 Mich. App. 258, 337 N.W.2d 332 (1983)

BURNS, J.

The parties were married on June 27, 1970, after plaintiff had graduated from Central Michigan University with a bachelor's degree in secondary education and defendant had graduated from Lansing Community College with an

---

[12]842 S.W.2d 588 (Tenn. 1992).

associate degree. They then moved to Jonesville, where plaintiff worked as a teacher and coach for the high school and defendant worked as a nursery school teacher in Hillsdale. In the fall of 1973, they sold their house, quit their jobs, and moved to Detroit, where plaintiff attended Wayne State Law School. Three years later, they moved to Lansing where plaintiff took and passed the bar exam and accepted a job as a research attorney with the Court of Appeals. Plaintiff is now a partner in a Lansing law firm.

The basic issue in this case is whether or not plaintiff's law degree is marital property subject to distribution. The trial court held that it was, valued it at $20,000, and awarded this amount to defendant in payments of $2,000 over ten years. Plaintiff contends that his law degree is not such a marital asset. We disagree.

The facts reveal that plaintiff's law degree was the end product of a concerted family effort. Both parties planned their family life around the effort to attain plaintiff's degree. Toward this end, the family divided the daily tasks encountered in living. While the law degree did not pre-empt all other facets of their lives, it did become the main focus and goal of their activities. Plaintiff left his job in Jonesville and the family relocated to Detroit so that plaintiff could attend law school. In Detroit, defendant sought and obtained full-time employment to support the family.

We conclude, therefore, that plaintiff's law degree was the result of mutual sacrifice and effort by both plaintiff and defendant. While plaintiff studied and attended classes, defendant carried her share of the burden as well as sharing vicariously in the stress of the experience known as the "paper chase."

We believe that fairness dictates that the spouse who did not earn an advanced degree be compensated whenever the advanced degree is the product of such concerted family investment. The degree holder has expended great effort to obtain the degree not only for himself or herself, but also to benefit the family as a whole. The other spouse has shared in this effort and contributed in other ways as well, not merely as a gift to the student spouse nor merely to share individually in the benefits but to help the marital unit as a whole. . . .

[W]e also agree that divorce courts cannot recompense expectations. However, we are not talking about an expectation here. Defendant is not asking us to compensate for a failed expectation that her husband would become a wealthy lawyer and subsequently support her for the rest of her life. Instead, she is merely seeking her share of the fruits of a degree which she helped him earn. We fail to see the difference between compensating for a degree which she helped him earn and compensating her for a house in his name which her earnings helped him buy.

The third argument against including an advanced degree as marital property is that its valuation is too speculative. . . .

However, future earnings due to an advanced degree are not "too speculative." While a degree holder spouse might change professions, earn less than projected at trial, or even die, courts have proved adept at measuring future earnings in such contexts as personal injury, wrongful death, and workers' compensation actions. In fact, pain and suffering, professional goodwill and mental distress, within these general legal issues, have similar valuation "problems". . . .

The last argument is that these matters are best considered when awarding alimony rather than when distributing the property. . . . However, alimony is basically for the other spouse's support. . . . The considerations for whether or not a spouse is entitled to support are different than for dividing the marital property. *McLain v. McLain,* 108 Mich. App. 166; 310 N.W.2d 316 (1981), listed 11 factors that the trial judge is to consider in determining whether or not to award alimony. Some of these deal with the parties' financial condition and their ability to support themselves. If the spouse has already supported the other spouse through graduate school, he or she is quite possibly already presently capable of supporting him or herself. Furthermore, MCL 552.13; MSA 25.93 gives the trial court discretion to end alimony if the spouse receiving it remarries. We do not believe that the trial judge should be allowed to deprive the spouse who does not have an advanced degree of the fruits of the marriage and award it all to the other spouse merely because he or she has remarried. Such a situation would necessarily cause that spouse to think twice about remarrying. . . .

CASE DISCUSSION QUESTIONS

1. In deciding how much to compensate the wife, the *Woodworth* court stated that there were two basic methods. The award could be a percentage share of the present value of the future earnings attributable to the law degree, or the award could be limited to the amount of money the wife actually contributed to the cost of earning the degree. Which formulation would you argue for if you were representing the wife? The husband? The court chose the first method. What problems do you foresee this created in this and future cases?

2. The court noted that some courts have held that

> [a]n education degree, such as an M.B.A., is simply not encompassed by the broad views of the concept of 'property.' It does not have an exchange value or any objective transferable value on an open market. It is personal to the holder. It terminates on death of the holder and is not inheritable. It cannot be assigned, sold, transferred, conveyed, or pledged. An advanced degree is a cumulative product of many years of previous education, combined with diligence and hard work. It may not be acquired by the mere expenditure of money. It is simply an intellectual achievement that may potentially assist in the future acquisition of property. In our view, it has none of the attributes of property in the usual sense of that term.[13]

Should the outcome of this and similar cases be determined by whether an education degree is "property"? On what other factors might the court base its decision?

(3) Alimony/maintenance agreements

Alimony, also referred to as **maintenance** or **support,** was traditionally awarded to the wife, who had stayed at home and raised the children, while the husband was working outside the home to provide the income needed to support the family's needs. The primary rationale for alimony was that the divorced wife needed continued support from the former husband because she either lacked the skills and/or experience to support herself after the divorce or should not be expected to have to go to work outside the home. In its 1979 decision in *Orr v. Orr*[14] the U.S. Supreme Court ruled that gender-based alimony violated the equal protection clause of the Fourteenth Amendment and that the court must decide solely on the basis of the educational backgrounds and job opportunities of both spouses.

In determining alimony the court looks to many of the same factors that are used in equitable property division. Also, the court may take into account the lifestyle to which the parties have become accustomed.

The trend in recent years has been to award rehabilitative or limited-term support rather than a permanent alimony for an indefinite time period. In many cases the nonworking spouse will be given support for a specific amount of time to return to school and reestablish job skills. After that period has expired, the spouse has to provide for his or her own support.

---

[13]Id. at 334.
[14]440 U.S. 268 (1979).

Alimony can also be paid in one lump sum rather than over time. Psychologically a lump sum payment may allow the parties to "get on with their lives." However, there might be severe tax consequences for the recipient, who might have to pay taxes on the entire amount when received.

Legal Reasoning Exercise

2. Michael and Bonnie were married. The couple separated, and Michael began living with Donna. Bonnie filed for divorce. On February 10 a hearing was held to end the marriage, but because Bonnie's attorney sent Michael a notice with the wrong date, a new hearing date was set. In the meantime Michael and Donna won a $2.2 million jackpot in the Arizona state lottery. At the rescheduled hearing Bonnie claimed an interest in one-half of the winnings. Should the judge award it to her? *Note:* Arizona is a community property state. Would your answer be different if it was not?

(4) Custody, visitation, and child support

Child custody and visitation rights often become two of the most contentious and difficult issues to deal with in a divorce case. Ideally the divorcing couple puts their own selfish interests aside and works with a professional mediator to arrive at an arrangement that is in the best long-term interests of the children. All too often, however, the issues of custody and visitation are decided in an atmosphere of acrimony and retribution. Sometimes those ill feelings can even lead to false charges of child abuse. Nothing can compare to the emotional trauma felt by everyone involved in a contested child custody dispute.

(a) Custody Custody can be either legal or physical, and it can be either sole or joint. Traditionally, it was common for the mother to get sole legal and physical custody. The trend today is toward joint legal custody, regardless of who has physical custody.

Physical custody determines with whom the child will live and who will supervise the child's day-to-day activities. **Legal custody** relates to who will have authority to make legal decisions for the child relating to such things as health care and education. If one party to the divorce is given **sole custody,** that parent has both physical and legal custody of the child until either the child reaches the age of majority or the court decides that it is in the best interests of the child to change this custody arrangement. **Joint legal custody** allows both parents to have an equal say in making major decisions—for example, decisions regarding the education of the child. Joint physical custody is also possible, allowing the child to spend a significant amount of time with each parent. When parents live in different states, they often have **split custody,** whereby one parent has both physical and legal custody during the school year and then the other parent gets both physical and legal custody during designated vacation periods. The

Physical custody
The child lives with and has day-to-day activities supervised by the designated parent or guardian.

Legal custody
The designated parent or guardian has authority to make legal decisions for the child relating to such matters as health care and education.

term **split** or **divided custody** can also refer to those rare situations when the court separates the children so that each parent is awarded custody of one or more of the children.

If the parents cannot agree on a mutually acceptable custody arrangement, the court holds a hearing at which interested parties give testimony regarding the child's needs and the fitness of each parent. The court should consider the wishes of the parents and the child; the child's adjustment to his or her home, school, and community; and the mental and physical health of all involved. The court may appoint a **guardian ad litem,** usually an attorney or a social worker, to speak for the interests of the child.

(b) Visitation In addition to determining which parent will be given custody of any children, the court must determine the extent to which the noncustodial parent can visit the child. Normally, when physical custody is given to one parent, the noncustodial parent is given visitation rights and ordered to pay support. However, the right to visit is not tied directly to the obligation to support. Therefore, if the custodial parent wrongfully denies the other parent access to the children, that does not relieve the noncustodial parent of the obligation to provide support. Likewise, if the support payments are late, that does not give the custodial parent the right to deny visitation. The appropriate response in either case is to return to court and ask for a court-ordered remedy. This is often a difficult concept for divorced couples to grasp, as evidenced by the following case.

Carroll v. Carroll
593 So. 2d 1131 (Fla. Dist. Ct. App. 1972)

PARKER, Judge.

Jane Carroll, the former wife of Ira Carroll, Sr., appeals a supplemental final judgment which temporarily suspended child support based upon her sixteen-year-old son, Hunter Carroll, refusing to visit his father, Mr. Carroll. Although we sympathize with a trial judge dealing with an almost impossible situation, we reverse that portion of the judgment suspending the father's child support obligation, concluding that the noncustodial parent's child support obligation does not cease upon the child refusing to visit the noncustodial parent.

A review of this court file reflects that for six years following a final judgment of dissolution of marriage, there has been bitter strife between Mr. and Mrs. Carroll over Mr. Carroll's rights of visitation with their three children. Two things happened to involve this court. The first was that the parties' sixteen-year-old child filed a motion

through his mother's attorney to have the trial judge terminate the requirement that he visit his father. The trial court granted the son's motion. The next thing to occur was the trial court, on its own motion, terminated Mr. Carroll's child support obligation for that child on a temporary basis until visitation was reinstituted.

We recognize the dilemma of the trial judge and quote from his order denying Mrs. Carroll's motion for rehearing:

The Former Wife's position is that the Court erred in tying a child support obligation to a visitation issue. Ordinarily, the Former Wife would be correct, and as a general rule it is clear that both Chapter 61 and the apposite case law provide that child support cannot be conditioned upon visitation. However, the instant case defies, in many ways, the general rule.

It would serve no useful purpose, except for appellate review, to expend the labor necessary to fully lay out the post judgment etiology of this case. The file speaks for itself. By the time the temporary visitation order was entered in the fall of last year, the parties and the child in question had reached a point justifying not only a temporary cessation of visitation, but also support for that child. Hunter Carroll and his father had become adversaries in about every sense of the word. They had escalated their enmity to the point of a physical confrontation. Hunter referred to his father as "Mr. Carroll," and indicated no respect whatsoever for him. Hunter actively resisted visitation with his father and in fact was the movant himself in the motion to terminate visitation. Hunter Carroll is a very sophisticated, bright, articulate sixteen year old boy who has, as he so forcefully points out, reached an age of discretion which all but insures that if he doesn't want to have meaningful visitation, it simply will not occur. He believes he has been driven to this emotional juncture by his father's behavior; the father believes his son's attitude is a by-product of the poisonous relationship between him and his former wife who is the custodial parent. Whatever the truth, it appears to the Court that where a child of sufficient maturity and intellect and discretion moves to terminate visitation, and where the motion is granted, this conduct justifies the suspension of support on a temporary basis. Of course support will be automatically and immediately re-instated once visitation re-commences.

We first note that this record contains no findings by the trial judge that Mrs. Carroll orchestrated her son's motion to terminate visitation. We do not have to address today what this court's position would be if that were the case. Although Mr. Carroll feels strongly that the wife and maternal grandparents have caused these problems, the trial judge made no such findings. Florida Statutes do provide a remedy for a noncustodial parent who is denied his or her visitation rights by the custodial parent.

Both natural parents share a duty to support a minor child, even though the trial court, under section 61.13(1)(a), may order either or both parents to pay child support upon dissolution of the marriage. Thus if this animosity had developed between the father and child while the parents were still married, the father still would have a duty of support of his family, including Hunter.

This court has recognized that ordinarily, if a parent supports his child, he has the right to visit the child. However, this court has further recognized that there are instances where a former spouse has a duty of support when visitation would not be advisable for various "sociological, psychiatric and other reasons." . . .

[W]e are unwilling to say that conduct by a child, not shown to be orchestrated by one of the parents, should relieve a parent of his or her duty to support the child. This seems to punish only the other parent's ability to pay for that child's needs.

The all too familiar tragedy in this case is, as stated by the guardian ad litem, that "this appears to be a classic case of parental strife affecting the dependent children; the children are always the losers." Instead of two parents working with one another and their child to deal with his concerns regarding visitation, we have instead the young man employing an attorney to file motions which require court resolution. And throughout this scenario, quality time between a child and his father is being lost which can never be replaced. The parents also should consider the effect this may have upon the other children.

While fully understanding the trial court's attempt to do equity in this case, we reverse and remand with directions for the trial court to order the payment of all of the suspended child support payments.

CASE DISCUSSION QUESTIONS

1. Do you agree with the *Carroll* court's decision in this case? Why?
2. Should the court have considered the needs of the two other children in reaching its decision?
3. Do you think the court would have reached a different result if it had found that Mrs. Carroll had "orchestrated" her son's decision to terminate visitation? Most courts will not relieve a parent of his or her obligation to supply child support solely on the basis that the custodial parent had denied that parent

his or her court-ordered visitation rights. Do you agree with this? Why should the noncustodial parent have to continue to pay child support if he or she is being denied visitation rights?

(c) Custody and visitation rights of others   Until recently the only party with standing to request custody or visitation rights after divorce was the noncustodial parent. Today, however, in some cases courts have expanded those rights to encompass unwed fathers, grandparents, stepparents, and gay and lesbian partners.

(i) Unwed fathers   In contradistinction to the legal protections offered unwed mothers, with regard to unwed fathers the U.S. Supreme Court has stated that the "mere existence of a biological link" is not enough to merit protection. For example, an unwed father who has not participated in the rearing of his child or given any financial support is not entitled to a hearing before his child can be adopted by the stepfather.[15] However, if an unwed father has demonstrated a full commitment to parental responsibilities, then his desire for personal contact with his child will acquire substantial protection under the due process clause of the Fourteenth Amendment. For example, where the father had lived with the mother and his children off and on for eighteen years, the unwed father was entitled to a hearing before the state could take his children from him.[16]

(ii) Grandparents   Traditionally, grandparents had no legal rights to visitation. In recent years, however, the courts have been more willing to grant visitation rights if the children are no longer living in an intact home with both parents and if it can be shown to be in the best interests of the children.

By 1999 a majority of the states had enacted legislation allowing third parties, such as grandparents, to petition for visitation, at least in situations where the parental unit was no longer intact due to divorce, separation, or death. In *Troxel v. Granville*[17] the U.S. Supreme Court was asked to rule on the constitutionality of a Washington state statute that allowed any third party to petition for visitation if it was in the "best interests" of the child. The Supreme Court held that the Constitution protects the interest of parents in the care, custody, and control of their children and that the Washington statute unconstitutionally infringed on that right. The Court noted that the statute was "breathtakingly broad" in that it allowed *any* person (with no requirement that the person have established a substantial relationship to the child) to petition the court for visitation at *any* time (with no requirement that the parent first be deemed unfit, that evidence be introduced showing that the child would be adversely affected by the lack of visitation, or that the parent first have unreasonably denied visitation). Under the statute a trial court had the power to grant visitation rights if the court determined it was in the best interests of the child. The Court was troubled by all of these statutory provisions as well as the lack of according at least a rebuttable presumption of validity to the parent's decision regarding visitation. Although the Court invalidated the Washington statute, it limited its decision to the specifics of that statute and declined to address the validity of the statutes enacted by the other forty-nine states. Nor did the Court clearly delineate what the Washington legislature would need to do to amend the

---

[15]Lehr v. Robertson, 463 U.S. 248 (1983).

[16]Stanley v. Illinois, 405 U.S. 645 (1972).

[17]530 U.S. 57 (2000).

statute to cure its constitutional problems. Therefore, because the Court did not lay down any clear guidelines, we should expect to see a great deal of litigation in which parents challenge the validity of the other state statutes that grant grandparents and others the right to petition for visitation.

(iii) Stepparents   When divorced parents remarry, their children often form very strong "parental" bonds with the new stepparent. However, if stepparents do not take the necessary steps to adopt the child of the new spouse, they may have no visitation rights if they divorce or their spouse dies. Sometimes visitation is allowed if the court determines that the person has become a "de facto parent" through prolonged contact and care for the child. However, it is not safe to rely on this exception, as evidenced by a recent Vermont case. In *Titchenal v. Dexter*[18] the court held that even though a woman was a "de facto parent" to a child she had raised with her lesbian partner, she had no visitation rights. The court stated that allowing such visitation rights raised the potential danger that parents would be forced to defend against visitation claims by anyone who had formed a strong bond with the child. The court stated that if the "de facto parent" wanted to preserve her rights, the proper approach would have been to adopt the child. However, adoption is not always a viable option. For example, in *In re EWB Applying for Adoption*[19] a stepfather was denied the right to adopt his wife's daughter even though he was "an ideal father figure" and the girl only occasionally saw her natural father, who owed unpaid child support. The court determined that it was in the best interest of the child to have "the best of both worlds" and denied the adoption request.[20]

In an unusual case an Oregon court granted custody to a stepfather. In *Fenimore v. Smith*[21] a twelve-year-old girl was present when her mother died of heart failure. Experts testified that the girl suffered great guilt because she felt the mother died as a result of being upset over an argument between her and her half-sister. In addition, the girl did not administer CPR and called her father rather than dialing 911. In those circumstances the court ruled it would be an additional loss for the girl to be taken away from her stepfather and half-sister. However, other courts have held the opposite, stating that unless the biological parent has abused or neglected the child, the award of custody must be to the natural parent. For example, in the case of *In re A.R.A.*[22] the parents, Tracy and Bill, were married for six years. During that time A.R.A. was born. When she was nineteen months old, they divorced, and Tracy was given custody. A year later Tracy married Patrick, and they had a son. Then Tracy died in a plane crash. In her will Tracy named Patrick A.R.A.'s guardian. When Bill came to pick up A.R.A., Patrick refused. The trial court determined that there was a close relationship between Patrick and A.R.A., that she was attached to her half-brother, that Patrick's parenting skills were better than Bill's, and that A.R.A. would be adversely affected by changing schools and homes. The court awarded custody to Patrick. The Montana Supreme Court reversed. It stated that the "best interest of the child" test can be used only after a showing of dependency or

---

[18] 693 A.2d 682 (Vt. 1997).

[19] 441 So. 2d 478 (La. App. 1983).

[20] Id. at 483.

[21] 930 P.2d 892 (O. App. 1997).

[22] 919 P.2d 388 (Mont. 1996).

abuse and neglect by the natural parent. Because there was no such showing here, the natural parent should be awarded custody.[23]

(iv) Gay and lesbian partners   The rights of homosexual parents constitute an emerging issue in family law. Traditionally, a homosexual parent had difficulty being awarded custody, as the court often thought that the parent's choice of lifestyle would have a bad influence on the child. As recently as 1996, a headline in the National Law Journal could proclaim: "Mom's a Lesbian, Dad's a Killer. Judge: She's Unfit." The article reported how a Florida judge, looking at the following facts, found the mother unfit. An eleven-year-old daughter had been living with her mother for the past five years, ever since her parents' separation. When the mother went to court seeking past-due child support, her ex-husband responded by suing for custody. He had served eight years in jail for killing his first wife and was currently living with his fourth wife. Because the mother was living with a female partner, the judge sent the daughter to live with the father. The judge noted that the daughter should be "given the opportunity and the option to live in a non-lesbian world."[24]

In another well-publicized case the Virginia Supreme Court upheld a trial court's decision to allow a grandmother to seek custody of her grandson on the grounds that her daughter was a lesbian. The court noted that "living daily under conditions stemming from active lesbianism practiced in the home may impose a burden upon a child by reason of the 'social condemnation' attached to such an arrangement, which will inevitably afflict [sic] the child's relationships with its 'peers and with the community at large.' "[25]

At the other end of the spectrum, many courts hold that, absent evidence that the child is being harmed, a parent's sexual orientation should not be a significant factor in custody cases. For example, in *Bezio v. Patenaude*[26] the court noted that "[b]oth parties introduced evidence to the effect that a mother's sexual preference per se is irrelevant to a consideration of her parental skills."[27] The court went on to hold that the "State may not deprive parents of custody of their children 'simply because their household fails to meet the ideals approved by the community' . . . [or] simply because the parents embrace ideologies or pursue life-styles at odds with the average."[28]

Child support
Money that the non-custodial parent contributes to assist the custodial parent in paying for a child's food, shelter, clothing, medical care, and education.

(d) Child support   The level of **child support** that the noncustodial parent will be required to contribute is another frequently contentious aspect of divorce proceedings. These determinations require a careful balancing of such factors as the parents' income and standard of living, the child's age, and the child's health and educational needs. The courts retain jurisdiction over this aspect of the divorce decree and often modify the support order based on changes in a parent's job status or remarriage.

---

[23]Id. at 392.

[24]National Law Journal, Feb. 12, 1996, at A9.

[25]Bottoms v. Bottoms, 457 S.E.2d 102, 108 (Va. 1995).

[26]410 N.E.2d 1207 (Mass. 1980).

[27]Id. at 1215.

[28]Id.

The basic child support obligation, based on the income of the noncustodial parent, is as follows:

Gross Weekly Income	Number of Children		
	1	2	3
$0–$100	Discretion of the court, but not less than $80 per month		
$101–$280	21%	24%	27%
$281–$750	$59 + 23% (% refers to all dollars over $280)	$67 + 28%	$76 + 31%
$751–max.	$167 + 25% (% refers to all dollars over $750)	$199 + 30%	$222 + 33%

Exhibit 14-2   Massachusetts Child Support Guidelines

Every state has guidelines to help the courts determine how much the child support payments should be. Exhibit 14-2 shows the 2004 guidelines for Massachusetts. These are only guidelines, and the court has discretion to either increase or decrease these amounts based on a number of factors.

As you can see, payments are dependent on the income of the parents and the number of children. These guidelines assume traditional custody and visitation arrangements. They do not apply when the parents share physical custody or have split custody—that is, when each parent has physical custody of one or more children. They also do not apply if the combined gross income of the parents exceeds $100,000.

One of the biggest problems with child support is collecting it. The problem of "deadbeat dads" has been widely publicized in recent years and has resulted in significant legislation at both the state and the national levels. In most states the custodial parent can attach the wages of the delinquent parent. Through a process called **garnishment** a court can require an employer to withhold money from an employee's wages and turn this money over to the party to which a debt is owed. Some states assist in the collection of child support by requiring that the payments be made directly to the local clerk of the court.

If the parent with a child support obligation moves to another state, two uniform laws come into play: the Uniform Reciprocal Enforcement of Support Act (URESA), adopted by all fifty states, and the Uniform Interstate Family Support Act (UIFSA), adopted by approximately half the states. Both allow an order for support issued in one state to be enforced in another state. A major difference in the two laws is whether the enforcing state is allowed to modify the original support order. Under URESA it can; under UIFSA it cannot. The federal Child Support Recovery Act of 1992[29] authorizes **extradition**—that is, the return of delinquent parents for criminal prosecution—in states that make willful failure to pay child support a crime.

Garnishment
A process through which a court can require an employer to withhold money from an employee's wages and turn this money over to the party to whom a debt is owed.

Extradition
The transportation of an individual from one state to another so that person can be tried on criminal charges.

---

[29]18 U.S.C. § 228 (2004).

DISCUSSION QUESTIONS

12. A husband and wife decided to try in vitro fertilization. They signed an agreement that provided that, in the event of their separation, the wife could use the embryos. The procedure was successful, and the wife gave birth to twins. When the couple separated, the wife sought "custody" of the remaining frozen embryos. The father objected. How do you think the court ruled?

13. In settling custody issues the courts are supposed to use a "best interest of the child" standard. To what extent do you think it is appropriate for the courts to take into consideration such things as a parent's gender, age, or religion? In determining custody how much, if any, consideration should be given to the fact that one of the parents smokes and would therefore be exposing the child to secondhand smoke? What if the new partner of one of the parents is of a different race than the child? What if one of the parents openly lives with his or her new homosexual partner?

14. To what extent should children at various ages be permitted to help determine which parents should have custody?

15. What should the court do if a child refuses to visit the noncustodial parent? In the case of *In re Marriage of Marshall,* 663 N.E.2d 1113 (Ill. App. 1996), nine-year-old Rachel and thirteen-year-old Heidi flatly refused to visit their father. The court "found both Rachel and Heidi to be in direct civil contempt. The court 'grounded' Rachel, and ordered that she not leave her mother's home. Rachel could not watch television or have friends over to the house, but she could read and do crafts. The court ordered [the mother] to enforce these measures. The court placed Heidi in a juvenile detention facility until she agreed to go to North Carolina. The judge indicated that the girls' conduct arose from the efforts of adults to manipulate the system." Id. at 1119. Do you agree that such sanctions are appropriate? What other remedies do you think the court could have pursued?

16. Which of the following two provisions for child visitation do you prefer? Do you think your answer might vary depending on the couple involved? Why?

- The parties shall determine visitation schedules between them. At a minimum the husband will see the children at least two weekends a month and one day or early evening during the week.
- The husband will have visitation with the three children every other weekend, commencing at 6:00 P.M. on Friday evening, when he will pick up the children at the wife's home. He will return them at 6:00 P.M. on Sunday evening.

B. THE PARENT-CHILD RELATIONSHIP

Having discussed the legal nature of the marital relationship, we now turn to a second major area of family law—the relationship between parents and their children. In this section we will cover the procedure for establishing paternity, adoption, surrogacy, parental rights, child neglect and abuse, and the status of minors.

1. Establishing the Relationship

In most cases the parent-child relationship is legally established at the point at which the names of the mother and father are recorded on a child's birth certificate, either at the time of birth or later through an adoption proceeding. While there have always been situations in which the identity of the father has not been clear, because of current advances in the scientific methods for treating infertility, both legal (as opposed to biological) paternity and legal maternity may be difficult to establish. For example, in the case of an anonymous sperm donor, state statutes cut off all rights of the donor and vest paternity in the married husband. However, if an unmarried woman has knowledge of a sperm donor's identity, then the donor may later be in a position to assert paternity rights. Another difficult situation occurs when an infertility clinic artificially combines a man's sperm with a woman's egg and then implants that fertilized egg into the womb of a second woman. The result is a genetic mother and a gestational mother. In this section we will discuss how parental rights are established through paternity actions, adoption, and surrogacy arrangements.

a. Paternity Actions

The need to establish paternity usually arises when the mother wishes her child to receive court-ordered support payment from the alleged father. As one aspect of recent attempts at "welfare reform," many states have become much more aggressive at identifying fathers of children born out of wedlock. Regulations in some states require the mother to name the child's father as a condition of qualifying for welfare benefits. The government itself then takes the lead in filing petitions to establish paternity that require the alleged father to submit to blood tests and to pay child support if found to have fathered the child.

An increasingly common occurrence is the case of a presumptive father who voluntarily desires to establish paternity in order to gain custody or visitation rights. For unwed fathers who wish to voluntarily assert their paternity, some states have established a putative fathers' registry. Signing the registry ensures that the father will be notified before any court determination regarding adoption of the child.

When a man wishes to establish himself as a child's father and he was not wed to the mother at the time of birth, he may run into a presumption that a husband who was living with his wife at the time of the birth is the father of the child. Such presumptions sometimes can be overcome if evidence shows the husband is impotent or sterile or if a blood test shows the child could not be his. However, some courts treat this presumption as a conclusive presumption and will not allow paternity to be established even through DNA testing.

An example of a court allowing the father to overcome such a presumption in favor of the husband is the case of *Comino v. Kelley*.[30] In that case the evidence established that although the child's mother, Stephanie Kelley, was legally married to Jeffrey Moyer, the marriage had been a mutually convenient "business relationship" that involved living in separate bedrooms. When Kelley became pregnant after having had intercourse with Paul Comino, she told him that he was the father, and prior to the birth she moved into Comino's home. Comino attended at least one Lamaze childbirth class with Kelley, was present at

---

[30]25 Cal. App. 4th 678 (1994).

the birth, and was identified as the father on the birth certificate. After the birth Kelley, Comino, and the baby all returned to Comino's house, and birth announcements were sent identifying him as the father. More than two years later Kelley moved out of Comino's home. When she threatened to restrict his access to the child, Comino went to court to formally establish his parental relationship and to obtain joint physical and legal custody. Kelley, in turn, asserted that "as a matter of law" Moyer was presumed to be the child's father because she had been married to him at the time the child was conceived.

In ruling in Comino's favor the California appellate court found that Comino's fatherhood was established by another section of the California Code that provides a presumption for paternity when a man "receives the child into his home and openly holds out the child as his natural child."[31] The court ruled, in effect, that this statutory presumption took precedence over the one on which Kelley relied.

DISCUSSION QUESTIONS

17. Do you agree with a policy that denies welfare assistance to a child because the mother refuses to cooperate with authorities in identifying the child's father?

18. A fifteen-year-old girl was raped and found herself pregnant. She decided not to have an abortion but to give the child up for adoption. The rapist, however, had other plans. He threatened to assert his paternity rights by signing the state's putative fathers' registry unless the girl dropped the charges against him. What actions do you think a state can take to protect the rights of unwed fathers, while preventing such abuses of the system?

19. Do you think the courts should continue to follow the conclusive presumption that a child born of married parents is their child?

b. Adoption

Adoption is the legal process by which someone other than a child's natural parent assumes the legal rights and responsibilities as a parent for the child. The new adoptive parent literally takes the place of the child's natural parent. Therefore, before the new parent-child relationship can be established, either the child's natural parent must voluntarily relinquish his or her parental rights, or a court of competent jurisdiction must terminate such rights. For example, if a woman remarries and her new husband wishes to adopt her child from her previous marriage, he cannot do so until the child's natural father either voluntarily gives up his parental rights or has them terminated by a court.

Although they are still few and far between, there have been some cases in which a child has sought to "divorce" his or her parents so that the child could be adopted by someone else. One such highly publicized case occurred in 1992 in Florida, where a state circuit court in Orlando allowed Gregory Kingsley to terminate the parental rights of his natural parents so that he could be adopted by the foster parents with whom he had been living. There is also a process for adult adoptions, which allows one adult to adopt another adult as a son or daughter. Such an adoption requires the consent of both parties and is designed

---

[31]Id. at 685.

to establish certain rights under the probate laws. The remainder of this section will focus on the more common occurrence of infant adoption.

Most states have different procedures and rules for agency adoptions and independent adoptions. Many **agency adoptions** involve children born out of wedlock to parents who do not feel they are prepared to accept the responsibilities of parenthood. Licensed agencies assume responsibility for these children, providing temporary foster care, and screen individuals and couples who wish to adopt. An **independent adoption** is one that involves a private agreement between the birth parents and the adoptive parents. Such adoptions still require investigations by approval agencies and formal actions by the courts.

Agency adoption
An adoption in which a licensed agency assumes responsibility for screening adoptive parents and matching them with available children.

Some states have adopted formal criteria that are to be used in selecting among potential adoptive parents. In California, for example, the first choice is a relative. If that is not possible or is not in the child's best interest, the foster parents as well as others can be considered. In making that determination the cultural, ethnic, racial, and religious background of the child may be taken into account. However, the agency may not delay or deny the placement "solely on the basis of the race, color, or national origin of the adoptive parent or the child involved."[32] When a match is made, the new parent or parents are given temporary custody of the child for a trial period, during which the agency monitors the new parents' care of the child. During this time a social worker or other official conducts a home study to determine whether they are fit to adopt.

Independent adoption
An adoption that involves a private agreement between the birth parents and the adoptive parents.

Before an adoption can be finalized, the birth parents must sign a document agreeing to give up their parental rights. Usually, this release cannot be signed prior to the baby's birth. Once it is signed, however, normally the birth parents cannot take back their relinquishment of parental rights unless they can show their consent was obtained by fraud. After the birth parents have released their parental rights and the adoptive parents are deemed fit, the adoptive parents must go to court to have the adoption finalized. Therefore, the child can live with the adoptive parents for a lengthy period before the adoption is finalized by the court.

DISCUSSION QUESTIONS

20. Do you agree with the placement criteria included in the California statute discussed above? What is the justification for matching the child's racial and ethnic characteristics with those of the adoptive parents? Should these factors take preference over the economic and lifestyle advantages that an alternative placement might have?

21. Should children be allowed to "divorce" their parents so that they can be adopted by others?

The importance of obtaining and documenting the consent of the child's natural parents to an adoption is illustrated in a highly controversial Illinois Supreme Court decision, the "Baby Richard" case, excerpted below.

---

[32]Cal. Fam. Code § 8708.

In re Petition of John Doe and Jane Doe, Husband and Wife, to Adopt Baby Boy Janikova
159 Ill. 2d 347, 638 N.E.2d 181 (1994)

Justice HEIPLE delivered the opinion of the court:

John and Jane Doe filed a petition to adopt a newborn baby boy. The baby's biological mother, Daniella Janikova, executed a consent to have the baby adopted four days after his birth without informing his biological father, Otakar Kirchner, to whom she was not yet married.

The mother told the father that the baby had died, and he did not find out otherwise until 57 days after the birth. The trial court ruled that the father's consent was unnecessary because he did not show sufficient interest in the child during the first 30 days of the child's life. The appellate court affirmed with one justice dissenting. We granted leave to appeal and now reverse.

Otakar and Daniella began living together in the fall of 1989, and Daniella became pregnant in June of 1990. For the first eight months of her pregnancy, Otakar provided for all of her expenses.

In late January 1991, Otakar went to his native Czechoslovakia to attend to his gravely ill grandmother for two weeks. During this time, Daniella received a phone call from Otakar's aunt saying that Otakar had resumed a former romantic relationship with another woman.

Because of this unsettling news, Daniella left their shared apartment, refused to talk with Otakar on his return, and gave birth to the child at a different hospital than where they had originally planned. She gave her consent to the adoption of the child by the Does, telling them and their attorney that she knew who the father was but would not furnish his name. Daniella and her uncle warded off Otakar's persistent inquiries about the child by telling him that the child had died shortly after birth.

Otakar found out that the child was still alive and had been placed for adoption 57 days after the child was born. He then began the instant proceedings by filing an appearance contesting the Does' adoption of his son. As already noted, the trial court ruled that Otakar was an unfit parent under section 1 of the Adoption Act because he had not shown a reasonable degree of interest in the child within the first 30 days of his life. Therefore, the father's consent was unnecessary under section 8 of the Act.

The finding that the father had not shown a reasonable degree of interest in the child is not supported by the evidence. In fact, he made various attempts to locate the child, all of which were either frustrated or blocked by the actions of the mother. Further, the mother was aided by the attorney for the adoptive parents, who failed to make any effort to ascertain the name or address of the father despite the fact that the mother indicated she knew who he was. Under the circumstances, the father had no opportunity to discharge any familial duty.

In the opinion below, the appellate court, wholly missing the threshold issue in this case, dwelt on the best interests of the child. Since, however, the father's parental interest was improperly terminated, there was no occasion to reach the factor of the child's best interests. That point should never have been reached and need never have been discussed.

Unfortunately, over three years have elapsed since the birth of the baby who is the subject of these proceedings. To the extent that it is relevant to assign fault in this case, the fault here lies initially with the mother, who fraudulently tried to deprive the father of his rights, and secondly, with the adoptive parents and their attorney, who proceeded with the adoption when they knew that a real father was out there who had been denied knowledge of his baby's existence. When the father entered his appearance in the adoption proceedings 57 days after the baby's birth and demanded his rights as a father, the petitioners should have relinquished the baby at that time. It was their decision to prolong this litigation through a lengthy, and ultimately fruitless, appeal.

The adoption laws of Illinois are neither complex nor difficult of application. Those laws intentionally place the burden of proof on the adoptive parents in establishing both the relinquishment and/or unfitness of the natural parents and, coincidentally, the fitness and the right to adopt of the adoptive parents. In addition, Illinois law requires a good-faith effort to notify the natural parents of the adoption proceedings. These laws are designed to protect natural parents in their preemptive rights to their own children wholly apart from any consideration of the so-called best interests of the child. If it were otherwise, few parents would be secure in the custody of their own children. If best interests of the child were a sufficient qualification to determine child custody, anyone with superior income, intelligence, education, etc., might challenge and deprive the parents of their right to their own children. The law is otherwise and was not complied with in this case.

Accordingly, we reverse. . . .

Justice HEIPLE, writing in support of the denial of rehearing: . . .

I have been a judge for over 23 years. In that time, I have seldom before worked on a case that involved the spread of so much misinformation, nor one which dealt with as straightforward an application of law to fact. . . .

As for the child, age three, it is to be expected that there would be an initial shock, even a longing for a time in the absence of the persons whom he had viewed as parents. This trauma will be overcome, however, as it is every day across this land by children who suddenly find their parents separated by divorce or lost to them through death. It will not be an insurmountable trauma for a three-year-old child to be returned, at last, to his natural parents who want to raise him as their own. It will work itself out in the fullness of time. As for the adoptive parents, they will have to live with their pain and the knowledge that they wrongfully deprived a father of his child past the child's third birthday. They and their lawyer brought it on themselves.

This much is clear. Adoptive parents who comply with the law may feel secure in their adoptions. Natural parents may feel secure in their right to raise their own children. If there is a tragedy in this case, as has been suggested, then that tragedy is the wrongful breakup of a natural family and the keeping of a child by strangers without right. We must remember that the purpose of an adoption is to provide a home for a child, not a child for a home.

CASE DISCUSSION QUESTIONS

1. The trial court stated: "Fortunately, the time has long past when children in our society were considered the property of their parents. . . . [W]e start with the premise that Richard is not a piece of property with property rights belonging to either his biological or adoptive parents. Richard 'belongs' to no one but himself. . . . A child's best interest is not part of an equation. It is not to be balanced against any other interest." Obviously, the Illinois Supreme Court disagreed. Articulate the standard adopted by the Illinois Supreme Court. Which standard, that of the trial court or that of the supreme court, produces the more just result? Just to whom?

2. The Illinois Supreme Court's decision in the "Baby Richard" case brought on a great deal of negative media coverage, including Chicago Tribune columns by Bob Greene entitled "Damn Them All," "The Sloppiness of Justice Heiple," and "Supreme Injustice for a Little Boy." Following Greene's columns the governor publicly backed legislation designed to change the court's decision. Do you think this is the type of decision that should be left to the courts, or could it be better handled through legislation? Why?

3. If you were drafting a statute to cover the type of situation that occurred in this case, what balance would you strike between the parents' rights to their natural-born children and the rights of adoptive parents? In drafting your statute

consider the proper balance between the natural parents' rights to keep their children and the "best interest of the child."

4. In January 1997 it was reported that Otakar Kirchner had moved out of his home, leaving custody of Baby Richard to his birth mother. Does this have any impact on your view as to whether the court reached a just decision in this case?

(1) Adoption records

Once a child is adopted, the original birth certificate is placed in the court records, and a new birth certificate is issued with the names of the adoptive parents. Those records are then sealed to protect the privacy of all the parties. In recent years many adults who were adopted as children have sought access to such records to learn the identity of their natural parents. In response to this "desire to know," some states have developed a registry system whereby adopted children and birth parents can let a state agency know they desire to be reunited. If both sides contact the agency, then the agency will facilitate such a reunion. In addition, records may be opened if the adoptee can show a compelling medical need. However, in the absence of such a procedure or a medical need the courts have been reluctant to open adoption records, as evidenced in the following case.

In re Roger B.
84 Ill. 2d 323, 418 N.E.2d 751, 49 Ill. Dec. 731 (1981)

Mr. Justice MORAN delivered the opinion of the court.

The circuit court of Cook County dismissed the amended petition of plaintiff, Roger B., which sought a judgment declaring section 18 of the Adoption Act (Section) (Ill. Rev. Stat. 1977, ch. 40, par. 1522) unconstitutional. That statute places adoption records and original birth records under seal. The appellate court, in a two-to-one decision, affirmed. . . .

The facts are uncontradicted. Plaintiff, who was born in 1949, filed an amended petition in the circuit court, asserting that his status as an adult adoptee who had feelings of inadequacy and uncertainty as to his background permitted access to his adoption records. Alternatively, plaintiff alleged that the Section is unconstitutional. At the hearing, plaintiff testified that he had been searching for his biological family for three years. Plaintiff regarded himself as "emotionally, physically, and financially comfortable." He testified that his search was

not based on any psychiatric or medical need. Rather, the search emanated from plaintiff's desire to know "information which pertains to [him] as a person." . . .

Plaintiff contends that the right to know his own identity is a fundamental right. He argues that the Section infringes upon his right without serving a compelling State interest, thereby violating the equal protection clause of the Federal Constitution. Plaintiff maintains that the right to determine one's natural identity finds its basis under one's right to privacy. He relies on several Supreme Court cases involving familial relationships, rights of family privacy, and freedom to marry and reproduce: *Roe v. Wade* (1973), (woman's right to terminate her pregnancy); *Eisenstadt v. Baird* (1972), (matters involving contraception); *Loving v. Virginia* (1967), (freedom to marry); *Prince v. Massachusetts* (1944), (matters involving child rearing); *Skinner v. Oklahoma ex rel. Williamson* (1942), (the right to procreate).

These cases concern the most intimate areas of personal and marital privacy. The Supreme Court has been very hesitant in expanding the list of fundamental rights. . . . Several courts, however, have found that the right asserted here is not a fundamental right. . . .

Inasmuch as a fundamental right is not involved, the statute will be upheld if it is not arbitrary and bears a rational relationship to a legitimate State objective. . . .

Section 18 and its related statutes represent a considered legislative judgment that confidentiality promotes the integrity of the adoption process. Confidentiality is needed to protect the right to privacy of the natural parent. The natural parents, having determined it is in the best interest of themselves and the child, have placed the child for adoption. This process is done not merely with the expectation of anonymity, but also with the statutory assurance that his or her identity as the child's parent will be shielded from public disclosure. Quite conceivably, the natural parents have established a new family unit with the expectation of confidentiality concerning the adoption that occurred several years earlier. . . . These interests of the natural parents do not cease when the adoptee reaches adulthood. . . .

The statute, by providing for release of adoption records only upon issuance of a court order, does no more than allow the court to balance the interests of all the parties and make a determination based on the facts and circumstances of each individual case.

We find the statute to be rationally related to the legitimate legislative purpose of protecting the adoption process. Consequently, the Section does not unconstitutionally infringe upon an adoptee's right to discover his own identity. . . .

In this case, plaintiff's attempt to have his adoption records released did not result from any physical or psychological medical need. It arose from plaintiff's desire to discover his natural identity. Further, the record does not show that the natural parents have ever waived their privacy right by consenting to divulgence of the information. We find that the trial court did not abuse its discretion in concluding that plaintiff's desire to obtain release of the records should not prevail over the potential infringement of the rights of other parties. Accordingly, the judgment of the appellate court is affirmed.

CASE DISCUSSION QUESTIONS

1. Do you agree with the Illinois Supreme Court's ruling? Why? What do you think the proper balance should be between the adopted child's interest in knowing about his or her parents and the natural parents' interest in protecting their privacy?

2. What, if any, types of medical conditions justify giving a child or a child's guardians access to sealed adoption records?

In recent years a few states have changed this traditional approach by enacting laws allowing adult adoptees access to their birth records. Such laws have created an emotional debate. On the one side are the adoptees who feel they have an absolute right to find out "who they are and where they came from." On the other side are the birth parents who wish to remain anonymous and who do not want to be contacted by the children they gave up for adoption. While birth parents have attempted to have such laws invalidated on the grounds that they violate their right to privacy, to date no court has done so.

(2) Tort of wrongful adoption

Although adoption is a lifelong commitment from which the parents cannot escape, recently several states have developed a new tort of wrongful adoption.

For example, in the case of *Mohr v. Commonwealth*[33] the court held that an adoption agency must notify the prospective parents of information that would enable them to make a knowledgeable decision about whether to adopt the child. In that case the social worker had not told the parents that the birth mother was hospitalized for schizophrenia and that the child had been diagnosed with mental retardation. While this would not form the basis for revoking the adoption, it would provide grounds for the recovery of resulting medical and educational expenses. States vary as to whether they require an act of intentional fraud on the part of the agency or whether negligent failure to disclose will suffice.

c. Surrogacy

Surrogacy contract
A document in which a woman agrees to conceive and give birth to a child, deliver the child to its natural father, and terminate her parental rights so the father's wife can become its adoptive mother.

A **surrogacy contract** is one in which a woman agrees to conceive a child, usually through artificial insemination; deliver the child to its natural father after birth; and then terminate her parental rights so the father's wife can become its adoptive mother. Such surrogacy agreements are typically used by couples who wish to have a baby that is genetically related to the husband in situations where the mother is infertile or medically unable to give birth. Opponents argue that such surrogacy agreements amount to "baby selling" and that they exploit women.

The "Baby M" case in New Jersey drew national attention to this issue in the mid-1980s. William Stern entered into a surrogacy contract in which Mary Beth Whitehead agreed to be artificially inseminated with Mr. Stern's sperm, to carry any resulting pregnancy to term, to turn the baby over to Mr. Stern after birth, and to terminate her maternal rights so that Mrs. Stern could then adopt the child. In return, Mr. Stern agreed to pay Ms. Whitehead $10,000 after the child was delivered to him. After an uneventful pregnancy, a baby girl was born on March 27, 1986, and turned over to the Sterns three days later. However, after having left the baby at the Sterns, Ms. Whitehead returned later in the evening and begged to be able to keep her for an additional week. The Sterns gave permission for her to keep the baby for one more week because Ms. Whitehead appeared so depressed that they feared she might commit suicide.

In the Matter of Baby M
109 N.J. 396, 537 A.2d 1227 (1988)

WILENTZ, C.J.

We invalidate the surrogacy contract because it conflicts with the law and public policy of this State. While we recognize the depth of the yearning of infertile couples to have their own children, we find the payment of money to a "surrogate" mother illegal, perhaps criminal, and potentially degrading to women. Although in this case we grant custody to the natural father, the evidence having clearly proved such custody to be in the best interests of the infant, we void both the termination of the surrogate mother's parental rights and the adoption of the child by the wife/stepparent. We thus restore the

---

[33]653 N.E.2d 1104 (Mass. 1995).

"surrogate" as the mother of the child. We remand the issue of the natural mother's visitation rights to the trial court, since that issue was not reached below and the record before us is not sufficient to permit us to decide it de novo. . . .

. . . The contract's basic premise, that the natural parents can decide in advance of birth which one is to have custody of the child, bears no relationship to the settled law that the child's best interests shall determine custody. . . .

The surrogacy contract guarantees permanent separation of the child from one of its natural parents. Our policy, however, has long been that to the extent possible, children should remain with and be brought up by both of their natural parents. . . . A child, instead of starting off its life with as much peace and security as possible, finds itself immediately in a tug-of-war between contending mother and father.[9] . . .

Under the contract, the natural mother is irrevocably committed before she knows the strength of her bond with her child. She never makes a totally voluntary, informed decision, for quite clearly any decision prior to the baby's birth is, in the most important sense, uninformed, and any decision after that, compelled by a preexisting contractual commitment, the threat of a lawsuit, and the inducement of a $10,000 payment, is less than totally voluntary. Her interests are of little concern to those who controlled this transaction. . . .

Worst of all, however, is the contract's total disregard of the best interests of the child. There is not the slightest suggestion that any inquiry will be made at any time to determine the fitness of the Sterns as custodial parents, of Mrs. Stern as an adoptive parent, their superiority to Mrs. Whitehead, or the effect on the child of not living with her natural mother.

This is the sale of a child, or, at the very least, the sale of a mother's right to her child, the only mitigating factor being that one of the purchasers is the father. Almost every evil that prompted the prohibition on the payment of money in connection with adoptions exists here. . . .

In the scheme contemplated by the surrogacy contract in this case, a middle man, propelled by profit, promotes the sale. Whatever idealism may have motivated any of the participants, the profit motive predominates, permeates, and ultimately governs the transaction. The demand for children is great and the supply small. The availability of contraception, abortion, and the greater willingness of single mothers to bring up their children has led to a shortage of babies offered for adoption. . . .

Intimated, but disputed, is the assertion that surrogacy will be used for the benefit of the rich at the expense of the poor. In response it is noted that the Sterns are not rich and the Whiteheads not poor. Nevertheless, it is clear to us that it is unlikely that surrogate mothers will be as proportionately numerous among those women in the top twenty percent income bracket as among those in the bottom twenty percent. Put differently, we doubt that infertile couples in the low-income bracket will find upper income surrogates. . . .

The point is made that Mrs. Whitehead agreed to the surrogacy arrangement, supposedly fully understanding the consequences. Putting aside the issue of how compelling her need for money may have been, and how significant her understanding of the consequences, we suggest that her consent is irrelevant. There are, in a civilized society, some things that money cannot buy. In America, we decided long ago that merely because conduct purchased by money was "voluntary" did not mean that it was good or beyond regulation and prohibition. Employers can no longer buy labor at the lowest price they can bargain for, even though that labor is "voluntary," or buy women's labor for less money than paid to men for the same job, or purchase the agreement of children to perform oppressive labor, or purchase the agreement of workers to subject themselves to unsafe or unhealthful working conditions. There are, in short, values that society

---

[9] And the impact on the natural parents, Mr. Stern and Mrs. Whitehead, is severe and dramatic. The depth of their conflict about Baby M, about custody, visitation, about the goodness or badness of each of them, comes through in their telephone conversations, in which each tried to persuade the other to give up the child. The potential adverse consequences of surrogacy are poignantly captured here—Mrs. Whitehead threatening to kill herself and the baby, Mr. Stern begging her not to, each blaming the other. The dashed hopes of the Sterns, the agony of Mrs. Whitehead, their suffering, their hatred—all were caused by the unraveling of this arrangement.

deems more important than granting to wealth whatever it can buy, be it labor, love, or life. Whether this principle recommends prohibition of surrogacy, which presumably sometimes results in great satisfaction to all of the parties, is not for us to say. We note here only that, under existing law, the fact that Mrs. Whitehead "agreed" to the arrangement is not dispositive.

The long-term effects of surrogacy contracts are not known, but feared—the impact on the child who learns her life was bought, that she is the offspring of someone who gave birth to her only to obtain money; the impact on the natural mother as the full weight of her isolation is felt along with the full reality of the sale of her body and her child; the impact on the natural father and adoptive mother once they realize the consequences of their conduct. . . .

Beyond that is the potential degradation of some women that may result from this arrangement. In many cases, of course, surrogacy may bring satisfaction, not only to the infertile couple, but to the surrogate mother herself. The fact, however, that many women may not perceive surrogacy negatively but rather see it as an opportunity does not diminish its potential for devastation to other women. . . .

We have found that our present laws do not permit the surrogacy contract used in this case. Nowhere, however, do we find any legal prohibition against surrogacy when the surrogate mother volunteers, without any payment, to act as a surrogate and is given the right to change her mind and to assert her parental rights. Moreover, the Legislature remains free to deal with this most sensitive issue as it sees fit, subject only to constitutional constraints. . . .

The judgment is affirmed in part, reversed in part, and remanded for further proceedings consistent with this opinion.

But at the end of this extra week Ms. Whitehead not only refused to turn the baby back over to the Sterns but also fled with the baby to Florida. When the Sterns discovered Ms. Whitehead's location, they started legal actions to carry out the terms of the surrogacy contract.

CASE DISCUSSION QUESTIONS

1. Opponents of surrogacy contracts argue that they should be outlawed because they amount to baby selling. Defenders of surrogacy contracts claim such contracts do not involve the purchase of a baby—they merely provide compensation to the surrogate mother for her time and expenses. With which position do you agree? Did the judges in the "Baby M" case treat this as a case about the "sale of a child"?

2. Opponents of surrogacy contracts also argue that they should be outlawed because they exploit women. Defenders counter that they are not exploitive because the women who agree to be surrogate mothers do so voluntarily and wish to help other women have babies of their own. Whose arguments do you find most persuasive and why? What kind of protections, if any, could be built into surrogacy contracts to prevent exploitation?

3. Why did the court think the surrogate mother's consent to the arrangement was irrelevant?

4. If you lived in New Jersey and wanted the court to uphold a surrogacy arrangement like the one in this case, what avenues would be open to you to change the law? Under what circumstances would the court enforce a surrogacy arrangement? How should the surrogacy contract be drafted to be enforceable?

DISCUSSION QUESTION

22. Jane and John Doe entered into an arrangement with a surrogate mother. The result of that arrangement was the birth of a girl. Since birth she has lived with Jane and John Doe. However, there was never any legal termination of the parental rights by the surrogate mother and her husband. Jane and John Doe are now divorcing. The girl is thirteen years old. Through blood testing John Doe was determined to be the natural father. The surrogate mother, not Jane Doe, is the natural mother. Both Jane and John Doe are seeking custody or, in the alternative, visitation rights. How do you think the court should rule?

Legal Reasoning Exercise

3. Mark and Chris Cooley were unable to have children because Chris had undergone a hysterectomy. They decided to enter into a surrogacy arrangement whereby a zygote formed of the gametes of the husband and the wife would be implanted in the uterus of Anna Johnson. Therefore, Mark and Chris were the natural parents of the child, and Anna served as the host surrogate. Anna was a co-worker of Chris's and had volunteered to serve as the surrogate. In return for agreeing to act as surrogate, the Cooleys agreed to reimburse Anna for her medical expenses and any loss of wages for time she had to take off from work, both during and after the pregnancy. In return, Anna agreed to relinquish all parental rights to the child. Shortly before she was to give birth, Anna announced that she would not go through with the agreement unless the Cooleys gave her an additional $20,000. The Cooleys responded with a lawsuit asking that they be declared the parents of the unborn child. Evaluate the arguments both for and against having the court rule in favor of the Cooleys. Base your arguments on *In the Matter of Baby M*, as well as on any additional policy considerations that you think should matter to the court.

2. Parental Rights, Responsibilities, and Liabilities

Parents have traditionally been given a great deal of discretion with respect to how they raise their children. Although they are required to provide an education, they can choose public schools, private schools, or in some states "home schooling." Parents can also decide the religious tradition and value structure in which they wish to raise their children. And short of crossing the line into child abuse, they can determine how they wish to discipline their children.

Parents are normally not liable for their child's negligent acts unless the injury was caused by the parents' own negligent failure to properly supervise the child. In addition, if a child intentionally harms someone, the parent can be held responsible if the parent was negligent in supervising the child's activities. Section 316 of the Restatement of the Law of Torts, Second describes a duty to exercise reasonable care to control one's minor children to prevent them from intentionally harming others. However, the comments point out that a parent is only responsible for a child's conduct insofar as the parent had the ability to control it.

Most states also have statutes making parents strictly liable for the intentional torts of their children. However, when only property is damaged, there is often a liability cap, usually set to a relatively low amount of no more than a few thousand dollars.

3. Child Neglect and Abuse

The state imposes responsibilities on parents to provide food, shelter, medical care, and other basic needs for their children. It also prohibits parents from physically or mentally abusing their children. Unfortunately there are often differences of opinion as to when one crosses the line between a parent's right to discipline a child and the state's right to protect that child from abuse.

As a society we have been reluctant to criminalize family law issues for several reasons. First, the courts are already struggling to manage their caseloads and are naturally cautious about adding to them by criminalizing family law issues. Second, law enforcement personnel have often been hesitant to arrest those who abuse family members. This is due both to a concern that an arrest will escalate the tension and to an awareness that frequently the victim will later refuse to prosecute, thereby eliminating any possibility that the abuser can be convicted. Third, what constitutes child neglect or abuse is colored by time and culture. For example, corporal punishment has been viewed with varying degrees of approval over time and across cultures. Fourth, as a society we are torn by the conflict between our belief that parents should have the right to raise their children as they see fit and our desire to protect those children. For example, if a parent's refusal to allow his or her child to receive needed medical treatment is based on strongly held religious views, should the state be allowed to interfere with that decision?

Child neglect
The negligent failure to provide a child with the necessaries of life.

Child abuse
Intentional harm to a child's physical or mental well-being.

Generally, **child neglect** can be defined as the negligent failure to provide a child with necessaries, such as food, clothing, shelter, and education. **Child abuse** involves intentional misconduct. However, in specific cases it is often difficult to determine where neglect stops and abuse begins. For example, the failure to feed a child breakfast occasionally might be seen as neglect. The failure to feed a child breakfast every day might be seen as abuse.

Evidence of abuse or neglect triggers state intervention, which can begin a multiyear process of trying to meet the needs of both the child and the parents. Normally the state first becomes aware of a potential neglect or abuse situation when someone reports suspicions of child neglect or abuse. Every state requires that those in a position of trust or authority with regard to children, such as teachers and doctors, report any suspected abuse. Because the state has the power to protect its citizens, including its children, it has the right to investigate such reports. Usually, the first step is to try to get voluntary compliance. If that is not possible, the investigating agency may request court-ordered physical examinations of the child, visits to the home, and a general psychological evaluation of the family. During this process the court may appoint a **guardian ad litem** to represent the child. If the end result of the investigation is a determination that the child is in danger, the court may remove the child from the home and place the child in foster care. The final and most drastic remedy is termination of parental rights.

NETNOTE

"Concerned over making decisions about abused and neglected children's lives without sufficient information, a Seattle judge conceived the idea of using trained community volunteers to speak for the best interests of these children in court. So successful was this Seattle program that soon judges across the country began utilizing citizen advocates." This program is now known as CASA, Court Appointed Special Advocates. To learn more about CASA and how to train as a volunteer, go to its national web site at *www.nationalcasa.org*.

A state must have **"clear and convincing"**evidence before parental rights can be terminated. A clear and convincing standard is something more than a preponderance of the evidence (used in most civil suits) but less than beyond a reasonable doubt (used in criminal cases).

Child advocates argue that this standard is too difficult to meet, thereby allowing children to remain with abusive or neglectful parents. Those representing parents, however, argue that, short of incarceration or death, there is no harsher penalty that the state can impose than removing children from a parent's care. Therefore, they argue the standard is not efficiently stringent to protect parental rights.

Evidence of the lack of parental fitness can result from direct actions of the parent, as well as from a parent's refusal to act to protect a child. For example, when a mother did nothing to protect her child from the abuse of her third husband (the child was found naked in a filthy motel room with multiple bruises and cigarette burns), the court involuntarily terminated her rights.[34]

Clear and convincing
An evidentiary standard that requires more than a preponderance of the evidence but less than beyond a reasonable doubt.

DISCUSSION QUESTIONS

23. To what extent should child abuse protection laws apply to the actions of pregnant women? Should the fact that a pregnant woman smokes or drinks alcoholic beverages be treated as child abuse?

24. When deciding whether to terminate parental rights, some argue that a "clear and convincing" standard gives abused children too little protection. They would advocate a "preponderance of the evidence" standard. On the other hand, parent advocates argue that termination of parental rights is such a final determination that parents should be judged unfit only if the court can find them so "beyond a reasonable doubt." Which standard do you think best balances the needs of the children and the parents?

25. Recently a New York judge ordered a couple to abstain from procreating until they could prove they can take care of their children. The mother had four children between 1998 and 2003. As newborns, all four babies tested positive for cocaine and were placed in foster care. The judge ruled the woman could not be a mother again until she could prove that she could care for the children

---

[34]In the Interest of B.R.S., 402 S.E.2d 281 (Ga. App. 1991).

she already had. A representative of the American Civil Liberties Union argued that this ruling was inconsistent with fundamental principles of privacy and autonomy. What do you think about the judge's ruling? Can you think of other approaches to the problems presented by pregnant women suffering from drug addiction and poverty?

4. Legal Status of Minors

Minor
A child who is under the age of legal competence.

From the time they are born until they reach the age of majority (eighteen in most states), children are classified as **minors**. Being classified as a minor has both its benefits and its detriments. Although they have legal rights, minors must rely on their parents or other guardians to act on their behalf in enforcing those rights. For example, minors cannot file lawsuits on their own.

Also, minors have more limited rights than do adults in regard to making major life decisions, such as whether to obtain an abortion. A minor who wants an abortion may be required to get the consent of a parent or the authorization of a trial court judge.

As we discussed in Chapter 11, Contract Law, one of the benefits of being a minor is that when he or she enters into a contract, it is considered to be "voidable." The minor may either enforce the terms of the contract or "disaffirm" it within a reasonable time period. In some states this has been modified so that contracts for necessaries may be enforced, at least as to their reasonable value. Also, some states have developed special laws to change this principle as it applies to contracts for things such as artistic performances and sports as long as the contract has court approval.

If a minor commits a crime, the case is ordinarily handled by a special juvenile court system, which is designed to be less punitive and more focused on rehabilitation. However, if the crime is a violent felony, in some states the minor is automatically transferred to the regular court system and is tried as an adult. In other states the judge holds a transfer hearing to determine whether the child should be treated as an adult.

Once minors have reached the age of majority, they are no longer legally subject to parental authority. They become adults and at that point trade in the special protections and liabilities they had as minors for the full set of legal rights and responsibilities given to adults.

Emancipated minor
Someone who is still under the legal age of adulthood but who has nevertheless been released from parental authority and given the legal rights of an adult.

An **emancipated minor** is someone who is still under the legal age of adulthood but who has nevertheless been released from parental authority and given the legal rights of an adult. Such emancipated status is usually given when a minor has entered into a valid marriage or is on active duty in the armed services. It can also be given at the discretion of the courts in situations where the minor is living independently, physically and financially, from his or her parents.

‖‖ SUMMARY

Marriage, traditionally viewed as the union of a man and woman, is categorized as either a solemnized or a common-law marriage. If the proper grounds exist, either type of marriage can be ended through annulment or divorce. An annulment is usually granted because of factors, such as fraud, that existed before the couple was married. A divorce can be based either on grounds or on no fault. Under no-fault divorce neither party is blamed for the divorce. As part of the divorce process the parties must reach agreement as to property division, alimony, child custody, child support, and child visitation rights. Once the parties enter into a settlement agreement, the court can finalize the divorce. If the parties are unable to agree, the case proceeds to trial.

A rapidly changing area of family law relates to child visitation and custody rights for persons other than the natural parents. In recent years grandparents, stepparents, and gay and lesbian partners have all received more receptive hearings from the courts than they have in the past.

Finally, family law deals with many issues relating to the parent-child relationship, including establishing the relationship through paternity actions, adoption, or surrogacy and defining parental rights and liabilities. In this latter category child neglect and abuse have received national attention as the legal system continues to struggle with these concerns.

REVIEW QUESTIONS

Pages 483 through 496

1. What are some of the legal benefits of marriage?
2. What is the difference between solemnized and common-law marriages?
3. What requirements does the state usually impose before allowing a couple to marry?
4. What is the purpose of a prenuptial agreement? What restrictions are placed on the enforceability of such agreements?

Pages 496 through 506

5. What is the difference between void and voidable marriages?
6. How does an annulment differ from a divorce?
7. What are some of the "costs" of divorce?
8. Describe the basic procedural steps involved in obtaining a divorce.
9. How do courts determine what qualifies as marital property and how it should be divided at divorce?
10. When dividing marital property how have the courts handled professional degrees?

Pages 506 through 514

11. What is the difference between physical custody and legal custody?
12. Is the right to visitation directly tied to the obligation to provide support payments? Why?
13. How are the courts handling the requests of nonparents for visitation and custody?

Pages 514 through 528

14. What must happen to the natural parents' rights before a child can be freed for adoption?
15. Why are adoption records normally sealed? Are there any exceptions?
16. What is a surrogacy contract? What factors would tend to make such a contract enforceable? Unenforceable?
17. When are parents responsible for the negligent acts of their children? When are they liable for the intentional torts of their children?
18. What is the difference between child neglect and child abuse?
19. Describe the normal procedure that is followed when child neglect or abuse is suspected.
20. In what ways does the law favor the rights of minors? In what ways are minors legally disadvantaged?
21. Who is an emancipated minor?

Chapter 15

Criminal Law and Procedure

The real significance of crime is in its being a breach of faith with the community of mankind.
Joseph Conrad

INTRODUCTION

Almost any time you turn on your television you can see someone's interpretation of how our criminal justice system works, or fails to work. Real-life court cases intertwine in the public's mind with fictitious courtroom battles and send mixed messages. It seems that more people question the criminal justice system than believe in it, and they raise fundamental questions: How far should police go to capture suspected criminals and to construct cases against them? Can defense attorneys and prosecutors protect the rights of criminal defendants and still respond to the needs of crime victims? How can criminal defense attorneys represent defendants who they know are guilty? Is it really better to let ten guilty people go free than to have one innocent person sent to jail? Are some innocent persons being sent to jail in spite of all our system's due process guarantees? Hardly any aspect of our legal system is as dynamic as the study of crime and criminals. Reacting to the fears and concerns of society, this field of law changes rapidly.

Criminal law defines for society what behaviors are illegal and determines how lawbreakers should be punished. As you read this chapter, keep in mind our earlier discussions of the differences between criminal and civil law. Also

Crime
An activity that has been prohibited by the legislature as violating a duty owed to society and hence prosecutable, with the possibility of resulting incarceration or the payment of a fine.

Rules of criminal procedure
Federal and state rules that regulate how criminal proceedings are conducted.

remember that while some behavior might be considered morally or ethically wrong, it is not a crime unless the law makes it a crime. Therefore, no act is a **crime** unless the legislature has written a statute explicitly prohibiting that behavior. This principle is expressed by the Latin maxim *nullum crimen, nulla poena sine lege* ("there can be no crime and no punishment without the law").

Criminal procedure dictates the methods the criminal justice system must follow to achieve the goal of protecting all society, even alleged criminals, from unjust prosecutions. As you will recall, one method for ensuring this is to require the prosecution to prove each element of the crime beyond a reasonable doubt. The federal and state **rules of criminal procedure** govern everything from investigation and arrest through sentencing and appeals. The federal and state **rules of evidence** regulate what types of evidence can be used in the trial and how it must be presented. The participants are also bound by a code of ethics, which helps to regulate their behavior. The American Bar Association Standards for Criminal Justice and the Code of Professional Responsibility or Rules of Professional Conduct govern the ethical behavior of the prosecutor, the defense attorney, and the judge. In addition, most states have separate codes of judicial conduct.

A. THE CRIMINAL JUSTICE SYSTEM

The term **criminal justice system** is used to refer to a combination of legislative, administrative, and judicial agencies that are involved in the development and enforcement of criminal law in the United States. These include Congress and state legislatures; law enforcement agencies; the judicial system, including prosecutors and defense attorneys; and the penal system.

The role of Congress and state legislative bodies is to define what constitutes criminal behavior. They also establish ranges of punishments for those crimes.

Law enforcement agencies of the federal, state, and local governments are responsible for maintaining order, investigating crimes, and apprehending offenders. The Federal Bureau of Investigation (FBI) is the most notable law enforcement agency on the federal level, and perhaps in the world. Through its system of field and foreign offices the FBI investigates crimes, works to uncover episodes of espionage, and assists state and local police departments with access to records and forensic resources. Other federal law enforcement agencies are responsible for investigating abuses related to the postal regulations; the customs and immigration laws; the possession, use, and sale of tobacco, alcohol, and firearms; labor; the possession and distribution of legal and illegal drugs; communication; transportation; and many other areas. State and local law enforcement agencies provide similar services within their own jurisdictions.

NETNOTE

The FBI maintains a web site at *www.fbi.gov*, where you can find a great deal of information, including the "ten most wanted" list.

Once law enforcement personnel have identified and arrested someone they believe to have committed a crime, the case moves into the judicial system. The **prosecuting attorney's** office takes over responsibility for presenting evidence in court of criminal wrongdoing. At the federal level these prosecutors are called **United States attorneys**; at the state and local levels they are often called **district attorneys** or **state's attorneys**. Prosecutors are the representatives of the people and the voices of the victims of crime. They have an ethical duty to seek justice— not just to convict defendants. In addition to preparing and presenting the prosecution's case in court, prosecutors are often responsible for deciding what charges should be brought against which defendant and making sentencing recommendations if the defendant is convicted. However, prosecutors must also decide when to dismiss or reduce charges against a defendant if investigation determines that the defendant is not guilty of a particular crime or any other included offenses. Being responsible to the people and the victims, while working to ensure justice, makes the prosecutors' role a difficult one.

Defense attorneys are often perceived as hired guns who will do anything to protect their clients. Part of that perception is true. Defense attorneys are required to represent their clients zealously within the confines of the law, regardless of any admissions of guilt or protestations of innocence from their clients. It is even improper for a defense attorney to advise a client to plead guilty to a crime merely because that defendant has admitted guilt to the attorney. Because defendants are presumed innocent until proven guilty by the courts, criminal defendants are entitled to the best representation possible. Regardless of any client admissions, the defense must explore all the relevant material and evidence. Due process protects everyone, not just the innocent. Defense attorneys are expected to ensure that even guilty defendants are protected from overreaching by the criminal justice system.

It is unethical, however, for an attorney to allow a client to commit **perjury**, lying to the court while under oath, or to assist or allow the client to engage in any activity that is illegal or fraudulent. In practice, this may put a defense attorney in an untenable position. For example, if the attorney thinks it is essential that the defendant take the stand and yet knows the defendant will lie under oath, the defense attorney is placed in a no-win situation.

Defense attorneys may be retained and paid by the client or assigned by a judge or the public defender's office. A **public defender** is an attorney who is paid by the government, on either a full-time or a part-time basis, to provide legal counsel to defendants who cannot afford to pay for an attorney. An **assigned counsel** is a private attorney who is paid on a contractual basis to represent a specific defendant.

Prosecuting attorney
The attorney responsible for presenting the state's evidence against the defendant; called **United States attorneys** on the federal level and **district attorneys** or **state's attorneys** on the state level.

Public defender
An attorney employed by the state to represent indigent defendants.

Assigned counsel
A private attorney paid by the state on a contractual basis to represent an indigent client.

As we learned in Chapter 9, no member of the criminal defense team may betray a client's confidence. This confidential information includes what the client tells the attorney and also includes what the attorney learns from other sources while investigating the case.

Ethics Alert

Perpetrator
A person who commits a crime.

Restitution
Repaying the victim for harm caused.

Penal system
Also known as the **correctional system**; the system of jails, prisons, and other places of confinement, as well as the pardon and parole systems.

Probation
An alternative sentence to incarceration that releases the defendant upon agreeing to certain conditions.

Parole
Conditional early release from custody.

Although a victims' rights movement has focused more attention on the plight of the criminal victim in recent years, it is the government's responsibility to investigate the crime, present the case in court, and punish the **perpetrator**. Other than receiving the psychological satisfaction of seeing the criminal fined, incarcerated, or possibly executed, the victim seldom receives any direct benefit from a criminal prosecution unless the criminal defendant is required to compensate the victim through **restitution** as part of a plea agreement or sentencing order. However, most criminals are simply too poor to be able to make any kind of meaningful restitution. Therefore, some states have special victim compensation laws that use general tax money to assist crime victims and their families with costs such as medical and counseling expenses and lost wages. In some jurisdictions a victim impact statement provides victims and their family members with a chance to address the sentencing judge or jury.

The **penal system**, also known as the **correctional system**, is responsible for carrying out the court-imposed sentences. It includes **jails**, most often belonging to the city or county, which are usually reserved for those who commit less serious offenses, and **prisons**, which usually house inmates convicted of more serious sentences, mandating longer periods of incarceration. Many penal systems offer alternatives to incarceration that include probation and parole.

With **probation** the defendant is released from custody after agreeing to comply with a series of court-ordered conditions. These conditions might include daily reporting, drug or alcohol tests, or psychological treatment and may also include vocational training or transitional employment. If the defendant fails to comply with those conditions, he or she may be returned to the court for a violation of probation. The defendant may then be sentenced to jail or prison. **Probation officers**, usually trained in criminal justice, social work, or sometimes even paralegal or legal studies, administer the probation system and work to ensure that probationers meet the conditions of their probation plans. Alternatives to probation include serving time only on weekends, making restitution to the victims for damage the defendant caused, or participating in a day-reporting system. A day-reporting system usually involves the wearing of an electronic device on the ankle or wrist. While leaving the defendant free to work, the defendant's location can be monitored. Finally, **parole** may be granted to inmates after a certain period of their sentences has been served. Inmates may be released from jail or prison if they meet the parole board's criteria after a review of their situation.

B. SUBSTANTIVE CRIMINAL LAW

In this section we will explore the origins of criminal law and how it is currently classified. We will also take a closer look at a concept we introduced in Chapter 3, the required elements of mens rea and actus reus. Finally, we will highlight some of the more common defenses to criminal activity, such as the insanity defense.

1. Common-Law Heritage and Model Penal Code

We inherited our system of criminal laws from many sources. The earliest influences came from religious origins. The Hebrews, the Greeks, the Romans, and the Catholics of the Middle Ages all contributed toward our understanding of what was "right" and "wrong," "moral" and "immoral," "legal" and "criminal."

Our most significant contributor by far, however, was the English, who, influenced by all these prior lawmakers, developed the system of common law that defined and classified crimes, defenses, and punishments. Over the years our American legislative bodies have clarified and added to these common-law crimes and enacted them into systems of formal criminal statutes on both the state and the federal levels.

By putting our criminal laws in statutory form, we provide all citizens with written notice as to what behaviors may result in prosecution and punishment. This notice helps contribute to **due process** as it is guaranteed to all citizens through the Fifth and Fourteenth Amendments to the U.S. Constitution.

Due process
Fifth and Fourteenth Amendments guarantee that notice and a hearing must be provided before depriving someone of property or liberty.

Amendment V

No person shall be . . . deprived of life, liberty, or property, without due process of law. . . .

Amendment XIV

[N]or shall any State deprive any person of life, liberty, or property, without due process of law. . . .

Although the principles of due process require the federal government and each of the states to set out their criminal laws in written form, there is no requirement for uniformity among the states. Thus while lotteries or casino gambling may be legal in some states, they may be illegal in others.

In 1956 the American Law Institute assembled a group of law professors and practicing lawyers to attempt to rectify this problem and simplify American criminal law by creating a **Model Penal Code and Commentaries**, which would be adopted in all fifty-one jurisdictions. However, this hoped-for uniformity was never achieved. While many of the provisions of the Model Penal Code have been adopted and incorporated into the laws of various states, the Code itself has not led to a uniform set of criminal laws in all states. Significant variations continue to exist among the state criminal codes.

Model Penal Code and Commentaries
The American Law Institute's proposal for a uniform set of criminal laws; not the law unless adopted by a state's legislature.

Discussion Questions

1. Think back to the last movie or television program you watched about the criminal justice system. Was the system portrayed in a realistic light? How would you describe the portrayal of the attorneys' behavior, both prosecutors and defense attorneys? If the system did not work in that instance, who was portrayed as being at fault? Do you agree?

2. What would you say to a friend who comments on your desire to work for a defense firm by stating, "But why would you want to do that? Defense attorneys are just hired guns."

3. A "Victim's Rights Amendment" has been introduced in Congress that would give victims the right to be present at court and parole proceedings, to be heard at sentencing, and to be notified about the release or escape of a defendant or prisoner. Would you support such an amendment? Some 450 law professors submitted a letter saying the amendment would hamper prosecutions by placing new burdens on law enforcement agencies. What do you think would be the basis for reaching such a conclusion?

2. Classification of Crimes

Crimes are classified in a number of ways. They are commonly classified on the basis of the severity of the punishment, the type of harm done to the victim, and whether they involve federal, state, or local law.

a. Severity of Punishment

One way that crimes are classified is according to the severity of the punishment the defendant faces upon conviction. Offenses that are considered to be serious crimes, such as murder, rape, armed robbery, and aggravated assault, are classified as **felonies** and call for the severest sanctions. Less serious offenses, such as disorderly conduct, shoplifting, and trespassing, are categorized as **misdemeanors**. Sometimes the same basic activity, such as drug possession, can be either a felony or a misdemeanor, depending on the drug and the quantity involved. For example, while possession of a single marijuana cigarette might be only a misdemeanor, possession of a large quantity of heroin would certainly qualify as a felony. Legislators determine whether a given act is to be considered a felony or a misdemeanor at the time they enact the statute making it a crime.

Felonies generally involve a punishment that can include a year or more in a state prison. Some felonies are also classified as **capital crimes**, those for which a death sentence, or capital punishment, can be imposed. The crimes for which the death penalty is typically authorized include multiple murders, murder of a police officer, murder of a child, and murder perpetrated during a rape or kidnapping. The penalty for a misdemeanor is usually less than one year in a county jail or some alternate form of punishment, such as a fine, probation, or restitution. While these types of crimes are not considered serious, they have a serious impact on the judicial system in terms of the time and other resources it takes to process these crimes.

Legislatures often subdivide felonies and misdemeanors into different classes with different ranges of imprisonment. For example, most states have divided murder into murder in the first degree, often carrying a maximum life sentence, and murder in the second degree, carrying a lesser sentence. The Model Penal Code also divides felonies into first-, second-, and third-degree felonies, with punishment linked to the degree. The MPC classifies all forms of murder as a felony of the first degree. Misdemeanors are sometimes also subdivided into classes that reflect greater or lesser degrees of punishment.

Although the state criminal code usually can be divided neatly into felonies and misdemeanors, there are some other types of quasi-criminal law situations of which you need to be aware. For example, traffic laws are usually codified in a different part of the state's statutes, and violations of these laws do not carry the same stigma as do violations of the criminal law. Nevertheless, the judicial proceedings used to enforce these traffic laws are criminal in nature. The state prosecutes offenders who, in turn, must be found guilty beyond a reasonable doubt. Some juvenile proceedings are also criminal in nature. Local ordinances covering matters like garbage disposal and barking dogs are also enforced through quasi-criminal proceedings. Violations of these types of administrative regulations and ordinances that involve only fines are often simply referred to as violations rather than as crimes.

Felony
A serious crime, usually carrying a prison sentence of one or more years.

Misdemeanor
A minor crime not amounting to a felony, usually punishable by a fine or a jail sentence of less than a year.

Capital crime
A crime for which the death sentence can be imposed.

b. Type of Harm

The criminal codes of most states further classify crimes according to the type of harm caused to society. The more severe the harm, the more serious the crime. Offenses involving physical harm to a person are considered more serious than offenses involving damage to someone's property. Figure 15-1 illustrates how some of the more familiar crimes fit within the major harm-based classifications. They include harm to the person, harm to property and home, harm to society's health and safety, and crimes against the government itself.

Offenses against the person include various types of homicides, kidnapping, and acts involving the infliction of bodily harm. A **homicide** is the killing of one human being by another. As we will discuss further later in this chapter, the circumstances under which the killing takes place and what the defendant was thinking at the time of the killing determine whether it was a first-degree murder, manslaughter, negligent homicide, or not a crime at all. Criminal assault and battery are similar to the torts of the same names. As you will recall, a **battery** is a wrongful physical contact with a person that entails some injury or offensive touching. An assault is conduct that places another person in reasonable apprehension of receiving a battery. **Kidnapping** is similar to the tort of false imprisonment in that it involves unlawful confinement. However, in most states asportation, or movement of the victim, must also occur. How much movement is required is often an issue in cases involving charges of criminal kidnapping. **Robbery** is a theft of personal property in circumstances that involve either the infliction of serious bodily injury or the threat of such injury. **Stalking** is a relatively

Homicide
The killing of one human being by another.

Figure 15-1   Classifications of Crime Based on Harm

Harm to Persons	Homicide crimes	
	Murder	
	Manslaughter	
	Negligent homicide	
	Other crimes against persons	
	Assault	
	Battery	
	Child abandonment	
	Kidnapping	
	Rape	
	Robbery	
	Stalking	
Crimes against Habitations and Property	Arson	Receiving stolen property
	Burglary	Shoplifting
	Forgery	Theft
		Trespass
Crimes against the Public Health, Safety, or Decency	Alcohol offenses	Drug offenses
	Child pornography	Obscenity
	Disorderly conduct	Prostitution
Crimes Affecting Governmental Functions	Bribery	
	Perjury	
	Treason	

NETNOTE

The U.S. Department of Justice maintains statistics about crimes and victims at *www.ojp.usdoj.gov/bjs,* as does the University of Michigan through its National Archive of Criminal Justice Data (NACJD) project at *www.icpsr.umich.edu/ NACJDd/archive.html.*

new crime. It is committed when a person intentionally or knowingly engages in a course of conduct that causes a reasonable person to fear the imminent physical injury or death of himself or herself or of a member of that person's family.

Crimes against habitations and property involve harm to or the taking of another's property without consent. **Arson** is the malicious burning of the house or property of another. Despite frequent misuse of the term, **burglary** is not synonymous with theft. Burglary involves breaking into and entering a building with the intent of committing a felony. That felony could be theft, but it also could be some other felony, such as rape. **Theft**, also known as **larceny**, is the act of "stealing"—that is, taking property without the owner's consent. To be found guilty of **receiving stolen property**, the state must prove that the property was stolen, that the defendant knew the property was stolen, and that the defendant knowingly had the stolen property in his or her possession. **Forgery** involves the alteration or falsification of documents with the intent to defraud. **Trespass** is an unauthorized intrusion or invasion of the premises or land of another.

Crimes affecting the public health, safety, and decency cover a wide variety of crimes, ranging from alcohol and drug abuse to obscenity and prostitution. This is one of the most controversial areas of the criminal law. As "victimless crimes" many of the laws in this category are criticized for interfering with basic civil liberties. Offenses covering alcohol and drugs include the possession, use, and sale of these substances. Some drugs are totally outlawed, while others can be sold or possessed only when prescribed by a licensed physician. Alcohol regulation can range from the establishment of a minimum drinking age to complete prohibition. **Prostitution** involves participation, or offering to partici-pate, in sexual activity for a fee, and **obscenity** regulations restrict the availability of sexually explicit books, magazines, movies, videos, and live performances.

Crimes affecting governmental functions include bribery, perjury, and treason. Historically, **bribery** involved offering something of value to a public official that, if accepted, would cause that public official to act in such a way as to violate the public trust. Today there is also commercial bribery. Perjury

PRACTICAL TIP

Because crimes vary from state to state, never rely on a general description of criminal law. Always consult your state statutes to determine the elements of particular crimes in your state.

involves knowingly making a false statement while under oath. Finally, **treason** consists of either attempting to overthrow the government or betraying the government to a foreign power.

c. Federal or State Law

Criminal law can also be classified according to its source. Most criminal behavior is defined by state statutes; the federal criminal law tends to focus on interstate activities. Nevertheless, there are numerous situations in which a single act could be prosecuted as either a federal or a state crime. For example, in the early 1970s the federal government enacted the Racketeer Influenced and Corrupt Organizations Act, also known as **RICO**, to help stop the spread of organized crime in the United States.

RICO
The federal Racketeer Influenced and Corrupt Organizations Act.

For a RICO conviction the United States must prove that the defendant obtained or received money from a pattern of racketeering and invested it in enterprises (business activities) that had an effect on interstate commerce. A defendant convicted under RICO can be forced to pay stiff penalties, which could include up to three times the damages, called treble damages, and forfeiture. While a **fine**, or money payment, is intended to make the defendant pay financially for the crime committed, a **forfeiture** allows the government to take additional money and property from the defendant. The government may take any property connected to the commission of the crime. This could include real property, such as land on which illegal drugs were grown; personal property, such as a boat on which there was illegal gambling; and any money or items found to have been connected to the criminal activity, such as a defendant's bank accounts and jewelry.

Forfeiture
The loss of money or property as a result of committing a criminal act.

3. Elements of the Crime

In order for a crime to take place, someone with a "guilty intent" (mens rea) must commit a "guilty act" (actus reus) that causes specified harmful results.

a. Actus Reus

The Model Penal Code and every criminal statute in every jurisdiction requires the defendant to do some act to be found guilty of a crime. This act, referred to as the **actus reus** of the crime, must be voluntary. The act in itself need not do any harm. For example, just possessing some substances, such as an illegal drug, may be a sufficient action to satisfy the actus reus.

Actus reus
Bad act.

Consider the following crimes from the Illinois Criminal Code.

720 Ill. Comp. Stat. 5/18-1 Robbery

(a) A person commits robbery when he or she takes property, except a motor vehicle covered by Section 18-3 or 18-4, from the person or presence of another by the use of force or by threatening the imminent use of force.

720 Ill. Comp. Stat. 5/18-2 Armed Robbery

(a) A person commits armed robbery when he or she violates Section 18-1 while he or she carries on or about his or her person or is otherwise armed with a dangerous weapon.

Therefore, to be found guilty of robbery in the state of Illinois, a defendant must

1. take property, except a motor vehicle,
2. from the person or presence of another
3. by the use of force *or*
4. by threatening the imminent use of force.

A prosecutor must prove all portions of the statute (1, 2, and either 3 or 4) before the defendant may be found guilty. These individual portions, referred to as the elements, include the actus reus of this crime—the taking of property. A defendant would be found not guilty if the prosecutor failed to prove any part or element of the statute or if the finder of fact had a reasonable doubt about any part of the prosecutor's proof. The more serious offense of armed robbery shares all of the elements of the robbery statute plus the added action or element of

5. carrying on or about his or her person or otherwise being armed with a dangerous weapon.

Lesser included offense
A crime whose elements are contained within a more serious crime. Theft is a lesser included offense of robbery.

Inchoate crimes
Attempted crimes.

Because all the robbery elements are contained in the armed robbery statute, robbery is called a **lesser included offense** of armed robbery. Typically, a defendant may be charged with both crimes, but if found guilty of the more serious offense, the lesser included offense usually will be dismissed.

Sometimes the criminal is prevented from completing the crime. Therefore, because there is no required actus reus, the defendant cannot be charged with having committed that crime. Such attempts, however, can form the basis for a separate conviction. Such attempts are classified as **inchoate crimes**. To be

Legal Reasoning Exercise

1. Review the robbery and armed robbery statutes from the Illinois Criminal Code. What crimes were committed under the following circumstances?

a. Martin waited until the bartender turned her head. Then he slipped $10 from the cash register into his pocket.

b. Kamil broke the lock on the kickstand and stole a bicycle while the owner was in the grocery store.

c. David drove his car slightly behind a woman walking on the side of the road. When she stopped for the light, David reached out of the car window and grabbed her purse. The set of knives that David just won while playing bingo was on the front passenger seat of the car.

d. After everyone left the party, Rosie took a fur coat that had been left behind, hid it in a shopping bag, left the apartment, and pushed the doorman as she left the building.

found guilty of an attempt, the state must prove the defendant intended to commit the crime. To satisfy the actus reus requirement, the state also must prove that the defendant did some overt act in furtherance of that intent that went beyond mere preparation. For example, the Model Penal Code lists several acts that indicate an intent to commit the crime, such as "possession of materials to be employed in the commission of the crime, which are specially designed for such unlawful use or which can serve no lawful purpose of the actor under the circumstances."[1]

Two other inchoate crimes are solicitation and conspiracy. **Solicitation** involves requesting or encouraging someone to commit a crime. For example, if a wife encourages her boyfriend to kill her husband, she could be found guilty of the crime of solicitation. **Conspiracy** involves an agreement between two or more persons to commit an unlawful act. The state must show that they intended to enter into an agreement and that they had the specific intent to commit some crime. Unlike an attempt, where mere preparation is not enough of an overt act to satisfy the actus reus requirement, in many states preparation is sufficient to prove conspiracy. In others the defendants must take substantial overt steps to be found guilty.

Solicitation
Encouraging someone to commit a crime.

Conspiracy
An agreement to commit an unlawful act.

b. Mens Rea

The **mens rea**, the nature of a person's intent, is also a critical factor in the definition of most crimes. The difference between innocently bumping into someone on a crowded street and the commission of the crime of battery depends for the most part on the state of mind of the person who initiated the contact. In order for the act to be considered a crime, there has to be evidence of a "guilty mind."

Under the common law, intent was divided between general and specific intent. If the defendant intended to act only, without regard to causing the results of the act, then the defendant had **general intent**. If the defendant did the act *and* intended to cause the harm that resulted from the act, then the defendant possessed **specific intent**. For example, as mentioned earlier, most states divide murder into first- and second-degree murder. To be found guilty of first-degree murder, most state statutes require that the defendant's actions be "willful, deliberate, and premeditated." As such, first-degree murder is a specific intent crime. That is, the defendant must not only intend to do the act, such as shooting a gun, but also intend that the victim die. States differ as to whether willfulness (also referred to as malice aforethought), deliberation, and premeditation are synonymous or whether they refer to three separate elements. While some courts have held that one or more of the terms are synonymous, others separately define *willfulness* as the specific intent to kill, *premeditation* as having enough time to plan, and *deliberation* as carrying out that plan with a cool head.

In the following case the court grappled with a new issue: whether someone diagnosed with the HIV virus had the specific intent to kill when he attempted to rape his robbery victim.

Mens rea
Bad intent.

General intent
An intention to act without regard to the results of the act.

Specific intent
An intention to act and to cause a specific result.

---

[1]Model Penal Code § 5.01(2)(c).

Smallwood v. State
106 Md. App. 1, 661 A.2d 747 (1995)

BISHOP, J.

... The agreed-upon statement of facts related by the State to the trial court reveals that, in July of 1991, appellant was incarcerated at the Prince George's County Detention Center, where he voluntarily agreed to be tested for the presence of the Human Immunodeficiency Virus ("HIV"). On August 29, 1991, appellant was diagnosed as being infected with HIV, the virus that causes Acquired Immune Deficiency Syndrome ("AIDS")....

On September 28, 1993, appellant and an accomplice approached a woman exiting her car, ordered her, at gunpoint, to drive them to an automated teller machine, and forced her to withdraw $300.... [A]ppellant attempted to rape the woman after robbing her....

Appellant seeks reversal of his convictions for assault with intent to murder and attempted second degree murder, arguing that one cannot be convicted of those crimes simply because one knowingly engages in sexual behavior that places his partner at risk of being infected with HIV. According to appellant, the evidence adduced was insufficient to support the trial court's verdict....

I.

"The crime of attempt consists of a specific intent to commit a particular offense coupled with some overt act in furtherance of the intent that goes beyond mere preparation." *State v. Earp*, 319 Md. 156, 162, 571 A.2d 1227 (1990). "The required specific intent in the crime of attempted murder is a specific intent to murder." Id. at 163.... The trier of fact may infer the existence of the requisite intent to kill from the surrounding circumstances. For example, in *State v. Jenkins*, 307 Md. 501, 514, 515 A.2d 465 (1986), the Court of Appeals held that an intent to kill may, under proper circumstances, be inferred from the use of a deadly weapon directed at a vital part of the human body.

Whether an intent to kill may, under proper circumstances, be inferred from attempted first degree rape which is likely to result in the transmission of HIV to the victim, and whether, under the proper circumstances, attempted first degree rape constitutes an overt act necessary to support a conviction for the crime of attempted murder present issues of first impression in Maryland. We, therefore, look to other jurisdictions for guidance.

In *Weeks v. State*, 834 S.W.2d 559 (Tex. Ct. App. 1992) the Court of Appeals of Texas held that the evidence was sufficient to support the appellant's conviction for attempted murder where appellant, who was HIV positive, spit in the face of a prison guard....

In *State v. Smith*, 262 N.J. Super. 487, 621 A.2d 493 (N.J. Super. Ct. App. Div. 1993) ... the defendant-appellant, a county jail inmate, knew he had HIV, and, prior to biting and puncturing the skin of a corrections officer's hand, repeatedly threatened that he would kill the corrections officers by spitting at them or biting them....

Similarly, in *State v. Haines*, 545 N.E.2d 834, 839 (Ind. Ct. App. 1989), the Court of Appeals of Indiana reviewed whether an HIV infected appellee could be convicted of attempted murder. In *Haines*, after a failed suicide attempt, the appellee scratched, bit, and spit at emergency technicians and police officers who came to his aid, and threatened to give them the AIDS virus.... The appellee was charged with three counts of attempted murder.... The Court of Appeals ... held: "from the evidence in the record before us we can only conclude that [the appellee] had knowledge of his disease and that he unrelentingly and unequivocally sought to kill the persons helping him by infecting them with AIDS." ...

In the case sub judice, the trial court ruled that malice and "the requisite intent to kill" could be inferred from appellant's knowledge that he was infected with HIV, his knowledge that HIV, a fatal disease, could be transmitted through sexual intercourse.... Appellant proffered no evidence suggesting that he did not understand that HIV could be transmitted through sexual contact. . . . "It is a reasonable inference that 'one intends the natural and probable consequences of his act.'" *Ford v. State*, 330 Md. 682, 704, 625 A.2d 984 (1993). "Relying upon that inference, the trial judge could rationally find, beyond a reasonable doubt," that appellant was guilty of attempted second degree murder. *Raines*, 326 Md. at 593. "Although a different trier of fact may have viewed the evidence as establishing [merely the crime of reckless endangerment], the trial court's decision was not clearly erroneous." Id. Accordingly, we affirm appellant's conviction for attempted second degree murder. . . .

BLOOM, J., dissenting.

. . . I agree with the majority opinion that an intent to kill the victims can be inferred from the agreed facts. Appellant was HIV positive and knew it. . . . He was, therefore, aware that in raping his victims he might infect them with a deadly and incurable disease. It is a well established principle of law that, in the absence of evidence to the contrary, one may be inferred to have intended that which is the natural consequences of his acts.

The difficulty is that from those same agreed facts an inference may also be drawn by a somewhat different state of mind: an intent to rape each of the victims, with a reckless disregard for the risk of infecting them with the deadly virus he carried. That is not the same as an intent to kill; it is the wanton, reckless indifference that signifies a depraved heart and that justified appellant's conviction for reckless endangerment. It is not the state of mind required for a conviction of either attempted murder or assault with intent to murder. Those are specific intent crimes,
the specific intent required being an intent to murder. . . .

The question then arises as to whether one may properly be convicted of a crime requiring a specific intent upon evidence from which the trier of fact can infer either that specific intent or a general malevolence. . . .

A reasonable trier of fact, either a judge or jury, may reasonably choose to draw an inference consistent with the guilt of the accused if it is stronger, i.e., more logical and more reasonable, than the alternative inference consistent with innocence. In this case, however, the inference of murderous intent is not a stronger, more reasonable inference than the alternative inference of depraved heart reckless indifference. Indeed, the inference of intent to murder by infecting his victims with a deadly incurable disease is, I suggest, far weaker and less reasonable than the alternative. Appellant was armed with a gun, which he used to accomplish both the robbery and the rape of each of his victims by threatening to shoot them. There was, undoubtedly, an intent to rob and an intent to rape. But is it more or less likely that one infected with a deadly, incurable disease and armed with a gun, intending to murder as well as to rape and to rob his victim, would choose to murder her by the transmission of the disease, which is far from a sure and certain method of killing someone, instead of shooting the victim in the head or the heart? Even the use of the gun as a bludgeon would be a more logical, sure, and certain method of killing a rape victim than the bare possibility of transmitting the virus, which may or may not develop into full-blown AIDS. . . .

I do not believe that a reasonable trier of fact can reasonably draw the weaker inference and thus be persuaded of appellant's guilt beyond a reasonable doubt.

CASE DISCUSSION QUESTIONS

1. In general, what must the state prove to show attempted murder?
2. Why did the majority in *Smallwood* believe the defendant's conviction for attempted second-degree murder should be sustained? Do you agree, or do you think the dissent was correct in saying that he did not have the specific intent required for a murder conviction?

The Model Penal Code abandoned the use of general and specific intent. Instead it divides intent into four categories that illustrate the defendant's state of mind: purposeful, knowing, reckless, and negligent.

When the defendant's acts are **purposeful**, they are specifically intended by the defendant. Notice the old standard of specific intent included here. The defendant must desire to cause the harm that resulted from the actions taken. For example, the defendant shoots a gun with the intent to harm one particular person. This is the highest level of intent, and when found, the defendant usually pays the highest price. If the judge or jury finds that the defendant acted **knowingly**, they determine that the defendant knew or had reason to know that harm would be caused by the actions taken even if the specific harm was not the objective of the defendant. For example, a defendant who shoots a gun into a crowded room would know that the action would cause harm (knowingly) even though the defendant was unaware that the action would harm one particular victim (purposeful).

Under the Model Penal Code, for a defendant to act knowingly, he or she need not literally "know" that a certain result will occur. For example, in *United States v. Jewell*[2] the issue was whether the defendant "knowingly" concealed marijuana in a secret compartment between his trunk and rear seat. It was undisputed that the defendant knew of the secret compartment and that something was inside. There was also evidence that the defendant had taken steps to avoid any actual positive knowledge of the contents of the secret compartment. The court stated that the term *knowingly* "includes a mental state in which the defendant is aware that the fact in question is highly probable but consciously avoids enlightenment."[3] Actual knowledge is not necessary. If that were not so, those who transport drugs could always avoid conviction by simply testifying that they did not "know" what they were carrying.

A defendant is said to have acted **recklessly** when he or she disregards a substantial and unjustifiable risk that harm will result from that action. For example, the defendant shoots a gun into the air while walking through a park at night, and the bullet strikes a person sitting on a bench. The defendant's intent is said to be **negligent** when he or she simply fails to be aware of that substantial and unjustifiable risk. For example, negligence could be found if, when cleaning a gun, a defendant forgets to check the bullet chamber, accidentally pulls the trigger, and shoots someone.

Compare how the Model Penal Code treats the various forms of homicide. Notice how the same act, the death of another human being, can result in different crimes based on the intent of the defendant.

Purposeful
Intending to cause a specific harm.

Knowingly
Not intending to cause a specific harm but being aware that such harm would be caused.

Recklessness
Disregarding a substantial and unjustifiable risk that harm will result.

Negligence
The failure to act reasonably under the circumstances.

Definitions of Specific Crimes

Offenses Involving Danger to the Person
Article 210. Criminal Homicide

Section 210.1   Criminal Homicide

(1) A person is guilty of criminal homicide if he purposely, knowingly, recklessly or negligently causes the death of another human being.

(2) Criminal homicide is murder, manslaughter or negligent homicide.

---

[2]532 F.2d 697 (9th Cir. 1976).
[3]Id. at 704.

Section 210.2   Murder

(1) Except as provided in Section 210.3(1)(b), criminal homicide constitutes murder when

(a) it is committed purposely or knowingly; or

(b) it is committed recklessly under circumstances manifesting extreme indifference to the value of human life. Such recklessness and indifference are presumed if the actor is engaged or is an accomplice in the commission of, or an attempt to commit, or flight after committing or attempting to commit robbery, rape or deviate sexual intercourse by force or threat of force, arson, burglary, kidnapping or felonious escape.

Section 210.3   Manslaughter

(1) Criminal homicide constitutes manslaughter when:

(a) it is committed recklessly; or

(b) a homicide which would otherwise be murder is committed under the influence of extreme mental or emotional disturbance for which there is reasonable explanation or excuse. The reasonableness of such explanation or excuse shall be determined from the viewpoint of a person in the actor's situation under the circumstances as he believes them to be.

(2) Manslaughter is a felony of the second degree.

Section 210.4   Negligent Homicide

(1) Criminal homicide constitutes negligent homicide when it is committed negligently.

(2) Negligent homicide is a felony of the third degree.

Section 210.5   Causing or Aiding Suicide

(1) A person may be convicted of criminal homicide for causing another to commit suicide only if he purposely causes such suicide by force, duress or deception.

(2) A person who purposely aids or solicits another to commit suicide is guilty of a felony of the second degree if his conduct causes such suicide or an attempted suicide, and otherwise of a misdemeanor.

As you might suspect, without a direct statement from the defendant that explains what he or she was thinking at the time of the incident, proving mental state is a difficult task. However, as we saw in *Smallwood v. State*, the law assumes that people know the probable consequences of their acts. A person who strikes another may be presumed to have intended the infliction of harm in that such a result naturally flows from hitting another. Also, during a criminal trial the judge or the jury is allowed to draw **inferences**. After looking at the facts of the case presented during the trial, including any statements and actions of the defendant and other prosecution or defense witnesses, the jury is allowed to reach a conclusion about the defendant's intent and to draw an inference about the defendant's state of mind, as well as what most likely occurred. For example, in *Commonwealth v. Gilbert*[4] a man was charged with having murdered his roommate by beating her with his cane. He told the police that she had died from an overdose of painkillers. Based on the testimony that the victim had been beaten, that there were no traces of any painkillers found during the autopsy, that the victim and the defendant had been having difficulties, and that the defendant was the only individual in the apartment at the time of the victim's death, the court held that it was reasonable for the jury to conclude he had deliberately premeditated his roommate's death and hence was guilty of first-degree murder.

Inference
A conclusion reached based on the facts given.

---

[4]673 N.E.2d 46 (Mass. 1996).

Every state defines murder and manslaughter in slightly different ways. For example, in California murder is defined as an unlawful killing with malice aforethought.[5] Malice can be shown through a deliberate intention to kill or can be implied when "the circumstances attending the killing show an abandoned and malignant heart."[6] In contrast, voluntary manslaughter occurs when the actions that cause the death occur because of the failure to use "due caution and circumspection."[7]

A controversial application of these statutes occurred in the 2002 California conviction of Marjorie Knoller. The jury surprised many legal commentators by finding the defendant guilty of second degree murder after her two dogs killed a neighbor in the hallway of their San Francisco apartment building.[8] The jury concluded that Ms. Knoller had acted recklessly in not properly restraining the dogs when she knew them to be vicious and dangerous. In gaining its conviction, the state had presented evidence that the dogs had been bred to fight and that they had not been properly trained to be around people. Through witness testimony the state established that Ms. Knoller had failed to restrain the dogs properly even though there had been more than thirty prior incidents in which the dogs had lunged at or otherwise shown overly aggressive behavior toward other people. In addition to her being found guilty of murder, Ms. Knoller was also convicted of involuntary manslaughter and owning a mischievous animal that caused a death.

On the day Ms. Knoller was to be sentenced, however, the trial court judge reversed the jury's verdict on the second-degree murder count by granting the defendant's motion for a new trial. Although the judge thought Knoller's actions were "despicable," he did not think that her mental state was sufficient to satisfy the murder statute's requirement for malice. The judge stated, "I cannot say as a matter of law that she subjectively knew on January 26 that her conduct would cause death."[9]

4. Parties to the Crime

When more than one person commits a crime, the perpetrators may be classified as principals, accomplices, or accessories. The person who commits a criminal act is a **principal** in the first degree. A principal in the second degree, also referred to as an **accomplice**, assists the principal in the first degree during the commission of the crime. That person could literally be standing next to the principal in the first degree or be waiting close by, for example, in a get-away car. An **accessory** is someone who assisted in the preparation of the crime but was not present during the crime. An accessory can also be referred to as an accomplice. The MPC defines *accomplice* in the context of when a person should be held accountable for the conduct of another:

Principal
The person who commits the crime.

Accomplice
Also known as a **principal in the second degree**; a person who assists the principal with the crime or with the preparation of the crime.

Section 2.06   Liability for Conduct of Another; Complicity
> (2) A person is legally accountable for the conduct of another person when: . . .
>> (c) he is an accomplice of such other person in the commission of the offense.

---

[5]Cal. Pen. Code § 187.

[6]Cal. Pen. Code § 188.

[7]Cal. Pen. Code § 192.

[8]"Dogs' keepers guilty in mauling," USA Today, Friday, March 22, 2002, p. 3A.

[9]"Dog-Mauling Murder Conviction Overturned," abcNews.com, June 17, 2002.

(3) A person is an accomplice of another person in the commission of an offense if:

   (a) with the purpose of promoting or facilitating the commission of the offense, he

     (i) solicits such other person to commit it; or

     (ii) aids or agrees or attempts to aid such other person in planning or committing it; or

     (iii) having a legal duty to prevent the commission of the offense, fails to make proper effort so to do. . . .

(6) Unless otherwise provided by the Code or by the law defining the offense, a person is not an accomplice in an offense committed by another person if: . . .

   (c) he terminates his complicity prior to the commission of the offense and

     (i) wholly deprives it of effectiveness in the commission of the offense; or

     (ii) gives timely warning to the law enforcement authorities or otherwise makes proper effort to prevent the commission of the offense.

Finally, an **accessory after the fact** is someone who aided the principal after the commission of the crime. When it comes to punishment, principals of any degree and accessories are all treated the same. Accessories after the fact are not punished as severely as are principals and accomplices.

Legal Reasoning Exercises

2. Apply the Model Penal Code, Article 210, Criminal Homicide, to each of the following situations. What crimes, if any, have been committed?

a. Sam, a hired assassin, pulls out a gun and points it at Mary's head. He pulls the trigger, the bullet strikes Mary in the temple, and she is killed instantly.

b. Janet, to protest what she views as the increasing decadence of modern society, leaves a bomb in an empty adult movie theater. Later that night the bomb goes off and kills the janitor, who was there cleaning the theater.

c. Rita accompanies John while he robs a store owner at gunpoint. The gun goes off, and the owner is killed by the gunshot.

d. Five boys are playing a game of "chicken" in which they pass a partially loaded gun (one of the six chambers contains a live bullet) around the circle. Each player takes a turn spinning the cylinder, pointing the gun at his head, and pulling the trigger. When Dan takes his turn, the gun goes off, and he dies instantly.

3. Your firm represents Jimmy Jones. He and his best friend, Bobby Smith, are both twenty-year-old high school dropouts. They have held several part-time jobs in the past but are currently unemployed.

Last Saturday night Jimmy and Bobby, along with their friend Doris, were restless with nothing to do. Bobby then had a brainstorm, and what started out as a frolic has since ended in a nightmare for Jimmy.

For "fun" and money the three decided to hold up the local 7-11 store. Doris volunteered the information that the only person on duty at that time of night would be an elderly gentleman who would give them no trouble. Shortly before leaving for the store Doris had a change of heart and told the other two that she would not be coming along.

Neither Jimmy nor Bobby owns a gun. Unbeknown to Jimmy, Bobby decided to take along his kid brother's very realistic looking water pistol. When they got to the store, no customers were present. Jimmy and Bobby went up to the counter and demanded that the clerk hand over the money in the cash register. When the clerk simply stared at them, Bobby pulled out the water pistol, which had been concealed under his jacket. He said, "Hand over the money, old man, or I'll spray you with acid." Actually, the gun only had water in it. The clerk, who was an elderly, overweight man, began to perspire and shake. He placed the money on the counter. Then he suddenly clutched his chest and fell to the floor. Bobby grabbed the money and ran from the store.

Although very frightened by the turn of events Jimmy decided to stay and try to help the clerk. He called the police, telling them to send an ambulance right away. When the police arrived, Jimmy turned himself in. Unfortunately on his way to the hospital the store clerk died.

    a. With what crimes do you think Bobby could be charged?

    b. What would be the major weaknesses in the prosecution's case?

    c. Do you think Doris could be convicted of any crimes? If so, which ones?

    d. What about Jimmy?

4. Apply the Model Penal Code, Article 210, Criminal Homicide, to the following situations. Have any homicide crimes been committed?

Last summer Willie Albano stabbed and killed Roberto Basso during an argument outside of a convenience store. Willie was apprehended by police only ten minutes later and one block away from the scene. A knife, the alleged murder weapon, was recovered at the scene and only the defendant's fingerprints were on it.

Two months later the victim's parents, Peter and Maria Basso, and their only other child, Michael, attended a pretrial hearing. At the hearing the Bassos discovered that the police department had lost the knife, and the judge agreed to dismiss all charges against Willie Albano. The defendant turned toward the family and smiled. He slowly walked toward the Bassos, leaned over them, and said, "Too bad. Better luck next time—after I kill your other son." To Michael he said, "Watch out, buddy. You're next."

    a. Mr. Basso jumped from his courtroom seat and grabbed the defendant's neck with a force so great that they both fell to the floor. A few seconds later Willie Albano was dead from a broken neck and other injuries inflicted by Mr. Basso.

    b. After Willie's comments Mr. Basso walked next to Willie out of the courtroom. Once outside the building Mr. Basso grabbed Willie by the neck and strangled him.

    c. Mr. Basso stayed in his seat as Willie walked past. When Willie exited the courtroom, Mr. Basso was waiting with a loaded pistol he had stolen from an unsuspecting guard. He aimed the gun at Willie but shot and killed the prosecutor, who was standing near Willie.

d. Mr. Basso waited in his seat until Willie left the courthouse, and then he brought his family home. The next day he purchased a rifle from the local sporting goods store. Later that day he waited outside of Willie's apartment, and when Willie returned, Mr. Basso called out, "You'll never touch anyone in my family again." He then pulled the trigger and killed Willie.

e. Three days after the hearing Mr. Basso waited with his shotgun outside Willie's apartment for several hours. While he was waiting, Mr. Basso drank six cans of beer and two small bottles of whisky. Finally giving up on his plan, Mr. Basso sped away from the apartment. He failed to notice a stop sign and killed a pedestrian with his car. The pedestrian was Willie Albano.

f. Mr. Basso arrived at Willie's apartment and forced his way inside. While he held a gun to Willie's head, Willie slit his own wrists with a kitchen knife. Willie died from those wounds six hours later.

5. Defenses

Although most people accused of crimes eventually agree to plead guilty to either the crime with which they were originally charged or to some lesser offense, many still go to court, asserting either that they did not do whatever it is they are accused of doing or that their actions were justified under the law.

If believed by the judge or jury, some defenses are **complete defenses** to a crime, and the defendant will be found not guilty. **Partial defenses** may reduce a crime to a lesser included offense.

In this section we will briefly discuss the alibi defense, status defenses (including infancy, insanity, and intoxication), duress and necessity, entrapment, reactive defenses, statutes of limitations, and constitutional defenses.

a. Alibi Defense

An **alibi defense** is one in which the defense attempts to show that the defendant could not have committed the crime because the defendant was in a specified place at a specific time that would make it impossible for him or her to have committed the crime. For example, if four witnesses testify that they were playing poker with the defendant at a home on the east side of town, then the defendant could not have been the person who robbed a liquor store on the west side of town at that time.

b. Ignorance or Mistake

We have all heard that ignorance of the law is no excuse. Generally, that is true. On the other hand, ignorance or mistake as to facts can form the basis for a defense if it can be shown that the defendant's ignorance or mistake negated the requisite mens rea. For example, if you left a classroom with

Complete defense
A defense that, if proven, relieves the defendant of all criminal responsibility.

Partial defense
A defense that reduces a crime to a lesser included offense.

Alibi defense
A defense requiring proof that the defendant could not have been at the scene of the crime.

a classmate's textbook, thinking it was your own, you would be mistaken as to the fact of ownership. Therefore, you could not be prosecuted for theft, as you did not have the required mens rea, the intent to steal the property of another.

The Model Penal Code places the following conditions on the use of the defense of ignorance or mistake:

> **Section 2.04   Ignorance or Mistake**
>   (1) Ignorance or mistake as to the matter of fact or law is a defense if:
>   (a) the ignorance or mistake negatives the purpose, knowledge, belief, recklessness or negligence required to establish a material element of the offense. . . .
>   (3) A belief that conduct does not legally constitute an offense is a defense to a prosecution for that offense based upon such conduct when:
>   (a) the statute or other enactment defining the offense is not known to the actor and has not been published or otherwise reasonably made available prior to the conduct alleged; or
>   (b) he acts in reasonable reliance upon an official statement of the law, afterward determined to be invalid or erroneous. . . .

c. Status: Infancy, Insanity, and Intoxication

The defenses in this group all involve excusing people from the criminal consequences of their actions because their status or condition renders them incapable of formulating the required element of mens rea.

Under the common law, children under the age of seven were conclusively presumed to be incapable of forming criminal intent, while there was a rebuttable presumption that those between the ages of seven and fourteen were not capable of forming such intent. The juvenile court system was created to provide a noncriminal alternative for processing juveniles who are accused of acts that are considered crimes if they are committed by adults. In recent years, however, especially with the increase in violent, gang-related crimes, there has been a movement to waive juvenile court jurisdiction and apply adult standards to the prosecution of these juvenile offenders.

As noted above, the **insanity defense** is based on the assertion that the defendant was incapable of formulating the required element of mens rea. In addition, many people believe that it is not appropriate to punish someone for actions over which the individual had no control. While most jurisdictions have the insanity defense available to criminal defendants, there is disagreement among the states and the federal circuits about the standard that should be used to determine insanity. The three alternative standards are the M'Naghten test, the irresistible impulse test, and the Model Penal Code Substantial capacity test. These tests are summarized in Figure 15-2.

The oldest of the standards, the **M'Naghten test**, originated in the 1840s in an English case where Daniel M'Naghten was tried for killing the secretary to the prime minister of England. M'Naghten mistook the secretary for the prime minister, whom M'Naghten thought to be engaged in a plot to kill him. The court found M'Naghten not guilty due to insanity because, at the time of the killing, he suffered from a defect or disease of the mind and could not understand whether the act was right or wrong. This test, or standard, is commonly known as either

Insanity defense
A defense requiring proof that the defendant was not mentally responsible.

M'Naghten test
A test that provides that the defendant is not guilty due to insanity if, at the time of the killing, the defendant suffered from a defect or disease of the mind and could not understand whether the act was right or wrong.

**P R A C T I C A L
T I P**

Jurisdictions differ greatly on how children should be treated when they commit acts that would be crimes if committed by adults.

M'Naghten or "Right from Wrong" Test

"[T]o establish insanity sufficient to relieve the defendant of guilt, it must be proved that, at the time of the commission of the act, the defendant was laboring under such a defect of reason, from disease of the mind as not to know the nature and quality of the act he was doing, or if he did know it, that he did not know that what he was doing was wrong." *M'Naghten's Case,* 8 Eng. Rep. 718, 722 (1843).

Irresistible Impulse Test

One is not guilty by reason of insanity if it is determined that the defendant has a mental disease that kept the defendant from controlling his or her conduct.

Substantial Capacity Test (Model Penal Code)

(1) A person is not responsible for criminal conduct if at the time of such conduct, as a result of mental disease or defect, he or she lacks substantial capacity to appreciate the criminality (wrongfulness) of his or her conduct or to conform that conduct to the requirements of law.

(2) The terms *mental disease* and *mental defect* do not include an abnormality manifested only by repeated criminal or otherwise antisocial conduct.

Figure 15-2 Insanity Tests

---

the M'Naghten test (sometimes also spelled McNaughten, M'Naughten, and M'Naughton) or the "right from wrong" test.

Under this test a defendant is not considered guilty of the crime if, at the time of committing the actus reus, the defendant was suffering from a defect or disease of the mind and could not understand whether the act was right or wrong. However, the court did not define what constituted a disease or defect of the mind.

Under the M'Naghten test a defendant will be found sane if he or she knew that a certain action was wrong but could not stop from taking that action. Therefore, some jurisdictions use both the M'Naghten standard and a variation of what is commonly known as the **irresistible impulse test**. With this test the focus is on the defendant's ability to control his or her own actions. If a mental disease robs the individual of control over his or her conduct, the person is not guilty by reason of insanity.

The drafters of the American Law Institute's Model Penal Code developed a third test, which combines elements of the other two. This ALI test is known as the **substantial capacity test**. It requires that the defendant "appreciate," rather than "know," the wrongfulness of his or her actions. Under the two options provided in this test defendants can lack either the ability to understand that their acts were wrong or the ability to control their behavior. Although the complete Model Penal Code has not been widely adopted, this section has been accepted as the test for insanity in a majority of jurisdictions.

Unfortunately, for Andrea Yates, Texas is not one of those states. In 2002 in a highly publicized trial, a jury in Houston, Texas, rejected Andrea Yates's insanity defense. She had drowned her five young children in the bathtub. In a

Irresistible impulse test A test that provides that the defendant is not guilty due to insanity if, at the time of the killing, the defendant could not control his or her actions.

Substantial capacity test Part of the Model Penal Code; a test that provides that the defendant is not guilty due to insanity if, at the time of the killing, the defendant lacked either the ability to understand that the act was wrong or the ability to control the behavior.

three-week-long trial, psychiatrists, relatives, and friends testified that Yates suffered from severe post-partum depression and that she heard voices telling her to kill her children in order to "save them from Satan."[10] However, Texas law follows the M'Naghten test that requires a showing that the defendant did not know right from wrong at the time of the crime. The prosecution argued, and the jury apparently accepted, that Yates's prompt action in reporting the drowning to the police established that she did know that what she had done was wrong.

The following case illustrates the role of both jurors and psychiatrists in determining insanity. In this appellate court opinion Justice Schauer explains why the court upholds a jury finding that the defendant was sane even though four psychiatrists testified at the trial that he suffered from "schizophrenia" and was therefore insane at the time he murdered his mother.

People v. Wolff
61 Cal. 2d 795, 394 P.2d 959, 40 Cal. Rptr. 271 (1964)

SCHAUER, Justice.

Defendant appeals from a judgment imposing a sentence of life imprisonment (with recommendation that he be placed in a hospital for the criminally insane) after he pleaded not guilty by reason of insanity to a charge of murder, the jury found that he was legally sane at the time of the commission of the offense, and the court determined the killing to be murder in the first degree. . . .

The defendant, a 15-year-old boy at the time of the crime, was charged with the murder of his mother. The juvenile court found him to be "not a fit subject for consideration" under the Juvenile Court Law, and remanded him to the superior court for further proceedings in the criminal action. . . .

The California M'Naughton Rule

On the issue of insanity the jury were instructed in terms of the California rule; i.e., the so-called M'Naughton rule as that rule has been developed by statute and decision in California. . . . "The test of sanity is this: First, did the defendant have sufficient mental capacity to know *and understand* what he was doing, and

second, did he know *and understand* that it was wrong *and a violation of the rights of another?* To be sane and thus responsible to the law for the act committed, the defendant must be able to know *and understand* the nature and quality of his act *and* to distinguish between right and wrong at the time of the commission of the offense." (Italics added.) . . .

The Sufficiency of the Evidence of Sanity

Turning now to defendant's more specific contentions, it is first urged that "As a matter of law, [defendant] was legally insane at the time of the commission of the offense." In support of this proposition defendant stresses the fact that each of the four psychiatrists who testified at the trial stated (1) that in his medical opinion defendant suffers from a permanent form of one of the group of mental disorders generically known as "schizophrenia" and (2) that defendant was also legally insane at the time he murdered his mother. . . .

However impressive this seeming unanimity of expert opinion may at first appear, . . . our inquiry on this just as on other factual issues is necessarily limited at the appellate level to a

---

[10]"Jury to Decide Yates' Sentence," USA Today, March 14, 2002, p. 3A.

determination whether there is substantial evidence in the record to support the jury's verdict of sanity ... under the law of this state. ...

Conduct of Defendant as Evidence of Legal Sanity

[T]here was evidence that in the year preceding the commission of the crime defendant "spent a lot of time thinking about sex." He made a list of the names and addresses of seven girls in his community whom he did not know personally but whom he planned to anesthetize and then either rape or photograph nude. One night about three weeks before the murder he took a container of ether and attempted to enter the home of one of these girls through the chimney, but he became wedged in and had to be rescued. In the ensuing weeks defendant apparently deliberated on ways and means of accomplishing his objective and decided that he would have to bring the girls to his house to achieve his sexual purposes, and that it would therefore be necessary to get his mother (and possibly his brother) out of the way first.

The attack on defendant's mother took place on Monday, May 15, 1961. On the preceding Friday or Saturday defendant obtained an axe handle from the family garage and hid it under the mattress of his bed. At about 10 P.M. on Sunday he took the axe handle from its hiding place and approached his mother from behind, raising the weapon to strike her. She sensed his presence and asked him what he was doing; he answered that it was "nothing," and returned to his room and hid the handle under his mattress again. The following morning defendant ... ate the breakfast that his mother prepared, then went to his room and obtained the axe handle from under the mattress. He returned to the kitchen, approached his mother from behind and struck her on the back of the head. She turned around screaming and he struck her several more blows. They fell to the floor, fighting. She called out her neighbor's name and defendant began choking her. She bit him on the hand and crawled away. He got up to turn off the water running in the sink, and she fled through the dining room. He gave chase, caught her in the front room, and choked her to death with his hands. Defendant then took off his shirt and hung it by the fire, washed the blood off his face and hands, read a few lines from a Bible or prayer book lying upon the dining room table, and walked down to the police station to turn himself in. Defendant told the desk officer, "I have something I wish to report. ... I just killed my mother with an axe handle." The officer testified that defendant spoke in a quiet voice and that "His conversation was quite coherent in what he was saying and he answered everything I asked him right to a T."

Defendant's counsel repeatedly characterizes as "bizarre" defendant's plan to rape or photograph nude the seven girls on his list. Certainly in common parlance it may be termed "bizarre"; likewise to a mature person of good morals, it would appear highly unreasonable. But many a youth has committed—or planned—acts which were bizarre and unreasonable. This defendant was immature and lacked experience and judgment in sexual matters. But it does not follow therfrom that the jury were precluded as a matter of law from finding defendant legally sane at the time of the murder. From the evidence set forth hereinabove the jury could infer that defendant had a motive for his actions (gratification of his sexual desires), that he planned the attack on his mother for some time (obtaining the axe handle from the garage several days in advance; abortive attempt to strike his mother with it on the evening before the crime), that he knew that what he was doing was wrong (initial concealment of the handle underneath his mattress; excuse offered when his mother saw him with the weapon on the evening before the crime; renewed concealment of the handle under the mattress), that he persisted in the fatal attack (pursuit of his fleeing mother into the front room; actual infliction of death by strangling rather than bludgeoning), that he was conscious of having committed a crime (prompt surrender to the police), and that he was calm and coherent (testimony of desk officer and others). ...

It is contended that the foregoing evidence of defendant's conduct and declarations is equally consistent with the type of mental illness (i.e., a form of "schizophrenia") from which, according to the psychiatric witnesses, defendant is said to be suffering. But this consistency establishes only that defendant is suffering from the diagnosed mental illness—a point that the prosecution readily concedes; it does not compel the conclusion that on the very different issue of legal sanity the evidence is insufficient as a matter of law to support the verdict. To hold otherwise would be in effect to substitute a trial by "experts" for a trial by jury, for it would require that the jurors accept the psychiatric testimony as conclusive on an issue—the legal sanity of the defendant—which under our present law is exclusively within the province of the trier of fact to determine. . . . [T]he evidence adequately supports the jury's verdict. . . .

Case Discussion Questions

1. Why did the *Wolff* court refuse to accept the testimony of the experts regarding the defendant's sanity? Do you agree that there should be a difference between the legal and the medical definitions of insanity? Why?

2. Do you think the result would have been different in this case if the court had been following the standard for insanity set out in the Model Penal Code?

A successful insanity defense results in a "not guilty" verdict, which relieves the defendant from any criminal responsibility. The defendant can then be set free or be committed to a mental health facility for treatment. Then, if and when the defendant is no longer considered to be insane, he or she will be released back into society. In recent years some states have adopted a "guilty, but mentally ill" verdict. The defendant who receives this verdict is considered guilty, sentenced to a prison term, and then sent to a health facility or hospital. If the defendant completes the treatment, he or she is then sent to prison to serve whatever time remains on the criminal sentence.

Even if a defendant was sane at the time the crime was committed, he or she can be considered legally incompetent at the time of trial. If a defendant cannot understand the legal process or assist in his or her own defense by, for example, talking about the case with the attorney or testifying meaningfully at trial, the defendant may not be tried and therefore may not be found guilty.

Intoxication defense
A defense requiring proof that the defendant was not able to form the requisite mens rea due to intoxication.

The third defense of this type is the **intoxication defense**. In some jurisdictions and under some circumstances, being under the influence of drugs or alcohol is considered a valid defense. Here the argument is that the intoxicating substance interfered with the defendant's ability to form the required mens rea. Although intoxication cannot be used as a defense for charges involving reckless behavior (such as drunk driving or criminal damage to property), it can generally be used as a defense for crimes requiring a specific intent, such as murder.

Discussion Questions

4. If children engage in criminal behavior, how old do you think they should be before being treated the same as adult criminals? Do you think that answer should change based on the crime committed?

5. Why do you think we have not been able to settle on one definition of legal insanity?

6. Do you think anyone should ever be found not guilty on the basis of insanity? If so, under what circumstances?

Legal Reasoning Exercise

5. Working as a member of the defense team, apply each of the three tests for insanity to determine whether this defendant might succeed with an insanity defense.

Emanuel Jones had been on medication for several years to stop the voices he heard in his head. He recently stopped taking his medication because it made him feel sleepy. Five days ago, during a visit with his best friend, Sam, Emanuel became angry and confused. He attacked Sam with a golf club and chased him from room to room as he tried to escape. He hit Sam several times with the golf club, and Sam died as the result of the wounds he sustained.

a. Emanuel walked out of the house and stopped at a nearby restaurant for a hamburger. When the waiter asked him how Sam was, Emanuel replied that he thought Sam was at home sleeping.

b. Before leaving the house Emanuel put the golf club and his bloody clothes in the bath tub and filled the tub with water. He changed his clothes and ran home.

c. When the police questioned Emanuel the next day and asked him about Sam, he replied, "I killed him. He'll be back tomorrow."

d. When the police questioned Emanuel the next day and asked him about Sam, he replied, "I killed him. I tried to stop, but he just kept laughing at me."

e. Several weeks after the incident and his return to his medication Emanuel expressed great grief and guilt over the death of Sam.

Consider the same facts as a member of the prosecution team. Do you come to the same conclusions?

d. Duress and Necessity

Because one of the fundamental principles of criminal law is that criminal behavior must be the result of a voluntary act, the law recognizes both duress and necessity as legitimate defenses. If a defendant can establish that the criminal act was committed because he or she was forced to carry it out, that individual is not held accountable for the criminal act.

Section 2.09 of the Model Penal Code defines *duress* as coercion through "the use of, or a threat to use, unlawful force against his person or the person of another, which a person of reasonable firmness in his situation would have been unable to resist." Therefore, if someone held a gun to your head and forced you to commit a criminal act, you would be entitled to use the defense of **duress**.

To assert this defense, you must prove that you reasonably believed that you were threatened with your death, the death of another person, or serious injury to yourself or others unless you committed the crime. In a highly publicized case in the mid-seventies Patty Hearst, the daughter of a millionaire newspaper publisher, was placed on trial for bank robbery. Approximately a

Duress
A defense requiring proof that force or a threat of force was used to cause a person to commit a criminal act.

year before the robbery took place she had been kidnapped by a radical group calling itself the Symbionese Liberation Army. When members of this same group robbed a bank, Ms. Hearst appeared to be a willing participant. At her trial, attorney F. Lee Bailey argued that Ms. Hearst had been "brainwashed" by her Symbionese Liberation Army kidnappers and had been coerced into participating in the robbery. The state countered with evidence that showed that Ms. Hearst had passed up opportunities to flee and call police and argued that this showed she was a willing participant who was acting voluntarily. The jury agreed with the prosecution and convicted her of armed robbery.

Necessity
A defense requiring proof that the defendant was forced to take an action to avoid a greater harm.

The **necessity** defense is similar to the duress defense except the force is exerted by nature rather than by another person. For example, you may be forced to trespass across a neighbor's yard to escape a fire in your home. In addition, this defense may be used in a more general way to exonerate otherwise criminal conduct when a person believes that such conduct is necessary to avoid a greater injury. An example would be where a motorist chooses to crash an automobile into a building in order to avoid hitting a child who runs into the street.

e. Entrapment

Entrapment
A defense requiring proof that the defendant would not have committed the crime but for police trickery.

The defense of **entrapment** arises when a defendant believes that he or she was tricked or led to commit a crime by a law enforcement agency when the defendant would not have committed the crime without the government's enticement. It is not entrapment if the government agents provide a person with the opportunity to commit a crime that he or she was already contemplating. The key is whether the defendant had a predisposition to commit the crime before the government agents contacted the person.

f. Reactive Defenses

This category includes defenses such as self-defense and the use of force in law enforcement. As to **self-defense**, individuals are allowed to use force in defending themselves or others and in defending their dwellings and other property. There is significant variation among the states as to the amount of force that can be used and the circumstances under which one is required to retreat when that is a viable option.

Self-defense
The justified use of force to protect oneself or others.

Generally, however, this right to use force is valid only as long as the following conditions are met. First, the person claiming self-defense must not have been the initiator of the violence. Second, the threat of bodily harm must be immediate. Third, once the threatening party ceases the threatening behavior, the right to self-defense disappears. Fourth, the amount of force used must be no more than is reasonably necessary to repel the attack. **Deadly force**, a force that would cause serious bodily injury or death, can be used only when the danger faced includes fear of serious bodily injury or death.

Deadly force
A force that would cause serious bodily injury or death.

In the mid-1980s a man named Bernhard Goetz made headlines when he took out a gun and shot four youths who had been attempting to rob him while on a subway in New York City. In the following excerpts from an appellate court decision in this case, the court reviews the facts of the case and the New York law on self-defense.

People v. Goetz
68 N.Y.2d 96, 497 N.E.2d 41, 506 N.Y.S.2d 18 (1986)

Chief Judge WACHTLER.

A Grand Jury has indicted defendant on attempted murder, assault, and other charges for having shot and wounded four youths on a New York City subway train after one or two of the youths approached him and asked for $5. The lower courts, concluding that the prosecutor's charge to the Grand Jury on the defense of justification was erroneous, have dismissed the attempted murder, assault and weapons possession charges. We now reverse and reinstate all counts of the indictment.

I. . . .

On Saturday afternoon, December 22, 1984, Troy Canty, Darryl Cabey, James Ramseur, and Barry Allen boarded an IRT express subway train in The Bronx and headed south toward lower Manhattan. The four youths rode together in the rear portion of the seventh car of the train. Two of the four, Ramseur and Cabey, had screwdrivers inside their coats, which they said were to be used to break into the coin boxes of video machines.

Defendant Bernhard Goetz boarded this subway train at 14th Street in Manhattan and sat down on a bench towards the rear section of the same car occupied by the four youths. Goetz was carrying an unlicensed .38 caliber pistol loaded with five rounds of ammunition in a waistband holster. The train left the 14th Street station and headed towards Chambers Street. . . .

According to Goetz's statement, the first contact he had with the four youths came when Canty, sitting or lying on the bench across from him, asked "how are you," to which he replied "fine." Shortly thereafter, Canty, followed by one of the other youths, walked over to the defendant and stood to his left, while the other two youths remained to his right, in the corner of the subway car. Canty then said "give me five dollars." Goetz stated that he knew from the smile on Canty's face that they wanted to "play with me." Although he was certain that none of the youths had a gun, he had a fear, based on prior experiences, of being "maimed."

Goetz then established "a pattern of fire," deciding specifically to fire from left to right. His stated intention at that point was to "murder [the four youths], to hurt them, to make them suffer as much as possible." When Canty again requested money, Goetz stood up, drew his weapon, and began firing, aiming for the center of the body of each of the four. Goetz recalled that the first two he shot "tried to run through the crowd [but] they had nowhere to run." Goetz then turned to his right to "go after the other two." One of these two "tried to run through the wall of the train, but . . . he had nowhere to go." The other youth (Cabey) "tried pretending that he wasn't with [the others]" by standing still, holding on to one of the subway hand straps, and not looking at Goetz. Goetz nonetheless fired his fourth shot at him. He then ran back to the first two youths to make sure they had been "taken care of." Seeing that they had both been shot, he spun back to check on the latter two. Goetz noticed that the youth who had been standing still was now sitting on a bench and seemed unhurt. As Goetz told the police, "I said '[you] seem to be all right, here's another,'" and he then fired the shot which severed Cabey's spinal cord. Goetz added that "if I was a little more under self-control . . . I would have put the barrel against his forehead and fired." He also admitted that "if I had had more [bullets], I would have shot them again, and again, and again." . . .

III.

Penal Law article 35 recognizes the defense of justification, which "permits the use of force under certain circumstances." One such set of circumstances pertains to the use of force in defense of a person, encompassing both self-defense and defense of a third person. Penal Law § 35.15(1) sets forth the general principles governing all such uses of force: "[a] person may . . . use physical force upon another person when and to the extent he *reasonably believes* such to be necessary to defend himself or a third person from what he *reasonably believes* to be the use or imminent use of unlawful physical force by such other person" (emphasis added).

Section 35.15(2) sets forth further limitations on these general principles with respect to the use of "deadly physical force": "A person may not use deadly physical force upon another person under circumstances specified in subdivision one unless (a) He *reasonably believes* that such other person is using or about to use deadly physical force . . . or (b) He *reasonably believes* that such other person is committing or attempting to commit a kidnapping, forcible rape, forcible sodomy or robbery" (emphasis added).

Because the evidence before the second Grand Jury included statements by Goetz that he acted to protect himself from being maimed or to avert a robbery, the prosecutor . . . properly instructed the grand jurors to consider whether the use of deadly physical force was justified to prevent either serious physical injury or a robbery, and, in doing so, to separately analyze the defense with respect to each of the charges. . . .

As expressed repeatedly in the Appellate Division's plurality opinion, because section 35.15 uses the term "he reasonably believes," the appropriate test, according to that court, is whether a defendant's beliefs and reactions were "reasonable to him." Under that reading of the statute, a jury which believed a defendant's testimony that he felt that his own actions were warranted and were reasonable would have to acquit him, regardless of what anyone else in defendant's situation might have concluded. Such an interpretation defies the ordinary meaning and significance of the term "reasonably" in a statute, and misconstrues the clear intent of the Legislature, in enacting section 35.15, to retain an objective element as part of any provision authorizing the use of deadly physical force.

Penal statutes in New York have long codified the right recognized at common law to use deadly physical force, under appropriate circumstances, in self-defense. These provisions have never required that an actor's belief as to the intention of another person to inflict serious injury be correct in order for the use of deadly force to be justified, but they have uniformly required that the belief comport with an objective notion of reasonableness. . . .

In 1961 the Legislature established a Commission to undertake a complete revision of the Penal Law and the Criminal Code. The impetus for the decision to update the Penal Law came in part from the drafting of the Model Penal Code by the American Law Institute, as well as from the fact that the existing law was poorly organized and in many aspects antiquated. . . . While using the Model Penal Code provisions on justification as general guidelines, however, the drafters of the new Penal Law did not simply adopt them verbatim.

The provisions of the Model Penal Code with respect to the use of deadly force in self-defense reflect the position of its drafters that any culpability which arises from a mistaken belief in the need to use such force should be no greater than the culpability such a mistake would give rise to if it were made with respect to an element of a crime. Accordingly, under Model Penal Code § 3.04(2)(b), a defendant charged with murder (or attempted murder) need only show that he "[*believed*] that [the use of deadly force] was necessary to protect himself against death, serious bodily injury, kidnapping or [forcible] sexual intercourse" to prevail on a self-defense claim (emphasis added). If the defendant's belief was wrong, and was recklessly, or negligently formed, however, he may be convicted of the type of homicide charge requiring only a reckless or negligent, as the case may be, criminal intent. . . .

New York did not follow the Model Penal Code's equation of a mistake as to the need to use deadly force with a mistake negating an element of a crime, choosing instead to use a single statutory section which would provide either a complete defense or no defense at all to a defendant charged with any crime involving the use of deadly force. The drafters of the new Penal Law adopted in large part the structure and content of Model Penal Code § 3.04, but, crucially, inserted the word "reasonably" before "believes" . . . .

We cannot lightly impute to the Legislature an intent to fundamentally alter the principles of justification to allow the perpetrator of a serious crime to go free simply because that person believed his actions were reasonable and necessary to prevent some perceived harm. To completely exonerate such an individual, no matter how aberrational or bizarre his thought patterns, would allow citizens to set their own standards for the permissible use of force. It would also allow a legally competent defendant suffering from delusions to kill or perform acts of violence with impunity, contrary to fundamental principles of justice and criminal law.

We can only conclude that the Legislature retained a reasonableness requirement to avoid giving a license for such actions. . . .

Goetz also argues that the introduction of an objective element will preclude a jury from considering factors such as the prior experiences of a given actor and thus, require it to make a determination of "reasonableness" without regard to the actual circumstances of a particular incident. This argument, however, falsely presupposes that an objective standard means that the background and other relevant characteristics of a particular actor must be ignored. To the contrary, we have frequently noted that a determination of reasonableness must be based on the "circumstances" facing a defendant or his "situation." Such terms encompass more than the physical movements of the potential assailant. As just discussed, these terms include any relevant knowledge the defendant had about that person. They also necessarily bring in the physical attributes of all persons involved, including the defendant. Furthermore, the defendant's circumstances encompass any prior experiences he had which could provide a reasonable basis for a belief that another person's intentions were to injure or rob him or that the use of deadly force was necessary under the circumstances. . . .

Accordingly, the order of the Appellate Division should be reversed, and the dismissed counts of the indictment reinstated.

CASE DISCUSSION QUESTIONS

1. The *Goetz* case gives an excellent example of how critical the choice can be as to which standard, objective or subjective, to apply. First, define each standard, and then discuss which standard you think should be applied to similar situations in the future.

2. How does the New York penal law differ from the Model Penal Code on the use of deadly force in self-defense? Which do you think is the better approach?

3. After nearly eight weeks of trial, Goetz was acquitted of attempted murder but convicted of illegal gun possession. If you could read the jurors' minds, what do you think was a determining factor in their verdict?

This right to defend oneself does not extend to all people at all times. In fact, it does not even extend to all people who find themselves in dangerous positions. Most jurisdictions include a **retreat exception** to the right to self-defense. This doctrine of retreat generally requires a person in danger to get away from the danger, or give up possessions, before resorting to the use of deadly force. If the victim can avoid danger but chooses instead to use deadly force, that victim may be prosecuted for any crime committed. Potential victims need not retreat if they are in their own homes or if retreating would create additional danger for them. Potential victims using nondeadly force need not retreat.

Retreat exception
The rule that in order to claim self-defense there must have been no possibility of retreat.

In most jurisdictions the rights and requirements of self-defense can also be applied to a person's right to protect another person. The defense of others permits you to use reasonable force to protect another person if you believe that the threat of bodily harm is immediate and that the amount of force used is reasonable.

You may also act against another person in defense of property. Rarely can deadly force be applied to protect property. Generally, we value human life over property even when the human life in question is trying to steal property. However, the right to self-defense extends inside of the home, and deadly force is still permitted if the home intruder is attempting to do great bodily harm.

Battered woman's or spouse's syndrome. Being the victim of repeated attacks, self-defense is sometimes allowed to the victim, even when the victim is not in immediate danger.

One recent change to the self-defense rule in a few jurisdictions is the addition of the **battered woman's or spouse's syndrome.** This defense allows a person who has been the victim of repeated attacks the right to self-defense even when there may not be immediate danger at the exact moment that the right to self-defense is exercised. Experts believe that, especially for battered women, the fear of immediate harm extends beyond individual episodes of violence and becomes a part of everyday life. Based on that theory, fear of immediate harm is always present. However, not all states have been willing to accept this defense, as the woman's actions usually are not taken in the face of "imminent" death or great bodily harm. The effects of the battered woman's syndrome may be used, however, to reduce the charge from murder to manslaughter.

Finally, it should be noted that law enforcement and military personnel are given special exemptions from the law to take actions that are required as part of their official duties. Soldiers killing enemy soldiers in battle and police officers killing an escaping felon fall under the category of justifiable homicide.

g. Statutes of Limitations and Speedy Trial Acts

Many crimes, like civil actions, are covered by statutes of limitations. Under these statutes the government cannot prosecute an individual after a designated number of years have passed since either the date of the crime or the discovery of the crime. However, there are some crimes, such as murder, for which there usually is no time limit on when charges may be brought.

The Speedy Trial Act of 1974[11] requires that defendants in federal court be brought to trial within one hundred days of their being charged with a crime. Many state legislatures have also set down specific time limits. While defendants usually can waive these time limits if added time is needed to prepare for the trial, prosecutors cannot claim the same privilege. Speedy trial statutes may require that the charges be dismissed if defendants are not brought to trial within a given number of days. Therefore, as is true with statutes of limitations, failure to comply with these dates can become a basis for having the charges dismissed.

h. Constitutional Defenses

A criminal conviction can sometimes be challenged on the grounds that the statute on which the conviction was based was unconstitutional.

---

[11]18 U.S.C. § 3161 (2004).

Once a statute is found to be unconstitutional, a defendant cannot be legally convicted or punished for violating it. The most common constitutional grounds for challenging criminal statutes are that they are vague or overbroad or that they violate the First Amendment protections of freedom of speech and religion.

When the First Amendment protections guaranteeing freedom of religion are used as a basis for challenging a statute, the courts look to whether the state's interest, as evidenced by the statute, is greater than the impediment to religious freedom. For example, the U.S. Supreme Court refused to find unconstitutional a statute prohibiting polygamy, despite an argument from the Mormon defendant that polygamous marriage was part of his religion.[12] However, the Supreme Court did invalidate a city ordinance prohibiting the ritual sacrifice of animals on the grounds that the governmental interest served by the ordinance did not justify targeting religious activity. In that case the Court held that the purpose of the ordinance was to suppress the Santeria religion's central element, animal sacrifice.[13] The First Amendment protection of freedom of speech can also form the basis for a constitutional challenge. For example, you may recall the case of *Texas v. Johnson*,[14] in which the Supreme Court held that a Texas statute prohibiting the burning of an American flag unconstitutionally restricted protected political speech.

The due process clauses of the Fifth and Fourteen Amendments can form the basis for a **void for vagueness** or **overbreadth** argument. For example, the Texas stalking statute made it illegal to engage in conduct that is "reasonably likely to harass, annoy, alarm, abuse, torment, or embarrass" someone. The highest Texas criminal appellate court found the statute to be unconstitutionally vague on its face.[15] Recently the overbreadth argument has been used to challenge city ordinances aimed at stopping gang activity. Such ordinances empower the police to order groups of loiterers to disperse if an officer reasonably believes one of the loiterers is a gang member. Obviously, such ordinances have the potential for abuse and for interfering with lawful activities. Therefore, because they cover both criminal activity and protected activity, these ordinances can be challenged as overbroad.

In cases involving the Fifth Amendment **double jeopardy clause**, defendants challenge the constitutionality of their prosecutions rather than that of the criminal laws under which they are being charged. They argue that they cannot be prosecuted because they have previously been tried for the same offense. Once jeopardy attaches, a defendant cannot be tried for the same offense again. Generally, jeopardy attaches once a jury has been selected. However, the same action can sometimes constitute two different criminal offenses. An act that is prosecuted as a homicide in state court may also be prosecuted as a violation of civil rights in federal court. Furthermore, double jeopardy does not prevent a civil action for damages that arose from the criminal action. Finally, if the defendant appeals a conviction and wins the appeal, the appellate court may remand the case for a new trial.

Void for vagueness
A reason for invalidating a statute where a reasonable person could not determine a statute's meaning.

Overbreadth
A reason for invalidating a statute where it covers both protected and criminal activity.

Double jeopardy
A constitutional protection against being tried twice for the same crime.

---

[12]Reynolds v. United States, 98 U.S. 611 (1878).

[13]Church of Lukumi Babalu Aye, Inc. v. Hialeah, 508 U.S. 520 (1993).

[14]411 U.S. 397 (1989).

[15]Long v. State, 931 S.W.2d 285 (Tex. 1996).

NETNOTE

To read about recent developments and issues involving criminal justice, go to the American Civil Liberties Union site at *www.aclu.org/CriminalJustice/ CriminalJusticeMain.cfm.*

6. Dynamic Change

State legislatures frequently revise our complex system of crimes, defenses, and punishments as they react to specific incidents in our society, such as a particularly gruesome episode of crime or changes in societal opinions about a particular crime. In some instances, such as the nonmedicinal use of alcohol and the use of birth control, statutes have been changed to decriminalize conduct. More often we have added new crimes to cover new concerns.

The most frequent change in criminal statutes, however, usually involves the penalties. As society continues to be afraid of the consequences of crime, many think that if the penalties get stiffer, the incidents of crime may decrease. For example, in Massachusetts several years ago a person who was convicted of driving an automobile while intoxicated only had to pay a fine of not more than $25, no matter how many such offenses that person had committed. In response to the public's growing concern about alcohol-related traffic accidents, the legislature significantly increased the penalties associated with drunk driving. Now, even for a first offense, the defendant who is arrested for operating a motor vehicle under the influence of an alcoholic beverage may face a driver's education program, loss of his or her driver's license for a specified number of days, probation for up to one year, and a fine in excess of $1,500. Subsequent offenses may include a more lengthy, or permanent, loss of license and jail time.

C. CRIMINAL PROCEDURE

Whereas **criminal law** defines for society what behaviors are illegal and determines how lawbreakers should be punished, **criminal procedure** specifies the rules and procedures governing the manner in which alleged criminals are prosecuted and punished. The federal and state rules of criminal procedure are designed to protect the rights of the accused, ensure a just result, and keep the system running smoothly. They cover the actions of law enforcement, the court system, defense attorneys and prosecutors, and the guidelines by which convicted criminals are sentenced.

The U.S. Supreme Court has ruled that state, as well as federal, prosecutions must be consistent with the constitutional protections of the Bill of Rights. Therefore, although approximately 95 percent of criminal prosecutions occur in state courts, the U.S. Constitution has a significant impact on how these prosecutions are conducted.

Figure 15-3 provides an overview of the stages in a criminal prosecution. Be warned, however, that the details of criminal procedure vary greatly among

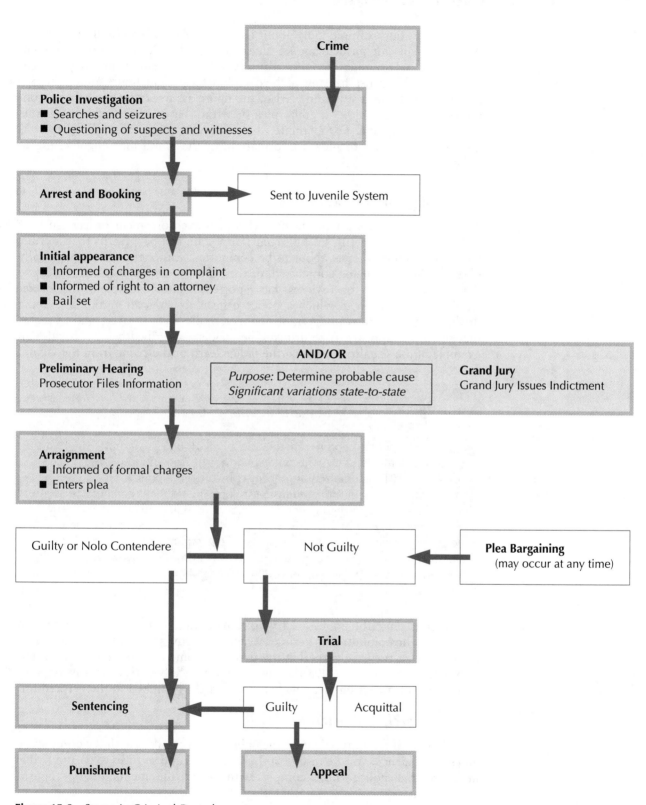

Figure 15-3 Stages in Criminal Procedure

jurisdictions. For example, only about half the states have a grand jury system. Also, especially for misdemeanors, the stages may be accelerated or even combined. The only mandated uniformity is the U.S. Supreme Court requirement that a probable cause hearing be held within forty-eight hours after a person is arrested without a warrant.[16] Also, the figure assumes that the process continues until there is either a guilty plea or a trial. However, the charges can be dropped at any time. For example, the prosecutor might decide that there is insufficient evidence to file an information, or the grand jury might refuse to indict.

1. Investigation of the Crime

The criminal process usually begins when a law enforcement officer (such as a police officer, a sheriff, an FBI agent, or a state trooper) learns that a crime has been committed or is about to be committed. Either the officer personally observes the crime being committed, or the officer is sent to investigate a crime that either the victim or a witness has reported. A good example of the former would be a situation in which a police officer observes an automobile being driven in a dangerous and erratic manner, pulls the car over, and observes that the driver appears to be drunk. The incident described below provides an example of the situation in which the police learn of the crime from the victim.

Stage I: *People v. Grant*

When Stephen Joseph returned home about 10:00 P.M. on April 30, he discovered that the window of his porch door was broken and someone had taken his stereo, VCR, and television. Mr. Joseph called the police.

The police took information from Mr. Joseph, and they searched the scene for additional clues. The next door neighbor, Pat Baker, remembered seeing a van parked in Mr. Joseph's driveway earlier in the evening. According to the neighbor, the van had *Grant's Audiovisual Equipment* written on the side. She saw two men in dark clothes standing at the end of the driveway. When the police finished at the scene, they left the Joseph home.

At this stage the police are trying to determine if a crime was committed and, if so, who committed the crime. When police investigate a crime and search a crime scene, they are gathering the first, and sometimes the most important, information needed to solve the case. They typically interview any possible witnesses and collect physical evidence that might be linked to the perpetrator.

a. *Search and Seizure*

As part of their investigation the police will typically search the crime scene and seize evidence. For the results of those searches and seizures to be admissible in court, the police must comply with the requirements of the Fourth Amendment.

---

[16]County of Riverside v. McLaughlin, 500 U.S. 44 (1991).

Amendment IV

The right of the people to be secure in their persons, houses, papers, and effects, against unreasonable searches and seizures, shall not be violated, and no Warrants shall issue, but upon probable cause, supported by Oath or affirmation, and particularly describing the place to be searched, and the persons or things to be seized.

As you can see, the Fourth Amendment requires that all searches and seizures be "reasonable." There are literally thousands of cases in which the courts have interpreted whether certain types of searches or seizures were "reasonable."

(1) Stop and frisk

If the police suspect criminal behavior, they are entitled to **stop** (detain) an individual for a brief period of time, to ask a few questions, and to **frisk** (pat down the outside of a suspect's clothes). The origin of this right dates back to 1963, when an Ohio police officer thought that a group of individuals was hanging around a street corner to plan a "stick-up." The officer asked the men to identify themselves. Then the officer patted down the men's clothing. The officer uncovered two guns. After one of the men was convicted of carrying a concealed weapon, he appealed to the U.S. Supreme Court. In *Terry v. Ohio*[17] the Supreme Court declared that the officer's stop and frisk was a search and seizure covered by the Fourth Amendment of the Constitution, giving the people the right "to be secure in their persons, houses, papers and effects, against unreasonable searches and seizures." However, because the intrusion into the person's privacy was slight, there was no Fourth Amendment violation.

But as suggested above the police cannot stop and frisk any individual they want at any time they want. An individual may be stopped only when the officer has a **reasonable suspicion** that the individual has committed, is in the process of committing, or is about to commit a crime. According to *Terry*, that reasonable suspicion must be based on "specific and articulable facts which, taken together with rational inferences from those facts, reasonably warrant that intrusion."[18]

If such a reasonable suspicion exists, however, the police can stop, "frisk," and ask individuals to identify themselves. But what if those individuals do not wish to identify themselves? A decade after the *Terry* decision, the Court held that if the police officer was not involved in a lawful "Terry stop," that is, if the police officer did not have reasonable suspicion of criminal activity, and the individuals refused to identify themselves, the police officer could not arrest them for remaining silent.[19] But what if the police officer was engaged in a lawful "Terry stop"? It was only recently in *Hiibel v. Nevada*[20] that the Supreme Court answered that question.

A Nevada police officer was investigating a possible assault. He asked a rancher he suspected of having committed the crime to identify himself. The rancher refused, and he was arrested. The police officer was responding to a call reporting that a man had assaulted a woman. The officer found the

Stop and frisk
The right of the police to detain an individual for a brief period of time and to search the outside of the person's clothing if the police have a reasonable suspicion that the individual has committed or is about to commit a crime.

Reasonable suspicion
A suspicion based on specific facts; less than probable cause.

---

[17]392 U.S. 1 (1968).
[18]Id. at 21.
[19]Brown v. Texas, 443 U.S. 47 (1979).
[20]124 S. Ct. 2451 (2004).

defendant standing outside a parked truck, the truck matched the description that the police had been given, and a woman was inside the truck. On these facts, the Court concluded that the officer had reasonable suspicion to stop the defendant and to ask him to identify himself.[21] When the defendant did not do so, the police were justified in arresting him.[22] Therefore, in states such as Nevada that have "stop and identify" statutes, police officers may detain persons under suspicious circumstances, ask them to identify themselves, and arrest them if they refuse to do so, without violating their Fourth Amendment rights. The Court also noted that asking an individual to reveal his or her name does not violate the Fifth Amendment right against self-incrimination.[23]

Again, before making a "Terry stop," keep in mind that an officer cannot simply guess that an individual is a suspect. The officer must be able to tell the court about the facts that led to the suspicion. Consider what happened next in *People v. Grant*.

Stage II: *People v. Grant*

As the police were returning to the station to file a report, they noticed two men in dark clothes walking about ten blocks from the Joseph home. The police turned on their cruiser lights and pulled up behind the men. After briefly questioning the men and patting down their clothes to make sure that they did not carry any weapons, the police determined that these men were late-night joggers and not related to the crime.

Because of the information the police had gathered, they would argue they had reasonable suspicion that the men might be involved in the crime. First, the neighbor's description of the men matched their appearances. Second, they were two in number. Finally, they wore dark clothes, and they were in the neighborhood of the crime late at night.

The court will also look at the circumstances of the stop. The length of time that the officers detain the suspect cannot be long. The longer the period of time is, the closer the court will look at the intrusiveness of the search. The court will also look at the number and the type of questions the police ask. If the questions become detailed or the officers begin to accuse the suspect of committing a crime, then the court may consider the stop too intrusive.

The court will also look carefully at the circumstances of a frisk. Because the purpose of the frisk is to protect the officers and to aid in the detection and prevention of crime, the officers may frisk the suspect only if officers, in their experience, believe that the suspect is carrying a weapon. The frisk may take place outside the suspect's clothes. The officers are not allowed to search the inside clothing or pockets of the suspect. If a motorist is stopped, the officer may pat down the areas within the suspect's immediate control, such as the car's seat.

---

[21] Id. at 2457.

[22] Id. at 2460.

[23] Id. at 2461.

(2) Arrest

Persons are under **arrest** when their freedom is restrained by law enforcement officers **and** they are charged with a crime. If the officers want to arrest or completely search a suspect, they must either have an **arrest warrant** or be able to prove independently that there is **probable cause**, a higher standard than "reasonable suspicion." To determine probable cause, the police can rely on their knowledge of the suspect and information provided by witnesses and victims. In the above example a stop and frisk was probably justified. There was not enough evidence, however, to establish probable cause for a full body search or an arrest.

Police can arrest a suspect with or without a warrant so long as there is probable cause to believe the suspect committed the crime. If, however, the arrest is to be made at a person's home, then generally an arrest warrant must first be obtained unless an exception exists, as when the police are in "hot pursuit" of a suspect.

Arrest
Occurs when the police restrain a person's freedom and charge the person with a crime.

Probable cause
Not susceptible to a precise definition; a belief based on specific facts that a crime has been or is about to be committed; more than a reasonable suspicion.

(3) Searches and seizures of evidence

Searches of a suspect's home, business, or automobile and seizures of property from those locations are crucial law enforcement tools. Through legal searches and seizures officers may uncover items that are illegal on their face, such as illegal drugs or weapons. Officers may also locate the fruits of crime, such as stolen property, or the instruments of crime, such as burglary tools, weapons, and plans.

Because the Fourth Amendment protects only against unreasonable searches, the court must first determine whether the police activity constituted a search. To determine whether a search has taken place, the court evaluates the defendant's expectation of privacy. Some areas, such as a suspect's bedroom closet and the inside of a suspect's refrigerator, are private places where the suspect expects people will enter only by the suspect's invitation. Other areas, such as the license plate of a suspect's automobile and the outside stairs of a suspect's home, are less private. The suspect expects that these areas will be seen by anyone passing by. Therefore, it is not a "search" to write down a speeding car's license plate number. Entering the private places in the suspect's life, however, constitutes a search for which the police must show probable cause.

Searches and seizures, if supported by probable cause, may be conducted with or without warrants. A **warrant** is the court's prior permission for the officers to search and seize. However, because the suspect's right to privacy is so important, the courts prefer that officers search with a warrant. The officers must show probable cause to the court that the items they seek are located where the officers intend to search. Read Stage III of *People v. Grant*.

Warrant
A court's prior permission for the police to search and seize.

Stage III: *People v. Grant*

After some investigation the officers determined that Bruce Grant is the owner of Grant's Audiovisual Equipment. By checking with the motor vehicle department the police also discovered that the vehicle was registered to Bruce Grant, age forty-two. The business is located at 17 Hastings Street. When they checked Mr. Grant's record, they discovered that he had twice been convicted of stealing audiovisual equipment and selling the stolen goods.

The officers wanted to search the business premises to look for Mr. Joseph's missing goods. They wanted to be able to take those goods, and any other stolen goods, from Mr. Grant's place of business to be used against him at a trial.

The officers went to court and told the judge what their investigation has produced. They told the judge exactly what they wanted to search (Grant's place of business and the inside of the van), and they told the judge exactly what they expected to find there (Mr. Joseph's stolen items). The judge determined that there was probable cause and issued the warrant to search.

The officers must show that they are looking for specific items and are not just going on a hunt to find something incriminating. The officers must show probable cause to believe that the items they seek are connected to criminal activity. In our case it would probably not be appropriate for the officers to simply ask the court for a warrant to search for TV sets because the business could have several TVs for sale that are not the products of the crime. The officers should list the specific brands, models, model numbers if they are known, and any other specific characteristics of the stolen items. Where the police are looking for illegal drugs, however, they need not be as specific. They can indicate on the warrant that they are looking for heroin because there is no legal heroin that can be found by mistake. The officers should also be as specific as possible about the location, noting street address, apartment number, or level. This not only makes the officers' probable cause stronger but also assists the officers who execute the warrant.

Execute
To perform.

The search warrant must be **executed**—that is, the search must actually be carried out—within a specific period of time. The officers must announce themselves as police officers and execute the warrant during the daytime unless the warrant specifically allows other arrangements. They must inventory and describe in writing all the items they seize, and usually they must give the suspect a receipt.

No-knock warrant
A warrant that allows the police to enter without announcing their presence in advance.

Under special conditions the courts will sometimes issue **no-knock warrants**, which allow the police to enter at night without announcing their presence in advance. In order to receive one of these special search warrants, the police must convince the judge that evidence is likely to be destroyed or that the police administering the warrant will be in danger.

Plain view doctrine
Without the need for a warrant, the police may seize objects that are openly visible.

One exception to the warrant requirement is the **plain view doctrine**. Because the Fourth Amendment is designed to protect one's privacy, it is reasoned that police have the right to seize contraband items or evidence of a crime when they see such items "in plain view." Therefore, when an officer looks in the driver's window of a car that has been stopped for a minor traffic offense, that police officer can seize a partially filled beer can she observes sitting on the automobile's front seat.

But what if the driver stops at a police "checkpoint" rather than being stopped for a traffic violation? It depends on the purpose for the stop. If the checkpoint was established for the specific purpose of finding evidence of illegal drugs and the police did not have either probable cause or a reasonable suspicion to stop any given driver, then such a stop is illegal.[24] Any evidence of criminal

---

[24]Indianapolis v. Edmond, 531 U.S. 32 (2000).

activity that the police found could not be used in court. On the other hand, if the police established the checkpoint for a valid purpose, then the stop might be legal. In *Illinois v. Lidster*,[25] police officers stopped motorists in an attempt to obtain information concerning a hit-and-run accident that had occurred nearby. They only stopped each vehicle for 10 to 15 seconds, asked the occupants whether they had seen anything happen there the previous weekend, and handed each driver a flyer requesting information about the accident. As one driver approached the checkpoint, his van swerved, nearly hitting an officer. The officer smelled alcohol on the driver's breath. After failing a sobriety test, the driver was arrested and later convicted for driving under the influence of alcohol. To determine the reasonableness of the checkpoint, the Court relied on three factors it had used in the past to determine whether a stop is constitutional: (1) the reason for the stop; (2) the degree to which it advances the public interest; and (3) the severity of the interference with individual liberty.[26] Applying the first two criteria, the Court characterized this investigation into a recent death as grave and, given the timing and location, found that it advanced the public interest in investigating a possible crime. Most important to the Court, however, was the third criteria. The Court held that the stop "interfered only minimally with the liberty of the sort the Fourth Amendment seeks to protect."[27] Therefore, the checkpoint was constitutional, and the driver's conviction was affirmed.

In addition to the "plain view" exception, there are several other situations in which the police are not required to obtain a warrant prior to conducting a search. Figure 15-4 lists the various **exigent circumstances** that allow for warrantless searches, the rationales behind them, and how they would affect the search in our case.

If one of the exigent circumstances applies to our case, then the officers may enter and search for or seize items from Grant's Audiovisual Equipment without a warrant. If the defendant objects to the search, the court will look carefully at the search by considering the totality of the circumstances—that is, all the facts that the officers and the defendant believe are true. The court will then decide whether the search was valid and whether the information found because of the search can be used against the defendant.

Exigent circumstances Generally, an emergency situation that allows a search to proceed without a warrant.

DISCUSSION QUESTIONS

7. Which of the following areas do you think should be considered "private" and therefore require a warrant to be searched?
   a. your bedroom in your parents' home
   b. your garage
   c. your office at work
   d. your school locker
   e. your garbage that you have placed at your roadside curb

---

[25]124 S. Ct. 885 (2004).

[26]Id. at 887.

[27]Id.

Exigent Circumstance	Rationale	Impact on Our Case
Plain view	The suspect leaves the item where it can be seen. The officers may not touch or move the item for a better view.	If the officers can see the Joseph equipment by looking into the windows of the shop, they may enter and seize it.
Consent	The suspect voluntarily invites the officers into the premises or lets the officers search his or her person. The suspect consents to the scope of the search, and the officers cannot exceed the scope.	If Mr. Grant allows the officers to search, they can seize anything they have probable cause to believe is related to the crime. Mr. Grant can limit their search to an area of any size and can demand that they stop searching at any time.
Third-party consent	If a person shares access and control of a location with the suspect, that person may give consent for the suspect.	If Mr. Grant has a partner who shares access to and control of the business, the partner can consent to the search.
Emergency (plain view items only)	The officers enter a premises to answer a call for help or to assist an emergency vehicle, such as an ambulance.	If Mr. Grant calls for help or suffers another emergency, the police cannot be expected to ignore illegal items in plain view.
Preservation of evidence	When evidence might be destroyed if the officers wait for the court to issue a warrant, they may act without one.	If the officers see Mr. Grant taking the Joseph equipment apart or otherwise destroying it, they can seize it.
Hot pursuit	When officers are chasing a suspect, they do not have to stop the chase when the suspect enters a building. They should enter, secure the location, and then get a warrant before searching.	If Mr. Grant runs from the scene of the crime with the police chasing him, the police can follow him into the store and arrest him but should not search until they get a warrant.
Incident to lawful arrest (vehicles and persons)	When a suspect is arrested, the officers need not get a warrant before searching the suspect's person or impounding and doing an inventory of the suspect's vehicle so that evidence is not destroyed or lost and the officers' lives are not endangered. The officers probably cannot search a locked glove box or trunk without a warrant.	If Mr. Grant is arrested and booked for a crime, the officers do not have to get a warrant before emptying his pockets.
Prisoners	Safety and security outweigh the privacy interests of prisoners. The Fourth Amendment does not apply to prisoners.	If Mr. Grant is in prison, his person and his room can be searched and items can be seized.

Figure 15-4 Exigent Circumstances Justifying Warrantless Searches

8. How "plain" does plain view have to be? For example, in which of the following situations do you think marijuana would be in plain view?
   a. Using a helicopter, the police fly over your fenced backyard and see it growing in pots on your back patio.
   b. Standing across the street, the police use binoculars and see it growing inside your sunroom.
   c. Walking down the street, the police dog that has been specially trained to smell marijuana and other illegal drugs "points" to your briefcase.
   d. Aiming a thermal-imaging device at your house, the police find suspicious "hot spots," indicating the probable presence of marijuana growing within your home.

b. Questioning Suspects

As previously noted, police officers usually investigate criminal activity by questioning victims and witnesses. As is well illustrated on TV shows, the interrogation of the leading suspects is one of the most glamorous parts of the investigation. In many cases the suspects will reveal information that can then be used against them in a trial. In some cases they even confess. If the suspects did not commit the crime, they may be able to help the officers refocus their investigation.

Stage IV: *People v. Grant*

When the search warrant was executed, the police found the stolen items in an unlocked cabinet in the rear of the store. The officers seized the equipment, gave Mr. Grant a receipt for the items they seized, and filed a report with the court. The police officers then asked Mr. Grant to come to the station to talk to them about the equipment. Mr. Grant rode along with them in the back seat of one of the patrol cars.

On the ride to the station one of the officers asked Mr. Grant where he had been on the evening of April 30. He replied that he and his cousin had gone to a movie. The officer then asked him what movie they had seen and what time it had started. Mr. Grant said they had gone to an 8 o'clock showing of *Star Wars*. Next the officer asked him where he had gotten the electronic equipment that they had seized from his store. He replied that he had taken it as a trade-in as part of a sale of a big-screen TV.

When they arrived at the police station, the officers took Mr. Grant into an interrogation room and read him his *Miranda* rights. He responded that he did not want to talk to them unless he had an attorney present. When they gave him a telephone so he could call his attorney, he told them he wanted a court-appointed attorney because he could not afford to hire one on his own.

Both the Fifth and Sixth Amendments to the Constitution are relevant to interrogation situations. The Fifth Amendment prohibits law enforcement agents from forcing defendants to give testimonial evidence that would tend to incriminate them. Note that this applies only to testimonial evidence and does not protect a suspect from having to take a breathalizer test, to be fingerprinted, or to provide a handwriting sample. The Sixth Amendment guarantees a right to be represented by an attorney.

Amendment V

No person shall . . . be compelled in any criminal case to be a witness against himself. . . .

Amendment VI

In all criminal prosecutions, the accused shall enjoy the right to . . . have the assistance of counsel for his defense.

Miranda warnings
The requirement that defendants be notified of their rights to remain silent and to have an attorney present prior to being questioned by the police.

In the landmark cases of *Escobedo v. Illinois*[28] and *Miranda v. Arizona*[29] the U.S. Supreme Court ruled that the privilege against self-incrimination and the right to assistance of counsel apply to the interrogation stage, as well as to the trial. The Court reasoned that the right to counsel at trial would not benefit the defendant if the defendant had already confessed before meeting with an attorney and that the presence of an attorney during an interrogation would help to ensure that any statements given would be truly voluntary rather than coerced. The famous *Miranda* **warnings** are designed to notify defendants of their rights and to explain those rights in language they will understand.

Miranda Warnings

Prior to custodial interrogation, the suspect must be told of these rights:

1. The right to remain silent.
2. That anything said can be used against the suspect in a court of law.
3. The right to the presence of an attorney.
4. That if the suspect cannot afford an attorney, one will be appointed prior to any questioning.[30]

Once these *Miranda* warnings are given, the police cannot interrogate the suspect further unless he or she waives these rights.

Although the *Miranda* warnings are now firmly entrenched in our criminal justice system, at the time it was announced the *Miranda* decision was quite controversial. Prior to *Miranda* courts had judged the admissibility of a suspect's

---

[28]378 U.S. 478 (1964).
[29]384 U.S. 436 (1966).
[30]Id. at 479.

confession under a voluntariness test. Under that approach, the voluntary nature of a confession and hence its admissibility as evidence of guilt was judged based on all of the circumstances, rather than being subject to exclusion solely because the suspect was not advised of his or her rights. Two years after *Miranda* was decided, Congress enacted a law that was intended to nullify the *Miranda* decision and to return the requirement to the voluntariness test that prevailed prior to *Miranda*. This federal statute was largely ignored until the late 1990s when the United States Court of Appeals for the Fourth Circuit held that *Miranda* was not required by the Constitution. Thus Congress had the power by statute to have the final say on the question of the admissibility of confessions. According to the Fourth Circuit, the totality-of-the-circumstances test outlined in the statute and not the *Miranda* warnings were to be used by courts to determine the voluntary nature and hence admissibility of confessions. The Supreme Court disagreed. In *Dickerson v. United States*, the Court held that "*Miranda*, being a constitutional decision of this Court, may not be in effect overruled by an Act of Congress."[31] Therefore, *Miranda* and not the federal statute continues to govern the admissibility of statements made during custodial interrogations in both state and federal courts.

In the *People v. Grant* case we have been discussing, the police read Mr. Grant his *Miranda* rights before they began questioning him at the police station. However, they questioned him in the car about his activities on the night of the burglary before they informed him of his *Miranda* rights. Did this questioning in the car constitute an interrogation, and were the police required to have read the *Miranda* rights before they questioned him in the car?

The answer depends on the definition of a **custodial interrogation**. Suspects are in police **custody** when they feel that their freedom has been deprived in a significant way. It does not matter whether the suspects have been arrested (formally charged with a crime), although an arrest might indicate that the suspects are not free to leave. When suspects are in police custody *and* are questioned by the police, it is difficult, and maybe even frightening, for them to say, "No, thank you," to police questions. Therefore, before beginning this custodial interrogation (questioning of suspects when they feel that their liberty has been deprived), the police are *required* to tell the suspects about their rights. However, what constitutes "interrogation" is not always clear, as you can see from reading the following U.S. Supreme Court opinion.

Custodial interrogation
Questioning that occurs after a defendant has been deprived of his or her freedom in a significant way.

Custody
Occurs when the defendant has been deprived of freedom in a significant way.

Rhode Island v. Innis
446 U.S. 291 (1980)

Mr. Justice STEWART delivered the opinion of the Court.

In *Miranda v. Arizona*, 384 U.S. 436, 474, the Court held that, once a defendant in custody asks to speak with a lawyer, all interrogation must cease until a lawyer is present. The issue in this case is whether the respondent was "interrogated" in violation of the standards promulgated in the *Miranda* opinion.

I

On the night of January 12, 1975, John Mulvaney, a Providence, R.I., taxicab driver, disappeared after being dispatched to pick up a

---

[31]Dickerson v. U.S., 530 U.S. 428 (2000).

customer. His body was discovered four days later buried in a shallow grave in Coventry, R.I. He had died from a shotgun blast aimed at the back of his head.

On January 17, 1975, shortly after midnight, the Providence police received a telephone call from Gerald Aubin, also a taxicab driver, who reported that he had just been robbed by a man wielding a sawed-off shotgun. Aubin further reported that he had dropped off his assailant near Rhode Island College in a section of Providence known as Mount Pleasant. While at the Providence police station waiting to give a statement, Aubin noticed a picture of his assailant on a bulletin board. Aubin so informed one of the police officers present. The officer prepared a photo array, and again Aubin identified a picture of the same person. That person was the respondent. Shortly thereafter, the Providence police began a search of the Mount Pleasant area.

At approximately 4:30 A.M. on the same date, Patrolman Lovell, while cruising the streets of Mount Pleasant in a patrol car, spotted the respondent standing in the street facing him. When Patrolman Lovell stopped his car, the respondent walked towards it. Patrolman Lovell then arrested the respondent, who was unarmed, and advised him of his so-called *Miranda* rights. While the two men waited in the patrol car for other police officers to arrive, Patrolman Lovell did not converse with the respondent other than to respond to the latter's request for a cigarette. Within minutes, Sergeant Sears arrived at the scene of the arrest, and he also gave the respondent the *Miranda* warnings. Immediately thereafter, Captain Leyden and other police officers arrived. Captain Leyden advised the respondent of his *Miranda* rights. The respondent stated that he understood those rights and wanted to speak with a lawyer. Captain Leyden then directed that the respondent be placed in a "caged wagon," a four-door police car with a wire screen mesh between the front and rear seats, and be driven to the central police station. Three officers, Patrolmen Gleckman, Williams, and McKenna, were assigned to accompany the respondent to the central station. They placed the respondent in the vehicle and shut the doors. Captain Leyden then instructed the officers not to question the respondent or intimidate or coerce him in any way. The three officers then entered the vehicle, and it departed.

While en route to the central station, Patrolman Gleckman initiated a conversation with Patrolman McKenna concerning the missing shotgun. As Patrolman Gleckman later testified:

> At this point, I was talking back and forth with Patrolman McKenna stating that I frequent this area while on patrol and [that because a school for handicapped children is located nearby,] there's a lot of handicapped children running around in this area, and God forbid one of them might find a weapon with shells and they might hurt themselves. App. 43-44.

Patrolman McKenna apparently shared his fellow officer's concern:

> A. I more or less concurred with him [Gleckman] that it was a safety factor and that we should, you know, continue to search for the weapon and try to find it. Id., at 53.

While Patrolman Williams said nothing, he overheard the conversation between the two officers:

> A. "He [Gleckman] said it would be too bad if the little—I believe he said a girl—would pick up the gun, maybe kill herself." Id., at 59.

The respondent then interrupted the conversation, stating that the officers should turn the car around so he could show them where the gun was located. At this point, Patrolman McKenna radioed back to Captain Leyden that they were returning to the scene of the arrest, and that the respondent would inform them of the location of the gun. At the time the respondent indicated that the officers should turn back, they had traveled no more than a mile, a trip encompassing only a few minutes.

The police vehicle then returned to the scene of the arrest where a search for the shotgun was in progress. There, Captain Leyden again advised the respondent of his *Miranda* rights. The respondent replied that he understood those rights but that he "wanted to get the gun out of the way because of the kids in the area in the school."

The respondent then led the police to a nearby field, where he pointed out the shotgun under some rocks by the side of the road.

On March 20, 1975, a grand jury returned an indictment charging the respondent with the kidnaping, robbery, and murder of John Mulvaney. Before trial, the respondent moved to suppress the shotgun and the statements he had made to the police regarding it. . . . [T]he trial court sustained the admissibility of the shotgun and testimony related to its discovery. That evidence was later introduced at the respondent's trial, and the jury returned a verdict of guilty on all counts.

On appeal, the Rhode Island Supreme Court, in a 3-2 decision, set aside the respondent's conviction. . . .

II

. . . In the present case, the parties are in agreement that the respondent was fully informed of his *Miranda* rights and that he invoked his *Miranda* right to counsel when he told Captain Leyden that he wished to consult with a lawyer. It is also uncontested that the respondent was "in custody" while being transported to the police station.

The issue, therefore, is whether the respondent was "interrogated" by the police officers in violation of the respondent's undisputed right under *Miranda* to remain silent until he had consulted with a lawyer. In resolving this issue, we first define the term "interrogation" under *Miranda* before turning to a consideration of the facts of this case.

The starting point for defining "interrogation" in this context is, of course, the Court's *Miranda* opinion. There the Court observed that "[by] custodial interrogation, we mean *questioning* initiated by law enforcement officers after a person has been taken into custody or otherwise deprived of his freedom of action in any significant way." Id., at 444 (emphasis added). This passage and other references throughout the opinion to "questioning" might suggest that the *Miranda* rules were to apply only to those police interrogation practices that involve express questioning of a defendant while in custody.

We do not, however, construe the *Miranda* opinion so narrowly. The concern of the Court in *Miranda* was that the "interrogation environment" created by the interplay of interrogation and custody would "subjugate the individual to the will of his examiner" and thereby undermine the privilege against compulsory self-incrimination. . . .

This is not to say, however, that all statements obtained by the police after a person has been taken into custody are to be considered the product of interrogation. As the Court in *Miranda* noted:

> Confessions remain a proper element in law enforcement. Any statement given freely and voluntarily without any compelling influences is, of course, admissible in evidence. The fundamental import of the privilege while an individual is in custody is not whether he is allowed to talk to the police without the benefit of warnings and counsel, but whether he can be interrogated. . . . Volunteered statements of any kind are not barred by the Fifth Amendment and their admissibility is not affected by our holding today.

It is clear therefore that the special procedural safeguards outlined in *Miranda* are required not where a suspect is simply taken into custody, but rather where a suspect in custody is subjected to interrogation. "Interrogation," as conceptualized in the *Miranda* opinion, must reflect a measure of compulsion above and beyond that inherent in custody itself. . . .

We conclude that the *Miranda* safeguards come into play whenever a person in custody is subjected to either express questioning or its functional equivalent. That is to say, the term "interrogation" under *Miranda* refers not only to express questioning, but also to any words or actions on the part of the police (other than those normally attendant to arrest and custody) that the police should know are reasonably likely to elicit an incriminating response from the suspect. The latter portion of this definition focuses primarily upon the perceptions of the suspect, rather than the intent of the police. This focus reflects the fact that the *Miranda* safeguards were designed to vest a suspect in custody with an added measure of protection against coercive police practices, without regard to objective proof of the underlying intent of the police. . . .

Turning to the facts of the present case, we conclude that the respondent was not "interrogated" within the meaning of *Miranda*. It is undisputed that the first prong of the definition of "interrogation" was not satisfied, for the conversation between Patrolmen Gleckman and McKenna included no express questioning of the respondent. Rather, that conversation was, at least in form, nothing more than a dialogue between the two officers to which no response from the respondent was invited.

Moreover, it cannot be fairly concluded that the respondent was subjected to the "functional equivalent" of questioning. It cannot be said, in short, that Patrolmen Gleckman and McKenna should have known that their conversation was reasonably likely to elicit an incriminating response from the respondent. . . . Given the fact that the entire conversation appears to have consisted of no more than a few offhand remarks, we cannot say that the officers should have known that it was reasonably likely that Innis would so respond. . . . It is our view, therefore, that the respondent was not subjected by the police to words or actions that the police should have known were reasonably likely to elicit an incriminating response from him. . . .

For the reasons stated, the judgment of the Supreme Court of Rhode Island is vacated, and the case is remanded to that court for further proceedings not inconsistent with this opinion.

Mr. Justice MARSHALL, with whom Mr. Justice BRENNAN joins, dissenting.

I am substantially in agreement with the Court's definition of "interrogation" within the meaning of *Miranda v. Arizona*, 384 U.S. 436 (1966). . . . Thus the Court requires an objective inquiry into the likely effect of police conduct on a typical individual, taking into account any special susceptibility of the suspect to certain kinds of pressure of which the police know or have reason to know.

I am utterly at a loss, however, to understand how this objective standard as applied to the facts before us can rationally lead to the conclusion that there was no interrogation. Innis was arrested at 4:30 A.M., handcuffed, searched, advised of his rights, and placed in the back seat of a patrol car. Within a short time he had been twice more advised of his rights and driven away in a four-door sedan with three police officers. Two officers sat in the front seat and one sat beside Innis in the back seat. Since the car traveled no more than a mile before Innis agreed to point out the location of the murder weapon, Officer Gleckman must have begun almost immediately to talk about the search for the shotgun.

The Court attempts to characterize Gleckman's statements as "no more than a few offhand remarks" which could not reasonably have been expected to elicit a response. Ante, at 303. If the statements had been addressed to respondent, it would be impossible to draw such a conclusion. The simple message of the "talking back and forth" between Gleckman and McKenna was that they had to find the shotgun to avert a child's death.

One can scarcely imagine a stronger appeal to the conscience of a suspect—any suspect—than the assertion that if the weapon is not found an innocent person will be hurt or killed. And not just any innocent person, but an innocent child—a little girl—a helpless, handicapped little girl on her way to school. The notion that such an appeal could not be expected to have any effect unless the suspect were known to have some special interest in handicapped children verges on the ludicrous. As a matter of fact, the appeal to a suspect to confess for the sake of others, to "display some evidence of decency and honor," is a classic interrogation technique.

Gleckman's remarks would obviously have constituted interrogation if they had been explicitly directed to respondent, and the result should not be different because they were nominally addressed to McKenna. This is not a case where police officers speaking among themselves are accidentally overheard by a suspect. These officers were "talking back and forth" in close quarters with the handcuffed suspect, traveling past the very place where they believed the weapon was located. They knew respondent would hear and attend to their conversation, and they are chargeable with knowledge of and responsibility for the pressures to speak which they created. . . .

CASE DISCUSSION QUESTIONS

1. How did the *Innis* court define *interrogation*?
2. Applying that definition of interrogation, why did the Court believe the officers' remarks were not a form of interrogation? Do you agree with the Court's decision?

Although suspects have the right not to answer questions during custodial interrogation, this does not mean that they have to remain silent. Suspects may waive their *Miranda* rights as long as they do so voluntarily, knowingly, and intelligently. To determine whether a suspect waived his or her rights, the court will look carefully at all the circumstances. The court will consider the educational level of the suspect, language barriers, the existence of a mental condition or impairments, addictions to alcohol or illegal substances, the suspect's prior court experiences, the duration and intensity of the questioning period, and any other facts brought to the court's attention. The prosecution has the burden of proving that the defendant made a proper waiver.

To avoid confusion about whether a suspect received *Miranda* warnings or about whether there were proper waivers of the suspect's rights, law enforcement agencies usually require defendants to sign a card that lists the suspect's rights and asks the defendant questions, such as these:

1. Do you understand these rights as they have been explained to you?
2. Understanding these rights, do you wish to speak to me now?
3. Please sign this card indicating that you understand the above information.

In addition to the *Miranda* cards, many police departments videotape or tape-record the suspects as they receive their rights and consider waiving their rights. Then if the suspects later claim that they did not receive their rights or that they did not understand the waiver of their rights, the police have documentation to show to the court.

Once a suspect decides to remain silent, the police cannot continue the questioning and must give the suspect an opportunity to communicate with an attorney. The police cannot try to continue questioning at a later time unless an attorney is present. A suspect can waive his or her *Miranda* rights at a later interrogation.

Juvenile suspects are also entitled to be given their *Miranda* rights. In addition to a right to speak to an attorney, juvenile suspects are given the right to talk to an interested adult, such as a parent or guardian, before deciding to waive

---

PRACTICAL TIP

Many police stations now videotape the booking process. This protects the police from allegations of abuse and protects defendants from the misuse of police powers at booking. These tapes may also provide evidence of a defendant's physical or mental condition at booking.

their rights. Because of their age or in some circumstances because of their lack of experience with the criminal justice system, juveniles may need extra help making such important decisions. Just as parents or guardians may help juveniles with other life decisions, the court recognizes that a juvenile needs the extra protection that talking to a trusted adult may provide.

Because Mr. Grant told police that he did not wish to be questioned without his lawyer being present and because he indicated that he could not afford to hire a lawyer, the police must withhold any further questioning until they can arrange to have a public defender present or have the court appoint counsel.

Legal Reasoning Exercise

6. Using the standard discussed in this chapter, did custodial interrogation take place during the following incidents?

a. A suspect ran up to the police officer and cried, "Help! I killed him. I killed him. I didn't mean to do it!"

b. An officer walked up to a group of boys hanging around a street corner and said, "Hey, guys. What are you doing here?"

c. While at the police station the suspect explained how he stole the car from the parking lot down the street.

d. As an officer asked questions, the suspect wrote answers on a piece of paper.

e. In the case scenario being used in this chapter the police questioned Bruce Grant on the ride to the police station.

2. The Court System

A suspect's involvement with the court system begins with the initial appearance and then continues through a series of stages, eventually leading to either a guilty or a not guilty plea. If a guilty plea is entered, the case moves into the sentencing phase. If a not guilty plea is entered, the case is scheduled for trial. Finally, in some situations either the defendant or the prosecution may appeal the results of a court proceeding.

a. Formal Charges, Initial Appearances, and Bail

The formal process of charging someone with a crime begins by notifying the person that he or she is being placed under arrest. How a defendant actually discovers that he or she must answer to criminal charges depends on the circumstances of the case. In some cases, especially when the crime is a misdemeanor, the defendant may be notified by mail to appear at court to answer criminal charges. When the defendant is caught in the act or shortly thereafter, he or she may be arrested on the spot without a warrant. Otherwise, officers must obtain a warrant for arrest.

Normally a defendant who is arrested is brought to the police facility and booked. The **booking process** usually includes taking the defendant's personal information, giving the defendant an opportunity to read and sign a *Miranda* card, and allowing the defendant the opportunity to use a telephone. Additionally, the police may take photographs, or "mug shots," of the defendant for identification purposes. The police may also require the defendant to be fingerprinted. Fingerprints may then be compared to fingerprints found at the scene of the crime or saved to be compared to prints found at future crime scenes. The defendant is then searched, and his or her belongings are inventoried and stored by the police.

Some defendants are released by the police after the booking process is completed. They are usually given the date of their first court appearances and instructed that they must appear at court or risk a court default. Other defendants may give the police a fee and promise to appear as instructed to face criminal charges. The process of giving money and promising to appear as instructed is called **posting bail**. Usually, when the case is over, the court will return the bail money to the defendants. Persons can also be released prior to the trial date on a **personal recognizance bond**, by which defendants personally promise to appear in court when instructed to do so. These defendants are indebted to pay a specified amount if they fail to fulfill the conditions of the bond. In many states one's driver's license is accepted in lieu of a cash bail for most traffic offenses. Other defendants may be held in the police facility until the next possible court session, when they are delivered by the police into the custody of the court.

Booking
The process after arrest that includes taking the defendant's personal information, giving the defendant an opportunity to read and sign a *Miranda* card, and allowing the defendant the opportunity to use a telephone.

Bail
Money or something else of value that is held by the government to ensure the defendant's appearance in court.

Personal recognizance bond
A defendant's personal promise to appear in court.

Stage V: *People v. Grant*

On the basis of the witness's testimony about seeing the Grant's Audiovisual Equipment van and the evidence seized from Mr. Grant's store, the police were convinced that Mr. Grant had burglarized Stephen Joseph's home. They therefore informed him that he was under arrest and began the process of fingerprinting and booking him.

The following morning he was taken to court to have bail set and to determine if he was qualified to have a public defender appointed. At this initial appearance the judge told Mr. Grant of the charges being brought against him, set bail at $5,000, and denied his request for a public defender because he appeared to have enough assets in his business to be able to afford to hire his own attorney.

His case was then bound over to the grand jury to determine if there was sufficient evidence to proceed to trial.

After an individual has been placed in custody, the law requires that he or she be brought before a judge or magistrate without unnecessary delay. At this initial appearance the defendant must be told of the charges being brought against him or her, be advised of the right to counsel, and have bail set. In some states the amount of bail is preset for minor offenses, and the accused can post bail at the police station prior to this initial appearance.

At the initial appearance a defendant who cannot afford the services of a private attorney will usually have either a public defender or a member of the private bar appointed to provide representation. Most courts have developed local guidelines that take into consideration the income and assets of the defendant, as well as the nature of the offense. In *Scott v. Illinois*[32] the U.S. Supreme Court ruled that attorneys do not have to be provided in all misdemeanor cases but that indigent defendants cannot be given jail sentences unless they either were provided with counsel or waived their right to such representation.

b. Preliminary Hearings and Grand Juries

A defendant in a felony case cannot be put through the ordeal of a trial solely on the authority of the prosecutor. The evidence must be tested independently to determine whether sufficient probable cause exists to justify placing the individual on trial. This independent testing of the evidence often occurs through a preliminary hearing or the use of the grand jury.

The Fifth Amendment to the U.S. Constitution requires that "[n]o person shall be held to answer for a capital, or otherwise infamous crime, unless on a presentment or indictment of a Grand Jury. . . ." Although this applies only to federal cases, about half the states require the use of a **grand jury**. Other states allow the prosecutor the option of using or not using a grand jury; some do not use grand juries at all.

Grand jury
A group of people, usually twenty-three, whose function is to determine if probable cause exists to believe that a crime has been committed and that the defendant committed it.

Historically, grand juries were seen as a protection against arbitrary governmental prosecutions. Today, however, there are many who advocate abolition of the grand jury system. Critics point out that the government, in the form of the prosecutors, has too much control over the proceedings. It is the prosecutor who presents witnesses and evidence. The defendant is not even allowed to attend, and the proceedings are kept secret. Generally, the use of grand juries does appear to be declining. The federal government and most states that do use grand juries follow the common-law format of having twenty-three persons serve during a term and requiring at least twelve votes for an **indictment**.

Indictment
A grand jury's written accusation that a given individual has committed a crime.

As an aside, the grand jury also can serve as an investigative arm of the government and can be especially useful when it comes to investigating organized crime or corruption in the government's own bureaucracy. The Watergate grand jury is probably the most famous example of a grand jury used for such investigations. The ability to subpoena and give immunity to key witnesses makes the grand jury an effective weapon in the hands of a well-trained prosecutor. When the grand jury takes on this type of investigative role, its investigations frequently include people who are not yet under arrest. If the grand jury decides that those people should be brought to trial, arrest warrants are issued on the basis of the grand jury's indictment. Defendants arrested in this manner go directly from the initial appearance stage to the arraignment.

Information
A prosecutor's written accusation that a given individual has committed a crime.

In sum, the main function of a preliminary hearing or a grand jury proceeding is to review the government's case to determine whether there is enough evidence to justify holding the defendant for trial. If a grand jury is used and the decision is to proceed, an indictment is issued. If the same decision is reached after a preliminary hearing, the prosecutor files an **information**.

---

[32] 440 U.S. 367 (1979).

Finally, not all states require either a preliminary hearing or a grand jury indictment. In some instances, especially for misdemeanors, after the initial court appearance the prosecutor can simply file the information.

Stage VI: *People v. Grant*

Two weeks later the grand jury heard testimony from the police officers who had taken the report of what had been stolen from Mr. Joseph's home and had interviewed the witness about seeing the Grant's Audiovisual Equipment truck there. It also heard from the officer who was involved in executing the search warrant and had heard Mr. Grant say that he had been watching *Star Wars* at the local theater that night. In addition to describing the goods they had seized, the officer reported that when he checked with the local theaters, he discovered that none had been showing *Star Wars* on April 30. The grand jury never heard any testimony from Mr. Grant.

The grand jury then followed the prosecuting attorney's suggestion and indicted Bruce Grant for possession of stolen property, selling stolen property, and larceny.

---

c. Arraignments, the Exclusionary Rule, and Pretrial Motions

At the **arraignment** the court informs the defendant of the charges contained in the indictment or the information. The judge then asks the defendant to answer the charges by pleading guilty or not guilty. If the defendant wishes to plead guilty, the judge must speak with the defendant to be sure that he or she understands the nature of the charge, the minimum and maximum sentences prescribed by law, and that by entering a guilty plea he or she waives the right to have a trial and to confront and cross-examine witnesses. The prosecution usually reads the facts of the case, and the defendant agrees that the facts are true. If the court determines that the defendant is aware of the guilty plea and is voluntarily pleading guilty, usually the court will ask the prosecution to recommend the sentence. The judge may either pronounce the sentence at that time or set a specific time for a sentencing hearing at some later date.

Arraignment
A criminal proceeding at which the court informs the defendant of the charges being brought against him or her and the defendant enters a plea.

The plea is the defendant's decision, *not* the attorney's decision.

Plea bargaining
A process whereby the prosecutor and the defendant's attorney agree for the defendant to plead guilty in exchange for the prosecutor's promise to charge him or her with a lesser offense, drop some additional charges, or request a lesser sentence.

Nolo contendere
A defendant's plea meaning that the defendant neither admits nor denies the charges.

Sometimes the prosecution and the defense negotiate the defendant's punishment. This negotiation is called **plea bargaining**. In plea bargaining the defendant may agree to plead guilty to the crime, or to a lesser included offense of the crime, in exchange for the prosecution's recommendation for a lighter sentence. The judge may consider the results of the plea bargain but is not required to accept it. If the defendant enters a not guilty plea, a tentative date is set for the trial based on whether the defendant requests a jury trial or a bench trial.

Defendants usually have a third option at arraignment. They may plead **nolo contendere**. This Latin phrase means "no contest." A defendant neither admits nor denies the charges. He or she simply agrees that if the case went to trial, the prosecution would have sufficient evidence to prove its case beyond a reasonable doubt. This plea is not considered an admission of guilt and so cannot be used later against the defendant at a civil trial. However, for purposes of the arraignment the case proceeds as though the defendant had pleaded guilty.

Stage VII: *People v. Grant*

Mr. Grant was released from custody after posting his bond, and he arrived at his arraignment with a private attorney he had hired. The judge informed him that he had been charged with possessing stolen property, selling stolen property, and committing larceny. Following his attorney's advice Mr. Grant pleaded not guilty and demanded a jury trial. The judge accepted his plea and assigned the case to the next jury calendar.

At this point Mr. Grant's attorney filed a motion to require the state to turn over police notes regarding interviews with witnesses. She also moved to suppress the statements her client had made in the back of the police car about his activities on the night of the crime.

Inculpatory evidence
Evidence that suggests the defendant's guilt.

Exculpatory evidence
Evidence that suggests the defendant's innocence.

As in civil proceedings, the parties in a criminal case have an opportunity to use various discovery devices to avoid "trial by ambush." Although the particulars vary from one jurisdiction to another, the defense generally has a right to discover all the evidence that the prosecution intends to use at trial, including such things as the names, addresses, and statements of persons that the prosecution intends to call as witnesses; transcripts of any electronic surveillance; and physical evidence, such as a gun, a knife, illegal drugs, or the results of scientific tests. In addition to turning over **inculpatory evidence**, which suggests the defendant's guilt, the prosecution is required to produce **exculpatory evidence**, which suggests that the defendant did not commit the crime. If the prosecution refuses to provide discovery to the defense, the defense team may file motions to compel the evidence and ask the court to force the prosecution to supply the evidence. The prosecution, in turn, has a right to have the defendant appear in line-ups, give handwriting samples, provide names and addresses of people who will be called as defense witnesses, and provide results of laboratory and medical reports to be used as evidence.

The most common pretrial motions relate to facilitating the discovery process and preventing certain types of evidence from being used at the trial. Figure 15-5

Type of Motion	Goal	Rationale
Motion to suppress	To eliminate all or some of the evidence against the defendant	Without evidence, the state cannot meet its burden of proof. Evidence obtained during an illegal search and seizure, or other improper behavior, may be suppressed.
Motion to dismiss	To dismiss all or some of the charges against the defendant	The best way for the defense team to win is to get the case (or at least a few charges) dismissed before subjecting the defendant to the dangers of trial.
Motion to compel	To force the opposition to provide evidence that has been refused	There is no more trial by ambush. The prosecution must disclose inculpatory *and* exculpatory evidence.
Motion to server	To try multiple defendants at separate trials	If several defendants are tried together, they may be deprived of certain defenses that point to another defendant as more culpable, and the jury may be overwhelmed and confused about what evidence pertains to each defendant. Through this motion the court attempts to eliminate undue prejudice.
Motion to bifurcate	To isolate the charges against a defendant and try each charge at a separate trial	If the jury would be misled by alternative charges, the defendant would benefit by defending against one charge at a time. Prejudice and unfairness are considered proper grounds under most circumstances.
Motion for a bill of particulars	To force the prosecution to provide specific information regarding the case	The defense team is entitled to know the details of the case with as much specificity as possible.
Motion to sequester witnesses	To keep witnesses out of the courtroom until after they testify	The testimony of one witness or the questioning tactics used by the attorneys may influence the testimony of witnesses yet to testify. Keeping witnesses outside the courtroom may help keep their testimony pure.

Figure 15-5 Typical Pretrial Motions

(continues)

Type of Motion	Goal	Rationale
Motion to rescue	To remove a particular judge from a case	If a judge knows a victim or defendant in a case, publicly voices an opinion about the outcome of the case, or otherwise has a conflict of interest, the judge should step down, and another judge should proceed.
Motion for funds	To allow indigent defendants access to funds from the state	An indigent defendant has the same legal needs for trial preparation as a wealthy defendant. Money may be made available through the court for expert witnesses, scientific tests, or other investigatory needs.
Motion for change of venue	To achieve an impartial jury panel through a request for a change of the location for trial	Sometimes a defendant cannot get a fair trial in the location where the crime was committed. Pretrial publicity or local prejudice may inhibit justice.
Motion to continue	To change the date of trial, usually to postpone to a later date	The parties may require more time to prepare or to allow witnesses to travel to the trial. Attorneys, witnesses, or the defendant could fall ill. When the trial cannot proceed as scheduled, this motion should be filed. Motions of this type, if not abused, are usually allowed.
Motion in limine	To make evidentiary and trial decisions prior to the beginning of trial	Some decisions, such as the order of witnesses, the scope of examination or cross-examination, and the admission of certain documents, may be decided by the parties prior to the start of trial. This speeds up the trial process and avoids bickering in front of the jury.
Motion for a view	To let the jury visit the scene of the crime	A viewing can give the jury members a better understanding of the crime scene than they could otherwise gain from witness testimony alone.

Figure 15-5   *(concluded)*

lists the motions you are most likely to encounter. Note, however, that not all of these are available in every jurisdiction. You need to check local court rules to determine the availability and format of specific motions. The federal and state rules of criminal procedure typically require that motions be accompanied by a memorandum of law, analyzing how the courts have decided similar motions in past cases and arguing how the motions should be decided in this case.

Because criteria for presenting and proving each motion depend on the jurisdiction, not all of these motions are available to every defendant and prosecutor in every jurisdiction. Other pretrial motions may also be available. The format and requirements for each motion, such as the requirement to file a memorandum of law to accompany the motion, will also depend on the jurisdiction. Remember, nothing in the table of typical motions, or in this chapter, takes the place of your research in your own jurisdiction.

Because these pretrial motions are designed to significantly influence the course of the case, defending against pretrial motions is a crucial job. Carefully dissect the factual analysis, legal research, and legal reasoning of your opponent's motion and, if applicable, the supporting memoranda of law. Do not take any detail or citation for granted.

DISCUSSION QUESTION

9. How do you reconcile the purpose behind a motion for a view with the traditional belief that jurors are supposed to base their decision solely on what they hear and see in the courtroom?

A **motion to suppress**, the first type of motion listed in Figure 15-5, is a request to have the court prohibit the use of certain evidence at the trial. Motions to suppress are based on what is known as the exclusionary rule. Under the terms of the **exclusionary rule**, evidence that has been obtained in violation of an individual's constitutional rights cannot be used against that individual in a criminal trial. Furthermore, the **fruit of the poisonous tree doctrine** holds that evidence that is spawned by or directly derived from an illegal search or illegal interrogation is inadmissible against the defendant by virtue of being tainted by the original illegality. If the tree (the primary evidence) has been poisoned from the illegal search, then all the fruit (collateral or additional evidence) must also be suppressed. The application of this doctrine does not invalidate the arrest or prevent the defendant from being convicted on the basis of independent evidence. Nor does it prohibit officers from later conducting legal searches and gathering additional evidence as long as that evidence was gathered without the aid of knowledge gained from the tainted evidence that was suppressed.

The exclusionary rule, which remains one of the most controversial aspects of constitutional law, applies to state as well as federal court cases. The exclusionary rule, as applied to the states, was established in the following landmark case.

Motion to suppress
A request that the court prohibit the use of certain evidence at the trial.

Exclusionary rule
A rule that states that evidence obtained in violation of an individual's constitutional rights cannot be used against that individual in a criminal trial.

Fruit of the poisonous tree doctrine
Evidence that is derived from an illegal search or interrogation is inadmissible.

Mapp v. Ohio
367 U.S. 643 (1961)

Mr. Justice CLARK delivered the opinion of the Court.

Appellant stands convicted of knowingly having had in her possession and under her control certain lewd and lascivious books, pictures, and photographs in violation of § 2905.34 of Ohio's Revised Code. As officially stated in the syllabus to its opinion, the Supreme Court of Ohio found that her conviction was valid though "based primarily upon the introduction in evidence of lewd and lascivious books and pictures unlawfully seized during an unlawful search of defendant's home. . . ."

On May 23, 1957, three Cleveland police officers arrived at appellant's residence in that city pursuant to information that "a person [was] hiding out in the home, who was wanted for questioning in connection with a recent bombing. . . . Miss Mapp and her daughter by a former marriage lived on the top floor of the two-family dwelling. . . . . When Miss Mapp did not come to the door immediately, at least one of the several doors to the house was forcibly opened and the policemen gained admittance. . . . It appears that Miss Mapp was halfway down the stairs from the upper floor to the front door when the officers, in this high-handed manner, broke into the hall. . . . Running roughshod over appellant, a policeman "grabbed" her, "twisted [her] hand," and she "yelled [and] pleaded with him" because "it was hurting." Appellant, in handcuffs, was then forcibly taken upstairs to her bedroom where the officers searched a dresser, a chest of drawers, a closet and some suitcases. They also looked into a photo album and through personal papers belonging to the appellant. The search spread to the rest of the second floor including the child's bedroom, the living room, the kitchen and a dinette. The basement of the building and a trunk found therein were also searched. The obscene materials for possession of which she was ultimately convicted were discovered in the course of that widespread search.

At the trial no search warrant was produced by the prosecution, nor was the failure to produce one explained or accounted for. . . .

The State says that even if the search were made without authority, or otherwise unreasonably, it is not prevented from using the unconstitutionally seized evidence at trial, citing *Wolf v. Colorado*, 338 U.S. 25 (1949), in which this Court did indeed hold "that in a prosecution in a State court for a State crime the Fourteenth Amendment does not forbid the admission of evidence obtained by an unreasonable search and seizure." At p. 33. On this appeal, of which we have noted probable jurisdiction, it is urged once again that we review that holding.

I.

[T]his Court, in *Weeks v. United States*, 232 U.S. 383 (1914), stated that

the Fourth Amendment . . . put the courts of the United States and Federal officials, in the exercise of their power and authority, under limitations and restraints [and] . . . forever secure[d] the people, their persons, houses, papers and effects against all unreasonable searches and seizures under the guise of law . . . and the duty of giving to it force and effect is obligatory upon all entrusted under our Federal system with the enforcement of the laws.

Specifically dealing with the use of the evidence unconstitutionally seized, the Court concluded:

If letters and private documents can thus be seized and held and used in evidence against a citizen accused of an offense, the protection of the Fourth Amendment declaring his right to be secure against such searches and seizures is of no value, and, so far as those thus placed are concerned, might as well be stricken from the Constitution. The efforts of the courts and their officials to bring the guilty to punishment, praiseworthy as they are, are not to be aided by the sacrifice of those great principles established by years of endeavor and suffering which have resulted in their embodiment in the fundamental law of the land.

Finally, the Court in that case clearly stated that use of the seized evidence involved "a denial of the constitutional rights of the accused." At p. 398. Thus, in the year 1914, in the *Weeks* case, this Court "for the first time" held that "in a federal prosecution the Fourth Amendment barred the use of evidence secured through an illegal search and seizure." . . .

IV.

Since the Fourth Amendment's right of privacy has been declared enforceable against the States through the Due Process Clause of the Fourteenth, it is enforceable against them by the same sanction of exclusion as is used against the Federal Government. Were it otherwise, then just as without the *Weeks* rule the assurance against unreasonable federal searches and seizures would be "a form of words," valueless and undeserving of mention in a perpetual charter of inestimable human liberties, so too, without that rule the freedom from state invasions of privacy would be so ephemeral and so neatly severed from its conceptual nexus with the freedom from all brutish means of coercing evidence as not to merit this Court's high regard as a freedom "implicit in the concept of ordered liberty." . . .

Moreover, our holding that the exclusionary rule is an essential part of both the Fourth and Fourteenth Amendments is not only the logical dictate of prior cases, but it also makes very good sense. There is no war between the Constitution and common sense. Presently, a federal prosecutor may make no use of evidence illegally seized, but a State's attorney across the street may, although he supposedly is operating under the enforceable prohibitions of the same Amendment. Thus the State, by admitting evidence unlawfully seized, serves to encourage disobedience to the Federal Constitution which it is bound to uphold. . . .

There are those who say, as did Justice (then Judge) Cardozo, that under our constitutional exclusionary doctrine "the criminal is to go free because the constable has blundered." In some cases this will undoubtedly be the result. But, as was said in *Elkins*, "there is another consideration—the imperative of judicial integrity." 364 U.S. at 222. The criminal goes free, if he must, but it is the law that sets him free. Nothing can destroy a government more quickly than its failure to observe its own laws, or worse, its disregard of the charter of its own existence. As Mr. Justice Brandeis, dissenting, said in *Olmstead v. United States*, 277 U.S. 438, 485 (1928): "Our Government is the potent, the omnipresent teacher. For good or for ill, it teaches the whole people by its example. . . . If the Government becomes a lawbreaker, it breeds contempt for law; it invites every man to become a law unto himself; it invites anarchy." . . .

Twenty-three years later in *United States v. Leon*[33] the U.S. Supreme Court curtailed its broad holding in *Mapp*. That case involved the admissibility of drugs seized by police after executing a search warrant. Leon's defense attorney filed a motion to suppress the drugs based on the theory that the affidavit on which the warrant was based was insufficient to establish the probable cause needed to justify its issuance. The trial judge found that the affidavit had been insufficient but that the officer who filed it had done so in good faith. Therefore, he rejected the motion to suppress the evidence. The Supreme Court agreed, noting that "substantial social costs [have been] exacted by the exclusionary rule."[34] The Court held that evidence obtained by officers "acting in reasonable reliance on a search warrant issued by a detached and neutral magistrate but ultimately found to be unsupported by probable cause"[35] should not be excluded from the prosecution's case.

---

[33] 468 U.S. 897 (1984).

[34] Id. at 907.

[35] Id.

CASE DISCUSSION QUESTIONS

1. According to the Supreme Court, what is the main justification for the exclusionary rule?

2. What negative consequences arise out of application of the exclusionary rule?

3. What problems would be created by having one set of rules for the federal courts and a separate set of rules for the state courts?

4. The dissenting justices in *Leon* saw that decision as a step toward the destruction of the Fourth Amendment. They wrote that "[t]he right to be free from the initial invasion of privacy and the right of exclusion are coordinate components of the central embracing right to be free from unreasonable searches and seizures."[36] Do you agree?

Legal Reasoning Exercise

7. Suppose someone fired a bullet through the floor of an apartment into the apartment below. The police entered the shooter's apartment looking for the shooter, for other weapons, and possibly for victims. While they were in the apartment, the police discovered weapons and a stocking cap. The police also noticed stereo equipment and, suspecting it was stolen, recorded the serial numbers. In order to read all the numbers, the police moved some of the equipment. When the police headquarters notified the police that the equipment was stolen, the police officers seized it.

   a. If you worked for the defense team, what arguments would you make to convince the court to suppress the evidence?

   b. If you worked for the prosecution, what arguments would you make to convince the court that the search was legal?

   c. Which side has the most persuasive arguments?

d. Plea Bargaining

Stage VIII: *People v. Grant*

After several continuances had pushed back the original court date, the judge announced that he would tolerate no further delays in the case and that both attorneys needed to be ready to begin the trial on January 10. Shortly before Christmas Mr. Grant's attorney called the assistant prosecutor that had been assigned to the case to discuss the terms of a possible plea bargain.

---

[36]Id. at 935.

The prosecutor offered to drop the larceny charges if Mr. Grant would plead guilty to possession of stolen property. Mr. Grant's attorney then proceeded to inquire as to what the prosecutor would recommend for jail time if her client accepted this offer. When the prosecutor said five years, she countered with one year. The prosecutor then laughed and said that his absolute minimum offer was four years. She responded that she would discuss the offer with her client but that she doubted he would accept. When she discussed the matter with Mr. Grant, he told her he would rather take his chances with a trial.

Plea bargaining was mentioned briefly above in the context of arraignment. However, a plea bargain can happen at any time in the process. Ninety percent of criminal cases never reach trial, as they are settled through a plea bargain. The defendant agrees to plead guilty to a criminal charge in exchange for a reduction in the charges or the sentence. The incentives offered by the government can include reducing the severity of the charge (for example, the prosecutor can settle for a guilty plea on a robbery charge where the original charge was for the more serious offense of armed robbery), dropping related counts (for example, an original indictment may include three counts of burglary, but the prosecutor may agree to drop two of them in return for a guilty plea to the third), and recommending the minimum sentence or even a suspended sentence rather than going for the maximum authorized by the law.

Prosecutors are willing to make these types of bargains for a variety of reasons. Because most prosecutors' offices are understaffed and overworked, plea bargaining provides a way to more efficiently manage their workloads and produce high conviction rates. Many prosecutors are willing to settle for a sure conviction on the record with at least some jail time for the defendant rather than risking an uncertain conviction for the sake of longer jail time. In *Santobello v. New York*[37] the U.S. Supreme Court spoke of the benefits of encouraging plea bargaining in a case in which the government tried to change the terms of a bargain after the defendant had entered a guilty plea. The Court stated that this was improper. Once a deal has been struck and the defendant has entered a guilty plea, the state cannot change the terms of the agreement.

e. The Right to a Jury Trial

The Sixth Amendment to the U.S. Constitution creates a right to trial by an impartial jury in federal criminal cases. The due process clause of the Fourteenth Amendment applies the right to a trial by jury to defendants in state criminal actions who face possible incarceration of six months or more.[38]

The U.S. Constitution requires that criminal juries at the federal level consist of twelve members and that their verdicts be unanimous. The U.S. Supreme Court has ruled that six-member juries are permissible at the state level,[39] as are less-than-unanimous verdicts.[40] It is left to the states to select which of these options they wish to use.

> **PRACTICAL TIP**
>
> Many prosecutors and defense teams hire jury specialists who can create "perfect" juror profiles to assist with jury selection.

---

[37] 404 U.S. 257 (1971).

[38] Baldwin v. New York, 399 U.S. 66 (1970).

[39] Williams v. Florida, 399 U.S. 78 (1970).

[40] Apodaca v. Oregon, 406 U.S. 404 (1972).

One of the most frequently misunderstood principles of the jury system is the concept of being tried before a jury of one's peers. This does not mean that the jury must consist of a group of people who are similar to the defendant. Rather the jury simply must be broadly representative of the community in which the trial takes place.

If the defendant waives the right to a jury trial, a bench trial is held, in which the judge serves as the fact finder, as well as the presiding officer.

f. Trial Procedures

There are few, but very important, differences between civil and criminal trials. The major difference is that the prosecutor in a criminal case must bear the burden of a higher standard of proof, beyond a reasonable doubt, as opposed to preponderance of the evidence. The defense is not required to put the defendant, or any other witnesses, on the stand. If the defendant chooses not to testify, the prosecution cannot comment or otherwise draw attention to it during any part of the trial.

The prosecution goes first, presenting all the information necessary to meet its burden of proof beyond a reasonable doubt. Through witnesses and the introduction of evidence the prosecution attempts to prove each element of each charge. With cross-examination of the prosecution's witnesses, the defense attempts to discredit their testimony.

Motion to require a finding of not guilty
The defense's request that the court find the prosecution failed to meet its burden and that it remove the case from the jury by finding the defendant not guilty.

When the prosecution has completed its case, it "rests." At that time, in most jurisdictions, the defense may make a **motion to require a finding of not guilty** for some or all of the charges. Outside of the hearing of the jury the defense may argue that the prosecution failed to meet its burden and that the court should remove the case from the jury by finding the defendant not guilty. The judge looks at the evidence presented and evaluates it in the light most favorable to the prosecution. If the judge grants this defense motion, the defendant can be found not guilty of the individual charges or the entire case. There is no penalty if the judge does not allow this motion. The jury returns and simply resumes hearing the case.

As mentioned above, the defense is not required to put witnesses on the stand. If the defense calls witnesses, the defense examines and the prosecution cross-examines each witness, again with an eye toward credibility.

Once the defense has rested its case, the defense may renew the motion for a required finding of not guilty. This time the judge looks at the motion in the light most favorable to the defendant. If the motion is allowed, the case never goes to the jury for a verdict. If the motion is denied, the court process begins again. The attorneys deliver their closing arguments to the jury, and the judge informs the jurors of the law that they need to know to make their decision, which is called

PRACTICAL TIP

The opening and closing arguments are not considered evidence. But they are the first and last statements that the jury hears. Therefore, they may be the most effective method the attorneys have to present their case.

charging the jury. Once they are charged and sworn to do their duty, the jury members are released from the courtroom to deliberate. They may bring any items entered into evidence into the jury room with them to help them decide, and they can come back into the courtroom to ask questions.

Nothing can describe the waiting period while the jury is deliberating. It is too late to change anything, too soon to know whether your strategy worked. Many attorneys spend this time discussing possible outcomes with their clients or evaluating their trial performances. There is no set length of time that a jury can deliberate and no special process that a jury must follow. If the defendant is found not guilty, the case is over. If the defendant is found guilty, then the case moves into the sentencing phase.

Charging the jury
The judge informs the jurors of the law they need to know to make their decision.

DISCUSSION QUESTION

10. Criminals are guaranteed a jury of their peers. If you were on trial for a criminal offense, what factors would you consider when trying to select a jury of your peers? Is there really such a thing?

3. Sentencing

The jury usually has no role to play in the sentencing process. Once the jury has found the defendant guilty of a specified crime, the judge is usually responsible for determining what the sentence will be. An exception occurs in capital punishment cases, where statutes frequently give the defendant the option of having the jury decide if the death penalty should be imposed.

After the guilty verdict the judge usually holds a special sentencing hearing, in which evidence can be presented "in aggravation and mitigation." At such a hearing both the prosecution and the defense have an opportunity to present evidence that was not relevant to whether the defendant committed the crime but is relevant to the nature of the punishment that is to be imposed. The judge also receives a presentence report, which reviews the defendant's criminal record, work record, family background, and other factors considered relevant in determining the appropriate punishment. The judge may also be willing to listen to the victim impact statements, in which the victim of the crime describes how it negatively affected his or her life and the lives of family members.

Most state statutes give the judge a broad range of discretion between the minimum and the maximum sentences for the crime in question. Under the Model Penal Code, for example, the sentence for murder can range from one year to life imprisonment. Furthermore, judges often have the power to sentence defendants to **probation**, to give them a conditional discharge, or to suspend their sentences altogether. Because some fear that allowing so much discretion results in uneven results, the federal government and some state legislatures have passed sentencing guidelines. These guidelines give much less sentencing discretion to the trial judge.

When the legislators determine the range of punishments applicable to each criminal offense, they are motivated by the theory that punishment is the most effective way to enforce criminal laws and to stop crime. There are at least five theories of punishment that help explain what society hopes to gain from punishing criminal offenders. See Figure 15-6.

Theory of Punishment	Rationale
Specific deterrence	The perpetrator of a crime is punished so that *this individual* will not commit other crimes.
General deterrence	The perpetrator of a crime is punished so that *other* individuals will not commit this or other crimes.
Incapacitation	The perpetrator of a crime is isolated in a prison so that *this individual* will not be able to commit any crimes during the length of the incarceration.
Rehabilitation	The perpetrator of a crime is given treatment so that *this individual* will have no need or desire to commit crimes in the future.
Retribution	The perpetrator of a crime is punished to exact revenge on behalf of the victim or the victim's family.

Figure 15-6   Theories of Punishment

General and specific deterrence are both designed to prevent future crime by convincing would-be criminals that any benefits they might get from carrying out criminal acts will be outweighed by the punishments they will receive. The difference between general and specific deterrence is that specific deterrence applies to the person who has already committed a crime, while general deterrence is directed at others who might be tempted to commit a similar crime. Both versions of deterrence theory rely on the assumption that would-be criminals will consciously weigh the benefits of committing crimes against the punishments they will receive if they are caught. Critics point out that criminals often act on emotion rather than reason and that they usually believe they will not be caught.

Incapacitation of criminals keeps individuals who commit crimes separated from society and limits their opportunities to commit further crimes. Criminals who are incarcerated or executed are not deterred from committing crimes; they are simply denied the opportunity to commit criminal acts. Instead of incarceration, criminals who are not citizens of the United States may be deported back to their countries of origin.

Rehabilitation involves efforts to reduce crime by changing the perpetrator of a crime so that he or she will have no need or desire to commit crimes in the future. Programs designed to rehabilitate criminals usually include education and job skill development that will help these persons become productive members of society who do not need to turn to crime for financial support. They may also include psychological counseling to help the criminals understand the difference between right and wrong and to appreciate the harm their crimes produce. Through the successful completion of these retraining and reshaping programs, society hopes that criminals will alter the patterns of their behavior and return to society without further episodes of criminal activity.

Retribution is based on society's desire for revenge. Many people wish to have the government enforce the Biblical admonition that punishment should involve "an eye for an eye, a tooth for a tooth." The theory is that it is better to have the government administer retribution than to leave it up to the victims to seek their own vengeance, thereby starting a cycle of retaliation involving friends and relatives.

Criminals who do continue to commit crimes after their first offenses are called **recidivists**. In an attempt to attack the problem of recidivism approximately one-half of the states, as well as the federal government, have enacted "three strikes," or habitual offender, statutes. Typically these statutes mandate required prison sentences for third-time offenders. As these statutes remove a great deal of the sentencing discretion from the hands of judges, some believe that they can create unfair results in individual cases. For example, a man in California was sentenced to twenty-five years to life under the state's "three strikes" law. His crime? Attempting to steal three golf clubs, worth $399 apiece. He challenged the length of his sentence arguing that the Eighth Amendment's prohibition against cruel and unusual punishment required greater proportionality between the crime and the punishment. In a 5-4 decision, the U.S. Supreme Court disagreed, declaring that such "three strikes" provisions do not violate the Eighth Amendment.[41]

Another force at work in decreasing sentencing discretion has been the adoption of formal sentencing guidelines designed to bring uniformity and reduce bias based on the defendant's race, religion, wealth, or other extraneous factors. On the federal level Congress enacted the Federal Sentencing Guidelines. These guidelines have evolved over the last twenty years and use a complicated, points-based system that requires the judge to set the sentence within a fixed range. Each crime is assigned a base offense level, which can be adjusted according to the particular circumstances of that crime. For example, the judge can take into account aggravating facts that were not considered by the jury. Recently this system was called into doubt based on a case that started in Washington state.

Ralph Blakely pleaded guilty to kidnapping his estranged wife. Washington's statutory maximum sentence for second-degree kidnapping is ten years, but the state's statutory sentencing guidelines, similar to the federal guidelines described above, set a presumptive range of 49 to 53 months. At sentencing, the judge imposed a 90-month sentence after finding that Blakely had acted with deliberate cruelty. The U.S. Supreme Court held that Blakely's sentence was imposed in a manner inconsistent with the Sixth Amendment right to a jury trial because the guidelines allowed the judge to increase the length of the sentence based on facts the defendant had not admitted and that had not been proven beyond a reasonable doubt to a jury.[42] Because similar provisions exist in the Federal Sentencing Guidelines and those of approximately fourteen other states, this decision raises questions not only about the constitutionality of such guidelines but also about the convictions of the people sentenced under them. Within two weeks of the decision, judges across the country had begun to shorten sentences, and Congress had started discussing proposed amendments to the federal guidelines.[43]

---

[41]Ewing v. California, 538 U.S. 11 (2003).

[42]Blakely v. Washington, 124 S. Ct. 2531 (2004).

[43]Dan Eggen and Jerry Markon, "High Court Ruling Sows Confusion," Washington Post, July 13, 2004, at A01.

DISCUSSION QUESTIONS

11. How might you respond to your neighbor who says the judicial system is "falling apart" because of plea bargaining?

12. "It is better that ten guilty men go free than one innocent man be convicted" is an often-quoted legal expression. Do you agree or disagree?

13. Discuss the manner in which the death penalty serves each of the major theories of punishment. Do you support or oppose the use of capital punishment? Why?

14. How much discretion should the judge have in sentencing? Why?

15. On November 4, Leandro Andrade stole five videotapes worth $84.70 from a Kmart store. Fourteen days later, Andrade entered a different Kmart store and placed four videotapes worth $68.84 in the rear waistband of his pants. (The tapes included "Batman Forever" and "Cinderella.") The police arrested Andrade for these crimes. At trial, Andrade was found guilty of two counts of petty theft. The jury also made a special finding that he had previously been convicted of three counts of first-degree residential burglary. (One case involved his attempt to steal a bicycle.) Each of his petty theft convictions for stealing the videotapes triggered a separate application of the three-strikes law. Therefore, the judge sentenced him to two consecutive terms of 25 years to life, with no chance for parole. Does it seem as though his punishment was proportionate to his crime? How would you argue that his case is similar to or different from the *Ewing* case discussed above?

4. Appeal

As with parties who want to pursue civil appeals, a criminal defendant who wishes to appeal a conviction must file the appropriate post-trial motions, usually accompanied by a notice of appeal. There is a specified time during which an appeal may be filed. The Fifth Amendment protection against double jeopardy prohibits the state from trying a defendant more than once for the same crime and prevents the government from appealing an acquittal. It does not prevent a prosecutor from appealing the dismissal of a case on technical grounds or from appealing a lower appellate court ruling to a higher court.

Writ of habeas corpus
A request that the court release the defendant because of the illegality of the incarceration.

After the appeal period has expired, the only avenue for relief is through a **writ of habeas corpus**, a request that the court review the legality of the incarceration. The convicted defendant argues that the incarceration is illegal because of a defect in the case. It is uncommon for this tactic to be successful.

|||| SUMMARY

Criminal law defines what behaviors are illegal and what punishments convicted defendants are to receive. Criminal procedure governs how the criminal process works.

Crimes can generally be divided into felonies, crimes that usually involve punishment by incarceration for a year or more, and misdemeanors. For any crime the government must prove that the defendant had the requisite mens rea while committing the actus reus. Common defenses include alibi, ignorance or mistake, infancy, insanity, intoxication, duress, necessity, entrapment, self-defense, and defense of others. In addition, a defendant may challenge a prosecution on the basis of a statute of limitations or the Constitution.

The rules governing criminal procedure begin with the criminal investigation and continue in force thorough trial and any possible appeal. The Fourth Amendment requires that all searches and seizures be reasonable. The court-crafted exclusionary rule provides that any evidence unlawfully seized may not be used in court against the defendant. The Fifth Amendment protects defendants against self-incrimination, and the Sixth Amendment guarantees a right to an attorney. While every defendant has a right to a trial, most cases end through a negotiated plea bargain.

If a trial does occur, the prosecution bears the burden of proving guilt beyond a reasonable doubt. The defense attorney is not required to put the defendant, or any other witnesses, on the stand. If the defendant chooses not to testify, the prosecution cannot comment or otherwise draw attention to the defendant's silence.

If the jury finds the defendant guilty, the judge is usually responsible for determining what the sentence will be. Most state statutes give the judge a broad range of discretion between a minimum and a maximum sentence for the crime. In recent years, however, this discretion has been severely curtailed through the enactment of sentencing guidelines.

If a criminal defendant wishes to appeal a conviction, he or she may do so. The Fifth Amendment protection against double jeopardy prohibits the state from trying a defendant twice for the same crime and prevents the government from appealing an acquittal. It does not, however, prevent a prosecutor from appealing the dismissal of a case on technical grounds or from appealing a lower appellate court ruling to a higher court.

REVIEW QUESTIONS

Pages 531 through 534

1. Why is "[n]o behavior a crime unless the law makes it a crime"?
2. Who has the burden of proving a criminal case? Why is the standard of proof not the same in criminal and civil cases?
3. What alternatives are there to incarceration?

Pages 534 through 539

4. What is the Model Penal Code? What was the intent of its drafters? Has that intent been accomplished?
5. What are the differences between felonies and misdemeanors?

Pages 539 through 549

6. What is the actus reus of a crime? What is the mens rea of a crime?
7. How do you determine whether one crime is a lesser included offense of another crime?
8. What is an inchoate crime?
9. What is the difference between general intent and specific intent?
10. Define and describe the categories of intent used by the Model Penal Code.
11. Who is the principal of a crime? What is the difference between the principal and the accessory to a crime?

Pages 549 through 562

12. What defense(s) might be available to the following individuals?
    a. The Elliots complained to the police that the son of their next-door neighbor broke their garage windows with rocks. They wanted him arrested. The police went next door to arrest the boy, and they discovered that he is seven years old. They arrested him and brought him to the police station. He was charged with destroying the Elliots' property.
    b. Marcus was arrested for the murder of his cousin Michael. At the time that Michael was killed Marcus claimed that he was on a business trip 300 miles away.

    c. Every day on the way to school Rosa pushed Carmen to the ground and stole her lunch. On Tuesday Carmen hid behind a car on the way to school, and when she saw Rosa walking toward her, she jumped out and hit her. Rosa pushed Carmen to the ground and walked away without taking her lunch.

    d. As Paula walked toward her car after work, she was confronted by Terry, who pointed a realistic toy gun at Paula and demanded that Paula hand over her wallet. Paula took a gun out of her purse and shot and killed Terry.

    e. After his car was forced off the road, Patrick tried to stop the bleeding on his wife's face. When she passed out, Patrick ran to a nearby home, jumped over the fence, and banged on the front door. When the occupants would not let him in, Patrick broke a window of the house, climbed through, and ran toward the telephone. The homeowner grabbed a rifle and shot Patrick in the back.

    f. During a grocery store robbery a thief held a gun to a customer's head and demanded that he put all the money from the store safe into a bag, which he did. When the police arrived, they arrested the customer for robbery.

    g. During the last five years of their marriage David beat his wife, Mary, so severely that she was hospitalized four times. About six months after the last beating Mary stabbed David to death while he was sleeping. She was arrested for murder.

    h. Officer Kaplan responded to an emergency call for a store robbery in progress. When the masked thief shot at the officer, Officer Kaplan shot and killed the thief. The man's family wanted Officer Kaplan charged with murder.

13. What is the difference between a complete defense and a partial defense?
14. Describe the various tests that have been developed to determine whether a defendant was insane at the time he or she committed the crime.
15. What are the possible results of successfully proving an insanity defense?
16. What is the difference between the duress and the necessity defenses?
17. What does a defendant have to show to prove entrapment?
18. When can a potential victim use deadly force to protect himself or herself?
19. What is the retreat exception to the self-defense doctrine?
20. What problems arise with using battered woman's syndrome as the basis for a self-defense argument?
21. What protections are afforded by the double jeopardy clause?
22. When might a statute be challenged for vagueness? For overbreadth?

Pages 562 through 571

23. What is a stop-and-frisk search?
24. What is the difference between reasonable suspicion and probable cause? Why does it matter?
25. Why does the court consider the suspect's expectation of privacy when evaluating a search?
26. What is a warrant?
27. List some specific facts that must be included when police officers apply for a warrant to search a suspect's home.
28. What is a no-knock warrant?
29. What exigent circumstances may allow the police to search without a warrant?

Pages 571 through 578

30. What are the *Miranda* warnings, when are the police required to give them, and under what circumstances might a defendant waive them?
31. What extra protection do juveniles usually get when they are given their *Miranda* rights?

Pages 578 through 589

32. What might a defendant expect to occur during booking?
33. What is the exclusionary rule?

34. How do motions to suppress affect the prosecution's case against defendants?
35. What are the differences between a guilty plea and a plea of nolo contendere?
36. If you worked for the prosecution, would you consider the following items to be potentially inculpatory or exculpatory? Could this evidence be potentially inculpatory *and* exculpatory?
    a. the fingerprints of a second person on the murder weapon
    b. a statement that the defendant gave to the police shortly after the arrest disclosing the location of the missing body
    c. samples of hair and skin found at the scene of the crime
37. If the following facts are true, what pretrial motions might you file on behalf of the defendants?
    a. All the local papers have reported that the judge on the case used to be married to the victim.
    b. Each of the two defendants claims that the other defendant was the sole assassin.
    c. The defendant, who was represented by a public defender, needs to conduct an independent drug evaluation, especially since the defendant alleged the green, leafy substance was oregano bought to add spice to spaghetti sauce.
    d. Four of the seven witnesses prepared to testify at trial are related by blood or marriage.
    e. The police stopped the defendant for speeding and then proceeded to search the glove compartment, in which they found a bag of heroin.

Pages 589 through 595

38. Describe the basic steps that occur in a criminal trial.
39. Why is there no requirement that the defendant take the stand?
40. What is the purpose of charging the jury?
41. What are the theories of punishment? Which theory or theories do you think are the most effective in eliminating crime in society?
42. What are the U.S. Sentencing Guidelines, and why are they controversial?
43. Why is it not double jeopardy for the prosecutor to appeal an intermediate-appellate-level decision?

Appendixes

Appendices

Appendix A

Excerpts from the United States Constitution

Preamble

We the People of the United States, in Order to form a more perfect Union, establish Justice, insure domestic Tranquility, provide for the common defence, promote the general Welfare, and secure the Blessings of Liberty to ourselves and our Posterity, do ordain and establish this Constitution for the United States of America.

Article I

Section 1. All legislative Powers herein granted shall be vested in a Congress of the United States, which shall consist of a Senate and House of Representatives.

Section 2. [*Section 2 describes the composition of and qualifications for the House of Representatives.*]

Section 3. [*Section 3 describes the composition of and the qualifications for the Senate.*]

Section 4. The Times, Places and Manner of holding Elections for Senators and Representatives, shall be prescribed in each State by the Legislature thereof; but the Congress may any time by Law make or alter such Regulations, except as to the Places of chusing Senators. . . .

Section 5. [*Section 5 discusses quorums and the development of procedural rules in the House and the Senate.*]

Section 6. [*Section 6 discusses compensation and legislative privileges.*]

Section 7. [*Section 7 establishes procedures for the passage of laws and presidential vetoes.*]

Section 8. The Congress shall have Power To lay and collect Taxes, Duties, Imposts and Excises, to pay the Debts and provide for the common Defence and general Welfare of the United States; but all Duties, Imposts and Excises shall be uniform throughout the United States;

To borrow Money on the credit of the United States;

To regulate Commerce with foreign Nations, and among the several States, and with the Indian Tribes;

To establish an uniform Rule of Naturalization, and uniform Laws on the subject of Bankruptcies throughout the United States; . . .

To constitute Tribunals inferior to the supreme Court;

To define and punish Piracies and Felonies committed on the high Seas, and Offenses against the Law of Nations; . . .

To make all Laws which shall be necessary and proper for carrying into Execution the foregoing Powers, and all other Powers vested by this Constitution in the Government of the United States, or in any Department or Officer thereof.

Section 9. [*Section 9 imposes several limitations on the federal government, including restrictions against preventing states from importing slaves prior to 1808; suspending the writ of habeas corpus; passing bills of attainder, ex post facto laws, and capitation taxes; and granting titles of nobility.*]

Section 10. [*Section 10 places limitations on the states that include not allowing them to enter into treaties, coin money, tax exports, or engage in war.*]

Article II

Section 1. [*Section 1 describes the qualifications for and procedures to be used in selecting the president. It also discusses compensation and succession if the president dies, resigns, or is unable to perform the duties of the office.*]

Section 2. The President shall be Commander in Chief of the Army and Navy of the United States, and of the Militia of the several States, when called into the actual Service of the United States; he may require the Opinion, in writing, of the principal Officer in each of the executive Departments, upon any Subject relating to the Duties of their respective Offices, and he shall have Power to grant Reprieves and Pardons for Offenses against the United States, except in Cases of Impeachment.

He shall have Power, by and with the Advice and Consent of the Senate, to make Treaties, provided two thirds of the Senators present concur; and he shall nominate, and by and with the Advice and Consent of the Senate, shall appoint Ambassadors, other public Ministers and Consuls, Judges of the supreme Court, and all other Officers of the United States, whose Appointments are not herein otherwise provided for, and which shall be established by Law; but the Congress may by Law vest the Appointment of such inferior Officers, as they think proper, in the President alone, in the Courts of Law, or in the Heads of Departments. . . .

Section 3. [*Section 3 lists duties of the president, including developing a state of the union message to Congress, receiving ambassadors from other countries, and "faithfully execut[ing]" the laws of the country.*]

Section 4. The President, Vice President and all civil Officers of the United States, shall be removed from Office on Impeachment for, and Conviction of, Treason, Bribery, or other high Crimes and Misdemeanors.

Article III

Section 1. The judicial Power of the United States, shall be vested in one supreme Court, and in such inferior Courts as the Congress may from time to time ordain and establish. The Judges, both of the supreme and inferior Courts, shall hold their Offices during good Behaviour, and shall, at stated Times, receive for their Services, a Compensation, which shall not be diminished during their Continuance in Office.

Section 2. The judicial Power shall extend to all Cases, in Law and Equity, arising under this Constitution, the Laws of the United States, and Treaties made, or which shall be made, under their Authority;—to all Cases affecting Ambassadors, other public Ministers and Consuls;—to all Cases of admiralty and maritime Jurisdiction;—to Controversies to which the United States shall be a Party;—to Controversies between two or more States;—between a State and Citizens of another State;—between Citizens of different States;—between Citizens of the same State claiming Lands under Grants of different States, and between a State, or the Citizens thereof, and foreign States, Citizens or Subjects.

In all Cases affecting Ambassadors, other public Ministers and Consuls, and those in which a State shall be Party, the supreme Court shall have original Jurisdiction. In all the other Cases before mentioned, the supreme Court shall have appellate Jurisdiction, both as to Law and Fact, with such Exceptions, and under such Regulations as the Congress shall make.

The Trial of all Crimes, except in Cases of Impeachment, shall be by Jury; and such Trial shall be held in the State where the said Crimes shall have been committed; but when not committed within any State, the Trial shall be at such Place or Places as the Congress shall by Law have directed.

Section 3. Treason against the United States, shall consist only of levying War against them, or in adhering to their Enemies, giving them Aid and Comfort. No Person shall be convicted of Treason unless on the Testimony of two Witnesses to the same overt Act, or on Confession in open Court. . . .

Article IV

Section 1. Full Faith and Credit shall be given in each State to the public Acts, Records, and judicial Proceedings of every other State; And the Congress may by general Laws prescribe the Manner in which such Acts, Records, and Proceedings shall be proved, and the Effect thereof.

Section 2. [*Section 2 discusses extradition for crimes (including escaped slaves).*]

Section 3. [*Section 3 discusses admission of new states into the Union.*]

Section 4. The United States shall guarantee to every State in this Union a Republican Form of Government, and shall protect each of them against Invasion; and on Application of the Legislature, or of the Executive (when the Legislature cannot be convened) against domestic Violence.

Article V

The Congress, whenever two thirds of both Houses shall deem it necessary, shall propose Amendments to this Constitution, or, on the Application of the Legislatures of two thirds of the several States, shall call a Convention for proposing Amendments, which, in either Case, shall be valid to all Intents and Purposes, as Part of this Constitution, when ratified by the Legislatures of three fourths of the several States, or by Conventions in three fourths thereof, as the one or the other Mode of Ratification may be proposed by the Congress. . . . [*This article also contains language designed to protect the importation of slaves until 1808.*]

Article VI

[*Article VI states that debts incurred by the national government under the former Articles*

of Confederation will be assumed by the new government.]

This Constitution, and the Laws of the United States which shall be made in Pursuance thereof; and all Treaties made, or which shall be made, under the Authority of the United States, shall be the supreme Law of the Land; and the Judges in every State shall be bound thereby, any Thing in the Constitution or Laws of any State to the Contrary notwithstanding.

[N]o religious Test shall ever be required as a Qualification to any Office or public Trust under the United States.

Article VII

The Ratification of the Conventions of nine States, shall be sufficient for the Establishment of this Constitution between the States so ratifying the Same. . . .

Amendment I[1]

Congress shall make no law respecting an establishment of religion, or prohibiting the free exercise thereof; or abridging the freedom of speech, or of the press, or the right of the people peaceably to assemble, and to petition the Government for a redress of grievances.

Amendment II

A well regulated Militia, being necessary to the security of a free State, the right of the people to keep and bear Arms, shall not be infringed.

Amendment III

No Soldier shall, in time of peace be quartered in any house, without the consent of the Owner, nor in time of war, but in a manner prescribed by law.

Amendment IV

The right of the people to be secure in their persons, houses, papers, and effects, against

---

[1]The first ten amendments were ratified in 1791.

unreasonable searches and seizures, shall not be violated, and no Warrants shall issue, but upon probable cause, supported by Oath or affirmation, and particularly describing the place to be searched, and the persons or things to be seized.

Amendment V

No person shall be held to answer for a capital, or otherwise infamous crime, unless on a presentment or indictment of a Grand Jury, except in cases arising in the land or naval forces, or in the Militia, when in actual service in time of War or public danger; nor shall any person be subject for the same offence to be twice put in jeopardy of life or limb, nor shall be compelled in any criminal case to be a witness against himself, nor be deprived of life, liberty, or property, without due process of law; nor shall private property be taken for public use without just compensation.

Amendment VI

In all criminal prosecutions, the accused shall enjoy the right to a speedy and public trial, by an impartial jury of the State and district wherein the crime shall have been committed, which district shall have been previously ascertained by law, and to be informed of the nature and cause of the accusation; to be confronted with the witnesses against him; to have compulsory process for obtaining witnesses in his favor, and to have the assistance of counsel for his defence.

Amendment VII

In Suits at common law, where the value in controversy shall exceed twenty dollars, the right of trial by jury shall be preserved, and no fact tried by a jury shall be otherwise re-examined in any Court of the United States, than according to the rules of the common law.

Amendment VIII

Excessive bail shall not be required, nor excessive fines imposed, nor cruel and unusual punishments inflicted.

Amendment IX

The enumeration in the Constitution of certain rights shall not be construed to deny or disparage others retained by the people.

Amendment X

The powers not delegated to the United States by the Constitution, nor prohibited by it to the States, are reserved to the States respectively, or to the people.

Amendment XI

(ratified in 1798)

The Judicial power of the United States shall not be construed to extend to any suit in law or equity, commenced or prosecuted against one of the United States by Citizens of another State, or by Citizens or Subjects of any Foreign State.

Amendment XII

(ratified in 1804)

[*Amendment XII revises the way in which the electoral college, and in some cases the Congress, votes for the offices of president and vice president.*]

Amendment XIII

(ratified in 1865)

Section 1. Neither slavery nor involuntary servitude, except as a punishment for crime whereof the party shall have been duly convicted, shall exist within the United States, or any place subject to their jurisdiction.

Section 2. Congress shall have power to enforce this article by appropriate legislation.

Amendment XIV

(ratified in 1868)

Section 1. All persons born or naturalized in the United States and subject to the jurisdiction thereof, are citizens of the United States and of the State wherein they reside. No State shall make or enforce any law which shall abridge the privileges or immunities of citizens of the United States; nor shall any State deprive any person of life, liberty, or property, without due process of law; nor deny to any person within its jurisdiction the equal protection of the laws.

Section 2. [*Section 2 counts former slaves as equal to all other residents in terms of apportioning representation in the House of Representatives.*]

Section 3. [*Section 3 disqualifies those who participate in an insurrection or rebellion against the United States (e.g., the Civil War) from holding public office in the federal government unless Congress votes by a two-thirds majority to remove this disability.*]

Section 4. [*Section 4 states that neither Congress nor any state can be held responsible for debts incurred in aid of an insurrection (e.g., the Civil War).*]

Section 5. The Congress shall have power to enforce, by appropriate legislation, the provisions of this article.

Amendment XV

(ratified in 1870)

Section 1. The right of citizens of the United States to vote shall not be denied or abridged by the United States or by any State on account of race, color, or previous condition of servitude.

Section 2. The Congress shall have power to enforce this article by appropriate legislation.

Amendment XVI

(ratified in 1913)

The Congress shall have power to lay and collect taxes on incomes, from whatever source derived, without apportionment among the several States, and without regard to any census or enumeration.

Amendment XVII

(ratified in 1913)

[*Article XVII changed the method of selecting senators from appointment by state legisla-*

tures to direct election by the people of that state.]

Amendment XVIII

(ratified in 1919)

[*Amendment XVIII the "Prohibition Amendment" prohibited the manufacture, sale, or transportation of intoxicating liquors.*]

Amendment XIX

(ratified in 1920)

Section 1. The right of citizens of the United States to vote shall not be denied or abridged by the United States or by any State on account of sex.

Section 2. Congress shall have power to enforce his article by appropriate legislation.

Amendment XX

(ratified in 1933)

[*Amendment XX changed the starting dates for presidential, vice presidential, and congressional terms. It also sets out procedures for situations in which the president elect dies before he or she actually takes office.*]

Amendment XXI

(ratified in 1933)

[*Amendment XXI repeals Amendment XVIII (Prohibition) but allows states to continue to prohibit the importation of intoxicating liquors across their own borders.*]

Amendment XXII

(ratified in 1951)

[*Amendment XXII imposes a two-term limit on the office of president.*]

Amendment XXIII

(ratified in 1961)

[*Amendment XXIII gives residents of the District of Columbia electors in the electoral college so they are on equal footing with residents of the states in "voting" for the president.*]

Amendment XXIV

(ratified in 1964)

Section 1. The right of citizens of the United States to vote in any primary or other election for President or Vice President, for electors for President or Vice President, or for Senator or Representative in Congress, shall not be denied or abridged by the United States or any State by reason of failure to pay any poll tax or other tax.

Section 2. The Congress shall have power to enforce this article by appropriate legislation.

Amendment XXV

(ratified in 1967)

[*Amendment XXV establishes procedures for selecting a new vice president when the vice president moves up to president upon the death or resignation of a president or when the vice president resigns or dies in office. It also sets out procedures for determining when a sitting president is temporarily unable to fulfill the duties of office.*]

Amendment XXVI

(ratified in 1971)

Section 1. The right of citizens of the United States, who are eighteen years of age or older, to vote shall not be denied or abridged by the United States or by any State on account of age.

Section 2. The Congress shall have power to enforce this article by appropriate legislation.

Amendment XXVII

(ratified in 1992)

No law varying the compensation for the services of the Senators and Representatives shall take effect, until an election of Representatives shall have intervened.

Appendix B

Fundamentals of Good Writing

*I have made this letter longer than usual, only because
I have not had the time to make it shorter.*
Blaise Pascal

INTRODUCTION

How you say something is often as important as what you say. No matter how insightful and intelligent your thoughts are, if your writing is filled with misspellings and grammar errors, the reader will very likely discount the value of what you are saying. In legal writing, good writing is especially important because people's fortunes often rest on what a lawyer has written. In legal writing therefore it is simply too costly to write in any style other than one that is clear, concise, and grammatically correct.

To be an effective writer, follow these simple rules:

Rule 1 Develop a clear, readable writing style that is appropriate for the audience to whom it is directed. This partly depends on an awareness of the ways in which legal writing differs from more informal writing and speech.

Rule 2 Always use good grammar and proper punctuation. Like it or not, most lawyers, judges, and clients are grammar snobs. If you do not follow the basic conventions of correct spelling and grammar, they will assume you are lazy or stupid, or both.

Rule 3   Carefully proofread what you have written. Take advantage of any spell-checking or grammar programs associated with the word processing software you use, but do not rely on these programs alone. A spell checker will not find correctly spelled but misused words. For example, a spell checker would find nothing wrong with this sentence: "The witness recounted the hole story."

Rule 4   Write and rewrite and then rewrite again. There is no such thing as good writing, only good rewriting. For those of you who suffer from writer's block, this is actually good news. Sometimes people are afraid to start writing because they assume what they initially write will be the final product. It is not.

This appendix is designed to help you improve the style and technical quality of your writing so that your work will be as professional looking as possible.

PART I: GRAMMAR

Good legal writing starts by being good writing. Therefore, to rate as good legal writing, the document must follow the normal rules of grammar and punctuation. The following suggestions should help you correct the most common grammar errors.

A. Use Proper Sentence Structure

Using proper sentence structure will make your writing easier to comprehend. Proper sentence structure means using simple sentence construction, avoiding sentence fragments and run-ons, and using parallel constructions.

1. Use Simple Sentence Construction

Whenever possible, stick to simple sentences. Legal writing is hard enough to read without complicating it further through long, convoluted sentences. Follow these guidelines:

a. Use normal sentence order

Unless there is a good reason to do otherwise, follow normal sentence order: noun, verb, object.

b. One thought per sentence

Have one main thought in a sentence.

c. Limit sentences to twenty-five words

Vary the sentence length but the average sentence should be no longer than twenty-five words.

d. Use tabulations

Divide long sentences using **tabulations**. If the items are complete sentences, use the following format:

1. Begin each item with an upper-case letter.
2. End each item with a period.

If the items are not complete sentences, use the following format:

1. a lower-case letter at the beginning of each item,
2. a semicolon or comma after each item, and
3. an "or" or "and" before the last item.

e. Avoid intrusive phrases

Do not let phrases or clauses intrude between the subject and verb. These **intrusive phrases** disrupt the sentence's logical flow and make it difficult for the reader to follow what is being said.

> **Example:** The interrogatories sent to our client and received by him at his home three days ago force us to reformulate our defense strategy.

Fourteen words separate the subject, *interrogatories*, from the verb, *force*. This writing style creates several problems. First, until the reader reaches the verb, he or she must wait in suspense as to what is going on with the subject, the interrogatories. Second, the reader must process the new information contained in the intrusive clause while remembering that the main point of the sentence relates to the interrogatories.

If you find yourself writing particularly long sentences, check to see whether your reader may get lost between the beginning and the end. If so, you may have inserted intrusive phrases between your subject and verb. There are two solutions. First, you can simply divide the sentence and create two sentences.

> **Revised:** Three days ago our client received interrogatories. The interrogatories force us to reformulate our defense strategy.

The other solution is to take the intrusive phrase out of the middle and put it at the beginning or the end.

> **Revised:** Sent to our client and received by him at his home three days ago, the interrogatories force us to reformulate our defense strategy.

NETNOTE

To find online exercises on run-ons, fragments, and more, go to Grammar Bytes!, *www.chompcomp.com/menu.htm.*

2. Avoid Sentence Fragments

An obvious corollary to the rule that you should use simple sentence construction is the requirement that you write in sentences. A sentence contains a subject and a verb and can stand alone as a complete thought. A sentence can be a single independent clause, two independent clauses joined with a coordinating conjunction, or an independent and a dependent clause.

> **Example:** The man yelled for help.
> (*independent clause*)
>
> The man yelled for help, and the police came running.
> (*two independent clauses*)
>
> Even though the man yelled for help, no one came to his assistance.
> (*dependent clause followed by independent clause*)

Sentence fragment
An incomplete sentence.

Sentence fragments are incomplete sentences and cannot stand alone. One type of sentence fragment is the phrase with no verb.

> **Example:** The doctor in white. (Did what?)

Another type of sentence fragment is the prepositional phrase standing alone.

> **Example:** By six o'clock. (What will happen?)

To correct the first type of fragment, insert a verb.

> **Revised:** The doctor in white *said* that I could go home.

To correct the second type of fragment, attach the prepositional phrase to the rest of the sentence.

> **Revised:** By six o'clock *we should have heard from the doctor.*

The most common type of sentence fragment is the **dependent clause** standing alone. The writer thinks she has written a complete sentence when she has not. The dependent clause does contain a subject and verb, but it cannot stand alone and make sense, as it does not contain a complete thought. When you read a dependent clause that is standing alone, it is as though you are waiting for the other shoe to drop.

Dependent clause
A clause that contains a subject and a verb but that cannot stand alone, as it does not contain a complete thought. A dependent clause always begins with a subordinating conjunction.

> **Example:** Although the defense attorney asked for a finding of not guilty. (What happened?)

Dependent clauses always begin with what is known as a **subordinating conjunction**: *after, although, as, because, before, even though, if, since, unless, when, where, whereas,* and *while*. To correct a sentence fragment created by a dependent clause standing alone, drop the subordinating conjunction and turn the dependent clause into an independent clause, or add an independent clause.

Subordinating conjunction
Dependent clauses always begin with subordinating conjunctions: *after, although, as, because, before, even though, if, since, unless, when, where, whereas,* and *while.*

> **Revised:** The defense attorney asked for a finding of not guilty. (subordinating conjunction dropped)
>
> Although the defense attorney asked for a finding of not guilty, the jury brought in a guilty verdict. (independent clause added)

3. Avoid Run-On Sentences (Fused Sentences and Comma Splices)

The **run-on sentence** is the opposite of the sentence fragment. Instead of being half a sentence, it is actually two sentences. It can occur either as a comma splice (two independent clauses joined by a comma) or as a fused sentence (two independent clauses with no separating punctuation).

Run-on sentence
Two sentences written as one. It can occur either as a common splice (two independent clauses joined by a comma) or as a fused sentence (two independent clauses with no separating punctuation).

> **Examples:** The man cried for help, the police came running. (*comma splice*)
>
> The man cried for help the police came running. (*fused sentence*)

Run-on sentences can be corrected in any of the following ways:

> **Revised:** The man cried for help. The police came running. (divided into two sentences)
>
> The man cried for help; the police came running. (two independent clauses separated by a semicolon, not a comma)
>
> The man cried for help, and the police came running. (two independent clauses joined by a comma and a coordinating conjunction)

Coordinating conjunction
A coordinating conjunction can join two independent clauses; examples include *and, but, for, nor, or,* and *yet.*

As seen above, a comma and a coordinating conjunction can join two independent clauses. **Coordinating conjunctions** include *and, but, for, nor, or,* and *yet.*

However, you cannot use conjunctive adverbs to join two independent clauses. Examples of **conjunctive adverbs** are *also, consequently, furthermore, however, moreover, nevertheless, then,* and *therefore.*

A very common error is to try to use *however* or *therefore* to join two independent clauses. Do not do it.

Conjunctive adverbs
Examples include *also, consequently, furthermore, however, moreover, nevertheless, then,* and *therefore.* These should not be used to join two independent clauses.

Incorrect:	The holding in the *Lane* decision would appear to be against our client, however, we do have one counterargument.
Revised:	The holding in the *Lane* decision would appear to be against our client. We do, however, have one counterargument.

4. Use Parallel Construction

Parallel construction
Using the same grammatical structure for clauses or phrases that bear the same relationship to some major idea.

Clauses or phrases that bear the same relationship to some major idea should have parallel grammatical structure. When writing lists, be particularly careful about not drifting into variations that lack **parallel construction.**

Incorrect:	The boy ate, he went horseback riding, and he was swimming.
Revised:	The boy ate, went horseback riding, and swam.
Incorrect:	My objections are that the complaint was filed late, no valid cause of action, and the wrong defendant.
Revised:	My objections are that the complaint was filed late, that it does not contain a valid cause of action, and that the plaintiff has sued the wrong defendant.

B. Use the Proper Verb Tense

In legal writing there are two common problems with verb tense: making inappropriate shifts between verb tenses and using present tense for events that happened in the past. The first problem, inappropriate shifts, occurs when a writer begins describing an event in one tense but then, perhaps realizing the wrong tense is being used, switches to another tense. When proofreading, be sure to check for this potential problem.

To correct the second problem, inappropriately using present tense, remember that past tense should always be used for actions that happened in the past. In legal writing these include

1. the facts that make up your client's story,
2. the events that occurred in the cases you read, and
3. what the court said in those cases.

Incorrect:	1. In *Bennett* Mrs. Brown runs home . . . ;
	2. In *Bennett* a woman sues . . . ; and
	3. In *Bennett* the court holds that. . . .
Revised:	1. In *Bennett* Mrs. Brown ran home . . . ;
	2. In *Bennett* a woman sued . . . ; and
	3. In *Bennett* the court held that. . . .

But use present tense when describing a rule of law.

Incorrect:	In *Bennett* the court held that minors *were* allowed to void contracts that they have signed.
Revised:	In *Bennett* the court held that minors *are* allowed to void contracts that they have signed.

C. Make Sure Pronouns and Antecedents Agree

When you do not want to use a noun, you use a **pronoun** as a substitute. In the following sentence *Mary* is the noun and *her* is the pronoun.

Example:	Mary reviewed her testimony with her attorney.

Because a pronoun (*hers, her, his, him, it, its, them, their, theirs*) substitutes for a noun that has preceded it, the noun is known as an **antecedent**. The pronoun and its antecedent must match as to gender and number. This often becomes a problem when the writer is trying to avoid sexist writing.

Incorrect:	The new computer user may find after many attempts at installing the software by themselves that they need help.

Sometimes you can correct this by making the noun plural.

Revised:	New computer users may find after many attempts at installing the software by themselves that they need help.

Another possibility is to drop the pronoun.

Revised:	The new computer user may find after many attempts at installing the software that help is needed.

Finally, you may need to resort to a "he or she," "his or hers," or "her or him" combination.

> **Revised:** The new computer user may find after many attempts at installing the software that he or she needs help.

D. Put Modifying Words Close to What They Modify

Misplaced modifiers are a very common problem. Sometimes the result is merely humorous, as in the following example:

> **Example:** The college has all the money from students deposited in the bank.

Obviously, the college has deposited the money and not the students. Other times, however, a misplaced modifier could cause serious interpretation problems and even litigation. Consider the following example taken from a lease provision:

> **Example:** If through no fault of Tenant, the apartment becomes uninhabitable, Landlord shall be notified immediately to provide alternative dwelling.

Does this mean that the landlord must be notified immediately or that the landlord must provide an alternative dwelling immediately? In this last example the word *immediately* is referred to as a squinting modifier because you cannot tell if the writer means for it to modify the word that precedes it or the word that follows it. Frequently this happens with the placement of the word *only*.

> **Example:** You may talk with the witness only today.

Does this mean that you can talk with the witness but not with anyone else, such as the defendant, or does this mean that you can talk to the witness today only? Depending on what you mean, you could rewrite the sentence as follows:

> **Example:** You may talk with only the witness today.
> You may talk with the witness today only.

E. Avoid Punctuation Problems

One area of grammar that may seem the most boring and useless is the area of punctuation. Nothing could be further from the truth. There are too many cases where a comma, or the lack of one, has been the focus of litigation. One example should suffice to emphasize the importance of being careful with punctuation. A will contained the following provision:

> I bequeath and devise my entire estate, both personal and real, . . . in equal shares, absolutely and in fee to my cousin, the said Walter Cassidy; Robert Jamison and William Stivers, tenants on my farm; George E. Smith, who rents my property on Bland Avenue, Shelbyville, Kentucky; and the Kentucky Society for Crippled Children.[1]

Jamison and Stivers argued that they should each receive one-fifth of the bequest. The other three beneficiaries argued that the two men should share one-fourth. Semicolons separated each of the other beneficiaries, whereas Jamison and Stivers were not separated. How would you decide this case? The court awarded the two men one-fifth each. Was the court correct? Only the dead testator knows for sure.

1. Use the Serial Comma

As suggested above, the punctuation problem that gets more attorneys into trouble than any other is the one regarding the **serial comma**. In a series of three or more items, use a comma after each item until you reach the final conjunction.

> **Serial comma**
> In a series of three or more items use a comma after each item until you reach the final conjunction.

Incorrect:	The boy swam, ran and played.
Revised:	The boy swam, ran, and played.

By always including that final comma you will never have to face the following interpretation problem:

> Sally went to the bookstore to buy book covers in green, red, blue and yellow.

Does this mean she bought three covers: one green, one red, and one blue and yellow? Or did she buy four book covers: one green, one red, one blue, and one yellow?

2. Do Not Use a Comma with Compound Verbs or between a Subject and Its Verb

Do not use a comma with compound subjects, verbs, or objects. Also do not let a comma separate your subject and its verb. Legal writers most often mispunctuate compound verbs.

Incorrect:	The boy ran, and fell down.
Revised:	The boy ran and fell down.

---

[1]Cassidy v. Vanattas, 242 S.W.2d 619, 620 (Ky. App. 1951).

3. Use Commas to Set Off Phrases Containing Nonessential Information

Nonrestrictive phrase
A phrase that is not essential to the sense of a sentence; it should be set off with commas.

Grammarians say that we must set off **nonrestrictive phrases** with commas. What that means is that if the sentence would make sense without the phrase, the phrase is nonrestrictive (i.e., nonessential) and should be set off with commas.

Incorrect:	In the leading case *Dillon v. Legg* the court held that a mother can recover for emotional distress.
Revised:	In the leading case, *Dillon v. Legg*, the court held that a mother can recover for emotional distress.

The sentence would retain its meaning and still make sense without the phrase *Dillon v. Legg*.

A **restrictive phrase** contains essential information.

Restrictive phrase
A phrase that contains essential information; it should not be set off with commas.

Incorrect:	All students, who do not register on time, must pay a $20 late fee.
Revised:	All students who do not register on time must pay a $20 late fee.

Without the phrase "who do not register on time," the sentence reads: "All students must pay a $20 late fee." The phrase contains essential information, the absence of which alters the sentence's meaning. Therefore, it should not be set off with commas.

As a general rule of thumb, use "that" with restrictive phrases and "which" with nonrestrictive phrases.

Example of restrictive:	Courts that recognize spousal immunity usually base their decision on a desire to promote family harmony. (Only some courts recognize spousal immunity.)
Example of nonrestrictive:	Courts, which are forums for justice, decide cases based on the facts presented to them. (All courts are forums for justice.)

4. Forming the Possessive

To form the possessive for singular nouns, use '*s* unless the noun ends in an *s* and it would make the possessive hard to pronounce.

Examples:	child's Bob's James's witness's

Traditionally, however, you should drop the *s* after the apostrophe with some proper names that both end in *s* and have an internal *s* sound.

Examples:	Jesus' life

To form the possessive for plural nouns, use *'s* for nouns that do not end in *s* but only an apostrophe for those that end in *s*.

Examples:	children's witnesses'

5. Combining Quotation Marks with Other Punctuation

Periods and commas always belong inside the closing quotation mark.

Examples:	The court stated that "the case should be remanded for a new trial."
	The court stated that "the case should be remanded for a new trial," and then it reprimanded the prosecuting attorney for his delay tactics.

Semicolons and colons always belong outside the closing quotation mark.

Example:	The court stated that "the case should be remanded for a new trial"; the court also reprimanded the prosecuting attorney for his delay tactics.

When they are part of the quotation, place dashes, question marks, and exclamation points inside the closing quotation mark.

Example:	The attorney asked his client, "Should we proceed?" before entering the courtroom.

Otherwise, place those marks outside the closing quotation mark.

Example:	Did the court state that "the case should be remanded for a new trial"?

PART II: STYLE

Accident Report

The party of the first part hereinafter known as Jack . . . and . . . The party of the second part hereinafter known as Jill . . . Ascended or caused to be ascended an elevation of undetermined height and degree of slope, hereinafter referred to as "hill." Whose purpose it was to obtain, attain, procure, secure, or otherwise gain acquisition to, by any and/or all means available to them a receptacle or container, hereinafter known as "pail," suitable for the transport of a liquid whose chemical properties shall be limited to hydrogen and oxygen, the proportions of which shall not be less than or exceed two parts for the first mentioned element and one part for the latter. Such combination will hereinafter be called "water." On the occasion stated above, it has been established beyond reasonable doubt that Jack did plunge, tumble, topple, or otherwise be caused to lose his footing in a manner that caused his body to be thrust into a downward direction. As a direct result of these combined circumstances, Jack suffered fractures and contusions of his cranial regions. Jill, whether due to Jack's misfortune or not, was known to also tumble in similar fashion after Jack. (Whether the term, "after," shall be interpreted in a spatial or time passage sense, has not been determined.)[2]

Besides following the basic rules of grammar, there are various techniques you can use to increase the clarity and effectiveness of your writing. These techniques include avoiding long paragraphs, using transitions, being concise by eliminating unnecessary words and introductory phrases and by saying it only once, and avoiding the passive voice. This section concludes with some special techniques peculiar to legal writing.

A. Avoid Long Paragraphs

Of course, there is no mechanical rule as to paragraph length. Nonetheless, if you find you have written a paragraph that is over half a page in length, consider whether it is too long. Check to be sure that you have only one major idea in the paragraph.

Trying to develop more than one theme in each paragraph can confuse the reader and require her or him to reread the paragraph. A good check is to

NETNOTE

At the following site, you can find help organized by level: word and sentence, paragraph, and paper: *www.ccc.commnet.edu/grammar/*.

---

[2]The Legal Guide to Mother Goose 7-11 (Don Sandburg trans., 1978).

go back over your document and see whether you can find a topic sentence in each paragraph that states the theme for that paragraph. Then, reading just those sentences from each paragraph, you should be able to follow your argument as it develops throughout your document.

B. Do Not Bury Your Points

A common error is to start a paragraph with "In the case of. . . ." This is a poor writing style for two reasons. First, a reader pays the most attention to the first and last sentences of a paragraph. Therefore, you should place your most important points there rather than burying them in the middle of the paragraph. Second, if you simply start your paragraph with a case description, you have failed to tell the reader why the case is relevant. No one (or at least no one we know) enjoys reading about case law in the abstract. In order to be interested in what you have to say about a given case, the reader must first understand why it is relevant. Lead off with a sentence or clause that will help the reader understand why you will be discussing the next case. At a minimum let the reader know that it is the leading case, the only case, the most recent case, or the like, and place the case citation at the end of the sentence.

> **Incorrect:** In <u>Bennett v. Bennett</u>, 186 N.E.2d 85 (Mass. 1988), the plaintiff sued to have a contract set aside, arguing that she was only sixteen years old when she signed it.
>
> **Revised:** Several cases have dealt with the issue of whether a contract can be set aside if one of the parties was a minor when the contract was signed. For example, in one recent case the plaintiff sued to have the contract set aside, arguing that she was only sixteen years old when she signed it. <u>Bennett v. Bennett</u>, 186 N.E.2d 85 (Mass. 1988).

C. Use Transitions

The type of case introduction in the prior example is one form of **transition**. Transitions help your reader follow the flow of your argument. They provide the link from where you have been to where you are going. On the simplest level, transitions can indicate a sequence: "The first point to be made is. . . . The second point to be made is. . . ." On a more sophisticated level, transitions artfully tie together the preceding thought and the one that follows. Assume a writer has written a paragraph analyzing *Bennett v. Bennett* and the paragraph concludes with the following sentence:

Transition
In writing, a technique used to help your reader move from one thought to the next and to see the connections between them.

> The court therefore held that as the plaintiff was only sixteen at the time she signed the contract, the contract should be set aside as void.

The next paragraph could pick up on the theme presented in the first paragraph by beginning with the following sentence:

> Because Margaret was only fifteen at the time of the contract's formation, her position that her contract should be set aside is consistent with that of the court in <u>Bennett</u>.

D. Be Concise

A taxpayer testified, "As God is my judge, I do not owe this tax." The judge answered, "He's not, I am; and you do."[3] While this may be an extreme example of brevity, it is always a good idea to write concisely so as not to bore your reader. But it is particularly important for lawyers to do so.

One major reason for being as concise as possible is that every unnecessary word serves as a source of potential ambiguity. If you write "null and void" instead of simply "void," you raise the issue of whether there is a difference between something that is only "void" and something that is both "null and void."

Second, those who read an attorney's writing are usually very busy people. Judges, other lawyers, and clients have little time to waste. They want to hear what you have to say and be done with it.

You should remember three guidelines when reviewing something you have written: Eliminate unnecessary words, remove unnecessary introductory phrases, and say it once. By following these guidelines you can condense your writing without sacrificing any of the content.

1. Eliminate Unnecessary Words

There are many compound word combinations that you can replace with a single word. Here are some examples:

At this point in time	Now
At that point in time	Then
Notwithstanding the fact that	Although
There is no doubt but that	Doubtless
The reason why is that	Because
The fact that	(Usually no replacement necessary)

> **Incorrect:** Because of the fact that John shot the victim, he will be found guilty.
>
> **Revised:** Because John shot the victim, he will be found guilty.

---

[3] Judge J. Edgar Murdock of the United States Tax Court, quoted in Brison v. Commissioner of Internal Revenue, T.C. Memo 1983-01, 11.

Finally, there is the attorney's favorite word: *clearly*—as in "Clearly the defendant was negligent." Either the defendant was or was not negligent. Saying the issue is clear will not make it so. In fact, this word often acts as a red flag, raising the reader's suspicions. After all, if you have to bootstrap your argument with words such as *clearly*, perhaps your argument is not that clear.

2. Remove Unnecessary Introductory Phrases

Phrases such as "It is interesting to note that . . ." and "It should be noted in this connection that . . ." are unnecessary filler. When writing a first draft, these phrases are often just what the writer needs to make the pen start moving across the page (or to cause the words to start appearing on the computer monitor). Use these phrases for that purpose, but then go back and strike them out. A good test is this: If the sentence makes sense without the introduction, cross it out.

3. Say It Once

If you find phrases such as "in other words" sprinkled throughout your writing, check to make sure that you are not engaging in some unnecessary duplication. Often a writer will finish a sentence and then think of a better way to say the same thing. We all have doubts now and then about just how clear our points are. Therefore, when this better approach occurs to us, instead of recognizing it as the better alternative we leave in both sentences. Instead try to combine the two approaches, or simply pick the better one and drop the other.

E. Avoid the Passive Voice

Use the active voice whenever possible. The **passive voice** is a weaker form of writing. In the passive voice the subject is acted on, but it is often unclear who is doing the acting.

Passive voice
A form of writing where the subject of the sentence is being acted on; opposite of **active voice.**

> **Examples:**   The ball was thrown by Mary. (*passive voice*)
> The ball was thrown. (*passive voice with actor missing so that it is unclear who threw the ball*)
>
> The ruling was made by the trial judge that the defendant was guilty. (*passive voice*)
> The ruling was made that the defendant was guilty. (*passive voice with actor missing so that it is unclear who made the ruling*)

Such ambiguity has its place in legal writing but only if you plan it.

The best clues that you are using the passive voice are the "by" construction, as in the first and third examples ("by Mary," "by the trial judge") and the absence of the actor entirely, as in the second and fourth examples.

Active voice
A form of writing where the subject of the sentence does the acting; opposite of **passive voice**.

Active voice is just that—active. In the **active voice** the subject of the sentence acts.

> **Examples:**   Mary threw the ball.
>   The trial judge ruled that the defendant was guilty.

Avoid the passive voice whenever possible. Usually, because of the "by" construction, it adds needless weight to your writing through the addition of useless words. When, to solve that problem, the writer omits the "by" construction, ambiguity often results. Consider the following lease provision, and try to determine who must report what to whom:

> When conditions affecting the habitability of the rental property are discovered, they must be promptly reported and failure to do so shall constitute a material breach of this lease.

Does the landlord have to report defects to the tenant, or does the tenant have to disclose conditions that affect the habitability to the landlord? Perhaps each party must disclose such conditions to the other party. Ambiguity such as this is an open invitation to a lawsuit.

The third reason for avoiding the passive voice is that it is a less powerful form. This becomes particularly important to the legal writer in advocacy writing, but it is something to keep in mind for any form of writing.

There are times when the passive voice is appropriate. But you must know when those times are and then use the passive voice by design and not by inadvertence. Specifically, there are four occasions when you may wish to use the passive voice:

1. When the writer wants to highlight the action instead of the actor.

> **Example:**   The man had been murdered.

2. When the actor is unknown.

> **Example:**   The dead body had been left in the woods.

3. When the writer wants to state a general principle.

> **Example:**   All men are created equal.

4. When the writer wants to disassociate the actor from the statement.

> **Example:**   The victim was robbed.
> **Not:**   Our client robbed the victim.

F. Special Rules for Legal Writing

As we mentioned at the beginning of this appendix, good legal writing is simply good writing. If you possess a clear, understandable style, you are well on your way to being a good legal writer. However, because you will be writing about the law and the legal system, you need to know a few special rules.

1. Avoid Legalese

Avoid the temptation to use "legalese," archaic legal terminology, to impress your reader. Several states have passed legislation requiring that all legal documents be written in plain English. Although many attorneys are still resisting the plain English movement, you should avoid legalese whenever possible.

Whenever you find yourself tempted to use legal sounding words, such as *wherefore, aforesaid,* and especially **said**, ask yourself if there is a less stilted English word that can serve your purpose better. Consider the following example, and ask yourself whether the word *said* adds anything or actually creates ambiguity.

> **Example:**   The defendant was seated inside a station wagon. Parked next to
>   him was a Corvette. Said car was green.

Usually, words such as *said* only give the illusion of precision and bog down the writing with heavy-sounding legal words.

2. Make the Court and Not the Court Opinion the Actor

You can avoid another common writing error if you remember that inanimate objects cannot act. Always make the court and not the court opinion do the holding.

> **Incorrect:** <u>Lewis</u> held that. . . .
> **Revised:**   The court in <u>Lewis</u> held that. . . .

3. Avoid Unnecessary Variation

If you have written "the car" four times in a paragraph, you may be tempted to switch to "the motor vehicle." Avoid the temptation. You may leave your reader wondering if you are talking about both a car and a motor vehicle. As this example illustrates, variation can cause serious interpretation problems if your reader thinks you mean to refer to two separate objects when you mean to refer to only one.

4. Do Not Use the First Person

The generally accepted rule in legal writing is to avoid using the first person. You want the emphasis to be on what you are saying and not on the fact that it is you who is saying it. Whenever you find yourself starting a sentence with a phrase such as "I think the court will hold that . . . ," go back and delete the first two words. Because you are the author, the reader already knows that these are your thoughts and no one else's. The reader also knows that there is no way that you can be 100 percent certain of what you write. Therefore, there is no need to soften the certitude with which you write by inserting "I think."

The one time when you can use the first person is when you are referring to one of your firm's clients, as in "Our client wishes to settle." However, even in that case some purists would prefer to use the client's name, as in "Ms. Brown wishes to settle."

5. Do Not Use Contractions

Legal writing is formal writing, and in formal writing there is no place for contractions. Contractions are acceptable only when you are writing an informal note for someone within the firm or, depending on the policy of your firm, occasionally a letter to a client.

6. Do Not Ask Your Reader Questions

It is your job to provide answers, not to ask your reader questions. There is nothing more annoying than to be reading someone's legal analysis only to be stopped by a series of questions.

> **Example:** The court in <u>Lewis</u> held that liability is limited to automobile accidents. Will that court extend its holding to our client's facts? Will the court limit its holding to exclude our client's facts?

The reader will probably be thinking, "I don't know. That's what I'm paying you to tell me." When you find yourself posing questions, simply rephrase them as issues.

> **Revised:** The court in <u>Lewis</u> held that liability is limited to automobile accidents. That raises the issue of whether the court will extend that holding to our client's facts or limit it to the facts of <u>Lewis</u>.

7. That Case/This Case

The convention is to refer to a cited case as **that case** and to your client's case as **this case**.

That case
A case that you are citing.

This case
Your client's case.

> **Example:** The court in <u>Lewis</u> held that liability is limited to automobile accidents. In that case the husband had been driving and the wife was a passenger when the accident occurred.

8. Written Numbers versus Numerals

There are times when you should write out numbers as opposed to using numerals. In text you write out the following numbers:

- zero to ninety-nine;
- any round number, such as one hundred; and
- any number that begins a sentence.

In footnotes you follow the same rules except you write out only the numbers zero through nine. When you have a series of numbers in a sentence, some of which you should write out and some of which you should give as numerals, use all numerals.

> **Example:** There were 2 attorneys, 40 witnesses, and 105 documents.

9. Do Not Eliminate the Articles "A," "An," and "The"

Leaving out articles makes your writing choppy and hard to follow. This style probably comes from students mistakenly thinking that their writing will appear more "lawyerly" if they adopt a headnote style of writing.

> **Example:** A person injured in fall from automobile parking floor to ground below while seeking shelter from rain was at most gratuitous or bare licensee.
>
> **Revised:** A person injured in *a* fall from *an* automobile parking floor to *the* ground below while seeking shelter from *the* rain was at most *a* gratuitous or bare licensee.

PART III: CORRECT WORD USAGE

Correct word usage simply means choosing the correct word to say exactly what you mean. At times this may require you to consult a dictionary or thesaurus. The following is a list of the most commonly misused words.

And/Or

There is much debate as to whether the *and/or* combination is acceptable. Many writers believe it is cumbersome and requires the reader to do too much work to understand its meaning. For example, in the phrase "the husband and/or the wife," the reader must translate that to mean the husband, the wife, or both. Therefore, many writers prefer it to be written just that way.

Because/Since

Because denotes a causal relationship. *Since* refers to time. Using *since* to also denote a causal relationship can cause ambiguity.

Examples:	Because he admitted his guilt, he has been held without bail. (The reason he is being held without bail is that he admitted his guilt.)
	Since he admitted his guilt, he has been held without bail. (Since the time he admitted his guilt, he has been held without bail.)

Court/court

Unless it starts a sentence, the word *Court* stands for the U.S. Supreme Court. Use *court* when referring to other courts.

Have/Of

In speech it often sounds as though someone is saying "of" when it really is "have." In writing, always use *would have, could have, should have,* not *would of, could of, should of.*

Its/It's

Its is a pronoun. *It's* is a contraction for *it is*.

Examples:	The car wobbled on its loose axle.
	It's a beautiful day.

That/Which

That is used for restrictive or essential phrases.

Example:	He went to the store that was around the corner to buy some bread.

The phrase "that was around the corner" describes which store and is essential for identifying the store.

> **Example:** He went to George's Grocery, which was around the corner, to buy some bread.

The phrase "which was around the corner" simply further describes the store that was already clearly identified as George's Grocery. Therefore, it provides nonessential information.

Their/There/They're   *Their* is a possessive pronoun. *There* represents a place. *They're* is a contraction for *they are*.

> **Example:** They're going to their house. Once they are there, they will have supper.

Which/Who
Who's/Whose   Use *which* for things and *who* for people.
Who's is a contraction for *who is*. *Whose* is a possessive pronoun.

> **Examples:** Who's going to the store?
>
> Whose jacket is this?

Your/You're   *Your* is a possessive pronoun. *You're* is a contraction for *you are*.

> **Example:** You're going to have to finish your report.

SUMMARY

Good legal writing starts with good writing. Follow the basic rules of grammar by using proper sentence structure, avoiding sentence fragments and run-on sentences, and using parallel construction. Also use the proper verb tense. Make sure your pronouns agree with your antecedents. Put modifying words close to what they modify, and be aware of common punctuation problems.

While you are encouraged to develop your own style, you should follow certain style guidelines. Avoid long paragraphs, and be careful that you do not bury your points in the middle of your paragraphs. Use transitions between paragraphs. Be concise by eliminating unnecessary words and phrases. Because the active voice is stronger, use it whenever possible. And when engaged in legal writing, do not fall into the trap of using legalese. Keep the court and not the court opinion the subject of your sentences. Avoid unnecessary variation and the use of the first person. In formal writing do not use contractions, and do not ask your reader questions. Be aware of the differences between "that case" and "this case." Know when to use numerals and when to write numbers out. Finally, do not write like a headnote editor. Include the articles—*a, an,* and *the.*

‖‖‖ REVIEW QUESTIONS

Pages 607 through 614

Correct the following sentences.

1. On any given day a paralegal can be asked to perform any of the following tasks, to interview clients, research in the library, drafting of documents, filed pleadings, or writing client letters.
2. The complaint, which contains theories based on both tort and contract law, alleging that the product was defective, was filed with the wrong court.
3. Even though the attorney made a long-winded and impassioned plea to the jury at the end of the trial.
4. The attorney made a long-winded and impassioned plea to the jury at the end of the trial the jury found the defendant guilty.
5. In *Jones*, a child is injured by his father's negligence. The court decides that children were able to sue for parental negligence.
6. Even though a criminal defendant may engage in plea bargaining, they still may receive a different sentence from the judge.
7. The judge, denied the plaintiff's request, ordered a new trial and set the new trial date.
8. All paralegals, who are members of the local paralegal association, have access to the job bank information.
9. He went over to Bob Browns house where he saw the Browns collection of stamps.
10. The witness stated that "he ran away from the accident", and he testified that he was "scared".

Pages 615 through 623

Correct the following sentences.

11. In *Black* the court held that only involuntary intoxication could be a defense to the formation of a contract. (first sentence in a paragraph)
12. It is interesting to note that notwithstanding the fact that the defendant was found guilty, at that point in time clearly the defendant still felt his attorney had done a good job of defending him.
13. The decision by the jury to convict the defendant surprised no one.

Pages 623 through 625

Correct the following sentences.

14. In *Jones v. Warner* the court felt that only those who were involuntarily intoxicated could be excused from their contractual obligations.
15. Said court also stated that two beers wouldn't be sufficient to prove intoxication.
16. Will the court in our case say that four beers are sufficient to prove intoxication? Would six be enough? What of two whiskeys?
17. There are 5 cases that deal with intoxication.
18. Defendant driving car after drinking five beers was found to be intoxicated.

Pages 625 through 627

Correct the following sentences.

19. The plaintiff can bring suit for negligence against the city for injuries he sustained in the accident. Even though his contributory negligence may bar him from recovery.

20. The woman was frightened by a man she described as seedy, it was only after she struck him with a rock that she discovered he was an undercover police officer.

21. During an autopsy, looking for the cause of death, the deceased is examined by the pathologist.

22. The new computer system offers four advantages for our firm:
    1. it includes 15 software packages
    2. the warranty extends to 160 days
    3. provides a full-scale training program
    4. state-of-the-art features are included.

23. The enclosed forms should be completed by you no later than August 15.

24. The depositions proved to be very revealing, however, our client has decided to settle.

25. *Dillon* holds that under certain circumstances a bystander may recover for emotional distress.

Appendix C

The Basics of Citation Form

When thou enter a city abide by its customs.
The Talmud

INTRODUCTION

In legal writing you must support everything you say by some authority other than yourself. The two most common sources of authority are case law (court opinions) and statutory law. When you tell your reader on what authority you relied, you must do so in such a way that the reader can take that information, go to the library, and locate it.

Increasingly "go to the library" is coming to mean sitting down at a computer and using an online service to conduct research. For the next few years, however, you can expect that most of your citations will still have to take the form of references to books. Therefore, the emphasis of this appendix is on learning the traditional methods for citing to books. In Part III of this appendix, we discuss how new technology may be changing those traditional citation rules.

Over the years a convention known as **citation** form has developed as a standardized way of communicating that information. It has its own grammar, syntax, and style. "*Jones v. Smith*, 75 P.2d 417 (Or. Ct. App. 1951)" is as much a sentence as "The dog ran up the hill." You would never say, "(Or. Ct. App. 1951) 75 P.2d 417, *Smith v. Jones*," for the same reason that you would not say, "Ran the dog the hill up."

Citation
A stylized form for giving the reader information about a legal authority. For court opinions, a citation includes the name of the case, where it can be located, the court that decided it, and the year it was decided. The Bluebook and the ALWD Citation Manual give precise rules as to how citations are to be written.

631

The purpose of this chapter is to introduce you to some basic rules about citation form. For a detailed explanation of citation form you should consult either the Bluebook or the ALWD citation Manual.

The Bluebook: A Uniform System of Citation, also known as the **Bluebook**, was originally written by a group of law students to provide a uniform method for citations in law reviews. It has been revised a number of times. In addition to containing the rules developed specifically for law review footnotes, it has a separate section entitled **Practitioners' Notes**. The Practitioners' Notes contain information on the correct citation forms to use in letters, memoranda, and other documents that an attorney submits to a court. The Bluebook also includes many useful tables, including Table T.1, which gives examples of how to cite court opinions and statutes for each of the fifty state systems and the federal system. (As one example of the type of information included in Table T.1 of the Bluebook, Figure C-1 contains the Massachusetts listing.) In addition, there are tables listing commonly used abbreviations for such things as words appearing in case, periodical, and court names. Finally, inside the back cover you will find a very helpful quick reference guide, with examples of the most common citation forms for court documents.

Bluebook
A book originally written by a group of law students to provide a uniform method for citations in law reviews; contains detailed rules for all forms of citation.

Figure C-1   Bluebook Table T.1, Showing Massachusetts Citation Form

Massachusetts

Supreme Judicial Court (Mass.): In documents submitted to Massachusetts state courts, cite to Mass. and to N.E. or N.E.2d if therein. In all other documents, cite only to N.E. or N.E.2d, if therein; otherwise, cite to Mass.

Massachusetts Reports		
97 Mass. to date	1867–date	Mass.
Allen	1861–1867	e.g., 83 Mass. (1 Allen)
Gray	1854–1860	e.g., 67 Mass. (1 Gray)
Cushing	1848–1853	e.g., 55 Mass. (1 Cush.)
Metcalf	1840–1847	e.g., 42 Mass. (1 Met.)
Pickering	1822–1839	e.g., 18 Mass. (1 Pick.)
Tyng	1806–1822	
Williams	1804–1805	Mass. (1 Will.)
North Eastern Reporter	1884–date	N.E., N.E.2d

Appeals Court (Mass. App. Ct.): In documents submitted to Massachusetts state courts, cite to Mass. App. Ct. if therein and to N.E.2d if therein. In all other documents, cite only to N.E.2d, if therein; otherwise cite to Mass. App. Ct.

Massachusetts Appeals Court Reports	1972–date	Mass. App. Ct.
North Eastern Reporter	1972–date	N.E.2d

District Court (Mass. Dist. Ct.): Cite to Mass. App. Div. if therein and to Mass. Supp. or Mass. App. Dec. if therein; otherwise cite to Mass. App. Div. Adv. Sh.

Appellate Division Reports	1936–1950	Mass. App. Div.
	1980–date	

Massachusetts Reports Supplement	1980–1983	Mass. Supp.
Appellate Division Advance Sheets	1975–1979	19xx Mass. App. Div. Adv. Sh. xxx
Appellate Decisions	1941–1977	Mass. App. Dec.

Statutory compilations: Cite to MASS. GEN. L. if therein.

General Laws of the Commonwealth of Massachusetts (Mass. Bar Assn./West)	MASS. GEN. L. ch. x, § x (19xx)
Massachusetts General Laws Annotated (West)	MASS. GEN. LAWS. ANN. ch. x, § x (West 19xx)
Annotated Laws of Massachusetts (Lexis Law Pub.)	MASS. ANN. LAWS ch. x § x (Lexis Law Pub. 19xx)

Session laws: Cite to Mass. Acts if therein.

Acts and Resolves of Massachusetts	19xx Mass. Acts xxx
Massachusetts Advance Legislative Service (Law. Co-op.)	19xx Mass. Adv. Legis. Serv. xxx (Law. Co-op.)
Massachusetts Legislative Service (West)	

Administrative compilation

| Code of Massachusetts Regulations | MASS. REGS. CODE tit. x, § x (1988) |

Administrative register

| Massachusetts Register | Mass. Reg. |

Figure C-1[1]

The **ALWD Citation Manual** was developed by the Association of Legal Writing Directors to provide a single consistent set of rules for all forms of legal writing. Like the Bluebook, it presents information on the format and content of legal citations, gives examples, and contains tables and appendices with detailed information on each state's specialized requirements. However, it provides greater coverage of electronic sources than does the Bluebook. It also includes an especially helpful section on how to change the settings in your word processor to make it easier to prepare correct legal citations. "Sidebars" contain additional information on key concepts, caveats about common mistakes, and tips for creating specific sources. Figure C-2 contains the Massachusetts listing as found in Appendix 1 of the ALWD Citation Manual. Take a moment to compare it to the Bluebook listings found in Figure C-1. As you can see, most of the

ALWD Citation Manual
A citation manual created by the Association of Legal Writing Directors that provides a single consistent set of rules for all forms of legal writing.

---

[1]Although this table shows the use of large and small letters in statutory abbreviations, this is the convention for law review footnotes. In normal law office writing you can use an initial capital letter followed by lowercase letters.

Court system and reporters:

Massachusetts Supreme Judicial Court (Mass.)

Reporter	Abbreviation	Dates	Status
Massachusetts Reports	Mass.	1804–present	Official
North Eastern Reporter	N.E.	1884–1936	Unofficial
Second Series	N.E.2d	1936–present	Unofficial
Massachusetts Decisions (West offprint)	N.E. or N.E. 2d	1884–present	Unofficial

Massachusetts Appeals Court (Mass. App.)

Reporter	Abbreviation	Dates	Status
Massachusetts Appeals Court Reports	Mass. App.	1972–present	Official
North Eastern Reporter, Second Series	N.E. 2d	1972–present	Unofficial
Massachusetts Decisions (West offprint)	N.E. 2d	1972–present	Unofficial

Massachusetts District Court, Appellate Division (Mass. Dist. App. Div.)

Reporter	Abbreviation	Dates	Status
Massachusetts Appellate Division Reports	Mass. App. Div.	1936–1950 1980–present	Official Official
Massachusetts Appellate Decisions	Mass. App. Dec.	1941–1977	Unofficial
Massachusetts Supplement	Mass. Supp.	1980–1983	Unofficial

Statutory compilations:

★General Laws of the Commonwealth of Massachusetts	Mass. Gen. Laws ch. chapter number, § section number (Year)
Massachusetts General Laws Annotated	Mass. Gen. Laws Ann. ch. chapter number, § section number (West Year)
Annotated Laws of Massachusetts	Mass. Ann. Laws ch. chapter number, § section number (Lexis L. Publg. Year)

Session Laws:

Acts and Resolves of Massachusetts	Year Mass. Acts page number

Administrative compilation:

Code of Massachusetts Regulations	Three-digit agency number Code Mass. Regs. chapter number, section number (Year) (e.g., 106 Code Mass. Regs. 303.510 (1998))

Administrative register:

Massachusetts Register	Issue number Mass. Register page number (Month, Day, Year)

Figure C-2 ALWD Citation Manual: Massachusetts Citation Form

NETNOTE

You can keep current on any change to the information contained in the ALWD Citation Manual by going to the ALWD web site at *www.alwd.org.*

citation formats are identical with those found in the Bluebook, but there are differences, such as in how to cite to the older Massachusetts Reports, the Massachusetts Appeals Court Reporter, the General Laws, the Code of Massachusetts Regulations, and the Massachusetts Register.

Throughout this appendix, unless we indicate otherwise, our examples will reflect rules common to the Bluebook and the ALWD Citation Manual. When those rules differ, we will give examples for both the Bluebook and the ALWD Citation Manual formats.

PART I: COURT OPINION CITATION FORM

Generally, you will cite only to appellate court decisions. Trial court decisions are recorded in the official case files and stored at the local courthouse, but they are usually not printed in reporters available to the public. Although these decisions are of great consequence to the parties involved, they usually have little significance for others and therefore do not need to be published.[2] The decisions of appellate courts, on the other hand, usually involve legal issues, rather than factual issues, and ordinarily are accompanied by a detailed justification of the court's decision. These decisions can serve as **precedents;** that is, later courts will use them to help them reach decisions. Therefore, it is important that these decisions be readily available to the general legal community. To accomplish this, they are published in case reporters.

Precedent
One or more prior court decisions.

A. Case Reporters

Case reporters, consisting of hundreds of volumes, are books that contain copies of court opinions. They are usually arranged in chronological order and divided into volumes according to the court that rendered the opinion. Thus, opinions of the Massachusetts Supreme Judicial Court, the highest appellate court in Massachusetts, are found in Massachusetts Reports. Likewise, those of the highest appellate court in Illinois are reported in Illinois Reports.[3] The federal government publishes U.S. Supreme Court decisions in United States Reports.

Case reporters
Books that contain court decisions. There are both official and unofficial reporters.

---

[2]There are occasions when trial courts, especially the U.S. district courts, will produce opinions involving significant legal issues. Those opinions are published in the same manner as are the appellate court decisions.

[3]Most states publish a reporter that contains the decisions from that state's highest appellate court, and that reporter carries the name of that state.

NETNOTE

You can find a terrific site that will walk you through the basics of citation form at *www.law.cornell.edu/citation*. There you will find information on the purpose of legal citation, instruction on how to cite, and many examples of correct citation form.

National Reporter System
The West system for reporting court decisions from every state and the federal courts.

Federal Supplement
The West reporter that contains decisions from the U.S. district courts.

Federal Reporter
The West reporter that contains decisions from the U.S. circuit courts of appeals.

Official reporter
A governmental publication of court opinions.

Unofficial reporter
A private publication of court opinions—for example, the regional reporters, such as N.E. 2d, published by West.

United States Reports
The official federal government publication of U.S. Supreme Court decisions.

While many states and the federal government publish their own opinions, **West Group** has become a major publisher of case reporters. The West **National Reporter System** covers all appellate court decisions in the fifty states, as well as federal district court, court of appeals, and U.S. Supreme Court decisions. For state court decisions West developed a regional reporter system, whereby it assigned each state to a region and to that region's reporter. In Figure C-3 is a map showing which states belong to each of West's regions.

On the federal side West publishes U.S. district court decisions in the **Federal Supplement**, opinions from the U.S. courts of appeals in the **Federal Reporter**, and U.S. Supreme Court decisions in the **Supreme Court Reporter**. Figure C-4 describes the complete West system for the federal courts.

The decisions of selected courts are also reported by other private publishing houses, principally **Lexis Law Publishing** and the **Bureau of National Affairs (BNA)**. For example, Lexis Law Publishing prints **United States Supreme Court Reports, Lawyers' Edition**, and BNA publishes U.S. Supreme Court opinions in a loose-leaf service entitled **United States Law Week**.

Reporters are generally divided into two categories—official and unofficial. They are **official** when published at the direction of state or federal statutes. All others are **unofficial**. The texts of the opinions published in the unofficial reporters are the same as those in the official ones. What differs are the editorial features, such as case summaries, that are added by the publishers of the unofficial reporters.

B. The Essentials of Case Citation

The citation for a court opinion has three essential parts:

1. the case name,
2. the volume and page of the case reporter where the case can be found, and
3. the parenthetical containing the date and sometimes the name of the court that decided the case.

In addition, some citations contain a fourth part, called the case history. When more than one appellate court has heard a case, the case is said to have a case history. Anything decided before the appellate court decision that you are citing

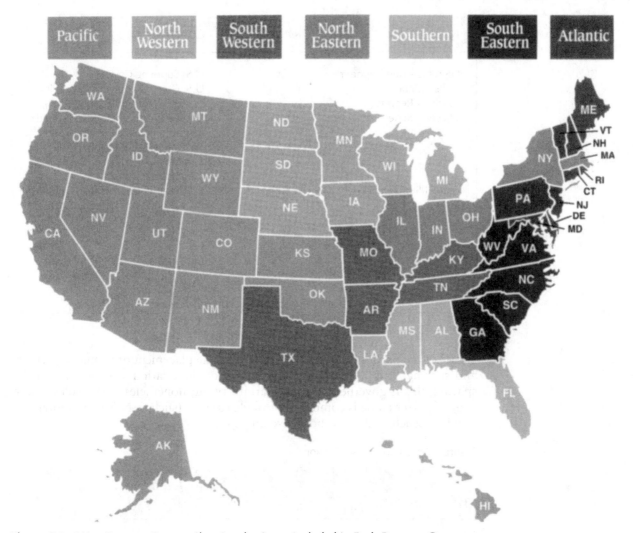

Figure C-3   West Reporter System, Showing the States Included in Each Reporter Group

is known as **prior case history**. Anything that was decided after the appellate court decision that you are citing is known as **subsequent case history**. For example, assume you want to cite to a case from the U.S. Court of Appeals for the First Circuit. Anything that happened in the district court would be prior history. If the decision from the First Circuit court was appealed to the U.S. Supreme Court, that would be subsequent history. The general rule is to cite subsequent history but not prior history.

Here is a typical citation for a state court case:

Callow v. Thomas, 322 Mass. 550, 78 N.E.2d 637 (1948)

The various parts of this citation are diagrammed in Figure C-5. Starting at the left, notice that the case name is underlined and that the "v." separating the

Prior case history Information about what happened procedurally to the cited case before it was heard by the cited court. Do not include this information in a citation.

Subsequent case history Information about what happened procedurally to the litigation after the case cited. Include this information in a citation.

Name of Case Reporter	Abbreviation	Courts Covered
Supreme Court Reporter	S. Ct.	U.S. Supreme Court
Federal Reporter; Federal Reporter, Second Series	F. F.2d	U.S. Courts of Appeals (formerly U.S. Circuit Courts of Appeals), District Courts before 1933, and some specialized federal courts, such as the U.S. Claims Court and the U.S. Court of Customs and Patent Appeals
Federal Supplement	F. Supp.	U.S. District Courts after 1932 and some decisions of the U.S. Customs Court and the U.S. Court of Claims
Federal Rules Decisions	F.R.D.	U.S. District Court opinions involving the Federal Rules of Civil Procedure and the Federal Rules of Criminal Procedure

Figure C-4   West Federal Case Reporters

names of the parties is lower case. Next note the placement of commas, periods, and spacing: It is all part of the grammar of the citation sentence. As to the spacing, this is governed by totally arbitrary but nonetheless strict rules. If the court reporter name is composed of single capitals (such as N.E.) and individual numbers (such as 2d), do not leave any spaces.

Figure C-5   Sample Case Citation

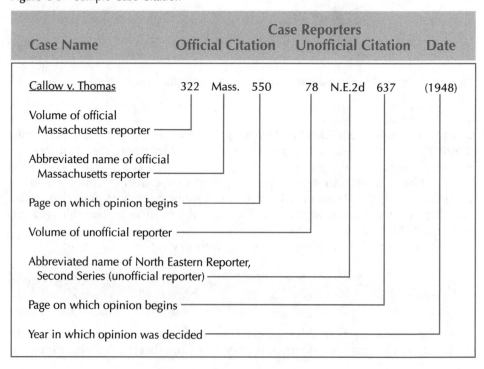

In all other situations, or when it would otherwise cause confusion, leave a space.

We have exaggerated the spacing in these examples for purposes of demonstration. Normally leave just one space.

The following is a more in-depth look at the main parts of the case citation.

C. Case Name

A case citation begins with the names of the parties to the litigation. The party bringing the appeal (the **appellant** or **petitioner**) is usually listed first, and the opposing side (the **appellee** or **respondent**) is listed second.[4] The party bringing the appeal is not necessarily the party who originated the litigation at the trial level.

The case title is usually printed in prominent letters at the very beginning of the opinion. In determining the format for this first part of the citation, the major problem usually centers on which parts of the title you should omit from the citation. Keep in mind that the general purpose of a citation is not only to give the reader information about the case but also to do it in the least amount of space possible. The following are some general rules to follow when trying to decide what to include in the case name.

Appellant or petitioner
The party in a lawsuit who brings an appeal.

Appellee or respondent
The party in a lawsuit against whom an appeal has been filed.

1. Omit First Names

Always omit the first names and initials of individuals. Muriel Callow and Frederick Thomas become simply *Callow v. Thomas*.

Example:	Callow v. Thomas
Not:	Muriel Callow v. Frederick Thomas

On the other hand, include first names or initials that are part of corporate names.

Example:	Williams v. D. L. Lewis & Co.
Not:	Williams v. Lewis & Co.

---

[4]Some states follow the practice of listing the name of the original plaintiff first, no matter which party brings the appeal.

2. Omit Descriptive Terms

Similarly, omit descriptive terms, such as administrator.

> **Example:** <u>Woods v. Lancet</u>
> **Not:** <u>Robert C. Woods, an Infant, by Estelle Woods, His Guardian Ad Litem v. Joseph Lancet</u>

3. Omit All but the First Parties' Names

When there is more than one party on any side to a dispute or when several cases have been consolidated, use only the name of the first party listed on each side or the first case listed. Never use the abbreviation *et al.* to indicate that more than one party is involved. If that information is important, you include it in the text of your argument but not in the citation.

> **Example:** <u>Smith v. Jones</u>
> **Not:** <u>Smith, Rogers, & Doe v. Jones</u>
> **Not:** <u>Smith, et al. v. Jones</u>

4. Use Abbreviations

To further shorten the title, you can use such common abbreviations as Co., Bd., Inc., and Natl. But do not abbreviate the first word of a party's name unless the abbreviation is widely recognized, such as NAACP. Never abbreviate United States.

> **Example:** <u>Smith Co. v. Morgan</u>
> **Not:** <u>Smith Company v. Morgan</u>
>
> **Example:** <u>United States v. Smith</u>
> **Not:** <u>U.S. v. Smith</u>

Also, you should omit Inc. or Ltd. from a company name if the name also includes an abbreviation such as Co., Corp., or Assn., which already indicates that it is a business.

> **Example:** <u>Smith & Wesson, Co. v. Rogers</u>
> **Not:** <u>Smith & Wesson, Co., Inc. v. Rogers</u>

Finally, you can abbreviate procedural phrases such as "on behalf of" to *ex rel.* and "in the matter of" or "petition of" to *In re.*

> **Example:** <u>In re Smith</u>
> **Not:** <u>In the matter of Smith</u>

5. The State as Part of the Citation

When the state is a party to a case in one of its own state courts, it is usually listed as *People v., State v.,* or *Commonwealth v.* On the other hand, if a state is a party to a suit in a federal or another state's court, the listing would be *The Name of the State v. . . .* According to the ALWD Citation Manual the state name should be abbreviated.

> **Examples:** Commonwealth v. Smith (in a Massachusetts state court)
> Massachusetts v. Smith (in a federal court or a court in another state)—Bluebook format
> Mass. v. Smith (in a federal court or a court in another state)—ALWD Citation Manual format

You can usually resolve any questions about what names to use by consulting the table of cases. You will find it at the beginning of the case reporter. You can also refer to the headings on the pages where the case is located to see how the editors of the reporter abbreviated the case. When still in doubt, consult the Bluebook, especially Table T.6, Case Names.

D. Case Reporter

This second part of the citation tells the reader where to go to find the citation. It does that by giving the volume and page number of the case reporter in which the opinion is published.

1. The Parallel Citation

Notice that *Callow v. Thomas* is published in two different volumes. It has an official citation—322 Mass. 550—and an unofficial one as well—78 N.E.2d 637. Every state except Alaska has at some time published an official reporter that bears the name of that state. For example, as you have seen, the Massachusetts reporter is called Massachusetts Reports; likewise, the California reporter is called California Reports. In addition, West publishes state court opinions in a set of unofficial reporters (called unofficial because they are not published by an official body, such as a state government) that cover specific regions of the country. Until recently the rule was that if the decision you are citing is published in an official reporter, you must cite to that reporter. Your reader, however, may have the unofficial rather than the official reporter in his or her library. Therefore, as a convenience to your reader, you must also cite to the unofficial reporter. This is known as giving the **parallel citation**.

Prior to the publication of the Fifteenth Edition of the Bluebook legal writers were expected to include two reporter citations: one to the official reporter and one to the unofficial reporter. However, the Fifteenth Edition of the Bluebook changed this rule, so that parallel citations are required only in documents submitted to state courts. The ALWD Citation Manual directs that unless local rules require otherwise, you should cite to only one source, with a preference for a citation to the unofficial West reporter.[5]

Parallel citation
When reference to two or more reporters is required, each citation is known as a parallel citation. For example, 333 Mass. 99 is the parallel citation for 89 N.E.2d 488; the reverse is also true.

---

[5]This is an example of how citation rules change over time. The "publication" of legal materials in electronic format, such as over the Internet, has created new challenges. See Part IV: Citations in the Electronic Era.

Examples: <u>Callow v. Thomas</u>, 322 Mass. 550, 78 N.E.2d 637 (1948) (in a brief submitted to a Massachusetts court)—Bluebook format

<u>Callow v. Thomas</u>, 78 N.E.2d 637 (Mass. 1948) (in a brief submitted to a New York court)—Bluebook and ALWD Citation Manual format

<u>Callow v. Thomas</u>, 78 N.E.2d 637 (Mass. 1948) (in an office memorandum or client letter)—Bluebook and ALWD Citation Manual format

<u>Callow v. Thomas</u>, 322 Mass. 550 (in a brief submitted to a Massachusetts court)—Massachusetts local rule

Because these rules can be quite confusing, you may find that many attorneys still prefer to see the parallel citations. The moral of the story? Always check with your supervising attorney to see whether your firm follows the Bluebook or ALWD Citation Manual format. And *always* check the local court rules to see if they provide a specific format that you *must* follow when a document is being submitted to that court. Finally, whenever there is a chance that the information in an office memorandum may someday be used in a court document, the prudent researcher will include parallel citations from the start so as not to have to return to the library later to ferret them out.

There are two situations when it is impossible to find a parallel citation. The first is when the state is no longer publishing an official reporter. Many states have given up on the practice of reporting their decisions in favor of letting West do it for them. If that is the case, then you can only cite to the unofficial regional reporter, but you must alert your reader to the source of the opinion by including the state abbreviation in the parenthetical.

Figure C-6   State Abbreviations

Ala.	Alaska
Ariz.	Ark.
Cal.	Colo.
Conn.	Del.
D.C.	Fla.
Ga.	Haw.
Idaho	Ill.
Ind.	Iowa
Kan.	Ky.
La.	Me.
Md.	Mass.
Mich.	Minn.
Miss.	Mo.
Mont.	Neb.
Nev.	N.H.
N.J.	N.M.
N.Y.	N.C.
N.D.	Ohio
Okla.	Or.
Pa.	R.I.
S.C.	S.D.
Tenn.	Tex.
Utah	Vt.
Va.	Wash.
W. Va.	Wis.
Wyo.	

Example: <u>James v. Williams</u>, 79 So. 2d 43 (Ala. 1981)

Unfortunately, you cannot assume that the proper state abbreviation is the two-letter post office version. The Bluebook uses the state abbreviations shown in Figure C-6.

The second situation when you do not use a parallel citation is in citing federal cases. Federal district court and court of appeals decisions are reported in only one reporter each: the Federal Supplement for district court decisions and the Federal Reporter for court of appeals decisions. Therefore, there is no parallel cite.

Examples: <u>Smith v. Brown</u>, 98 F. Supp. 439 (D. Mass. 1982)
<u>Brown v. Brown</u>, 33 F.2d 999 (1st Cir. 1991)

Again, notice that an indication of the court that decided the case is given in the parenthetical.

2. A Special Rule for the U.S. Supreme Court

There is one situation where you could give a parallel citation, but you are not supposed to do so, and that is for U.S. Supreme Court cases. Unlike the other federal cases mentioned above, Supreme Court cases are reported in more than one reporter. In fact, Supreme Court cases are reported in no fewer than four reporters:

1. United States Law Week (U.S.L.W.), a loose-leaf reporter in which the new decisions are first reported;
2. the Supreme Court Reporter (S. Ct.), an unofficial reporter published by West.
3. the United States Supreme Court Reports, Lawyers' Edition (L. Ed.), an unofficial reporter published by Lexis Law Publishing; and
4. United States Reports (U.S.), the official reporter published by the U.S. government.

Some legal writers cite all three reporters. The official rule, however, is that if the decision is in the United States Reports, you cite only to that reporter.

Example: Smith v. Jones, 73 U.S. 68 (1960)
Not: Smith v. Jones, 73 U.S. 68, 102 S. Ct. 446, 378 L. Ed. 998 (1960)

The only time you cite to the Supreme Court Reporter is if the decision has not yet appeared in the official reporter but is in the Supreme Court Reporter.

Example: Black v. Brown, 84 S. Ct. 88 (1989)

If the decision is too recent to have been published yet in either of those two reporters, you cite to United States Law Week.

Example: White v. Green, 51 U.S.L.W. 4076 (U.S. July 7, 1989)

3. Advance Sheets, Westlaw, and Lexis

After an appellate court decides a case, it is usually several months before it is published in a hardbound reporter volume. Until then, it is published in what are known as **advance sheets**. Sometimes these are literally loose sheets of paper kept in three-ring binders. Other times they are softbound pamphlets. As the pagination is the same in the advance sheets as it will be in the hardbound reporter, you merely follow normal citation form.

Normally, the fastest way to obtain new court opinions is through an online service, such as **Westlaw** and **Lexis**. Until such opinions are available in a published reporter, you cite to the Westlaw or Lexis source.

Advance sheets
The first printing of a court decision before it appears in a hardbound reporter.

Westlaw
An on-line legal database containing court decisions and statutes from the entire country, as well as secondary authority; a competitor to Lexis.

Lexis
An on-line legal database containing court decisions and statutes from the entire country, as well as secondary authority; a competitor to Westlaw.

> **Examples:**   <u>Smith v. Green</u>, No. 95-2465, 1997 U.S. App. LEXIS 5444 (1st Cir. Apr. 11, 1997)
>
> <u>Smith v. Green</u>, No. 95-2465, 1997 WL 45302 (1st Cir. Apr. 11, 1997)

4. Cite to Specific Pages

If you cite an authority for a particular proposition, whether you are paraphrasing or quoting, you must indicate the particular page where that proposition appears. If you are citing using a parallel citation, you must give the specific page references for both citations. In the following example from Massachusetts Reports, 249 is the beginning page, and 250 is the page on which the quotation appears.

> **Example:**   <u>Jones v. Goodrow</u>, 173 Mass. 249, 250, 76 N.E.2d 48, 49 (1973)

In a Westlaw or Lexis cite, if screen or page numbers have been assigned, you precede that number by the word "at" and an asterisk.

> **Example:**   <u>Smith v. Green</u>, No. 95-2465, 1997 U.S. App. LEXIS 5444, at *4 (1st Cir. Apr. 11, 1997)

E. Parenthetical

Parenthetical
The parenthetical that occurs at the end of a court citation always contains the year of decision and also the name of the court if that information is not obvious from the name of the reporter.

Persuasive decisions
Court decisions from an equal or a lower court from the same jurisdiction or from a higher court in a different jurisdiction.

Mandatory decisions
Court decisions from a higher court in the same jurisdiction.

In the **parenthetical** you will *always* include the date the opinion was decided. Without the date your reader will have no idea as to how much significance to place on the decision. Especially if the area of law being discussed is one that is rapidly changing, citing to a 1943 case is quite different from citing to a 1993 decision. In addition to the date, if you cannot tell which court decided the opinion from the name of the case reporter, you must give that information in the parenthetical. You must always include information about which court decided the case so that the reader will know whether the decision will be **mandatory** or only **persuasive**. Mandatory decisions are those decisions from a higher court within the same jurisdiction.

Because most official case reporters report only the opinions of their highest courts, by naming the reporter you are also telling the reader which court decided the case. For example, the citation 124 Mass. 79 tells the reader not only that the case is located in Massachusetts Reports but also that the case was decided by the Massachusetts Supreme Judicial Court. That is because "everyone knows" that only Massachusetts Supreme Judicial Court decisions are reported in Massachusetts Reports, only California Supreme Court decisions are reported in California Reports, and so on. Similarly, "everybody knows" that the only decisions reported in the United States Reports are U.S. Supreme Court decisions; there is no need to repeat that information in the parenthetical.

Therefore, whenever you have included a citation to an official reporter, usually you have also told your reader the court that decided the case. When you cite only to an unofficial reporter (other than to a United States Supreme Court Reporter), however, you have told your reader where to find the opinion but not who decided it. For example, look at the following citation: *James v. Williams*, 70 So. 2d 43 (1981). The decisions from four different states are reported in the Southern Reporter. If you do not include the name of the state in the parenthetical, the reader has no way of knowing which state court decided that case. Similarly, look at these citations: *Smith v. Brown*, 98 F. Supp. 439 (1982) and *Jones v. Baker*, 406 F.2d 933 (1980). The decisions from almost a hundred different district courts are reported in F. Supp. and all thirteen courts of appeals in F.2d. Without more of a clue, once again your reader will not know which court decided each of these cases. Leaving the court out of the parenthetical is probably the single most common and most serious citation error.

In summary, here are some examples of the types of information that you should include in a parenthetical.

1. The year the case was decided is *always* in the parenthetical.
2. For federal court of appeals cases put the circuit before the date.

> **Example:**   Jones v. Smith, 510 F.2d 870 (2d Cir. 1975)

3. For federal district court cases put the district and state before the date.

> **Example:**   Baker v. Brown, 372 F. Supp. 416 (D. Mass. 1987)

As mentioned above, you must include the court in the last two examples, as the reader seeing only a cite to F.2d or F. Supp. would have no idea which court of appeals or which district court decided the case. As you know, the location of the court determines whether the case is mandatory or persuasive authority. If the reader does not know where the case was decided, the case might be ignored or discounted.

4. If a state court reporter publishes opinions from more than one court and you cannot tell which court decided the case from the name of the reporter, you should include the name of the court in the parenthetical.

> **Examples:**   White v. Black, 87 N.M. 121, 59 P.2d 44 (Ct. App. 1980) (a state court of appeals decision)
>
> Gray v. Bennett, 87 N.M. 140, 59 P.2d 50 (1980) (a state supreme court decision)

5. If you give only the unofficial citation (for example, because the state has discounted publishing its official reporter), you must indicate the state in the parenthetical.

> **Example:**   Abbott v. Jones, 312 So. 2d 901 (Fla. 1981)

F. Case History

If the case has subsequent case history, you must include that information in your citation. Subsequent history occurs when there were further appeals from the case you are citing.

> **Example:**   Jackson v. Clark, 48 F.2d 99 (2d Cir. 1983), cert. denied, 444 U.S. 98 (1984).

This citation indicates that the case was first decided by the U.S. Court of Appeals for the Second Circuit and can be found in F.2d. The U.S. Supreme Court decision not to grant certiorari is reported in volume 444 of the United States Reports. The information beginning with "*cert. denied*" describes the type of subsequent history that occurred. In this case certiorari was denied. It constitutes subsequent history because it is something that happened after the Second Circuit decision.

If the date of the subsequent history is the same as the date for the original cite, give the date once.

> **Example:**   Smith v. Brown, 88 F. Supp. 402 (D. Mass.), aff'd, 102 F.2d 45 (1st Cir. 1990).

Common examples of subsequent history are included in Figure C-7.

Although generally you must include subsequent history (what happened later to the litigants), you need not include prior history (what happened to the litigants before they reached the present court). This makes quite a bit of sense. If your citation is not to the last court that dealt with these litigants, your reader will always want to know what happened later to them, the subsequent history. Reading the decision you have cited will not give the reader that information. Therefore, you must include this history in your citation. However, if you are citing to the last case in a line of appeals, reading that case will give the reader information about what happened to the case before it reached that court. Therefore, there is no need to include this prior history.

History	Abbreviation
affirmed	aff'd,
appeal denied	appeal denied,
certiorari denied	cert. denied,
certiorari granted	cert. granted,
modified	modified,
overruled by	overruled by
reversed	rev'd,
reversed on other ground	rev'd on other ground

Figure C-7   Subsequent History Abbreviations

PART II: ENACTED LAW CITATION FORM

Today elected officials create most of the law that governs our daily activities, and you usually can find the law governing a given situation by reading **statutes**, regulation or local ordinates.

A. Statutory Citation

State and federal statutes are usually published in three primary forms: individual slip laws, periodic compilations of new laws passed within a certain time period, and unified codes.

When laws are first officially enacted, they are usually published individually as **slip laws**. Federal slip laws are available at libraries designated as official depositories and can be ordered directly from the U.S. Government Printing Office. State slip laws are usually available at larger libraries in the various states and from the state governments themselves.

At the end of a legislative term the federal and most state governments publish the laws passed during that term as one or more volumes in a continuing set. They are usually arranged in chronological order by date of passage and are called either **statutes at large** or **session laws**.

The above publications are arranged chronologically by date of passage and contain only those laws passed during a particular time period. **Codes,**[6] on the other hand, are arranged by subject matter and contain all public laws currently in force. The **United States Code (U.S.C.)** is the official codification of federal statutes and is printed and distributed by the U.S. Government Printing Office. The United States Code Annotated and the United States Code Service

Statute
A law enacted by a state legislature or Congress.

Slip laws
A form in which statutes are published; they are printed individually at the time they are first enacted.

Statutes at large or session laws
The chronological publication of statutes at the end of a legislative session.

Code
A compilation of statutes arranged by subject matter.

United States Code (U.S.C.)
Federal statutes arranged by subject matter.

---

[6]The formal names for these codes differ from one state to another. In addition to "codes," they may be called "revised statutes," "consolidated statutes," or "compiled statutes."

Annotated codes
Private publications that include not only the statutes arranged by subject matter but also editorial material, such as legislative history and summaries of court decisions interpreting the statutes.

are published by West and Lexis Law Publishing, respectively. In addition to the text of the laws themselves, these two **annotated** versions of the code have information about the legislative history and references to court decisions that have interpreted the statutes. Many state statutes are also published by West or another private publisher in an annotated form.

Local ordinances are usually published as individual slip laws and then kept in a loose-leaf binder. They are commonly found in local libraries and at the administrative offices of the governmental unit involved.

You should follow a reference to a specific statute or ordinance with the appropriate citation so that others can easily locate and check the source. As with case citations, in the absence of special instructions from a court or publisher to the contrary, The Bluebook: A Uniform System of Citation is generally accepted as the guide for determining the proper format for citations.

1. Federal Statutes

For federal statutes currently in force, cite to the **United States Code (U.S.C.)**, the official publication. If that set is unavailable, cite to either unofficial publication: **United States Code Annotated (U.S.C.A.)**, published by West, or **United States Code Service (U.S.C.S.)**, published by Lexis Law Publishing. Include the statute's name only if it is commonly cited that way. Otherwise simply cite to the code title and section.

Examples: Administrative Procedure Act, 5 U.S.C. § 552(b)(3) (1994)

42 U.S.C. § 1983 (1988)

42 U.S.C.A. § 1983 (West 1993)

42 U.S.C.S. § 1983 (Lexis Law Pub. 2000)—Bluebook format

42 U.S.C.S. § 1983 (LEXIS L. Publg. 2000)—ALWD Citation Manual format

---

U.S.C. stands for United States Code. The number preceding the U.S.C. designation indicates the title. The § symbol stands for section. Note the spacing. There is a space between the § symbol and the section number.

The date in parentheses refers to the latest date when the code was updated, *not* the date the statute was enacted. With a little thought you will see why it is the code's last publication date and not the date of enactment that is important. Until a statute is amended or repealed, it remains good law. Therefore, it is irrelevant whether it was passed in 1882 or 1982. Whenever a statute is amended or repealed, that change is reflected the next time the statutory code is updated. If a statute is repealed, it will be eliminated from the next publication of the code.[7]

---

[7]This is unlike the publication method for court opinions. Court opinions can be changed through future court or legislative action, but the original opinion is never removed from the case reporter in which it was published.

Therefore, it is vital to know that the volume of the code you are reading is up to date, as that is your assurance that it contains any recent changes to legislation. To determine the correct year to cite, first examine the spine of the volume, and use the year that appears there. If none appears, use the year that appears on the title page or, if none appears there either, the latest copyright year.

If the material you are citing appears in a supplement, such as a pocket part, you must indicate that in the parenthetical.

Examples:	19 U.S.C. § 101 (Supp. V 1993)—Bluebook format
	19 U.S.C. § 105 (1982 & Supp. V 1993)—Bluebook format
	19 U.S.C. § 101 (Supp. 1999)—ALWD Citation Manual format
	19 U.S.C. § 105 (1988 & Supp. 1993)—ALWD Citation Manual format

By way of summary, Figure C-8 lists the most common federal statutory publications and their abbreviations.

2. State Statutes

Citations to state statutes follow the same general format as that used for federal statutes. If a state has both an official and unofficial code, when possible you should cite to the official code. Otherwise, cite to a current unofficial code. As with case reporters, the words *official* and *unofficial* simply refer to whether the code was published by the government or by a private publisher. As an example, Massachusetts statutory law is published in three separate sets: Massachusetts General Laws (official), Massachusetts General Laws Annotated (unofficial, published by West), and the Annotated Laws of Massachusetts

Figure C-8 Common Publications Containing the Texts of Federal Statutes

Publication	Abbreviation	Coverage
United States Code	U.S.C.	Official codification of federal statutes arranged by subject matter.
United States Code Annotated	U.S.C.A.	West's unofficial codification of federal statutes arranged by subject matter with annotations.
United States Code Service	U.S.C.S.	Lexis Law Publishing's unofficial codification of federal statutes arranged by subject matter with annotations.
United States Statutes at Large	Stat.	Federal statutes arranged chronologically by session enacted.
United States Law Week	U.S.L.W.	Loose-leaf service containing the most recently enacted federal statutes.

(unofficial, published by Lexis Law Publishing). The preferred method is to cite to the official code, the General Laws of the Commonwealth of Massachusetts.

> **Example:**   Mass. Gen. Laws ch. 53, § 2 (1993)

Notice the spacing. There is a space between ch. (which stands for chapter) and the chapter number and between the § symbol and the section number.

If it is not possible to cite to the official publication, you can cite to either of the unofficial sources.

> **Examples:**   Mass. Gen. Laws Ann. ch. 53, § 2 (West 1985)
>
> Mass. Gen. Laws Ann. ch. 87, § 5 (West Supp. 2000)
>
> Mass. Gen. Laws Ann. ch. 9, § 23 (West 1989 & Supp. 2000)
>
> Mass. Ann. Laws ch. 53, § 2 (Lexis Law Pub. 1985)—Bluebook format
>
> Mass. Ann. Laws ch. 53, § 2 (Lexis Law Pub. Supp. 2000)—Bluebook format
>
> Mass. Ann. Laws ch. 53, § 2 (LEXIS L Publg. Supp. 2000)—ALWD Citation Manual format

As with federal statutes, for state citations the date in parentheses refers to the date of the volume, *not* the date the statute was enacted. A date standing by itself indicates that the statute is located in the main volume. The date preceded by the word *Supp.* indicates that the statute is located in the pocket part.

You can include the statute's name if it is commonly cited that way:

> **Example:**   Cannabis Control Act, Ill. Rev. Stat. ch. 56[42], § 701 (1973)

By way of summary, Figure C-9 lists examples of state statutory publications and their abbreviations.

B. Local Ordinances

Local ordinance citations follow the same general format as that for statutes. According to the Bluebook at the beginning of the citation give the name of the city or county and the abbreviated state name. If the ordinance is codified, then you should include the name of the code followed by the subdivision (art., ch., §, etc.) and the year of the code.

> **Example:**   Portland, Or., Police Code art. 30 (1953)

Publication	Abbreviation	Coverage
Alabama Code	Ala. Code	Official codification of Alabama statutes arranged by subject matter.
West's Annotated California Code, Business and Professions	Cal. Bus. & Prof. Code	West's unofficial codification of California statutes relating to business and the professions with annotations.
General Laws of the Commonwealth of Massachusetts	Mass. Gen. L.	Official codification of Massachusetts statutes arranged by subject matter.
Massachusetts General Laws Annotated	Mass. Gen. Laws Ann.	West's unofficial codifications of Massachusetts statutes with annotations arranged by subject matter.

Figure C-9 Examples of State Statutory Publications and Their Abbreviations

If the ordinance is not codified, give its number; if it is not numbered, give its name and date of adoption.

Example: Belchertown, Mass., Ordinance 44,505 (June 13, 1984)

To follow the ALWD Citation Manual format for local ordinances, you should give the abbreviated name of the code, followed by the state abbreviation in parentheses, the pinpoint reference, and finally the date in parentheses.

Example: Portland Police Code (Or.) art. 30 (1953)

A citation to an uncodified ordinance should contain the name of the political subdivision, the state abbreviation, the ordinance number or name, and the date in parentheses.

Example: Belchertown, Mass., Ordin. 44,505 (June 13, 1984)

C. Administrative Law

Because legislatures often delegate considerable lawmaking authority to administrative agencies, it is frequently necessary to look beyond the statutes to **administrative regulations** promulgated by these agencies. These materials are published in formats that resemble those used for statutes.

Administrative regulations
Rules, regulations, orders, and decisions created by administrative agencies under their authority to interpret specific statutes.

Federal Register
A daily newspaper in which proposed federal regulations are first printed.

Code of Federal Regulations (C.F.R.)
A compilation of federal administrative regulations arranged by agency.

Federal administrative regulations and decisions are published in the **Federal Register** (Fed. Reg.). This publication is issued daily (except Sundays, Mondays, and the days following holidays). The **Code of Federal Regulations** (**C.F.R.**) is analogous to the United States Code in that it contains only those regulations that are of a general permanent nature and currently in force. It is organized based on the same fifty titles as the United States Code.

Some states publish codes of regulations that correspond to the C.F.R. In other states you must obtain the regulations from each individual agency. At both the state and the federal levels some private publishers issue loose-leaf reporters that contain administrative regulations in specialized areas, such as taxes and labor law.

Citations for administrative regulations follow a form that is analogous to statutes.

Example: 49 C.F.R. § 6.1 (2000)

The 49 stands for Title 49 and the 6.1 for Section 6.1. Each title of the C.F.R. is revised and reprinted on at least an annual basis. The year in the parentheses is the date of the latest publication. It is not the year the regulation was enacted.

Most states follow a similar procedure for citing to their regulations, but to be on the safe side always check Table T.1 in the Bluebook.

In addition to issuing regulations, administrative agencies hold hearings. Cite adjudicative decisions in the following manner:

Example: Electric Bond and Share Co., 11 S.E.C. 1146 (1942)

The abbreviation S.E.C. stands for the agency involved—in this case the Securities and Exchange Commission.

D. Constitutions

Legal researchers are most likely to cite to a constitutional provision when they are seeking to challenge an objectionable statute or the manner in which government agents conducted themselves (such as a Fourth Amendment challenge to an allegedly unreasonable search).

State and federal constitutions are usually included in the above mentioned compilations of statutes. The U.S. Constitution can be found in the U.S.C., U.S.C.A., and U.S.C.S. The Library of Congress also publishes a separated annotated edition of the Constitution. A state statute compilation usually includes a copy of its state constitution, and a few even feature a copy of the U.S. Constitution with annotations to their own state court decisions.

Sections of constitutions are cited as follows:

> **Examples:**   U.S. Const. art. I, § 8, cl. 3
>
>   U.S. Const. amend. XX, § 3
>
>   Ill. Const. art. IV, § 2(b)

When referring to the U.S. Constitution in your text, use initial capitalization.

> **Example:**   First Amendment
>
>   Bill of Rights
>
>   Article I, Section 8, Clause 3 of the Constitution

PART III: USING CITATIONS IN YOUR LEGAL WRITING

In this section we will explore how the citation can either form an independent sentence or appear as a clause within a sentence. You will also learn the trick to using a shortened citation form. The section concludes with an example of citations integrated into text and a table summarizing the most common citation forms.

A. The Citation as a Sentence or Clause

Standing alone, view the citation as a sentence. It begins with a capital letter and ends with a period.

> **Example:**   The court stated that the test is scope of employment.
>   <u>Smith v. Jones</u>, 217 F. Supp. 421, 425 (E.D.N.Y. 1971).

This is the procedure to follow when the citation supports the entire preceding sentence. If the citation supports only part of a sentence, treat the citation as a clause, set off by commas or semicolons.

> **Example:**   Relevant constitutional restraints apply as much to the withdrawal of public assistance benefits as to disqualification for unemployment compensation, <u>Sherbert v. Verner</u>, 374 U.S. 398 (1963); denial of a tax exemption, <u>Speiser v. Randall</u>, 357 U.S. 513 (1958); or discharge from public employment, <u>Slowchower v. Board of Higher Education</u>, 350 U.S. 551 (1956).

1. String Citations

String citation
A series of citations in a row.

If you give more than one authority to support a proposition, you are string citing. Generally, avoid **string citations**. It is better to thoroughly discuss a few cases than to overwhelm your reader with a long list of citations. However, there are times when you can use string citations to emphasize that the great weight of authority is on your side. When string citing, separate each cite with a semicolon, listing federal cases first. Within that category Supreme Court cases are followed by court of appeals and then district court cases. Next, list state cases, in alphabetical order by state. If there is more than one case from the same court, list them in reverse chronological order.

> **Example:** That the statute of limitations begins to run from the moment the plaintiff discovers the malpractice is well established by American case law. <u>Smith v. Rowan</u>, 99 U.S. 483 (1945) (medical malpractice); <u>Black v. Sanders</u>, 94 S.E.2d 109 (Ga. 1933) (medical malpractice); <u>Harper v. Lee</u>, 334 N.E.2d 87 (Mass. 1989) (medical malpractice); <u>White v. Brown</u>, 234 S.W.2d 890 (Tex. 1960) (attorney malpractice); <u>Gagnon v. Spoon</u>, 212 S.W.2d 89 (Tex. 1958) (accountant malpractice).

2. Explanatory Parentheticals

Explanatory parenthetical
A parenthetical located at the end of a case citation containing information about the case.

The parentheticals following the dates are known as **explanatory parentheticals**. They can be very useful in giving the reader a quick indication of why you have cited the case. They can be short phrases as shown above, or they can begin with a present participle.

> **Example:** Many states have analogized the situation of spousal immunity to that of parental immunity. <u>See, e.g., Lewis v. Lewis</u>, 351 N.E.2d 526 (Mass. 1976) (explaining that the same policy considerations support the abolition of spousal immunity as supported the abolition of parental immunity).

3. Signals

Signals
A word or a phrase that precedes a citation to indicate why you are citing the case.

The *See, e.g.,* is known as a signal. **Signals** are a shorthand method for alerting your reader as to why you are citing a case. You will often notice signals in court opinions. As a beginning legal writer, you are generally better advised to avoid signals, as it is easy to misuse them and not all of your readers may be familiar with their use.

Short citation form
A partial citation that may be used after you have given a complete citation.

B. Authority Previously Cited—Short Citing

The first time you cite to an authority use the basic citation form discussed so far. If you cite to the same authority a second time, however, it is not necessary to repeat the full citation. There are several **short citation forms** that you can use.

First, for case citations, if you are citing to the immediately preceding case and to the same page in that opinion, you may simply use the word **id**. Assume that you have just given the following citation, *Brown v. Smith*, 29 Mass. 54, 55, 443 N.E.2d 56, 57 (1960), and that you want to cite to it again, referring to the same pages as before. Simply type *Id.* If it is to the same authority, but to another page, you may use *Id.* followed by the new page number.

Id.
A short citation form indicating reference is to the immediately preceding authority.

> **Example:** The court stated that the statute of limitations had run. <u>Brown v. Smith</u>, 29 Mass. 54, 55, 443 N.E.2d 56, 57 (1960). The plaintiff had no valid justification for failing to file her complaint. <u>Id.</u> at 57, 443 N.E. 2d at 60.

Second, if you are citing to a case previously cited but not the immediately preceding case, use what is known as the short form.

> **Example:** <u>Brown</u>, 29 Mass. at 58, 443 N.E.2d at 60

Some short form, you say. Well, it is shorter than the original. First, only one of the parties' names appears. Second, you include only a specific page reference and not the beginning page reference. Third, the parenthetical information is omitted.

Follow the same general guidelines for statutes. For example, assume you have cited Labor Management Relations (Taft-Hartley) Act § 301(a), 29 U.S.C. § 185(a) (2000). If your next citation is to 29 U.S.C. § 185(b) (2000), you can give the citation as follows: *Id.* § 185(b). If the use of *Id.* is not appropriate, you can use any short form that clearly identifies the statute.

> **Examples:** 29 U.S.C. § 185(a)
>
> Taft-Hartley Act § 301(a)

Finally, in court opinions you will sometimes see the word **supra**, meaning that this is a reference to a previously cited authority. You can use it to refer to preceding secondary authority, such as books. Do not use supra when referring to previously cited court opinions, statutes, constitutions, or other primary authority.

Supra
Above; used to refer to authority already cited in the document. May not be used with citations to cases, statutes, or constitutions.

C. Example of Citations Integrated into Text

The following is an example of citations as they would appear in a law office memorandum.

> On September 15 Michael Zink was arrested for breaking and entering a deserted farmhouse in violation of Mass. Gen. Laws ch. 48, § 3 (1990). While attempting to escape from the police, Mr. Zink tripped over a wire that caused a hidden shotgun to discharge. The shotgun blast severed a portion

> of his lower leg. Mr. Zink now wants to sue the owner of the farmhouse for his injuries, basing his arguments on <u>Smith v. Fields</u>, 99 N.E.2d 893 (Mass. 1960). In that case the court held that the owner of a barn can be liable for setting a "lethal trap." <u>Id.</u> at 895. However, in a more recent decision, <u>Jones v. Bartlett</u>, 230 N.E.2d 88 (Mass. 1980), the court distinguished <u>Smith</u> by stating that the same rules should not be applied to barns as to habitable conditions. <u>Id.</u> at 90. Nonetheless, if the court should find that the deserted farmhouse is more like a barn than like a habitable building, it will follow the rule laid down in <u>Smith</u> that an owner can be responsible for harm done by "lethal traps." <u>Smith</u>, 99 N.E.2d at 896.

D. Summary of the Most Common Citation Forms

Figure C-10 lists examples of some of the most common citation forms. Feel free to add to this list with examples from your own state. As you become more comfortable with citation form, you will find that such a quick reference is often all that you will need.

PART IV: CITATIONS IN THE ELECTRONIC ERA

More and more, research no longer means going to law books. Rather it means finding your primary authority either on a specialized Internet service, such as Westlaw or Lexis, or on a public web site, such as Findlaw. Section 17.3.3 of the Bluebook and Rule 40 of the ALWD Citation Manual provide that when citing to material you find on the Internet, you should include the title or top-level heading and the uniform resource locator (URL) in angled brackets. The URL is the electronic address for the cite where you found your information. For example, you can retrieve Supreme Court opinions from *www.findlaw.com*. In that instance "*www.findlaw.com*" is the URL. If available, for point citations you should refer to paragraph numbers.

The problem with this approach is that most court opinions are published electronically as they appear in their parallel print medium. Cases do not carry unique identifying numbers or individualized paragraph numbers. Therefore, the researcher must still cite as though the case were found in a bound volume and include those volume and page numbers in the citation. Also, because the individual paragraphs are not numbered, the researcher must rely on the on-line service to include star paging. Star paging is a method for indicating in the electronic version where the page breaks occur in the printed version.

In recognition of the growing prevalence of electronic publishing and the difficulties of citing to it, in the summer of 1996 the American Bar Association recommended that courts adopt a "medium neutral citation" system. The opinions for each year would be numbered sequentially, and each paragraph would be numbered. Citations would be to the case name, the year of the opinion, the court, the opinion number, and, if necessary for pinpoint citing, a specific paragraph number. This method would be used no matter where the researcher found the decision: in a printed volume or from an on-line service.

Examples of Federal Court Citations

<u>Brown v. Brown</u>, 33 F.2d 999 (1st Cir. 1991)
Other circuits: (2d Cir. 1991), (3d Cir. 1991), (D.C. Cir. 1991)
<u>Black v. Black</u>, 888 F. Supp. 25 (D. Mass. 1991)
Other districts: (M.D. Pa. 1991), (S.D.N.Y. 1991), (D.D.C. 1991)
<u>White v. White</u>, 88 U.S. 1093 (1991).

Examples of Federal Statutory Citations

Administrative Procedure Act, 5 U.S.C. § 552(b)(3) (2000)
19 U.S.C. § 101 (Supp. v. 1993) — Bluebook format
19 U.S.C. § 105 (1988 & Supp. v. 1993) — Bluebook format
19 U.S.C. § 105 (1988 & Supp. 1993) — ALWD Citation Manual format

Examples of Federal Regulatory Citations

Atomic Energy Commn. Rules of Practice § 2.701, 21 Fed. Reg. 805 (1956)
49 C.F.R. § 6.1 (2000)

Examples of State Cases

In a brief submitted to a Massachusetts court:
<u>Callow v. Thomas</u>,322 Mass. 550, 78 N.E.2d 637 (1948)

In a brief submitted to a New York court:
<u>Callow v. Thomas</u>, 78 N.E.2d 637 (Mass. 1948)

In a law office memorandum or client letter:
<u>Callow v. Thomas</u>, 78 N.E.2d 637 (Mass. 1948)

Examples of State Statutes

Mass. Gen. L. ch. 53, § 2 (1993)
Mass. Gen. Laws Ann. ch. 53, § 2 (West 1985)
Mass. Gen. Laws Ann. ch. 87, § 5 (West Supp. 2000)

Examples of Secondary Authority

Books: Deborah L. Rhode, <u>Justice and Gender</u> (1989)

Journals: Patricia J. Williams, <u>Alchemical Notes: Reconstructed Ideals from Decon-</u><u>structed Rights</u>, 22 Harv. L. Rev. 401 (1987)

Journals (student articles): Dawn M. Johnsen, Note, <u>The Creation of Fetal Rights: Con-</u><u>flicts with Women's Constitutional Rights of Liberty, Privacy, and Equal Protec-</u><u>tion</u>, 95 Yale L.J. 1419 (1990) (book review)

Figure C-10   A Quick Reference for Common Citation Forms

The ABA committee also strongly encouraged use of a book-based parallel citation during a transition period. The committee gave the following example:

<u>Smith v. Jones</u>, 1996 5 Cir 15, ¶ 18, 22 F.3d 955

The *Smith v. Jones* case was the fifteenth case that the U.S. Court of Appeals for the 5th Circuit decided in 1996. The citation is to the eighteenth paragraph. The book-based parallel cite is 22 F.3d 955.

No matter how the rules of citation form evolve, keep in mind the two basic reasons for giving citations. They are to reassure the reader that your arguments are based on precedent and to allow the reader to quickly and easily find that precedent. So long as those two goals are met, the actual form the citation rules take should not matter. In the meantime be sure to check with your local court rules to find the method that your jurisdiction currently follows.

SUMMARY

Citation form governs how you refer to legal authority, such as court opinions and statutes. When citing court opinions, include the names of the parties, the volume and page numbers of the court reporter, and a parenthetical including the date and the name of the court if the name of the court cannot be discerned from the reporter name alone. Also include subsequent case history. When citing statutes, include the chapter or title number, the section number, and the copyright date of the volume you are consulting, not the date the statute was enacted. While these citation rules have been followed for years, they may be changing soon due to the increased use of electronically published materials.

REVIEW QUESTIONS

Pages 631 through 647

Give the correct citation for each of the following.

1. A 1988 Massachusetts Supreme Judicial Court decision. The appellant was James Bennett; the appellee was William Buckley. The opinion begins on page 55 of volume 108 of the North Eastern Reporter, Second Series, and on page 119 of volume 329 of Massachusetts Reports.
2. A 1993 Illinois Supreme Court decision. The appellants were Sally Field and James Connor; the appellee was the Fine Gun Shooting Gallery Company, Inc. The opinion begins on page 999 of volume 109 of North Eastern Reporter, Second Series, and on page 40 of volume 232 of Illinois Reports. You want to direct the reader to a specific page within the opinion: page 1001 in the North Eastern Reporter, Second Series, and page 43 in Illinois Reports.
3. A 1989 Massachusetts Appeals Court decision. The appellant was Matthew Brown; the appellee was Christine White. The opinion begins on page 225 of volume 555 of Massachusetts Appeals Court Reports and page 1019 of volume 446 of the North Eastern Reporter, Second Series.
4. A 1980 Massachusetts federal district court decision. The appellant was Janet Smith; the appellee was Judy Green. The opinion begins on page 448 of volume 509 of the Federal Supplement.
5. A 1979 First Circuit decision. The appellant was Frank Pierce; the appellee was Grant Coleman. The opinion begins on page 1058 of volume 559 of the Federal Reporter, Second Series.

6. A 1960 U.S. Supreme Court decision. The petitioner was Shirley Temple; the respondent was Sylvia Porter. The opinion begins on page 45 of volume 354 of United States Reports, on page 558 of volume 997 of the Supreme Court Reporter, and on page 68 of volume 199 of United States Supreme Court Reports.

7. A 1988 Minnesota Supreme Court decision. The appellant was Robert Recht; the appellee was Louise Wrong. The opinion begins on page 787 of volume 556 of the North Western Reporter, Second Series. Minnesota stopped publishing its official reports in 1977.

Pages 647 through 653

Give the correct citation for each of the following. Use the information contained in this appendix and especially the examples for Massachusetts state statutory and regulatory citations as found on page 632.

8. The 1973 Massachusetts statute on comparative negligence. You have located it in Lexis Law Publishing's Massachusetts Annotated Laws hardbound volume. The copyright date on the inside page of that hardbound volume is 2001. The statute is Chapter 231, Section 85 of Massachusetts General Laws.

9. The 1963 Massachusetts statute on spousal immunity. It is Chapter 209, Section 6 of Massachusetts General Laws. You have located it in the 2005 pocket part of volume 34 of West's Massachusetts General Laws Annotated, beginning on page 174.

10. A 1964 federal statute. It is Section 108 found in Title 29. You have located it in volume 42 of the United States Code Annotated. The copyright date on the inside page of that hardbound volume is 2004.

11. A federal regulation that you found in the 2005 edition of the Code of Federal Regulations. It is Title 47, Section 73.609.

12. A Massachusetts regulation. It is Title 603, Section 7.00. In Massachusetts the regulations are published in a loose-leaf binder. As changes are made to the regulations, new pages replace older ones. At the bottom of the pages you can see the effective date of the new provision: 12/31/00.

13. The federal Constitution, Article two, Section two.

Pages 653 through 658

Give the correct citation for each of the following.

14. Assume you have cited to *Smith v. Brown*, 99 Mass. 432, 301 N.E.2d 404 (1983). You have cited no other authority. You want to cite to the opinion as a whole again. What would be the easiest way to do that?

15. Assume you next cite to an Illinois court decision. You now want to cite to the Massachusetts court decision in question 14 again, but now referring specifically to material located on page 435 in Massachusetts Reports and page 406 in the North Eastern Reporter, Second Series. What would be the easiest way to do that?

Appendix D

Finding the Law

I have found that a great part of the information I have was acquired by looking for something and finding something else on the way.
Franklin P. Adams

INTRODUCTION

In Chapters 6 and 7 we described how you can locate statutory materials and court cases when you have a formal citation. In this appendix we will introduce you to some of the basic researching aids that will help you find and better understand both primary and secondary legal materials.

This appendix begins with a research strategy that assumes the researcher knows very little about the particular area involved. A legal professional who comes to a legal problem with a more complete background can eliminate some of the preliminary stages of the researching process. One caution: If you feel overwhelmed by the amount of material in this appendix, do not despair. It takes years of experience to become a truly competent legal researcher, but it can be done.

In this appendix we will follow the process that you might use to research the issue of spousal immunity. Recall the situation on Janice Miller, who was injured while working in her backyard with her husband, George. Because the problem of Janice and George occurred in Springfield, Massachusetts, we will focus our research on Massachusetts law. However, the principles that we will be discussing can be applied to research in any state. Because the purpose of this appendix is to introduce you to the many researching resources, our journey will be more all-inclusive than would be typical of a normal researching session.

A. OVERVIEW OF THE RESEARCHING PROCESS

Primary authority
The law itself, such as statutes and court opinions.

Your main goal in conducting legal research is to look for and find **primary authority**—that is, court opinions and enacted law (such as statutes and regulations) governing the situation. Your starting point for your research will depend on what you already know about the facts of the case and the law in that general area.

If, for example, you have the citation for a statute or court opinion, you can go directly to the appropriate volume of the code or reporter and proceed to read the cited document. Even if you do not have a citation, if you are fairly familiar with the area of law, you might go directly to primary sources. For example, if you knew that a statute governed the situation but did not know its citation, you could go directly to the statutes and search the index for the relevant citation. If you knew that the problem was governed by case law but did not have a citation, you could not go directly to the court reporters. Unlike statutes, which are organized by subject matter and contain their own indexes, court opinions are organized chronologically, being published in the order in which they are decided. To solve the problem of locating a court opinion by subject matter, West Group has provided us with a master index to all court opinions, the **digests**. These are organized by subject matter and will help you find relevant court opinions.

Digest
A book that contains court opinion headnotes arranged by subject matter.

Secondary authority
Information about the law, such as that contained in encyclopedias and law review articles.

If, on the other hand, you have no information other than the client's facts, you may have absolutely no idea if the situation will be covered by statutes or court opinions or both. Your best approach then might be to begin your work in the **secondary sources** and read general background information on your topic. Secondary sources tell you about the law. Secondary sources, such as legal encyclopedias, are a great resource because they have done much of the preliminary research for you. While your goal is to find primary sources, secondary sources

Figure D-1 Primary and Secondary Authority

Books That Contain the Law (Primary Authority)	Books about the Law (Secondary Authority)	Books That Index (Help You Locate) the Law (Secondary Authority)

Statutory codes	**Encyclopedias**
	General
	  Am. Jr 2d
	  C.J.S.
	State Specific
	  Ex.: Mass. Practice
		Digests

Case reporters	**Scholarly publications**
	Law school journals
	  Ex.: Harvard Law Review
	Bar Association Journals
	  Ex.: ABA Journal
		American Law Reports

Regulations	**Newspapers**
	National
	  Ex.: National Law Journal
	State Specific
	  Ex.: Mass. Lawyer's Weekly
		Shepard's

are a great beginning point. Not only will they give you general background information, but also they will often include references to relevant primary authority. Figure D-1, page 662, gives you a listing of the types of books you will encounter in a law library.

B. THE FIVE STEPS OF LEGAL RESEARCH

Legal research involves five basic steps:

1. Identify your search terms.
2. Go to secondary authority (optional).
3. Go to primary authority.
4. Update your research.
5. Decide when to stop researching.

Step two is labeled optional because, for example, a researcher already familiar with spousal immunity law would know that issues of spousal immunity involve state tort law and, after identifying the relevant search terms, could proceed directly to finding state statutes and court opinions. A researcher not familiar with the law in this area might first turn to secondary sources in order to learn some of the basic principles of spousal immunity law and decide where to begin researching in primary authority.

1. Identify Your Search Terms

Because much of your research will begin with indexes, you need to develop a list of words to describe your client's facts and the legal issues. These will be the words that you will look for in the indexes. Several techniques have been developed to help you think of words to look for. They include TAPP—*Thing, Acts, Person,* or *Place* (developed by Lawyers Co-operative)—and TARP—*Thing, Cause of Action, Relief, Parties* (developed by Jacobstein & Mersky). The function of these acronyms is simply to suggest words that you could look for in an index. Once you have thought of words that fit these categories, you should try to enlarge your search possibilities by thinking of synonyms, antonyms, broader words, and narrower words. For example, in a case involving possible malpractice by a pediatrician, for Person or Parties you would certainly think of *physician.* Synonyms would include *doctor* and perhaps *surgeon.* A broader term might be *medical professional* or *practitioner,* while narrower terms would include *pediatrician* and *pediatric neurologist.*

In analyzing Janice's situation we can see that the central research issue concerns her ability to sue her husband. We begin by developing a list of words that indexers might use to categorize this problem. In this case Cause of Action (as well as defenses) and Person or Parties seem to be the most likely categories. Possible words to look for in indexes include

> | | |
> |---|---|
> | **Cause of Action or Defenses:** | Tort, Negligence, Action, Interspousal Immunity, Immunity, Spousal Immunity |
> | **Person or Parties:** | Spouses, Marriage, Husband, Wife |

Can you think of other words?

> **P R A C T I C A L T I P**
>
> Always think through your proposed researching project *before* entering the library or going on-line.

It is always best to enter the library with too many rather than too few possibilities. There is a strange library fog that settles on many researchers that prevents them from thinking. If you have thought of only a few words before entering the library and then you do not find them in an index, be assured that this mysterious fog will settle in and prevent you from thinking of any alternative approaches. Therefore, do your brainstorming *before* entering the library. Assume you will not be able to find any of your initial words in an index. To handle that eventuality, come to the library armed with a long list of possible words. Also think of several synonyms for each word. Alternatively, if you can find nothing in one source, try a different one. Different indexers use different words to categorize the same topic.

As an example, let's assume you wished to start your research in a general legal encyclopedia, such as Am. Jur. 2d. (We discuss legal encyclopedias more fully below.) To locate the appropriate sections to research, you would begin by consulting the index. The index is printed in separate volumes at the end of the series. The procedure is similar to that used in reading any normal index. The key is to determine the correct words to locate. Exhibit D-1 demonstrates that if you look up the word *Spouse* in the Am. Jur. 2d index, you will find that this is not the correct word. However, the indexers for Am. Jur. 2d anticipated that this is a word you might use and direct you to the topic Husband and Wife in the index, reproduced here as Exhibit D-2 on page 666.

As this index entry shows, you may find what appear to be too many listings. Should you write down all of them or try to be selective? At this stage of your research your best approach is to write down all the possibilities and check them all. It is better to include too many possibilities than to eliminate a potentially relevant section. If you have no luck finding index entries in one source, you can switch to another source, and you may have more success.

Although indexes can be very frustrating to use, once you have found relevant information in one source, you will rarely have to start from scratch with a new resource. This is because many resources cross-reference each other. If you are lucky enough to have a cross-reference from another source, simply go to the proper section in that source, and read about your topic.

2. Go to Secondary Authority (Optional)

Secondary authority is helpful because it contains general overviews of various areas of the law, as well as citations to primary authority. You can find general overviews of various areas of the law in encyclopedias, treatises, articles in periodicals, and annotations.

Treatises, periodical articles, and annotations usually focus on a specific topic. Encyclopedias provide a broader overview of the general language and principles of the law.

a. National Legal Encyclopedias

There are two major national encyclopedias: **American Jurisprudence Second,** most commonly referred to and cited as **Am. Jur. 2d,** and **Corpus Juris Secundum,** referred to as **C.J.S.** Each encyclopedia is divided into hundreds of separate topics, ranging from abandoned property to zoning and planning. Each topic is broken down into numerous subtopics. Each subtopic contains a

AMERICAN JURISPRUDENCE 2d

SPLITTING CAUSES OF ACTION —Cont'd
Wages, claims for payment, **Actions § 120**
Waiver of rule against splitting, **Actions § 113**
Wrongful death actions. Death and death actions, above

SPLITTING CLAIMS
Courts, effect on amount in controversy, **Courts § 127**
Trusts, **Trusts § 659**

SPLITTING COMMISSIONS OR FEES
Notaries public, **Notaries § 25**
Partnerships, **Partn § 234**
Physicians and surgeons, **Phys & S § 82, 157**
Profit Sharing (this index)

SPLITTING OF CORPORATE STOCK
Corporations (this index)

SPLITTING OF MOTIONS
Generally, **Motions § 6**

SPLITTING PROFITS
Profit Sharing (this index)

SPLIT TRIAL
Joint or Separate Action or Trial (this index)

SPLIT WEEK PLANS, OVERTIME, Labor § 4341

SPOILAGE OF GOODS
Contamination (this index)

SPOLIATION
Alteration of Instruments (this index)
Evidence, **Evid § 244**
Property. **Destruction of Property** (this index)

SPONATSKI RULE
Workers' compensation, **Work C § 344**

SPONGES
Malpractice By Medical Profession (this index)

SPONSORS
Cooperative Apartments (this index)
Supplemental Security Income (SSI) (this index)

SPONSORS OR SPONSORED AFFAIRS
Aliens and Citizens (this index)
Copyright and literary property, **Copy & Lit P § 199**
Penal and correctional institutions, religious services sponsor, **Penal Inst § 37, 41**

SPONSORS OR SPONSORED AFFAIRS—Cont'd
Pensions and Retirement (this index)
Recall election or petition, **Pub Off § 214**
Statutes, statements by sponsors of bill as aid to construction, **Stat § 177**
Workers' compensation, sponsorship of recreational activities, **Work C § 287, 288**

SPONTANEITY
Homicide, res gestae. **Homi § 325**

SPONTANEOUS COMBUSTION
Insurance, **Ins § 685**
Ships and shipping, **Ins § 685; Ship § 841**

SPONTANEOUS DECLARATIONS
Res Gestae (this index)

SPONTANEOUS REMARKS OF AGENTS, Labor § 998

SPONTANEOUS RESCUE
Generally. **Negl § 1089**

SPONTANEOUS UTTERANCES
Carriers, personal injuries, **Carriers § 1183**

SPORADIC ACTS
Casual or Occasional Acts or Matters (this index)

SPORADIC PURSUITS
Social security. **Soc Sec § 555**

SPORTS
Entertainment and Sports Law (this index)

SPORTS AND ATHLETICS
Gambling on sports events. **Gambl § 79**
Highways, Streets, and Bridges (this index)
Hotels and motels, premises liability, **Hotels § 116**

SPORTS ARENAS
Civil rights. **Civ R § 260**

SPORTSHIRTS
Contempt, **Contempt § 73**

SPOT REMOVER
Expert and opinion evidence, spot remover causing hepatitis. **Expert § 252**

SPOTS AND STAINS
Bloodstains (this index)
Expert and opinion evidence, **Expert § 293. 294**

SPOT ZONING
Generally, **Zoning § 146-159**
For detailed treatment, see index topic **Zoning and Planning** (this index)

SPOUSAL SUPPORT
Divorce and Separation (this index)

SPOUSE
Husband and wife (this index)

SPOUT
Downspout (this index)

SPRAINS
Damages (this index)

SPRAY OR SPRAYING
Adjoining landowners. Adj L § 38
Aerosol Containers (this index)
Aviation
generally, **Avi § 169**
Dusting Crops or Vegetation (this index)
Premises liability, **Prem Liab § 558**
Zoning and planning. **Zoning § 493**

SPRAY TRUSTS
Trusts, **Trusts § 11**

SPREADING VEGETATION
Adjoining landowners. **Adj L § 30**

SPRING GUN
Nuisances. **Nuis § 222**
Premises liability, generally, **Prem Liab § 195, 196**

SPRING GUNS
Homicide. **Homi § 76**

SPRINGING AND SHIFTING USES
Trusts (this index)

SPRINGS
Water Pollution (this index)

SPRINGS-WATERS
Waters (this index)

SPRINKLER SYSTEMS
Building regulations, **Bldgs § 28**
Fixtures, **Fixt § 106, 107**

SPRINKLING AND SPRINKLER DEVICES OR SYSTEMS
Automatic Sprinkler System or Fire Extinguisher (this index)
Expert and opinion evidence. **Expert § 344**
Highways, Streets, and Bridges (this index)
Insurance, **Ins § 479, 521, 1198, 1244, 1245**
Telecommunications. **Telecom § 200**
Warehouses (this index)

SPRINKLING TRUSTS
Trusts, **Trusts § 11**

SPURIOUS CLASS ACTION
Class Actions or Proceedings (this index)

512 For assistance using this index, call 1-800-328-4880

Exhibit D-1 American Jurisprudence Second, Index

narrative description of the general rules in that area. Wherever different states follow conflicting rules, the encyclopedia points out the conflict and briefly explains both positions. In addition to this type of general narrative discussion, Am. Jur. 2d provides various cross-references with citations to specific court cases, selected law review articles, other sections of Am. Jur. 2d, and annotations in American Law Reports Annotated. This latter reference is abbreviated as

Once you look under the topic **Husband and Wife** and then the subtopic **Immunity from suit, Interspousal,** you will find several likely entries.

To find the first entry, you would go to the main volume (not the index) that contains the topic Husband & Wife and look for Section 291. (§ stands for section.)

In an index you may notice the use of the words **infra, supra,** and **et seq.** In this index, the word below is used instead of infra and the word above is used instead of supra. Et seq. simply means "and following."

AMERICAN JURISPRUDENCE 2d

HUSBAND AND WIFE—Cont'd
Governing law, **Marr § 63**
Governing law. **Conflict of Laws** (this index)
Grandchildren or Grandparents (this index)
Grounds. Alimony, support, or maintenance without divorce, suit for, above
Guardian and ward
  mental incompetent, marriage of, **Marr § 23**
  minor, consent to marriage of, **Marr § 17**
Guardian and Ward (this index)
Guilt or innocence, adultery and fornication, innocent spouse, **Adult § 8, 9**
Habeas corpus, restraint without judicial order, **Hab Corp § 89**
Harboring criminals, **Harb § 2**
Head of family, rights of husband as, **Husb & W § 10**
Health
  Annulment of Marriage (this index)
  Breach of Promise (this index)
Heart Balm Statutes (this index)
Home, obligation to provide, **Husb & W § 171**
Homestead (this index)
Homicide (this index)
Husband and Wife (this index)
Husband's duty to support. Support, duty of, below
Idiots or imbeciles. Insane or other incompetent persons, below
Illegality. Unlawful or irregular marriages, below
Illegitimate Children (this index)
Illicit sexual relations, interference with family relationships by soliciting another's wife for sexual intercourse. **Torts § 33**
Immunity from suit, interspousal
  generally, **Husb & W § 291-302**
  abrogation or modification of doctrine generally, **Husb & W § 292-294**
  statute, by, **Husb & W § 293**
  annulment of marriage, separation, or divorce, effect of, **Husb & W § 297**
  application of rule in particular circumstances, **Husb & W § 296-302**
  community property, abrogation in jurisdictions following doctrine of, **Husb & W § 294**
  employer's liability for married employee's tort, **Husb & W § 300**
  estate of tortfeasor, action against, **Husb & W § 299**
  insurer's liability, **Husb & W § 301**
  intentional torts, **Husb & W § 302**
  law governing existence of interspousal immunity, **Husb & W § 295**
  motor vehicle, action for negligent operation of, **Husb & W § 302**
  negligence, immunity abolished, **Negl § 1800**
  statute, abrogation or modification of doctrine by, **Husb & W § 293**
  tort committed prior to marriage. **Husb & W § 296**
  trials. **Trial § 503**

HUSBAND AND WIFE—Cont'd
Immunity from suit, interspousal—Cont'd
  wrongful death, action for, **Husb & W § 298**
Impairment of Contracts (this index)
Impediments to lawful marriage
  capacity to marry, above
Impediments to marriage
  generally, **Marr § 47-61**
  common law marriage. **Marr § 44**
  divorce, waiting period after. **Marr § 47**
  family relationship of parties. **Incest** (this index)
  incarceration. **Marr § 48**
  same sex of parties. **Marr § 49, 50**
  sex change surgery. **Marr § 50**
  waiting period after divorce, **Marr § 47**
Implied contractual liability for goods and services, **Husb & W § 181**
Impotence, **Marr § 25**
Impotency (this index)
Imprisonment for debt, **Const L § 631**
Improper relations, alienation of affections and criminal conversation. **Husb & W § 274**
Improvements
  agency, improvements to property, **Husb & W § 156**
  community property, liability for debts of other spouse, **Husb & W § 166**
  separately held property, improvement of or service to property of other spouse, **Husb & W § 110**
Imputed negligence
  generally, **Negl § 1773, 1799-1802**
  agency, **Negl § 1799**
  community property, **Negl § 1813**
  instructions to jury, **Negl § 1758**
  joint interest in recovery, **Negl § 1802**
  joint venture or enterprise, **Negl § 1775, 1801**
  loss of consortium, imputation of impaired spouse's negligence to spouse seeking recovery for, **Husb & W § 261**
  nominal plaintiff. **Negl § 1780**
  questions of law and fact. **Negl § 1757**
  statutory abolition, **Negl § 1800**
Incarceration. **Marr § 48**
Incest, husband or wife as witness against spouse. **Incest § 21**
Incest (this index)
Incidental relief. Alimony, support, or maintenance without divorce, suit for, above
Incidental rights and liabilities, partnership. **Husb & W § 163**
Incompetency. Insane or incompetent persons, below
Incompetents. Insane or incompetent persons, below
Indemnity, validity of contract for indemnification of husband for support of wife and children, **Support Per § 7**
Index of conveyance, inclusion of names in, **Records § 94**
Indians, **Marr § 77, 78**
Inducement of marriage
  generally, **Marr § 93-97**

HUSBAND AND WIFE—Cont'd
Inducement of marriage—Cont'd
  criminal liability, **Marr § 97**
  damages, **Marr § 96**
  third person, liability of. **Marr § 95**
In equity, suit for alimony, support, or maintenance without divorce. **Husb & W § 212**
Infants. Children, above
Inferences. Presumptions, inferences, and burden of proof, below
Injunctions, **Inj § 90**
  transactions with third persons, **Husb & W § 90**
Insane or incompetent persons
  adjudication of insanity
    capacity to marry, **Marr § 23**
  Annulment of Marriage (this index)
  capacity to marry, above
  effect of, duty of support, **Husb & W § 177**
  necessaries. **Husb & W § 337, 338, 368; Incom P § 99 (Special Pamphlet)**
Insolvency (this index)
Insurance (this index)
Intent
  alienation of affections and criminal conversation, **Husb & W § 276**
  common law marriage, **Marr § 37, 43**
  interspousal immunity from suit, intentional torts, **Husb & W § 302**
Interracial marriages. Miscegenation, below
Interspousal debts and liabilities, generally, **Husb & W § 17**
Interspousal immunity from suit. Immunity from suit, interspousal, above
Intoxicating Liquors (this index)
Intoxication. **Marr § 21**
Invalidity. Validity, below
Irregular marriages. Unlawful or irregular marriages, below
Issuance of licenses. Marriage licenses, below
Jest or mock marriage
  annulment of marriage, lack of intent to enter into binding marriage as grounds for, **Annul § 3**
Job Discrimination (this index)
Joinder of parties to action
  husband, **Husb & W § 76**
  loss of consortium. **Husb & W § 269**
  wife, **Husb & W § 77-79**
Joint deposits and accounts, **Banks § 685**
Joint enterprise. **Negl § 1775, 1801**
Joint interest in recovery, negligence. **Negl § 1802**
Jointly committed torts, liability for, right of action against husband or wife or both, **Husb & W § 242**
Joint ownership. Cotenancy and joint ownership, above
Joint Ventures (this index)
Jones Act, **Husb & W § 258**
Judges (this index)
Judgments and decrees
  alimony, support, or maintenance without divorce, suit for, above
  assignment of judgments, **Judgm § 482**

For assistance using this index, call 1-800-328-4880

Exhibit D-2 American Jurisprudence Second, Index

A.L.R. and is discussed in greater detail beginning on page 674. C.J.S. includes cross-references to the key number system used in West's digests. (Beginning on page 687 there is an explanation of key numbers and the digest system.)

Am. Jur. 2d tends to take a fairly selective approach to case inclusion. C.J.S. attempts to be more all-inclusive. You will notice the difference when you compare the amount of textual material with the amount of footnote material.

Because C.J.S. includes more case citations, the footnote material tends to dominate its pages.

Our work in the Am. Jur. 2d index (Exhibit D-2) indicated we should go to the volume containing the topic Husband and Wife and look under sections 291-302. Exhibit D-3 takes you to volume 41 of Am. Jur. 2d and the topic of Husband and Wife. Section 290 begins on page 192 of Am. Jur. 2d. Look at the way in which Am. Jur. 2d begins its discussion of the right of spouses to sue each other. Notice that the footnotes are full of citations to court opinions that support the textual narrative. They are arranged in alphabetical order by state. However, one of the disadvantages of the way Am. Jur. 2d cites cases is that no date is included.

On page 193 of Am. Jur. 2d note the references to A.L.R. annotations. A.L.R. stands for American Law Reports. We discuss it beginning on page 674 in this chapter. Notice the reference to *Lewis v. Lewis* in footnote 89.

Exhibit D-4 on page 670 shows how C.J.S. discusses the same issue of the right of one spouse to sue the other. Each section begins with bold text. This is the **black letter law** in the area, that is, the generally accepted legal principles. Also locate the references to the digest topic and key numbers. Finally, notice that the number of footnotes exceeds what you would find in Am. Jur. 2d because C.J.S. claims to be all-inclusive. As with Am. Jur. 2d, all cases in the footnotes are listed in alphabetical order by state. Also, once again the dates of the decisions are omitted.

Black letter law
Generally accepted legal principles.

Like most secondary legal reference books, Am. Jur. 2d and C.J.S. are kept current with the publication of **pocket part** supplements. New material is organized to correspond with the section, page, and footnote numbers used in the bound volume. It is then inserted in a special pocket at the back of the volume. When these pocket supplements get too thick and unwieldy, the publisher issues a replacement volume.

Pocket part
A pamphlet inserted into the back of a book containing information new since the volume was published.

b. State-Specific Encyclopedias

Am. Jur. 2d and C.J.S. cover cases from all fifty states. This is useful when you want to compare and contrast the differences between the laws of various states. Usually, however, you will find that only the laws of your state are relevant. In those situations you should use a local encyclopedia specifically geared to your state.

These local encyclopedias carry names such as California Jurisprudence 2d, Michigan Law and Practice, and Pennsylvania Law Encyclopedia. They are usually arranged by topics that parallel those in the national encyclopedias. They have subject analysis sections, indexes, and supplements that also closely resemble those in Am. Jur. 2d and C.J.S. Unfortunately, such local encyclopedias are not published in some states, while other states have two publishers vying for your business. For example, Massachusetts has both the Massachusetts Practice Series and Massachusetts Jurisprudence.

Exhibit D-5 on page 671 shows the type of discussion that can occur in a state encyclopedia. Notice the cross-references to Westlaw, West's on-line database containing court opinions and statutes from around the country. References to Massachusetts General Laws Annotated are also included. As with national encyclopedias, the textual material is supported by references to case law, here with the focus on Massachusetts state law. Also, as with national encyclopedias, most state encyclopedias are supplemented with pocket parts.

§ 288 HUSBAND AND WIFE 41 Am Jur 2d

criminal conversation, to show the motives, feelings, emotions, and relations of the parties with respect to the loss of affection or consortium or the desertion of the plaintiff by his or her spouse,[80] and in an action for alienation of affections to show affection or lack of affection between the spouses at the time of the alienation.[81]

§ 289. Competence of spouse as witness; maritally privileged communications

The plaintiff in an action for alienation of affection or criminal conversation is generally competent to testify as to the conduct of his or her spouse. A statute which provides that one spouse is not competent to give evidence for or against the other spouse in an action in consequence of adultery or criminal conversation does not bar a spouse's testimony where the other spouse is not a party to the action.[82] A communication between a husband and wife may, however, be privileged under applicable rules of evidence pertaining to marital privilege.[83]

XIII. INTERSPOUSAL IMMUNITY FROM SUIT [§§ 290–301]

A. IN GENERAL [§§ 290–294]

Research References
ALR Digest: Husband and Wife §§ 148-154
ALR Index: Husband and Wife; Privileges and Immunities; Torts

---

§ 290. Generally

The common law established interspousal tort immunity as a consequence of the legal identity of husband and wife: the husband and wife were one person, and that person was the husband, so it was both morally and conceptually objectionable to permit a tort suit between spouses.[84] The doctrine has been justified on the grounds that immunity is necessary to preserve marital harmony

SW2d 470; Turner v PV International Corp. (Tex App Dallas) 765 SW2d 455, writ den (Tex) 778 SW2d 865, rehg of writ of error overr on other grounds (Nov 22, 1989).
Practice References: 1 Am Jur Proof of Facts 237, Adultery.

80. Blaylock v Strecker, 291 Ark 340, 724 SW2d 470.

81. Giltner v Stark (Iowa) 219 NW2d 700; Shaw v Stringer, 101 NC App 513, 400 SE2d 101.

82. Scott v Kiker, 59 NC App 458, 297 SE2d 142 (criticized on other grounds by Cannon v Miller, 71 NC App 460, 322 SE2d 780).

83. Scott v Kiker, 59 NC App 458, 297 SE2d 142 (criticized on other grounds by Cannon v Miller, 71 NC App 460, 322 SE2d 780) (defendant waived privilege by failing to object to testimony by plaintiff husband concerning conversation he had with his wife).

As to marital privilege, generally, see 81 Am Jur 2d, Witnesses §§ 296-336.

84. Hamilton v Hamilton, 255 Ala 284, 51 So 2d 13 (noting that under statute, actions at law between spouses may be maintained); Rains v Rains, 97 Colo 19, 46 P2d 740; Saunders v Hill (Sup) 57 Del 519, 202 A2d 807 (criticized on other grounds as stated in Hudson v Hudson (Del Super) 532 A2d 620) and (ovrld in part on other grounds by Beattie v Beattie (Del Sup) 630 A2d 1096); Taylor v Vezzani, 109 Ga App 167, 135 SE2d 522; Perkins v Blethen, 107 Me 443, 78 A 574 (ovrld in part on other grounds by Moulton v Moulton (Me) 309 A2d 224); Ex parte Badger, 286 Mo 139, 226 SW 936, 14 ALR 286; Mertz v Mertz, 271 NY 466, 3 NE2d 597, 108 ALR 1120; Shaw v Lee, 258 NC 609, 129 SE2d 288 (superseded by statute on other grounds as stated in Henry v Henry, 291 NC

192

Exhibit D-3 American Jurisprudence Second, Volume 41 *(continues)*

41 Am Jur 2d   HUSBAND AND WIFE   § 291

by shutting off interspousal disputes[85] and to prevent fraud and collusion between parties to an interspousal suit.[86]

Common-law interspousal tort immunity has withstood a variety of constitutional challenges relating to due process, equal protection, and the availability of remedies generally.[87]

▌▌▌▌ *Practice guide:* The defense of interspousal tort immunity must be affirmatively pleaded and may be waived by failure to include it in the answer.[88]

§ 291. Abrogation or modification of doctrine; generally

In some jurisdictions, the common law relating to interspousal immunity has been judicially abrogated or modified.[89] Other authority, however, holds that such change is outside the sphere of proper judicial action and that any change in the common-law rule is a matter for the legislature.[90] Courts willing to abrogate the doctrine have done so on the grounds that interspousal immunity

156, 229 SE2d 158) (by statute, spouses may sue each other); Lillienkamp v Rippetoe, 133 Tenn 57, 179 SW 628; Vigilant Ins. Co. v Bennett, 197 Va 216, 89 SE2d 69 (ovrld in part on other grounds by Surratt v Thompson, 212 Va 191, 183 SE2d 200) (statute permits suits between spouses).

The common-law immunity of a husband from action by his wife was based on the conception of husband and wife as one, and the disqualification of the wife from owning property and maintaining actions independently of the husband. Welch v Davis, 410 Ill 130, 101 NE2d 547, 28 ALR2d 656.

Annotations: Modern status of interspousal tort immunity in personal injury and wrongful death actions, 92 ALR3d 901 § 8.

85. Burns v Burns, 111 Ariz 178, 526 P2d 717 (ovrld in part on other grounds by Fernandez v Romo, 132 Ariz 447, 646 P2d 878); Sturiano v Brooks (Fla) 523 So 2d 1126, 13 FLW 224; Shoemake v Shoemake, 200 Ga App 182, 407 SE2d 134, 102-136 Fulton County D R 14B; Counts v Counts, 221 Va 151, 266 SE2d 895.

Annotations: 92 ALR3d 901 § 9.

86. Burns v Burns, 111 Ariz 178, 526 P2d 717 (ovrld in part on other grounds by Fernandez v Romo, 132 Ariz 447, 646 P2d 878); Sturiano v Brooks (Fla) 523 So 2d 1126, 13 FLW 224.

Annotations: 92 ALR3d 901 § 10.

87. Paiewonsky v Paiewonsky (CA3 VI) 446 F2d 178, cert den 405 US 919, 30 L Ed 2d 788, 92 S Ct 944 (applying Virgin Islands law); Harris v Harris, 252 Ga 387, 313 SE2d 88; Heckendorn v First Nat'l Bank, 19 Ill 2d 190, 166 NE2d 571, cert den 364 US 882, 5 L Ed 2d 104, 81 S Ct 172 and (ovrld on other grounds as stated in Farmers Ins. Group v Nudi (1st Dist) 108 Ill

App 3d 151, 63 Ill Dec 897, 438 NE2d 1260); Williams v Williams (3d Dist) 108 Ill App 3d 936, 64 Ill Dec 390, 439 NE2d 1055, mod 98 Ill 2d 128, 74 Ill Dec 495, 455 NE2d 1388.

88. De Guido v De Guido (Fla App D3) 308 So 2d 609.

The defense of interspousal immunity can be waived, because it does not involve subject-matter jurisdiction. Policino v Ehrlich, 478 Pa 5, 385 A2d 968.

89. Brooks v Robinson, 259 Ind 16, 284 NE2d 794; Ebert v Ebert, 232 Kan 502, 656 P2d 766; Boblitz v Boblitz, 296 Md 242, 462 A2d 506; Lewis v Lewis, 370 Mass 619, 351 NE2d 526, 92 ALR3d 890; Beaudette v Frana, 285 Minn 366, 173 NW2d 416; Rupert v Stienne, 90 Nev 397, 528 P2d 1013; Maestas v Overton, 87 NM 213, 531 P2d 947; Shearer v Shearer, 18 Ohio St 3d 94, 18 Ohio BR 129, 480 NE2d 388 (ovrld on other grounds as stated in Petrie v Nationwide Mut. Ins. Co. (Ohio App, Franklin Co) 1994 Ohio App LEXIS 6072); Digby v Digby, 120 RI 299, 388 A2d 1; Davis v Davis (Tenn) 657 SW2d 753; Freehe v Freehe, 81 Wash 2d 183, 500 P2d 771 (ovrld in part on other grounds by Brown v Brown, 100 Wash 2d 729, 675 P2d 1207).

Annotations: Modern status of interspousal tort immunity in personal injury and wrongful death actions, 92 ALR3d 901 § 18.

90. Paiewonsky v Paiewonsky (CA3 VI) 446 F2d 178, cert den 405 US 919, 30 L Ed 2d 788, 92 S Ct 944 (applying Virgin Islands law); Burns v Burns, 111 Ariz 178, 526 P2d 717 (ovrld in part on other grounds by Fernandez v Romo, 132 Ariz 447, 646 P2d 878); Luna v Clayton (Tenn) 655 SW2d 893.

Annotations: 92 ALR3d 901 § 6.

193

Exhibit D-3   American Jurisprudence Second, Volume 41 *(concluded)*

---

41 C.J.S.   **HUSBAND AND WIFE § 112**

longer entitled to such presumption.[74]

Thus, when a wife is coerced by her husband to perpetrate an illegal act, she remains exempt from punishment, just as would anyone who could demonstrate that the crime was committed under duress,[75] and the same rules of proof are applied to duress or coercion by a husband as are applied to duress or coercion by anyone else.[76]

VI. ACTIONS

§ 111. In General

A married woman may sue and be sued in her own name as if she were unmarried.

> **Library References**
> Husband and Wife ⊜203, 203½.

The rule at early common law that a married woman could not sue or be sued as a feme sole,[77] is no longer adhered to.[78]

It is now the rule that a married woman may sue and be sued,[79] in her own name,[80] as if she were unmarried.[81]

What law governs.

A number of different choice of law rules or tests have been used to determine whether one spouse has the capacity to sue the other in tort, or is instead barred from doing so by interspous- al tort immunity, including the most significant relationship test,[82] the government interest analysis,[83] and the place-of-the wrong rule.[84] Where the most significant relationship test is employed, the applicable law will usually be the local law of the state of the married couple's domicile.[85]

Depending on the applicable choice of law rule, whether one spouse has a right of action for loss of consortium or loss of care, consideration and society, has been determined to be governed by the lex loci delicti,[86] or by the law of the married couple's domicile.[87]

§ 112. Right of Action Between Husband and Wife

Except where prohibited by statute or by the doctrine of interspousal tort immunity, suit may be brought by one spouse against the other.

---

74. N.C.—State v. Smith, 235 S.E.2d 860, 33 N.C.App. 511, certiorari denied Smith v. North Carolina. 98 S.Ct. 1267, 434 U.S. 1076, 55 L.Ed.2d 782.

Doctrine outdated

Independence of women in political, social, and economic matters renders the doctrine of coercion outdated and inapplicable to modern society.

Pa.—Commonwealth v. Santiago, 340 A.2d 440, 462 Pa. 216.

75. N.C.—State v. Smith, 235 S.E.2d 860, 33 N.C.App. 511, certiorari denied Smith v. North Carolina, 98 S.Ct. 1267, 434 U.S. 1076, 55 L.Ed.2d 782.

Pa.—Commonwealth v. Santiago, 340 A.2d 440, 462 Pa. 216.

76. Mass.—Commonwealth v. Barnes, 340 N.E.2d 863, 369 Mass. 462.

77. Fla.—McGill v. Cockrell, 88 So. 268, 81 Fla. 463.

Ga.—Heyman v. Heyman, 92 S.E. 25, 19 Ga.App. 634.

N.J.—Klinger v. Steffens, 6 A.2d 217, 17 N.J.Misc. 118.

78. Alaska—Cramer v. Cramer, 379 P.2d 95.

Ark.—Leach v. Leach, 300 S.W.2d 15, 227 Ark. 599.

Cal.—Self v. Self, 26 Cal.Rptr. 97, 376 P.2d 65, 58 C.2d 683.

Hawaii—Peters v. Peters, 634 P.2d 586, 63 Haw. 653.

Ohio—Kobe v. Kobe, 399 N.E.2d 124, 61 Ohio App.2d 67, 15 O.O.3d 86.

Tex.—Broadway Drug Store of Galveston, Inc. v. Trowbridge. 435 S.W.2d 268.

79. Alaska—Cramer v. Cramer, 379 P.2d 95.

Ark.—Leach v. Leach, 300 S.W.2d 15, 227 Ark. 599.

Mich.—Hosko v. Hosko, 187 N.W.2d 236, 385 Mich. 39.

Neb.—Imig v. March, 279 N.W.2d 382, 203 Neb. 537.

Ohio—Shearer v. Shearer, 480 N.E.2d 388, 18 Ohio St.3d 94, 18 O.B.R. 129.

W.Va.—Coffindaffer v. Coffindaffer, 244 S.E.2d 338, 161 W.Va. 557.

80. Cal.—Self v. Self, 26 Cal.Rptr. 97, 376 P.2d 65, 58 C.2d 683.

W.Va.—Coffindaffer v. Coffindaffer, 244 S.E.2d 338, 161 W.Va. 557.

81. Alaska—Cramer v. Cramer, 379 P.2d 95.

Ark.—Leach v. Leach, 300 S.W.2d 15, 227 Ark. 599.

Mich.—Hosko v. Hosko, 187 N.W.2d 236, 385 Mich. 39.

Neb.—Imig v. March, 279 N.W.2d 382, 203 Neb. 537.

Ohio—Shearer v. Shearer, 480 N.E.2d 388, 18 Ohio St.3d 94, 18 O.B.R. 129.

W.Va.—Coffindaffer v. Coffindaffer, 244 S.E.2d 338, 161 W.Va. 557.

82. Ill.—Nelson v. Hix, 522 N.E.2d 1214, 119 Ill.Dec. 355, 122 Ill.2d 343, certiorari denied 109 S.Ct. 309, 488 U.S. 925, 102 L.Ed.2d 328.

Mo.—Huff v. LaSieur, App., 571 S.W.2d 654.

Tex.—Robertson v. McKnight's Estate, 609 S.W.2d 534.

83. N.J.—Veazey v. Doremus, 510 A.2d 1187, 103 N.J. 244.

84. N.C.—Henry v. Henry, 229 S.E.2d 158, 291 N.C. 156.

Va.—McMillan v. McMillan, 253 S.E.2d 662, 219 Va. 1127.

85. Ill.—Nelson v. Hix, 522 N.E.2d 1214, 119 Ill.Dec. 355, 122 Ill.2d 343, certiorari denied 109 S.Ct. 309, 488 U.S. 925, 102 L.Ed.2d 328.

Mo.—Huff v. LaSieur, App., 571 S.W.2d 654.

Tex.—Robertson v. McKnight's Estate, 609 S.W.2d 534.

86. U.S.—Madison v. Deseret Livestock Co., C.A.Utah, 514 F.2d 1027.

Miller v. Holiday Inn's, Inc., D.C.Va., 436 F.Supp. 460.

87. U.S.—Linnell v. Sloan, C.A.Va., 636 F.2d 65.

407

Exhibit D-4   Corpus Juris Secundum, Volume 41

Review the sample pages from a Massachusetts encyclopedia in Exhibit D-5. Note the footnoted references to M.G.L.A. c. 209 §§ 2, 6 (a common but incorrect way of citing to Mass. Gen. Laws Ann.), to *Callow*, and to *Lewis*. You will also find references to other publications: C.J.S. and the digest system, as well as the Restatement of the Law of Torts.

Ch. 9   DOMESTIC RELATIONS   **§ 151**

contract with each other and may bring an action against each other on the contract.[5]

Actions by and between the spouses founded on negligence, once outlawed on the grounds of public policy, even after divorce or annulment,[6] are now maintainable.[7] Courts with equitable jurisdiction will entertain actions between husband and wife (1) to secure her separate property; (2) to prevent fraud; (3) to relieve from coercion; (4) to enforce trusts; (5) to establish other conflicting interests.[8]

Interspousal immunity was diminished in Brown v. Brown,[9] where the wife fell on property owned by her and her husband as tenants by the entirety. The court could find no reason to bar the wife's claim where it was argued that the husband had control of the premises and was responsible for maintaining it after a snowstorm and where the court was persuaded by the argument that

order has health insurance on a group plan available to him through an employer or organization that may be extended to cover the spouse for whom support is ordered. When said court has determined that the obligor has such insurance, said court shall include in the support order a requirement that the obligor exercise the option of additional coverage in favor of such spouse.

See also, M.G.L.A. c. 208 § 1. Cf. Bianco v. Bianco, 371 Mass. 420, 358 N.E.2d 243 (1976).

→ 5. M.G.L.A. c. 209 §§ 2, 6 provide:

§ 2. Married Woman; Power to Contract

A married woman may make contracts, oral and written, sealed and unsealed, in the same manner as if she were sole, and may make such contracts with her husband.

§ 6. Married Woman; Power to Sue and Be Sued

A married woman may sue and be sued in the same manner as if she were sole; but this section shall not authorize suits between husband and wife except in connection with contracts entered into pursuant to the authority contained in section two.

Gahm v. Gahm, 243 Mass. 374, 375, 137 N.E. 876 (1922).

6. Callow v. Thomas, 322 Mass. 550, ← 78 N.E.2d 637 (1948).

As to immunities, see Restatement, Second, Torts § 895F.

7. Lewis v. Lewis, 370 Mass. 619, ← 629–630, 351 N.E.2d 526, 532–533 (1976).

Restatement, Second, Torts § 895F provides:

§ 895F. Husband and Wife

(1) A husband or wife is not immune from tort liability to the other solely by reason of that relationship.

(2) Repudiation of general tort immunity does not establish liability for an act or omission that, because of the marital relationship, is otherwise privileged or is not tortious.

8. Gahm v. Gahm, 243 Mass. 374, 376, 137 N.E. 876 (1922).

9. 381 Mass. 231, 232–233, 409 N.E.2d 717, 718–719 (1980).

Exhibit D-5   Massachusetts Practice, Chapter 9   (continues)

§ 151   INTENTIONAL TORTS ·   Ch. 9

the tortious conduct did not invade the more private aspects of married life.

> The Court has not changed the traditional immunity as to intentional torts. The spouses are not permitted to maintain actions for personal torts against each other such as assault and battery, false imprisonment, malicious prosecution, defamation and the like.[10]

The Restatement recognizes a cause of action for a fraudulent nondisclosure of physical conditions making marital relations dangerous to the other's health [11] and for fraud in inducing the plaintiff to contract marriage when the defendant is not free to marry.[12]

Spouses have always been criminally liable for offenses against each other.

> **Library References:**
> C.J.S. Husband and Wife § 163.
> West's Key No. Digests, Husband and Wife ⬤═53.

10. Thompson v. Thompson, 218 U.S. 611, 31 S.Ct. 111, 54 L.Ed. 1180 (1910).

Nogueira v. Nogueira, 388 Mass. 79, 80–82, 444 N.E.2d 940, 941–942 (1983) (However, the doctrine of interspousal immunity was inapplicable to a spouse's claim for libel and intentional infliction of emotional distress once the marriage was terminated by divorce and even upon the entry of the judgment of divorce nisi).

Garrity v. Garrity, 399 Mass. 367, 370–372 & n. 9, 504 N.E.2d 617, 619–620 (1987) (Interspousal immunity inapplicable to wife's claim against husband for violation of fiduciary duties with respect to their close corporation and for fraudulently conveying property in which plaintiff had an interest).

→ **11. Restatement, Second, Torts**

§ 554. Fraudulent Nondisclosure of Physical Conditions Making Marital Relation Dangerous

A husband or wife who fraudulently conceals from the other a physical condition that makes cohabitation dangerous to the health of the other spouse is subject to liability to the other spouse for the harm suffered as a result.

12. Restatement, Second, Torts

§ 555. Fraudulent Misrepresentation or Nondisclosure Inducing Recipient to Enter Into Meretricious Relations With the Maker or Third Person

One who by fraudulent misrepresentation that he or she is free to contract a lawful marriage or by a failure to disclose a bar to the marriage induces another to cohabit as husband and wife is subject to liability to the other for any harm suffered as a result of the cohabitation.

Restatement, Second, Torts

§ 556. Fraudulent Misrepresentation of a Third Person's Fitness for or Freedom to Marry

One who by fraudulent misrepresentation that a third person is physically fit and legally free to marry intentionally induces another to enter into a marriage with the third person is subject to liability to the other for any harm caused to the other by the misrepresentation.

260

Exhibit D-5   Massachusetts Practice, Chapter 9 *(concluded)*

Legal Reasoning Exercise

1. Read the paragraph in Exhibit D-5 that begins, "The Court has not changed. . . ." Given what the court said about negligence actions in *Lewis*, do you agree with the analysis, which states that "spouses are not permitted to maintain actions for personal torts against each other such as assault"? If the court no longer thinks spousal immunity is a bar in negligence cases, do you think that the court would keep it as a bar when one spouse intentionally hurts the other?

c. Special Subject Encyclopedias, Treatises, and Restatements

In addition to the types of encyclopedias discussed above, other sources of general background information include special subject encyclopedias, treatises, and restatements. Special subject encyclopedias focus on a single topic, such as contracts or evidence. They bear names like Fletcher's Cyclopedia of the Law of Private Corporations.

A **treatise** summarizes, interprets, and evaluates the law. This differentiates a treatise from an encyclopedia, which simply summarizes the law. Although some treatises are published as multivolume sets, most look just like standard library books. In addition to the usual table of contents, text, and index, legal treatises usually contain a table of cases, and many are also supplemented with pocket parts. They are given regular library call numbers and can be found in the standard library card catalog. Two well-known treatises are Corbin on Contracts and Wigmore on Evidence.

Restatements represent still another source of general background information. In 1923 a group of prominent law professors, judges, and lawyers founded the American Law Institute (ALI) and began a series of books—the Restatements of the Law—to summarize the basic principles of the common law in several major areas. Recognizing that there was disagreement among the courts on the meaning of some of these principles, the ALI sought to present what its experts thought were the best rules. These are printed in the Restatements in boldface type as relatively short statements. Each principle is then followed by an explanation of the situations in which it should be applied. Restatements have been published in the areas of agency, conflict of laws, foreign relations, torts, and trusts.

d. Legal Periodicals and Newspapers

Law reviews and other types of legal periodicals are still another source for researching the meaning of the law. Law reviews, published by law schools and edited by law students, contain a wealth of thoroughly researched information about specific areas of the law. The lead articles are usually expansive pieces, often written by law professors. A comments or notes section contains contributions of the student editors. Because the law review staffs are traditionally made up of the brightest students, their work has earned a high reputation. Other periodicals are often more specialized and practitioner oriented and also can contain articles of great value.

There are also weekly newspapers devoted to legal topics. Two that are national in scope are the National Law Journal and Lawyers Weekly USA. Many states also have state-specific newspapers. For example, the same publisher that prints Lawyers Weekly USA prints Massachusetts Lawyers Weekly. Not only will these newspapers keep you up to date on current developments in the legal field, but also they will frequently provide background information on specific topics.

e. American Law Reports Annotated

American Law Reports Annotated is similar to an encyclopedia in that it provides you with information from around the country on selected topics. It differs from an encyclopedia, however, in that only selected topics are covered. In addition, those topics are covered in much more depth than you will find in an encyclopedia. The approach of the A.L.R. is to select a timely topic, reprint a leading case in that area, and then follow it with a discussion of related cases and an analysis of any trends that appear to be developing. If you find a pertinent A.L.R. annotation, you will have a good overview of the law in that given area. However, because the coverage of the A.L.R. is not encyclopedic, there may not be an A.L.R. annotation covering your area.

Many other publications contain cross-references to one of the A.L.R. series. If you do not have such a reference, begin your research with the A.L.R. Quick Index.

f. Citing Secondary Authority

In terms of citation value all secondary sources are not created equal. Unless you have absolutely nothing else on which to rely, you should never cite to an encyclopedia. Encyclopedias give you valuable background information, but once you have that, you should then proceed with your research into primary authority. It is appropriate to cite to other types of secondary authority, especially if they evaluate and analyze the law rather than simply describe it. Of the secondary sources that we have discussed the most authoritative and hence the most valuable to cite are Restatements, law review articles written by known authorities in the field, and treatises. Generally, you should not cite to A.L.R. annotations except when giving general information, such as the number of states that have held a certain way on a particular legal issue. Finally, you can cite to newspaper articles if you cannot find that information in any other source.

g. Ending Your Secondary Research and Relying on Secondary Sources

How do you know when you have done enough background researching and you are ready to move on to primary sources? There is no magic litmus test, but generally it will be time to move on when you start finding references to the same court decisions in each of the secondary sources you consult.

PRACTICAL TIP

Be warned: Secondary sources provide only descriptions of the author's view of the law. Never rely only on a secondary source. Always read and analyze the primary authority yourself.

3. Go to Primary Authority

Your ultimate goal in conducting research is to find statutes, administrative regulations, and court opinions. Secondary sources are designed to help you find and understand this primary authority. As mentioned earlier, there will be times when you will dispense altogether with these secondary sources.

As we discussed in Chapter 2, there are three basic sources of law: legislatures, administrative agencies, and courts. Legislatures enact statutes, administrative agencies enact and enforce regulations, and courts write court opinions. Figure D-2 summarizes the sources of primary authority for Massachusetts. Most states follow a similar approach.

When litigants ask a trial court to rule on a legal issue, the trial court will look to statutes and prior appellate court decisions from its own state for guidance. For example, in Massachusetts on a Massachusetts state law issue, appellate court decisions from the Massachusetts Appeals Court and the Massachusetts Supreme Judicial Court are binding on all Massachusetts trial courts. This is known as mandatory authority—that is, a statute or court opinion from a higher court in

Figure D-2   Sources of Law: Massachusetts Primary Authority

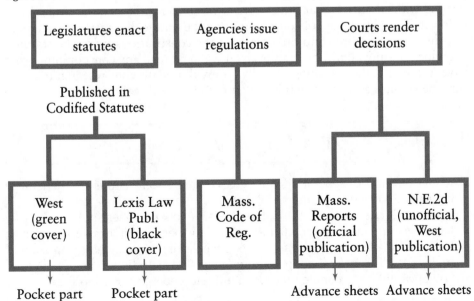

NETNOTE

You can find the text of most state and federal statutes and regulations on government web sites. A good place to start your search is at the home page of Findlaw: *www.findlaw.com*. From there, for federal and state statutes and regulations, click on "US Law: Cases & Codes." Then for federal materials click on "US Code" or "Code of Federal Regulations." For state statutes and regulations select your state.

the same state (jurisdiction). Appellate decisions from other states and the federal system can be influential, but they are not binding on Massachusetts trial courts and hence are known as persuasive authority. Therefore, if you are working in a Massachusetts law firm and are assigned to research the question of whether or not a wife can sue her husband, you will begin with the realization that the trial court assigned to decide your case will be looking primarily to Massachusetts statutes and appellate decisions for guidance.

When beginning research into primary resources, statutes and court opinions, first think about whether the facts of your client's case suggest that the situation will be governed by a statute or by the common law. For example, if your client has been charged with a crime, you know that for something to be a crime, there must be a statute prohibiting that behavior. Therefore, you will begin with the statutes. On the other hand, if your client wants to sue someone for negligence, you know that most of tort law is still common law, and you will want to start with the court opinions.

If you are unsure as to whether to start your research with statutes or court decisions, you will usually begin your research with the statutes. The reason for starting with statutes is that if a statute governs your problem, the courts must follow it. The courts may, of course, interpret the statute, but they cannot ignore it. (This assumes there is no problem with the constitutionality of the statute.) After locating any applicable statutes, you will next read any court opinions that have interpreted those statutes. Finally, you will update your research to make sure the statutes and court opinions you found are still valid.

PRACTICAL TIP

Recall that in our federal system of government state courts and federal courts are co-equal partners. Except in matters of federal law, federal court decisions are not mandatory on state courts. Therefore, when a federal court decides a matter of state law because it has jurisdiction based on diversity of citizenship, its decision is *not* mandatory on state trial courts. The federal court is merely guessing as to how state appellate courts would have handled the issue if it had been presented to them.

a. A Note on Lawbook Publishers

Traditionally, two commercial publishers published most of the materials you use when doing legal research: West Publishing Company and Lawyers Co-operative. Generally, they published the same materials but added their own specialized editorial features and did not cross-reference each other's publications. In most states the state statutes were published by one or both of these companies. Then in 1996 Thomson Legal Publishing Company became the owner of both West and Lawyers Co-operative. As a result, most of the titles that were published by either West Publishing Company or Lawyers Co-operative are now owned and published by a subsidiary of Thomson, known as West Group. However, because of possible antitrust problems, West Group has and is still in the process of divesting itself of some of its publications, such as the United States Code Service, now owned by Michie Company, a subsidiary of Lexis Law Publishing.

These changes in the publishing industry should not greatly impact the way in which you conduct your research. However, it may mean that you will see more cross-referencing between the various books. Also, as individual volumes need to be replaced, on the replacement book's spine you will see the designation for the new publisher.

Many states also publish an official version of their statutes. As a researching tool, the main disadvantage to using the official statutes is that they usually do not contain any editorial features, such as summaries of court opinions that have interpreted the statutes.

When researching a state that has annotated statutes published by more than one publisher, feel free to begin your research with either version. Before proceeding to read court decisions, however, you should always consult the case summaries located in both versions. You will usually find summaries of the same court decisions in each publication—but not always. That is because the editors at the different publishing companies decide which opinions to summarize and to include after the statute.

To begin your research into the question of spousal immunity, you could start with one of the two privately published versions of the Massachusetts statutes annotated. You could also begin your research in the official Massachusetts General Laws, but then you would not receive the benefit of the annotations provided by the private publishers.

b. Finding Statutes

Each year as legislatures enact new laws, they are compiled and published in statutory codes. The codes are generally arranged by subject matter, and if the code is annotated, it will also include such editorial features as historical notes and summaries of court opinions that have interpreted the statute.

NETNOTE

For current information on federal legislation a good source is *http://thomas.loc .gov/* provided by the Library of Congress. You can also find information on the legislative branch at *http://thomas.loc.gov/home/legbranch/legbranch.html*.

(1) Starting with the citation

The simplest way to begin statutory research is with a citation to a relevant statute. For example, your boss might know that Mass. Gen. L. ch. 209 § 6 governs suits between spouses and might merely want you to check whether the legislature has recently amended the statute. Or if you were lucky during your background research, as we were with the information we found in Massachusetts Practice, you may have found a statutory reference in one of those secondary sources.

If you have the citation for a statute, you know its chapter and section number. You can simply go to the appropriate volume and locate the statute. Remember that the citation gives chapter numbers, not volume numbers. The chapter numbers are printed on the spine of the statutory code volumes.

(2) Starting with an index

If you do not know the citation, you will have to use a subject matter index. Both the Massachusetts General Laws Annotated and the Annotated Laws of Massachusetts have subject matter indexes, called the General Index, which can be used to find the citation for any statute that might govern our problem.

As with indexes for secondary sources, before consulting a statutory index you should always try to think of several words or phrases that might pertain to your problem. Sometimes the indexes will help you out by trying to second-guess the words you might use. For example, if you look under the word *Spouse* in the Massachusetts General Laws Annotated index, it will send you to Husband and Wife. Exhibit D-6 shows what you will find in the index, once you go to the topic Husband and Wife. Under the subtopic Actions and proceedings, notice the reference to "Between husband and wife, 209 § 6." You should follow the same process of working with the index to find the statute's citation in the index for the Annotated Laws of Massachusetts.

PRACTICAL TIP

Different publishers may use different words to describe the same concept (for example, car instead of motor vehicle). Therefore, if you cannot find what you are looking for in one index, look in a competitor's index.

---

(3) Reading an annotated statute

Exhibit D-7 on pages 680–681 shows you what you will find once you locate chapter 209, section 6. Under the statute you will see the heading Historical Note. This contains information about when the statute was amended. The years, such as 1845 and 1902, refer to the years in which the statute was amended. The other numbers, such as c. 208 § 5, refer to the chapter numbers of the statute as it was enacted by the legislature before it was codified—that is, placed in the statute books with other statutes dealing with similar subject matter. At the bottom of the page are references to law review articles.

Codification
The process of organizing statutes by subject matter.

HUNTER

1470

Exhibit D-6 Index to Massachusetts General Laws Annotated

HUSBAND AND WIFE   **209 § 6**

Who may be appointed trustee, competency, see M.P.S. vol. 22, Lombard, § 1346.

WESTLAW Electronic Research

See WESTLAW guide following the Foreword of this volume.

Notes of Decisions

In general 2
Prior law 1

1. Prior law

Under St.1783, c. 24, § 19, the marriage of a
single woman, who was sole administratrix,
did not terminate her authority, but made her
husband joint administrator with her. Barber
v. Bush (1812) 7 Mass. 510.

2. In general

Where A., a married woman, during the lifetime of her husband and before the passage of
St.1855, c. 304, deposited in a savings bank a
sum of money in her name as "trustee for B,"
and A., until her death, retained possession of
the deposit book, and at times drew out portions of the money, and A.'s executor took
possession of the deposit book, charged himself with the amount of the deposit in his
inventory, and about two years after her death
paid it over to B., who until then had no
knowledge of the deposit, the deposit was a
part of A.'s estate and was improperly paid to
B. Jewett v. Shattuck (1878) 124 Mass. 590.

---

§ 6. Married woman; power to sue and be sued

A married woman may sue and be sued in the same manner as if she were
sole; but this section shall not authorize suits between husband and wife
except in connection with contracts entered into pursuant to the authority
contained in section two.

Amended by St.1963, c. 765, § 2.

Historical Note

St.1845, c. 208, § 5.   G.S.1860, c. 108, § 8.   P.S.1882, c. 147, § 7.
St.1855, c. 304, §§ 2, 4.   St.1871, c. 312.   R.L.1902, c. 153, § 6.
St.1857, c. 249, § 3.   St.1874, c. 184, § 3.

St.1963, c. 765, § 2, approved Oct. 22, 1963,
added the exception.

Cross References

Recovery of money or goods lost at gaming; limitations, see c. 137, § 1.

Law Review Commentaries

Collateral-source rule. William Schwartz
(1961) 41 Boston U.L.Rev. 348.

Consortium damages in Massachusetts.
John E. Hannigan 21 Boston U.L.Rev. 452
(1941).

Contracts between husband and wife. Frederick M. Hart, 10 Annual Survey of Mass. Law,
Boston College, p. 57 (1963).

Equity jurisdiction in Massachusetts, the
wife's equity in money advanced to the husband. Frank W. Grinnell (1946) 31 Mass.L.Q.
No. 2, p. 47.

Domestic relations, foreign decrees. William J. Greenler, Jr., 6 Annual Survey of Mass.
Law, Boston College, p. 74 (1959).

Husband and wife, contract for married
woman's services. William J. Greenler, Jr., 3
Ann.Surv.Mass.L. 81 (1956).

Husband and wife tort actions. Monroe L.
Inker, 11 Annual Survey of Mass. Law, Boston
College, p. 76 (1964).

Interspousal contracts. (1974) 9 Suffolk U.L.
Rev. 185.

Interspousal immunity: Application of domi-
ciliary law. Francis J. Nicholson. 13 Annual

351

Exhibit D-7   Massachusetts General Laws Annotated ch. 209, §6   *(continues)*

209 § 6   **DOMESTIC RELATIONS**

Survey of Mass. Law, Boston College, p. 136 (1966).

Interspousal immunity, conflict of laws. Francis J. Nicholson, S. J., 15 Annual Survey of Mass. Law, Boston College, p. 122 (1968).

Law affecting interspousal immunity. Francis J. Nicholson, 11 Annual Survey of Mass. Law, Boston College, p. 91 (1964).

Right of husband to recover for expenses of future medical care of wife. 43 Harvard L.Rev. 661 (1930).

Suits between husband and wife. Harry Zarrow (1957) 4 Ann.Surv.Mass.L. 109.

Wife's liability as husband's surety, disability to sue spouse. Bernard A. Riemer and William E. Hogan, 2 Ann.Surv.Mass.L. 81, 82 (1955).

Written contracts between husband and wife. (1945) 30 Mass.L.Q. No. 4, p. 20.

Library References

Husband and Wife ⬅203, 204.
C.J.S. Husband and Wife § 389 et seq.

Comments.
Actions between husband and wife, marshalling of assets, see M.P.S. vol. 31, Nolan, § 316.
Antenuptial agreements and contracts, probate, see M.P.S. vol. 23, Lombard, § 1626.
Capacity, husband and wife, defendant's case, the obligation in tort, see M.P.S. vol. 17, Bishop, § 465.
Capacity of parties to contract, see M.P.S. vol. 14, Simpson and Alperin, § 301 et seq.
Capacity to be party, proceedings involving husband and wife, see M.P.S. vol. 9, Nolan, § 155.
Capacity to contract, husband and wife, the plaintiff's case, see M.P.S. vol. 17, Bishop, § 11.
Contracts and suits directly between husband and wife, see M.P.S. vol. 2, Lombard, § 1256.
Contracts between husband and wife, see M.P.S. vol. 3, Lombard, § 2161.

Contracts between husband and wife and trustees, separation agreements, see M.P.S. vol. 2, Lombard, § 1255.
Married women, capacity, contracts, see M.P.S. vol. 14, Simpson and Alperin, § 308.
Married women, capacity, torts, see M.P.S. vol. 14A, Simpson and Alperin, § 1711.
Property and property rights, see M.P.S. vol. 3, Lombard, § 2141 et seq.
Spouse vs. Spouse, actionable tort, see M.P.S. vol. 11, Martin and Hennessey, § 93.
Suits between husband and wife, particular relationships, see M.P.S. vol. 14, Simpson and Alperin, § 771.
Torts between the spouses, see M.P.S. vol. 37, Nolan, § 121.

Forms.
Action by husband against wife to recover savings bank deposit, complaints, pleadings and motions, see M.P.S. vol. 10, Rodman, § 1699.
Agreement between husband and wife, effect of reconciliation, form, see M.P.S. vol. 2, Lombard, § 1306.

WESTLAW Electronic Research

See WESTLAW guide following the Foreword of this volume.

Notes of Decisions

In general 1
Abortions, actions between husband and wife 30
Accounting, equitable proceedings between husband and wife 40
Actions between husband and wife 28–37
    In general 28
    Abortions 30
    Foreign judgments 37
    Marriage settlements 31
    Prior law 29
    Probate proceedings 32
    Professional services 33
    Torts, generally 34

Actions between husband and wife—Cont'd
    Trusts 36
    Vehicular torts, generally 35
Agency, liability of wife 17
Alienation of affections, right of action by wife 9
Burden of proof 55
Clean hands doctrine, equitable proceedings between husband and wife 41
Common law 3
Consortium
    Generally 51
    Right of action by wife 10
Contracts, right of action by wife 6

352

Exhibit D-7   Massachusetts General Laws Annotated ch. 209, § 6 *(concluded)*

Also notice the references on the second page to other resources: the relevant digest topic and key number, C.J.S., M.P.S. (Massachusetts Practice Series), and Westlaw. Finally, at the bottom of the second page notice the index to the case summaries, called Notes of Decisions.

Many cases are summarized following the statute. One such case is *Lewis*. In Exhibit D-8 on page 683 notice how the citation following the summary for *Lewis* lists the North Eastern Reporter citation first. Remember that when you cite, you should always give the official citation (in this case Massachusetts Reports) first.

You could also have conducted your research in the Annotated Laws of Massachusetts. The statutory language is identical to what you found in the Massachusetts General Laws Annotated. However, the cross-references differ. Also occasionally you will find a case listed in one source but not the other. Therefore, before leaving the annotated statutes, it is worthwhile to take the time to check both sets for case summaries.

(4) Checking the pocket part

Any changes to the statute that have occurred since the time the hardbound volume was printed will be found in the pocket part. Always check the pocket part. In addition to any statutory changes, the pocket part will include any recent court opinions that have interpreted the statute. Exhibit D-9 on page 684 shows the changes to chapter 209 contained in the pocket part for West's Massachusetts General Laws Annotated. As you can see, there has been a change to the statutory language in section 1A. There has been no change to the language of section 6, but two new court decisions have been added since the main volume was printed.

c. Finding State Agency Regulations

Once you have located a state statute, you should check to see whether any state agency has issued regulations interpreting that statute. Unfortunately, research into state regulations is often a hit-or-miss affair. Some states have compiled their agency regulations into codes, similar to the statutory codes, complete with a subject matter index. Some states, however, make no attempt to publish all their state regulations in one location. Finally, some states, such as Massachusetts, are somewhere in between. Massachusetts publishes a Code of Massachusetts Regulations. However, it is organized by agency rather than by subject matter, and there is no index for the series. Instead, the researcher must know the name of the agency involved, find the volume of the code that covers that agency, and then search through the table of contents for that agency to find the desired information.

For state administrative regulation questions you are often best advised to consult directly with the agency on the most convenient source for this type of information. In Massachusetts there are no state agency regulations governing the topic of spousal immunity.

d. Finding Court Opinions

Court opinions are published in court reporters. If the reporter is published by a private publishing company, such as West, it will also include editorial features, such as the **headnotes** added by West at the beginning of each case.

Most state court decisions are published in both an official government-published reporter and an unofficial regional reporter, published by West.

P R A C T I C A L
T I P

Always check the pocket part!

Headnote
A summary of one legal point in a court opinion; written by the editors at West.

rectly, without intervention of a trustee. Charney v. Charney (1944) 55 N.E.2d 917, 316 Mass. 580.

Where, if final and absolute decree of divorce had been entered, remedy of wife to sue at law for alimony awarded would be complete; in action to recover alimony under interlocutory order entered in foreign state, law of forum governed, where laws of foreign state did not appear and under R.L.1902, c. 153, § 6, and St.1910, c. 576, wife could not sue husband in Massachusetts for alimony awarded by interlocutory order. Golder v. Golder (1920) 126 N.E. 382, 235 Mass. 261.

A foreign sister state which by statute conferred jurisdiction upon its courts over nonresidents by service upon them in respective places of their residence within sister states, for causes of action which arose from business transactions within the enacting state, enabled courts of that state to render a judgment against a non-resident husband who entered into and breached a marriage settlement agreement with his wife while they were both domiciled there and where she was still domiciled. Spitz v. Spitz (1965) 31 Mass.App.Dec. 124.

3. Common law

This section which provides that a married woman may sue and be sued in same manner as if she were sole, but provides that this section does not authorize suit between husband and wife except in connection with certain contracts, left interspousal immunity rule in its common-law status susceptible to reexamination and alteration by Supreme Judicial Court. Lewis v. Lewis (1976) 351 N.E.2d 526, 370 Mass. 619.

At common law, one spouse could not sue the other in an action at law. Zwick v. Goldberg (1939) 22 N.E.2d 661, 304 Mass. 66.

At common law, husband, by one action, might recover for wife's personal injuries and expenses and other damage resulting to husband therefrom. Thibeault v. Poole (1933) 186 N.E. 632, 283 Mass. 480.

In the case of Fowle v. Torrey (1883) 135 Mass. 87, the court said: "While the Legislature has removed from a wife many of the disabilities she was under at common law, and has authorized her to hold property as a feme sole, to deal with it as such, and to sue and be sued in relation thereto, it has carefully provided always, in the acts by which this has been done, that nothing therein contained shall be construed as authorizing contracts between husband and wife, conveyances or gifts to each other (except by the husband to a limited amount), or as giving the right to either to sue or be sued by the other. Gen.Sts. c. 108, § 1. Sts.1874, c. 184; 1879, c. 133. Whatever rights

they had in these respects remain as they stood at common law before this legislation commences."

4. Retroactive effect

St.1871, c. 312, providing that any married woman could be sued in an action of tort as if she were sole, and her husband should not be liable to pay the judgment against her in any such suit, did not apply to actions against husband and wife for the wife's tort, begun before the passing of the statute. Hill v. Duncan (1872) 110 Mass. 238.

5. Right of action by wife—In general

By divorce, the marriage was so far suspended that the wife could maintain her rights by suit upon causes which arose after the divorce, and she was to the same extent liable to be sued alone. Chase v. Chase (1856) 72 Mass. 157, 6 Gray 157; Dean v. Richmond (1827) 22 Mass. 461, 5 Pick. 461.

Wife's right to sue "in the same manner as if she were sole" refers both to extent of rights to be established and mode of ascertaining and declaring those rights. Cassidy v. Constantine (1929) 168 N.E. 169, 269 Mass. 56.

In the case of MacKeown v. Lacey (1909) 86 N.E. 799, 200 Mass. 437, 21 L.R.A.,N.S., 683, 16 Ann.Cas. 220, the court said: "The indorsements operated as assignments of the notes to the plaintiff (Hill v. Lewis, 1 Salk. 132; 2 Ames' Cases on Bills and Notes, 100, note 1), and under St.1897, p. 378, c. 402 (Rev.Laws, c. 173, § 4), which was in force at the time of the transfer and of the bringing of the action, the assignee could sue in her own name."

Where a man and woman living in another state came into this commonwealth for the purpose of being married, and were married here, and a few days afterwards, while they were living here at an inn, she wrote to a broker in that state, with whom before the marriage she had deposited property earned by her, to send her a sum of money by an expressman, which the broker did and instructed the expressman to deliver it to her upon her personal receipt; but the expressman delivered it to the husband, who absconded with it, under St.1855, c. 304, she could maintain an action in her own name against the expressman for the money, if she had not authorized her husband to receive it, or held him out as her agent to collect money. Read v. Earle (1859) 78 Mass. 423, 12 Gray 423.

The desertion of a wife by her husband which would enable her to sue, and render her liable to be sued, as a feme sole, should be an absolute and complete desertion by his continued absence from the commonwealth, and a voluntary separation from and abandonment

354

Exhibit D-8   Massachusetts General Laws Annotated ch. 209, § 6

---

*   *   *

→ **§ 1A.   Tenants by entirety under older deed; electing treatment of tenancy**

Tenants by the entirety holding under a deed dated prior to February eleventh, nineteen hundred and eighty may elect to have their tenancy treated as being subject to the provisions of chapter seven hundred and twenty-seven of the acts of nineteen hundred and seventy-nine; provided, however, that such election is made in writing, identifying the real estate with reference to the book and page of the registry of deeds wherein such deed is filed. Such election shall be executed by the grantees named as tenants by the entirety on the deed who are electing to be subject to this section, duly notarized, and recorded in said registry.

Added by St.1989, c. 283.

Historical and Statutory Notes

1989 Legislation

St.1989, c. 283, was approved July 25, 1989.

*   *   *

→ **§ 6.   Married woman; power to sue and be sued**

Library References

Comments.

Actions between husband and wife, marshalling of assets, see M.P.S. vol. 31, Nolan and Sartorio, §§ 316, 317.

Capacity, husband and wife, defendant's case, the obligation in tort, see M.P.S. vol. 17, Bishop, § 546.

Capacity to contract, husband and wife, the plaintiff's case, see M.P.S. vol. 17, Bishop, § 22.

Consequential damages, see M.P.S. vol. 17, Bishop, § 589.

Domestic immunities, see M.P.S. vol. 37A, Nolan and Sartorio, § 553.

Notes of Decisions

34. —— Torts, generally, actions between husband and wife

Wife was not prohibited by this section from bringing suit against her husband to recover damages for bodily injuries sustained incident to an assault and battery allegedly committed by the husband.   Knobel-Aronova v. Knobel (App. Div. 1987) 1987 Mass.App.Div. 75.

35. —— Vehicular torts, generally, actions between husband and wife

Coster v. Coster, 1943, 46 N.E.2d 509, 289 N.Y. 438, [main volume] motion denied 49 N.E.2d 621, 290 N.Y. 662.

Exhibit D-9   Pocket Part, Massachusetts General Laws Annotated ch. 209, § 6

As you can see from this map, the North Eastern Reporter contains court decisions from Illinois, Indiana, New York, and Ohio, as well as Massachusetts. Because many attorneys are not interested in purchasing out-of-state court decisions, West also publishes condensed versions of its regional reporters, containing the decisions from just one state. For example, West offers an abbreviated version of N.E.2d that contains just Massachusetts decisions, called, appropriately enough, Massachusetts Decisions. This can be a confusing book to use. First, because the decisions from the other states are missing, West is able to combine three to four volumes of the North Eastern Reporter into each volume of Massachusetts Decisions. When trying to locate decisions in a combined reporter, such as the Massachusetts Decisions, first make sure that you are in the correct portion of the volume. Second, because the out-of-state cases are missing, there are also missing pages in the condensed volumes.

The wording of the court decisions found in West's North Eastern Reporter and the Massachusetts Reports is identical. Their differences lie in the editorial features. The most useful West editorial feature is the headnotes located at the beginning of each decision. These headnotes summarize the court opinion. Never forget that these are a West editorial feature written by West. They are not part of the court decision. The decision itself begins with the justice's name who wrote the opinion.

If you have the full citation to a case, it is relatively easy to locate the text of that case in a reporter. If you do not have the citation, but you do have other information, there are three different approaches you can use. First, if you have only a name, you can use a table of cases to find the full citation. Second, if you know a case interprets a specific statute, you can look up the statute in an annotated version of the statutes and get the citation from that source. Third, you can use a digest to locate relevant cases by their subject matter.

(1) Starting with a citation or name

If you are given a citation by your boss or a co-worker or if you find it through your own research in secondary sources, it is relatively easy to find the case.

A typical Massachusetts Supreme Judicial Court decision cite would be as follows:

Mounsey v. Ellard, 363 Mass. 693, 297 N.E.2d 43 (1973).

It tells us that the name of the case is *Mounsey v. Ellard* and that it can be found either on page 693 of volume 363 of the Massachusetts Reports or on page 43 of volume 297 of the North Eastern Reporter, Second Series.

More often, however, you will know the name but not the citation. For example, now that you have worked with the problem of spousal immunity, you will probably remember that one decision dealing with this problem is *Callow v. Thomas*. You will probably not remember its citation. Because this is a common problem, West has come up with a solution. West publishes a series of books called the Massachusetts Digest, summarizing all Massachusetts court decisions decided before 1933, and the Massachusetts Digest 2d, summarizing all Massachusetts court decisions from 1933 to date. Contained in each of those series is a volume entitled Table of Cases.

Exhibit D-10 on page 686 shows a page from the Massachusetts Digest 2d Table of Cases listing *Callow v. Thomas*. In addition to the citation, you will see a listing of the West topics that are discussed in that opinion. These are the same topics listed at the beginning of the headnotes to *Callow v. Thomas*. This can be very helpful in locating the right case. For example, assume you are looking for a negligence case called *Callahan v. Somebody*. The Massachusetts Digest Table of Cases lists many *Callahan* cases but only one with the topic of libel. Notice that once again a publisher has given you an incomplete citation by omitting the date.

30 Mass D 2d—233   **CAMBEX**

See Guidelines for Arrangement at the beginning of this Volume

Callahan; Nelson v., CA1 (Mass), 721 F2d 397.—Crim Law 273.1(1), 273.1(4); Hab Corp 85.1(2), 85.2(1), 85.5(4), 90.3(5).

Callahan; Nguyen v., DMass, 997 FSupp 179.—Social S 175.25, 175.30.

Callahan; N.O. v., DMass, 110 FRD 637.—Fed Civ Proc 1559, 1598, 1600(4), 1623, 1653; Mental H 51.5, 486, 487, 490; Witn 184(1), 212.

Callahan; O. v., DMass, 110 FRD 637. See N.O. v. Callahan.

Callahan; Reddick v., DMass, 587 FSupp 880.—Crim Law 1030(1), 1178; Hab Corp 45.3(1.30), 45.3(4).

Callahan; Ricci v., DMass, 646 FSupp 378.—Fed Civ Proc 2397.6.

Callahan; Ricci v., DMass, 576 FSupp 415.—Inj 210.

Callahan; Ricci v., DMass, 97 FRD 737.—Fed Civ Proc 219.

Callahan; Richard v., CA1 (Mass), 723 F2d 1028.—Crim Law 273(4), 273.1(1); Hab Corp 113(12); Homic 234(5), 354.

Callahan; Richard v., DMass, 564 FSupp 511, aff 723 F2d 1028.—Const Law 270(1); Fed Cts 386; Hab Corp 45.1(4).

Callahan; Robinson v., CA1 (Mass), 694 F2d 6.—Crim Law 778(5), 789(13).

Callahan; Setian v., DMass, 973 FSupp 16.—Social S 140.85, 148.1.

Callahan; Sheffield v., DMass, 9 FSupp2d 75.—Social S 140.10, 143.60, 148.15.

Callahan; Shoobridge v., Mass, 39 NE2d 429, 310 Mass 632.—App & E 989; Autos 242(8); Evid 589; Refer 99(4), 99(6).

Callahan; Subilosky v., CA1 (Mass), 689 F2d 7, cert den 103 SCt 1788, 460 US 1090, 76 LEd2d 356.—Const Law 269; Crim Law 938(1); Hab Corp 45.2(4), 45.2(7), 85.2(1).

Callahan v. Superior Court, Mass, 570 NE2d 1003, 410 Mass 1001.—Mand 1, 3(1), 4(4), 31, 176.

Callahan v. Town of Athol, Mass, 188 NE2d 571, 345 Mass 572.—Towns 29.

Callahan v. U.S. I.R.S., BkrtcyDMass, 168 BR 272. See Callahan, In re.

Callahan; Watkins v., CA1 (Mass), 724 F2d 1038.—Crim Law 412.1(4), 667(1); Hab Corp 45.3(1.40), 90.2(6); Homic 8; Witn 2(1).

Callahan v. Westinghouse Broadcasting Co., Inc., Mass, 363 NE2d 240, 372 Mass 582.—Libel 112(2), 124(2); Trial 295(5).

Callahan; Woods v., CA1 (Mass), 172 F2d 179.—Fed Civ Proc 2505; Land & Ten 149; War 210, 220.

Callahan; Young v., CA1 (Mass), 700 F2d 32, cert den 104 SCt 194, 464 US 863, 78 LEd2d 170.—Crim Law 637, 1166.8.

Callahan; Zeigler v., CA1 (Mass), 659 F2d 254.—Const Law 268(5); Crim Law 553, 627.8(6), 627.9(2.1), 1171.8(1); Hab Corp 25.1(8).

Callahan & Sons, Inc. v. Board of Appeals of Lenox, MassAppCt, 565 NE2d 813, 30 MassAppCt 36. See Maurice Callahan & Sons, Inc. v. Board of Appeals of Lenox.

Callan v. Winters, Mass, 534 NE2d 298, 404 Mass 198.—Const Law 93(1); Statut 174; Wills 498.

Callanan, In re. BkrtcyDMass, 190 BR 137.—Bankr 2702.1.

Callanan v. International Fidelity Ins. Co., BkrtcyDMass, 190 BR 137. See Callanan, In re.

Callanan v. Personnel Adm'r for Com., Mass, 511 NE2d 525, 400 Mass 597.—Inj 231; Mun Corp 197; Offic 11.7, 11.8.

Calledare v. Sawyer, Mass, 225 NE2d 367, 352 Mass 769.—Theaters 6(19).

Callen; Com. v., MassAppCt, 521 NE2d 861, 26 MassAppCt 920, review den 531 NE2d 1274, 403 Mass 1105.—Autos 144.2(8).

Callender; Com. v., Mass, 673 NE2d 22, 423 Mass 771. See Mendonza v. Com.

Calligaris' Case, Mass, 198 NE 607, 292 Mass 397.—App & E 843(2); Work Comp 2215.

Callinan v. Larsen, MassAppDiv, 1979 MassAppDiv 186.—Judgm 97.

Callow v. Thomas, Mass, 78 NE2d 637, 322 Mass 550, 2 ALR2d 632.—Divorce 313; Hus & W 205(2); Marriage 57, 67.

Callum; Liberty Leather Corp. v., CA1 (Mass), 653 F2d 694.—Fed Civ Proc 839.1, 2146, 2152; Fed Cts 615, 907; Fraud 12, 20, 50, 58(2), 58(3), 58(4); Torts 10(1), 28.

Callum; Liberty Leather Corp. v., DMass, 86 FRD 550.—Fed Civ Proc 2736, 2738.

Calnan; Becker v., Mass, 48 NE2d 668, 313 Mass 625.—App & E 870(5); Equity 417; Labor 107, 109, 114, 122, 127, 763, 769; Plead 8(1), 34(3); Stip 14(3).

Calnan; Weeks v., MassAppCt, 658 NE2d 173, 39 MassAppCt 933.—Damag 23; Land & Ten 164(1).

Calore Exp. Co. v. U. S., CA1 (Mass), 351 F2d 596.—Autos 128.

Calore Exp. Co., Inc., In re, DMass, 226 BR 727, opinion after grant of writ 228 BR 338, opinion after grant of writ 228 BR 338.—Atty & C 54; Mand 1, 29, 51, 53.

Calore Exp. Co., Inc., In re. BkrtcyDMass, 199 BR 424.—Bankr 2156, 2671, 2674, 2675, 2679, 2680; Sec Tran 138, 147.

Calvanese v. A. S. W. Taxi Corp., MassAppCt, 405 NE2d 1001, 10 MassAppCt 817.—Autos 244(36.1), 246(1); Pretrial Proc 3; Refer 91, 99(6); Witn 379(10).

Calvanese v. W. W. Babcock Co., Inc., MassAppCt, 412 NE2d 895, 10 MassAppCt 726.—App & E 1067; Damag 166(1); Evid 150, 350, 547, 547.5; Pretrial Proc 383; Prod Liab 54, 83, 97; Sales 1.5; Witn 347.

Calvary Holdings, Inc. v. Chandler, CA1 (Mass), 948 F2d 59.—Fed Civ Proc 2553; Fed Cts 643; Sec Reg 53.15.

Calvert-Distillers Corp.; Jackman v., Mass, 28 NE2d 430, 306 Mass 423.—Courts 91(1); Trade Reg 93, 97, 98, 99, 251, 257, 485, 736.

Calvine Mills, Inc.; Prudhomme v., Mass, 225 NE2d 592, 352 Mass 767.—Neglig 1130, 1173, 1177.

Calvin Hosmer, Stolte Co. v. Paramount Cone Co., Mass, 189 NE 192, 285 Mass 278.—App & E 992, 1050.1(10); Contracts 352(1); Damag 78(6), 175; Evid 213(1), 213(4); Sales 177, 371, 383; Trial 260(9).

Calvo; Com. v., MassAppCt, 668 NE2d 846, 41 MassAppCt 903.—Crim Law 982.9(5).

Camacho v. Board of Selectmen of Stoughton, MassAppCt, 535 NE2d 1290, 27 MassAppCt 178.—Towns 18, 49.

Camaioni, Case of, MassAppCt, 389 NE2d 1028, 7 MassAppCt 927.—Work Comp 1738, 1950.

Camara v. Board of Appeals of Tewksbury, MassAppCt, 662 NE2d 719, 40 MassAppCt 209.—Evid 43(4).

Camara v. Capeto, MassAppCt, 446 NE2d 91, 15 MassAppCt 955.—Mun Corp 710.

Camara; Smola v., MassAppCt, 449 NE2d 678, 16 MassAppCt 908.—Int Rev 4790; Receivers 29(1).

Camara; U.S. v., CA1 (Mass), 451 F2d 1122, cert den 92 SCt 1513, 405 US 1074, 31 LEd2d 808.—Armed S 20.1(2), 20.8(1), 40.1(7); Crim Law 1031(3), 1115(1), 1186.1; Gr Jury 8.

Camar Corp. v. Preston Trucking Co., Inc., DMass, 18 FSupp2d 112.—Carr 111, 133, 134, 135, 147, 153, 155, 158(1); Evid 351.

Camarra; Bowie v., MassAppDiv, 36 MassAppDec 105.—App & E 192(1); Damag 118; New Tr 74.

Cambara; U.S. v., CA1 (Mass), 902 F2d 144.—Consp 33(1), 47(6); Crim Law 742(1), 1159.2(7), 1166.18.

Cambex Corp.; Greenstone v., CA1 (Mass), 975 F2d 22.—Fed Civ Proc 636.

Cambex Corp.; Greenstone v., DMass, 777 FSupp 88, aff 975 F2d 22.—Fed Civ Proc 636; Sec Reg 60.28(2.1), 60.28(4), 60.28(13).

For Later Case History Information, see KeyCite on WESTLAW

Exhibit D-10   Massachusetts Digest, Table of Cases

If you remember the defendant's name but not the plaintiff's name, West has a solution for that, too. In the volume following the Table of Cases is a Defendant-Plaintiff Table, listing all the cases with defendant's name first.

Exhibit D-11 on page 688 shows the first page of *Callow*. Take a look at the headnote topics at the beginning of *Callow*, and compare them to those listed in the Table of Cases. For example, the first topic listed in the Table of Cases for *Callow* is Divorce 313. That corresponds to headnote 3.

Finally, if you do not have the name for the opinion, but you do have the citation to one reporter, and your library only contains the other reporter, you can use a book called Shepard's Citations to help you find the parallel citation.

Take a look at a page from Shepard's in Exhibit D-12 on page 689. Assume you have the North Eastern Reporter citation for *Callow v. Thomas*, 78 N.E.2d 637, but are missing the Massachusetts Reports citation. You would look in the Shepard's volume that contains information on cases reported in volume 78 of the North Eastern Reporter, Second Series, for the North Eastern Reporter cite 78 N.E.2d 637. Look in the first column for the reference to page 637, listed as —637—. Immediately under the —637— you will see the name of the case—Callow v. Thomas—and then (322Mas550). That is the Massachusetts Reports citation for *Callow*. Shepard's indicates this is the parallel citation by including it in parentheses. Do not be put off by the seemingly endless list of numbers on the Shepard's page. These are simply case citations in a very abbreviated format. We will talk about the purpose of these other citations later in the chapter when we discuss updating your research.

(2) Using a summary following a statute

As you have already seen, if you have found a statute governing your problem, an annotated version of those statutes will contain a summary of court opinions interpreting it. This summary will include a citation so that you can locate it in the case reporters.

(3) Using a digest

Court opinions are published in chronological order, not by subject matter. Therefore, if there is no statute governing your problem and if you do not know the citation for any court decision relevant to your problem, absent a better way to find relevant court decisions, you would simply have to begin reading court decisions until you stumbled on one that related to your problem. Fortunately, West developed its digest system to help us locate cases more efficiently. A digest is a collection of court decision summaries arranged by subject matter. These summaries are in reality the headnotes located at the beginning of cases "cut and pasted" into the right digest locations.

West has organized the law into hundreds of legal topics. Each topic is then subdivided into key numbers, or sections. The job of the West editor who is read-ing a new decision is to categorize each aspect of the decision by labeling it with a West topic name and key number. If a given case involves five different points of law, it will be listed in five different parts of the digest. If it contains ten different points of law, it will be listed in ten different parts of the digest, and so on. Take another look at the headnotes to *Callow v. Thomas* in Exhibit D-11. Each head-note summarizes one aspect of that decision. Each headnote is also labeled with a legal topic, such as Divorce; a key symbol; and then a number (known as the key

CALLOW v. THOMAS
Cite as 78 N.E.2d 637

Mass. 637

N.E.2d 729, 731. Consequently, no error of fact or of law being made to appear, we cannot modify this provision of the decree.

The matter of allowance of attorney's fees, briefs and expenses in this court will be settled by a separate order of a single justice upon presentation of an itemized list of the expenses.

Decree affirmed.

CALLOW v. THOMAS.

Supreme Judicial Court of Massachusetts. Middlesex.

April 1, 1948.

1. Husband and wife ⊜205(2)

No cause of action arises in favor of either spouse for a tort committed by the other during coverture.

2. Husband and wife ⊜205(2)

Where either spouse commits a tort upon the other during coverture recovery is denied, not merely because of the disability of one spouse to sue the other during coverture, but because of the marital relationship, no cause of action ever came into existence.

3. Divorce ⊜313

After divorce, no action can be maintained by either spouse for a tort committed by the other during coverture.

4. Marriage ⊜57, 67

Generally an "annulment" is distinguished from a "divorce" in that annulment is not a dissolution of the marriage but is a judicial declaration that no marriage has ever existed, and decree of annulment makes the marriage void ab initio even though the marriage be voidable only at the instance of the injured party. G.L.(Ter.Ed.) c. 207, § 14.

See Words and Phrases, Permanent Edition, for all other definitions of "Annulment" and "Divorce".

5. Marriage ⊜67

Where marriage was voidable and not void and so was valid until set aside by decree of nullity, wife could not after annulment, recover for a tort committed upon her by husband during coverture because of his gross negligence in operation of automobile in which wife was a guest passenger. G.L.(Ter.Ed.) c. 207, § 14.

6. Marriage ⊜67

Where a voidable marriage has been annulled things which have been done during the period of the supposed marriage ought not be undone or reopened after the decree of annulment. G.L.(Ter.Ed.) c. 207, § 14.

———

Report from Superior Court, Middlesex County.

Action by Muriel Callow against Frederick Thomas for injuries sustained when plaintiff was riding as a gratuitous passenger in an automobile owned and operated by defendant. The case was reported to Supreme Judicial Court without decision.

Judgment for defendant.

Before QUA, C. J., and LUMMUS, DOLAN, WILKINS, and SPALDING, JJ.

M. Harry Goldburgh and J. Finks, both of Boston, for plaintiff.

K. C. Parker, of Boston, for defendant.

SPALDING, Justice.

The plaintiff and the defendant were married in this Commonwealth on August 6, 1944, and thereafter lived together here as husband and wife. On November 9, 1944, while riding as a "gratuitous passenger" in an automobile owned and operated by the defendant, the plaintiff was injured when the automobile, due to the gross negligence of the defendant, ran into a tree. The plaintiff was in the exercise of due care. The accident occurred on a public way in this Commonwealth and the defendant's automobile was registered in accordance with the laws thereof. On June 28, 1945, upon the petition of the plaintiff to annul the marriage because of the defendant's fraud, the Probate Court decreed that the marriage was "null and

Exhibit D-11 *Callow v. Thomas* (First Page)

Vol. 78	NORTHEASTERN REPORTER, 2d SERIES (Massachusetts Cases)

—629—
Wright v
Health
Commissioner
of Boston
1948

(322Mas535)
107NE[1]775
157NE228
360NE[4]1060
387NE188

—633—
Watson's Case
1948

(322Mas581)
d 85NE[4]75
88NE[3]639
102NE[4]415
116NE[4]128
120NE[4]756
127NE[4]193
d 138NE[4]288
138NE[3]633
138NE[7]751
148NE[4]373
154NE[4]605
155NE[4]790
f 173NE[4]644
232NE[4]927
258NE[1]927
363NE[4]1336
373NE[7]1178
408NE[8]894
Cir. 5
186F2d277

—637—
Callow v
Thomas
1948

(322Mas550)
173NE[4]269
178NE[4]283
178NE[5]283
236NE[4]201
351NE[2]528
373NE[6]358
373NE[6]358
489NE[4]673
574NE[4]405
Cir. 1
504FS[4]654

—641—
Joyce v
Devaney
1948

(322Mas544)
95NE[1]175
103NE[1]322

115NE[1]495
116NE[2]155
141NE[1]516
142NE[1]405
146NE[2]514
165NE[1]116
224NE[1]224
372NE[1]283
372NE[4]283

—644—
Massachusetts
v Hall
1948

(322Mas523)
82NE[3]10
87NE[6]202
178NE[3]267
317NE[3]831
334NE[2]616
366NE[2]726
421NE[2]761
421NE[1]764
440NE[5]769
d 595NE[1]777
58USLW4925

—649—
Franklin
Square House
v Siskind
1948

(322Mas556)
124NE[5]231
183NE[5]291
226NE[5]196

—651—
Provost's Case
1948

(322Mas604)

—652—
Rosenthal
v Maletz
1948

(322Mas586)
80NE[5]15
84NE552
97NE[17]171
99NE[1]927
d 103NE[4]251
105NE[1]248
126NE[1]531
129NE[10]906
140NE[15]646
163NE[10]160
170NE[4]839
170NE[10]840
247NE[1]393
q 342NE[13]717

---

d 374NE[10]350
Cir. 1
331F2d33
97FS[17]777

—697—
Massachusetts
v Farrell
1948

(322Mas606)
85NE[2]451
95NE[10]541
109NE[18]174
126NE[18]808
132NE[20]303
142NE[10]389
182NE[1]128
201NE[18]832
216NE[18]426
226NE[14]210
235NE[14]800
265NE[4]382
314NE[4]450
326NE[6]714
334NE[1]648
337NE711
344NE[16]927
348NE[18]820
355NE478
363NE[7]1316
370NE[7]1026
370NE[14]1026
373NE[14]1126
383NE[20]1121
387NE[7]164
389NE[10]762
402NE[6]1056
402NE[6]1057
f 402NE[12]1060
406NE[6]419
406NE[6]421
417NE[6]980
422NE[4]452
436NE[6]1217
436NE[6]1223
457NE[12]624
471NE[7]1358
487NE[8]1370
504NE[13]615
509NE[7]304
522NE[6]6
547NE944
564NE[5]378
574NE[7]344
576NE[12]711
594NE[14]868
23MJ325

Vol. 79

—1—
King v
Tewksbury
1948

(322Mas668)
cc 81NE737

—2—
Morin v
Trailways
of New
England Inc.
1948

(322Mas744)

—3—
Wagstaff v
Director of the
Division of
Employment
Security
1948

(322Mas664)
82NE[1]2
84NE[1]544
85NE[1]780
86NE[1]57
89NE[1]782
92NE[1]253
96NE[2]862
97NE640
98NE[1]362
99NE[1]59
106NE[3]422
117NE[1]165
118NE[1]774
197NE[4]597
344NE[2]895
382NE[2]201
454NE[4]95

—5—
Kubilius
v Hawes
Unitarian
Congregational
Church
1948

(322Mas638)
87NE[1]214
154NE[6]601
244NE[4]279
244NE[6]279
Cir. 1
735FS[6]1097

—10—
Royal v Royal
1948

(322Mas662)
s 87NE850
j 133NE[1]240

—11—
Seltmann v
Seltmann
1948

(322Mas650)
85NE[3]442
q 146NE[2]499
294NE[1]557
316NE[1]763

—13—
Herald v Rich
1948

(322Mas659)

—15—
Goff v Hickson
1948

(322Mas655)
88NE[1]337
89NE[3]1
91NE[4]235
91NE[4]927
104NE[1]495

—17—
Ryder v Ryder
1948

(322Mas645)
269NE[6]94
412NE[7]917

—185—
Delgreco v
Delgreco
1948

(322Mas706)
145NE[2]688
215NE[3]670

—187—
General v
Woburn
1948

(322Mas634)
85NE[1]230
86NE[1]645
99NE[1]43
111NE[2]671

---

e 115NE[5]149
129NE[1]895
175NE[2]916
208NE[1]234
214NE[1]43
252NE[1]213
252NE[1]896
269NE[1]233
438NE[5]91
461NE771
556NE[4]117

—189—
Connolly v
John Hancock
Mutual Life
Insurance Co.
1948

(322Mas678)
116NE[4]678
129NE[1]619
141NE[4]513
141NE[4]726
d 174NE[1]38
258NE[1]20
Cir. 1
201F2d[4]422
282FS[4]376

—192—
McCartin
v School
Committee
of Lowell
1948

(322Mas624)
111NE[3]750
q 184NE[3]43
217NE[1]769
294NE211
d 294NE[3]212
d 310NE[2]336
335NE[2]655
336NE752
356NE[2]263
378NE[2]1376
378NE[3]1376
384NE[2]230
384NE[3]230
417NE[2]461
486NE46
486NE[3]47

—195—
Owens-Illinois
Glass Co. v
Bresnahan
1948

(322Mas629)
d 110NE[2]125
142NE[2]762

Exhibit D-12   Massachusetts Shepard's

number). For example, when reading *Callow,* the editor thought that the second legal point raised in the case dealt with the topic of Husband and Wife.

There are 354 separate subtopics under Husband and Wife. The editor thought this particular point belonged under key number 205(2). To find out what all the possible subtopics under Husband and Wife are, you could consult the Analysis section, located at the beginning of the Husband and Wife topic in the Massachusetts Digest.

Exhibit D-13 on page 691 shows a copy of that Analysis page. Note that key number 205(2) comes under the general heading VI. ACTIONS. Following the Analysis is a further breakdown, showing the subject matter of each key number.

Once the West editor has finished labeling the headnotes and writing the one-paragraph headnote summaries, they are placed at the beginning of the decision, and the decision is published in the appropriate regional reporter. For Massachusetts cases that would be the North Eastern Reporter. In addition, each headnote is published in a state digest along with the headnotes from all other decisions from that state relating to the same topic. In state digests West lists the summaries as follows: (1) Federal cases that originated in that jurisdiction (if there are any) are listed before state cases; (2) the highest courts are listed before the intermediate appellate courts; and (3) the cases are listed in reverse chronological order, with the newest cases listed first.

Exhibit D-14 on page 692 shows a page from the Massachusetts Digest 2d on the topic Husband and Wife, key number 205(2). Find the summaries of *Callow v. Thomas.* Then compare them to headnotes 1 and 2 of the *Callow* decision on page 688. They are identical. Similarly, you could read an exact duplicate of headnote 3 in the Massachusetts Digest by looking under the topic Divorce and the key number 313.

The beauty of the digest system is this: Once you know that the West editors think your problem is categorized under the topic Husband and Wife, key number 205(2), you can go to the Massachusetts Digest and look under that topic and key number to find every other Massachusetts case that West thinks has dealt with that topic. Look again at the digest page, Exhibit D-13. What other decision do you see summarized there? *Lewis*! If you compare those summaries with headnotes 1 and 6 in *Lewis*, located on page 200, you will see that once again the digest summaries and headnotes are identical.

As you can see by looking at the digest page, there have also been more recent decisions on your topic. If you were researching this problem in the real world, you would want to read those decisions also. As with the secondary sources, digests are kept current with annual pocket parts and six-month interim supplements. Always check the pocket parts and interim supplements.

If you already know the topic and key number that you are interested in (for example, by having read *Callow v. Thomas* and thereby knowing that the topic

---

PRACTICAL TIP

Use headnotes and digest summaries to help you locate relevant opinions. But, *never* quote from or rely on the headnote or digest language. Always read the case for yourself.

HUSBAND AND WIFE

SUBJECTS INCLUDED

The marital relation; rights, powers, duties and liabilities of married persons as between themselves and as to others, incident to the existence of the relation or arising from conveyances or agreements in consideration or in consequence of marriage

Disabilities and privileges of married women by reason of their coverture, and protection of their persons and property

Legal proceedings affecting husbands and wives and their property

Abandonment, community property and separate maintenance

Tort liability for interference with the marriage relation, as by enticing and alienating or by criminal conversation

SUBJECTS EXCLUDED AND COVERED BY OTHER TOPICS

Adultery and bigamy as criminal offenses, see ADULTERY, BIGAMY

Contracts to marry, see BREACH OF MARRIAGE PROMISE

Contracts to procure marriage or in restraint of marriage, see CONTRACTS

Divorce and judicial separation, see DIVORCE

Marriage and annulment thereof, see MARRIAGE

Surviving spouse's property rights, see DOWER AND CURTESY, HOMESTEAD, DESCENT AND DISTRIBUTION, WILLS

Testamentary capacity of married women, see WILLS

Witnesses, competency of husband and wife for or against each other and privileged communications, see WITNESSES

For detailed references to other topics, see Descriptive-Word Index

---

Analysis

I. MUTUAL RIGHTS, DUTIES, AND LIABILITIES, ☞1–25(6).

II. MARRIAGE SETTLEMENTS, ☞26–35.

*   *   *

VI. ACTIONS.—Continued.

    205. Rights of action between husband and wife.
        (1). Nature and form of remedy.
        (2). Rights of action in general.
        (3). Actions on contract in general.
        (4). Actions in respect to wife's separate property.
        (5). Intervention of prochein ami or next friend.
        (6). Allowance to wife to maintain action.
    206. Rights of action by husband or wife or both.
    207. —— In general.
    208. —— On contracts.
    209. —— For torts.

Exhibit D-13 Analysis Page from Massachusetts Digest

13 Mass D 2d—623

HUSBAND & WIFE ☞**205(2)**

For references to other topics, see Descriptive-Word Index

that statute shall not authorize suits between husband and wife. M.G.L.A. c. 209, § 6.

Patuleia v. Patuleia, 127 F.Supp. 60.

Mass. 1980. Common–law rule of interspousal immunity did not bar action in which it was alleged that husband was in control of premises and responsible for sanding, salting or shoveling after snowstorm, that his failure to do so caused wife to fall, and that she suffered fractures and incurred medical expenses in excess of $2,500.

Brown v. Brown, 409 N.E.2d 717, 381 Mass. 231.

Mass. 1978. Common-law doctrine of interspousal immunity did not protect husband as host driver from liability to his wife as passenger for injuries sustained in collision and, hence, did not preclude owner and operator of other vehicle, named as defendants in main action by wife, from seeking to recover in third-party action against husband for contribution as a joint tort-feasor. M.G.L.A. c. 231B § 1 et seq.

Hayon v. Coca Cola Bottling Co. of New England, 378 N.E.2d 442, 375 Mass. 644.

Mass. 1976. Arguments that tort actions between husband and wife would tend to disrupt peace and harmony of family and that such actions would tend to promote fraud and collusion on part of husband and wife for purpose of reaping undeserved financial reward at expense of family's liability insurer are insufficient to justify common-law rule of interspousal immunity.

Lewis v. Lewis, 351 N.E.2d 526, 370 Mass. 619, 92 A.L.R.3d 890.

Wife's action against her husband for personal injuries sustained in automobile accident was not barred by common-law rule of interspousal immunity.

Lewis v. Lewis, 351 N.E.2d 526, 370 Mass. 619, 92 A.L.R.3d 890.

Mass. 1974. Supreme Judicial Court had jurisdiction over suit by estranged husband seeking declaratory and injunctive relief against his pregnant wife, who intended to procure an abortion over his objection, as against contention of wife that there was no jurisdiction because of statute relating to suits between husband and wife. M.G.L.A. c. 209 § 6.

Doe v. Doe, 314 N.E.2d 128, 365 Mass. 556, 62 A.L.R.3d 1082.

Mass. 1959. Purpose of statute to effect that probate court shall have jurisdiction to enforce foreign judgments for support of wife against husband who is resident or inhabitant of commonwealth was to enable wife to enforce in commonwealth a foreign judgment for support against husband, provided he resides in or was an inhabitant of commonwealth but

right to enforce such judgment must be exercised solely in probate court. M.G.L.A. c. 209 § 6; c. 215 § 6.

Adams v. Adams, 157 N.E.2d 405, 338 Mass. 776.

Mass. 1958. Where bank books and bonds had stood in joint names of husband and wife and husband evidenced intent to give his wife a one half interest in deposits and bonds if she returned to live with him by saying "that they would belong to both equally", wife's interest in deposits and bonds upon return to live with husband was that of a tenant in common, and as such wife could maintain a suit in equity against husband who had converted the property held in common to his own use and by his appropriation of it had finally precluded her from any future enjoyment of it.

Arsenault v. Arsenault, 148 N.E.2d 662, 337 Mass. 189.

Mass. 1952. A wife had no cause of action against husband for past nonsupport which could be the subject of set-off in proceeding by husband for accounting of his property and business which wife took over upon husband's commitment to hospital as mental patient.

Peteros v. Peteros, 104 N.E.2d 149, 328 Mass. 416.

Husband was entitled to recover his property or its value and was entitled to an accounting of profits derived therefrom by wife during period husband was committed to hospital as a mental patient, but wife was entitled to credit for her services in operating the business during such period.

Peteros v. Peteros, 104 N.E.2d 149, 328 Mass. 416.

Mass. 1948. No cause of action arises in favor of either spouse for a tort committed by the other during coverture.

Callow v. Thomas, 78 N.E.2d 637, 322 Mass. 550, 2 A.L.R.2d 632.

Where either spouse commits a tort upon the other during coverture recovery is denied, not merely because of the disability of one spouse to sue the other during coverture, but because of the marital relationship, no cause of action ever came into existence.

Callow v. Thomas, 78 N.E.2d 637, 322 Mass. 550, 2 A.L.R.2d 632.

Mass. 1947. Jurisdiction in equity exists to adjudicate conflicting rights of husband and wife concerning property.

Yurkanis v. Yurkanis, 73 N.E.2d 598, 321 Mass. 375.

Mass. 1945. The fact that parties are husband and wife does not in general enable them to maintain against each other in equity equiv-

see **Massachusetts General Laws Annotated**

13 Mass.Dig.2d—21

Exhibit D-14 Massachusetts Digest Case Summaries

Husband and Wife governs your issue), you can access a digest by looking up that key number topic. If you do not already know the topic or key number, you need to consult the subject matter index, just as you did with the statutes.

West places headnotes on *all* cases, federal and state. West then organizes these headnotes by subject matter in several different digests, including the American digest system (all cases, federal and state, from 1658 to the present time), regional digests (cases from a particular region), state digests (federal and state cases from a particular state), and federal digests (all federal cases). The topic and key number system is the same in all these digests. As we have seen, if you look under Husband and Wife, key number 205(2), in the Massachusetts Digest, you will find Massachusetts cases dealing with whether spouses can sue each other. If you want to know how another state handles that same problem, you simply go to the state digest for that state and look under the topic Husband and Wife, key number 205(2). If you want to find recent cases from around the country, you go to the most recent general digest.

When seeking court opinions through the West digest system, you first have to decide what types of cases you want and what time period you want to cover. The first question to ask yourself is whether you want federal or state cases. If you want federal, do you want all federal cases or only Supreme Court cases and cases from your circuit and district? If you want state cases, do you want them from only your state, your region, a mixture of states, or all states? Second, do you want cases from the beginning of time or only the most recent cases? Depending on your answers you will select one or more of the available digests. See Figure D-3.

Figure D-3   Summary of Available Digests

If you want	Use
only U.S. Supreme Court decisions	the U.S. Supreme Court Digest.
recent federal cases	the Federal Practice Digest 4th.
older federal cases	the Federal Digest, the Modern Federal Practice Digest, or the Federal Practice Digest 2d or 3d.
individual states cases, along with federal cases that originated in federal courts in that state or that were appealed from state court to the federal courts	the state digest (available for all states except Delaware, Nevada, and Utah). State digests may also be organized by date. For example, the Massachusetts Digest covers decisions before 1933, while the Massachusetts Digest 2d includes cases from 1933 to date.
a group of state and the federal cases that originated in federal courts in that region or that were appealed from a state court in that region to the federal courts	a number of individual state digests or a regional digest (available for all regions except the Northeast, South, and Southwest). Regional digests may also be organized by date. For example, the Atlantic Digest covers decisions up to 1938, and the Atlantic Digest 2d covers cases from 1938 to date.
all cases, both federal and state	the Decennials and General Digest.

e. Summary of the Steps for Locating Primary Authority

Figure D-4 presents a checklist summarizing the main approaches that we have been discussing for locating statutes and court opinions.

4. Update Your Research

Reverse
A decision is reversed when an appellate court overturns or negates the decision of a lower court.

Overrule
A decision is overruled when a court in a later case changes the law so that its prior decision is no longer good law.

In order to feel confident about your researching results, you must do everything you can to make sure your results are as up to date as possible. If you do not do this, there will always be the possibility that one of the cases you are relying on has been reversed or overruled. Recall that we say a case is **reversed** when the litigants appeal the decision and a higher court overturns or negates the decision of the lower court. A case is **overruled** when the court in a later case changes the law as it was found in a prior appellate decision. Finally, even if the case has not been reversed or overruled, a later court decision may explain the earlier case in such a way as to change its meaning. It is hard to imagine any more terrible researching nightmare than to turn over the results of your research to someone else and then to have that someone else rely on those results, only to find out that a recent case you did not find invalidates your conclusions. Making sure that your researching results are complete and up to date is vital.

Figure D-4   Summary of Steps for Locating Primary Authority

1. **Look for Relevant Statutes**
   A. Locate the statutes.
      ■ If you have the citation, go immediately to the correct chapter and section number.
      ■ If you do not have a citation, locate it by
         —using the subject matter index,
         —finding it in a secondary source, or
         —seeing it in a case decision.
   B. Update the statutes by checking the pocket parts.
   C. Read the case annotations.
      ■ If your state has more than one set of annotated statutes, check them both.
      ■ Check the pocket part.

2. **Look for Relevant Court Opinions**
   A. If you have the citation, go immediately to the correct volume and page number.
   B. If you do not have a citation, locate it by
      ■ looking up one of the party's names in the Digest Table of Cases or Defendant/Plaintiff's Table,
      ■ using Shepard's to locate a parallel citation if you have only one of the citations,
      ■ searching the summaries following a relevant statute,
      ■ doing background research in a secondary source, or
      ■ looking in a digest under the appropriate topic and key number.
   Locate the appropriate topic and key number either
      —by using the same topic and key number as found in another relevant case or
      —by searching in the subject matter index for your issue.

The following is a discussion of two of the main methods to update your researching results: checking the regional reporter "mini-digests" and using Shepard's Citations. In the last section of this chapter we will discuss a third method, conducting on-line research. Computerized on-line databases, such as Westlaw and Lexis, are definitely much more current than any printed materials used for updating. In fact, both Westlaw and Lexis claim to have most court decisions in their computers, and hence accessible to researchers, within twenty-four to forty-eight hours after they are decided. National law journals and newspapers, such as Lawyers Weekly USA, and state-specific newspapers, such as Massachusetts Lawyers Weekly, are also good resources for keeping current with legal changes.

a. Using the Digest Topics and Key Numbers

This method will help you find all recent court opinions that have been digested under the particular topic and key number that you have been using when doing your research. Recall that West reviews all new court decisions in order to summarize the key legal points in headnotes. The headnotes are then arranged by subject matter in the digest. Headnotes from older cases are found in the hardbound volumes of the digest. Headnotes from more recent cases are found in the pocket parts of the digest. Therefore, when doing research, once you have found a pertinent case, you must read the headnotes to determine which ones are relevant to the issues you are researching. Those headnotes will be labeled with topics and key numbers. You then go to the digest's hardbound volume *and* pocket part under those topics and key numbers and check for additional cases.

Pocket parts are published only once a year. These are supplemented halfway through the publication year with a paperback supplement. Check to see whether your library contains the interim supplement. If there is such a supplement, check it for cases that have been published since the pocket parts were printed.

In order to bring your research up to date, you must take one further step: You must check for cases that have been decided since the pocket part or supplement was published. To do that, you check the first page of the digest pocket part or supplement. On that page is a list that states when this particular pocket part was printed and which volumes of which reporters are included. We will be referring to this list as the closing table.

For example, if you checked the first page of the pocket part of the Massachusetts Digest 2d volume covering Husband and Wife, you would find a list similar to the following:

Closing with Cases Reported in

North Eastern Reporter, Second Series . . . 788 N.E.2d 1116
Supreme Court Reporter . . . . 123 S. Ct. 1964
Federal Reporter, Second Series 329 F.2d 183
Federal Supplement. . . . . 262 F. Supp. 2d

This listing tells you that when this particular pocket part was printed, the North Eastern Reporter, Second Series, was current through volume 679. This means that all court decisions that have been printed through that volume are summarized in the digest. The cases published in volume 680 and later, however, have not been summarized, as they did not exist at the time the pocket part was printed.

Unfortunately for you, a case published in volume 680 or later might be just the one you need. One method to bring the research up to date would be to read through every court decision that has been published in those volumes from volume 680 on. There is a better method, however.

In every hardbound volume of court decisions West includes a minidigest. That mini-digest includes headnotes from only those cases published in that hardbound volume. Therefore, instead of having to read through each case that has been published since the digest pocket part was printed, you can scan through the mini-digests in the recently published hardbound volumes for your topic and key number and then note only the relevant cases for further study. In addition, prior to publishing cases in the hardbound volumes West issues a few opinions at a time in pamphlets called advance sheets. These pamphlets also contain mini-digests of just the cases in those pamphlets. Therefore, to complete your updating, you will want to search in these advance sheet mini-digests as well.

Exhibit D-15 on page 697 shows what such a mini-digest looks like. Notice that in this particular advance sheet there are no cases on the topic Husband and Wife.

Figure D-5 on page 698 summarizes the steps that you need to take when updating your research using the digest topic and key number method.

b. Using Shepard's

Subsequent case history
Information about what happened procedurally to the litigation after the case cited. Include this information in a citation. There is no entry for the topic Husband and Wife.

Researchers use Shepard's Citations for several purposes. First, as we explained earlier, it is a source of parallel citations. For example, if you have only the Massachusetts citation for a court opinion, Shepard's will give you the North Eastern Reporter citation. It also works in the opposite direction; that is, if you have only the North Eastern Reporter citation, Shepard's will provide you with the Massachusetts citation.

The second major reason for using Shepard's is to find **subsequent history** for your case. Subsequent history includes such actions as an appellate court modifying, affirming, or reversing your case. For example, assume you find a Massachusetts intermediate appellate court decision that harms your client. You will be delighted if the Massachusetts Supreme Judicial Court (Massachusetts's highest appellate court) reversed that decision. That is an example of how you can use subsequent history, and Shepard's will give you that information.

Treatment
How subsequent cases have affected the case you are Shepardizing. It is sometimes indicated by a one-letter abbreviation before the Shepard's citation.

The third reason for using Shepard's is to find out what later courts, deciding cases involving different litigants, have had to say about your case. In Shepard's this is called the **treatment** of your case. Assume you **Shepardized** a Massachusetts appellate court decision that harms your client, and it was affirmed by the Massachusetts Supreme Judicial Court. Things look bleak for your client. But there is always the possibility that the Massachusetts Supreme Judicial Court changed its mind regarding the legal issue involved and in a later decision, involving other litigants, overruled that earlier opinion. While this will not affect the outcome of the original case (as subsequent history does), it will have an effect on the precedential value of that case for future cases. Shepard's will also give you that information.

Shepardizing
The process of using Shepard's citations to check a court citation to see whether there has been any subsequent history or treatment by other court decisions.

HOMICIDE—Cont'd

VIII. TRIAL.

(C) INSTRUCTIONS.

☞294.2. Intoxication.

Ind. 2002. Capital murder defendant was not entitled to jury instruction on defense of voluntary intoxication, where evidence at trial did not indicate, and counsel did not argue, that defendant had been so intoxicated at time of murder as to have been unable to form intent required for murder.— Saylor v. State, 765 N.E.2d 535.

☞300(7). Applicability to issues and evidence in general.

Mass. 2002. Instructing jurors that original aggressor had no right to self defense unless he withdrew from conflict in good faith and announced his intention of abandoning the fight was warranted by evidence in murder prosecution indicating that defendant initiated confrontation.— Com. v. Garrey, 765 N.E.2d 725, 436 Mass. 422.

☞305. Principals and accessories.

Ind. 2002. State's proffered accomplice liability instruction in murder prosecution was at least marginally supported by evidence, and its allowance was not abuse of trial court's discretion, despite fact that only evidence at trial indicating that someone other than defendant was the killer was third party's hearsay testimony to effect that such other person confessed to being the killer, declarant was not unavailable within scope of exception to hearsay rule for statements against penal interest, and evidence was allowed only upon stipulation that declarant would have denied having confessed had he testified. Rules of Evid., Rule 804.—Smith v. State, 765 N.E.2d 578.

XI. SENTENCE AND PUNISHMENT.

☞354(2). Life sentence.

N.Y. 2002. Defendant who pleaded guilty to first degree murder could be sentenced to life imprisonment without the possibility of parole, although People never filed notice of intent to seek the death penalty. McKinney's CPL §§ 250.40, 400.27; McKinney's Penal Law §§ 60.06, 70.00, subd. 5.—People v. Mower, 765 N.E.2d 839, 97 N.Y.2d 239.

Authority to impose a sentence of life imprisonment without parole exists whether a defendant's conviction is by guilty plea or jury verdict. McKinney's CPL §§ 250.40, 400.27; McKinney's Penal Law §§ 60.06, 70.00, subd. 5.—Id.

HOSPITALS

☞7. Liabilities of proprietors, officers, and employees.

N.Y. 2002. Actions of physician who improperly touched patient, for purposes of his own sexual gratification, while patient was recovering from surgery, were not in furtherance of the business of hospital which employed physician, or within the scope of his employment, and thus could not form basis for recovery by patient against hospital under doctrine of respondeat superior; physician was not charged with patient's care, and his actions could not be characterized as an "examination," as an internal pelvic examination as contraindicated in light of nature of surgery patient had undergone.— N.X. v. Cabrini Medical Center, 765 N.E.2d 844, 97 N.Y.2d 247.

HOSPITALS—Cont'd

A sexual assault perpetrated by a hospital employee is not in furtherance of hospital business and is a clear departure from the scope of employment, having been committed for wholly personal motives, and thus may not form basis for imposition of liability against hospital under doctrine of respondeat superior.—Id.

A hospital has a duty to safeguard the welfare of its patients, even from harm inflicted by third persons, measured by the capacity of the patient to provide for his or her own safety; however, this sliding scale of duty is limited, and does not render a hospital an insurer of patient safety or require it to keep each patient under constant surveillance.— Id.

As with any liability in tort, the scope of a hospital's duty to safeguard the welfare of its patients is circumscribed by those risks which are reasonably foreseeable.—Id.

Observations and information known to or readily perceivable by hospital staff that there is a risk of harm to a patient under the circumstances can be sufficient to trigger duty on part of hospital to protect the patient's welfare.—Id.

IMPLIED AND CONSTRUCTIVE CONTRACTS

◀—— There is no entry for the topic Husband and Wife.

I. NATURE AND GROUNDS OF OBLIGATION.

(A) IN GENERAL.

☞3. —— Unjust enrichment.

Ind.App. 2002. To prevail on a claim of unjust enrichment, plaintiff must establish that a measurable benefit has been conferred on defendant under circumstances in which defendant's retention of the benefit without payment would be unjust.— Encore Hotels of Columbus, LLC v. Preferred Fire Protection, 765 N.E.2d 658.

Principles of equity prohibit unjust enrichment where a party accepts unrequested benefits another provides despite having opportunity to decline those benefits.—Id.

Under the theory of quasi-contracts, the court may impose liability, though the parties have not mutually assented to a contract, to prevent one party's unjust enrichment at the expense of the other.—Id.

(C) SERVICES RENDERED.

☞33.1. —— In general.

Ind.App. 2002. Owner, who contracted with general contractor for construction of a hotel, was liable to subcontractor on unjust enrichment theory after owner failed to pay general contractor or subcontractor for work performed; subcontractor completed several weeks' worth of work on project for benefit of owner, owner never complained regarding quality of work and even asked subcontractor to come back to finish project, and reason for subcontractor's failure to complete project was owner's failure to give guarantee that it would pay subcontractor additional cost for overtime or that it would pay subcontractor for unpaid work it had already done.—Encore Hotels of Columbus, LLC v. Preferred Fire Protection, 765 N.E.2d 658.

Exhibit D-15   Example of a Digest Page Located in Regional Reporters and Their Advance Sheets

1. **Check the Digest's Main Volume, Supplement, and Pocket Part.**
   Use the relevant topics and key numbers to check the pocket part (and supplement if it exists) for recent decisions.

2. **Check the Closing Table.**
   Check the listing on the first page of the most recent digest pocket part or supplement to determine the last volume of your regional reporter covered in that pocket part.

3. **Check Recent Hardbound Reporter Volumes.**
   Check the mini-digest located in each hardbound volume of your regional reporter published since the digest pocket part or most recent supplement was printed (as determined by the digest closing table).

4. **Check the Pamphlets Containing the Advance Sheets.**
   Check the mini-digest located in each advance sheet of your regional reporter published since the digest pocket part or most recent supplement was printed (as determined by the digest closing table).

Figure D-5   Summary of Steps for Updating through the Digest Topic and Key Number Method

(In addition to using Shepard's for updating case law, you can use it to determine whether a statutory provision is still in force.)

Shepard's is comprised of several red hardbound volumes, supplemented with red, gold, and white paper pamphlets. Using Shepard's is a very straightforward process, but it requires that you be absolutely precise. When Shepardizing, there is no room for even the slightest mistake in writing the citation because all of Shepard's is based on numbers: the numbers that make up the case citation.

To see how Shepard's works, assume that in the course of your research you located *Callow v. Thomas*, 322 Mass. 550, 78 N.E.2d 637 (1948), and that you would like to find additional cases that have discussed the topic of spousal immunity. Using Shepard's would be a good approach because, having read *Callow*, you would assume recent decisions that have discussed spousal immunity would mention *Callow* somewhere in the course of their discussion. Shepard's will give you the citation for every case (known as the **citing case**) that mentions the case you are Shepardizing (known as the **cited case**).

Citing case
A case listed in Shepard's that cites your case.

Cited case
The case you are Shepardizing.

As the first step in Shepardizing, you would write down the citation for *Callow*. It is essential that you write down the correct volume number, page number, and reporter. It is also important to include the date so you will know with which Shepard's you need to begin your research.

Shepard's will inform you of whether a later case has dealt with your case as a whole or whether it has treated only specific issues. Therefore, the second step is to review the headnotes at the beginning of the case you want to Shepardize. In order to avoid finding cases that have cited your case but for irrelevant points, you need to write down the relevant headnote numbers from your case. For example, turn to page 688. The *Callow* headnotes that relate to the topic of spousal immunity are headnotes 1, 2, and 3. You do not want to find every case that has cited *Callow*. For example, you do not want to find cases that have cited *Callow* for what the court said regarding annulment. That topic is discussed in headnotes 4, 5, and 6. Therefore, you would write down just those headnote numbers that relate to your issue of whether spouses can sue each other: headnotes 1, 2, and 3. Your notes would now look like the following:

Callow v. Thomas, 322 Mass. 550, 78 N.E.2d[1,2,3] 637 (1948)

The third step is to select the appropriate Shepard's volumes. There is a Shepard's for each state, for each region covered by West's regional reporters, and for each level in the federal court system. Which volumes you select will depend on your goal in Shepardizing. The state Shepard's will give you references to that state's state and federal court decisions that have cited your case. A regional Shepard's will give you references to *all* state and federal court decisions that have cited your case. Therefore, in Shepardizing *Callow*, if you want to find recent Massachusetts court decisions, the appropriate Shepard's would be the Massachusetts Shepard's volumes. If you want to find court decisions from around the country, the appropriate Shepard's would be the North Eastern Shepard's.

Once you have determined which Shepard's set to use, you must find the most recent paper supplement updating the hardbound Shepard's volumes for that set. On the front cover of that supplement you will see a box indicating how many hardbound volumes and supplements you will have to consult. A new paper supplement is issued each month. Depending on the month you may find anywhere from one to three paper supplements to the hardbound volumes. These could include an annual or a semiannual supplement, a cumulative supplement, and a white advance sheet. In March of 2000, the "What Your Library Should Contain" box on the latest Massachusetts Shepard's supplement contained the following information:

WHAT YOUR LIBRARY SHOULD CONTAIN

1993 Bound Volume, Cases (Parts 1-4)[*]
1993 Bound Volume, Statutes (Parts 1 and 2)[*]
1993-2002 Bound Supplement, Cases and Statutes

[*]*Supplemented with*
—December 2003 Annual Cumulative Supplement Vol. 96 No. 12
—May 2004 Cumulative Supplement Vol. 97 No. 5

DISCARD ALL OTHER ISSUES

Of course, as of the time you are reading this text, the information in the "What Your Library Should Contain" box will have changed to reflect the current status of the Shepard's supplements.

Now you are finally ready to begin the process of Shepardizing. Look for your citation in either the first Shepard's that could contain references to your case or the most recent Shepard's. Usually, you will want to start with the most recent Shepard's to save yourself from unnecessary work. For example, if you are

Shepardizing a case that was overruled six months ago, you could find that information fairly quickly by starting in the most recent Shepard's supplement. If you had started in the hardbound volume, you would have noted many citations that would no longer be relevant given the recent decision.

You can use either the North Eastern Reporter citation or the Massachusetts Reports citation. If you use the North Eastern Reporter citation, you will get North Eastern Reporter citations. If you use the Massachusetts Reports citation, you will get Massachusetts Reports citations. You will also get citations to some additional sources, such as law reviews, if you use the Massachusetts Reports citation. However, if you are relying on headnote numbers from the case as printed in the North Eastern Reporter to focus your search, be sure to use the North Eastern Reporter citations. Otherwise, the raised numbers you see in Shepard's will not match the numbers on the North Eastern Reporter headnotes.

For our example problem first we will use the N.E.2d cite, and we will start with the first Shepard's that could contain references to *Callow*. Because *Callow* is a 1948 decision, that would be the 1993 hardbound volume of Shepard's. Take a look at the page from the hardbound volume of Shepard's reproduced as Exhibit D-16 on page 701.

First, notice that we are in the right part of Shepard's, as the words NORTHEASTERN REPORTER, 2d SERIES (Massachusetts Cases) appear centered at the top of the page. Second, find the reference to Vol. 78 in the left-hand corner. This means we have located the right volume number. Next look in the first column for —637—, our page number.

The first citation following —637— is (322Mas550). This is the parallel citation for *Callow*. The parallel citation will always be the first reference, and it will always be surrounded by parentheses. Shepard's will give you this citation only once: in the first Shepard's that contains references to your case. Because *Callow* is a 1948 case, the parallel citation is found in the hardbound volume. For cases decided after 1993, the parallel citation will be in the first paper pamphlet to contain references to that case.

Following the parallel citation Shepard's always gives references to case history *if there is any*, and it will *always* be preceded by a letter. There is none for *Callow*. If you had seen a listing, such as D335US849, that would be a reference to case history. The *D* means that the appeal of the case was dismissed by the U.S. Supreme Court.

Look once again at the citations for *Callow* under —637—. Following the parallel citation are nine citations. Notice the raised numbers that follow some of the N.E.2d abbreviations. These numbers refer to the headnotes in our cited case, *Callow*. Again, this is Shepard's way of helping you narrow your research so that you can search for cases that cited your case on a specific topic as referenced in a particular headnote. Based on this information we see that only one of the listed cases, $351NE2d^2528$, pertains to our issue.

Finally, under *Callow* you will see one reference to a federal case. *FS* stands for Federal Supplement. A state Shepard's, such as the one for Massachusetts, will tell you about federal cases that originated in that state.

Notice that some of the citations on the Shepard's page are *preceded* by a letter. For example, the first citation under 78 N.E.2d 633 is preceded by the letter *d*. A listing of the letters used and what they mean can be found at the beginning of each Shepard's volume. For example, *d* means distinguished and *f* means followed. Three letters are of particular concern: *r* for reversed, *o* for overruled, and *q* for

| Vol. 78 | NORTHEASTERN REPORTER, 2d SERIES (Massachusetts Cases) | | | | |

—629—

Wright v
Health
Commissioner
of Boston
1948

(322Mas535)
107NE¹775
157NE228
360NE⁶1060
387NE188

—633—

Watson's Case
1948

(322Mas581)
d 85NE⁶75
88NE³639
102NE⁴415
116NE⁴128
120NE⁴756
127NE⁴193
d 138NE⁴288
138NE³633
138NE⁷751
148NE⁴373
154NE⁴605
155NE⁴790
f 173NE⁴644
232NE⁴927
258NE⁴927
363NE⁴1336
373NE⁷1178
408NE⁶894
Cir. 5
186F2d277

—637—

Callow v
Thomas
1948

(322Mas550)
173NE⁴269
178NE⁴283
178NE⁸283
236NE⁴201
351NE²528
373NE⁴358
373NE⁶358
489NE⁴673
574NE⁴405
Cir. 1
504FS⁴654

—641—

Joyce v
Devaney
1948

(322Mas544)
95NE¹175
103NE¹322

115NE¹495
116NE²155
141NE¹516
142NE¹405
146NE²514
165NE¹116
224NE¹224
372NE¹283
372NE⁴283

—644—

Massachusetts
v Hall
1948

(322Mas523)
82NE³10
87NE⁶202
178NE³267
317NE³831
334NE²616
366NE²726
421NE²761
421NE¹764
440NE⁶769
d 595NE¹777
58USLW4925

—649—

Franklin
Square House
v Siskind
1948

(322Mas556)
124NE²231
183NE⁸291
226NE⁸196

—651—

Provost's Case
1948

(322Mas604)

—652—

Rosenthal
v Maletz
1948

(322Mas586)
80NE⁶15
84NE552
97NE¹⁷171
99NE¹927
d 103NE⁴251
105NE¹248
126NE¹531
129NE¹⁰906
140NE¹⁶646
163NE¹⁰160
170NE⁴839
170NE¹⁹840
247NE¹393
q 342NE¹³717

---

d 374NE¹⁰350
Cir. 1
331F2d33
97FS¹⁷777

—697—

Massachusetts
v Farrell
1948

(322Mas606)
85NE²451
95NE¹⁸541
109NE¹⁸174
126NE¹⁸808
132NE²⁰303
142NE¹⁰389
182NE¹128
201NE¹⁸832
216NE¹⁸426
226NE¹⁴210
235NE¹⁴800
265NE⁴382
314NE⁴450
326NE⁶714
334NE¹648
337NE711
344NE¹⁶927
348NE¹⁸820
355NE478
363NE⁷1316
370NE⁷1026
370NE¹⁴¹1026
373NE¹⁴¹1126
383NE²⁰1121
387NE⁷164
389NE¹⁰762
402NE⁶1056
402NE⁶1057
f 402NE¹²¹1060
406NE⁶419
406NE⁴421
417NE⁶980
422NE⁴452
436NE⁶1217
436NE⁶1223
457NE¹²624
471NE⁷1358
487NE⁸1370
504NE¹³615
509NE⁷304
522NE⁶6
547NE944
564NE⁸378
574NE⁷344
576NE¹²711
594NE¹⁴868
23MJ325

Vol. 79

—1—

King v
Tewksbury
1948

(322Mas668)
cc 81NE737

—2—

Morin v
Trailways
of New
England Inc.
1948

(322Mas744)

—3—

Wagstaff v
Director of the
Division of
Employment
Security
1948

(322Mas664)
82NE¹2
84NE¹544
85NE¹780
86NE¹57
89NE¹782
92NE¹253
96NE²862
97NE640
98NE¹362
99NE¹59
106NE³422
117NE¹165
118NE¹774
197NE⁴597
344NE²895
382NE²201
454NE⁴95

—5—

Kubilius
v Hawes
Unitarian
Congregational
Church
1948

(322Mas638)
87NE¹214
154NE⁸601
244NE⁴279
244NE⁶279
Cir. 1
735FS⁶1097

—10—

Royal v Royal
1948

(322Mas662)
s 87NE850
j 133NE¹240

—11—

Seltmann v
Seltmann
1948

(322Mas650)
85NE³442
q 146NE²499
294NE¹557
316NE¹763

—13—

Herald v Rich
1948

(322Mas659)

—15—

Goff v Hickson
1948

(322Mas655)
88NE¹337
89NE³1
91NE⁴235
91NE⁴927
104NE¹495

—17—

Ryder v Ryder
1948

(322Mas645)
269NE⁶94
412NE⁷917

—185—

Delgreco v
Delgreco
1948

(322Mas706)
145NE²688
215NE³670

—187—

General v
Woburn
1948

(322Mas634)
85NE¹230
86NE¹645
99NE¹43
111NE²671

---

e 115NE⁵149
129NE¹895
175NE²916
208NE¹234
214NE¹43
252NE¹213
252NE¹896
269NE¹233
438NE⁸91
461NE771
556NE⁴117

—189—

Connolly v
John Hancock
Mutual Life
Insurance Co.
1948

(322Mas678)
116NE⁴678
129NE¹619
141NE⁴513
141NE⁴726
d 174NE¹38
258NE¹20
Cir. 1
201F2d⁴422
282FS⁴376

—192—

McCartin
v School
Committee
of Lowell
1948

(322Mas624)
111NE³750
q 184NE³43
217NE¹769
294NE211
d 294NE³212
d 310NE²336
335NE²655
336NE752
356NE³263
378NE²1376
378NE³1376
384NE²230
384NE³230
417NE²461
486NE46
486NE²47

—195—

Owens-Illinois
Glass Co. v
Bresnahan
1948

(322Mas629)
d 110NE²125
142NE²762

318

Exhibit D-16   Massachusetts Shepard's

History of a Case	
a	(affirmed on appeal)
D	(appeal dismissed)
m	(modified on appeal)
r	(reversed on appeal)
s	(same case)
US cert den	(Certiorari denied by U.S. Supreme Court)

Treatment of a Case	
c	(criticized)
d	(case distinguished from cited case)
e	(case explains cited case)
f	(case follows cited case)
j	(dissenting judge refers to cited case)
l	(limited)
o	(case expressly overrules cited case)
q	(soundness of decision or reasoning questioned)

Figure D-6 Shepard's Analysis Abbreviations

questioned. Figure D-6 summarizes the one-letter abbreviations most commonly seen in Shepard's.

Before leaving this page of Shepard's, you should write down any citations that meet the requirements listed above—that is, any decision that is preceded by a letter, that contains a raised number corresponding to one of your decision's relevant headnote numbers, or that contains no raised headnote numbers. For our example there is only one citation that meets those requirements, and that is 351N.E.2d^2528.

Next you need to repeat this process for each of the other supplements and hardbound volumes in the Shepard's set you are using. Once this is done, the last step is to find the cases for which you have found citations. To find the case that corresponds to the citation 351N.E.2d^2528, take a look in your text on page 202. This is where we have reproduced page 528 from *Lewis*. Can you find the reference to *Callow*? Notice that Shepard's takes you right to the page on which the citing case cites the decision that you are Shepardizing. To correctly cite the citing case, in this instance *Lewis*, remember that you need to include the beginning page number.

If you had Shepardized using the official state citation, all the citing case references would also have used the official Massachusetts citations. You would also have found references to law review articles and American Law Reports Annotated. You can find ALR annotations and law review articles only if you Shepardize using the official state citation.

In addition to state Shepard's, there are also regional Shepard's. The advantage to using regional Shepard's is that they include references to cases from around the country. Exhibit D-17 on page 703 shows what such a regional listing looks like. This North Eastern Reporter edition of Shepard's shows citations to *Callow* from several states, including California and Wisconsin.

In conclusion, Shepard's is an invaluable resource. However, to be successful in using Shepard's, you must pay attention to every detail, such as the number of volumes and supplements to check. Use Figure D-7 on page 704 to assist you with this process. It summarizes the steps you must take when using Shepard's to update your research.

c. Using Both Digests and Shepard's

Finally, you may be wondering why a researcher would use both methods of updating: the digest topic/key number method and Shepard's. The reason is that you may find different cases using the different methods. The digest method will only help you find cases that West thinks should be categorized as your case has been categorized. For example, the digest method will not work if you are researching spousal immunity cases under the topic Husband and Wife, key number 205(2), and a West editor categorizes a newer and relevant case as Torts, key number 168. On the other hand, Shepardizing will help you find all recent court opinions that have *cited* your decision whether or not they are digested under the same topic and key number. To be found through Shepard's, however, the more recent opinion must have cited your opinion. If the opinion simply discusses the same topic without citing your case, you will not find out about that more recent case using Shepard's.

Vol. 78	NORTHEASTERN REPORTER, 2nd Series

—611—
Case 3
Anchor Trading Corp. v Ryerson & Son Inc. 1948
(297NY817)
s 69 NYS2d844
83 NYS2d876
Cir. 5
119FS817
Calif
225 P2d960

—612—
Case 1
Spinelli v Arthur Tickle Engineering Works Inc. 1948
(297NY818)
s 67 NYS2d713
s 74 NYS2d11
261 NYS2d625

—612—
Case 2
New York Central Railroad Co. v New York and Harlem Railroad Co. 1948
(297NY820)
s 56 NYS2d712
s 72 NYS2d404
s 72 NYS2d830
s 85 NYS2d112
s 90 NYS2d309
cc 93 NE451
h 85 NYS2d270
132 NYS2d24
Cir. 2
203F2d707
Cir. 3
d 354FS741
354FS769
f 354FS772
Cir. 5
403F2d550
Md
86 A2d488

—613—
Eisemann v Fidelity & Deposit Company of Maryland 1948
(297NY822)
s 71 NYS2d186
s 87 NYS2d333

—614—
Case 1
Ruina v Commercial Travelers Mutual Accident Association of America 1948
(297NY824)
s 73 NYS2d641
182 NYS2d921
208 NYS2d325
j 467 NYS2d651

—614—
Case 2
New York State ex rel Whitney v Chambers 1948
(297NY826)
s 69 NYS2d360

—614—
Case 3
Ginsberg v Horvath 1948
(297NY827)
s 66 NYS2d631
s 67 NYS2d701
s 74 NYS2d409

—616—
Broman v Byrne 1948
(322Mas578)
82 NE[5]882
95 NE[4]186
j 107 NE[6]26
q 156 NE[6]805

j 314 NE[6]137
344 NE[2]907
555 NE[3]875
Ill
125 NE[4]648
N H
82 A2d603
Wyo
276 P2d466
35 A2d681n
47 A2d848n

—618—
Sullivan v Municipal Court of the Roxbury District 1948
(322Mas566)
85 NE[2]217
87 NE[2]21
89 NE[1]782
97 NE[11]183
101 NE[1]890
103 NE[3]697
130 NE[7]692
131 NE[6]748
142 NE[10]344
171 NE[1]276
171 NE[2]282
174 NE[10]448
174 NE[4]659
174 NE[3]660
205 NE[4]709
d 205 NE[1]710
214 NE[2]736
243 NE[2]925
247 NE[4]381
f 268 NE[1]348
f 268 NE[2]348
f 268 NE[3]348
f 269 NE[2]451
f 269 NE[3]451
271 NE[2]591
303 NE129
309 NE[10]890
332 NE[1]904
332 NE[2]904
332 NE[3]904
337 NE[2]685
337 NE[3]685
338 NE[2]833
343 NE[2]368
375 NE[11]343
389 NE[2]434
f 396 NE[2]995
396 NE[7]995
407 NE[10]368
451 NE445
d 471 NE[1]66
502 NE[3]958
Mont
530 P2d465
Tex
422 SW147

—623—
Broussard v Melong 1948
(322Mas560)
92 NE255
384 NE205
389 NE438
402 NE[2]1020

—624—
National Shawmut Bank of Boston v Hallett 1948
(322Mas596)
f 143 NE[8]535
149 NE[7]370
212 NE[7]560
292 NE[4]32
298 NE839
345 NE[3]924
Cir. 1
808FS[7]64

—629—
Wright v Health Commissioner of Boston 1948
(322Mas535)
107 NE[1]775
157 NE228
360 NE[9]1060
387 NE188

—633—
Watson's Case 1948
(322Mas581)
d 85 NE[8]75
88 NE[3]639
102 NE[4]415
116 NE[4]128
120 NE[4]756
127 NE[4]193
d 138 NE[4]288
138 NE[3]633
138 NE[7]751
148 NE[4]373
154 NE[4]605
155 NE[4]790
f 173 NE[4]644
232 NE[4]927
258 NE[1]927
363 NE[4]1336
373 NE[7]1178
408 NE[8]894

Cir. 5
186F2d277
N M
237 P2d355

—637—
Callow v Thomas 1948
(322Mas550)
(2A2632)
173 NE[4]269
178 NE[4]283
178 NE[5]283
236 NE[4]201
351 NE[2]528
373 NE[4]358
373 NE[6]358
489 NE[4]673
574 NE[4]405
Cir. 1
504FS[4]654
Calif
240 P2d1006
283 P2d347
Conn
137 A2d355
142 A2d528
Kan
239 P2d934
Me
216 A2d32
Mo
331 SW656
478 SW337
N H
156 A2d133
193 A2d439
216 A2d782
241 A2d373
260 A2d98
279 A2d586
N M
269 P2d750
N D
68 NW665
Tenn
336 SW26
Utah
384 P2d391
Wis
95 NW823
43 A2d637n
43 A2d653n
92 A2d945n

—641—
Joyce v Devaney 1948
(322Mas544)
95 NE[1]175
103 NE[1]322

115 NE[1]495
116 NE[2]155
141 NE[1]516
142 NE[1]405
146 NE[2]514
165 NE[1]116
224 NE[1]224
372 NE[1]283
372 NE[4]283
N Y
137 NYS2d327
Conn
109 A2d589
Md
142 A2d819

—644—
Massachusetts v Hall 1948
(322Mas523)
82 NE[3]10
87 NE[6]202
178 NE[3]267
317 NE[3]831
334 NE[2]616
366 NE[2]726
421 NE[2]761
421 NE[1]764
440 NE[5]769
d 595 NE[1]777
617 NE[1]613
111LE254
N Y
462 NYS2d116
Calif
140 CaR289
140 CaR293
Iowa
124 NW721
Md
596 A2d661
Mich
208 NW660
S D
134 NW109
Utah
585 P2d63
Va
141 SE714
61 A3d1210n
61 A3d1217n

—649—
Franklin Square House v Siskind 1948
(322Mas556)
124 NE[5]231
183 NE[5]291
226 NE[5]196

Exhibit D-17   Northeastern Shepard's

1. **Start with the Full Citation.**
   Write down the full citation of the decision you want to Shepardize.

2. **Note the Relevant Headnotes.**
   Write down the relevant headnote numbers of the decision you want to Shepardize.

3. **Locate the Appropriate Shepard's.**
   Select the appropriate Shepard's volumes.

4. **Find the Most Recent Shepard's.**
   Find the most recent paper supplement updating the hardbound Shepard's volumes for that set. Then look on the front cover of that supplement to see how many hardbound volumes and supplements you will have to consult.

5. **Using the Most Recent Supplement, Find Your Citation.**
   Look for your citation in the most recent Shepard's.
   a. Make sure you are in the *right part* of Shepard's for your reporter; for example, looking in the N.E. section for an N.E.2d cite is fatal.
   b. Make sure you have the *right volume number*.
   c. Make sure you have the *right page number*.
   d. Write down the citation for any decision that is preceded by a letter, that contains a raised number corresponding to one of your decision's relevant headnote numbers, or that contains no raised headnote numbers.

6. **If Necessary, Repeat Step 5.**
   Repeat this process for each of the other supplements and hardbound volumes in the Shepard's set you are using.

7. **Locate Your Citations.**
   Remember that Shepard's will take you to the page on which your case is mentioned.

Figure D-7   Summary of Steps for Updating Using Shepard's

5. Decide When to Stop Researching

This can often be one of the most difficult parts of a researching assignment. How can you know when to stop? Usually, you will know it is time to stop when you keep finding the same references in different resources. For example, you may find the same court opinion mentioned in an encyclopedia, a state digest, and an annotated code. When looking at more resources no longer gives you new citations to add to your list, stop.

C. RESEARCH INVOLVING FEDERAL STATUTES AND REGULATIONS

Up to this point we have been discussing how you perform state law research. Research into federal law follows a similar pattern. Assume you are representing Diane, the waitress whom we met in Chapter 2 whose boss fired her when he discovered she was pregnant. If she wants to sue for sex discrimination, which is prohibited by federal law, you will want to begin your research in the federal statutes.

The official publication for the federal statutes is the United States Code (U.S.C.). It is organized by subject matter into fifty titles. Like its official state counterparts it does not contain summaries of court decisions. Therefore, most researchers will begin with one of the two private publications: the United States Code Annotated (U.S.C.A.), published by West Group, or the United States Code Service (U.S.C.S.), published by Lexis Law Publishing.

As with state law research, you first need to think of words to describe your client's situation. Next you should consult an index.

In addition to using an index, you might be able to find a citation by looking in a popular name table. Some statutes are commonly referred to by the names of the sponsors (the Taft-Hartley Act) or a descriptive title (the Truth in Lending Act). All three publications—U.S.C., U.S.C.A., and U.S.C.S.—contain **popular name tables**, which give the formal citations for these acts. In addition, Shepard's Acts and Cases by Popular Names, Federal and State provides a convenient source for both federal and state legislation. The U.S. Supreme Court Reports Digest also contains a popular name table. In Diane's situation the statute that governs unlawful employment practices was enacted as part of the Civil Rights Act of 1964. It is codified in the United States Code in title 42, beginning at section 2000.

Popular name table Located in most codified statutes, this table lists statutes by their popular names along with their citations.

A few pages of 42 U.S.C.S. § 2000e-2, the part of the statute that outlaws certain employment practices, are reproduced in Exhibit D-18. As with annotated state codes, in the federal annotated codes following each statute there is some basic information about the law's legislative history. The United States Code Service also includes cross-references to the Code of Federal Regulations, as well as to other publications, such as Am. Jur. 2d. Finally, the annotated codes also include summaries of court decisions.

Just as when doing state-based research, once you have located and analyzed a federal statute, you must determine whether an administrative agency has interpreted the statute through regulations. Like the United States Code, the Code of Federal Regulations is organized by subject matter into fifty titles. Unfortunately, however, those fifty titles are not the same as those used in the United States Code. Therefore, your first step is to find the correct citation for any applicable regulation. To assist you, the Code of Federal Regulations contains a table of all those sections of the C.F.R. that have been promulgated under the authority of a particular statute.

You can also begin your research with the subject index to C.F.R., using it in the same way you would use the subject index of a statutory code. Exhibit D-19 on page 707 presents a portion of the text of the Code of Federal Regulations covering sexual harassment. Notice the reference to 42 U.S.C. 2000e, the enabling statute that gives the Equal Employment Opportunity Commission authority to issue regulations setting out what constitutes sexual harassment.

In order to be as up to date as possible, you should also check the latest issues of the Federal Register. The Federal Register is published on a daily basis and contains any newly proposed regulations, as well as any proposed amendments to old regulations.

Unfortunately, there is no clear pattern for the publication of agency rulings (as opposed to agency regulations). Some loose-leaf services provide administrative regulations and rulings in such special-interest areas as employment, taxation, and commerce. When available, they are a particularly useful source.

EQUAL EMPLOYMENT OPPORTUNITIES   42 USCS § 2000e-2

*   *   *

§ 2000e-2. Unlawful employment practices

(a) **Employer practices.** It shall be an unlawful employment practice for an employer—

(1) to fail or refuse to hire or to discharge any individual, or otherwise to discriminate against any individual with respect to his compensation, terms, conditions, or privileges of employment, because of such individual's race, color, religion, sex, or national origin; or

(2) to limit, segregate, or classify his employees or applicants for employment in any way which would deprive or tend to deprive any individual of employment opportunities or otherwise adversely affect his status as an employee, because of such individual's race, color, religion, sex, or national origin.

*   *   *

(July 2, 1964, P. L. 88-352, Title VII, § 703, 78 Stat. 255; Mar. 24, 1972, P. L. 92-261, § 8(a), (b), 86 Stat. 109.)

HISTORY; ANCILLARY LAWS AND DIRECTIVES

References in text:

"The Subversive Activities Control Act of 1950", referred to in subsec. (f) of this section, is Act Sept. 23, 1950, c. 1024, Title I, and appears as 18 USCS §§ 792 note, 793, note prec. 1501, 1507; 22 USCS § 618; 50 USCS §§ 781 et seq., 788 et seq.

Effective date of section:

Section 716(a) and (b) of Act July 2, 1964, provided: "(a) This title [42 USCS §§ 2000e et seq.] shall become effective one year after the date of its enactment.

"(b) Notwithstanding subsection (a), sections of this title other than sections 703, 704, 706, and 707 [42 USCS §§ 2000e-2, 2000e-3, 2000e-5, 2000e-6] shall become effective immediately.".

Amendments:

1972. Act Mar. 24, 1972, in subsec. (a), in paragraph (2), inserted "or applicants for employment"; and, in subsec. (c), in paragraph (2), inserted "or applicants for membership".

CODE OF FEDERAL REGULATIONS

Nondiscrimination requirements, 12 CFR Part 528.
Bureau of Indian Affairs, Department of the Interior; roads of the Bureau of Indian Affairs, 25 CFR Part 170.
Pennsylvania Avenue Development Corporation, Affirmative Action policy and procedure, 36 CFR Part 906.

RESEARCH GUIDE

Federal Procedure L Ed:

12 Fed Proc, L Ed, Evidence, § 33:66.

21 Fed Proc, L Ed, Job Discrimination, §§ 50:1, 16, 85, 127, 144, 176, 270, 275, 480, 488, 558, 576.

33 Fed Proc, L Ed, Trial, § 77:256.

Am Jur:

3A Am Jur 2d, Aliens and Citizens § 2001.

452

Exhibit D-18   United States Code Service tit. 42, § 2000e-2

Equal Employment Opportunity Comm.   **Pt. 1604, App.**

§ 1604.11 Sexual harassment.

(a) Harassment on the basis of sex is a violation of section 703 of title VII.[1] Unwelcome sexual advances, requests for sexual favors, and other verbal or physical conduct of a sexual nature constitute sexual harassment when (1) submission to such conduct is made either explicitly or implicitly a term or condition of an individual's employment, (2) submission to or rejection of such conduct by an individual is used as the basis for employment decisions affecting such individual, or (3) such conduct has the purpose or effect of unreasonably interfering with an individual's work performance or creating an intimidating, hostile, or offensive working environment.

(b) In determining whether alleged conduct constitutes sexual harassment, the Commission will look at the record as a whole and at the totality of the circumstances, such as the nature of the sexual advances and the context in which the alleged incidents occurred. The determination of the legality of a particular action will be made from the facts, on a case by case basis.

(c) Applying general title VII principles, an employer, employment agency, joint apprenticeship committee or labor organization (hereinafter collectively referred to as "employer") is responsible for its acts and those of its agents and supervisory employees with respect to sexual harassment regardless of whether the specific acts complained of were authorized or even forbidden by the employer and regardless of whether the employer knew or should have known of their occurrence. The Commission will examine the circumstances of the particular employment relationship and the job junctions performed by the individual in determining whether an individual acts in either a supervisory or agency capacity.

(d) With respect to conduct between fellow employees, an employer is responsible for acts of sexual harassment in the workplace where the employer (or its agents or supervisory employees) knows or should have known of the

conduct, unless it can show that it took immediate and appropriate corrective action.

(e) An employer may also be responsible for the acts of non-employees, with respect to sexual harassment of employees in the workplace, where the employer (or its agents or supervisory employees) knows or should have known of the conduct and fails to take immediate and appropriate corrective action. In reviewing these cases the Commission will consider the extent of the employer's control and any other legal responsibility which the employer may have with respect to the conduct of such non-employees.

(f) Prevention is the best tool for the elimination of sexual harassment. An employer should take all steps necessary to prevent sexual harassment from occurring, such as affirmatively raising the subject, expressing strong disapproval, developing appropriate sanctions, informing employees of their right to raise and how to raise the issue of harassment under title VII, and developing methods to sensitize all concerned.

(g) Other related practices: Where employment opportunities or benefits are granted because of an individual's submission to the employer's sexual advances or requests for sexual favors, the employer may be held liable for unlawful sex discrimination against other persons who were qualified for but denied that employment opportunity or benefit.

(Title VII, Pub. L. 88–352, 78 Stat. 253 (42 U.S.C. 2000e *et seq.*))

[45 FR 74677, Nov. 10, 1980]

APPENDIX TO PART 1604—QUESTIONS AND ANSWERS ON THE PREGNANCY DISCRIMINATION ACT, PUBLIC LAW 95–555, 92 STAT. 2076 (1978)

INTRODUCTION

On October 31, 1978, President Carter signed into law the *Pregnancy Discrimination Act* (Pub. L. 95–955). The Act is an amendment to title VII of the Civil Rights Act of 1964 which prohibits, among other things, discrimination in employment on the basis of sex. The *Pregnancy Discrimination Act* makes it clear that "because of sex" or "on

---

[1] The principles involved here continue to apply to race, color, religion or national origin.

183

Exhibit D-19   Code of Federal Regulations tit. 29, § 1604.11

D. COMPUTER-ASSISTED RESEARCH

Two great advantages of computers are their abilities to store large amounts of information and to rapidly sort through and retrieve this information. These characteristics make computers valuable tools for legal researchers. Through the Internet and direct connections to Lexis, Westlaw, or LoisLaw, law offices and libraries can access legal research materials that are stored on large mainframe computers. When connected to an on-line legal database, your computer can provide you with instant access to legal information that goes far beyond what the normal law firm can maintain in the form of traditional books and journals.

1. Major On-line Providers

On-line research via the Internet is rapidly becoming the principal, if not the primary, type of legal and factual research. Internet-based research shares many of the advantages of research using CD-ROMs. First, with an Internet connection and a laptop computer the law library becomes instantly portable. Second, the researcher can search for information by citation or by conduct a full-text search. Third, Internet-based research is becoming increasingly cost effective and sometimes, aside from the cost of the Internet connection itself, is free.

The major law-related Internet based research providers fall into two general categories. The first are commercial operations that charge a fee for their services, such as Lexis, Westlaw, and Loislaw. The second includes various governmental agencies educational institutions, and private enterprises that provide both primary and secondary resources at minimal or even no cost.

a. The Major Commercial Databases: Lexis, Westlaw, and LoisLaw

Until recently, Lexis and Westlaw were the only two major competing sources for on-line legal information. In 1996, LoisLaw joined them as a lower cost Internet-based alternative. All three services are accessed through their Internet site. To use any one of the three, a law firm must pay a subscription fee.

(1) Lexis

Lexis
An on-line legal database containing court decisions and statutes from the entire country, as well as secondary authority; a competitor to Westlaw.

The **Lexis** database includes the full text of federal and state court cases, statutes, and administrative regulations and of various specialized legal publications. The inclusion of Shepard's citations makes Lexis particularly useful to a researcher. Shepard's in FULL format provides the same information that can be obtained from the print volumes. You use Shepard's in KWIC format to check the accuracy of your case citation and to locate cases that directly affect your case's validity as precedent.

(2) Westlaw

Westlaw
An on-line legal database containing court decisions and statutes from the entire country, as well as secondary authority; a competitor to Lexis.

Westlaw covers the same types of materials contained in the Lexis database. Perhaps the most significant difference is that in addition to the full text of appellate court cases, Westlaw contains the headnotes and key numbers that appear in West's National Reporter System. This feature can simplify the search process for some users and makes it easier to coordinate the results with materials gathered from West's regular publications.

To verify the continuing validity of court decisions, Westlaw also includes KeyCite, a service similar to Shepard's. In Westlaw you can also search for additional cases on the basis of West key numbers.

(3) LoisLaw

LoisLaw is the newest entrant into on-line delivery of legal researching materials. While the materials contained in its database are not nearly as extensive as those you can find in Lexis and Westlaw, the service is also considerably less expensive. LoisLaw does contain all of the primary researching material from the federal and state systems, and is constantly adding new sources of information, such as treatises and news sources.

LoisLaw includes GlobalCite as its citation verification service. Once you have completed a search, you click on the GlobalCite button and LoisLaw produces a list of all primary and secondary materials in its database that contain a reference to your search result.

LoisLaw
An on-line legal database containing court decisions and statutes from the entire country. While its coverage of other legal materials is not as extensive as that of Westlaw and Lexis, it is also less expensive.

b. Other Internet-Based Resources

Within the last five years, there has been an explosion of legal materials on the Internet. The **Internet** is a worldwide network of networks—that is, a number of smaller regional networks all linked together. The Internet has been likened to the superhighways that connect large cities. From these large cities smaller freeways link smaller towns, where travelers move on slower, narrower side streets.

Internet
A worldwide network of computer networks.

Many Internet sites contain legal materials, such as federal statutes, regulations, and Supreme Court opinions. The federal government, as well as many state and local governments, now maintains **web sites**, where they publish official documents on their **web pages**. In addition to combining text, pictures, and sometimes even sound, these web pages often contain **hypertext links** to other web pages with related information.

Hypertext links
Computer codes that, when clicked on with a mouse, connect the user to other web pages with related information.

The major newspapers and television networks have web sites that cover law-related news. In the future we expect to see even more materials available through the Internet. However, while most of the information on the Internet is now free, it is not always as reliable or complete as the materials accessed through commerial providers such as Lexis, Westlaw, and LoisLaw.

2. Computer Search Techniques

Fortunately, the same general principles apply to all computer searches, whether they are done using a commercial service such as Lexis or Westlaw, or other Internet-based sources. The most difficult part of computerized research is learning how to define and limit the nature of the search. You would not begin traditional legal research by going to the law library and simply paging through the books in the order that they appear on the shelf. You would first think of key terms to look for in the appropriate legal indexes. Similarly, when you approach the computer terminal, you should already have carefully thought out the nature of the issues and have identified key words or phrases that will become the basis of your computer search. Although the computer can process information at dazzling speeds, computerized research can still be expensive. Also, the old computer adage "garbage in, garbage out" is particularly applicable to computerized legal research. Because commercial on-line services often charge by the minute or by the search, you should develop your research strategy before you actually sign on.

a. Determining Which Database to Use

If you have access to Lexis, Westlaw, or Loislaw, you will probably utilize one of these commercial services because they are generally more reliable and up to date than web sites on the Internet. However, once you have decided to use one of these service providers, you need to determine which of their many databases you wish to search. For example, if you are searching for court cases, you can search a particular district or circuit court in a specific state, all courts within a particular state, or all state courts in all fifty states. Then you have to decide if you also want to search federal court decisions and, if so, in which states or circuits.

When you first sign on to one of the commercial databases, you will be asked to designate which database you wish to use. Although the list of databases or "libraries" you can choose from will be shown on the computer screen, it is a good idea to make your decision before you go on-line.

You should limit your search to the smallest database that will accomplish your goal. Searching in too large a database, for example selecting all state cases when you are only looking for Florida case law, can result in extra on-line charges and may cause you to retrieve a very sizeable and therefore unmanageable list of cases.

Web browser
A computer program that allows users to access and search the web with the click of a mouse.

If you are using other sources on the Internet, you can "surf the web" to locate legal databases. This surfing is done through a **web browser program**, such as Netscape or Microsoft Explorer. These browsers give you access to many popular **search engines**, such as Google, Excite, Yahoo, and AltaVista. However, while all search engines are intended to perform the same task, each goes about it in a slightly different way, and they often produce very different results.

Search engine
A computer program that allows the user to retrieve web documents that match the key words entered by the searcher.

b. Searching within a Database

One of the main advantages of using a computerized database is that you are not limited to indexes. Instead, you can search the full text of the statutes court opinions, and other materials contained in the on-line database. There are two main methods for conducting **full-text searches** in a computerized database. The first is known as terms and connectors. To use that method, you must first think of terms to describe your legal issues and then connect those terms with Boolean operators, such as *or* and *and*, or proximity connectors. The second method is known as natural language. When you use that method, you simply tell the computer what you want it to find using a normal English sentence.

Full-text search
A computer search that identifies every place in which the search term appears in the actual text of the document being searched.

(1) Terms and connectors

There are two basic steps in using the terms and connectors approach. First, you must determine which words best describe the legal issue you are researching. Then you must connect those words. The most critical step in this process is the first one: entering key words and phrases that tell the computer for what it is to search. Because the cost of computer research is often based on the number of searches conducted, there is a clear incentive to be as prepared as possible before the meter starts running.

The two most common errors in conducting computerized research are making your search request too general, resulting in hundreds of cases, or making it too narrow, potentially eliminating the very case you want. For example, if you instruct the computer to search for a single key word, frequently you will get back an overwhelming number of cases, with many of them not even relevant to your legal issue. For example, a list of all cases that include a term as general as *negligence* is not helpful. One solution is to substitute narrower terms, such as *legal malpractice*. Also you can search for combinations of terms appearing together within a specifically defined space, such as *assumption* and *risk* appearing together or *store, wet, floor*, and *negligent* all appearing within the same paragraph.

The second problem, finding too few cases, usually occurs when too specific a term is used. For example, if you are searching for cases dealing with malpractice by a pediatric oncologist for failure to diagnose leukemia, you could certainly search by typing in *pediatric oncologist*. However, if there is a case directly on point but the court referred to the defendant simply as a pediatrician, then you would not find it. Therefore, you should always enter synonyms. In this example your search might be for *pediatrician* or *pediatric oncologist* or *physician* or *doctor* or *surgeon*.

In addition to using synonyms, in most computer databases you can also broaden your search by asking the computer to locate any word with a specific root, such as *pediatric*. In Westlaw and Lexis you do this by using the root expander: !. If you typed in *pediatric!* in either Lexis or Westlaw, you would get cases referring to *pediatric* or *pediatrician*. Other services, such as LoisLaw, use the asterisk (*) as the root expander. Therefore, in LoisLaw you would type *pediatric**. Be careful with root expanders. Entering the search *child!* (or *child** in LoisLaw) would get you references to *child* and *children*, but it would also retrieve *childish, childhood, childlike*, and so on.

Once you have determined the words to use, you must select your connectors. There are two types of connectors, Boolean (or logical) and proximity. The two most common Boolean connectors are *or* and *and*. You use or to find alternatives, such as in the example given above of *pediatrician* or *pediatric oncologist* or *physician*. You use *and* to require that both terms appear somewhere within the opinion: *pediatrician and negligence*.

Please note that in all three main commercial providers you can use the word *or* to indicate alternatives. However, in Westlaw a space also equals *or*. Therefore, in Lexis or LoisLaw the search *pediatric oncologist* would find the phrase *"pediatric oncologist."* In Westlaw the same search would find cases that contained either the word *"pediatric"* or the word *"oncologist."* In any of the three systems you can ensure that you are searching for a phrase by including the words in quotation marks: *"pediatric oncologist."*

As indicated above, the use of *and* will require that both terms occur somewhere within the opinion. However, to ensure that the terms are related to each other, you should use a proximity connector, such as w/s or w/p for within the same sentence or paragraph. For the "s" or "p" you can also substitute a precise number, such as w/10 to find two terms that occur within ten words of each

PRACTICAL TIP

When using the terms and connectors method of searching, you will often find yourself with either too few or too many cases.

If you find too few or no cases:

- ■ If you found no cases, the first thing to do is to check your spelling. If you typed *grandfater* when you meant *grandfather*, you will get no search results.
- ■ Run your search in a larger database. For example, if you were searching in the database that covered cases from only the state's highest court, expand your search to cases from all of the courts of that state.
- ■ Either eliminate some terms or use less-restrictive terms. Instead of *poodle*, search for *dog*. Instead of *dog*, search for *pet*.
- ■ Use less-restrictive connectors. Instead of w/10, use w/25. Instead of w/p, use "and."
- ■ Use more synonyms. Instead of *doctor*, use "*doctor or physician or surgeon or medical.*"

If you find too many cases:

- ■ Run the search in a smaller database. If you were looking at all state courts, change to the highest state courts or to all courts in a specific state.
- ■ Add additional terms or use more-restrictive terms. For example, change *negligence* to *malpractice* and add the term *legal*.
- ■ Use more-restrictive connectors. Change a w/p to a w/s.
- ■ Add a date restriction to find just the most recent cases.

other. Some Internet services, including LoisLaw, use the proximity connector "near." Depending on the service, "near" may mean anything between ten and fifty words. In LoisLaw "near" by itself means within twenty words. You can also specify an exact number. For example, "near2" requires the terms to be within two words of each other.

Finally, the computer will allow you to limit your search so that you retrieve only cases decided before or after a certain date or opinions authored by a particular judge. This power to limit your request means that you can perform searches that would be far too time consuming if using conventional means. Imagine trying to use the hardbound reporters to find all cases decided by a particular judge, such as Justice Scalia, and involving a specific issue, such as freedom of religion. A task that would take hours using books only can be done in seconds using a computerized on-line service.

Once you have entered a terms and connectors search, you will be presented with a list of cases, arranged by most recent case first, that match your search criteria. Keep in mind that the computer can work only with the information you give it. As noted above, the use of synonyms is crucial if you want to retrieve all cases that deal with a similar fact pattern.

(2) Natural language

Both Lexis and Westlaw also include a "natural language query" method. You can phrase your search request as a normal English sentence, and the computer program will translate it into the type of search request the computer can understand. For example, for the problem discussed above you could type:

> When can a pediatric oncologist be sued for malpractice because of a failure to diagnose leukemia?

Unlike a terms and connectors search, in a natural language search there is no requirement that every term (not connected with *or*) be found in every case. Rather, the computer first evaluates the search, looking for the most unique terms, and then lists those cases that have the greatest number of those terms. Finally, it ranks the results by relevance; that is, the first case listed will be the case the computer determines will most likely answer the question you asked.

(3) Variation among services

One of the challenges in conducting on-line research is that the various on-line researching services have not developed a uniform method for conducting a search. For example, as noted above, in both Westlaw and Lexis, the exclamation point is used as a root expander. However, LoisLaw uses the asterisk for the same purpose. As another example, in AltaVista, a popular general search engine, simple searches are essentially treated like natural language searches, and the results are listed with those documents contained the most unique terms listed first. To make a term mandatory, you insert a "+" before the word. When in doubt about how to conduct a search, read the help section for that service.

3. Updating with Lexis, Westlaw, and LoisLaw

Another major advantage of using computer programs is the ease with which you can update your research. Using the electronic version of Shepard's is much simpler than using the books and supplemental pamphlets. You simply type in

NETNOTE

There are various search engines that can assist you with your Internet legal research. Two that have been designed specifically for legal research include

www.lawcrawler.com and

http://gsulaw.gsu.edu/metaindex.

the citation, and the results from all volumes of Shepard's, including the pamphlet updates, are automatically displayed for you. You can also limit the displayed results to cases that negatively treated the cited opinion or that deal with topics from specific headnotes in the cited case. In Westlaw, KeyCite performs a similar function, while LoisLaw use GlobalCite.

4. Beyond Researching Primary Authority

Westlaw and Lexis are becoming increasingly useful because of the types of information they store in addition to federal and state statutes and court decisions. For example, in the Nexis part of Lexis a researcher can find full-text versions of news articles from major newspapers, jury verdicts, secretary of state filings, and asset information. While legal researchers have traditionally relied on primary law sources, these other sources are becoming increasingly important. Because most cases settle and hence never make it to a trial court, let alone an appellate court, you may not be able to find a published court opinion discussing the product that harmed your client. However, by searching news articles you may find that the product manufacturer recently settled a similar case.

If a lawyer has access to a commercial service, such as Lexis, Westlaw, or LoisLaw, and does not use it to update research, that may be grounds for a malpractice action.

Legal Reasoning Exercise

PRACTICAL TIP

When deciding whether to research state or federal case law, remember that even state law issues can end up in federal court under diversity jurisdiction.

2. Assume you work for a law firm in Pennsylvania. One of your firm's clients, Melba Street, had a pet poodle, Suzie, whom she dearly loved. She left the poodle one weekend at the local kennel. On Saturday a new kennel worker accidentally let Suzie loose in the fenced-in yard with Butch, a vicious German shepard. Unfortunately, that was the end of Suzie. Melba would like to sue the kennel for the emotional distress she suffered in having her pet killed.

a. What terms and connectors search would you construct to try to find cases that would indicate whether she can recover for her emotional distress?

b. What natural language search would you construct?

1. Identify Search Terms.

2. Check Secondary Authority (Optional).
   ■ Look for references to relevant statutes and court opinions.

3. Decide Whether to Research State or Federal Law or Both.

4. Check Statutes and Their Pocket Parts.
   ■ Look for cases that have interpreted the statute.
   ■ Look for references to administrative regulations.

5. Check Court Opinions.
   ■ Check for any references to relevant statutes and other court opinions.
   ■ Note the relevant headnote topics and key numbers.
     – Use them to find more cases in the digests.
     – Use them to find more cases in Shepard's.

6. Update Your Research.
   ■ Check the pocket parts.
   ■ Use Shepard's.
   ■ Check the digest interim supplement and recent hardbound volumes and the advance sheets of regional reporters for recent cases.
   ■ Use on-line services, such as Lexis, Westlaw, and LoisLaw.

Figure D-8   Summary Checklist for Legal Research

E. THE INTERRELATIONSHIP OF RESEARCHING MATERIALS

It may seem that there is a lot to learning how to conduct legal research—and there is. However, the more researching you do, the more comfortable you will become with the process. Also always keep in mind one of the major tricks of legal researching: Once you have found *one* relevant authority, you can proceed from there just by following up on the leads that your first authority gives you. For example, if you find a relevant section in Am. Jun. 2d, the footnotes will give you references to the A.L.R. and to cases. Even if none of the cases is from your jurisdiction, look one of them up in a regional reporter. Read the headnotes, and write down the appropriate key numbers. You can then go to your state's digest to find cases from your state. Figure D-8 contains a summary checklist for conducting legal research.

SUMMARY

The goal of legal research is to find relevant primary authority, court opinions, and enacted law, such as statutes and regulations. Secondary sources, such as legal encyclopedias and law review articles, can provide valuable background information.

The first step in legal research is to identify search terms. If you are unfamiliar with the area of law, you may next want to consult secondary sources. However, you can also go directly to primary authority. Never forget to update your research by consulting pocket parts and supplements, by checking Shepard's, and, if available, by using on-line resources, such as the commercial providers and other Internet-based sources.

Computer-assisted research programs are becoming more sophisticated, and the number of decided cases continues to increase. Thus, the need for legal researchers to become proficient in computer-assisted research also continues to grow.

REVIEW QUESTIONS

Pages 661 through 664

1. What is your main goal when conducting legal research?
2. In what type of books can you read general background information on a particular legal topic?
3. What is the difference between primary and secondary authority?
4. What are TAPP and TARP, and how do they aid a legal researcher?

Pages 664 through 674

5. What are the two major legal encyclopedias? In what ways are they the same, and how do they differ?
6. Why should you never end your research with an encyclopedia?
7. What is a law review, and what types of articles does it contain?
8. How do you locate relevant law review articles?
9. How does the A.L.R. differ from an encyclopedia?
10. Why do you think the general rule is that it is appropriate to cite to a law review article but not to an encyclopedia?

Pages 675 through 694

11. When researching primary authority, should you generally begin your research with statutes or court opinions? Why?
12. What makes an annotated statutory code "annotated"?
13. How are digest summaries and headnotes similar? What is the function of each?
14. Assume you are researching the topic of whether minors can get out of their contractual obligations and that you have found a New Hampshire case directly on point. That case's third headnote lists the topic as Contracts 211. How would you go about locating a Kansas case dealing with that same issue?

Pages 694 through 707

15. What is the difference between saying a case has been reversed and saying it has been overruled?
16. When using the digest topic method, what steps do you need to take to make sure your research is up to date?
17. What are the three main reasons for using Shepard's?
18. In Shepard's what is subsequent history, and what is the treatment of a case?
19. In Shepard's, to what do the terms *citing case* and *cited case* refer?
20. Your boss has asked you to Shepardize 89 N.E. 542.
    a. What is your first step? What do you do next?

b. In Shepardizing you found the following information. What does it mean? Is there any history of the case? How do you know?

—542—
(203Mas364)
f90NE^{2}864
94NE^{1}691
129NE718

21. Your boss has asked you to Shepardize a case giving you only the official citation. Describe the steps you would take to Shepardize the case.

22. Your boss knows of a California case, *Tarasoff v. The Regents of the University of California*, 551 P.2d 334 (Cal. 1976), that stands for the proposition that if a psychiatrist knows a patient is a threat to another person, the psychiatrist must warn that person. If you want to find out whether any New York cases have followed the *Tarasoff* decision, which Shepard's would you use and why? (*Note:* California is in the Pacific region, and New York is in the Northeast region.)

23. Last month the police saw your client Bill Johnson exchange money for a packet of white powder. Without a warrant the police placed an electronic tracking device on your client's car. The police then followed him to an alley where he handed the packet to a woman who gave him money in return. They arrested your client for selling illegal drugs. Your boss would like to make a motion to have the evidence excluded by arguing that it was unlawful for the police to put the electronic tracking device on your client's car without a warrant.

Assume that in the course of your research you have found *Commonwealth v. Boven*, 413 Mass. 755, 306 N.E.2d 222 (1986). The headnotes in the North Eastern Reporter, Second Series, appear as follows:

1. Searches and Seizures [Key] 7(26)
   Defendant did not have standing to challenge X-ray search of suitcase, where the suitcase belonged to his co-defendant.
2. Searches and Seizures [Key] 7(10)
   Utilization of electronic tracking device, without prior court approval, may be justified by probable cause and exigent circumstances.
3. Criminal Law [Key] 1144.13
   On appeal from jury conviction, Court must view evidence, both direct and circumstantial, and all reasonable inferences to be drawn therefrom.
4. Criminal Law [Key] 696(1)
   Trial court did not err in failing to grant defense motion to strike testimony of agent, although all of agent's investigatory notes had been destroyed.

Using the information *from the headnotes*, describe how you would go about finding out whether there are any other court opinions in Massachusetts dealing with the subject of when police officers can place electronic surveillance devices on cars without first obtaining a warrant. Describe the steps you would take in as much detail as possible. Include a description of how you would bring your research up to date, using both the digest and the Shepard's approaches.

24. In updating your research what is the advantage of using the digest method over Shepardizing? In using Shepard's over the digests?

25. Your boss asks you to Shepardize *Brown v. Smith*, 322 Mass. 89, 78 N.E.2d 640 (1946). You determine that headnotes 4 and 8 are most relevant to your client's problem. In Shepard's you find the following information:

—640—
99 N.E.2d^3 888
99 N.E.2d 904
q101 N.E.2d 44
102 N.E.2d^8 99
102 N.E.2d^1 301

Explain which citations you would look up, in what order, and why.

Pages 708 through 715

26. How does the use of on-line research differ from traditional book research?
27. What are the two main methods for conducting full-text research in an on-line database, and how do those two methods differ from each other?
28. You need to find cases dealing with free speech, and using the terms and connectors method, you type in the following search: *free speech*. How do you think Westlaw, Lexis, and Lioslaw would differ in the ways they would interpret that search request?
29. Your boss represents a client who was injured when his Handy Hardy riding tractor tipped over. You searched through the on-line sources that contained primary authority but did not find any appellate decisions involving the Handy Hardy riding tractor. In what other types of on-line databases might you want to search and why?

⚜ Appendix E

NetNotes

BUSINESS INFORMATION

Business ownership information, such as the names of the resident agent and the corporate officers—Go to *www.westlaw.com* (Westlaw) or *www.lexis.com* (Lexis).

The Electronic Data Gathering, Analysis, and Retrieval (EDGAR) system—Go to either *www.sec.gov/edgar.shtml* or *www.freeedgar.com*.

Information on the Americans with Disabilities Act—Go to the U.S. Department of Justice site at *www.usdoj.gov/crt/ada/adahom1.htm* or the Americans with Disabilities Act Document Center at *www.jan.wvu.edu/links/adalinks.htm*.

CITATION RULES

You can find additional material, examples, updates, and a Frequently Asked Questions list at the ALWD Citation Manual's web site, *www.alwd.org*.

"Introduction to Basic Legal Citation," an on-line tutorial designed to teach the Bluebook rules—Go to *www.law.cornell.edu/citation*.

COMMERCIAL ON-LINE PROVIDERS

Lexis—*www.lexis.com*.

Westlaw—*www.westlaw.com*.

Findlaw—*www.findlaw.com*.

VersusLaw—*www.versuslaw.com*.

LoisLaw—*www.loislaw.com*.

GOVERNMENT SITES

The EEOC home page is located at *www.eeoc.gov.*

The FBI maintains a web site at *www.fbi.gov.*

The U.S. Department of Justice maintains statistics about crimes and victims at *www.ojp.usdoj.gov/bjs.*

GRAMMAR

Grammar Bytes! at *www.chompchomp.com/menu.htm.*

Help organized by level: word and sentence, paragaph, and paper at *www.ccc.commnet.edu/grammar/.*

INFORMATION ON THE COURT SYSTEM

Map of the federal circuits with links to their cases—Go to *www.law.emory.edu/FEDCTS.* Note that FEDCTS must be typed in all caps.

Biographies of the U.S. Supreme Court justices—Go to *http://supremecourtus.gov/about/biographiescurrent.pdf.*

Information on specific state courts—Go to the National Center for State Courts, *www.ncsconline.org/D_KIS/info_court_web_sites.html.*

Information on federal courts—Go to either the federal judiciary home page at *www.uscourts.gov* or the Federal Judicial Center home page at *www.fjc.gov.*

The U.S. Supreme Court—Go to *www.supremecourtus.gov.*

Read about and see video clips of current trials at *www.courttv.com.*

LEGAL ETHICS

Developments in legal ethics and links to the states' Rules of Professional Conduct or Code of Professional Responsibility and to their ethics opinions— Go to *www.law.cornell.edu/ethics* and *www.legalethics.com.*

You can locate the ABA Model Rules of Professional Conduct at *www.abanet.org/cpr/mrpc/mrpc_toc.html.*

LEGAL NEWS

Start at Findlaw: *www.findlaw.com.* Click on "Latest News."

LEGAL SEARCH ENGINES

There are various search engines that can assist you with your Internet legal research. Two that have been designed specifically for legal research are *www.lawcrawler.com* and *http://gsulaw.gsu.edu/metaindex*.

ORGANIZATIONS

American Arbitration Association—*www.adr.org*.

American Bar Association (ABA)—*www.abanet.org*.

American Civil Liberties Union—*www.aclu.org*.

Court Appointed Special Advocates (CASA)—*www.nationalcasa.org*.

PRIMARY MATERIAL

U.S. Supreme Court opinions dating back to the 1800s—Start at Findlaw: *www.findlaw.com*. On Findlaw's home page click on "US Law: Cases & Codes." Then click on "US Supreme Court - Opinions & Web Site."

Federal appellate court opinions—Start at Findlaw: *www.findlaw.com*. Click on "US Law: Cases & Codes." Click on "Federal and State Courts." Select your circuit.

State court opinions—Start at Findlaw: *www.findlaw.com*. Under "US Law: Cases & Codes" click on "States." Select your state.

Federal statutes and regulations—Start at Findlaw: *www.findlaw.com*. Click on "US Law: Cases & Codes." Select the US Code or the Code of Federal Regulations.

State statutes and regulations—Start at Findlaw: *www.findlaw.com*. Under "US Law: Cases & Codes" click on "States." Select your state.

Current information on federal legislation—A good source is *http://thomas .loc.gov*, provided by the Library of Congress. You can also find information on the legislative branch at *http://thomas.loc.gov/home/legbranch/legbranch.html*.

The Declaration of Independence—Go to the National Archives web site: *www.archives.gov/national_archives_experience/charters/declaration.html*.

The Constitution at *www.archives.gov/national_archives_experience/charters/ constitution.html* or *http://caselaw.findlaw.com/data/constitution/articles.html*.

The Bill of Rights at *www.archives.gov/national_archieves_experience/charters/ bill_of_rights.html* or *http://caselaw.findlaw.com/data/Constitution/amendments .html*.

TORTS

Expert witnesses—A feature of Findlaw, go to *http://marketcenter/findlaw.com/expert_witness.html*.

Medical information—You can find current medical news at *www.medscape.com*. The Cancer Web at *cancerweb.ncl.ac.uk/omd* contains an on-line medical dictionary.

Consumer Product Safety Commission—*www.cpsc.gov*.

UNIFORM LAWS

The Uniform Commercial Code as revised through 1992—Go to *www.law.cornell.edu/ucc/ucc.table.html*.

The Uniform Probate Code—Go to *www.law.cornell.edu/uniform/probate.html*.

Various uniform laws governing the family, such as the Uniform Child Custody Jurisdiction Act, the Uniform Interstate Family Support Act, the Uniform Premarital Agreement Act, and the Uniform Marriage and Divorce Act—Go to *www.law.cornell.edu/uniform/vol9.html*.

Glossary

Abstract A condensed history of the title to real property, which includes the chain of ownership and a record of all liens, taxes, or other encumbrances that may impair the title.

Abuse of process Misusing the criminal or civil court process.

Accessory Also referred to as an **accomplice**; a person who assists the principal in the preparation of the crime.

Accessory after the fact A person who aids the principal after the commission of the crime.

Accomplice Also known as a *principal in the second degree;* a person who assists the principal with the crime or with the preparation of the crime.

Accord and satisfaction An accord is an agreement to do something different than originally promised. The satisfaction is the performance of the accord.

Acquit To determine that a criminal defendant is not guilty of the crime with which he or she is charged.

Active voice A form of writing where the subject of the sentence does the acting; opposite of **passive voice.**

Actual cause Also known as **cause in fact**; this is measured by the "but for" standard: But for the defendant's actions, the plaintiff would not have been injured.

Actual damages See **Compensatory damages.**

Actus reus Bad act.

Adhesion contract A contract formed where the weaker party has no realistic bargaining power. Typically a form contract is offered on a "take it or leave it" basis.

Adjudicatory hearing A mechanism through which parties to a dispute can present arguments and evidence about their case to an administrative law judge.

Administrative law Rules and regulations created by administrative agencies.

Administrative law judge Another name for a **hearing officer.**

Administrative regulations Rules, regulations, orders, and decisions created by administrative agencies under their authority to interpret specific statutes.

Administrator/administratrix A person appointed by the court to carry out the directions and requests of someone's will.

ADR See **Alternative dispute resolution.**

Advance sheets The first printing of a court decision before it appears in a hardbound reporter.

Adverse possession A transfer of real property rights that occurs after someone other than the owner has had actual, open, adverse, and exclusive use of the property for a statutorily determined number of years.

Affinity Persons related to the decedent by marriage.

Affirm A decision is affirmed when the litigants appeal the trial court decision and the higher court agrees with what the lower court has done.

Affirmative defense A defense whereby the defendant offers new evidence to avoid judgment.

Agency adoption An adoption in which a licensed agency assumes responsibility for screening adoptive parents and matching them with available children.

Agent Someone who has the power to act in the place of another.

Alibi defense   A defense requiring proof that the defendant could not have been at the scene of the crime.

Alien corporation   A corporation formed in another country.

Alimony   Also known as **maintenance** or **support**; financial support and other forms of assistance required to supply the "necessities" of life.

Alternative dispute resolution (ADR)   Techniques for resolving conflicts that are alternatives to full-scale litigation. The two most common are **arbitration** and **mediation**.

American Association for Paralegal Education (AAfPE)   A national organization of paralegal programs that promotes high standards for paralegal education.

American Bar Association (ABA)   A national voluntary organization of lawyers.

American Bar Association approval   A voluntary process; approval by the American Bar Association indicates that a paralegal program meets ABA standards.

American Jurisprudence Second (Am. Jur. 2d)   A general legal encyclopedia that summarizes the entire body of American law.

American Law Reports (ALR)   ALR contains the full text of leading court opinions, followed by a discussion of the issue with references to cases from around the country. Only selected topics are covered, but they are covered in more depth than you will find in an encyclopedia.

Amicus curiae   Someone who, with the court's permission, intervenes in litigation, usually on appeal, to influence the decision. Also known as a **friend of the court.**

Analogize   To find similarities between two situations.

Analogous   Similar; analogous cases involve similar facts and rules of law.

Annotated codes   Private publications that include not only the statutes arranged by subject matter but also editorial material, such as legislative history and summaries of court decisions that have interpreted the statutes.

Annotated statutes   See **Annotated codes.**

Annotations   Editorial features, such as court decision summaries and references to other sources of information, added by the editor to assist the researcher.

Annulment   A legal (or religious) judgment that a valid marriage never existed.

Answer   The defendant's reply to the complaint. It may contain statements of denial, admission, or lack of knowledge and affirmative defenses.

Antecedent   When a pronoun (*hers, her, his, him, it, its, them, their, theirs*) substitutes for a noun that has preceded it, the noun is known as an antecedent.

Anti-heart-balm statute   A law that prohibits lawsuits for such things as breach of a promise of marriage, alienation of affection, and seduction of a person over the legal age of consent.

Appeal   To ask a higher court to review the actions of a lower court.

Appealable issues   Questions that can form the basis for an appeal.

Appellant or **petitioner**   The party in a lawsuit who has initiated an appeal.

Appellate brief   An attorney's written argument presented to an appeals court, setting forth a statement of the law as it should be applied to the client's facts.

Appellate courts   Courts that determine whether lower courts have made errors of law.

Appellate jurisdiction   The power of a higher court to review and modify the decision of a lower court.

Appellee or **respondent**   The party in a lawsuit against whom an appeal has been filed.

Appropriation   An intentional unauthorized exploitive use of another person's personality, name, or picture for the defendant's benefit.

Arbitration   An ADR mechanism whereby the parties submit their disagreement to a third party whose decision is binding.

Arraignment   A criminal proceeding at which the court informs the defendant of the charges being brought against him or her and the defendant enters a plea.

Arrest   Occurs when the police restrain a person's freedom and charge the person with a crime.

Arrest warrant   A court order directing the arrest of a person.

Arson   The malicious burning of the house or property of another.

Articles of incorporation   The primary document needed to form a corporation.

Artisan's lien   The right to retain an interest in property until a worker has been paid for his or her labor.

Assault   An intentional act that creates a reasonable apprehension of an immediate harmful or offensive physical contact.

Assigned counsel   A private attorney paid by the state on a contractual basis to represent an indigent client.

Assignee   A person to whom contract rights are assigned.

Assignment   The transfer by one of the original parties to the contract of part or all of his or her interest to a third party.

Assignor   A person who assigns contract rights.

Assumption In logic, a belief that justifies one in arguing a conclusion.

Assumption of the risk Voluntarily and knowingly subjecting oneself to danger.

At-will employment When an employee has not signed a formal contract with the employer governing the employment relationship.

Attachment If a creditor either possesses the collateral or has a signed **security agreement,** and gave something of value and if the debtor has rights in the collateral, the creditor's interest in the security is said to have attached.

Attorney Lawyer; a person licensed by a court to practice law.

Attorney-client privilege A rule of evidence that prevents an attorney or a paralegal from being compelled to testify about confidential client information.

Attorney general The chief legal officer of the federal or a state government.

Bail Money or something else of value that is held by the government to ensure the defendant's appearance in court.

Bailee The party taking temporary control of personal property during a bailment.

Bailiff An officer of the court who is responsible for maintaining order in the courtroom.

Bailment A temporary transfer of personal property to someone other than the owner for a specified purpose.

Bailor The owner of the personal property that is being temporarily transferred as part of a bailment.

Bankruptcy judges Appointed for set terms, they handle bankruptcy matters.

Battered woman's or spouse's syndrome Being the victim of repeated attacks, self-defense sometimes is allowed to the victim, even when the victim is not in immediate danger.

Battery An intentional act that creates a harmful or offensive physical contact. Can form the basis for either a tort or a criminal action.

Bearer paper Has written on its front a statement that it is payable to cash or payable to the bearer, or has a signature on the back, causing it to be indorsed in blank.

Bench trial A trial conducted without a jury.

Beneficiary The person named in a will, insurance policy, or trust who receives a benefit.

Bequest Also known as a **legacy;** a gift of personal property in a will.

Beyond a reasonable doubt The standard of proof used in criminal trials. The proof must be so conclusive and complete that all reasonable doubts regarding the facts are removed from the jurors' minds.

Bilateral contract A contract where a promise is exchanged for a promise.

Bill A proposed law as presented to a legislature.

Bill of Rights The first ten amendments to the U.S. Constitution.

Black letter law Generally accepted legal principles.

Bluebook A book originally written by a group of law students to provide a uniform method for citations in law reviews; contains detailed rules for all forms of citation.

Board of directors The group responsible for the management of a corporation.

Boilerplate Standard language found in a particular type of legal document.

Bona fide occupational qualification (BFOQ) A defense to an overt discrimination claim, alleging that the qualification is necessary to the essence of the business operation.

Booking The process after arrest that includes taking the defendant's personal information, giving the defendant an opportunity to read and sign a *Miranda* card, and allowing the defendant the opportunity to use a telephone.

Bribery Offering something of value to a public official with the purpose of influencing that official's actions.

Brief Either a short written summary of a court opinion or a written argument presented to a court. See **Appellate brief.**

Brief answer In a law office memorandum, the brief answer gives the reader a short, specific answer to the question presented.

Broad holding A statement of the court's decision in which the facts are either omitted or given in very general terms so that it will apply to a wider range of cases.

Burden of production The necessity to produce some evidence, but it need not be so strong as to convince the trier of fact of its truth.

Burden of proof The necessity of proving the truth of the matter asserted.

Bureau of National Affairs (BNA) A private publishing company that publishes legal materials, including United States Law Week.

Burglary Breaking into and entering a building with the intent of committing a felony.

"But for" standard See **Actual cause.**

Buyer in the ordinary course of business   Someone who buys a product in good faith and without knowledge that someone else has a security interest in the goods.

Canons of construction   General principles that guide the courts in their interpretation of statutes.

Capital crime   A crime for which the death sentence can be imposed.

Caption   The heading section of a pleading that contains the names of the parties, the name of the court, the title of the action, the docket or file number, and the name of the pleading.

Case briefing   A method for summarizing court opinions.

Case citation   Information that tells the reader the name of the case, where it can be located, the court that decided it, and the year it was decided. The Bluebook gives precise rules as to how case citations are to be written.

Case history   Either prior or subsequent procedural history of the case cited.

Case management   Managing the flow of paperwork involved in handling client cases.

Case of first impression   A type of case that the court has never faced before.

Case reporters   Books that contain appellate court decisions. There are both official and unofficial reporters.

Cause of action   A claim that based on the law and the facts is sufficient to support a lawsuit. If the plaintiff does not state a valid cause of action in the complaint, the court will dismiss it.

Cause in fact   See **Actual cause.**

Caveat emptor   Let the buyer beware.

Censure   A public or private statement that an attorney's conduct violated the code of ethics.

Certificated   The status of having received a certificate documenting that the person has successfully completed an educational program.

Certification   A method of recognizing accomplishment administered by nongovernmental bodies.

Certified   The status of being formally recognized by a nongovernmental organization for having met special criteria, such as fulfilling educational requirements and passing an exam, established by that organization.

Certified Legal Assistant   A registered trademark of the National Association of Legal Assistants.

Certiorari   See **Writ of certiorari.**

Challenge for cause   A method for excusing a prospective juror based on the juror's inability to serve in an unbiased manner.

Charging the jury   The judge informs the jurors of the law they need to know to make their decision.

Charitable immunity   The prohibition against suing charitable institutions.

Chattel   Personal property.

Check   A specialized form of a draft in which a bank depositor names a specific payee to whom funds are to be paid from the drawer's account.

Checks and balances   Division among governmental branches so that each branch acts as a check on the power of the other two, thereby maintaining a balance of power among the three branches.

Child abuse   Intentional harm to a child's physical or mental well-being.

Child neglect   The negligent failure to provide a child with the necessaries of life.

Child support   Money that the noncustodial parent contributes to assist the custodial parent in paying for a child's food, shelter, clothing, medical care, and education.

Citation   A stylized form for giving the reader information about a legal authority, generally including the name of the authority, its date, and specifics such as volume and page numbers to help the reader locate it. For court opinions, a citation includes the name of the case, where it can be located, the name of the court that decided it, and the year it was decided. A statutory citation is a formalized method for referring to a statute's chapter (or title) and section numbers. The Bluebook gives precise rules as to how citations are to be written. See **Bluebook.**

Cited case   The case you are Shepardizing.

Citing case   A case listed in Shepard's that cites your case.

Civil action   A lawsuit brought to enforce an individual right or gain payment for an individual wrong.

Civil law   Law that deals with harm to an individual.

Class action suit   A lawsuit brought by a person as a representative for a group of people who have been similarly injured.

Clear and convincing   An evidentiary standard that requires more than a preponderance of the evidence but less than beyond a reasonable doubt.

Clear title   Also known as **marketable title;** an ownership right that is free from encumbrances or other defects.

Clearly erroneous   Standard used by appellate courts when reviewing a trial court's findings of fact.

Client confidentiality   An ethical rule requiring that attorneys and paralegals maintain their clients' secrets.

Client trust account   A bank account used to hold money belonging to a client or to a third party.

Closely held corporation   A relatively small business operation in which one person or the members of a family own all the stock.

Closing statement An itemized allocation of all the costs and moneys exchanged among the various parties, including financial institutions and real estate brokers, when a property is sold.

Closing table A table located in digest volumes and pocket parts indicating the last volume and page numbers for the reporters included in that digest.

Code A compilation of federal or state statutes in which the statutes are organized by subject matter rather than by year of enactment.

Code of Federal Regulations (C.F.R.) A compilation of federal administrative regulations arranged by agency.

Code of Massachusetts Regulations A compilation of Massachusetts administrative regulations arranged by agency.

Codicil A supplement or addition to a will that modifies, explains, or adds to its provisions.

Codification The process of organizing statutes by subject matter.

Codification of the common law The process of legislative enactment of areas of the law previously governed solely by the common law.

Collateral heir One who has the same ancestors, but does not descend from the decedent.

Comma splice A type of run-on sentence; two independent clauses joined by a comma.

Commercial impracticability An argument that a contract has become too costly for one of the parties.

Commercial paper A written promise or order to pay a certain sum of money.

Committee hearing Legislative committees often hold public hearings where interested parties can testify about a proposed law. The transcript of the hearing becomes a part of the statute's legislative history.

Committee report When a legislative committee holds public hearings on proposed legislation, the result of those hearings is sometimes published in a committee report, which becomes part of the statute's legislative history.

Common law Law created by the courts.

Common-law marriage A marriage that has not been solemnized but in which the parties have mutually agreed to enter into a relationship in which they accept all the duties and responsibilities that correspond to those of marriage.

Community property states States that classify all property acquired by either the husband or the wife during the marriage, with the exception of gifts or inheritance, as marital property to be equally distributed between the spouses at the time of the divorce.

Comparative negligence A method for measuring the relative negligence of the plaintiff and the defendant, with a commensurate sharing of the compensation for the injuries.

Compensatory damages Money awarded to a plaintiff in payment for his or her actual losses. Compare **punitive damages**.

Complaint The pleading that begins a lawsuit.

Complete defense A defense that, if proven, relieves the defendant of all criminal responsibility.

Compulsory joinder When a person must be brought into a lawsuit as either a plaintiff or a defendant.

Concluding paragraph The final paragraph in a written legal analysis that summarizes the writer's conclusions.

Concurrent conflict of interest Simultaneously representing adverse clients.

Concurrent jurisdiction When more than one court has jurisdiction to hear a case.

Concurring opinion An opinion that agrees with the majority's result but disagrees with its reasoning.

Conditional fee estate The current owner of the land retains ownership only as long as certain conditions are met.

Cone of silence See **Ethical wall**.

Confidentiality The ethical rule prohibiting attorneys and paralegals from disclosing information regarding a client or a client's case.

Conflict of interest The ethical rule prohibiting attorneys and paralegals from working for opposing sides in a case.

Conjunctive adverbs Examples include *also, consequently, furthermore, however, moreover, nevertheless, then,* and *therefore.* These should not be used to join two independent clauses.

Consanguinity See **Kindred**.

Consequential damages See **Special damages**.

Consideration Something of value exchanged to form the basis of a contract; each side must give consideration for a valid contract to exist.

Consortium See **Loss of consortium**.

Conspiracy An agreement to commit an unlawful act.

Constitutional court A court established by Article III of the U.S. Constitution.

Constitutional law The study of the U.S. Constitution, the legal framework it established, and the rights it protects.

Constructive Not factually true, but accepted by the courts as being legally true.

Constructive delivery When actual delivery is impossible but the court decides that enough was done to prove intent to relinquish title and control.

Constructive eviction An act by a landlord that makes the premises unfit or unsuitable for occupancy.

Constructive knowledge Not actual knowledge but the knowledge the person should have if reasonable care is taken to be informed.

Contextual analysis A form of statutory analysis in which meaning is inferred from the statement of legislative purpose and other sections of the statute.

Contingency fee Attorney compensation as a percentage of the amount recovered rather than a flat amount of money or an hourly fee.

Contract An agreement supported by consideration.

Contract reformation An equitable remedy that allows the courts to "rewrite" contract provisions.

Contributory negligence Negligence by the plaintiff that contributed to his or her injury. Normally, any finding of contributory negligence acts as a complete bar to the plaintiff's recovery. See **Comparative negligence**.

Conversion The taking of someone else's property with the intent of permanently depriving the owner; the civil side of theft.

Coordinating conjunction A coordinating conjunction can join two independent clauses; examples include *and, but, for, nor, or*, and *yet*.

Copyright An author or artist's right to control the use of his or her works.

Corporation A business entity formed by an association of shareholders.

Corpus Juris Secundum (C.J.S.) West's law encyclopedia. Contains cross-references to West digest topics and key numbers.

Count In a complaint, one cause of action.

Counterclaim A claim by the defendant against the plaintiff. A compulsory counterclaim relates to the facts alleged in the complaint. A permissive counterclaim can relate to an entirely different factual setting.

Court A unit of the judicial branch of government that has the authority to decide legal disputes.

Court clerk A court official responsible for keeping the court files in proper condition and ensuring that the various motions filed by lawyers and the actions taken by judges are properly recorded.

Court commissioner A title given in some states to a public official with limited judicial powers.

Court of record A court where a permanent record is kept of the testimony, lawyers' remarks, and judges' rulings.

Court reporter A person trained to take a verbatim transcript of a courtroom proceeding or deposition.

Covenant not to compete A promise not to compete within a given geographical area for a specific time period.

Cover Finding substitute goods.

Crime An activity that has been prohibited by the legislature as violating a duty owed to society and hence prosecutable, with the possibility of resulting incarceration or the payment of a fine.

Criminal complaint A document charging a person with a crime.

Criminal justice system Used to refer to a combination of legislative, administrative, and judicial agencies that are involved in the development and enforcement of criminal law in the United States.

Criminal law Law that deals with harm to society as a whole.

Criminal procedure The way in which criminal prosecutions are handled; governed by the federal or state rules of criminal procedure.

Critical Legal Studies (CLS) An offshoot of legal realism that seeks to identify ways in which the law protects certain groups and ideas at the expense of others.

Cross-claim A claim by one defendant against another defendant or by one plaintiff against another plaintiff.

Cross-examination The questioning of an opposing witness.

Custodial interrogation Questioning that occurs after a defendant has been deprived of his or her freedom in a significant way.

Custody Occurs when the defendant has been deprived of freedom in a significant way.

Damages Monetary compensation, including compensatory, punitive, and nominal damages.

Deadly force A force that would cause serious bodily injury or death.

Decedent A person who died.

Deductive reasoning A form of logical reasoning based on a major premise, a minor premise, and a conclusion.

Deed The legal document that formally conveys title to the property to the new owner.

Defamation The publication of false statements that harm a person's reputation.

Defamation per se Remarks considered to be so harmful that they are automatically viewed as defamatory.

Default judgment A judgment entered against a party who fails to complete a required step, such as answering the complaint.

Defendant In a lawsuit, the person who is sued; in a criminal case, the person who is charged with a crime.

Defense A fact or legal argument that would relieve the defendant of liability in a civil case or guilt in a criminal case.

Delegatee A person who owes an obligation to the obligee in a contractual situation.

Delegation The transfer by one of the original parties to the contract of his or her obligations to a third party.

Delegator A person who delegates duties under a contract.

Demand letter A letter from an attorney demanding that some action be taken, with either an implicit or an explicit threat to take the matter to court if the requested action is not forthcoming.

Dependent clause A clause that contains a subject and a verb but that cannot stand alone, as it does not contain a complete thought. Dependent clauses always begin with subordinating conjunctions.

Deponent The person who is being asked questions at a deposition.

Deposition The pretrial oral questioning of a witness under oath.

Derogation of the common law Used to describe legislation that changes the common law.

Descendants Also known as issue; lineal heirs who descend from, or issue from, the decedent, such as children and grandchildren.

Detrimental reliance See **Promissory estoppel**.

Devise A gift of real estate that is given to someone through a will.

Dicta Plural of dictum.

Dictum A statement in a judicial opinion not necessary for the decision of the case.

Digest A book that contains court opinion headnotes arranged by subject matter.

Direct appellate review Occurs when the courts think a case is so significant that the middle step of going through an intermediate appellate court should be skipped; the case proceeds directly from a trial court to the highest appellate court.

Direct examination The questioning of your own witness.

Directed verdict A verdict ordered by a trial judge if the plaintiff fails to present a prima facie case or if the defendant fails to present a necessary defense.

Disability Under the Americans with Disabilities Act, a physical or mental impairment that substantially limits a major life activity. An individual with a disability is one who has such an impairment, has a record of such an impairment, or is regarded as having such an impairment.

Disaffirm The ability to take back one's contractual obligations.

Disbarment The revocation of an attorney's license.

Disclosure The intentional publication of embarrassing private affairs.

Discovery The modern pretrial procedure by which one party gains information from the adverse party.

Disillusionment See **divorce**.

Dismissal with prejudice A court order that ends a lawsuit; the suit cannot be refiled by the same parties.

Dismissal without prejudice A court order that ends a lawsuit; the suit can be refiled by the same parties.

Disparate impact The legal theory applied when the use of a neutral standard has a disproportionate impact on one protected group.

Disparate treatment The legal theory applied when a rejected applicant claims the reason for rejection was based on a discriminatory intent but the employer alleges a nondiscriminatory reason.

Disposition The result reached in a particular case.

Dissenting opinion An opinion that disagrees with the majority's decision and reasoning.

Distinguish To find differences (distinctions) between two situations.

Distinguishable Different; distinguishable cases involve dissimilar facts and/or rules of law.

District attorney An attorney appointed to prosecute crimes.

Diversity jurisdiction The power of the federal courts to hear matters of state law if the opposing parties are from different states and the amount in controversy exceeds $75,000.

Divided custody A situation in which the court separates the children so that each parent is awarded custody of one or more of the children.

Dividend A distribution of the corporate profit as ordered by the board of directors.

Divorce Also called disillusionment; a legal judgment that dissolves a marriage.

Doctrine of equitable distribution A system for distributing property acquired during a marriage on the basis of such factors as the contributions of the spouses, the length of the marriage, the age and health of the spouses, and their ability to make a living.

Doctrine of implied powers Powers not stated in the Constitution but that are necessary for Congress to carry out other, expressly granted powers.

Documents clerk Someone who organizes and files legal documents.

Domestic corporation A corporation doing business in its own state.

Donor Also known as a **grantor** or **settlor**; a person who creates a trust.

Double jeopardy A constitutional protection against being tried twice for the same crime.

Draft A three-party instrument in which the **drawer** orders the drawee, usually a bank, to pay money to the **payee**.

Dramshop laws Statutes making bar owners responsible if intoxicated patrons negligently injure third parties.

Drawee On the face of a check or draft, the party that is ordering payment to be made.

Drawer On the face of a check or draft, the party that is ordered to pay.

Due process Fifth and Fourteenth Amendment guarantees that notice and a hearing must be provided before depriving someone of property or liberty.

Durable power of attorney See **Health care proxy**.

Duress In criminal law, a defense requiring proof that force or a threat of force was used to cause a person to commit a criminal act. In contract law, pressure that is so great as to overwhelm the contracting party's ability to make a free choice.

Earnest money The money the buyer turns over to the real estate agent to be applied to the purchase price of property.

Easement A right to use property owned by another for a limited purpose.

Ejusdem generis A canon of construction meaning "of the same class."

Element A separable part of a statute that must be satisfied for the statute to apply.

Emancipated minor Someone who is still under the legal age of adulthood but who has nevertheless been released from parental authority and given the legal rights of an adult.

Eminent domain The power of government to take private property for public purposes.

Employee A person working for another. Compare **Independent contractor**.

En banc When an appellate court that normally sits in panels sits as a whole.

Enabling act A statute establishing and setting out the powers of an administrative agency.

Encumbrance A lien or other type of security interest that signifies that some other party has a legitimate claim to the property.

Entrapment A defense requiring proof that the defendant would not have committed the crime but for police trickery.

Equity Fairness; a court's power to do justice. Equity powers allow judges to take action when otherwise the law would limit their decisions to monetary awards. Equity powers include a judge's ability to issue an injunction and to order specific performance.

Escheat A reversion of property to the state when there are no heirs.

Escrow account A bank account used to hold money belonging to a client or a third party.

Estate An interest in or title to real property. In probate law, the total property of whatever kind, both real and personal, that a person owns at the time of his or her death.

Ethical wall Also known as a **screen** or **cone of silence**; a system developed to shield an attorney or a paralegal from a case that otherwise would create a conflict of interest.

Evict To remove a tenant from possession of rental property.

Evidence The way in which a question of fact is established. Evidence can consist of witness testimony or documents and exhibits. It is the proof presented at a trial.

Evolutionary approach An approach to constitutional interpretation in which judges seek to determine the underlying purpose that the drafters had in mind at the time they wrote the law and the modern-day option that best advances that purpose.

Exception An attorney's objection to a trial court's ruling in order to preserve it as grounds for an appeal.

Exclusionary rule A rule that states that evidence obtained in violation of an individual's constitutional rights cannot be used against that individual in a criminal trial.

Exclusive jurisdiction when only one court has the power to hear a case.

Exculpatory clause A provision that purports to waive liability.

Exculpatory evidence Evidence that suggests the defendant's innocence; opposite of **inculpatory evidence**.

Execute To perform or to sign; in contract law an executed contract is one that has been completely performed.

Executor/executrix A person appointed by the testator to carry out the directions and requests in his or her will.

Executory contract A contract that has not been fully performed.

Exemplary damages See **Punitive damages**.

Exhaustion The requirement that certain preliminary steps be taken.

Exhaustion of administrative remedies The requirement that relief be sought from an administrative agency before proceeding to court.

Exigent circumstances   Generally, an emergency situation that allows a search to proceed without a warrant.

Explanatory parenthetical   A parenthetical located at the end of a case citation containing information about the case.

Express contracts   Contracts that are formed through words, either oral or written.

Express warranty   An express warranty or promise can be created by an affirmation of fact or a promise made by the seller, a description of the goods being sold (including technical specifications and blueprints), or a sample or model provided.

Extradition   The transportation of an individual from one state to another so that person can be tried on criminal charges.

Fact bound   When even a minor change in the facts can change the outcome.

False arrest   Occurs when a person is arrested (by either a law officer or a citizen) without probable cause and the arrest is not covered by special privilege.

False imprisonment   Occurs whenever one person, through force or the threat of force, unlawfully detains another person against his or her will.

False light   The intentional false portrayal of someone in a way that would be offensive to a reasonable person.

Family law   The area of the law that covers marriage, divorce, and parent-child relationships.

Federal courts of appeals   The intermediate appellate courts in the federal system.

Federal district courts   The trial courts in the federal system.

Federal question jurisdiction   The power of the federal courts to hear matters of federal law.

Federal Register   A daily newspaper in which proposed federal regulations are first printed.

Federal Reporter   The West reporter that contains decisions from the U.S. courts of appeals.

Federal Rules of Civil Procedure   The rules governing the stages of civil litigation in federal courts.

Federal Supplement   The West reporter that contains decisions from the U.S. district courts.

Federalism   A system of government in which the authority to govern is split between a single, nationwide central government and several regional governments that control specific geographical areas.

Fee simple absolute estate   An ownership of land that is free from any conditions or restrictions.

Felony   A serious crime, usually carrying a prison sentence of one or more years.

Fiduciary   A person who has a legally imposed obligation to act in the best interests of another party.

Fiduciary duty   A legally imposed obligation to act in the best interests of the party to whom the duty is owed.

Financing statement   A public record of a security interest.

Fine   A penalty requiring the payment of money.

Floating lien   A security interest in proceeds or after-acquired property.

Floor debate   Debate that takes place in the legislature before a vote is taken on a proposed statute. It becomes part of the statute's legislative history.

Follow precedent   When a court bases its decision on prior similar cases.

Forcible entry and detainer   In some states, a summary civil action by a landlord to regain possession of the premises from a tenant who disputes the landlord's right to possession. Also, an action by anyone with the right to possession who has been unlawfully evicted.

Foreclosure   The process by which a creditor who holds a mortgage or some other form of a lien on real property can force the sale of that property in order to satisfy the debt to the mortgagee or lien holder.

Foreign corporation   A corporation incorporated in one state doing business in another state.

Forfeiture   The loss of money or property as a result of committing a criminal act.

Forgery   The alteration or falsification of documents with the intent to defraud.

Formal contract   A contract requiring certain formalities, such as a seal, to be valid.

Formal will   A will that has been prepared on a word processor or typewriter and that has been properly signed by the testator and the required witnesses.

Fourth branch of government   Administrative agencies.

Fraud   A false representation of facts or intentional perversion of the truth to induce someone to take some action or give up something of value.

Freehold estate   A right of title or ownership to real property that extends for life or some other indeterminate period of time.

Freelance paralegal   A paralegal who works as an independent contractor rather than as an employee of a law firm or corporation.

Friend of the court   See **Amicus curiae**.

Fruit of the poisonous tree doctrine   Evidence that is derived from an illegal search or interrogation is inadmissible.

Full-text search   A computer search that identifies every place in which the search term appears in the actual text of the document being searched.

Fused sentence A type of run-on sentence; two independent clauses with no separating punctuation.

Garnishment A process through which a court can require an employer to withhold money from an employee's wages and turn this money over to the party to whom a debt is owed.

General damages Damages that you would naturally expect to occur given the type of harm suffered.

General intent An intention to act without regard to the results of the act.

General jurisdiction A court's power to hear any type of case arising within its geographical area.

General partnership A type of partnership in which all partners have the right to manage the business.

Grand jury A group of people, usually twenty-three, whose function is to determine if probable cause exists to believe that a crime has been committed and that the defendant committed it.

Grantor The prior owner.

Guardian A person appointed by the court to manage the affairs or property of a person who is incompetent due to age or some other reason.

Guardian ad litem Someone appointed by the court to speak for the interests of a child.

Guilty Convicted of a crime.

Harmless error A trial court error that is not sufficient to warrant reversing the decision.

Headnote A summary of one legal point in a court opinion; written by the editors at West.

Health care proxy Also known as a **durable power of attorney**; a document in which an individual delegates legal authority to make medical or financial decisions for that person if he or she is too incapacitated to make such decisions.

Hearing officer Holds administrative hearings, administers oaths, issues subpoenas, oversees depositions, and holds settlement conferences.

Hearsay Testimony or evidence introduced in court regarding what someone said out of court for the purpose of establishing the truth of what was said.

Heir Someone entitled to inherit property left by the decedent.

History The prior or subsequent history of the case you are Shepardizing. It is always preceded by a one-letter abbreviation.

Holder Someone who receives negotiable paper through proper delivery.

Holder in due course Someone who gives value in good faith (a subjective standard) and without notice that the instrument is overdue or has been dishonored or has any claims against it or defenses to it (an objective standard).

Holding In a case brief, the court's answer to the issue presented to it; the new legal principle established by a court opinion.

Holographic will A will that was handwritten by the testator, without the witness signatures necessary for a formal will; an informal will.

Home page The first page of a web site that has multiple links to other places on the web site and to other web sites.

Homicide The killing of one human being by another.

Hostile work environment Occurs when unwelcome sexual conduct has the purpose or effect of unreasonably interfering with an individual's work performance or creating an intimidating, hostile, or offensive working environment.

Hypertext links Computer codes that, when clicked on with a mouse, connect the user to other web pages with related information.

Id. A short citation form indicating reference is to the immediately preceding authority.

Immunity For policy reasons, protection from being sued for negligent acts.

Implied warranty of fitness An implied promise that the goods being sold will satisfy a special purpose.

Implied warranty of habitability A requirement that property be fit for the purpose for which it is being rented. Owners are required to repair and maintain the premises at certain minimum levels.

Implied warranty of merchantability An implied promise that the goods being sold will be usable for the purpose for which they were sold.

Implied-in-fact contracts Contracts formed through conduct.

Inchoate crimes Attempted crimes.

Incidental beneficiary Someone who the original contracting parties did not explicitly intend to benefit from the contract.

Inculpatory evidence Evidence that suggests the defendant's guilt; opposite of **exculpatory evidence**.

Independent adoption An adoption that involves a private agreement between the birth parents and the adoptive parents.

Independent clause A clause that contains a subject and a verb and that can stand alone as a sentence.

Independent contractor A person who works for another but who retains the right to control the manner of producing the end result; not an employee.

Independent paralegal A paralegal working under the supervision of an attorney in a contractual relationship. Sometimes used to refer to a paralegal providing legal services directly to the public without being under the supervision of an attorney.

Indictment A grand jury's written accusation that a given individual has committed a crime. Compare **Presentment.**

Indorsement in blank When an indorser simply signs his or her name and does not specify to whom the instrument is payable.

Infant In the law, a name sometimes used to mean any minor child.

Inference A conclusion reached based on the facts given.

Inferior courts In the federal system, all courts other than the U.S. Supreme Court.

Informal contract A contract not requiring any particular formalities to be valid.

Information A prosecutor's written accusation that a person has committed a crime.

Infra Below; used to refer to authority cited later in the document. May not be used with citations to cases, statutes, or constitutions.

Initial appearance The first court hearing for a person charged with committing a crime.

Injunction A court order requiring a party to perform a specific act or to cease doing a specific act.

Insanity defense A defense requiring proof that the defendant was not mentally responsible.

Intangible property Personal property that cannot be touched.

Intellectual property Intangible assets, such as trademarks, copyrights, and patents.

Intended beneficiary A person the contractual parties intend to benefit.

Intentional infliction of emotional distress An intentional tort that occurs through an extreme and outrageous act that causes severe emotional distress.

Intentional tort A tort committed by one who intends to do the act that creates the harm.

Inter vivos trust A trust that is created before a person's death.

Interference with a contractual relationship An intentional tort that occurs if someone induces a party to breach a contract or interferes with the performance of a contract.

Internet A worldwide network of computer networks.

Interrogatories Written questions sent by one side to the opposing side, answered under oath.

Intestate When a person dies without a valid will.

Intoxication defense A defense requiring proof that the defendant was not able to form the requisite mens rea due to intoxication.

Intrusion The intentional unjustified encroachment into another person's private activities.

Intrusive phrase A phrase placed between a sentence's subject and verb.

Invasion of privacy An intentional tort that covers a variety of situations, including disclosure, intrusion, appropriation, and false light.

IRAC A method for organizing legal writing: issue, rule, analysis, and conclusion.

Irresistible impulse test A test that provides that the defendant is not guilty due to insanity if, at the time of the killing, the defendant could not control his or her actions.

Irrevocable trust A form of inter vivos trust that the grantor cannot alter.

Issue Arises when the law is applied to specific facts and the result is not obvious. In a case brief, the statement of the problem facing the court. In an IRAC analysis, the statement of the client's problem. In probate law, a lineal heir; see **Decedent.**

Issue of first impression An issue that the court has never faced before.

Jails City or county places of confinement.

J.N.O.V. Shorthand for **judgment notwithstanding the verdict.**

Joint and several liability Liability shared collectively and individually.

Joint legal custody Both parents have an equal say in making major decisions, such as those regarding the education of the child.

Joint liability Shared liability, so that if one party is sued, others must be sued also.

Joint tenancy Ownership by two or more persons who have equal rights in the use of that property. When a joint tenant dies, that person's share passes to the other joint tenant(s).

Joint tenancy with right of survivorship Another term for **joint tenancy.**

Judge A court official who presides over courtroom proceedings and decides all legal questions. In a bench trial the judge also decides the facts.

Judgment The decision of the court regarding the claims of each side. It may be based on a jury's verdict.

Judgment notwithstanding the verdict (J.N.O.V.) A judgment that reverses the verdict of the jury when the verdict had no reasonable factual support or was contrary to law.

Judgment proof   When the defendant does not have sufficient money or other assets to pay the judgment.

Judicial activism   A judicial philosophy that supports an active role for the judiciary in changing the law.

Judicial history   See **Procedural facts.**

Judicial restraint   A judicial philosophy that supports a limited role for the judiciary in changing the law, including deference to the legislative branch.

Judicial review   The court's power to review statutes to decide if they conform to the U.S. Constitution.

Jurisdiction   The power of a court to hear a case.

Jurisprudence   The study of law and legal philosophy.

Jury trial   When a jury decides the facts and determines liability or guilt.

Just compensation   The amount of money the government must pay the owner of property it seizes through eminent domain.

Justice of the peace   A title given to the presiding officer (judge) in limited jurisdiction minor courts operated by some states.

Kidnapping   An unlawful movement and confinement of the victim.

Kindred   Also known as **consanguinity**; persons related to the decedent by blood.

Knowingly   Not intending to cause a specific harm but being aware that such harm would be caused.

Land contract   An installment contract for the sale of land.

Landmark decision   A court opinion that establishes new law in an important area.

Larceny   Another term for **theft.**

Last clear chance   The doctrine that states that despite the plaintiff's contributory negligence, the defendant should still be liable if the defendant was the last one in a position to avoid the accident.

Law clerk   A law student or a recent law school graduate whose duties usually focus on legal research.

Law office memorandum   An unbiased analysis of the client's situation.

Law review   A journal generally published by a law school editorial board or by a bar association. The articles usually contain in-depth analyses of current legal topics.

Laws   Rules of conduct promulgated and enforced by the government, based on policy decisions that determine legal rights and duties between people or between people and the government.

Lay advocate   A nonlawyer who provides legal services directly to the public without being under the supervision of an attorney; also known as a **legal technician.** Absent a statute allowing this activity, it constitutes the unauthorized practice of law.

Leading question   A question that suggests the answer; generally, leading questions may not be asked during direct examination of a witness.

Lease   An agreement in which the property owner gives someone else the right to use that property for a designated period of time.

Leasehold   A parcel of real estate held under a lease.

Leasehold estate   A right to use real property for a limited period of time.

Legacy   See **Bequest.**

Legal aid services   See **Legal Services Corporation.**

Legal analysis   The process of applying the law to a client's facts. Also known as **legal reasoning.**

Legal assistant   Synonym for **paralegal**; may also refer to other nonlawyers who assist attorneys.

Legal Assistant Management Association (LAMA)   A national association of legal assistant managers.

Legal custody   The designated parent or guardian who has authority to make legal decisions for the child relating to such matters as health care and education.

Legal fiction   An assumption that something that is not real is real—for example, assuming that a corporation is a person for purposes of its being able to sue and be sued.

Legal formalism   A legal theory that views the law as a complete and autonomous system of logically consistent principles within which judges find the correct result by simply making logical deductions.

Legal malpractice   The failure of an attorney to act reasonably.

Legal positivism   A legal theory whose proponents believe that the validity of a law is determined by the process through which it was made rather than by the degree to which it reflects natural law principles.

Legal realism   A legal philosophy whose proponents think that judges decide cases based on factors other than logic and preexisting rules, such as economic and sociological factors.

Legal reasoning   The application of legal rules to a client's specific factual situation; also known as **legal analysis.**

Legal research   The process of finding the law.

Legal scrivener   The provider of a typing service.

Legal Services Corporation   A federally funded program to deliver legal assistance to the indigent.

Legal technician   A nonlawyer who provides legal services directly to the public without being under the supervision of an attorney; also known as a **lay advocate.**

Absent a statute allowing this activity, it constitutes the unauthorized practice of law.

Legal writing Examples of legal writing include case briefs, law office memoranda, and documents filed with the court.

Legislative courts Courts created under Congress's Article I powers.

Legislative history The background documents created during the process of a bill becoming a statute. These documents can include alternative versions of the legislation, proceedings of committee hearings, committee reports, and transcripts of floor debates.

Legislative intent The purpose of the legislature at the time it enacted a statute. In interpreting statutes the role of the court is to try to discover the intent of the legislature at the time it enacted the statute.

Lessee or tenant The person with right of possession during the term of the lease.

Lesser included offense A crime whose elements are contained within a more serious crime. Theft is a lesser included offense of robbery.

Lessor or landlord The owner of the property being leased.

Lexis An on-line legal database containing court decisions and statutes from the entire country, as well as secondary authority; a competitor to **Westlaw**.

Liable A finding in a civil suit that a defendant is responsible.

Libel Written defamation.

Liberal construction An approach whereby the courts give a statute a broad interpretation.

Licensing Governmental permission to engage in a profession.

Life estate An ownership right to real property that lasts only as long as that person, or some other named individual, lives.

Life tenant A person who has ownership under a life estate.

Limited jurisdiction A court's power to hear only specialized cases.

Limited liability company (LLC) A new form of business ownership that gives small businesses the advantage of liability limited to the amount of the owner's investment along with single taxation.

Limited liability partnership (LLP) A form of business ownership similar to a general partnership except the partners do not have unlimited personal liability for the wrongful acts of other partners. Unlike a limited liability company, however, the partners remain personally liable for other business debts, such as rent and utilities.

Limited partnership A partnership of at least one general partner and one or more limited partners. The limited partners' liability is limited to their investments so long as they do not participate in management decisions.

Lineal heir Someone who is a grandparent, parent, child, grandchild, or great-grandchild of the decedent.

Liquidated damages clause A contract provision that specifies what will happen in case of breach.

Listing agreement A document that spells out the nature of the services a real estate agent will perform with respect to selling real property and how the agent will be compensated for those services.

Litigation A lawsuit; a controversy to be settled in a court.

Living Constitution Judicial philosophy that seeks to interpret the Constitution in light of existing societal values.

Living trust A form of inter vivos trust that allows a person, while still living, to benefit another.

Living will Also known as a **medical directive**; a document expressing a person's wishes regarding the withholding or withdrawal of life-support equipment and other heroic measures to sustain life if the individual has an incurable or irreversible condition that will cause death.

Loss of consortium The loss by one spouse of the other spouse's companionship, services, or affection.

Magistrate A title sometimes given to a public official exercising limited judicial power.

Magistrate judges In the federal district courts they supervise court calendars, hear procedural motions, issue subpoenas, hear minor criminal offense cases, and conduct civil pretrial hearings.

Maintenance See **Alimony**.

Major premise In deductive reasoning, the statement of a broad proposition that forms the starting point; in law, the statement of a legal rule that you can find in a statute or court opinion.

Majority opinion An opinion in which a majority of the court joins.

Maker On the face of a note, the person who signs, promising to pay.

Malice Making a defamatory remark either knowing the material was false or acting with a "reckless disregard" for whether or not it was true.

Malicious prosecution A lawsuit that can be brought against someone who unsuccessfully and maliciously brought an action without probable cause.

Mandatory authority or decisions Court decisions from a higher court in the same jurisdiction.

Marital property Property that is subject to court distribution upon termination of the marriage.

Market share theory A legal theory that allows plaintiffs to recover proportionately from a group of manufacturers when the identity of the specific manufacturer responsible for the harm is unknown.

Marketable title See **Clear title.**

Massachusetts Decisions The unofficial reporter published by West covering court decisions from Massachusetts also found in the North Eastern Reporter. The pages containing the court decisions from the other four states reported in the North Eastern Reporter are removed.

Massachusetts Digest A West publication; the digest is a collection of Massachusetts court decision summaries arranged by subject matter.

Massachusetts Digest table of cases An alphabetical listing of court decisions arranged by the plaintiff's last name, giving the citation and relevant topics and key numbers. There is also a defendant-plaintiff table, an alphabetical listing by the defendant's last name.

Massachusetts Practice Series (M.P.S.) A West publication; the Massachusetts equivalent of a legal encyclopedia. Contains cross-references to C.J.S. and Massachusetts Digest topics and key numbers.

Massachusetts Register A biweekly publication listing proposed and new Massachusetts regulations.

Massachusetts Reports The official reporter published by the state of Massachusetts covering Massachusetts Supreme Judicial Court decisions.

Master In law, the name that is sometimes given to an employer.

Material breach Such a grave failure to fulfill the contractual terms that the other party is relieved of all contractual obligations.

Mechanic's lien A claim filed by a contractor or repair person who had done work on a building for which he or she has not been fully paid.

Mediation An ADR mechanism whereby a neutral third party assists the parties in reaching a mutually agreeable, voluntary compromise.

Medical directive See **Living will.**

Mens rea Bad intent.

Merchant's firm offer An offer made by a merchant in a signed writing that assures the buyer that the offer will remain open for a specific period of time. It does not require consideration to be binding.

Mini-digest A digest located in an advance sheet pamphlet or hardbound volume of court decisions published by West. It contains the headnotes for the cases in that single publication.

Minimum contacts A constitutional fairness requirement that a defendant have at least a certain minimum contact with a state before the state courts can have jurisdiction over the defendant.

Minor A child who is under the age of legal competence.

Minor premise In deductive reasoning, the second proposition, which along with the major premise leads to the conclusion; in law, the minor premise consists of the client's facts.

Miranda warnings The requirement that defendants be notified of their rights to remain silent and to have an attorney present prior to being questioned by the police.

Mirror image rule The requirement that the acceptance exactly mirror the offer or the acceptance will be viewed as a counteroffer.

Misdemeanor A minor crime not amounting to a felony, usually punishable by a fine or a jail sentence of less than a year.

Misfeasance Acting in an improper or a wrongful way.

Mistrial A trial ended by the judge because of a major problem, such as a prejudicial statement by one of the attorneys.

Mitigation of damages The requirement that the nonbreaching party take reasonable steps to limit his or her damages.

M'Naghten test A test that provides that the defendant is not guilty due to insanity if, at the time of the killing, the defendant suffered from a defect or disease of the mind and could not understand whether the act was right or wrong.

Model Code of Professional Responsibility An older set of standards governing attorney ethics developed by the American Bar Association.

Model Penal Code and Commentaries The American Law Institute's proposal for a uniform set of criminal laws; not the law unless adopted by a state's legislature.

Model Rules of Professional Conduct A set of ethical rules developed by the American Bar Association in the 1980s. The Model Rules have been adopted by more than half the states.

Motion A request made to the court.

Motion for acquittal A request that the court end the trial by finding for the defendant.

Motion for a continuance A request that the court postpone the proceeding to a later time.

Motion for a directed verdict A request that the court find for the moving party because either the plaintiff failed to present a prima facie case or the defendant failed to present a necessary defense.

Motion for further appellate review   In Massachusetts, the process whereby the Supreme Judicial Court agrees to hear a case.

Motion for judgment notwithstanding the verdict   A request that the court reverse the jury's verdict when the verdict had no reasonable factual support or was contrary to law.

Motion for leave to obtain further appellate review   In Massachusetts, a request that the Supreme Judicial Court hear a case.

Motion in limine   A request that the court order that certain information not be mentioned in the presence of the jury.

Motion for a new trial   A request that the court order a rehearing of a lawsuit because irregularities, such as errors of the court or jury misconduct, make it probable that an impartial trial did not occur.

Motion to require a finding of not guilty   The defense's request that the court find the prosecution failed to meet its burden and that it remove the case from the jury by finding the defendant not guilty.

Motion to suppress   A request that the court prohibit the use of certain evidence at the trial.

Narrow holding   A statement of the court's decision that contains many of the case's specific facts, thereby limiting its future applicability to a narrow range of cases.

National Association of Legal Assistants (NALA)   A national paralegal association.

National Federation of Paralegal Associations (NFPA)   A national association of paralegal associations.

National Reporter System   West's system for reporting court decisions from every state and the federal courts.

Natural law   A legal philosophy whose proponents think there are ideal laws that can be discovered through careful thought and humanity's innate sense of right and wrong.

Necessaries   Normally food, clothing, shelter, and medical treatment.

Necessity   A defense requiring proof that the defendant was forced to take an action to avoid a greater harm.

Negligence   The failure to act reasonably under the circumstances.

Negotiable instrument   Commercial paper that can be transferred by indorsement or delivery. It must meet the requirements of UCC § 3-104 to be negotiable. If it does not, a transferee cannot become a holder, but only gets the rights along with the liabilities of a contract assignee.

New trial   A rehearing of a lawsuit granted when irregularities such as errors of the court or jury misconduct make it probable that an impartial trial did not occur.

Next friend   A person who represents the interests of someone in court without being that person's legal guardian.

No-fault divorce   A form of divorce that allows a couple to end their marital relationship without having to assess blame for the breakup.

No-knock warrant   A warrant that allows the police to enter without announcing their presence in advance.

Nolo contendere   A defendant's plea meaning that the defendant neither admits nor denies the charges.

Nominal damages   A token sum awarded when liability has been found but monetary damages cannot be shown.

Nonfeasance   Failing to act.

Nonrestrictive phrase   A phrase that is not essential to the sense of a sentence; it should be set off with commas.

North Eastern Reporter   An unofficial regional reporter published by West covering court decisions from Massachusetts, as well as four other states.

Note   A promise to pay money.

Notice   Being informed of some act done or about to be done.

Notice pleading   A method adopted by the federal rules in which the plaintiff simply informs the defendant of the claim and the general basis for it.

Novation   In a contract, when a third party is substituted for one of the original parties.

Nuncupative will   An oral will.

Obiter dictum   See **Dictum.**

Obligee   A person owed a contractual benefit.

Obligor   A person under a contractual obligation.

Obscenity   Sexually explicit material without redeeming artistic, scientific, or political worth.

Official reporter   A governmental publication of court opinions.

On all fours   A term used to describe two cases that are almost identical, with similar facts and legal issues.

On point   A term used to describe a case that is similar to another case.

Option contract   A contract in which the buyer gives the seller consideration to keep the offer open for a stated period of time.

Order paper   An instrument that is payable to the order of a specific party.

Ordinance   A local law.

Originalism   An approach to constitutional interpretation that narrowly interprets the text of the Constitution in a manner that is consistent with what most people understood those words to mean at the time that they were written.

Original jurisdiction   The authority of a court to hear a case when it is initiated, as opposed to appellate jurisdiction.

Output contract   A contract in which one party agrees to deliver its entire output of a particular product to the other party.

Overbreadth   A reason for invalidating a statute where it covers both protected and criminal activity.

Overrule   A decision is overruled when a court in a later case changes the law so that its prior decision is no longer good law. Compare with **Reverse**.

Overt discrimination   When an employer openly refuses to treat all applicants or employees equally.

Paralegal   A person who assists an attorney and, working under the attorney's supervision, does tasks that, absent the paralegal, the attorney would do. A paralegal cannot give legal advice or appear in court.

Parallel citation   When reference to two or more reporters is required, each citation is known as a parallel citation. For example, 333 Mass. 99 is the parallel citation for 89 N.E.2d 488; the reverse is also true.

Parallel construction   Using the some grammatical structure for clauses or phrases that bear the same relationship to some major idea.

Parental immunity   The prohibition against allowing children to sue their parents.

Parenthetical   The parenthetical that occurs at the end of a court citation always contains the year of decision and also the name of the court if that information is not obvious from the name of the reporter.

Parol evidence rule   An evidentiary rule that a written contract cannot be modified or changed by prior verbal agreements.

Parole   Conditional early release from custody.

Partial defense   A defense that reduces a crime to a lesser included offense.

Partnership   A business run by two or more persons as co-owners.

Partnership by estoppel   A partnership created by the words or actions of persons acting as though they were a partnership.

Passive voice   A form of writing where the subject of the sentence is being acted on; opposite of **active voice**.

Patent   A right to exclude others from making, using, or selling one's invention.

Pattern jury instructions   A set of standardized jury instructions.

Payee   The person who will receive payment.

Penal system   Also known as the *correctional system*; the system of jails, prisons, and other places of confinement, as well as the pardon and parole systems.

Per stirpes   Also known as the **right of representation**; a method of dividing an intestate estate whereby a person takes in place of the dead ancestor.

Peremptory challenge   A method for excusing a prospective juror; no reason need be given.

Perfect tender rule   The requirement that the goods delivered exactly meet the contractual specifications.

Perfected security interest   A creditor's interest in security is perfected if the creditor possesses the security, files a financing statement, or gives money to purchase consumer goods.

Perfection   In secured transactions, a security interest is perfected when notice of an attached security interest has been given, usually by filing a financing statement, thereby protecting the secured party from claims of third parties.

Periodic tenancy   A tenancy established at a set interval, such as week to week, month to month, or year to year. At the end of each rental period the lease can be terminated with proper notice.

Perjury   Lying to the court while under oath.

Perpetrator   A person who commits a crime.

Personal defense   In negotiable instrument law, a defense that is good against everyone except a holder in due course. Compare **Real defense**.

Personal jurisdiction   The power of a court to force a person to appear before it.

Personal property   All property that is not **real property**.

Personal recognizance bond   A defendant's personal promise to appear in court.

Persuasive authority or decisions   Court decisions from an equal or a lower court from the same jurisdiction or from a higher court in a different jurisdiction. Also includes secondary authority.

Petitioner   A person who initiates an appeal.

Physical custody   The child lives with and has day-to-day activities supervised by the designated parent or guardian.

Piercing the corporate veil   When a court sets aside the unlimited liability protection normally given to corporate shareholders.

Pinpoint cite   The reference to a particular page within an opinion.

Plain meaning   A method for interpreting statutes in which the ordinary meaning of the statute's language is examined.

Plain view doctrine Without the need for a warrant, the police may seize objects that are openly visible.

Plaintiff A person who initiates a lawsuit.

Plea bargaining A process whereby the prosecutor and the defendant's attorney agree for the defendant to plead guilty in exchange for the prosecutor's promise to charge him or her with a lesser offense, drop some additional charges, or request a lesser sentence.

Pleading in the alternative Including more than one count in a complaint; the counts do not need to be consistent.

Pleadings The papers that begin a lawsuit—generally, the complaint and the answer.

Pocket part A pamphlet inserted into the back of a book containing information new since the volume was published.

Popular name table Located in most codified statutes, this table lists statutes by their popular names along with their citations.

Potential conflict A situation in which a conflict of interest may arise in the future—for example, representing business partners.

Power of judicial review A court's power to review statutes to decide if they conform to the federal or state constitution.

Power of sale clause A clause authorizing a private foreclosure sale that does not require court action.

Practice of law An activity that requires professional judgment, or the educated ability to relate law to a specific legal problem.

Practitioners' Notes A section of the Bluebook devoted to citation information for the practicing attorney.

Precedent One or more prior court decisions.

Preemption The power of the federal government to prevent the states from passing conflicting laws, and sometimes even to prohibit states from passing any laws on a particular subject.

Prejudicial error A trial court error so serious as to require reversal of the trial court's decision.

Preliminary hearing The first time a judge considers the criminal charge and decides whether there is enough evidence for the government to continue with the case.

Prenuptial agreement Also known as an antenuptial agreement; a document that prospective spouses sign prior to marriage regarding financial and other arrangements should the marriage end.

Preponderance of the evidence The standard of proof used in civil trials. The proof must indicate that it is more likely than not that the defendant committed the wrong.

Presentment Acting on its own initiative, a grand jury's charging a person with a crime. Compare **Indictment**.

Pretrial conference A meeting of the attorneys and the judge prior to the beginning of the trial.

Pretrial motion A motion brought before the beginning of a trial either to eliminate the necessity for a trial or to limit the information that can be heard at the trial.

Prima facie case What the prosecution or the plaintiff must be able to prove in order for the case to go to the jury—that is, the elements of the prosecution's case or the plaintiff's cause of action.

Primary authority The law itself, such as statutes and court opinions.

Principal In agency law, a person who permits or directs another person to act on the principal's behalf; in criminal law, the person who commits the crime.

Prior case history Information about what happened procedurally to the cited case before it was heard by the cited court. Do not include this information in a citation.

Prisons Places of confinement for those convicted of the more serious crimes.

Privity of contract The relationship that exists between the contracting parties.

Pro bono work Legal representation done without charge.

Pro se One who represents himself or herself in a legal action.

Probable cause Not susceptible to a precise definition; a belief based on specific facts that a crime has been or is about to be committed; more than a reasonable suspicion.

Probate The process of court supervision over the distribution of a deceased person's property.

Probation An alternative sentence to incarceration that releases the defendant upon agreeing to certain conditions.

Probation officers Government employees who administer the probation system.

Procedural facts In a case brief, the facts that relate to what happened procedurally in the lower courts or administrative agencies before the case reached the court issuing the opinion and how the appellate court disposed of the case. Examples include aff'd and rev'd.

Procedural law Law that regulates how the legal system operates.

Product misuse When the product was not being used for its intended purpose or was being used in a dangerous manner; it is a defense to a products liability claim so long as the misuse was not foreseeable.

Products liability   The theory holding manufacturers and sellers liable for defective products when the defects make the products unreasonably dangerous.

Professional judgment   The educated ability to apply law to specific facts.

Promissory estoppel   Occurs when the courts allow detrimental reliance to substitute for consideration.

Pronoun   A word that substitutes for a noun: *hers, her, his, him, its, them, their, theirs.*

Property   A tangible object or a right or ownership interest.

Property law   Law dealing with ownership.

Prosecuting attorney   The attorney responsible for presenting the state's evidence against the defendant; called *United States attorneys* on the federal level and **district attorneys** or **state's attorneys** on the state level.

Prostitution   Participating in sexual activity for a fee.

Protected categories   Under Title VII, race, color, religion, sex, and national origin.

Protection order   A court order issued in domestic violence and abuse cases to keep one spouse away from the other, the children, or the home.

Proving a case within a case   The requirement in a legal malpractice case that the plaintiff-client prove that but for the attorney's negligence, the client would have won.

Proximate cause   Once actual cause is found, as a policy matter, the court must also find that the act and the resulting harm were so foreseeably related as to justify a finding of liability.

Public defender   An attorney employed by the state to represent indigent defendants.

Punitive damages   Money awarded to a plaintiff in cases of intentional torts in order to punish the defendant and serve as a warning to others.

Purchase money security interest   Arises when a seller gives credit to a debtor so that the debtor can purchase an item.

Purposeful   Intending to cause a specific harm.

Qualified individual   Under the Americans with Disabilities Act, someone who can perform the essential job functions.

Quasi-contract   Although no contract was formed, the courts will fashion an equitable remedy to avoid unjust enrichment.

Question of fact   Relates to what happened: who, what, when, where, and how. Disputed factual issues are normally for the jury or trial court to decide and cannot be appealed.

Question of law   Relates to the application or interpretation of the law. Disputed legal issues are initially for the trial court to decide but can be appealed.

Question presented   In a law office memorandum, the question presented states the legal issue raised by the facts of the problem in as concrete a fashion as possible.

Quid pro quo sexual harassment   A situation involving an exchange of sexual favors for employment benefits.

Quiet enjoyment   The tenant's right to be free from interference from the landlord with respect to how the property is used.

Quitclaim deed   A deed in which the grantor gives up any claims to the property without making any assertions about there being a clear title.

Ratio decidendi   The court's reasoning for its decision.

Real defense   In negotiable instrument law, a defense inherent in the instrument itself, such as forgery. Compare **Personal defense.**

Real estate closing   A meeting at which the buyer and the seller or their representatives sign and deliver a variety of legal documents associated with the sale and transfer of the property.

Real property   Also known as *real estate;* land and items growing on or permanently attached to that land.

Reasonable accommodation   Under the Americans with Disabilities Act, an accommodation that would not create an undue hardship for the employer.

Reasonable suspicion   A suspicion based on specific facts; less than probable cause.

Receiving stolen property   Knowingly possessing stolen property.

Recidivist   A repeat offender; one who continues to commit more crimes.

Recklessness   Disregarding a substantial and unjustifiable risk that harm will result.

Reformation   An equitable remedy whereby the court rewrites a contract.

Registered agent   The person designated to receive service of legal documents.

Registration   The process by which individuals or organizations have their names placed on an official list kept by some private organization or governmental agency.

Regulation   A law promulgated by an administrative agency.

Remand   When an appellate court sends a case back to the trial court for a new trial or other action.

Remedial statute   A statute enacted to correct a defect in prior law or to provide a remedy where none existed.

Removal   The transfer of a case from one state court to another or from state court to federal court.

Reporters   Books that contain court decisions. There are both official and unofficial reporters.

Reprimand or censure   A public or private statement that an attorney's conduct violated the code of ethics.

Request for admissions   A document that lists statements regarding specific items for the other party to admit or deny.

Request for documents   A discovery tool whereby one party asks for documents in the other party's possession or control.

Requirements contract   A contract in which one party agrees to buy all its requirements for a particular product from the other party.

Res ipsa loquitur   "The thing speaks for itself"; the doctrine that suggests negligence can be presumed if an event happens that would not ordinarily happen unless someone was negligent.

Rescission   The act of canceling the contract and returning the parties to the positions they were in prior to the contract having been formed.

Respondeat superior   The tort theory that an employer can be sued for the negligent acts of its employees.

Respondent   The party in a lawsuit against whom an appeal has been filed.

Restatement of the Law of Torts, Second   An authoritative secondary source, written by a group of legal scholars, summarizing the existing common law, as well as suggesting what the law should be.

Restatements   A series of books—the Restatements of the Law—summarizing the basic principles of the common law, written by the American Law Institute (ALI).

Restitution   Repaying the victim for harm caused.

Restrictive covenant   A provision in a deed that prohibits specified uses of the property.

Restrictive phrase   A phrase that contains essential information; it should not be set off with commas.

Retreat exception   The rule that in order to claim self-defense there must have been no possibility of retreat.

Reversal   When an appellate court reverses a lower court decision.

Reverse   A decision is reversed when an appellate court overturns or negates the decision of a lower court. Compare with **Overrule**.

Reversible error   An error made by the trial judge sufficiently serious to warrant reversing the trial court's decision.

Revocable trust   A form of inter vivos trust that the grantor can alter.

RICO   The federal Racketeer Influenced and Corrupt Organizations Act.

Right of representation   See **Per stirpes**.

Road map paragraph   An introductory paragraph listing issues to be discussed in the order they are to be discussed.

Robbery   Theft through the use of force.

Rule   In a case brief, the general legal principle in existence before the case began.

Rule 8   The rule of civil procedure that sets forth the general pleading requirements.

Rule 11   A requirement that attorneys sign a pleading only after conducting a reasonable inquiry into the circumstances supporting it.

Rule 56 motion (summary judgment motion)   A request that the court grant judgment in favor of the moving party because there is no genuine issue as to any material fact and the moving party is entitled to judgment as a matter of law. It is similar to a **12(b)(6) motion** except that the court also considers matters outside the pleadings.

Rulemaking hearing   An administrative agency hearing that resembles a legislative hearing in which interested parties present evidence and arguments to an administrative agency about what the general law should be.

Rules of criminal procedure   Federal and state rules that regulate how criminal proceedings are conducted.

Rules of evidence   Federal and state rules that govern the admissibility of evidence in court.

Run-on sentence   Two sentences written as one. It can occur either as a comma splice (two independent clauses joined by a comma) or as a fused sentence (two independent clauses with no separating punctuation).

Said   Legalese for "the."

Screen   See **Ethical wall**.

Search engine   A computer program that allows the user to retrieve web documents that match the key words entered by the searcher.

Secondary authority   Information about the law, such as that contained in encyclopedias and law review articles.

Secured transaction   An arrangement whereby a creditor asks for and receives a guarantee of repayment from the debtor in the form of collateral.

Security agreement   An agreement granting a creditor a security interest in specific property.

Security deposit   An amount of money, usually equal to one month's rent, that is collected at the time the lease is signed and then held by the landlord to cover the cost of repairs that may be needed when the tenant moves out.

Security interest   A security interest is created when a debtor agrees to put up something as collateral that the creditor can then claim if the debtor fails to pay the debt.

Self-defense   The justified use of force to protect oneself or others.

Self-proving clause   A notarized affidavit, signed by the attesting witnesses, that may eliminate the need to call witnesses during the probate process to attest to the validity of the will.

Sentence fragment   An incomplete sentence.

Sentencing hearing   A hearing held after a finding of guilt to determine the appropriate sentence.

Separation of powers   The division of governmental power among the legislative, executive, and judicial branches.

Serial comma   In a series of three or more items use a comma after each item until you reach the final conjunction.

Servant   In law, an archaic term sometimes used to mean employee.

Service   The delivery of a pleading or other paper in a lawsuit to the opposing party.

Service mark   A mark used to identify a service-oriented business.

Service of process   See **Service.**

Session laws   Statutes that are enacted and published for a particular session of the legislature

Settlement   An agreement between the parties to end the lawsuit on mutually satisfactory terms.

Settlement agreement   A document that contains the arrangements agreed on by the parties to a dispute.

Settlor   See **Donor.**

Shareholders   The owners of a corporation.

Shepardizing   The process of using **Shepard's Citations** to check a court citation to see whether there has been any subsequent history or treatment by other court decisions.

Shepard's Citations   A book that contains nothing but citations. It serves three purposes: (1) as a source for parallel citations; (2) as a source for subsequent history for a case or statute; and (3) as a source for treatment by later courts of the case or statute you are Shepardizing.

Short citation form   A partial citation that may be used after you have given a complete citation.

Signal   A word or a phrase that precedes a citation to indicate the purpose for which the citation is being given.

Simultaneous death clause   A clause that states that if a person named as a beneficiary in the will dies within a short period of time after the decedent dies, it will be assumed for purposes of the will that the person in question failed to survive the decedent.

Slander   Spoken defamation.

Slip laws   A form in which statutes are published; they are printed individually at the time they are first enacted.

Sole custody   An individual has both physical and legal custody of the child.

Sole proprietorship   A business owned by a single owner.

Solemnized marriage   A marriage in which the couple has obtained the proper marriage license from a local government official and has then taken marriage vows before either a recognized member of the clergy or a judge and a designated number of witnesses.

Solicitation   Encouraging someone to commit a crime.

Sovereign immunity   The prohibition against suing the government without the government's consent.

Special damages   Indirect damages that must be foreseeable to be recovered.

Specific intent   An intention to act and to cause a specific result.

Specific performance   When money damages are inadequate, a court may use this equitable remedy and order the breaching party to perform his or her contractual obligations.

Split custody   One parent has both physical and legal custody during one part of the year, and the other parent gets both physical and legal custody during the rest of the year.

Spousal immunity   The prohibition against one spouse suing the other.

Stalking   The intentional or knowing course of conduct that places a person in fear of imminent physical injury or death to that person or that person's family.

Standing   The principle that courts cannot decide abstract issues or render advisory opinions; rather they are limited to deciding cases that involve litigants who are personally affected by the court's decision.

Stare decisis   The doctrine stating that normally once a court has decided one way on a particular issue in the past, it and other courts in the same jurisdiction will decide the same way on that issue in future cases given a similar set of facts unless they can be convinced of the need for change.

State's attorney   A law officer who represents the state in criminal cases. Also known as a **district attorney.**

Statute   A law enacted by a state legislature or by Congress.

Statute in derogation of the common law   A statute that changes the common law.

Statute of frauds A statutory requirement that in order to be enforceable certain contracts must be in writing.

Statute of limitations The law that sets the length of time from when something happens to when a lawsuit must be filed before the right to bring it is lost.

Statutes at large or session laws The chronological publication of statutes at the end of a legislative session.

Statutory element A separable part of a statute that must be satisfied for the statute to apply.

Stay the judgment A suspension of the judgment. It is often requested when the trial court judgment is being appealed.

Stipulate To agree.

Stop and frisk The right of the police to detain an individual for a brief period of time and to search the outside of the person's clothing if the police have a reasonable suspicion that the individual has committed or is about to commit a crime.

Strict construction An approach whereby the courts give a statute a narrow interpretation.

Strict liability Liability without having to prove fault.

String citation A series of citations in a row.

Subject matter jurisdiction The power of a court to hear a particular type of case.

Subordinating conjunction Dependent clauses always begin with subordinating conjunctions: *after, although, as, because, before, even though, if, since, unless, when, where, whereas,* and *while.*

Subpoena A court order requiring a person to appear to testify at a trial or deposition. (Administrative agencies also usually have subpoena powers.)

Subpoena duces tecum A court order that a person who is not a party to litigation appear at a trial or deposition and bring requested documents.

Subsequent case history Information about what happened procedurally to the litigation after the case cited. Include this information in a citation.

Substantial capacity test Part of the Model Penal Code; a test that provides that the defendant is not guilty due to insanity if, at the time of the killing, the defendant lacked either the ability to understand that the act was wrong or the ability to control the behavior.

Substantial performance Although a breach of contract, performance of all the essential terms of the contract will entitle the breaching party to the contractual price minus any damages caused by the breach.

Substantive facts In a case brief, facts that deal with what happened to the parties before the litigation began.

Substantive law Law that creates rights and duties.

Successive conflict of interest Representing someone who is in a position adverse to a prior client.

Summary judgment A judgment based on a finding that there is no genuine issue as to any material fact and that the moving party is entitled to judgment as a matter of law.

Summary judgment motion A request for a summary judgment.

Summary jury trial A nonbinding process in which attorneys for both sides present synopses of their cases to a jury, which renders an advisory opinion on the basis of these presentations.

Summons A notice informing the defendant of the lawsuit and requiring the defendant to respond or risk losing the suit.

Superseding cause In negligence, an intervening cause that relieves the defendant of liability.

Support See **Alimony.**

Supra Above; used to refer to authority already cited in the document. May not be used with citations to cases, statutes, or constitutions.

Supreme Court Reporter A West publication containing U.S. Supreme Court decisions.

Surrogacy contract A document in which a woman agrees to conceive and give birth to a child, deliver the child to its natural father, and terminate her parental rights so the father's wife can become its adoptive mother.

Suspension A determination that an attorney may not practice law for a set period of time.

Syllabus A summary of a court opinion that appears at the beginning of the case.

Synthesis The process of integrating a series of cases in such a way that their interrelationship is explained to the reader.

Tabulation A method for writing lists.

Tangible personal property Also known as **chattel;** personal property that can be touched and moved.

Temporary restraining order (TRO) A court order of limited duration designed to maintain the status quo pending further court action at a later date.

Tenancy in common Ownership by two or more people. Ownership shares do not have to be equal, but each has an undivided interest in the property. When a tenant in common dies, that person's share passes either by will or by intestate statute.

Tenancy by the entirety A special type of joint tenancy applicable only to married couples.

Tenancy at sufferance A situation in which the person in possession of the land has no legal right to be there.

Tenancy for a term or estate for years A right to control real property for a set period of time.

Tenancy at will An arrangement in which no time period is specified and the lessee can leave or the lessor can reclaim the land at any time.

Testamentary capacity The mental capacity, also known as *sound mind*, whereby the testator understands the nature of his or her property and the identity of those most closely related to him or her.

Testamentary trust A trust that is created by a will and does not become effective until after the testator's death.

Testator/testatrix The person making a will to direct how his or her assets will be distributed at death.

That case A case that you are citing.

Theft Also known as **larceny**; the taking of another's property with the intent to permanently deprive the owner.

Third-party claim A claim by a defendant against someone in addition to the persons the plaintiff has already sued.

This case Your client's case.

Title insurance Insurance against any loss due to a defective title.

Title search An examination of documents recording title to a property to ensure the owner has a clear title.

Tort Harm to a person or a person's property.

Tort law Law that deals with harm to a person or a person's property.

Tortfeasor A person who commits a tort.

Trademark A name, combination of letters or numbers, or logo that identifies a particular product.

Transferred intent A legal fiction that if a person directs a tortious action toward A but instead harms B, the intent to act against A is transferred to B.

Transition In writing, a technique used to help your reader move from one thought to the next and to see the connections between them.

Treason Attempting to overthrow the government or betraying the government to a foreign power.

Treatise A book that summarizes, interprets, and evaluates the law.

Treatment How subsequent cases have affected the case you are Shepardizing. It is sometimes indicated by a one-letter abbreviation before the Shepard's citation.

Trespass The unauthorized intrusion onto the land of another.

Trespass to personal property Occurs when someone harms or interferes with the owner's exclusive possession of the property but has no intention of keeping the property.

Trial The process of deciding a dispute by presenting evidence and witness testimony either to a jury or to a judge.

Trial courts Courts that determine the facts and apply the law to the facts.

Trust A legal relationship in which one party holds property for the benefit of another.

Trustee The person appointed to administer a trust.

12(b)(6) motion A request that the court find the plaintiff has failed to state a valid claim and dismiss the complaint.

Ultrahazardous activities Those activities that have an inherent risk of injury and therefore may result in strict liability.

Unauthorized practice of law When nonlawyers do things that only lawyers are allowed to do. In most states this is a crime.

Unconscionable contract A contract formed between parties of very unequal bargaining power where the terms are so unfair as to "shock the conscience."

Undue influence When one party is in a position of trust and misuses that trust to influence the actions of another.

Unenforceable contract A valid contract that cannot be enforced, for example, because the statute of limitations has passed.

Uniform Commercial Code (UCC) Originally drafted by the National Conference of Commissioners on Uniform State Law, it governs commercial transactions and has been adopted by all states entirely or in part.

Uniform Partnership Act (UPA) Known as a gap filler, the UPA comes into play only if terms are left out of a partnership agreement.

Unilateral contract A contract where a promise is exchanged for an act.

United States Code (U.S.C.) Federal statutes arranged by subject matter.

United States Code Annotated (U.S.C.A.) Federal statutes arranged by subject matter, published by West.

United States Code Service (U.S.C.S.) Federal statutes arranged by subject matter, published by Lexis Law Publishing.

United States Constitution Drafted in 1787, it established the structure of the federal government and the relationship between the federal and state governments.

United States courts of appeals The intermediate appellate courts in the federal system.

United States district courts The general jurisdiction trial courts in the federal system.

United States Law Week BNA's publication of U.S. Supreme Court decisions.

United States Reports The official federal government publication of U.S. Supreme Court decisions.

United States Sentencing Guidelines Government guidelines that specify an appropriate range of sentences for each class of convicted persons based on factors related to the offense and the offender.

United States Supreme Court The highest appellate court in the federal system; consists of nine appointed members; established by Article III of the U.S. Constitution.

United States Supreme Court Reports, Lawyers' Edition U.S. Supreme Court decisions published by Lexis Law Publishing.

Unlawful detainer A civil action brought to recover use of property.

Unofficial reporter A private publication of court opinions—for example, the regional reporters, such as N.E.2d, published by West.

Valid In logic, an argument is considered to be valid or sound if the assumptions underlying the argument are true.

Valid contract A contract having all the essential elements needed for a binding agreement.

Verdict The opinion of a jury on a question of fact.

Verification An affidavit signed by the client indicating that he or she has read the complaint and that its contents are correct.

Vicarious representation The rule whereby all members of a law firm are treated as though they had represented the former client.

Void In law, if an action is void, it has no legal effect.

Void contract A contract that is invalid even if it is not repudiated by either party; for example, a contract formed for an illegal purpose.

Void for vagueness A reason for invalidating a statute where a reasonable person could not determine a statute's meaning.

Void marriage A marriage that is invalid from its inception and that does not require court action for the parties to be free of any marital obligations.

Voidable A valid contract that can be set aside at the option of one of the parties.

Voidable contract A contract that can be disaffirmed by one of the parties.

Voidable marriage A marriage that was valid when it was entered into and that remains valid until either party obtains a court order dissolving it.

Voir dire An examination of a prospective juror to see if he or she is fit to serve as a juror.

Warrant A court's prior permission for the police to search and seize.

Warranty A guarantee, made by the seller or implied by law, regarding the character, quality, or title of the goods being sold.

Warranty deed A deed in which the seller promises clear title to the property.

Web An abbreviation for the World Wide Web, a subset of the Internet. Web sites combine text, pictures, and sometimes even sound with hypertext links to other web pages with related information.

Web browser A computer program that allows users to access and search the web with the click of a mouse.

Web page A computer page, accessible on the Internet, that contains links to other pages.

Web site A location on the Internet that contains a series of web pages that are linked to a home page.

West Group A major private publisher of legal materials. Its logo is the key symbol.

Westlaw An on-line legal database containing court decisions and statutes from the entire country, as well as secondary authority; a competitor to **Lexis.**

Will The document used to express a person's wishes as to how his or her property should be distributed upon death.

Writ A judge's order requiring that something be done.

Writ of certiorari A means of gaining appellate review; in the U.S. Supreme Court the writ is discretionary and will be issued to another court to review a federal question if four of the nine justices vote to hear the case.

Writ of execution A court order authorizing a sheriff to take property in order to enforce a judgment.

Writ of habeas corpus A request that the court release the defendant because of the illegality of the incarceration.

Wrongful birth Also known as *wrongful life;* liability for negligently causing a child's birth.

Table of Cases

Index